CONCISE MAJOR 21ST-CENTURY WRITERS

A Selection of Sketches from *Contemporary Authors*

Tracey L. Matthews, Project Editor

Volume 5: Sc-Z

Detroit • New York • San Francisco • New Haven, Conn. • Waterville, Maine • London • Munich

Concise Major 21st-Century Writers

Project Editor
Tracey L. Matthews

Editorial
Michelle Kazensky, Josh Kondek, Lisa Kumar, Julie Mellors, Joyce Nakamura, Mary Ruby

Composition and Electronic Capture
Carolyn A. Roney

Manufacturing
Rita Wimberley

For more information, contact
Thomson Gale
27500 Drake Rd.
Farmington Hills, MI 48331-3535
Or you can visit our internet site at
http://www.gale.com

Library of Congress Control Number: 2006929297

ISBN 0-7876-7539-3 (hardcover : set), ISBN 0-7876-7540-7 (v. 1), ISBN 0-7876-7541-5 (v. 2), ISBN 0-7876-7542-3 (v. 3), ISBN 0-7876-7543-1 (v. 4), ISBN 0-7876-7544-X (v. 5)

Printed in the United States of America
10 9 8 7 6 5 4 3 2 1

Contents

Introduction

Concise Major 21st-Century Writers (*CMTFCW*) is an abridgement of the 2004 eBook-only edition of Thomson Gale's *Major 21st-Century Writers* (*MTFCW*), a set based on Thomson Gale's award-winning *Contemporary Authors* series. *CMTFCW* provides students, educators, librarians, researchers, and general readers with a concise yet comprehensive source of biographical and bibliographical information on 700 of the most influential and studied authors at the turn of the twenty-first century as well as emerging authors whose literary significance is likely to increase in the coming decades.

CMTFCW includes sketches on approximately 700 authors who made writing literature their primary occupation and who have had at least part of their oeuvre published in English. Thus novelists, short story writers, nonfiction writers, poets, dramatists, genre writers, children's writers, and young adult writers of about sixty nationalities and ethnicities are represented. Selected sketches of authors that appeared in the 2004 edition of *MTFCW* are completely updated to include information on their lives and works through 2006. About thirty authors featured in *CMTFCW* are new to this set evidencing Thomson Gale's commitment to identifying emerging writers of recent eras and of many cultures.

How Authors Were Chosen for *CMTFCW*

The preliminary list of authors for *MTFCW* was sent to an advisory board of librarians, teaching professionals, and writers whose input resulted in informal inclusion criteria. In consultation with the editors, the list was narrowed to 700 authors for the concise edition plus criteria were established for adding authors. Criteria our editors used for adding authors not previously published in the last edition of *MTFCW* include:

- Authors who have won major awards
- Authors whose works are bestsellers
- Authors whose works are being incorporated into curricula and studied at the high school and/or college level

Broad Coverage in a Single Source

CMTFCW provides detailed biographical and bibliographical coverage of the most influential writers of our time, including:

- *Contemporary Literary Figures*: Mitch Albom, Sherman Alexie, Maya Angelou, Margaret Atwood, Dan Brown, Michael Chabon, J.M. Coetzee, Don DeLillo, Joan Didion, Dave Eggers, Gabriel Garcia Marquez, Nadine Gordimer, Khaled Hosseini, Toni Morrison, Joyce Carol Oates, Thomas Pynchon, J.K. Rowling, Salman Rushdie, Amy Tan, and John Updike, among many others.

- *Genre Writers*: Ray Bradbury, Tom Clancy, Philip K. Dick, Neil Gaiman, Sue Grafton, Dennis Lehane, Stephen King, Walter Mosley, Christopher Paolini, Anne Rice, Nora Roberts, Art Spiegelman, and Jane Yolen, among many others.

- *Novelists and Short Story Writers*: James Baldwin, Charles Baxter, Peter Carey, Carlos Fuentes, Graham Greene, Sebastian Junger, Sue Monk Kidd, John le Carré, Yann Martel, Rick Moody, Chuck Palahniuk, and Zadie Smith, among many others.

- *Dramatists*: Edward Albee, Samuel Beckett, Athol Fugard, Tony Kushner, David Mamet, Arthur Miller, Neil Simon, Tom Stoppard, Wendy Wasserstein, Alfred Uhry, Paula Vogel, and Tennessee Williams, among many others.

- *Poets*: Gwendolyn Brooks, Allen Ginsburg, Louise Glück, Jorie Graham, Seamus Heaney, Ted Kooser, Mary Oliver, Kenneth Rexroth, Adrienne Rich, Derek Walcott, and C.K. Williams, among many others.

How Entries Are Organized

Each *CMTFCW* biography begins with a series of rubrics that outlines the author's personal history, including information on the author's birth, death, family life, education, career, memberships, and awards. The *Writings* section lists a bibliography of the author's works along with the publisher and year published. The *Sidelights* section provides a biographical portrait of the author's development; information about the critical reception of the author's works; and revealing comments, often by the author, on personal interests, motivations, and thoughts on writing. The *Biographical/Critical Sources* section features a useful list of books, articles, and reviews about the author and his or her work. This section also includes citations for all material quoted in the *Sidelights* essay.

Other helpful sections include *Adaptations*, which lists the author's works that have been adapted by others into various media, including motion pictures, stage plays, and television or radio broadcasts, while the *Work in Progress* section lists titles or descriptions of works that are scheduled for publication by the author.

Using the Indexes

CMTFCW features a Nationality/Ethnicity index as well as a Subject/Genre index. More than sixty nations are represented in the Nationality/Ethnicity index, reflecting the international scope of this set and the multinational status of many authors. The Subject/Genre index covers over fifty genres and subject areas of fiction and nonfiction frequently referenced by educators and students, including social and political literature, environmental issues, and science fiction/science fantasy literature.

Citing *CMTFCW*

Students writing papers who wish to include references to information found in *CMTFCW* may cite sources in their bibliographies using the following format. Teachers adhering to other bibliographic formats may request that their students alter the citation below, which should only serve as a guide:

"Margaret Atwood." *Concise Major 21st-Century Writers.* Ed. Tracey L. Matthews. Detroit: Thomson Gale, 2006, pp. 214-223.

Comments Are Appreciated

CMTFCW is intended to serve as a useful reference tool for a wide audience, so your comments about this work are encouraged. Suggestions for authors to include in future editions of *CMTFCW* are also welcome. Send comments and suggestions to: *Concise Major 21st-Century Writers*, Thomson Gale, 27500 Drake Rd., Farmington Hills, MI 48331-3535; call at 1-248-699-4253; or fax at 1-248-699-8070.

Concise Major 21st-Century Writers Advisory Board

In preparation for the first edition of *Major 20th-Century Writers* (*MTCW*), the editors of *Contemporary Authors* conducted a telephone survey of librarians and mailed a survey to more than 4,000 libraries to help determine the kind of reference resource the libraries wanted. Once it was clear that a comprehensive, yet affordable source of information on twentieth-century writers was needed to serve small and medium-sized libraries, a wide range of resources was consulted: national surveys of books taught in American high schools and universities; British secondary school syllabi; reference works such as the *New York Library Desk Reference, Reading Lists for College-Bound Students: The Books Most Recommended by America's Top Colleges, The List of Books, E.D. Hirsch's Cultural Legacy*, and volumes in Thomson Gale's Literacy Criticism and Dictionary of Literary Biography series. From these resources and with advice of an international advisory board, the author list for the first edition of *MTCW* was finalized, the sketches edited, and the volume published.

For the eBook edition of *Major 21st-Century Writers* (*MTFCW*), the editors compiled a preliminary author list based largely upon a list of authors included in the second print edition of *MTCW* with recommendations based on new inclusion criteria. This list was sent to an advisory board of librarians, authors, and teaching professionals in both the United States and Britain. In addition to vetting the submitted list, the advisors suggested other noteworthy writers. Recommendations made by the advisors ensure that authors from all nations and genres are represented.

Concise Major 21st-Century Writers (*CMTFCW*) is an abridgement of the eBook-only edition of *MTFCW*. The editors built upon the work of past advisors of the eBook edition to create a concise version and added authors who have earned increased recognition since the publication of *MTFCW*. The advisory board for *MTFCW* played a major role in shaping the author list for *CMTFCW*, and the editors wish to thank them for sharing their expertise. The twenty-seven member advisory board includes the following individuals:

- **Carl Antonucci,** Director of Library Services, Capital Community College, Hartford, Connecticut
- **Barbara Bibel,** Reference Librarian, Oakland Public Library, Oakland, California
- **Beverly A. Buciak,** Librarian, Brother Rice High School, Chicago, Illinois
- **Mary Ann Capan,** District Library Media Specialist, Sherrard Jr. Sr. High School, Sherrard, Illinois
- **Linda Carvell,** Head Librarian, Lancaster Country Day School, Lancaster, Pennsylvania
- **Anne Christensen,** Librarian II, Phoenix Public Library, Phoenix, Arizona
- **Peggy Curran,** Adult Services Librarian, Naperville Public Library, Naperville, Illinois
- **Eva M. Davis,** Youth Services Manager, Ann Arbor District Library, Ann Arbor, Michigan
- **Thomas Eertmoed,** Librarian, Illinois Central College, East Peoria, Illinois
- **Lucy K. Gardner,** Director, Howard Community College, Columbia, Maryland

- **Christine C. Godin,** Director of Learning Resources, Northwest Vista College, San Antonio, Texas
- **Francisca Goldsmith,** Senior Librarian, Berkeley Public Library, Berkeley, California
- **Nancy Guidry,** Reference Librarian, Bakersfield College, Bakersfield, California
- **Jack Hicks,** Administrative Librarian, Deerfield Public Library, Deerfield, Illinois
- **Charlie Jones,** School Library Media Specialist, Plymouth High School Library Media Center, Canton, Michigan
- **Carol M. Keeler,** Upper School Media Specialist, Detroit Country Day School, Beverly Hills, Michigan
- **Georgia Lomax,** Managing Librarian, King County Library System, Covington, Washington
- **Mary Jane Marden,** Librarian, M.M. Bennett Library, St. Petersburg College, Pinellas Park, Florida
- **Frances Moffett,** Materials Selector, Fairfax County Public Library, Chantilly, Virginia
- **Ruth Mormon,** Upper School Librarian, The Meadows School, Las Vegas, Nevada
- **Bonnie Morris,** Upper School Media Specialist, Minnehaha Academy, Minneapolis, Minneapolis
- **Nancy Pinkston,** English Teacher, Sherrard Jr. Sr. High School, Sherrard, Illinois
- **Robert Reginald,** Head of Technical Services and Collection Development, California State University, San Bernadino, California
- **Janet P. Sarratt,** Library Media Specialist, John E. Ewing Middle School, Gaffney, South Carolina
- **Brian Stableford,** 0.5 Lecturer in Creative Writing, University College, Winchester (formerly King Alfred's College), Reading, England
- **Stephen Weiner,** Director, Maynard Public Library, Maynard, Massachusetts
- **Hope Yelich,** Reference Librarian, College of William and Mary, Williamsburg, Virginia

Concise Major 21st-Century Writers

VOLUME 1: A-Cl

Abbey, Edward 1927-1989

Abe, Kobo 1924-1993

Achebe, Chinua 1930-

Ackroyd, Peter 1949-

Adams, Alice 1926-1999

Adams, Douglas 1952-2001

Affabee, Eric
See Stine, R.L.

Aghill, Gordon
See Silverberg, Robert

Albee, Edward 1928-

Albom, Mitch 1958-

Aldiss, Brian W. 1925-

Aldrich, Ann
See Meaker, Marijane

Alegría, Claribel 1924-

Alexie, Sherman 1966-

Allan, John B.
See Westlake, Donald E.

Allen, Paula Gunn 1939-

Allen, Roland
See Ayckbourn, Alan

Allende, Isabel 1942-

Allison, Dorothy E. 1949-

Alvarez, A. 1929-

Alvarez, Julia 1950-

Amado, Jorge 1912-2001

Ambrose, Stephen E. 1936-2002

Amichai, Yehuda 1924-2000

Amis, Kingsley 1922-1995

Amis, Martin 1949-

Anand, Mulk Raj 1905-2004

Anaya, Rudolfo A. 1937-

Anderson, Laurie Halse 1961-

Anderson, Poul 1926-2001

Andrews, Elton V.
See Pohl, Frederik

Angelou, Maya 1928-

Anouilh, Jean 1910-1987

Anthony, Peter
See Shaffer, Peter

Anthony, Piers 1934-

Archer, Jeffrey 1940-

Archer, Lee
See Ellison, Harlan

Ard, William
See Jakes, John

Arenas, Reinaldo 1943-1990

Arias, Ron 1941-

Arnette, Robert
See Silverberg, Robert

Aronson, Marc 1948-

Ashbery, John 1927-

Ashbless, William
See Powers, Tim

Asimov, Isaac 1920-1992

Atwood, Margaret 1939-

Axton, David
See Koontz, Dean R.

Ayckbourn, Alan 1939-

Bachman, Richard
See King, Stephen

Bainbridge, Beryl 1934-

Baker, Nicholson 1957-

Baker, Russell 1925-

Baldacci, David 1960-

Baldwin, James 1924-1987

Ballard, J.G. 1930-

Bambara, Toni Cade 1939-1995

Banat, D.R.
See Bradbury, Ray

Banks, Iain M. 1954-

Banks, Russell 1940-

Baraka, Amiri 1934-

Barclay, Bill
See Moorcock, Michael

Barclay, William Ewert
See Moorcock, Michael

Barker, Clive 1952-

Barnes, Julian 1946-

Baron, David
See Pinter, Harold

Barrington, Michael
See Moorcock, Michael

Barthelme, Donald 1931-1989

Bashevis, Isaac
See Singer, Isaac Bashevis

Bass, Kingsley B., Jr.
See Bullins, Ed

Baxter, Charles 1947-

Beagle, Peter S. 1939-

Beattie, Ann 1947-

Beauvoir, Simone de 1908-1986

Beckett, Samuel 1906-1989

Beldone, Phil "Cheech"
See Ellison, Harlan

Bell, Madison Smartt 1957-

Bellow, Saul 1915-2005

Benchley, Peter 1940-2006

Benitez, Sandra 1941-

Berendt, John 1939-

Berger, Thomas 1924-

Berry, Jonas
See Ashbery, John

Berry, Wendell 1934-

Bethlen, T.D.
See Silverberg, Robert

Binchy, Maeve 1940-

Bird, Cordwainer
See Ellison, Harlan

Birdwell, Cleo
See DeLillo, Don

Blade, Alexander
See Silverberg, Robert

Blais, Marie-Claire 1939-

Bliss, Frederick
See Card, Orson Scott

Block, Francesca Lia 1962-

Bloom, Amy 1953-

Blount, Roy, Jr. 1941-

Blue, Zachary
See Stine, R.L.

Blume, Judy 1938-

Bly, Robert 1926-

Boland, Eavan 1944-

Böll, Heinrich 1917-1985

Boot, William
See Stoppard, Tom

Borges, Jorge Luis 1899-1986

Bowles, Paul 1910-1999

Box, Edgar
See Vidal, Gore

Boyle, Mark
See Kienzle, William X.

Boyle, T. Coraghessan 1948-

Brackett, Peter
See Collins, Max Allan

Bradbury, Edward P.
See Moorcock, Michael

Bradbury, Ray 1920-

Bradley, Marion Zimmer 1930-1999

Bragg, Rick 1959-

Brashares, Ann 1967-

Breslin, Jimmy 1930-

Brink, André 1935-

Brodsky, Iosif Alexandrovich 1940-1996

Brodsky, Joseph
See Brodsky, Iosif Alexandrovich

Brodsky, Yosif
See Brodsky, Iosif Alexandrovich

Brookner, Anita 1928-

Brooks, Cleanth 1906-1994

Brooks, Gwendolyn 1917-2000

Brooks, Terry 1944-

Brown, Dan 1964-

Brown, Dee Alexander 1908-2002

Brown, Rita Mae 1944-

Brown, Sterling Allen 1901-1989

Brownmiller, Susan 1935-

Bruchac, Joseph, III 1942-

Bryan, Michael
See Moore, Brian

Buckley, William F., Jr. 1925-

Buechner, Frederick 1926-

Bukowski, Charles 1920-1994

Bullins, Ed 1935-

Burke, Ralph
See Silverberg, Robert

Burns, Tex
See L'Amour, Louis

Busiek, Kurt

Bustos, F.
See Borges, Jorge Luis

Butler, Octavia E. 1947-2006

Butler, Robert Olen 1945-

Byatt, A.S. 1936-

Cabrera Infante, Guillermo 1929-2005

Cade, Toni
See Bambara, Toni Cade

Cain, G.
See Cabrera Infante, Guillermo

Caldwell, Erskine 1903-1987

Calisher, Hortense 1911-

Calvino, Italo 1923-1985

Camp, John 1944-

Campbell, Bebe Moore 1950-

Capote, Truman 1924-1984

Card, Orson Scott 1951-

Carey, Peter 1943-

Carroll, James P. 1943-

Carroll, Jonathan 1949-

Carruth, Hayden 1921-

Carter, Nick
See Smith, Martin Cruz

Carver, Raymond 1938-1988

Cavallo, Evelyn
See Spark, Muriel

Cela, Camilo José 1916-2002

Cela y Trulock, Camilo José
See Cela, Camilo José

Cesaire, Aimé 1913-

Chabon, Michael 1963-

Chang, Iris 1968-2004

Chapman, Lee
See Bradley, Marion Zimmer

Chapman, Walker
See Silverberg, Robert

Charby, Jay
See Ellison, Harlan

Chávez, Denise 1948-

Cheever, John 1912-1982

Chevalier, Tracy 1962-

Childress, Alice 1920-1994

Chomsky, Noam 1928-

Cisneros, Sandra 1954-

Cixous, Hélène 1937-

Clancy, Tom 1947-

Clark, Carol Higgins 1956-

Clark, Curt
See Westlake, Donald E.

Clark, John Pepper
See Clark Bekederemo, J.P.

Clark, Mary Higgins 1929-

Clark Bekederemo, J.P. 1935-

Clarke, Arthur C. 1917-

Clarke, Austin C. 1934-

Clavell, James 1925-1994

Cleary, Beverly 1916-

Clifton, Lucille 1936-

Clinton, Dirk
See Silverberg, Robert

Clowes, Daniel 1961-

VOLUME 2: Co-Gr

Codrescu, Andrei 1946-

Coe, Tucker
See Westlake, Donald E.

Coetzee, J.M. 1940-

Coffey, Brian
See Koontz, Dean R.

Coleman, Emmett
See Reed, Ishmael

Collins, Billy 1941-

Collins, Max Allan 1948-

Colvin, James
See Moorcock, Michael

Condé, Maryse 1937-

Connell, Evan S., Jr. 1924-

Conroy, Pat 1945-

Cook, Roy
See Silverberg, Robert

Cooper, J. California

Cooper, Susan 1935-

Coover, Robert 1932-

Cormier, Robert 1925-2000

Cornwell, Patricia 1956-

Corso, Gregory 1930-2001

Cortázar, Julio 1914-1984

Courtney, Robert
See Ellison, Harlan

Cox, William Trevor
See Trevor, William

Craig, A.A.
See Anderson, Poul

Creeley, Robert 1926-2005

Crews, Harry 1935-

Crichton, Michael 1942-

Crowley, John 1942-

Crutcher, Chris 1946-

Cruz, Victor Hernández 1949-

Culver, Timothy J.
See Westlake, Donald E.

Cunningham, E.V.
See Fast, Howard

Cunningham, J. Morgan
See Westlake, Donald E.

Cunningham, Michael 1952-

Curtis, Price
See Ellison, Harlan

Cussler, Clive 1931-

Cutrate, Joe
See Spiegelman, Art

Dahl, Roald 1916-1990

Dale, George E.
See Asimov, Isaac

Danticat, Edwidge 1969-

Danziger, Paula 1944-2004

Davies, Robertson 1913-1995

Davis, B. Lynch
See Borges, Jorge Luis

Deighton, Len 1929-

Delany, Samuel R. 1942-

DeLillo, Don 1936-

Demijohn, Thom
See Disch, Thomas M.

Denis, Julio
See Cortázar, Julio

Denmark, Harrison
See Zelazny, Roger

dePaola, Tomie 1934-

Derrida, Jacques 1930-

Desai, Anita 1937-

DeWitt, Helen 1957-

Dexter, Colin 1930-

Dexter, John
See Bradley, Marion Zimmer

Dexter, N.C.
See Dexter, Colin

Dexter, Pete 1943-

Diamond, Jared 1937-

Dick, Philip K. 1928-1982

Didion, Joan 1934-

Dillard, Annie 1945-

Disch, Thomas M. 1940-

Disch, Tom
See Disch, Thomas M.

Doctorow, E.L. 1931-

Domecq, H. Bustos
See Borges, Jorge Luis

Domini, Rey
See Lorde, Audre

Dorris, Michael 1945-1997

Douglas, Leonard
See Bradbury, Ray

Douglas, Michael
See Crichton, Michael

Dove, Rita 1952-

Doyle, John
See Graves, Robert

Doyle, Roddy 1958-

Dr. A.
See Asimov, Isaac

Dr. Seuss
See Geisel, Theodor Seuss

Drabble, Margaret 1939-

Drummond, Walter
See Silverberg, Robert

Druse, Eleanor
See King, Stephen

Dubus, Andre, III 1959-

Due, Linnea A. 1948-

Due, Tananarive 1966-

Duke, Raoul
See Thompson, Hunter S.

Duncan, Lois 1934-

Duncan, Robert 1919-1988

Dunn, Katherine 1945-

Durang, Christopher 1949-

Dworkin, Andrea 1946-2005

Dwyer, Deanna
See Koontz, Dean R.

Dwyer, K.R.
See Koontz, Dean R.

Eco, Umberto 1932-

Edelman, Marian Wright 1939-

Edmondson, Wallace
See Ellison, Harlan

Eggers, Dave 1971-

Ehrenreich, Barbara 1941-

Eisner, Will 1917-2005

Eliot, Dan
See Silverberg, Robert

Elkin, Stanley L. 1930-1995

Elliott, Don
See Silverberg, Robert

Elliott, William
See Bradbury, Ray

Ellis, Alice Thomas 1932-

Ellis, Bret Easton 1964-

Ellis, Landon
See Ellison, Harlan

Ellison, Harlan 1934-

Ellison, Ralph 1914-1994

Ellroy, James 1948-

Emecheta, Buchi 1944-

Endo, Shusaku 1923-1996

Enger, L.L.
See Enger, Leif

Enger, Leif 1961-

Epernay, Mark
See Galbraith, John Kenneth

Erdrich, Louise 1954-

Erickson, Steve 1950-

Erickson, Walter
See Fast, Howard

Ericson, Walter
See Fast, Howard

Ernaux, Annie 1940-

Erwin, Will
See Eisner, Will

Esquivel, Laura 1951-

Estleman, Loren D. 1952-

Eugenides, Jeffrey 1960-

Everett, Percival L. 1956-

Fadiman, Anne 1953-

Faludi, Susan 1959-

Farmer, Philip José 1918-

Fast, Howard 1914-2003

Ferlinghetti, Lawrence 1919-

Ferré, Rosario 1938-

Fielding, Helen 1958-

Fitch, John, IV
See Cormier, Robert

Fitzgerald, Penelope 1916-2000

Fleur, Paul
See Pohl, Frederik

Flooglebuckle, Al
See Spiegelman, Art

Fo, Dario 1926-

Foer, Jonathan Safran 1977-

Foote, Horton 1916-

Foote, Shelby 1916-2005

Forché, Carolyn 1950-

Ford, Michael Thomas 1969-

Ford, Richard 1944-

Forsyth, Frederick 1938-

Fowler, Karen Joy 1950-

Fowles, John 1926-2005

Francis, Dick 1920-

Franzen, Jonathan 1959-

Fraser, Antonia 1932-

Frayn, Michael 1933-

Frazier, Charles 1950-

French, Marilyn 1929-

French, Paul
See Asimov, Isaac

Frey, James 1969-

Friedan, Betty 1921-2006

Friedman, Thomas L. 1953-

Frisch, Max 1911-1991

Fry, Christopher 1907-

Fuentes, Carlos 1928-

Fugard, Athol 1932-

Fundi
See Baraka, Amiri

Gaddis, William 1922-1998

Gaiman, Neil 1960-

Gaines, Ernest J. 1933-

Galbraith, John Kenneth 1908-

Gallant, Mavis 1922-

Garcia, Cristina 1958-

Garcia Marquez, Gabriel 1928-

Gardner, John 1933-1982

Gardner, Miriam
See Bradley, Marion Zimmer

Gardons, S.S.
See Snodgrass, W.D.

Garner, Alan 1934-

Gass, William H. 1924-

Gates, Henry Louis, Jr. 1950-

Gee, Maggie 1948-

Geisel, Theodor Seuss 1904-1991

Genet, Jean 1910-1986

Gibbons, Kaye 1960-

Gibson, William 1948-

Gibson, William2 1914-

Gilchrist, Ellen 1935-

Ginsberg, Allen 1926-1997

Ginzburg, Natalia 1916-1991

Giovanni, Nikki 1943-

Glück, Louise 1943-

Godwin, Gail 1937-

Golden, Arthur 1956-

Golding, William 1911-1993

Goodkind, Terry 1948-

Gordimer, Nadine 1923-

Goryan, Sirak
See Saroyan, William

Gottesman, S.D.
See Pohl, Frederik

Gould, Stephen Jay 1941-2002

Goytisolo, Juan 1931-

Grafton, Sue 1940-

Graham, Jorie 1950-

Grant, Skeeter
See Spiegelman, Art

Grass, Günter 1927-

Graves, Robert 1895-1985

Graves, Valerie
See Bradley, Marion Zimmer

Gray, Alasdair 1934-

Gray, Francine du Plessix 1930-

Gray, Spalding 1941-2004

Greeley, Andrew M. 1928-

Green, Brian
See Card, Orson Scott

Greene, Graham 1904-1991

Greer, Richard
See Silverberg, Robert

Gregor, Lee
See Pohl, Frederik

Grisham, John 1955-

Grumbach, Doris 1918-

VOLUME 3: Gu-Ma

Guest, Judith 1936-

Gump, P.Q.
See Card, Orson Scott

Guterson, David 1956-

Haddon, Mark 1962-

Hailey, Arthur 1920-2004

Halberstam, David 1934-

Hall, Donald 1928-

Hall, Radclyffe 1886-1943

Hamilton, Franklin
See Silverberg, Robert

Hamilton, Jane 1957-

Hamilton, Mollie
See Kaye, M.M.

Hamilton, Virginia 1936-2002

Handke, Peter 1942-

Hardwick, Elizabeth 1916-

Hargrave, Leonie
See Disch, Thomas M.

Harjo, Joy 1951-

Harris, E. Lynn 1957-

Harris, Robert 1957-

Harris, Thomas 1940-

Harson, Sley
See Ellison, Harlan

Hart, Ellis
See Ellison, Harlan

Harvey, Jack
See Rankin, Ian

Hass, Robert 1941-

Havel, Vaclav 1936-

Hawkes, John 1925-1998

Hawking, S.W.
See Hawking, Stephen W.

Hawking, Stephen W. 1942-

Haycraft, Anna
See Ellis, Alice Thomas

Hayes, Al
See Grisham, John

Hazzard, Shirley 1931-

Head, Bessie 1937-1986

Heaney, Seamus 1939-

Hébert, Anne 1916-2000

Hegi, Ursula 1946-

Heinlein, Robert A. 1907-1988

Heller, Joseph 1923-1999

Hellman, Lillian 1906-1984

Helprin, Mark 1947-

Hempel, Amy 1951-

Henley, Beth 1952-

Herbert, Frank 1920-1986

Hersey, John 1914-1993

Hiaasen, Carl 1953-

Highsmith, Patricia 1921-1995

Hijuelos, Oscar 1951-

Hill, John
See Koontz, Dean R.

Hillenbrand, Laura 1967-

Hillerman, Tony 1925-

Hinojosa, Rolando 1929-

Hinton, S.E. 1950-

Hoban, Russell 1925-

Hochhuth, Rolf 1931-

Høeg, Peter 1957-

Hoffman, Alice 1952-

Hollander, Paul
See Silverberg, Robert

Homes, A.M. 1961-

hooks, bell 1952-

Hosseini, Khaled 1965-

Houellebecq, Michel 1958-

Houston, Jeanne Wakatsuki 1934-

Howard, Maureen 1930-

Howard, Warren F.
See Pohl, Frederik

Hoyle, Fred 1915-2001

Hubbell, Sue 1935-

Hudson, Jeffrey
See Crichton, Michael

Hughes, Ted 1930-1998

Humes, Edward

Hwang, David Henry 1957-

Ionesco, Eugene 1912-1994

Irving, John 1942-

Isaacs, Susan 1943-

Isherwood, Christopher 1904-1986

Ishiguro, Kazuo 1954-

Ives, Morgan
See Bradley, Marion Zimmer

Jakes, John 1932-

James, Mary
See Meaker, Marijane

James, P.D. 1920-

James, Philip
See Moorcock, Michael

Janowitz, Tama 1957-

Jarvis, E.K.
See Ellison, Harlan

Jarvis, E.K.2
See Silverberg, Robert

Jenkins, Jerry B. 1949-

Jhabvala, Ruth Prawer 1927-

Jiang, Ji-li 1954-

Jimenez, Francisco 1943-

Jin, Ha 1956-

Johnson, Adam 1967-

Johnson, Angela 1961-

Johnson, Charles 1948-

Jones, Diana Wynne 1934-

Jones, Edward P. 1950-

Jones, Gayl 1949-

Jones, LeRoi
See Baraka, Amiri

Jong, Erica 1942-

Jorgensen, Ivar
See Ellison, Harlan

Jorgenson, Ivar2
See Silverberg, Robert

Judd, Cyril
See Pohl, Frederik

Junger, Sebastian 1962-

Karageorge, Michael A.
See Anderson, Poul

Karr, Mary 1955-

Kastel, Warren
See Silverberg, Robert

Kaufman, Moises 1963-

Kavanagh, Dan
See Barnes, Julian

Kaye, M.M. 1908-2004

Kaye, Mollie
See Kaye, M.M.

Keillor, Garrison 1942-

Kelly, Lauren
See Oates, Joyce Carol

Keneally, Thomas 1935-

Kennedy, William 1928-

Kennilworthy Whisp
See Rowling, J.K.

Kerr, M.E.
See Meater, Marijane

Kerry, Lois
See Duncan, Lois

Kesey, Ken 1935-2001

Keyes, Daniel 1927-

Kidd, Sue Monk

Kienzle, William X. 1928-2001

Kincaid, Jamaica 1949-

King, Stephen 1947-

King, Steve
See King, Stephen

Kingsolver, Barbara 1955-

Kingston, Maxine Hong 1940-

Kinnell, Galway 1927-

Kinsella, Thomas 1928-

Kinsella, W.P. 1935-

Kizer, Carolyn 1925-

Knight, Etheridge 1931-1991

Knowles, John 1926-2001

Knox, Calvin M.
See Silverberg, Robert

Knye, Cassandra
See Disch, Thomas M.

Koch, Kenneth 1925-2002

Kogawa, Joy 1935-

Kolb, Edward W. 1951-

Kolb, Rocky
See Kolb, Edward W.

Koontz, Dean R. 1945-

Kooser, Ted 1939-

Kosinski, Jerzy 1933-1991

Kozol, Jonathan 1936-

Krakauer, Jon 1954-

Kumin, Maxine 1925-

Kundera, Milan 1929-

Kunitz, Stanley 1905-

Kushner, Tony 1956-

L'Amour, Louis 1908-1988

L'Engle, Madeleine 1918-

La Guma, Alex 1925-1985

Lahiri, Jhumpa 1967-

Lamb, Wally 1950-

Lange, John
See Crichton, Michael

Laredo, Betty
See Codrescu, Andrei

Laurence, Margaret 1926-1987

Lavond, Paul Dennis
See Pohl, Frederik

Leavitt, David 1961-

le Carré, John 1931-

Lee, Don L.
See Madhubuti, Haki R.

Lee, Harper 1926-

Lee, Stan 1922-

Le Guin, Ursula K. 1929-

Lehane, Dennis 1965-

Leonard, Elmore 1925-

LeSieg, Theo.
See Geisel, Theodor Seuss

Lessing, Doris 1919-

Lester, Julius 1939-

Lethem, Jonathan 1964-

Levi, Primo 1919-1987

Levin, Ira 1929-

Levon, O.U.
See Kesey, Ken

Leyner, Mark 1956-

Lindbergh, Anne Morrow 1906-2001

Lively, Penelope 1933-

Lodge, David 1935-

Logan, Jake
See Smith, Martin Cruz

Long, David 1948-

Loos, Anita 1893-1981

Lorde, Audre 1934-1992

Louise, Heidi
See Erdrich, Louise

Lowry, Lois 1937-

Lucas, Craig 1951-

Ludlum, Robert 1927-2001

Lynch, B. Suarez
See Borges, Jorge Luis

M.T.F.
See Porter, Katherine Anne

Macdonald, Anson
See Heinlein, Robert A.

MacDonald, John D. 1916-1986

Mackay, Shena 1944-

MacKinnon, Catharine A. 1946-

MacLeish, Archibald 1892-1982

MacLeod, Alistair 1936-

Maddern, Al
See Ellison, Harlan

Madhubuti, Haki R.

Maguire, Gregory 1954-

Mahfouz, Naguib 1911-

Mailer, Norman 1923-

Makine, Andreï 1957-

Malabaila, Damiano
See Levi, Primo

Malamud, Bernard 1914-1986

Malcolm, Dan
See Silverberg, Robert

Malouf, David 1934-

Mamet, David 1947-

Mara, Bernard
See Moore, Brian

Marchbanks, Samuel
See Davies, Robertson

Marías, Javier 1951-

Mariner, Scott
See Pohl, Frederik

Markandaya, Kamala 1924-2004

Markham, Robert
See Amis, Kingsley

Marshall, Allen
See Westlake, Donald E.

Marshall, Paule 1929-

Martel, Yann 1963-

Martin, Webber
See Silverberg, Robert

Mason, Bobbie Ann 1940-

Mason, Ernst
See Pohl, Frederik

Mass, William
See Gibson, William2

Massie, Robert K. 1929-

Mathabane, Mark 1960-

Matthiessen, Peter 1927-

Maupin, Armistead 1944-

Mayo, Jim
See L'Amour, Louis

VOLUME 4: Mc-Sa

McBride, James 1957-

McCaffrey, Anne 1926-

McCall Smith, Alexander 1948-

McCann, Edson
See Pohl, Frederik

McCarthy, Cormac 1933-

McCourt, Frank 1930-

McCreigh, James
See Pohl, Frederik

McCullough, Colleen 1937-

McCullough, David 1933-

McDermott, Alice 1953-

McEwan, Ian 1948-

McGuane, Thomas 1939-

McInerney, Jay 1955-

McKie, Robin

McKinley, Robin 1952-

McLandress, Herschel
See Galbraith, John Kenneth

McMillan, Terry 1951-

McMurtry, Larry 1936-

McNally, Terrence 1939-

McPhee, John 1931-

McPherson, James Alan 1943-

Meaker, M.J.
See Meaker, Marijane

Meaker, Marijane 1927-

Mehta, Ved 1934-

Members, Mark
See Powell, Anthony

Méndez, Miguel 1930-

Merchant, Paul
See Ellison, Harlan

Merrill, James 1926-1995

Merriman, Alex
See Silverberg, Robert

Merwin, W.S. 1927-

Michener, James A. 1907-1997

Miéville, China 1973-

Miller, Arthur 1915-

Millett, Kate 1934-

Millhauser, Steven 1943-

Milosz, Czeslaw 1911-2004

Min, Anchee 1957-

Mitchell, Clyde
See Ellison, Harlan

Mitchell, Clyde2
See Silverberg, Robert

Momaday, N. Scott 1934-

Monroe, Lyle
See Heinlein, Robert A.

Moody, Anne 1940-

Moody, Rick 1961-

Moorcock, Michael 1939-

Moore, Alan 1953-

Moore, Brian 1921-1999

Moore, Lorrie
See Moore, Marie Lorena

Moore, Marie Lorena 1957-

Mora, Pat 1942-

Morgan, Claire
See Highsmith, Patricia

Mori, Kyoko 1957-

Morris, Mary McGarry 1943-

Morrison, Chloe Anthony Wofford
See Morrison, Toni

Morrison, Toni 1931-

Morrow, James 1947-

Mortimer, John 1923-

Mosley, Walter 1952-

Motion, Andrew 1952-

Mowat, Farley 1921-

Mukherjee, Bharati 1940-

Munro, Alice 1931-

Murdoch, Iris 1919-1999

Murray, Albert L. 1916-

Myers, Walter Dean 1937-

Myers, Walter M.
See Myers, Walter Dean

Nafisi, Azar 1950-

Naipaul, Shiva 1945-1985

Naipaul, V.S. 1932-

Narayan, R.K. 1906-2001

Naylor, Gloria 1950-

Nemerov, Howard 1920-1991

Newt Scamander
See Rowling, J.K.

Ngugi, James T.
See Ngugi wa Thiong'o

Ngugi wa Thiong'o 1938-

Nichols, John 1940-

Nichols, Leigh
See Koontz, Dean R.

North, Anthony
See Koontz, Dean R.

North, Milou
See Dorris, Michael

North, Milou2
See Erdrich, Louise

Nosille, Nabrah
See Ellison, Harlan

Novak, Joseph
See Kosinski, Jerzy

Nye, Naomi Shihab 1952-

O'Brian, E.G.
See Clarke, Arthur C.

O'Brian, Patrick 1914-2000

O'Brien, Edna 1932-

O'Brien, Tim 1946-

O'Casey, Brenda
See Ellis, Alice Thomas

O'Faolain, Sean 1900-1991

O'Flaherty, Liam 1896-1984

Oates, Joyce Carol 1938-

Oates, Stephen B. 1936-

Oe, Kenzaburo 1935-

Okri, Ben 1959-

Olds, Sharon 1942-

Oliver, Mary 1935-

Olsen, Tillie 1912-

Ondaatje, Michael 1943-

Osborne, David
See Silverberg, Robert

Osborne, George
See Silverberg, Robert

Osborne, John 1929-1994

Oz, Amos 1939-

Ozick, Cynthia 1928-

Packer, Vin
See Meaker, Marijane

Paglia, Camille 1947-

Paige, Richard
See Koontz, Dean R.

Pakenham, Antonia
See Fraser, Antonia

Palahniuk, Chuck 1962-

Paley, Grace 1922-

Paolini, Christopher 1983-

Parfenie, Marie
See Codrescu, Andrei

Park, Jordan
See Pohl, Frederik

Parker, Bert
See Ellison, Harlan

Parker, Robert B. 1932-

Parks, Gordon 1912-2006

Pasternak, Boris 1890-1960

Patchett, Ann 1963-

Paton, Alan 1903-1988

Patterson, James 1947-

Payne, Alan
See Jakes, John

Paz, Octavio 1914-1998

Peretti, Frank E. 1951-

Petroski, Henry 1942-

Phillips, Caryl 1958-

Phillips, Jayne Anne 1952-

Phillips, Richard
See Dick, Philip K.

Picoult, Jodi 1966-

Piercy, Marge 1936-

Piers, Robert
See Anthony, Piers

Pinsky, Robert 1940-

Pinta, Harold
See Pinter, Harold

Pinter, Harold 1930-

Plimpton, George 1927-2003

Pohl, Frederik 1919-

Porter, Katherine Anne 1890-1980

Potok, Chaim 1929-2002

Powell, Anthony 1905-2000

Powers, Richard 1957-

Powers, Tim 1952-

Pratchett, Terry 1948-

Price, Reynolds 1933-

Prose, Francine 1947-

Proulx, E. Annie 1935-

Puig, Manuel 1932-1990

Pullman, Philip 1946-

Pygge, Edward
See Barnes, Julian

Pynchon, Thomas, Jr. 1937-

Quindlen, Anna 1953-

Quinn, Simon
See Smith, Martin Cruz

Rampling, Anne
See Rice, Anne

Rand, Ayn 1905-1982

Randall, Robert
See Silverberg, Robert

Rankin, Ian 1960-

Rao, Raja 1909-

Ravenna, Michael
See Welty, Eudora

Reed, Ishmael 1938-

Reid, Desmond
See Moorcock, Michael

Rendell, Ruth 1930-

Rensie, Willis
See Eisner, Will

Rexroth, Kenneth 1905-1982

Rice, Anne 1941-

Rich, Adrienne 1929-

Rich, Barbara
See Graves, Robert

Richler, Mordecai 1931-2001

Ríos, Alberto 1952-

Rivers, Elfrida
See Bradley, Marion Zimmer

Riverside, John
See Heinlein, Robert A.

Robb, J.D.
See Roberts, Nora

Robbe-Grillet, Alain 1922-

Robbins, Tom 1936-

Roberts, Nora 1950-

Robertson, Ellis
See Ellison, Harlan

Robertson, Ellis2
See Silverberg, Robert

Robinson, Kim Stanley 1952-

Robinson, Lloyd
See Silverberg, Robert

Robinson, Marilynne 1944-

Rodman, Eric
See Silverberg, Robert

Rodríguez, Luis J. 1954-

Rodriguez, Richard 1944-

Roquelaure, A.N.
See Rice, Anne

Roth, Henry 1906-1995

Roth, Philip 1933-

Rowling, J.K. 1965-

Roy, Arundhati 1960-

Rule, Ann 1935-

Rushdie, Salman 1947-

Russo, Richard 1949-

Rybczynski, Witold 1943-

Ryder, Jonathan
See Ludlum, Robert

Sábato, Ernesto 1911-

Sacco, Joe 1960-

Sacks, Oliver 1933-

Sagan, Carl 1934-1996

Salinger, J.D. 1919-

Salzman, Mark 1959-

Sanchez, Sonia 1934-

Sanders, Noah
See Blount, Roy, Jr.

Sanders, Winston P.
See Anderson, Poul

Sandford, John
See Camp, John

Saroyan, William 1908-1981

Sarton, May 1912-1995

Sartre, Jean-Paul 1905-1980

Satterfield, Charles
See Pohl, Frederik

Saunders, Caleb
See Heinlein, Robert A.

VOLUME 5: Sc-Z

Schaeffer, Susan Fromberg 1941-

Schulz, Charles M. 1922-2000

Schwartz, Lynne Sharon 1939-

Scotland, Jay
See Jakes, John

Sebastian, Lee
See Silverberg, Robert

Sebold, Alice 1963-

Sedaris, David 1957-

Sendak, Maurice 1928-

Seth, Vikram 1952-

Shaara, Jeff 1952-

Shaara, Michael 1929-1988

Shackleton, C.C.
See Aldiss, Brian W.

Shaffer, Peter 1926-

Shange, Ntozake 1948-

Shapiro, Karl Jay 1913-2000

Shepard, Sam 1943-

Shepherd, Michael
See Ludlum, Robert

Shields, Carol 1935-2003

Shreve, Anita 1946-

Siddons, Anne Rivers 1936-

Silko, Leslie 1948-

Sillitoe, Alan 1928-

Silverberg, Robert 1935-

Silverstein, Shel 1932-1999

Simic, Charles 1938-

Simon, David 1960-

Simon, Neil 1927-

Simpson, Louis 1923-

Singer, Isaac
See Singer, Isaac Bashevis

Singer, Isaac Bashevis 1904-1991

Škvorecký, Josef 1924-

Smiley, Jane 1949-

Smith, Martin
See Smith, Martin Cruz

Smith, Martin Cruz 1942-

Smith, Rosamond
See Oates, Joyce Carol

Smith, Wilbur 1933-

Smith, Zadie 1976-

Snicket, Lemony 1970-

Snodgrass, W.D. 1926-

Snyder, Gary 1930-

Solo, Jay
See Ellison, Harlan

Solwoska, Mara
See French, Marilyn

Solzhenitsyn, Aleksandr I. 1918-

Somers, Jane
See Lessing, Doris

Sontag, Susan 1933-2004

Soto, Gary 1952-

Soyinka, Wole 1934-

Spark, Muriel 1918-

Sparks, Nicholas 1965-

Spaulding, Douglas
See Bradbury, Ray

Spaulding, Leonard
See Bradbury, Ray

Spencer, Leonard G.
See Silverberg, Robert

Spender, Stephen 1909-1995

Spiegelman, Art 1948-

Spillane, Mickey 1918-

Stack, Andy
See Rule, Ann

Stacy, Donald
See Pohl, Frederik

Stancykowna
See Szymborska, Wislawa

Stark, Richard
See Westlake, Donald E.

Steel, Danielle 1947-

Steig, William 1907-

Steinem, Gloria 1934-

Steiner, George 1929-

Steiner, K. Leslie
See Delany, Samuel R.

Stephenson, Neal 1959-

Sterling, Brett
See Bradbury, Ray

Sterling, Bruce 1954-

Stine, Jovial Bob
See Stine, R.L.

Stine, R.L. 1943-

Stone, Robert 1937-

Stone, Rosetta
See Geisel, Theodor Seuss

Stoppard, Tom 1937-

Straub, Peter 1943-

Styron, William 1925-

Swenson, May 1919-1989

Swift, Graham 1949-

Swithen, John
See King, Stephen

Symmes, Robert
See Duncan, Robert

Syruc, J.
See Milosz, Czeslaw

Szymborska, Wislawa 1923-

Talent Family, The
See Sedaris, David

Talese, Gay 1932-

Tan, Amy 1952-

Tanner, William
See Amis, Kingsley

Tartt, Donna 1964-

Taylor, Mildred D. 1943-

Tenneshaw, S.M.
See Silverberg, Robert

Terkel, Studs 1912-

Theroux, Paul 1941-

Thomas, D.M. 1935-

Thomas, Joyce Carol 1938-

Thompson, Hunter S. 1937-2005

Thornton, Hall
See Silverberg, Robert

Tiger, Derry
See Ellison, Harlan

Tornimparte, Alessandra
See Ginzburg, Natalia

Tremblay, Michel 1942-

Trevor, William 1928-

Trillin, Calvin 1935-

Trout, Kilgore
See Farmer, Philip José

Turow, Scott 1949-

Tyler, Anne 1941-

Tyree, Omar

Uchida, Yoshiko 1921-1992

Uhry, Alfred 1936-

Uncle Shelby
See Silverstein, Shel

Updike, John 1932-

Urban Griot
See Tyree, Omar

Uris, Leon 1924-2003

Urmuz
See Codrescu, Andrei

Vance, Gerald
See Silverberg, Robert

Van Duyn, Mona 1921-2004

Vargas Llosa, Mario 1936-

Verdu, Matilde
See Cela, Camilo José

Vidal, Gore 1925-

Vile, Curt
See Moore, Alan

Vine, Barbara
See Rendell, Ruth

Vizenor, Gerald Robert 1934-

Vogel, Paula A. 1951-

Voigt, Cynthia 1942-

Vollmann, William T. 1959-

Vonnegut, Kurt, Jr. 1922-

Vosce, Trudie
See Ozick, Cynthia

Wakoski, Diane 1937-

Walcott, Derek 1930-

Walker, Alice 1944-

Walker, Margaret 1915-1998

Wallace, David Foster 1962-

Walley, Byron
See Card, Orson Scott

Ware, Chris 1967-

Warren, Robert Penn 1905-1989

Warshofsky, Isaac
See Singer, Isaac Bashevis

Wasserstein, Wendy 1950-2006

Watson, James D. 1928-

Watson, John H.
See Farmer, Philip José

Watson, Larry 1947-

Watson, Richard F.
See Silverberg, Robert

Ways, C.R.
See Blount, Roy, Jr.

Weldon, Fay 1931-

Wells, Rebecca

Welty, Eudora 1909-2001

West, Edwin
See Westlake, Donald E.

West, Owen
See Koontz, Dean R.

West, Paul 1930-

Westlake, Donald E. 1933-

White, Edmund 1940-

Wideman, John Edgar 1941-

Wiesel, Elie 1928-

Wilbur, Richard 1921-

Williams, C.K. 1936-

Williams, Juan 1954-

Williams, Tennessee 1911-1983

Willis, Charles G.
See Clarke, Arthur C.

Wilson, August 1945-2005

Wilson, Dirk
See Pohl, Frederik

Wilson, Edward O. 1929-

Winterson, Jeanette 1959-

Wolf, Naomi 1962-

Wolfe, Gene 1931-

Wolfe, Tom 1931-

Wolff, Tobias 1945-

Woodiwiss, Kathleen E. 1939-

Woodson, Jacqueline 1964-

Wouk, Herman 1915-

Wright, Charles 1935-

Wright, Judith 1915-2000

Xingjian, Gao 1940-

Yolen, Jane 1939-

York, Simon
See Heinlein, Robert A.

Zelazny, Roger 1937-1995

Zindel, Paul 1936-2003

Sc

SCHAEFFER, Susan Fromberg 1941-

PERSONAL: Born March 25, 1941, in Brooklyn, NY; daughter of Irving (a clothing manufacturer) and Edith (Levine) Fromberg; married Neil Jerome Schaeffer (a college English professor), October 11, 1970; children: Benjamin Adam, May Anna. *Education:* Attended Simmons College; University of Chicago, B.A., 1961, M.A. (with honors), 1963, Ph.D. (with honors), 1966. *Religion:* Jewish.

ADDRESSES: *Office*—Department of English, Brooklyn College of the City University of New York, Brooklyn, NY 11210. *Agent*—Timothy Seldes, Russell & Volkening, Inc., 50 West 29th St., New York, NY 10001.

CAREER: Novelist and poet. Wright Junior College, Chicago, IL, instructor in English, 1963-64; Illinois Institute of Technology, Chicago, assistant professor of English, 1964-67; Brooklyn College of the City University of New York, Brooklyn, NY, assistant professor, 1967-73, associate professor, 1973-75, professor of English, 1975—, Broeklundian Professor of English, 1985—. Guest lecturer at University of Chicago, Cornell University, University of Arizona, and University of Maine. Has given readings of work at Yale University, University of Massachusetts, University of Texas, University of Houston, and other universities.

MEMBER: Modern Language Association of America, PEN, Authors Guild, Authors League of America, Poetry Society of America.

AWARDS, HONORS: Edward Lewis Wallant Award, 1974, and Friends of Literature Award, both for *Anya;* National Book Award nomination, 1974, for *Granite Lady;* O. Henry Award, 1977, for "The Exact Nature of the Plot"; Lawrence Award, *Prairie Schooner,* 1984; Guggenheim fellowship, 1984-85; *Centennial Review* award for poetry, 1985.

WRITINGS:

The Witch and the Weather Report (poetry), Seven Woods Press, 1972.

Falling (novel), Macmillan (New York, NY), 1973.

Anya (novel), Macmillan (New York, NY), 1974.

Granite Lady (poetry), Macmillan (New York, NY), 1974.

The Rhymes and Runes of the Toad (poetry), Macmillan (New York, NY), 1975.

Alphabet for the Lost Years (poetry), Gallimaufry, 1976.

The Red, White, and Blue Poem, Ally Press, 1977.

Time in Its Flight (novel), Doubleday (New York, NY), 1978.

The Bible of the Beasts of the Little Field (poetry), Dutton (New York, NY), 1980.

The Queen of Egypt (short fiction), Dutton (New York, NY), 1980.

Love (novel), Dutton (New York, NY), 1980.

The Madness of a Seduced Woman (novel), Dutton (New York, NY), 1983.

Mainland (novel), Linden Press, 1985.

The Dragons of North Chittendon (children's novel), Simon & Schuster (New York, NY), 1986.

The Injured Party (novel), St. Martin's Press (New York, NY), 1986.

Buffalo Afternoon (novel), Knopf (New York, NY), 1989.

First Nights (novel), Knopf (New York, NY), 1993.

The Golden Rope (novel), Knopf (New York, NY), 1996.

The Autobiography of Foudini M. Cat, Knopf (New York, NY), 1997.
The Snow Fox (novel), Norton (New York, NY), 2004.

Contributor of critical articles to numerous periodicals, including *Centennial Review, Modern Fiction Studies, Great Ideas Today, London Review of Books,* and *New York Times.*

ADAPTATIONS: The film rights to *The Madness of a Seduced Woman* have been purchased.

SIDELIGHTS: Although highly respected for both her poetry and shorter pieces of fiction, Susan Fromberg Schaeffer is perhaps more widely known for her novels. As Elizabeth Ward observed in the *Washington Post Book World,* Schaeffer is "a born storyteller, with a rare ability to transport the reader bodily into her various fictional worlds, all criticism suspended. [She has a] genuinely original voice, at once light, versatile, stylish and informed by a sharp eye and ear for the life-giving detail." Sybil S. Steinberg added in *Publishers Weekly* that reading Schaeffer's novels "is rather like falling into a time warp and experiencing events through total immersion in the mind of the protagonist. So carefully does she build character, so meticulously does she convey details of time and place and social mores that one wonders with each new novel if the author is writing autobiography in the guise of fiction."

Schaeffer's first novel, *Falling,* was very well received by critics, and its author was hailed as a novelist with much promise. In *Falling* the reader watches a young Jewish graduate student, Elizabeth Kamen, as she slowly rises from a near-suicidal existence to a hopeful future; a *Time* reviewer called *Falling* "the blunt but quietly humorous story of a New York girl who lifts herself out of depression by her own pantyhose." Wayne C. Booth stated in the *New York Times Book Review:* "I love this novel—first reading, second reading, browsing. . . . [Elizabeth's] journey is not only convincing, it is for the most part very funny. I can't think of any other treatment of 'the way those young people live now' that has made me laugh so much." And Pearl K. Bell wrote in the *New Leader* that Schaeffer "is a writer of uncommon talent and honesty blessed with a natural command of humor and perception, and she has crafted one of the most engaging and genuinely funny books I've read in years. . . . *Falling* is at once poignant, hilarious and luminous."

In *Falling,* as in many of her subsequent works, Schaeffer effectively and dramatically uses the narrative voice to draw the reader deeper into the plot. As Cynthia MacDonald explained in a review for the *Washington Post Book World:* Schaeffer "is a fine storyteller. You care about her characters and want to know what is going to happen next. . . . Description functions as a part of character so it is never extraneous, never like those paste wedding cake decorations, something to remove before eating." In his review of *Falling* Booth remarked that the reader remains "engaged with remarkable intensity in this young woman's fight for a life of her own; somehow . . . the very possibility of life in such a world seems at stake. As we catch through her eyes occasional images of beauty and mystery, images that transform the intellectual deciphering into promises of meaning, we come to care very much about whether this sharp-eyed lost woman can find a way to live without self-deception, in acceptance of all that has been done against her and all that she has done to destroy herself."

Schaeffer's second novel, *Anya,* explores the plight of a Jewish woman trying to survive in a turbulent era. The book begins in the 1930s and takes Anya through the Nazi massacre of Jews in Poland up to the present day in America. As such, maintained Judith Thurman in a review for *Ms., Anya* "is one of the few 'Holocaust' novels to begin long enough before the war to give us a full, material sense of what was lost." D.A. Parente similarly believed *Anya* is unique because it transforms the "reader into a totally involved participant." In a *Best Sellers* review Parente wrote: "Anya, the narrator, becomes of course our most intimate acquaintance and those to whom she is the closest . . . are portrayed in depth. . . . This novel is a thoroughly worthwhile experience on all levels—moral, psychological, social, historical, and artistic. . . . It is perhaps, however, the final tribute to Mrs. Schaeffer's artistry that she has created a life experience so realistic and convincing that we can only believe at the end that it is a reproduction of a historical life."

In the *Washington Post Book World,* Mary Richie similarly commented that in *Anya,* "A writer of remarkable power . . . has taken on the biggest moral questions, made us see the Holocaust anew as if we had never heard of it." Continued the critic: "*Anya* unfolds before us like a superb film, so detailed it seems many minds and hands must have gone into decorating the set, clothing the performers, and detailing the dialogue. It is like a *makimono,* those narrative scrolls to be unrolled slowly from one ivory cylinder to another so that the panoramic story is experienced image by image, as it was envisioned. It is a vision, set down by a fearless, patient poet, a fabulist who knows that whatever is created never dies, that it is truly good to see and tell."

Just as with *Falling,* many reviewers have credited Schaeffer's powerful characterization aided by the use of a convincing narrative voice for making *Anya* especially moving. Thurman believed that "the compelling horror of the [Holocaust] does not distract us from the real business of the book—of any fiction—to create an awareness of character which grows, changes, and deepens. *Anya*'s power as a novel is its extraordinary specificity. Its focus is the woman herself—who she was, what happened to her, and because of that, what she became." Thurman commented further: "I have read few books that are more tangible. The reality is solid—it bears the full weight of one's trust. The story is told in the first person, with a depth of vision that seems to be memory, that imitates memory, but is really something much less passive and more interesting: an author in possession of someone she has fully imagined."

Another of Schaeffer's historical novels, *Time in Its Flight,* is a family saga set in nineteenth-century New England that covers several generations over more than a hundred years. As Clifton Fadiman wrote in the *Book-of-the-Month Club News* magazine, in *Time in Its Flight* "Schaeffer contrives to turn time backward in its flight, to give us the feeling, the shape of a whole stubborn Yankee rural culture. This she manages not merely through vivid details of manners and dress, but by an extraordinary photographic genius. These are real voices, dozens of them, using the idiom of their time and place, but always colored by a precise notation of individuality. In a way we do not read this book. We hear it, or overhear it."

Webster Schott, however, remarked in the *New York Times Book Review* that *Time in Its Flight* "will satisfy if you need to kill time or want to know how the rural rich once lived in America. But it's a poor intellectual companion. It's capriciously organized and confusing without purpose." "Schaeffer has a teeming imagination, and scatters ideas, anecdotes, and descriptions with a prodigal hand," Lynne Sharon Schwartz commented in *Saturday Review.* "Unfortunately, only a portion of these contribute to any formal design or movement. Similarly, Schaeffer's attempt to render a photographic reality of affectionate family life yields tedium." In contrast, a reviewer for the *New Yorker* wrote that "the abundant dialogue and reminiscences are entertaining and informative. Articulate women abound . . . and Mrs. Schaeffer manages to keep her characters and readers curious about what the future has in store for them."

As Cynthia MacDonald observed of *Time in Its Flight,* however, Schaeffer's saga is perhaps too all-encompassing to be entirely successful. Explained the critic in the *Washington Post Book World:* the author's "ambition is to incorporate a whole world, take it into the body of the novel and into each character. Much of the ambition is realized, much in the novel is wonderful, but there is too much. More shaping, more order, more discarding were needed. Yet I would say read this book; Susan Fromberg Schaeffer is a good enough writer to make even a flawed book worth reading."

Schaeffer's fourth novel, *Love,* is the story of two generations of Jewish families, the Lurias and the Romanoffs, beginning with events in Russia and ending with a new life in America. Susanne Freeman wrote in the *Washington Post* of *Love* that the novelist "takes us trudging through Russian snows, dancing through Jewish weddings, noshing in Brooklyn kitchens. She gives us childbirth, divorce and nightmares that come true. She serves up murder, pogroms and talking dogs. This can all be pretty steamy stuff—the thick soup of family life in a story that spans a hundred years—but Schaeffer is too clever for that. Family sagas are her specialty, and she knows just how to spoon them out—in short dream passages as thin as broth, followed by meatier scenes, just dense and sweet enough to make us wish for more."

Love also met with mixed reviews similar to those of *Time in Its Flight.* Dorothy Wickenden, for instance, remarked in *Saturday Review* that "Schaeffer knows what ingredients insure a novel's commercial success. *Love* captures Jewish family tradition, celebrates the lives of the hardworking and the obscure, and is punctuated with wry anecdotes about daily domestic crises. Still, Schaeffer's glimmers of wit aren't enough to sustain one throughout this overwritten and carelessly edited novel." Nevertheless, critics once again praised Schaeffer's skillful use of the narrative voice. For example, Lore Dickstein remarked in the *New York Times Book Review* that "Schaeffer has constructed this novel in large sections of flashback interspersed with narratives written in the voices of the characters, a device she has used in previous novels. Although many of these first-person accounts sound very much like verbatim transcripts of tape-recorded interviews, they are quite wonderful in the way they foretell and retell the story and they save the novel from mediocrity. Only in these sections can one hear distinctly individual voices, a quiet chuckle, and ironic comment."

The idea behind Schaeffer's next book, *The Madness of a Seduced Woman,* germinated for almost twenty years before the author wrote a novel concerning, as she once explained, "the spectacle of a body gone to war with the mind." While doing research for *Time in Its Flight,* Schaeffer came across five newspaper articles describing the murder trial of a woman accused of killing another woman after discovering they were both engaged to the same man. Following the shooting, the young woman attempted suicide, but failed and was put on trial for her crime. As the author recalled to a contributor to *Publishers Weekly:* "I thought then: what an awful fate, that no matter what she did to herself she was destined to go on living. And that led me to speculate about any usual person finding happiness in life, especially one with an obsessive determination to change the nature of reality. And the seductive possibility of being able to visualize a better world than the one you were given by birth or inheritance."

Julie Greenstein wrote in *Ms.* that *The Madness of a Seduced Woman,* "set at the turn of the [twentieth] century in New England, possesses the subtle allure of an Andrew Wyeth painting. Beautifully constructed and intelligently written, *Madness* is a Gothic tale of romance, passion, and oddly enough, feminism." Mary Kathleen Benet commented in the *Times Literary Supplement* that Schaeffer "has written not so much a novel as an example of the sort of novel women really ought to be reading." And Edmund White remarked in his *Nation* review that "at the heart of the novel beats the fibrillating pulse of an obsession. . . . Many books (trashy ones) blandly accept the genre of romantic fiction without a pause—they repeat every cliche. But serious books, such as this honest, intelligent novel, re-examine the cliches by observing even the most hackneyed situations with a deeper, more powerful vision." *The Madness of a Seduced Woman* "is much more complex and satisfying than its romantic plot suggests," Rosellen Brown likewise stated in the *New York Times Book Review.* "Schaeffer's earnest exploration of questions of mind versus body, family history versus personal freedom, does distance her novel from the common run of good reads about the travails of beautiful wantons. But in the end, the story of Agnes, who 'would love the world if she didn't have to live in it,' is an absorbing, wonderfully inventive psychological tale of a woman imagined as we would never dare, or want, to be."

Schaeffer's novel *Mainland* tells the story of Eleanor, a forty-six-year-old college professor who, after undergoing cataract surgery, takes a look at her seemingly happy marriage and family and decides she is no longer content with her life. After embarking on an affair with her Chinese chauffeur, Eleanor begins to undergo a slow transformation and finds real happiness at last. As Susan Allen Toth asked in her review for the *New York Times Book Review:* "Who wants to read another novel about an upper-middle-class New York City wife, unhappy despite (or because of) her prosperous husband and bright, healthy children? . . . In bare outline, Susan Fromberg Schaeffer's *Mainland* sounds tediously familiar. But this short, lilting novel offers many delightful surprises, not only in its underlying optimism but in its fresh, funny and often poetic prose." While Alice Kavounas reported in the *Times Literary Supplement* that "it's debatable whether the author intended *Mainland* to be more than the enjoyable read it is," she also pointed out that Schaeffer "keeps the pace of the narrative lively" and "endows her central character with [a] special brand of self-deprecating wit."

Schaeffer takes on a difficult subject and an unconventional one for a female writer in *Buffalo Afternoon.* It is the story of Pete Bravado, an Italian-American youth who becomes a combat soldier in Vietnam. Narrated by both Bravado and Li, a Vietnamese girl who eventually mothers the American's child, it is a haunting tale told without the cloud of politics. *Buffalo Afternoon* received mixed reviews from critics, Elizabeth Becker writing in the *Los Angeles Times Book Review* that the novel is inferior due to its lack of political analysis. Schaeffer "tells Bravado's story as if documents such as 'The Pentagon Papers' did not exist; as if Gen. William C. Westmoreland had not written 'A Soldier Reports' to give his side of the story; as if there were no way to get at the answers behind the war." Conversely, Nicholas Proffitt in the *New York Times Book Review* hailed the book as "one of the best treatments of the Vietnam War to date, and all the more impressive for the fact that its author never heard a shot fired in anger or set foot in that country." Proffitt, who served as a *Newsweek* correspondent in Vietnam, found Schaeffer's prose "evocative, often haunting," but cited in particular "the details that ultimately convince. All the Vietnam material is authentic." Jack Fuller in Chicago's *Tribune Books* also praised Schaeffer's "rich rendering of realistic detail. She is anything but a minimalist. Her stories proceed through the accumulation of vivid incident and description, through the presentation of conversation and internal states of mind. Hers are not tight, shapely narratives. They sprawl like a landscape, like the passage of time." Yet Fuller also noted that Schaeffer slips as she takes Bravado into a lengthy hallucinatory episode at the end: "so long and elaborate that it violates the basic terms of the relationship she has established with the reader." She returns the reader to more solid footing by the end of the novel, causing Fuller to conclude: "It is a relief to return to the daylight world, but a shame to have left it at all."

The protagonists of Schaeffer's novel *First Nights,* are a Swedish actress modeled after Greta Garbo, and the actress's West Indian housekeeper. "'Inspired' by Garbo is not really the right word, though, 'totally based on, down to the smallest detail' might be a better description," argued Robert Plunket in the *New York Times Book Review.* The actress, Anna, and the housekeeper, Ivy, have nothing in common at first glance, but over the fifteen years of their relationship, the reader views the parallels between them. As Plunket continued: *First Nights* "is beautifully and gracefully written with many of its stories delightful to read, but it lacks dramatic tension." This, Plunket argued, is due to the Garbo character: "The problems faced by the most beautiful woman in the world are not the sort that trouble the average reader, and it is not until the conclusion of the book, in an ending both effective and affecting, that Anna becomes a real human being." Susan Issacs, writing for the Chicago *Tribune Books,* had a similar comment, calling the novel "quite long, and there is too much of Anna being the melancholy Swede." Issacs found the ending "satisfying," however, and commented that "Here, Schaeffer draws together all her motifs with elegance and ease. It is a moment of first-rate art, but it is a moment that has been too long in coming." Pam Houston, reviewing for the *Los Angeles Times Book Review,* noted of the novel that there are "moments when I believed *First Nights* could have been 100 pages shorter and equally successful." Regardless, she praised Schaeffer's efforts, calling the book "honest and wise" and adding that "what it takes on is so huge and all encompassing that I am more than willing to indulge the author's excess. *First Nights* dances, strong and gracefully, on the philosophical boundaries between words and silence."

Because of her insightful and sensitive treatment of much of her subject matter and the background of many of her main characters, many critics have described Schaeffer as a "Jewish-American writer." As William Novack explained in the *New York Times Book Review,* changing literary trends in the later twentieth century "reflect . . . a growth in the Jewish-American consciousness. Writers like Cynthia Ozick and Arthur A. Cohen, together with some of their younger colleagues, have begun to produce a literature about Jews which is more identifiably Jewish than anything we have seen until now in the work of American-born authors. This new writing is more concerned with Jewish history, culture and even theology than with questions of how Jews live in American society." According to Novack, Schaeffer's *Anya* in particular is "a perhaps unintentional part of this phenomenon" that "represents a new stride toward maturity in Jewish-American writing. The novel looks history straight in the eye, engaging it with a stubborn fierceness. It is a triumph of realism in art."

Although many of her characters are Jewish, Schaeffer takes issue with reviewers labeling her as a "Jewish-American writer." As she explained to interviewer Harold U. Ribalow in *The Tie That Binds: Conversations with Jewish Writers,* "Partly the reason I wouldn't call myself a Jewish writer is because I'm not trying deliberately to write on Jewish themes." According to Susan Kress in the *Dictionary of Literary Biography,* while Schaeffer's "primary concerns are not Jewish themes and Jewish identity. . . . Nevertheless, her Jewish identity is important . . . ; in her own words, she regards her Jewishness as 'like the wallpaper in every room [she has] ever been in.'"

BIOGRAPHICAL AND CRITICAL SOURCES:

BOOKS

Contemporary Literary Criticism, Thomson Gale (Detroit, MI), Volume 6, 1976, Volume 11, 1979, Volume 22, 1982.

Dictionary of Literary Biography, Volume 28: *Twentieth-Century American-Jewish Fiction Writers,* Thomson Gale (Detroit, MI), 1984.

Ribalow, Harold U., editor, *The Tie That Binds: Conversations with Jewish Writers,* A.S. Barnes, 1980.

PERIODICALS

American Book Review, January-February, 1981.

Antioch Review, fall, 1981.

Best Sellers, October 1, 1974, review of *Anya.*

Booklist, August, 1986, p. 1694; May 1, 1996, review of *The Golden Rope,* p. 1470.

Book-of-the-Month Club News, July, 1978, review of *Time in Its Flight.*

Chicago Tribune Book World, January 27, 1980, review of *Love;* May 3, 1981; April 17, 1983.

Kirkus Reviews, August 1, 1986, p. 1154.

Library Journal, September 15, 1974; June 15, 1978, review of *Time in Its Flight.*

London Review of Books, November 20, 1986, p. 13.

Los Angeles Times, July 24, 1983; August 20, 1985.

Los Angeles Times Book Review, March 15, 1981; June 11, 1989, p. 1; May 30, 1993, Pam Houston, review of *First Nights,* p. 249.

Ms., March, 1975; November, 1975; February, 1980, review of *Love;* July, 1983.

Nation, July 9-16, 1983.

New Leader, August 6, 1973.

New Yorker, July 31, 1978.

New York Times Book Review, May 20, 1973, Wayne C. Booth, review of *Falling;* July 14, 1974, review of *Anya;* October 20, 1974; March 20, 1975; May 18, 1975; August 13, 1978, review of *Time in Its Flight;* February 24, 1980, Lore Dickstein, review of *Love;* January 11, 1981; May 22, 1983; July 8, 1984; July 7, 1985; November 16, 1986, p. 15; May 21, 1989, p. 7; December 15, 1991, p. 32; May 30, 1993, Robert Plunket, review of *First Nights,* p. 21.
Open Places, fall, 1975-76.
Partisan Review, fall, 1973, review of *Falling.*
Poetry, July, 1975.
Prairie Schooner, fall, 1977.
Publishers Weekly, April 8, 1983; June 27, 1986, p. 91; March 10, 1989, p. 75; May 6, 1996, review of *The Golden Rope,* p. 69.
Saturday Review, June 24, 1978, review of *Time in Its Flight;* January, 1981.
Time, July 18, 1973; December 31, 1973; October 14, 1974.
Times Literary Supplement, March 23, 1984; January 17, 1986.
Tribune Books (Chicago, IL), May 7, 1989, p. 1; May 2, 1993, review of *First Nights,* p. 6.
Washington Post, January 26, 1981; October 17, 1986.
Washington Post Book World, August 11, 1974; November 17, 1974; June 18, 1978; February 3, 1980; June 12, 1983; April 18, 1983.

* * *

SCHULZ, Charles M. 1922-2000 (Charles Monroe Schulz)

PERSONAL: Born November 26, 1922, in Minneapolis, MN; died of colon cancer, February 12, 2000, in Santa Rosa, CA; son of Carl (a barber) and Dena (Halverson) Schulz; married Joyce Halverson, April 18, 1949 (divorced, 1972); married Jean Clyde (some sources say last name was Forsyth), 1973; children: (first marriage) Meredith, Charles Monroe, Craig, Amy, Jill. *Education:* Studied cartooning in art school, 1940. *Hobbies and other interests:* Outdoor sports, especially ice hockey and golf.

CAREER: Cartoonist and illustrator. Art instructor at Art Instruction Schools, Inc. (correspondence school), Minneapolis, MN; cartoonist, *St. Paul Pioneer Press* and *Saturday Evening Post,* 1948-49; creator of syndicated comic strip, "Peanuts," 1950. *Military service:* U.S. Army, 1943-45, served with Twentieth Armored Division in Europe; became staff sergeant.

AWARDS, HONORS: Reuben Award as outstanding cartoonist of the year, National Cartoonists' Society, 1955 and 1964; Yale Humor Award as outstanding humorist of the year, 1956; School Bell Award, National Education Association, 1960; L.H.D., Anderson College, 1963; Peabody Award and Emmy Award, both 1966, for CBS cartoon special, "A Charlie Brown Christmas"; D.H.L., St. Mary's College of California, 1969; named International Cartoonist of the Year, International Pavilion of Humor (Montreal, Canada), 1978; Charles M. Schulz Award, United Feature Syndicate, 1980, for his contribution in the field of cartooning; Ordre des arts et des lettres (France), 1990; named one of top twenty-five newspaper people of the twentieth century, *Editor and Publisher,* 1999; Lifetime Achievement Award, National Cartoonists' Society, 2000; Congressional Gold Medal, 2000.

WRITINGS:

CARTOON BOOKS

Peanuts, Rinehart (New York, NY), 1952.
More Peanuts, Rinehart (New York, NY), 1954.
Good Grief, More Peanuts!, Rinehart (New York, NY), 1956.
Good Ol' Charlie Brown, Rinehart (New York, NY), 1957.
Snoopy, Rinehart (New York, NY), 1958.
Young Pillars, Warner Press (Anderson, IN), 1958.
But We Love You, Charlie Brown, Rinehart (New York, NY), 1959.
Peanuts Revisited: Favorites Old and New, Rinehart (New York, NY), 1959.
You're out of Your Mind, Charlie Brown, Rinehart (New York, NY), 1959.
"Teenager" Is Not a Disease, Warner Press (Anderson, IN), 1961.
Happiness Is a Warm Puppy, Determined Productions (San Francisco, CA), 1962, enlarged edition, 1979.
Security Is a Thumb and a Blanket, Determined Productions (San Francisco, CA), 1963, reprinted, 1983.
Christmas Is Together-Time, Determined Productions (San Francisco, CA), 1964.
I Need All the Friends I Can Get, Determined Productions (San Francisco, CA), 1964, reprinted, 1981.
What Was Bugging Ol' Pharaoh?, Warner Press (Anderson, IN), 1964.
A Charlie Brown Christmas (adapted from the television production), World Publishing (Cleveland, OH), 1965, reprinted, Miniature Editions (Philadelphia, PA), 2003.

Love Is Walking Hand in Hand, Determined Productions (San Francisco, CA), 1965.

Charlie Brown's All-Stars (adapted from the television production), World Publishing (Cleveland, OH), 1966.

Home Is on Top of a Doghouse, Determined Productions (San Francisco, CA), 1966, reprinted, 1982.

Charlie Brown's Reflections, Hallmark (Kansas City, MO), 1967.

Happiness Is a Sad Song, Determined Productions (San Francisco, CA), 1967.

It's the Great Pumpkin, Charlie Brown (adapted from the television production), World Publishing (Cleveland, OH), 1967.

Teenagers, Unite!, Bantam (New York, NY), 1967.

"He's Your Dog, Charlie Brown!" (adapted from the television production), World Publishing (Cleveland, OH), 1968.

Suppertime!, Determined Productions (San Francisco, CA), 1968.

You're in Love, Charlie Brown (adapted from the television production), World Publishing (Cleveland, OH), 1968.

Charlie Brown's Yearbook (includes *"He's Your Dog, Charlie Brown!"; It's the Great Pumpkin, Charlie Brown; You're in Love, Charlie Brown;* and *Charlie Brown's All-Stars*), World Publishing (Cleveland, OH), 1969.

Peanuts School Year Date Book, 1969-1970, Determined Productions (San Francisco, CA), 1969.

For Five Cents, Determined Productions (San Francisco, CA), 1970.

It Was a Short Summer, Charlie Brown (adapted from the television production), World Publishing (Cleveland, OH), 1970.

It Really Doesn't Take Much to Make a Dad Happy, Determined Productions (San Francisco, CA), 1970.

Peanuts Date Book 1972, Determined Productions (San Francisco, CA), 1970.

It's Fun to Lie Here and Listen to the Sounds of the Night, Determined Productions (San Francisco, CA), 1970, reprinted, Ballantine (New York, NY), 2002.

The World according to Lucy, Hallmark (Kansas City, MO), 1970.

Winning May Not Be Everything, But Losing Isn't Anything!, Determined Productions (San Francisco, CA), 1970.

Play It Again, Charlie Brown (adapted from the television production), World Publishing (Cleveland, OH), 1971.

You're Elected, Charlie Brown, World Publishing (Cleveland, OH), 1972.

Snoopy's Secret Life, Hallmark (Kansas City, MO), 1972.

The Peanuts Philosophers, Hallmark (Kansas City, MO), 1972.

Love à la Peanuts, Hallmark (Kansas City, MO), 1972.

It's Good to Have a Friend, Hallmark (Kansas City, MO), 1972.

A Charlie Brown Thanksgiving, Random House (New York, NY), 1974.

There's No Time for Love, Charlie Brown (adapted from the television production), Random House (New York, NY), 1974.

It's a Mystery, Charlie Brown, Random House (New York, NY), 1975.

Be My Valentine, Charlie Brown, Random House (New York, NY), 1976.

It's the Easter Beagle, Charlie Brown (adapted from the television production), Random House (New York, NY), 1976.

You're a Good Sport, Charlie Brown, Random House (New York, NY), 1976.

Hooray for You, Charlie Brown, Random House (New York, NY), 1977.

It's Another Holiday, Charlie Brown, Random House (New York, NY), 1977.

Summers Fly, Winters Walk, Volumes I-II, Holt (New York, NY), 1977, Volume III, Fawcett, 1980.

It's Arbor Day, Charlie Brown (adapted from the television production), Random House (New York, NY), 1977.

The Loves of Snoopy, Hodder & Stoughton (London, England), 1978.

Lucy Rules OK?, Hodder & Stoughton (London, England), 1978.

The Misfortunes of Charlie Brown, Hodder & Stoughton (London, England), 1978.

Snoopy and His Friends, Hodder & Stoughton (London, England), 1978.

What a Nightmare, Charlie Brown, Random House (New York, NY), 1978.

It's Your First Kiss, Charlie Brown (adapted from the television production), Random House (New York, NY), 1978.

Bon Voyage, Charlie Brown, and Don't Come Back! (adapted from the film production), Random House (New York, NY), 1980.

You're Not Elected, Charlie Brown, Scholastic (New York, NY), 1980.

Life Is a Circus, Charlie Brown (adapted from the television production), Random House (New York, NY), 1981.

She's a Good Skate, Charlie Brown (adapted from the television production), Random House (New York, NY), 1981.

Also author of *Snoopy on Wheels,* 1983; *Snoopy and the Twelve Days of Christmas,* 1984; *Peanuts at School,* 1986; and *If Beagles Could Fly,* 1990.

PUBLISHED BY HOLT (NEW YORK, NY)

Go Fly a Kite, Charlie Brown, 1960.
Peanuts Every Sunday, 1961.
It's a Dog's Life, Charlie Brown, 1962.
Snoopy Come Home, 1962.
You Can't Win, Charlie Brown, 1962.
You Can Do It, Charlie Brown, 1963.
As You Like It, Charlie Brown, 1964.
We're Right behind You, Charlie Brown, 1964.
There's a Vulture Outside, 1965.
Sunday's Fun Day, Charlie Brown, 1965.
You Need Help, Charlie Brown, 1965.
Snoopy and the Red Baron, 1966.
The Unsinkable Charlie Brown, 1966.
What's Wrong with Being Crabby?, 1966, reprinted, 1992.
Who's the Funny-Looking Kid with the Big Nose?, 1966.
You're Something Else, Charlie Brown: A New Peanuts Book, 1967.
It's a Long Way to Tipperary, 1967.
You'll Flip, Charlie Brown, 1967.
Peanuts Treasury (American Library Association Notable Book), foreword by Johnny Hart, 1968.
You're You, Charlie Brown: A New Peanuts Book, 1968.
A Boy Named Charlie Brown (adapted from the film production), 1969.
You've Had It, Charlie Brown: A New Peanuts Book, 1969.
Snoopy and His Sopwith Camel, 1969.
Peanuts Classics, 1970.
Snoopy and "It Was a Dark and Stormy Night," 1970.
You're Out of Sight, Charlie Brown: A New Peanuts Book, 1970.
You've Come a Long Way, Charlie Brown: A New Peanuts Book, 1971.
"Ha Ha, Herman," Charlie Brown: A New Peanuts Book, 1972.
Snoopy's Grand Slam, 1972.
The "Snoopy, Come Home" Movie Book (adapted from the film production), 1972.
Thompson Is in Trouble, Charlie Brown: A New Peanuts Book, 1973.
You're the Guest of Honor, Charlie Brown: A New Peanuts Book, 1973.
The Snoopy Festival, 1974.
Win a Few, Lose a Few, Charlie Brown: A New Peanuts Book, 1974.
Speak Softly, and Carry a Beagle: A New Peanuts Book, 1975.
Don't Hassle Me with Your Sighs, Chuck, 1976.
"I Never Promised You an Apple Orchard": The Collected Writings of Snoopy, Being a Compendium of His Puns, Correspondence, Cautionary Tales, Witticisms, Titles Original and Borrowed, with Critical Commentary by His Friends, and, Published for the First Time in Its Entirety, the Novel "Toodleoo, Caribou!," a Tale of the Frozen North, 1976.
Always Stick Up for the Underbird: Cartoons from "Good Grief, More Peanuts!," and "Good Ol' Charlie Brown," 1977.
It's Great to Be a Superstar: Cartoons from "You're Out of Sight, Charlie Brown," and "You've Come a Long Way, Charlie Brown," 1977.
How Long, Great Pumpkin, How Long?: Cartoons from "You're the Guest of Honor, Charlie Brown," and "Win a Few, Lose a Few, Charlie Brown," 1977.
It's Hard Work Being Bitter: Cartoons from "Thompson Is in Trouble, Charlie Brown," and "You're the Guest of Honor, Charlie Brown," 1977.
There Goes the Shutout: Cartoons from "More Peanuts" and "Good Grief, More Peanuts!," 1977.
My Anxieties Have Anxieties: Cartoons from "You're You, Charlie Brown," and "You've Had It, Charlie Brown," 1977.
Sandlot Peanuts, introduction by Joe Garagiola, 1977.
A Smile Makes a Lousy Umbrella: Cartoons from "You're Something Else, Charlie Brown," and "You're You, Charlie Brown," 1977.
Stop Snowing on My Secretary: Cartoons from "You've Come a Long Way, Charlie Brown," and "Ha Ha, Herman, Charlie Brown," 1977, reprinted, 1992.
The Beagle Has Landed, 1978.
Race for Your Life, Charlie Brown (adapted from the television production), 1978.
Snoopy's Tennis Book: Featuring Snoopy at Wimbledon and Snoopy's Tournament Tips, introduction by Billie Jean King, 1979.
And a Woodstock in a Birch Tree, 1979.
Here Comes the April Fool!, 1980.
Things I Learned after It Was Too Late (and Other Minor Truths), 1981.
Dr. Beagle and Mr. Hyde 1981.
You're Weird, Sir!, 1982.
Classroom Peanuts, 1982.
Kiss Her, You Blockhead!, 1983.
And the Beagles and the Bunnies Shall Lie Down Together: The Theology in Peanuts, 1984.
Things I've Had to Learn Over and Over and Over: (Plus a Few Minor Discoveries), 1984.
I'm Not Your Sweet Babboo!, 1984.
Big League Peanuts, 1985.

The Way of the Fussbudget Is Not Easy, 1986.
Don't Hassle Me with Your Sighs, Chuck, 1993.
Duck, Here Comes Another Day!, 1994.
Snoopy's Love Book, 1994.
The Cheshire Beagle, 1994.
Nothing Echoes Like an Empty Mailbox, 1995.
Sarcasm Does Not Become You, Ma'am, 1995.
I Heard a D Minus Call Me, 1995.

Also author of *A Kiss on the Nose Turns Anger Aside, The Mad Punter Strikes Again, Thank Goodness for People, What Makes Musicians So Sarcastic?,What Makes You Think You're So Happy?,* and *Fly, You Stupid Kite, Fly.*

PUBLISHED BY FAWCETT (NEW YORK, NY)

Good Ol' Snoopy (contains selections from *Snoopy*), 1958.
Wonderful World of Peanuts (contains selections from *More Peanuts*), 1963.
Hey, Peanuts! (contains selections from *More Peanuts*), 1963.
Good Grief, Charlie Brown! (contains selections from *Good Grief, More Peanuts!*), 1963.
For the Love of Peanuts (contains selections from *Good Grief, More Peanuts!*), 1963.
Fun with Peanuts (contains selections from *Good Ol' Charlie Brown*), 1964.
Here Comes Charlie Brown (contains selections from *Good Ol' Charlie Brown*), 1964.
Very Funny, Charlie Brown! (contains selections from *You're Out of Your Mind, Charlie Brown!*), 1965.
What Next, Charlie Brown? (contains selections from *You're Out of Your Mind, Charlie Brown!*), 1965.
Here Comes Snoopy (contains selections from *Snoopy*), 1966.
We're On Your Side, Charlie Brown (contains selections from *But We Love You, Charlie Brown*), 1966.
You Are Too Much, Charlie Brown (contains selections from *But We Love You, Charlie Brown*), 1966.
You're a Winner, Charlie Brown (contains selections from *Go Fly a Kite, Charlie Brown*), 1967.
Let's Face It, Charlie Brown (contains selections from *Go Fly a Kite, Charlie Brown*), 1967.
Who Do You Think You Are, Charlie Brown? (contains selections from *Peanuts Every Sunday*), 1968.
You're My Hero, Charlie Brown (contains selections from *Peanuts Every Sunday*), 1968.
This Is Your Life, Charlie Brown (contains selections from *It's a Dog's Life, Charlie Brown*), 1968.
Slide, Charlie Brown, Slide (contains selections from *It's a Dog's Life, Charlie Brown*), 1968.
All This and Snoopy, Too (contains selections from *You Can't Win, Charlie Brown*), 1969.
Here's to You, Charlie Brown (contains selections from *You Can't Win, Charlie Brown*), 1969.
Nobody's Perfect, Charlie Brown (contains selections from *You Can Do It, Charlie Brown*), 1969.
You're a Brave Man, Charlie Brown (contains selections from *You Can Do It, Charlie Brown*), 1969.
Peanuts for Everybody (contains selections from *We're Right behind You, Charlie Brown*), 1970.
You've Done It Again, Charlie Brown (contains selections from *We're Right behind You, Charlie Brown*), 1970.
We Love You, Snoopy (contains selections from *Snoopy, Come Home*), 1970.
It's for You, Snoopy (contains selections from *Sunday's Fun Day, Charlie Brown*), 1971.
Have It Your Way, Charlie Brown (contains selections from *Sunday's Fun Day, Charlie Brown*), 1971.
You're Not for Real, Snoopy (contains selections from *You Need Help, Charlie Brown*), 1971.
You're a Pal, Snoopy (contains selections from *You Need Help, Charlie Brown*), 1972.
What Now, Charlie Brown? (contains selections from *The Unsinkable Charlie Brown*), 1972.
You're Something Special, Snoopy! (contains selections from *The Unsinkable Charlie Brown*), 1972.
You've Got a Friend, Charlie Brown (contains selections from *You'll Flip, Charlie Brown*), 1972.
Who Was That Dog I Saw You With, Charlie Brown? (contains selections from *You're You, Charlie Brown*), 1973.
There's No One Like You, Snoopy (contains selections from *You're You, Charlie Brown*), 1973.
It's All Yours, Snoopy (contains selections from *You've Come a Long Way, Charlie Brown*), 1975.
Peanuts Double, Volume I, 1976, Volume II, 1978.
Watch out, Charlie Brown (contains selections from *You're Out of Sight, Charlie Brown*), 1977.
You've Got to Be You, Snoopy (contains selections from *You've Come a Long Way, Charlie Brown*), 1978.
You're on Your Own, Snoopy (contains selections from *"Ha Ha, Herman," Charlie Brown*), 1978.
You Can't Win Them All, Charlie Brown (contains selections from *"Ha Ha, Herman," Charlie Brown*), 1978.
It's Your Turn, Snoopy (contains selections from *You're the Guest of Honor, Charlie Brown*), 1978.
You Asked for It, Charlie Brown (contains selections from *You're the Guest of Honor, Charlie Brown*), 1978.

It's Show Time, Snoopy (contains selections from *Speak Softly, and Carry a Beagle*), 1978.
You've Got to Be Kidding, Snoopy, 1978.
They're Playing Your Song, Charlie Brown, 1978.
You're So Smart, Snoopy (contains selections from *You're Out of Sight, Charlie Brown*), 1978.
Charlie Brown and Snoopy (contains selections from *As You Like It, Charlie Brown*), 1978.
You're the Greatest, Charlie Brown (contains selections from *As You Like It, Charlie Brown*), 1978.
Try It Again, Charlie Brown (contains selections from *You're Something Else, Charlie Brown*), 1978.
Your Choice, Snoopy (contains selections from *You're Something Else, Charlie Brown*), 1978.
Take It Easy, Charlie Brown (contains selections from *You'll Flip, Charlie Brown*), 1978.
You've Got It Made, Snoopy (contains selections from *You've Had It, Charlie Brown*), 1978.
Don't Give Up, Charlie Brown (contains selections from *You've Had It, Charlie Brown*), 1978.
That's Life, Snoopy (contains selections from *Thompson Is in Trouble, Charlie Brown*), 1978.
You've Come a Long Way, Snoopy (contains selections from *Thompson Is in Trouble, Charlie Brown*), 1979.
Play Ball, Snoopy (contains selections from *Win a Few, Lose a Few, Charlie Brown*), 1979.
Let's Hear It for Dinner, Snoopy, 1979.
Keep Up the Good Work, Charlie Brown, 1979.
Think Thinner, Snoopy, 1979.
Stay with It, Snoopy (contains selections from *Summers Fly, Winters Walk,* Volume III), 1980.
Sing for Your Supper, Snoopy, 1981.
Snoopy, Top Dog (contains selections from *The Beagle Has Landed*), 1981.
You're Our Kind of Dog, Snoopy (contains selections from *And a Woodstock in a Birch Tree*), 1981.

Also author of *Love and Kisses, Snoopy.*

"SNOOPY'S FACTS AND FUN BOOK" SERIES

Snoopy's Facts and Fun Book about Boats, Random House (New York, NY), 1979.
Snoopy's Facts and Fun Book about Houses, Random House (New York, NY), 1979.
Snoopy's Facts and Fun Book about Planes, Random House (New York, NY), 1979.
Snoopy's Facts and Fun Book about Seasons, Random House (New York, NY), 1979.
Snoopy's Facts and Fun Book about Farms, Random House (New York, NY), 1980.
Snoopy's Facts and Fun Book about Nature, Random House (New York, NY), 1980.
Snoopy's Facts and Fun Book about Seashores, Random House (New York, NY), 1980.
Snoopy's Facts and Fun Book about Trucks, Random House (New York, NY), 1980.

OTHER

Peanuts Project Book, Determined Productions (San Francisco, CA), 1963.
(With Kenneth F. Hall) *Two-by-Fours: A Sort of Serious Book about Small Children,* Warner Press (Anderson, IN), 1965.
(Contributor) Jeffrey H. Loria and others, *What's It All about, Charlie Brown?: Peanuts Kids Look at America Today,* Holt (New York, NY), 1968.
(Contributor) Robert L. Short, *The Parables of Peanuts,* Harper (New York, NY), 1968.
(With Lee Mendelson) *Charlie Brown and Charlie Schulz: In Celebration of the Twentieth Anniversary of Peanuts,* World Publishing (Cleveland, OH), 1970.
(Author of foreword) Morrie Turner, *Nipper,* Westminster (Philadelphia, PA), 1970.
(With Kathryn Wentzel Lumley) *Snoopy's Secret Code Book* (spelling and pronunciation guide), Holt (New York, NY), 1971.
The Charlie Brown Dictionary, Random House (New York, NY), 1973.
Peanuts Jubilee: My Life and Art with Charlie Brown and Others, Holt (New York, NY), 1975.
Charlie Brown's Super Book of Things to Do and Collect: Based on the Charles M. Schulz Characters, Random House (New York, NY), 1975.
Charlie Brown's Super Book of Questions and Answers about All Kinds of Animals from Snails to People!, Random House (New York, NY), 1976.
Charlie Brown's Second Super Book of Questions and Answers: About the Earth and Space from Plants to Planets!, Random House (New York, NY), 1977.
Charlie Brown's Third Super Book of Questions and Answers: About All Kinds of Boats and Planes, Cars and Trains, and Other Things That Move!, Random House (New York, NY), 1978.
Charlie Brown's Fourth Super Book of Questions and Answers: About All Kinds of People and How They Live!, Random House (New York, NY), 1979.
(With Lee Mendelson) *Happy Birthday, Charlie Brown,* Random House (New York, NY), 1979.
(With R. Smith Kiliper) *Charlie Brown, Snoopy and Me: And All the Other Peanuts Characters,* Doubleday (Garden City, NY), 1980.

Charlie Brown's Fifth Super Book of Questions and Answers: About All Kinds of Things and How They Work!, Random House (New York, NY), 1981.

Someday You'll Find Her, Charlie Brown, Random House (New York, NY), 1982.

It's Magic, Charlie Brown, Random House (New York, NY), 1982.

Charlie Brown's Encyclopedia of Energy: Based on the Charles M. Schulz Characters: Where We've Been, Where We're Going, and How We're Getting There, Random House (New York, NY), 1982.

Is This Good-Bye, Charlie Brown?, Random House (New York, NY), 1984.

Snoopy's Getting Married, Charlie Brown, Random House (New York, NY), 1986.

Happy New Year, Charlie Brown, Random House (New York, NY), 1986.

Dogs Don't Eat Dessert, Topper Books (New York, NY), 1987.

You're on the Wrong Foot Again, Charlie Brown, Topper Books (New York, NY), 1987.

By Supper Possessed, Topper Books (New York, NY), 1988.

Sally, School Is My World, Sparkler Books (New York, NY), 1988.

Talk Is Cheep, Charlie Brown, Topper Books (New York, NY), 1988.

Snoopy, My Greatest Adventures, Sparkler Books (New York, NY), 1988.

Schroeder, Music Is My Life, Sparkler Books (New York, NY), 1988.

Get in Shape, Snoopy!, Western Pub. Co. (Racine, WI), 1989.

I Take My Religion Seriously, Warner Press (Anderson, IN), 1989.

It Doesn't Take Much to Attract a Crowd, Topper Books (New York, NY), 1989.

Brothers and Sisters, It's All Relative: A Peanuts Book, Topper Books (New York, NY), 1989.

Snoopy around the World, photographs by Alberto Rizzo, H.N. Abrams (New York, NY), 1990.

Why, Charlie Brown, Why?: A Story about What Happens When a Friend Is Very Ill, Topper Books (New York, NY), 1990.

An Educated Slice: Starring Snoopy As the World Famous Golfer, Topper Books (New York, NY), 1990.

Don't Be Sad, Flying Ace, Topper Books (New York, NY), 1990.

You're a Star, Snoopy!, Western Publishing (Racine, WI), 1990.

Could You Be More Pacific?, Topper Books (New York, NY), 1991.

Dr. Snoopy's Advice to Pet Owners, illustrations by Charles M. Schulz, Andrews & McMeel (Kansas City, MO), 1993.

Mischief on Daisy Hill: Featuring the Daisy Hill Puppies, Determined Productions (San Francisco, CA), 1993.

Creatures, Large and Small, Derrydale Books (New York, NY), 1994.

The Cheshire Beagle, Holt (New York, NY), 1994.

Around the World in 45 Years: Charlie Brown's Anniversary Celebration, Andrews & McMeel (Kansas City, MO), 1994.

Land and Space, Derrydale Books (New York, NY), 1994.

Being a Dog Is a Full-Time Job: A Peanuts Collection, Andrews & McMeel (Kansas City, MO), 1994.

People and Customs of the World, Derrydale Books (New York, NY), 1994.

Make Way for the King of the Jungle: A Peanuts Collection, Andrews & McMeel (Kansas City, MO), 1995.

Pop! Goes the Beagle, HarperFestival (New York, NY), 1996.

Life's Answers (and Much, Much More), Collins Publishers (San Francisco, CA), 1996.

Bah, Humbug!, Collins Publishers (San Francisco, CA), 1996.

Snoopy's Christmas Tree, HarperFestival (New York, NY), 1996.

Your Dog Plays Hockey?, HarperFestival (New York, NY), 1996.

Friends for Life, Collins Publishers (San Francisco, CA), 1996.

Way beyond Therapy, Collins Publishers (San Francisco, CA), 1996.

Trick or Treat, Great Pumpkin, HarperFestival (New York, NY), 1996.

Kick the Ball, Marcie!, HarperFestival (New York, NY), 1996.

Love Isn't Easy, Collins Publishers (San Francisco, CA), 1996.

Dogs Are from Jupiter, Cats Are from the Moon, Collins Publishers (San Francisco, CA), 1996.

Happy Birthday! (And One to Glow On), Collins Publishers (San Francisco, CA), 1996.

It's Christmas!, Collins Publishers (San Francisco, CA), 1996.

Somebody Loves You, Collins Publishers (San Francisco, CA), 1996.

Me, Stressed Out?, Collins Publishers (San Francisco, CA), 1996.

I Love You!, Collins Publishers (San Francisco, CA), 1996.

Season's Greetings!, Collins Publishers (San Francisco, CA), 1996.

See You Later, Litigator!, Collins Publishers (San Francisco, CA), 1996.

Birthdays Are No Piece of Cake, Collins Publishers (San Francisco, CA), 1996.

Snoopy, Not Your Average Dog, Collins Publishers (San Francisco, CA), 1996.

You Can Count on Me, Collins Publishers (San Francisco, CA), 1996.

'Tis the Season to Be Crabby, Collins Publishers (San Francisco, CA), 1996.

Have Another Cookie (It'll Make You Feel Better), Collins Publishers (San Francisco, CA), 1996.

Sally's Christmas Miracle, HarperFestival (New York, NY), 1996.

A Good Caddie Is Hard to Find, Collins Publishers (San Francisco, CA), 1996.

Happy Valentine's Day, Sweet Babboo!, HarperFestival (New York, NY), 1997.

Insights from the Outfield, Collins (New York, NY), 1997.

Born Crabby, HarperCollins (New York, NY), 1997.

Life Is Like a Ten-Speed Bicycle, Collins (New York, NY), 1997.

You're Divine, Valentine!, Collins (New York, NY), 1997.

Charlie Brown: Not Your Average Blockhead, HarperCollins (New York, NY), 1997.

Love Is in the Air, Collins (New York, NY), 1997.

Lucy, Not Just Another Pretty Face, HarperHorizon (New York, NY), 1998.

Happy New Year!, HarperHorizon (New York, NY), 1998.

Have Fun at Beanbag Camp!, HarperHorizon (New York, NY), 1998.

Aaugh! A Dog Ate My Book Report, HarperCollins (New York, NY), 1998.

I've Been Traded for Pizza?, HarperHorizon (New York, NY), 1998.

Beware of the Snoring Ghost!, HarperCollins (New York, NY), 1998.

Bon Voyage!, HarperCollins (New York, NY), 1998.

My Best Friend, My Blanket, HarperHorizon (New York, NY), 1998.

Punt, Pass, and Peanuts, HarperHorizon (New York, NY), 1998.

The Round-Headed Kid and Me, HarperHorizon (New York, NY), 1998.

Travels with My Cactus, HarperHorizon (New York, NY), 1998.

The Doctor Is In(sane), HarperHorizon (New York, NY), 1998.

Everyone Gets Gold Stars but Me!, HarperCollins (New York, NY), 1998.

Our Lines Must Be Crossed!, HarperHorizon (New York, NY), 1998.

You're Our New Mascot, Chuck!, HarperCollins (New York, NY), 1998.

You're the Tops, Pops!, HarperCollins (New York, NY), 1998.

Leaf It to Sally Brown, HarperHorizon (New York, NY), 1998.

Lighten Up, It's Christmas!, HarperHorizon (New York, NY), 1998.

Sally's Christmas Play, HarperHorizon (New York, NY), 1998.

You Have a Brother Named Spike?, HarperCollins (New York, NY), 1998.

A Flying Ace Needs Lots of Root Beer, HarperHorizon (New York, NY), 1998.

Calling All Cookies!, HarperHorizon (New York, NY), 1999.

Dogs Are Worth It!, HarperPerennial (New York, NY), 1999.

Good Grief! Gardening Is Hard Work!, HarperHorizon (New York, NY), 1999.

I Told You So, You Blockhead, HarperPerennial (New York, NY), 1999.

Shall We Dance, Charlie Brown?, HarperHorizon (New York, NY), 1999.

It's Baseball Season, Again!, HarperHorizon (New York, NY), 1999.

Now That's Profound, Charlie Brown, HarperPerennial (New York, NY), 1999.

Peanuts: A Golden Celebration: The Art and the Story of the World's Best-Loved Comic Strip, HarperCollins (New York, NY), 1999.

The World Is Filled with Mondays, HarperPerennial (New York, NY), 1999.

Peanuts 2000, Ballantine (New York, NY), 2000.

It's a Big World, Charlie Brown, Ballantine (New York, NY), 2001.

It's a Dog's Life, Snoopy, Ballantine (New York, NY), 2001.

A Peanuts Christmas, Ballantine (New York, NY), 2002.

A Peanuts Valentine, Ballantine (New York, NY), 2003.

TELEPLAYS

A Charlie Brown Christmas, CBS-TV, December 9, 1965.

Charlie Brown's All-Stars, CBS-TV, June 8, 1966.

It's the Great Pumpkin, Charlie Brown, CBS-TV, October 27, 1966.

You're in Love, Charlie Brown, CBS-TV, June 12, 1967.

He's Your Dog, Charlie Brown!, CBS-TV, February 14, 1968.

It Was a Short Summer, Charlie Brown, CBS-TV, September 27, 1969.

Play It Again, Charlie Brown, CBS-TV, March 28, 1971.

It's the Easter Beagle, Charlie Brown, CBS-TV, 1972.

You're Elected, Charlie Brown, CBS-TV, October 29, 1972.

There's No Time for Love, Charlie Brown, CBS-TV, March 11, 1973.

Race for Your Life, Charlie Brown, CBS-TV, January, 1976.

It's Arbor Day, Charlie Brown, CBS-TV, March 16, 1976.

It's Your First Kiss, Charlie Brown, CBS-TV, 1978.

Life Is a Circus, Charlie Brown, CBS-TV, 1981.

She's a Good Skate, Charlie Brown, CBS-TV, 1981.

Also writer of screenplays for feature-length animated films, *A Boy Named Charlie Brown,* National General Pictures, 1969,*Snoopy, Come Home,* National General Pictures, 1972, and *Bon Voyage, Charlie Brown, and Don't Come Back!,* Paramount, 1980.

ILLUSTRATOR

Art Linkletter, *Kids Say the Darndest Things,* Prentice-Hall (Englewood Cliffs, NJ), 1957.

Art Linkletter, *Kids Still Say the Darndest Things,* Geis (New York, NY), 1961.

Bill Adler, compiler, *Dear President Johnson,* Morrow (New York, NY), 1964.

Fritz Ridenour, editor, *I'm a Good Man, But . . . ,* Regal Books (Glendale, CA), 1969.

June Dutton, *Peanuts Cookbook,* Determined Productions (San Francisco, Ca), 1969.

June Dutton, *Peanuts Lunch Bag Cookbook,* Determined Productions (San Francisco, CA), 1970.

All I Want for Christmas Is . . . : Open Letters to Santa, Hallmark (Kansas City, MO), 1972.

Evelyn Shaw, *The Snoopy Doghouse Cook Book,* Determined Productions (San Francisco, CA), 1979.

Tubby Book Featuring Snoopy, Simon & Schuster (New York, NY), 1980.

Monica Bayley, *The Snoopy Omnibus of Fun Facts from the Snoopy Fun Fact Calendars,* Determined Productions (San Francisco, CA), 1982.

J.C. Suares, editor and designer, *The Snoopy Collection,* introduction by Nancy Smart, photographs by Don Hamerman, Stewart, Tabori & Chang (New York, NY), 1982.

June Dutton, *Snoopy and the Gang out West,* Determined Productions (San Francisco, CA), 1982.

Nancy Hall, *Snoopy's ABC's,* background illustrations by Art and Kim Ellis, Golden Books (New York, NY), 1987.

Nancy Hall, *Snoopy's Book of Shapes,* background illustrations by Art and Kim Ellis, Golden Books (New York, NY), 1987.

Nancy Hall, *Snoopy's 1, 2, 3,* background illustrations by Art and Kim Ellis, Golden Books (New York, NY), 1987.

Harry Coe Verr, *Let's Fly a Kite, Charlie Brown!: A Book about the Seasons,* background illustrations by Art and Kim Ellis, Golden Books (New York, NY), 1987.

Justine Korman, *Snoopy's A Little Help from My Friend,* background illustrations by Art and Kim Ellis, Golden Books (New York, NY), 1987.

Nancy Hall, *Snoopy's Book of Colors,* background illustrations by Art and Kim Ellis, Golden Books (New York, NY), 1987.

Nancy Hall, *Snoopy's Book of Opposites,* background illustrations by Art and Kim Ellis, Golden Books (New York, NY), 1987.

Norman Simone, *Come Back, Snoopy,* background illustrations by Art and Kim Ellis, Golden Books (New York, NY), 1987.

Abraham J. Twerski, *When Do the Good Things Start?,* Topper Books, 1988.

Margo Lundell, *Where's Woodstock?,* background illustrations by Art and Kim Ellis, Golden Books (New York, NY), 1988.

Justine Korman, *It's How You Play the Game,* background illustrations by Art and Kim Ellis, Golden Books (New York, NY), 1988.

Marci McGill, *Snoopy, the World's Greatest Author,* background illustrations by Art and Kim Ellis, Golden Books (New York, NY), 1988.

Justine Korman, *Snoopy's Two-Minute Stories,* background illustrations by Art and Kim Ellis, Western Publishing (Racine, WI), 1988.

Margo Lundell, *Charlie Brown's Two Minute Stories,* background illustrations by Art and Kim Ellis, Western Publishing (Racine, WI), 1988.

Diane Namm, *A Charlie Brown Christmas,* background illustrations by Art and Kim Ellis, Golden Books (New York, NY), 1988.

Robert L. Short, *Short Meditations on the Bible and Peanuts,* Westminster/John Knox Press (Louisville, KY), 1990.

Abraham J. Twerski, *Waking Up Just in Time: A Therapist Shows How to Use the Twelve-Steps Approach to Life's Ups and Downs,* Topper Books (New York, NY), 1990.

Abraham J. Twerski, *I Didn't Ask to Be in This Family: Sibling Relationships and How They Shape Adult Behavior and Relationships,* Holt (New York, NY), 1996.

ADAPTATIONS: The following titles were based on the "Peanuts" comic strip by Shulz, and were published by Little Simon (New York, NY): *Friends Forever, Snoopy,* adapted by Tricia Boczkowski, 2001; *Kick the Football, Charlie Brown,* adapted by Judy Katschke, 2001; *A Charlie Brown Valentine,* adapted by Justine and Ron Fontes, art adapted by Paige Braddock, 2001; *It's Time for School, Charlie Brown,* adapted by Judy Katschke, art adapted by Nick LoBianco, 2002; *A Charlie Brown Thanksgiving,* adapted by Justine and Ron Fontes, art adapted by Tom Brannon, 2002; *Lucy's Advice,* adapted by Nancy Krulik, art adapted by Peter LoBianco, 2003; *Puppy Days,* adapted by Lizzie Mack, art adapted by Tom Brannon, 2003.

SIDELIGHTS: Charles M. Schulz, the world-renowned creator of the "Peanuts" comic strip, loved his job. During his lifetime, he maintained that all he "really ever wanted was to be a cartoonist." When the "Peanuts" comic strip began in 1950, Schulz had no idea the phenomenon it would become. A great admirer of Roy Crane, George Herriman, Al Capp, and Milt Caniff in his youth, he had a hard time selling his own comic strip at first; United Feature Syndicate finally bought it in 1950 and named it "Peanuts." Schulz, who wanted to name the strip "Li'l Folks," never really liked the title. "Peanuts" started in just eight newspapers and gradually grew. At the time of his death in 2000, Schulz's comic strip was read by more than 335 million people everyday. It appeared in 2,600 newspapers and 75 countries. Reprints of the comic strip still appear in newspapers today.

Schulz named his Charlie Brown character after a friend at Art Instruction Schools named Charles Frances Brown. Charlie Brown's dog, Snoopy, was modeled after Schulz's own childhood pet, Spike. Many of the other characters in the strip were also based on friends and acquaintances of Schulz. The popularity of the strip is often credited to its ability to relate to almost anyone. "Charlie Brown was the quintessence of ordinariness," reported the *Encyclopedia of World Biography.*

Lee Mendelson pointed out in his biography of Schulz, "Charlie Brown has become *the* symbol of mid-century America . . . because [he is] a basic reflection of his time," the "Mr. Anxious" of the age. Richard R. Lingeman wrote in the *New York Times* that the "Peanuts" children "precociously know that life can be lousy and their popularity from the late fifties on may be due to their reflecting a secret, self-doubting, self-questioning mood abroad in the nation: Charlie Brown is everybody's loser because everybody is a loser much of the time. "Peanuts" offers a gentle philosophy of human relations, of stoically coping with existence, that is the underside of the preachments of those eupeptic middle-class yeasayers from Norman Vincent Peale to *How to Be Your Own Best Friend.*" Commenting on the universality of the appeal of Charlie Brown, the perpetual loser, Schulz said in *Peanuts Jubilee: My Life and Art with Charlie Brown and Others,* "Readers are generally sympathetic toward a lead character who is rather gentle, sometimes put upon, and not always the brightest person. Perhaps this is the kind of person who is easiest to love. Charlie Brown has to be the one who suffers because he is a caricature of the average person. Most of us are much more acquainted with losing than we are with winning. Winning is great, but it isn't funny."

Newsmakers 2000 noted, "'Peanuts' opened a new chapter in comics for its focus on the insecurities that everyone faces in life." Unlike many cartoonists, Schulz did all of the work on the comic strip by himself, often drawing material for the strip from his own childhood memories and from his experiences in raising five children. According to *Contemporary Heroes and Heroines,* "His own youthful disappointments in love, athletics, and school" became part of his comic strip. His personal touch set it apart from other comic strips. Schulz was the only cartoonist ever to have won the Reuben Award (the cartoonist's equivalent of the Oscar, designed by and named after Rube Goldberg) twice, in 1955 and again in 1964.

The popularity of the strip "cuts across every kind of classification for all kinds of special reasons," wrote John Tebbel in a *Saturday Review* article titled "The Not-So-Peanuts World of Charles M. Shulz." Tebbel continued, "Schroeder, the Beethoven-loving character who is usually seen playing the piano when he isn't playing baseball, appeals to people who had never heard of Beethoven before. The little tyrant Lucy is seen by the small fry as a deliciously contrary girl. . . . Linus, with his security blanket, seems to speak to everyone who would like to have a blanket of his own in troubled times. And Snoopy, the beagle who has Van Goghs hanging in his doghouse and a World War I aviator's helmet on his head, is the kind of fantasy dog everyone would like to own." Nonetheless, Schulz contended that there really was no specific "philosophy" behind the strip, and that his "chief purpose" was "to get the strips done in time to get down to the post office" before it closed.

The "Peanuts" comic strip developed well beyond the pages of the newspaper. In 1965, Schulz introduced the lovable characters to television, and during his lifetime, wrote many memorable animated shows about Charlie Brown and his pals, including classic favorites such as *A Charlie Brown Christmas* and *It's the Great Pumpkin, Charlie Brown.* He also wrote several feature-length animated films about the "Peanuts." But, the "Peanuts" industry does not stop there. "Peanuts" characters adorn T-shirts, lunchboxes, stationery, furniture, and much more. The "Peanuts" cartoon propelled Schulz to fame, and spawned books and documentaries about the cartoonist. Broadway and Off-Broadway musicals were created based on "Peanuts" characters.

Even the National Aeronautics and Space Administration (NASA) has shown its love for the "Peanuts" cartoon. Snoopy made international history as the official name of the Lunar Excursion Module (LEM) of the Apollo 10 manned flight to the moon in 1969. Great Pumpkin sightings are reported almost as often as UFO's, and Schroeder and his toy piano have been immortalized in the stained glass window of the Westminster Presbyterian Church in Buffalo, New York, along with Bach, Martin Luther, Duke Ellington, and Dr. Albert Schweitzer. Through his "Peanuts" cartoon, and Charlie Brown's "everyman" appeal, Schulz touched many lives. "The reader knew [Charlie Brown], knew his fears, sympathized with his sense of inferiority and alienation," noted the Charles M. Schulz Museum Web site.

The award-winning cartoonist laid down his crow-quill pen and announced his retirement on December 14, 1999, after suffering a stroke and a battle with colon cancer. According to the Charles M. Schulz Museum Web site, Schulz said, "I never dreamed that this would happen to me." In the months following his retirement, his office was flooded with letters from fans, lauding the cartoonist for his work. "Charles Schulz has shown us that a comic strip can transcend its small space on the page. It can uplift; it can challenge; it can educate its readers even as it entertains us," said President Bill Clinton in a farewell to Schulz.

Schulz would not live to see his last original Sunday cartoon in print, set to run on February 13, 2000. Schulz passed away in his sleep on February 12, 2000. The Charles M. Schulz Museum Web site noted, "As soon as he ceased to be a cartoonist, he ceased to be."

BIOGRAPHICAL AND CRITICAL SOURCES:

BOOKS

Berger, Arthur Asa, *The Comic-Stripped American,* Walker (New York, NY), 1973.

Contemporary Heroes and Heroines, Book IV, Thomson Gale (Detroit, MI), 2000.

Contemporary Literary Criticism, Volume 12, Thomson Gale (Detroit, MI), 1980.

Encyclopedia of World Biography, 2nd edition, Thomson Gale (Detroit, MI), 1998.

Gross, Theodore L., editor, *Representative Men,* Free Press, 1970.

Johnson, Rheta Grimsley, *Good Grief: The Story of Charles M. Schulz,* Pharos Books (New York, NY), 1989.

Kidd, Chip, editor, *Peanuts: The Art of Charles M. Schulz,* Pantheon (New York, NY), 2001.

Mascola, Marilyn, *Charles Schulz, Great Cartoonist,* Rourke Enterprises (Vero Beach, FL), 1989.

Mendelson, Lee, *A Charlie Brown Christmas: The Making of a Tradition,* HarperResource (New York, NY), 2000.

Mendelson, Lee, and Charles Schulz, *Charlie Brown and Charlie Schulz: In Celebration of the Twentieth Anniversary of Peanuts,* World Publishing (Cleveland, OH), 1970.

Newsmakers 2000, Issue 3, Thomson Gale (Detroit, MI), 2000.

Reitberger, Reinhold, and Wolfgang Fuchs, *Comics: Anatomy of a Mass Medium,* translated by Nadia Fowler, Studio Vista (London, England), 1972.

Richards, Carmen, *Minnesota Writers,* Denison (Minneapolis, MN), 1961.

Schulz, Charles M., *Around the World in 45 Years: Charlie Brown's Anniversary Celebration,* Andrews & McMeel (Kansas City, MO), 1994.

Schulz, Charles M., *I Take My Religion Seriously,* Warner Press (Anderson, IN), 1989.

Schulz, Charles M., *Peanuts Jubilee: My Life and Art with Charlie Brown and Others,* Holt (New York, NY), 1975.

Schulz, Charles M., *Peanuts Treasury,* foreword by Johnny Hart, Holt (New York, NY), 1968.

Schulz, Charles M., *Snoopy around the World,* photographs by Alberto Rizzo, Abrams (New York, NY), 1990.

Schulz, Charles M., *Things I've Had to Learn Over and Over and Over: (Plus a Few Minor Discoveries),* Holt, Rinehart, & Winston (New York, NY), 1984.

Schulz, Charles M., *You Don't Look 35, Charlie Brown!,* Holt, Rinehart, and Winston (New York, NY), 1985.

Schulz, Monte, and Jody Millward, *The Peanuts Trivia and Reference Book,* Holt (New York, NY), 1986.

Short, Robert L., *The Gospel according to Peanuts,* John Knox (Louisville, KY), 1965.

Short, Robert L., *The Parables of Peanuts,* Harper (New York, NY), 1968.

Trimboli, Giovanni, editor, *Charles M. Schulz: Forty Years Life and Art,* preface by Umberto Eco, Pharos Books (New York, NY), 1990.

PERIODICALS

Appraisal, spring, 1982, review of *Charlie Brown's Fifth Super Book of Questions and Answers,* p. 62; spring, 1983, review of *Charlie Brown's Encyclopedia of Energy,* p. 47.

Art in America, March-April, 1976.

Booklist, November 1, 1974; February 1, 1983, reviews of *Charlie Brown's Super Book of Questions and Answers, Charlie Brown's Second Super Book of Questions and Answers, Charlie Brown's Third Super Book of Questions and Answers,* and *Charlie Brown's Fourth Super Book of Questions and Answers,* p. 740, and review of *Charlie Brown's Fifth Super Book of Questions and Answers,* p. 741; September 1, 1983, review of *Charlie Brown Dictionary,* p. 97; December 15, 1985, review of *You Don't Look 35, Charlie Brown!,* p. 603; January 15, 1990, review of *Charlie Brown Dictionary,* p. 1034; April 15, 1999, review of *Why, Charlie Brown, Why?,* p. 1625; December 15, 1999, review of *Peanuts: A Golden Celebration,* p. 750.

Books for Keeps, September, 1991, review of *Why, Charlie Brown, Why?,* p. 11.

Bulletin of the Center for Children's Books, December, 1982, review of *Charlie Brown's Encyclopedia of Energy,* p. 76.

Business World, December 20, 1969.

Christian Science Monitor, November 29, 1968; November 11, 1970.

Curriculum Review, October, 1983, review of *Charlie Brown's Encyclopedia of Energy,* p. 76.

Detroit Free Press, February 14, 2000, p. A1; October 14, 2001, review of *It's the Great Pumpkin, Charlie Brown,* p. 5E.

Globe and Mail, December 18, 1999, review of *Peanuts: A Golden Celebration,* p. D15; November 24, 2001, review of *Peanuts: The Art of Charles Schulz,* p. D34.

Journal of Youth Services in Libraries, fall, 1987, review of *Is This Good-Bye, Charlie Brown?,* p. 72.

Junior Bookshelf, October, 1991, review of *Why, Charlie Brown, Why?,* p. 219.

Kliatt, spring, 1983, review of *It's Chow Time, Snoopy,* p. 54; winter, 1983, review of *You're Weird, Sir!,* p. 80; fall, 1984, review of *And the Beagles and the Bunnies Shall Lie Down Together,* p. 54; winter, 1985, review of *I'm Not Your Sweet Babboo!,* p. 77; fall, 1986, review of *The Way of the Fussbudget Is Not Easy,* p. 77; winter, 1986, review of *You Don't Look 35, Charlie Brown!,* p. 72; January, 1989, review of *Talk Is Cheep, Charlie Brown,* p. 61; April, 1989, review of *Brothers and Sisters: It's All Relative,* p. 66; January, 1990, review of *Things I've Had to Learn Over and Over and Over,* p. 49, and review of *It Doesn't Take Much to Attract a Crowd,* p. 49; April, 1990, review of *If Beagles Could Fly,* p. 52; September, 1990, review of *An Educational Slice,* p. 53; September, 1991, review of *Could You Be More Pacific?,* p. 66.

Learning: The Magazine for Creative Teaching, April, 1990, review of *Why, Charlie Brown, Why?,* p. 76.

Life, March 17, 1967.

Look, July 22, 1958.

Los Angeles Times Book Review, October 20, 1996, review of *Trick or Treat, Great Pumpkin,* p. 8; February 3, 2002, review of *Peanuts: The Art of Charles M. Schulz,* p. 12.

New Republic, December 7, 1974.

Newsweek, March 6, 1961; December 27, 1971.

New Yorker, March 18, 1967.

New York Times, May 26, 1969; June 2, 1971.

New York Times Book Review, March 12, 1967; December 7, 1975; December 11, 1977; October 26, 1980.

New York Times Magazine, April 16, 1967.

Publishers Weekly, July 7, 1975; July 27, 1990, review of *Snoopy around the World,* p. 219; June 24, 1996, reviews of *Your Dog Plays Hockey?, Kick the Ball, Marcie!, It's the First Day of School!,* and *I'll Be Home Soon, Snoopy,* p. 62; September 30, 1996, review of *Trick or Treat, Great Pumpkin,* p. 86, review of *Snoopy's Christmas Tree,* p. 93, review of *Sally's Christmas Miracle,* p. 93; October 4, 1999, review of *Peanuts: A Golden Celebration,* p. 59; December 3, 2001, review of *A Charlie Brown Valentine,* p. 62.

Punch, February 7, 1968.

Redbook, December, 1967.

Reflections . . . The Wanderer Review of Literature, summer, 1986, review of *Me and Charlie Brown, Volume 1,* p. 24.

Saturday Evening Post, January 12, 1957; April 25, 1964.

Saturday Review, April 12, 1969.

School Library Journal, January, 1982, review of *Charlie Brown's Fifth Super Book of Questions and Answers,* p. 74; February, 1982, review of *Dr. Beagle and Mr. Hyde,* p. 72; March, 1983, review of *Charlie Brown's Encyclopedia of Energy,* p. 172; May, 1983, review of *Someday You'll Find Her, Charlie Brown,* p. 66; December, 1983, review of *Snoopy on Wheels,* p. 59; January, 1985, review of *Is This Good-Bye, Charlie Brown?,* p. 80; April, 1986, review of *You Don't Look 35, Charlie Brown!,* p. 109; February, 2002, review of *It's a Big World, Charlie Brown,* p. 157.

Science Books and Films, May, 1982, review of *Charlie Brown's Fifth Super Book of Questions and Answers,* p. 273; March, 1983, review of *Charlie Brown's Encyclopedia of Energy,* p. 207; March, 1985, review of *Snoopy's Facts and Fun Book about Seasons,* p. 215.

Seventeen, January, 1962.

Time, March 3, 1957; April 9, 1965; January 5, 1970.

Times Educational Supplement, December 14, 1984, review of *Snoopy and the Twelve Days of Christmas,* p. 24.

Times Literary Supplement, December 3, 1976.

U.S. Catholic, July, 1969.

Valuator, spring, 1969.

Village Voice, March 16, 1967.

Voice of Youth Advocates, February, 1982, review of *Dr. Beagle and Mr. Hyde,* p. 44; April, 1986, review of *You Don't Look 35, Charlie Brown!,* p. 54.

Wall Street Journal, October 21, 1999, review of *Peanuts: A Golden Celebration,* p. W8.

Washington Post, April 4, 1970.

Washington Post Book World, September 16, 1979; March 24, 2002, review of *Peanuts: The Art of Charles M. Schulz,* p. 9.

ONLINE

Charles M. Shulz Museum Web site, http://www.charlesmschulzmuseum.org/ (June 2, 2003), biography of Charles M. Schulz.

Minnesota Author Biographies Project Web site, http://people.mnhs.org/authors/ (June 2, 2003), "Charles M. Schulz."

* * *

SCHULZ, Charles Monroe
See SCHULZ, Charles M.

* * *

SCHWARTZ, Lynne Sharon 1939-

PERSONAL: Born March 19, 1939, in Brooklyn, NY; daughter of Jack M. (a lawyer and accountant) and Sarah (Slatus) Sharon; married Harry Schwartz (a city planner), December 22, 1957; children: Rachel Eve, Miranda Ruth. *Education:* Barnard College, B.A., 1959; Bryn Mawr College, M.A., 1961; graduate study at New York University, 1967-72.

ADDRESSES: Home—50 Morningside Dr., New York, NY 10025. *Agent*—c/o Counterpoint, 387 Park Avenue South, New York, NY 10016

CAREER: Full-time writer. *Writer* (magazine), Boston, MA, associate editor, 1961-63; Operation Open City (civil rights-fair housing organization), New York City, writer, 1965-67; Hunter College of the City University of New York, New York City, lecturer, 1970-75. Taught fiction workshops at University of Iowa, 1982-83, Columbia University, 1983-84, 1985, Boston University, 1984-85, Rice University, 1987, University of California at Irvine, 1991, and University of Hawaii at Manoa, 1994.

MEMBER: PEN American Center, Authors Guild, Authors League of America, National Book Critics Circle.

AWARDS, HONORS: James Henle Award, Vanguard Press, 1974, for "Lucca"; Lamport Award, Lamport Foundation, 1977, for short story "Rough Strife"; American Book Award nomination for first novel, 1981, for *Rough Strife;* fellowship, National Endowment for the Arts, 1985; Guggenheim fellowship, 1986; New York State Foundation for the Arts fellowship; PEN/Faulkner Award nominee, 1990, and Harold Ribalow Award, 1990, both for *Leaving Brooklyn;* PEN/Renato Puggioli Translation award, 1991, for *Smoke Over Birkenau.*

WRITINGS:

Rough Strife (novel), Harper (New York, NY), 1980.

Balancing Acts (novel), Harper (New York, NY), 1981.

Disturbances in the Field (novel), Harper (New York, NY), 1983.

Acquainted with the Night (short stories), Harper (New York, NY), 1984.

We Are Talking about Homes: A Great University against Its Neighbors (nonfiction), Harper (New York, NY), 1985.

The Melting Pot and Other Subversive Stories, Penguin (New York, NY), 1987.

Leaving Brooklyn (novel), Bantam (New York, NY), 1989.

The Four Questions (children's book), paintings by Ori Sherman, Dial (New York, NY), 1989.

A Lynne Sharon Schwartz Reader: Selected Prose and Poetry, University Press of New England (Hanover, NH), 1992.

(Translator) Millu, Liana, *Smoke Over Birkenau,* Jewish Publication Society (Philadelphia, PA), 1991.

The Fatigue Artist: A Novel, Scribner (New York, NY), 1995.

Ruined by Reading: A Life in Books, Beacon Press (Boston, MA), 1996.

In the Family Way: An Urban Comedy (novel), Morrow (New York, NY), 1999.

Face to Face: A Reader in the World, Beacon Press (Boston, MA), 2000.

Referred Pain: And Other Stories, Counterpoint (New York, NY), 2004.

Work represented in anthologies, including *Best American Short Stories, 1978; Best American Short Stories, 1979; Banquet,* Penmaen Press (Great Barrington, MA), 1979, *O. Henry Prize Stories, 1979,* and *Imagining America,* 1992. Contributor of stories, articles, translations, and reviews to literary journals and popular magazines, including *Ontario Review, Harper's, New York Times Book Review, Washington Post Book World, Ploughshares, Redbook,* and *Chicago Review.*

SIDELIGHTS: Lynne Sharon Schwartz's short stories and novels magnify the subtleties of human relationships. In her first novel, *Rough Strife,* she documents in extreme detail the development and growth of a long marriage from the wife's point of view. Following the premise that "the unexamined life is not worth living," Schwartz creates characters who seek a complete understanding of themselves and the world around them. Her other novels, including *Disturbances in the Field* and *Balancing Acts,* also portray dynamic, intelligent female characters whose searches for fulfillment are affected by events beyond their control. "She writes of those things that constitute our lives," commented James Kaufmann in the *Los Angeles Times,* that "show us how what we do and what's done to us slowly accumulate to make us what we are."

Although Schwartz knew from an early age that she wanted to be a writer, she did not begin taking her work seriously until she was over thirty. While working on her Ph.D. at New York University, she realized the time was right: "Suddenly it dawned on me: I was a little over 30, and if I was going to write, I'd better write," Schwartz told Wendy Smith in a *Publishers Weekly* interview. Realizing that she no longer had to live "the way it was done" she told Smith, she abandoned her graduate studies and concentrated solely on fiction writing. Though she considered herself a short story writer, her publisher urged her to first write novels because they tend to sell better than collections of stories. Schwartz's first attempt produced *Rough Strife,* an expanded version of a prize-winning short story. Schwartz related the key objective of all her writing to Smith: "Beneath all the layers of dailiness, the commonplace that I write about, I really try to get at these things that nobody wants to look at."

In *Rough Strife,* Caroline recounts the ups and downs of her twenty-year marriage to Ivan. Through courtship, marriage, careers, and rearing children, Caroline and Ivan retain their commitment to one another. They transcend personal differences, arguments, and infidelities to make their relationship survive. Lore Dickstein wrote in *Ms.* that though Caroline's retreat into feminism in face of her conflicting roles as wife, mother, and professional seems forced, Schwartz nevertheless has "written an American 'Scenes from a Marriage'. . . . [T]he author traces the slow and subtle changes . . . between Caroline and Ivan, and it all rings true: the crises and dull spells, the falling in and out of love with the same person, the struggle of creating an enduring partnership." Katha Pollit stated in the *New York Times Book Review* that though the "relentless focus begins to seem claustrophobic," Schwartz "registers the fluctuations of marital feeling with the fidelity of a Geiger counter." Anne Tyler noticed this feeling of claustrophobia as well in a *Book World* review, but praised the effect as being "as convoluted and intense as marriage itself." Jonathan Yardley, also writing in *Book World,* wrote that *Rough Strife* is a "remarkably mature examination of the tensions and satisfactions of marriage."

Similarly, *Disturbances in the Field* focuses on the dynamics of another marital relationship. Lydia enjoys her relationship with her husband, Victor, her four children, and her career as a classical pianist. Her social life revolves around her old college friends, with whom she discusses philosophy on a regular basis. She has had various extramarital affairs and remains on good terms with one of her lovers, a successful psychotherapist. When two of her children are killed in a bus accident, Lydia's life deteriorates into chaos and pain. She questions her beliefs and loses interest in the things in which she used to find pleasure.

Some critics have expressed irritation with Lydia, a heroine whose life seems too idyllic. "The culture for her heroine is both peculiarly specific and chillingly impersonal," wrote Carolyn See in the *New York Times Book Review.* "It's ironic that only when tragedy strikes do these characters begin to sound real," See continues. Yardley also commented that Lydia fails to become a sympathetic character, mainly because of her smug complacency about her ideal life. Noting Lydia's frequent conversations about Greek philosophers such as Aristotle, Heraclitus, and Leucippus, Yardley stated that "the idea, apparently, is to show how intimate the relationship is between the words of philosophy and the events of ordinary life." Carole Cook of *Commonweal* regarded the work as "the execution of an entire, unique world out of a generous accumulation of detail, character, and incident." Furthermore, Cook continued, though "the novel cannot explain reality, it can nonetheless embody its frustrations and limitations."

In *Balancing Acts,* Schwartz examines a different kind of relationship: an intergenerational one. Alison is a precocious thirteen-year-old who sees in seventy-four-year-old Max an escape from the constraints of her traditional suburban upbringing. Max is a retired circus performer and widower who resents Alison's intrusion into his life because he wants to grow old peacefully. Alison befriends Max in hopes of emulating his unconventional lifestyle. In a *Book World* review, Anne Tyler remarked that Alison's background does not provide sufficient explanation for her actions and that "when Max calls her a 'pest,' we tend to agree, although we're not supposed to." Bill Greenwell, however, praised the personality conflict in the *New Statesman:* "Lynne Sharon Schwartz handles the clash of Max and Alison beautifully, with one thumbing her nose at the conventions of adolescence, the other snubbing a senility into which he seems expected to lapse." Judith Gies stated in the *Saturday Review* it is a relationship in which "one of them learns to accept life and the other to relinquish it. . . . Each is looking for transcendence."

Schwartz's 1995 novel *The Fatigue Artist* has some autobiographical elements. Its protagonist is a novelist, Laura, who—like Schwartz—has suffered from Chronic Fatigue Symptom (CFS), a vague, mysterious illness that brings on bouts of exhaustion, aches, and other symptoms. CFS forms "the backdrop for the book's narrative, which really deals with a woman's struggle to come to terms with loss, middle-age and loneliness," explained Beth Weinhouse in *New Leader.* Laura's CFS has set in just after the violent death of her husband, a policeman who was shot on the job. The malaise of the illness mingles with her struggle to make a normal life again. Spending long hours in bed, she muses on the lukewarm quality of her marriage, the meaning of her various affairs, and the nature of illness. Traditional doctors are no help to her, and she eventually puts her trust in a "witch" who acts as a kind of therapist. As Laura's understanding of her own feelings deepens and her sense of control is reestablished, her weariness slowly leaves her.

Reviewers were generally enthusiastic about *The Fatigue Artist.* Donna Seaman, a *Booklist* contributor, found that "there's an incredible intimacy to Schwartz's prose, that precious feeling of connectedness you experience only with the very closest of friends. . . . Schwartz sustains that mood on every beautifully rendered page so that we become deeply involved with and fond of her heroine." And Weinhouse declared: "Her novel compellingly and entertainingly recounts the story of modern urban life, where exhaustion, violence, stress, and loneliness are commonplace, but not invincible." A *Publishers Weekly* reviewer concurred, "Schwartz's painstaking, literary prose and her sensitive exploration of the themes of illness and healing create a resonant picture of a woman confronting the chaos of contemporary life with humor and intelligence."

Schwartz's next novel was more comic than *The Fatigue Artist.* As one reviewer notes, *In the Family Way* "takes on the flavor of a Woody Allen film or an intelligent sitcom as it exposes the unsettled morals and mores of sophisticated, liberal urbanites." Set in an apartment building on New York's Upper West Side, the book centers on Roy, a psychotherapist, and the extended family that shares the building with him. The group includes his first, second, and third wives and their various parents, children, and lovers. "Schwartz . . . masterfully orchestrates," asserted the *Publishers Weekly* reviewer, "providing enough outrageous situations and ironic twists to keep the reader chuckling appreciatively throughout." *Library Journal* contributor Amanda Fung also approved of *In the Family Way,* writing: "The dialog is in-your-face and intimate. Schwartz . . . successfully tells the story of people in search of love and sexual gratification through humor and short scenes that accurately portray relationships in contemporary society."

In addition to her works of adult fiction, Schwartz has written a children's book and some nonfiction work. *The Four Questions* is an illustrated children's book that explains the significance of the Jewish Passover celebration and the symbolism of the Seder meal. Schwartz's text appears in both Hebrew and English and is illustrated by Ori Sherman's drawings of animals. The book explains Jewish history, including the slavery and plagues they endured that led to their exodus from Egypt, as it pertains to the rituals of Passover. *The Four Questions* was well-received by children's book critics; David Gale in the *School Library Journal* called it "an elegant, accessible retelling of the Four Questions," and a *Publishers Weekly* reviewer, noting Schwartz's background as a novelist, stated that her attempt "to bring a simple, yet sophisticated poetic countenance to the story" is often successful.

We Are Talking about Homes: A Great University against Its Neighbors is an account of Schwartz's landlord-tenant dispute with Columbia University following a fire in her New York City apartment building—a building owned by the university. When Schwartz and her neighbors were displaced following a minor fire in 1983, she suspected that Columbia intended to renovate the building for its own use, leaving its former tenants out in the cold. Schwartz "provides a reasonably balanced account" of the tenants' housing predicament, stated Slewyn Raab in *New York Times Book Review,* but "at times . . . her reporting is too understated." Diane K. Harvey of the *Library Journal* cited as the most interesting part of the study the "vivid descriptions of the texture of New York apartment life." In another nonfiction work, *Ruined by Reading: A Life in Books,* Schwartz reflects on her life as a reader, which began at age four. Highly personal, the book is also an intelligent meditation on the value of reading. According to *Booklist*'s Donna Seaman, "She segues confidently from personal memories to moral inquiries and questions of aesthetics, muses over the value of reading randomly and indulgently rather than dutifully, and celebrates the sensuous aspects of time spent with a book."

Schwartz's other publications include the short story collections *Acquainted with the Night* and *The Melting Pot and Other Subversive Stories,* and the novel *Leaving Brooklyn,* a coming-of-age story that parallels Schwartz's own experiences. Schwartz has the ability "to move deeply into her characters's psyches," wrote Jay Parini in *Book World,* "to bring them shimmeringly to life in a remarkably short space within her short stories." Smith remarks in *Publishers Weekly* that these stories "demonstrate that Schwartz can juggle the minutiae of daily life and serious philosophical themes as easily in a 15-page story as she [does] in [her] novels." In a review of *The Melting Pot, New York Times Book Review*'s Perri Klass remarked that "whether she is being sharp and satirical or affectionately comic . . . Lynne Sharon Schwartz writes cleanly and with compassion. Her voice is strong, even as her stories are varied, and her images are compelling."

BIOGRAPHICAL AND CRITICAL SOURCES:

BOOKS

Contemporary Literary Criticism, Volume 31, Thomson Gale (Detroit, MI), 1985.

Schwartz, Lynne Sharon, *Ruined by Reading: A Life in Books,* Beacon Press, 1996.

PERIODICALS

America, April 5, 2004, Sharon Locy, review of *Referred Lives,* p. 35.

Booklist, January 15, 1993, p. 872; June 1, 1995, Donna Seaman, review of *The Fatigue Artist,* p. 1731; April 15, 1996, Donna Seaman, review of *Ruined by Reading,* p. 1409; September 15, 1999, review of *In the Family Way,* p. 234; February 15, 2004, Donna Seaman, review of *Referred Pain,* p. 1038.

Book World, June 21, 1981; October 2, 1983; September 30, 1984; April 15, 1996, p. 1409.

Chicago Tribune, February 15, 2004, Michael Upchurch, review of "Referred Pain," p. 3.

Commonweal, November 4, 1983.

Kirkus Reviews, March 15, 1996, review of *Ruined by Reading.*

Library Journal, November 15, 1985; April 15, 1995, p. 117; April 15, 1996, p. 89; September 1, 1999, Amanda Fung, review of *In the Family Way,* p. 235; February 1, 2004, Diana McRae, review of *Referred Pain,* p. 127.

Los Angeles Times, September 1, 1983; February 23, 2004, Merle Rubin, review of *Referred Pain,* p. Part E.

Ms., June, 1980.

New Leader, October 9, 1995, Beth Weinhouse, review of *The Fatigue Artist,* p. 18.

New Statesman, March 12, 1982.

New York Times Book Review, June 15, 1980; November 6, 1983; November 24, 1985; October 11, 1987; April 16, 1989, p. 26; April 30, 1989, p. 16; July 30, 1995, Anna Shapiro, "No Place Like Bed," p. 16; April 18, 2004, Wendy Smith, review of *Referred Pain,* p. 4.

People, May 15, 1989, p. 33.

Present Tense, September-October, 1989, p. 64.

Publishers Weekly, August 3, 1984; February 10, 1989; August 23, 1991, p. 53; November 23, 1992, p. 58; May 8, 1995, review of *The Fatigue Artist,* p. 287; March 11, 1996, review of *Ruined by Reading,* p. 47; August 23, 1999, review of *In the Family Way,* p. 44; March 27, 2000, review of *Face to Face: A Reader in the World,* p. 66; January 19, 2004, Jeff Zaleski, review of *Referred Pain,* p. 53.

Saturday Review, June, 1981.

School Library Journal, April, 1989; August, 2004, review of Silvana Gandolfi's *Aldabra: Or the Tortoise Who Loved Shakespeare,* translated from the Italian by Lynne Sharon Schwartz, p. 122.

Smithsonian, December, 1996, Kathleen Burke, review of *Ruined by Reading,* p. 137.

Tikkun, September-October, 1989, p. 67.
Variety, June 13, 1990, p. 82.

* * *

SCOTLAND, Jay
See JAKES, John

* * *

SEBASTIAN, Lee
See SILVERBERG, Robert

* * *

SEBASTIAN OWL
See THOMPSON, Hunter S.

* * *

SEBOLD, Alice 1963(?)-

PERSONAL: Born c. 1963; married Glen David Gold (a writer). *Education:* Studied at Syracuse University, 1980-c.84; graduated from University of Houston; University of California—Irvine, M.F.A., 1998.

ADDRESSES: Home—CA. *Agent*—c/o Henry Dunow, Dunow & Carlson Literary Agency, 27 W. 20th Street, Ste. 1003, New York, NY 10011. *E-mail*—henry@dunowcarlson.com.

CAREER: Writer and teacher. Appears on television news shows, such as *NBC News,* to discuss her writing.

AWARDS, HONORS: Bram Stoker Award for best first novel and nomination for best novel, Horror Writers Association, both 2002, for *The Lovely Bones.*

WRITINGS:

Lucky (memoir), Scribner (New York, NY), 1999.
The Lovely Bones: A Novel, Little, Brown (Boston, MA), 2002.

Contributor of stories and articles to popular press, including *Washington Post.*

ADAPTATIONS: The Lovely Bones was adapted as a screenplay to be directed by Peter Jackson and produced in conjunction with FilmFour.

SIDELIGHTS: Alice Sebold's first published book was a memoir of her rape as an eighteen-year-old college freshman. Titled *Lucky* because one of the policemen told her that she was lucky to be alive—not long before Sebold's attack, another young woman had been killed and dismembered in the same tunnel—the book was many years in the making. Sebold returned to Syracuse University, the scene of the rape, and finished her education. She studied writing, and wanted to write her story then, but kept failing. "I wrote tons of bad poetry about it and a couple of bad novels about it—lots of bad stuff," Sebold told Dennis McLellan of the *Los Angeles Times.* She explained to McLellan why the novels were not successful: "I felt the burden of trying to write a story that would encompass all rape victims' stories and that immediately killed the idea of this individual character in the novel. So [the novels] tended to be kind of fuzzy and bland, and I didn't want to make any political missteps."

Sebold continued trying to write after graduation and moved to New York City, where she lived for ten years. "I worked a lot of different jobs and became a competent New Yorker, which is no small task, and went through a lot of stuff and rediscovered reading on my own and I became more honest to who I was, which matters a lot. I went out a lot. I would go to a lot of readings. I did a lot of things that I'm not particularly proud of and that I can't believe I did," she recalled in a talk she gave at the University of California—Irvine (UCI) as recorded by Ehzra Cue on the UCI Web site. At that talk, Sebold presented climbing to the top of the Manhattan Bridge as an example of something she can't believe she did; in other forums, she has also discussed the three years during which she used heroin while she was living in New York.

Lucky began to take shape in the late 1990s, when Sebold was studying fiction writing at a graduate program at UCI. A ten-page assignment sparked her to write forty pages about the rape. Although none of that writing was itself included in the final book, the experience was the impetus for Sebold to begin doing research and putting her memoir together. She read through old letters and journal entries, the transcripts of her rapist's trial, and even returned to Syracuse and talked to the former assistant district attorney who had helped to prosecute the man, allowing her, even fifteen years after the attack, to tell the story in great detail. The result is "a remarkable personal look at a crime all too common in our out-of-whack society," wrote *Toronto Sun* reviewer Yvonne Crittenden. Despite her dark subject matter, "Sebold's wit is as powerful as her searing candor," remarked a *Publishers Weekly* contributor.

Sebold's second book, *The Lovely Bones: A Novel,* is similarly dark in topic. Its narrator, fourteen-year-old Susie Salmon, is raped and killed by a neighbor at the beginning of the book. She narrates the story of her death—and of her family, her friends, and herself coming to terms with it—in the first person from her omniscient seat in heaven. This is "Sebold's most dazzling stroke," declared a *Publishers Weekly* reviewer, as it "provid[es] the warmth of a first-person narration and the freedom of an omniscient one." That omniscience is necessary, since Susie's tale encompasses several different stories: Susie's mother's search to build a new life away from the family after the murder; her father's quest to find the real killer, into which Susie's teenage sister Lindsay is drawn and which puts her at great risk from the same killer; and Susie's vicarious living-out of her own teen and young adult years through Lindsay. "What might play as a sentimental melodrama in the hands of a lesser writer becomes in this volume a keenly observed portrait of familial love and how it endures and changes over time," Michiko Kakutani declared in the *New York Times.* The popularity of *The Lovely Bones* in the U.S. and abroad made Alice Sebold a celebrated writer and "the disaster memoir . . . an American literary genre all its own," wrote Anne-Marie O'Connor of the *Los Angeles Times.*

In an interview with *Publishers Weekly,* Sebold said that writing *The Lovely Bones* "was a delight, because I loved my main character so much and I liked being with her. It was like having company. I was motivated to write about violence because I believe it's not unusual. I see it as just a part of life, and I think we get in trouble when we separate people who've experienced it from those who haven't. Though it's a horrible experience, it's not as if violence hasn't affected many of us."

BIOGRAPHICAL AND CRITICAL SOURCES:

PERIODICALS

ARTVOICE, July 16, 2003, Melissa Sandor, review of *Lovely Bones.*

Buffalo News (Buffalo, NY), August 15, 1999, Louise Continelli, "Victims' Advocate and Author Is Doomed to Live with the Nightmare of Being Raped," p. C2.

Herald (Glasgow, Scotland), September 15, 2001, "Glen David Gold," p. 2; June 26, 2004, Hannah McGill, "The Fight Over the Bones," p. 10.

Kirkus Reviews, May 1, 2002, review of *The Lovely Bones: A Novel,* p. 608.

Library Journal, June 15, 1999, Janice Dunham, review of *Lucky,* p. 92.

Los Angeles Times, September 15, 1999, Dennis McLellan, "Memoir Frees Writer from Dark Days of Her Past," p. 2; September 26, 2003, Anne-Marie O'Connor, "The Power of Having a Little Hope," p. E.1; July 7, 2004, an article about L.A.-based novelists, p. A2.

New Statesman, June 30, 2003, Andrea Dworkin, review of *Lucky,* p. 51.

New York Times, June 18, 2002, Michiko Kakutani, "The Power of Love Leaps the Great Divide of Death," p. E1.

Publishers Weekly, June 21, 1999, review of *Lucky,* p. 44; June 17, 2002, review of *The Lovely Bones,* p. 40, Anne Darby, "PW Talks with Alice Sebold," p. 41.

Sunday Herald (Glasgow, Scotland), February 10, 2002, "Hollywood Break for Lynne's *Lovely Bones,*" p. 11.

Toronto Sun, October 23, 1999, Yvonne Crittenden, "Not So Lucky."

ONLINE

Random House Web site, http://www.randomhouse.com/ (June 18, 2004), "Boldtype: Conversation with Aimee Bender and Alice Sebold."

University of California—Irvine Web site, http://www.uci.edu/ (June 18, 2004), Ehzra Cue, "Alice Sebold's 'An Evening of Fiction'"; Michaela Baltasar, "UCI MFA Graduate Says She Is *Lucky.*"

* * *

SEDARIS, David 1957-
(The Talent Family, a joint pseudonym)

PERSONAL: Surname pronounced "seh- *dar*-iss;" born 1957, in Raleigh, NC; son of Lou and Sharon Sedaris; partner of Hugh Hamrick (a painter). *Education:* Attended Kent State University; School of the Art Institute of Chicago, attained degree in 1987.

ADDRESSES: *Home*—Kensington, London, England. *Agent*—Steven Barclay, 321 Pleasant St., Petaluma, CA 94952.

CAREER: Diarist, radio commentator, essayist, and short story writer. Has taught writing at the School of the Art Institute of Chicago, Chicago, IL; appeared on *Milly's Orchid Show,* Chicago; appeared on *The Wild Room,* WBEZ radio, Chicago; appeared on *This America Life,* National Public Radio; has held numerous part-time jobs, including employment as a performance artist, a moving company worker, an office worker, an elf in SantaLand at Macy's department store, a housepainter, an apple-picker, and an apartment cleaner; volunteered with English Language Library for the Blind in Paris, France, and Age Concern in London, England.

AWARDS, HONORS: Obie Award, *Village Voice,* 1995, for *One Woman Shoe;* Humorist of the Year, *Time* magazine, 2001; Thurber Prize for American Humor; Grammy Award nomination for Best Spoken Word Album, 2005, for *Dress Your Family in Corduroy & Denim;* Grammy Award nomination for Best Comedy Album, 2005, for *David Sedaris: Live at Carnegie Hall.*

WRITINGS:

AUTOBIOGRAPHICAL ESSAYS

Origins of the Underclass, and Other Stories, Amethyst Press (Washington, DC), 1992.
Barrel Fever, Little, Brown (Boston, MA), 1994.
Naked, Little, Brown (Boston, MA), 1997.
Holidays on Ice, Little, Brown (Boston, MA), 1997.
Me Talk Pretty One Day, Little, Brown (Boston, MA), 2000.
Dress Your Family in Corduroy and Denim, Little, Brown (Boston, MA), 2004.

PLAYS

Jamboree, produced at Theatre for the New City (New York, NY), 1991.
Stump the Host, produced at La MaMa ETC (New York, NY), March, 1993.
(With sister, Amy Sedaris, as The Talent Family) *One Woman Shoe,* produced at La MaMa ETC (New York, NY), 1995.
(With Joe Mantello) *The SantaLand Diaries,* produced off-Broadway, November, 1996, published as *SantaLand Diaries and Seasons Greetings: Two Plays,* Dramatists Play Service (New York, NY), 1998.
(With Amy Sedaris, as The Talent Family) *Little Freida Mysteries,* produced at La MaMa ETC (New York, NY), February, 1997.
(With Amy Sedaris, as The Talent Family) *Incident at Cobbler's Knob,* produced at the Fiorello H. LaGuardia High School of Music and Art (New York, NY), 1997.
(With Amy Sedaris, as The Talent Family) *The Book of Liz,* (produced at Greenwich House Theater, New York, 2001), Dramatists Play Service (New York, NY), 2002.

Also, with Amy Sedaris, author of the play *Stitches;* author of three plays produced in Chicago, IL, prior to 1991.

COMEDY ALBUMS

Barrel Fever and Other Stories, Time Warner Audio, 2001.
(With Amy Sedaris and Ann Magnuson) *The David Sedaris Box Set,* Time Warner Audio, 2002.
David Sedaris Live at Carnegie Hall, Time Warner Audio, 2003.

OTHER

(Editor and author of introduction) *Children Playing before a Statue of Hercules,* Simon & Schuster (New York, NY), 2005.
Also author of commentaries for *This American Life* and other National Public Radio programs, 1992—. *This American Life* commentaries included in collections, including *This American Life: Lies, Sissies, and Fiascos,* Rhino Records, 1999; *Crimebusters and Crossed Wires: Stories from This American Life,* Sony, 2003; and *Committed: Men Tell Stories of Love, Commitment and Marriage,* Bloomsbury, 2005. Contributor to periodicals, including *Esquire.*

ADAPTATIONS: "Diary of a Smoker," an essay from *Barrel Fever,* was adapted by Matthew Modine into a thirteen-minute film shown at the Sundance Film Festival and on the Public Broadcasting System (PBS), 1994. Audiobook versions of *Naked* and *Holidays on Ice* were released by Time Warner Audio Books in 1997; an audiobook version of *Dress Your Family in Corduroy and Denim* was released by Time Warner Audiobooks in 2004.

SIDELIGHTS: "Thank God for the maladjusted lives of Lou and Sharon Sedaris," Hannah Sampson wrote in the *Miami Herald.* "Their home may have been frenzied and their six children destined for therapy, but they gave us the shrewd and unconventional David Sedaris, who has created a successful career of telling hilarious, heartbreaking stories about his dysfunctional family." Sedaris has published several books of essays about his life, including the *New York Times* best-sellers *Me Talk Pretty One Day* and *Dress Your Family in Corduroy and Denim.* Also, in collaboration with his sister Amy Sedaris (best known for her appearances on the cable show *Strangers with Candy*), Sedaris has written several satiric plays, including the Obie Award-winning *One Woman Shoe.* "No one puts the fun into function quite like Sedaris," Kim Harwell wrote in the *Dallas Morning News.*

Sedaris grew up in North Carolina and moved to Chicago while in his twenties, where he attended school and performed readings from his diaries for audiences. In the audience at one reading was Ira Glass, of the National Public Radio (NPR) programs *The Wild Room* and *This American Life.* After Sedaris moved to New York in 1991, Glass called and asked him if he had any holiday-themed essays for a program Glass was putting together. Sedaris did—"SantaLand Diaries"—and this piece launched his career. Sedaris began reading excerpts from his diaries on the air, where his "nicely nerdy, quavering voice," in the words of *Newsweek* commentator Jeff Giles, delivered monologues praised for their acerbic wit and dead-pan delivery. Commenting about Sedaris's early commentaries in the *New York Times,* John Marchese wrote: "Sedaris has shown remarkable skill as a mimic and the ability to mix the sweet and the bitter: to be naive and vulnerable and at the same time, jaded and wickedly funny." Because of these radio pieces, Sampson continued, Sedaris has "become the closest thing public radio has to Elvis, so popular that his appearances at concert halls sell out."

Sedaris's comic, and often satirical, monologues draw primarily on his experiences in the odd day-jobs that he held before his work with NPR heated up his artistic career. Of his long-standing position as an apartment cleaner, Sedaris told Marchese in the *New York Times:* "I can only write when it's dark, so basically, my whole day is spent waiting for it to get dark. Cleaning apartments gives me something to do when I get up. Otherwise, I'd feel like a bum." As a result of his appearances on NPR, Sedaris has received numerous job offers, both for cleaning and for writing—as well as a two-book contract with Little, Brown, who in 1994, published *Barrel Fever,* a collection of Sedaris's essays and short stories.

Barrel Fever includes several pieces that brought Sedaris to national attention when he read them on the radio, including "Diary of a Smoker," in which the author declares that the efforts of nonsmokers to extend his life by not allowing him to smoke in front of them only gives him more time to hate nonsmokers, and "SantaLand Diaries," in which the author chronicles his amorous and aggravating experiences playing one of Santa's elves at Macy's one Christmas. Critics remarked on the humorously exaggerated self-delusion of Sedaris's narrators in the short stories, including a man who brags on talk- shows about his affairs with such stars as rock singer Bruce Springsteen and boxer Mike Tyson, and a gay man with a persecution complex who "bemoans his suffering at the hands of society in a style so over-the-top as to be laughable," according to a critic in *Kirkus Reviews.*

Critical response to *Barrel Fever* was generally positive, with reviewers appreciating Sedaris's humorous yet accurate portrayal of such American foibles as the commercialism of Christmas and the self-righteousness of health fanatics. "Without slapping the reader in the face with a political diatribe," wrote a critic for *Kirkus Reviews,* "the author skewers our ridiculous fascination with other people's tedious everyday lives." A contributor to *Publishers Weekly* commented: "Sedaris ekes humor from the blackest of scenarios, peppering his narrative with memorable turns of phrase and repeatedly surprising with his double-edged wit." And although *Newsweek* critic Giles found some of Sedaris's commentary relatively shallow, he nonetheless concluded: "This is a writer who's cleaned our toilets and will never look at us the same way."

Sedaris's second collection of essays, *Naked,* appeared in 1997. These essays, according to a reviewer for *Publishers Weekly,* reveal that "Sedaris can hardly be called a humorist in the ordinary sense . . . . Sedaris is instead an essayist who happens to be very funny." In his characteristic deadpan style, Sedaris tells stories "about nutty or bizarre experiences, like volunteering at a hospital for the insane," Craig Seligman observed in the *New York Times Book Review.* Other essays include Sedaris on hitchhiking, working in Oregon, his personal battle with his childhood nervous disorders, and the title piece, about his sojourn at a nudist colony. But, for Seligman, "the funniest [essays], and ultimately the saddest, have to do with the writer's family." In these autobiographical tales, wrote Margot Mifflin in *Entertainment Weekly,* "Sedaris covers an impressive emotional range . . . . from the comically corrosive title piece . . . to 'Ashes,' his account of his mother's death from cancer—a direct, unsentimental hit to the heart." As Ira Glass told Peter Ames Carlin in a *People* profile, "People come to his work because he's funny . . . . But there's a complicated moral vision there."

In *Me Talk Pretty One Day,* Sedaris tells more stories of his family, but also writes several essays about living in Paris with his partner, painter Hugh Hamrick. (Sedaris moved to Paris after becoming too recognizable in the United States. "It's harder to spy on people when someone is shouting 'Loved you on Letterman!,'" he told *Entertainment Weekly* reviewer Nancy Miller. Then, after he started to become famous in Paris as well, Sedaris moved on to London.) "Although amusing, Sedaris' tales of life in France now that he's happy don't have the bite of those in the first half of the book, many of them dealing with his eccentric father, an IBM engineer who ruins miniature golf with dissertations on wind trajectory," argued Nancy Pate in *Knight Ridder/Tribune News Service.* Lisa Schwarzbaum concluded in *Entertainment Weekly:* "These days Sedaris glitters as one of the wittiest writers around, an essayist and radio commentator who only appears to be telling simple then-what-happened anecdotes."

The trend towards a softer side in Sedaris's stories continued in *Dress Your Family in Corduroy and Denim,* many critics thought. "You get the sense that Sedaris is thinking, 'This is one screwed-up family, but it's my screwed-up family,'" commented *Knight Ridder/Tribune News Service* contributor David Tarrant. His late mother particularly benefits from Sedaris's new-found sympathetic side; in *Dress Your Family in Corduroy and Denim* she "emerges as one of the most poignant and original female characters in contemporary literature," declared a *Publishers Weekly* contributor. As Jason Rowan commented in *Lambda Book Report,* "It's moving to revisit their prickly relationship from a softer and more compassionate place." The fact that Sedaris "can see the ridiculousness in his family's misadventures, yet relate them with tenderness," Marta Salij wrote in the *Detroit Free Press,* makes *Dress Your Family in Corduroy and Denim* "an even richer pleasure than Sedaris' earlier books."

BIOGRAPHICAL AND CRITICAL SOURCES:

PERIODICALS

Advocate, February 25, 1992, Sarah Schulman, review of *Origins of the Underclass, and Other Stories,* pp. 82-84; December 10, 1996, Robert L. Pela, review of *The SantaLand Diaries,* p. 54; March 18, 1997, Robert L. Pela, review of *Naked,* pp. 76-77; June 20, 2000, Robert L. Pela, review of *Me Talk Pretty One Day,* p. 133.

American Theatre, July-August, 1993, Michael Broder, "David Sedaris: Welcome to the Talent Family," pp. 48-50.

Back Stage, June 23, 1995, David Sheward, review of *One Woman Shoe,* p. 29; November 29, 1996, Eric Grode, review of *The SantaLand Diaries,* p. 28; February 28, 1997, Robert Simonson, review of *The Little Frieda Mysteries,* p. 60; July 18, 1997, Robert Simonson, review of *Incident at Cobbler's Knob,* p. 40.

Berkshire Eagle (Berkshire County, MA), April 24, 1998, Seth Rogovoy, "David Sedaris: Just a Writer."

Book, September, 2000, Rochelle O'Gorman, review of *Me Talk Pretty One Day,* p. 85; March-April, 2003, review of *The David Sedaris Box Set,* p. 78, interview with Sedaris, p. 78.

Booklist, June 1, 1994, Benjamin Segedin, review of *Barrel Fever,* p. 1762; February 15, 1997, Donna Seaman, review of *Naked,* p. 996; May 1, 2004, Donna Seaman, review of *Dress Your Family in Corduroy and Denim,* p. 1482; May 1, 2005, Donna Seaman, review of *Children Playing before a Statue of Hercules,* p. 1568.

Chicago Tribune, February 2, 1996, sec. 7, p. 2.

Commonweal, June 15, 2001, Francis DeBernardo, review of *Me Talk Pretty One Day,* p. 24.

Dallas Morning News, June 29, 2004, Kim Harwell, "What We Like: David Sedaris."

Detroit Free Press, June 23, 2004, Marta Salij, review of *Dress Your Family in Corduroy and Denim.*

Entertainment Weekly, July 29, 1994, Margot Mifflin, review of *Barrel Fever,* p. 55; December 13, 1996, Kip Cheng, "Elf Awareness" (interview with Sedaris), p. S10; March 21, 1997, Margot Mifflin, review of *Naked,* p. 68; May 10, 2002, review of *Holidays on Ice,* p. 74; June 2, 2000, Lisa Schwarzbaum, review of *Me Talk Pretty One Day,* p. 72; January 23, 2004, review of *Dress Your Family in Corduroy and Denim,* p. 68; June 4, 2004, Augusten Burroughs, review of *Dress Your Family in Corduroy and Denim,* p. 84; June 11, 2004, Nancy Miller, "Where in the World Is David Sedaris? He Just Fled Paris for London, but America's Most Wanted Humorist Can't Outrun Success," p. 73.

Esquire, June, 2000, Ira Glass, review of *Me Talk Pretty One Day,* p. 38.

Fortune, June 12, 2000, review of *Me Talk Pretty One Day,* p. 358.

Gay and Lesbian Review, January, 2001, Lewis Whittington, review of *Me Talk Pretty One Day,* p. 46.

Independent (London, England), February 9, 2001, Steve Jelbert, "How to Take the World By Charm" (interview with Sedaris), section S, page 9.

Kirkus Reviews, April 1, 1994, p. 430; April 15, 2004, review of *Dress Your Family in Corduroy and Denim,* p. 384.

Knight Ridder/Tribune News Service, June 20, 2001, Nancy Pate, review of *Me Talk Pretty One Day,* p. K6846; July 18, 2001, Robert K. Elder, "Cult Writer David Sedaris Finds Mainstream Success with Acerbic Tales of the Absurd," p. K2674; August 5, 2004, David Tarrant, review of *Dress Your Family in Corduroy and Denim,* p. K3038.

Lambda Book Report, September, 1997, David Tedhams, review of *Naked,* pp. 37-38; May, 2004, Jason Rowan, review of *Dress Your Family in Corduroy and Denim,* p. 8.

Library Journal, May 1, 1994, Thomas Wiener, review of *Barrel Fever,* p. 104; April 1, 1997, Mary Paumier, review of *Naked,* p. 93; July, 1997, Dana C. Bell-Russel, review of *Naked* (audiobook), p. 143; May 15, 2000, A.J. Anderson, review of *Me Talk Pretty One Day,* p. 95; October 15, 2000, Gloria Maxwell, review of *Me Talk Pretty One Day* (audiobook), p. 124; June 15, 2004, Robin Imhof, review of *Dress Your Family in Corduroy and Denim,* p. 72.

Los Angeles Times Book Review, October 16, 1994, p. 6; July 2, 1995, p. 11.

Miami Herald, June 13, 2004, Hannah Sampson, review of *Dress Your Family in Corduroy and Denim.*

Nation, September 8, 1997, Laurie Stone, review of *Incident at Cobbler's Knob,* pp. 32- 33.

Newsweek, August 15, 1994, Jeff Giles, review of *Barrel Fever,* pp. 66- 67.

New York Times, February 19, 1997, p. C14; March 2, 2001, Jesse McKinley, review of *The Book of Liz,* section B, page 2, section E, page 2; March 28, 2001, Ben Brantley, review of *The Book of Liz,* section B, page 1, section E, page 1.

New York Times Book Review, July 4, 1993, p. 5; March 16, 1997, p. 10; June 16, 2000, Michiko Kakutani, review of *Me Talk Pretty One Day;* June 20, 2004, Stephen Metcalf, review of *Dress Your Family in Corduroy and Denim,* p. 7.

Orlando Sentinel, June 28, 2000, Nancy Pate, review of *Me Talk Pretty One Day.*

O, The Oprah Magazine, June, 2004, Lisa Kogan, review of *Dress Your Family in Corduroy and Denim,* p. 148.

People, March 24, 1997, Paula Chin, review of *Naked,* pp. 35-37; October 20, 1997, Peter Ames Carlin, "Elf-Made Writer: Former Santa's Helper David Sedaris Turns His Odd Life into Literature," p. 129; June 26, 2000, review of *Me Talk Pretty One Day,* p. 20; June 7, 2004, Sean Daly, review of *Dress Your Family in Corduroy and Denim,* p. 50.

Publishers Weekly, April 25, 1994, review of *Barrel Fever,* p. 58; January 27, 1997, review of *Naked,* p. 88; April 7, 1997, p. 22; May 5, 1997, review of *Naked* (audiobook), pp. 40-41; November 24, 1997, review of *Holidays on Ice,* p. 55; May 8, 2000, review of *Me Talk Pretty One Day,* p. 212; June 19, 2000, Kathie Bergquist, interview with Sedaris, p. 54; August 7, 2000, review of *Me Talk Pretty One Day* (audiobook), p. 42; October 6, 2003, Shannon Maughan, "Him Talk Pretty on Audiobooks" (interview with Sedaris), pp. 26-27; December 1, 2003, review of *David Sedaris Live at Carnegie Hall,* p. 21; May 24, 2004, review of *Dress Your Family in Corduroy and Denim,* p. 56; June 14, 2004, Daisy Maryles, "Sedaris Scores," p. 24; July 5, 2004, review of *Dress Your Family in Corduroy and Denim* (audiobook), p. 18; June 6, 2005, review of *Children Playing before a Statue of Hercules,* p. 60.

Sarasota Herald Tribune, December 14, 2001, Jay Handelman, review of *SantaLand Diaries,* p. 28.

South Florida Sun-Sentinel, August 11, 2004, Oline H. Cogdill, review of *The David Sedaris Box Set.*

Time, June 19, 2000, interview with Sedaris, p. 139; July 2, 2001, Belinda Luscombe, "That's Signing, Not Singing," p. 79; September 17, 2001, Walter Kirn, "Wry Slicer: Neurotic, Self-Absorbed and Laugh-Out-Loud Funny, David Sedaris Takes Readers on a Wild Ride Through His Improbable Life," p. 86; June 21, 2004, Josh Tyrangiel, "Ten Questions for David Sedaris," p. 8.

Variety, November 11, 1996, Greg Evans, review of *The SantaLand Diaries,* p. 66; April 2, 2001, Charles Isherwood, review of *The Book of Liz,* p. 30.

Wall Street Journal, June 2, 2000, Robert J. Hughes, review of *Me Talk Pretty One Day,* p. W10.

Washington Post, March 22, 1997, p. B1.

Whole Earth Review, winter, 1995, Allison Levin, review of *Barrel Fever,* p. 63.

ONLINE

January Magazine, http://www.januarymagazine.com/ (August 12, 2004), Linda Richards, "January Interview: David Sedaris."

Stephen Barclay Agency Web Site, http://www.barclayagency.com/ (August 12, 2004), "David Sedaris."

SENDAK, Maurice 1928-
(Maurice Bernard Sendak)

PERSONAL: Born June 10, 1928, in Brooklyn, NY; son of Philip (a dressmaker) and Sarah (Schindler) Sendak. *Education:* Attended Art Students' League, New York, NY, 1949-51.

ADDRESSES: Home—Ridgefield, CT. *Office*—c/o HarperCollins Children's Books, 1350 Avenue of the Americas, New York, NY 10019. *Agent*—Steven Barclay Agency, 12 Western Ave., Petaluma, CA 94952.

CAREER: Writer and illustrator of children's books, 1951—. Worked for comic book syndicate All American Comics part-time during high school; Timely Service (window display house), New York, NY, window display artist, 1946; F.A.O. Schwartz, New York, NY, display artist, 1948-51. Co-founder and artistic director of Night Kitchen (national children's theater), 1990—. Parsons School of Design, Yale University, former instructor; May Hill Arbuthnot Honor Lecturer, 2003. Set and costume designer for opera productions in the United States and Great Britain, including Mozart's *The Magic Flute,* for Houston Grand Opera, 1980; Leos Janacek's *The Cunning Little Vixen,* for New York City Opera, 1981; Serge Prokofiev's *Love for Three Oranges,* for Glyndebourne Opera, 1982; Mozart's *The Goose of Cairo,* for New York City Opera, c. 1984; *Idomeneo,* for Los Angeles Opera, 1988; and Maurice Ravel's *L'enfant et les sortileges* and *L'heure espagnol,* both for New York City Opera, both 1989; designer for *The Nutcracker: The Motion Picture,* 1986. Has appeared in film *The Lively Art of Picture Books,* c. 1965, and "Mon Cher Papa" (episode of television series *American Masters*), Public Broadcasting Service, 1987. Executive producer, *Little Bear* animated television series, Canadian Broadcasting Corporation, 1995. Sendak's illustrations have been displayed in one-man shows at the School of Visual Arts, New York, NY, 1964, Rosenbach Foundation, Philadelphia, PA, 1970 and 1975, Trinity College, 1972, Galerie Daniel Keel, Zurich, Switzerland, 1974, Ashmolean Museum, Oxford University, 1975, American Cultural Center, Paris, France, 1978, and J. Pierpont Morgan Library, New York, NY, 1981. Lecturer at schools and libraries; Arbuthnot Lecturer, 2003.

MEMBER: Authors Guild, Authors League of America.

AWARDS, HONORS: New York Times Best Illustrated Book award, 1952, for *A Hole Is to Dig,* 1954, for *I'll Be You and You Be Me,* 1956, for *I Want to Paint My Bathroom Blue,* 1957, for *The Birthday Party,* 1958, for *What Do You Say, Dear?,* 1959, for *Father Bear Comes Home,* 1960, for *Open House for Butterflies,* 1962, for *The Singing Hill,* 1963, for *Where the Wild Things Are,* 1964, for *The Bat-Poet,* 1965, for *The Animal Family,* 1966, for *Zlateh the Goat and Other Stories,* 1968, for *A Kiss for Little Bear,* 1969, for *The Light Princess,* 1970, for *In the Night Kitchen,* 1973, for *The Juniper Tree and Other Tales from Grimm* and *King Grisly-Beard,* 1976, for *Fly by Night,* 1981, for *Outside over There,* and 1984, for *The Nutcracker;* Caldecott Medal runner-up, American Library Association, 1954, for *A Very Special House,* 1959, for *What Do You Say, Dear?,* 1960, for *The Moon Jumpers,* 1962, for *Little Bear's Visit,* 1963, for *Mr. Rabbit and the Lovely Present,* 1971, for *In the Night Kitchen,* and 1982, for *Outside over There;* Spring Book Festival honor book, 1956, for *Kenny's Window;* Caldecott Medal, and Lewis Carroll Shelf award, both 1964, International Board on Books for Young People award, 1966, Art Books for Children award, 1973, 1974, 1975, *Redbook* Best Young Picture Books Paperback Award, 1984, and Children's Choice award, 1985, all for *Where the Wild Things Are;* Chandler Book Talk Reward of Merit, 1967; Hans Christian Andersen International Medal, 1970, for body of illustration work; Art Books for Children award, 1973, 1974, 1975, and *Redbook* award, 1985, for *In the Night Kitchen;* American Book Award nomination, 1980, for *Higglety Pigglety Pop!; or, There Must Be More to Life; Boston Globe/Horn Book* award, and *New York Times* Outstanding Book designation, both 1981, and American Book Award, 1982, all for *Outside over There;* Laura Ingalls Wilder Award, Association for Library Service to Children, 1983, for "substantial and lasting contribution to children's literature;" National Medal of the Arts from President Bill Clinton, 1996; Visual Arts Award, National Foundation for Jewish Culture, 1998; L.H.D., Boston University, 1977; honorary degrees from University of Southern Mississippi, 1981, and Keene State College, 1986.

WRITINGS:

FOR CHILDREN; SELF-ILLUSTRATED

Kenny's Window, Harper (New York, NY), 1956, reprinted, 2004.

Very Far Away, Harper (New York, NY), 1957.

The Acrobat, privately printed, 1959.

The Sign on Rosie's Door, Harper (New York, NY), 1960, reprinted, 2002.

Nutshell Library (verse; contains *Chicken Soup with Rice: A Book of Months, One Was Johnny: A*

Counting Book, Alligators All Around: An Alphabet, and *Pierre: A Cautionary Tale*), Harper (New York, NY), 1962.

Where the Wild Things Are, Harper (New York, NY), 1963, 25th anniversary edition, 1988, miniature edition, HarperFestival (New York, NY), 1992.

Hector Protector and As I Went over the Water: Two Nursery Rhymes, Harper (New York, NY), 1965.

Higglety Pigglety Pop!; or, There Must Be More to Life, Harper (New York, NY), 1967.

In the Night Kitchen, Harper (New York, NY), 1970.

Ten Little Rabbits: A Counting Book with Mino the Magician, Philip H. Rosenbach, 1970.

Pictures by Maurice Sendak, Harper (New York, NY), 1971.

Maurice Sendak's Really Rosie (based on the television program of the same title; also see below), Harper (New York, NY), 1975.

(With Matthew Margolis) *Some Swell Pup; or, Are You Sure You Want a Dog?,* Farrar, Straus (New York, NY), 1976.

Outside over There, Harper (New York, NY), 1981.

We Are All in the Dumps with Jack and Guy: Two Nursery Rhymes with Pictures, HarperCollins (New York, NY), 1993.

ILLUSTRATOR:

M.L. Eidinoff and Hyman Ruchlis, *Atomics for the Millions* (for adults), McGraw (New York, NY), 1947.

Robert Garvey, *Good Shabbos, Everybody!,* United Synagogue Commission on Jewish Education, 1951.

Marcel Ayme, *The Wonderful Farm,* Harper (New York, NY), 1951.

Ruth Krauss, *A Hole Is to Dig: A First Book of Definitions,* Harper (New York, NY), 1952.

Ruth Sawyer, *Maggie Rose: Her Birthday Christmas,* Harper (New York, NY), 1952.

Beatrice Schenck de Regniers, *The Giant Story,* Harper (New York, NY), 1953.

Meindert de Jong, *Hurry Home, Candy,* Harper (New York, NY), 1953.

Meindert de Jong, *Shadrach,* Harper (New York, NY), 1953.

Ruth Krauss, *A Very Special House,* Harper (New York, NY), 1953, reprinted, 2002.

Hyman Chanover, *Happy Hanukkah, Everybody,* United Synagogue Commission on Jewish Education, 1954.

Ruth Krauss, *I'll Be You and You Be Me,* Harper (New York, NY), 1954.

Edward Tripp, *The Tin Fiddle,* Oxford University Press, 1954.

Marcel Ayme, *Magic Pictures,* Harper (New York, NY), 1954.

Betty MacDonald, *Mrs. Piggle-Wiggle's Farm,* Lippincott (Philadelphia, PA), 1954.

Meindert de Jong, *The Wheel on the School,* Harper (New York, NY), 1954.

Ruth Krauss, *Charlotte and the White Horse,* Harper (New York, NY), 1955, reprinted, 2002.

Meindert de Jong, *The Little Cow and the Turtle,* Harper (New York, NY), 1955.

Jean Ritchie, *Singing Family of the Cumberlands,* Oxford University Press (Oxford, England), 1955.

Beatrice Schenck de Regniers, *What Can You Do with a Shoe?,* Harper (New York, NY), 1955, reprinted, Alladin (New York, NY), 2001.

Jack Sendak, *The Happy Rain,* Harper (New York, NY), 1956, reprinted, 2002.

Meindert de Jong, *The House of Sixty Fathers,* Harper (New York, NY), 1956.

Ruth Krauss, *I Want to Paint My Bathroom Blue,* Harper (New York, NY), 1956, reprinted, 2002.

Ruth Krauss, *Birthday Party,* Harper (New York, NY), 1957.

Jack Sendak, *Circus Girl,* Harper (New York, NY), 1957, reprinted, 2002.

Ogden Nash, *You Can't Get There from Here,* Little, Brown (New York, NY), 1957.

Else Holmelund Minarik, *Little Bear,* Harper (New York, NY), 1957.

Meindert de Jong, *Along Came a Dog,* Harper (New York, NY), 1958.

Else Holmelund Minarik, *No Fighting, No Biting!,* Harper (New York, NY), 1958.

Ruth Krauss, *Somebody Else's Nut Tree,* Harper (New York, NY), 1958.

Sesyle Joslyn, *What Do You Say, Dear?: A Book of Manners for All Occasions,* W.R. Scott, 1958.

Else Holmelund Minarik, *Father Bear Comes Home,* Harper (New York, NY), 1959.

Janice Udry, *The Moon Jumpers,* Harper (New York, NY), 1959.

Hans Christian Andersen, *Seven Tales,* Harper (New York, NY), 1959.

Wilhelm Hauff, *Dwarf Long-Nose,* Random House (New York, NY), 1960.

Else Holmelund Minarik, *Little Bear's Friend,* Harper (New York, NY), 1960.

Ruth Krauss, *Open House for Butterflies,* Harper (New York, NY), 1960, reprinted, 2002.

Janice Udry, *Let's Be Enemies,* Harper (New York, NY), 1961.

Clemens Brentano, *The Tale of Gockel, Hinkel, and Gackeliah,* Random House (New York, NY), 1961.

Else Holmelund Minarik, *Little Bear's Visit,* Harper (New York, NY), 1961.

Sesyle Joslyn, *What Do You Do, Dear?,* Young Scott Books, 1961.

Clemens Brentano, *Schoolmaster Whackwell's Wonderful Sons,* Random House (New York, NY), 1962.

Charlotte Zolotow, *Mr. Rabbit and the Lovely Present,* Harper (New York, NY), 1962.

Meindert de Jong, *The Singing Hill,* Harper (New York, NY), 1962.

Leo Tolstoy, *Nikolenka's Childhood,* Harper (New York, NY), 1963.

Robert Keeshan, *She Loves Me, She Loves Me Not,* Harper (New York, NY), 1963.

Randall Jarrell, *The Bat-Poet,* Collier (London, England), 1964.

Amos Vogel, *How Little Lori Visited Times Square,* Harper (New York, NY), 1964.

Jan Wahl, *Pleasant Fieldmouse,* Harper (New York, NY), 1964.

William Engvick, editor, *Lullabies and Night Songs,* Pantheon (New York, NY), 1965.

Randall Jarrell, *The Animal Family,* Pantheon (New York, N), 1965.

Isaac Bashevis Singer, *Zlateh the Goat and Other Stories,* Harper (New York, NY), 1966.

George Macdonald, *The Golden Key,* Harper (New York, NY), 1967, second edition, Farrar, Straus (New York, NY), 1984.

William Blake, *Poems from William Blake's Songs of Innocence,* Bodley Head (London, England), 1967.

Robert Graves, *The Big Green Book,* Crowell (New York, NY), 1968.

Frank Stockton, *Griffin and the Minor Canon,* Collins (London, England), 1968.

Else Holmelund Minarik, *A Kiss for Little Bear,* Harper (New York, NY), 1968.

George Macdonald, *The Light Princess,* Bodley Head (London, England), 1969, revised edition, Farrar, Straus (New York, NY), 1969.

Frank Stockton, *The Bee-Man of Orn,* Holt (New York, NY), 1971.

Doris Orgel, *Sarah's Room,* Bodley Head (London, England), 1971.

Jakob Grimm and Wilhelm Grimm, *The Juniper Tree, and Other Tales from Grimm,* Farrar, Straus (New York, NY), 1973.

Marie Catherine Jumelle de Berneville Aulnoy, *Fortunia: A Tale by Mme. D'Aulnoy,* translated by Richard Schaubeck, Frank Hallman, 1974.

Randall Jarrell, *Fly by Night,* Farrar, Straus (New York, NY), 1976.

Jakob Grimm and Wilhelm Grimm, *King Grisly-Beard: A Tale from the Brothers Grimm,* Harper (New York, NY), 1978.

E.T.A. Hoffman, *The Nutcracker,* translated by Ralph Manheim, Crown (New York, NY), 1984.

Philip Sendak, *In Grandpa's House,* translated and adapted by Seymour Barofsky, Harper (New York, NY), 1985, reprinted, 2002.

Dear Mili: An Old Tale by Wilhelm Grimm (based on a letter by Wilhelm Grimm), translated by Ralph Manheim, Michael Di Capua Books/Farrar, Straus (New York, NY), 1988.

(With Garth Williams) Jerome Griswold, *The Children's Books of Randall Jarrell,* University of Georgia Press (Athens, GA), 1988.

Iona and Peter Opie, *I Saw Esau: The Schoolchild's Pocket Book,* Candlewick Press (Cambridge, MA), 1992.

Arthur Yorinks, *The Miami Giant,* HarperCollins (New York, NY), 1995.

Herman Melville, *Pierre; or, The Ambiguities,* HarperCollins (New York, NY), 1996.

Heinrich von Kleist, *Penthesilia: A Tragic Drama* (verse drama), translated by Joel Agee, HarperCollins (New York, NY), 1996.

James Marshall, *Swine Lake,* HarperCollins (New York, NY), 1999.

Else Holmelund Minarik, *Little Bear and the Missing Pie,* HarperFestival (New York, NY), 2002.

Else Holmelund Minarik, *Little Bear's Wagon,* HarperFestival (New York, NY), 2002.

Else Holmelund Minarik, *Little Bear's Egg,* HarperFestival (New York, NY), 2002.

Also illustrator of *Little Stories* by Gladys B. Bond, Anti-Defamation League of B'nai B'rith. Contributor of illustrations to *McCall's* and *Ladies' Home Journal.*

OTHER

Fantasy Sketches (published in conjunction with one-man show at Rosenbach Foundation), Philip H. Rosenbach, 1970.

(Editor and author of introduction) *Maxfield Parrish Poster Book,* Crown (New York, NY), 1974.

(Author of appreciation) *The Publishing Archive of Lothar Meggendorfer,* Schiller, 1975.

(And director and lyricist) *Really Rosie, Starring the Nutshell Kids* (animated television special; based on characters from *The Nutshell Library* and *The Sign on Rosie's Door;* broadcast on Columbia

Broadcasting System, 1975; also see below), music composed and performed by Carol King, Harper (New York, NY), 1975.

(Editor) *The Disney Poster Book,* illustrated by Walt Disney Studios, Harper (New York, NY), 1977.

(Lyricist and set designer) *Really Rosie* (musical play; revised from the television special of the same title), music by Carol King, first produced in London, England, then Washington, DC, 1978, produced off-Broadway, 1980.

(Lyricist and set and costume designer) *Where the Wild Things Are* (opera; based on his book of the same title), music by Oliver Knussen, first produced by Opera Nationale, Belgium, 1980; produced by New York City Opera with Mozart's *The Goose from Cairo,* 1984.

(Author of introduction) Jean de Brunhoff, *Babar's Anniversary Album,* Random House (New York, NY), 1981.

Collection of Books, Posters, and Original Drawings, Schiller, 1984.

(With Frank Corsaro) *The Love for Three Oranges: The Glyndebourne Version* (dialogue), Farrar, Straus (New York, NY), 1984.

(Librettist and set and costume designer) *Higglety, Pigglety, Pop!* (opera), first produced by Glyndebourne Opera, Glyndebourne, England, 1984.

(Author of commentary) Jonathan Cott, editor, *Masterworks of Children's Literature,* Volume 7, Chelsea House (Broomall, PA), 1984.

(Photographer) Rudolf Tesnohlidek, *The Cunning Little Vixen,* Farrar, Straus (New York, NY), 1985.

(Author of introduction) Jonathan Cott, *Victorian Color Picture Books,* Stonehill Publishing/Chelsea House (Broomall, PA), 1985.

Posters, Harmony Books (New York, NY), 1986.

(Author of foreword) John Canemaker, *Winsor McCay: His Life and Art,* Abbeville Press, 1987.

Caldecott & Co.: Notes on Books and Pictures, Michael Di Capua Books/Farrar, Straus (New York, NY), 1988.

(Author of introduction) *Mickey Mouse Movie Stories,* Abrams, 1988.

Maurice Sendak Book and Poster Package: Wild Things, Harper (New York, NY), 1991.

(With others) *Worlds of Childhood: The Art and Craft of Writing for Children,* Houghton Mifflin (Boston, MA), 1998.

(With others) *HarperCollins Treasury of Picture Book Classics,* HarperCollins (New York, NY), 2002.

Many of Sendak's books have been translated into foreign languages; *Where the Wild Things Are* has been translated into sixteen languages. Collections of Sendak's manuscripts are kept at the Museum of the Philip H. and A.S.W. Rosenbach Foundation, Philadelphia, PA, and in the Kerlan Collection at the University of Minnesota, Minneapolis.

ADAPTATIONS: Film strips with cassettes were produced by Weston Woods of *Where the Wild Things Are,* 1968, and *Pierre, Chicken Soup with Rice, Alligators All Around,* and *One Was Johnny,* all 1976; *Where the Wild Things Are* was adapted as a ballet, music by Randall Woolf, produced by American Repertory Ballet, 1997, and was also made into an audio cassette, Caedmon, 1988; a film of *In the Night Kitchen* was produced by Weston Woods, 1988; *Higglety Pigglety Pop!* was adapted as a Braille book and a record by Caedmon Records; toy "Wild Thing" dolls were created by Harper; a television series produced by Nelvana (Canada) was based on the "Little Bear" books with accompanying videos produced by Alliance Video; *Where the Wild Things Are* was scheduled to be produced by Universal Studios in 2004. *Seven Little Monsters,* by Arthur Yorinks, is based on Sendak's characters and published by Hyperion in 2003. A series of books based on the *Little Bear Movie,* with illustrators chosen by Sendak and text by Else Holmelund Minarik, were published by HarperCollins in 2002: *A Present for Mother Bear, The Search for Spring, To Grandmother's House, Father's Flying Flapjacks, Little Bear's Valentine,* and *Little Bear's New Friend.*

SIDELIGHTS: The first American to win a Hans Christian Andersen International Medal, Maurice Sendak developed, during the course of his long career, into a major figure in the evolution of children's literature during the second half of the twentieth century. With books such as his Caldecott-winning *Where the Wild Things Are,* Sendak has led the way in trying to create more realistic child characters who are not the nostalgic models of innocence and sweetness that inhabited children's books before the 1960s. By creating drawings inspired by everything from nineteenth-century illustrators to twentieth-century cartoon artists, Sendak has also demonstrated an artistic adaptability that is unconventional. Because of these deviations from what were once considered acceptable forms of writing and illustrating for children, despite his popularity among readers, Sendak has also been the object of some controversy. However, Jill P. May observed in *Journal of Popular Culture* that "although Sendak's works seem disgusting to some U.S. educators, librarians, and parents, his books are found in most public libraries and elementary school libraries." And authorities such as writer and critic John Rowe Townsend, author of *Written for Children: An Outline of English-Language Children's Literature,* consider Sendak "the greatest creator of picture books in the hundred-odd years' history of the form."

Critics of Sendak's work often argue that youngsters are not ready for the themes and images he presents. "Sendak has forthrightly confronted such sensitive subject matters as childhood anger, sexuality, or the occasionally murderous impulses of raw sibling rivalry," explained Selma G. Lanes in *The Art of Maurice Sendak.* This "honesty has troubled or frightened many who would wish to sentimentalize childhood—to shelter children from their own psychological complexity or to deny that this complexity exists," commented *Dictionary of Literary Biography* contributor John Cotham. For the artist this exploration of children's feelings has been more of a personal quest than a desire to break new ground in juvenile literature. Many of his books refer—to a greater or lesser degree—to his own past experiences. "Primarily," Sendak revealed in Steven Heller's *Innovators of American Illustration,* "my work was an act of exorcism, an act of finding solutions so that I could have peace of mind and be an artist and function in the world as a human being and a man. My mind doesn't stray beyond my own need to survive."

The son of Jewish immigrants from Poland, Sendak grew up in a poor Brooklyn neighborhood with his older brother, Jack, and sister, Natalie. A number of factors in the artist's early life prevented him from having a normal, stable childhood. One problem was that his family never stayed in one neighborhood for very long, moving from apartment to apartment every time their landlords painted, because Sendak's mother could not stand the smell of fresh paint. Sendak had a hard time making friends not only because of this, but also because he was very sickly—he suffered from measles, double pneumonia, and scarlet fever between the ages of two and four. Because his parents were reluctant to let their son go outside and play for fear he would become sick and die, young Sendak spent much of his time in bed, looking out his bedroom window at the other children playing and becoming obsessed with the idea that he might not have long to live. "I was a miserable kid," he confessed to Lanes.

Fortunately, Sendak found escape through drawing, books, movies, music, and his own imagination. Contrary to what one might think a future writer and artist would read as a child, Sendak mostly read comic books—especially those featuring Mickey Mouse and other Disney characters—and his artwork clearly reflects this early influence. He also loved to go to the local theater and watch musicals and comedies like the Stan Laurel and Oliver Hardy films. One area where Sendak did deviate in his tastes for popular American culture was in his love of classical music, especially the music of Mozart. He often listened to classical music on the radio, and he would have taken piano lessons except that his parents could only afford lessons for his older brother, Jack.

Sendak found an inexpensive way to express his creativity in drawing and writing stories. During his many long days spent sick in bed, the young artist sketched the people and houses in his neighborhood, dreaming up fantasies for them to be in. "There is not a book I have written or picture I have drawn that does not, in some way, owe [those neighborhood children] its existence," the artist revealed in Lanes's *Down the Rabbit Hole: Adventures and Misadventures in the Realm of Children's Literature.* He learned to make up stories from his father, who amused his children with fantastic tales he would improvise. "Sendak feels that his father's stories were the first important source from which his work developed," explained Cotham. When he was about seven years old, Sendak and his brother, Jack, started writing down stories on cardboard discarded from shirt wrappings. Later, Jack also became a children's author, and two of his books have been illustrated by Sendak.

Sendak's first step toward becoming a professional illustrator came in high school when he worked on backgrounds for the comic strips "Mutt and Jeff," "Tippy," and "Captain Stubbs"; he also wrote his own comic strip for his school newspaper and illustrated a physics book, *Atomics for the Millions,* for one of his teachers. After he graduated, Sendak did not go to college as his father wished because he hated school and was eager to leave the strictures of the classroom as soon as possible. Instead, he worked for two years in a warehouse in Manhattan. Leaving that job in 1948, Sendak designed mechanical wooden toys with Jack, and they tried to sell them to the famous New York toy company F.A.O. Schwartz. Their plan did not succeed, but Sendak was hired to work on the store's window displays. One of his displays was seen by noted illustrator Leonard Weisgard, who offered Sendak a commission to illustrate *Good Shabbos, Everybody.*

At the same time Sendak was working for Schwartz he attended the Art Student's League, where he received encouragement from one of his instructors, John Groth, who told him that his time would be better spent if he left school and actively practiced his art in the real world. This idea appealed to Sendak. He left the art school and tried submitting his drawings to publishing houses, but was rejected many times by editors who saw his work as old-fashioned. Indeed, Sendak had been influenced very early by such nineteenth-century illustrators as George Cruikshank, John Tenniel, Wilhelm Busch, and Louis Maurice Boutet de Monvel, the last whose intricate, cross-hatching style was nothing like the simpler style preferred by book editors in the 1940s and 1950s.

Then F.A.O. Schwartz's children's book department head Frances Christie introduced Sendak to Harper and Brothers editor Ursula Nordstrom. It was Nordstrom who gave Sendak his education in the business of book publishing, and she also carefully selected books for the artist to illustrate that would help him develop his craft and reputation. "I loved her on first meeting," Sendak remembered in *The Art of Maurice Sendak.* "My happiest memories, in fact, are of my earliest career, when Ursula was my confidante and best friend. She really became my home and the person I trusted most." Nordstrom arranged for Sendak to be the illustrator for Ruth Krauss's *A Hole Is to Dig,* the book that first established Sendak as an important illustrator. *A Hole Is to Dig* was such a popular and critical success that Sendak was able to quit his job at F.A.O. Schwartz and work as a freelancer.

During the 1950s Sendak learned how to be flexible and adapt his drawings to the texts they accompanied. Many illustrators of that time period were not able to do so, the artist told Heller: "That's what doomed a lot of the illustrators working then. And that was the one thing Ursula was absolutely not going to let happen to me. . . . I was going to learn how to draw in a variety of styles. I think my books are identifiable, but they all look different because illustrators are secondary to the text. If you insist on being primary to the text, then you're a bad illustrator." Sendak's illustrations have thus varied from the line drawings of *Kenny's Window* and *Where the Wild Things Are* to the cartoonish style of *In the Night Kitchen* to the highly detailed, cross-hatching style found in *Outside over There* and his drawings for the books by the Brothers Grimm.

To make ends meet, the artist illustrated as many books as he could, so at first he did not have much time to do any of his own writing. Nordstrom, who had done so much for his career as an illustrator, also later encouraged Sendak to write his own children's books. His first two efforts, *Kenny's Window* and *Very Far Away,* did not satisfy the artist completely. He later called *Kenny's Window* "overwritten" and "not well illustrated;" and although Sendak liked the story in *Very Far Away,* he eventually considered reillustrating the book. With *The Sign on Rosie's Door,* however, the artist created his first memorable character. Rosie is based on a real girl whom Sendak remembers from his Brooklyn childhood. The book draws from the sketches he once made of Rosie and her friends in 1948 and 1949, and the story line uses some actual events and quotes the real Rosie directly in some cases. The fictional Rosie became the model for the typical Sendak character: strong-willed, honest, and—above all—imaginative.

"Rosie personifies Sendak's ability to empathize with the triumphs and terrors of childhood," observed John Lahr in *New York Times. The Sign on Rosie's Door* is a simple story about a group of children with nothing to do on a long summer day in the city. Rosie, a somewhat bossy, but friendly and highly imaginative ten-year-old girl, shows her friends how to use fantasy to chase away their boredom. Later, Rosie became a television star when Sendak wrote, directed, and composed lyrics for a half-hour animated special that aired in 1975; and this led in turn to the artist's first venture into live theater when he designed the sets and wrote lyrics for a stage version produced in 1980.

Sendak's next work, *The Nutshell Library,* features some of the characters from *The Sign on Rosie's Door.* Comprised of an alphabet book, a counting book, a book about the seasons, and a cautionary tale—all measuring only two-and-one-half by four inches—*The Nutshell Library* books have been highly praised for Sendak's skill "at integrating text, design, and illustrations," according to Cotham. Today, they are still considered by many critics to be one of the artist's most successful efforts.

After illustrating several picture books for other authors, Sendak decided to write some picture books himself as a way of controlling the wordiness he felt prevented him from expressing what he wanted to say in his illustrated books. "I finally came to grips with what my theme was and found the form most suitable to me as a writer and illustrator," he said in Heller's book. Picture books differ from illustrated books in that they consist mostly of illustrations accompanied by only short passages of text, while illustrated books are mostly text with only a few illustrations. During the following years, Sendak composed three picture books that he considers to form a loose trilogy: *Where the Wild Things Are, In the Night Kitchen,* and *Outside Over There.* Although the three stories seem unrelated, the artist said in *The Art of Maurice Sendak* that they "are all variations on the same theme: how children master various feelings—anger, boredom, fear, frustration, jealousy—and manage to come to grips with the realities of their lives."

One common aspect of these books is that they all involve the main character's voyaging into some type of fantasy world. In *Where the Wild Things Are* Max has an argument with his mother and is sent to his room without supper. He deals with his anger by imagining himself sailing to an island ruled by enormous, frightening monsters and becoming their king. However, Max soon becomes lonesome for his family and decides to return home. The fantasy world of *In the Night Kitchen* is a place that looks like a New York City skyline except that the buildings are made up of 1930s-era food boxes, bottles, and kitchen utensils. Here, bakers who all resemble the comedian Oliver Hardy work all night making goodies. When Mickey—who is named after Mickey Mouse—finds himself in the Night Kitchen he saves the day by finding milk for the bakers' cake. *Outside Over There,* which was marketed as both a children's and adult book, has a much more serious tone than *In the Night Kitchen.* It tells how Ida, who is very jealous of her baby brother, neglects him, until one day goblins kidnap the baby and take him to another world "outside over there." By traveling to this other world Ida reaffirms her love for her brother and manages to rescue him from the goblins.

Just as Sendak's characters resolve any crises they might have by traveling to a world of imagination, Sendak himself uses his imagination in some of these books as a means of releasing some of his own private conflicts. Depending on the book, this is true to a greater or lesser extent. For example, the monsters in *Where the Wild Things Are* were inspired by the artist's hated Brooklyn relatives. "I wanted the wild things to be frightening," Sendak remarked in *The Art of Maurice Sendak.* "But why? It was probably at this point that I remembered how I detested my Brooklyn relatives as a small child. . . . [They'd] lean way over with their bad teeth and hairy noses, and say something threatening like 'You're so cute I could eat you up.' And I knew if my mother didn't hurry up with the cooking, they probably would."

The events that preceded the writing of *In the Night Kitchen* had an even greater role in the creation of that book. In 1967 Sendak suffered a heart attack, lost his mother and beloved Sealyham terrier, Jennie, to cancer, and, two years later, his father also died. After these tragic events, the artist left New York City and moved to Connecticut. *In the Night Kitchen* was a way for Sendak "to do a book that would say goodbye to New York," he told Martha Shirk in a *Chicago Tribune* article, "and say goodbye to my parents, and tell a little bit about the narrow squeak I had just been through." In the story, Mickey's brush with death when he is nearly baked in a cake symbolizes Sendak's own close call. *In the Night Kitchen,* the artist concluded in a *New York Times* article by Lisa Hammel, is about his "victory over death."

Although *In the Night Kitchen* is an important book to Sendak, he has called *Outside over There* his most personal work. "The book is obviously related to my own babyhood when my sister, Natalie, Ida's age, took care of me," he revealed to Jean F. Mercier in *Publishers Weekly.* The tale has its roots in the real-life story of the kidnapping of famous American pilot Charles Lindbergh's baby in 1932. Sendak recalled in his *New York Times Book Review* article how at the time he was "[four] years old, sick in bed and somehow confusing myself with this baby. I had the superstitious feeling that if he came back I'd be O.K., too. Sadly, we all know the baby didn't come back. It left a peculiar mark in my mind." *Outside over There* "is really a homage to my sister, who is Ida," the artist later added. Sendak has never directly revealed the deep personal turmoils that his books at times express, but whatever they are *Outside over There* has been the most therapeutic work for him. "I think it's the best thing I've done in my life," he once admitted. "It's the book I've searched for and scratched for. . . . What I got was as close to the realization of vision as I've ever experienced in my creative life. . . . It's a personal salvation and recovery of vision," he later added.

Because of the personal value of *Outside over There* to Sendak the relatively smaller sales of the book have not been a great concern to him. The problems that some of his other books have caused him have been much more troubling. Sendak first became a controversial figure with the publication of *Where the Wild Things Are.* Many critics and educators complained that the monsters were too frightening for small children. Critics like Bruno Bettelheim even felt that the book could cause psychological damage to sensitive children. In a *Ladies' Home Journal* piece he wrote that Sendak "failed to understand . . . the incredible fear it evokes in the child to be sent to bed without supper, and this by the first and foremost giver of food and security—his mother." Sendak responded to this criticism in Mark I. West's *Trust Your Children: Writers against Censorship in Children's Literature* by pointing out that Bettelheim had not even read the book. "He simply based his judgment on someone else's summary of it. Because of his article, all sorts of people said that the book was psychologically harmful to children. This hurt the book, and it hurt me. Since then Bettelheim has come full circle, but the damage had already been done."

A number of other books by Sendak have been criticized and even censored for various reasons. *In the Night Kitchen* was attacked by some reviewers because of its use of cartoon-style illustrations. Some people "dismiss comic books as vulgar trash," observed Sendak. But most of the objections have been aimed at the illustration in the book that shows Mickey completely nude from the front. Many librarians defaced the book by drawing diapers or underwear on Mickey to hide his genitals. "It's as if my book contains secret information that kids would be better off not knowing. This whole idea, of course, is ridiculous," said Sendak, pointing out that children are naturally open about their bodies until adults teach them to be ashamed of them. Another censored book by Sendak is *Some Swell Pup; or, Are You Sure You Want a Dog?,* a realistic guide to taking care of puppies, which was flagged because of an illustration showing a dog defecating. According to Sendak in a *New York Times* article by Bernard Holland, censoring books that portray some of the facts of life to children is more for the benefit of the adult than the child: "Children are willing to expose themselves to experiences. We aren't. Grown-ups always say they protect their children, but they're really protecting themselves. Besides, you can't protect children. They know everything."

After moving to Connecticut, Sendak found peace and quiet by living in virtual isolation during much of the 1970s. Here, in a ten-room stone and clapboard house a few miles outside of Ridgefield, he worked ten to eleven hours a day in a room he converted into a studio. Many of the books he worked on at this time were picture books for other authors, as well as his own *Outside over There.* Sendak felt that with this book he had gone about as far as he could go with picture books and he needed to move on to something else. In 1980, after "years spent on picture books, Sendak was ready to get out of his 'solitary confinement' and do his first opera project," noted *Theatre Crafts* contributor Ellen Levene.

After designing the sets and costumes for Mozart's *The Magic Flute,* Sendak then worked on the designs for such operas as *The Cunning Little Vixen* and *The Love of Three Oranges,* as well as the stage and film versions of *The Nutcracker.* He also wrote the lyrics and did designs for his own *Where the Wild Things Are* (also adapted as a ballet in 1997) and wrote a libretto for *Higglety, Pigglety, Pop!* As a classical music fan since his boyhood, Sendak had always wanted to get closer to the works of the masters, especially Mozart. Often, while writing and illustrating his books he would listen to Mozart for inspiration, and he has consequently memorized many of Mozart's compositions. The image of Mozart has even entered into some of Sendak's illustrations, but this was never enough for the artist. "That is why the operas are so important," Sendak explained, "because by costuming and setting them I have come as close to the music as I ever have in my life. I'm now literally on the stage, and I'm coloring Mozart, illustrating him in the way I used to illustrate people's stories."

Sendak wanted to do more with his work in the opera than repeat what others had done before him. Discussing his stage version of *Where the Wild Things Are* with *Horn Book* interviewer David E. White, the artist observed: "There are too many operas called children's operas. Most of them suffer for this very reason. They are written down to children, as though children could not appreciate the full weight of good musical quality. So I want *Wild Things* to be an opera which is comical and quite serious, a work that will satisfy adults as well as children." The same is true of the previously produced operas and ballet with which Sendak has been involved. For example, when Sendak was asked to help with a new production of *The Nutcracker* he refused because he did not like the almost plotless story that had been used in earlier performances. However, he accepted the job when his own version of the stage drama was accepted. It was truer to the original book by E.T.A. Hoffman, which centers on the sexual and emotional coming-of-age of a young girl.

In order to have more freedom in the type of work he wanted to do for the theater, Sendak cofounded—with fellow writer Arthur Yorinks—a national theater for children in 1990 that he named The Night Kitchen. As the artistic director of the theater, he hoped to produce new versions of such plays as *Peter Pan* and *Hansel and Gretel* that will not talk down to children. "Our work is very peculiar, idiosyncratic . . . ," Sendak told *New York Times* contributor Eleanor Blau. "I don't believe in things literally *for* children. That's a reduction." Believing that children and adults should be treated with equal respect, he later added: "Children are more open in their hearts . . . for what you're doing. . . . They're the best audience in town."

Following a hiatus of several years from writing and illustrating children's books, Sendak became inspired to return to this activity through his collaboration with editors Iona and Peter Opie on a compilation of children's verses titled *I Saw Esau: The Schoolchild's Pocket Book.* Reviewers emphasized the significance of the collection for adults interested in folklore, children's literature, and illustration, as the book compiles a variety of poems and songs originating from contemporary American and British children at play, most of which would not be sanctioned by adults. Commentators remarked on the uniqueness of Sendak's illustrations, which often help to explicate the otherwise opaque meanings of certain verses. *New York Times Book Review* critic Alison Lurie, for example, found Sendak's drawings "as entrancing—and sometimes as shocking—as the text."

Sendak also received praise for his illustrated edition of a relatively unpopular book by Herman Melville, *Pierre.* Jed Perl asserted in *New Republic* that the "stylized histrionics of Sendak's illustrations underline the fascination of this psychological fable of deluded innocence and suicidal experience. Sendak embraces the book's dark, loopy mood and makes it his own." Perl emphasized in particular Sendak's successful decision to eschew historical accuracy in his rendering of characters in favor of a more whimsical, expressive style that reflects the diverse moods and themes of Melville's text.

Demonstrating the full impact of Sendak's realistic approach to children's literature, the picture book *We Are All in the Dumps with Jack and Guy* combines two cryptic and little-known Mother Goose verses with scenes depicting homelessness and poverty among children. Sendak explained that the inspiration for the story came from his research into the communities of abandoned and runaway children that surround many cities. He subsequently decided to set *We Are All in the Dumps* in a cardboard shanty town located beneath the Brooklyn Bridge that is inhabited by children. The format of the book reveals the influence of Sendak's extensive experience in the theater: "The Mother Goose lines, set at the top of the spreads, read like supertitles, while a shallow visual plane recalls a stage set, and the characters, issuing their lines in dialogue balloons, seem more like actors," commented Elizabeth Devereaux in *Publishers Weekly.* While Brian Alderson cautioned in *New York Times Book Review* against forcing children to view the "pain and deprivation" that are the subject of *We Are All in the Dumps with Jack and Guy, Wilson Library Bulletin* reviewer Judith Rovenger lauded the courage of Sendak's social commentary regarding America's underclass and the power of the book's visual imagery. "This is a picture book that makes demands," she commented. "It is provocative and disturbing; it is not a book to cuddle with."

His later years have seen no slowdown in interest in Sendak. Between 2000 and 2001, corresponding with the fiftieth anniversary of his first book for Harper, the artist's longtime publisher reissued some twenty-two of his books. "We went through all that was buried and decided what was worth unburying," Sendak told Sally Lodge of *Publishers Weekly.* "A lot of the books I love, and some, quite frankly, I wrote to earn money. We decided what were the best books from any given period and discarded others." Among the titles slated to reach a new generation of readers include perennial bestsellers such as *Where the Wild Things Are* and *In the Night Kitchen;* they join such volumes as *A Very Special House, Charlotte and the White Horse,* and *Open House for Butterflies.* As Sendak admitted, he was most pleased with the reissue of a 1954 Ruth Krauss collaboration, *I'll Be You and You Be Me,* which he described to Lodge as "Ruth at her sweetest, most optimistic and imaginative."

Sendak's original publications in the late 1990s include two books designed to appeal to audiences of all ages. The hero of *The Miami Giant* is an explorer, Giaweeni, who leaves Italy to sail for China but lands instead in Florida, where he encounters the natives—Jewish retirees of Miami Beach "in all their primitive splendor," as Hazel Rochman described it in *Booklist.* In 1999 Sendak illustrated the whimsical parody *Swine Lake.* The very image of a hungry wolf infiltrating a porcine ballet (at the New Hamsterdam Theater) with designs on devouring the cast caught the delighted attention of some critics. "Just a look at the dust jacket and you know you're in for fun," declared Ilene Cooper of *Booklist.* Sendak's "irrepressible art makes the most of [James] Marshall's understated text," remarked a *Publishers Weekly* critic, who pointed to such hidden pleasures as "an obviously bored, sailor-suit-clad young pig in the audience who sticks his tongue out at readers."

In addition, a new series of "Little Bear" books, based on characters created by author Else Minarik and illustrated by Sendak in the 1950s and 1960s was created by Sendak and published to coincide with a "Little Bear" animated television series, which was first produced by the Canadian Broadcasting Corporation in 1995, and broadcast later on the Nickelodeon cable channel in the United States.

Sendak has never had children of his own or been married, but he maintained that having contact with children is not necessary for him to write tales that young audiences can appreciate. What is important is what he called the "peculiar relationship with myself that allows me to dip endlessly into feelings which are not available to most people." By maintaining contact with the child within him, Sendak can easily relate to children while also touching on subjects and feelings that can stir recognition in adults. "We've all passed the same places," said the artist. "Only I remember the geography, and most people forget it."

The connection with the imagination and fantasy of childhood has always been Sendak's primary motivation in all that he has done. "The writing and the picture-making are merely a means to an end," he said in *Down the Rabbit Hole.* He then remarked, "It has never been for me a graphic matter—or even, for that matter, a word matter! To discuss a children's book in terms of its pictorial beauty—or prose style—is not to the point. It is the particular nugget of magic it achieves—if it achieves. It has always only been a means—a handle with which I can swing myself into—somewhere or other—the place I'd rather be."

BIOGRAPHICAL AND CRITICAL SOURCES:

BOOKS

Arbuthnot, May Hill, and Zena Sutherland, *Children and Books,* fourth edition, Scott, Foresman, 1972.

Bader, Barbara, *American Picturebooks from Noah's Ark to the Beast Within,* Macmillan (New York, NY), 1976, pp. 495-524.

Berg, Julie, *Maurice Sendak,* Abdo & Daughters (Minnesota), 1993.

Cech, John, *Angels and Wild Things: The Archetypal Poetics of Maurice Sendak,* Pennsylvania State University Press, 1995.

Children's Literature Review, Thomson Gale (Detroit, MI), Volume 1, 1976, Volume 17, 1989.

Contemporary Theatre, Film, and Television, Volume 11, Thomson Gale (Detroit, MI), 1994.

Dictionary of Literary Biography, Volume 61: *American Writers for Children since 1960: Poets, Illustrators, and Nonfiction Authors,* Thomson Gale (Detroit, MI), 1987.

Dictionary of Twentieth-Century Culture, Thomson Gale (Detroit, MI), 1994.

Dooley, Patricia, editor, *The First Steps: Best of the Early "ChLA Quarterly,"* ChLA Publications, 1984, pp. 135-139.

Georgiou, Constantine, *Children and Their Literature,* Prentice-Hall, 1969.

Heller, Steven, editor, *Innovators of American Illustration,* Van Nostrand, 1986, pp. 70-81.

Hopkins, Lee Bennett, *Books Are by People,* Citation Press (New York, NY), 1969.

Kingman, Lee, editor, *Newbery and Caldecott Medal Books: 1956-1965,* Horn Book (Boston, MA), 1956.

Kushner, Tony, *The Art of Maurice Sendak: 1980 to Present,* Abrams (New York, NY), 2003.

Lacy, Lyn Ellen, *Art and Design in Children's Picture Books: An Analysis of Caldecott Award-winning Illustrations,* American Library Association, 1986, pp. 104-143.

Lanes, Selma G., *Down the Rabbit Hole: Adventures and Misadventures in the Realm of Children's Literature,* Atheneum (New York, NY), 1971, pp. 67-78.

Lanes, Selma G., *The Art of Maurice Sendak,* Abrams (New York, NY), 1980.

St. James Guide to Children's Writers, fifth edition, St. James Press (Detroit, MI), 1999.

Smith, Jeffrey Jon, *A Conversation with Maurice Sendak,* Smith, 1974.

Townsend, John Rowe, *Written for Children: An Outline of English-Language Children's Literature,* revised edition, Lippincott (Philadelphia, PA), 1974, p. 310.

West, Mark I., *Trust Your Children: Writers against Censorship in Children's Literature,* Neal-Schuman (New York, NY), 1988, pp. 87-91.

PERIODICALS

Appraisal, spring-summer, 1984, pp. 4-9.

Australian Book Review, December, 1993, review of *We Are All in the Dumps with Jack and Guy,* p. 70.

Booklist, April 15, 1992, Hazel Rochman, review of *I Saw Esau,* p. 1529; June 15, 1992, Hazel Rochman, "Maurice Sendak" (author interview), p. 1848; September 15, 1993; March 15, 1994, review of *We Are All in the Dumps with Jack and Guy,* p. 1355; Carolyn Phelan, review of *We Are All in the Dumps with Jack and Guy,* p. 156; June 1, 1995, review of *Where the Wild Things Are,* p. 1761; October 1, 1995, Hazel Rochman, review of *The Miami Giant,* p. 328; December 15, 1995, Michael Cart, "The 'Stinky Cheese Man' Goes to College," p. 695; May 1, 1999, Ilene Cooper, review of *Swine Lake,* p. 1590.

Books and Bookmen, June, 1969; December, 1974, pp. 74-75.

Books for Keeps, March, 1992, review of *One Was Johnny, Alligators All Round* and *Chicken Soup with Rice,* p. 7; November, 1993, review of *We Are All in the Dumps with Jack and Guy,* p. 32.

Books for Your Children, summer, 1992, review of *Where the Wild Things Are,* p. 3.

Center for Children's Books, October, 1993, review of *We Are All in the Dumps with Jack and Guy,* p. 56.

Chicago Tribune, July 17, 1980; January 29, 1990.

Chicago Tribune Book World, May 3, 1981.

Children's Book Review, June, 1971, p. 84; October, 1993, review of *We Are All in the Dumps with Jack and Guy,* p. 17.

Children's Bookwatch, April, 1996, review of *Where the Wild Things Are,* p. 5.

Children's Literature, Volume 6, 1977, pp. 130-140; Volume 10, 1982, pp. 178-182; Volume 12, 1984, pp. 3-24; Volume 13, 1985, pp. 139-153; annual, 1996, Elizabeth Goodenough, "One Was Maurice," p. 235.

Children's Literature Association Quarterly, fall, 1985, pp. 122-127; winter, 1997, review of *Where the Wild Things Are,* p. 26.

Children's Literature in Education, November, 1971, p. 48; spring, 1982, pp. 38-43; summer, 1988, pp. 86-93; September, 1993, review of *Where the Wild Things Are,* p. 223; March, 1994, review of *We Are All in the Dumps with Jack and Guy,* p. 29.

Choice, September, 1992, H.F. Stein, "Maurice Sendak," p. 119.

Christian Science Monitor, November 5, 1993, review of *We Are All in the Dumps with Jack and Guy,* p. 10.

Commonweal, November 20, 1998, review of *Caldecott and Company,* p. 24.

Elementary English, February, 1971, pp. 262-263; November, 1971, pp. 825-832, 856-864.

Emergency Librarian, November, 1992, review of *Where the Wild Things Are,* p. 27.

Entertainment Weekly, February 28, 1992, Susan Stewart, review of *Where the Wild Things Are* (sound recording) p. 66.

Five Owls, November, 1993, review of *We Are All in the Dumps with Jack and Guy,* p. 29.

Guardian (London, England), November 9, 1999, review of *What Can You Do with a Shoe?,* p. 4.

Horn Book, December, 1970, pp. 642-646; October, 1976, p. 495; June, 1977, p. 303; April, 1980, pp. 145-155; August, 1983, pp. 474-477; May-June, 1986, pp. 305-313; May-June, 1987; September-October, 1992, Mary Burns, review of *I Saw Esau,* p. 602; May-June, 1993, p. 291; January-February, 1994, review of *We Are All in the Dumps with Jack and Guy,* p. 92; January-February, 1996, p. 70; January-February, 1997, Roger Sutton, review of *Frank and Joey Eat Lunch* and *Frank and Joey Go to Work,* p. 53; March, 1997, review of *Where the Wild Things Are,* p. 187; July, 1999, review of *Swine Lake,* p. 457; November, 2000, Karla Kuskin, review of *Where the Wild Things Are,* p. 778.

Hungry Mind Review, summer, 1993, review of *We Are All in the Dumps with Jack and Guy,* p. 16C.

Instructor, November, 1992, review of *Seven Little Monsters, Some Swell Pup, Outside over There, Hector Protector* and *As I Went over the Water, Higglety Pigglety Pop!,* and *Where the Wild Things Are,* p. 67.

Journal of Popular Culture, summer, 1978, Jill P. May, pp. 30-35.

Junior Bookshelf, April, 1966, pp. 103-111; February, 1968, p. 30; August, 1970, pp. 205-206; June, 1971, pp. 165-166.

Kirkus Reviews, August 15 1993, review of *We Are All in the Dumps with Jack and Guy,* p. 1080.

Ladies' Home Journal, March, 1969, Bruno Bettelheim, review of *Where the Wild Things Are,* p. 48.

Library Talk, November, 1993, review of *We Are All in the Dumps with Jack and Guy,* p. 63; January, 1994, review of *We Are All in the Dumps with Jack and Guy,* p. 13; May, 1994, review of *We Are All in the Dumps with Jack and Guy,* p. 27.

Los Angeles Times Book Review, February 6, 1981; December 10, 1982; October 3, 1993, review of *We Are All in the Dumps with Jack and Guy,* p. 1.

Magpies, September, 1993, review of *We Are All in the Dumps with Jack and Guy,* p. 24.

Monkeyshines on Great American Authors, January, 1996, "Maurice Sendak," p. 28.

National Observer, November 27, 1967.

New Advocate, spring, 1994, review of *Where the Wild Things Are,* p. 37.

New Republic, March 18, 1996, Jed Perl, review of *Pierre,* p. 30.

Newsweek, May 18, 1981.

New Yorker, January 22, 1966; November 23, 1992, p. 75; September 27, 1993, Art Spiegelman, "In the Dumps," p. 80.

New York Review of Books, December 17, 1970.

New York Times, November 1, 1967; December 9, 1970; January 5, 1973; October 12, 1980; October 15, 1980; April 11, 1981; June 1, 1981; November 30, 1981; October 24, 1985; November 8, 1987; October 25, 1990; December 2, 1993, Christopher Lehmann-Haupt, review of *We Are All in the Dumps with Jack and Guy,* p.

New York Times Book Review, October 16, 1960, p. 40; October 22, 1967; November 1, 1970; February 29, 1976, p. 26; April 29, 1979; April 26, 1981, pp. 49, 64-65; October 9, 1983; May 17, 1987; May 17, 1992, Alison Lurie, review of *I Saw Esau,* p. 23; November 14, 1993, Brian Alderson, review of *We*

Are All in the Dumps with Jack and Guy, p. 17; November 12, 1995, Sean Kelly, review of *The Miami Giant,* p. 24; November 16, 1997, review of *Where the Wild Things Are,* p. 26; May 16, 1999, Peter Marks, review of *Swine Lake,* p. 21.

New York Times Magazine, June 7, 1970.

Observer (London, England), November 28, 1993, review of *We Are All in the Dumps with Jack and Guy,* p. 11.

Parabola, fall, 1981, pp. 88-91.

Parenting, May, 1992, Leonard Marcus, review of *I Saw Esau,* p. 30; October, 1993, Marcus, "Why Is Maurice Sendak So Incredibly Angry?," p. 78.

Parents, November, 1992, Sara Evans, "The Wild World of Sendak," p. 365; reviews of *Very Far Away, Pierre: A Cautionary Tale, The Sign on Rosie's Door, Very Far Away, Outside over There, One Was Johnny, Kenny's Window, In the Night Kitchen, Higglety Pigglety Pop!, Dear Mili, Chicken Soup with Rice, Caldecott and Co., Alligators All Around,* and *Where the Wild Things Are,* pp. 366-367; June, 1997, review of *Alligators All Around,* p. 189.

Parents' Choice, spring, 1995, review of *We Are All in the Dumps with Jack and Guy,* p. 3.

People, December 2, 1985, pp. 215-216.

Publishers Weekly, April 10, 1981, pp. 45-46; May 25, 1992, review of *I Saw Esau,* p. 55; June 8, 1992, p. 26; August 16, 1993, review of *We Are All in the Dumps with Jack and Guy,* p. 104; November 1, 1993, review of *We Are All in the Dumps with Jack and Guy,* p. 28; July 31, 1995, review of *The Miami Giant,* p. 80; May 3, 1999, review of *Swine Lake,* p. 74; May 28, 2001, Sally Lodge, "Unearthing Sendak Treasures," p. 33; June 4, 2001, "Vintage Sendak," p. 82; July 23, 2001, review of *What Can You Do with a Shoe?,* p. 79; November 19, 2001, "Sendak Is Back," p. 69.

Quarterly Journal of the Library of Congress, Volume 28, number 4, 1971.

Rolling Stone, December 30, 1976.

Saturday Review, December 14, 1963.

School Library Journal, December, 1970; May, 1976, p. 54; June, 1992, Shirley Wilton, review of *I Saw Esau,* p. 110; October, 1993, p. 119; November, 1995, Karen Radtke, review of *The Miami Giant,* p. 86; February, 1999, Brian Wilson, review of *Maurice Sendak's Little Bear,* p. 148; March, 1999, Kristina Aaronson, review of *Maurice Sendak's Little Bear* (video), p. 148; July, 1999, Julie Cummins, review of *Swine Lake,* p. 77; September, 2001, Kathleen Simonetta, "Maurice Sendak," p. 244 and "An Animated Sendak Classic," p. 20.

Signal, September, 1986, pp. 172-187.

Spectator, November 28, 1998, review of *Where the Wild Things Are,* p. 46.

Theatre Crafts, April, 1984, Ellen Levene, pp. 43-45, 75-78.

Time, July 6, 1981; July 28, 1986, p. 50; October 4, 1993, review of *We Are All in the Dumps with Jack and Guy,* p. 93; December 20, 1993, review of *We Are All in the Dumps with Jack and Guy,* p. 64.

Times Educational Supplement, December 17, 1993, William Feaver, review of *We Are All in the Dumps with Jack and Guy,* p. 24; May 19, 2000, Ted Dewan, review of *Swine Lake.*

Times Literary Supplement, July 2, 1971; March 27, 1981.

Top of the News, June, 1970, pp. 366-369.

Tribune Books (Chicago, IL), November 14, 1993, review of *We Are All in the Dumps with Jack and Guy,* p. 6.

TV Guide, November 11, 1978.

Vogue, September, 1993, Jed Perl, review of *We Are All in the Dumps with Jack and Guy,* p. 104.

Washington Post, November 1, 1978; November 20, 1981.

Washington Post Book World, May 10, 1981, pp. 1-2; October 10, 1993, review of *We Are All in the Dumps with Jack and Guy,* p. 11; December 8, 1996, review of *Nutshell Library,* p. 20.

Wilson Library Bulletin, January, 1994, Judith Rovenger, review of *We Are All in the Dumps with Jack and Guy,* p. 31.

ONLINE

American Masters, http://www.pbs.org/ (January 6, 2002), "Maurice Sendak."

Educational Paper Association, http://www.eduppaperback.org/ (January 6, 2002), "Maurice Sendak."

Falcon, http://falcon.jmu.edu/ (January 6, 2002), Carol Gregory and Inez Ramsey, "Maurice Sendak."

First Person Book Page, http://wwww.bookpage.com/ (May 1, 1999), Alice Cary, "Swine Lake: A Night at the Ballet with Maurice Sendak."

National Foundation for Jewish Culture, http://wwwjewishculture.org/ (May 18, 1998), "Maurice Sendak Visual Arts Award."

Write News, http://writenews.com/ (December 7, 2001), "Maurice Sendak Creates New 'Little Bear' Story."

OTHER

Maurice Sendak (film), Weston Woods, 1986.

SENDAK, Maurice Bernard
See SENDAK, Maurice

* * *

SETH, Vikram 1952-

PERSONAL: Surname is pronounced "sate"; born June 20, 1952, in Calcutta, India; son of Premnath (a consultant) and Leila (a judge) Seth. *Education:* Corpus Christi College, Oxford, B.A. (with honors), 1975, M.A., 1978; Stanford University, M.A., 1977; Nanjing University, China, graduate diploma, 1982.

ADDRESSES: *Home*—8 Rajaji Marg, New Delhi, India 110 011. *Agent*—c/o Irene Skolnick Agency, 22 West 23rd St., 5th Floor, New York, NY 10010-5211; c/o Giles Gordon, Curtis Brown, 37 Queensferry St., Edinburgh EH2 4QS.

CAREER: Poet, novelist, and travel writer. Stanford University Press, Stanford, CA, senior editor, 1985-86.

AWARDS, HONORS: Thomas Cook Travel Book Award, 1983, for *From Heaven Lake: Travels through Sinkiang and Tibet;* Commonwealth Poetry Prize, Asian Region, 1985, for *The Humble Administrator's Garden;* Ingram Merrill fellowship, 1985-86; Quality Paperback Book Club New Voice Award and Commonwealth Poetry Prize, both 1986, for *The Golden Gate: A Novel in Verse;* Guggenheim fellowship, 1986-87; W.H. Smith Award, 1994, for *A Suitable Boy: A Novel;* Commonwealth Writer's Prize, 1994.

WRITINGS:

Mappings (poems), Writers Workshop (Calcutta, India), 1980.

From Heaven Lake: Travels through Sinkiang and Tibet, illustrated with own photographs, Chatto and Windus (London, England), 1983, Vintage (New York, NY), 1987.

The Humble Administrator's Garden (poems), Carcanet (Manchester, England), 1985.

The Golden Gate: A Novel in Verse, Random House (New York, NY), 1986.

All You Who Sleep Tonight: Poems, Knopf (New York, NY), 1990.

Beastly Tales from Here and There, illustrated by Ravi Shankar, Viking (New Delhi), 1992, HarperCollins (New York, NY), 1994.

(Translator) *Three Chinese Poets: Translations of Poems by Wang Wei, Li Bai, and Du Fu,* HarperPerennial (New York, NY), 1992.

A Suitable Boy: A Novel, HarperCollins (New York, NY), 1993.

The Poems, 1981-1994, Penguin (New York, NY), 1995.

Arion and the Dolphin, illustrations by Jane Ray, Dutton (New York, NY), 1995.

An Equal Music, Broadway Books (New York, NY), 1999.

SIDELIGHTS: Vikram Seth will "no doubt . . . be proclaimed the reinventor of narrative verse in America," predicted X.J. Kennedy in a review of *The Golden Gate: A Novel in Verse* for *Los Angeles Times Book Review.* "I don't know when a versifier has proved better versed in verse-form than Seth," continued the reviewer, declaring that such mastery of poetry "probably hasn't been heard in English since Alexander Pope." Seth's studies in economics and literature, in addition to travel and residency in eastern Asia and west-coast America, have given him ample and uncommon background for his writings, and he has acquired a reputation as a skillful poet who exhibits unique cultural understanding in all of his works.

From Heaven Lake: Travels through Sinkiang and Tibet is Seth's account of his 1981 hitchhiking adventure from Nanjing University in eastern China through Tibet and Nepal to his home in Delhi, India. In what Jonathan Mirsky in *New Statesman* deemed "the perfect travel book," Seth tells of his episodes of loneliness, illness, and danger as well as the pleasures he took from visiting various civilizations, encountering interesting people along the way. Intermittently, he reflects—with both lament and satire—on the Chinese Cultural Revolution, the annihilation of Tibetan temples, and the treatment of foreigners by the Chinese. Mirsky noted that with his ability to read and speak Chinese, his attention to detail, and his acceptance of cultural differences, Seth is "a wonderful companion," able to manage better than the average tourist. "Very few foreigners have spent the night in Chinese truck parks and country inns," the reviewer added. "Few have had even a meal with a Chinese family. . . . Seth has, and he notices everything and tells us about it."

Seth conveys more of his cultural diversity through the medium of poetry in *The Humble Administrator's Garden.* Like his previous book, the collection of poems contains material gleaned from Seth's visits to both Eastern and Western countries. "Given the exotic nature of his background," noted Tom D'Evelyn in *Christian Science Monitor,* the poet could have gone "toward the specialized feeling and idea, toward myth and cultural arcana, toward anthropology." Instead Seth goes in the other direction, continued the reviewer, choosing "to represent in his poems feeling of the widest applicability." Divided into three sections—on China, India, and California (with occasional references to England)—the book was hailed by Raymond Tong in *British Book News* as an "impressive" collection in which "a high level is generally maintained throughout."

As with *From Heaven Lake,* critics liked *The Humble Administrator's Garden* for the unassuming tone Seth presents in the work. Dick Davis in *Listener,* for example, found the collection to be "modest, ordered, well-mannered and well-planned, with a trace of deprecatory self-pity." In his review in *Times Literary Supplement,* Claude Rawson praised Seth's "fastidious probing language," noting that the work includes "small masterpieces of delicate verbal and emotional discipline, observant of pathos, of ironies of behaviour, of the unexpected small exuberances of life." Extolling Seth's talent as a disciplined poet, the critic observed that "Seth focuses on the mundane with unusual clarity," and he added that Seth "is one of the few young poets who has taken the trouble to learn, really learn, the disciplines of meter."

Seth's widest acclaim as a technically solid poet came with *The Golden Gate,* his 1986 verse novel, which many critics hailed as a tour de force. Containing nearly six hundred sonnets of iambic tetrameter, Seth's long narrative poem is set in present-day San Francisco and concerns the lives of young, urban professionals, or "yuppies." The story introduces John Brown, a twenty-six-year-old computer expert working for a defense contractor, who suddenly comes to the realization that his life is meaningless. He has lunch with his old girlfriend Janet Hayakawa—a sculptor and a drummer in a punk-rock band called Liquid Sheep—after which Janet, unbeknownst to John, submits an advertisement on John's behalf to a lonely hearts column. The action is a catalyst for the presentation of *The Golden Gate*'s other characters: Liz Dorati, an attractive lawyer; Phil Weiss, a divorced single parent, philosopher, and peace demonstrator; and Ed, an advertising executive. In addition to incorporating timely concerns within the novel—such as a long scene at an anti-nuclear demonstration and a dialogue between two homosexual men on sex and celibacy—Seth places his characters in typically modern situations, such as singles bars and wine-making parties. Seth "knows these people inside out," noted Kennedy, and he consequently "conducts us on a psychological safari through five interesting souls."

Deemed "one of the curiosities of the season" by John Gross in *New York Times, The Golden Gate* struck many critics as unusual in its portrayal of modern yuppies conveyed through narrative verse, a form that is a "throwback to our literary past," Raymond Mungo pointed out in *New York Times Book Review.* Seth once told *CA* interviewer Jean W. Ross that he patterned the style of *The Golden Gate* after Russian poet Aleksandr Pushkin's *Eugene Onegin,* a work exhibiting intricately rhymed and metered sonnets. Expecting little, Seth found in reading *Eugene Onegin* that "I was reading it as I would read a novel. That was something that intrigued me, because the idea of a novel in verse had at first struck me as some curious hybrid, something that would not work. Here was something that *did* work, and that not only worked, but moved me and amused me and made me want to write something in a similar form set in my time and in a place that I knew." According to Alan Hollinghurst in *Times Literary Supplement,* the Pushkin stanza is "a form whose inner counterpoint gives it both gravity and levity." Moreover, the reviewer judged the unconventionality of Seth's novel entirely appropriate, declaring, "It is hard to imagine a better vehicle for social verse narrative which aims to be both reflective and lightly comic."

It took Seth years to complete and publish his next novel, *A Suitable Boy,* described by Michele Field of *Publishers Weekly* as "the longest single-volume work of English fiction since Samuel Richardson's *Clarissa* was published in 1747." At a dense 1,349 pages and weighing four pounds, *A Suitable Boy* is Seth's "magnum opus," according to Robert Worth of *Commonweal.* Seth completed several other works while *A Suitable Boy* was in progress: the poetry collections *Beastly Tales from Here and There* and *All You Who Sleep Tonight,* and the translation of a collection of Chinese poetry titled *Three Chinese Poets: Translations of Poems by Wang Wei, Li Bai, and Du Fu.*

A Suitable Boy is the story of the arranged marriage of Lata Mehra, an upper-class Indian woman rebelling against the traditional customs imposed upon her by her mother and Indian society at large. The widow Mehra, Lata's mother, is determined to find her daughter a husband of appropriate caste, color, religion, and financial stability—a "suitable boy." However, after attending her older sister's wedding at the beginning of the novel, Lata becomes skeptical of marriage and of the Indian traditions inherent in arranged matrimony. The plot centers on four families—the Mehras, Kapoors, Chatterjis, and Khans—yet Seth reaches beyond the limits of their experiences: "He chose to tell the whole story, producing for all time the whole world of Lata Mehra, with all the intermingled levels of North Indian culture," Schuyler Ingle remarked in *Los Angeles Times Book Review.* While the action in *A Suitable Boy* takes place in the fictional northern city of Brahmpur in the 1950s, not long after India's 1947 independence from England, Seth describes in great detail the political, religious, and cultural shifts gripping postcolonial India in a multitude of subplots.

New Republic reviewer Richard Jenkyns acknowledged the tendency of long books to "be spoken of, whether for praise or blame, in superlatives," which may seem to leave only one conclusion: "Since *A Suitable Boy* is not obviously a bad book, it must be a marvel. What we do not expect, with something so massive, is to speak in neutral, colorless terms: pleasant, mostly unpretentious, some pale charm, some gentle humor, readable but a bit flat and dull. But such, I think, is the judgment that we should return on this book." *Vanity Fair*'s Christopher Hitchens noted, "Those who aren't so keen on Seth's blockbuster say that it's more like [English writer John] Galsworthy than [Russian epic novelist Leo] Tolstoy, a jolly giant of a saga with lots of characters and speaking parts but no darkness or depth and no real consciousness of evil and suffering." Robert Towers, writing in *New York Times Book Review,* found that "in his drive toward inclusiveness" the author "has sacrificed intensity," and he concluded, "In the end, *A Suitable Boy* succeeds less as a novel than as a richly detailed documentary focused upon a crucial era in the history of an endlessly fascinating country." *London Review of Books* contributor John Lanchester found, however, that the author succeeds in his quest for "complete transparency: all his energies are concentrated on making the prose a vehicle for the characters and the action." He further added, "The prose is intended not to distract. The resulting structural clarity is remarkable—you never don't know what's happening, why, where, and to whom. . . . It's a considerable technical feat." In *Los Angeles Times Book Review,* Ingle noted the many hours required to read a novel of such length but concluded that "*A Suitable Boy* is a book that pays readers back, and richly, for their nightly effort."

As critics debated the issue of the book's length, some found it a hindrance, and others deemed it appropriate, though unwieldy. According to Jill Rachlin of *People,* although the author intended *A Suitable Boy* to be the first novel of a set of five, his first draft was close to two thousand pages. "After cutting it by a third," Rachlin reported, "he tried to divide it into two or three separate books. 'It didn't break in any right point,' he says with a laugh, 'so I was stuck with this monster.'" In a *Newsweek* review, Laura Shapiro remarked, "Surprisingly, it makes very easy reading. What you can't do is *hold* the damn thing." She further observed, "Very few novels demand extraordinary length, and this isn't one of them. But Seth's publishers aren't entirely crazy: there is something strangely appealing about *A Suitable Boy.*" Pico Iyer, writing for *Times Literary Supplement,* observed, "Every single page of *A Suitable Boy* is pleasant and readable and true; but the parts are better crafted, and so more satisfying, than the whole. . . . [I]t is not immediately evident that its some 1,400 pages make it four times better than it would have been at 350." Yet Ingle found the book's length logical: "In a land of 900 million people, Seth seems to be saying, no one person can possibly be singled out: Their connections must be taken into account as well."

Arion and the Dolphin, a 1995 children's book based on Seth's libretto for an opera, is a blend of prose and verse that retells an ancient Greek legend: the story of a young musician whose life is saved by a dolphin. Cruel fisher folk imprison Arion and put his dolphin friend on display; the dolphin soon dies. Though the book is meant for children, its message that humans can find love, liberation, and mercy in the natural world may be overpowered for them by the sadness of the dolphin's death. The opera on which the book is based, with music by Alec Roth, was first performed in 1994 in Plymouth, England. A flyer from the Singapore opera, where the work was performed in 1996, notes that the cast totaled two hundred people, the most ambitious production ever undertaken by the company.

Seth's novel, *An Equal Music,* is a love story between Michael and Julia who are both immersed, by vocation, in the world of Western classical music. It is the story of a resurrected love between the two protagonists who meet by chance years later. Writing for *Time,* Elizabeth Gleick opined, "*An Equal Music* is almost unbearably sudsy, a huge disappointment for the legions of *A Suitable Boy* fans waiting to see what magic Seth could possibly spin next." However, Donna Seaman of *Booklist* was much more enthusiastic, "Seth has moved from the symphonic scope of his best-selling *A Suitable Boy* (1993) to a love story set to chamber music. . . . Replete with feverish drama and elegant characters, staccato dialogue, and sweeping emotions, Seth's irresistible novel is destined to please diverse readers as it artfully bridges the divide between popular and literary fiction."

BIOGRAPHICAL AND CRITICAL SOURCES:

BOOKS

Agarwalla, Shyam S., *Vikram Seth's "A Suitable Boy": Search for an Indian Identity,* Prestige Books, 1995.

Contemporary Literary Criticism, Thomson Gale (Detroit, MI), Volume 43, 1987, Volume 90, 1996.

Contemporary Novelists, St. James Press, (Detroit, MI), 1996.

Dictionary of Literary Biography, Volume 120: *American Poets since World War II, Third Series,* Thomson Gale (Detroit, MI) 1992, pp. 281-285.

Kirpal, Viney, editor, *The New Indian Novel in English,* Allied Publishers (New Delhi, India), 1990, pp. 91-100.

Parker, Peter, editor, *A Reader's Guide to Twentieth-Century Writers,* Oxford University Press, (Oxford, England), 1996.

Riggs, Thomas, editor, *Contemporary Poets,* St. James Press, (Detroit, MI), 1996.

Serafin, Steven R., editor, *Encyclopedia of American Literature,* Continuum Publishing, (New York, NY), 1999.

Stringer, Jenny, editor, *The Oxford Companion to Twentieth-Century Literature in English,* Oxford University Press, (Oxford, England), 1996.

PERIODICALS

ACLALS Bulletin, 1989, Makarand R. Paranjape, "'The Golden Gate' and the Quest for Self-Realization."

American Poetry Revue, November-December, 1986, Marjorie Perloff, "'Homeward Ho!' Silicon Valley Pushkin."

Arkansas Philological Association, fall, 1996, Jay Curlin, "'The World Goes On:' Narrative Structure and the Sonnet in Vikram Seth's 'The Golden Gate.'"

Booklist, March 15, 1999, Donna Seaman, review of *An Equal Music,* p. 1261.

Books, summer, 1999, review of *An Equal Music,* p. 20.

British Book News, November, 1983; September, 1985.

Chicago Tribune, April 20, 1986; February 3, 1988.

Christian Science Monitor, August 21, 1985; June 10, 1999, review of *An Equal Music,* p. 16.

Commonweal, May 21, 1993, Robert Worth, review of *A Suitable Boy,* pp. 25-26.

Economist, May 15, 1999, review of *An Equal Music,* p. 12.

Entertainment Weekly, June 4, 1999, review of *An Equal Music,* p. 79.

Five Owls, January, 1996, p. 52.

Globe and Mail (Toronto, Ontario, Canada), May 15, 1999, review of *An Equal Music,* p. D16.

Horn Book Guide, fall, 1995, p. 281.

Island, winter, 1995, J.H. Walker, "Trunks of the Banyan Tree: History, Politics and Fiction."

Kirkus Reviews, March 15, 1999, review of *An Equal Music,* p. 404.

Library Journal, April 15, 1999, Shirley N. Quan, review of *An Equal Music,* p. 146.

Listener, December 5, 1985, Dick Davis, review of *The Humble Administrator's Garden.*

Literary Criterion, 1986, Rowena Hill, "Vikram Seth's 'The Golden Gate.'"

London Review of Books, April 22, 1993, p. 9; April 29, 1999, review of *An Equal Music,* p. 15.

Los Angeles Times Book Review, April 6, 1986; May 23, 1993, pp. 4, 11; May 30, 1999, review of *An Equal Music,* p. 10.

New Republic, April 21, 1986, John Hollander, review of *The Golden Gate,* p. 32; June 14, 1993, Richard Jenkyns, review of *A Suitable Boy,* pp. 41-44; July 12, 1999, Karl Miller, review of *An Equal Music,* p. 44.

New Statesman, October 7, 1983, Kathy O'Shaughnessy, "From Heaven Lake: Travels Through Sinkiang and Tibet," p. 25; May 3, 1999, Tom Holland, review of *An Equal Music,* p. 58.

Newsweek, April 14, 1986, David Lehman, review of *The Golden Gate,* p. 74; May 24, 1993, Laura Shapiro, review of *A Suitable Boy,* p. 62; May 3, 1999, review of *An Equal Music,* p. 72.

New Yorker, July 14, 1986, Whitney Balliett, review of *The Golden Gate,* p. 82; June 7, 1999, David Denby, review of *An Equal Music,* p. 91.

New York Review of Books, July 15, 1999, review of *An Equal Music,* p. 20.

New York Times, April 14, 1986, John Gross, review of *The Golden Gate,* p. 18.

New York Times Book Review, May 11, 1986, Raymond Mungo, review of *The Golden Gate,* p. 11; May 9, 1993, Robert Towers, review of *A Suitable Boy,* pp. 3, 16; June 13, 1999, review of *An Equal Music,* p. 34.

Observer (London, England), September 12, 1993, p. 54; March 28, 1999, review of *An Equal Music,* p. 11; December 30, 2001, audio book review of *Beastly Tales from Here and There,* p. 14; January 27, 2002, review of *The Golden Gate,* p. 18; March 31, 2002, audio book review of *A Suitable Boy,* p. 16.

People, June 30, 1986, Cutler Durkee, review of *The Golden Gate,* p. 82; May 24, 1993, Jill Rachlin, review of *A Suitable Boy,* pp. 29-30.

Publishers Weekly, May 10, 1993, Michele Field, review of *A Suitable Boy,* pp. 46-47; June 26, 1995, review of *Arion and the Dolphin,* p. 106; April 12, 1999, review of *An Equal Music,* p. 53.

Rosyjska Ruletka, 1995, Roumiana Deltcheva, review of *The Golden Gate.*

School Library Journal, July, 1995, Cheri Estes, review of *Arion and the Dolphin,* p. 74.

Spectator, February 11, 1984; April 10, 1999, review of *An Equal Music,* p. 30.

Time, May 31, 1999, Elizabeth Gleick, review of *An Equal Music,* p. 98.

Times Literary Supplement, February 7, 1986; July 4, 1986; September 21-27, 1990, p. 1007; March 19, 1993, p. 20.

Vanity Fair, June, 1993, Christopher Hitchens, review of *A Suitable Boy,* pp. 36-40.

Wall Street Journal, May 14, 1999, review of *An Equal Music,* p. W9.

Washington Post, May 17, 1986.

Washington Post Book World, March 23, 1986; July 22, 1990, p. 4; December 2, 1990, p. 9; May 9, 1999, review of *An Equal Music,* p. 15.

Whole Earth Review, winter, 2001, review of *A Suitable Boy,* p. 6.

World Literature Today, spring, 1993, John Oliver Perry, review of *Beastly Tales from Here and There,* pp. 447-448.

ONLINE

Atlantic Unbound, http://www.theatlantic.com/ (June 23,1999), interview with Seth.

Connect Online, http://www.connectmagazine.com/ (November 20, 2003), overview of Seth.

Emory University Web site, http://www.emory.edu/ (June 19,2002), "Vikram Seth."

Four Elephants Web site, http://www.fourelephants.com/ (May 1, 2000), Samantha Brown, review of *An Equal Music.*

Illinois Institute of Technology Web site, http://www.iit.edu/ (November 20, 2003).

January Online, http://www.januarymagazine.com/ (November 20, 2003), interview with Seth.

Random House Web site, http://www.randomhouse.com/ (May, 2003).

Salon.com, http://archive.salon.com/ (May 13,1999), Akash Kapur, review of *An Equal Music.*

Seattle Arts and Lectures Web site, http://www.lectures.org/seth.html/ (November 19, 2003), "Vikram Seth."

University of California, Santa Cruz Web site, http://www.ucsc.edu/ (October 8, 2001), John Newman, overview of Seth.

* * *

SHAARA, Jeff 1952-

PERSONAL: Born February 21, 1952, in New Brunswick, NJ; son of Michael (a novelist) and Helen (Krumwiede) Shaara; married wife Lynne, October 3, 1992. *Education:* Florida State University, B.S. (criminology), 1973.

ADDRESSES: Office—P.O. Box 16445, Missoula, MT 59808. *E-mail*—email@jeffshaara.com.

CAREER: Historical novelist. Coin dealer in Tampa, FL, 1968-88.

WRITINGS:

(Reviser) Michael Shaara, *The Noah Conspiracy* (revision of *The Herald*), 1994.

Gods and Generals, Ballantine Books (New York, NY), 1996.

The Last Full Measure, Ballantine Books (New York, NY), 1998.

Gone for Soldiers: A Novel of the Mexican War, Ballantine (Books New York, NY), 2000.

Rise to Rebellion, Ballantine Books (New York, NY), 2001.

The Glorious Cause, Ballantine Books (New York, NY), 2002.

To the Last Man, Ballantine Books (New York, NY), 2004.

ADAPTATIONS: Gods and Generals, Rise to Rebellion, The Glorious Cause, The Last Full Measure, and *Gone for Soldiers* were recorded for audio cassette; *Gods and Generals* was adapted into a film, directed by Ronald Maxwell from his screenplay, starring Stephen Lang, Jeff Daniels, and Robert Duvall, and released by Warner Bros. in 2003.

SIDELIGHTS: Although technically a first-time novelist, Jeff Shaara was far from unfamiliar with the writing trade when his book *Gods and Generals* was published, for he is the son of Pulitzer Prize-winning historical novelist Michael Shaara, author of 1974's *The Killer Angels.* Indeed, for his first fictional outing, Shaara, a former rare-coin dealer who eventually took over management of his father's literary estate, chose to write a prequel to his father's prize-winning book. While *The Killer Angels* deals with the military engagement at Gettysburg during the American Civil War, *Gods and Generals* portrays the years 1858 to 1863, which led up to the decisive battle.

Shaara did not expect to become a writer. He decided to write *Gods and Generals,* he said, after getting to know Ronald Maxwell, who directed *Gettysburg,* the film based on *The Killer Angels,* and who thought someone should continue the story. As Shaara explained to *Insight on the News* interviewer Kelly Patricia O'Meara:

"Listening to Ron, I thought, 'Maybe I can do this. I don't know, but if someone is going to continue the story—continue my father's words—maybe it should be the son.' I wasn't afraid because I had no expectations." With the blessing of his mother and sister, he went ahead.

Shaara wrote *Gods and Generals* from the narrative viewpoints of two Southern and two Northern generals: Robert E. Lee and Thomas "Stonewall" Jackson, and Joshua Lawrence Chamberlain and Winfield Scott Hancock, respectively. All except Jackson—who died before the battle of Gettysburg—are also characters in *The Killer Angels,* which like *Gods and Generals* tells its story from various participants' perspectives. *Gods and Generals* received "vast publisher promotion," in the words of *Booklist* contributor Brad Hooper, and earned a critical response to match. Hooper, referring to Shaara's genre as "superior historical fiction," averred that *Gods and Generals* offers readers a "splendidly detailed witness" to the war. Shaara, Hooper observed, explores the four generals' inner lives sufficiently to describe social and political issues in a meaningful fashion, resulting in "an impressive achievement."

A *Publishers Weekly* reviewer expressed similar views, particularly praising Shaara's exploration of the mind of Stonewall Jackson and complimenting the novel as a whole for being "impressive in its sweep, depth of character and historic verisimilitude." In short, wrote a *Publishers Weekly* critic, "the Shaara genes, it seems, are in fine shape." Thomas L. Kilpatrick, writing in *Library Journal,* also had positive words for the novel's exploration of the four generals' characters. "Considered together, the two novels by father and son present a powerful portrait of the generals who won and lost the Civil War," Kilpatrick remarked.

After the success of *Gods and Generals,* a closing chapter to the fictional trilogy, titled *The Last Full Measure,* was "a natural," according to *Booklist* reviewer Gilbert Taylor. The story begins with Lee's retreat from Gettysburg and concludes with his surrender at Appomattox. The general depicted here is a man "haunted by Stonewall Jackson's ghost," noted a *Publishers Weekly* critic, while his rival, Ulysses S. Grant, "more concerned about his supply of cigars than battle losses, comes across as a dolt." J. Edwin Smith, writing in the *Chicago Tribune,* had a different view, stating that the author "accomplished something that no writer before him has—put a human face and a compassionate heart within one of the war's most vilified warriors, Ulysses S. Grant." The focus on Grant was no coincidence, Shaara explained in an online *Bookpage* interview with David Madden. "I loved writing about that man. I wanted to shatter the myths about him and tell his story fully and truthfully. I liked being able to bring out the differences between Lee and Grant. People are emotional about Lee, a beloved figure, an inspiring figure. But Grant is cool and aloof, so I wanted to bring him alive for the reader."

In *Gone for Soldiers* Shaara turns to the Mexican War; this 1840s conflict involved many of the men who would go on to be Civil War leaders, including Lee, Grant, Longstreet, and Jackson. "All the way through the research on the Civil War characters they kept drawing attention to the war with Mexico," Shaara told O'Meara. "Down the roster all of them refer to that experience in Mexico during their maturing—in their growing up—as the one that really made them soldiers." Shaara's telling of their story is "respectable if uneven," commented a *Publishers Weekly* reviewer, who found the battle scenes in *Gone for Soldiers* "fluid and compelling" but character development lacking. *Library Journal* contributor David Keymer, however, thought the book "wonderful" in its portrayal of "eminently human heroes" fighting a "muddied" war.

Shaara examines the roots of the Revolutionary War in *Rise to Rebellion,* his fourth novel in five years. The novel covers the period from to 1770 to 1776, beginning with the Boston Massacre and ending with the Declaration of Independence. It depicts such historical figures as John and Abigail Adams, George Washington, and Benjamin Franklin. Shaara shows much more sympathy for these colonials than for their British rulers, observed Keymer in *Library Journal,* but all his characters are "complicated human beings" and he is able to bring their stories to "vibrant life." A *Publishers Weekly* critic also praised the book, writing that Shaara "demonstrates an ever-growing level of literary competence" and imbues the historical narrative with "vigor and passion."

A second volume on the American Revolution, *The Glorious Cause,* traces the conflict to its end. Once more presenting history from the viewpoints of the various people who lived it, "Shaara reaches new heights here, with a narrative that's impossible to put down," commented a *Publishers Weekly* reviewer. Robert Conroy, writing in *Library Journal,* praised the novelist's historical accuracy as well as his characterizations, and summed up *The Glorious Cause* as "rich, exciting, and compelling."

Shaara has said that despite his use of multiple viewpoints, his writing style is different from his father's; it is more action-oriented, among other things. When he began *Gods and Generals,* he told O'Meara, "My only conscious decision was to continue the format of *The Killer Angels*—going back and forth between characters, from one point of view to the other. In any case, there's absolutely no way to mimic my father's writing style. No matter how hard you try to write like someone else you'll run out of gas pretty quickly—you'll end up spending so much energy copying the style that you lose the substance." He added, "I understand what a classic *Killer Angels* is. I will never stand up and say I'm as good a writer as my father because I don't believe it, so it is hard for me to imagine that anyone could confuse our writing styles."

BIOGRAPHICAL AND CRITICAL SOURCES:

BOOKS

Contemporary Literary Criticism, Volume 119: *Yearbook 1998,* Thomson Gale (Detroit, MI), 1999.

PERIODICALS

Booklist, April 15, 1996, p. 1395; May 1, 1998, Gilbert Taylor, review of *The Last Full Measure,* p. 1478.

Chicago Tribune, June 12, 1998, J. Edwin Smith, "Bringing the Civil War to a Heartfelt End," sec. 5, p. 3.

Christian Science Monitor, June 18, 1998, Keith Henderson, "How Civil War Generals Thought and Fought," p. B7.

Insight on the News, September 11, 2000, Kelly Patricia O'Meara, "Shaara Makes Good on His Literary Legacy" (interview), p. 36.

Kirkus Reviews, May 1, 1996, review of *Gods and Generals,* p. 633.

Library Journal, May 1, 1996, Thomas L. Kilpatrick, review of *Gods and Generals,* p. 134; June 1, 1998, Charles Michaud, review of *The Last Full Measure,* p. 161; May 15, 2000, David Keymer, review of *Gone for Soldiers,* p. 126; March 15, 2001, David Keymer, review of *Rise to Rebellion,* p. 106; October 1, 2002, Robert Conroy, review of *The Glorious Cause,* p. 129.

Publishers Weekly, May 13, 1996, review of *Gods and Generals,* p. 55; April 20, 1998, review of *The Last Full Measure,* p. 44; April 3, 2000, review of *Gone for Soldiers,* p. 62; May 21, 2001, review of *Rise to Rebellion,* p. 78; September 30, 2002, review of *The Glorious Cause,* p. 45.

School Library Journal, August, 1997, Barry Williams, review of *Gods and Generals,* p. 190.

ONLINE

Bookpage, http://www.bookpage.com/ (August 14, 2004), David Madden, "With *The Last Full Measure,* the Trilogy Concludes but the Legacy Lives On" (interview with Shaara).

Jeff Shaara Web site, http://www.jeffshaara.com/ (August 11, 2004).

* * *

SHAARA, Michael 1929-1988
(Michael Joseph Shaara, Jr.)

PERSONAL: Born June 23, 1929, in Jersey City, NJ; died of a heart attack, May 5, 1988, in Tallahassee, FL; son of Michael Joseph, Sr. (a union organizer) and Alleene (Maxwell) Shaara; married Helen Krumweide, September 16, 1950 (divorced, June, 1980); children: Jeff, Lila Elise. *Education:* Rutgers University, B.A., 1951; graduate study at Columbia University, 1952-53, and University of Vermont, 1953-54.

CAREER: Writer. Worked as merchant seaman, 1948-49; St. Petersburg Police Department, St. Petersburg, FL, police officer, 1954-55; short story writer, 1955-61; Florida State University, Tallahassee, associate professor of English, 1961-73. Guest lecturer at universities. *Military service:* U.S. Army, 1946-49, paratrooper in 82nd Airborne Division; became sergeant. U.S. Army Reserve, 1949-53.

MEMBER: International Platform Association, Authors Guild, Omicron Delta Kappa, Gold Key.

AWARDS, HONORS: Award from American Medical Association, 1966, for article "In the Midst of Life"; Pulitzer Prize for fiction, 1975, for *The Killer Angels;* short story awards include Dikty's best science fiction of the year awards and citations from Judith Merrill.

WRITINGS:

The Broken Place (novel), New American Library (New York, NY), 1968.

The Killer Angels (novel), McKay (New York, NY), 1974, reprinted, Modern Library (New York, NY), 2004.

The Herald (novel), McGraw (New York, NY), 1981, revised edition with additions by son, Jeff Shaara, published as *The Noah Conspiracy,* Pocket Books (New York, NY), 1994.

Soldier Boy (short stories), Pocket Books (New York, NY), 1982.

For Love of the Game (novel), Carroll & Graf (New York, NY), 1991.

Author of screenplay *Billy Boy,* 1980. Contributor of stories to magazines, including *Saturday Evening Post, Playboy, Galaxy, Redbook,* and *Cosmopolitan,* as well as to various newspapers.

ADAPTATIONS: The Killer Angels was adapted into the film *Gettysburg,* directed by Ronald Maxwell from his screenplay, starring Tom Berenger, Jeff Daniels, and Martin Sheen, and produced by Turner Pictures, 1993. *The Killer Angels* was also recorded in an unabridged audio version by Books on Tape, 1985. *For Love of the Game* was adapted into a feature film, directed by Sam Raimi from a screenplay by Dana Stevens, starring Kevin Costner and Kelly Preston, and released by Universal, 1999.

SIDELIGHTS: Michael Shaara published his first story while still an undergraduate at Rutgers University, even though his creative writing teacher had been less than impressed with his manuscript and urged him instead to write "literature." His professor's criticism notwithstanding, Shaara continued to publish many more stories and four novels, one of which, *The Killer Angels,* won the Pulitzer Prize for fiction in 1975.

Shaara became a full-time writer after working for a year on the police department in St. Petersburg, Florida; while at Rutgers, he had attended a lecture by author John O'Hara, who commented that being a police officer or a doctor would be good preparation for a writing career. Shaara's first success as a writer came with science fiction and fantasy stories that he sold to several magazines in the 1950s. These early works have since been collected in the volume *Soldier Boy,* which a *Publishers Weekly* reviewer thought showed Shaara to be "a master of a particularly humanistic brand of SF." Shaara's humanistic bent is also evident in his novels, the first of which, *The Broken Place,* owes a debt to Ernest Hemingway. Like much of Hemingway's work, it follows a man emotionally scarred by war whose psychological return to society is attained by grueling physical trials—boxing in the case of Shaara's Tom McClain. McClain searches for meaning in a world that seems devoid of it: "In all this world there are no signs and no miracles and nobody watching over and nobody caring," he tells a friend. "But I believe anyway." Shaara's novel was received favorably by several critics; John C. Pine of *Library Journal* praised it for "a natural rhythm that is unmistakable."

By this point in his career Shaara was teaching at Florida State University in Tallahassee. He had joined the faculty in 1961 as writer-in-residence, and he was soon promoted to associate professor. He was popular with students and encouraged them in their creative writing efforts, but the university would not promote him beyond associate professor because he lacked a graduate degree. This was a source of ongoing friction between Shaara and the university administration.

In 1971 Shaara, inspired by visits to the Gettysburg battlefield in Pennsylvania and by eyewitness accounts of the U.S. Civil War, finished *The Killer Angels,* his second novel, which was published in 1974 and won the Pulitzer Prize the following year. *The Killer Angels* recounts the events of the July, 1863, battle in which nearly 50,000 men lost their lives. Historians have often considered Gettysburg a turning point in the Civil War, as Union forces, often beaten by the Confederates up to then, were able to turn back a Confederate incursion into Union territory. Shaara's goal in writing the novel, he once told *New York Times* interviewer Thomas Lask, was to know "what is was like to *be* there, what the weather was like, what men's faces looked like." To do this, he deployed multiple points of view, from generals Lee and Longstreet of the Confederacy to General John Buford and Colonel Joshua Chamberlain for the Union. He also blended two fictional elements, according to Lask: "a careful expository description of strategy and tactics, . . . and a graphic evocation of the clashes themselves." *Best Sellers* reviewer L.C. Smith praised the former, making note of Shaara's "particularly good description of the military problems caused by the terrain at Gettysburg." Lask praised the latter, observing that "The pages in which Win Hancock, the Union general, canters slowly along in the very hell of battle looking after his men, is not a passage a reader will soon forget." Thomas LeClair, writing in the *New York Times Book Review,* added that Shaara's "achievement is combining these passages of apocalyptic immediacy with smaller scenes that dramatize the historian's cultural understandings."

Although it was not a significant commercial success at first, *The Killer Angels* was reprinted several times and has proved enduringly popular with Civil War enthusiasts. It was also adapted into the 1993 film *Gettysburg.* A paperback edition was on the *New York Times* best-seller list for several weeks following the film's release. Years after the novel's initial publication, on the occasion of Shaara's death, *Washington Post* writer Hank Burchard commented that *The Killer Angels* is "what many consider to be the best book ever written about the Civil War" and reported that it "is so meticulously true to the facts that it is used as a source book in many history departments." Shaara's son, writer Jeff Shaara, has written a prequel and sequel to *The Killer Angels*—*Gods and Generals* and *The Last Full Measure.*

Shaara's literary achievement with *The Killer Angels* came against a backdrop of difficulties in his personal life. On a trip to Italy in 1972, he was involved in a motorcycle accident in which he suffered severe head injuries that left him unable to write or teach for a year and a half. He also had a dispute with Florida State University over disability benefits. After his recovery, he managed to lecture, travel, and write again, although some reviewers felt his later work did not meet the high standard set by *The Killer Angels.*

Shaara's next novel, *The Herald,* was a departure from *The Killer Angels* in terms of subject matter. The story's hero, Nick Tesla, lands his plane in a town devastated by a scientist whose goal is to kill most of the world's inhabitants in his efforts to create a master race. Some dismissed the book's ideas as simplistic, including a *Science Fiction Review* contributor who wondered "how Michael Shaara could have won a Pulitzer Prize." But others saw philosophical import in the novel; Algis Budrys, writing in the *Magazine of Fantasy and Science Fiction,* called it "a must-read book that raises a profound question."

Shaara's last novel, *For Love of the Game,* was published posthumously, the book's manuscript only uncovered by his children while in the process of settling his estate. *For Love of the Game* is the tale of an aging baseball pitcher who, even as his life is falling apart, pitches a perfect game. As in Shaara's first novel, the story's central character plays out his emotional crises in the crucible of an all-out athletic challenge. Also as with Shaara's first novel, *For Love of the Game* garnered praise for its intense psychological exploration of an athlete pushed to his limits. Though criticized by some as falling short of Shaara's greatest work—a reviewer for *Publishers Weekly* noted that "one feels he might have liked to give it a rewrite"—Bill Brashler wrote in the *Chicago Tribune* that "Shaara obviously had a love of the game, of its tradition and natural grace, and he left it this lovely token."

Shaara once commented: "I have written almost every known type of writing, from science fiction through history, through medical journalism and *Playboy* stories, always because I wrote only what came to mind, with no goal and little income, always for the joy of it, and it has been a great joy. The only trouble comes from the 'market mind' of the editor when the work is done. I have traveled over most of the world, lived three years in South Africa, two years in Italy, speak some foreign languages, and love airplanes, almost as much as women. I enjoyed teaching, because it taught me a lot."

BIOGRAPHICAL AND CRITICAL SOURCES:

BOOKS

Dictionary of Literary Biography Yearbook: 1983, Thomson Gale (Detroit, MI), 1983.

Scribner Encyclopedia of American Lives, Volume 2, 1986-1990, Scribner (New York, NY), 1999.

Shaara, Michael, *The Broken Place,* New American Library (New York, NY), 1968.

PERIODICALS

American Heritage, October, 1992, p. 103; April, 1994, p. 116.

American Spectator, December, 1988, p. 17; December, 1989, p. 28; December, 1993, p. 25.

Analog, August, 1982, p. 125.

Atlantic Monthly, October, 1974, p. 118; April, 1975, p. 98; August, 1981, p. 86.

Best Sellers, September 15, 1974, p. 281.

Booklist, June 1, 1968, p. 1129; May 15, 1981, p. 1214; May 1, 1982, p. 1148; May 15, 1991, p. 1781.

Chicago Tribune, April 7, 1991, section 14, p. 5.

Fantasy Review, August, 1984, p. 26.

Forbes, October 19, 1992, p. 28; March 15, 1993, p. 172.

Inc., January, 1987, p. 64.

Kirkus Reviews, January 15, 1968, p. 72; July 1, 1974, p. 702; April 1, 1981, p. 457; March 15, 1991, p. 358.

Kliatt, fall, 1984, p. 19; September, 1992, p. 16; November, 1994, p. 65.

Library Journal, February 15, 1968, p. 772; September 1, 1974, p. 2091; June 1, 1981, p. 1246; March 15, 1982, p. 653; April 1, 1991, p. 156; February 1, 1992, p. 144; February 1, 1993, p. 132; October 1, 1994, p. 130.

Los Angeles Times Book Review, April 7, 1991, p. 6.
Magazine of Fantasy and Science Fiction, May, 1982, p. 33; September, 1984, p. 52.
New Republic, November 8, 1993, p. 32.
New Yorker, June 26, 1995, p. 57.
New York Times, May 10, 1975, p. 27.
New York Times Book Review, April 7, 1968, p, 36; October 20, 1974, Thomas LeClair, review of *The Killer Angels,* p. 38; June 12, 1994, p. 20.
Observer (London, England), August 14, 1977, p. 23.
Publishers Weekly, January 15, 1968, p. 84; July 8, 1974, p. 69; June 2, 1975, p. 57; May 15, 1981, p. 49; January 29, 1982, p. 64; April 12, 1991, p. 44.
San Francisco Chronicle, May, 1986, p. 38.
School Library Journal, April, 1995, p. 91.
Science Fiction and Fantasy Book Review, June, 1982, p. 32.
Science Fiction Review, November, 1981, p. 54.
Tallahassee Democrat, September 15, 1974, pp. 410-411.
Times Literary Supplement, June 20, 1997, p. 25.
USA Today, July 10, 1991, p. D5.
Washington Post, September 29, 1982, p. B15.

ONLINE

Jeff Shaara Web site, http://www.jeffshaara.com/ (August 14, 2004).

* * *

SHAARA, Michael Joseph, Jr.
See SHAARA, Michael

* * *

SHACKLETON, C.C.
See ALDISS, Brian W.

* * *

SHAFFER, Peter 1926-
(Peter Anthony, a joint pseudonym, Peter Levin Shaffer)

PERSONAL: Born May 15, 1926, in Liverpool, England; son of Jack (a real estate agent) and Reka (Fredman) Shaffer. *Education:* Trinity College, Cambridge, B.A., 1950. *Politics:* "Conservative anarchist." *Religion:* Humanist. *Hobbies and other interests:* Music, architecture.

ADDRESSES: Home—173 Riverside Dr., New York, NY 10024-1615. *Office*—The Lantz Office, 888 7th Ave., Ste. 2500, New York, NY 10010-6000. *Agent*—c/o McNaughton-Lowe Representation, 200 Fulham Rd., SW10, England.

CAREER: Playwright and critic. Worked in the New York Public Library, New York, NY, 1951-54, and for Boosey & Hawkes (music publishers), London, England, 1954-55; literary critic for *Truth,* 1956-57; music critic for *Time and Tide,* 1961-62. *Military service:* Served as a conscript in coal mines in England, 1944-47.

MEMBER: Royal Society of Literature (fellow), Dramatists Guild, Garrick Club (London).

AWARDS, HONORS: Evening Standard Drama Award, 1958, and New York Drama Critics Circle Award, 1960, both for *Five Finger Exercise;* Antoinette Perry Award (Tony) for Best Play, Outer Critics Circle Award, and New York Drama Critics Circle Award, all 1975, all for *Equus;* Tony Award, 1981, and best play of the year award from *Plays and Players,* both for *Amadeus;* New York Film Critics Circle Award, Los Angeles Film Critics Association Award, and Academy Award of Merit (Oscar) from the Academy of Motion Picture Arts and Sciences, all 1984, all for screenplay adaptation of *Amadeus;* named Commander of the British Empire, 1987; *Evening Standard* Drama Award for Best Comedy, 1988, for *Lettice and Lovage: A Comedy;* Hamburg Shakespeare Prize, 1989; William Inge Award for Distinguished Achievement in the American Theatre, 1992; knighted by the Queen of England, 2001.

WRITINGS:

PLAYS

Five Finger Exercise (produced on the West End, London, England, at the Comedy Theatre, July 16, 1958; produced on Broadway, New York, NY, at the Music Box Theater, December 2, 1959; also see below), Hamish Hamilton (London, England), 1958, Harcourt (San Diego, CA), 1959.
The Private Ear [and] *The Public Eye* (two one-acts; produced on the West End, London, England, at the Globe Theatre, May 10, 1962; produced on Broadway, New York, NY, at the Morosco Theater, October 9, 1963; also see below), Hamish Hamilton (London, England), 1962, Stein & Day (Briarcliff Manor, NY), 1964.

The Merry Rooster's Panto, produced on the West End, London, England, at Wyndham's Theatre, December, 1963.

The Royal Hunt of the Sun: A Play Concerning the Conquest of Peru (produced by the National Theater Company at the Chichester Festival, Chichester, England, July 7, 1964; produced on Broadway, New York, NY, at the ANTA Theatre, October 26, 1965), Samuel French (London, England), 1964, Stein & Day (New York, NY), 1965.

Black Comedy (one-act; produced by the National Theatre Company at the Chichester Festival, Chichester, England, July 27, 1965 [also see below], produced on Broadway, New York, NY, at the Ethel Barrymore Theater with *White Lies* [also see below], February 12, 1967; produced on the West End, London, England, at the Lyric Theatre as *Black Comedy* [and] *The White Liars* [also see below], 1968), Samuel French (New York, NY), 1967.

A Warning Game, produced in New York, NY, 1967.

The White Liars, Samuel French (New York, NY), 1967.

Black Comedy [and] *White Lies,* Stein & Day (New York, NY), 1967, published as *The White Liars* [and] *Black Comedy,* Hamish Hamilton (London, England), 1968, published as *The White Liars and Black Comedy: Two One-Act Plays,* Samuel French (New York, NY), 1995.

It's about Cinderella, produced in London, England, 1969.

Equus (produced by the National Theatre Company on the West End, London, England, at the Old Vic Theatre, July 26, 1973; produced on Broadway, New York, NY, at the Plymouth Theater, October 24, 1974; also see below), Deutsch (London, England), 1973, Samuel French (New York, NY), 1974.

Shrivings (three-act; produced on the West End, London, England, at the Lyric Theatre as *The Battle of Shrivings,* February 5, 1970; also see below), Deutsch (London, England), 1974.

Equus [and] *Shrivings,* Atheneum (New York, NY), 1974.

Three Plays (contains *Five Finger Exercise, Shrivings,* and *Equus*), Penguin (New York, NY), 1976.

Four Plays (contains *The Private Ear, The Public Eye, White Liars,* and *Black Comedy*), Penguin (New York, NY), 1981.

Amadeus (produced on the West End, London, England, by the National Theatre Company at the Olivier Theatre, November 2, 1979; produced on Broadway, New York, NY, at the Broadhurst Theater, December 17, 1980; also see below), Deutsch, 1980, Harper (New York, NY), 1981, published as *Peter Shaffer's Amadeus,* with an introduction by Sir Peter Hall and a new preface by Shaffer, Perennial (New York, NY), 2001.

Collected Plays of Peter Shaffer, Crown (New York, NY), 1982.

Yonadab: The Watcher, produced on the West End, London, England, by the National Theatre Company at the Olivier Theatre, December 4, 1985, published as *Yonadab: A Play,* Harper (New York, NY), 1988.

Lettice and Lovage: A Comedy (produced on the West End, London, England, at the Globe Theatre, 1987; produced on Broadway, New York, NY, at the Ethel Barrymore Theater, March 25, 1990), HarperCollins (New York, NY), 1990.

The Gift of the Gorgon: A Play (produced at the Barbican, 1992), Viking (New York, NY), 1993.

NOVELS; WITH BROTHER, ANTHONY SHAFFER

(Under joint pseudonym Peter Anthony) *Woman in the Wardrobe,* Evans Brothers (London, England), 1951.

(Under joint pseudonym Peter Anthony) *How Doth the Little Crocodile?,* Evans Brothers (London, England), 1952, published under names Peter Shaffer and Anthony Shaffer, Macmillan (New York, NY), 1957.

Withered Murder, Gollancz (London, England), 1955, Macmillan (New York, NY), 1956.

SCREENPLAYS

(With Peter Brook) *Lord of the Flies,* Walter Reade, 1963.

The Pad (and How to Use It) (adaptation of *The Private Ear*), Universal, 1966.

Follow Me!, Universal, 1971.

The Public Eye (based on Shaffer's play of the same title), Universal, 1972.

Equus (based on Shaffer's play of the same title), United Artists, 1977.

Amadeus (based on Shaffer's play of the same title), Orion Pictures, 1984, released as *Amadeus: Director's Cut* on DVD, with commentary by Shaffer and Milos Forman, Warner Home Video, 2002.

OTHER

The Salt Land (television play), Independent Television Network (London, England), 1955.

The Prodigal Father (radio play), British Broadcasting Corp. (London, England), 1955.

Balance of Terror (television play), British Broadcasting Corp. (London, England), 1957.

(Editor) *Elisabeth Frink Sculpture: Catalogue Raisonne,* Trafalgar Square (London, England), 1988.

Whom Do I Have the Honor of Addressing?, Deutsch (London, England), 1990.

Contributor of articles to periodicals, including *Theatre Arts, Atlantic, Encore,* and *Sunday Times.*

ADAPTATIONS: Five Finger Exercise was filmed by Columbia Pictures in 1962; *The Royal Hunt of the Sun: A Play Concerning the Conquest of Peru* was filmed by CBS's Cinema Center Films.

SIDELIGHTS: "Whatever else Peter Shaffer may lack, it isn't courage, it isn't derring-do. His plays traverse the centuries and the globe, raising questions that have perplexed minds from Job to Samuel Beckett," Benedict Nightingale wrote in the *New York Times.* Shaffer examines the conflict between atheism and religion in *The Royal Hunt of the Sun: A Play Concerning the Conquest of Peru;* the nature of sanity and insanity in modern society in *Equus;* the role of genius in *Amadeus;* and Old Testament ethics in *Yonadab: The Watcher.* These epic plays are always a visual spectacle, but some critics have felt that Shaffer's spectacles mask superficial stories. *Newsweek* contributor Jack Kroll characterized the typical Shaffer play as "a large-scale, large-voiced treatment of large themes, whose essential superficiality is masked by a skillful theatricality reinforced by . . . extraordinary acting." Despite such criticism, Shaffer's plays are enormously popular—both *Equus* and *Amadeus* had Broadway runs of more than 1,000 performances each.

Shaffer's first major success was *The Royal Hunt of the Sun,* based on Francisco Pizarro's sixteenth-century expedition to the Incan Empire of Peru. To force the Incan people to give him the gold he desired, Pizarro took their leader, Atahuallpa, prisoner. But Atahuallpa refused to concede defeat and the resulting battle between Pizarro's forces and the Incan Indians proved disastrous for his people. In the ensuing battle, Atahuallpa is killed, but Pizarro had befriended the Incan leader. When Atahuallpa dies, Pizarro renounces Catholicism to adopt the Incan religion.

The Royal Hunt of the Sun is considered unique because of its historical subject and its stylized theatrical techniques, including mime and adaptations of Japanese Kabuki theater. To enhance the visual spectacle of the play, Shaffer specified that the Indians wear dramatic Inca funeral masks during Atahuallpa's death scene; many in the audience later claimed to have seen the masks change expression during the production. "They hadn't, of course," Shaffer told Richard Schickel in *Time.* "But the audience invested so much emotion in the play that it looked as if they had."

Despite this positive emotional response from audiences, some critics felt the play's language and theatrical devices are not effective. *Drama*'s Ronald Hayman thought that Shaffer borrows from so many different traditions and uses so many theatrical devices that "instead of unifying to contribute to the same effect, the various elements make their effects separately and some of them are superfluous and distracting." Warren Sylvester Smith in the *Dictionary of Literary Biography* indicated that the language "sometimes fail[s] to achieve the magnitude of the characters or to match the scope of the events." And Hayman faulted the dialogue for being "lustreless, tumbling into cliches and even pleonasms like 'trapped in time's cage' when nothing less than poetry would take the strain Shaffer is putting on it."

But other critics, and many playgoers, had a more generous response to *The Royal Hunt of the Sun.* These reviewers mentioned that the elaborate sets and costumes, the epic story, and the innovative rendition of history were exciting additions to the contemporary dramatic scene. John Russell Taylor wrote in *Peter Shaffer* that as a "piece of sheer theatrical machinery the play is impeccable." He concluded that *The Royal Hunt of the Sun* is "at once a spectacular drama and a thinkpiece."

In Shaffer's 1973 play, *Equus,* he confronts the question of sanity in the modern world. Despite its morbid focus, *Equus* was so well-liked that the opening-night Broadway audience gave it a five-minute standing ovation. "It's never happened to me before," Shaffer told Schickel. "I cry every time I think about it." Shaffer got the idea for *Equus* from a newspaper report of a boy who blinded several horses in a north England stable. He only used the boy's act of blinding the horses, the rest of the play is his creation.

The play revolves around psychiatrist Martin Dysart's treatment of the boy, Alan Strang, for the offense he committed. During his examination of the boy, Dysart discovers that Strang is a pagan who believes that horses are gods. When a stable girl attempts to seduce him in front of the horses, Strang is impotent. In frustrated rage that they have seen his failure, Strang blinds the horses. Dysart tries to treat him in a conventional manner, but eventually finds that he prefers Strang's primitive passion to his own rational, controlled personality. Brendan Gill noted in the *New Yorker* that Dysart "poses questions that go beyond the sufficiently puzzling matter of the boy's conduct to the infinitely puzzling matter of why, in a world charged with insanity, we should seek to 'cure' anyone in the name of sanity."

Equus brought complaints from some reviewers who argued that it superficially portrays insanity and psychoanalysis. *Equus,* John Simon suggested in *New York,* "falls into that category of worn-out whimsy wherein we are told that insanity is more desirable, admirable, or just saner than sanity." *Commentary* contributor Jack Richardson stated that *Equus* seems to be a "perfect case-study in the mediocrity of insight necessary nowadays for a play to enjoy a popular reputation for profundity." Simon concluded that no "amount of external embellishment can overcome the hollowness within."

Shaffer's next play, *Amadeus,* is based on the life of eighteenth-century composer Wolfgang Amadeus Mozart. Richard Christiansen of the *Chicago Tribune* believed that the characters in *Amadeus* and *Equus* are similar, remarking that "here again, as in *Equus,* an older, learned man of the world is struck and amazed by the wild inspiration of a much younger man who seemingly is possessed with divine madness." The older man in *Amadeus* is Antonio Salieri, portrayed as a second-rate composer who is consumed by jealousy because of the young Mozart's greater talent.

Shaffer became interested in the rivalry between Mozart and Salieri upon reading material about Mozart's mysterious death. Shaffer at first suspected that Salieri might have murdered the composer, but further research proved this to be wrong. "But by then the cold eyes of Salieri were staring at me," Shaffer told Roland Gelatt in the *Saturday Review.* "The conflict between virtuous mediocrity and feckless genius took hold of my imagination, and it would not leave me alone."

In *Amadeus,* Salieri has made a bargain with God. He is to remain pious in return for being made the most popular composer of his time. As court composer in Vienna, Salieri is satisfied that his bargain with God has been kept. But then Mozart arrives at the court, playing music Salieri considers to be the finest he has ever heard. And in contrast to Salieri's piety, Mozart is a moral abomination—a bastard, a womanizer, and an abrasive man with a scatological sense of humor. Salieri feels cheated and angry, and begins to sabotage Mozart's budding career by spreading rumors about him. These rumors, along with Mozart's contentious personality, serve to ostracize him from polite society and cause him to lose his pupils. Eventually Mozart becomes ill and dies, and the play asks whether he was killed by Salieri or died from natural causes.

"*Amadeus* . . . is about the ravaging of genius by mediocrity," Robert Brustein wrote in the *New Republic.* Some critics believed Shaffer handled his material in much the same manner, charging him with a superficial portrayal of Mozart's life. Brustein argued that "at the same time that the central character—a second-rate kapellmeister named Antonio Salieri—is plotting against the life and reputation of a superior composer named Wolfgang Amadeus Mozart, a secondary playwright named Peter Shaffer is reducing this genius, one of the greatest artists of all time, to the level of a simpering, braying ninny."

Despite complaints from reviewers, audiences received *Amadeus* enthusiastically, and it played in many European cities. Bernard Levin, writing in the London *Times,* summed up the feelings of many theatergoers by writing that "those who go to [*Amadeus*] prepared to understand what it is about will have an experience that far transcends even its considerable value as drama." Impressed with the play's serious intentions, Gelatt wrote that "*Amadeus* gives heartening evidence that there is still room for the play of ideas." Perhaps Shaffer's most famous work is the screenplay adaptation of *Amadeus,* written in collaboration with director Milos Forman and producer Saul Zaentz. This 1984 film won several Academy Awards, including best screenplay adaptation and best picture of the year.

Amadeus was filmed with Shaffer's characteristic visual spectacle in the centuries-old cathedrals and churches of Prague, Czechoslovakia (now the Czech Republic). Geoff Brown commented in the London *Times* on the ambience of the production, writing that "so many films lie on the screen today looking shrivelled or inert; *Amadeus* sits there resplendent, both stately and supple, a compelling, darkly comic story of human glory and human infamy."

In December of 1985, Shaffer's play *Yonadab: The Watcher* opened to mixed reviews. Based on the Old Testament account of King David's reign in ancient

Jerusalem, the play focuses on court hanger-on Yonadab, who believes an ancient superstition that incest committed between members of the royal family promotes wisdom in government. He convinces Amnon, King David's son, to rape his own sister, Tamar. Commenting on the strikingly different subject matter of this play, Shaffer told Higgins: "I never want to repeat myself, so it is essential to come up in a different place every time."

Although some critics expressed many of the same complaints about *Yonadab: The Watcher* that they had about previous Shaffer plays—historical inaccuracies, superficial treatment of theme, lack of character development—Shaffer remained undaunted. Dan Sullivan reported in the *Los Angeles Times* that Shaffer told the Associated Press's Matt Wolf: "Audiences are very excited by the play; that's the main thing."

Audience reaction to 1987's *Lettice and Lovage: A Comedy* was also positive. Wolf wrote in the *Chicago Tribune* that the play, "an overtly commercial, out-and-out comedy," was winning "nightly bravos and may even get an award or two." Shaffer wrote the play as a gift for actress Maggie Smith, who starred in his earlier work *Black Comedy* and played the lead role of Lettice, a middle-aged woman and would-be actress who finds herself working as a tour guide in an English mansion. To make her job more interesting, Lettice makes up stories about what happened in the house. "The play is a bitingly funny satire on English attitudes towards their national heritage," David Sheward noted in *Back Stage;* mixed in with the humor, "serious points are made on the British penchant for worshipping the past and yet destroying great architectural landmarks and replacing them with ugly, modern skyscrapers."

Like many of Shaffer's earlier plays, and in sharp contrast to the comedy of *Lettice and Lovage, The Gift of the Gorgon* is a serious, philosophical work that "asks more questions than it answers," as Sam Abel wrote in *Theatre Journal.* "*The Gift of the Gorgon,* like its predecessors," Abel continued, "is essentially a mystery story, where the plot revolves around the discovery of the motivations behind a horrible crime, but where the 'whodunnit' aspect of the story is ultimately subsumed within larger moral and psychological issues." In this play, the crime is the death of playwright Edward Damson, who fell—or was pushed—off of a cliff near his retirement home on a Greek island. After he dies, his illegitimate son, who never met his father, asks Edward's wife Helen if she can help him write a biography of his father. The play then unfolds through flashbacks, as Helen describes Edward's life to his son.

The Gift of the Gorgon opened in London with a stellar cast, including Michael Pennington as Edward and Judi Dench as Helen, and their performances were widely praised. The tension in the play comes from their love-hate relationship, which is based on the attraction of opposites. Edward is a flamboyant playwright who sees the world through the prism of Greek tragedy, with its emphasis on the redemptive potential of vengeance. Helen, on the other hand, is a meeker academic who puts her faith in reason and mercy. In the play's Greek frame of reference, Edward personifies the Dionysian hero Perseus and Helen, the Apollonian goddess Athena. *The Gift of the Gorgon* "is drenched in stage blood, Greek mythology and high rhetoric about creativity, violence and justice," Christopher Porterfield wrote in *Time,* and "once again, Shaffer somehow makes riveting drama out of it all."

The fact that audiences are excited by Shaffer's plays is a testament to his popularity and staying power. Smith concluded that though Shaffer is sometimes slighted by critics, "none of [his] imputed failings has inhibited the lines at the box office or deterred serious theatergoers from expressing gratitude for the revitalization [he] has brought to contemporary drama."

BIOGRAPHICAL AND CRITICAL SOURCES:

BOOKS

Benet's Reader's Encyclopedia, 3rd edition, Harper (New York, NY), 1987.

Brustein, Robert, *The Third Theatre,* Knopf (New York, NY), 1969.

Concise Dictionary of British Literary Biography, Volume 8, Thomson Gale (Detroit, MI), 1991.

Contemporary Dramatists, 6th edition, St. James Press (Detroit, MI), 1999.

Contemporary Literary Criticism, Thomson Gale (Detroit, MI), Volume 5, 1976; Volume 14, 1980; Volume 18, 1981; Volume 37, 1986; Volume 60, 1990.

Contemporary Theatre, Film and Television, Volume 13, Thomson Gale (Detroit, MI), 1995.

Cooke, Virginia, and Malcolm Page, editors, *File on Shaffer,* Methuen (London, England), 1987.

Crystal, David, editor, *Cambridge Biographical Encyclopedia,* Cambridge University Press (Cambridge, England), 1998.

Dictionary of Literary Biography, Volume 13: *British Dramatists since World War II,* Thomson Gale (Detroit, MI), 1982.

Drama Criticism, Volume 7, Thomson Gale (Detroit, MI), 1997.

Encyclopedia of World Biography, 2nd edition, Thomson Gale (Detroit, MI), 1998.

Encyclopedia of World Literature in the Twentieth Century, 3rd edition, Volume 4, St. James Press (Detroit, MI), 1998.

Gianakaris, C. J., *Peter Shaffer,* Macmillan (London, England), 1992.

Kamm, Anthony, *Biographical Companion to Literature in English,* Scarecrow Press (Lanham, MD), 1997.

Klein, Dennis A., *Peter Shaffer,* Twayne (Boston, MA), 1979.

Lumley, Frederick, *New Trends in Twentieth-Century Drama,* Oxford University Press (Oxford, England), 1967.

MacMurraugh-Kavanagh, M. K., *Peter Shaffer: Theatre and Drama,* Macmillan (London, England), 1998.

Magill, Frank N., *Critical Survey of Drama,* revised edition, Salem Press (Pasadena, CA), 1994.

Magill, Frank N., *Cyclopedia of World Authors,* 3rd edition revised, Salem Press (Pasadena, CA), 1997.

McCrindle, J. F., editor, *Behind the Scenes,* Holt (New York, NY), 1971.

Modern British Literature, 2nd edition, St. James Press (Detroit, MI), 2000.

Ousby, Ian, *The Cambridge Guide to Literature in English,* Cambridge University Press (Cambridge, England), 1988.

Parry, Melanie, *Chambers Biographical Dictionary,* 6th edition, Larousse (New York, NY), 1997.

Plunka, Gene A., *Peter Shaffer: Roles, Rites and Rituals in the Theater,* Fairleigh Dickinson University Press (Teaneck, NJ), 1988.

Reference Guide to English Literature, 2nd edition, St. James Press (Detroit, MI), 1991.

Taylor, John Russell, *Anger and After,* Methuen (London, England), 1962.

Taylor, John Russell, *Peter Shaffer,* Longman (London, England), 1974.

Twentieth-Century Crime and Mystery Writers, 3rd edition, St. James Press (Detroit, MI), 1991.

Wynne-Davies, Marion, editor, *Bloomsbury Guide to English Literature,* Prentice-Hall (New York, NY), 1990.

PERIODICALS

America, January 24, 1981, Catharine Hughes, review of *Amadeus,* p. 62; October 13, 1984, Richard A. Blake, review of *Amadeus,* p. 210; April 21, 1990, Thomas P. O'Malley, review of *Lettice and Lovage,* p. 410; January 29, 1994, Joseph J. Feeney, review of *The Gift of the Gordon,* pp. 23-26.

American Scholar, winter, 1992, review of *Amadeus,* p. 49.

Back Stage, December 25, 1981, Jennie Schulman, review of *The Public Eye* and *The Private Ear,* p. 108; March 30, 1990, David Sheward, review of *Lettice and Lovage,* p. 48; January 29, 1993, Roy Sander, review of *The Gift of the Gorgon,* p. 41; July 16, 1993, Rob Stevens, review of *Equus,* section W, p. 8; September 10, 1993, Martin Schaeffer, review of *Black Comedy* and *White Liars,* p. 44.

Back Stage West, April 21, 1994, Rob Stevens, review of *Lettice and Lovage,* p. 9; May 30, 1996, Lesley Jacobs, review of *Lettice and Lovage,* p. 21; June 25, 1998, Charlene Baldridge, review of *Lettice and Lovage,* p. 15; July 9, 1998, Paul Birchall, review of *Lettice and Lovage,* p. 13; January 28, 1999, Judy Richter, review of *Amadeus,* p. 14; February 28, 2002, Les Spindle, review of *Black Comedy,* p. 29.

Booklist, March 15, 1960, review of *Five Finger Exercise;* November 15, 1974, review of *Equus* and *Shrivings,* p. 315; April 15, 1981, review of *Amadeus,* p. 1135; March 15, 1983, review of *The Collected Plays of Peter Shaffer,* p. 942; June 1, 1990, review of *Lettice and Lovage,* p. 1871.

Bookmark, November, 1959, review of *Five Finger Exercise.*

British Book News, September, 1980, review of *Amadeus,* p. 563; September, 1981, review of *The Royal Hunt of the Sun,* p. 521.

Chicago Tribune, March 7, 1983; September 19, 1984; November 15, 1987, Matt Wolf, review of *Lettice and Lovage.*

Choice, March, 1975, review of *Equus* and *Shrivings,* p. 78; September, 1981, review of *Amadeus,* p. 1135.

Classical and Modern Literature, summer, 1995, review of *The Gift of the Gorgon,* p. 345.

Commentary, February, 1975, Jack Richardson, review of *Equus.*

Commonweal, April 25, 1975; June 15, 1990, Gerald Weales, review of *Lettice and Lovage,* pp. 388-389.

Comparative Drama, summer, 1998, review of *Lettice and Lovage,* p. 145.

Drama, autumn, 1970; autumn, 1977, review of *White Liars,* p. 80; January, 1980; autumn, 1981, review of *The Royal Hunt of the Sun* and *Four Plays,* p. 51.

Encounter, January, 1975, review of *Shrivings* and *Equus,* p. 65.

Film Comment, September-October, 1984; January-February, 1985.

Globe and Mail (Toronto, Ontario, Canada), June 13, 1987.

Guardian, August 6, 1973.
Harper's, July, 1981.
Hollywood Reporter, April 8, 2002, David Hunter, review of *Amadeus: Director's Cut,* p. 18; September 26, 2002, Glenn Abel, review of *Amadeus: Director's Cut,* p. 57.
Hudson Review, summer, 1967.
Kliatt Paperback Book Guide, fall, 1981, review of *Amadeus,* p. 29.
Library Journal, January 15, 1960, review of *Five Finger Exercise;* April 1, 1981, review of *Amadeus,* p. 811.
Listener, February 12, 1970; December 12, 1985.
Los Angeles Times, December 5, 1982, Martin Bernheimer, review of *Amadeus,* p. 63; December 10, 1982, Dan Sullivan, review of *Amadeus,* p. 1; September 16, 1983, Dan Sullivan, review of *Amadeus,* p. 1; September 19, 1984, Sheila Benson, review of *Amadeus,* p. 1; October 6, 1984, Charles Champlin, review of *Amadeus,* p. 1.
Maclean's, October 1, 1984, Mark Czarnecki, review of *Amadeus,* p. 83; May 28, 1990, Patricia Hluchy and Brian D. Johnson, review of *Lettice and Lovage,* pp. 62-63.
Manchester Guardian, February 20, 1959, Gerard Fay, review of *Five Finger Exercise,* p. 5.
Modern Drama, September, 1978; March, 1985.
Monthly Film Bulletin, January, 1985.
Nation, February 27, 1967; January 17, 1981, Stephen Harvey, review of *Amadeus,* pp. 59-60; May 7, 1990, Thomas M. Disch, review of *Lettice and Lovage,* p. 644.
National Review, October 19, 1984, John Simon, review of *Amadeus,* pp. 56-57.
New Leader, February 27, 1967; January 26, 1981, Leo Sauvage, review of *Amadeus,* pp. 17-18.
New Republic, January 17, 1981, Robert Brustein, review of *Amadeus,* pp. 62-63; October 22, 1984, Stanley Kauffmann, review of *Amadeus,* pp. 30-32.
New Statesman, February 13, 1970; April 25, 1985, John Coleman, review of *Amadeus,* p. 37; July 5, 1985, Andrew Rissik, review of *The Royal Hunt of the Sun,* p. 35; December 13, 1985, Benedict Nightingale, review of *Yonadab,* pp. 31-32.
New Statesman & Society, December 11, 1992, Kate Bassett, review of *The Gift of the Gorgon,* pp. 32-33.
Newsweek, February 20, 1967; November 4, 1974; December 29, 1980, T.E. Kalem, review of *Amadeus,* p. 57; September 20, 1984, David Ansen, review of *Amadeus,* p. 85; April 2, 1990, Jack Kroll, review of *Lettice and Lovage,* p. 54.
New York, November 11, 1974, John Simon, review of *Equus;* September 24, 1984, David Denby, review of *Amadeus,* pp. 93-95; April 9, 1990, John Simon, review of *Lettice and Lovage,* pp. 102-103; September 6, 1993, John Simon, review of *Black Comedy* and *White Liars,* p. 63.
New Yorker, February 25, 1967; November 4, 1974; March 10, 1980; December 29, 1980, Brendan Gill, review of *Amadeus,* p. 54; October 29, 1984, Pauline Kael, review of *Amadeus,* pp. 122-123; April 9, 1990, Edith Oliver, review of *Lettice and Lovage,* p. 80; September 13, 1993, Edith Oliver, review of *Black Comedy,* p. 120.
New York Times, September 29, 1968; December 23, 1979; December 18, 1980, Frank Rich, review of *Amadeus,* p. 21, section C, p. 16; January 4, 1981, Walter Kerr, review of *Amadeus,* section D, p. 3; March 2, 1980, Harold C. Schonberg, review of *Amadeus,* section D, p. 21; June 1, 1982, Frank Rich, review of *Amadeus,* p. 24, section C, p. 10; September 16, 1984; September 19, 1984, Vincent Canby, review of *Amadeus,* p. 22, section C, p. 23; September 23, 1984, Donal Henehan, review of *Amadeus,* section H, p. 1; December 22, 1985, Benedict Nightingale, review of *Yonadab,* section H, p. 5; February 13, 1987; November 22, 1987, Benedict Nightingale, review of *Lettice and Lovage,* section H, p. 5; March 26, 1990, Frank Rich, review of *Lettice and Lovage,* section B, p. 1, section C, p. 11; December 23, 1992, Frank Rich, review of *The Gift of the Gorgon,* section B, p. 3, section C, p. 9; September 2, 1993, Ben Brantley, review of *White Liars* and *Black Comedy,* section B, p. 3, section C, p. 13; December 16, 1999, Ben Brantley, review of *Amadeus,* section B, p. 1, section E, p. 1; January 16, 2000, Vincent Canby, review of *Amadeus,* section AR, p. 7; September 27, 2002, Peter M. Nichols, review of *Amadeus: Director's Cut,* section B, p. 23, section E, p. 25.
New York Times Magazine, August 17, 1973; October 25, 1974; October 27, 1974; April 13, 1975.
Observer, February 25, 1968; December 8, 1985.
Partisan Review, spring, 1966.
People, October 1, 1984, review of *Amadeus,* p. 14.
Punch, February 28, 1968.
Rocky Mountain Review of Language and Literature, Volume 40, number 1, 1986, review of *Yonadab* and *Amadeus,* p. 52.
Saturday Review, February 25, 1967; November, 1980, Roland Gelatt, review of *Amadeus,* pp. 11-14; February, 1981.
School Library Journal, April, 1983, review of *The Collected Plays of Peter Shaffer,* p. 134.
South Atlantic Quarterly, autumn, 1980.
Spectator, March 1, 1968.
Theatre Journal, December, 1993, Sam Abel, review of *The Gift of the Gorgon,* pp. 549-552.
Time, November 11, 1974; December 29, 1980; April 2, 1990, William A. Henry, III, review of *Lettice and*

Lovage, p. 71; March 15, 1993, Christopher Porterfield, review of *The Gift of the Gorgon,* pp. 69-70; September 20, 1993, William A. Henry, III, review of *Black Comedy* and *White Liars,* p. 84.

Times (London, England), January 9, 1985; January 18, 1985; November 28, 1985; December 6, 1985; November 17, 1988.

Times Educational Supplement, February 24, 1984, review of *The Royal Hunt of the Sun* and *Equus,* p. 29; June 22, 1984, review of *Amadeus,* p. 28; September 4, 1987, review of *The Royal Hunt of the Sun,* p. 29.

Times Literary Supplement, January 2, 1959, review of *Five Finger Exercise,* p. 5; December 25, 1992, Oliver Reynolds, review of *The Gift of the Gorgon,* p. 17.

Variety, November 19, 1980, review of *Amadeus,* p. 84; December 24, 1980, review of *Amadeus,* p. 62; December 23, 1981, review of *Amadeus,* p. 70; March 28, 1990, review of *Lettice and Lovage,* pp. 103-104; May 11, 1992, Markland Taylor, review of *Lettice and Lovage,* p. 126; January 11, 1993, Matt Wolf, review of *The Gift of the Gorgon,* p. 72; September 13, 1993, Jeremy Gerard, review of *Black Comedy* and *White Liars,* p. 35; May 25, 1998, Matt Wolf, review of *Black Comedy,* pp. 68-69.

Voice of Youth Advocates, December, 1993, review of *Equus,* p. 285.

Washington Post, July 5, 1979; November 9, 1980; November 13, 1980; November 23, 1980; December 15, 1982, David Richards, review of *Equus,* section C, p. 1;December 3, 1984, Jonathan Yardley, review of *Amadeus,* section C, p. 2; March 27, 1985, Edwin M. Yoder, Jr., review of *Amadeus,* section A, p. 23; March 26, 1990; September 8, 1993, Edwin Wilson, review of *Black Comedy,* section A, pp. 10, 12; April 22, 1998, William Triplett, review of *Amadeus,* section D, p. 14; April 27, 1999, Nelson Pressley, review of *Equus,* section C, p. 5.

Yale Review, autumn, 1983, J.D. McClatchy, review of *Amadeus,* p. 115.

* * *

SHAFFER, Peter Levin
See SHAFFER, Peter

* * *

SHANGE, Ntozake 1948-

PERSONAL: Born Paulette Linda Williams October 18, 1948, in Trenton, NJ; name changed 1971; pronounced "En-to-zaki Shong-gay"; daughter of Paul T. (a surgeon) and Eloise (a psychiatric social worker and educator) Williams; married second husband, David Murray (a musician), July, 1977 (divorced); children: Savannah. *Ethnicity:* Black *Education:* Barnard College, B.A. (with honors), 1970; University of Southern California, Los Angeles, M.A., 1973, and graduate study. *Hobbies and other interests:* Playing the violin.

ADDRESSES: Home—402 McCarty C, P.O. Box 115900, Gainesville, FL 32611. *Agent*—c/o Author Mail, St. Martin's Press, 175 5th Ave, New York, NY 10010-7703.

CAREER: Writer, performer, and teacher. Faculty member in women's studies, California State College, 1973-75, Sonoma Mills College, 1975, University of California Extension, 1972-75, City College of the City University of New York, New York, NY, 1975, Douglass College, New Brunswick, NJ, 1978; University of Houston, Houston, TX, associate professor of drama, 1983-2001; University of Florida, professor, African American Studies Program and the Center for Women's Studies and Gender Research, 2000—. Visiting professor at DePaul University, visiting artist at Brown University, artist in residence, New Jersey State Council on the Arts, and creative writing instructor, City College of New York. Lecturer at Douglass College, 1978, and at many other institutions, including Yale University, Howard University, Detroit Institute of Arts, and New York University.

Dancer with Third World Collective, Raymond Sawyer's Afro-American Dance Company, Sounds in Motion, West Coast Dance Works, and For Colored Girls Who Have Considered Suicide (Shange's own dance company); has appeared in Broadway and off-Broadway productions of her own plays, including *For Colored Girls Who Have Considered Suicide/When the Rainbow Is Enuf* and *Where the Mississippi Meets the Amazon.* Director of productions, including *The Mighty Gents,* produced by the New York Shakespeare Festival's Mobile Theatre, 1979, *A Photograph: A Study in Cruelty,* produced in Houston's Equinox Theatre, 1979, and June Jordan's *Lovers-in-Motion,* Houston, 1979, *The Issue* and *The Spirit of Sojourner Truth,* 1979. Actress in plays, including *The Lady in Orange,* New York, 1976, *Where the Mississippi Meets the Amazon,* New York, 1977, and *Mouths,* New York, 1981. Has given many poetry readings.

MEMBER: Actors Equity, National Academy of Television Arts and Sciences, Dramatists Guild, PEN American Center, Academy of American Poets, Poets and Writers, Women's Institute for Freedom of the Press, New York Feminist Arts Guild, Writers Guild.

AWARDS, HONORS: NDEA fellow, 1973; Obie Award, Outer Critics Circle Award, Audience Development Committee (Audelco) Award, Mademoiselle Award, and Tony, Grammy, and Emmy award nominations, all 1977, all for *For Colored Girls Who Have Considered Suicide/When the Rainbow Is Enuf;* Frank Silvera Writers' Workshop Award, 1978; *Los Angeles Times* Book Prize for Poetry, 1981, for *Three Pieces;* Guggenheim fellowship, 1981; Medal of Excellence, Columbia University, 1981; Obie Award, 1981, for *Mother Courage and Her Children;* Nori Eboraci Award, Barnard College, 1988; Lila Wallace-Reader's Digest Fund annual writer's award, 1992; Paul Robeson Achievement Award, 1992; Arts and Cultural Achievement Award, National Coalition of 100 Black Women (Pennsylvania chapter), 1992; Taos World Poetry Heavyweight Champion, 1992, 1993, 1994; Living Legend Award, National Black Theatre Festival, 1993; Claim Your Life Award, WDAS-AM/FM, 1993; Monarch Merit Award, National Council for Culture and Art; Pushcart Prize.

WRITINGS:

NOVELS

Sassafrass, Shameless Hussy Press (San Lorenzo, CA), 1976, revised edition published as *Sassafrass, Cypress, and Indigo,* St. Martin's Press (New York, NY), 1982.

For Colored Girls Who Have Considered Suicide/ When the Rainbow Is Enuf, Shameless Hussy Press (San Lorenzo, CA), 1976.

Betsey Brown, St. Martin's Press (New York, NY), 1985.

Liliane: Resurrection of the Daughter, St. Martin's Press (New York, NY), 1994.

If I Can Cook You Know God Can, Beacon Press, 1998.

FOR CHILDREN

Whitewash, illustrated by Michael Sporn, Walker (New York, NY), 1997.

Float Like a Butterfly: Muhammad Ali, the Man Who Could Float Like a Butterfly and Sting Like a Bee, Jump at the Sun (New York, NY), 2002.

Ellington Was Not a Street, Simon & Schuster (New York, NY), 2003.

Daddy Says, Simon & Schuster (New York, NY), 2003.

PLAYS

For Colored Girls Who Have Considered Suicide/When the Rainbow Is Enuf: A Choreopoem, (first produced in New York, NY, at Studio Rivbea, July 7, 1975; produced off-Broadway at Anspacher Public Theatre, 1976; produced on Broadway at Booth Theatre, September 15, 1976), Shameless Hussy Press (San Lorenzo, CA), 1975, revised edition, Macmillan (New York, NY), 1976.

A Photograph: A Study of Cruelty (poem-play; first produced off-Broadway at Public Theatre, December 21, 1977; revised and produced as *A Photograph: Lovers in Motion* in Houston, TX, at the Equinox Theatre, November, 1979), S. French (New York, NY), 1981.

(With Thulani Nkabinde and Jessica Hagedorn) *Where the Mississippi Meets the Amazon,* first produced in New York, NY, at Public Theatre Cabaret, December 18, 1977.

From Okra to Greens: A Different Kinda Love Story; A Play with Music and Dance (first produced in New York, NY, at Barnard College, November, 1978), S. French (New York, NY), 1985, revised edition published as *Mouths,* The Kitchen, (New York, NY), 1981.

Boogie Woogie Landscapes (in *Poetry at the Public* series; produced at Shakespeare Festival (New York, NY), 1978; revised as *Black and White Two-Dimensional Planes,* produced at Sounds in Motion Studio Works, New York, February, 1979; revised and produced on Broadway, at Symphony Space Theater, 1979; produced in Washington, DC, at John F. Kennedy Center for the Performing Arts, 1980), St. Martin's Press (New York, NY), 1978.

Spell No.7: A Geechee Quick Magic Trance Manual (produced on Broadway at Joseph Papp's New York Shakespeare Festival Public Theater, July 15, 1979), published as *Spell No.7: A Theatre Piece in Two Acts,* S. French (New York, NY), 1981.

(Adapter) Bertolt Brecht, *Mother Courage and Her Children,* first produced off- Broadway at the Public Theatre, April, 1980.

Three Pieces: Spell No.7; A Photograph: Lovers in Motion; Boogie Woogie Landscapes, St. Martin's Press (New York, NY), 1981.

It Has Not Always Been This Way: A Choreopoem, (revision of *From Okra to Greens: A Different Kinda Love Story*), in collaboration with the *Sounds in Motion Dance Company,* Symphony Space Theater, (New York, NY), 1981.

Triptych and Bocas: A Performance Piece, (revision of *From Okra to Greens: A Different Kinda Love Story*) Mark Taper Forum (Los Angeles, CA), 1982

Three for a Full Moon [and] *Bocas,* first produced in Los Angeles, CA, at the Mark Taper Forum Lab, Center Theatre, April 28, 1982.

(Adapter) Willy Russell, *Educating Rita* (play), first produced in Atlanta, GA, by Alliance Theatre Company, 1982.

Three Views of Mt. Fuji (play), first produced at the Lorraine Hansberry Theatre, June, 1987, produced in New York, NY, at the New Dramatists, October, 1987.

Betsey Brown: A Rhythm and Blues Musical, produced in Philadelphia, PA, at American Music Theater Festival, 1989.

The Love Space Demands: A Continuing Saga, produced in New Brunswick, NJ, at Crossroads Theater, March 1992; in Philadelphia, PA, at Painted Bride Art Center, 1993.

Whitewash (video screenplay), First Run Features, 1994.

Author of the operetta *Carrie,* produced in 1981. Has written for a television special starring Diana Ross, and appears in a documentary about her own work for WGBH-TV (Boston, MA).

POETRY

Melissa and Smith, Bookslinger (St. Paul, MN), 1976.

Natural Disasters and other Festive Occasions (prose and poems), Heirs International (San Francisco, CA), 1977.

A Photograph: Lovers in Motion: A Drama, S. French (New York, NY), 1977.

Nappy Edges, St. Martin's Press (New York, NY), 1978.

Some Men (poems), 1981.

A Daughter's Geography, St. Martin's Press (New York, NY), 1983.

From Okra to Greens, Coffee House Press (Minneapolis, MN), 1984.

Ridin' the Moon in Texas: Word Paintings (responses to art in prose and poetry), St. Martin's Press (New York, NY), 1987.

The Love Space Demands: A Continuing Saga, St. Martin's Press (New York, NY), 1991.

Three Pieces, St. Martin's Press (New York, NY), 1992.

I Live in Music, edited by Linda Sunshine, illustrated by Romare Bearden, Stewart, Tabori & Chang (New York, NY), 1994.

The Sweet Breath of Life: A Poetic Narrative of the African-American Family, photographs by the Kamoinge Workshop, Atria Books (New York, NY), 2004.

PROSE AND ESSAYS

See No Evil: Prefaces, Essays and Accounts, 1976-1983, Momo's Press (San Francisco, CA), 1984.

(Author of foreword) Robert Mapplethorpe, *The Black Book,* St. Martin's Press (New York, NY), 1986.

Plays, One, Methuen (London, England), 1992.

(Author of preface) Francoise Kourilsky and Catherine Temerson, editors, *Plays by Women, Book Two: An International Anthology,* Ubu Repertory Theater Publications (New York, NY), 1994.

(Contributor) Jules Feiffer, *Selected from Contemporary American Plays: An Anthology,* Literacy Volunteers of New York City (New York, NY), 1990.

(Editor) *The Beacon Best of 1999: Creative Writing by Women and Men of All Colors,* Houghton Mifflin (New York, NY), 1999.

Contributor to anthologies, including *Love's Fire: Seven New Plays Inspired by Seven Shakespearean Sonnets,* introduction by Mark Lamos, Quill, (New York, NY), 1998; *"May Your Days Be Merry and Bright" and Other Christmas Stories by Women,* edited by Susan Koppelman, Wayne State University Press (Detroit, MI), 1988; *New Plays for the Black Theatre,* edited by Woodie King, Jr., Third World Press (Chicago, IL), 1989; *Breaking Ice: An Anthology of Contemporary African American Fiction,* edited by Terry McMillan, Penguin Books (New York, NY), 1990; *Yellow Silk: Erotic Arts and Letters,* edited by Lily Pond and Richard Russo, Harmony Books (New York, NY), 1990; *Daughters of Africa: An International Anthology,* edited by Margaret Bushby, Pantheon (New York, NY), 1992; *Erotique Noire—Black Erotica,* edited by Miriam DeCosta-Willis, Reginald Martin, and Roseann P. Bell, Anchor (New York, NY), 1992; *Resurgent: New Writing by Women,* edited by Lou Robinson and Camille Norton, University of Illinois Press (Champaign, IL), 1992; *Wild Women Don't Wear No Blues: Black Women Writers on Love, Men, and Sex,* edited by Marita Golden, Doubleday (New York, NY), 1993; and *Moon Marked and Touched by Sun: Plays by African-American Women,* edited by Sydne Mahone, Theater Communications Group (New York, NY), 1994.

Contributor to periodicals, including *Black Scholar, Third World Women, Ms.,* and *Yardbird Reader.*

ADAPTATIONS: A musical-operetta version of Shange's novel *Betsey Brown* was produced by Joseph Papp's Public Theater in 1986.

SIDELIGHTS: Ntozake Shange—originally named Paulette Williams—was raised with the advantages of the black middle class. Yet the roles she chose for herself—including war correspondent and jazz musician—were dismissed as "no good for a woman," she told Stella Dong in a *Publishers Weekly* interview. Frustrated and hurt after separating from her first husband, Shange attempted suicide several times before focusing her rage against the limitations society imposes on black women. While earning a master's degree in American Studies from the University of Southern California, she reaffirmed her personal strength based on a self-determined identity and took her African name, which means "she who comes with her own things" and she "who walks like a lion." Since then she has sustained a triple career as an educator, a performer/director, and a writer whose works draw heavily on her experiences of being a black female in America. "I am a war correspondent after all," she told Dong, "because I'm involved in a war of cultural and esthetic aggression."

Shange became famous for her play *For Colored Girls Who Have Considered Suicide/When the Rainbow Is Enuf.* A unique blend of poetry, music, dance and drama called a "choreopoem," it "took the theatre world by storm" in 1975 noted Jacqueline Trescott in the *Washington Post,* as it "became an electrifying Broadway hit and provoked heated exchanges about the relationships between black men and women . . . . Its form—seven women on the stage dramatizing poetry—was a refreshing slap at the traditional, one-two-three-act structures." Mel Gussow, writing in the *New York Times.* stated that "Miss Shange was a pioneer in terms of her subject matter: the fury of black women at their double subjugation in white male America."

In *For Colored Girls,* poems dramatized by the women dancers recall encounters with their classmates, lovers, rapists, abortionists, and latent killers. The women survive the abuses and disappointments put upon them by the men in their lives and come to recognize in each other, dressed in the colors of Shange's personal rainbow, the promise of a better future. As one voice, at the end, they declare, "i found god in myself / and i loved her / . . . fiercely." To say this, remarked Carol P. Christ in *Diving Deep and Surfacing: Women Writers on Spiritual Quest,* is "to say . . . that it is all right to be a woman, that the Black woman does not have to imitate whiteness or depend on men for her power of being." "The poetry," said Marilyn Stasio in *Cue,* "touches some very tender nerve endings. Although roughly structured and stylistically unrefined, this fierce and passionate poetry has the power to move a body to tears, to rage, and to an ultimate rush of love."

While some reviewers are enthusiastic in their praise for the play, others are emphatically negative. "Some Black people, notably men, said that . . . Shange broke a taboo when her *For Colored Girls . . .* took the theatre world by storm," Connie Lauerman reported in the *Chicago Tribune.* "[Shange] was accused of racism, of 'lynching' the black male." But the playwright does not agree. She told Lauerman, "Half of what we discussed in *For Colored Girls* about the dissipation of the family, rape, wife-battering and all that sort of thing, the U.S. Census Bureau already had . . . . We could have gone to the Library of Congress and read the Census reports and the crime statistics every month and we would know that more black women are raped than anyone else. We would know at this point that they think forty-eight percent of our households are headed by single females . . . . My job as an artist is to say what I see."

"Shange's poems aren't war cries," Jack Kroll wrote in a *Newsweek* review of the Public Theatre production of *For Colored Girls.* "They're outcries filled with a controlled passion against the brutality that blasts the lives of 'colored girls'—a phrase that in her hands vibrates with social irony and poetic beauty. These poems are political in the deepest sense, but there's no dogma, no sentimentality, no grinding of false mythic axes." Critic Edith Oliver of the *New Yorker* remarked, "The evening grows in dramatic power, encompassing, it seems, every feeling and experience a woman has ever had; strong and funny, it is entirely free of the rasping earnestness of most projects of this sort. The verses and monologues that constitute the program have been very well chosen—contrasting in mood yet always subtly building."

Reviews of Shange's next production, *A Photograph: A Study of Cruelty,* were less positive, although critics were generally impressed with the poetic quality of her writing. "Miss Shange is something besides a poet but she is not—at least not at this stage—a dramatist," Richard Eder explained in a *New York Times* review. He continued, "More than anything else, she is a troubadour. She declares her fertile vision of the love and pain between black women and black men in outbursts full of old malice and young cheerfulness. They are short outbursts, song-length; her characters are perceived in flashes, in illuminating vignettes."

Shange's next play, *Spell No.7: A Geechee Quick Magic Trance Manual,* more like *For Colored Girls* in structure, elicited a higher recommendation from Eder. Its nine characters in a New York bar discuss the racism black artists contend with in the entertainment world. At one point, the all-black cast appears in overalls and minstrel-show blackface to address the pressure placed on the black artist to fit a stereotype in order to succeed. "That's what happens to black people in the arts no matter how famous we become . . . . Black Theatre is not moving forward the way people like to think it is. We're not free of our paint yet," Shange told Claudia Tate in *Black Women Writers at Work.* "On another level, *Spell No.7* deals with the image of a black woman as a neutered workhorse, who is unwanted, unloved, and unattended by anyone," noted Elizabeth Brown in the *Dictionary of Literary Biography.*"The emphasis is still on the experiences of the black woman but it is broadened and deepened, and it ventures more boldly across the sexual divide," Eder wrote in the *New York Times.* Don Nelson, writing in the *New York Daily News,* deemed the show "black magic . . . . The word that best describes Shange's works, which are not plays in the traditional sense, is power."

Shange's poetry books, like her theater pieces, are distinctively original. *Washington Post Book World* critic Harriet Gilbert believed *Nappy Edges,* containing fifty poems, is too long. However, Gilbert praised the author, saying, "Nothing that Shange writes is ever entirely unreadable, springing, as it does, from such an intense honesty, from so fresh an awareness of the beauty of sound and of vision, from such mastery of words, from such compassion, humor and intelligence." Alice H.G. Phillips related in the *Times Literary Supplement,* "Comparing herself to a jazzman 'takin' a solo, she lets go with verbal runs and trills, mixes in syncopations, spins out evocative hanging phrases, variations on themes and refrains. Rarely does she come to a full stop, relying instead on line breaks, extra space breaking up a line, and/or oblique strokes . . . . She constantly tries to push things to their limit, and consequently risks seeming overenthusiastic, oversimplistic or merely undisciplined . . . . But at its best, her method can achieve both serious humour and deep seriousness."

In her poetry, Shange takes many liberties with the conventions of written English, using nonstandard spellings and punctuation. Some reviewers feel that these innovations present unnecessary obstacles to the interested readers of *Nappy Edges, A Daughter's Geography,* and *From Okra to Greens: Poems.* Explaining her "lowercase letters, slashes, and spelling" to Tate, Shange said that "poems where all the first letters are capitalized" bore her; "also, I like the idea that letters dance. . . . I need some visual stimulation, so that reading becomes not just a passive act and more than an intellectual activity, but demands rigorous participation." Her idiosyncratic punctuation assures her "that the reader is not in control of the process." She wants her words in print to engage the reader in a kind of struggle, and not be "whatever you can just ignore." The spellings, she said, "reflect language as I hear it. . . . The structure is connected to the music I hear beneath the words."

Shange takes liberties with the conventions of fiction writing with her first full-length novel, *Sassafrass, Cypress, and Indigo.* "The novel is unusual in its form—a tapestry of narrative, poetry, magic spells, recipes and letters. Lyrical yet real, it also celebrates female stuff—weaving, cooking, birthing babies," related Lauerman. Its title characters are sisters who find different ways to cope with their love relationships. Indigo, the youngest sister, retreats into her imagination, befriending her childhood dolls, seeing only the poetry and magic of the world. The music she plays on her violin becomes a rejuvenating source for her mother and sisters. "Probably there is a little bit of all three sisters in Shange," Lauerman suggested, "though she says that her novel is not autobiographical but historical, culled from the experiences of blacks and from the information of my feelings."

Critics agree that Shange's poetry is more masterfully wrought than her fiction, yet they find much in the novel to applaud. Wrote Doris Grumbach in the *Washington Post Book World,* "Shange is primarily a poet, with a blood-red sympathy for and love of her people, their folk as well as their sophisticated ways, their innocent, loving goodness as much as their lack of immunity to powerful evil . . . . But her voice in this novel is entirely her own, an original, spare and primary-colored sound that will remind readers of Jean Toomer's *Cane.*" In Grumbach's opinion, "Whatever Shange turns her hand to she does well, even to potions and recipes."

In *The Love Space Demands,* a choreopoem published in 1991, Shange returned to the blend of music, dance, poetry and drama that characterized *For Colored Girls Who Have Considered Suicide.* "I've gone back to being more like myself," Shange explained to *Voice Literary Supplement* interviewer Eileen Myles. "I'm working on my poetry with musicians and dancers like I originally started." Described by Myles as "a sexy, discomfiting, energizing, revealing, occasionally smug, fascinating kind of book," *The Love Space Demands* includes poems on celibacy and sexuality, on black women's sense of abandonment by black men, on a crack-addicted mother who sells her daughter's virginity for a hit and a pregnant woman who swallows cocaine, destroying her unborn child, to protect her man from arrest. The lead poem of the book, "irrepressibly bronze, beautiful and mine," was inspired by Robert Mapplethorpe's photographs of black and white gay men. The artist's task, Shange told Myles, is "to keep our sensibilities alive . . . . To keep people alive so they know they can feel what is happening as opposed to simply trying to fend it off." "I would rather you not think about how the poem's constructed but simply be in it with me," she added. "That's what it's for, not for the construction, even for the wit of it. It's for actual, visceral responses."

Shange's novel *Liliane: Resurrection of the Daughter* again finds the author exploring the issues of race and gender in contemporary America. The protagonist, Liliane Lincoln, undergoes psychoanalysis in an attempt to better understand the events of her life, particularly her mother's decision to abandon Liliane and her father for a white man when Liliane was a child. As Clarence Major noted in the *Washington Post Book World,* the story is presented "through twelve monologue- performance pieces narrated in turn by [Liliane] and her friends and lovers." Shange "offers a daring portrait of a black woman artist re-creating herself out of social and psychological chaos," remarked Kelly Cherry in the *Los Angeles Times Book Review.* Cherry added, "Shange has written a novel that manages to be both risky and stylish." While some reviewers praised the author for her lush and unusual prose, others felt that Shange's stylistic density occasionally "up-ends the narrative," in the words of *New Statesman and Society* reviewer Andrea Stuart. Nevertheless, commented Valerie Sayers in the *New York Times Book Review,* the book "is a dense, ambitious, worthy song." And Major concluded, "A standing ovation for Ntozake Shange. This is her finest work of fiction so far."

"In the tradition of M.F.K. Fisher," according to the publisher, *If I Can Cook You Know God Can* is a "generous banquet" of essays steeped in "lyrical originality and musical patois." These conversational essays take the reader to the tables of African Americans, Nicaraguans, Londoners, Barbadoans, Brazilians, and Africans. A *Booklist* reviewer noted that the recipes are interwoven with a "fervent, richly impassioned chronicle of African-American experience" that examines political turmoil and relates "how connections are made beyond issues of class or skin color."

Shange's *The Sweet Breath of Life: A Poetic Narrative of the African-American Family,* with photographs by the Kamoinge Workshop, is another of her multi-media approaches to poetry. The volume is an homage to *The Sweet Flypaper of Life,* which was published in 1955 by poet Langston Hughes and photographer Roy DeCarava. The Hughes and DeCarava edition features poems paired with photographs, and the book is renowned for portraying the lives of African Americans in mid-twentieth-century Harlem, New York. Shange's volume follows the same format but seeks to expand the theme away from location and into a broader exploration of the African-American experience. Critics, however, again gave Shange's work mixed reviews. *Black Issues Book Review* contributor Patricia Spears Jones complained that Shange's poems "directly respond to the photographs in such a manner that they feel more like journalism than poetry." Yet *Booklist* reviewer Janet St. John responded to this issue in very different terms, stating that the poems and images are "inherently intertwined and equally expressive." A *Publishers Weekly* writer agreed by concluding that the "style complements the unadorned and intimate images."

In addition to poetry, novels, essays, and screenplays, Shange has taken on the field of children's literature with the publication of four books for children: *Whitewash, Float Like a Butterfly, Ellington Was Not a Street,* and *Daddy Says.* Receiving lukewarm praise and mixed critical reviews, Shange's children's fiction was not as well received among critics as her poetry. In a review of *Daddy Says* for the *School Library Journal,* Carol Edwards concluded, "Despite strong characters and a lively setting, this novel is disjointed and unsatisfying, which is a shame since Shange is clearly capable of portraying rivalry and competitive spirit realistically." However, a *Publishers Weekly* reviewer described *Float Like a Butterfly* a biographical tribute to boxer Muhammad Ali, as work that "nicely characterizes this modern-day hero, with poster- like illustrations and punchy text."

Shange as an editor is fully in her purview, as demonstrated by the positive critiques that greeted the release of *The Beacon Best of 1999,* a collection of poems, short stories, and essays written by lesser-known men and women of color. Vanessa Bush in *Booklist* called it "an eclectic group of works, reflecting on racial and sexual relations in the context of everyday life and self-discovery." A *Publishers Weekly* reviewer claimed, "Shange has been careful not to surrender to ideology or dogma in her selection of material for this expansive collection, which deserves pride of place on the crowded shelf of literary anthologies." Shange defines the work of writers she profiled in *Beacon's Best* as "artful glimpses of life at the end of the twentieth century," which perhaps also describes Shange's work at its most acclaimed and creative.

BIOGRAPHICAL AND CRITICAL SOURCES:

BOOKS

Adell, Sandra, editor, *Dictionary of Twentieth-Century Culture,* Volume 5: *African American Culture,* Gale (Detroit, MI), 1996.

Andrews, William L., Frances Smith Foster, and Trudier Harris, editors, *The Oxford Companion to African American Literature,* Oxford University Press (New York, NY), 1997.

Arata, Esther Spring, editor, *More Black American Playwrights,* Scarecrow Press (Metuchen, NJ), 1978.

Authors and Artists for Young Adults, Volume 9, Gale (Detroit, MI), 1992.

Berney, K.A., editor, *Contemporary Dramatists,* St. James Press (London, England), 1993.

Berney, K.A., editor, *Contemporary American Dramatists,* St. James Press (London, England), 1994.

Berney, K.A., editor, *Contemporary Women Dramatists,* 5th edition, St. James Press (London, England), 1994.

Betsko, Kathleen, and Rachel Koenig, editors, *Interviews with Contemporary Women Playwrights,* Beech Tree Books, 1987.

Black Literature Criticism, Gale (Detroit, MI), 1992.

Brater, Enoch, editor, *Feminine Focus: The New Women Playwrights,* Oxford University Press (New York, NY), 1989.

Chevalier, Tracy, editor, *Contemporary Poets,* 5th edition, St. James Press (Chicago, IL), 1991.

Christ, Carol P., *Diving Deep and Surfacing: Women Writers on Spiritual Quest,* Beacon Press (Boston, MA), 1980.

Christian, Barbara T., *Black Feminist Criticism: Perspectives on Black Women Writers,* Pergamon Press (New York, NY), 1985.

Contemporary Literary Criticism, Gale (Detroit), Volume 8, 1978, Volume 25, 1983, Volume 38, 1986, Volume 74, 1993.

Coven, Brenda,*American Women Dramatists of the Twentieth Century,* Scarecrow Press (Metuchen, NJ), 1982.

Davis, Thadious M., and Trudier Harris, editors,*Dictionary of Literary Biography,* Volume 38: *Afro-American Writers after 1955: Dramatists and Prose Writers,* Gale (Detroit, MI), 1985.

Drama Criticism, Volume 3, Gale (Detroit, MI), 1993.

Easthope, Antony, editor, *Contemporary Poetry Meets Modern Theory,* University of Toronto Press (Toronto, Canada), 1991.

Geis, Deborah R., "Distraught at Laughter: Monologue in Shange's Theatre Pieces," in *Feminine Focus: New Playwrights,* Oxford University Press (New York, NY), pp. 210- 225.

Green, Carol Hurd, and Mary Grimley Mason, editors, *American Women Writers,* Volume 5: Supplement, Continuum Publishing (New York, NY), 1994.

Halloway, Karla F.C., *Moorings and Metaphors: Figures of Culture and Gender in Black Women's Literature,* Rutgers University Press (Brunswick, NJ), 1992.

Hart, Lynda, *Making a Spectacle: Feminist Essays on Contemporary Women's Theatre,* University of Michigan Press (Ann Arbor, MI), 1989.

Hine, Darlene Clark, editor, *Black Women in America: An Historical Encyclopedia,* Carlson Publishing (Brooklyn, NY), 1993.

Kester-Shelton, Pamela, editor, *Feminist Writers,* St. James Press (Detroit, MI), 1996.

Kirkpatrick, D.L., editor, *Contemporary Dramatists,* 4th edition, St. James Press (Chicago, IL), 1988.

Lester, Neal A., *Ntozake Shange: A Critical Study of the Plays,* Garland (New York, NY), 1995.

Magill, Frank N., *Critical Survey of Drama,* revised edition, Salem Press (Pasadena, CA), 1994.

Magill, Frank N., *Great Women Writers,* Henry Holt (New York, NY), 1994.

Magill, Frank N., *Survey of American Literature,* Marshall Cavendish (North Bellmore, NY), 1992.

Martin, Tucker, editor, *Modern American Literature,* Volume 6, third supplement, Continuum Publishing (New York, NY), 1997.

Modern American Literature, 5th edition, St. James Press (Detroit, MI), 1997.

Modern Black Writers, 2nd edition, St. James Press (Detroit, MI), 2000.

Olaniyan, Tejumola, *Scars of Conquest/Masks of Resistance: The Invention of Cultural Identities in African- American, and Caribbean Drama,* Oxford University Press (New York, NY), 1995.

Page, James A., and Jae Min Roh, compilers,*Selected Black American, African, and Caribbean Authors,* 2nd edition, Libraries Unlimited (Littleton, CO), 1985.

Peck, David, editor,*Identities and Issues in Literature,* Salem Press (Pasadena, CA), 1997.

Pendergast, Tom and Sara Pendergast, editors, *St. James Guide to Young Adult Writers,* 2nd edition, St. James Press (Detroit, MI), 1999.

Reinelt, Janelle, and Joseph Roach, *Critical Theory and Performance,* University of Michigan Press (Ann Arbor, MI), 1992.

Riggs, Thomas, editor, *Contemporary Poets,* 6th edition, St. James Press (Detroit, MI), 1996

Riggs, Thomas, editor, *Reference Guide to American Literature,* 4th edition, St. James Press (Detroit, MI), 2000

Robinson Lillian S., compiler and editor, *Modern Women Writers,* Continuum Publishing (New York, NY), 1996.

Schlueter, June, editor, *Modern American Drama: The Female Canon,* Fairleigh Dickinson University Press, 1990.

The Schomburg Center Guide to Black Literature, Gale (Detroit, MI), 1996.

Serafin, Steven R., editor, *Encyclopedia of American Literature,* Continuum Publishing (New York), 1999.

Shelton, Pamela L., editor, *Contemporary Women Poets,* St. James Press (Detroit, MI), 1998.

Smith, Valerie, Lea Baechler, and Walton Litz, *African American Writers,* Scribner (New York, NY), 1991.

Spradling, Mary Mace, editor, *In Black and White,* Gale (Detroit, MI), 1980.

Squier, Susan Merrill, editor, *Women Writers and the City: Essays in Feminist Literary Criticism,* University of Tennessee Press (Knoxville, TN), 1984.

Stringer, Jenny, editor, *The Oxford Companion to Twentieth-Century Literature in English,* Oxford University Press (New York, NY), 1996.

Tate, Claudia, editor, *Black Women Writers at Work,* Continuum (New York, NY), 1983.

Vaught, Jacqueline Brogan and Cordelia Chavez Candelaria, editors, *Women Poets of the Americas: Toward a Pan- American Gathering,* University of Notre Dame Press (Notre Dame, IN), 1999.

PERIODICALS

African American Review, spring, 1992, Neal A. Lester, "Ntozake Shange," pp. 322-325; summer, 1992, and Neal A. Lester, "Shange's Men: *For Colored Girls* revisited, and Movement Beyond," pp. 319-328.

American Black Review, September, 1983; March, 1986.

Black American Literature Forum, winter, 1979, Henry Blackwell, "An Interview with Ntozake Shange," pp. 134-138; summer, 1981, Sandra Hollin Flowers, "*Colored Girls*: Textbook for the Eighties," p. 51; summer, 1983, Sandra L. Richards, review of *Spell No. 7,* pp. 74-75; fall, 1990; winter, 1990, Neal A. Lester, "At the Heart of Shange's Feminism: An Interview," pp. 717-730.

Black Issues Book Review, November-December, 2002, Clarence V. Reynolds, review of "For Colored Girls Who Have Considered Fairy Tales," p. 42; March-April, 2003, review of *Daddy Says,* p. 66; November-December, 2004, Patricia Spears Jones, review of *The Sweet Breath of Life: A Poetic Narrative of the African-American Family,* p. 46.

Black Scholar, March, 1979; October, 1979, Robert Staples, "The Myth of Black Macho: A Response to Angry Black Feminists," pp. 24-33; March, 1981; December, 1982; July, 1985; winter, 1996, p. 68; summer, 1996, p. 67.

Booklist, April 15, 1987; May 15, 1991; January 1, 1998; October 15, 1999, Vanessa Bush, review of *The Beacon Best of 1999,* p. 410; June 1, 2001, review of *Betsey Brown,* p. 1837; March 15, 2003, Hazel Rochman, review of *Daddy Says,* p. 1317; October 15, 2004, Janet St. John, review of *The Sweet Breath of Life,* p. 382.

Boston Review, November 14, 1994, Laurel Elkind, review of *Lilliane: Resurrection of the Daughter,* p. 38.

Chicago Tribune, October 21, 1982.

Chicago Tribune Book World, July 1, 1979; September 8, 1985.

Christian Science Monitor, September 9, 1976; October 8, 1982; May 2, 1986.

College Language Association Journal, June, 1996, Jane Splawn, "Rites of Passage in the Writing of Ntozake Shange: The Poetry, Drama, and Novels," p. 1989; June 1986, Jane Splawn, "New World Consciousness in the Poetry of Ntozake Shange and June Jordan: Two African-American Women's Response to Expansionism in the Third World."

Cue, June 26, 1976.

Detroit Free Press, October 30, 1978; October 30, 1979, Laura Berman, "The Last Angry Woman? Playwright-Poet Isn't Running from the Rage That Inspires Her," p. C1.

Early Childhood Education Journal, fall, 1999, review of *Whitewash,* p. 36.

Entertainment Weekly, March 10, 1995, p. 65.

Essence, November, 1976; May, 1985, Marcia Ann Gillespie, "Ntozake Shange Talks with Marcia Ann Gillespie," pp. 122-123; June, 1985; August, 1991.

Freedomways, 1976, Jean Carey Bond, review of *For Colored Girls Who Have Considered Suicide,* pp. 187-191.

Horizon, September, 1977.

Journal of American Culture, fall, 1987, Jean Strandness, review of *Sassafrass, Cypress, and Indigo,* p. 11.

Journal of Ethnic Studies, spring, 1978, Erskine Peters, "Some Tragic Propensities of Ourselves: The Occasion of Ntozake Shange's *For Colored Girls Who Have Considered Suicide/When the Rainbow Is Enuf,*" pp. 79-85.

Kirkus Reviews, September 1, 1999, review of *The Beacon Best of 1999,* p. 69; September 1, 2002, review of *Float Like a Butterfly: Muhammad Ali, the Man Who Could Float Like a Butterfly and Sting Like a Bee,* p. 1320; December 1, 2002, review of *Daddy Says,* p. 1773.

Kliatt Young Adult Paperback Book Guide, January, 1989.

Library Journal, May 1, 1987; October 15, 1999, review of *The Beacon Best of 1999,* p. 70.

Los Angeles Times, October 20, 1982; June 11, 1985; July 28, 1987.

Los Angeles Times Book Review, August 22, 1982; October 20, 1982; January 8, 1984; July 29, 1984; June 11, 1985; July 19, 1987; December 18, 1994, p. 12.

Massachussetts Review, autumn, 1981, Andrea Benton Rushing, "For Colored Girls, Suicide or Struggle," pp. 539-550; winter, 1987, Brenda Lyons, "Interview with Ntozake Shange," pp. 687-696.

MELUS, fall, 1994, Barbara Frey Waxman, "Dancing out of Form, Dancing into Self: Genre and Metaphor in Marshall, Shange, and Walker," pp. 91-107.

Modern Drama, March, 1995, Timothy Murray, "Screening the Camera's Eye: Black and White Confrontations of Technological Representations," pp. 110-124; 1986, P. Jane Splawn, "Change the Joke[r] and Slip the Yoke: Boal's *Joker* System in Ntozake Shange's *For Colored Girls* and *Spell No. 7,* " pp. 386-398.

Mother Jones, January- February, 1995, p. 69.

Ms., September, 1976; December, 1977, "Ntozake Shange Interviews Herself"; June, 1985; June, 1987.

Newsday, August 22, 1976.

New Statesman, October 4, 1985.

New Statesman and Society, May 19, 1995, p. 37.

Newsweek, June 14, 1976; July 30, 1979.

New York Daily News, July 16, 1979.

New Yorker, June 14, 1976; August 2, 1976; January 2, 1978.

New York Times, June 16, 1976; December 22, 1977; June 4, 1979; June 8, 1979; July 16, 1979; July 22, 1979; May 14, 1980; June 15, 1980, Frank Rich, " *Mother Courage* Transplanted," p. D5; January 1, 1995, Valerie Sayers, "A Life in Collage," p. 38; September 3, 1995, Andrea Stevens, "*For Colored Girls* May Be for the Ages," p. H5.

New York Times Book Review, June 25, 1979; July 16, 1979; October 21, 1979; September 12, 1982; May 12, 1985; April 6, 1986; January 1, 1995, p. 6; October 15, 1995, p. 36; February 25, 1996, p. 32.

New York Times Magazine, May 1, 1983.

Phylon, fall, 1987, Elizabeth Brown-Guillory, "Black Women Playwrights: Exorcising Myths," pp. 229-239.

Plays and Players, June, 1985, Carole Woddis, review of *Spell No. 7,* pp. 230-248.

Publishers Weekly, May 3, 1985; November 14, 1994, review of *I Live in Music,* p. 65; January 1, 1996, p. 69; September 20, 1999, review of *The Beacon Best of 1999,* p. 65; September 16, 2002, review of *Float Like a Butterfly,* p. 68; August 2, 2004, review of *The Sweet Breath of Life,* p. 66.

Saturday Review, February 18, 1978; May-June, 1985.

School Library Journal, February, 2003, Carol A. Edwards, review of *Daddy Says,* p. 148.

Social Studies, January, 2001, review of *Whitewash,* p. 39.

Studies in American Drama, 1989, "The Poetry of a Moment: Politics and the Open Forum in the Drama of Ntozake Shange," pp. 91-101, Neal A. Lester, "An Interview with Ntozake Shange," pp. 42-66.

Time, June 14, 1976; July 19, 1976; November 1, 1976.

Times (London, England), April 21, 1983.

Times Literary Supplement, December 6, 1985; April 15-21, 1988.

Umoja, spring, 1980, Linda Lee Talbert, "Ntozake Shange: Scarlet Woman and Witch/Poet," pp. 5-10.

Variety, July 25, 1979.

Village Voice, August 16, 1976, Michelle Wallace, "For Colored Girls, the Rainbow Is Not Enough," pp. 108-109; July 23, 1979; June 18, 1985.

Voice Literary Supplement, August, 1991; September, 1991.

Washington Post, June 12, 1976; June 29, 1976; February 23, 1982; June 17, 1985.

Washington Post Book World, October 15, 1978; July 19, 1981; August 22, 1982; August 5, 1984; February 5, 1995, p. 4.

Wilson Library Bulletin, October, 1990.

Women's Review of Books, November, 1985, Evelyn C. White "Growing Up Black," p. 11.

World Literature Today, summer, 1995, Deirdre Neilen, review of *Liliane: Resurrection of the Daughter,* p. 584.

ONLINE

Academy of American Poets Web site, http://www.poets.org/poets/ (February 21, 2001), "Ntozake Shange."

African American Literature Book Club Web site, http://aalbc.com/ (November 18, 2003), "Ntozake Shange."

Open Book Systems Web site, http://archives.obsus.com/obs/ (November 18, 2003), "Ntozake Shange."

University of Florida Web site, http://web.wst.ufl.edu/ (November 18, 2003), "Ntozake Shange."

Women of Color, Women of Words Web site, http://www.scils.rutgers.edu/~cybers/shange2.html/ (November 18, 2003), "Ntozake Shange."

* * *

SHAPIRO, Karl Jay 1913-2000

PERSONAL: Name legally changed to Karl Shapiro in 1920; born Carl Shapiro, November 10, 1913, in Baltimore, MD, USA; died May 14, 2000, in New York, NY; son of Joseph (in business) and Sarah (Omansky) Shapiro; married Evalyn Katz (a secretary), March 25, 1945 (divorced, January, 1967); married Teri Kovach, July 31, 1967 (divorced, July, 1982); married Sophie Wilkins, April 25, 1985; children: (first marriage) Katharine, John Jacob, Elizabeth. *Education:* Attended University of Virginia, 1932-33, Johns Hopkins University, 1937-39, and Enoch Pratt Library School, 1940. *Politics:* Republican.

CAREER: Library of Congress, Washington, DC, consultant in poetry, 1946-47; Johns Hopkins University, Baltimore, MD, associate professor of writing, 1947-50; *Poetry,* Chicago, IL, editor, 1950-56; University of Nebraska, Lincoln, professor of English, 1956-66; University of Illinois at Chicago Circle, professor of English, 1966-68; University of California, Davis, professor of English, 1968-85. Lecturer in India, summer of 1955, for U.S. Department of State. Visiting professor or lecturer at University of Wisconsin, 1948, Loyola University, 1951-52, Salzburg Seminar in American Studies, 1952, University of California, 1955-56, and Indiana University, 1956-57. Member, Bollingen Prize Committee, 1949. *Military service:* U.S. Army, 1941-45.

MEMBER: National Institute of Arts and Letters, American Academy of Arts and Sciences (honorary), Phi Beta Kappa, PEN.

AWARDS, HONORS: Fellow in American Letters, Library of Congress; Jeanette S. Davis Prize and Levinson prize, both from *Poetry* in 1942; *Contemporary Poetry* prize, 1943; American Academy of Arts and Letters grant, 1944; Guggenheim Foundation fellowships, 1944, 1953; Pulitzer Prize in poetry, 1945, for *V-Letter and Other Poems;* Shelley Memorial Prize, 1946; Kenyon School of Letters fellowship, 1956-57; Eunice Tietjens Memorial Prize, 1961; Oscar Blumenthal Prize, *Poetry,* 1963; Bollingen Prize, 1968; Robert Kirsch Award L.A. Times, 1989; Charity Randall Citation, 1990; Library of Congress fellowship.

WRITINGS:

English Prosody and Modern Poetry, Johns Hopkins Press (Baltimore, MD), 1947, reprinted, Folcroft Library Editions, 1975.

A Bibliography of Modern Prosody, Johns Hopkins Press (Baltimore, MD), 1948, reprinted, Folcroft Library Editions (Folcroft, PA), 1976.

(Editor with Louis Untermeyer and Richard Wilbur) *Modern American and Modern British Poetry,* Harcourt (New York, NY), 1955.

(Author of libretto) *The Tenor* (opera; music by Hugo Weisgall), Merion Music (Bryn Mawr, PA), 1956.

(Editor) *American Poetry* (anthology), Crowell (New York, NY), 1960.

(Editor) *Prose Keys to Modern Poetry,* Harper & Row (New York, NY), 1962.

(With Robert Beum) *Prosody Handbook,* Harper & Row (New York, NY), 1965.

Edsel (novel), B. Geis Associates (New York, NY), 1970.

(Editor with Robert Phillips) *Letters of Delmore Schwartz,* Ontario Review Press/Persea Books (New York, NY), 1984.

The Younger Son: Poet; An Autobiography in Three Parts; The Youth and War Years of a Distinguished American Poet, Algonquin Books (Chapel Hill, NC), 1988.

Reports of My Death: An Autobiography, Algonquin Books (Chapel Hill, NC), 1990.

POETRY

Poems, Waverly Press (Baltimore, MD), 1935.

(Contributor) *Five Young American Poets,* New Directions, 1941.

Person, Place, and Thing, Reynal & Hitchcock (New York, NY), 1942.

The Place of Love, Comment Press, 1942.

V-Letter and Other Poems, Reynal & Hitchcock (New York, NY), 1944.

Essay on Rime, Secker & Warburg (London, England), 1945.

Trial of a Poet and Other Poems, Reynal & Hitchcock (New York, NY), 1947.

(Contributor) *Poets at Work,* Harcourt (New York, NY), 1948.

Poems: 1940-1953, Random House (New York, NY), 1953.

The House, privately printed, 1957.

Poems of a Jew, Random House (New York, NY), 1958.

The Bourgeois Poet, Random House (New York, NY), 1964.

Selected Poems, Random House (New York, NY), 1968.

White-Haired Lover, Random House (New York, NY), 1968.

Adult Book Store, Random House (New York, NY), 1976.

Collected Poems: 1948-1978, Random House (New York, NY), 1978.

Love and War, Art and God, Stuart Wright, 1984.

Adam and Eve, edited by John Wheatcroft, Bucknell University, Press of Appletree Alley (Lewisburg, PA), 1986.

New and Selected Poems, 1940-1986, University of Chicago Press (Chicago, IL), 1987.

The Wild Card: Selected Poems, Early and Late, edited by Stanley Kunitz and David Ignatow, University of Illinois Press (Urbana, IL), 1998.

Essay on Rime; with Trial of a Poet, edited with afterword by Robert Phillips, University of Michigan Press (Ann Arbor, MI), 2003.

Selected Poems, edited by John Updike, Library of American (New York, NY), 2003.

Creative Glut: Selected Essays of Karl Shapiro, edited and with introduction by Robert Phillips, Ivan R. Dee (Chicago, IL), 2004.

LITERARY CRITICISM

Beyond Criticism, University of Nebraska Press (Lincoln, NE), 1953, published as *A Primer for Poets,* 1965.

In Defense of Ignorance, Random House (New York, NY), 1960.

(With James E. Miller, Jr., and Beatrice Slote) *Start it with the Sun: Studies in Cosmic Poetry,* University of Nebraska Press (Lincoln, NE), 1960.

(With Ralph Ellison) *The Writer's Experience,* Library of Congress (Washington, D.C.), 1964.

Randall Jarrell, Library of Congress (Washington, D.C.), 1967.

To Abolish Children and Other Essays, Quadrangle Books (Chicago, IL), 1968.

The Poetry Wreck: Selected Essays, 1950-1970, Random House (New York, NY), 1975.

AUTHOR OF INTRODUCTION

Pawel Majewski, editor, *Czas Niepokoju* (anthology; title means "Time of Unrest"), Criterion, 1958.

Jack Hirschman, *A Correspondence of Americans,* Indiana University Press (Bloomington, IN), 1960.

Bruce Cutler, *The Year of the Green Wave,* University of Nebraska Press (Lincoln, NE), 1960.

Also author of screenplay "Karl Shapiro's America," 1976. Work appears in anthologies. Contributor of articles, poetry, and reviews to *Partisan Review, Poetry, Nation, Saturday Review,* and other periodicals. Editor, *Poetry,* 1950-56, *Newberry Library Bulletin,* 1953-55, and *Prairie Schooner,* 1956-66. Some of Shapiro's papers are held in the Library of Congress's Archival Manuscript Materials Collection.

SIDELIGHTS: Karl Jay Shapiro's poetry received early recognition, winning a number of major poetry awards, including the Pulitzer prize, during the 1940s. Strongly influenced by the traditionalist poetry of W.H. Auden, Shapiro's early work was "striking for its concrete but detached insights," Alfred Kazin wrote in *Contemporaries.* "It is witty and exact in the way it catches the poet's subtle and guarded impressions, and it is a poetry full of clever and unexpected verbal conceits. It is a very professional poetry—supple and adaptable." Stephen Stepanchev noted in *American Poetry since 1945: A Critical Survey,* that Shapiro's poems "found impetus and subject matter in the public crises of the 1940's and all have their social meaning."

Although his early traditionalist poetry was successful, Shapiro doubted the value and honesty of that kind of poetry. In many of his critical essays, he attacked the assumptions of traditionalist poetry as stifling to the poet's creativity. "What he wants," Paul Fussell, Jr., commented in *Partisan Review,* "is a turning from received and thus discredited English and European techniques of focus in favor of honest encounters with the stuff of local experience." In lectures and essays, Shapiro championed the works and poetic theories of Walt Whitman and William Carlos Williams, two poets who broadened the possibilities of American poetry by defending new prosodies of open form.

In the poetry of both Whitman, which he memorized in his youth, and the Beat poets, Shapiro found a confirmation of his own idea of feeling over form. In his collection *The Bourgeois Poet,* Shapiro broke with his traditional poetic forms in favor of the free verse of Whitman and the Beats and the new poems also contained insights and an apocalyptic tone that was shocking compared to other poetry being published at that time.

Person, Place and Thing, containing poems that had won the Levinson prize when published in *Poetry* magazine, was applauded by the critics. Directly confronting subjects such as love, the history of the South in which Shapiro grew up an outsider, or the war in the South Pacific in which he served as a medical corps clerk, the poems were received as palpable "attacks." His most frequent target in the poems, related Ross Labrie in the *Dictionary of Literary Biography,* was the "dehumanized technocracies" that fostered urban decadence and sent men and women to war without regard for their worth as persons. In a *Poetry* review of a later book, *Love and War, Art and God,* David Wojahn commented that social criticism had always been part of Shapiro's work. Wojahn wrote, "From the very beginning, Shapiro identified himself as an iconoclast, and his outsider's role extended beyond his attacks on social injustice. At a time before it was fashionable to do so, he proudly proclaimed his Jewishness and set himself against the main trends of Modernism."

Coming of age in the United States had much to do with Shapiro's development as an iconoclast. In his introduction to *Poems of a Jew,* he wrote, "As a third generation American I grew up with the obsessive idea of personal liberty which engrosses all Americans except the oldest and richest families." In a *Paris Review* interview, Shapiro explained how being both a Jew and a poet also partly accounted for his point of view as an "outsider": "I've always had this feeling—I've heard other Jews say—that when you can't find any other explanation for the Jews, you say, 'Well, they are poets.' . . . The poet is in exile whether he is or he is not. Because of what everybody knows about society's idea of the artist as a peripheral character and a potential bum. Or a troublemaker. . . . Like the way most artists probably feel in order to survive—you have to at least pretend that you are 'seriously' in the world. Or actually perform in it while you know that in your own soul you are not in it at all." Wojahn pointed out that Shapiro's stance as a social critic did not make the poems cynical. "For all his stridency, Shapiro could be a wonderfully tender poet. . . . This side . . . materializes in empathic portraits like 'The Leg' and 'The Figurehead,' as well as in the poems that focus on Shapiro's experience in the military during World War II."

Shapiro published the Pulitzer prize-winning volume *V-Letter and Other Poems* in 1944 while serving with the U.S. Army in New Guinea. V-letters were letters written by American soldiers and microfilmed by censors before delivery to the United States. The poems recreate the tension between the intensity of wartime experiences and a sense of detachment from events that many soldiers felt while trying to conduct their personal lives over the obstacles of distance and the added obstacle of the censors. Though he appreciated what the award would do to establish his career as a writer, Shapiro felt more honored when he found out that copies of *V-Letter and Other Poems* had been placed in all U.S. Navy ship libraries.

In 1988, Shapiro published the first volume in a planned three-volume autobiography. This volume, titled *The Younger Son,* details Shapiro's childhood and early manhood, including his World War II experience and the beginnings of his literary career. While "the poet," as Shapiro referred to himself throughout the volume, divulges little information about his relationship with his parents and the experiences of his youth, he is more expansive when discussing his wartime tour of duty, when he managed a prodigious poetic output while caring for wounded soldiers. Shapiro arrived home in 1945 having just been awarded the Pulitzer Prize for *V-Letter.* Commenting on the author's use of the third person in the book and the resulting detachment from his life that is implied, *Sewanee Review* contributor David Miller noted that "The mood is an eerie one of diminishment and distance." However, Miller concluded that "*The Younger Son* is beautifully styled, honest, and fascinating."

Shapiro continued his autobiography with 1990's *Reports of My Death,* the title referring to inaccurate media reports in the 1980s that Shapiro had committed suicide. The volume covers the period between 1945, when Shapiro returned home from World War II, and 1985, chronicling the process of Shapiro's literary development; his stints as editor of *Poetry* and *Prairie Schooner;* his controversial decision to vote against Ezra Pound as recipient of the first Bollingen Prize for poetry; and his gradual fading from the literary limelight during the 1970s and 1980s. Again referring to himself in the third person, Shapiro openly discusses his numerous extramarital affairs, his disgust with the American literary scene, and his frustration at being dropped from the prestigious *Oxford Book of American Verse.* "Shapiro has written a beautiful book, not only tracing the long career of 'the poet' but doing so in dreamy, mellifluous sentences that sometimes left me feeling euphoric," remarked Morris Dickstein in the *Washington Post Book World.* Several critics expressed disappointment with Shapiro's decision not to date important events and not to identify people who figure prominently in his story. *World Literature Today* critic John Boening felt that "such indirectness may make the book rough going for future generations." Nevertheless, Chicago *Tribune Books* reviewer Larry Kart declared that Shapiro's two volumes of autobiography "not only rank with Shapiro's finest poetic achievements but also will come to occupy . . . a high place in the canon of American autobiography."

New York Times contributor Laurence Leiberman saw Shapiro as one of "a generation of poets who . . . wrote a disproportionate number of superbly good poems in early career, became decorated overnight with honors . . . and spent the next twenty-odd years trying to outpace a growing critical notice of decline." Leiberman found *The Bourgeois Poet* to be Shapiro's attempt to "recast the poetic instrument to embody formerly intractable large sectors of his life" and to win "a precious freedom to extend the limits of his art." Leiberman saw the two styles in Shapiro's poetry, the traditionalist and free verse, as enhancing each other. He believed that Shapiro's "future work stands an excellent chance of merging the superior qualities of two opposite modes: the expressiveness of candid personal confession and the durability of significant form."

BIOGRAPHICAL AND CRITICAL SOURCES:

BOOKS

Contemporary Authors Autobiography Series, Volume 6, Thomson Gale (Detroit, MI), 1987.

Contemporary Literary Criticism, Thomson Gale (Detroit, MI), Volume 4, 1975, Volume 8, 1978, Volume 15, 1980, Volume 53, 1989.

Dictionary of Literary Biography, Volume 48: *American Poets, 1880-1945, Second Series,* Thomson Gale (Detroit, MI), 1986.

Jarrell, Randall, *The Third Book of Criticism,* Farrar, Straus & Giroux (New York, NY), 1969.

Kazin, Alfred, *Contemporaries,* Little, Brown (Boston, MA), 1962.

Nemerov, Howard, *Poetry and Fiction,* Rutgers University Press (New Brunswick, NJ), 1963.

Rosenthal, M. L., *The Modern Poets: A Critical Introduction,* Oxford University Press (New York, NY), 1960.

Scannell, Vernon, *Not without Glory,* Woburn Press (London, England), 1976.

Shapiro, Karl, *Poems of a Jew,* Random House (New York, NY), 1958.

Spears, Monroe K., *Dionysus and the City,* Oxford University Press (New York, NY), 1970.

Stepanchev, Stephen, *American Poetry since 1945: A Critical Survey,* Harper & Row (New York, NY), 1965.

White, William, *Karl Shapiro: A Bibliography,* Wayne State University Press (Detroit, MI), 1960.

PERIODICALS

America, January 7, 1989, p. 14.

Antioch Review, Volume 31, number 3, 1971.

Books, March, 1964.

Book Week, August 2, 1964.

Book World, July 28, 1968.

Carleton Miscellany, spring, 1965.

Christian Science Monitor, July 3, 1968.

College English, February, 1946.

Commonweal, September 19, 1958; January 20, 1960; October 4, 1968.

Esquire, April, 1968.

Harper's, August, 1964.

Hollins Critic, December, 1964.

Hudson Review, autumn, 1975; summer, 1988.

Kenyon Review, winter, 1946.

Literary Times, June, 1967.

Los Angeles Times, July 7, 1968; May 18, 2000, p. B8.

Nation, July 5, 1958; September 24, 1960; August 24, 1964; November 11, 1978.

New Republic, November 24, 1958.

New Yorker, November 7, 1964.

New York Herald Tribune Book Review, May 8, 1960.

New York Times, July 29, 1968; January 6, 1969; October 4, 1971.

New York Times Book Review, September 7, 1958; May 8, 1960; July 14, 1968; August 18, 1968; July 25, 1976; March 31, 1985, Richard Tillinghast, review of *Love and War—Art and God,* p. 14; November 27, 1988, Wendy Brumer, review of *The Younger Son: Poet; An Autobiography in Three Parts; The Youth and War Years of a Distinguished American Poet,* p. 23; May 13, 1990, Evelyn Toynton, review of *Reports of My Death,* p. 25.

Paris Review, spring, 1986, interview with Karl Shapiro.

Partisan Review, winter, 1969.

Poetry, June, 1965; April, 1969; July, 1969; February, 1970; June, 1985.

Prairie Schooner, winter, 1965.

Publishers Weekly, March 2, 1990, p. 67.

Saturday Review, September 27, 1958; April 15, 1978.

Sewanee Review, winter, 1965; April, 1989, David Miller, review of *The Younger Son,* p. 283.

Southern Review, winter, 1973.

Time, August 2, 1968.

Tribune Books (Chicago, IL), October 30, 1988; July 15, 1990, Larry Kart, review of *Reports of My Death,* p. 3.

Village Voice, March 29, 1976.

Virginia Quarterly Review, winter, 1969.

Wall Street Journal, July 7, 1976.

Washington Post, January 4, 1980; December 9, 1988.
Washington Post Book World, July 1, 1990, Morris Dickstein, review of *Reports of My Death,* p. 1.
Western Review, spring, 1954.
World Literature Today, winter, 1992, John Boening, review of *Reports of My Death,* p. 139.
Yale Review, winter, 1954; June, 1975.

ONLINE

Bucknell University, http://www.bucknell.edu/ (September, 2004), "Karl Shapiro."

OTHER

Poets in Person. Karl Shapiro with Joseph Parisi. Poets in Person. Maxine Kumin with Alicia Ostriker, Modern Poetry Association (Chicago, IL), sound cassette, 1991.

* * *

SHEPARD, Sam 1943- (Samuel Shepard Rogers, VII)

PERSONAL: Given name Samuel Shepard Rogers VII; born November 5, 1943, in Fort Sheridan, IL; son of Samuel Shepard (a teacher and farmer) and Elaine (Schook) Rogers; married O-Lan Johnson Dark (an actress), November 9, 1969 (divorced); currently living with Jessica Lange (an actress and film producer); children: (first marriage) Jesse Mojo; (with Lange) Hannah Jane, Samuel Walker. *Education:* Attended Mount Antonio Junior College, California, 1960-61. *Hobbies and other interests:* Polo, rodeo.

ADDRESSES: Office—Sam Shepard, International Creative Management, 8942 Wilshire Blvd., Beverly Hills, California, CA 90211-1934. *Agent*—Toby Cole, 234 West 44th St., New York, NY 10036.

CAREER: Writer, 1964—. Conley Arabian Horse Ranch, Chino, CA, stable hand, 1958-60; Bishop's Company Repertory Players (touring theatre group), actor, 1962-63; Village Gate, New York, NY, busboy, 1963-64. Rock musician (drums and guitar) with Holy Modal Rounders, 1968-71; playwright in residence at Magic Theatre, San Francisco, CA, 1974-84; actor in feature films, including *Days of Heaven,* 1978, *Resurrection,* 1980, *Raggedy Man,* 1981, *Frances,* 1982, *The Right Stuff,* 1983, *Country,* 1984, *Fool for Love,* 1985, and *Crimes of the Heart,* 1986, *Baby Boom,* 1987, *Steel Magnolias,* 1989, *The Hot Spot,* 1990, *Defenseless,* 1991, *Voyager,* 1991, *Thunderheart,* 1992, *The Pelican Brief,* 1993, *Silent Tongue,* 1994, *Safe Passage,* 1994, and *Black Hawk Down,* 2002; director of feature film *Far North,* 1988.

MEMBER: American Academy and Institute of Arts and Letters, 1992.

AWARDS, HONORS: Obie Awards from *Village Voice* for best plays of the Off-Broadway season, 1966, for *Chicago, Icarus's Mother,* and *Red Cross,* 1967, for *La Turista,* 1968, for *Forensic and the Navigators* and *Melodrama Play,* 1973, for *The Tooth of Crime,* 1975, for *Action,* 1977, for *Curse of the Starving Class,* 1979, for *Buried Child,* and 1984, for *Fool for Love*; grant from University of Minnesota, 1966; Rockefeller foundation grant and Yale University fellowship, 1967; Guggenheim foundation memorial fellowships, 1968 and 1971; National Institute and American Academy award for literature, 1974; Brandeis University creative arts award, 1975-76; Pulitzer Prize for drama, 1979, for *Buried Child*; Academy Award for best supporting actor nomination from Academy of Motion Picture Arts and Sciences, 1984, for *The Right Stuff*; Golden Palm Award from Cannes Film Festival, 1984, for *Paris, Texas*; New York Drama Critics' Circle Award, 1986, for *A Lie of the Mind*; American Academy of Arts and Letters Gold Medal for Drama, 1992; Theater Hall of Fame, 1994; Antoinette Perry Award Nomination for best play, 1996, for *Buried Child;* revised version of *True West,* first produced off-Broadway in 1980, nominated for a Tony Award for best play, 2000.

WRITINGS:

PLAYS

Cowboys (one-act), first produced Off-Off-Broadway at St. Mark Church in-the-Bowery, October 16, 1964.
The Rock Garden (one-act; also see below), first produced Off-Off-Broadway at St. Mark Church in-the-Bowery, October 16, 1964.
4-H Club (one act; also see below), first produced Off-Broadway at Cherry Lane Theatre, 1965.
Up to Thursday (one-act), first produced Off-Broadway at Cherry Lane Theatre, February 10, 1965.

Dog (one-act), first produced Off-Broadway at La Mama Experimental Theatre Club, February 10, 1965.

Chicago (one-act; also see below), first produced Off-Off-Broadway at St. Mark Church in-the-Bowery, April 16, 1965.

Icarus's Mother (one-act; also see below), first produced Off-Off-Broadway at Caffe Cino, November 16, 1965.

Fourteen Hundred Thousand (one-act; also see below), first produced at Firehouse Theater, Minneapolis, MN, 1966.

Red Cross (one-act; also see below), first produced Off-Broadway at Martinique Theatre, April 12, 1966.

La Turista (two-act; first produced Off-Broadway at American Place Theatre, March 4, 1967; also see below), Bobbs-Merrill (Indianapolis, IN), 1968.

Cowboys #2 (one-act; also see below), first produced Off-Broadway at Old Reliable, August 12, 1967.

Forensic and the Navigators (one-act; also see below), first produced Off-Off-Broadway at St. Mark Church in-the-Bowery, December 29, 1967.

(Contributor) *Oh! Calcutta!,* first produced on Broadway at Eden Theatre, 1969.

The Unseen Hand (one-act; also see below), first produced Off-Broadway at La Mama Experimental Theatre Club, December 26, 1969.

Holy Ghostly (one-act; also see below), first produced in New York, NY, 1970.

Operation Sidewinder (two-act; first produced Off-Broadway at Vivian Beaumont Theatre, March 12, 1970; also see below), Bobbs-Merrill, 1970.

Shaved Splits (also see below), first produced Off-Broadway at La Mama Experimental Theatre Club, July 29, 1970.

Mad Dog Blues (one-act; also see below), first produced Off-Off-Broadway at St. Mark Church in-the-Bowery, March 4, 1971.

(With Patti Smith) *Cowboy Mouth* (also see below), first produced at Transverse Theatre, Edinburgh, Scotland, April 2, 1971, produced Off-Broadway at American Place Theatre, April 29, 1971.

Back Bog Beast Bait (one-act; also see below), first produced Off-Broadway at American Place Theatre, April 29, 1971.

The Tooth of Crime (two-act; also see below), first produced at McCarter Theatre, Princeton, NJ, 1972, produced Off-Off-Broadway at Performing Garage, March 7, 1973.

Blue Bitch (also see below), first produced Off-Off-Broadway at Theatre Genesis, February, 1973.

(With Megan Terry and Jean-Claude van Itallie) *Nightwalk* (also see below), first produced Off-Off-Broadway at St. Clement's Church, September 8, 1973.

Geography of a Horse Dreamer (two-act; also see below), first produced at Theatre Upstairs, London, England, February 2, 1974.

Little Ocean, first produced at Hampstead Theatre Club, London, England, March 25, 1974.

Action (one-act; also see below), first produced Off-Broadway at American Place Theatre, April 4, 1975.

Killer's Head (one-act; also see below), first produced Off-Broadway at American Place Theatre, April 4, 1975.

Angel City (also see below), first produced at Magic Theatre, San Francisco, CA, 1976.

Curse of the Starving Class (two-act; also see below), first produced Off-Broadway at Newman/Public Theatre, March, 1978.

Buried Child (two-act; also see below), first produced Off-Broadway at Theatre of the New City, November, 1978.

Seduced (also see below), first produced Off-Broadway at American Place Theatre, February 1, 1979.

Suicide in B-flat (also see below), first produced Off-Off-Broadway at Impossible Ragtime Theatre, March 14, 1979.

Tongues, first produced at Eureka Theatre Festival, CA, 1979, produced Off-Off-Broadway at The Other Stage, November 6, 1979.

Savage/Love, first produced at Eureka Theater Festival, CA, 1979, produced Off-Off-Broadway at The Other Stage, November 6, 1979.

True West (two-act; first produced Off-Broadway at Public Theatre, December 23, 1980), Doubleday, 1981.

(Also director of original production) *Fool for Love* (one-act; also see below), first produced at Magic Theatre, San Francisco, 1983, produced Off-Broadway by Circle Repertory Company, May 27, 1983.

The Sad Lament of Pecos Bill on the Eve of Killing His Wife (one-act; also see below), first produced Off-Broadway at La Mama Experimental Theatre Club, September 25, 1983.

Superstitions (one-act), first produced Off-Broadway at La Mama Experimental Theatre Club, September 25, 1983.

(Also director of original production) *A Lie of the Mind* (three-act; first produced Off-Broadway at Promenade Theatre, December, 1985), published with *The War in Heaven* (also see below), New American Library (New York, NY), 1987.

Hawk Moon, produced in London, England, 1989.

States of Shock, produced in New York, NY, 1991.

Simpatico, Dramatists Play Service (New York, NY), 1995.

Curse of the Starving Class, Dramatists Play Service (New York, NY), 1997.

Eyes for Consuela, from the story "The Blue Bouquet" by Octavio Paz, Dramatists Play Service (New York, NY), 1999.

The Late Henry Moss, produced at the Signature Theater in New York, NY, 2001; revived at the Creative Place Theater in New York, NY, 2005.

(And director) *The God of Hell,* produced Off-Broadway at the New School University in New York, NY, 2004.

PLAY COLLECTIONS

Five Plays by Sam Shepard (contains *Icarus's Mother, Chicago, Melodrama Play, Red Cross,* and *Fourteen Hundred Thousand*), Bobbs-Merrill (Indianapolis, IN), 1967.

The Unseen Hand and Other Plays (contains *The Unseen Hand, 4-H Club, Shaved Splits, Forensic and the Navigators, Holy Ghostly,* and *Back Bog Beast Bait*), Bobbs-Merrill (Indianapolis, IN), 1971.

Mad Dog Blues and Other Plays (includes *Mad Dog Blues, The Rock Garden, Cowboys #2, Cowboy Mouth, Blue Bitch,* and *Nightwalk*), Winter House (New York, NY), 1972.

The Tooth of Crime [and] *Geography of a Horse Dreamer,* Grove (New York, NY), 1974.

Angel City, Curse of the Starving Class and Other Plays (includes *Angel City, Curse of the Starving Class, Killer's Head,* and *Action*), Urizen Books (New York, NY), 1976.

Buried Child, Seduced, Suicide in B-flat, Urizen Books (New York, NY), 1979.

Four Two-Act Plays by Sam Shepard (contains *La Turista, The Tooth of Crime, Geography of a Horse Dreamer,* and *Operation Sidewinder*), Urizen Books (New York, NY), 1980.

Chicago and Other Plays, Urizen Books (New York, NY), 1981.

The Unseen Hand and Other Plays, Urizen Books (New York, NY), 1981.

Seven Plays by Sam Shepard, Bantam (New York, NY), 1981.

Fool for Love [and] *The Sad Lament of Pecos Bill on the Eve of Killing His Wife,* City Lights Books (San Francisco, CA), 1983.

Fool for Love and Other Plays, Bantam (New York, NY), 1984.

The Unseen Hand and Other Plays, Bantam (New York, NY), 1986.

States of Shock, Far North, [and] Silent Tongue, Vintage (New York, NY), 1993.

The Late Henry Moss, Eyes for Consuela, [and] When the World Was Green, Vintage (New York, NY), 2002.

SCREENPLAYS

(With Michelangelo Antonioni, Tonino Guerra, Fred Graham, and Clare Peploe) *Zabriskie Point* (produced by Metro-Goldwyn-Mayer, 1970), Cappelli (Bologna, Italy), 1970, published with Antonioni's *Red Desert,* Simon & Schuster (New York, NY), 1972.

(With L.M. Kit Carson) *Paris, Texas,* Twentieth Century-Fox, 1984.

Fool for Love (based on Shepard's play of the same title), Golan Globus, 1985.

Far North, Alive, 1988.

Silent Tongue, Trimark, 1992.

OTHER

Hawk Moon: A Book of Short Stories, Poems, and Monologues, Black Sparrow Press (Santa Barbara, CA), 1973.

Rolling Thunder Logbook, Viking (New York, NY), 1977.

Motel Chronicles, City Lights Books (San Francisco, CA), 1982.

(With Joseph Chaikin) *The War in Heaven* (radio drama; first broadcast over WBAI in January, 1985), published with *A Lie of the Mind,* New American Library (New York, NY), 1987.

Joseph Chaikin and Sam Shepard: Letters and Texts, 1972-1984, edited by Barry V. Daniels, New American Library (New York, NY), 1989.

Cruising Paradise: Tales, Knopf (New York, NY), 1996.

Great Dream of Heaven: Stories, Knopf (New York, NY), 2002.

Also author, with Robert Frank, of *Me and My Brother,* and with Murray Mednick, of *Ringaleerio.*

ADAPTATIONS: Fourteen Hundred Thousand was filmed for NET *Playhouse,* 1969; *Blue Bitch* was filmed by the British Broadcasting Corporation (BBC), 1973; *True West* was filmed for the Public Broadcasting Service (PBS) series *American Playhouse.*

SIDELIGHTS: Sam Shepard has devoted more than two decades to a highly eclectic—and critically acclaimed—career in the performing arts. He is considered the pre-eminent literary playwright of his generation. Shepard has also directed plays of his authorship, played drums and guitar in rock bands and jazz ensembles, and acted in major feature films. His movie appearances include leading roles in *The Right Stuff* and *Country,* but acting is a sideline for the man *Newsweek*'s Jack Kroll called "the poet laureate of America's emotional Badlands." Despite his success in Hollywood, Shepard is primarily a playwright whose dramas explore mythic images of modern America in the nation's own eccentric vernacular.

Shepard established himself by writing numerous one-act plays and vignettes for the Off-Off-Broadway experimental theatre. Although his audiences have grown and his plays have been widely produced in America and abroad, he has yet to stage a production on Broadway. *New Republic* contributor Robert Brustein, who found Shepard "one of our most celebrated writers," contends that the lack of attention from Broadway "has not limited Shepard's powers." Brustein added: "Unlike those predecessors who wilted under such conditions, Shepard has flourished in a state of marginality. . . . Shepard's work has been a model of growth and variety." From his early surreal one-acts to his more realistic two-and three-act plays, Shepard has stressed artistic integrity rather than marketability. As a result, Kroll contended, Shepard plays have "overturned theatrical conventions and created a new kind of drama filled with violence, lyricism and an intensely American compound of comic and tragic power."

Shepard has won eleven Obie Awards for best Off-Broadway plays, a Pulitzer Prize for *Buried Child,* and a New York Drama Critics' Circle Award in 1986 for *A Lie of the Mind.* Richard A. Davis wrote in *Plays and Players* magazine that Shepard has both "a tremendous ability to make words bring the imagination of an audience to life" and "a talent for creating with words alone extremely believable emotional experiences."

According to *Village Voice* correspondent Michael Feingold, Shepard "has the real playwright's gift of habitually transposing his feelings and visions into drama as a mere matter of praxis. He speaks through the theatre as naturally as most of us speak through the telephone." Shepard's plays use modern idiomatic language as well as such prevailing themes of American popular culture, particularly the American West, Hollywood and the rock-and-roll industry. "No one knows better than Sam Shepard that the true American West is gone forever," wrote Frank Rich in the *New York Times,* "but there may be no writer alive more gifted at reinventing it out of pure literary air."

Shepard's modern cowboys, drifters, farmers, and other offspring of the frontier era yearn for a purer past that may never have existed as they quarrel with family members. *Journal of Popular Culture* contributor George Stambolian maintained that, like many of his fellow playwrights, Shepard "knows that the old frontier myths of America's youth are no longer a valid expression of our modern anxieties, even though they continue to influence our thoughts." Stambolian said Shepard seeks "a new mythology that will encompass all the diverse figures of our cultural history together with the psychological and social conditions they represent. . . . Shepard's greatest contribution to a new American mythology may well be his elaboration of a new myth of the modern artist."

Sam Shepard's theater is marked by "a spirit of comedy that tosses and turns in a bed of revulsion," as Richard Eder wrote in the *New York Times.* Malicious mischief and comic mayhem intensify Shepard's tragic vision; in many of his plays, inventive dialogue supplements vigorous action. As David Richards wrote in the *Washington Post,* actors and directors "respond to the slam-bang potential in [Shepard's] scripts, which allows them to go for broke, trash the furniture, and generally shred the scenery. Whatever else you've got, you've got a wild and wooly fight on your hands." The theatrical fisticuffs, sometimes physical, sometimes verbal, is on the overriding American musical rhythms. *New York Times* theatre critic Clive Barnes said: "Mr. Shepard writes mythic plays in American jazz-poetry. . . . He is trying to express truths wrapped up in legends and with the kind of symbolism you often find nowadays in pop music. His command of language is daring and inventive—some of the words sound new, and quite a few of them actually are." Richard L. Homan makes a similar point in *Critical Quarterly:* "Shepard's vivid use of language and flair for fantasy have suggested something less like drama and more like poetry in some unfamiliar oral tradition."

While Shepard's subjects—nostalgia, power struggles, family tensions—may seem simple at first, his plays remain "extraordinarily resistant to thematic exegesis," Richard Gilman wrote in his introduction to *Seven Plays by Sam Shepard.* Gilman added that standard criticism of Shepard is inadequate because the dramatist "slips out of all the categories" and seems to have come "out of no literary or theatrical tradition at all but precisely for the breakdown or absence—on the level of art if not of commerce—of all such traditions in America." Gilman added that several of the plays "seem like fragments, chunks of various sizes thrown out from some mother lode of urgent and heterogeneous imagination in which [Shepard] has scrabbled with pick, shovel, gunbutt and hands. The reason so many of them seem incomplete is that they lack the clear boundaries as artifact, the internal order, the progress toward a denouement . . . and the consistency of tone and procedure that ordinarily characterize good drama."

In *American Dreams: The Imagination of Sam Shepard,* Michael Earley said Shepard "seems to have forged a whole new kind of American play that has yet to receive adequate reckoning." Earley called the playwright "a true American primitive, a literary naif coursing the stage of American drama as if for the first time" who brings to his work "a liberating interplay of word, theme and image that has always been the hallmark of the romantic impulse. His plays don't work like plays in the traditional sense but more like romances, where the imaginary landscape (his version of America) is so remote and open that it allows for the depiction of legend, adventure, and even the supernatural." *Partisan Review* contributor Ross Wetzsteon contended that viewers respond to Shepard's plays "not by interpreting their plots or analyzing their characters or dissecting their themes, but simply by experiencing their resonance. . . . Shepard's arias seek to soar into a disembodied freedom, to create emotions beyond rational structure, to induce in both player and audience a trancelike state of grace."

Shepard, born in Fort Sheridan, Illinois, was given the name his forebears had used for six generations—Samuel Shepard Rogers. His father was a career army officer, so as a youngster Shepard moved from base to base in the United States and even spent some time in Guam. When Shepard's father retired from the service, the family settled on a ranch in Duarte, California, where they grew avocados and raised sheep. Although the livelihood was precarious, Shepard enjoyed the atmosphere on the ranch and liked working with horses and other animals. Influenced by his father's interest in Dixieland jazz, Shepard gravitated to music; he began to play the drums and started what *Dictionary of Literary Biography* contributor David W. Engel called "his lifelong involvement with rock-and-roll music and its subculture." He graduated from Duarte High School in 1960 and spent one year studying agricultural science at the local junior college, but his family situation deteriorated as his father began drinking excessively. Shepard fled by joining a touring theatrical group called the Bishop's Company Repertory Players. At age nineteen, he found himself in New York, determined to seek his fortune with only a few months' acting experience.

By chance Shepard encountered a high school friend in New York, Charles Mingus, Jr., son of the renowned jazz musician. Mingus found Shepard a job at The Village Gate, a jazz club, and the two young men became roommates. While working at The Village Gate, Shepard met Ralph Cook, founder of the Off-Off-Broadway company Theatre Genesis. Cook encouraged Shepard to write plays, and Shepard produced *Cowboys* and *The Rock Garden,* two one-acts that became part of the first Theatre Genesis show at St. Mark Church in-the-Bowery. Though Engel notes that most of the critics regarded Shepard's first two works as "bad imitations of Beckett," the *Village Voice* columnist "gave the plays a rave review." Shepard began to rapidly turn out one-act pieces, many performed Off-Off-Broadway; they attracted a cult following within that theatrical circuit. Shepard also continued his association with jazz and rock music, incorporating the rhythms into his dialogue and including musical riffs in the scripts. He reminisced about his early career in *New York* magazine: "When I arrived in New York there was this environment of *art* going on. I mean, it was really tangible. And you were right *in* the thing, especially on the Lower East Side. La Mama, Theatre Genesis, . . . all those theaters were just starting. So that was a great coincidence. I had a place to go and put something on without having to go through a producer or go through the commercial network. All of that was in response to the tightness of Broadway and Off-Broadway, where you couldn't get a play done."

Shepard told *New York* he did his early work hastily. "There wasn't much rewriting done," he said. "I had this whole attitude toward that work that it was somehow violating it to go back and rework it. . . . Why spend the time rewriting when there was another one to do?" Kroll said: "The true artist starts with his obsessions, then makes them ours as well. The very young Sam Shepard exploded his obsessions like firecrackers; in his crazy, brilliant early plays he was escaping his demons, not speaking to ours." *New York Times* correspondent Mel Gussow, who has monitored Shepard's career, calls the playwright's early works "a series of mystical epics (on both a large and small scale) mixing figures from folklore with visitors from the outer space of fantasy fiction." The Shepard one-acts, still frequently performed at theatre festivals and universities, juxtapose visual and verbal images with dramatic collage. Stambolian said the technique "forces the spectator to view the surface, so to speak, from behind, from within the imagination that conceived it."

"Shepard draws much of his material from popular culture sources such as B-grade westerns, sci-fi and horror films, popular folklore, country and rock music and murder-mysteries," *Modern Drama* critic Charles R.

Bachman wrote. "In his best work he transforms the original stereotyped characters and situations into an imaginative, linguistically brilliant, quasi-surrealistic chemistry of text and stage presentation which is original and authentically his own." According to Stanley Kauffmann in the *New Republic,* the deliberate use of movie types "is part of Shepard's general method: the language and music of rock, spaceman fantasies, Wild West fantasies, gangster fantasies—pop-culture forms that he uses as building blocks, rituals of contemporary religion to heighten communion."

Some critics have dismissed Shepard's early work as undisciplined and obscure. *Massachusetts Review* essayist David Madden found the plays "mired in swampy attitudes toward Mom and Dad. Their main line of reasoning seems to be that if Mom and Dad's middle class values are false, that if they and the institutions they uphold are complacent and indifferent, the only alternative is some form of outlaw behavior or ideology." Other national drama critics have evaluated the one-act plays quite differently. In the *New York Review of Books,* Robert Mazzocco wrote: "If one is content to follow this hard-nosed, drug-induced, pop-flavored style, this perpetual retuning of old genres and old myths, one encounters, finally, a profuse and unique panorama of where we are now and where we have been." Stambolian said that Shepard "is in fact showing to what extent the mind, and particularly the modern American mind, can become and has become entrapped by its own verbal and imaginative creations." And, according to Barnes, Shepard "is so sweetly unserious about his plays, and so desperately serious about what he is saying. . . . There is more in them than meets the mind. They are very easy to be funny about, yet they linger oddly in the imagination." In his own assessment of his first plays, Shepard told *New York* he thinks of them as "survival kits, in a way. They were explosions that were coming out of some kind of inner turmoil in me that I didn't understand at all. There are areas in some of them that are still mysterious to me."

Shepard's first major production, *Operation Sidewinder,* premiered at the Vivian Beaumont Theatre in 1970. Engel described the two-act play as "an excellent example of how [Shepard] combines the roles of poet, musician, and playwright." Set in the Hopi Indian country of the American Southwest, *Operation Sidewinder* follows the attempts to control a huge, mechanical rattlesnake originally designed to trace unidentified flying objects. Air force commandos, Hopi snake-worshippers, black power activists, and even a beautiful but foolish blonde named Honey try to use the computerized sidewinder for their own ends. Engel notes that the "playful and satiric action is amplified by Shepard's production techniques. He assaults the senses of the audience by the use of intense sound and lights, and by various chants and songs." Shepard himself performed music in the play with a rock band, the Holy Modal Rounders. Although Engel said "the psychological resonance of stylized production, and not its sociological satire, is Shepard's aim," some critics called the work overly moralistic and stylistically confusing. "The difficulty of the play is in the writing," Barnes said. "The symbolic progression, while clearly charting the progress to atomic holocaust, is altogether too symbolic." Kroll maintains that the play's energy "has congealed in a half-slick pop machine with the feel of celluloid and the clackey sound of doctrinaire contemporaneity." Martin Gottfried viewed the play differently in *Women's Wear Daily.* "Everything about Sam Shepard's *Operation Sidewinder* is important to our theatre," Gottfried wrote. "More than any recent major production, it is built upon exactly the style and the mentality energizing the youth movement in America today."

In 1971 Shepard took his wife and infant son and moved to England. Having long experimented with drugs, the playwright sought escape from the abusive patterns he saw destroying fellow artists in New York. He also hoped to become more involved with rock music, still a central obsession. He did not accomplish that goal, but as Engel noted, he did "write and produce some of his finest works" while living in London. Gussow wrote: "As the author became recognized as an artist and found himself courted by such unearthly powers as Hollywood, he went through a Faustian phase. The result was a series of plays about art and the seduction of the artist." Plays such as *Angel City, Geography of a Horse Dreamer,* and *The Tooth of Crime* explore various aspects of the artist/visionary's dilemma when faced with public tastes or corporate profit-taking. Mazzocco felt that at this stage in his career Shepard chose to examine "not so much in political or economic parallels as in those of domination and submission, the nature of power in America. Or, more precisely, the duplicitous nature of 'success' and 'failure,' where it's implied that a failure of nerve and not that of a 'life' is at the basis of both." The playwright also discovered, as Richard A. Davis wrote, that "it is only within the individual mind that one finds his 'shelter' from the world; and even this shelter is not permanent, for the mind and body are tied together. To a great extent, Shepard's dramas have all been caught in this continual exploration of the same human problem."

The Tooth of Crime further strengthened Shepard's literary reputation. A two-act study of rock-and-roll stars who fight to gain status and "turf," the play "depicts a society which worships raw power," in Engel's words. London *Times* reviewer Irving Wardle wrote: "Its central battle to the death between an aging superstar and a young pretender to his throne is as timeless as a myth . . . and . . . has proved a durably amazing reflection of the West Coast scene. If any classic has emerged from the last 20 years of the American experimental theatre, this is it."

"Moving freely from gangster movies of the 40's to punk rock of the 70's, Mr. Shepard speaks in a language that is vividly idiomatic," Gussow wrote. Mazzocco called *The Tooth of Crime* "undoubtedly the quintessential Shepard play" and "a dazzlingly corrosive work . . . one of the most original achievements in contemporary theater. It is also the play that best illustrates the various facets—at once highly eclectic and highly singular—of [Shepard's] genius."

The Tooth of Crime, represented a stylistic departure for Shepard. Bachman contended that the work "utilizes . . . the traditional dramatic values of taut, disciplined structure, vivid and consistent characterization, and crescendo of suspense." The transition, however, from modernist to traditional style has hardly been smooth. According to Richard L. Homan in *Critical Quarterly,* Shepard has learned "to express the outrage, which gave rise to the experimental theatre, in plays which work through realistic conventions to challenge our everyday sense of reality." Shepard told *New York* that he sees a growing emphasis on character in his plays since 1972. "When I started writing," he said, "I wasn't interested in character at all. In fact, I thought it was useless, old-fashioned, stuck in a certain way. . . . I preferred a character that was constantly unidentifiable, shifting through the actor, so that the actor could almost play anything, and the audience was never expected to identify with the character. . . . But I had broken away from the idea of character without understanding it." Shepard's more recent plays explore characters—especially idiosyncratic and eccentric ones—for dramatic effect.

Gussow believed Shepard's new phase of writing reflects the changes in his own life. The playwright increasingly seeks to expose "the erosion and the conflagration of the ill-American family," Gussow said. Mazzocco said Shepard has "turned from the game to the trap, from the trail back to the hearth, from warfare in a 'buddy culture' to warfare among kith and kin." Four of Shepard's plays, *Buried Child, Curse of the Starving Class, True West,* and *A Lie of the Mind,* document in scenes of black humor the peculiar savagery of modern American family life. *New York Times* contributor Benedict Nightingale found these plays peopled by a "legion of the lost," whose "essential tragedy . . . seems . . . to be that they are simultaneously searching for things that are incompatible and possibly not attainable anyway: excitement and security, the exhilaration of self-fulfillment and a sense of belonging, freedom and roots."

Buried Child and *A Lie of the Mind,* separated by seven years, examine disturbed families. In *Buried Child,* David Richards wrote in the *Washington Post,* Shepard "delivers a requiem for America, land of the surreal and home of the crazed. . . . Beyond the white frame farmhouse that contains the evening's action, the amber waves of grain mask a dark secret. The fruited plain is rotting and the purple mountain's majesty is like a bad bruise on the landscape." In *Buried Child,* son Vince arrives at his midwestern farm home after a long absence. A dangerous cast of relatives confronts him, harboring secrets of incest and murder. Richard Christiansen, in the *Chicago Tribune,* called the Pulitzer Prize-winning play "a Norman Rockwell portrait created for *Mad Magazine,* a scene from America's heartland that reeks with 'the stench of sin.'" Similarly, *A Lie of the Mind* presents a tale of "interior domestic violence, the damage that one does to filial, fraternal and marital bonds—and the love that lingers in the air after the havoc has run its natural course," Gussow wrote. In that work, two families are galvanized into violence when a jealous husband beats his wife, almost fatally. *A Lie of the Mind* won the New York Drama Critics' Circle Award for best new Off-Broadway play of 1985, and Shepard himself directed the original production.

Fool for Love, which Shepard also directed, is probably his best-known work. The one-act piece has been produced for the stage and has also been made into a feature film in which Shepard starred. *Fool for Love* alternates submission and rejection between two lovers who may also be half-brother and half-sister. New York *Daily News* critic Douglas Watt said the ninety-minute, nonstop drama "is Sam Shepard's purest and most beautiful play. An aching love story of classical symmetry, it is . . . like watching the division of an amoeba in reverse, ending with a perfect whole." *Fool for Love,* wrote *New York Times* reviewer Frank Rich, "is a western for our time. We watch a pair of figurative gunslingers fight to the finish—not with bullets, but with piercing words that give ballast to the weight of a nation's buried dreams. . . . As Shepard's people race verbally through the debris of the West, they search for the identities and familial roots that have disappeared with the landscape of legend." In the *New Republic,*

Brustein found "nothing very thick or complicated about either the characters or the plot" and a lack of resolution to the play's ending. Still, the critic concluded that *Fool for Love* is "not so much a text as a legend, not so much a play as a scenario for stage choreography, and under the miraculous direction of the playwright, each moment is rich with balletic nuances."

Since 1978 Shepard has taken a major movie role each year, and was nominated for an Academy Award for his performance in *The Right Stuff.* He has, despite his discomfort with the image, assumed a certain matinee idol status. "Shepard did not become famous by writing plays," Stephen Fay wrote in *Vogue.* "Like it or not, acting [has] made him a celebrity." Shepard does *not* like to be considered a screen celebrity; his attitude toward film work is ambivalent, and public scrutiny has made him a recluse. He told *New York:* "There's a definite fear about being diminished through film. It's very easy to do too much of it, to a point where you're lost. Image-making is really what film acting is about. It's image-making, as opposed to character-making, and in some cases it's not true." But *Film Comment* essayist David Thomson contended that Shepard's long-standing fascination with movies lures him into that sort of work. "His sternness wants to be tested against their decadence," Thomson wrote. "His restraint struggles to reconcile a simultaneous contempt and need for movies. The uneasiness hovers between passion and foolishness, between the lack of skill and a monolith of intractability."

Shepard has often contradicted his own persona. In *Country,* for instance, he portrays a farmer who wilts under pressure when threatened with foreclosure, and in *Fool for Love* he appears as a womanizing, luckless rodeo rider. According to Thomson, Shepard brings the same sort of integrity to his movie roles that he brings to his writing. "For five years or so," Thomson wrote, "he has been prowling around the house of cinema, coming in a little way, armored with disdain, slipping out, but coming back, as if it intrigued and tempted his large talent. And movies need him. . . . But as with all prowlers, there remains a doubt as to whether this roaming, wolfen, mongrel lurcher wants to live in the house or tear it to pieces with his jaws and then howl at the desert moon, queen of dead worlds." Shepard told *New York:* "I'm a writer. The more I act, the more resistance I have to it. Now it seems to me that being an actor in films is like being sentenced to a trailer for twelve weeks."

In 1983, German director Wim Wenders commissioned Shepard to write a screenplay based loosely on the playwright's book *Motel Chronicles.* The resulting work, *Paris, Texas,* was a unanimous winner of the Golden Palm Award at the 1984 Cannes Film Festival. The film recasts many of Shepard's central concerns—broken families, the myth of the loner, and the elegy for the old West—in a story of reunion between a father and a son. In *People* magazine, Peter Travers called *Paris, Texas* the "most disturbing film ever about the roots of family relationships. Shepard's words and Wenders' images blend in a magical poetry." *New York* reviewer David Denby found the film "a lifeless art-world hallucination—a movie composed entirely of self-conscious flourishes," but most other critics praised the work.

For all his work in other media, Shepard is still most highly regarded for his playwriting. "He is indeed an original," wrote Edith Oliver in the *New Yorker,* "but it might be pointed out that the qualities that make him so valuable are the enduring ones—good writing, wit, dramatic invention, and the ability to create characters." Stambolian added, "It is certain that in a society drifting rapidly into the escapism of a permanent, and often instant, nostalgia, Shepard's plays are a sign of artistic health and awareness, and are, therefore, worthy of our attention." John Lahr elaborated on this idea in *Plays and Players:* "Shepard, who has put himself outside the killing commercial climate of American life and theatre for the last few years, seems to be saying . . . that the only real geography is internal." And, as *New York Times* correspondent Walter Kerr concludes, "everyone's got to admire [Shepard's] steadfast insistence on pursuing the vision in his head."

Shepard himself sees room for growth in his writing. "I guess I'm always hoping for one play that will end my need to write plays," he told *Vogue.* "Sort of the definitive piece, but it never happens. There's always disappointment, something missing, some level that hasn't been touched, and the more you write the more you struggle, even if you are riding a wave of inspiration. And if the piece does touch something, you always know you haven't got to the depths of certain emotional territory. So you go out and try another one." According to *New Statesman* reviewer Benedict Nightingale, "we can rely on [Shepard] to continue bringing a distinctively American eye, ear and intelligence to the diagnosis of what are, if you think about it, universal anxieties."

The playwright told the *New York Times* that he has no plans to stop. "I want to do the work that fascinates me," he said.

BIOGRAPHICAL AND CRITICAL SOURCES:

BOOKS

Almanac of Famous People, 6th edition, Thomson Gale (Detroit, MI), 1998.

Auerbach, Doris, *Sam Shepard, Arthur Kopit, and the Off Broadway Theater,* Twayne (Boston, MA), 1982.

Banham, Martin, editor, *The Cambridge Guide to World Theatre,* Cambridge University Press (New York, NY), 1988.

Bowman, John S., editor, *Cambridge Dictionary of American Biography,* Cambridge University Press (New York, NY), 1996.

Contemporary Dramatists, 6th edition, St. James (Detroit, MI), 1999.

Contemporary Literary Criticism, Thomson Gale (Detroit, MI), Volume 4, 1975, Volume 6, 1976, Volume 17, 1981, Volume 34, 1985, Volume 41, 1987, Volume 44, 1987.

Contemporary Theatre, Film, and Television, Volume 25, Thomson Gale (Detroit, MI), 2000,

Dictionary of Literary Biography, Volume 8: *Twentieth-Century American Dramatists,* 1981, Volume 212: *Twentieth-Century American Western Writers, Second Series,* 1999, Thomson Gale (Detroit, MI).

Drabble, Margaret, editor, *The Oxford Companion to English Literature,* 6th edition, Oxford University Press (New York, NY), 2000.

Drama Criticism, Volume 5, Thomson Gale (Detroit, MI), 1995.

Drama for Students, Volume 14, Greg Barnhisel, "Critical Essay on *Curse of the Starving Class,*" Thomson Gale (Detroit, MI), 2002.

Earl Blackwell's Celebrity Register 1990, Thomson Gale (Detroit, MI), 1990.

Encyclopedia of World Biography, 2nd edition, Thomson Gale (Detroit, MI), 1998.

Encyclopedia of World Literature in the 20th Century, Volume 4, St. James (Detroit, MI), 1999.

Graham, Laura, *Sam Shepard: Theme, Image, and the Director,* Lang (New York, NY), 1995.

Greasley, Philip, editor, *Dictionary of Midwestern Literature,* Volume 1: *The Authors,* Indiana University Press (Bloomington, IN), 2001.

Hart, James D., editor, *The Oxford Companion to American Literature,* 6th edition, Oxford University Press (New York, NY), 1995.

International Dictionary of Films and Filmmakers, Volume 3: *Actors and Actresses,* St. James (Detroit, MI), 1996.

International Dictionary of Theatre, Volume 2: *Playwrights,* St. James (Detroit, MI), 1993.

Magill, Frank N., editor, *Critical Survey of Drama,* revised edition, Volume 6, Salem Press (Pasadena, CA), 1994.

Magill, Frank N., editor, *Cyclopedia of World Authors,* revised 3rd edition, Volume 5, Salem Press (Pasadena, CA), 1997.

Magill, Frank N., editor, *Magill's Survey of American Literature,* Volume 5, Marshall Cavendish (New York, NY), 1991.

Marranca, Bonnie, editor, *American Dramas: The Imagination of Sam Shepard,* Performing Arts Journal Publications (New York, NY), 1981.

Mottram, Ron, *Inner Landscapes: The Theater of Sam Shepard,* University of Missouri Press (Columbia, MO), 1984.

Newsmakers 1996, Issue 4, Thomson Gale (Detroit, MI), 1996.

New York Times Theatre Reviews, New York Times Company (New York, NY), 1971.

Oumano, Ellen, *Sam Shepard: The Life and Work of an American Dreamer,* St. Martin's Press (New York, NY), 1986.

Parker, Peter, editor, *A Reader's Guide to Twentieth-Century Writers,* Oxford University Press (New York, NY), 1996.

Patraka, Vivian M., and Siegel, Mark, *Sam Shepard,* Boise State University (Boise, ID), 1985.

Peck, David, editor, *Identities and Issues in Literature,* Volume 3, Salem Press (Pasadena, CA), 1997.

Riggs, Thomas, editor, *Reference Guide to American Literature,* 4th edition, St. James (Detroit, MI), 2000.

St. James Encyclopedia of Popular Culture, St. James (Detroit, MI), 2000.

Schlueter, Paul and June, editors, *Modern American Literature,* Volume 5, second supplement to the 4th edition, *A Library of Literary Criticism,* Continuum (New York, NY), 1985.

Serafin, Steven R., editor, *Encyclopedia of American Literature,* Continuum (New York, NY), 1999.

Shepard, Sam, *Five Plays by Sam Shepard,* Bobbs-Merrill (Indianapolis, IN), 1967.

Shepard, Sam, *Mad Dog Blues and Other Plays,* Winter House, 1972.

Shepard, Sam, *Seven Plays by Sam Shepard,* Bantam (New York, NY), 1981.

Shewey, Don, *Sam Shepard,* Dell (New York, NY), 1985.

Tucker, Martin, editor, *Modern American Literature,* Volume 6, supplement to the 4th edition, *A Library of Literary Criticism,* Continuum (New York, NY), 1985.

Tucker, Martin, editor, *Literary Exile in the Twentieth Century: An Analysis and Biographical Dictionary,* Greenwood (New York, NY), 1991.

Trussler, Simon, *File on Shepard,* Methuen (London, England), 1989.

Wallflower Critical Guide to Contemporary North American Directors, Columbia University Press (New York, NY), 2001.

Weales, Gerald, *The Jumping-Off Place: American Drama in the 1960's,* Macmillan (New York, NY), 1969.

PERIODICALS

After Dark, June, 1975.

America, November 5, 1983.

American Film, October, 1984.

American Theatre, October, 2000, "Alma Pater," p. 40.

Back Stage, May 3, 1996, Daniel Sheward, review of *Buried Child,* p. 48; May 16, 1997, Peter Shaughnessy, review of *Curse of the Starving Class,* p. 64; March 24, 2000, Eric Grode, review of *True West,* p. 64; October 26, 2001, David Sheward, review of *The Late Henry Moss,* p. 56.

Back Stage West, September 28, 2000, Kristina Mannion, review of *Simpatico,* p. 18; January 18, 2001, Michael Green, review of *Fool for Love,* p. 14.

Booklist, April 15, 1996, Donna Seaman, review of *Cruising Paradise,* p. 1422.

Books, December, 1997, review of *Cruising Paradise,* p. 20.

Canadian Forum, March, 1985.

Chicago Tribune, December 15, 1978; December 7, 1979; July 2, 1980; April 23, 1982; December 16, 1985; December 18, 1985.

Christian Century, November 21, 1984.

Christian Science Monitor, June 9, 1983.

Commonweal, June 14, 1968; May 8, 1970; November 30, 1984; July 12, 1991.

Cosmopolitan, January, 1985.

Critical Quarterly, spring, 1982.

Cue, April 11, 1970; July 18, 1970; February 17, 1973; March 31, 1973; March 18, 1978.

Daily News (New York), May 27, 1983.

Drama, winter, 1965; spring, 1969; autumn, 1973; summer, 1976.

Educational Theatre Journal, October, 1977.

Entertainment Weekly, May 31, 1996, Margot Mifflin, review of *Cruising Paradise,* p. 54.

Esquire, February, 1980; November, 1988.

Film Comment, November-December, 1983; June, 1984.

Globe and Mail (Toronto), December 21, 1985.

Guardian, February 20, 1974.

Harper's Bazaar, September, 1985; November, 1994, p. 98.

Hollywood Reporter, August 12, 2002, Barry Garron, review of *True West,* pp. 33-34.

Hudson Review, spring, 1979; spring, 1984.

Interview, September, 1988.

Journal of Popular Culture, spring, 1974.

Kirkus Reviews, March 15, 1996, review of *Cruising Paradise,* p. 403; August 1, 2002, review of *Great Dream of Heaven,* p. 1071.

Kliatt, November, 1996, review of *Cruising Paradise* (audio recording), p. 47.

Library Journal, May 15, 1996, review of *Cruising Paradise* (audio recording), p. 100; June 15, 1996, review of *Cruising Paradise,* p. 95, reviews of *Simpatico* and *The Unseen Hand and Other Plays,* p. 97.

Listener, September 26, 1974.

London Magazine, December, 1968.

Los Angeles Magazine, March, 1988.

Los Angeles Times, May 12, 1982; February 12, 1983; October 1, 1983; December 12, 1983; March 14, 1984; November 16, 1984; September 25, 1985; December 6, 1985; January 25, 1986; April 11, 1986; August 11, 1986.

Los Angeles Times Book Review, July 28, 1996, review of *Cruising Paradise,* p. 6.

Maclean's, October 29, 1984; December 24, 1984; January 13, 1986; January 18, 1988; November 21, 1988; October 2, 2000, "Actor, Playwright, Cowboy," p. 74.

Mademoiselle, March, 1985.

Massachusetts Review, autumn, 1967.

Modern Drama, December, 1976, March, 1979; March, 1981.

Ms., November, 1984.

Nation, February 21, 1966; April 4, 1966; March 30, 1970; March 26, 1973; May 3, 1975; January 10, 1976; February 24, 1979; January 31, 1981; October 27, 1984; December 29, 1984; January 5, 1985; January 11, 1986; February 22, 1986.

New Leader, April 10, 1967.

New Republic, April 21, 1973; April 8, 1978; January 31, 1981; June 27, 1983; October 29, 1984; December 3, 1984; December 23, 1985; September 29, 1986; February 2, 1987; November 28, 1988, Stanley Kauffmann, review of *Far North,* pp. 22-23; July 15, 1995, p. 27.

New Statesman, August 24, 1984; October 12, 1984; March 1, 1985; July 4, 1986; October 30, 1987; February 9, 1990; September 6, 1991; July 23, 2001, Katherine Duncan-Jones, "A Little Legend about Love" (review of *A Lie of the Mind*), p. 45.

Newsweek, March 23, 1970; January 5, 1981; June 6, 1983; October 1, 1984; November 19, 1984; November 11, 1985; December 16, 1985.

New York, November 27, 1978; February 19, 1979; June 13, 1983; December 5, 1983; October 15, 1984; November 19, 1984; December 9, 1985; May 27, 1991; May 13, 1996, p. 64.

New Yorker, May 11, 1968; March 21, 1970; March 17, 1973; May 5, 1975; December 22, 1975; November 29, 1982; October 1, 1984; September 2, 1985; January 27, 1986; December 15, 1986; June 3, 1991; April 22, 1996, p. 84; May 27, 1996, p. 138.

New York Post, May 27, 1983.

New York Review of Books, April 6, 1967; May 9, 1985.

New York Times, February 11, 1965; April 13, 1966; May 28, 1968; April 13, 1969; March 15, 1970; April 2, 1970; March 8, 1971; June 28, 1971; March 7, 1973; September 17, 1977; March 3, 1978; April 28, 1978; November 7, 1978; December 10, 1978; February 2, 1979; March 4, 1979; March 14, 1979; April 17, 1979; June 3, 1979; February 7, 1980; March 12, 1980; December 24, 1980; November 9, 1981; January 6, 1982; October 18, 1982; March 2, 1983; May 27, 1983; June 5, 1983; September 20, 1983; September 25, 1983; May 27, 1983; January 29, 1984; September 28, 1984; September 30, 1984; November 9, 1984; November 14, 1984; November 18, 1984; November 22, 1984; November 29, 1984; November 30, 1984; August 15, 1985; October 1, 1985; October 4, 1985; November 14, 1985; December 1, 1985; December 15, 1985; January 12, 1986; January 21, 1986; April 13, 1986; May 17, 1996, review of *Cruising Paradise,* p. B12; June 16, 1996, review of *Buried Child,* p. H5.

New York Times Book Review, June 23, 1996, review of *Cruising Paradise,* p. 23; September 7, 1997, review of *Cruising Paradise,* p. 40.

Partisan Review, Volume XLI, number 2, 1974; Volume XLIX, number 2, 1982.

People, December 26, 1983; January 2, 1984; October 15, 1984; November 5, 1984; December 9, 1985; January 6, 1986; June 10, 1996, p. 15; November 14, 1988, Peter Travers, review of *Far North,* p. 24.

Plays and Players, June, 1970; October-November, 1971; April, 1974; May, 1974; November, 1974; April, 1979.

Publishers Weekly, April 1, 1996, review of *Cruising Paradise,* p. 38; April 15, 1996, review of *Cruising Paradise,* p. 48; September 9, 2002, review of *Great Dream of Heaven,* pp. 40-41.

Quill & Quire, February, 1980.

Rolling Stone, August 11, 1977; December 18, 1986; February 24, 1994.

Saturday Review, December, 1984.

Spectator, November 16, 1996, review of *Cruising Paradise,* p. 51.

Theatre Journal, March, 1984.

Theatre Quarterly, August, 1974.

Time, November 27, 1972; June 6, 1983; October 8, 1984; August 12, 1985; December 2, 1985; December 16, 1985; November 7, 1988, Richard Corliss, review of *Far North,* pp. 108-109; May 20, 1996, Richard Zoglin, review of *Buried Child,* p. 77.

Times (London), September 24, 1983; September 26, 1983; October 6, 1984; January 7, 1986.

Times Literary Supplement, November 24, 1978; March 1, 1985; November 22, 1996, review of *Cruising Paradise,* p. 22.

Variety, September 14, 1988; May 20, 1991; February 8, 1993; September 19, 1994; May 5, 1997, Robert L. Daniels, review of *Curse of the Starving Class,* p. 213; February 16, 1998, Greg Evans, review of *Eyes for Consuela,* p. 68; July 16, 2001, Matt Wolf, review of *A Lie of the Mind,* p 25.

Village Voice, April 4, 1977; August 15, 1977; February 12, 1979.

Vogue, February, 1984; February, 1985.

Washington Post, January 14, 1979; June 2, 1979; March 5, 1983; April 22, 1983; October 23, 1983; April 12, 1985; October 15, 1985; May 1, 1986; September 12, 1986.

Western American Literature, fall, 1989, review of *True West,* p. 225.

Women's Wear Daily, March 13, 1970; May 27, 1983.

World Literature Today, winter, 1997, review of *Cruising Paradise,* p. 152.

ONLINE

Moonstruck Drama Bookstore Web site, http://www.imagi-nation.com/moonstruck/ (March 5, 2003), biography of Sam Shepard.

Pegasos Web site, http://www.kirjasto.sci.fi/ (March 5, 2003), biography of Sam Shepard.

Thespian Net Web site, http://www.thespiannet.com/ (March 5, 2003), biography of Sam Shepard.

* * *

SHEPHERD, Michael
See LUDLUM, Robert

* * *

SHIELDS, Carol 1935-2003
(Carol Ann Shields)

PERSONAL: Born June 2, 1935, in Oak Park, IL; died from complications from breast cancer, July 16, 2003, in Victoria, British Columbia, Canada; daughter of Robert E. and Inez (Selgren) Warner; married Donald Hugh Shields (a professor), July 20, 1957; children: John, Anne, Catherine, Margaret, Sara. *Education:* Hanover College, B.A., 1957; University of Ottawa, M.A., 1975.

CAREER: Canadian Slavonic Papers, Ottawa, Ontario, editorial assistant, 1972-74; writer, 1974-2003; University of Manitoba, professor, 1980-2000; Chancellor University of Winnipeg, 1996-2000.

MEMBER: Writers' Union of Canada, Writers Guild of Manitoba, PEN, Jane Austen Society, Royal Society of Canada.

AWARDS, HONORS: Winner of young writers' contest sponsored by Canadian Broadcasting Corp. (CBC), 1965; Canada Council grants, 1972, 1974, 1976; fiction prize from Canadian Authors Association, 1976, for *Small Ceremonies;* CBC Prize for Drama, 1983; National Magazine Award, 1984, 1985; Arthur Ellis Award, 1988; Marian Engel Award, 1990; Governor General's Award for English-language fiction, National Book Critics Circle Award for fiction, 1994, and Pulitzer Prize for fiction, 1995, all for *The Stone Diaries;* Orange Prize, 1998, for *Larry's Party;* Guggenheim fellow, 1999; Chevalier de l'Ordre des Arts et des Lettres (France), 2000; shortlisted for Booker Prize and James Tait Black Memorial Prize for fiction, both 2002, and Orange Prize for fiction nomination, 2003, all for *Unless;* Charles Taylor Prize for literary nonfiction, 2002, for *Jane Austen;* named Author of the Year, Book Expo Canada, 2003. Honorary doctorates from University of Ottawa, 1995; Hanover College, 1996; University of Winnipeg, 1996; Queen's University, 1996; University of British Columbia, 1997; Concordia University, 1997; University of Toronto, 1998; University of Western Ontario, 1998; Carleton University, 2000; Mount St. Vincent University, 2000; and Wilfrid Laurier University, 2000.

WRITINGS:

Others (poetry), Borealis Press (Ottawa, Ontario, Canada), 1972.

Intersect (poetry), Borealis Press (Ottawa, Ontario, Canada), 1974.

Susanna Moodie: Voice and Vision (criticism), Borealis Press (Ottawa, Ontario, Canada), 1976.

Small Ceremonies (novel), McGraw-Hill (New York, NY), 1976, reprinted, Penguin (New York, NY), 1996.

The Box Garden (novel), McGraw-Hill (New York, NY), 1977, reprinted, Penguin (New York, NY), 1996.

Happenstance (novel; also see below), McGraw-Hill (New York, NY), 1980.

A Fairly Conventional Woman (novel; also see below), Macmillan (Toronto, Ontario, Canada), 1982.

Various Miracles (short stories), Stoddart (Don Mills, Canada), 1985, Penguin (New York, NY), 1989.

Swann: A Mystery (novel), General, 1987, Viking (New York, NY), 1989.

The Orange Fish (short stories), Random House (Toronto, Ontario, Canada), 1989, Viking (New York, NY), 1990.

Departures and Arrivals, Blizzard (Winnipeg, Ontario, Canada), 1990.

(With Blanche Howard) *A Celibate Season* (novel), Coteau (Regina, Canada), 1991, Penguin (New York, NY), 1999.

The Republic of Love (novel), Viking (New York, NY), 1992.

Coming to Canada (poetry), Carleton University Press (Ottawa, Canada), 1992.

Happenstance (contains the novels *Happenstance* and *A Fairly Conventional Woman*), Random House (Toronto, Ontario, Canada), 1993, Viking, 1994.

The Stone Diaries (novel), Random House (Toronto, Ontario, Canada), 1993, Viking (New York, NY), 1994.

Thirteen Hands (drama), Blizzard (Winnipeg, Ontario, Canada), 1993.

(With Catherine Shields) *Fashion, Power, Guilt, and the Charity of Families,* Blizzard (Winnipeg, Ontario, Canada), 1995.

Mary Swann, Fourth Estate (London, England), 1996.

Larry's Party (novel), Viking (New York, NY), 1997.

(With David Williamson) *Anniversary* (play), Blizzard (Winnipeg, Ontario, Canada), 1998.

(Editor) *Scribner's Best of the Fiction Workshops 1998,* Scribner, 1998.

Dressing up for the Carnival (short stories), Viking (New York, NY), 2000.

Jane Austen (biography), Viking (New York, NY), 2001.

(Editor with Marjorie Anderson) *Dropped Threads: What We Aren't Told,* Vintage Canada (Toronto, Ontario, Canada), 2001.

Unless (novel), Fourth Estate (New York, NY), 2002.

(Editor with Marjorie Anderson) *Dropped Threads 2: More of What We Aren't Told,* Vintage Canada (Toronto, Ontario, Canada), 2003.

Collected Stories, Fourth Estate (New York, NY), 2005.

Author of *The View,* 1982, *Women Waiting,* 1983, and *Face Off,* 1987.

Shields's works have been translated into other languages, including Swedish, Italian, French, Chinese, Norwegian, German, Spanish, Danish, Korean, Japanese, and Polish.

ADAPTATIONS: Swann: A Mystery was adapted for a film starring Miranda Richardson, 1996; several of Shields's novels were adapted as audiobooks.

SIDELIGHTS: "The extraordinariness of ordinary people was Carol's forte," novelist Margaret Atwood noted in an *Entertainment Weekly* remembrance of Pulitzer Prize-winning author Carol Shields. Shields, who died of cancer in 2003, is best remembered for her 1993 novel *The Stone Diaries,* as well as for her highly acclaimed biography of English writer Jane Austen. Praising Shields for her "intellectual daring" and "unambiguous prose," *New Statesman* contributor Rachel Cusk noted that "reading Shields is like talking to a good friend, someone reassuring and wise who, out of modesty or sympathy, keeps her own heart a secret."

Shields was born in Oak Park, Illinois, the youngest of three children. Her mother was a former teacher, and her father managed a candy factory. After graduating from Hanover College, she met Donald Shields while they both studied in England. They married and moved to Vancouver a year later. She began writing while raising her family, and in 1965 submitted a poem to a young writers' competition, which she won.

When her husband landed a job at the University of Ottawa, Shields began to work toward a Master of Arts degree. Urged by professors who recognized her talent, she put together her first book of poems, which was published in 1972. Four years later she was offered an editing position with a small journal, *Canadian Slavonic Papers.* As Shields once said, "it was a jobette, really. I worked in a spare room upstairs. I became the Mother who Typed." Shields's first book, *Small Ceremonies,* was written, in part, from research she did for her thesis on Susanna Moodie. With its publication, she began her long and distinguished writing and teaching career.

Critics have sometimes divided Shields's career as a writer into two distinct phases. Her first four novels—*Small Ceremonies, The Box Garden, Happenstance,* and *A Fairly Conventional Woman*—are portrayals of everyday life, where her protagonists struggle to define themselves and make human connections in their close relationships. Kathy O'Shaughnessy wrote in *Observer* that *Small Ceremonies* "is a novel of ideas: about privacy, knowledge of others, about how we perceive each other, and are perceived by others," while *London Review of Books* writer Peter Campbell, in a review of *Happenstance,* stated that "Shields writes well about decent people, and her resolutions are shrewder than those in the self-help books."

The next phase of Shields's career is marked by risk taking. With her first short-story collection, 1985's *Various Miracles,* she began to experiment more with form by using a variety of voices, while continuing to portray ordinary people in everyday situations. *Books* contributor Andrea Mynard asserted that Shields's "robust realism is typical of the growing sorority of Canadian writers, including Margaret Atwood and Alice Munro, who have been gaining a strong reputation. . . . In her accessibly simple and lucid style, Carol intelligently grasps the minutiae of everyday life and illuminates the quirks of human nature. Her observations of contemporary dilemmas are brilliant."

In her 1987 novel *Swann: A Mystery* Shields continues her experimentation by using four distinct voices to tell the story. In this novel she also develops the theme that will be used in her subsequent work: the mysterious nature of art and creation. *Swann,* noted Danny Karlin in *London Review of Books,* "is a clever book, self-conscious about literature, fashionably preoccupied with questions of deconstruction, of the 'textuality' of identity, of the powers and powerlessness of language. This impression is confirmed by its confident and playful manipulation of different narrative modes." Some critics, however, castigated what they considered the author's simple characterizations. *New York Times Book Review* writer Josh Robins noted that "the characters remain too one-dimensional, often to the point of caricature, to support sporadic attempts at psychological portraiture." The book, which first brought Shields to the attention of U.S. publishers, was later adapted as a film.

Shields took another risk by attempting the genre of the romance novel in 1992's *The Republic of Love,* but made the form her own by making her main characters wade through the coldness and problems of the twentieth century before reaching the happy ending. "Shields has created a sophisticated [romance] story," stated *Books in Canada* contributor Rita Donovan. "And the 'happy ending,' so traditional to the romance novel, is here refurbished, updated, and—most happily—earned."

Shields's early novels, while popular with readers, were not taken seriously by critics. Some have argued that in the early part of her career Shields was underestimated as a stylist and her works were dismissed as being naturalistic. Critics generally praised Shields when she began experimenting more with form. Some of her risks were originally considered failures, as in the case of the last section of *Swann,* in which she attempts to bring all four voices together in a screenplay form. More recent critical appraisal of her works has found more appreciation for such experimentation.

The Stone Diaries is the fictional biography of Daisy Goodwill Flett, whose life spans eight decades and includes time spent in both Canada and the United States. Written in both the first and third person, the story begins with her birth in 1905 in rural Manitoba, Canada. Daisy's mother, extremely obese and unaware that she is pregnant, dies moments later. Unable to care for his daughter, the infant's father, Cuyler Goodwill, convinces his neighbor Clarentine Flett to raise the child. Soon afterward, Clarentine leaves her husband and, taking Daisy with her, travels to Winnipeg, where she moves in with her son, Barker. Cuyler later takes Daisy to Bloomington, Indiana, where he has become a highly successful stonecarver. There, Daisy marries a wealthy young man who dies during their honeymoon. In 1936 she marries Barker, who has become renowned for his agricultural research, and resettles in Canada. In her role as wife and mother, Daisy appears quiet and content, but after her husband dies, she takes over a gardening column for *Ottawa Recorder,* writing as Mrs. Greenthumb. Her joy—she finds the work incredibly meaningful and fulfilling—is short-lived however, as the editor decides to give the column to a staff writer, despite Daisy's protests. She eventually recovers from the disappointment and lives the remainder of her life in Sarasota, Florida, where she amuses herself playing bridge.

Critical reaction to *The Stone Diaries,* which won Canada's Governor General's Award, the National Book Critics Circle Award, and the Pulitzer Prize, and was also short-listed for the Booker Prize, was overwhelmingly favorable. Commentators have praised Shields for exploring such universal problems as loneliness and lost opportunities and for demonstrating that all lives are significant and important no matter how banal and confined they appear. Others have lauded the novel as a brilliant examination of the divergence between one's inner and outer self, and of the relations between fiction, biography, and autobiography. As Allyson F. McGill wrote in *Belles Lettres,* "Shields and Daisy challenge us to review our lives, to try and see life honestly, even while 'their' act of authorship only reveals how impossible it is to see and speak objective truth." A *Canadian Forum* reviewer noted that "Shields demonstrates there are no small lives, no lives out of which significance does not shine. She makes us aware that banality, ultimately, is in the eye of the beholder."

Shields's follow-up to *The Stone Diaries* was a second award-winning novel, *Larry's Party,* published in 1997. Shields structures this novel thematically; each chapter covers a different area of Larry's life: his marriages and relationships, his friends, and his children. However, readers also follow Larry as he grows from an awkward adolescent to a somewhat settled, typical middle-aged white male. The "party" is one given by Larry and his girlfriend in honor of his forty-seventh birthday, and which is attended by both of his former wives. *Time* reviewer Paul Gray wrote that Shields "captures an unremarkable man in a remarkable light."

What is not typical about Larry is his job. After working as a floral designer for twenty years, he develops an interest in, and becomes an expert at, building elaborate mazes out of shrubbery. According to Michiko Kakutani in *New York Times,* these mazes "become a metaphor for the path his own life has taken, full of twists and turns and digressions. They also become a metaphor for Ms. Shields's own looping narrative, a narrative that repeatedly folds back on itself to gradually disclose more and more details about Larry's past." Commentators have remarked that in *Larry's Party* Shields portrays Everyman, much as she portrayed Everywoman in *The Stone Diaries.* Verlyn Klinkenborg, in reviewing *Larry's Party* for *New York Times Book Review,* said of Shields that "the mood in which she writes is that of the final act of *A Midsummer Night's Dream*—a mood of complicity and withdrawal, affection and mockery. Like Larry, and like God, she sees the perfect sense that mazes make 'when you look down on them from above.'"

Shields began to attract an international following in the early 1990s, particularly after the American publication of *The Stone Diaries.* Many of her early novels were published for the first time in the United States and England to much popular and critical acclaim. *A Celibate Season,* written with Blanche Howard and originally published in 1991, is the story of Jocelyn "Jock" and Charles "Chas" Selby, a couple married for twenty years, who are separated when Jock takes a temporary government job. They make the decision not to communicate by telephone, but rather keep in touch with letters, in which they talk about their lives, children, and marriage. Shields wrote the letters from Chas, and Howard those from Jock. A *Publishers Weekly* reviewer called the authors "skillful writers, and the epistolary form adds dimension to their thoughtful novel of love, marriage, and forgiveness."

In *Unless,* Shields's final novel, writer Reta Winter should be excited about the response to her first novel; instead she is preoccupied over the reticence of her oldest daughter, Nora. Nora, seemingly withdrawing from life, also withdraws from college, leaving Reta frustrated and looking for reasons, and answers, to Nora's seeming pain. Although a writer, she is voiceless, writing letters she doesn't send, having empty conversations with casual friends, and succumbing to the demands of editors to silence the women's voice in her second novel, a work-in-progress, in favor of a more assertive male presence. "Pain is never far: it's the book's frozen, icy core," Lev Grossman wrote of the novel in *Time,* "and the most vivid moments in *Unless* demonstrate the oblique, unexpected angles at which agony can enter our lives—as when Reta impulsively scrawls MY HEART IS BROKEN in the ladies' room of a bar." *New Statesman* contributor Cusk described *Unless* as "a formidable meditation on reality: it takes the vessel of fiction in its hands and hurls it to the floor." Praising the novel, Cusk added that the novel "speaks without pretension about its strange and singular subject: the relationship between women and culture, the nature of artistic endeavour, and the hostility of female truth to representations of itself."

Dressing up for the Carnival is a collection of twenty-two stories, many of them previously published. "And yet," wrote Paul Gray in *Time,* "the result is not as random or eclectic as might be anticipated. Shields . . . displays in all her writing, long or short, a consistently whimsical ruefulness toward her characters and the dilemmas they face, some of which, in this collection, are engagingly bizarre." In the title story, eleven people choose clothing and accessories to take them through the day. *Maclean's* reviewer John Bemrose wrote that Shields "also specializes in a kind of breezy essay-story—call it Borges-lite—that wittily investigates such topics as keys, inventors, and the cooking habits of an imaginary kingdom. These pieces are heavily theme-driven." In "Dying for Love," three women, who are individually contemplating suicide over love gone wrong, decide that life is worth living. In "Windows" two artists cover their windows to keep daylight from entering when the government institutes a window tax.

"Many of the stories are light and breezy but not unsatisfying," said a *Publishers Weekly* contributor of *Dressing up for the Carnival,* "because the characters are winning even in their mostly cameo-like appearances." *Time International* reviewer Francine Prose wrote that for the couple in "Mirrors," for example, "the decision not to put mirrors in their summer cottage becomes a metaphor for the shifting balance between partnership and solitude, contentment and dissatisfaction, intimacy and concealment." Prose noted that Shields "does a fine job of gauging and charting the subtle but volatile chemistry of domestic happiness, and of depicting the inner lives of her characters."

Prior to her death, Shields also collaborated with fellow editor Marjorie Anderson on *Dropped Threads: What We Aren't Told,* as well as a continuation volume, each containing over thirty essays by noted Canadian women writers. Inspirational in tone, the collections serve to "celebrate . . . the strength of the female spirit in the face of public and private challenges," explained *Catholic New Times* contributor Colleen Crawley. As Shields noted in her afterword to *Dropped Threads 2; More of What We Aren't Told:* "Frequently we discover that what we believe to be singular is, in fact, universally experienced. No wonder Holocaust survivors seek each other out. No wonder those who have lost a child turn to others who have endured the same loss. We need these conversations desperately." *Dropped Threads 2* was published shortly after Shields's death in July of 2003, following the author's five-year battle with cancer.

BIOGRAPHICAL AND CRITICAL SOURCES:

BOOKS

Contemporary Literary Criticism, Thomson Gale (Detroit, MI), Volume 91, 1996, Volume 113, 1999.

Shields, Carol, and Marjorie Anderson, editors, *Dropped Threads 2: More of What We Aren't Told,* Vintage Canada (Toronto, Ontario, Canada), 2003.

PERIODICALS

Belles Lettres, spring, 1991, p. 56; summer, 1992, p. 20; fall, 1994, pp. 32, 34.

Book, May-June, 2002, Beth Kephart, review of *Unless,* p. 76.

Booklist, July, 1997, Donna Seaman, review of *Larry's Party,* p. 1777; April 15, 2000, Donna Seaman, review of *Dressing up for the Carnival,* p. 1525; January 1, 2003, p. 793.

Books in Canada, October, 1979, pp. 29-30; May, 1981, pp. 31-32; November, 1982, pp. 18-19; October, 1985, pp. 16-17; October, 1987, pp. 15-16; May,

1989, p. 32; January-February, 1991, pp. 30-31; April, 1992, p. 40; February, 1993, pp. 51-52; September, 1993, pp. 34-35; October, 1993, pp. 32-33.
Books in Review, summer, 1989, pp. 158-60.
Books Magazine, November-December, 1994, p. 12.
Canadian Forum, July, 1975, pp. 36-38; November, 1993, pp. 44-45; January-February, 1994, pp. 44-45; January, 1996, Christine Hamelin, "Coming to Canada," p. 46; November, 1997, Merna Summers, review of *Larry's Party,* p. 38.
Canadian Literature, summer, 1989, pp. 158-60; autumn, 1991, pp. 149-50; spring, 1995.
Catholic New Times September 7, 2003, Colleen Crawley, review of *Dropped Threads 2,* p. 18.
Chatelaine, April, 1996, Leslie Hughes, "The Shields Diaries," p. 110; May, 2003, Bonnie Schiedel, review of *Dropped Threads 2,* p. 36.
Christian Science Monitor, December 7, 1990, pp. 10-11.
Critique, spring, 2003, p. 313.
Detroit Free Press, September 7, 1997.
Entertainment Weekly, September 19, 1997, Vanessa V. Friedman, review of *Larry's Party,* p. 78; May 31, 2002, Karen Valby, "No Tears" (interview), p. 70.
Kirkus Reviews, May 1, 1976, p. 559; March 15, 2000, review of *Dressing up for the Carnival,* p. 328.
Library Journal, August, 1997, Ann Irvine, review of *Larry's Party,* p. 135; June 15, 1998, Jo Carr, review of *Larry's Party,* p. 122.
London Review of Books, September 27, 1990, pp. 20-21; March 21, 1991, p. 20; May 28, 1992, p. 22; September 9, 1993, p. 19.
Los Angeles Times Book Review, August 20, 1989, p. 2; April 17, 1994, pp. 3, 7.
Maclean's, October 11, 1993, p. 74; September 29, 1997, Diane Turbide, "The Masculine Maze: Carol Shields Gets Inside the Head of the Ordinary Guy," p. 82; March 20, 2000, John Bemrose, "Enriching a Fictional Universe: In Her New Collection of Short Stories, Carol Shields Proves Adept at Finding Wonder in the Unremarkable," p. 66.
Ms., January-February, 1996, Sandy M. Fernandez, reviews of *Small Ceremonies* and *The Box Garden,* p. 90.
New Statesman, August 20, 1993, p. 40; April 29, 2002, Rachel Cusk, review of *Unless,* p. 47.
Newsweek, October 6, 1997, Laura Shapiro, review of *Larry's Party,* p. 76.
New York, March 7, 1994.
New Yorker, May 20, 2002, review of *Unless,* p. 113.
New York Review of Books, June 29, 2000, Joyce Carol Oates, review of *Dressing up for the Carnival,* p. 38.
New York Times, July 17, 1989, p. C15; May 10, 1995.
New York Times Book Review, August 6, 1989, p. 11; August 12, 1990, p. 28; March 1, 1992, pp. 14, 16; March 14, 1992; March 27, 1994, pp. 3, 14; January 7, 1996, Claire Messud, "Why So Gloomy?," p. 12; August 26, 1997, Michiko Kakutani, "Br'er Rabbit, Ordinary in Nearly Every Way;" September 7, 1997, Verlyn Klinkenborg, "A Maze Makes Sense from Above," p. 7; June 20, 1999, Michael Porter, review of *A Celibate Season,* p. 16; June 11, 2000, David Willis McCullough, "Itemize This."
Observer (London, England), February 19, 1995, Kathy O'Shaughnessy, p. 19.
People, October 6, 1997, Paula Chin, review of *Larry's Party,* p. 43.
Performing Arts & Entertainment in Canada, winter, 1998, Karen Bell, "Carol Shields: All These Years Later, Still Digging," p. 4.
Publishers Weekly, February 28, 1994; August 11, 1997, review of *Larry's Party,* p. 383; April 26, 1999, review of *A Celibate Season,* p. 55; February 28, 2000, review of *Dressing up for the Carnival,* p. 56.
Quill and Quire, January, 1981, p. 24; September, 1982, p. 59; August, 1985, p. 46; May, 1989, p. 20; August, 1993, p. 31.
Scrivener, spring, 1995.
Spectator, March 21, 1992, pp. 35-36; September 24, 1994, p. 41; May 4, 2002, p. 39.
Time, September 29, 1997, Paul Gray, review of *Larry's Party,* p. 92; May 29, 2000, Paul Gray, review of *Dressing up for the Carnival,* p. 82; May 27, 2002, Lev Grossman, "Turning over the Last Page," p. 61.
Time International, February 28, 2000, Francine Prose, "Acts of Redemption: Carol Shields' Book of Stories Brings a Master's Eye to the Transfiguring Aspects of the Everyday," p. 52.
Times (London, England), January 23, 2000, Hilary Mantel, "Full of Domestic Surprises," p. 44.
Times Literary Supplement, August 27, 1993, p. 22; February 17, 1995.
West Coast Review, winter, 1988, pp. 38-56, pp. 57-66.
Women's Review of Books, May, 1994, p. 20.
World Literature Today, October-December, 2003, W.M. Hagen, review of *Unless,* p. 95.
Writer, July, 1998, Carol Shields, "Framing the Structure of a Novel," p. 3.

* * *

SHIELDS, Carol Ann
See SHIELDS, Carol

SHREVE, Anita 1946-

PERSONAL: Born 1946; daughter of an airline pilot and a homemaker; married John Osbourne (an insurance agent); two previous marriages failed. *Education:* Attended Tufts University. *Hobbies and other interests:* Knitting, architecture.

ADDRESSES: *Home*—Longmeadow, MA. *Agent*—Virginia Barber, 101 5th Ave., New York, NY 10003.

CAREER: Freelance journalist and short story writer; high school English teacher; Amherst College, Amherst, MA, instructor in creative writing; formerly deputy editor of *Viva* magazine, editor for *US* magazine, and special issue writer for *Newsweek;* spent three years as a journalist in Nairobi, Kenya.

AWARDS, HONORS: O. Henry Award, 1976, for "Past the Island, Drifting"; PEN/L. L. Winship Award, 1998; New England Book Award for fiction, 1998.

WRITINGS:

NONFICTION

(With Patricia Lone) *Working Woman: A Guide to Fitness and Health,* Mosby (St. Louis, MO), 1986.
Remaking Motherhood: How Working Mothers Are Shaping Our Children's Future, Viking (New York, NY), 1987.
Women Together, Women Alone: The Legacy of the Consciousness-Raising Movement, Viking (New York, NY), 1989.

NONFICTION; WITH LAWRENCE BALTER

Dr. Balter's Child Sense: Understanding and Handling the Common Problems of Infancy and Early Childhood, Simon & Schuster (New York, NY), 1985.
Dr. Balter's Baby Sense, Poseidon Press (New York, NY), 1985.
Who's in Control?: Dr. Balter's Guide to Discipline without Combat, Poseidon Press (New York, NY), 1988.

NOVELS

Eden Close, Harcourt (New York, NY), 1989.
Strange Fits of Passion (New York, NY), 1991.
Where or When, Harcourt (New York, NY), 1993.
Resistance, Little, Brown (Boston, MA), 1995.
The Weight of Water, Little, Brown (Boston, MA), 1997.
The Pilot's Wife, Little, Brown (Boston, MA), 1998.
Fortune's Rocks, Little, Brown (Boston, MA), 2000.
The Last Time They Met, Little, Brown (Boston, MA), 2001.
Sea Glass, Little, Brown (Boston, MA), 2002.
All He Ever Wanted, Little, Brown (Boston, MA), 2003.
Light on Snow, Little, Brown (Boston, MA), 2004.
A Wedding in December, Little, Brown (Boston, MA), 2005.

Contributor to periodicals, including *The New York Times Magazine, Seventeen,* and *Ball State Forum.*

ADAPTATIONS: *The Weight of Water* was adapted as a film, written by Alice Arlen and Christopher Kyle, and directed by Kathryn Bigelow, for Lions Gate Films in 2002; *The Pilot's Wife* was adapted as a television movie, starring Christine Lahti.

SIDELIGHTS: Anita Shreve is the author of novels and nonfiction works highlighting women's issues and exploring themes of violence and loss. Her 1989 book *Women Together, Women Alone: The Legacy of the Consciousness- Raising Movement* is based on sixty-five interviews the author conducted with women, aged thirty-four to fifty-five, who were involved in the consciousness-raising movement of the early 1970s. Consciousness- raising, which Shreve abbreviates as "CR," involved small groups of women who discussed their feelings about being female in a male-dominated society and explored the oppression that had isolated them from one another. Shreve discusses the movement's history and its implications for women's lives. She attempted to learn how the women she interviewed had felt about the experience at the time, as well as what it means to them today. Shreve found that while they were involved in consciousness-raising, most of the women felt extremely passionate about it, believing it could change their lives in meaningful ways. When interviewed, however, most believed that the same problems still exist, and that some new ones—such as competition between women and the need for affordable, quality child care—have been added.

Many of the women with whom Shreve spoke are struggling: competing for jobs, trying to balance career and family, and feeling trapped by stringent beauty standards. Their new career opportunities have left them isolated and over-committed. Many are bitter toward the feminist movement, which, they say, promised changes that are still unrealized. The author, too, faults the feminist movement with ending women's isolation and then recreating it. As she writes in *Women Together, Women Alone,* "In preparing the ground for greater career opportunities," the movement "sowed the seeds of its own demise," in that "women who combine career and family life simply don't have any time left to devote to feminism or CR or activist issues." Critics appreciated Shreve's information concerning consciousness-raising groups, but some found her analysis flawed. Although *New York Times Book Review* contributor Alix Kates Shulman considered the author's presentation "balanced and lively," the reviewer disagreed with Shreve's conclusions, commenting that, "not the beleaguered women's movement but public institutions are responsible for the scandal of inadequate child care." Gayle Greene, writing in the *Nation,* called Shreve's interviews "fascinating," but felt that the author "attributes too much negative power to [consciousness-raising] and ends up blaming feminism for the faults of the system feminism is trying to change."

Shreve's first novel, *Eden Close,* deals with violence toward women in a nonpolitical manner. The main characters, Andrew and Eden, grew up living next door to one another in a farming community in upstate New York. The two were good friends as children, and as teenagers were on the verge of a potential love affair when Eden was raped by an intruder who permanently blinded her with gunshot. Her father was murdered by the same gun. While Andrew went on to college, marriage, and a career as an advertising executive in New York, Eden remained idle at home with her cruel mother. Now Andrew, divorced and in his mid-thirties, returns home for his own mother's funeral. He visits Eden and brings her gifts, and the two begin to rekindle their friendship while Andrew attempts to discover the identity of Eden's attacker. A *Publishers Weekly* reviewer lauded "Shreve's evocative prose and elegiac voice," while *New York Times Books Review* contributor Carolyn Banks commented that the work's "insights are keen, its language measured and haunting."

In her 1991 novel, *Strange Fits of Passion,* Shreve takes a different view of the subject of violence against women and also explores the issue of journalistic integrity. Intending to produce another nonfiction work, the author spent more than ten years conducting hundreds of interviews, many of which focused on women's issues. She was particularly drawn to the stories victims of domestic violence had shared with her. But when it came time to write the book, Shreve felt she could portray the facts about battered women more honestly by allowing a fictitious character to relate a set of experiences. The work begins with vague references to a woman's murder of her husband, who has physically and emotionally abused her. The events that led up to this act are then revealed in a series of transcripts narrated by different characters, including the accused woman, Maureen, and a reporter, Helen Scofield, who observes Maureen over a six-week period. Other characters introduce Maureen's husband Harrold, who repeatedly gets drunk, accuses Maureen of infidelity, brutalizes her, apologizes, and then repeats the cycle. Finally Maureen, accused of murder, escapes with their baby to St. Hilaire, a village in Maine, where she begins a new life under an assumed name and has a brief affair with a sympathetic lobsterman. Helen composes a magazine piece about Maureen's life, but the article conflicts with Maureen's version of the story. Appraising *Strange Fits of Passion,* reviewers praised Shreve's descriptive style, although some found the plot predictable and questioned the credibility of the characters' actions.

Throughout the remainder of the 1990s, Shreve published four novels that examine the themes of failed marriage and adultery from various perspectives. In many of them, as a *Publishers Weekly* critic noted in a review of *All He Ever Wanted,* "Shreve . . . reveal[s] an impeccably sharp eye and a generous sensitivity in describing the moment when a man and a woman become infatuated." Susan Isaacs, writing in the *New York Times Book Review,* described one of these books, *Where or When,* as "a novel of middle-aged obsession and lust in the most decorous literary fashion." Sian and Charles, both trapped in loveless marriages, rekindle a three-decade-old infatuation they experienced while adolescents at summer camp. Since they are both lapsed Catholics, guilt quickly becomes a part of their relationship. "In less skillful hands," observes Regina Weinreich in *Washington Post Book World,* "this material could yield up the worst sort of nostalgia." Shreve avoids this pitfall by the depth and subtlety of her portrayal. The perspective of the book shifts back and forth between the viewpoints of the two central characters, revealing their feelings about both their current affair and the past. As Isaacs notes, Sian and Charles "are not presented in isolation, enveloped by a cloud of concupiscence. Instead, they are placed against a richly drawn background that encompasses everything from the grim reality of a deteriorating economy to the thin black dirt of the Richards farm."

Shreve's *Resistance* takes place in Europe against the backdrop of World War II. Comparing the book to the works of writers Helen MacInnes and Erich Maria Remarque, Rollene Saal in the *New York Times Book Review* remarked: "We don't see much of this kind of romantic suspense anymore." The action of the plot concerns an American pilot, Ted Brice, who is downed over Nazi- occupied Belgium. Brice is saved, hidden, and nursed back to health by Claire Daussois, a member of the Belgian resistance movement. After Claire's husband Henri is captured by the Nazis, Shreve's theme of adultery surfaces again as Brice and Claire become lovers. "If this sounds familiar," Saal notes, "it doesn't matter . . . . Shreve adds subtle gray shadings to a familiar morality tale of good and evil, bravery and betrayal."

In *The Weight of Water* Shreve returns to New England to relate a dual story, both contemporary and historical. A photojournalist, Jean, is given the assignment to photograph the Isle of Shoals, off the New Hampshire coast, where an infamous nineteenth- century double murder took place. Traveling there on a sloop with her husband Thomas, their daughter, her brother-in-law and his girlfriend, Jean discovers firsthand documents that seem to contradict the jury's decision in the case. The narrative moves back and forth between Jean's unraveling of the historical truth and the stresses that threaten to envelop her modern-day marriage. Maureen McLane, in Chicago *Tribune Books,* called *The Weight of the Water* a "spare, tightly plotted and compactly written novel," while Susan Kenney of the *New York Times Book Review* praised it as "a cryptic long-lost narrative inside an impending family tragedy wrapped in a true-crime murder mystery framed by the aftermath of all of the above."

Like *Resistance,* Shreve's *The Pilot's Wife* begins with a downed aircraft, only in this case the setting is contemporary, the plane is a commercial jet, and no one survives the crash, which may have been an act of suicide on the part of the pilot. Kathryn Lyons is awakened by a phone call informing her that her husband Jack's plane has exploded off the coast of Ireland. In the subsequent investigation of the crash, Kathryn uncovers Jack's double life, including a mistress he kept in England. She also becomes romantically involved with one of the men investigating the incident. Noting Kathryn's failure to analyze "her own complicity" in "Jack's mendacity," Lucinda Ballantyne in the *Boston Globe* felt that *The Pilot's Wife* "doesn't know what it wants to be. Psychological study of a woman in crisis, or suspense romance?" On the other hand, Barbara Hoffert, in *Library Journal,* characterized the novel as "good solid reading for popular audiences."

In *Fortune's Rocks,* set at the turn of the twentieth century, Shreve returns "to her forte—a literary novel set in a historical framework," according to Beth Gibbs in *Library Journal.* The book takes its name from a small town in coastal New Hampshire, the town where, many years later, *The Pilot's Wife* is set. There a fifteen- year-old girl named Olympia and her family are spending their summer. Olympia meets a friend of her father's, John Haskell, an eminent physician, twenty-six years older than her and with a wife and four children. The two begin an affair, which goes horribly wrong when Olympia becomes pregnant. "As sexy as their taboo liaisons are," Gilbert Taylor and Donna Seaman wrote in *Booklist,* "Shreve is just as compelling in her descriptions of Olympia's solitary suffering in their aftermath." Because of the moral standards of the day, Olympia is forced to give the child up and is ostracized, but she eventually goes to court and fights to get her child back. "The level of suspense never falters," wrote a *Publishers Weekly* reviewer, but it "becomes breathtaking" during this custody battle.

Sea Glass is set in the same house as *The Pilot's Wife* and *Fortune's Rocks,* in the year 1929. Twenty- year-old Honora has just married Sexton, a traveling salesman whom, she later discovers, is frequently dishonest. He lies to get them a mortgage for the run- down house, just before the bottom falls out of the stock market and their finances. Fortunately Sexton is able to get another job at the local textile mill, which thrusts the couple into a looming labor dispute. They begin holding union meetings at their house, which brings Honora in contact with an attractive, idealistic mill worker named McDermott. The two begin to fall in love, although McDermott, honorable as he is, does not want to admit that he is attracted to a married woman.

Reviewers particularly praised Shreve's supporting cast in *Sea Glass,* which include a Boston socialite named Vivian and young Alphonse, an eleven-year-old millworker whom McDermott takes under his wing. These "vibrant characters, coupled with a graceful writing style," as Nancy Pearl wrote in *Library Journal,* make *Sea Glass* "perfect for readers who appreciate multilayered stories with a social conscience." "This is one of Shreve's best," concluded a *Publishers Weekly* critic.

The Last Time They Met sees the return of Thomas from Shreve's earlier novel, *The Weight of Water.* The story moves backwards through time, telling of the passionate, lifelong love affair Thomas has had with fellow poet Linda Fallon, even though he has only encountered her infrequently. "While the backwards progression is confusing at times and can necessitate some rereading," Beth Gibbs noted in *Library Journal,* "it is time well spent." Linda and Thomas meet for the third time when they are both in their fifties, at a literary convention where they are both speaking. Their second encounter, described in the middle section of the book, took place in Africa when they were in their mid-twenties, and they first met as high-school students in Massachusetts in the mid-1960s. The couple's initial meeting is described in the final section, and the dark secret behind their affair is not revealed until the final page, although it is hinted at throughout. The secrets revealed at the end of the book "transform what could be merely an overwrought tale of middle-aged Romeo and Juliet into a much more complex work about the interconnection of love, loss, imagination, and art," commented *Antioch Review* contributor Rosemary Hartigan.

All He Ever Wanted is a rarity among Shreve's books, a tale told from the point of view of a man. In 1899 New England English professor Nicholas Van Tassel meets a woman named Etna Bliss and convinces her to marry him. She does not love him and resents the loss of her freedom, but her financial situation is precarious and there are practical benefits to the union. At the beginning of their relationship Nicholas is too obsessed with Etna to care that she does not love him as he loves her, but as their marriage progresses Nicholas's jealousy becomes more and more of an issue. Desperate to regain some fragment of her former independence, Etna secretly uses a small inheritance she has received to buy a tiny house of her own, and this act, which Nicholas sees as utter betrayal, pushes him over the edge. Nicholas narrates this story in retrospect, "in the stilted and somewhat formal language of a pompous English professor," as Joanne Wilkinson noted in *Booklist.* In addition, explained a *Kirkus Reviews* critic, "Shreve lets her narrator damn himself by his own sanctimonious words."

Although she began as a journalist, "fiction is, and always has been, my first love," Shreve told *Writer* interviewer Robert Allen Papinchak. "I consider myself a better writer as a fiction writer, even though I have used a number of journalistic techniques in my fiction: shaping a story, trying to have a captivating first page, not being afraid of research."

Shreve's next novel, *Light on Snow,* portrays a widower and his young daughter who accidentally find an abandoned baby in the woods. The narrative is told from the point of view of the daughter as an adult, shifting frequently from past to present. It is also interesting to note that the book was quickly followed by the publication of Shreve's novel *A Wedding in December,* which relies more explicitly than its predecessor on the interplay between past and present. In it, a group of classmates who have not seen each other in decades meet for the wedding of a recently reunited school couple. The only person missing is Steven, who drowned during their senior year, and his absence is often obliquely alluded to by members of the party. According to *Library Journal* contributor Bette-Lee Fox, all of the "many what-ifs and might-have-beens" related to Steven's death and to the various missed opportunities for love between the classmates "come to a head" as the story progresses. Shreve creates "characters who are entirely convincing in their portrayals of human fallibility," Kim Dare commented in *School Library Journal.* Numerous other critics praised Shreve's skillful renderings. Indeed, a *Kirkus Reviews* writer particularly noted that the novel is "an impressive display of literary talent from Shreve."

BIOGRAPHICAL AND CRITICAL SOURCES:

BOOKS

Shreve, Anita, *Women Together, Women Alone: The Legacy of the Consciousness-Raising Movement,* Viking (New York, NY), 1989.

PERIODICALS

Antioch Review, spring, 1998, John Taylor, review of *The Weight of Water,* p. 243; winter, 2002, Rosemary Hartigan, review of *The Last Time They Met,* p. 163.

Atlanta Constitution, June 24, 1993, p. E6.

Atlantic, April, 2001, review of *The Last Time They Met,* pp. 105- 106.

Book, March, 2001, E. Beth Thomas, review of *The Last Time They Met,* p. 78; May-June, 2002, Beth Kephart, review of *Sea Glass,* p. 78; March-April, 2003, Adam Langer, "What Lies Beneath: For Novelist Anita Shreve, Passion and Turmoil Simmer underneath Seemingly Unremarkable Exteriors," pp. 50-51.

Booklist, March 15, 1993, Denise Perry Donavin, review of *Where or When,* p. 1276; April 1, 1995, Gilbert Taylor, review of *Resistance,* p. 1379; January 1, 1997, Emily Melton, review of *The Weight of Water,* p. 822; May 1, 1998, Joanne Wilkinson, review of *The Pilot's Wife,* p. 1504; August, 1999, review of *The Pilot's Wife,* p. 2025; October 1, 1999, Donna Seaman and Gilbert Taylor, review of *For-*

tune's Rocks, p. 308; August, 2000, Mary Frances Wilkens, review of *Fortune's Rocks,* p. 2164; February 1, 2001, Marlene Chamberlain, review of *The Last Time They Met,* p. 1020; October 1, 2001, Joyce Saricks, review of *The Last Time They Met,* p. 343; February 15, 2002, Joanne Wilkinson, review of *Sea Glass,* p. 971; February 1, 2003, Joanne Wilkinson, review of *All He Ever Wanted,* p. 956.

Boston Globe, May 10, 1998, p. F2.

Detroit Free Press, April 5, 2002, Emiliana Sandoval, review of *Sea Glass;* April 11, 2003, Emiliana Sandoval, review of *All He Ever Wanted.*

Entertainment Weekly, April 27, 2001, Rebecca Ascher-Walsh, "Past Imperfect: Acclaimed Writers Anita Shreve and Louise Erdrich Revisit Familiar Terrain, but Only Erdrich Finds Her Way," p. 110.

Kirkus Reviews, February 1, 2002, review of *Sea Glass,* pp. 136-137; February 1, 2003, review of *All He Ever Wanted,* pp. 175-176; August 1, 2004, review of *Light on Snow,* p. 712; August 15, 2005, review of *A Wedding in December,* p. 879.

Kliatt, May, 2003, Sherri Forgash, review of *Sea Glass,* p. 21; July, 2003, review of *The Weight of Water,* p. 5.

Knight Ridder/Tribune News Service, December 22, 1999, Nancy Klingener, review of *Fortune's Rocks,* p. K2277.

Library Journal, May 15, 1985, Jo Kibbee, review of *Dr. Balter's Baby Sense: Understanding and Handling the Common Problems of Infancy and Early Childhood,* p. 68; October 1, 1986, Carol Spielman Lezak, review of *Working Woman: A Guide to Fitness and Health,* p. 105; May 15, 1987, Janice Arenofsky, review of *Remaking Motherhood: How Working Mothers Are Shaping Our Children's Future,* p. 89; June 1, 1989, Barbara Bibel, review of *Women Together, Women Alone: The Legacy of the Consciousness-Raising Movement,* pp. 132-133; August, 1989, Heidi Schwartz, review of *Eden Close,* p. 166; May 15, 1995, Kathy Ingels Helmond, review of *Resistance,* p. 98; October 15, 1996, Starr E. Smith, review of *The Weight of Water,* p. 91; March 15, 1998, Barbara Hoffert, review of *The Pilot's Wife,* p. 96; November 1, 1999, Beth Gibbs, review of *Fortune's Rocks,* p. 125; March 15, 2000, Rochelle Ratner, review of *Fortune's Rocks,* p. 145; February 15, 2001, Beth Gibbs, review of *The Last Time They Met,* p. 203; March 15, 2002, review of *Sea Glass,* p. 110; March 15, 2003, Nanci Milone Hill, review of *All He Ever Wanted,* p. 117; September 1, 2005, Bette-Lee Fox, review of *A Wedding in December,* p. 134.

Los Angeles Times, April 19, 2002, Carmela Ciuraru, review of *Sea Glass,* p. E3.

Los Angeles Times Book Review, January 19, 1997, p. 7.

Nation, April 29, 1991, Gayle Greene, review of *Women Together, Women Alone,* pp. 562-567.

New York Times, August 25, 1989, Michiko Kakutani, review of *Eden Close,* p. B7, p. C30; June 6, 1993, p. 50; May 14, 1995, p. 17; January 19, 1997, p. 30; December 9, 1999, Christopher Lehmann-Haupt, review of *Fortune's Rocks,* p. B11; April 19, 2001, Janet Maslin, review of *The Last Time They Met,* p. B9; April 8, 2002, Janet Maslin, review of *Sea Glass,* p. B6.

New York Times Book Review, August 13, 1989, Alix Kates Shulman, review of *Women Together, Women Alone,* p. 10; September 3, 1989, Carolyn Banks, review of *Eden Close,* p. 6; June 6, 1993, Susan Isaacs, review of *Where or When,* p. 50; May 14, 1995, Rollene Saal, review of *Resistance,* p. 17; January 19, 1997, Susan Kenney, review of *The Weight of Water,* p. 30; June 7, 1998, Laura Jamison, review of *The Pilot's Wife,* p. 37; December 26, 1999, Alberto Mobilio, review of *Fortune's Rocks,* p. 21; April 22, 2001, Tom Shone, review of *The Last Time They Met,* p. 34; June 2, 2002, review of *Sea Glass,* p. 24; January 26, 2003, Scott Veale, review of *Sea Glass,* p. 28.

People, April 15, 1991, Joanne Kaufman, review of *Strange Fits of Passion,* p. 26; June 14, 1993, Louisa Ermelino, review of *Where or When,* p. 41; January 1, 2000, Jill Smolowe, review of *Fortune's Rocks,* p. 41; May 7, 2001, Erica Sanders, review of *The Last Time They Met,* p. 47; April 15, 2002, Michelle Vellucci, review of *Sea Glass,* p. 43; April 28, 2003, Michelle Vellucci, review of *All He Ever Wanted,* p. 43.

Psychology Today, October, 1987, Beryl Lieff Benderly, review of *Remaking Motherhood,* pp. 69-70.

Publishers Weekly, April 26, 1985, Genevieve Stuttaford, review of *Dr. Balter's Baby Sense,* p. 76; July 18, 1986, Penny Kaganoff, review of *Working Woman,* p. 76; March 13, 1987, Genevieve Stuttaford, review of *Remaking Motherhood,* p. 79; December 11, 1987, Genevieve Stuttaford, review of *Who's in Control? Dr. Balter's Guide to Discipline without Combat,* p. 54; July 7, 1989, Sybil Steinberg, review of *Eden Close,* p. 47; January 25, 1991, Sybil Steinberg, review of *Strange Fits of Passion,* pp. 47-48; April 12, 1991, Christina Frank, "Anita Shreve: Her Nonfiction Books Have Feminist Themes, but in Fiction She Portrays Women as Victims," pp. 40-41; March 22, 1993, review of *Where or When,* p. 68; March 6, 1995, review of *Resistance,* p. 57; October 14, 1996, review of *The Weight of Water,* p. 61; March 16, 1998, review of *The Pilot's Wife,* p. 52; September 13, 1999, John F. Baker, "Shrevetide," p. 14; October 4, 1999, p. 61; November 1, 1999, review of *Fortune's Rocks,* p. 47; January 3, 2000, review of *Fortune's Rocks,* p. 40; March 19, 2001, review of *The Last Time They Met,* p. 74; February 11, 2002, review of *Sea Glass,* p. 160; August 5, 2002, review of *Sea Glass,* pp. 26- 27; March 17, 2003, review of *All He Ever Wanted,* p. 50; April 28, 2003, Daisy Maryles and Dick Donahue, "Anita Turns Ten," p. 22; September 20, 2004, review of *Light on Snow,* p. 44.

School Library Journal, November, 2005, Kim Dare, review of *A Wedding in December,* p. 182.

Spectator, May 18, 2002, Sara Maitland, review of *Sea Glass,* p. 45.

Times Literary Supplement, January 17, 1992, Glyn Brown, review of *Strange Fits of Passion,* p. 23; February 11, 2000, Stephen Henighan, review of *Fortune's Rocks,* p. 21; March 23, 2001, Sylvia Brownrigg, review of *The Last Time They Met,* p. 12; April 5, 2002, review of *Sea Glass,* p. 26; July 18, 2003, Sara K. Crangle, review of *All He Ever Wanted,* p. 23.

Tribune Books (Chicago, IL), January 19, 1997, p. 1.

Washington Post, January 23, 1997, p. D2.

Washington Post Book World, August 29, 1993, p. 6; May 6, 2001, Susan Dooley, review of *The Last Time They Met,* p. 8.

Writer, November, 2001, Robert Allen Papinchak, review of "Testing the Water" (interview), p. 26.

ONLINE

Time Warner Web Site, http://www.twbookmark.com/ (August 13, 2004).

* * *

SIDDONS, Anne Rivers 1936-
(Sybil Anne Rivers Siddons)

PERSONAL: Born January 9, 1936, in Atlanta, GA; daughter of Marvin (an attorney) and Katherine (a secretary; maiden name, Kitchens) Rivers; married Heyward L. Siddons (a business partner and creative director), 1966; children: (stepsons) Lee, Kemble, Rick, David. *Education:* Auburn University, B.A.A., 1958; attended Atlanta School of Art, c. 1958. *Hobbies and other interests:* Swimming, cooking, reading, cats.

ADDRESSES: Home—3767 Vermont Rd. NE, Atlanta, GA 30319; (summer) Osprey Cottage, Brooklin, ME 04616. *Agent*—Jennifer Rudolph Walsh, William Morris Agency, 1325 Avenue of the Americas, New York, NY 10019.

CAREER: Writer. Worked in advertising with Retail Credit Co., c. 1959, Citizens & Southern National Bank, 1961-63, Burke-Dowling Adams, 1967-69, and Burton Campbell Advertising, 1969-74. Senior editor, *Atlanta,* 1964-67. Full-time writer, 1974—. Member of governing board, Woodward Academy; member of publications board and arts and sciences honorary council, Auburn University, 1978-83.

MEMBER: Chevy Chase Club, Every Saturday Club, Ansley Golf Club, Tri-Delt sorority.

AWARDS, HONORS: Alumna achievement award in arts and humanities, Auburn University, 1985; Georgia Author of the Year, 1988; honorary doctorate in Humanities, Oglethorpe University, 1991.

WRITINGS:

NOVELS

Heartbreak Hotel, Simon & Schuster (New York, NY), 1976.

The House Next Door (horror), Simon & Schuster (New York, NY), 1978.

Fox's Earth, Simon & Schuster (New York, NY), 1981.

Homeplace, Harper (New York, NY), 1987.

Peachtree Road, Harper (New York, NY), 1988.

King's Oak, Harper (New York, NY), 1990.

Outer Banks, HarperCollins (New York, NY), 1991.

Colony, HarperCollins (New York, NY), 1992.

Hill Towns, HarperCollins (New York, NY), 1993.

Downtown, HarperCollins (New York, NY), 1994.

Fault Lines, HarperCollins (New York, NY), 1995.

Up Island, HarperCollins (New York, NY), 1997.

Low Country, HarperCollins (New York, NY), 1998.

Nora, Nora, HarperCollins (New York, NY), 2000.

Islands, HarperCollins (New York, NY), 2004.

Sweetwater Creek, HarperCollins (New York, NY), 2005.

NONFICTION

John Chancellor Makes Me Cry (essays), Doubleday (New York, NY), 1975, HarperCollins (New York, NY), 1992.

Go Straight on Peachtree (guide book), Dolphin Books (New York, NY), 1978.

Contributor to *Gentleman's Quarterly, Georgia, House Beautiful, Lear's, Reader's Digest, Redbook,* and *Southern Living.*

ADAPTATIONS: Heartbreak Hotel was adapted as the film *Heart of Dixie,* Orion Pictures, 1989.

SIDELIGHTS: Novelist Anne Rivers Siddons identifies herself as an author of the South—an author of Atlanta in particular. "Everything I know and do is of here, of the South," she said in an interview in *Southern Living.* Her novels are most often concerned with the lives of Southern women; her later books have occasionally transplanted these characters to other locales. Wherever they find themselves, however, Siddons's women must explore more than their surroundings: they must come to terms with their own lives and gain strength in the process. A *Booklist* reviewer once noted, "Siddons has had a solid winning streak with her seductive portrayals of plucky southern gals holding their own in alien territory . . . . What's intriguing about Siddons is how much she transcends the usual parameters of fluff fiction, both in terms of literary finesse and penetrating intelligence."

Oddly enough, the famed fiction writer's first book, *John Chancellor Makes Me Cry,* is a collection of essays. The book chronicles one year of her life in Atlanta, humorously reflecting on the frustrations and joys of day-to-day living—serving jury duty, hosting parties, and taking care of a husband suffering with the flu. The author's style in *John Chancellor Makes Me Cry* has been favorably compared to that of Erma Bombeck, whose own review of the book praised Siddons: "She is unique. She's an original in her essays that combine humor, intimacy, and insight into a marriage." Bombeck found the most "poignant and very real" chapter to be the one describing "the month [Siddons's] husband lost his job, her Grandmother died, a Siamese cat they were keeping for a friend was hit by a car, their house was burgled and their Persian cat contracted a fifty-dollar-a-week disease."

Siddons soon found a home in fiction. *The House Next Door,* Siddons's tale of an affluent couple whose lives are changed by the mysterious evils occurring in a neighboring house, was praised by Stephen King. In *Stephen King's Danse Macabre,* King's critique on the horror genre, King devoted an entire chapter to an analysis of *The House Next Door,* comparing it to Shirley Jackson's *Haunting of Hill House.* Siddons, in an interview in *Publishers Weekly,* called the book "something of a lark. It's different from anything I've ever written, or probably ever will. But I like to read occult, supernatural stories. Some of the world's great writers have written them, and I guess I wanted to see what I could do with the genre." In the *St. James Guide to Horror, Ghost, and Gothic Writers,* Brian Stableford called the book "a far more adventurous and interesting work than the rash of schlocky haunted-house movies which came soon after."

Siddons novels such as *Homeplace* and *Peachtree Road,* won greater favor with critics and became best-sellers. Noted Bob Summers in *Publishers Weekly, Homeplace* "struck a national chord" with its account of an independent Southern-born woman returning home after more than twenty years. *Peachtree Road* is Siddons's "love letter to Atlanta," according to *Chicago Tribune* contributor Joyce Slater. "Siddons does an admirable job of tracing the city's rebirth after World War II without idealizing it." Slater concluded that *Peachtree Road* is Siddons's "most ambitious [book] to date."

Siddons's first novel set outside the South, *Colony,* is the saga of the family of a Carolinian woman who has been transplanted by marriage into the Brahmin milieu of a coastal Maine retreat. As a young bride, heroine Maude Gascoigne detests her new summer home and its people, but with the passing decades she grows to love it enough to fight hard to pass it on to her granddaughter. Joan Mooney, writing in the *New York Times Book Review,* called Maude "a match for anything that's thrown her way—and plenty is." Others have also praised Siddons's development of character in *Colony.* A reviewer for *Publishers Weekly* deemed the novel "a page-turner by virtue of realistic characters who engage the reader's affection and concern," though *Booklist* contributor Denise Blank observed that "although her verbal artistry cannot be denied, Siddons never quite captures the feel of a place or a person—one is left with the impression of a very pretty painting that looks much like other very pretty paintings."

In her next novel, *Hill Towns,* Siddons again sends a Southern woman into new territory, this time even farther afield. Cat Gaillard suffers from what *Chicago Tribune* reviewer Joyce R. Slater termed "reverse acrophobia." She is only comfortable at heights that allow her to see for miles around her. She is also agoraphobic and is finally lured from a hermetic existence in her Appalachian lookout by an invitation to a wedding in Italy. Rome, Venice, and Tuscany have the expected loosening effect on Cat, though she and her husband "will not be corrupted by decadent Europeans, but by their fellow countrymen altered by extended sojourns abroad," according to Elaine Kendall in the *Los Angeles Times.* Among these are a famous expatriate painter and his wife, who work their separate wiles on Cat and her husband, Joe. Yet Cat pulls back from the brink. In the words of Slater, "Italy and the charismatic painter, Sam Forrest, are nearly Cat's undoing. Nearly."

Many reviewers identify Siddons's greatest strength in *Hill Towns* as her characterization. Writing for the *Washington Post,* Natalie Danford claimed that the author's "portrayals of people . . . are often stunning." Slater too praised Siddons in this regard, writing that she "sensitively describes the confusion of a woman who opts to travel from an existence of academic, almost Elysian perfection to one of the steamiest, most chaotic cities in the world."

Downtown, Siddons's 1994 novel set in the mid-1960s, is admittedly autobiographical. The circumstances that surround its main character, Smoky O'Donnell, a twenty-six-year-old ingenue with the dream and drive to succeed as a writer for Atlanta's trendiest magazine, mirror those of Siddons's own past. As a writer for *Downtown* magazine, Smoky sees the ups and downs of life in Atlanta at a time when "promises . . . hung in the bronze air like fruit on the eve of ripeness." For Smoky some of these promises are kept, but others, such as the promise that brightens within her growing awareness of the civil rights movement, are shot down as the decade approaches its close.

Critical reaction to *Downtown* was mixed. A reviewer for *Publishers Weekly* wrote of being "disappointed in [Siddons's] uninspired and often pretentious story line," and Jean Hanff Korelitz complained in the *Washington Post Book World* that Smoky's "responses are so predictable and her path to adulthood so well-worn that we can't escape feeling that we have already read this novel, that only the names and locations have been changed." Both reviewers nevertheless responded favorably to Siddons's evocation of the ambience of Atlanta in the 1960s.

One recurring theme in Siddons's work is the family crisis that forces a "comfortable" woman to assess the silent damage done by untreated psychic wounds. In *Fault Lines,* for instance, Merritt Fowler is caught in a series of midlife crises: her husband is a possibly philandering workaholic, her sixteen-year-old anorexic daughter, Glynn, is caught up in teenage rebellion, and her mother-in-law is afflicted with Alzheimer's and needs constant care. When Glynn runs away to her Aunt Laura's home in Northern California, Merritt follows, determined to save her daughter and herself. When Merritt, Laura, and Glynn unite, they take a trip to the Santa Cruz mountains in an attempt to leave their troubles behind. The trip marks a shift in Merritt's life as she begins to evolve out of the dutiful wife mindset. The earth shifts as well, and as the three women seek safety, they learn valuable lessons about themselves and each other. One reviewer wrote in *Contemporary Southern Writers,* "In *Fault Lines,* Siddons avoids fluff fiction with her excellent landscapes and characters, who are believable and for whom we care." Siddons's thirteenth novel, *Low Country,* reveals how socialite Caroline Venable is forced to choose between her marriage and privileged lifestyle and her deep devotion to Peacock Island, a wild, offshore island on which her grandfather had lived. Carol's husband of twenty-five years, Clay, owns a land-developing business and wants to turn her family's native tribal settlement land into a theme park. When she discovers his plan, she must fight him to protect the beloved wild ponies that grace her island. She also struggles with the accidental drowning of her daughter, five years prior, and the desire to drink away her problems. "Familiar ground for the prolific Siddons . . . though her latest saga of the South replaces gothic melodrama with well-honed emotion," observed a *Kirkus Reviews* correspondent in a critique of *Low Country.* The correspondent described the book as "a delicate, compelling tale, full of real feeling and lush description."

In a 1994 interview for the *Atlanta Journal & Constitution,* Siddons hinted that she was finished writing about Atlanta, although she toyed with the possibility of setting a future book in the nearby affluent enclave of Cobb County. Since then she has shown little inclination to cut her ties to the South, and—with hardcover and paperback sales in the millions—she has reason to stay the course. Stableford commended the author for her ability "to flay the skin of illusion from the moral pretensions of the American south" in her best work. In *Southern Living* Siddons commented, "I have found I can move anywhere in my fiction. If I take it from the point of view of a Southerner traveling there, it's still an honest point of view."

True to her word, Siddons's millennium novel *Nora, Nora* is set instead in the small, 1960s, segregated town of Lytton, Georgia. The main character is a twelve-year-old girl named Peyton McKenzie. Peyton endures many internal struggles, the biggest of which is the guilt she feels for "killing her mother" when she first came into the world. Peyton is a member of the Losers

Club, whose other two members are the town grave keeper and the black housekeeper's handicapped son. It is only in this environment, and with this definition of herself, that she feels comfortable. Then her twenty-nine-year-old distant cousin Nora Findlay comes to Lytton to teach, and sets in motion the upheaval of Peyton's—and Lytton's—world. Nora is much different than anyone Peyton has known in her limited experience. Nora smokes, drinks, and engages in several other behaviors considered improper for a woman of her time, including advocating for drastic changes in the small town. Her bold red hair, pink Thunderbird convertible, and radical, integrated classrooms draw negative attention from Lytton citizens, who impatiently wait for Nora to self-destruct so they may be rid of her. But to Peyton, Nora's presence is a valuable one, as Peyton needs a catalyst to set her in motion and on the way to adulthood. Nora unearths qualities Peyton never realized she possessed: beauty, writing talent, and the possibility of a happy life. Nora removes Peyton's guilt and begins to teach Peyton how to love, beginning with herself. Even Peyton's father, who has lived in a shell since his wife's death, starts to come around.

"Siddons's prose is so graceful, and lovely, that after diving in, the reader is carried along effortlessly and with great pleasure," praised Carol J. Bissett in a review of *Nora, Nora* for *Library Journal.* Bissett also pointed out the book's similarities and reference to Harper Lee's *To Kill a Mockingbird* and called the book "a completely satisfying and nourishing read, containing both style and substance." Not all critics were satisfied with Siddons's thematic distance from her previous novels. "Though Siddons doesn't deliver any thematic surprises in the well-worn genre," commented a *Publishers Weekly* reviewer, "she does offer a neatly competent and engrossing story that captures the reader's sympathies despite its quality of déjà vu, as she conjures up the social and racial attitudes of a small Southern town in the 1960s." In *Booklist,* Vanessa Bush described *Nora, Nora* as "a solid novel about growing up, daring to love, and weathering life's disappointments."

Siddons's next books, *Islands* and *Sweetwater Creek,* are both set in the Carolinas, the region her writing is famous for portraying. The latter novel is similar to *Nora, Nora* because in both stories, noted Bissett in *Library Journal,* "a strong-willed young woman enter[s] the scene both to disturb and to enrich." The young protagonist in *Sweetwater Creek* is Emily Parmenter, who is the same age as Peyton (twelve) and is motherless by abandonment (instead of by death). Nevertheless, Emily lives with her reticent father and mourns instead the loss of her older brother who committed suicide. The catalyst in this story is Lulu Foxworth, who visits the family's dog farm and decides to live there. Lulu, it turns out, is an alcoholic entangled in an intense love affair. Given the novel's similarity to its predecessor, a *Publishers Weekly* contributor felt that "the plot follows formula." Yet *Booklist* critic Maria Hatton was far more impressed by the story. She stated that the "haunting, lyrical prose and complex characters . . . will captivate any reader."

Though many reviewers have compared Siddons's writing and subject matter to those of Margaret Mitchell, Siddons doesn't see her writings as romanticized, but rather realistic. "It's like an old marriage or a long marriage," she once said about her relationship with the South and its portrayal in her novels. "The commitment is absolute, but the romance has long since worn off. . . . I want to write about it as it really is."

BIOGRAPHICAL AND CRITICAL SOURCES:

BOOKS

Contemporary Popular Writers, St. James Press (Detroit, MI), 1997.

Contemporary Southern Writers, St. James Press (Detroit, MI), 1999.

King, Stephen, *Stephen King's Danse Macabre,* Everest House (New York, NY), 1981.

St. James Guide to Horror, Ghost, and Gothic Writers, St. James Press (Detroit, MI), 1998.

PERIODICALS

Atlanta Journal & Constitution, October 9, 1988; July 14, 1991, p. N8; June 26, 1992, p. P1; June 28, 1992, p. N9; June 5, 1994, p. M1, p. N10.

Booklist, May 1, 1987, p. 948; July, 1988, p. 1755; August, 1990, p. 2123; June 1, 1991, p. 1843; November 15, 1991, p. 638; April 15, 1992, Denise Blank, review of *Colony,* p. 1643; March 15, 1993, p. 1369; May 1, 1993, p. 1548; February 15, 1994, Nancy McCray, sound recording review of *Heartbreak Hotel,* p. 1100; May 15, 1994, Donna Seaman, review of *Downtown,* p. 1645; May 15, 1995, Nancy McCray, sound recording review of *John Chancellor Makes Me Cry,* p. 1664; September 1, 1995, Joanne Wilkinson, review of *Fault Lines,* p. 7; April 15, 1997, Mary Frances Wilkins, review of *Up Island,* p. 1365; June 1, 1998, Brad Hooper, review of *Low Country,* p. 1671; June 1, 2000, Vanessa Bush, review of *Nora, Nora,* p. 1799; March 1, 2001, audiobook review of *Nora, Nora,* p. 1296; July, 2005, Maria Hatton, review of *Sweetwater Creek,* p. 1877.

Bookwatch, October, 1991, p. 6; August, 1992, p. 6.

Chicago Tribune, June 14, 1987; November 11, 1988, Joyce Slater, review of *Peachtree Road*; July 25, 1993, p. 6.

Chicago Tribune Book World, June 28, 1981.

Christian Science Monitor, July 1, 1994, p. 10.

Entertainment Weekly, November 3, 1995, Rebecca Ascher-Walsh, review of *Fault Lines,* p. 61; June 6, 1997, Vanessa V. Friedman, review of *Up Island,* p. 63; August 11, 2000, "The Week," review of *Nora, Nora,* p. 76.

Kirkus Reviews, April 1, 1987, p. 510; August 1, 1988, p. 1093; August 1, 1990, p. 1038; June 1, 1991, p. 692; May 1, 1992, p. 564; April 15, 1993, p. 484; May 1, 1994, p. 587; June 1, 1998.

Kliatt, spring, 1985, p. 18; July, 1994, p. 89; January, 1995, p. 52; March, 1995, p. 53; September, 2001, audiobook review of *Nora, Nora,* p. 54.

Library Journal, June 15, 1975, p. 1211; April 1, 1987, p. 165; August, 1990, p. 145; October 1, 1991, p. 159; September 15, 1992, p. 108; August, 1993, p. 178; October 15, 1993, p. 110; June 15, 1994, p. 97; November 15, 1994, p. 106; October 1, 1998, Mark Pumphrey, sound recording review of *Low Country,* p. 150; July, 2000, Carol J. Bissett, review of *Nora, Nora,* p. 143; October 1, 2000, Lane Anderson, review of *The House Next Door,* p. 176; January 1, 2001, Adrienne Furness, audiobook review of *Nora, Nora,* p. 186; January, 2004, Carol J. Bissett, review of *Islands,* p. 160; August 1, 2005, Carol J. Bissett, review of *Sweetwater Creek,* p. 72.

Locus, January, 1990, p. 52.

Los Angeles Times, September 3, 1993, p. E6.

Los Angeles Times Book Review, September 18, 1988, p. 10; September 16, 1990, p. 8; August 4, 1991, p. 3; October 3, 1993, p. 8; July 10, 1994, p. 14.

New York Times, September 16, 1989.

New York Times Book Review, April 13, 1975, p. 18; September 12, 1976; October 23, 1977; December 10, 1978; August 30, 1987, Robin Bromley, review of *Homeplace,* p. 20; August 14, 1988, p. 26; January 1, 1989, p. 14; November 4, 1990, Gene Lyons, "She Didn't Hate Herself in the Morning," p. 33; August 2, 1992, p. 20; December 10, 1995, Sarah Ferguson, review of *Fault Lines.*

People, September 16, 1991, Cynthia Sanz, "Ring out the Belles," pp. 101-102; May 5, 1997, review of *Up Island,* p. 194; June 9, 1997, Kim Hubbard, review of *Up Island,* p. 33; July 31, 2000, "Pages," Erica Sanders, review of *Nora, Nora,* p. 41.

Publishers Weekly, May 1, 1987, p. 55; August 5, 1988, p. 72; November 18, 1988, Bob Summer, interview with Siddons, pp. 55-56; November 3, 1989, p. 88; February 2, 1990, sound recording review of *Peachtree Road,* p. 50; August 3, 1990, Sybil Steinberg, review of *King's Oak,* p. 62; May 31, 1991, review of *Outer Banks,* p. 61; March 30, 1992, pp. 21-26; May 18, 1992, p. 57; May 25, 1992, review of *Colony,* p. 57; May 24, 1993, review of *Hill Towns,* p. 67; May 23, 1994, review of *Downtown,* pp. 76-77; August 14, 1995, review of *Fault Lines,* p. 69; May 5, 1997, review of *Up Island,* p. 194; May 25, 1998, review of *Low Country* p. 63; June 12, 2000, review of *Nora, Nora,* p. 52; July 31, 2000, Daisy Maryles, "Women, Women, Women," p. 21; January 5, 2004, review of *Islands,* p. 37; August 15, 2005, review of *Sweetwater Creek,* p. 33.

Reader's Digest, January, 1987, pp. 53-55.

Southern Literary Journal, spring, 1985, Lamar York, "From Hebe to Hippolyta: Anne River Siddons's Novels," pp. 91-99.

Southern Living, October, 1987, p. 96; March, 1991, p. 118; December, 1991, p. 83; September, 1994, Dianne Young, "Words of Home," pp. 100-102.

Town & Country, March, 1993, p. 76.

Tribune Books (Chicago, IL), June 14, 1987, p. 7; November 25, 1990, p. 4; July 25, 1993, p. 6.

USA Today, July 17, 1991, p. D5; August 1, 1991, p. D1.

Washington Post, August 3, 1987; July 28, 1991, p. July 13, 1993, p. E2.

Washington Post Book World, July 28, 1991, p. 1; June 12, 1994, Jean Hanff Korelitz, review of *Downtown,* p. 8; June 17, 2001, review of *Colony,* p. 4.

Woman's Journal, February, 1995, p. 13.

ONLINE

AllReaders.com, http://www.allreaders.com/ (November 17, 2003), Jennifer Kirkman, reviews of *Up Island, King's Oak, Fox's Earth, Colony, Nora, Nora,* and *Outer Banks.*

Book Haven, http://thebookhaven.homestead.com/ (November 17, 2003), Amy Coffin, review of *Nora, Nora.*

BookPage.com, http://www.bookpage.com/ (November 17, 2003), Lynn Hamilton, review of *Nora, Nora*; Alice Cary, "Anne Rivers Siddons Preserves Natural Treasures in *Low Country*" (interview).

BookReporter.com, http://www.bookreporter.com/ (November 17, 2003), "Anne Rivers Siddons."

HarperCollins Web site, http://www.harpercollins.com/ (November 17, 2003).

SIDDONS, Sybil Anne Rivers
See SIDDONS, Anne Rivers

* * *

SILKO, Leslie 1948-
(Leslie Marmon Silko)

PERSONAL: Born March 5, 1948, in Albuquerque, NM; daughter of Lee H. Marmon (a photographer); children: two sons. *Education:* University of New Mexico, received B.A. (summa cum laude), 1969.

ADDRESSES: *Home*—8000 West Camireo Del Certo, Tucson, AZ 85705.

CAREER: Novelist, poet, and essayist; schoolteacher, Keresan cultural historian; teacher, Navajo Community College, Tsaile, AZ; was associated with the University of New Mexico, Albuquerque, NM; former assistant professor of English and fiction writing at University of Arizona, Tucson; founder, Laguna Film Project.

AWARDS, HONORS: Grant from National Endowment for the Arts and poetry award from *Chicago Review,* both 1974; Rosewater Foundation grant; Pushcart Prize for poetry, 1977; American Book Award, Before Columbus Foundation, 1980, for *Ceremony;* National Endowment for the Humanities grant, 1980; John D. and Catherine T. MacArthur Foundation *genius grant,* 1983; Native Writers' Circle of the Americas Lifetime Achievement Award, 1994; named a *Living Cultural Treasure,* New Mexico Humanities Council; Lannan Literary Award for Fiction, 2000.

WRITINGS:

NOVELS

Ceremony, Viking (New York, NY), 1977.
Almanac of the Dead, Simon & Shuster (New York, NY), 1991.
Gardens in the Dunes, Simon & Schuster (New York, NY), 1999.

POETRY

Laguna Woman, Greenfield Review Press (Greenfield Center, NY), 1974.
Storyteller (includes short stories), Seaver Books (New York, NY), 1981.
Voices under One Sky (poems) Crossing Press (Freedom, CA), 1994.
Rain (poems), Library Fellows of the Whitney Museum of American Art and Grenfell Press (New York, NY), 1996.

OTHER

(With Frank Chin) *Lullaby* (a play adaptation of a story by Silko), produced in San Francisco, 1976.
Arrowboy and the Witches (film), Video Tape Co. (North Hollywood CA), 1980.
(With James A. Wright) *Delicacy and Strength of Lace: Letters between Leslie Marmon Silko and James Wright,* Graywolf Press (Minneapolis, MN), 1985.
Yellow Woman (criticism), edited by Melody Graulich, Rutgers University Press (New Brunswick, NJ), 1993.
Sacred Water: Narratives and Pictures, Flood Plain Press (Tuscon, AZ), 1993.
Rooster and the Power of Love (correspondence), W.W. Norton (New York, NY), 1995.
Yellow Woman and a Beauty of the Spirit: Essays on Native American Life Today, Simon & Schuster (New York, NY), 1996.
Conversations with Leslie Marmon Silko, edited by L. Arnold, University Press of Mississippi (Jackson, MS), 2000.
(With Vine Deloria, Jr., and George E. Tinker), *God Is Red: A Native View of Religion, 30th Anniversary Edition,* Fulcrum Publishing (Golden, CO), 2003.

Author of stories, including "Bravura," "Humaweepi, the Warrior Priest," "Laughing and Loving," "Lullaby," "Private Property," and "Tony's Story." Work represented in anthologies, including *The Man to Send Rainclouds,* Viking (New York, NY), 1974, and *Norton Anthology of Women's Literature,* 5th edition, second volume, W.W. Norton, (New York, NY), 1998. Contributor to periodicals, including *New York Times Book Review. Almanac of the Dead* has been translated into German.

SIDELIGHTS: As a novelist, poet, and essayist, Leslie Silko has earned acclaim for her writings about Native Americans. Although her first book published was the 1974 volume of poems called *Laguna Woman,* Silko received wide and substantial critical attention in 1977 with her novel *Ceremony.* Her novels, as well as her poems, are shaped by her Native American heritage. In her writings, Silko draws from many of the traditional oral stories that she heard growing up at Laguna Pueblo

Indian reservation in northern New Mexico. Her works primarily focus on the alienation of Native Americans in a white society and on the importance of native traditions and community in helping them cope with modern life. She has been noted as a major contributor to the Native American literary and artistic renaissance, which began in the late 1960s.

In *Ceremony,* Silko tells of a half-breed war veteran's struggle for sanity after returning home from World War II. The veteran, Tayo, has difficulties adjusting to civilian life on a New Mexico Indian reservation. He is haunted by his violent actions during the war and by the memory of his brother's death in the same conflict. Deranged and withdrawn, Tayo initially wastes away on the reservation while his fellow Native American veterans drink excessively and rail against racism. After futilely exploring Navajo rituals in an attempt to discover some sense of identity, Tayo befriends a wise old half-breed, Betonie, who counsels him on the value of ceremony. Betonie teaches Tayo that ceremony is not merely formal ritual but a means of conducting one's life. With the old man's guidance, Tayo learns that humanity and the cosmos are aspects of one vast entity, and that ceremony is the means to harmony within that entity.

With its depiction of life on the Indian reservation and its exploration of philosophical issues, *Ceremony* established Silko as an important Native American writer and marked her as the first Native American woman novelist. Charles R. Larson, writing in *Washington Post Book World,* called *Ceremony* a novel "powerfully conceived" and attributed much of the book's success to Silko's incorporation of Native American elements. "Tayo's experiences may suggest that *Ceremony* falls nicely within the realm of American fiction about World War II," Larson wrote. "Yet Silko's novel is also strongly rooted within the author's own tribal background and that is what I find especially valuable here." Similarly, Frank MacShane wrote in the *New York Times Book Review* that Silko skillfully incorporates aspects of Native American storytelling techniques into *Ceremony.* "She has used animal stories and legends to give a fabulous dimension to her novel," he declared. MacShane added that Silko was "without question . . . the most accomplished Indian writer of her generation."

Some critics considered *Ceremony* a powerful confirmation of cosmic order. Elaine Jahner, who reviewed the novel for *Prairie Schooner Review,* wrote that the book "is about the power of timeless, primal forms of seeing and knowing and relating to all of life." She observed that the Native American storytelling tradition provided the novel with both theme and structure and added that Tayo eventually "perceives something of his responsibilities in shaping the story of what human beings mean to each other." Peter G. Beidler focused on the importance of storytelling in *Ceremony* by writing in *American Indian Quarterly* that the novel is both "the story of a life [and] the life of a story." Beidler called *Ceremony* "a magnificent novel" that "brings life to human beings and makes readers care about them."

After the publication of *Ceremony,* Silko received greater recognition for her earlier short stories. Among her most noteworthy stories were "Lullaby," "Yellow Woman," and "Tony's Story." "Lullaby" is an old woman's recollection of how her children were once taken away for education and how they returned to a culture that no longer seemed familiar or comfortable. Writing in the *Southwest Review,* Edith Blicksilver called "Lullaby" Silko's "version of the Native American's present-day reality." This story was included in *Norton Anthology of Women's Literature,* with Silko being the youngest writer to be included in this work. "Yellow Woman" concerns a Navajo woman who is abducted by a cattle ranger; she begins to believe that she is both herself and acting in the role of the mythical Yellow Woman, while the stranger is also whom she suspects to be the embodiment of a *ka'tsina* spirit. In *MELUS* A. LaVonne Ruoff wrote that "'Yellow Woman' is based on traditional abduction tales, [but] it is more than a modernized version." Ruoff attributed the difference to Silko's emphasis on "the character's confusion about what is real and what is not." "'Tony's Story'" is about an Indian who kills a vicious policeman. In *MELUS,* Ruoff noted Silko's ability to equate the murder with the Pueblo exorcism ritual. "Tony's Story," Ruoff declared, "deals with the return to Indian ritual as a means of coping with external forces."

Some of Silko's stories were included in the anthology *The Man to Send Rainclouds,* which derives its title from Silko's humorous tale of conflict between a Catholic priest and Pueblo Indians during a Native American funeral. Silko also included some of her early stories in her 1981 collection *Storyteller,* which features her poetry as well. In the *New York Times Book Review,* N. Scott Momaday called *Storyteller* "a rich, many-faceted book." Momaday acknowledged Silko's interests in ritual and the Native American storytelling tradition and her ability to portray characters and situations. "At her best," Momaday contended, "Leslie Silko is very good indeed. She has a sharp sense of the way in which the profound and the mundane often run together." James Polk gave similar praise in *Saturday Review* when he wrote that Silko's "perceptions are accurate, and her style reflects the breadth, the texture, the mortality of her subjects."

In 1983 Silko received an award from the prestigious MacArthur Foundation for her small but influential body of work. The award—for 176,000 dollars—was particularly appreciated by Silko, who produced most of her writings while also working as an English professor. Acknowledging her cash prize, she told *Time* that she was now "a little less beholden to the everyday world." Indeed, Silko used that money to work on an epic novel, *Almanac of the Dead,* that eventually took ten years to complete. Published in 1991, the novel "ranges over five centuries of the struggle between Native Americans and Europeans and focuses upon a half-breed Tucson family voyaging to Africa and Israel," noted John Domini in the *San Francisco Review of Books.* In addition to its wide scope, the novel contains a multitude of original, colorful characters. As *Bloomsbury Review* contributor M. Annette Jaimes explained, "Throughout the book, this entire wondrous and seedy spectrum of humanity parades itself endlessly across the knotted tightrope of a world gone hopelessly, splendidly, and quite believably mad."

Some reviewers of *Almanac of the Dead* felt that this array of characters was the novel's weakest aspect. Writing in the *Los Angeles Times Book Review,* Paul West remarked that the author's "myth remains unforgettable, whereas her characters—too many, introduced too soon and then abandoned for long stretches—remain invisible and forgettable." Silko herself acknowledged that she experimented with characterization in the novel. In an interview with Linda Niemann for the *Women's Review of Books,* Silko commented: "I was trying to give history a character. It was as if native spirits were possessing me, like a spell. . . . I knew I was breaking rules about not doing characters in the traditional way, but this other notion took over—and I couldn't tell you rationally why. I knew it was about time and about old notions of history, and about narrative being alive." While West called the book "an excellent work of myth and a second-rate novel," Jaimes concluded, "*Almanac* must be ranked as a masterpiece."

Silko's third novel, *Gardens in the Dunes,* directly contrasts the traditional world of Native Americans with the European and American upper-class culture through the story of Sister Salt and Indigo, members of the ancient Sand Lizard tribe. After witnessing a miraculous and disturbing appearance of the Messiah along with his Holy Mother and eleven children, the girls are eventually separated. After running away from a government school, Indigo is taken in by a white couple, who take Indigo to New York and then to Europe. The surrogate mother, Hattie, is rebellious of the staid Victorian culture yet tries to bring Indigo up as a well-bred white American child. But Indigo's world-view is still steeped in her native American culture, and Hattie has as much to learn from Indigo as the young girl does from her. As another plot device, Indigo saves the seeds and roots that she gathers from around the world, leading to, as Donna Seaman noted in *Booklist,* "musings on the cultivation of plants and the exploitation of the earth." A contributor to *Publishers Weekly* said that Silko "soars beyond the simpler categorizations that might circumscribe her virtuosic and visionary work." The reviewer also noted, "Silko's integration of glorious details into her many vivid settings and intense characters is a triumph of the storyteller's art." In *Booklist* Seaman called the novel "an intricate, mesmerizing, and phantasmagorical tale, rooted in Silko's passionate involvement with history, deep thinking about the spiritual consequences of our ravaging of the planet, and astoundingly fertile imagination."

Silko began writing poetry based on traditional stories and legends she learned from her family. For example, in the poem "Bear Story," she uses characters from Laguna and other Southwestern Indian stories to tell the tale of how bears can bring people to them and help them become bears. Her poems highlight many of the same themes found in her prose, including the Native Americans' non-Western sense of time, the strength of women, and the need for change.

Silko's other works include *Delicacy and Strength of Lace,* which features correspondence between Silko and Pulitzer Prize-winning poet James Wright. Writing a review in the journal *Standards,* Emmanuela de Léon noted that the two "shared a personal admiration for one another's work, as well as a kinship developed through shared experiences of their individual employment as lecturers . . . and their struggles with health and family matters. When these simple commonalities are expressed in the form of an ongoing epistolary exchange between two of our greatest literary talents, the private dialogue becomes a source of true literary enrichment." Silko self-published her multi-genre book *Sacred Water: Narratives and Pictures* under her own imprint (Flood Plain Press). As a result, she was able to experiment with the text's physical form and the use of handmade materials. Her collection of essays *Yellow Woman and a Beauty of the Spirit: Essays on Native American Life Today,* focuses on the spirit and voice of Native Americans, from her exploration of literature and language in Native American heritage to the wisdom of her ancestors to the racist treatment of Native Americans.

Silco was also a contributor to the thirtieth anniversary edition of *God Is Red: A Native View of Religion,* whose main author is Vine Deloria, Jr. This book compares Christianity to the nature-oriented religions of Native Americans and reminds us, ". . . we are a part of nature, not a transcendent species with no responsibilities to the natural world," as summarized by its publisher, Fulcrum Publishing. The book is considered by many critics to be a classic. An *Awke:kon Journal* review called the work "a trenchant and often witty critique on non-Native religion through Native eyes." In a review of the second edition of this work for *The American Indian Quarterly,* George Tinker called this work "a critical reflection on western thought and culture."

Considered by many as one of the most important contemporary Native American writers, Silko has received the Native Writers' Circle of the Americas Lifetime Achievement Award and was named a *Living Cultural Treasure,* by the New Mexico Humanities Council. As a writer who bridges cultures, Silko had this to say, "I see myself as a member of the global community," Silko told Thomas Irmer for an interview in the *Write Stuff.* "My old folks who raised me saw themselves as citizens of the world. We see no borders. When I write I am writing to the world, not to the United States alone. I do believe that the things I am talking about will finally, maybe not in my lifetime . . . turn out."

BIOGRAPHICAL AND CRITICAL SOURCES:

BOOKS

Allen, Paula Gunn, editor, *Studies in American Indian Literature: Critical Essays and Course Designs,* Modern Language Association of America, 1983, pp. 127-33.

Barnard, Anja, and Anna Sheets Nesbitt, editors, *Short Story Criticism,* Volume 37, Thomson Gale (Detroit, MI), 2000.

Contemporary Literary Criticism, Thomson Gale (Detroit, MI), Volume 23, 1983, Volume 74, 1993, Volume 114, 1999, pp. 282-344.

Contemporary Poets, 7th edition, St. James Press (Detroit, MI), 2001.

Dictionary of Literary Biography, Volume 143: *American Novelists since World War II, Third Series,* Thomson Gale (Detroit, MI), 1994, Volume 175: *Native American Writers of the United States,* 1997.

Encyclopedia of World Biography, 2nd edition, Thomson Gale (Detroit, MI), 1998.

Native North American Literature, Thomson Gale (Detroit, MI), 1994.

Patraka, Vivian, and Louise A. Tilly, editors, *Feminist Re-Visions: What Has Been and Might Be,* University of Michigan Press (Ann Arbor, MI), 1983, pp. 26-42.

Riggs, Thomas, editor, *Reference Guide to American Literature,* 4th Edition, St. James Press (Detroit, MI), 2000.

Scholer, Bo, editor, *Coyote Was Here: Essays on Contemporary Native American Literary and Political Mobilization,* Seklos, 1984, pp. 116-23.

Seyerstad, Per, *Leslie Marmon Silko,* Boise State University, 1980, pp. 45-50.

Velie, Alan R., *Four American Indian Literary Masters: N. Scott Momaday, James Welch, Leslie Marmon Silko, and Gerald Vizenor,* University of Oklahoma Press, 1982, pp. 106-21.

PERIODICALS

American Indian Quarterly, winter, 1977-78, Peter G. Beidler, review of *Ceremony;* fall, 1988, pp. 313-28; fall, 1990, pp. 367-77; spring, 1990, pp. 155-59; George Tinker, review of *God Is Red: A Native View of Religion,* fall, 1994, p. 546; summer, 1999, p. 24; winter, 2000, p. 1.

Arizona Quarterly, spring, 1988, pp. 86-94.

Bloomsbury Review, April/May, 1992, M. Annette Jaimes, review of *Almanac of the Dead,* p. 5.

Booklist, February 15, 1996, p. 988; February 1, 1999, Donna Seaman, review of *Gardens in the Dunes,* p. 942; December 15, 2000, Donna Seaman, review of *Gardens in the Dunes,* p. 787.

Chicago Tribune, December 1, 1991, p. 30.

College Literature, fall, 2000, p. 88; winter, 2001, review of *Almanac of the Dead* and *Storyteller,* p. 29.

Critique, spring, 1983, pp. 158-72.

Denver Quarterly, winter, 1980, pp. 22-30.

Explicator, fall, 2001, p. 54.

Genre, fall, 1988, pp. 307-19.

Harper's, June, 1977.

Journal of the Southwest, autumn, 1988, pp. 281-316.

Los Angeles Times, January 13, 1992, pp. E1, E3.

Los Angeles Times Book Review, January 4, 1987; February 2, 1992, Paul West, review of *Almanac of the Dead,* p. 8.

MELUS, winter, 1978; summer, 1981; winter, 1983, pp. 37-48; spring, 1985, pp. 25-36 and 65-78; spring, 1988, pp. 83-95; summer, 1993, pp. 47-60.

Ms., July, 1981.

New Leader, June 6, 1977.
Newsweek, July 4, 1977, pp. 73-4; November 18, 1991, p. 84.
New York Times, May 25, 1981.
New York Times Book Review, June 12, 1977, Frank MacShane, review of *Ceremony;* May 24, 1981, N. Scott Momaday, review of *Storyteller;* December 22, 1991, p. 6; April 18, 1999, review of *Gardens in the Dunes,* p. 31.
Prairie Schooner Review, winter, 1977-78, Elaine Jahner, review of *Ceremony.*
Publishers Weekly, March 1, 1999, review of *Gardens in the Dunes,* p. 59.
San Francisco Review of Books, fall, 1992, John Domini, review of *Almanac of the Dead,* p. 18.
Saturday Review, May, 1981.
Southern Folklore, no. 2, 1989, pp. 133-46.
Southwest Review, spring, 1979, Edith Blicksilver, review of "Lullaby."
Time, August 8, 1983; May 3, 1999, review of *Gardens in the Dunes,* p. 78.
Village Voice Literary Supplement, November, 1991, pp. 17-18.
Washington Post Book World, April 24, 1977, Charles R. Larson, review of *Ceremony.*
Western American Literature, February, 1994, pp. 301-12; spring, 1999, review of *The Delicacy and Strength of Lace,* p. 48.
Women's Review of Books, July, 1992, Linda Niemann, interview with Silko, p. 10.

ONLINE

Fulcrum Publishing Web site, http://www.fulcrum-books.com/ (August 8, 2004), "*God Is Red: A Native View of Religion, 30th Anniversary Edition.*"
Internet Public Library Web site, http://www.ipl.org/div/ (August 8, 2004), "Native American Authors Project;" "Online Literary Criticism Collection."
Lannan Foundation Web site, http://www.lannan.org/literary/fiction.htm/ (August 8, 2004), "Lannan Literary Awards and Fellowships for Fiction."
Lopez Bookseller Web site, http://www.lopezbooks.com/ (August 8, 2004), "Leslie Marmon Silko."
Pace University Web site, http://csis.pace.edu/amlit/proj1d/silko.htm/ (August 8, 2004), "A Native Struggle, Short Summary of Leslie Silko's *Lullaby.*"
Standards, http://www.colorado.edu/journals/standards/ (January 28, 2003), Volume 6, Emmanuela de Léon, review of *Delicacy and Strength of Lace: Letters between Leslie Marmon Silko and James Wright.*
Student Books Online Web site, http://studentbooksonline.net/ (August 8, 2004), "*God Is Red: A Native View of Religion, 30th Anniversary Edition.*"
University of Richmond Web site, http://oncampus.richmond.edu/˜rnelson/ (August 8, 2004), "Leslie Silko, Storyteller."
Voices from the Gaps, http://voices.cla.umn.edu/ (October 9, 2002), "Biography-Criticism" of Leslie Marmon Silko.
Write Stuff, http://www.altx.com/interviews/ (October 9, 2002), Thomas Irmer, "An Interview with Leslie Marmon Silko."

* * *

SILKO, Leslie Marmon
See SILKO, Leslie

* * *

SILLITOE, Alan 1928-

PERSONAL: Born March 4, 1928, in Nottingham, England; son of Christopher (a laborer) and Sabina (Burton) Sillitoe; married Ruth Fainlight (a poet, writer, and translator), November 19, 1959; children: David Nimrod, Susan (adopted). *Education:* Left school at age fourteen. *Hobbies and other interests:* Travel, shortwave radio.

ADDRESSES: *Home*—14 Ladbroke Terrace, London W11 3PG, England.

CAREER: Worked in a bicycle plant, 1942-46, in a plywood mill, and as a capstan-lathe operator; air traffic control assistant, 1945-46; freelance writer, 1948—. *Military service:* Royal Air Force, radio operator in Malaya, 1946-49.

MEMBER: Society of Authors, Royal Geographical Society (fellow), Writers Action Group, Savage Club.

AWARDS, HONORS: Author's Club prize, 1958, for *Saturday Night and Sunday Morning;* Hawthornden Prize for Literature, 1960, for *The Loneliness of the Long-Distance Runner;* honorary fellow, Manchester Polytechnic, 1977; honorary doctorates, Nottingham Polytechnic, 1990, Nottingham University, 1994, and De Montfort University (Leicester, England), 1998.

WRITINGS:

POEMS

Without Beer or Bread, Outpost Publications (London, England), 1957.

The Rats and Other Poems, W.H. Allen (London, England), 1960.

A Falling Out of Love and Other Poems, W.H. Allen (London, England), 1964.

Shaman and Other Poems, Turret (London, England), 1968.

Love in the Environs of Voronezh, and Other Poems, Macmillan (London, England), 1968, Doubleday (New York, NY), 1969.

(With Ruth Fainlight and Ted Hughes) *Poems,* Rainbow Press (London, England), 1971.

Canto Two of the Rats, Ithaca (London, England), 1973.

Storm: New Poems, W.H. Allen (London, England), 1974.

Barbarians and Other Poems, Turret (London, England), 1974.

(With Ruth Fainlight) *Words Broadsheet Nineteen,* Words Press (Bramley, Surrey, England), 1975.

Snow on the North Side of Lucifer, W.H. Allen (London, England), 1979.

More Lucifer, Booth (Knotting, Bedfordshire, England), 1980.

Israel: Poems on a Hebrew Theme, Steam Press (London, England), 1981.

Sun before Departure, Grafton Books (London, England), 1984.

Tides and Stone Walls, Grafton Books (London, England), 1986.

Collected Poems, HarperCollins (London, England), 1993.

NOVELS

Saturday Night and Sunday Morning (also see below), W.H. Allen (London, England), 1958, Knopf (New York, NY), 1959, revised edition, with an introduction by the author and commentary and notes by David Craig, Longmans, Green (London, England), 1968, new edition, HarperCollins (London, England), 1995.

The General (also see below), W.H. Allen (London, England), 1960, Knopf (New York, NY), 1961, published as *Counterpoint,* Avon (New York, NY), 1968.

Key to the Door, W.H. Allen (London, England), 1961, Knopf (New York, NY), 1962.

The Death of William Posters (first volume of trilogy), Knopf (New York, NY), 1965.

A Tree on Fire (second volume of trilogy), Macmillan (London, England), 1967, Doubleday (New York, NY), 1968.

A Start in Life, W.H. Allen (London, England), 1970, Scribner (New York, NY), 1971.

Travel in Nihilon, W.H. Allen (London, England), 1971, Scribner (New York, NY), 1972.

Raw Material, W.H. Allen (London, England), 1972, Scribner (New York, NY), 1973.

The Flame of Life (third volume of trilogy), W.H. Allen (London, England), 1974.

The Widower's Son, W.H. Allen (London, England), 1976, Harper (New York, NY), 1977.

The Storyteller, W.H. Allen (London, England), 1979, Simon & Schuster (New York, NY), 1980.

Her Victory, F. Watts (New York, NY), 1982.

The Lost Flying Boat, Little, Brown (New York, NY), 1983.

Down from the Hill, Granada, 1984.

Life Goes On (sequel to *A Start in Life*), Grafton Books (London, England), 1985.

Out of the Whirlpool, Hutchinson (London, England), 1987.

The Open Door, HarperCollins (London, England), 1988.

Last Loves, Grafton Books (London, England), 1990, Chivers (Boston, MA), 1991.

Leonard's War: A Love Story, HarperCollins (London, England), 1991.

Snowstop, HarperCollins (London, England), 1994.

The Broken Chariot, Flamingo (London, England), 1998.

The German Numbers Woman, Flamingo (London, England), 2000.

Birthday, Flamingo (London, England), 2001.

A Man of His Time, Flamingo (London, England), 2004.

SHORT STORIES

The Loneliness of the Long-Distance Runner (includes "The Loneliness of the Long-Distance Runner," "The Match," and "Uncle Ernest"; also see below), W.H. Allen (London, England), 1959, Knopf (New York, NY), 1960, bound with *Sanctuary,* by Theodore Dreiser, and related poems, edited by Roy Bentley, Book Society of Canada, 1967.

The Ragman's Daughter and Other Stories (also see below), W.H. Allen (London, England), 1961, Knopf (New York, NY), 1964.

Guzman Go Home and Other Stories, Macmillan (London, England), 1968, Doubleday (New York, NY), 1969.

A Sillitoe Selection, Longmans, Green (London, England), 1968.

Men, Women, and Children, W.H. Allen (London, England), 1973, Scribner (New York, NY), 1974.

The Second Chance and Other Stories, Simon & Schuster (New York, NY), 1981.

The Far Side of the Street, W.H. Allen (London, England), 1988.

Collected Stories (includes "The Loneliness of the Long-Distance Runner," "Fishing Boat Picture," "Mr. Raynor the School Teacher," and "The Magic Box"), HarperCollins (London, England), 1995.

Alligator Playground (includes "Alligator Playground," "Ron Delph and His Fight with King Arthur," and "A Matter of Teeth"), Flamingo (London, England), 1998.

New and Collected Stories, Robson Books (London, England), 2003.

SCREENPLAYS

Saturday Night and Sunday Morning (based on his novel of the same title), Continental, 1960.

The Loneliness of the Long-Distance Runner (based on his short story of the same title), Continental, 1961.

The Ragman's Daughter (based on short story of same title), Penelope Films, 1972.

Also author of *Che Guevara,* 1968.

PLAYS

(Translator and adapter, with Ruth Fainlight) Lope de Vega, *All Citizens Are Soldiers* (two-act; first produced at Theatre Royal, Stratford, London, 1967), Macmillan (London, England), 1969, Dufour (Chester Springs, PA), 1970.

The Slot Machine (also see below), first produced as *This Foreign Field,* in London, England, at Round House, 1970.

Pit Strike (also see below), produced by British Broadcasting Corporation, 1977.

The Interview (also see below), produced at the Almost Free Theatre, 1978.

Three Plays: The Slot Machine, The Interview, Pit Strike, W.H. Allen (London, England), 1978.

JUVENILE

The City Adventures of Marmalade Jim, Macmillan (London, England), 1967.

Big John and the Stars, Robson Books (London, England), 1977.

The Incredible Fencing Fleas, Robson Books (London, England), 1978.

Marmalade Jim on the Farm, Robson Books (London, England), 1979.

Marmalade Jim and the Fox, Robson Books (London, England), 1985.

TRAVEL

Road to Volgograd, Knopf (New York, NY), 1964.

The Saxon Shore Way, Hutchinson (London, England), 1983.

Nottinghamshire, photography by David Sillitoe, Grafton Books (London, England), 1987.

Leading the Blind: A Century of Guide Book Travel, 1815-1914, Picador (New York, NY), 1995.

OTHER

(Author of introduction) Arnold Bennett, *Riceyman Steps,* Pan Books (London, England), 1964.

(Author of introduction) Arnold Bennett, *The Old Wives' Tale,* Pan Books (London, England), 1964.

Mountains and Caverns: Selected Essays, W.H. Allen (London, England), 1975.

Down to the Bone (collection), Wheaton (Exeter, England), 1976.

Day Dream Communiqué, Sceptre (Knotting, Bedfordshire, England), 1977.

Every Day of the Week: An Alan Sillitoe Reader, W.H. Allen (London, England), 1987.

Life without Armour (autobiography), Macmillan (London, England), 1995.

A Flight of Arrows: Opinions, People, Places, Robson Books (London, England), 2003, Robson Books/Parkwest Publications (New York, NY), 2004.

SIDELIGHTS: "I was twenty years old when I first tried to write, and it took ten years before I learned how to do it," remarked Alan Sillitoe in reference to *Saturday Night and Sunday Morning,* the novel that catapulted the thirty-year-old, self-educated Briton into the literary limelight. Described by *New Yorker* critic Anthony West as a "brilliant first book," *Saturday Night and Sunday Morning* broke new ground with its portrayal of "the true robust and earthy quality characteristic of English working-class life." Only one year later, Sillitoe was again the center of critical attention, this time for "The Loneliness of the Long-Distance Runner," the title novella in a collection of short stories that also contained some frank representations of working-class life in Britain. Although he has since written numerous novels and short stories, as well as poems and plays, Sillitoe has almost always been evaluated in terms of these first two works.

On a thematic level, Sillitoe's works often center on an individual isolated from society, studying what the *Guardian* 's Roy Perrot called "the spirit of the outsider, the dissenter, the man apart." But instead of limiting himself strictly to the psychological confines of this one person and allowing the rest of the world to remain somewhat shadowy, Sillitoe places his rebellious outsider in a gritty, distinctive milieu—Nottingham, an English industrial town—and the author's birthplace—where, as Charles Champlin explained in the *Los Angeles Times,* "the lower-middle and working classes rub, where breaking even looks like victory, and London is a long way South." This strong regionalism, reminiscent of the regionalism common in nineteenth-century British fiction, is one of the most noted features of Sillitoe's writing.

Sillitoe's world is populated with factory workers, shop girls, and other types not often depicted in English literature. Whether they are at home, at work, or relaxing in the pubs, these characters reveal themselves to be "unfamiliar with the great world of London or country houses or what is called high culture," explained Kendall Mitchell in Chicago's *Tribune Books.* "And they don't care—they have their lives to live, their marriages to make and wreck, their passions to pursue." As Champlin noted, "The cumulative impression of Sillitoe's people is of their strength and will to survive, however forces beyond their control blunt their prospects."

These "forces beyond their control" play a major role in the author's fiction; Sillitoe's conception of fate, however, differs from the classical one in that economic and social factors, not the whim of the gods, determine one's destiny. As James Jack Gindin wrote in *Postwar British Fiction: New Accents and Attitudes:* "Nothing really changes Sillitoe's jungle world. A man may win or lose, depending on the wheel of chance, but he cannot control the wheel or change his position. Often, too, the wheel is rigged, for the same numbers keep coming up as privilege and power keep reinforcing themselves." In short, commented Saul Maloff in *Contemporary British Novelists,* "for Sillitoe, class is fate."

Though his characters are rough-edged and his world is harsh, *Washington Post*'s Daniel O'Neill credited the author with an "ability to blend cold-blooded rendering of the exterior world with insightful and sensitive representation of the inner workings of the characters' minds." According to Max Cosman of *Commonweal,* "such is Mr. Sillitoe's interest in his fellow man and such [is] his skill in compelling attention, that ignoble, or subnormal as his Nottinghamites are, they can [bring] forth compassion even in the midst of disapproval."

Sillitoe's practice of speaking through less "sophisticated" narrators has resulted in a style many critics have trouble classifying. As Champlin noted, "at times the essayist, social historian, and social reporter in Sillitoe seems simply to have chosen fiction as the best carrier of impressions he wants to leave and points he wants to make." Consequently, remarked Stanley Kauffmann in the *New York Review of Books,* his writing "fluctuates from straight hard prose to Nottingham slang to the most literary effusions, often all on the same page." Many reviewers, including *Times Literary Supplement* contributor John Lucas, have commented that in most other respects, Sillitoe's style is "peculiarly artless" in that "even the best of [the stories] work in a manner that is unusual or unorthodox." There is, for example, no particularly strong emphasis on plot in a Sillitoe story, no "half hidden thread that can be traced," no sudden flash or insight that makes everything clear; as Lucas stated, "nothing happens: there is no revelation, the story hardly seems to be a story at all." West also noticed that Sillitoe's stories are "so firmly rooted in experience, and so ably handled, that they do not seem to have been written at all; they seem to be occurrences of a most engrossing and absorbing kind." Gene Baro reached a similar assessment of the author, writing in the *New York Herald Tribune Book Review* that "Sillitoe exhibits . . . lucid design, pace, a gift for salty vernacular, an unerring eye for the telling gesture, a robust and yet a restrained sense of the comic. . . . All is achieved simply, matter-of-factly, without apparent striving for effect."

A *Times Literary Supplement* critic was especially impressed by Sillitoe's "integrity of style that never falsifies the writer's role—which is why, for instance, he refuses to go on 'like a penny-a-liner to force an ending' if inspiration stops before he knows what to do with the character he has created. There may not even *be* an ending to a Sillitoe story." John Updike noticed this same feature in Sillitoe's writing, pointing out in a *New Republic* article that his stories "have a wonderful way of going on, of not stopping short . . . that lifts us twice, and shows enviable assurance and abundance in the writer."

P.H. Johnson, writing in the *New Statesman,* also regarded Sillitoe as "highly gifted technically: he is an excellent story-teller, and his style is perfectly adapted to his subject-matter; he has literary tact and a sense of design." *Saturday Review* critic James Yaffe reported that among Sillitoe's "many wonderful qualities" are "a fluent, often brilliant command of language, an acute ear for dialect, [and] a virtuoso ability to describe the sight, sound, and smell of things."

Critics have often discussed Sillitoe's works in terms of whether he belonged to the literary tradition of his contemporaries, the "Angry Young Men" of 1950s and 1960s Britain, or of an earlier age, notably the American proletarian novelists of the 1930s. The Angry Young Men were known for their bitter attacks on the political and social establishment, which critics found comparable with Sillitoe's depictions of the struggles of the working class. Other critics, however, have noted that Sillitoe writes with an emphasis on compassion, which, they believe, makes him less an Angry Young Man with a special talent for describing the plight of the proletariat than a sentimentalist who idealizes the lives of his working-class heroes. Kauffmann felt Sillitoe to be a victim of the cultural "timelag" between the United States and England, and therefore rediscovered the themes that American writers such as John Steinbeck, Erskine Caldwell, Theodore Dreiser, and John Dos Passos dealt with in their fiction during the 1930s. In *Contemporary British Novelists,* Saul Maloff wrote that Sillitoe's similarities to these authors made him "a historical surprise. In the utterly changed circumstances of the fifties and sixties, he has partially validated as art the 'proletarian novel' of the thirties; and standing eccentrically against the current driven by his defter contemporaries, he has made a working-class novel."

Allen R. Penner, writing in *Contemporary Literature,* noted the traces of old-fashioned literary tradition in Sillitoe's works, but pointed out their modern twist: "'The Loneliness of the Long-Distance Runner' . . . is written in a tradition in English fiction which dates at least from Elizabethan times, in . . . the rogue's tale, or thief's autobiography." In his opinion Sillitoe "has reversed the formula of the popular crime tale of fiction, wherein the reader enjoys vicariously witnessing the exploits of the outlaw and then has the morally reassuring pleasure of seeing the doors of the prison close upon him in the conclusion. Sillitoe begins his tale in prison, and he ends it before the doors have opened again, leaving us with the unsettling realization that the doors will indeed open and that the criminal will be released unreformed." This emphasis on unrepentant rebellion, wrote Penner, proves that "Sillitoe was never, really, simply an 'angry young man.' His hostility was not a transitory emotion of youth, but a permanent rancor well grounded in class hatred. 'The Loneliness of the Long-Distance Runner' contains the seeds of the revolutionary philosophy which would eventually attain full growth in his works."

Other critics have not been so quick to dismiss Sillitoe's connections to the Angry Young Men. Commenting in the *New York Times Book Review,* Malcolm Bradbury noted that "if the heroes of some . . . English novels are angry young men, Mr. Sillitoe is raging; and though he doesn't know it, he is raging for much the same reasons." Champlin remarked that Sillitoe's emergence was "a sharp signaling of an end to quiet acceptance of the way things are. It was a protest, fueled by the war, against the stratified status quo. . . . Unlike some of Britain's angry young men who have matured and prospered into more conservative postures, Sillitoe remains the poet of the anonymous millions in the council flats and the cold-water attached houses, noting the ignored, remembering the half-forgotten."

Though John R. Clark of the *Saturday Review* also saw Sillitoe as an Angry Young Man, he felt that "his anger and fictions have altered with time. In [his] early work there was something single-minded and intense in the actions and scenes, particularly in the shorter novels." On the other hand, more recent "novels reveal a broader social and political horizon. Sillitoe's characters not only privately rebel but become dedicated to larger 'movements.'" Sillitoe told Igor Hajek in a *Nation* interview that he is not at all dismayed by the fact that he is best known for his earliest works, especially *Saturday Night and Sunday Morning* and "The Loneliness of the Long-Distance Runner." "I think those people [who remember me primarily as the author of 'The Loneliness of the Long-Distance Runner'] are absolutely right," he said. "This story of a working-class youth is at the same time the statement of my artistic integrity. I shall never write anything to uphold this Establishment and this society. And I'm ready to stick to my principles even to a self-damaging extent."

Some thirty years after the publication of *Saturday Night and Sunday Morning* and its sequel, *Key to the Door,* Sillitoe returned to the characters introduced in those books. *The Open Door* centers on Brian Seaton, the older brother of *Saturday Night*'s protagonist Arthur Seaton. Brian is "the most closely autobiographical of Sillitoe's characters," according to *World Literature Today* reviewer William Hutchings. Like the author, Brian escapes his working-class home town by joining the army and serving as a radio operator in Malaya. Also like Sillitoe, Brian discovers upon his return to England that he has contracted tuberculosis. "His illness dominates the first two-thirds of the novel, as . . . Brian gains a heightened awareness of his own mortality," related Hutchings. Parallels to Sillitoe's life continue as Brian uses his convalescence to read voraciously and to realize his ambition to become a writer. Hutchings found that together, *Key to the Door* and *The Open Door* "constitute an extraordinarily intimate fictional 'portrait of the artist as a young man.'" Brian Morton also commented very favorably on the book, writing in the *Times Literary Supplement* that *The Open Door* "is an extraordinary, almost symphonic development of deceptively familiar materials, and confirms [Sillitoe's] standing as one of Britain's most powerful and sophisticated fiction-writers."

In 1995, Sillitoe published the memoir *Life without Armour,* relating in nonfiction form the story of his childhood, his military service, his struggle with tuberculosis, and his eventual triumph as a writer. Ironically, his illness provided the means for him to realize his artistic dreams, as his small disability pension made it possible for him to support himself in the days before his writing sold. Several reviewers note that the autobiography's early sections are its best; John Melmoth noted in *Times Literary Supplement* that "the squalor of [Sillitoe's] upbringing is captured with a novelistic verve that later sections of the book fail to match. Deprivation makes good copy; hard work and dedication—as ever—write white." Nicholas Wollaston found the author's life story inspirational, and comments that it is "the more impressive for being told in a simple, almost biblical voice. . . . There was iron in his soul as faith and energy drove him on, fighting solitude and publishers' indifference."

Sillitoe's *Collected Stories* also came out in 1995, featuring works such as "The Loneliness of the Long-Distance Runner," "Mr. Raynor the School Teacher," and "The Magic Box." "Taken individually," wrote a reviewer for *Publishers Weekly,* "the stories in this collection are searing and dead-on. Taken collectively, they render Sillitoe's pessimism and vitriol hard to take." The situations in which Sillitoe places his characters are difficult; Mr. Raynor, for example, is a teacher who ogles his students, and one of them is later murdered by her boyfriend. In "The Magic Box" and "Fishing Boat Picture," couples have to deal with the difficulties of marriage. Brad Hooper, writing for *Booklist,* declared the collection "a needed roundup of a master's work."

Though best known for his fiction, Sillitoe has also produced a number of travel guides. He became a collector of guide books from the nineteenth century, and has used those texts to create *Leading the Blind: A Century of Guide Book Travel, 1815-1914.* "Sillitoe has selected some of the choiciest bits of advice from a wide array of guide books to give us the flavour of travel," wrote Richard Mullen in *Contemporary Review.* The reviewer noted that Sillitoe chose to leave out the colored illustrations from more-modern guide books, inspiring the reader to use more of their intellect and imagination. "This is a delightful book," Mullen concluded, "either for the bedside traveller or a real traveller."

In 1998, Sillitoe returned to fiction with a novella and collection of short stories titled *Alligator Playground.* The title story deals with the promiscuous social scene of London's literati, and the eventual marriage of a misogynist and a former lesbian. "The result," commented James Urquhart in *New Statesman & Society,* "has the circularity of a morality tale but lacks any sense of empathy or moral structure." Despite this complaint, Urquhart continued, "Happily the other eight tales restore faith." The stories, including "Ron Delph and His Fight with King Arthur," a tale of adolescent anxieties, and "A Matter of Teeth," which justifies simultaneous affairs, explore a more middle-class terrain than his previous works.

The German Numbers Woman, Sillitoe's 2000 novel, casts a blind short-wave radio operator as a hero who undermines a drug smuggling scheme and rescues the girl at the end. Howard, a World War II Royal Air Force veteran, blinded in combat, has become a stoic, and almost resents the attentions of his wife. Instead of focusing on life, he turns his passions toward Morse code and eavesdrops on conversations over his short-wave radio. His wife introduces him to a drug runner, and when Howard discovers that one of the voices he hears on the radio will be put in danger by one of the latest drug schemes, he asks to be taken along. Patrick Sullivan, writing for *Library Journal,* called *The German Numbers Woman* an "ambitious but flawed novel," but a reviewer from *Publishers Weekly* stated that Sillitoe's "alienated hero—older, wizened, subdued—is still a marvelous creation."

In his *Nation* interview, Sillitoe declared his opinion that "a writer never stands still. When you are young, everything is simple, but I am not young any more, [which] means that I am leaving a lot of simplicities behind. Basic beliefs stay, but things now look more complex." In short, concluded Sillitoe, "Each individual has to make a choice: either to accept this society or stand up against it. . . . In this country, as in any other, a writer is liked if he is loyal to the system. But it is the writer's duty in a sense to be disloyal. In the modern world, he is one of the few people who are listened to, and his primary loyalty should be to his integrity and to his talent. He can speak up in many ways; the best way is to write a book."

Sillitoe's *Birthday* is the fourth novel about the family of his best-known character, the "notoriously rowdy working-class protagonist Arthur Seaton." A contributor to *Publishers Weekly* decreed that the writing shows that "Sillitoe is no longer the aggressive, take-no-prisoners writer who brought these characters to life so provocatively half a century ago, but his craftsmanship remains high and his insights are always sharp." Although in *Birthday* Sillitoe "does meander some," the critic added, "in this novel the literary journey more than justifies the occasional side trip." Allan Massie, in a review for *Spectator,* declared *Birthday* to be "a humane book, often funny; an affirmation of the—provincial?—values of hard work, decency, respect for others, honesty between people."

BIOGRAPHICAL AND CRITICAL SOURCES:

BOOKS

Atherton, Stanley S., *Alan Sillitoe: A Critical Assessment,* W.H. Allen (London, England), 1979.

Gerard, David, *Alan Sillitoe: A Bibliography,* Meckler (Westport, CT), 1988.

Gindin, James Jack, *Postwar British Fiction: New Accents and Attitudes,* Greenwood Press (Westport, CT), 1976.

Hanson, Gillian Mary, *Understanding Alan Sillitoe,* University of South Carolina Press (Columbia, SC), 1997.

Penner, Richard, *Alan Sillitoe* ("English Author" series), Twayne (New York, NY), 1972.

Sawkins, John, *The Long Apprenticeship: Alienation in the Early Work of Alan Sillitoe,* Peter Lang (Oxford, England), 2001.

Shapiro, Charles, editor, *Contemporary British Novelists,* Southern Illinois University Press (Carbondale, IL), 1965.

Vaverka, Ronald Dee, *Commitment as Art: A Marxist Critique of a Selection of Alan Sillitoe's Political Fiction,* Almqvist & Wiksell (Stockholm, Sweden), 1978.

PERIODICALS

Booklist, September 15, 1996, Brad Hooper, review of *Collected Stories,* p. 222.

Books and Bookmen, December, 1973, pp. 42-46.

British Book News, April, 1985, p. 237.

Commonweal, September 4, 1959; April 29, 1960; March 27, 1964.

Contemporary Literature, Volume X, number 2, 1969; October, 1987, p. 214.

Contemporary Review, February, 1996, Richard Mullen, review of *Leading the Blind: A Century of Guide Book Travel, 1815-1914,* p. 110.

Dalhousie Review, autumn, 1968, pp. 324-331.

Four Quarters, November, 1971, pp. 3-10.

Globe and Mail (Toronto, Ontario, Canada), September 7, 1985.

Guardian, September 25, 1959.

Journal of Narrative Technique, number 3, 1980, pp. 170-185.

Library Journal, September 15, 1996, Albert E. Wilhelm, review of *Collected Stories,* p. 100; February 15, 2000, Patrick Sullivan, review of *The German Numbers Woman,* p. 200.

Listener, November 11, 1982, p. 27.

Literature and Language, spring, 1962, pp. 35-48.

Literature-Film Quarterly, number 3, 1981, pp. 161-188.

London Review of Books, November 17, 1983, pp. 12-13; December 5, 1985, pp. 22-23; December 20, 1985, pp. 19-20.

Los Angeles Times, October 1, 1980; April 21, 1981.

Los Angeles Times Book Review, November 21, 1982.

Milwaukee Journal, November 10, 1974.

Nation, January 27, 1969, Igor Hajek, interview with Alan Sillitoe.

Neophilologus, April, 1981, pp. 308-319.

New Republic, August 24, 1959; May 9, 1960.

New Statesman, October 3, 1959; January 30, 1998, review of *Alligator Playground,* p. 47.

New Statesman & Society, March 10, 1989, p. 36; July 21, 1995, p. 39; July 30, 1998, James Urquhart, review of *Alligator Playground,* p. 47.

New Yorker, September 5, 1959, Anthony West, review of *Saturday Night and Sunday Morning;* June 11, 1960; September 22, 1980, review of *The Storyteller,* p. 157.

New York Herald Tribune Book Review, August 16, 1959; May 29, 1960.

New York Review of Books, March 5, 1964, review by Stanley Kauffmann.

New York Times Book Review, August 16, 1959; April 10, 1960; December 14, 1969, pp. 44-45; September 28, 1980; April 19, 1981, pp. 6, 25; December 12, 1982, pp. 15, 28; April 24, 1988, p. 34.

Observer (London, England), February 26, 1989, p. 47; May 13, 1990, p. 58; September 29, 1991, p. 61; July 23, 1995, p. 14.

Prairie Schooner, winter, 1974-75, review by Robert S. Haller, pp. 151-158.

Publishers Weekly, August 1, 1980, review of *The Storyteller,* p. 45; August 12, 1996, review of *Life without Armour,* p. 74; August 26, 1996, review of *Collected Stories,* p. 90; January 3, 2000, review of *The German Numbers Woman,* p. 59; April 22, 2002, review of *Birthday,* p. 51.

San Francisco Chronicle, November 29, 1959; May 1, 1960.

Saturday Review, September 5, 1959; April 16, 1960; January 25, 1964; November 22, 1969, p. 86; October 16, 1971; September, 1980, David Bell, review of *The Storyteller,* p. 72.

Sewanee Review, summer, 1975.

Spectator, September 25, 1959; April 7, 2001, Allan Massie, review of *Birthday,* p. 32.

Studies in Short Fiction, number 4, 1966-67, pp. 350-351; winter, 1975, pp. 9-14.

Studies in the Novel, winter, 1973, pp. 469-482.

Sunday Times (London, England), February 26, 1989, p. G6.

Sunday Times Magazine (London, England), March 1, 1989, pp. 36, 38.

Time, April 18, 1960.

Times (London, England), November 10, 1983; November 15, 1984; October 10, 1985; February 23, 1989, p. 19.

Times Educational Supplement, July 4, 1993, p. 10; July 7, 1995, p. 12.

Times Literary Supplement, October 2, 1959; October 24, 1968, p. 1193; October 19, 1973; January 15, 1981; January 23, 1981, p. 76; October 15, 1982; November 11, 1983; November 16, 1984, p. 1301; June 7, 1985; December 6, 1985, p. 1407; April 7, 1989, Brian Morton, review of *The Open Door,* p. 364; May 18, 1990, D.A.N. Jones, review of *Last Loves,* p. 535; October 11, 1991, Candice Rodd, review of *Leonard's War,* p. 24; May 14, 1993, Sean O'Brien, review of *Snowstop,* p. 23; August 12, 1994, John Lucas, review of *Collected Poems,* p. 24; August 18, 1995, John Melmoth, review of *Life without Armour* and *Collected Stories,* p. 22; January 16, 1998, Henry Hitchings, review of *Alligator Playground,* p. 21; October 16, 1998, Neil Powell, review of *The Broken Chariot,* p. 24.

Tribune Books (Chicago, IL), October 26, 1980; August 31, 1981.

Washington Post, June 2, 1981; December 10, 1982; April 13, 1988, p. 8.

Washington Post Book World, October 26, 1980.

World Literature Today, summer, 1990, p. 465; spring, 1991, pp. 304-305; summer-autumn, 2002, p. 94.

Yale Review, September, 1959.

SILVERBERG, Robert 1935-

(Gordon Aghill, a joint pseudonym, Robert Arnette, a house pseudonym, T.D. Bethlen, Alexander Blade, a house pseudonym, Ralph Burke, a joint pseudonym, Walker Chapman, Dirk Clinton, Roy Cook, Walter Drummond, Dan Eliot, Don Elliott, Richard Greer, a house pseudonym, Franklin Hamilton, Paul Hollander, E.K. Jarvis, a house pseudonym, Ivar Jorgenson, Warren Kastel, a house pseudonym, Calvin M. Knox, Dan Malcolm, Webber Martin, Alex Merriman, Clyde Mitchell, a house pseudonym, David Osborne, George Osborne, Robert Randall, a joint pseudonym, Ellis Robertson, a joint pseudonym, Lloyd Robinson, Eric Rodman, Lee Sebastian, Leonard G. Spencer, a house pseudonym, S.M. Tenneshaw, a house pseudonym, Hall Thornton, Gerald Vance, a house pseudonym, Richard F. Watson)

PERSONAL: Born January 15, 1935, in New York, NY; son of Michael (an accountant) and Helen (Baim) Silverberg; married Barbara H. Brown (an engineer), August 26, 1956 (separated, 1976; divorced, 1986); married Karen L. Haber, 1987. *Education:* Columbia University, B.A., 1956.

ADDRESSES: Home—P.O. Box 13160, Station E, Oakland, CA 94661-0160. *Agent*—Ralph Vicinanza, 111 Eighth Ave., No. 1501, New York, NY 10011. *E-mail*—ragberg@attglobal.net.

CAREER: Writer, 1956—; president, Agberg Ltd., 1981—.

MEMBER: Science Fiction Writers of America (president, 1967-68), Hydra Club (chair, 1958-61).

AWARDS, HONORS: Hugo Awards, World Science Fiction Convention, best new author, 1956, best novella, 1969, for *Nightwings,* best novella, 1987, for *Gilgamesh in the Outback,* and best novelette, 1990, for *Enter a Soldier. Later: Enter Another; New York Times* best hundred children's books citation, 1960, for *Lost Race of Mars;* Spring Book Festival Awards, *New York Herald Tribune,* 1962, for *Lost Cities and Vanished Civilizations,* and 1967, for *The Auk, the Dodo, and the Oryx: Vanished and Vanishing Creatures;* National Association of Independent Schools award, 1966, for *The Old Ones: Indians of the American Southwest;* Nebula Award nominations, Science Fiction Writers of America, best novel, 1967, for *Thorns,* best novella,

1967, for *Hawksbill Station,* best novella, 1968, for *Nightwings,* best novel, 1969, for *Up the Line,* best novella, 1969, for *To Jorslem,* best novel, 1970, for *Tower of Glass,* best novel, 1972, for *The Book of Skulls,* best novel, 1972, for *Dying Inside,* best novel, 1975, for *The Stochastic Man,* best novel, 1976, for *Shadrach in the Furnace,* best short story, 1982, for "The Pope of Chimps," best novella, 1983, for *Homefaring,* best novella, 1986, for *Gilgamesh in the Outback,* best novella, 1987, for *The Secret Sharer,* and best novelette, 1989, for *Enter a Soldier. Later: Enter Another;* Hugo Award nominations, best novel, 1968, for *Thorns,* best novella, 1968, for *Hawksbill Station,* best novel, 1970, for *Up the Line,* best short story, 1970, for "Passengers," best novella, 1970, for *To Jorslem,* best novel, 1971, for *Tower of Glass,* best short story, 1971, for "The World Outside," best novel, 1972, for *A Time of Changes,* best novel, 1972, for *The World Inside,* best novel, 1973, for *The Book of Skulls,* best novel, 1973, for *Dying Inside,* best short story, 1973, for "When We Went to See the End of the World," best novella, 1975, for *Born with the Dead,* best short story, 1975, for "Schwartz between Galaxies," best novel, 1976, for *The Stochastic Man,* best novel, 1977, for *Shadrach in the Furnace,* best novel, 1981, for *Lord Valentine's Castle,* best short story, 1981, for "Our Lady of the Sauropods," best novella, 1986, for *Sailing to Byzantium,* best novella, 1988, for *The Secret Sharer,* best novella, 1993, for *Thebes of the Hundred Gates,* best short story, 1995, for "Via Roma," and best short story, 1996, for "Hot Times in Magma City"; Guest of Honor, World Science Fiction Convention, 1970; Nebula Awards, Science Fiction Writers of America, best short story, 1970, for "Passengers," best short story, 1972, for "Good News from the Vatican," best novel, 1972, for *A Time of Changes,* best novella, 1975, for *Born with the Dead,* and best novella, 1986, for *Sailing to Byzantium;* John W. Campbell Memorial Award, 1973, for excellence in writing; Jupiter Award, best novella, 1973, for *The Feast of St. Dionysus;* Prix Apollo, novel, 1976, for *Nightwings;* Milford Award, 1981, for editing; *Locus* Awards, best fantasy novel, 1982, for *Lord Valentine's Castle,* and best anthology, 1999, for *Legends: Short Novels by the Masters of Modern Fantasy.*

WRITINGS:

SCIENCE FICTION

Master of Life and Death (also see below), Ace Books (New York, NY), 1957.

The Thirteenth Immortal (bound with *This Fortress World* by J.E. Gunn), Ace Books, 1957.

Invaders from Earth (bound with *Across Time* by D. Grinnell), Ace Books, 1958, published separately, Avon, 1968, published as *We, the Marauders* (bound with *Giants in the Earth* by James Blish under joint title *A Pair in Space*), Belmont (New York, NY), 1965.

Stepsons of Terra (bound with *A Man Called Destiny* by L. Wright), Ace Books, 1958, published separately, 1977.

The Planet Killers (bound with *We Claim These Stars!*) by Poul Anderson), Ace Books, 1959.

Collision Course, Avalon (New York, NY), 1961.

Next Stop the Stars (story collection) [and] *The Seed of Earth* (novel), Ace Books, 1962, published separately, 1977.

Recalled to Life, Lancer Books (New York, NY), 1962.

The Silent Invaders (bound with *Battle on Venus* by William F. Temple), Ace Books, 1963, published separately, 1973.

Godling, Go Home! (story collection), Belmont, 1964.

Conquerors from the Darkness, Holt (New York, NY), 1965.

To Worlds Beyond: Stories of Science Fiction, Chilton, 1965.

Needle in a Timestack (story collection), Ballantine (New York, NY), 1966, revised edition, Ace Books, 1985.

Planet of Death, Holt, 1967.

Thorns, Ballantine, 1967.

Those Who Watch, New American Library (New York, NY), 1967.

The Time-Hoppers, Doubleday (New York, NY), 1967.

To Open the Sky (story collection), Ballantine, 1967.

Hawksbill Station, Doubleday, 1968, published as *The Anvil of Time,* Sidgwick & Jackson (London), 1968.

The Masks of Time, Ballantine, 1968, published as *Vornan-19,* Sidgwick & Jackson, 1970.

Dimension Thirteen (story collection), Ballantine, 1969.

The Man in the Maze, Avon (New York, NY), 1969.

Nightwings, Avon, 1969.

(Contributor) *Three for Tomorrow: Three Original Novellas of Science Fiction,* Meredith Press, 1969.

Three Survived, Holt, 1969.

To Live Again, Doubleday, 1969.

Up the Line, Ballantine, 1969, revised edition, 1978.

The Cube Root of Uncertainty (story collection), Macmillan (New York, NY), 1970.

Downward to the Earth, Doubleday, 1970.

Parsecs and Parables: Ten Science Fiction Stories, Doubleday, 1970.

A Robert Silverberg Omnibus (contains *Master of Life and Death, Invaders from Earth,* and *The Time-Hoppers*), Sidgwick & Jackson, 1970.

Tower of Glass, Scribner (New York, NY), 1970.

Moonferns and Starsongs (story collection), Ballantine, 1971.

Son of Man, Ballantine, 1971.

A Time of Changes, New American Library, 1971.

The World Inside, Doubleday, 1971.

The Book of Skulls, Scribner, 1972.

Dying Inside, Scribner, 1972, recorded by the author, Caedmon, 1979.

The Reality Trip and Other Implausibilities (story collection), Ballantine, 1972.

The Second Trip, Doubleday, 1972.

(Contributor) *The Day the Sun Stood Still,* Thomas Nelson, 1972.

Earth's Other Shadow: Nine Science Fiction Stories, New American Library, 1973.

(Contributor) *An Exaltation of Stars: Transcendental Adventures in Science Fiction* (includes short story *"The Feast of St. Dionysus"*), edited by Terry Carr, Simon & Schuster, 1973.

(Contributor) *No Mind of Man: Three Original Novellas of Science Fiction,* Hawthorn, 1973.

Unfamiliar Territory (story collection), Scribner, 1973.

Valley beyond Time (story collection), Dell (New York, NY), 1973.

Born with the Dead: Three Novellas about the Spirit of Man, Random House, 1974.

Sundance and Other Science Fiction Stories, Thomas Nelson (Nashville), 1974.

The Feast of St. Dionysus: Five Science Fiction Stories, Scribner, 1975.

The Stochastic Man, Harper (New York, NY), 1975.

The Best of Robert Silverberg, Volume 1, Pocket Books (New York, NY), 1976, Volume 2, Gregg, 1978.

Capricorn Games (story collection), Random House, 1976.

Shadrach in the Furnace, Bobbs-Merrill (Indianapolis), 1976.

The Shores of Tomorrow (story collection), Thomas Nelson, 1976.

The Songs of Summer and Other Stories, Gollancz, 1979.

Lord Valentine's Castle, Harper, 1980.

The Desert of Stolen Dreams, Underwood-Miller, 1981.

A Robert Silverberg Omnibus (contains *Downward to the Earth, The Man in the Maze,* and *Nightwings*), Harper, 1981.

Majipoor Chronicles, Arbor House (New York, NY), 1982.

World of a Thousand Colors (story collection), Arbor House, 1982.

Valentine Pontifex (sequel to *Lord Valentine's Castle*), Arbor House, 1983.

The Conglomeroid Cocktail Party (story collection), Arbor House, 1984.

Sailing to Byzantium, Underwood-Miller, 1985.

Tom O'Bedlam, Donald I. Fine, 1985.

Beyond the Safe Zone: Collected Short Fiction of Robert Silverberg, Donald I. Fine, 1986.

Star of Gypsies, Donald I. Fine, 1986.

At Winter's End, Warner (New York, NY), 1988.

Born with the Dead (bound with *The Saliva Tree* by Brian W. Aldiss), Tor Books (New York, NY), 1988.

To the Land of the Living, Gollancz, 1989.

(With wife, Karen Haber) *The Mutant Season,* Foundation/Doubleday, 1989.

The New Springtime, Warner, 1990.

In Another Country: Vintage Season, Tor Books, 1990.

(With Isaac Asimov) *Nightfall,* Doubleday, 1990.

Time Gate II, Baen Books, 1990.

The Face of the Waters, Bantam, 1991.

(With Asimov) *Child of Time,* Gollancz, 1991.

(With Asimov) *The Ugly Little Boy,* Doubleday, 1992.

Thebes of the Hundred Gates, Pulphouse, 1992.

The Collected Stories of Robert Silverberg, Volume 1: Secret Sharers, Bantam, 1992, published in 2 volumes, Grafton (London), 1992.

(With Asimov) *The Positronic Man,* Doubleday, 1993.

Kingdoms of the Wall, Bantam, 1993.

Hot Sky at Midnight, Bantam, 1994.

The Mountains of Majipoor, Bantam, 1995.

Starborne, Bantam, 1996.

The Alien Years, HarperPrism, 1998.

Shadow on the Stars, Foxacre Press, 2000.

Cronos, I Books, 2001.

Longest Way Home, Gollancz, 2002.

Roma Eterna, Eos, 2003.

Also author of short story "Passengers," published in *Orbit 4,* edited by Damon Knight, 1969; of novella *To Jorslem,* published in the periodical *Galaxy,* February, 1969; of short story "The World Outside," published in *Galaxy,* October, 1970; of short story "Good News from the Vatican," published in *Universe 1,* edited by Terry Carr, 1971; of short story "When We Went to See the End of the World," published in *Universe 2,* edited by Terry Carr, 1972; of short story "Schwartz between the Galaxies," published in *Stellar 1,* edited by Judy Lynn del Rey, 1973; of short story "Our Lady of the Sauropods," published in the periodical *Omni,* September, 1980; of short story "The Pope of Chimps," published in *Perpetual Light,* edited by Alan Ryan, 1982; of novella *Homefaring,* published in the periodical *Amazing Stories,* November, 1983; of novella *Gilgamesh in the Outback,* published in the periodical *Asimov's Science Fiction,* July, 1986; of novella *The Secret Sharer,* published in *Asimov's Science Fiction,* September, 1987; of novella *Enter a Soldier. Later: Enter Another,* published in *Asimov's Science Fiction,* June, 1989; of short story "Via Roma," published in *Asimov's Science Fiction,* April, 1994; of short story "Hot Times in Magma City," published in *Asimov's Science Fiction,* December, 1995.

"LORD PRESTIMION" SERIES

Sorcerers of Majipoor, HarperPrism, 1996.
Lord Prestimion, HarperPrism, 1999.
King of Dreams, Eos (New York, NY), 2001.

JUVENILE FICTION

Revolt on Alpha C, Crowell, 1955.
Starman's Quest, Gnome Press, 1959.
Lost Race of Mars, Winston, 1960.
Regan's Planet, Pyramid Books, 1964, revised edition published as *World's Fair, 1992,* Follett, 1970.
Time of the Great Freeze, Holt, 1964.
The Mask of Akhnaten, Macmillan, 1965.
The Gate of Worlds, Holt, 1967.
The Calibrated Alligator and Other Science Fiction Stories, Holt, 1969.
Across a Billion Years, Dial, 1969.
Sunrise on Mercury and Other Science Fiction Stories, Thomas Nelson, 1975.
(Editor with Charles G. Waugh and Martin H. Greenberg) *The Science Fictional Dinosaur,* Avon, 1982.
Project Pendulum, Walker, 1987.
Letters from Atlantis, Macmillan, 1990.

CHAPBOOKS

Absolutely Inflexible, Alexandria Digital Entertainment, 1998.
Hunters in the Forest, Random House (London, England), 2001.
Seventh Shrine, Tor (New York, NY), 2004.

NONFICTION

First American into Space, Monarch, 1961.
Lost Cities and Vanished Civilizations, Chilton, 1962.
Empires in the Dust: Ancient Civilizations Brought to Light, Chilton, 1963.
The Fabulous Rockefellers: A Compelling, Personalized Account of One of America's First Families, Monarch Books, 1963.
Akhnaten: The Rebel Pharaoh, Chilton, 1964.
(Editor) *Great Adventures in Archaeology,* Dial, 1964.
Man before Adam: The Story of Man in Search of His Origins, Macrae Smith, 1964.
The Great Wall of China, Chilton, 1965, published as *The Long Rampart: The Story of the Great Wall of China,* 1966.
Scientists and Scoundrels: A Book of Hoaxes, Crowell, 1965.
Bridges, Macrae Smith, 1966.
Frontiers in Archaeology, Chilton, 1966.
The Auk, the Dodo, and the Oryx: Vanished and Vanishing Creatures, Crowell, 1967.
Light for the World: Edison and the Power Industry, Van Nostrand, 1967.
Men Against Time: Salvage Archaeology in the United States, Macmillan, 1967.
Mound Builders of Ancient America: The Archaeology of a Myth, New York Graphic Society, 1968.
The Challenge of Climate: Man and His Environment, Meredith Press, 1969.
The World of Space, Meredith Press, 1969.
If I Forget Thee, O Jerusalem: American Jews and the State of Israel, Morrow, 1970.
The Pueblo Revolt, Weybright & Talley, 1970.
Before the Sphinx: Early Egypt, Thomas Nelson, 1971.
Clocks for the Ages: How Scientists Date the Past, Macmillan, 1971.
To the Western Shore: Growth of the United States, 1776-1853, Doubleday, 1971.
The Longest Voyage: Circumnavigators in the Age of Discovery, Bobbs-Merrill, 1972.
The Realm of Prester John, Doubleday, 1972.
(Contributor) *Those Who Can,* New American Library, 1973.
Drug Themes in Science Fiction, National Institute on Drug Abuse, 1974.
(Contributor) *Hell's Cartographers: Some Personal Histories of Science Fiction Writers,* Harper, 1975.

JUVENILE NONFICTION

Treasures beneath the Sea, Whitman Publishing, 1960.
Fifteen Battles That Changed the World, Putnam, 1963.
Home of the Red Man: Indian North America before Columbus, New York Graphic Society, 1963.
Sunken History: The Story of Underwater Archaeology, Chilton, 1963.
The Great Doctors, Putnam, 1964.

The Man Who Found Nineveh: The Story of Austen Henry Layard, Holt, 1964.

Men Who Mastered the Atom, Putnam, 1965.

Niels Bohr: The Man Who Mapped the Atom, Macrae Smith, 1965.

The Old Ones: Indians of the American Southwest, New York Graphic Society, 1965.

Socrates, Putnam, 1965.

The World of Coral, Duell, 1965.

Forgotten by Time: A Book of Living Fossils, Crowell, 1966.

To the Rock of Darius: The Story of Henry Rawlinson, Holt, 1966.

The Adventures of Nat Palmer: Antarctic Explorer and Clipper Ship Pioneer, McGraw, 1967.

The Dawn of Medicine, Putnam, 1967.

The Morning of Mankind: Prehistoric Man in Europe, New York Graphic Society, 1967.

The World of the Rain Forest, Meredith Press, 1967.

Four Men Who Changed the Universe, Putnam, 1968.

Ghost Towns of the American West, Crowell, 1968.

Stormy Voyager: The Story of Charles Wilkes, Lippincott, 1968.

The World of the Ocean Depths, Meredith Press, 1968.

Bruce of the Blue Nile, Holt, 1969.

Vanishing Giants: The Story of the Sequoias, Simon & Schuster, 1969.

Wonders of Ancient Chinese Science, Hawthorn, 1969.

Mammoths, Mastodons, and Man, McGraw, 1970.

The Seven Wonders of the Ancient World, Crowell-Collier, 1970.

(With Arthur C. Clarke) *Into Space: A Young Person's Guide to Space,* Harper, revised edition, 1971.

John Muir: Prophet among the Glaciers, Putnam, 1972.

The World within the Ocean Wave, Weybright & Talley, 1972.

The World within the Tide Pool, Weybright & Talley, 1972.

EDITOR; SCIENCE FICTION

Earthmen and Strangers: Nine Stories of Science Fiction, Duell, 1966.

Voyagers in Time: Twelve Stories of Science Fiction, Meredith Press, 1967.

Men and Machines: Ten Stories of Science Fiction, Meredith Press, 1968.

Dark Stars, Ballantine, 1969.

Tomorrow's Worlds: Ten Stories of Science Fiction, Meredith Press, 1969.

The Ends of Time: Eight Stories of Science Fiction, Hawthorn, 1970.

Great Short Novels of Science Fiction, Ballantine, 1970.

The Mirror of Infinity: A Critics' Anthology of Science Fiction, Harper, 1970.

The Science Fiction Hall of Fame, Doubleday, Volume 1, 1970, published in two volumes, Sphere (London), 1972.

Worlds of Maybe: Seven Stories of Science Fiction, Thomas Nelson, 1970.

1977–78 *Alpha,* Volumes 1-6, Ballantine, Volumes 7-9, Berkley.

Four Futures, Hawthorn, 1971.

Mind to Mind: Nine Stories of Science Fiction, Thomas Nelson, 1971.

The Science Fiction Bestiary: Nine Stories of Science Fiction, Thomas Nelson, 1971.

To the Stars: Eight Stories of Science Fiction, Hawthorn, 1971.

Beyond Control: Seven Stories of Science Fiction, Thomas Nelson, 1972.

Invaders from Space: Ten Stories of Science Fiction, Hawthorn, 1972.

Chains of the Sea: Three Original Novellas of Science Fiction, Thomas Nelson, 1973.

Deep Space: Eight Stories of Science Fiction, Thomas Nelson, 1973.

Other Dimensions: Ten Stories of Science Fiction, Hawthorn, 1973.

Three Trips in Time and Space, Hawthorn, 1973.

Infinite Jests: The Lighter Side of Science Fiction, Chilton, 1974.

Mutants: Eleven Stories of Science Fiction, Thomas Nelson, 1974.

Threads of Time: Three Original Novellas of Science Fiction, Thomas Nelson, 1974.

Windows into Tomorrow: Nine Stories of Science Fiction, Hawthorn, 1974.

(With Roger Elwood) *Epoch,* Berkley, 1975.

Explorers of Space: Eight Stories of Science Fiction, Thomas Nelson, 1975.

The New Atlantis and Other Novellas of Science Fiction, Warner Books, 1975.

Strange Gifts: Eight Stories of Science Fiction, Thomas Nelson, 1975.

The Aliens: Seven Stories of Science Fiction, Thomas Nelson, 1976.

The Crystal Ship: Three Original Novellas of Science Fiction, Thomas Nelson, 1976.

Earth Is the Strangest Planet: Ten Stories of Science Fiction, Thomas Nelson, 1977.

Galactic Dreamers: Science Fiction as Visionary Literature, Random House, 1977.

The Infinite Web: Eight Stories of Science Fiction, Dial, 1977.

Triax: Three Original Novellas, Pinnacle, 1977.

Trips in Time: Nine Stories of Science Fiction, Thomas Nelson, 1977.

Lost Worlds, Unknown Horizons: Nine Stories of Science Fiction, Thomas Nelson, 1978.

The Androids Are Coming: Seven Stories of Science Fiction, Elsevier-Nelson, 1979.

(With Greenberg and Joseph D. Olander) *Car Sinister,* Avon, 1979.

(With Greenberg and Olander) *Dawn of Time: Prehistory through Science Fiction,* Elsevier-Nelson, 1979.

The Edge of Space: Three Original Novellas of Science Fiction, Elsevier-Nelson, 1979.

(With Greenberg) *The Arbor House Treasury of Great Science Fiction Short Novels,* Arbor House, 1980.

(With Greenberg) *The Arbor House Treasury of Modern Science Fiction,* Arbor House, 1980.

Randall Garrett, *The Best of Randall Garrett,* Pocket Books, 1982.

The Nebula Awards, Arbor House, 1983.

(With Greenberg) *The Arbor House Treasury of Science Fiction Masterpieces,* Arbor House, 1983.

(With Greenberg) *The Fantasy Hall of Fame,* Arbor House, 1983.

(With Greenberg) *The Time Travelers: A Science Fiction Quartet,* Donald I. Fine, 1985.

(With Greenberg) *Neanderthals,* New American Library, 1987.

Robert Silverberg's Worlds of Wonder, Warner, 1987.

(With Greenberg) *The Mammoth Book of Fantasy All-Time Greats,* Robinson, 1988.

Worlds Imagined: Fifteen Short Stories, Crown, 1989.

(With Haber) *Universe 1,* Foundation/Doubleday, 1990.

(With Haber) *Universe 2,* Bantam Books, 1992.

Alfred Bester, *Virtual Unrealities: The Short Fiction of Alfred Bester,* Vintage, 1997.

Legends: Short Novels by the Masters of Modern Fantasy, Tor Books, 1997.

A Century of Fantasy, 1980-1989, MJF Books, 1997.

A Century of Science Fiction, 1950-1959, MJF Books, 1997.

Far Horizons: All New Tales from the Greatest Worlds of Science Fiction, Avon Eos, 1999.

EDITOR; "NEW DIMENSIONS" SERIES

1980–81 *New Dimensions,* Volumes 1-5, Doubleday, Volumes 6-10, Harper, (with Marta Randall) Volumes 11-12, Pocket Books.

The Best of New Dimensions, Pocket Books, 1979.

UNDER PSEUDONYM WALKER CHAPMAN

The Loneliest Continent: The Story of Antarctic Discovery, New York Graphic Society, 1964.

(Editor) *Antarctic Conquest: The Great Explorers in Their Own Words,* Bobbs-Merrill, 1966.

Kublai Khan: Lord of Xanadu, Bobbs-Merrill, 1966.

The Golden Dream: Seekers of El Dorado, Bobbs-Merrill 1967, published as *The Search for El Dorado,* 1967.

UNDER PSEUDONYM DON ELLIOTT

Flesh Peddlers, Nightstand, 1960.

Passion Trap, Nightstand, 1960.

Backstage Sinner, Nightstand, 1961.

Lust Goddess, Nightstand, 1961.

Sin Cruise, Nightstand, 1961.

Kept Man, Midnight, 1962.

Shame House, Midnight, 1962.

Sin Hellion, Ember, 1963.

Sin Servant, Nightstand, 1963.

Beatnik Wanton, Evening, 1964.

Flesh Bride, Evening, 1964.

Flesh Prize, Leisure, 1964.

Flesh Taker, Ember, 1964.

Sin Warped, Leisure, 1964.

Switch Trap, Evening, 1964.

Nudie Packet, Idle Hour, 1965.

The Young Wanton, Sundown, 1965.

Depravity Town, Reed, 1973.

Jungle Street, Reed, 1973.

Summertime Affair, Reed, 1973.

Also author of eighty other novels, 1959-65, under pseudonyms Dan Eliot and Don Elliott.

OTHER

(With Randall Garrett, under joint pseudonym Robert Randall) *The Shrouded Planet,* Gnome Press, 1957, published under names Robert Silverberg and Randall Garrett, Donning, 1980.

(Under pseudonym Calvin M. Knox) *Lest We Forget Thee, Earth,*Ace Books, 1958.

(Under pseudonym David Osborne) *Aliens from Space,* Avalon, 1958.

(Under pseudonym Ivar Jorgenson) *Starhaven,* Avalon, 1958.

(Under pseudonym David Osborne) *Invisible Barriers,* Avalon, 1958.

(With Randall Garrett, under joint pseudonym Robert Randall) *The Dawning Light,* Gnome Press, 1959, published under names Robert Silverberg and Randall Garrett, Donning, 1981.

(Under pseudonym Calvin M. Knox) *The Plot against Earth,* Ace Books, 1959.

(Under pseudonym Walter Drummond) *Philosopher of Evil,* Regency Books, 1962.

(Under pseudonym Walter Drummond) *How to Spend Money,* Regency Books, 1963.

(Under pseudonym Franklin Hamilton) *1066,* Dial, 1963.

(Under pseudonym Calvin M. Knox) *One of Our Asteroids Is Missing,* Ace Books, 1964.

(Under pseudonym Paul Hollander) *The Labors of Hercules,* Putnam, 1965.

(Under pseudonym Franklin Hamilton) *The Crusades,* Dial, 1965.

(Under pseudonym Lloyd Robinson) *The Hopefuls: Ten Presidential Candidates,* Doubleday, 1966.

(Under pseudonym Roy Cook) *Leaders of Labor,* Lippincott, 1966.

(Under pseudonym Lee Sebastian) *Rivers,* Holt, 1966.

(Under pseudonym Franklin Hamilton) *Challenge for a Throne: The Wars of the Roses,* Dial, 1967.

(Under pseudonym Lloyd Robinson) *The Stolen Election: Hayes versus Tilden,* Doubleday, 1968.

(Under pseudonym Paul Hollander) *Sam Houston,* Putnam, 1968.

(Under pseudonym Lee Sebastian) *The South Pole,* Holt, 1968.

Robert Silverberg Reads "To See the Invisible Man" and "Passengers" (recording), Pelican Records, 1979.

Lord of Darkness (fiction), Arbor House, 1983.

Gilgamesh the King (fiction), Arbor House, 1984.

Reflections and Refractions: Thoughts on Science-Fiction, Science, and Other Matters, Underwood Books (Grass Valley, CA), 1997.

Contributor, sometimes under pseudonyms, to *Omni, Playboy, Amazing Stories Science Fiction, Fantastic Stories Science Fiction, Magazine of Fantasy and Science Fiction,* and other publications.

SIDELIGHTS: Robert Silverberg is among the best-known contemporary science-fiction writers in the United States. A prolific author, he has won the field's prestigious Nebula and Hugo awards and has received more award nominations for his work than any other writer in the genre. Interestingly, despite his prominence in the field, Silverberg's science fiction makes up only a portion of his total production—indeed, he has even left the field entirely to work in other genres on two separate occasions. Much of Silverberg's work has been nonfiction, reflecting his interests in such varied topics as archaeology, conservation, history, and the natural sciences. He has received awards for several of these nonfiction books, while his *Mound Builders of Ancient America: The Archaeology of a Myth* has been hailed as one of the standard works on the subject. Still, this considerable success in the nonfiction field is overshadowed by his continuing popularity among science-fiction fans. As George R.R. Martin, writing in the *Washington Post Book World,* admits, Silverberg "is best known and best regarded for his work within science fiction."

Silverberg began his writing career while still a student at Columbia University in the 1950s. He had decided to become a science-fiction writer because of his own reaction to the genre as a boy. He told Jeffrey M. Elliot in *Science Fiction Voices #2:* "When I was a boy, I read science fiction and it did wonderful things for me. It opened the universe to me. I feel a sense of obligation to science fiction to replace what I had taken from it, to add to the shelf, to put something there for someone else that would do for them what other writers had done for me." Silverberg's first sales were to the science fiction magazines of the 1950s, and his first book, *Revolt on Alpha C* (1955), was a juvenile science-fiction novel. Upon graduation from Columbia in 1956, he became a full-time freelance writer. His work was already so popular that the World Science Fiction Convention, a gathering of the genre's devotees, voted him the Hugo Award as the best new writer of 1955. At the time, Silverberg was only twenty years old.

During the 1950s Silverberg produced hundreds of stories for the science fiction magazines. His production was so voluminous that he was obliged to publish much of this work under a host of pseudonyms. Silverberg recalled that time to Charles Platt in *Dream Makers: The Uncommon People Who Write Science Fiction:* "I was courted by editors considerably back then, because I was so dependable; if they said, 'Give me a story by next Thursday,' I would." George W. Tuma characterizes these early stories in the *Dictionary of Literary Biography* as "conform[ing] closely to the conventions of science fiction: alien beings, technological gadgetry, standard plot devices, confrontations between [Earthlings] and extraterrestrial beings, and so forth."

In 1959 a downturn in sales forced many science-fiction magazines out of business. No longer able to support himself by writing for the genre—and somewhat disillusioned by the formulaic nature of the work desired by publishers—Silverberg instead turned to writing articles for popular magazines, maintaining his high level of production by turning out two pieces every working day. By the early 1960s he began writing juvenile nonfiction, a career transition he once recalled with some relief to *CA*. "I severed my connections with my sleazy magazine outlets and ascended into this new, astoundingly respectable and rewarding career," he explained. In a few years Silverberg established himself as one of the most successful nonfiction writers in the country, publishing books about Antarctica, ancient Egypt, the U.S. space program, medical history, and a host of other topics for young readers. "I was considered one of the most skilled popularizers of the sciences in the United States," the author remembered.

During the 1960s Silverberg maintained a rapid writing pace, publishing nearly two million words per year, not only juvenile nonfiction works but science-fiction novels, such as the highly praised *Collision Course,* 1963's *The Silent Invaders,* sci-fi short stories, and rewrites of many of his earlier novels. He told Elliot that he managed to write prolifically due to intense concentration. "I concentrated on a point source and the words just came out right," the author recalled. Barry M. Malzberg in the *Magazine of Fantasy and Science Fiction* allows that "the man is prolific. Indeed, the man may be, in terms of accumulation of work per working year, the most prolific writer who ever lived."

However, the years of prolific writing finally ended in the mid-1960s. Silverberg later cited two factors for the slowdown in his production at that time. The first was a hyperactive thyroid gland, brought on by prolonged overwork, which forced him in 1966 to slow his working pace considerably. The second factor was a fire in early 1968 at Silverberg's New York City home. This fire, he once told *CA,* "drained from me, evidently forever, much of the bizarre energy that had allowed me to write a dozen or more significant books in a single year."

Despite the drop in production, the late 1960s found the author embarking on more experimental science-fiction writing. In fact, it is the work from this period that most observers credit as the beginning of his serious fiction in the genre. Thomas D. Clareson, although noting in his book *Robert Silverberg* that "from the beginning, he was a skilled storyteller," marked 1969 to 1976 the period when Silverberg "conducted his most deliberate experiments and attained the most consistent command of his material." Malzberg claimed that "in or around 1965 Silverberg put his toys away and began to write literature."1967's *Thorns* has been cited as the author's transitional work through its focus on not only the physical universe, but the inner, psychic universe as reflected by philosophical, psychological, and social elements. In the novel, human protagonist Minner Burris has been physically altered to conform to beings on the planet Manipol. On Manipol, while now accepted for his appearance, Burris is emotionally isolated from native Manipolians due to his social, cultural, and psychological differences. Eventually returning to Earth, he finds himself rejected due to his unusual appearance. Burris's resulting alienation from human society is contrasted with that of other characters, whose circumstances have set them apart while their inner natures continue to need the contact of fellow humans.

In part, the change in Silverberg's science fiction of the late 1960s reflected shifts in the field as a whole. The New Wave, a movement of writers (including Silverberg) trying to break out of the pulp formulas of science fiction and utilize the techniques of modernist literature, had a powerful influence on many writers in the field. New subjects and approaches were suddenly suitable for commercial science fiction. Referring to such novels as *Nightwings* (1969) and *Hawksbill Station* (1968), in an article in the *New York Times Book Review,* Theodore Sturgeon maintains that Silverberg "changed into something quite new and different—his own man, saying his own things his own way, and doing it with richness and diversity." Tuma also saw a transformation in Silverberg's work, stating that the author finally "found his unique approach to science fiction, in terms of both content and writing style." And Russell Letson, writing in *Extrapolation,* found Silverberg's fiction "pursued the modernist themes of anxiety and alienation" while he "shaped science fiction materials to deal with themes that were not previously part of the American sf mainstream." Speaking of the novels *Thorns* and *Hawksbill Station,* as well as of the story "To See the Invisible Man," Stableford sees Silverberg as using "science fictional ideas to dramatize situations of extreme alienation."

As Silverberg sought to extend the range of science fiction his experiments with style and narrative structure continued into the 1970s. "Having already proved that he could write every kind of s.f. story at least as well as anyone else," Gerald Jonas comments in the *New York Times Book Review,* "Silverberg set out . . . to stretch both the genre and himself." In 1971's *Son of Man,* for example, Silverberg writes of a series of bizarre adventure sequences set on "not the physical planet Earth but the Earth of human perception—the model world of the mind," as Stableford relates. Clay, the novel's aptly named protagonist, time-shifts to the future, where he meets several species of humanoids that have evolved in differing directions. In this future world, communication between beings involves sexual contact, and Clay eventually experiences unity and transcendence through understanding the heightened significance of physical union. Sandra Miesel, writing in *Extrapolation,* calls *Son of Man* a "sensuous, didactic, and witty novel" in which "the dream fantasy is stretched to the breaking point."

Despite the fact that his new approach in his work put Silverberg in the forefront of the science fiction field—"By the 1970s Silverberg was writing science fiction much as such of his contemporaries as Barth, Reed, Bartheleme, and Coover were presenting their renditions of everyday American life," Clareson would write in *Voices for the Future: Essays on Major Science-Fiction Writers*—Silverberg was dissatisfied with the response to his work. His books won awards, but their sales were poor and they often met with uninformed critical comments from science fiction purists. "I was at first bewildered by the response I was getting from the audience," Silverberg told Platt. "There are passages in *Dying Inside* or in *Nightwings* which I think are sheer ecstatic song, but people would come up to me and say, Why do you write such depressing books? Something was wrong." By 1975 all of Silverberg's more serious books, upon which he had placed such importance, were out of print. At that point he announced his retirement from science fiction.

For the next four years Silverberg wrote no new science fiction. Instead, he devoted his time to the garden of his California home. "I had had my career," the author once recalled to *CA*. "Now I had my garden." But in 1978 he was pushed back into the field after he and his first wife separated and she required a house of her own. To raise the necessary money, Silverberg decided to write "one last book." The result, *Lord Valentine's Castle,* was a massive novel that set a record (for its time) when it was offered to publishers at auction. Harper & Row paid the largest sum ever given for a science fiction novel, $127,500. Silverberg was a writer again.

In *Lord Valentine's Castle* Silverberg mixes elements from science fiction and heroic fantasy. The science fiction elements include a far future setting, the imaginary planet of Majipoor, and a host of exotic alien life forms. However, the plot is common to the fantasy genre. It involves a quest by the exiled prince of a distant planet to regain the throne of Majipoor, right the ancient wrong of dispossession committed against the planet's original inhabitants, the primitive Metamorph peoples, and rejuvenate his own self-confidence. The clever combination of genre elements was praised by Jack Sullivan in the *New York Times Book Review.* Sullivan describes *Lord Valentine's Castle* as "an imaginative fusion of action, sorcery and science fiction, with visionary adventure scenes undergirded by scientific explanations." In his book *Robert Silverberg,* Clareson states that "whatever else it does, *Lord Valentine's Castle* demands that its readers re-examine the relationship between science fiction and fantasy, for in this narrative Silverberg has fused the two together."

The rich diversity of the planet Majipoor was remarked upon by several reviewers, including Patrick Parrinder of the *Times Literary Supplement.* "Silverberg's invention," Parrinder writes, "is prodigious throughout. The early sections . . . are a near-encyclopaedia of unnatural wonders and weird ecosystems. I suspect this book breaks all records in the coinage of new species." John Charnay of the *Los Angeles Times Book Review,* although believing the book "lacks depth of dialogue and emotion to match the grandeur of scenery and plot," still finds that "Silverberg's inventiveness is intriguing."

The success of *Lord Valentine's Castle* drew Silverberg back into the writing life. He began to write stories for *Omni* magazine, where several old friends were working. In 1982 he published *Majipoor Chronicles,* a novel fashioned from several short stories set on the planet introduced in *Lord Valentine's Castle.* Each story is an episode from Majipoor's history, which has been stored on an experience-record. By using a futuristic reading machine, a young boy is able to relive these historical events. "As a result," Michael Bishop comments in the *Washington Post Book World,* "the stories become something more than stories—vivid initiation experiences in the boy's struggle to manhood. A neat trick, this." Sturgeon, in his review of the book for the *Los Angeles Times Book Review,* expresses "absolute awe at Silverberg's capacity for creating images—wonder upon wonder, marvel upon marvel, all with verisimilitude. . . . This is a beautiful book."

With the novel *Valentine Pontifex,* Silverberg did what he had once vowed he would never do: write a sequel to *Lord Valentine's Castle.* Colin Greenland, of the *Times Literary Supplement,* who had maintained that *Lord Valentine's Castle* was a weak novel that "satisfied readers' wishes for a great big safe world where nice things flourish and evil succumbs to forgiveness," saw Silverberg's sequel as an "act of conscience for *Lord Valentine's Castle.* " In *Valentine Pontifex,* Lord Valentine, now restored to his position as ruler of Majipoor, faces opposition from the Piurivars, an aboriginal race dispossessed years before by Earthling colonists. The Piurivars release plagues and deadly bio-engineered creatures upon the humans. Finding that "the lazy pace through time and space" found in *Lord Valentine's Castle* gives way in this novel "to a dance of conflicting emotions and political intrigue," a reviewer for the *Voice Literary Supplement* regards *Lord Valentine's Castle, Majipoor Chronicles,* and *Valentine Pontifex* as related works forming a loose trilogy that "becomes a whole in a way that the form rarely achieves."

Silverberg continued the Majipoor series with *The Mountains of Majipoor, Sorcerers of Majipoor,* and *Lord Prestimion. The Mountains of Majipoor* "is a modest story," recounted Roland Green in *Booklist,* "but the marvelously well realized world of Majipoor and Silverberg's graceful prose carry it along in a fashion that most lovers of Majipoor will find highly satisfying." *Lord Prestimion,* published in 1999, was also well received by critics. Jackie Cassada in *Library Journal* writes: "Silverberg excels at balancing strong characters and complex plotting to achieve a rare example of epic fantasy told with a scientist's eye for detail."

In the years since his return from self-imposed "early retirement," Silverberg has continued his work in the genre with both novels and short stories that expand upon his view of future worlds. Among those are 1988's *At Winter's End,* the following year's *To the Land of the Living,* and *Kingdoms of the Wall,* which Silverberg published in 1993. Compared by one reviewer to the works of nineteenth-century fantasy writer Lord Dunsany, *Kingdoms of the Wall* follows the pilgrimage of a group of young alien beings to the summit of a daunting mountain range called Kosa Saag, or "the Wall." The purpose of the pilgrimage was to learn from the gods who live at that great height. Traditionally, few pilgrims ever returned from this annual trip, and none had ever returned sane. On the way, the group passes through numerous "worlds" at different levels of the mountains' ascent, at one point coming across a space traveler, an "Irtiman" (Earthman), who has been stranded on their planet. He is weak from hunger and eventually dies. Finally, nearing the summit, the surviving members of the group are tempted to end their quest when they discover a land of magic where they can remain perpetually young. *Analog* reviewer Tom Easton views Silverberg's tale as social allegory: "He is . . . hinting that those who persevere despite all the pressures upon them to conform do not find the satisfaction they crave. In fact, if they ever reach the goal of their quest, they are crashingly disillusioned." In contrast, *New York Times Book Review* critic Gerald Jonas viewed the work as a religious parable "about the dangers of seeking more intimate contact with the powers that control the universe." Disregarding the novel's social or spiritual implications, Paul Di-Filippo lauded *Kingdoms of the Wall* in his *Washington Post Book World* review "for its first two-thirds, pure witchery, a Bosch-like canvas of strange creatures and places. . . . *Kingdoms of the Wall* proves once more, if it needed proving, that scaling and comprehending Robert Silverberg is just as exciting as tackling Kosa Saag."

Many of Silverberg's works have been supplemented in bookstores by reprints and limited editions of earlier, often unpublished works. In addition, several collections have drawn together some of his best short fiction from the 1970s and 1980s. *The Conglomeroid Cocktail Party,* released in 1984, collects several short stories from the early 1980s that a *Sci-Fi Review* critic termed "very slick, very polished, and often [focusing on] substantial matters, but at the same time . . . perfunctory." However, Stan Gebler Davies disagrees in *Punch,* praising Silverberg's ability to portray time travel realistically. Citing included works, such as "Needles in a Timestack" and "Jennifer's Lover," Davies notes that "Silverberg is hooked on time-travel and comes as near as any writer to getting away with it." Also with the publication of the first part of *The Collected Stories of Robert Silverberg* in 1992, Silverberg devotees were able to sample twenty-four of his most critically acclaimed short stories of the 1980s. In addition to the novella *Sailing to Byzantium,* winner of the Nebula Award, and *Enter a Soldier. Later: Enter Another,* a Hugo winner, are lesser-known but equally well-written works, each prefaced by the author's own introduction, which puts the story into the context of the author's total oeuvre. "The end result," notes Gary K. Wolfe in *Locus,* "is not only a good lesson in craft and style, but a clear picture of a highly professional writer who knows exactly what he's doing—even when he plays it safe." James Sallis agrees in a *Los Angeles Times Book Review* piece. He comments that "This man who speaks so insistently of simple craftsmanship again and again delivers, surreptitiously and a little abashedly, it seems, a rare kind of art."

Over a writing career spanning several decades, Silverberg has produced an immense body of original fiction in several genres, authored numerous nonfiction works, and edited several highly praised collections, such as 1992's shared-world anthology titles *Murasaki,* featuring work by writers Frederik Pohl, Nancy Kress, and

Pohl Anderson. Commenting on Silverberg's diversity, Martin reflects that "few writers, past or present, have had careers quite as varied, dramatic, and contradictory as that of Robert Silverberg." As a writer of nonfiction, Silverberg has enjoyed success, but as a writer of science fiction, he is among a handful of writers who have helped to shape the field into what it is today. He is, Elliot declares, "a titan in the science fiction field." "Few science fiction readers," Elliot continues, "have not been enriched and inspired by his contributions to the genre, contributions which reflect his love of the field and his deep respect for its readers." Silverberg's contributions to the field, Clareson writes in the *Magazine of Fantasy and Science Fiction,* are of predictably high quality: "He will tell a good story, he will fuse together content and form, and he will add to our perception of the human condition."

In his introduction to *Galactic Dreamers: Science Fiction as Visionary Literature,* Silverberg explains what he has been striving to attain in his work: "To show the reader something he has never been able to see with his own eyes, something strange and unique, beautiful and troubling, which draws him for a moment out of himself, places him in contact with the vastness of the universe, gives him for a sizzling moment a communion with the fabric of space and time, and leaves him forever transformed, forever enlarged."

BIOGRAPHICAL AND CRITICAL SOURCES:

BOOKS

Aldiss, Brian, and Harry Harrison, editors, *Hell's Cartographers: Some Personal Histories of Science-Fiction Writers,* Harper, 1975.

Chapman, Edgar L., *The Road to Castle Mount: The Science Fiction of Robert Silverberg,* Greenwood Press, 1999.

Children's Literature Review, Volume 59, Thomson Gale (Detroit), 2000.

Clareson, Thomas D., editor, *Voices for the Future: Essays on Major Science Fiction Writers,* Volume 2, Bowling Green State University Popular Press, 1979.

Clareson, Thomas D., *Robert Silverberg,* Starmont House, 1983.

Clareson, Thomas D., *Robert Silverberg: A Primary and Secondary Bibliography,* G.K. Hall, 1983.

Contemporary Literary Criticism, Volume 7, Thomson Gale, 1977.

Dictionary of Literary Biography, Volume 8: *Twentieth-Century American Science Fiction Writers,* Thomson Gale, 1981.

Elliot, Jeffrey M., *Science Fiction Voices #2,* Borgo Press, 1979.

Magill, Frank N., editor, *Survey of Science Fiction,* Salem Press, 1979.

Platt, Charles, *Dream Makers: The Uncommon People Who Write Science Fiction,* Berkley, 1980.

Rabkin, Eric S., and others, editors, *No Place Else,* Southern Illinois University Press, 1983.

Schweitzer, Darrell, editor, *Exploring Fantasy Worlds: Essays on Fantastic Literature,* Borgo Press, 1985.

Silverberg, Robert, editor, *Galactic Dreamers: Science Fiction as Visionary Literature,* Random House, 1977.

Stableford, Brian M., *Masters of Science Fiction,* Borgo Press, 1981.

Staircar, Tom, editor, *Critical Encounters II,* Ungar, 1982.

Walker, Paul, *Speaking of Science Fiction: The Paul Walker Interviews,* Luna Press, 1978.

PERIODICALS

Analog Science Fiction/Science Fact, November, 1979; December, 1990; August, 1993, p. 162; July, 1994, p. 306.

Atlantic, April, 1972.

Booklist, September 1, 1992; February 1, 1995, p. 993; May 15, 1996, p. 1573; April 1, 1997, p. 1277; August, 1998, p. 1924; May 15, 1999, p. 1676.

Essays in Arts and Sciences, August, 1980.

Extrapolation, summer, 1979; winter, 1980; winter, 1982.

Fantasy Newsletter, June-July, 1983.

Library Journal, June 15, 1997, p. 101; August, 1998, p. 139; August, 1999, p. 147.

Locus, March, 1992, p. 60; April, 1992, p. 15; October, 1992, p. 33; January, 1993, pp. 22-23; February, 1994, p. 27.

Los Angeles Times Book Review, May 18, 1980; April 18, 1986; September 13, 1987; January 10, 1993.

Magazine of Fantasy and Science Fiction, April, 1971; April, 1974; May, 1988.

Megavore, March, 1981.

National Review, November 3, 1970.

New Statesman, June 18, 1976.

New York Times Book Review, May 9, 1965; November 3, 1968; March 5, 1972; August 24, 1975; August 3, 1980; August 4, 1985; November 23, 1986; July 24, 1988; December 31, 1989; May 13, 1990; December 9, 1990; May 3, 1992, p. 38; March 14, 1993; November 14, 1993; March 13, 1994 p. 30; June 30, 1996, p. 28.

Publishers Weekly, December 20, 1993, p. 54; January 16, 1995, p. 444; May 27, 1996, p. 69; January 27, 1997, p. 86; June 16, 1997, p. 49; June 29, 1998, p. 40; September 21, 1998, p. 78; April 12, 1999, p. 58; July 26, 1999, p. 68.

Punch, March 6, 1985, p. 54.

Rapport, Volume 18, number 2, 1994, p. 19.

Science Fiction: A Review of Speculative Literature, September, 1983.

Science Fiction Chronicle, January, 1985; May, 1985.

Sci-Fi Review, February, 1985, pp. 51-52.

Starship, November, 1982.

Times (London), November 19, 1988; August 2, 1990.

Times Literary Supplement, June 12, 1969; March 15, 1974; November 7, 1980; August 3, 1984; January 2, 1987.

Tribune Books (Chicago), December 30, 1990.

Voice Literary Supplement, December, 1983.

Voice of Youth Advocates, August, 1993, pp. 170-171; June, 1993, p. 104.

Washington Post Book World, February 28, 1982; May 8, 1983; September 28, 1986; September 27, 1987; May 27, 1990; March 28, 1993, p. 9.

Writer, November, 1977.

* * *

SILVERSTEIN, Shel 1932-1999
(Sheldon Allan Silverstein, Uncle Shelby)

PERSONAL: Born September 25, 1932, in Chicago, IL; died of a heart attack, May 8, 1999, in Key West, FL; son of Nathan and Helen Silverstein; divorced; children: Matthew.

CAREER: Cartoonist, composer, lyricist, folksinger, writer, and director. *Playboy,* Chicago, IL, writer and cartoonist, 1956-99. Appeared in film, *Who Is Harry Kellerman and Why Is He Saying Those Terrible Things about Me?,* 1971. *Military service:* Served with U.S. forces in Japan and Korea during 1950s; cartoonist for Pacific *Stars and Stripes.*

AWARDS, HONORS: New York Times Outstanding Book Award, 1974, Michigan Young Readers' Award, 1981, and George G. Stone Award, 1984, all for *Where the Sidewalk Ends: The Poems & Drawings of Shel Silverstein; School Library Journal* Best Books Award, 1981, Buckeye Award, 1983 and 1985, George G. Stone Award, 1984, and William Allen White Award, 1984, all for *A Light In the Attic;* International Reading Association's Children's Choice Award, 1982, for *The Missing Piece Meets the Big O.*

WRITINGS:

SELF-ILLUSTRATED

Now Here's My Plan: A Book of Futilities, foreword by Jean Shepherd, Simon & Schuster (New York, NY), 1960.

Uncle Shelby's ABZ Book: A Primer for Tender Young Minds (humor), Simon & Schuster (New York, NY), 1961.

Playboy's Teevee Jeebies (drawings), Playboy Press (Chicago, IL), 1963.

Uncle Shelby's Story of Lafcadio, the Lion Who Shot Back (juvenile), Harper (New York, NY), 1963.

The Giving Tree (juvenile), Harper (New York, NY), 1964, thirty-fifth anniversary edition, HarperCollins (New York, NY), 1999.

Uncle Shelby's Giraffe and a Half (verse; juvenile), Harper (New York, NY), 1964, published in England as *A Giraffe and a Half,* J. Cape (London, England), 1988.

Uncle Shelby's Zoo: Don't Bump the Glump! (verse; juvenile), Simon & Schuster (New York, NY), 1964.

(Under pseudonym Uncle Shelby) *Who Wants a Cheap Rhinoceros!* Macmillan (New York, NY), 1964, revised and expanded edition, Simon & Schuster (New York, NY), 2002.

More Playboy's Teevee Jeebies: Do-It-Yourself Dialog for the Late Late Show (drawings), Playboy Press (Chicago, IL), 1965.

Where the Sidewalk Ends: The Poems & Drawings of Shel Silverstein (poems), Harper (New York, NY), 1974, thirtieth anniversary edition, HarperCollins (New York, NY), 2004.

The Missing Piece (juvenile), Harper (New York, NY), 1976.

Different Dances (drawings), Harper (New York, NY), 1979, twenty-fifth anniversary edition, HarperCollins (New York, NY), 2004.

A Light in the Attic (poems), Harper (New York, NY), 1981.

The Missing Piece Meets the Big O (juvenile), Harper (New York, NY), 1981.

(With Cherry Potts) *Poetry Galore and More,* Upstart Library (New York, NY), 1993.

Falling Up: Poems and Drawings, HarperCollins (New York, NY), 1996.

Runny Babbit: A Billy Sook, HarperCollins (New York, NY), 2005.

PLAYS

The Lady or the Tiger Show (one-act; from the short story by Frank Stockton), first produced in New York, NY at Ensemble Studio Theatre, May, 1981.

(And director) *Gorilla,* first produced in Chicago, IL, 1983.

Wild Life (contains *I'm Good to My Doggies, Nonstop, Chicken Suit Optional,* and *The Lady or the Tiger Show*), first produced in New York, NY, 1983.

Remember Crazy Zelda? first produced in New York, NY, 1984.

The Crate, first produced in New York, NY, 1985.

The Happy Hour, first produced in New York, NY, 1985.

One Tennis Shoe, first produced in New York, NY, 1985.

Little Feet, first produced in New York, NY, 1986.

Wash and Dry, first produced in New York, NY, 1986.

The Devil and Billy Markham (drama; produced in New York, NY, at Lincoln Center, December, 1989, with David Mamet's *Bobby Gould in Hell* under the collective title *Oh, Hell*) published in *Oh, Hell!: Two One-Act Plays,* Samuel French (New York, NY), 1991.

(Contributor) Billy Aronson, editor, *The Best American Short Plays 1992-1993: The Theatre Annual since 1937,* Applause (Diamond Bar, CA), 1993.

OTHER

(Contributor) Myra Cohn Livingston, editor, *I Like You, If You Like Me: Poems of Friendship,* Margaret McElderry Books (New York, NY), 1987.

(With David Mamet) *Things Change* (screenplay), Grove Press (New York, NY), 1988.

Also composer and lyricist of songs, including "A Boy Named Sue," "One's on the Way," "The Unicorn," "Boa Constrictor," "So Good to So Bad," "The Great Conch Train Robbery," and "Yes, Mr. Rogers." Albums of Silverstein's songs recorded by others include *Freakin' at the Freakers Ball,* Columbia, 1972; *Sloppy Seconds,* Columbia, 1972; *Dr. Hook,* Columbia, 1972; and *Bobby Bare Sings Lullabys, Legends, and Lies: The Songs of Shel Silverstein,* RCA Victor, 1973. Albums of original motion picture scores include *Ned Kelly,* United Artists, 1970, and *Who Is Harry Kellerman and Why Is He Saying Those Terrible Things about Me?* Columbia, 1971. Other recordings include *Drain My Brain,* Cadet; *Dirty Feet,* Hollis Music, 1968; *Shel Silverstein: Songs and Stories,* Casablanca, 1978; *The Great Conch Train Robbery,* 1980; and *Where the Sidewalk Ends,* Columbia, 1984. *The Giving Tree* has been translated into French and Latin.

SIDELIGHTS: Shel Silverstein was best known for his collections of children's poetry *Where the Sidewalk Ends: The Poems & Drawings of Shel Silverstein* and *A Light in the Attic,* both of which enjoyed extended stays on the *New York Times* Bestseller List. Silverstein was also the author of the children's classic *The Giving Tree.* In addition to his writings for children, Silverstein served as a longtime *Playboy* cartoonist, wrote several plays for adults, and penned and recorded such country and novelty songs as Johnny Cash's "A Boy Named Sue."

Silverstein's talents were well-developed when he joined the U.S. armed forces in the 1950s. Stationed in Japan and Korea, he worked as a cartoonist for the Pacific edition of the military newspaper *Stars and Stripes.* After leaving the military, Silverstein became a cartoonist for *Playboy* in 1956, and his work for that magazine resulted in such collections as *Playboy's Teevee Jeebies* and *More Playboy's Teevee Jeebies: Do-It-Yourself Dialog for the Late Late Show.*

Silverstein's career as a children's author began with the 1963 publication of *Uncle Shelby's Story of Lafcadio, the Lion Who Shot Back.* In a *Publishers Weekly* interview, he confided to Jean F. Mercier: "I never planned to write or draw for kids. It was Tomi Ungerer, a friend of mine, who insisted. . . practically dragged me, kicking and screaming, into (editor) Ursula Nordstrom's office. And she convinced me that Tomi was right, I could do children's books." *Lafcadio* concerns a lion who obtains a hunter's gun and practices until he becomes a good enough marksman to join a circus. A *Publishers Weekly* reviewer called the book "a wild, free-wheeling, slangy tale that most children and many parents will enjoy immensely."

Although *Lafcadio* and *Uncle Shelby's Giraffe and a Half* met with moderate success, it was not until *The Giving Tree* that Silverstein first achieved widespread fame as a children's writer. The story of a tree that sacrifices its shade, fruit, branches, and finally its trunk to a little boy in order to make him happy, *The Giving Tree* had slow sales initially, but its audience steadily grew. As Richard R. Lingeman reported in the *New York Times Book Review,* "Many readers saw a religious symbolism in the altruistic tree; ministers preached sermons on *The Giving Tree;* it was discussed in Sunday schools." Despite its popularity as a moral or fable, the book was on occasion attacked by feminist critics for what they perceived as its inherent sexism; Barbara A. Schram noted in *Interracial Books for Children:* "By choosing the female pronoun for the all-giving tree and the male pronoun for the all-taking boy, it is clear that the author did indeed have a prototypical master/slave relationship in mind. . . How frightening that little boys and girls who read *The Giving Tree* will encounter this glorification of female selflessness and male selfishness."

In 1974 Silverstein published the collection of poems titled *Where the Sidewalk Ends.* Earning Silverstein favorable comparisons to Dr. Seuss and Edward Lear, *Where the Sidewalk Ends* contained such humorous pieces as "Sarah Cynthia Sylvia Stout / Would Not Take the Garbage Out," "Dreadful," and "Band-Aids." The collection and its 1981 successor, *A Light in the Attic,* continue to be popular with both children and adults; *Publishers Weekly* called the latter book "a big, fat treasure for Silverstein devotees, with trenchant verses expressing high-flown, exhilarating nonsense as well as thoughts unexpectedly sober and even sad."

Silverstein's 1976 *The Missing Piece,* like *The Giving Tree,* has been subject to varying interpretations. The volume chronicles the adventures of a circle who, lacking a piece of itself, goes along singing and searching for its missing part. But after the circle finds the wedge, he decides he was happier on the search—without the missing wedge—than he is with it. As Anne Roiphe explained in the *New York Times Book Review, The Missing Piece* can be read in the same way as "the fellow at the singles bar explaining why life is better if you don't commit yourself to anyone for too long—the line goes that too much togetherness turns people into bores—that creativity is preserved by freedom to explore from one relationship to another. . . . This fable can also be interpreted to mean that no one should try to find all the answers, no one should hope to fill all the holes in themselves, achieve total transcendental harmony or psychic order because a person without a search, loose ends, internal conflicts and external goals becomes too smooth to enjoy or know what's going on. Too much satisfaction blocks exchange with the outside." Silverstein published a sequel, *The Missing Piece Meets the Big O,* in 1981. This work is told from the missing piece's perspective, and as in the original, the book's protagonist discovers the value of self-sufficiency.

Beginning in 1981, Silverstein concentrated on writing plays for adults. One of his best known, *The Lady or the Tiger Show,* has been performed on its own and with other one-act works collectively entitled *Wild Life.* Updating a short story by American novelist and fiction writer Frank Stockton, *The Lady or the Tiger Show* concerns a game show producer willing to go to extreme lengths to achieve high ratings. Placed in a life-or-death situation, the contestant of the show is forced to choose between two doors; behind one door lies a ferocious tiger, while the girl of his dreams is concealed behind the other. The play was characterized in *Variety* as "a hilarious harpooning of media hype and show biz amorality."

With *Falling Up,* Silverstein returned to poetry for children (and adults) after a fifteen-year absence. This collection of 140 poems with drawings ranges in subject matter "from tattoos to sun hats to God to—no kidding—a garden of noses," wrote Susan Stark in the *Detroit News. Publishers Weekly* called the poems "vintage Silverstein," a work "cheeky and clever and often darkly subversive," focusing on the unexpected. Judy Zuckerman reported in the *New York Times Book Review,* "Mr. Silverstein's expressive line drawings are perfectly suited to his texts, extending the humor, and sometimes the strangeness of his ideas."

Silverstein also collaborated with American playwright, scriptwriter, director, and novelist David Mamet on several projects. The two cowrote the screenplay for Mamet's 1988 film *Things Change,* which starred Joe Mantegna and Don Ameche. Silverstein's play *The Devil and Billy Markham* and Mamet's *Bobby Gould in Hell* have also been published and produced together under the collective title *Oh, Hell.* Performed as a monologue, *The Devil and Billy Markham* relates a series of bets made between Satan and a Nashville songwriter and singer. Although the work received mixed reviews, William A. Henry III noted in *Time* that "Silverstein's script, told in verse with occasional bursts of music, is rowdy and rousing and raunchily uproarious, especially in a song about a gala party where saints and sinners mingle."

Silverstein died of a heart attack in May, 1999. According to an obituary in *Publishers Weekly,* Robert Warren, the editorial director of HarperCollins Children's Books and Silverstein's editor, commented that "He had a genius that transcended age and gender, and his work probably touched the lives of more people than any writer in the second half of the 20th century."

Roughly six years after his death, a previously unpublished work by Silverstein was released. *Runny Babbit: A Billy Sook,* which the author had been working on for more than twenty years, was met with generally positive reviews. Lee Bock, writing for *School Library Journal,* lauded the work for containing the "signature comical bold line drawings" common to Silverstein's work and referred to the book as "a treasure." The story introduces Runny Babbit and several of his companions, who make their way through a world of poems in which most words have been rearranged. In her review of *Runny Babbit* for *Horn Book Magazine,* Susan Dove Lempke wrote, "this new book is a surprising treat." Lempke concluded, "readers will find Runny both lovable and memorable." An obituary in the *Media Industry Newsletter* related that *Playboy* founder Hugh Hefner, the man credited with giving Silverstein his break, called him "a Renaissance man. He was a giant as a talent, a giant as a human being."

BIOGRAPHICAL AND CRITICAL SOURCES:

BOOKS

Children's Literature Review, Volume 5, Thomson Gale (Detroit), 1983, pp. 208-13.

Something about the Author, Thomson Gale, Volume 27, 1982, Volume 33, 1983, Volume 92, 1997.

Twentieth-Century Children's Writers, 3rd edition, St. James Press (Detroit), 1989, pp. 886-87.

PERIODICALS

Back Stage, May 21, 1999, p. 58.

Billboard, May 22, 1999, p. 93.

Book Week, March 21, 1965.

Detroit News, November 4, 1979; May 1, 1996.

Entertainment Weekly, May 21, 1999, p. 14.

Hollywood Reporter, May 12, 1999, p. 13.

Horn Book Magazine, May-June, 2005, Susan Dove Lempke, review of *Runny Babbit: A Billy Sook,* p. 343.

Independent, May 25, 1999, p. S7.

Interracial Books for Children, Volume 5, number 5, 1974.

Maclean's, May 24, 1999, p. 9.

Media Industry Newsletter, May 17, 1999.

Nation, January 29, 1990, pp. 141-44.

New Republic, January 29, 1990, pp. 27-28.

Newsweek, December 7, 1981.

New York, May 30, 1983, p. 75; December 18, 1989, pp. 105-7.

New Yorker, November 14, 1988, p. 89; December 25, 1989, p. 77.

New York Times, May 29, 1981; October 11, 1981.

New York Times Book Review, September 24, 1961; September 9, 1973; November 3, 1974; May 2, 1976; April 30, 1978; November 25, 1979; November 8, 1981; March 9, 1986, pp. 36-37; May 19, 1996, p. 29.

People Weekly, August 18, 1980; May 24, 1999, p. 64.

Publishers Weekly, October 28, 1963; February 24, 1975; September 18, 1981; April 29, 1996; May 17, 1999, p. 32.

Rolling Stone, June 24, 1999, p. 26.

Saturday Review, November 30, 1974; May 15, 1976.

School Library Journal, April, 2005, Lee Bock, review of *Runny Babbit,* p. 127.

Time, December 18, 1989, p. 78; May 24, 1999, p. 35.

United Press International, May 11, 1999.

Variety, May 11, 1983, p. 112; December 13, 1989, p. 89.

Washington Post Book World, April 12, 1981.

Wilson Library Bulletin, November, 1987, p. 65.

* * *

SILVERSTEIN, Sheldon Allan
See SILVERSTEIN, Shel

* * *

SIMIC, Charles 1938-

PERSONAL: Born May 9, 1938, in Belgrade, Yugoslavia; immigrated to the United States, 1954, naturalized citizen, 1971; son of George (an engineer) and Helen (Matijevic) Simic; married Helene Dubin (a designer), October 25, 1965; children: Anna, Philip. *Education:* New York University, B.A., 1967. *Religion:* Eastern Orthodox.

ADDRESSES: *Home*—P.O. Box 192, Strafford, NH 03884-0192. *Office*—Department of English, University of New Hampshire, Durham, NH 03824.

CAREER: Poet and educator. *Aperture* (photography magazine), New York, NY, editorial assistant, 1966-69; University of New Hampshire, Durham, associate professor of English, 1973—. Visiting assistant professor of English, State University of California, Hayward, 1970-73, Boston University, 1975, and Columbia University, 1979. *Military service:* U.S. Army, 1961-63.

AWARDS, HONORS: PEN International Award for translation, 1970; Guggenheim fellowship, 1972-73; National Endowment for the Arts fellowship, 1974-75, and 1979-80; Edgar Allan Poe Award from American Academy of Poets, 1975; National Institute of Arts and Letters and American Academy of Arts and Letters Award, 1976; National Book Award nomination, 1978, for *Charon's Cosmology;* Harriet Monroe Poetry Award from University of Chicago, Di Castignola Award from Poetry Society of America, 1980, and PEN translation award, all 1980; Fulbright traveling fellowship, 1982; Ingram Merrill fellowship, 1983-84; MacArthur Foundation fellowship, 1984-89; Pulitzer Prize nominations, 1986 and 1987; Pulitzer Prize, 1990, for *The World Doesn't End;* National Book Award finalist in poetry, 1996, for *Walking the Black Cat;* nominated for the National Book Award for poetry and for the *Los Angeles Times* Book Award for poetry, both 2003, both for *The Voice at 3:00 a.m.: Selected Late and New Poems.*

WRITINGS:

POETRY

What the Grass Says, Kayak (San Francisco, CA), 1967.

Somewhere among Us a Stone Is Taking Notes, Kayak (San Francisco, CA), 1969.

Dismantling the Silence, Braziller (New York, NY), 1971.

White, New Rivers Press, 1972, revised edition, Logbridge Rhodes (Durango, CO), 1980.

Return to a Place Lit by a Glass of Milk, Braziller (New York, NY), 1974.

Biography and a Lament, Bartholemew's Cobble (Hartford, CT), 1976.

Charon's Cosmology, Braziller (New York, NY), 1977.

Brooms: Selected Poems, Edge Press (Christchurch, NZ), 1978.

School for Dark Thoughts, Banyan Press (Pawlet, VT), 1978, sound recording of same title published by Watershed Tapes (Washington, DC), 1978.

Classic Ballroom Dances, Braziller (New York, NY), 1980.

Austerities, Braziller (New York, NY), 1982.

Weather Forecast for Utopia and Vicinity, Station Hill Press (Barrytown, NY), 1983.

Selected Poems, 1963-1983, Braziller (New York, NY), 1985.

Unending Blues, Harcourt (New York, NY), 1986.

Nine Poems, Exact Change (Cambridge, MA), 1989.

The World Doesn't End, Harcourt (New York, NY), 1989.

The Book of Gods and Devils, Harcourt (New York, NY), 1990.

Hotel Insomnia, Harcourt (New York, NY), 1992.

A Wedding in Hell: Poems, Harcourt (New York, NY), 1994.

Frightening Toys, Faber & Faber (New York, NY), 1995.

Walking the Black Cat: Poems, Harcourt (New York, NY), 1996.

Jackstraws: Poems, Harcourt (New York, NY), 1999, revised edition, Faber & Faber (New York, NY), 2000.

Selected Early Poems, Braziller (New York, NY), 2000.

Night Picnic, Harcourt (New York, NY), 2001.

The Voice at 3:00 a.m.: Selected Late and New Poems, Harcourt (New York, NY), 2003.

Aunt Lettuce, I Want to Peek under Your Skirt, Bloomsbury USA (New York, NY), 2005.

Contributor of poetry to more than one hundred magazines, including *New Yorker, Poetry, Nation, Kayak, Atlantic, Esquire, Chicago Review, New Republic, American Poetry Review, Paris Review,* and *Harvard Magazine.*

TRANSLATOR

Ivan V. Lalic, *Fire Gardens,* New Rivers Press (Moorhead, MN), 1970.

Vasko Popa, *The Little Box: Poems,* Charioteer Press (Washington, DC), 1970.

Four Modern Yugoslav Poets: Ivan V. Lalic, Branko Miljkovic, Milorad Pavic, Ljubomir Simovic, Lillabulero (Ithaca, NY), 1970.

(And editor, with Mark Strand) *Another Republic: Seventeen European and South American Writers,* Viking (New York, NY), 1976.

Vasko Popa, *Homage to the Lame Wolf: Selected Poems,* Field (Oberlin, OH), 1979.

(With Peter Kastmiler) Slavko Mihalic, *Atlantis,* Greenfield Review Press (Greenfield Center, NY), 1983.

Tomaz Salamun, *Selected Poems,* Viking (New York, NY), 1987.

Ivan V. Lalic, *Roll Call of Mirrors,* Wesleyan University Press, 1987.

Aleksandar Ristovic, *Some Other Wine or Light,* Charioteer Press (Washington, DC), 1989.

Stavko Janevski, *Bandit Wind,* Dryad Press (College Park, MD), 1991.

Novica Tadic, *Night Mail: Selected Poems,* Oberlin College Press (Oberlin, OH), 1992.

Horse Has Six Legs: Contemporary Serbian Poetry, Graywolf Press (Saint Paul, MN), 1992.

Aleksander Ristovic, *Devil's Lunch,* Faber & Faber (New York, NY), 1999.

Radmila Lazic, *A Wake for the Living,* Graywolf Press (Saint Paul, MN), 2003.

Gunter Grass, *The Gunter Grass Reader,* Harcourt (New York, NY), 2004.

OTHER

The Uncertain Certainty: Interviews, Essays, and Notes on Poetry, University of Michigan Press (Ann Arbor, MI), 1985.

Wonderful Words, Silent Truth, University of Michigan Press (Ann Arbor, MI), 1990.

Dime-Store Alchemy: The Art of Joseph Cornell, Ecco (New York, NY), 1992.

The Unemployed Fortune-Teller: Essays and Memoirs, University of Michigan Press (Ann Arbor, MI), 1994.

Orphan Factory: Essays and Memoirs, University of Michigan Press (Ann Arbor, MI), 1997.

A Fly in the Soup: Memoirs, University of Michigan Press (Ann Arbor, MI), 2000.

Metaphysician in the Dark (essays), University of Michigan Press (Ann Arbor, MI), 2003.

(Editor, with Don Paterson) *New British Poetry,* Graywolf Press (Saint Paul, MN), 2004.

Simic's works have been translated into several languages, including French, Dutch, Macedonian, Norwegian, Polish, Spanish, and German.

Contributor to anthologies, including *Young American Poets,* Follett, 1968; *Contemporary American Poets,* World Publishing, 1969; *Major Young American Poets,* World Publishing, 1971; *America a Prophesy,* Random House, 1973; *Shake the Kaleidoscope: A New Anthology of Modern Poetry,* Pocket Books, 1973; *The New Naked Poetry,* Bobbs-Merrill, 1976; *The American Poetry Anthology,* Avon, 1976; *A Geography of Poets,* Bantam, 1979; *Contemporary American Poetry, 1950-1980,* Longman, 1983; *The Norton Anthology of Poetry,* Norton, 1983; *Harvard Book of American Poetry,* Harvard University Press, 1985; and *The Harper American Literature,* Volume 2, Harper, 1987. Author of introductions, *Homage to a Cat: As It Were: Logscapes of the Lost Ages,* by Vernon Newton, Northern Lights, 1991, and *Prisoners of Freedom: Contemporary Slovenian Poetry,* edited by Ales Debeljak, Pedernal, 1992.

SIDELIGHTS: Charles Simic, a native of Yugoslavia who immigrated to the United States during his teens, has been hailed as one of his adopted homeland's finest poets. Simic's work, which includes *Unending Blues, Walking the Black Cat,* and *Hotel Insomnia,* has won numerous awards, among them the 1990 Pulitzer Prize and the coveted MacArthur Foundation "genius grant." Although he writes in English, Simic draws upon his own experiences of war-torn Belgrade to compose poems about the physical and spiritual poverty of modern life. *Hudson Review* contributor Liam Rector noted that the author's work "has about it a purity, an originality unmatched by many of his contemporaries."

The receipt of a Pulitzer Prize for *The World Doesn't End* may have widened Simic's audience, but the poet has never lacked admirers in the community of creative writers. In the *Chicago Review,* Victor Contoski characterized Simic's work as "some of the most strikingly original poetry of our time, a poetry shockingly stark in its concepts, imagery, and language." *Georgia Review* correspondent Peter Stitt wrote: "The fact that [Simic] spent his first eleven years surviving World War II as a resident of Eastern Europe makes him a going-away-from-home writer in an especially profound way. . . . He is one of the wisest poets of his generation, and one of the best." In a piece for the *New Boston Review,* Robert Shaw concluded that Simic "is remarkably successful at drawing the reader into his own creative moment."

Simic spent his formative years in Belgrade. His early childhood coincided with World War II; several times his family evacuated their home to escape indiscriminate bombing—or as he put it in an online interview for *Cortland Review,* "My travel agents were Hitler and Stalin." The atmosphere of violence and desperation continued after the war. Simic's father left the country for work in Italy, and his mother tried several times to follow, only to be turned back by authorities. In the meantime, young Simic was growing up in Belgrade, where he was considered a below-average student and a minor troublemaker.

When Simic was fifteen, his mother finally arranged for the family to travel to Paris. After a year spent studying English in night school and attending French public schools during the day, Simic sailed for America and a reunion with his father. He entered the United States at New York City and then moved with his family to Chicago, where he enrolled in high school. In a suburban school with caring teachers and motivated students, Simic began to take new interest in his courses, especially literature.

Simic also began to take a serious interest in poetry, though he admits that one reason he began exploring the art form was to meet girls. Talking on the *Artful*

Dodge home page, Simic compared his nascent interest in poetry to another early passion, jazz: "It's a music I've loved from the first time I heard it. . . . There was an American Armed Forces station in Italy and you could pick it up. And I remember my mother and I had a terrific, old German radio; it was a huge thing and I was playing with the dial, and I heard something and I wanted to figure out what the hell it was. It was Big Band music, a kind of bluesy thing. . . . I remember instantly liking it. I had no idea what it was."

Simic's first poems were published in 1959, when he was twenty-one. He also confesses that he started a novel at age twenty, a decision he has lived to regret: "You've got to be really stupid to start writing a novel at twenty," he told *Artful Dodge*. "I remember I wrote out a plot, to page 55. Then I ran out of ideas."

Between that year and 1961, when he entered the service, he churned out a number of poems, most of which he has since destroyed. Simic finally earned his bachelor's degree in 1966. His first full-length collection of poems, *What the Grass Says,* was published the following year. In a very short time, Simic's work, including both original poetry in English and translations of important Yugoslavian poets, began to attract critical attention. In *The American Moment: American Poetry in the Mid-Century,* Geoffrey Thurley noted that the substance of Simic's earliest verse—its material referents—"are European and rural rather than American and urban. . . . The world his poetry creates—or rather with its brilliant semantic evacuation decreates—is that of central Europe—woods, ponds, peasant furniture." *Voice Literary Supplement* reviewer Matthew Flamm also contended that Simic was writing "about bewilderment, about being part of history's comedy act, in which he grew up half-abandoned in Belgrade and then became, with his Slavic accent, an American poet."

Simic's work defies easy categorization. Some poems reflect a surreal, metaphysical bent and others offer grimly realistic portraits of violence and despair. *Hudson Review* contributor Vernon Young maintained that memory—a taproot deep into European folklore—is the common source of all of Simic's poetry. "Simic, a graduate of NYU, married and a father in pragmatic America, turns, when he composes poems, to his unconscious and to earlier pools of memory," the critic wrote. "Within microcosmic verses which may be impish, sardonic, quasirealistic or utterly outrageous, he succinctly implies an historical montage." Young elaborated: "His Yugoslavia is a peninsula of the mind. . . . He speaks by the fable; his method is to transpose historical actuality into a surreal key. . . . [Simic] feels the European yesterday on his pulses."

Some of Simic's best-known works challenge the dividing line between the ordinary and extraordinary. He gives substance and even life to inanimate objects, discerning the strangeness in household items as ordinary as a knife or a spoon. Shaw wrote in the *New Republic* that the most striking perception of the author's early poems was that "inanimate objects pursue a life of their own and present, at times, a dark parody of human existence." *Chicago Review* contributor Victor Contoski concluded: "Simic's efforts to interpret the relationship between the animate and inanimate have led to some of the most strikingly original poetry of our time, a poetry shockingly stark in its concepts, imagery, and language." As Anthony Libby put it in the *New York Times Book Review,* Simic "takes us to his mysterious target, the other world concealed in this one."

Childhood experiences of war, poverty, and hunger lie behind a number of Simic's poems. *Georgia Review* correspondent Peter Stitt claimed that the poet's most persistent concern "is with the effect of cruel political structures upon ordinary human life. . . . The world of Simic's poems is frightening, mysterious, hostile, dangerous." Thurley also declared that Simic "creates a world of silence, waiting for the unspeakable to happen, or subsisting in the limbo left afterwards. . . . The dimension of menace in Simic becomes metaphysics in itself." Simic tempers this perception of horror with gallows humor and an ironic self-awareness. Stitt averred: "Even the most somber poems . . . exhibit a liveliness of style and imagination that seems to recreate, before our eyes, the possibility of light upon the earth. Perhaps a better way of expressing this would be to say that Simic counters the darkness of political structures with the sanctifying light of art."

Critics find Simic's style particularly accessible, a substantial achievement for an author for whom English is a second language. According to Shaw, the "exile's consciousness still colors [Simic's] language as well as his view of existence. Having mastered a second language, Simic is especially aware of the power of words, and of the limits which words grope to overcome. His diction is resolutely plain: as with the everyday objects he writes about, he uncovers unexpected depth in apparently commonplace language." In the *New Letters Review of Books,* Michael Milburn remarked: "Charles Simic is a poet of original vision. . . . Simic practically taunts the reader with a familiarity bordering on cliche. He seems to challenge himself to write as plainly as possible, while still producing works of freshness and originality. [His works] literally beckon us off the street and into a world that at first looks indistinguishable from our own. . . . But a brilliant method lies behind Simic's plainness. . . . Casual, unobtrusive language expresses the most fantastic images." Milburn added that the poet "mines ingredients of language and experience that readers may take for granted, and fuses them in a singular music."

Since 1973 Simic has taught English, creative writing, and criticism at the University of New Hampshire. He describes the New England environment as ripe for producing original thinkers because, as he said on *Artful Dodge,* "[there] are these states like Maine and New Hampshire filled with little out-of-the-way places which have winter for nine months. You discover that these poor children in these places have inner lives, an inwardness, because there is nothing else to do but scrutinize the self. Introspection is a big thing, even though now cable TV has come into New England."

At the same time, Simic has reached out to students in urban settings, places where poetry isn't assumed to be part of daily life. But the students in New York City slums, he says, "had absolutely no difficulty understanding poetry. . . . I was reading them Whitman. I was reading them Emily Dickinson. And this happened repeatedly. I found that these kids understood poetry much better than the kids in [upscale] Westchester." As opposed to the inner-city youths who accepted the poetry on its own terms, Simic notes, the suburban students, "if you gave them the simplest poem, would want to know what it 'means'. . . . They did not know how to read poetry."

In 1996 Simic published another poetry collection, *Walking the Black Cat.* In this work, a *Publishers Weekly* reviewer found the poet's "short, taut lines" carve "dark-edged images" in passages that present the black cat—a traditional symbol of bad luck—as a "constant, even loved, companion." On the other hand, Paul Breslin of *Poetry* had more to criticize: While the best passages in *Black Cat* "won't submit to their own glibness altogether . . . on the whole I have the sense of a style running on automatic pilot, the urgencies that once called it into existence largely forgotten." (Responding to such criticism, the poet remarked to J.M. Spalding in the *Cortland Review:* "I would consider myself a total failure in life if Paul Breslin admired my work. Everything I have ever done as a poet was done in contempt of what he regards as 'good' poetry.")

In addition to poetry and prose poems, Simic has also written several works of prose nonfiction, including 1992's *Dime-Store Alchemy: The Art of Joseph Cornell.* A literary paean to one of the most innovative visual artists of the twentieth century, Simic's book highlights Cornell's work, which included minimalist sculptures using found objects to create intriguing surrealist collages, by creating verbal collages that are themselves composed of still smaller units of prose. "As in his poems, Simic's style in *Dime-Store Alchemy* is deceptively offhand and playful," noted Edward Hirsch in the *New Yorker,* "moving fluently between the frontal statement and the indirect suggestion, the ordinary and the metaphysical." Among Simic's essay collections is *Orphan Factory.* According to a *Publishers Weekly* reviewer, these essays and brief memoirs are at their best "when fragmentary and spontaneous ideas and images combine." The reviewer also praised the work for its "wisdom and humor."

The poetry collection *The Voice at 3:00 a.m.: Selected Late and New Poems* offers "oblique self-perceptions, metaphysical musings, inexplicable intimations and—not least—amorous affection," according to John Taylor of the *Antioch Review.* Donna Seaman of *Booklist* declared Simic a "unique and necessary voice in American poetry" whose "brooding lyrics are eloquently spare."

Diana Engelmann of the *Antioch Review* commented at length about Simic's poetry as being a dual voice that speaks both as an American and as an exile. She observed, "While it is true that the experiences of Charles Simic, the 'American poet,' provide a uniquely cohesive force in his verse, it is also true that the voices of the foreign and of the mother tongue memory still echo in many poems." Engelmann concluded, "Simic's poems convey the characteristic duality of exile: they are at once authentic statements of the contemporary American sensibility and vessels of internal translation, offering a passage to what is silent and foreign." Discussing his creative process, Simic commented on *Artful Dodge:* "When you start putting words on the page, an associative process takes over. And, all of a sudden, there are surprises. All of a sudden you say to yourself, 'My God, how did this come into your head? Why is this on the page?' I just simply go where it takes me."

BIOGRAPHICAL AND CRITICAL SOURCES:

BOOKS

Contemporary Authors Autobiography Series, Volume 4, Thomson Gale (Detroit, MI), 1986.

Contemporary Literary Criticism, Thomson Gale (Detroit, MI), Volume 6, 1976, Volume 9, 1978, Volume 22, 1982, Volume 49, 1988, Volume 68, 1991.
Thurley, Geoffrey, *The American Moment: American Poetry in the Mid-Century,* St. Martin's Press (New York, NY), 1978.
Weigl, Bruce, editor, *Charles Simic: Essays on the Poetry,* University of Michigan Press (Ann Arbor, MI), 1996.

PERIODICALS

America, January 13, 1996, p. 18.
Antioch Review, spring, 1977; John Taylor, review of *The Voice at 3:00 a.m.: Selected Late and New Poems;* winter, 2004, p. 176; winter, 2004, Diana Engelmann, "Speaking in Tongues: Exile and Internal Translation in the Poetry of Charles Simic," p. 44.
Booklist, October 1, 1997, review of *Walking the Black Cat,* p. 317; April 1, 2003, Donna Seaman, review of *The Voice at 3:00 a.m.,* p. 1370.
Boston Review, March-April, 1981; April, 1986.
Chicago Review, Volume 48, number 4, 1977.
Choice, March, 1975.
Gargoyle, number 22-23, 1983.
Georgia Review, winter, 1976; summer, 1986.
Hudson Review, spring, 1981; autumn, 1986.
Los Angeles Times Book Review, March 16, 1986; December 7, 1986; December 27, 1992, pp. 1, 8.
New Boston Review, March-April, 1981.
New Letters Review of Books, spring, 1987.
New Republic, January 24, 1976; March 1, 1993, p. 28.
New Yorker, December 21, 1992, pp. 130-135; June 28, 1993, p. 74.
New York Times, May 28, 1990.
New York Times Book Review, March 5, 1978; October 12, 1980; May 1, 1983; January 12, 1986; October 18, 1987; March 21, 1993, pp. 14, 16; April 16, 2000, review of *Selected Early Poems,* p. 23.
People, May 5, 1997, review of *Walking the Black Cat,* p. 40.
Ploughshares, Volume 7, number 1, 1981.
Poet and Critic, Volume 9, number l, 1975.
Poetry, December, 1968; September, 1971; March, 1972; February, 1975; November, 1978; July, 1981; October, 1983; July, 1987; April, 1996, p. 33; July, 1997, review of *Walking the Black Cat,* p. 226.
Poetry Review, June, 1983.
Publishers Weekly, November 2, 1990; September 21, 1992, p. 78; August 25, 1997, review of *Orphan Factory,* p. 54.
Stand, summer, 1984.
Tribune Books (Chicago, IL), June 12, 1983.
Village Voice, April 4, 1974; February 28, 1984.
Virginia Quarterly Review, spring, 1975.
Voice Literary Supplement, December, 1986.
Washington Post, April 13, 1990.
Washington Post Book World, November 2, 1980; April 13, 1986; May 7, 1989; January 3, 1993, pp. 9-10.

ONLINE

Artful Dodge, http://www.wooster.edu/ (August 24, 2000).
Cortland Review, http://www.cortlandreview.com/ (August 24, 2000).

* * *

SIMON, David 1960-

PERSONAL: Born September 2, 1960, in Washington, DC; son of Bernard (a public relations executive) and Dorothy (a homemaker; maiden name, Ligeti) Simon; married Kayle Tucker (a graphic artist), September 22, 1991; children: Ethan Simon. *Education:* University of Maryland—College Park, B.S., 1983. *Religion:* Jewish.

ADDRESSES: *Office*—c/o Author Mail, Broadway Books, Doubleday Broadway Group, 1540 Broadway, New York, NY 10036.

CAREER: Journalist. *University of Maryland Diamondback,* College Park, editor and reporter, 1978-81, editor-in-chief, 1981-82; *Baltimore Sun,* Baltimore, MD, correspondent, 1982-83, city reporter, 1983-95; writer and television producer of *Homicide: Life on the Street,* National Broadcasting Corporation (NBC), beginning 1995.

AWARDS, HONORS: Five national and thirteen regional newspaper-writing awards; Anthony Award, *True Crime,* 1992, for *Homicide: A Year on the Killing Streets.*

WRITINGS:

Homicide: A Year on the Killing Streets, Houghton (Boston, MA), 1991.
(With Edward Burns) *The Corner: A Year in the Life of an Inner-City Neighborhood,* Broadway Books (New York, NY), 1997.
The Wire (television series), Home Box Office, 2002.

WORK IN PROGRESS: The Detail, a novel about urban police work; a book about criminal defense attorneys.

SIDELIGHTS: Between 1983 and 1995 Maryland-based journalist David Simon covered the city beat for the *Baltimore Sun.* His 1991 book *Homicide: A Year on the Killing Streets* was the result of a special year-long assignment in 1988, during which he followed the officers of the city's homicide department, viewing crime scenes and emergency rooms, and witnessing police interrogations of murder suspects as well as the impact of violent crime upon the lives of others. During his year shadowing the work of eighteen police detectives, the city suffered 234 murders; "with empathy, psychological nuance, racy verbatim dialogue and razor-sharp prose," Simon provides readers with "the detective's tension-wracked world," noted a *Publishers Weekly* contributor. His book proved so compelling that it was later the basis for a television series.

Several years later, beginning in the winter of 1992, Simon joined with teacher and former-cop Edward Burns to take on a similar year-long chronicle, which they published in 1997 as *The Corner: A Year in the Life of an Inner-City Neighborhood.* "Against all the sanctions we can muster," the authors note at the outset of their 1997 book, "this new world is surviving, expanding, consuming everything in its path." Focusing on Baltimore's ethnically mixed Franklin Park neighborhood, a known hang-out for drug dealers, junkies, and residents too poor to escape the resulting violence, Simon and Burns spent countless hours following the activities at the intersection of Monroe and Fayette streets, a high-traffic area, where they became involved in the lives of people trapped in the cycle of addiction and crime, and recorded the history of the West Baltimore neighborhood and its disintegration, the efforts of police and social workers to battle the problems, and the efforts of many to escape while others died or succumbed to despair.

In *The Corner* the authors present "full portraits instead of caricatures" of their subjects, noted *Washington Monthly* contributor Steve Bogira, who credited the accomplishment to the authors' "willingess to stay close to their subjects for more than a year." Noting that "the people of the corner are obviously not saints," Bogira added that "as the authors show, most are not sociopaths either; they want a better life for themselves and their kin." Praising the authors for their ability to present a compassionate portrait of the human cost of the nation's drug war, a *Publishers Weekly* reviewer described the book as "part family neighborhood portrait, part political-social analysis."

The Corner is "a bracing read," according to an *Economist* critic, who noted that the inclusion of the sounds, jargon, and "incessant incidents of street life prove suspenseful. Its periodic sermonettes about addiction, the drug war, teen pregnancy and welfare dependency are crafted with such a hard-bitten, street-level sensibility—and without any preconceptions or ideology—that they exude immediate credibility." Calling *The Corner* "an important book sure to generate controversy," *Booklist* contributor Wes Lukowsky added that "Simon and Burns have put a human face on a national disgrace." "At 543 grim pages, [*The Corner*] is a challenge, sometimes a chore, to read," added Alex Tresniowski in a review for *People,* but "the reward is a deepened understanding of America's complex, intractable drug culture and, indeed, of human nature."

BIOGRAPHICAL AND CRITICAL SOURCES:

PERIODICALS

American Enterprise, May-June, 1998, Martin Morse Wooster, review of *The Corner: A Year in the Life of an Inner-City Neighborhood,* p. 83.

Booklist, July, 1997, Wes Lukowsky, review of *The Corner,* p. 1773.

Economist (U.S.), October 11, 1997, review of *The Corner,* p. 110.

Journal of the American Planning Association, winter, 1999, p. 127.

Library Journal, August, 1997, Paula Dempsey, review of *The Corner,* p. 113.

People, November 17, 1997, Alex Tresniowski, review of *The Corner,* p. 47.

Publishers Weekly, April 26, 1991, review of *Homicide: A Year on the Killing Streets,* p. 50; July 14, 1997, review of *The Corner,* p. 74.

Washington Monthly, October, 1997, Steve Bogira, review of *The Corner,* p. 55.

* * *

SIMON, Marvin Neil
See SIMON, Neil

* * *

SIMON, Neil 1927-
(Marvin Neil Simon)

PERSONAL: Born July 4, 1927, in Bronx, NY; son of Irving (a garment salesman) and Mamie Simon; married Joan Baim (a dancer), September 30, 1953 (died, 1973); married Marsha Mason (an actress), 1973 (divorced, 1982); married Diana Lander, 1987 (divorced, 1989; remarried, 1990; divorced, 1998); married Elaine Joyce, 1999; children: (first marriage) Ellen, Nancy; (third marriage) Bryn (adopted daughter). *Education:* Attended New York University, 1946, and University of Denver.

ADDRESSES: Office—c/o Gary N. Da Silva, 111 North Sepulveda Blvd., Ste. 250, Manhattan Beach, CA 90266-6850.

CAREER: Playwright. Warner Brothers, Inc., New York, NY, mail room clerk, 1946; Columbia Broadcasting System, Inc. (CBS), New York, NY, comedy writer for Goodman Ace, late 1940s; comedy writer for Robert W. Lewis *The Little Show,* radio, late 1940s; comedy writer for *The Phil Silvers Arrow Show,* National Broadcasting Co., Inc. (NBC-TV), 1948, *The Tallulah Bankhead Show,* NBC-TV, 1951, Sid Caesar's *Your Show of Shows,* NBC-TV, 1956-57, *The Phil Silvers Show,* CBS-TV, 1958-59, *The Garry Moore Show,* CBS-TV, 1959-60, and *The Jackie Gleason Show* and *The Red Buttons Show,* both CBS-TV, and for television specials. Producer of motion pictures, including *Only When I Laugh,* Columbia, 1981, *I Ought to Be in Pictures,* Twentieth Century- Fox, 1982, and *Max Dugan Returns,* Twentieth Century-Fox, 1983. Appearances on television programs, including *52nd Annual Academy Awards,* presenter, 1980; *Caesar's Writers,* as himself, Public Broadcasting Service, 1996; *Pitch,* as himself, Hollywood or Bust Productions, 1997; *Sid Caesar Collection,* as himself, Creative Light Entertainment, 2000-01. *Military service:* U.S. Army Air Force Reserve; sports editor of *Rev-Meter,* the base newspaper at Lowry Field, CO, 1946.

MEMBER: Dramatists Guild, Writers Guild of America.

AWARDS, HONORS: Academy of Television Arts and Sciences Award (Emmy), 1957, for Sid Caesar's *Your Show of Shows,* and 1959, for *The Phil Silvers Show;* Antoinette Perry Award (Tony) nomination, 1963, for *Little Me,* 1964, for best play for *The Odd Couple,* 1965, for *Barefoot in the Park,* 1966, for *Sweet Charity,* 1968, for *Plaza Suite,* 1969, for *Promises, Promises,* 1970, for *Last of the Red Hot Lovers,* 1972, for *The Prisoner of Second Avenue,* 1973, for *The Sunshine Boys,* 1978, for book of a musical for *They're Playing Our Song,* 1979, for *Chapter Two,* and 1987, for *Broadway Bound;* Tony Award for best playwright, 1965, for *The Odd Couple,* for best drama, 1985, for *Biloxi Blues,* and best play, 1991, for *Lost in Yonkers;* special Tony Award for overall contributions to the theater, 1975; Writers Guild Award nomination, 1967, for *Barefoot in the Park; Evening Standard* Drama Award, 1967, for *Sweet Charity;* Sam S. Shubert Foundation Award, 1968; Academy of Motion Picture Arts and Sciences Award (Oscar) nomination, 1968, for *The Odd Couple,* and 1978, for *California Suite;* Writers Guild Award, 1969, for *The Odd Couple,* 1970, for *Last of the Red Hot Lovers,* 1971, for *The Out-of-Towners,* and 1972, for *The Trouble with People;* named Entertainer of the Year, *Cue* magazine, 1972; Oscar nomination and Golden Globe Award nomination, 1975, for *The Sunshine Boys,* and 1977, for *The Goodbye Girl;* Writers Guild Award, 1975; Hollywood Foreign Press Association award, 1978, for *The Goodbye Girl;* Laurel Award, Writers Guild of America, 1979; L.H.D., Hofstra University, 1981; New York Drama Critics Circle Award, 1983, for *Brighton Beach Memoirs;* elected to the Theater Hall of Fame, Uris Theater, 1983; Lifetime Creative Achievement Award, American Comedy Awards, George Schlatter Productions, 1989; a Neil Simon tribute show was held at the Shubert Theatre, March 1, 1987; Pulitzer Prize for Drama, and Drama Desk Award, both 1991, both for *Lost in Yonkers;* Emmy nomination for Outstanding Made for Television Movie, 2001, for *Laughter on the 23rd Floor;* Neil Simon Endowment for the Dramatic Arts was established at Duke University; Apple Award, Nederlander Company and Wayne State University, 2001.

WRITINGS:

PLAYS

(With William Friedberg) *Adventures of Marco Polo: A Musical Fantasy* (music by Clay Warnick and Mel Pahl), Samuel French (New York, NY), 1959.

(Adaptor, with William Friedberg) *Heidi* (based on the novel by Johanna Spyri; music by Warnick), Samuel French (New York, NY), 1959.

(With brother, Danny Simon) *Come Blow Your Horn* (also see below; first produced in New Hope, PA, at the Bucks County Playhouse, August, 1960; produced on Broadway at the Brooks Atkinson Theatre, February 22, 1961; produced on London's West End at the Prince of Wales Theatre, February 17, 1962), Samuel French (New York, NY), 1961.

Barefoot in the Park (also see below; first produced, under title *Nobody Loves Me,* in New Hope, PA, at the Bucks County Playhouse, 1962; produced on Broadway at the Biltmore Theatre, October 23, 1963; produced on the West End, 1965), Random House (New York, NY), 1964.

The Odd Couple (also see below; first produced on Broadway at the Plymouth Theatre, March 10, 1965; produced on the West End at the Queen's Theatre, October 12, 1966; revised version first produced in Los Angeles at the Ahmanson Theatre, April 6, 1985; produced on Broadway at the Broadhurst Theatre, June, 1985; produced on Broadway at the Brooks Atkinson Theatre, 2005), Random House (New York, NY), 1966.

Sweet Charity (also see below; musical; based on the screenplay *The Nights of Cabiria* by Federico Fellini; music and lyrics by Cy Coleman and Dorothy Fields; first produced on Broadway at the Palace Theatre, January 29, 1966; produced on the West End at the Prince of Wales Theatre, October 11, 1967), Random House (New York, NY), 1966.

The Star-Spangled Girl (also see below; first produced on Broadway at the Plymouth Theatre, December 21, 1966), Random House (New York, NY), 1967.

Plaza Suite (also see below; three one-acts entitled *Visitor from Hollywood, Visitor from Mamaroneck,* and *Visitor from Forest Hills;* first produced on Broadway at the Plymouth Theatre, February 14, 1968; produced on the West End at the Lyric Theatre, February 18, 1969), Random House (New York, NY), 1969.

Promises, Promises (also see below; musical; based on the screenplay *The Apartment* by Billy Wilder and I. A. L. Diamond; music by Burt Bacharach; lyrics by Hal David; first produced on Broadway at the Shubert Theatre, December 1, 1968; produced on the West End at the Prince of Wales Theatre, October 2, 1969), Random House (New York, NY), 1969.

Last of the Red Hot Lovers (also see below; three acts; first produced in New Haven, CT, at the Shubert Theatre, November 26, 1969; produced on Broadway at the Eugene O'Neill Theatre, December 28, 1969; produced in London, 1979), Random House (New York, NY), 1970.

The Gingerbread Lady (also see below; first produced in New Haven, CT, at the Shubert Theatre, November 4, 1970; produced on Broadway at the Plymouth Theatre, December 13, 1970; produced in London, 1974), Random House (New York, NY), 1971.

The Prisoner of Second Avenue (also see below; first produced in New Haven, CT, at the Shubert Theatre, October 12, 1971; produced on Broadway at the Eugene O'Neill Theatre, November 11, 1971; reprised on London's West End, 1999), Random House (New York, NY), 1972.

The Sunshine Boys (also see below; first produced in New Haven, CT, at the Shubert Theatre, November 21, 1972; produced on Broadway at the Broadhurst Theatre, December 20, 1972; produced in London, 1975), Random House (New York, NY), 1973.

The Good Doctor (also see below; musical; adapted from stories by Anton Chekhov; music by Peter Link; lyrics by Simon; first produced on Broadway at the Eugene O'Neill Theatre, November 27, 1973), Random House (New York, NY), 1974.

God's Favorite (also see below; first produced on Broadway at the Eugene O'Neill Theatre, December 11, 1974), Random House (New York, NY), 1975.

California Suite (also see below; first produced in Los Angeles, CA, April, 1976; produced on Broadway at the Eugene O'Neill Theatre, June 30, 1976; produced in London, 1976), Random House (New York, NY), 1977.

Chapter Two (also see below; first produced in Los Angeles, CA, 1977; produced on Broadway at the Imperial Theatre, December 4, 1977; produced in London, 1981), Random House (New York, NY), 1979.

They're Playing Our Song (also see below; musical; music by Marvin Hamlisch; lyrics by Carol Bayer Sager; first produced in Los Angeles, CA, 1978; produced on Broadway at the Imperial Theatre, February 11, 1979; produced in London, 1980), Random House (New York, NY), 1980.

I Ought to Be in Pictures (also see below; first produced in Los Angeles, CA, 1980; produced on Broadway at the Eugene O'Neill Theatre, April 3, 1980; produced in London at the Offstage Downstairs, December, 1986), Random House (New York, NY), 1981.

Fools (also see below; first produced on Broadway at the Eugene O'Neill Theatre, April, 1981), Random House (New York, NY), 1982.

Brighton Beach Memoirs (also see below; first produced in Los Angeles, CA, at the Ahmanson Theatre, December, 1982; produced on Broadway at the Alvin Theatre, March 27, 1983), Random House (New York, NY), 1984.

Biloxi Blues (also see below; first produced in Los Angeles, CA, at the Ahmanson Theatre, December, 1984; produced on Broadway at the Neil Simon Theatre, March, 1985), Random House (New York, NY), 1986.

Broadway Bound (also see below; first produced at Duke University, October, 1986; produced on Broadway at the Broadhurst Theatre, December, 1986), Random House (New York, NY), 1987.

Rumors (first produced in San Diego, CA, at the Old Globe Theater in 1988; produced on Broadway at the Broadhurst Theatre, November 17, 1988), Random House (New York, NY), 1990.

Lost in Yonkers (first produced on Broadway at the Richard Rodgers Theatre, 1991), Plume (New York, NY), 1991.

Jake's Women (produced on Broadway at the Neil Simon Theatre, March 24, 1992), Samuel French (New York, NY), 1993, Random House (New York, NY), 1994.

Laughter on the 23rd Floor (produced on Broadway at the Richard Rodgers Theatre, November 22, 1993; produced on the West End, 1996), Random House (New York, NY), 1995.

London Suite (produced Off-Broadway at the Union Square Theatre, April 9, 1995), Samuel French (New York, NY), 1996.

OMNIBUS COLLECTIONS

The Comedy of Neil Simon (contains *Come Blow Your Horn, Barefoot in the Park, The Odd Couple, The Star-Spangled Girl, Promises, Promises, Plaza Suite,* and *Last of the Red Hot Lovers*), Random House (New York, NY), 1971, published as *The Collected Plays of Neil Simon,* Volume 1, New American Library (New York, NY), 1986.

The Collected Plays of Neil Simon, Volume 2 (contains *The Sunshine Boys, Little Me* [also see below], *The Gingerbread Lady, The Prisoner of Second Avenue, The Good Doctor, God's Favorite, California Suite,* and *Chapter Two*), Random House (New York, NY), 1979.

The Collected Plays of Neil Simon, Volume 3 (contains *Sweet Charity, They're Playing Our Song, I Ought to Be in Pictures, Fools, The Odd Couple—Female Version, Brighton Beach Memoirs, Biloxi Blues,* and *Broadway Bound*), Random House (New York, NY), 1992.

UNPUBLISHED PLAYS

1952–53(Contributor of sketches) *Tamiment Revue,* first produced in Tamiment, PA.

(Contributor of sketches, with Danny Simon) *Catch a Star!* (musical revue), first produced on Broadway at the Plymouth Theatre, November 6, 1955.

(Contributor of sketches, with Danny Simon) *New Faces of 1956,* first produced on Broadway at the Ethel Barrymore Theatre, June 14, 1956.

(Adaptor) *Little Me* (musical; based on the novel by Patrick Dennis), music by Coleman, first produced on Broadway at the Lunt-Fontanne Theatre, November 17, 1962, produced on the West End at the Cambridge Theatre, November 18, 1964, revised version produced in New York, 1981.

(Contributor of sketch) *Broadway Revue* (satirical musical revue), first produced in New York City at the Karmit Bloomgarden Theatre, November, 1968.

(Editor of book for musical) *Seesaw* (based on *Two for the Seesaw* by William Gibson), first produced on Broadway, March 18, 1973.

The Goodbye Girl (musical; based on Simon's screenplay), lyrics by David Zippel, music by Marvin Hamlisch, first produced on Broadway at the Marquis Theatre, March 4, 1993.

Forty-five Seconds from Broadway, produced on Broadway at the Richard Rogers Theatre, November 11, 2001.

The Dinner Party, produced at the Music Box Theatre, New York, NY, October 23, 2000.

Oscar and Felix: A New Look at the Odd Couple, produced in New York, NY, 2002.

Rose and Walsh, produced in Los Angeles, CA, at the Geffen Playhouse, January 28- February 9, 2003, also produced as *Rose's Dilemma,* in New York, NY, at the Manhattan Theatre Club, December 18-February 1, 2004.

SCREENPLAYS

Come Blow Your Horn (based on Simon's play of the same title), Paramount, 1963.

(With Cesare Zavattini) *After the Fox* (also known as *Caccia alla volpe*), United Artists, 1966.

Barefoot in the Park (based on Simon's play of the same title), Paramount, 1967.

The Odd Couple (based on Simon's play of the same title), Paramount, 1968.

The Out-of- Towners, Paramount, 1970.

Plaza Suite (based on Simon's play of the same title), Paramount, 1971.

(With Arnold Margolin and Jim Parker) *Star Spangled Girl,* Paramount, 1971.

Last of the Red Hot Lovers (based on Simon's play of the same title), Paramount, 1972.

The Heartbreak Kid (based on short story by Bruce Jay Friedman), Twentieth Century-Fox, 1972.

The Prisoner of Second Avenue (based on Simon's play of the same title), Warner Bros., 1975.

The Sunshine Boys (based on Simon's play of the same title), Metro- Goldwyn-Mayer, 1975.

Murder by Death, Columbia, 1976.

The Goodbye Girl, Warner Bros., 1977.

The Cheap Detective, Columbia, 1978.

California Suite (based on Simon's play of the same title), Columbia, 1978.

Chapter Two (based on Simon's play of the same title), Columbia, 1979.

Seems Like Old Times, Columbia, 1980.

Only When I Laugh (based on Simon's play *The Gingerbread Lady*), Columbia, 1981.

I Ought to Be in Pictures (based on Simon's play of the same title), Twentieth Century-Fox, 1982.

Max Dugan Returns, Twentieth Century-Fox, 1983.

(With Edward Weinberger and Stan Daniels) *The Lonely Guy* (based on the novel *The Lonely Guy's Book of Life,* by Bruce Jay Friedman), Universal, 1984.

The Slugger's Wife, Columbia, 1985.

Brighton Beach Memoirs (based on Simon's play of the same title), Universal, 1986.

Biloxi Blues (based on Simon's play of the same title), Universal, 1988.

The Marrying Man, Hollywood Pictures, 1991.

Lost in Yonkers (based on Simon's play of the same title), Columbia, 1993, published as *Neil Simon's Lost in Yonkers: The Illustrated Screenplay of the Film,* Newmarket Press (New York, NY), 1993.

Neil Simon's The Odd Couple II, Paramount Pictures, 1998.

The Odd Couple I and II: The Original Screen Plays, Simon & Schuster (New York, NY), 2000.

TELEPLAYS

The Trouble with People, NBC-TV, 1972.

Plaza Suite (based on Simon's play of the same title), ABC-TV, 1987.

Broadway Bound (based on Simon's play of the same title), ABC-TV, 1992.

Jake's Women (based on Simon's play of the same title), CBS-TV, 1996.

London Suite (based on Simon's play of the same title), NBC-TV, 1996.

The Sunshine Boys (based on Simon's play of the same title), Hallmark Entertainment, 1997.

Laughter on the 23rd Floor (based on Simon's play of the same title), Paramount Television/Showtime Network, 2001.

The Goodbye Girl (based on Simon's play of the same title), Turner Network Television, 2004.

Also coauthor of teleplay *Happy Endings,* 1975.

OTHER

Rewrites: A Memoir (autobiography), Simon & Schuster (New York, NY), 1996.

(Contributor) *Hold Fast Your Dreams,* edited by Carrie Boyko and Kimberly Colen, Scholastic (New York, NY), 1996.

Neil Simon Monologues: Speeches from the Works of America's Foremost Playwright, edited by Roger Karshner, Dramaline (Rancho Mirage, CA), 1996.

Neil Simon's Proposals, Samuel French (New York, NY), 1998.

The Play Goes On: A Memoir, Simon & Schuster, 1999.

Neil Simon Scenes: Scenes from the Works of America's Foremost Playwright, edited by Roger Karshner, Dramaline (Rancho Mirage, CA), 2000.

ADAPTATIONS: *Come Blow Your Horn* was filmed by Paramount in 1963; *Sweet Charity* was filmed by Universal in 1969; *The Star-Spangled Girl* was filmed by Paramount in 1971; *Barefoot in the Park* was adapted as a television series by American Broadcasting Co. (ABC) in 1970; *The Odd Couple* was adapted as a television series by ABC in 1970-75, as another television series, *The Oddball Couple,* 1975, as *The New Odd Couple,* ABC, in 1982-83, and a television movie, *The Odd Couple: Together Again* (also known as *The Odd Couple: One More Time*), CBS, 1993; *Laughter on the 23rd Floor* was adapted as a television movie.

SIDELIGHTS: Playwright Neil Simon "can look back on an incredibly productive career that shows no signs of faltering despite the usual diminution of energy brought about by advancing years," according to Jonathan Yardley, writing in the *Washington Post.* Since 1959 Simon's comedies have dominated the Broadway stage and have been adapted as popular Hollywood films as well. As David Richards explained in the *Washington Post,* Simon's comedies have run "forever on Broadway and made him pots of money, after which they were turned into movies that made him pots more." Such plays as *Barefoot in the Park, The Odd Couple, Plaza Suite, The Prisoner of Second Avenue, The Sunshine Boys,* and the autobiographical trilogy of *Brighton Beach Memoirs, Biloxi Blues,* and *Broadway Bound* have ensured Simon a position as "one of America's most popular and prolific playwrights" and "the most formidable comedy writer in American theatre," as Sheila Ennis Geitner reported in the *Dictionary of Literary Biography.* Yardley similarly noted that Simon's productions "have worked their way into the heart of twentiethth-century American culture."

Even though Simon's plays are often praised for their humor, in later years they have grown more serious, confronting issues of importance, the humor developing naturally from the characters and their interactions.

With these plays, Simon has gained a new respect for his own work. "Simon's mature theatre work," Robert K. Johnson wrote in *Neil Simon,* "combines comedy with moments of poignance and insight." Speaking of the Tony Award-winning *Biloxi Blues,* Frank Rich of the *New York Times* argued that Simon "at last begins to examine himself honestly, without compromises, and the result is his most persuasively serious effort to date."

Simon began his career as a radio writer in the 1940s. He and his brother Danny Simon worked as a team, writing comedy sketches for radio personality Goodman Ace. In the 1950s the pair graduated to television, working with such popular entertainers as Sid Caesar, Phil Silvers, and Jackie Gleason, and with such other writers as Mel Brooks and Woody Allen. But after some ten years in the business, Simon wanted out. "I hated the idea of working in television and having conferences with network executives and advertising executives who told you what audiences wanted and in what region they wanted it," Simon told the *New York Times Magazine.* With the success of his play *Come Blow Your Horn,* written with Danny, Simon was finally able to leave television and devote his efforts to the stage. He has never regretted the move. As he told Richards, "I would rather spend my nights writing for an audience of 1,000 than an audience of fourteen million."

Since the initial success of *Come Blow Your Horn,* which ran for eighty-four weeks on Broadway, Simon has seldom had a disappointing reception to his work. His second play, *Barefoot in the Park,* ran for over 1,500 performances on Broadway; *The Odd Couple* for over 900 performances; *Plaza Suite* for over 1,000 performances; and *Last of the Red Hot Lovers* and *The Prisoner of Second Avenue* ran for over 700 performances each. Richards noted that "all but a handful of Simon's plays" have made a profit, while Simon is reputedly "the richest playwright alive and arguably the richest ever in the history of the theater." "Most of Simon's plays," Richard Christiansen remarked in the *Chicago Tribune,* "have been good box office. [And] he still holds the record for having the most plays running simultaneously on Broadway (four)."

Although Simon's plays have dealt with a wide range of situations and characters, certain elements recur in all of them. The setting is usually Simon's hometown of New York, the characters are often native New Yorkers, and their problems are similar to those experienced by Simon himself. *Come Blow Your Horn,* for instance, is a thinly disguised version of Simon and brother Danny coming of age and leaving home, *The Odd Couple* stems from Danny's experience of sharing an apartment with a divorced friend, and *Chapter Two* concerns Simon's recovery following the death of his first wife in 1973. Simon explained to *New York Times* contributor Leslie Bennetts about how he has incorporated events from his own life into his plays: "The theme is me, my outlook on life. If you spread [my career] out like a map, you can chart my emotional life: some of the growth, some of the changes, some of the side trips."

Critics often point out that Simon has an admirable ability to accurately depict American domestic life. Writing in the *Humanist,* Julius Novick claimed that Simon immerses "himself in the minutiae of modern American upper-middle-class existence, which no one conveys with more authority—or, anyhow, more assiduity— than he."

Simon's plays usually focus on the members of one family or on a small group of friends, and often concern the more disruptive problems of modern life: divorce, urban crime and congestion, conflicts between children and parents, infidelity. These conflicts occur in a closed environment: an apartment or the family home. "Many of my plays [deal] with people being dumped together in a confined space, physically and emotionally," Bennetts quoted Simon as explaining. He uses this confined space with expert skill. David Kehr of the *Chicago Tribune* noted that Simon has "a kind of genius—a genius for stagecraft, the art of getting characters on and off a stage as unobtrusively as possible and of finding plausible, natural excuses for restricting a whole range of dramatic action to the confines of a single set. As a master of logistics, Simon is without peer."

Although Simon's plays are often concerned with domestic troubles, they nonetheless find humor in these painful situations. In his critique of *The Odd Couple* for the *Saturday Review,* Henry Hewes explained that Simon "makes comic cadenzas out of our bleats of agony." Simon's characters, Hewes maintained, "are blissfully unhappy but the pain of what they do to each other and to themselves is exploded into fierce humor."

In her *Neil Simon: A Critical Study,* Edythe M. McGovern argued that in his early plays Simon also advocated compromise and moderation. In *Barefoot in the Park,* for instance, a newly married couple are opposites: she is spontaneous; he is overly careful. Their different outlooks on life threaten to pull them apart. But by play's end, they have moderated their behavior so that they can live comfortably together. "Simon," McGovern wrote, "has made a point here regarding the desirability of following a middle course in order to live pleasurably without boredom, but with a sensible regard for responsibility."

The same theme is returned to in *The Odd Couple,* in which two divorced male friends share an apartment, only to find that the disagreeable personality traits which led them to get divorces also make their living together impossible. They are "two rather nice human beings who will never be able to communicate with one another simply because each man has a completely different way of viewing the world and is committed to what amounts to an extreme position with no intention of compromise," as McGovern explained. Their unyielding attitudes lead to an angry confrontation and eventual break. In showing the consequences of their inability to compromise, Simon again argues for "a middle course rather than an extremely polarized position," McGovern further commented. Speaking of Simon's handling of such important themes in his comedies, McGovern claimed that "to Neil Simon, . . . the comic form provides a means to present serious subjects so that audiences may laugh to avoid weeping."

But not all critics have been kind to Simon. Some believe his long string of hit comedies are filled with funny one-liners and little else. Jack Kroll of *Newsweek* referred to Simon's image as "Gagman Laureate." Writing in his *Uneasy Stages: A Chronicle of the New York Theater, 1963- 73,* John Simon felt that "the basic unit of [Simon's] playmaking is the joke. Not the word, the idea, the character, or even the situation, but the gag. It kills him if here and there a monosyllable resists funnying up, if now and then someone has to make a move that won't fracture the audience."

For many years, Simon was taken less than seriously even by critics who enjoyed his work. Geitner remarked that Simon's reputation as "the most formidable comedy writer in American theatre . . . prevented his being considered a serious dramatist by many critics."

Since the autobiographical trilogy *Brighton Beach Memoirs, Biloxi Blues,* and *Broadway Bound* in the 1980s, however, critical opinion about Simon's work has improved enormously. Speaking of the critical reception of *Brighton Beach Memoirs,* Richards explained that "the critics, who have sometimes begrudged the playwright his ability to coin more funny lines per minute than seems humanly possible, have now decided that he has a very warm heart." And *Biloxi Blues,* his twenty-first Broadway play, won Simon in 1985 his first Tony Award for best drama. (He had twenty years earlier won the Tony for best playwright.)

The trilogy is based on Simon's own childhood and youth in the 1930s and 1940s, although he told Charles Champlin of the *Los Angeles Times:* "I hate to call it autobiographical, because things didn't necessarily happen, or happen to me. It's an Impressionist painting of that era and that place. But there are bits and pieces of me in several of the characters." *Broadway Bound* is close enough to the truth, however, for *Time* critic William A. Henry III to report that both Simon "and his brother Danny have wept openly while watching it in performance."

Brighton Beach Memoirs is set in the Brooklyn of 1937 and tells of a Jewish family, the Jeromes, and their financial troubles during the Depression. When an aunt loses her job, she and her son move in with the Jeromes, and the family, now seven people in a cramped house, must survive their financial crisis and the aggravatingly close proximity to each other. Rich explained that "Simon uses the family's miseries to raise such enduring issues as sibling resentments, guilt-ridden parent-child relationships and the hunger for dignity in a poverty-stricken world." Simon's alter ego is the family's teenage son, Eugene, who comments on his family's problems in asides to the audience. Eugene, Richards commented, "serves as the play's narrator and [his] cockeyed slant on the family's tribulations keeps the play in comic perspective."

The play earned Simon some of the best reviews of his career. Brown wrote that *Brighton Beach Memoirs* has "plenty of laughs," but "Simon avoids the glib, tenderly probing the often- awkward moments where confused emotions cause unconscious hurts . . . . Simon's at his best, finding the natural wit, wisecracking and hyperbole in the words and wisdom of everyday people."

Eugene Jerome joins the Army in *Biloxi Blues,* the second play of the trilogy. The story follows Eugene through his ten weeks of basic training in Biloxi, Mississippi. During this training, one recruit is jailed for his homosexuality; one comes into constant conflict with his superior officers; and Eugene faces anti-Semitic insults from another soldier. Eugene, an aspiring writer, records these events faithfully in his diary, learning to examine his life and the lives of his friends honestly, and developing personal values in the process. Eugene's dream of becoming a writer is greatly furthered when he is assigned to work on an Army newspaper instead of being sent to the front, a fortunate turn of events that nonetheless makes him feel guilty.

Eugene's Army career is virtually identical to Simon's own stint in the military, and this self-examination was well received by the critics, who found that Simon realistically presents life in the Army. "For all the familiarity of its set pieces," Dan Sullivan of the *Los Angeles Times* said of *Biloxi Blues,* "it feels like life, not 'Gomer Pyle.'" Critics have also been impressed with how Simon subordinates the play's humor to its more serious concerns. Richards claimed that *Biloxi Blues* "may be the most touching play ever written about the rigors of basic training."

The story of Eugene Jerome continues in *Broadway Bound,* in which Eugene and his older brother, Stan, become comedy writers, leave home, and take jobs with a major network radio show. The breakup of their parents' marriage, the family's resistance to their new profession, and Eugene's realization that life does not contain the happy endings found in art form the basis of the plot. Danny Simon told Nina Darnton in the *New York Times* that *Broadway Bound* "is the closest in accuracy" of the three autobiographical plays.

Eugene's mother is the primary character in *Broadway Bound.* "Through much of the comedy," Christiansen noted, "she has been the needling, nagging Jewish mother who gets the old, familiar laughs. But by the end of the play, with her personal life a shambles, she has turned into a creature of great sorrow and weariness, as well." After recounting to Eugene the story of how she once danced with actor George Raft—an exhilarating and romantic moment she still recalls fondly—Eugene asks his mother to dance with him. "In this," Kroll observed, "perhaps the most delicate and highly charged moment in any Simon play, we feel the waste of a woman's unlived life and the shock of a young man who feels in his arms the repressed rhythm of that life." Eugene "sees that behind his mother's depressed exterior," Mel Gussow commented in the *New York Times,* "is the heart of a once vibrant and hopeful young woman; she is someone who has been defeated by the limits she has imposed on her life." Although he saw some flaws in *Broadway Bound,* Rich admitted that it "contains some of its author's most accomplished writing to date—passages that dramatize the timeless, unresolvable bloodlettings of familial existence as well as the humorous conflicts one expects."

Simon finally received critical recognition of his status as one of America's major playwrights in 1991, when his play *Lost in Yonkers* won both a Pulitzer Prize for drama and a Tony Award for best drama. The play, which tells the story of a dysfunctional Jewish-American family during World War II, is "closer to pure surrealism than anything Mr. Simon has hitherto produced," wrote David Richards in the *New York Times,* "and take[s] him several bold steps beyond the autobiographical traumas he recorded in *Brighton Beach Memoirs* and *Broadway Bound.*" "No longer content to dramatize divisive arguments around the family table," the critic continued, "he has pulled the family itself out of shape and turned it into a grotesque version of itself. These characters are not oddballs, they're deeply disturbed creatures. Were it not for his ready wit and his appreciation for life's incongruities, *Lost in Yonkers* could pass for a nightmare."

Lost in Yonkers is the story of how Eddie Kurnitz is forced by his economic circumstances to leave his two young sons, Arty and Jay, in the care of his severe, overbearing German-born Jewish mother. Grandma Kurnitz has tried to encourage self-reliance among her children by exercising strict discipline in her home, but she has only succeeded in scarring them emotionally. She continues to exert her authority over her gangster son Louie and her mentally impaired daughter Bella. "The two children," Richards declared in his *New York Times* review of the show, "are our sole connection to a world of conventional relationships and values." "During the eight months Jay and Arty spend with their relatives," Richards continued, "Bella takes it into her addled head that she's going to leave home, marry the usher at the local movie house, open a restaurant and have babies—more or less in that order." Grandma opposes Bella's show of individuality, and, with Arty's and Jay's help, Bella stages her own defiance of the family matriarch. "We are relieved, at the end, when the father reappears," wrote James S. Torrens in *America.* "And the youngsters, who have made it through the same ordeals as their parents . . . can be seen as having survived. *Lost in Yonkers* touches all the chords."

Critics have remarked on how Simon's later plays—including *Lost in Yonkers* and his autobiographical trilogy—turn from straight comedy toward the depiction of suffering. "Over the last decade," Richards wrote in a *New York Times Magazine* piece about the playwright, "pain has slowly crept into the comic world of Neil Simon. Although his popularity remains undiminished, his increasing willingness to recognize that the uproariously funny can also be ineffably sad may be freeing him from the taint of craven commercialism."

"He was already a past master at depicting the sundry ways people get on one another's nerves," the critic wrote in a *Washington Post* article on Simon's career. "What have surfaced increasingly in his mature works are the hurt, the sadness and the longings that possess his characters. In *Lost in Yonkers,* . . . the ache and the absurdity of living are inextricably interwoven." Richards further noted that the prestigious National Theater of Britain has performed *Brighton Beach Memoirs,* that *Time* magazine cited *Broadway Bound* as the "best American play of the 1980s," and that PBS had deemed him worthy of inclusion with luminaries such as Jasper Johns, Cole Porter, and Edward R. Murrow by profiling him in the *American Masters* television series. Summarizing the reasons for Simon's enduring popularity, Richards declared that he is "the least philosophical of playwrights and politics rarely intrudes upon his world . . . . What he returns to, time and again, are the dynamics and difficulties of personal relationships, as they transpire in an essentially middle-class society—a perspective that helps explain the loyalty of Broadway audiences."

After the high drama of *Lost in Yonkers,* Simon returned to straight comedy in two farces: *Rumors* (1988) and *Jake's Women* (1992). In both cases critics remarked that the plays seemed almost too lightweight after the successes of his autobiographical plays and *Lost in Yonkers. Rumors* is "a self-described farce," reported Frank Rich in the *New York Times,* "that has nothing on its mind except making the audience laugh. And not exactly in the Moliere manner. Maybe I've led a charmed life, but I can't recall hearing this many toilet jokes since the ninth grade." *Jake's Women* received "scathing" reviews in the *Los Angeles Times,* stated *New York Times* reporter Mervyn Rothstein, and "the San Diego critics said it needed a lot of work but had promise."

Jake's Women and Simon's next play, *Laughter on the 23rd Floor* (1993), both failed to make a profit, in part because of the expense of Broadway productions. When *Laughter on the 23rd Floor*—based on stories from Simon's life working on Sid Caesar's *Your Show of Shows*—met with good reviews and had a decent run but was less than a financial success, Simon declared his intention to open his next play Off-Broadway. *London Suite,* a series of four one-act plays, opened Off-Broadway in 1995 and later traveled successfully to Chicago.

With his year 2000 play *Dinner Party,* Simon is once again "simply out to have fun," according to Clifford A. Ridley in the *Knight Ridder/Tribune News Service.* Ridley thought even the set of the play was "funny," with dialogue "zestily peppered with insult and misunderstanding." Simon devises an intriguing dinner party: three men, unknown to one another, have been invited by a common acquaintance, the divorce lawyer who served each successfully. Three other places are also laid at the table; seats for these men's former wives. Ridley ultimately felt that Simon's "insights seldom have matched his obsessiveness," and that comedy is soon replaced by a "string of colloquies about love and marriage."

In his 2003 play about love and loss, *Rose and Walsh,* Simon "finally confronts the afterlife and its effects on loved ones left behind, creating his most rewarding play in years," wrote Phil Gallo in *Variety.* Rose is a hard-living, prize-winning writer facing not only the end of her career but life without Walsh, her husband and legendary writer, who died five years earlier. Walsh has, however, kept in contact in a ghostly manner with his wife, and now recommends that she finish one of his mystery novels and also that she bring in a ghost writer, Clancy, a seemingly washed-up writer, to do so. Added to this strange brew is Arlene, Rose's secret daughter from a fling many years ago, a young woman who has only been able to spend time with her mother since Walsh's death. Somewhat inspired by the real-life relationship between Dashiell Hammett and Lillian Hellman, *Rose and Walsh* "is ultimately about transitions," Gallo further commented. Diane Haithman, reviewing the play in the *Los Angeles Times,* found it a "quirky love story," but one very much still under construction. For Haithman, it was an "erratic effort that, despite a few bright moments, plot-twists slowly in the wind." Gallo, however, felt the play was "simple in its construction— an often-comical, eventually poignant ghost story—and refreshing in its logic." Gallo also felt that Simon managed to strike "that delicate balance between the comic . . . and the profound."

Although primarily known for his plays, Simon also has written a score of popular films. These include the screen adaptations of many of his own hit plays—including *Barefoot in the Park, The Odd Couple,* and *The Sunshine Boys*—as well as such original screenplays as *The Cheap Detective, Murder by Death,* and *The Goodbye Girl.* Simon's best screen work is found in films where he creates a desperate situation, Vincent Canby argued in the *New York Times.* Simon's "wisecracks define a world of mighty desperation," Canby wrote, "in which every confrontation, be it with a lover, a child, a husband, a friend or a taxi driver, becomes a last chance for survival. When he writes a work in which the desperation is built into the situations, Mr. Simon can be both immensely funny and surprisingly moving."

But not all critics appreciate Simon's film work. Simon's adaptations of his own plays, while often good box office, have sometimes been criticized for being too stagey, like "photographed plays," as Johnson put it. Yet, most of Simon's films, especially *The Heartbreak Kid* and *Only When I Laugh,* have been extremely popular with audiences and critics alike.

The Heartbreak Kid concerns a young couple who get divorced during their honeymoon in Florida after the husband meets another woman. Simon creates humor in this film, as Johnson allowed, "out of situations which are not basically surefire comedy material." It is this blend of the humorous and the essentially tragic—with the humor emerging naturally from the actions and speech of the characters—which makes *The Heartbreak Kid* "the best film created thus far from a Neil Simon script," Johnson believed.

Only When I Laugh was also a critical success for Simon. It tells the story of Georgia Hines, an alcoholic Broadway actress who, despite rehabilitation, cannot beat her dependence. Georgia "is one of the most interesting, complicated characters that Mr. Simon, the master of the sometimes self-defeating one-liner, has ever written," according to Canby. Johnson found *Only When I Laugh* "one of the most absorbing pieces of work that Simon has written."

Yet after all his film successes, Simon eventually came to feel "disenchantment with Hollywood," according to Richards. The movie-making industry, which used to "give him carte blanche . . . now subjects him to the same corporate humiliations as anyone else." After an unhappy alliance with Disney Studios for the film *The Marrying Man,* Simon observed to Richards: "With a play, I have only two people to please—myself and the director . . . . With this movie it was nineteen executives, plus a director who'd never done anything but animation before, and two stars who would tell you what lines they'd say and what lines they wouldn't say." Richards concluded that despite the troubles plaguing the New York theater scene, "Simon knows his place, and it's on Broadway. If he is not so sure what that means these days, he thinks it still denotes accessibility and craftsmanship. It has to do with refining every detail, every line, every moment, so that he can feel, as he rarely does on opening night, a momentary sense of completion, of coming in to land."

Simon did venture onto the screen again, however, with his 1998 update of the antics of his humorous couple, Oscar and Felix. *Odd Couple II* finds the unlikely duo long retired and en route to their children's wedding in California. "Getting there is all the fun," noted George Meyer in the *Sarasota Herald Tribune.* During the course of their journey, the two manage to lose their luggage, get lost and arrested, and "bicker and spat continuously," as Leah Rozen noted in *People.* Meyer felt that Simon came up with a "delightful comedy," and one that is "witty, insightful and some of the best Simon writing in years." Other critics were not so positive about the merits of the movie. Renee Graham, writing in the *Boston Globe,* thought the picture was a "time-worn mixture of road picture and buddy movie" with a "lousy" script. *Entertainment Weekly* critic Mike D'Angelo called the movie a "dire sequel" and a "feeble" comedy, and Rosen felt the adventures of Felix and Oscar were "more strained than amusing," making for "one mighty long, slow journey."

"Writing is an escape from a world that crowds me," Simon admitted to *New York Times* contributor John Corry. "I like being alone in a room. It's almost a form of meditation—an investigation of my own life." He explained to William A. Henry how he begins a play: "There's no blueprint per se. You just go through the tunnels of your mind, and you come out someplace." Accepting his success as a writer has also been difficult. "I was depressed for a number of years," Simon told Corry. The opening of a new play filled him with guilt. It took psychoanalysis, and a consultation with his second wife's swami, before Simon learned to enjoy his accomplishments.

Simon explores his life in writing in two memoirs, *Rewrites,* which traces his first forty-six years of life, up to the death of his wife Joan in 1973, and *The Play Goes On,* which continues from that point through his marriages to Marsha Mason and Diane Lander and the successes of the 1980s. Along the way, he recounts numerous behind-the-scenes anecdotes about plays and play-making. Christopher Lehmann-Haupt, writing in the *New York Times,* found *Rewrites* a "pleasant memoir," but with "surprisingly flat prose." For Everett Evans, writing in the *Houston Chronicle,* the same memoir was "frequently funny, occasionally poignant and resolutely unaffected." Similarly, *Billboard*'s Trudi Miller Rosenblum thought the first installment was a "fascinating and thoughtful autobiography." Reviewing the second portion of the memoir, 1999's *The Play Goes On,* Larry King noted in *USA Today* that "Simon writes books as well as he writes plays, and there aren't any better." Peter Marks, writing in the *New York Times Book Review,* however, felt that despite a few "entertaining anecdotes," the book as a whole "feels tossed off." It was "too bad," Marks concluded, "this master play doctor was not encouraged to perform a little more surgery on his own story." Celia Wren, writing in *American Theatre,* found more to like in the title. She praised Simon's "low-key wit . . . [and] insight into the creative process."

Simon writes on a daily basis, although much of his work is never completed. Richards reported that "Simon's desk overflows with the plays he's begun over the years. On an average, for every one he finishes, there are ten he abandons after fifteen or twenty pages." Generally, if Simon gets past page thirty-five he will finish the play, a process that takes four months for a first draft, longer for the final draft. *Come Blow Your Horn,* for example, was rewritten twenty times before Simon was satisfied with it. In *Broadway Bound,* Simon has his alter ego, Eugene, say: "I love *being* a writer. It's the writing that's hard."

Despite the difficulty involved in writing, Simon has managed to produce an impressive body of work. A new Simon comedy every theatrical season was a Broadway staple for well over three decades. Henry called him "America's foremost stage comedist" and placed Simon "in the top rank of American playwrights." Rich similarly called him "not just a show business success but an institution." After surveying Simon's many achievements during his long career as a writer for the stage and screen, Johnson concluded by dubbing him "one of the finest writers of comedy in American literary history."

BIOGRAPHICAL AND CRITICAL SOURCES:

BOOKS

Contemporary Literary Criticism, Gale (Detroit, MI), Volume 6, 1976, Volume 9, 1979, Volume 31, 1985, Volume 39, 1986, Volume 70, 1991.

Dictionary of Literary Biography, Volume 7: *Twentieth-Century American Dramatists,* Gale (Detroit, MI), 1981.

Johnson, Robert K., *Neil Simon,* Twayne (Boston, MA), 1983.

Kerr, Walter, *Thirty Plays Hath November,* Simon & Schuster (New York, NY), 1969.

Konas, Gary, *Neil Simon: A Casebook,* Garland (New York, NY), 1997.

McGovern, Edythe M., *Neil Simon: A Critical Study,* Ungar (New York, NY), 1979.

Monaco, James, *American Film Now,* Oxford University Press (New York, NY), 1979.

Simon, John, *Uneasy Stages: A Chronicle of the New York Theater, 1963-73,* Random House (New York, NY), 1975.

Simon, Neil, *Rewrites: A Memoir,* Simon & Schuster (New York, NY), 1996.

PERIODICALS

America, May 4, 1991, James S. Torrens, "Absent and Lost: Seasonal High Points," pp. 496-97.

American Theatre, December, 1999, Celia Wren, review of *The Play Goes On: A Memoir,* p. 80.

Billboard, January 11, 1997, Trudi Miller Rosenblum, review of *Rewrites: A Memoir,* p. 86.

Boston Globe, April 10, 1998, Renee Graham, review of *The Odd Couple II,* p. D7.

Chicago Sun Times, October 13, 1996, Bill Zwecker, "One on One with Bill Zwecker" p. 3NC.

Chicago Tribune, November 2, 1986, Richard Christiansen, "Neil Simon, Himself: *Broadway Bound* Bares Playwright's Heart and Soul," p. 4; December 13, 1992, Richard Christiansen, "The Goodbye Guy: You Can Make Book on Neil Simon's Musical Scripts," section 13, pp. 4-5; November 23, 1993, Richard Christiansen, "Laugh Factory Humor Flows from *23rd Floor,*" section 4, p. 20; October 8, 1995, Richard Christiansen, "Rewrite Specialist Even after 28 Plays, Neil Simon Is Still Fine-Tuning His Craft," section 7, p. 8.

Entertainment Weekly, October 9, 1998, Mike D'Angelo, review of *The Odd Couple II,* p. 90; November 12, 1999, Charles Winecoff, review of *The Play Goes On,* p. 74.

Financial Times, April 1, 1999, "Simon Is Just Too Cute for Words," p. 15.

Hollywood Reporter, June 21, 2002, Jay Reiner, "Oscar and Felix," pp. 22- 23.

Houston Chronicle, November 17, 1996, Everett Evans, review of *Rewrites,* p. 22.

Humanist, September- October, 1976, Julius Novick.

Knight Ridder, October 9, 1996, Pat Craig, review of *Rewrites,* p. 1009K5245.

Library Journal, December, 1996, Gordon Blackwell, review of *Rewrites,* p. 169.

Los Angeles Times, December 5, 1982, Charles Champlin, "Neil Simon Remembers When Times Were Tough," p. 1; December 15, 1984, Dan Sullivan, review of *Biloxi Blues,* p. 1; October 14, 1999, Jonathan Levi, review of *The Play Goes On,* p. 3; February 7, 2003, Diane Haithman, review of *Rose and Walsh,* p. E1.

Newsweek, April 14, 1980, Jack Kroll, "I Ought to Be in Pictures," p. 106; April 20, 1981, Jack Kroll, review of *Fools,* p. 104; December 15, 1986, Jack Kroll, review of *It Only Hurts When I Laugh,* p. 76; March 4, 1991, Jack Kroll, "Going Bonkers in Yonkers," p. 60; March 15, 1993, Jack Kroll, "This Goodbye Is a Bad Guy," p. 82; December 6, 1993, Jack Kroll, "When Laughter Wasn't Canned," p. 81; November 17, 1997, Jack Kroll, "The Forest of Simon," p. 94.

New York Times, April 5, 1981, John Corry, "Why Broadway's Fastest Writer Cannot Slow Down," p. 1; March 27, 1983, Leslie Bennetts, "Neil Simon Delves into His Past," p. H1; March 24, 1985, Nina Darnton, "From Neil Simon: A New Film, a New Play," p. H1; April 7, 1985, Frank Rich, review of *Biloxi Blues,* p. H1; December 5, 1986, Frank Rich, review of *Broadway Bound,* p. C3; December 26, 1986, Nina Darnton, "Danny Simon's View of Younger Brother Neil," p. C10; January 8, 1987, Frank Rich, "Neil Simon Takes On Neil Simon," p. C20; March 25, 1988, Vincent Canby, review of *Biloxi Blues,* p. C1; November 13, 1988, Mervyn Rothstein, "For Neil Simon, the Prescription Was Farce," pp. 13, 41; November 18, 1988, Frank Rich, review of *Rumors,* p. C3; March 3, 1991, David Richards, review of *Lost in Yonkers,* pp. 1, 7; April 5, 1992, David Richards, review of *Jake's Women,* pp. 5, 37; April 10, 1995, Vincent Canby, review of *London Suite,* pp. C9, C11; October 24, 1996, Christopher Lehmann-Haupt, review of *Rewrites,* p. C19.

New York Times Book Review, October 24, 1999, Peter Marks, review of *The Play Goes On,* p. 19.

New York Times Magazine, May 26, 1985, "The Craft of the Playwright: A Conversation between Neil Simon and David Rabe," p. 36; February 17, 1991, David Richards, "The Last of the Red Hot Playwrights," pp. 30-32, 36, 57, 64.

People, April 20, 1998, Leah Rozen, review of *The Odd Couple II,* p. 35.

Philippine Daily Inquirer, March 2, 2002, Noelani Torre, review of *Rewrites.*

Sarasota Herald Tribune (Sarasota, FL), April 10, 1998, George Meyer, review of *The Odd Couple II,* p. 15.

Saturday Review, March 27, 1965, Henry Hewes.

Time, December 15, 1986, William A. Henry III, "Reliving a Poignant Past," p. 72; November 28, 1988, William A. Henry III, "Theater: Falling Short," p. 94.

Times—Picayune (New Orleans, LA), November 15, 2002, David Cuthbert, review of *The Prisoner of Second Avenue,* p. L14.

USA Today, October 4, 1999, Larry King, review of *The Play Goes On,* p. D2; October 7, 1999, David Patrick Stearns, review of *The Play Goes On,* p. D8.

Variety, February 17- 23, 2003, Phil Gallo, review of *Rose and Walsh,* p. 48.

Washington Post, April 9, 1995, David Richards, "Simon: Give My Regards to Broadway; Economics Force Him to Think Small with New Play," p. G1; October 10, 1999, Jonathan Yardley, review of *The Play Goes On,* p. X2.

ONLINE

Kennedy Center Web site, http://www.kennedy-center.org/ (November 12, 2003), *Kennedy Centers Honors Profile for 1995.*

* * *

SIMPSON, Louis 1923-
(Louis Aston Marantz Simpson)

PERSONAL: Born March 27, 1923, in Kingston, Jamaica, British West Indies; United States citizen; son of Aston and Rosalind (Marantz) Simpson; married Jeanne Rogers, 1949 (divorced, 1954); married Dorothy Roochvarg, 1955 (divorced, 1979); married Miriam Butensky Bachner, 1985; children: (first marriage) Matthew; (second marriage) Anne, Anthony. *Education:* Columbia University, B.S., 1948, A.M., 1950, Ph.D., 1959.

ADDRESSES: *Home*—186 Old Field Rd., Setauket, New York, NY 11733-1636.

CAREER: Bobbs-Merrill Publishing Co., New York, NY, editor, 1950-55; Columbia University, New York, NY, instructor in English, 1953-59; New School for Social Research, instructor in English, 1955-59; University of California, Berkeley, 1959-67, began as assistant professor, became professor of English; State University of New York at Stony Brook, professor of English and comparative literature, 1967-91, distinguished professor, 1991-93, professor emeritus, 1993—. Has given poetry readings at colleges and poetry centers throughout the United States and Europe and on television and radio programs in New York, San Francisco, and London. *Military service:* U.S. Army, 1943-46; became sergeant; awarded Bronze Star with oak leaf cluster, Purple Heart (twice), Presidential Unit Citation.

MEMBER: American Academy in Rome.

AWARDS, HONORS: Fellowship in literature (Prix de Rome) at American Academy in Rome, 1957; *Hudson Review* fellowship, 1957; Columbia University, distinguished alumni award, 1960, Medal for Excellence, 1965; Edna St. Vincent Millay Award, 1960; Guggenheim fellowship, 1962, 1970; American Council of Learned Societies grant, 1963; Pulitzer Prize for poetry, 1964, for *At the End of the Open Road;* Medal for Excellence, Columbia University, 1965; Commonwealth Club of California poetry award, 1965; American Academy of Arts and Letters award in literature, 1976; D.H.L., Eastern Michigan University, 1977; Institute of Jamaica, Centenary Medal, 1980; Jewish Book Council, Award for Poetry, 1981; Elmer Holmes Bobst Award, 1987; Academy of American Poets, Harold Morton Landon Translation Award, 1998, for *Modern Poets of France;* Hampden Sydney College, D.Litt., 1990; nominated for the National Book Award for poetry, 2003, for *The Owner of the House: New Collected Poems;* Griffin Poetry Prize, 2004 for *The Owner of the House.*

WRITINGS:

The Arrivistes: Poems, 1940-49, Fine Editions, 1949.

Good News of Death and Other Poems, Scribner (New York, NY), 1955.

(Editor, with Donald Hall and Robert Pack) *The New Poets of England and America,* Meridian, 1957.

A Dream of Governors (poems), Wesleyan University Press (Middletown, CT), 1959.

Riverside Drive (novel), Atheneum, 1962.

James Hogg: A Critical Study, St. Martin's Press (New York, NY), 1962.

At the End of the Open Road (poems), Wesleyan University Press (Middletown, CT), 1963.

(Contributor) Thom Gunn and Ted Hughes, editors, *Five American Poets,* Faber (London, England), 1963.

Selected Poems, Harcourt (New York, NY), 1965.

(Editor) *An Introduction to Poetry,* St. Martin's Press (New York, NY), 1967, 2nd edition, 1972.

Adventures of the Letter I (poems), Harper (New York, NY), 1971.

North of Jamaica (autobiography), Harper (New York, NY), 1972, published as *Air with Armed Men,* London Magazine Editions, 1972.

Three on the Tower: The Lives and Works of Ezra Pound, T.S. Eliot and William Carlos Williams (literary criticism), Morrow, 1975.

Searching for the Ox (poems), Morrow, 1976.

A Revolution in Taste: Studies of Dylan Thomas, Allen Ginsberg, Sylvia Plath and Robert Lowell (literary criticism), Macmillan, 1978, published in England as *Studies of Dylan Thomas, Allen Ginsberg, Sylvia Plath and Robert Lowell,* Macmillan (New York, NY), 1979.

Armidale (poems), BOA Editions, 1979.

Out of Season (poems), Deerfield Press, 1979.

Caviare at the Funeral (poems), Franklin Watts, 1980.

A Company of Poets (literary criticism), University of Michigan (Ann Arbor, MI), 1981.

The Best Hour of the Night (poems), Ticknor & Fields, 1983.

People Live Here: Selected Poems, 1949-1983, BOA Editions, 1983.

The Character of the Poet (literary criticism), University of Michigan (Ann Arbor, MI), 1986.

An Introduction to Poetry, St. Martin's Press (New York, NY), 1986.

Collected Poems, Paragon House (New York, NY), 1988.

Selected Prose, Paragon House (New York, NY), 1988.

Selected Prose, Paragon House (New York, NY), 1989.

Wei Wei and Other Friends (poems), Typographeum, 1990.

In the Room We Share (poems), Paragon House (New York, NY), 1990.

Jamaica Poems, Press of Appletree Alley, 1993.

Ships Going into the Blue: Essays and Notes on Poetry, University of Michigan Press (Ann Arbor, MI), 1994.

The King My Father's Wreck (memoir), Story Line Press, 1994.

There You Are: Poems, Story Line (Brownsville, OR), 1995.

Modern Poets of France: A Bilingual Anthology (poems), Story Line Press, 1997.

(Translator) *The Legacy & The Testament,* Story Line Press, 2000.

The Owner of the House: New Collected Poems, BOA Editions, 2003.

Contributor of poems, plays, and articles to literary periodicals, including *American Poetry Review, Listener, Hudson Review, Paris Review,* and *Critical Quarterly.* Sound recordings include: *Louis Simpson Reading His Poems with Comment in New York City, Mar. 19, 1959,* 1959; *Louis Aston Marantz Simpson and James Wright Reading and Discussing Their Poetry in the Coolidge Auditorium, Dec. 5, 1966,* 1966.

SIDELIGHTS: Jamaican-born poet and educator Louis Simpson, author of poetry collections that include the Pulitzer Prize-winning *At the End of the Open Road,*

Searching for the Ox, and *There You Are,* is noted for simple, controlled verses that reveal hidden layers of meaning. Critic Yohma Gray wrote in praise of the poet's ability to make his readers heed that which usually passes undiscerned. "Even in the most mundane experience there is a vast area of unperceived reality," the critic noted, "and it is Louis Simpson's kind of poetry which brings it to our notice. It enables us to see things which are ordinarily all about us but which we do not ordinarily see; it adds a new dimension to our sensational perception, making us hear with our eyes and see with our ears." Gray maintained in "The Poetry of Louis Simpson" in *Poets in Progress* that poetry seeks the same goal as religious belief: "to formulate a coherent and significant meaning for life. The poetry of Louis Simpson offers us that meaning."

In a discussion of Simpson's early poetry, Gray commented that the author "never departs from traditional form and structure and yet he never departs from contemporary themes and concerns." Gray described one poem, for example, in which Simpson "handles a modern psychological situation in the delicate cadence of seventeenth-century verse." Ronald Moran in *Louis Simpson* made a similar comment in regard to *The Arrivistes,* Simpson's first book. Moran found that Simpson often sounds "like an Elizabethan song-maker or like a Cavalier poet." Gray argued that this juxtaposition of traditional form (ordered meter and rhyme) and modern subjects emphasizes, particularly in the poems about the world wars, the chaotic quality and the tensions of contemporary life. Gray found that Simpson neither complains nor moralizes about modern problems; rather he clarifies difficulties and presents rational insights.

After 1959, the publication date of *A Dream of Governors,* there was a perceived change in Simpson's work; reviewer Stephen Stepanchev contended in *American Poetry since 1945* that it changed for the better. Notes Stepanchev: "The prosaism of his early work—which required metrics and rhyme in order to give it character as verse—now gave way to rich, fresh, haunting imagery. His philosophical and political speculations achieved a distinction and brilliance that they had lacked before." A *Chicago Review* critic had more cautious praise for the shift in Simpson's poetry, writing that, "*A Dream of Governors* has wit, sophistication, perceptiveness, intelligence, variety, and knowingness, but it comes perilously close to being a poetry of chic." The reviewer went on to say that this early work lacks a depth of feeling.

However, he continued, "*At the End of the Open Road* . . . is a different story entirely. Simpson has found the secret of releasing the meaning and power of his themes. . . . It is not that his stanzas . . . are becoming more flexible and experimental: this in itself does not mean very much. . . . What is more fundamental, it seems to me, is that greater stylistic flexibility should be the sign of growth in the character and thought of the speaker. Simpson is becoming more able to be a part of what he writes about, and to make what he writes about more a part of him." *New York Time Book Review*'s Edward Hirsch agreed that the Pulitzer Prize-winning *At the End of the Open Road* indicates a growth and finesse in Simpson's poetry, opining, "It is not only a major breakthrough in his own work; it is also one of the tours de force of American poetry in the 60's." Hirsch described *At the End of the Open Road* as "a sustained meditation on the American character," noting, "The moral genius of this book is that it traverses the open road of American mythology and brings us back to ourselves; it sees us not as we wish to be but as we are."

Not all critics appreciated the change in Simpson's verse. In a review of 1965's *Selected Poems,* which contains twelve new poems in addition to selections of earlier work, Harry Morris stated that "Simpson's first three volumes are better" than his new poetry. Morris believed that Simpson's "new freedoms" have not helped him convey his themes more effectively. T. O'Hara, in a critique of *Adventures of the Letter I,* also questioned Simpson's new manner: "What has happened to Louis Simpson's energy? . . . It almost appears that success has mellowed the tough poetic instinct that once propelled him, for this present collection barely flexes a muscle." Yet Marie Borroff, speaking of the same book, avowed, "When the remaining decades of the twentieth century have passed ignominiously into history along with the 1960's, these stanzas and other gifts will remain to us." And Christopher Hope deemed *Adventures* "a work of pure, brilliant invention."

A mix of criticism continued in reviews of *Searching for the Ox.* Derwent May found the quiet, reflective mood of the poems attractive. Nikki Stiller, on the other hand, felt that "Louis Simpson's work now suggests too much comfort: emotional, physical, intellectual. He has stopped struggling, it seems, for words, for rhythms, for his own deepest self." Yet in contrast to this, Peter Stitt remarked that *Searching for the Ox* "is a tremendously refreshing book. . . . The style in which [the poems] are written presents us with no barriers—it is plain, direct and relaxed. Moreover, the poems tell a story, or stories, in which we can take a real interest."

Simpson's ability to have his poems relate stories of interest is evident as well in *Collected Poems.* Selections from his poetry created from 1940 through the 1980s, *Collected Poems* focuses on the lives of everday citizens. "For the last two decades [Simpson's] appetite has increasingly been for re-creating quintessentially American stories of ordinary people . . . living out lives of quiet desperation," found Hirsch, noting, "He has turned his ardor and ingenuity to uncovering the secret and public lives of people stripped of their expectations and bewildered by their fates." "Simpson takes part in the existence of other people, and pecks or picks about the shopping mall with them, or the redwoods and the Golden Gate, or Paris, or the battlefields of the Second World War which so nearly unmade him," observed the *Times Literary Supplement*'s William Scammell, adding, "And he manages to do this without relinquishing his own firm sense of identity, or slumping into a reverent pantheistic incoherence." Scammell concluded with praise for *Collected Poems* as "a masterclass for reader and writer alike, alive on every page." "But mastery is not the right metaphor to end on," he surmised, "for Simpson is someone who stands outside aestheticism, outside schools and movements."

In *There You Are: Poems,* the poet again "send[s] us into the lives of people and their stories," commented Mark Jarman in the *Hudson Review.* A *Publishers Weekly* contributor stated that in *There You Are* while "combining straightforward diction with oblique insights, Simpson limns people and stories with an irony tempered by compassion." Jarman hailed Simpson as "a poet of the American character and vernacular." Praising Simpson's storytelling skill and style, Jarman claimed "that no one writing today has a better understanding of narrative as a figure of speech. Each of his stories is like a piece standing for life as a whole, existing in a kind of chaste simplicity and yet, to paraphrase Simpson himself, giving off vibrations."

Simpson occasionally ventures from verse into other genres: novel, autobiography, and literary critical study. Robert Massie wrote of the poet's 1962 novel *Riverside Drive* in the *New York Times Book Review:* "Into fragments of dialogue, [Simpson] packs more meaning and drama than many novelists can bring off in a chapter. . . . As novels go, *Riverside Drive* is not a tragedy to shake the Gods—but it should stir most of its readers. From the first chapter to the last, it has the ring of truth." Concerning Simpson's literary critical study *A Revolution in Taste,* Paul Zweig commented that the author "has provided a series of engaging portraits of poets whom he presents less as cultural exemplars than as individuals struggling, as Baudelaire wrote, to absolve the pain of their lives with the grace of an enduring poem. It is the life narrowing intensely and heatedly into the act of writing that interests Simpson, the life pared to the poem. And this has enabled him to write a series of compact literary biographies that have the pithiness of a seventeenth-century 'character' and a literary good sense that reminds me of [Samuel] Johnson's *Lives of the Poets.*"

Simpson has also written several volumes of autobiography, including 1972's *North of Jamaica* and *The King My Father's Wreck,* published in 1994. The latter work recounts the poet's early years in Jamaica and his transition to adulthood and literary maturity through a selection of essays. Focusing on specific images from his past—his mother's disappearance from home when he was a young boy, his excitement at the prospect of becoming a U.S. citizen, a dissatisfying job working as an editor for a publishing house, the experiences he encountered in the armed forces during World War II that led to later protestations over the conflict in Vietnam, returning a book to his Jamaican school sixty years after borrowing it— *The King My Father's Wreck* is written in the same spare style that is characteristic of Simpson's verse. The poet's "insistent voice" imbues his reminiscences with "more dramatic emotional topography than most," commented a *Publishers Weekly* reviewer, thereby "rewarding adventurous readers."

His much-acclaimed anthology *The Owner of the House: New Collected Poems* represents a sixty-year career, in which Simpson has chosen to represent himself as a sociologist of suburbia's banalities. Although in poems like "Shoe-Fly Pie," he revisits the West Indies of his childhood, he always keeps one foot in his adopted country, never slipping into sentimentality. The outsider's perspective allows him to confront "the terror and beauty of life with a wry sense of humor and a mysterious sense of fate," wrote Edward Hirsch of the *Washington Post.* In his recent poems, there is a sense of an acceptance of life "here, on this street / where the houses from the outside / are all alike, and so are the people." In his review, David Orr of the *New York Times* stated, "If there's little Louis Simpson 'could learn from anyone' at this point, that's only because he's worked so hard and so long—and successfully—to learn it for himself."

BIOGRAPHICAL AND CRITICAL SOURCES:

BOOKS

Contemporary Literary Criticism, Thomson Gale (Detroit, MI), Volume 4, 1975, Volume 7, 1977, Volume 9, 1978, Volume 32, 1985.

Hungerford, Edward, editor, *Poets in Progress: Critical Prefaces to Thirteen Modern American Poets,* Northwestern University Press, 1967.
Lazer, Hank, editor, *On Louis Simpson: Depths beyond Happiness,* University of Michigan, 1988.
Lensing, George S., and Ronald Moran, *Four Poets and the Emotive Imagination,* Louisiana State University Press (Baton Rouge, LA), 1976.
Moran, Ronald, *Louis Simpson,* Twayne, 1972.
Roberson, William H., *Louis Simpson: A Reference Guide,* G.K. Hall, 1980.
Stepanchev, Stephen, *American Poetry since 1945,* Harper (New York, NY), 1965.
Stitt, Peter, *The World's Hieroglyphic Beauty: Five American Poets,* University of Georgia, 1985.

PERIODICALS

American Poetry Review, January-February, 1979.
Best Sellers, June 15, 1972.
Chicago Review, Volume XIX, number 1, 1966.
Christian Science Monitor, November 18, 2003, p. 17.
Harper's, October, 1965.
Hudson Review, autumn, 1996.
Listener, November 25, 1976.
London Magazine, February-March, 1977.
Los Angeles Times Book Review, April 30, 1995, p. 13.
Midstream, December, 1976.
New Statesman, January 31, 1964.
New York Herald Tribune Book Review, November 15, 1959; May 13, 1962.
New York Times Book Review, September 27, 1959; May 13, 1962; May 9, 1976; December 17, 1978; January 29, 1984; November 13, 1988; September 21, 2003, p. 17.
New York Times Magazine, May 2, 1965.
Parnassus, Volume 21, pp. 138-145.
Poetry, April, 1960.
Publishers Weekly, October 24, 1994, p. 58; July 31, 1995.
Saturday Review, May 21, 1960.
Saturday Review/World, April 3, 1976.
Sewanee Review, spring, 1969.
Time, May 18, 1962.
Times Literary Supplement, June 9, 1966; January 4, 1980; July 4, 1986; May 5, 1989.
Washington Post Book World, March 5, 1995, p. 12; October 26, 2003, article by Edward Hirsch, p. T12.
Yale Review, March, 1964; October, 1972.

* * *

SIMPSON, Louis Aston Marantz
See SIMPSON, Louis

SINGER, Isaac
See SINGER, Isaac Bashevis

* * *

SINGER, Isaac Bashevis 1904-1991
(Isaac Bashevis, Isaac Singer, Isaac Warshofsky)

PERSONAL: Born July 14, 1904, in Radzymin, Poland; immigrated to United States, 1935; naturalized U.S. citizen, 1943; died after several strokes, July 24, 1991, in Surfside, FL; son of Pinchos Menachem (a rabbi and author) and Bathsheba (Zylberman) Singer; married; wife's name Rachel (divorced); married Alma Haimann, February 14, 1940; children: (first marriage) Israel Zamir. *Education:* Attended Tachkemoni Rabbinical Seminary, Warsaw, Poland, 1920-23. *Religion:* Jewish.

CAREER: Novelist, short story writer, children's author, and translator. *Literarishe Bletter,* Warsaw, Poland, proofreader and translator, 1923-33; *Globus,* Warsaw, associate editor, 1933-35; *Jewish Daily Forward,* New York, NY, member of staff, 1935-91. Founder of the literary magazine *Svivah.* Appeared in films *Isaac in America* and *The Cafeteria* (based on one of his short stories), both Direct Cinema Limited Associates, 1986.

MEMBER: Jewish Academy of Arts and Sciences (fellow), National Institute of Arts and Letters (fellow), Polish Institute of Arts and Sciences in America (fellow), American Academy of Arts and Sciences, PEN.

AWARDS, HONORS: Louis Lamed Prize, 1950, for *The Family Moskat,* and 1956, for *Satan in Goray;* National Institute of Arts and Letters and American Academy award in literature, 1959; Harry and Ethel Daroff Memorial Fiction Award, Jewish Book Council of America, 1963, for *The Slave;* D.H.L., Hebrew Union College, 1963; Foreign Book prize (France), 1965; National Council on the Arts grant, 1966; *New York Times* best illustrated book citation, 1966, Newbery Honor Book Award, 1967, International Board on Books for Young People (IBBY) honor list, 1982, *Horn Book* "Fanfare" citation, and American Library Association (ALA) notable book citation, all for *Zlateh the Goat, and Other Stories;* National Endowment for the Arts grant, 1967; *Playboy* magazine award for best fiction, 1967; Newbery Honor Book Award, 1968, for *The Fearsome Inn;* Bancarella Prize, 1968, for Italian translation of *The Family Moskat;* Newbery Honor Book Award, 1969, ALA notable book citation, and *Horn*

Book honor list citation, all for *When Schlemiel Went to Warsaw, and Other Stories;* Brandeis University Creative Arts Medal for Poetry-Fiction, 1970; National Book Award for children's literature, 1970, and ALA notable book citation, both for *A Day of Pleasure;* Sydney Taylor Award, Association of Jewish Libraries, 1971; Children's Book Showcase Award, Children's Book Council, 1972, for *Alone in the Wild Forest;* D.Litt., Texas Christian University, 1972, Colgate University, 1972, Bard College, 1974, and Long Island University, 1979; Ph.D., Hebrew University, Jerusalem, 1973; National Book Award for fiction, 1974, for *A Crown of Feathers and Other Stories;* Agnon Gold Medal, 1975; ALA notable book citation, 1976, for *Naftali the Storyteller and His Horse, Sus, and Other Stories;* Nobel Prize for Literature, 1978; Kenneth B. Smilen/*Present Tense* Literary Award, *Present Tense* magazine, 1980, for *The Power of Light; Los Angeles Times* fiction prize nomination, 1982, for *The Collected Stories of Isaac Bashevis Singer; New York Times* outstanding book citation, and *Horn Book* honor list citation, both 1982, Parents' Choice Award, Parents' Choice Foundation, 1983, and ALA notable book citation, all for *The Golem; New York Times* notable book citation, and ALA notable book citation, both 1984, both for *Stories for Children;* Handel Medallion, 1986; PEN/Faulkner Award nomination, 1989, for *The Death of Methuselah and Other Stories;* Gold Medal for Fiction, American Academy and Institute of Arts and Letters, 1989; *Mazel and Shlimazel; or, The Milk of a Lioness* and *The Wicked City* received ALA notable book citations.

WRITINGS:

NOVELS; ORIGINALLY IN YIDDISH

Der Satan in Gorey, [Warsaw, Poland], 1935, translation by Jacob Sloan published as *Satan in Goray,* Noonday Press (New York, NY), 1955, reprinted, Farrar, Straus (New York, NY), 1996.

(Under name Isaac Bashevis) *Di Familie Mushkat,* two volumes, [New York, NY], 1950, translation by A.H. Gross published under name Isaac Bashevis Singer as *The Family Moskat,* Knopf (New York, NY), 1950.

The Magician of Lublin, translation by Elaine Gottlieb and Joseph Singer, Noonday Press (New York, NY), 1960.

The Slave (also see below), translation by author and Cecil Hemley, Farrar, Straus (New York, NY), 1962.

The Manor (also see below), translation by Elaine Gottlieb and Joseph Singer, Farrar, Straus (New York, NY), 1967.

The Estate (also see below), translation by Elaine Gottlieb, Joseph Singer, and Elizabeth Shub, Farrar, Straus (New York, NY), 1969.

Enemies: A Love Story (first published in *Jewish Daily Forward* under title *Sonim, di Geshichte fun a Liebe,* 1966; also see below), translation by Aliza Shevrin and Elizabeth Shub, Farrar, Straus (New York, NY), 1972.

Shosha (also see below), translation by Joseph Singer, Farrar, Straus (New York, NY), 1978.

Reaches of Heaven: A Story of the Baal Shem Tov, Farrar, Straus (New York, NY), 1980.

Isaac Bashevis Singer, Three Complete Novels (includes *The Slave, Enemies: A Love Story,* and *Shosha*), Avenel Books (Avenel, NJ), 1982, reprinted, Wings Books (New York, NY), 1995.

The Penitent, Farrar, Straus (New York, NY), 1983.

The King of the Fields, limited edition, Farrar, Straus (New York, NY), 1988.

Scum, translation by Rosaline D. Schwartz, Farrar, Straus (New York, NY), 1991.

The Certificate, translation by Leonard Wolf, Farrar, Straus (New York, NY), 1992.

Meshugah, translation by Nili Wachtel, Farrar, Straus (New York, NY), 1994.

Shootns baym Hodson, translation by Joseph Sherman published as *Shadows on the Hudson,* Farrar, Straus (New York, NY), 1998.

The Manor and the Estate University of Wisconsin Press (Madison, WI), 2004.

SHORT-STORY COLLECTIONS; ORIGINALLY IN YIDDISH

Gimpel the Fool, and Other Stories, translation by Saul Bellow and others, Noonday Press (New York, NY), 1957.

The Spinoza of Market Street, and Other Stories, translation by Elaine Gottlieb and others, Farrar, Straus (New York, NY), 1961.

Short Friday, and Other Stories, translation by Ruth Whitman and others, Farrar, Straus (New York, NY), 1964.

Selected Short Stories, edited by Irving Howe, Modern Library (New York, NY), 1966.

The Seance, and Other Stories, translation by Ruth Whitman, Roger H. Klein, and others, Farrar, Straus (New York, NY), 1968.

(And translator with others) *A Friend of Kafka, and Other Stories,* Farrar, Straus (New York, NY), 1970.

An Isaac Bashevis Singer Reader, Farrar, Straus (New York, NY), 1971.

(And translator with others) *A Crown of Feathers and Other Stories,* Farrar, Straus (New York, NY), 1973.

Passions, and Other Stories, Farrar, Straus (New York, NY), 1975.

Old Love, and Other Stories, Farrar, Straus (New York, NY), 1979.

The Collected Stories of Isaac Bashevis Singer, Farrar, Straus (New York, NY), 1982.

The Image, and Other Stories, Farrar, Straus (New York, NY), 1985.

Gifts, Jewish Publication Society of America (Philadelphia, PA), 1985.

The Death of Methuselah and Other Stories, Farrar, Straus (New York, NY), 1988.

Collected Stories: Gimpel the Fool to the Letter Writer, edited by Ilan Stavans, Library of America (New York, NY), 2004.

Collected Stories: A Friend of Kafka to Passions, edited by Ilan Stavans, Library of America (New York, NY), 2004.

Collected Stories: One Night in Brazil to The Death of Methuselah, edited by Ilan Stavans, Library of America (New York, NY), 2004.

FOR CHILDREN; ORIGINALLY IN YIDDISH; AND TRANSLATOR WITH ELIZABETH SHUB

Mazel and Shlimazel; or, The Milk of a Lioness, illustrated by Margot Zemach, Harper (New York, NY), 1966.

Zlateh the Goat, and Other Stories, illustrated by Maurice Sendak, Harper (New York, NY), 1966.

The Fearsome Inn, illustrated by Nonny Hogrogian, Scribner (New York, NY), 1967.

When Schlemiel Went to Warsaw, and Other Stories (also see below), illustrated by Margot Zemach, Farrar, Straus (New York, NY), 1968.

(Under pseudonym Isaac Warshofsky) *A Day of Pleasure: Stories of a Boy Growing up in Warsaw* (autobiography), photographs by Roman Vishniac, Farrar, Straus (New York, NY), 1969.

Elijah the Slave: A Hebrew Legend Retold, illustrated by Antonio Frasconi, Farrar, Straus (New York, NY), 1970.

Joseph and Koza; or, The Sacrifice to the Vistula, illustrated by Symeon Shimin, Farrar, Straus (New York, NY), 1970.

Alone in the Wild Forest, illustrated by Margot Zemach, Farrar, Straus (New York, NY), 1971.

The Topsy-Turvy Emperor of China, illustrated by William Pene du Bois, Harper (New York, NY), 1971, reprinted with illustrations by Julian Jusim, Farrar, Straus (New York, NY), 1996.

The Wicked City, illustrated by Leonard Everett Fisher, Farrar, Straus (New York, NY), 1972.

The Fools of Chelm and Their History, illustrated by Uri Shulevitz, Farrar, Straus (New York, NY), 1973.

Why Noah Chose the Dove, illustrated by Eric Carle, Farrar, Straus (New York, NY), 1974.

A Tale of Three Wishes, illustrated by Irene Lieblich, Farrar, Straus (New York, NY), 1975.

Naftali the Storyteller and His Horse, Sus, and Other Stories (also see below), illustrated by Margot Zemach, Farrar, Straus (New York, NY), 1976.

The Power of Light: Eight Stories for Hanukkah (also see below), illustrated by Irene Lieblich, Farrar, Straus (New York, NY), 1980.

The Golem, illustrated by Uri Shulevitz, Farrar, Straus (New York, NY), 1982.

Stories for Children (includes stories from *Naftali the Storyteller and His Horse, Sus, and Other Stories, When Schlemiel Went to Warsaw and Other Stories,* and *The Power of Light*), Farrar, Straus (New York, NY), 1984.

Shrewd Todie and Lyzer the Miser and Other Children's Stories, illustrated by Margot Zemach, Barefoot Books (Boston, MA), 1994.

AUTOBIOGRAPHY; ORIGINALLY IN YIDDISH; UNDER PSEUDONYM ISAAC WARSHOFSKY

Mayn Tatn's Bes-din Shtub, [New York, NY], 1956, translation by Channah Kleinerman-Goldstein published under name Isaac Bashevis Singer as *In My Father's Court,* Farrar, Straus (New York, NY), 1966.

A Little Boy in Search of God: Mysticism in a Personal Light (also see below), illustrated by Ira Moskowitz, Doubleday (Garden City, NY), 1976.

A Young Man in Search of Love (also see below), translation by Joseph Singer, Doubleday (Garden City, NY), 1978.

Lost in America (also see below), translation by Joseph Singer, paintings and drawings by Raphael Soyer, Doubleday (Garden City, NY), 1981.

Love and Exile: The Early Years: A Memoir (includes *A Little Boy in Search of God: Mysticism in a Personal Light, A Young Man in Search of Love,* and *Lost in America*), Doubleday (Garden City, NY), 1984.

More Stories from My Father's Court, translation by Curt Leviant, Farrar, Straus (New York, NY), 2000.

PLAYS; ORIGINALLY IN YIDDISH

The Mirror (also see below), produced in New Haven, CT, 1973.

(With Leah Napolin) *Yentl, the Yeshiva Boy* (adaptation of a story by Singer; produced on Broadway, 1974), Samuel French (New York, NY), 1978.

Schlemiel the First, produced in New Haven, CT, 1974.

(With Eve Friedman) *Teibele and Her Demon* (produced in Minneapolis at Guthrie Theatre, 1978, produced on Broadway, 1979), Samuel French (New York, NY), 1984.

A Play for the Devil (based on his short story "The Unseen"), produced in New York City at the Folksbiene Theatre, 1984.

TRANSLATOR INTO YIDDISH

Knut Hamsun, *Pan,* Wilno (Warsaw, Poland), 1928.

Knut Hamsun, *Di Vogler* (translation of *The Vagabonds*), Wilno (Warsaw, Poland), 1928.

Gabriele D'Annunzio, *In Opgrunt Fun Tayve* (translation of *In Passion's Abyss*), Goldfarb (Warsaw, Poland), 1929.

Karin Michaelis, *Mete Trap,* Goldfarb (Warsaw, Poland), 1929.

Stefan Zweig, *Roman Rolan,* Bikher (Warsaw, Poland), 1929.

Knut Hamsun, *Viktorya* (translation of *Victoria*), Wilno (Warsaw, Poland), 1929.

Erich Maria Remarque, *Oyfn Mayrev-Front Keyn Nayes* (translation of *All Quiet on the Western Front*), Wilno (Warsaw, Poland), 1930.

Thomas Mann, *Der Tsoyberbarg* (translation of *The Magic Mountain*), four volumes, Wilno (Warsaw, Poland), 1930.

Erich Maria Remarque, *Der Veg oyf Tsurik* (translation of *The Road Back*), Wilno (Warsaw, Poland), 1930.

Moshe Smilansky, *Araber: Folkstimlekhe Geshikhtn* (translation of *Arabs: Stories of the People*), Farn Folk (Warsaw, Poland), 1932.

Leon S. Glaser, *Fun Moskve biz Yerusholayim* (translation of *From Moscow to Jerusalem*), Jankowitz, 1938.

OTHER

(Editor with Elaine Gottlieb) *Prism 2,* Twayne (Boston, MA), 1965.

Visit to the Rabbinical Seminary in Cincinnati, [New York, NY], 1965.

(With Ira Moscowitz) *The Hasidim: Paintings, Drawings, and Etchings,* Crown (New York, NY), 1973.

Nobel Lecture, Farrar, Straus (New York, NY), 1979.

The Gentleman from Cracow; The Mirror, illustrated with water colors by Raphael Soyer, introduction by Harry I. Moore, Limited Editions Club, 1979.

Isaac Bashevis Singer on Literature and Life, University of Arizona Press (Tucson, AZ), 1979.

The Meaning of Freedom, United States Military Academy (West Point, NY), 1981.

My Personal Conception of Religion, University of Southwestern Louisiana Press (Lafayette, LA), 1982.

One Day of Happiness, Red Ozier Press, 1982.

Remembrances of a Rabbi's Son, translated by Rena Borrow, United Jewish Appeal-Federation Campaign, 1984.

(With Richard Burgin) *Conversations with Isaac Bashevis Singer,* Farrar, Straus (New York, NY), 1986.

The Safe Deposit and Other Stories about Grandparents, Old Lovers, and Crazy Old Men ("Masterworks of Modern Jewish Writing" series), edited by Kerry M. Orlitzky, Wiener, Markus (New York, NY), 1989.

Isaac Bashevis Singer: Conversations, edited by Grace Farrell, University Press of Mississippi (Jackson, MS), 1992.

Also author of works under name Isaac Singer. Author of the introduction for Knut Hamsun's *Hunger,* Farrar, Straus (New York, NY), 1967; of the preface for Ruth Whitman's *An Anthology of Modern Yiddish Poetry,* Workmen's Circle Education Department (New York, NY), 1979; and of the introduction and commentary for Richard Nagler's *My Love Affair with Miami Beach,* Simon & Schuster (New York, NY), 1991. Contributor to books, including *Tully Filmus,* edited by Anatol Filmus, Jewish Publication Society of America (Philadelphia, PA), 1971; and *Miami Beach,* by Gary Monroe, Forest & Trees, 1989. Contributor of stories and articles to periodicals in the United States and Poland, including *Die Yiddische Welt, Commentary, Esquire, New Yorker, Globus, Literarishe Bletter, Harper's,* and *Partisan Review.*

Sound recordings include *Isaac Bashevis Singer Reading His Stories* (contains *Gimpel the Fool* and *The Man Who Came Back*), and *Isaac Bashevis Singer Reading His Stories in Yiddish* (contains *Big and Little, Shiddah and Kuziba,* and *The Man Who Came Back*), both Caedmon Records, both 1967. Singer's works are housed in the Elman Collection, Arents Research Library, Syracuse University, and at the Butler Library, Columbia University.

ADAPTATIONS: Filmstrips based on Singer's short stories include: *Isaac Singer and Mrs. Pupko's Bread,* New Yorker, 1973, *Rabbi Leib and the Witch Cunnegunde,* Miller-Brody Productions, 1976, and *Shrewd Todie and Lyzer the Miser,* Miller-Brody Productions, 1976; works adapted into filmstrips by Miller-Brody Productions include *Zlateh the Goat, and Other Stories, When Schlemiel Went to Warsaw,* and *Why Noah Chose the Dove,* all 1975, and *Mazel and Shlimazel,* 1976. *Zlateh the Goat, and Other Stories* was adapted into a film by Weston Woods, 1973, and broadcast on National Broadcasting Company (NBC-TV), 1973. *The Magician of Lublin* was adapted into a film starring Alan Arkin, produced by Menahem Golan, 1978. *Gimpel the Fool* was adapted for the stage by David Schechter and produced by the Bakery Theater Cooperative of New York, 1982. *Yentl, the Yeshiva Boy* was adapted into the movie *Yentl,* starring Barbra Streisand, who also directed, and from a screenplay she wrote with Jack Rosenthal, and released by Metro-Goldwyn-Mayer/United Artists, 1983. *Enemies: A Love Story* was adapted into a film by Paul Mazursky and Roger L. Simon, directed by Mazursky and starring Ron Silver, Anjelica Huston, Lena Olin, and Margaret Sophie Stein, and released by Twentieth Century-Fox, 1989. *Meshugah* was adapted for the stage by playwright Emily Mann in a production directed by Loretta Greco at the Kirk Theater in New York, 2003. Works adapted into recordings read by Eli Wallach include: *When Schlemiel Went to Warsaw, and Other Stories,* Newbery Awards Records, 1974, *Zlateh the Goat, and Other Stories,* Newbery Award Records, 1974, *Eli Wallach Reads Isaac Bashevis Singer* (contains *Zlateh the Goat, and Other Stories* and *When Schlemiel Went to Warsaw, and Other Stories*), Miller-Brody Productions, 1976, and *Isaac Bashevis Singer* (contains *The Seance* and *The Lecture*), Spoken Arts, 1979. *The Family Moskat, The Slave, Satan in Goray, Passions, and Other Stories,* and *In My Father's Court* were adapted into audio cassettes; about twenty of Singer's works have been adapted into Braille editions; more than a dozen of Singer's works have been adapted into talking books.

SIDELIGHTS: Widely proclaimed to be one of the foremost writers of Yiddish literature, Isaac Bashevis Singer stood clearly outside the mainstream and basic traditions of both Yiddish and American literature. His work, translated into numerous languages, won him the Nobel Prize for Literature in 1978, as well as numerous other prestigious honors. "The river of words that flowed from Singer's pen is vast: hundreds of short stories, volumes of autobiography, a dozen novels and even more children's books," noted Lore Dickstein in the *New York Times Book Review.* Dickstein added, "He was embraced by a large, unlikely audience, including readers of *Playboy* and *The New Yorker,* most of them far removed from the lost world of Eastern European Jewry that Singer evoked so pungently." The critic also noted that Singer "is the most magical of writers, transforming reality into art with seemingly effortless sleight of hand. His deceptively spare prose has a pristine clarity that is stunning in its impact." Lee Siegel, also writing in the *New York Times Book Review,* deemed Singer "the creator of stories and novels that, at their best, are like hard diamonds of perfection."

Singer's writing has proven difficult to categorize, with critics attaching to the author various and sometimes contradictory labels in an attempt to define his work. He was called a modernist, although he personally disliked most contemporary fiction, and he was also accused of being captivated by the past, of writing in a dying language despite his English fluency, of setting his fiction in a world that no longer exists: the *shtetls* (Jewish ghettos) of Eastern Europe, which were destroyed by Hitler's campaign against the Jews. And despite the attention called to the mysticism, the prolific presence of the supernatural, and the profoundly religious nature of his writing, Singer was called both a realist and a pessimist. Undeniably a difficult author to place in critical perspective, Singer once addressed himself to the problems of labeling his work in an interview with Cyrene N. Pondrom for *Contemporary Literature:* "People always need a name for things, so whatever you will write or whatever you will do, they like to put you into a certain category. Even if you would be new, they would like to feel that a name is already prepared for you in advance. . . . I hope that one day somebody will find a new name for me, not use the old ones."

Whatever else he was, Singer was a storyteller. His works deal with crises of faith: having discarded their old traditions as inadequate to cope with modern society, his characters are engaged in a fruitless search for something to replace them. "Singer portrays men who are between faiths," Nili Wachtel explained in *Judaism.* "Having freed themselves from the bonds of God and community, they have also freed themselves from their very identities. With their God and their community, they knew who they were and what they were expected to do; now they know nothing as certain." Michael Wood similarly observed in the *New York Review of Books:* "Again and again in his fiction Singer evokes the destruction of a community, the crumbling of a whole social edifice, because people, one way or another, have averted their faces from a truth they used to know."

The key to Singer's work lies in his background, in his roots in the Polish, Yiddish-speaking, Jewish ghettos. "I was born with the feeling that I am part of an unlikely adventure, something that couldn't have happened, but happened just the same," Singer once remarked to a *Book Week* interviewer. Born in a small Polish town, Singer was the son of a Hasidic rabbi, and both his grandfathers were also rabbis. Visiting his maternal grandfather in the rural village of Bilgoray as a young boy, Singer learned of life in the *shtetl,* which would become the setting of much of his later work. The village was a "world of old Jewishness [in which] I found a spiritual treasure trove," the author was quoted as saying in the *Dictionary of Literary Biography Yearbook,* "Time seemed to flow backwards. I lived Jewish history."

The young Singer received a basic Jewish education, preparing him to follow his father's and grandfathers' steps into the rabbinical vocation. He studied the Torah, the Talmud, the Cabala, and other sacred Jewish books. An even stronger influence than his education and his parents' orthodoxy, however, was his older brother, the novelist I.J. Singer, who broke with the family's orthodoxy and began to write secular stories. Attempting to overcome the influence of his brother's rationalism and to strengthen the cause of religion, his parents told him stories of *dybbuks* (wandering souls in Jewish folklore believed to enter a human body and control its actions, possessions, and other spiritual mysteries). Singer once commented that he was equally fascinated by his parents' mysticism and his brother's rationalism. Although this duality would come to characterize much of his writing, eventually Singer would break from both traditions.

At seventeen Singer entered a seminary in Warsaw, but he left two years later to follow his brother into the world of arts and letters. He got a proofreading job with a Yiddish literary magazine, worked as a translator, and at twenty-three had his first piece of fiction published. Concerned about German aggression and the policies of Adolf Hitler, Singer left Poland in 1935 and joined his brother in New York City. There he married and began a long career as a journalist and writer for the *Jewish Daily Forward.* The periodical would serve as the first publisher of many of Singer's works—short stories, articles, and serialized novels in Yiddish.

Singer continued to do all of his writing in Yiddish, and much of his large body of writing remained untranslated after his death in 1991. Before he felt sufficiently fluent in English, Singer had to rely on other people to do the translations; his nephew Joseph Singer was responsible for much of it. Toward the end of his career, though, Singer usually did a rough translation into English himself and then had someone help him polish the English version and work on the idioms. The English translations were often a "second original," according to Singer, differing structurally from the Yiddish. "I used to play with the idea [of writing in English]," Singer once admitted in an interview with Joel Blocker and Richard Elman for *Commentary,* "but never seriously. Never. I always knew that a writer has to write in his own language or not at all."

Singer described Yiddish in his Nobel lecture as "a language of exile, without a land, without frontiers, not supported by any government, a language which possesses no words for weapons, ammunition, military exercises, war tactics; a language that was despised by both gentiles and emancipated Jews. . . . Yiddish has not yet said its last word. It contains treasures that have not been revealed to the eyes of the world. It was the tongue of martyrs and saints, of dreamers and cabalists—rich in humor and in memories that mankind may never forget. In a figurative way, Yiddish is the wise and humble language of us all, the idiom of the frightened and hopeful humanity."

Aside from believing that he must write in his native tongue, Singer also believed that the function of his fiction should be entertainment. "I never thought that my fiction—my kind of writing—had any other purpose than to be read and enjoyed by the reader," he commented to Sanford Pinsker in *The Schlemiel as Metaphor: Studies in the Yiddish and American Jewish Novel.* "I never sit down to write a novel to make a better world or to create good feelings towards the Jews or for any other purpose," he continued. "I knew this from the very beginning, that writing fiction has no other purpose than to give enjoyment to a reader. . . . I consider myself an entertainer. . . . I mean an entertainer of good people, of intellectual people who cannot be entertained by cheap stuff. And I think this is true about fiction in all times."

Singer's first novel, *Satan in Goray,* was first published in Yiddish in 1935. The novel's action takes place in a small Hasidic community in Poland during the seventeenth century. Cossacks have raided the closely knit community, and the *shtetl* easily accepts the promises of a false messiah, Sabbatai Zevi. As violations of religious law take place, a rash of strange, demonic occurrences erupts, eventually concentrating themselves in Zevi's chosen bride, who becomes pregnant with Satan's child. According to Ted Hughes, writing in the *New York Review of Books,* the novel is Singer's "weakest book—important, and with a stunning finish, but for the most part confusingly organized." Hughes added that the supernatural elements provide "an accurate metaphor for a cultural landslide that has destroyed all spiritual principles and duped an entire age into a cynical materialism emptied of meaning." In his critical work *Isaac Bashevis Singer: The Magician of West 86th Street* Paul Kresh described *Satan in Goray* as "rich in vivid, convincing descriptions of things, places and people [and] . . . haunting in its imagery."

The Family Moskat departs from its predecessor and offers a long, epic vision of a large family in a big Polish city. Radical changes are afoot, and the narrator, Asa Heshel, not only participates in them himself but also observes their effects upon the Moskat family. The story ends as the Nazis are about to invade, and Asa leaves his family behind to join the army. *Spectator* critic John Daniel called the work "a considerable novel" with "powerfully created characters; a deep sense of Warsaw as a city; and a real saturation in Jewish lore." In *Yiddish Literature* Charles A. Madison praised the novel's characterizations, concluding that the book "is an intensely conceived narrative pulsating with human life and revealing the inner emotional recesses of the individuals involved."

Turning to yet another format, the picaresque adventure *The Magician of Lublin* follows magician and acrobat Yasha Mazur as he courts several women—even though he already has a devoted wife and family. According to *Critical Quarterly* contributor David Seed, this novel "is certainly one of Singer's most concentrated and unified works," mainly because the disordered setting of the Warsaw streets matches the emotional crisis suffered by Yasha, whose conscience pains him even as he involves himself in trouble. In addition, Nili Wachtel observed in *Judaism* that Yasha's profession—magician and tightrope walker—reflects the dilemma of rootless modern man: "He is afraid to be fixed by a single and permanent identity. . . . He has no peace, he feels himself dangling; he is walking his tightrope, he feels, but always on the verge of disaster." Yasha finally reconciles his conscience with his actions by enclosing himself in a cell, locked away from the potential to misbehave. "That his singular behavior, which would normally seem queer, appears plausible is due to Singer's powers of exposition and characterization," Madison remarked, for the characters "are portrayed realistically, without affection or sympathy, but also without manipulation and artfulness."

Whether they feature sweeping historical events or the singular struggles of an individual, Singer's novels express his concern with issues of faith and freedom. Set in Poland in the seventeenth century, *The Slave* features the religious crises the protagonist, Jacob, suffers as he experiences various forms of freedom and slavery, some of them mirroring Biblical events. *New York Times Book Review* contributor Milton Hindus found the novel "overburdened . . . with too much allegorical suggestiveness" but allowed that "there is a lovely lyricism in some of the descriptive passages which makes them partake of the quality of expressionist paintings." Madison praised the appealing characters and setting, concluding that "all of this folklore, exotic atmosphere, and genuine emotion is depicted with an intimate knowledge and artistic sensuousness that combine to give the book major status as a work of fiction."

In *The Manor* and *The Estate* Singer once again took an epic approach in portraying an era of Polish-Jewish history. The two volumes cover the last third of the nineteenth century, a time of dramatic change. "As in his earlier novels," Madison related, "Singer deals at length and significantly with the events and salient thoughts and ideas of the time in which his characters live and function." Nili Wachtel remarked in *Judaism* that the central character's experience "gives voice to what it is that ails modern man. Alone, independent, free of any single influence or direction, modern man becomes aware of a chaotic world alive within him, a churning chaos of conflicting drives and ambitions." These two novels, according to Seed, "raise various theoretical issues (usually in explicit discussion) and one of their central themes is the notion of progress."

Later Singer works reflect his experiences living not just as an exile from his homeland, but also as one of the few survivors of a culture that was exterminated by the Holocaust. In *Enemies: A Love Story* Herman Broder is a Polish refugee whose entire family has perished in the death camps. He has immigrated to America, where he lives in New York with Yadwiga, the Polish woman who saved him from the Nazis by hiding him in her hayloft. Although Yadwiga has converted to Judaism for him, Herman has taken a mistress, the divorced Masha, who lives with her mother, a bitter survivor of a concentration camp. When Herman discovers that the wife he thought had perished during the war is actually alive and living in New York, it sets in motion a tragicomic series of events. *Enemies* "is a bleak, obsessive novel that offers neither release nor hope," Dickstein observed in the *New York Times Book Review.* Kresh, however, felt that the book "hangs together uncommonly well" and praised Singer's focus on the love story. He explained that the author concentrates "on the lines of force that bond his characters together, ironically, angrily, passionately, even though life has done everything to deprive them of their illusions and their appetites." *Newsweek* contributor Walter Clemons concluded, "Whether or not you accept its ending, *Enemies: A Love Story* is a brilliant, unsettling novel."

The author's most autobiographical novel, *Shosha,* "is filled with the usual Singer questions about demonic possession, free-floating souls, an archive of spirits, a world rife with secret powers and occult mysteries," reported Edward Hirsch in the *Saturday Review.* "But mostly it is a testament to the haunting power of the past." Taking place in the Warsaw of the 1920s and 1930s, *Shosha* follows the developing relationship between a rabbi's son and the title character, a somewhat simple and innocent girl. As the protagonist looks for his place and for meaning in the world, he wanders from woman to woman until he returns to his childhood friend. "Singer conveys a sense of the teeming particularities of Polish-Jewish life," Robert Alter remarked in the *New Republic.* Alter added, "Singer, here as elsewhere, is so *beguiling* a writer that one readily forgives the flaws of his work." In *Harper's,* Paul Berman wrote that *Shosha* is "an entertaining novel, for though Singer is an earnest writer, his earnestness steps lightly." Kresh declared *Shosha* a "powerful and important work," adding that while the characters and themes are familiar ground for Singer, "*Shosha* casts a fresh light on them, making their story one of the most poignant Isaac has ever written."

Several Singer novels have been translated and published posthumously, including *Scum, The Certificate, Meshugah,* and *Shadows on the Hudson.* A *dybbuk* and Polish Jewry figure in *Scum.* In 1906 Max Barabander has returned to Warsaw from Argentina some twenty years after leaving. Because of shady dealings, he now is a wealthy man, but he is impotent after the sudden death of his teenage son and his wife's isolation. In Warsaw he becomes a philanderer, convinced he is possessed by a *dybbuk,* and a master of language. "There is, as Singer warns, little of God's wisdom and mercy in this book, but the display of human perversity and sheer cussedness is enthralling," Paul Gray remarked in *Time.*

The Certificate "is a mildly engaging piece of work, more fictionalized memoir than anything else," commented Kenneth Turan in the *Los Angeles Times Book Review.* The protagonist is unpublished writer David Bendinger, whose father is a rabbi and brother is a writer. After four years in the country, Bendinger returns to Warsaw seeking a certificate from the British government that will allow him to immigrate to Palestine. Through Bendinger's relationships with three very different women, Singer subtly criticizes the Zionists, Communists, and the religious Jewish community and reveals Bendinger's anxieties. "It is impossible not to feel the charm of this book, which may be the most Jewish of all Singer's works. The warmest and the saddest too," remarked Chicago *Tribune Books* reviewer Elie Wiesel.

Originally titled *Lost Souls, Meshugah* (Yiddish for "crazy") describes the encounters that Polish exile Aaron Greidinger has with Holocaust survivors in early-1950s Manhattan. "The various survivors, all mourning loved ones, are indeed 'lost souls,' subject to melancholy, poisonous dreams and thoughts of suicide," Joel Conarroe pointed out in the *New York Times Book Review.* "As for the concept of *meshugah,*" Conarroe added, "Singer weaves into his narrative references to the innate craziness not only of his high-strung men and women, but of the mad events that have shaped their behavior." George Packer commented in *Washington Post Book World* that in *Meshugah* Singer uses his "familiar bag of tricks: love triangles and quadrangles, sudden reversals from disaster to fulfillment and back, relentless questions about good and evil." However, concluded Packer, "the concoction lacks Singer's customary zest." According to Mark Shechner in Chicago *Tribune Books,* the previously serialized story "is reminiscent of daytime television" because it is episodic and contains licentiousness and pathos. However, stressed Shechner, "its licentiousness, far from being a commercial pandering to the market, is a tragic metaphysics, warranted by the apocalypses of the 20th century."

Shadows on the Hudson once again is concerned with the lives of Jewish refugees in World War II-era Manhattan. Hertz Dovid Grein, a Polish native, struggles to reconcile his simultaneous passions for three women while wrestling with theological, philosophical, and political issues pertinent to the times. The novel, like most of Singer's other works, was published serially in *The Jewish Daily Forward;* unlike the others, however, its publication in novel form does not include editing of redundant or repetitive passages. The work is therefore long and—some critics felt—tedious in places. Siegel noted in the *New York Times Book Review* that the "shapeless lump does a keen disservice to the author of 'Gimpel the Fool.'" Concluding that the novel "would have been a failure under any circumstances," Siegel determined that it "would have been a respectable failure if only Singer's editors had striven in the slightest degree." *Commentary* reviewer Hillel Hakin, however, deemed the work "an absorbing novel," which "has the added value of showing us a Singer who, precisely because he seems more morally earnest and religiously anguished than the artful juggler of demons, dybbuks, and eccentric Jews that his American readers came to know him as, makes us realize how elaborately crafted was this impish mask of his later years." Rita D. Jacobs, critiquing the book for *World Literature Today,* allowed that Singer may have wanted "to sharpen his focus and his tale," but thought the novel was nevertheless "rich, various, evocative, and thought-provoking" and "well worth reading."

Although his novels were frequently noteworthy, Singer was perhaps better known as a master of the short story. Story-writing was his most effective and favorite genre because, as he once explained, it was more possible to be perfect in the short story than in a longer work. Furthermore, Singer did not think that the supernatural—which was his main element—lent itself well to longer, novelistic writing. Singer's style in the short story was simple, spare, and in the tradition of the spoken tale. In his *Commentary* interview, the author remarked: "When I tell a story, I tell a story. I don't try to discuss, criticize, or analyze my characters." *Nation* reviewer Dan Isaac commented that Singer's short stories "are far superior to his novels" because they more closely follow the Jewish literary tradition of "the proverb, the parable and the folk tale." In *Studies in Short Fiction,* John Lawrence Abbott declared, "The short story continues to remain Singer's most congenial turf. It is here that the economy of style and the deceptive simplicity of his vision can be most richly felt." Hughes also observed that Singer's stories "give freer play to his invention than the novels. At their best, they must be among the most entertaining pieces extant. Each is a unique exercise in tone, focus, style, form, as well as an unforgettable re-creation of characters and life." It was Singer's first collection of short fiction, *Gimpel the Fool, and Other Stories,* that first gained him a wider English-speaking audience. Part of the notoriety came from the collection's translator, for novelist Saul Bellow, himself a future Nobel laureate, was already critically acclaimed for his own fiction. But it was primarily the quality of the stories that captivated readers, particularly the title story about a supposed "fool" whose innocent faith protects him from the evil that harms others. Leon Wieseltier, writing in the *New York Review of Books,* felt that the collection "contains Singer's best work, his boldest and liveliest inventions. And it belies at once his familiar disclaimer that he is only a storyteller. He is not. His tales are thick with speculation and prejudice, and both are damaging." The 1961 compilation *The Spinoza of Market Street, and Other Stories* also won notice for its title piece, which concerns a Jewish scholar who eventually finds happiness in marriage, not philosophy. *New Republic* contributor Irving Howe remarked that the collection, while demonstrating nothing unexpected of Singer, is still the work of "a writer who has mastered his chosen form and keeps producing work often distinguished and always worthy of attention."

After his 1964 short story collection, *Short Friday, and Other Stories,* Singer's fiction began to show the influence of his adopted homeland. Many of the author's later stories featured Jews transplanted to America after World War II. The stories in *A Friend of Kafka,* for instance, "show this venerable master seriously extending his range," according to Jay L. Halio in *Southern Review.* Some stories still utilize Singer's popular Polish village settings, but there are many more following the lives of Jewish immigrants in America, Israel, and Argentina. *Time* correspondent Stefan Kanfer believed that "these twenty-one miraculous creations are, in the highest artistic tradition, true stories." Dan Isaac commented that the collection "is by far the best thing we have" from Singer, adding in his *Nation* review that the author "seems to go from strength to strength as though increasing age had become the generative force."

The 1974 National Book Award-winning collection *A Crown of Feathers* also demonstrated Singer's growing preoccupation with life in America. According to William Peden in *Sewanee Review,* "whether [Singer's] landscape be a Warsaw soup kitchen for intellectuals, an old world haunted by demons, imps, and *dybbuks* of the past, or a cafeteria in Coney Island, it is alive and vibrant with unforgettable people." While *Nation* writer Seymour Kleinberg found *A Crown of Feathers* "the least rewarding of Singer's . . . short-story collections," he acknowledged that "his literary craftsmanship and sophistication, and the special Singer voice, are here and gratifying; only in comparison with his past achievements does the book fall short." Crawford Woods concluded in his *New Republic* review, "These unusually fine stories take joy in paradox but not in irony, and they're often tragic but never sad. If their resemblance to each other makes the book seem long, it also makes it cut deep. What might be a sign of limitation in a lesser writer in Singer must be seen as wisdom. He is one of our best storytellers—'our' meaning everybody."

Later Singer collections garnered much the same praise as his previous works. In his *Studies in Short Fiction* review of *Passions, and Other Stories,* Timothy Evans maintained, "Here is passion in the art, an imaginative providence as prodigal as ever, a talent in its prime, a writer to be rejoiced in." *New York Times* columnist John Gross observed of *The Image, and Other Stories* that while the themes and subjects are familiar, "in another sense, virtually every story in the book comes as a surprise, with the freshness of a bold conception firmly imagined and confidently executed." Singer, the critic concluded, "remains a true storyteller—at every stage, you want to know what happens next—and there has been no falling-off in the quality of his writing."

Even into his eighties Singer continued to produce new works of short fiction at a rapid pace. The final collection published during his lifetime, *The Death of Methuselah and Other Stories,* demonstrates that "like a vintage wine, Isaac Bashevis Singer gets better with time," commented Lothar Kahn in *World Literature Today.* The stories include many of the same themes and supernatural occurrences that characterize his earlier fiction. In one, an exorcist eventually gives in to his own demons; in another, an artist discovers he has spent his creativity on love rather than art; in a third, a Florida retiree cannot give up his wheeler-dealer lifestyle even though it jeopardizes his health. *New Leader* contributor David Evanier thought that while "Singer does not here attain the heights he scaled three decades ago in *Gimpel the Fool, and Other Stories,* he remains one of our best short form writers . . . Singer instantly breathes life into his people. He makes them real and urgent. We are drawn irresistibly into their lives and turn the pages with eagerness." Believing that for Singer, the urge to create and learn was as tempting as sex, Robert Pinsky wrote in the *New York Times Book Review* that "Singer's stories both demonstrate the power and irresistible attraction of such [creative] secular arts, and question the moral force underneath the attraction."

In addition to his work for adult readers, Singer penned a number of acclaimed children's books. "Children are the best readers of genuine literature," Singer remarked in *Top of the News,* "In our epoch, when storytelling has become a forgotten art and has been replaced by amateurish sociology and hackneyed psychology, the child is still the independent reader who relies on nothing but his own taste. . . . Long after literature for adults will have gone to pieces, books for children will constitute that last vestige of storytelling, logic, faith in the family, in God and in real humanism."

Most of Singer's children's books are collections of short stories in which "religion and custom dominate life and a rich folktale tradition abounds," according to Sylvia W. Iskander in the *Dictionary of Literary Biography.* A number of his stories are set in the humorous Polish city of Chelm—a town that Yiddish people view as a place of fools. And they also include *schlemiel* (eternal loser) characters, who naturally reside in the city of Chelm. They are essentially fools, but are portrayed as being charming and engaging, as is the city itself. Aside from these humorous and silly tales, Singer also wrote stories about animals and such supernatural beings as witches, goblins, devils, and demons. "Certainly the union of stories by a Nobel laureate storyteller with illustrations by some of the finest artists in the field of children's literature has produced outstanding books," concluded Iskander. "But it is the content of the stories—the combination of folklore, fairy tale, religion, and imagination—that makes Singer's books unique and inimitable."

With so many of his fictional works finding a basis in the author's own experiences, it is not surprising that Singer also published several volumes of autobiography. These include *In My Father's Court, A Little Boy in Search of God, A Young Man in Search of Love, Lost in America,* and *More Stories from My Father's Court.* "Singer makes vivid a world triply gone," observed Jonathan Rosen in the *New York Times Book Review.* "He is evoking the world of childhood, which is always a lost world, as well as the culture of Judaism that produced his father but that was already breaking apart under the weight of assimilation. He is also recording the transitional realm of Jewish Poland that Singer himself was born into in 1904—a world that was destroyed by the Nazis, who murdered the Jewish prostitutes and the rabbis without distinction. Writing in the aftermath of that destruction, Singer pays his characters the high honor of recreating them in all their low reality, which in some paradoxical way seems like an act of profound humanism."

Although Singer died in 1991, most of his work is still in print, and new translations of Yiddish prose and fiction are continuing to appear. Some critics have suggested that the author's use of a vanishing language, traditional folklore, and "old country" settings belie a modern consciousness that could address issues central to universal human emotion. "Singer repetitively and compellingly focuses on the individual's struggle to find a viable faith in the age possessed by this very problem," Linda G. Zatlin commented in *Critique.* "Thus, the stories, despite their setting, . . . portray and explore this predominant problem of modern man with all its accompanying apprehension and tension." For *Commentary* contributor Joseph Epstein it was Singer's skill at recreating eras that made him noteworthy. "No modern writer in any literature that I know is so adept at setting his stories anywhere he wishes temporally," Epstein wrote. "This ability sets much of Singer's writing finally beyond time, which is of course where everyone who thinks himself an artist wishes to be." "Singer is one of the great tale-tellers of this century," Sean French observed in *New Statesman and Society.* "He has a skill for the gripping short narrative, the 'yarn' that is almost without precedent since the time of Kipling. . . . Singer is better than anyone else on the surfaces, sounds and smells of life, about worldly things—lust, acquisitiveness, magic, superstition."

Julia O'Faolain summed up Singer's accomplishment in her *New Review* piece on the Nobel laureate. "My pleasure in Singer's work comes from no fact he imparts," she stated. "The virtue is in the tale itself and the tale is his response to those riddles which excite such passion in him that he had to elaborate a narrative method for dealing with it. It is *his* own method and fits his themes. In other words, he has a voice of his own." Noting that Singer was "a remarkable storyteller, at once swift and complex," Peter S. Prescott concluded in *Newsweek,* "I believe that Singer, in his short and humorous tales drawn from an old tradition, celebrates the dignity, mystery and unexpected joy of living with more art and fervor than any other writer."

BIOGRAPHICAL AND CRITICAL SOURCES:

BOOKS

Alexander, Edward, *Isaac Bashevis Singer,* Twayne (Boston, MA), 1980.

Allentuck, Marcia, editor, *The Achievement of Isaac Bashevis Singer,* Southern Illinois University Press (Carbondale, IL), 1967.

Allison, Alida, *Isaac Bashevis Singer: Children's Stories and Memoirs,* Twayne (New York, NY), 1996.

Authors and Artists for Young Adults, Volume 29, Thomson Gale (Detroit, MI), 1999.

Authors in the News, Thomson Gale (Detroit, MI), Volume 1, 1976, Volume 2, 1976.

Biletzky, Israel Ch., *God, Jew, Satan in the Works of Isaac Bashevis-Singer,* University Press of America (Lanham, MD), 1995.

Buchen, Irving H., *Isaac Bashevis Singer and the Eternal Past,* New York University Press (New York, NY), 1968.

Children's Literature Review, Volume 1, Thomson Gale (Detroit, MI), 1976.

Concise Dictionary of American Literary Biography: The New Consciousness, 1941-1968, Thomson Gale (Detroit, MI), 1987.

Contemporary Literary Criticism, Thomson Gale (Detroit, MI), Volume 1, 1973, Volume 3, 1975, Volume 6, 1976, Volume 9, 1978, Volume 11, 1979, Volume 15, 1980, Volume 23, 1983, Volume 38, 1986, Volume 69, 1992.

Denman, Hugh, *Isaac Bashevis Singer: His Work and World,* Brill (Boston, MA), 2002.

Dictionary of Literary Biography, Thomson Gale (Detroit, MI), Volume 6: *American Novelists since World War II,* 1980, Volume 28: *Twentieth-Century American-Jewish Fiction Writers,* 1984, Volume 52: *American Writers for Children since 1960: Fiction,* 1986.

Dictionary of Literary Biography Yearbook 1991, Thomson Gale (Detroit, MI), 1992.

Farrell, Grace, editor, *Critical Essays on Isaac Bashevis Singer,* Hall (New York, NY), 1996.

Farrell Lee, Grace, *From Exile to Redemption: The Fiction of Isaac Bashevis Singer,* Southern Illinois University Press (Carbondale, IL), 1987.

Gibbons, Frances Vargas, *Transgression and Self-Punishment in Isaac Bashevis Singer's Searches,* Lang (New York, NY), 1995.

Goran, Lester, *The Bright Streets of Surfside: The Memoir of a Friendship with Isaac Bashevis Singer,* Kent State University Press (Kent, OH), 1994.

Hadda, Janet, *Isaac Bashevis Singer: A Life,* Oxford University Press (New York, NY), 1997.

Kazin, Alfred, *Bright Book of Life: American Novelists and Storytellers from Hemingway to Mailer,* Atlantic Monthly Press (Boston, MA), 1973.

Kresh, Paul, *Isaac Bashevis Singer: The Magician of West 86th Street,* Dial (New York, NY), 1979.

Madison, Charles A., *Yiddish Literature: Its Scope and Major Writers,* Ungar (New York, NY), 1968.

Malin, Irving, editor, *Critical Views of Isaac Bashevis Singer,* New York University Press (New York, NY), 1969.

Malin, Irving, *Isaac Bashevis Singer,* Ungar (New York, NY), 1972.

Pearl, Lila, *Isaac Bashevis Singer: The Life of a Storyteller,* illustrated by Donna Ruff, Jewish Publication Society (Philadelphia, PA), 1994.

Pinsker, Sanford, *The Schlemiel as Metaphor: Studies in the Yiddish and American Jewish Novel,* Southern Illinois University Press (Carbondale, IL), 1971.

Ran-Moseley, Fay, *The Tragicomic Passion: A History and Analysis of Tragicomedy and Tragicomic Characterization in Drama, Film, and Literature,* Lang (New York, NY), 1994.

St. James Guide to Children's Writers, 5th edition, St. James Press (Detroit, MI), 1999.

Short Story Criticism, Volume 3, Thomson Gale (Detroit, MI), 1989.

Siegel, Ben, *Isaac Bashevis Singer,* University of Minnesota Press (Minneapolis, MN), 1969.

Singer, Isaac Bashevis, *Nobel Lecture,* Farrar, Straus (New York, NY), 1979.

Stavans, Ilan, editor, *Isaac Bashevis Singer: An Album,* Library of America (New York, NY), 2004.

Telushkin, Dvorah, *Master of Dreams: A Memoir of Isaac Bashevis Singer,* Morrow (New York, NY), 1997.

Tuszyanska, Agata, *Lost Landscapes: In Search of Isaac Bashevis Singer and the Jews of Poland,* translated from the Polish by Madeline G. Levine, Morrow (New York, NY), 1998.

Wirth-Nesher, Hana, *City Codes: Reading the Modern Urban Novel,* Cambridge University Press (New York, NY), 1996.

Zamir, Israel, and Barbara Harshav, *Journey to My Father, Isaac Bashevis Singer,* Little, Brown (Boston, MA), 1995.

PERIODICALS

American Spectator, September, 1985, Anita Susan Grossman, review of *The Image and Other Stories,* pp. 43-44.

Atlantic, August, 1962; January, 1965; July, 1970; January, 1979.

Best Sellers, October 1, 1970.

Books and Bookmen, October, 1973; December, 1974.

Book Week, July 4, 1965, interview with Singer.

Book World, October 29, 1967; March 3, 1968; September 1, 1968; November 25, 1979.

Chicago Review, spring, 1980.

Chicago Tribune, October 25, 1980; June 23, 1987; July 25, 1991.

Chicago Tribune Book World, July 12, 1981; March 21, 1982; November 6, 1983; July 21, 1985.

Christian Science Monitor, October 28, 1967; September 5, 1978; September 18, 1978.

Commentary, November, 1958; October, 1960; November, 1963; February, 1965; February, 1979; November, 1991, Joseph Epstein, "Our Debt to I.B. Singer," pp. 31-37; December, 1992; June, 1998, Hillel Hakin, review of *Shadows on the Hudson,* p. 73.

Contemporary Literature, winter, 1969; summer, 1969, Cyrene N. Pondrom, interview with Singer.

Critical Quarterly, spring, 1976, David Seed, "The Fiction of Isaac Bashevis Singer," pp. 73-79.

Criticism, fall, 1963.

Critique, Volume 11, number 2, 1969, Linda G. Zatlin, "The Themes of Isaac Bashevis Singer's Short Fiction," pp. 40-46; Volume 14, number 2, 1972.

Detroit Free Press, July 25, 1991.

Globe & Mail (Toronto, Ontario, Canada), May 3, 1980; November 23, 1985; June 13, 1988.

Harper's, October, 1965; September, 1978, Paul Berman, review of *Shosha,* p. 94.

Horn Book, September-October, 1991, p. 654.

Hudson Review, winter, 1966-1967, Herbert Leibowitz, "A Lost World Redeemed," pp. 669-673; spring, 1974.

Jewish Currents, November, 1962.

Jewish Quarterly, winter, 1966-1967; autumn, 1972.

Judaism, fall, 1962, J.A. Eisenberg, "Isaac Bashevis Singer: Passionate Primitive or Pious Puritan?," pp. 345-356; winter, 1974; spring, 1977, Nili Wachtel, "Freedom and Slavery in the Fiction of Isaac Bashevis Singer," pp. 171-186; winter, 1979, Edward Alexander, "The Nobel Prize for I.B. Singer," pp. 8-13.

Kenyon Review, spring, 1964.

Library Journal, March 1, 1994, p. 120; August, 1999, Melody A. Moxley, p. 163.

London Review of Books, October 24, 1991, p. 17.

Los Angeles Times, November 8, 1978; December 28, 1981; November 18, 1983; March, 18, 1984; December 4, 1986; December 12, 1989.

Los Angeles Times Book Review, November 16, 1980; August 16, 1981; May 2, 1982; February 6, 1983; December 9, 1984; August 25, 1985; May 1, 1988; April 14, 1991, Jonathan Kirsch, "The Dybbuk Made Him Do It," p. 12; January 3, 1993, p. 7.

Nation, November 2, 1970, Dan Isaac, "The World of Jewish Gothic," pp. 438-440; November 19, 1973, Seymour Kleinberg, "The Last to Speak That Tongue," pp. 538-539; November 19, 1983.

New Leader, June 27, 1988, David Evanier, review of *The Death of Methuselah, and Other Stories,* p. 20.

New Republic, November 24, 1958; January 2, 1961; November 13, 1961, Irving Howe, "Stories: New, Old, and Sometimes Good," pp. 18-19, 22-23; June 18, 1962; November 3, 1973, Crawford Woods, "Worlds beyond Ours," pp. 28-29; October 25, 1975; September 16, 1978, Robert Alter, review of *Shosha,* pp. 20-22; October 21, 1978.

New Review, June, 1976, Julia O'Faolain, review of *Passions and Other Stories,* pp. 59-60.

New Statesman, September 13, 1974, Peter Straub, review of *A Crown of Feathers,* p. 355; April 19, 1985, Anne Smith, "Holy Fool," p. 30.

New Statesman & Society, July 14, 1989, Sean French, "Singer's Gods," pp. 42-43; October 18, 1991, p. 39.

Newsweek, June 26, 1972, Walter Clemons, "Herman's Three Wives," p. 86; November 12, 1973, Peter S. Prescott, "The Dance of Life," pp. 113-114; April 12, 1982; September 26, 1983; August 5, 1991.

New York, December 31, 1979.

New Yorker, August 17, 1981; December 21, 1992.

New York Review of Books, April 22, 1965, Ted Hughes, "The Genius of Isaac Bashevis Singer," pp. 8-10; February 7, 1974, Michael Wood, review of *A Crown of Feathers and Other Stories,* pp. 10-11; December 7, 1978, Leon Wieseltier, "The Revenge of I.B. Singer," pp. 6, 8.

New York Times, October 30, 1966; January 29, 1967; July 10, 1978; July 22, 1978; December 9, 1978; October 17, 1979; December 5, 1979; December 16, 1979; December 17, 1979; April 19, 1980; June 15, 1982; November 30, 1982; September 22, 1983; October 7, 1984; November 7, 1984; June 25, 1985, John Gross, review of *The Image and Other Stories,* pp. 43-44; October 30, 1985; November 17, 1985; June 24, 1986; September 28, 1986; November 8, 1986; July 6, 1987; April 12, 1988; May 18, 1989; July 30, 1989; December 10, 1989; December 13, 1989; April 9, 1991, Michiko Kakutani, "Trapped in a Somber Dialectic of Faith and Flesh," p. C14; July 26, 1991; May 30, 1996, p. B3; May 30, 1996, p. C13.

New York Times Book Review, December 29, 1957; June 26, 1960; October 22, 1961; June 17, 1962, Milton Hindus, "An Upright Man on an Eternal Landscape," p. 4; November 15, 1964; October 8, 1967, Hugh Nissenson, review of *The Fearsome Inn,* p. 38; February 1, 1970, Richard M. Elman, review of *A Day of Pleasure,* p. 30; June 25, 1972, Lore Dickstein, review of *Enemies: A Love Story,* pp. 4-5, 10; November 4, 1973; November 2, 1975; April 30, 1978, Andrew Bergman, review of *A Young Man in Search of Love,* p. 59; July 23, 1978; October 28, 1979; January 18, 1981; June 21, 1981, Mark Harris, "A Storyteller's Story," pp. 7, 28-29; January 31, 1982; March 21, 1982; November 14, 1982; September 25, 1983; November 11, 1984; June 30, 1985; October 27, 1985; October 16, 1988, Ewa Kuryluk, "Nightmares of the Poles and Lesniks," pp. 12-13; March 24, 1991, Bette Pesetsky, "Looking for Love on Krochmaina Street," p. 7; November 1, 1992, Lore Dickstein, "An Account Book Full of Humiliations," p. 7; April 10, 1994, Joel Conarroe, "'The World Is One Vast Madhouse,'" p. 9; January 25, 1998, Lee Siegel, "West Side Story"; December 24, 2000, Jonathan Rosen, "A World Triply Lost."

Paris Review, fall, 1968.

Publishers Weekly, February 18, 1983, interview with Singer; September 18, 2000, review of *More Stories from My Father's Court,* p. 93.

San Francisco Review of Books, Summer, 1991, pp. 15-16.

Saturday Review, January 25, 1958; November 25, 1961; June 16, 1962; November 21, 1964; September 19, 1970, Curt Leviant, review of *A Friend of Kafka,* pp. 36-37, 46; July 22, 1972; July 8, 1978, Edward Hirsch, review of *A Young Man in Search of Love* and *Shosha,* pp. 34-35.

School Library Journal, September, 1991; June, 1996, p. 124.

Sewanee Review, fall, 1974, William Peden, review of *A Crown of Feathers,* pp. 718-719.

Southern Review, spring, 1972; spring, 1973, Jay L. Halio, review of *A Friend of Kafka,* pp. 466-467.

Spectator, October 17, 1958; September 15, 1961; May 11, 1962; June 10, 1966, John Daniel, review of *The Family Moskat,* p. 734.

Studies in Short Fiction, summer, 1974, John Lawrence Abbott, review of *A Crown of Feathers,* pp. 311-312; fall, 1976, Timothy Evans, review of *Passions, and Other Stories,* pp. 528-529.

Tikkun, September-October, 1994, p. 79.

Time, October 20, 1967; September 21, 1970, Stefan Kanfer, "Sammler's Planetarians," p. 101; October 27, 1975, Stefan Kanfer, "Fiddler," pp. 78, 80; November 3, 1975; June 15, 1981; April 5, 1982; October 17, 1983; October 28, 1984; July 15, 1985; May 2, 1988; March 25, 1991, p. 70; August 5, 1991.

Times (London, England), April 10, 1980; March 8, 1984.

Times Literary Supplement, January 2, 1959; May 4, 1962; April 11, 1980; July 16, 1982; July 22, 1983; March 23, 1984; October 19, 1984; May 3, 1985; April 4, 1986; May 1, 1987; October 21, 1988; September 1, 1989.

Top of the News, November, 1972.

Tribune Books (Chicago), April 10, 1988; November 6, 1988; June 7, 1992, p. 2; November 1, 1992, p. 6; May 8, 1994, p. 5.

Washington Post, October 6, 1978; October 16, 1979; October 26, 1979; November 4, 1981; September 17, 1984; July 26, 1991.

Washington Post Book World, November 30, 1980; June 28, 1981, Helen Epstein, "Isaac Singer in Pursuit of Love and Literature," p. 4; March 28, 1982 (interview); November 7, 1982; July 7, 1985; September 21, 1986; October 23, 1988; March 3, 1991, Jonathan Yardley, "The Ills of the Flesh," p. 3; April 3, 1994, p. 9; January 25, 1998, Franklin Foer, "Survivors and Café Philosophers," p. 8.

World Literature Today, spring, 1979, Lothar Kahn, "The Talent of I.B. Singer, 1978 Nobel Laureate for Literature," pp. 197-201; autumn, 1988, Lothar Kahn, review of *The Death of Methuselah and Other Stories,* pp. 675-676; summer, 1998, Rita D. Jacobs, review of *Shadows on the Hudson,* p. 646; summer-autumn, 2001, James Knudsen, review of *More Stories from My Father's Court,* p. 200.

ONLINE

Books and Writers, http://www.kirjasto.sci.fi/ (August 15, 2004), "Isaac Bashevis Singer."

Nobel e-Museum, http://www.nobel.se/ (August 15, 2004), "Isaac Bashevis Singer."

Singer Centennial Web site, http://www.ibsinger100.org/ (August 15, 2004).

* * *

ŠKVORECKÝ, Josef 1924-
(Josef Vaclav Škvorecký)

PERSONAL: Surname pronounced "*Shquor*-et-skee"; born September 27, 1924, in Nachod, Czechoslovakia; immigrated to Canada, 1969; son of Josef Karel (a bank clerk) and Anna Marie (Kurazova) Škvorecký; married Zdenka Salivarova (a writer and publisher), March 31, 1958. *Education:* Charles University, Prague, Ph.D., 1951; postgraduate study at Masaryk University, 1991, University of Calgary, 1992, and University of Toronto, 1992. *Politics:* Progressive conservative. *Religion:* Roman Catholic. *Hobbies and other interests:* Film, jazz (Škvorecký plays the saxophone), American folklore.

ADDRESSES: *Home*—487 Sackville St., Toronto, Ontario, Canada M4X 1T6. *Agent*—Nicole Winstanley, Westwood Creative Artists, 94 Harbord St., Toronto, Ontario, Canada M5S 1G6.

CAREER: Odeon Publishers, Prague, Czechoslovakia, editor of Anglo-American department, 1953-56; *World Literature Magazine,* Prague, assistant editor-in-chief, 1956-59; freelance writer in Prague, 1963-69; University of Toronto, Erindale College, Mississawga, Ontario, special lecturer in English and Slavic drama, 1969-71, writer-in-residence, 1970-71, associate professor, 1971-75, professor of English, 1975-90, professor emeritus, 1990—. 68 Publishers, co-founder and editor-in-chief, 1972—. Advisor to Czech President Vaclav Havel. Founded Academy of Creative Writing in Prague, 2000. *Military service:* Czechoslovak Army (Tank Corps), 1951-53.

MEMBER: International PEN, International Association of Crime Writers, Authors Guild, Authors League of America, Mystery Writers of America, Royal Society of Canada (fellow), Crime Writers of Canada, Canadian Writers Union, Czechoslovak National Association of Canada, Czechoslovak Society of Arts and Letters (honorary member), Order of Canada.

AWARDS, HONORS: Literary Award of Czechoslovakian Writers Union, 1968; Neustadt International Prize for Literature, 1980; Guggenheim fellowship, 1980; Silver Awards for Best Fiction Publication in Canadian Magazines, 1980, 1981; nominated for the Nobel Prize in literature, 1982; Governor General's Award for Best Fiction, 1984, for *The Engineer of Human Souls;* City of Toronto Book Award 1985; Echoing Green Foundation Literature Prize, 1985; D.H.L., State University of New York, 1986, Masaryk University, Brno, 1991, University of Calgary, 1992, University of Toronto, 1992, and McMaster University, Hamilton, 1993; Czechoslovak Order of the White Lion, 1990; Order of Canada, appointed member, 1992; Chevalier de L'ordre des Arts et des Lettres, Republique Française, 1996; State Prize for Literature, Czechoslovakia, 1999; Pangea/Comenius Award, 2001.

WRITINGS:

Zbabelci (novel), Ceskoslovensky spisovatel (Prague, Czechoslovakia), 1958, 4th edition, Nase vojsko (Prague), 1968, translated by Jeanne Nemcova as *The Cowards,* Grove (New York, NY), 1970.

Legenda Emoke (novel; title means "The Legend of Emoke"), Ceskoslovensky spisovatel, 1963, second edition, 1965.

Sedmiramenny svicen (stories; title means "The Menorah"), Nase vojsko, 1964, 2nd edition, 1965.

Babylonsky pribeh (stories; title means "A Babylonian Story"), Svobodne Slovo (Prague, Czechoslovakia), 1965.

Napady ctenare detektivek (essays; title means "Reading Detective Stories"), Ceskoslovensky spisovatel, 1965.

Ze zivota lepsi spolecnosti (stories; title means "The Life of Better Society"), Mlada fronta (Prague, Czechoslovakia), 1965.

Smutek porucika Boruvka (stories), Mlada fronta, 1966, translated as *The Mournful Demeanor of Lieutenant Boruvka,* Gollancz (London, England), 1974.

Konec nylonoveho veku (novel; title means "The End of the Nylon Age"), Ceskoslovensky spisovatel, 1967.

O nich—o nas (essays; title means "About Them—Which Is about Us"), Kruh (Hradec Kralove), 1968.

(With Evald Schorm) *Fararuv Konec* (novelization of Skvorecký's filmscript "Konec farare"; title means "End of a Priest"; also see below), Kruh, 1969.

Lvice (novel), Ceskoslovensky spisovatel, 1969, translated as *Miss Silver's Past,* Grove (New York, NY), 1973.

Horkej svet: Povidky z let, 1946-1967 (title means "The Bitter World: Selected Stories, 1947-1967"), Odeon (Prague, Czechoslovakia), 1969.

Tankovy prapor (novel; title means "The Tank Corps"), 68 Publishers (Toronto, Ontario, Canada), 1971, translated as *Republic of Whores: A Fragment from the Time of the Cults,* Ecco (New York, NY), 1994.

All the Bright Young Men and Women: A Personal History of the Czech Cinema, translation by Michael Schonberg, Peter Martin Associates, 1971.

Mirakl, 68 Publishers (Toronto, Ontario, Canada), 1972, translated by Paul Wilson as *The Miracle Game,* Knopf (New York, NY), 1991.

Hrichy pro patera Knoxe, (novel), 68 Publishers (Toronto, Ontario, Canada), 1973, translated by Kaca Polackova-Henley as *Sins for Father Knox,* Norton (New York, NY), 1989.

Prima Sezona (novel), 68 Publishers (Toronto, Ontario, Canada), 1974, translated as *The Swell Season,* Ecco (New York, NY), 1986.

Konec porucika Boruvka (novel), 68 Publishers (Toronto, Ontario, Canada), 1975, translated as *The End of Lieutenant Boruvka,* Norton (New York, NY), 1990.

Pribeh inzenyra lidskych dusi (novel), 68 Publishers (Toronto, Ontario, Canada), 1977, translated as *The Engineer of Human Souls: An Entertainment of the Old Themes of Life, Women, Fate, Dreams, the Working Class, Secret Agents, Love, and Death,* Knopf (New York, NY), 1984.

The Bass Saxophone, translation by Kaca Polackova-Henley, Knopf (New York, NY), 1979.

Navrat porucika Boruvka (novel), 68 Publishers (Toronto, Ontario, Canada), 1980, translated by Paul Wilson as *The Return of Lieutenant Boruvka,* Norton (New York, NY), 1991.

Jiri Menzel and the History of the "Closely Watched Trains" (comparative study), University of Colorado Press (Boulder, CO), 1982.

Scherzo capriccioso (novel), 68 Publishers (Toronto, Ontario, Canada), 1984, translated as *Dvorak in Love,* Knopf (New York, NY), 1986.

Ze zivota ceskae spolecnosti, 68 Publishers (Toronto, Ontario, Canada), 1985.

Talkin' Moscow Blues (essays), Ecco (New York, NY), 1990.

Nevesta z Texasu (novel), 68 Publishers (Toronto, Ontario, Canada), 1992, translated as *The Bride of Texas,* Knopf (New York, NY), 1996.

The Bass Saxophone: Two Novellas (includes the memoir *Red Music,* and the novellas *The Bass Saxophone* and *Emoke*), Ecco (New York, NY), 1994.

Pribech newspesneno saxofonisty: vlastni zivotopis = Dichtung und Wahrheit, Bla izkaasetkani (Prague, Czech Republic), 1994.

Pribehy o Lize a mladem Wertherovi a jine povidky, Ivo Zelezny (Prague, Czech Republic), 1994.

Headed for the Blues: A Memoir, translated by Kaca Polackova-Henley, Ecco (New York, NY), 1996.

Nove canterburske povidky a jine pribehy, Ivo Zelezny (Prague, Czech Republic), 1996.

Povidky tenorsaxofonisty (stories), translated by Caleb Crain, Kaca Polackova-Henley, and Peter Kussi as *The Tenor Saxophonist's Story,* Ecco (New York, NY), 1997.

Nevysvetlitelny pribeh, aneb Vypraveni Questa Firma Sicula, (title means "An Unexplainable Story or The Narrative of Questus Firmus Siculus") Ivo Zelazny (Prague, Czech Republic), 1999, translation by Kaca Polackova-Henley as *An inexplicable story, or, The narrative of Questus Firmus Siculus,* Key Porter Books (Toronto, Ontario, Canada), 2002.

(With Zdena Salivarová) *Kratke setkani, s vrazdou,* (novel; title means "Brief Encounter, with Murder") Ivo Selezny (Prague, Czech Republic), 1999.

Two Murders in My Double Life: A Crime Novel in Two Interlocking Movements, Key Porter Books (Toronto, Ontario, Canada), 1999, Farrar, Straus (New York, NY), 2001.

When Eve Was Naked: Stories of a Life's Journey (stories), Key Porter Books (Toronto, Ontario, Canada), 2000.

(With Zdena Salivarová) *Setkani na konci ery, s vrazdou,* (novel; title means "Encounter at the End of an Era, with Murder") Ivo Selezny (Prague, Czech Republic), 2001.

(With Zdena Salivarová) *Setkani po letech, s vrazdou,* Ivo Zelezny (Prague, Czech Republic), 2001.

Pulchra: Pribeh o krasne planete, (science fiction) Petrov (Brno, Czech Republic), 2003.

Škvorecký's complete works in thirteen volumes were published by Ivo Zelezny (Prague, Czech Republic), 1998-99.

EDITOR

Selected Writings of Sinclair Lewis, Odeon, 1964–69.

(With P.L. Doruzka) *Tvar jazzu* (anthology; title means "The Face of Jazz"), Statni hudebni vydavatelstvi (Prague, Czechoslovakia), Part 1, 1964, Part 2, 1966.

Collected Writings of Ernest Hemingway, Odeon, 1965–69.

Three Times Hercule Poirot, Odeon, 1965.

(With P.L. Doruzka) *Jazzova inspirace* (poetry anthology; title means "The Jazz Inspiration"), Odeon, 1966.

Nachrichten aus der CSSR (title means "News from Czechoslovakia"), translation by Vera Cerna and others, Suhrkamp Verlag (Frankfurt, Germany), 1968.

Also author of afterword for *Indecent Dreams,* by Arnost Lustig, Northwestern University Press (Evanston, IL), 1990; author of introduction for *The Little Town Where Time Stood Still,* by Bohumil Hrabal, Pantheon (New York, NY), 1993. Author of movie screenplays, including *Zlocin v divci skole* (title means "Crime in a Girl's School"), 1966; *Zlocin v santanu* (title means "Crime in a Night Club"), 1968; *Konec farare* (title means "End of a Priest"), 1969; *Flirt se slecnou Stribrnou* (title means "Flirtations with Miss Silver"), 1969; and *Sest cernych divek* (title means "Six Brunettes"), 1969. Author of scripts for television programs. Author of prefaces and introductions to Czech and Slovak editions of the works of Saul Bellow, Bernard Malamud, Stephen Crane, Rex Stout, Dorothy Sayers, Charles Dickens, Sinclair Lewis, and others. Translator of numerous books from English to Czech, including the works of Ray Bradbury, Henry James, Ernest Hemingway, William Faulkner, Raymond Chandler, and others.

ADAPTATIONS: Tankovy prapor was produced as a feature film by BONTON Co. in Prague, 1991; several other works have been produced as films for Czech television.

SIDELIGHTS: "In his native country, Josef Škvorecký is a household word," fellow Czech author Arnost Lustig told the *Washington Post.* Skvorecký, whose idiomatic and highly colloquial fictions in his native language defy easy translation, is among the most noted twentieth-century expatriate Czech authors. His works provide a mordant commentary on the political and cultural differences between his war-weary homeland and his adopted nation, Canada, where he has lived since 1969. Škvorecký is also acclaimed as the founder and director of 68 Publishers, a Toronto-based publishing firm that has helped dissident Czech and Slovak writers get into print. According to Neil Bermel in the *New York Times Book Review,* Škvorecký is "the pre-eminent Czech interpreter of [the] theme of home and exile, in his life and in his work. . . . His refusal to bend his writing to official views eventually led to his leaving Czechoslovakia in 1969, and taking up residence in Canada." In 2000, Škvorecký set up the Academy of Creative Writing in Prague, the first institution of its kind in the Czech Republic, with the express aim of training new generations of Czech and Slovak writers.

Škvorecký wrote his first novel, *The Cowards,* in 1948 when he was twenty-four. Not published until 1958, the book caused a flurry of excitement that led to "firings in the publishing house, ragings in the official press, and a general purge that extended eventually throughout the arts," to quote Neal Ascherson in the *New York Review of Books.* The book was banned by Czech officials one month after publication, marking "the start of an incredible campaign of vilification against the author," a *Times Literary Supplement* reviewer reported. Škvorecký subsequently included a "cheeky and impenitent Introduction," Ascherson noted in the novel's second edition. "In spite of all the suppression," the *Times Literary Supplement* critic explained, "*The Cowards* became a milestone in Czech literature and Joseph Škvorecký one of the country's most popular writers." Formerly a member of the central committees of the Czechoslovak Writers' Union and the Czechoslovak Film and Television Artists, Škvorecký chose exile and immigrated to Canada following the Soviet invasion of his country.

Ascherson explained why *The Cowards* caused so much controversy: "It is not at all the sort of mirror official Czechoslovakia would wish to glance in. A recurring theme is . . . pity for the Germans, defeated and bewildered. . . . The Russians strike [the main character] as alluring primitives (his use of the word 'Mongolian' about them caused much of the scandal in 1958)." The *Times Literary Supplement* writer added that the novel "turned out to be anti-Party and anti-God at the same time; everybody felt himself a victim of the author's satire." Set in a provincial Bohemian town, the story's events unfold in May, 1945, as the Nazis retreat and the Russian army takes control of an area populated with "released prisoners of war, British, Italian, French and Russian (Mongolians, these, whom the locals do not find very clean), and Jewish women survivors from a concentration camp," wrote Stuart Hood in the *Listener.* The narrator, twenty-year-old Danny Smiricky, and his friends—members of a jazz band—observe the flux of power, human nature, and death around them while devoting their thoughts and energies to women and music. "These are, by definition, no heroes," stated Hood. "They find themselves caught up in a farce which turns into horror from one minute to the next." The group may dream of making a bold move for their country, but, as Charles Dollen noted in *Best Sellers,* "they never make anything but music."

Labeled *judeonegroid* (Jewish-Negro) and suppressed by the Nazis, jazz becomes political. To play blues or sing scat is to stand up for "individual freedom and spontaneity," stated Terry Winch in the *Washington*

Post Book World. "In other words, [jazz] stood for everything the Nazis hated and wanted to crush." Škvorecký, like his narrator, was a jazz musician during the Nazi "protectorate." The author wields this music as a "goad, the 'sharp thorn in the sides of the power-hungry men, from Hitler to Brezhnev,'" Saul Maloff declared in the *New York Times Book Review.* Described as a "highly metaphorical writer" by Winch, Škvorecký often employs jazz "in its familiar historical and international role as a symbol (and a breeding-ground) of anti-authoritarian attitudes," according to Russell Davies in the *Times Literary Supplement.*

Škvorecký follows the life of the semi-autobiographical character Danny Smiricky in *Tankovy prapor* ("The Tank Corps"), translated as *The Republic of Whores: A Fragment from the Time of the Cults; The Miracle Game; The Bass Saxophone; The Engineer of Human Souls: An Entertainment of the Old Themes of Life, Women, Fate, Dreams, the Working Class, Secret Agents, Love, and Death;* and *Two Murders in My Double Life: A Crime Novel in Two Interlocking Movements. The Republic of Whores* portrays Danny as a conscript in a Czechoslovakian tank division during the 1950s. This bitter satire exposes the hypocrisy and incompetence of the East Bloc military through Škvorecký's depiction of sadistic officers, idiotic interrogations, mock battles, habitual drunkenness, and sexual liaisons. "Mr. Škvorecký has made a reputation as one of the pre-eminent writers of postwar Europe. For him to have composed such a scathing fictional indictment of the Soviet military system while he was still within its jurisdiction was an act of considerable courage," declared James McManus in the *New York Times Book Review.* John-Paul Flintoff noted in the *Times Literary Supplement:* "Hard-boiled cynicism is not confined to the army, according to Škvorecký. The whole of Czechoslovakia is the same—nobody really cares about anything—hence the insistent reference to whoredom, in the [translator's] title and in the text."

Škvorecký builds on this theme in *The Miracle Game.* The novel opens in 1948 in a provincial Czechoslovakian town under Stalinist rule where Danny has secured employment as a teacher at a girl's school. While Danny is bedridden with gonorrhea and characteristically absent, a local priest claims that a statue of Saint Joseph has miraculously moved. Despite the unequivocal rejection of his claim by Communist authorities, the priest insists on the reality of the miracle until he is eventually tortured and killed by the police. In 1968, twenty years later, Danny returns to the place of this tragic mystery to investigate the veracity of the priest's sighting and to determine if it may have been a prank or a Communist ruse to discredit the church. "Danny is a self-described 'misguided counter-revolutionary of minor importance, re-educable, the author of librettos for musical comedies, of detective novels and comedy films, fearing God less than he feared the world, a skeptic,'" noted David Rieff in the *Washington Post Book World.* "In the end," Rieff added, "Danny both solves the riddle and lets the mystery stand. 'Every idea brought into fruition is awful,' he reflects somberly, even a miracle."

The Miracle Game recounts life during the dark years of Soviet hegemony over Czechoslovakia and alludes to the then-unforeseeable possibility of change. Stephanie Strom observed in the *New York Times Book Review,* "Josef Škvorecký began writing *The Miracle Game* when it seemed that a bloodless revolution installing a liberal intellectual at the helm of his native Czechoslovakia would require a miracle." Describing the significance of the miraculous statue in the novel, *New York Times Book Review* contributor Angela Carter maintained, "The statue, freshly painted in bright greens, blues and pinks by a devout toy maker, is an image of innocence, of faith, perhaps even hope, which emerges battered but unbowed from the long winter of Communist oppression and survives even the brutal suppression of the Prague Spring, in 1968, when, for a brief moment, it looked as if the system might renew itself." However, this hope vanished when Soviet tanks rolled into Czechoslovakia in 1968 to support the Communist Party. "The novel teems with well-drawn figures, from jazzmen to schoolgirls, intellectuals to priests, pious old ladies to true Communist believers," wrote Peter Sherwood in the *Times Literary Supplement.* "None the less," Sherwood added, "its high points are the manic set-pieces which encapsulate in all its painful absurdity life behind the Iron Curtain in the early 1950s and for far too long thereafter."

The Bass Saxophone contains a memoir and two novellas first published individually in Czechoslovakia during the 1960s. Like *The Cowards,* the memoir *Red Music,* observed Maloff, "evokes the atmosphere of that bleak time [during World War II], the strange career of indigenous American music transplanted abroad to the unlikeliest soil." Although it is only a "brief preface to the stories," Winch maintained that the memoir "in some ways is the more interesting section" of the book. Davies believed that the "short and passionate essay" shows how, "since [the jazz enthusiast in an Iron Curtain country] has sorrows other than his own to contend with, the music must carry for him not just a sense of isolation and longing but a bitterly practical political resentment."

Emoke, the novella that follows, is "fragile, lyrical, 'romantic'" and, like its title character, "fabulous: precisely the materials of fable," commented Maloff. Davies added that "in its poetic evocation of Emoke, a hurt and delicate creature with an array of spiritual cravings, . . . the story has a . . . depth of soul and concern." Winch, however, felt the woman "is not a vivid or forceful enough character to bear the burden of all she is asked to represent." The three critics believed that the title novella, *The Bass Saxophone,* is more successful, "perhaps because music, Škvorecký's real passion, is central to the narrative," Winch explained. Here, wrote Davies, music "emerges as a full symbolic and ideological force," whereas in *Emoke* it was "a mere undercurrent." The story of a boy playing music while under Nazi rule, claimed Maloff, is "sheer magic, a parable, a fable about art, about politics, about the zone where the two intersect." Writing in the *Atlantic,* Benjamin De Mott called *The Bass Saxophone* "an exceptionally haunting and restorative volume of fiction, a book in which literally nothing enters except the fully imagined, hence the fully exciting."

Škvorecký's writing continues to parallel his own life in subsequent novels and stories. Danny, again the main character in *The Engineer of Human Souls,* accepts a position at a small University of Toronto college. The ironic title alludes to Stalin's description of the writer's function. The main theme, brought out by the author's use of humor in the book, concerns the dangers of dogmatic thinking, the political naivete of Westerners, and the injustices of totalitarianism. Through flashback sequences and letters to other dissidents, Škvorecký juxtaposes Danny's past and present experiences in Czechoslovakia and Canada. *Quill and Quire* critic Mark Czarnecki asserted that as "an exhaustive, insightful document of modern society in both East and West, [*The Engineer of Human Souls*] has no equal." In a *Canadian Forum* review, Sam Solecki noted that *The Engineer of Human Souls* is also a "transitional novel for Škvorecký, in which we see him extending his imagination beyond his Czechoslovak past while still including it." Solecki also commented that this novel, which portrays Smiricky in his sixties, will probably bring "the Smiricky cycle to a close."

The Engineer of Human Souls is divided into seven long chapters named after American authors whom Danny discusses in class. Through commentary on major literary figures such as Mark Twain, Edgar Allen Poe, and Nathaniel Hawthorne, Škvorecký illustrates Danny's frustration over his students' misunderstanding of great literature, which uncomfortably recalls for him the uniformity and intolerance of the Communists. As Anthony Burgess noted in an *Observer* review, Danny's "students have no sense of history; for them the past contains events like the deaths of James Dean and Janis Joplin. Their response to art is glibly ideological, and Smiricky hears in their wretched little slogans the voices of his country's oppressors." According to Richard Eder in the *Los Angeles Times Book Review,* "Škvorecký calls *The Engineer of Human Souls* an entertainment. It is, in places, so entertaining that it would be dangerous to read it without laughing aloud; in other places it is sad or dismaying. What he has really written, though, is an epic of his country and its exiles." Though some critics found shortcomings in the novel's amorphous plot and narrative meanderings, as Burgess noted, acclaimed Czechoslovakian novelist Milan Kundera regarded *The Engineer of Human Souls* as "a magnum opus."

In his novel *Dvorak in Love* Škvorecký builds on the theme of music which is maintained throughout the Smiricky books. *Dvorak in Love* is a fictionalized account of Škvorecký's compatriot, composer Antonin Dvorak, and his visit to New York City. The life of Dvorak, whose music was influenced by black folk music and jazz, provided the author with the perfect subject for discussing the synthesis "of the two dominant musical cultures of our time—the classical European tradition . . . and the jazzy American tradition," as William French put it in a *Globe and Mail* review. Although some reviewers, like Barbara Black, have found the narrative structure of the opening chapters of *Dvorak in Love* too complicated to enjoy, the author's characteristic humor later enlivens the story. "Best of all" in this book, remarked Black, "Škvorecký celebrates Dvorak and the musical trail he blazed."

Škvorecký has also produced a series of detective stories featuring Lieutenant Josef Boruvka, a painfully sensitive Prague police officer whose ardent humanism is nearly a professional liability. He dislikes guns, disapproves of the death penalty, and carefully solves crimes, though not without experiencing deep sadness for the captured perpetrators. *The Mournful Demeanor of Lieutenant Boruvka* introduces the melancholic Boruvka through twelve interrelated stories centered around diverse themes including music, ballet, science, and mountain climbing. "Škvorecký's undeniable qualities as a fiction writer shine throughout the stories," wrote Alberto Manguel in *Books in Canada.* Manguel further contended that the stories lack enough convincing mystery to represent effective detective fiction. Citing elements of parody in Škvorecký's mysteries, Stewart Lindh observed in the *Los Angeles Time Book Review:* "Lurking at the side of every story is the following question: How can a detective find truth in a society concealing it? He can't." Summarizing Škvorecký's message, Lindh concluded that Boruvka "lives in a society that itself is guilty of a monstrous crime: the murder of truth."

Sins for Father Knox is a volume of ten detective stories in which Škvorecký deliberately sets out to violate the ten commandments of crime fiction writing as set down by Monsignor Ronald Knox, who lived between 1888 and 1957. Among his cardinal rules, Knox proclaimed that no more than one secret chamber or passage should exist in the story; that the detective must not have committed the crime himself; and that no previously unknown poisons should figure into the plot. Only two of the stories involve Lieutenant Boruvka, while the remainder feature Prague nightclub singer Eve Adam as she tours the Western world and solves crimes that leave the local police befuddled. D.J. Enright commented in the *New York Review of Books,* "In each tale the reader is challenged to spot both the guilty party and the commandment broken. Some of the mysteries are tricky in the extreme." Though praising the compelling characters, *Los Angeles Times Book Review* contributor Ross Thomas found the Father Knox premise and cryptic formulas "tedious and opaque." Comparing the volume to an excursion on the Orient Express, Michael Dibdin concluded in the *Observer* that the stories represent "an elaborately unconvincing blend of parody and pastiche which will delight those nostalgic for the days before the detective story was gentrified into crime fiction."

Additional Boruvka detective stories appeared with the publication of *The End of Lieutenant Boruvka* and *The Return of Lieutenant Boruvka. The End of Lieutenant Boruvka* includes five stories based on actual criminal cases from Czech police files in the 1960s. Each of the stories, as Kati Marton noted in the *New York Times Book Review,* "throws a beam of light on a different aspect of the state in an advanced stage of decay. Mr. Škvorecký's people, though mostly clear-eyed about their lot, must still pay lip service to the lie that they are living in an egalitarian society." Marton observed, "The air is foul with revolutionary stench." Commenting on the seriousness of the extended, more developed narratives in *The End of Lieutenant Boruvka,* Peter Lewis concluded in *Stand:* "In this Orwellian world, murder can easily be newspeaked into suicide or accidental death. Škvorecký is therefore using the crime story to make a political statement about the endemic corruption and falsification of Communist rule, under which there is one law for the Party and another law for everyone else."

In *The Return of Lieutenant Boruvka* Boruvka has escaped from a Czechoslovakian prison, where he was detained for political crimes, and reappears as an expatriate in Toronto where he finds employment as a parking lot attendant. The novel is narrated by an amateur Canadian detective who employs the expertise of Boruvka to solve the murder of a young woman whom Boruvka suspects was mistaken for the Czech editor of an anti-regime publication. After a second murder involving cyanide, Boruvka uncovers Old World divisions and malicious intrigue among a circle of wealthy exiles in the Czech émigré community. Though lamenting the diminished presence of Boruvka in the novel, *New York Times Book Review* contributor Marilyn Stasio noted the "preposterously funny, if poignant, tales of political intrigue and personal scandal" among the Eastern European population of Toronto. Christopher Wordsworth concluded in an *Observer* review that Škvorecký "is a fine novelist" whose depictions of "brain-sick politics are never outdated." Škvorecký turned to historical fiction in the 1990s with *The Bride of Texas,* a novel that recounts the adventures of Czech and Slovak immigrants who served in the Union army during the U.S. Civil War. The story opens near the end of the war with Czech troops assisting General William Tecumseh Sherman in his destructive campaign through the South. Inspired by his own research into the lives of actual immigrant troops, Škvorecký's complex subplots and flashbacks describe the lives of numerous characters in Europe and America before the war. "Mr. Škvorecký notes that nearly all of the characters here, including all but one of the Czech soldiers in the 26th Wisconsin, actually existed," wrote Verlyn Klinkenborg in the *New York Times Book Review.* "Yet," Klinkenborg continued, "*The Bride of Texas* is pure, exalted romance generated by the forces we think of as constituting history itself." The romantic element of the novel centers primarily around Moravian Lida Toupelik, a Czech immigrant who is forced by her lover's disapproving father to emigrate to the U.S. where she marries the son of a plantation owner in Texas.

Commenting on Škvorecký's historical portrayal of the U.S. Civil War, Donald McCraig wrote in *Washington Post Book World,* "His view of the war is the standard Northern view and unexceptional." Noting the difficulty of keeping track of the many plots and characters in the novel, McCraig added, "Page by page, anecdote by anecdote, Škvorecký is a fine writer, but his structure betrays his story." According to *Quill and Quire* reviewer Carol Toller, "Škvorecký has an obvious passion for U.S. history and the motley assortment of characters that have shaped it. But ultimately, his exhaustive research is as frustrating as it is enlightening: the novel's romantic tale seems overburdened by the weight of historical facts and figures heaped so liberally upon it." However, *Booklist* reviewer Donna Seaman praised the novel as "a colossal feat of imagination and cerebration . . . often hilarious and consistently engrossing." A *Publishers Weekly* reviewer similarly concluded, "Škvorecký's stunning novel shows us the Civil War, race relations, slavery and melting-pot America in a fresh and often startling light."

Danny Smiricky returns in *Two Murders in My Double Life,* the only novel Škvorecký has written in English. In a pair of plots that run simultaneously, Smiricky attempts to solve a murder at politically correct Edenvale College, while he also tries to clear his wife's name when virulent anti-communists accuse her of conspiring with the police during the Communist era in Czechoslovakia. The theme that unites the two disparate stories is the perplexity of the expatriate as he seeks reconciliation with his homeland and a sense of assimilation in his new environment. Bermel observed, "Škvorecký says a native land never disappears below the émigré's horizon. For his characters, and perhaps for himself, this seems a colossal understatement. The pull of events in a land half a world away is far stronger, far more compelling and, in some universal sense, far more important than those that occur in his comfortable, cosseted new Eden."

Reviewers of *Two Murders in My Double Life* generally lamented Škvorecký's style. Michiko Kakutani in the *New York Times* cited the work for "lumbering prose" and suggested that the narrative strategy "works to undermine, rather than build suspense." A *Kirkus Reviews* contributor likewise noted that the play-within-a-play form of the book leads to "results that fail to allay its own artificialities." *Los Angeles Times Book Review* reviewer Merle Rubin found the work to be "an odd book: playful in form, ruefully comic in tone, tragic in content." Rubin concluded, "Škvorecký is content to tell rather than show, to deliver wry, rather offhand comments rather than probe in depth. And so, we are left with a wistful, querulous plaint instead of a fully imagined work of fiction." In the *Washington Post Book World,* James Hynes wrote, "There's a general atmosphere of score-settling about both stories, the silly and the tragic, that eventually shuts out the sunlight of the author's considerable charm like an overcast sky, and vitiates the power of this book as art."

Summarizing the writer's accomplishments in all his works, Hood commented that Škvorecký "is a novelist of real stature, who writes without sentimentality about adolescence, war and death." Yet it is not plot that impressed Winch. He pointed out that Škvorecký "is a poetic writer whose work depends more on the interplay of words and images than on story-line." Maloff concluded, "We have had to wait a very long time for the . . . English translation and . . . American publication of [Škvorecký's] superlative, greatly moving works of art. . . . Fortunately, [his] work has lost none of its immediacy or luster, nor is it likely to for a long time to come." Škvorecký once stated "I'm an entertainer who, through no fault of mine but due to life's circumstances, occasionally had some important things to say."

BIOGRAPHICAL AND CRITICAL SOURCES:

BOOKS

Contemporary Authors Autobiography Series, Volume 1, Thomson Gale (Detroit, MI), 1984.

Contemporary Literary Criticism, Thomson Gale (Detroit, MI), Volume 15, 1980; Volume 39, 1986; Volume 63, 1991.

Galligan, Edward L., *The Truth of Uncertainty: Beyond Ideology in Science and Literature,* University of Missouri Press, 1998.

Solecki, Sam, *Josef Škvorecký and His Works,* ECW Press (Toronto, Ontario, Canada), 1997.

Solecki, Sam, *Prague Blues: The Fiction of Josef Škvorecký,* ECW Press, 1990.

Solecki, Sam, editor, *The Achievement of Josef Škvorecký,* University of Toronto Press (Toronto, Ontario, Canada), 1994.

Trensky, Paul I., *The Fiction of Josef Škvorecký,* St. Martin's Press (New York, NY), 1991.

PERIODICALS

Atlantic, March, 1979.

Best Sellers, November 1, 1970.

Booklist, December 15, 1995, p. 668.

Books in Canada, May, 1981, p. 40; February, 1983, pp. 13-14; November, 1986, pp. 17-18; June-July, 1987, p. 13; October, 1988, pp. 31-32; December, 1989, p. 9; June-July, 1990, pp. 24-26.

Canadian Forum, November, 1977, pp. 40-41; December-January, 1982-83, p. 40; August-September, 1984; April, 1994, p. 40.

Canadian Literature, spring, 1992, pp. 166-167, 212-214.

Chicago Tribune Book World, August 12, 1984; March 1, 1987.

Chicago Tribune Review, July 19, 1992, p. 8; August 21, 1994, p. 1; February 18, 1996, p. 6.
Encounter, July-August, 1985.
Globe and Mail (Toronto, Ontario, Canada), November 25, 1986; November 29, 1986; June 25, 1988; November 24, 1990.
Guardian May 1, 2004, essay, Central Europe's Writers Post-Communism, p. 16.
Kirkus Reviews, February 1, 2001, review of *Two Murders in My Double Life,* p. 140.
Library Journal, July, 1970; February 1, 1996, p. 100; April 15, 2001, Jim Coan, review of *Two Murders in My Double Life,* p. 133.
Listener, October 8, 1970; March 11, 1976; August 17, 1978.
London Review of Books, March 21, 1985, p. 19.
Los Angeles Times Book Review, July 1, 1984, p. 1; February 15, 1987, pp. 3, 8; August 23, 1987, p. 13; June 12, 1988; February 26, 1989, p. 1; May 10, 1991, p. 7; May 29, 2001, Merle Rubin, "Dark and Light Tales of Politics Played out in Academia," p. 3.
Maclean's, December 31, 1990, p. 47; December 4, 1995, p. 76.
Nation, August 4, 1984; March 25, 1991, p. 381.
New Republic, August 27, 1984.
New Statesman, October 2, 1970, p. 426; February 5, 1988, p. 33.
New Statesman & Society, March 1, 1991, p. 37.
Newsweek, August 13, 1984.
New York Review of Books, November 19, 1970, p. 45; April 5, 1973, pp. 34-35; September 27, 1984; May 18, 1989, p. 37; April 11, 1991, pp. 45-46.
New York Times, July 23, 1984; August 9, 1984; January 31, 1987, p. 13; June 8, 2001, Michiko Kakutani, "A Murder Mystery Bound up with the Killing of Souls," p. 37.
New York Times Book Review, September 21, 1975, p. 38; January 14, 1979, pp. 7, 35; November 25, 1979, p. 46; August 19, 1984; January 12, 1986; February 22, 1987; September 6, 1987, p. 16; March 12, 1989, p. 24; February 18, 1990, p. 14; February 10, 1991, p. 1; March 10, 1991, p. 21; July 19, 1992, p. 32; August 28, 1994, p. 9; December 15, 1995, p. 32; January 21, 1996, p. 14; May 20, 2001, Neil Bermel, "Dead Man on Campus"; July 28, 2002, Laura Secor, "Occupational hazard: In Josef Skvorecky's fiction, 20th-century history interferes with chasing girls," p. 9.
Observer (London, England), March 3, 1985, p. 26; January 3, 1988, p. 23; May 7, 1989, p. 44; February 10, 1991, p. 54; May 8, 1994, p. 17.
Publishers Weekly, June 22, 1984; January 26, 1990, Sybil Steinberg, review of *The End of Lieutenant Boruvka,* p. 404; December 14, 1990, Sybil Steinberg, review of *The Miracle Game,* p. 53; January 11, 1991, Sybil Steinberg, review of *The Return of Lieutenant Boruvka,* p. 94 July 11, 1994, review of *The Republic of Whores,* p. 65; December 4, 1995, review of *The Bride of Texas,* p. 53; May 7, 2001, review of *Two Murders in My Double Life,* p. 221.
Quill and Quire, May, 1984, p. 30; November, 1988, p. 18; October, 1989, p. 23; September, 1990, pp. 60-61; December, 1995.
Review of Contemporary Fiction, summer, 1997, Sam Solecki, An Interview with Josef Škvorecký, p. 82; summer, 1997, Steve Horowitz, review of *The Tenor Saxophonist's Stbory,* p. 281.
San Francisco Chronicle, June 23, 2002, Jonathan Curiel, "Reflecting on a life in exile," p. 2.
Sewanee Review, winter, 1993, pp. 107-115.
Stand, autumn, 1990, p. 76.
Time, July 30, 1984.
Times Literary Supplement, October 16, 1970; June 23, 1978; August 12, 1983; March 8, 1985, p. 256; January 23, 1987; November 30, 1990, p. 1300; March 8, 1991, p. 19; May 13, 1994, p. 20.
Tribune Books (Chicago, IL), June 9, 1987.
Washington Post, December 4, 1987.
Washington Post Book World, July 29, 1984; March 29, 1987; April 16, 1989, p. 8; February 17, 1991, p. 6; March 3, 1996, p. 8; May 6, 2001, James Hynes, "Paper Chases," p. 6; July 21, 2002, Zofia Smardz, review of *When Eve Was Naked,* p. T03.
World Literature Today, autumn, 1978; summer, 1979, p. 524; autumn, 1980, special Škvorecký issue; autumn, 1985, p. 622; summer, 1986, p. 489; autumn, 1987, pp. 652-653; summer, 1991, pp. 511-512; fall, 1996, Edward J. Czerwinski, review of *The Bride of Texas,* p. 988; winter, 1997, B.R. Bradbrook, review of *Nove canterburske povidky a jine pribehy,* p. 182.

ONLINE

Center for Book Culture, http://www.centerforbookculture.org/ (October 1, 2001), Sam Solecki, "An Interview with Josef Škvorecký."
Central European Review, http://www.ce-review.org/ (October 30, 2000), Julie Hansen, "All's Well That Ends Well: An Interview with Josef Škvorecký."
Internet Public Library Online Literary Criticism Collection, http://www.ipl.org/ (October 1, 2001), "Josef Škvorecký."
Writers' Academy of Josef Škvorecký Web site, http://www.lit.akad.cz/pages/zaklinfo.htm/ (October 16, 2004).

ŠKVORECKÝ, Josef Vaclav
See ŠKVORECKÝ, Josef

* * *

SMILEY, Jane 1949-
(Jane Graves Smiley)

PERSONAL: Born September 26, 1949, in Los Angeles, CA; daughter of James Laverne (in U.S. Army) and Frances Nuelle (a writer; maiden name, Graves) Smiley; married John Whiston, September 4, 1970 (divorced, November, 1975); married William Silag (an editor), May 1, 1978 (divorced, February, 1986); married Stephen M. Mortensen (a screenwriter), July 25, 1987 (marriage ended, 1997); children: (second marriage) Phoebe Graves Silag, Lucy Gallagher Silag; (third marriage) Axel James Mortensen. *Education:* Vassar College, B.A., 1971; University of Iowa, M.A., 1975, M.F.A., 1976, Ph.D., 1978. *Politics:* "Skeptical." *Religion:* "Vehement agnostic." *Hobbies and other interests:* Cooking, swimming, playing piano, quilting.

ADDRESSES: *Home*—California. *Agent*—Molly Friedrich, Aaron Priest Agency, 708 Third Ave., 23rd Floor, New York, NY 10017.

CAREER: Iowa State University, Ames, professor of English, 1981-90, distinguished professor of English, 1992-96. Visiting assistant professor at University of Iowa, 1981, 1987.

MEMBER: Authors Guild, Authors League of America, Screenwriters Guild.

AWARDS, HONORS: Fulbright fellowship, 1976-77; grants from National Endowment for the Arts, 1978 and 1987; Friends of American Writers Prize, 1981, for *At Paradise Gate;* O. Henry awards, 1982, 1985, and 1988; National Book Critics Circle Award nomination, 1987, for *The Age of Grief* and 1995 for *Moo;* Pulitzer Prize, National Book Critics Circle Award, and Heartland Award, all 1991, all for *A Thousand Acres;* Midland Authors Award, 1992.

WRITINGS:

Barn Blind (novel), Harper (New York, NY), 1980.

At Paradise Gate (novel), Simon & Schuster (New York, NY), 1981.

Duplicate Keys (mystery novel), Knopf (New York, NY), 1984.

The Age of Grief (novella and stories), Knopf (New York, NY), 1987, reprinted, 2002.

Catskill Crafts: Artisans of the Catskill Mountains (nonfiction), Crown (New York, NY), 1988.

The Greenlanders (historical novel), Knopf, 1988.

Ordinary Love; and Good Will (two novellas), Knopf, 1989.

The Life of the Body (short stories), Coffee House Press (Minneapolis, MN), 1990.

A Thousand Acres (novel), Knopf (New York, NY), 1991.

(With others) *The True Subject: Writers on Life and Craft,* Graywolf Press (St. Paul, MN), 1993.

Moo (novel), Knopf (New York, NY), 1995.

(Author of introduction) Carolyn Keene, *Nancy's Mysterious Letter,* Applewood Books, 1996.

The All-True Travels and Adventures of Lidie Newton (novel), Knopf (New York, NY), 1998.

(Editor, with Roger Rosenblatt and Bharati Mukherjee) *Consuming Desires: Consumption Culture and the Pursuit of Happiness,* Island Press, 1999.

(Contributor, with others) Yona Zeldis McDonough, editor, *The Barbie Chronicles: A Living Doll Turns Forty,* Simon & Schuster (New York, NY), 1999.

(Author of introduction) Thomas Hardy, *The Return of the Native,* Signet (New York, NY), 1999.

Horse Heaven (novel), Knopf (New York, NY), 2000.

(Author of preface) *The Sagas of Icelanders: A Selection,* introduction by Robert Kellogg, Viking Penguin (New York, NY), 2000.

(Author of introduction) Harriet Beecher Stowe, *Uncle Tom's Cabin,* Random House (New York, NY), 2001.

Charles Dickens, Viking (New York, NY), 2002.

(Author of afterword) George Eliot, *Mill on the Floss,* Signet Classics (New York, NY), 2002.

Good Faith, Knopf (New York, NY), 2003.

(Author of introduction, with William H. Gass) Michael Eastman, photographer, *Horses: Photographs,* Knopf (New York, NY), 2003.

(With Robert Gordon, Vicki Hearne, and John Yau) *Deborah Butterfield,* Harry N. Abrams (New York, NY), 2003.

(Editor) *Writers on Writing, Volume 2: More Collected Essays from The New York Times,* Holt (New York, NY), 2003.

A Year at the Races: Reflections on Horses, Humans, Love, Money, and Luck, Knopf (New York, NY), 2004.

Contributor to books, including *Pacific Light: Images of the Monterrey Peninsula,* edited by Douglas Steakley, Carmel Publishing, 2000; and to periodicals, including,

Vogue, New Yorker, Practical Horseman, Harper's, New York Times Magazine, Victoria, Mirabella, Allure, Nation, and others.

ADAPTATIONS: A Thousand Acres was adapted for film by Laura Jones and released by Touchstone Pictures, 1997; the novella *The Age of Grief* was adapted by Craig Lucas as the film *The Secret Lives of Dentists,* directed by Alan Rudolph and starring Hope Davis and Campbell Scott, and released by Manhattan Pictures International.

SIDELIGHTS: Even before her Pulitzer Prize-winning novel *A Thousand Acres,* Jane Smiley's fiction shared a concern for families and their troubles. As Joanne Kaufman remarked in *People,* Smiley "has an unerring, unsettling ability to capture the rhythms of family life gone askew." Smiley also possesses what Jane Yolen in the *Washington Post* called a "spare, yet lyric" prose. In addition, Yolen found Smiley to be "a true storyteller."

The theme of family life was present in Smiley's first book, *Barn Blind,* a "pastoral novel of smooth texture and—like the Middle Western summer in which it is set—rich, drowsy pace," as Michael Malone described it in the *New York Times Book Review.* The story revolves around Kate Karlson, a rancher's wife, and her strained relationships with her four teenaged children. "Smiley handles with skill and understanding the mercurial molasses of adolescence, and the inchoate, cumbersome love that family members feel for one another," according to Malone.

In her next book, *At Paradise Gate,* Smiley looked again at conflict between family members. In this story, elderly Anna Robinson faces the imminent death of her husband, Ike. The couple have had a rough marriage; Ike is an emotionally cold and violent person. When Anna's three daughters arrive to visit their dying father, old sibling rivalries are revived, tensions between the parents are renewed, and Anna must confront the failures and triumphs of her life. The story, explained Valerie Miner in the *New York Times Book Review,* "is not so much about Ike's death as about Anna's life—a retrospective on her difficult past and a resolution of her remaining years." *At Paradise Gate,* Susan Wood maintains in the *Washington Post,* "is a sensitive study of what it means to grow old and face death, and of the courage to see clearly what one's life has meant."

Smiley took a different tack with *Duplicate Keys,* a mystery novel set in Manhattan; and yet even in this book her concern for family relations holds firm. Laura Marcus of the *Times Literary Supplement* called *Duplicate Keys* a story about "marriages, affairs, friendships, growing up and growing older. . . . Smiley demonstrates a considerable sensitivity in the treatment of love and friendship." Lois Gould in the *New York Times Book Review* called the book only incidently a mystery. "More important and far more compelling," Gould noted, "is the anatomy of friendship, betrayal, the color of dusk on the Upper West Side, the aroma of lilacs in Brooklyn's Botanical Garden, of chocolate tortes at Zabar's, and the bittersweet smell of near success that is perhaps the most pungent odor in town." Alice Cromie in Chicago's *Tribune Books* concluded that *Duplicate Keys* is "a sophisticated story of friendships, loves, jealousies, drugs, celebrities and life in the fastest lane in Manhattan."

In 1987 Smiley published *The Age of Grief,* a collection of five stories and a novella, focusing on the joys and sorrows of married life. The title novella, according to Kaufman, "is a haunting view of a marriage from the inside, a tale told by a betrayed husband full of humor and sadness and sound and quiet fury." Michiko Kakutani, writing in the *New York Times,* found that the novella "opens out, organically, from a comic portrait . . . into a lovely and very sad meditation on the evanescence and durability of love." Speaking of the book as a whole, Roz Kaveney wrote in the *Times Literary Supplement* that "one of the major strengths of this quiet and unflashy collection . . . is that in [Smiley's] stories things actually do happen. These events are entirely in keeping with her strong vein of social realism, but they have too a quality of the unpredictable, a quality which gives an uninsistent but pervasive sense of the pain and surprise which lie beneath even the most conventional of lives." Anne Bernays, in her review for the *New York Times Book Review,* concluded: "The stories are fine; the novella is splendid." John Blades in the *Chicago Tribune* found that Smiley "speaks most confidently and affectingly [about] the delicate mechanics of marriage and family life, the intricate mysteries of love."

In 1988 Smiley published *The Greenlanders,* a "prodigiously detailed, haunting novel," as Howard Norman described it in the *New York Times Book Review.* A 500-page historical novel set in fourteenth-century Greenland, the book took Smiley five years to research and write. *The Greenlanders* is "a sprawling, multigenerational, heroic Norse narrative," according to Richard Panek in Chicago's *Tribune Books.* Based on old Viking sagas and, in particular, on surviving accounts of the colonies the Vikings established in Greenland, the story blends fact and fiction to create a modern novel with a traditional flavor. As Norman explained, the book "employs a 'folkloristic' mode with its stories overlapping other stories, folded into yet others." The technique, Yolen found, presents "more than an individual's story. It is the community's story, the land's." By telling the community's story, Smiley contrasts the tragic failure of the Greenland colonies to survive with our contemporary society and its problems. "The result," Panek wrote, "is a novel that places contemporary conflicts into the context of the ages."

As in her other novels, Smiley also focuses on family relations in *The Greenlanders,* tracing the effects of a curse on several generations of the Gunnarsson family, well-to-do farmers in Greenland. "Family matters . . . ," Yolen stated, "become both the focus and the subtext of the novel: the feuds, the curses, the marriages, the passions and the brutal deaths." Norman noted the complexity of the novel, citing the "hundreds of episodes and tributary episodes: the seasonal seal hunts and rituals, the travels over hazardous yet awe-inspiring terrain, the births and deaths. . . . Given the vast template of History, it is impressive how Ms. Smiley is able to telescope certain incidents, unravel personalities in a few paragraphs, [and] delve into a kind of folkloric metaphysics." Norman concluded that Smiley "is a diverse and masterly writer."

After the publication of the novellas *Ordinary Love; and Good Will,* and a short story collection, *The Life of the Body,* Smiley published *A Thousand Acres.* The subtle account of a family's disintegration emerges through a painstakingly detailed portrait of Midwestern farm life, just before much of it was lost during the wave of foreclosures in the 1980s. Donna Rifkind commented in her *Washington Post* review that the novel "has all the stark brutality, if not the poetic grandeur, of a Shakespearean tragedy."

The correlation to Shakespeare is no accident; as Smiley admitted, *A Thousand Acres* is a deliberate recasting of *King Lear,* the Elizabethan playwright's drama of an aged king bordering on madness and conspired against by three daughters plotting to take control of his kingdom. Reinterpreting the motivations of the daughters through a more jaundiced view of patriarchal control and feminine subjugation, Smiley puts the character of Lear's eldest daughter, Goneril in Shakespeare's work, now Ginny in her own, at the center of her family narrative. "Her feminist re-writing of Shakespeare's plot replaces the incomprehensibly malign sisters with real women who have suffered incomprehensible malignity," noted Diane Purkiss in a review for the *Times Literary Supplement.* "In giving Goneril a voice, Smiley joins the distinguished line of women's writers who have written new parts for Shakespeare's women."

For Jack Fuller, reworking the plot of *King Lear* has its dangers. "The large risk that Smiley runs, of course, is using the Lear story so explicitly," Fuller noted in Chicago's *Tribune Books.* "It could have turned the book into a kind of precious exercise or a literary curiosity. But Smiley avoids this by the mounting brilliance of her close observations and delicate rendering of human behavior."

Through Ginny's eyes, Smiley shows the deleterious impact of her father Larry's decision to divide his multimillion dollar farm among his three daughters, who include the embittered Rose and the emotionally distant Caroline. As the divided enterprise deteriorates, marriages fall apart and family relationships are crippled by suspicion and betrayal. Describing *A Thousand Acres* as "powerful" and "poignant," Ron Carlson wrote in the *New York Times Book Review* that "Smiley brings us in so close that it's almost too much to bear. She's good in those small places, with nothing but the family, pulling tighter and tighter until someone has to leave the table, leave the room, leave town."

As the Cook family saga unfolds, Smiley gently yet skillfully reveals her feminist and environmentalist sympathies. "In *A Thousand Acres,* men's dominance of women takes a violent turn, and incest becomes an undercurrent in the novel," wrote Martha Duffy in *Time.* "The magic of [the novel] is that it deals so effectively with both the author's scholarship and her dead-serious social concerns in an engrossing piece of fiction."

In her next work, *Moo,* Smiley leaves the strains of family relationships to poke some fun at campus life, which she explores at the fictitious Midwestern agricultural college, nicknamed Moo U. *Moo* received mixed reactions from reviewers. While critics found moments of brilliance in the work, some considered it flawed. In the *Washington Post Book World,* a reviewer compared *Moo* with another satire of academia, *Pictures from an Institution* by Randall Jarrell. "Stylistically, [Smiley] employs a prose and tone reminiscent of the dry, ironic, distanced manner Jarrell so masterfully adopted," the critic noted. "When it comes down to the essential business of satire, though, Smiley is ill-equipped to follow in Jarrell's train. This is not because she lacks humor but because, more tellingly, she lacks malice." While commenting that Smiley wields a "considerable wit" and "provocative intelligence," Richard Eder, in the *Los Angeles Times Book Review,* took the novel to task for being "a playful takeoff on too many things, all crowded together and happening at once." In contrast *New York Review of Books* contributor Cathleen Schine found *Moo* a social comedy closer to Victorian novelist Anthony Trollope's work than Jarrell's satire. As Schine noted, "Smiley subverts satire, making it sweeter and ultimately more pointed. She has written a generous and, therefore daring book. . . . Smiley has transformed the genre by embracing a different tradition altogether. . . . [She] has created what modern novel readers have until now been able only to dream about, that elusive, seemingly impossible thing: a fresh literary, modern twentieth-century nineteenth-century novel." A reviewer for *Publishers Weekly* offered praise for the work, writing that in *Moo* "Smiley delivers a surprising tour de force, a satire of university life that leaves no aspect of contemporary academia unscathed." Joanne Wilkinson sounded a similar positive note in her review for *Booklist,* citing her appreciation of the novel's ending: "Smiley's great gift here is the way she gently skewers any number of easily recognizable campus fixtures . . . while never failing to show their humanity."

Following *Moo,* Smiley returned to historical fiction with *The All-True Travels and Adventures of Lidie Newton,* which appeared in 1998. Discussing the novel with Lewis Burke Frumkes in *Writer,* Smiley explained that *Lidie Newton* "takes place in the mid-1850s, mostly in Kansas and Missouri. It's about a tall, plain woman without any prospects, and a man [Thomas Newton], associated with an abolitionist group from New England, who passes through Lidie's town in Illinois." Lidie and Thomas fall in love, are married, and settle in Kansas. There Lidie must confront primitive frontier living conditions, conflicts about free labor versus slavery, and the "worst winter in a hundred years." "I once read that every 19th-century American novel was actually a romance," Smiley told Frumkes, "so I wanted to write a romance, a story in which the protagonist sets out on a journey and sees many amazing things." Smiley credits Mark Twain's *Huckleberry Finn* and Harriet Beecher Stowe's *Uncle Tom's Cabin* as literary progenitors of *The All-True Travels and Adventures of Lidie Newton.* Starr E. Smith, reviewing the novel for *Library Journal,* found the book to be "believable period fiction," whereas Donna Seaman in *Booklist* credited it with exploring both "the bloody conflict over slavery and the simultaneous awakening of the feminist movement within in the parameters of a love story."

Smiley's 2000 volume *Horse Heaven* again demonstrates her interest in continually mining new fictional territory. In a novel described by Maxine Kumin in the *Women's Review of Books* as "exuberant, often hilarious," and by Bill Barich of the *New York Times Book Review* as "smart, warmhearted, winning," Smiley explores the contemporary world of thoroughbred horse racing at tracks throughout the world over a two-year period beginning in 1997. *Horse Heaven* is a big book—561 pages—encompassing a large cast of major characters—more than two dozen humans, a number of equines, and a dog—and a complex plot with many interweaving storylines. Trainers, jockeys, owners, gamblers, an animal communicator, horse fanciers, and assorted racetrack hangers-on share center stage, exploring their own lives and others through love affairs, business dealings, friendships, and betrayals.

Among Smiley's four-legged creations are the savage stallion Epic Steam, the delicate and insecure Froney's Sis, the aging Mr. T., and the five-year-old gelding, Justa Bob, the last characterized by Barich as a "joker at heart." Barich also found Smiley's research for the book to be "exemplary," remarking: "Its deeply satisfying to read a work of fiction so informed about its subject and so alive to every nuance and detail. . . . From veterinary surgery to the riding tactics of jockeys." As Paula Chin noted in *People,* "it is the hearts of the magnificent thoroughbreds that Smiley describes most movingly." Barich concurred, stating: "What's remarkable about Smiley's handling of horses as characters is that she manages to bring it off at all—and more, she does it brilliantly."

BIOGRAPHICAL AND CRITICAL SOURCES:

BOOKS

Contemporary Literary Criticism, Volume 76, Thomson Gale (Detroit, MI), 1993.

Sheldon, Barbara H., *Daughters and Fathers in Feminist Novels,* P. Lang (New York, NY), 1997.

PERIODICALS

Belles Lettres, summer, 1992, pp. 36-38.

Booklist, February 1, 1995, p. 971; November 1, 1995, p. 453; February 15, 2000, Donna Seaman, review of *Horse Heaven,* p. 1053; February 15, 2000, Donna Seaman, review of *The All-True Travels and Adventures of Lidie Newton,* p. 1078.

Chicago Tribune, November 6, 1987; November 24, 1991.

Library Journal, March 15, 2000, Starr E. Smith, review of *Horse Heaven,* p. 130.
London Review of Books, November 19, 1992; October 19, 1995, p. 38.
Los Angeles Times Book Review, March 18, 1984; October 18, 1987; April 2, 1995, pp. 3, 8.
Nation, May 8, 1995, p. 638.
New Leader, March 13, 1995, p. 18.
New Statesman and Society, June 9, 1995, p. 37.
Newsweek, April 17, 2000, Jeff Giles, "All the Pretty Racehorses," p. 68.
New York Review of Books, August 10, 1995, pp. 38-39.
New York Times, August 26, 1987.
New York Times Book Review, August 17, 1980; November 22, 1981; April 29, 1984; September 6, 1987; May 15, 1988; November 3, 1991; April 2, 1995, p. 1; April 5, 1998, p. 10; April 2, 2000, Bill Barich, "From the Horse's Mouth."
People, January 18, 1988; April 24, 1995, p. 29; January 15, 1996, p. 35; April 10, 2000, Paula Chin, review of *Horse Heaven,* p. 49.
Publishers Weekly, April 1, 1988; February 6, 1995, pp. 75-76.
Time, November 11, 1991; April 17, 1995, p. 68.
Times (London, England), February 4, 1988.
Times Literary Supplement, August 24, 1984; March 18, 1988; October 30, 1992.
Tribune Books (Chicago, IL), July 8, 1984; April 3, 1988; November 3, 1991.
Washington Post, October 27, 1981; May 13, 1988; October 27, 1991.
Washington Post Book World, March 26, 1995.
Women's Review of Books, June, 2000, Maxine Kumin, "More Equine the Others," p. 11.
Writer, May, 1999, Lewis Burke Frumkes, "A Conversation with . . . Jane Smiley," p. 20.
Yale Review, October, 1995, p. 135.

ONLINE

Random House Web site, http://www.randomhouse.com/ (October 23, 2003), "Jane Smiley."
Salon.com, http://www.salon.com/ (April 17, 2000), review of *Horse Heaven.*

* * *

SMILEY, Jane Graves
See SMILEY, Jane

* * *

SMITH, Alexander McCall
See McCALL SMITH, Alexander

SMITH, Martin
See SMITH, Martin Cruz

* * *

SMITH, Martin Cruz 1942-
(Nick Carter, Jake Logan, Simon Quinn, Martin Smith)

PERSONAL: Original name, Martin William Smith; born November 3, 1942, in Reading, PA; son of John Calhoun (a musician) and Louise (a jazz singer and Native American rights leader; maiden name, Lopez) Smith; married Emily Arnold (a chef), June 15, 1968; children: Ellen Irish, Luisa Cruz, Samuel Kip. *Education:* University of Pennsylvania, B.A., 1964.

ADDRESSES: *Home*—240 Cascade Dr., Mill Valley, CA 94941. *Agent*—c/o Knox Burger Associates Ltd., 425 Madison Avenue, Floor 10, New York, NY 10017. *E-mail*—mcsmith@literati.net.

CAREER: Writer. Worked for local television stations, newspapers, and as a correspondent for Associated Press; *Philadelphia Daily News,* Philadelphia, PA, reporter, 1965; Magazine Management, New York, NY, 1966-69, began as writer, became editor of *For Men Only.*

MEMBER: Authors League of America, Authors Guild.

AWARDS, HONORS: Edgar Award nomination, Mystery Writers of America, 1972, for *Gypsy in Amber,* 1976, for *The Midas Coffin,* 1978, for *Nightwing,* and 1982, for *Gorky Park;* Gold Dagger, Crime Writers Association, 1982, for *Gorky Park.*

WRITINGS:

NOVELS

Nightwing (also see below), Norton (New York, NY), 1977.
The Analog Bullet, Belmont-Tower, 1978.
Gorky Park, Random House (New York, NY), 1981.
Stallion Gate, Random House (New York, NY), 1986.
Polar Star, Random House (New York, NY), 1989.
Red Square, Random House (New York, NY), 1992.
Rose, Random House (New York, NY), 1996.

Havana Bay: A Novel, Random House (New York, NY), 1999.

December 6, Simon & Schuster (New York, NY), 2002.

NOVELS; UNDER NAME MARTIN SMITH

The Indians Won, Belmont-Tower, 1970, reprinted under name Martin Cruz Smith, Leisure Books, 1981.

Gypsy in Amber, Putnam (New York, NY), 1971.

Canto for a Gypsy, Putnam (New York, NY), 1972, reprinted under name Martin Cruz Smith, Ballantine (New York, NY), 1983.

NOVELS UNLESS NOTED OTHERWISE; UNDER PSEUDONYM SIMON QUINN

His Eminence, Death, Dell (New York, NY), 1974.

Nuplex Red, Dell (New York, NY), 1974.

The Devil in Kansas, Dell (New York, NY), 1974.

The Last Time I Saw Hell, Dell (New York, NY), 1974.

The Midas Coffin, Dell (New York, NY), 1975.

Last Rites for the Vulture, Dell (New York, NY), 1975.

The Human Factor (movie novelization), Dell (New York, NY), 1975.

The Adventures of the Wilderness Family (movie novelization), Ballantine (New York, NY), 1976.

NOVELS; UNDER HOUSE PSEUDONYM JAKE LOGAN

North to Dakota, Playboy Press, 1976.

Ride for Revenge, Playboy Press, 1977.

Slocum Bursts Out, Berkley (New York, NY), 1990.

Slocum, No. 150: Trail of Death, Berkley (New York, NY), 1991.

Slocum, No. 154: Slocum's Standoff, Berkley (New York, NY), 1991.

Slocum, No. 155: Death Council, Berkley (New York, NY), 1991.

Slocum, No. 156: Timber King, Berkley (New York, NY), 1992.

Slocum, No. 157: Railroad Baron, Berkley (New York, NY), 1992.

Slocum, No. 158: River Chase, Berkley (New York, NY), 1992.

Slocum, No. 159: Tombstone Gold, Berkley (New York, NY), 1992.

Slocum, No. 163: Slocum and the Bushwackers, Berkley (New York, NY), 1992.

Slocum, No. 165: San Angelo Shootout, Berkley (New York, NY), 1992.

Slocum, No. 166: Blood Fever, Berkley (New York, NY), 1992.

Revenge at Devil's Tower, Berkley (New York, NY), 1993.

Ambush at Apache Rocks, Berkley (New York, NY), 1993.

Slocum, No. 167: Helltown Trail, Berkley (New York, NY), 1993.

Slocum, No. 168: Sheriff Slocum, Berkley (New York, NY), 1993.

Slocum, No. 169: Virginia City Showdown, Berkley (New York, NY), 1993.

Slocum, No. 170: Slocum and the Forty Thieves, Berkley (New York, NY), 1993.

Slocum, No. 171: Powder River Massacre, Berkley (New York, NY), 1993.

Slocum, No. 173: Slocum and the Tin Star Swindle, Berkley (New York, NY), 1993.

Slocum, No. 174: Slocum and the Nightriders, Berkley (New York, NY), 1993.

Slocum, No. 176: Slocum at Outlaw's Haven, Berkley (New York, NY), 1993.

Pikes Peak Shoot-Out, Berkley (New York, NY), 1994.

Slocum and the Cow Town Kill, Berkley (New York, NY), 1994.

Slocum and the Gold Slaves, Berkley (New York, NY), 1994.

Slocum and the Invaders, Berkley (New York, NY), 1994.

Slocum and the Mountain of Gold, Berkley (New York, NY), 1994.

Slocum and the Phantom Gold, Berkley (New York, NY), 1994.

Slocum, No. 179: Slocum and the Buffalo Soldiers, Berkley (New York, NY), 1994.

Ghost Town, Berkley (New York, NY), 1994.

Blood Trail, Berkley (New York, NY), 1994.

OTHER

(Under name Martin Cruz Smith, with Steve Shagan and Bud Shrake) *Nightwing* (screenplay; based on novel of same title), Columbia, 1979.

(Editor) *Death By Espionage: Intriguing Stories of Betrayal and Deception,* Cumberland House (Nashville, TN), 1999.

Also author of several other genre novels under various pseudonyms, including Nick Carter. Contributor of stories to *Male, Stag,* and *For Men Only* and of book reviews to *Esquire. Gorky Park* has been translated into Russian.

ADAPTATIONS: The film *Gorky Park,* starring William Hurt and Lee Marvin, was released by Orion Pictures, 1983.

SIDELIGHTS: In 1972, a struggling young writer named Martin William Smith approached his publisher, G.P. Putnam, with an idea for a different sort of mystery. Inspired by a *Newsweek* review of *The Face Finder,* a nonfiction book recounting the efforts of Soviet scientists to reconstruct faces from otherwise unidentifiable human remains, Smith outlined a plot involving a partnership between a Soviet detective and his American counterpart as they attempt to solve an unusual murder. (As the author later revealed in the *Washington Post,* his original inclination was to portray a sort of "Butch Cassidy and the Sundance Kid, but one [partner would be] Russian.") Putnam liked Smith's proposal and agreed to pay him a 15,000 dollar advance.

For the next five years, Smith eked out a living writing several dozen paperback novels, often under one of his various pseudonyms. "I didn't want to be associated with those books," he told *Newsweek*'s Peter S. Prescott. Whenever he had accumulated enough to live on for awhile, he did research for his murder mystery; in 1973, he even managed to make a trip to Moscow, where he spent almost a week wandering through the city jotting down notes on how it looked and sketching scenes he hesitated to photograph. Later denied permission for a return visit, Smith instead spent hours pumping various Russian émigrés and defectors for details about life in the Soviet Union "on everything from the quality of shoes . . . to whether a ranking policeman would have to be a member of the Communist Party," as Arthur Spiegelman of the *Chicago Tribune* noted. "I would write a scene and show it to one of my Russian friends," Smith recalled. "If he would say that some Russian must have told me that, then I knew it was OK."

By this time, Smith knew he no longer wanted to write a conventional thriller. "I suddenly realized that I had something," he commented in the *Washington Post.* "This [was] the book that [could] set me free." He abandoned the idea of a partnership between detectives, deciding instead to focus on the challenge of making the Soviet detective his hero. Putnam, however, was less than enthusiastic about the change in plans, for the publisher doubted that such a book would have much commercial appeal. Smith was urged to stick to more marketable plots—namely, those featuring an American hero.

The year 1977 proved to be a turning point of sorts for Smith; he not only bought back the rights to his novel from Putnam, after a long and bitter battle, and changed his middle name from William to Cruz (his maternal grandmother's name), he also received approximately a half million dollars when *Nightwing,* his vampire bat horror-thriller, became a surprise success. *Nightwing,* featuring Hopi Indian characters caught up in a vampire bat legend, deals with Indian attitudes and folklore. In an interview with *CA,* Smith discussed his own Pueblo Indian heritage and acknowledged that he "relied on [his] own background and research" for the novel. The following period of financial security enabled Smith to put the finishing touches on his "simple detective story," which by now had grown into a 365-page novel. In 1980, Smith and his agent began negotiating with Random House and Ballantine for the publishing rights. Despite the lack of interest Putnam had shown in his work, Smith was confident that his book would indeed be published—and at a price *he* would name. As he remarked to Prescott: "Every time I looked at the novel I decided to double the price. When I wrote the last line, I *knew;* I have never been so excited in my life, except for the birth of children, as when I wrote the last line of [that book]. Because I knew it was just right. I had this marvelous book and I was *damned* if I was going to sell it for anything less than a marvelous price. The words 'one million' seemed to come to mind." Before the end of the year, Smith *was* one million dollars richer and Random House was preparing to gamble on an unusual 100,000-copy first printing of what soon would become one of the most talked-about books of 1981—*Gorky Park.*

The result of eight years of research and writing, *Gorky Park* chronicles the activities of homicide detective Arkady Renko as he investigates a bizarre murder. Three bullet-riddled bodies—two men and a woman—have been discovered frozen in the snow in Moscow's Gorky Park, their faces skinned and their fingertips cut off to hinder identification. Renko immediately realizes that this is no ordinary murder; his suspicions are confirmed when agents of the KGB arrive on the scene. But instead of taking over the investigation, the KGB suddenly insists that Renko handle the affair. From this point on, the main plot is complicated by an assortment of sub-plots and a large cast of characters, including a greedy American fur-dealer, a visiting New York City police detective who suspects one of the murder victims might be his radical brother, and a dissident Siberian girl with whom Renko falls in love. Before the end of the story, the detective has tracked the killer across two continents and has himself been stalked and harassed by the KGB, the CIA, the FBI, and the New York City police department.

Critics praised the novel for Smith's ability to portray exceptionally vivid Russian scenes and characters. Peter Andrews in the *New York Times Book Review* wrote, "Just when I was beginning to worry that the large-scale adventure novel might be suffering from a terminal case of the Folletts," he wrote, "along comes *Gorky Park* . . . , a book that reminds you just how satisfying a smoothly turned thriller can be." The *Washington Post Book World*'s Peter Osnos compared Smith to John Le Carré, maintaining that "*Gorky Park* is not at all a conventional thriller about Russians. It is to ordinary suspense stories what John Le Carré is to spy novels. The action is gritty, the plot complicated, the overriding quality is intelligence. You have to pay attention or you'll get hopelessly muddled. But staying with this book is easy enough since once one gets going, one doesn't want to stop." Perhaps because he is the protagonist, the character of Arkady Renko seems to have impressed reviewers the most, though Osnos, among others, pointed out that Smith avoids making *any* of his characters into the "sinister stick figures" common in other novels about the Soviets. Tamar Jacoby in the *New Republic* regarded the detective as an "unusual and winning . . . moral hero without a trace of righteousness, an enigmatic figure as alluring as the mystery he is trying to solve. . . . Smith sees to it that there is nothing easy or superior about the moral insight that Arkady earns."

In 1986, Smith published *Stallion Gate,* setting his fiction among the scientists and military personnel of the Manhattan Project, those men and women who gathered near Los Alamos, New Mexico, to develop and test the first atom bomb. "Where *Gorky Park*'s subject was Russian," wrote Stephen Pickles in the *Spectator,* "in this novel Martin Cruz Smith turns to something very American, taking on one of the 20th century's most crucial historical moments." Yet, even with this more familiar setting, Smith recognized the need to investigate his subject in order to reanimate the now famous scientists and to reconstruct the historical setting. Explained Pickles, Smith "researched the subject for 18 months, interviewing survivors and anyone who knew or worked with those involved with the Manhattan Project."

Though closer to home, the backdrop for Smith's novel of intrigue gives it an alien quality much as Moscow colored *Gorky Park.* Set in the desert, the novel blends native Indian allusions with modern, even futuristic images of scientists and their work. At the test site are J. Robert Oppenheimer, Edward Teller, Enrico Fermi, Brigadier General Leslie Groves, Harry Gold, and Klaus Fuchs. In a review of *Stallion Gate* for *Time,* R.Z. Sheppard observed that Smith "shapes images that contain haunting affinities: wild horses and Army jeeps; rattlesnakes and coils of electrical cable; the lustrous surfaces of ceremonial pottery and the polished plutonium core of the atom bomb." "Through the Indians, the author develops a magical dimension within the story," added Pickles. Through the chief of security, an army captain who suspects Oppenheimer of passing project secrets to the Soviets, Smith involves his main character and his readers in this story of suspense. Yet, in the view of *New York Review of Books* contributor Thomas R. Edwards, "This is only reluctantly a thriller. Smith, himself part Indian, is interested in the cultural collision between modern science and native beliefs and folkways of New Mexico." For this reason, as Edwards observed, "*Stallion Gate* is crammed with facts about the customs of the various Indian tribes that dwell in New Mexico, and of another tribe, this one composed of scientists." In a *Los Angeles Times Book Review* article on *Stallion Gate,* Tony Hillerman concluded, "Martin Cruz Smith, master-craftsman of the good read, has given us another dandy."

Smith resumed the adventures of *Gorky Park*'s hero, Russian inspector Arkady Renko, in 1989's *Polar Star,* and *Red Square,* published in 1992. Readers last saw Renko at the end of *Gorky Park* returning from America to his homeland, Russia. Upon his arrival, however, he is imprisoned in a mental hospital, escapes to Siberia, and lands a job as a second-class seaman on the Russian fishing ship *Polar Star,* bound for the Bering Sea. Once out to sea, the fishing nets haul in a dead body identified as crew member Zina Patiashvili. Renko is then ordered to investigate whether Patiashvili's death was suicide or murder.

Reviews of *Polar Star* were largely favorable; Robert Stuart Nathan, in the *New York Times Book Review* wrote, "The novel opens with a Conradian evocation of a ship at sea," he proclaimed, "and immediately we are reminded of just how skilled a storyteller Mr. Smith is, how supple and commanding his prose." Reid Beddow, in the *Washington Post Book World,* labeled the characterization of Renko as "terrific," adding that "Martin Cruz Smith writes the most inventive thrillers of anyone in the first rank of thriller-writers." Allen J. Hubin of *Armchair Detective* asserted that the book is "filled with graphic images and cinematic sequences, involving the ship and the frigid, ice-filled expanses of the Bering Sea." Likewise, T.J. Binyon, in the *Times Literary Supplement,* remarked that "Martin Cruz Smith does a magnificent job on the background," calling the work "wholly absorbing."

In Smith's 1992 novel *Red Square,* Renko operates in post-Communist Russia, a Moscow quite different, but every bit as threatening, as that of *Gorky Park.* In *Red Square,* Renko faces a new threat—the corrupt "Chechen" Mafia of Moscow. As black markets flourish in this new capitalist atmosphere, Renko seeks to solve the murder of his informant Rudy, who turns out to have had connections with the mob. Francis X. Clines in *New York Times Book Review* praised the work, focusing on Smith's finely detailed settings: "The great virtue of the book is its narrative rendering of the sleazy, miasmic environment of *fin-de-Communisme* Moscow . . . that slouching, unworkable 'Big Potato,' as its citizens call it." A *Washington Post Book World* critic welcomed back Smith's much-loved hero, Renko, as "an immensely complex and likeable man. Here his qualities stand out even more luminously." The critic added that Martin Cruz Smith's *Red Square* "is as good popular fiction should be, a novel that proceeds on many levels." Reid Beddow in the *Washington Post Book World* pointed to Smith's competence in dealing with varied subjects—everything from American Indians, forensic medicine, police procedures and atomic secrets, to life in Soviet Russia and the Commonwealth of Independent States. The reviewer concluded that "rather than relying on the repetition of a successful formula, [Smith] has constantly sought to freshen his material."

In *Rose,* published in 1996, Smith departed from Russia for an altogether different setting: 1870s Victorian England. The plot features Jonathan Blair, an engineer and explorer recently returned from Africa who journeys to the Lancashire town of Wigan to investigate a mystery. Wigan is a gritty, coal-mining town, and Blair sets about determining the whereabouts of the local curate, who has not been seen since the day when a mining accident killed seventy-six people. In attempting to discover what happened to the man, Blair finds himself bewitched by the "pit girls"—local women who work in the mines—and in conflict with several male miners. In particular, one pit girl, Rose, eventually comes to play a large role in the mystery—and in Blair's life as well. Reviewing the book in the *Washington Post Book World,* Bruce Cook praised the author's command of historical details in telling his story and noted that "This novel is blessed with the sort of strong narrative line that makes it a joy to read, yet it is about a good deal more than plot." While remarking that Smith's dialogue sometimes betrays a modern tone, *New York Times Book Review* contributor Eugen Weber declared that "Smith's tale is smartly told, engaging and worth reading."

Russian cop Arkady Renko is once again at the center of things in Smith's book *Havana Bay.* This time, Renko is in Cuba, investigating the death of a missing Russian embassy official who was an old friend. Although he comes from the fatherland of communism, Renko finds himself thwarted in his investigation by the Cuban bureaucracy, who now dislike Russians for abandoning communism and selling out. Jim Strader, writing in the *Pittsburgh Post-Gazette,* noted, "But as he did in relating Renko's past adventures, Smith exposes a culture and country literally foreign to most in the United States." Strader went on to call the novel "an engaging tale" that opens "a window to a distinctly different and intriguing place." In *Booklist,* contributor Bill Ott commented, "Smith's beautifully evoked Cuba—rusting idealism set against resurgent decadence—makes the perfect foil for a melancholic investigator who doesn't particularly believe in the very things he stubbornly defends." A contributor to *Publishers Weekly* noted that "Smith's vision of Havana is unforgettable." The reviewer also said, "Gripping, worldly wise and brimming with emotional intelligence, this novel showcases Smith at the top of his game."

Smith continued with his remarkable ability to evoke place with *December 6,* which is set in Japan on the eve of its infamous attack on Pearl Harbor. An American who grew up on the wild streets of Japan but feels comfortable in neither culture, Harry Niles is also a con man who owns a tea room in Tokyo. Aware of a possible attack by Japan on the United States, Niles sets out to possibly thwart the plan while playing both sides against the middle just in case. "In alternating narratives of Harry the boy juxtaposed against Harry the club owner, Smith paints an extraordinary picture of life in Japan . . . and captures the essence of that strange, exotic country on the brink of war," wrote Barbara Lipkien Gershenbaum in online *Bookreporter.* Calling the book a "superb thriller," *Booklist* contributor Bill Ott noted, "When Smith chooses a place to write about, he makes it his own." Barbara Conaty, writing in *Library Journal,* said that "the locale is as evocative as the cherry blossom itself."

In an interview for *Geographical,* Smith, who researches and visits all of his books' locales, noted that he likes to write about unfamiliar places. "If anything, it gives me a great advantage," he noted. "When I start, I'm aware of the extent of my ignorance, so I naturally question everything." Smith went on to comment, "There are things you experience that are so basic that people just don't tell you. It's a little bit like people telling you about going to sea—nobody bothers to tell you that it is salty. They always overlook the details."

BIOGRAPHICAL AND CRITICAL SOURCES:

BOOKS

Riggs, Thomas, editor, *Reference Guide to American Literature,* St. James Press (Detroit, MI), 2000.
St. James Guide to Horror, Ghost & Gothic Writers, St. James Press (Detroit, MI), 1998.

PERIODICALS

Armchair Detective, fall, 1990, pp. 422-423.
Booklist, May 1, 2000, Bill Ott, review of *Havana Bay,* p. 1590; August, 2002, Bill Ott, review of *December 6,* p. 1887.
Books Magazine, April, 1996, p. 14.
Chicago Tribune, March 25, 1981; July 19, 1992, p. 9.
Chicago Tribune Book World, April 19, 1981; May 11, 1986.
Geographical, December, 2002, interview with Martin Cruz Smith, p. 130.
Kirkus Reviews, June 15, 2002, review of *December 6,* p. 837.
Library Journal, May 1, 1999, Barbara Conaty, review of *Havana Bay,* p. 113; August, 2002, Barbara Conaty, review of *December 6,* p. 147.
London Review of Books, September 4, 1986, pp. 18-19; December 7 1989, p. 19.
Los Angeles Times Book Review, April 19, 1981; May 11, 1986; June 24, 1990.
Maclean's, May 4, 1981, p. 56.
Nation, April 4, 1981, pp. 406-407.
New Republic, May 9, 1981, pp. 37-38.
Newsweek, April 6, 1981; May 25, 1981; April 14, 1986; September 14, 1992, p. 70.
New Yorker, April 6, 1981, pp. 181-182.
New York Times, March 19, 1981; October 12, 1992, p. C20; May 1, 1996, p. B2.
New York Times Book Review, April 5, 1981; May 3, 1981; May 4, 1986; July 16, 1989, pp. 33-34; July 15, 1990, p. 32; October 18, 1992, pp. 45-46; June 16, 1996, p. 50.
People, June 3, 1996, p. 35.
Playboy, December, 1992, p. 34.
Publishers Weekly, May 3, 1999, review of *Havana Bay,* p. 68; August 5, 2002, review of *December 6,* p. 50.
Saturday Review, April, 1981, pp. 66-67.
Time, March 30, 1981; May 12, 1986; November 16, 1992, p. 98; June 3, 1996, p. 73.
Times Literary Supplement, June 5, 1981; December 8, 1989, p. 1369.
Wall Street Journal, May 18, 1981, p. 26; May 29, 1996, p. A16.
Washington Post Book World, March 29, 1981; April 30, 1986; July 2, 1989, p. 5; November 1, 1992, p. 3; May 5, 1996, p. 1.
West Coast Review of Books, 1986, p. 25.

ONLINE

Bookreporter.com, http://www.bookreporter.com/ (October 9, 2002), Barbara Lipkien Gershenbaum, review of *December 6;* interview with Martin Cruz Smith (April 30, 2003).
Martin Cruz Smith Home Page, http://literati.net/MCSmith/ (December 9, 2002).
Post-Gazette Web site (Pittsburgh, PA), http://www.post-gazette.com/ (October 9, 2002), Jim Strader, review of *Havana Bay,* August 22, 1999.
Salon.com, http://www.salon.com/ (October 9, 2002), "The Salon Interview: Working in a Coal Mine."

* * *

SMITH, Rolando (R.) Hinojosa
See HINOJOSA, Rolando

* * *

SMITH, Rosamond
See OATES, Joyce Carol

* * *

SMITH, Wilbur 1933-
(Wilbur Addison Smith)

PERSONAL: Born January 9, 1933, in Broken Hill, Northern Rhodesia (now Zambia); son of Herbert James and Elfreda (Lawrence) Smith; married Jewell Slabbert, August 28, 1964 (divorced); married Danielle Thomas, February 1971; children: two sons and one daughter. *Education:* Rhodes University, Bachelor of Commerce, 1954. *Hobbies and other interests:* Fishing and wildlife conservation.

ADDRESSES: *Home*—Sunbird Hill, 34 Klaassens Road, Constantia 7800, South Africa. *Agent*—Charles Pick Consultancy, Flat 3, 3 Bryanston Place, London W1H 7FN, England. *E-mail*—wilbur.smith\@stmartins.com.

CAREER: Affiliated with Goodyear Tire & Rubber Co., Port Elizabeth, South Africa, 1954-58, and H.J. Smith & Son, Ltd., Salisbury, Rhodesia (now Zimbabwe), 1958-63; full-time writer, 1964—.

MEMBER: Chartered Institute of Secretaries, South African Wildlife Society (trustee), Friends of Conservation (trustee), Rhodesian Wildlife Conservation Association, British Sub Aqua Club.

WRITINGS:

When the Lion Feeds, Viking (New York, NY), 1964.

The Train from Katanga, Viking (New York, NY), 1965, published as *The Dark of the Sun,* Heinemann (London, England), 1965.

Shout at the Devil, Coward (New York, NY), 1968.

Gold Mine, Doubleday (New York, NY), 1970.

The Diamond Hunters, Heinemann (London, England), 1971, Doubleday (New York, NY), 1972.

The Sunbird, Heinemann (London, England), 1972, Doubleday (New York, NY), 1973.

Eagle in the Sky, Doubleday (New York, NY), 1974.

Eye of the Tiger, Doubleday (New York, NY), 1974.

Cry Wolf, Doubleday (New York, NY), 1975.

A Sparrow Falls, Doubleday (New York, NY), 1976.

Hungry As the Sea, Doubleday (New York, NY), 1977.

Wild Justice, Doubleday (New York, NY), 1978.

A Falcon Flies, Doubleday, 1979 (New York, NY), published as *Flight of the Falcon,* Doubleday (New York, NY), 1982.

Men of Men, Doubleday (New York, NY), 1980.

The Delta Decision, Doubleday (New York, NY), 1981.

The Angels Weep, Doubleday (New York, NY), 1983.

The Leopard Hunts in Darkness, Doubleday (New York, NY), 1984.

The Burning Shore, Doubleday (New York, NY), 1985.

Power of the Sword, Little, Brown (Boston, MA), 1986.

Rage, Little, Brown (Boston, MA), 1987.

The Courtneys, Little, Brown (Boston, MA), 1988.

A Time to Die, Random House (New York, NY), 1989.

Golden Fox, Random House (New York, NY), 1990.

Elephant Song, Random House (New York, NY), 1991.

The Sound of Thunder, Fawcett (New York, NY), 1991.

River God, St. Martin's Press (New York, NY), 1994.

The Seventh Scroll, St. Martin's Press (New York, NY), 1995.

Birds of Prey, St. Martin's Press (New York, NY), 1997.

Monsoon, St. Martin's Press (New York, NY), 1999.

Warlock, Macmillan (New York, NY), 2001.

The Blue Horizon, St. Martin's Press (New York, NY), 2003.

Writer for British Broadcasting Corp. (BBC) programs.

ADAPTATIONS: The Dark of the Sun was filmed by Metro-Goldwyn-Mayer and released in 1968; *Gold Mine* was filmed by Hemdale and released in 1974; the film rights to *The Leopard Hunts in Darkness* have been purchased by Sylvester Stallone, as have the film rights of two of Smith's other novels. Most of Smith's novels have been adapted for audiocassette.

SIDELIGHTS: A writer of historical adventure sagas, Wilbur Smith is known for his "swashbuckling adventure novels set against the historical backdrop of Africa," as an essayist for *Contemporary Popular Writers* explained. His novels have sold some 100 million copies throughout the world. Smith once told *CA:* "I am essentially a writer of entertainment fiction. So far most of my work is against the background of southern Africa. My interests are the history of this land, its wildlife, and its people. . . . I speak Afrikaans and some African dialects, including Zulu."

Born in Northern Rhodesia, now Zambia, Smith was first discouraged from writing by his father, who thought the profession would not pay well. Speaking to Jonah Hull of the *Out There* Web site about his father, Smith explained: "He was a hard man, but a fair one, who wanted me to do something sensible with my life, like be an accountant. I actually was an accountant for a while in my twenties. That made him happy. When I got seriously into writing, though, he couldn't understand it. I think it puzzled him to his death. He wasn't a man who read many books. In fact, I seriously doubt if he actually read any of my books. Even the first one which I dedicated to him." Following a divorce, which brought on depression, Smith began to write fiction to take himself away from the realities of his daily life. While working a day job with the Rhodesian tax department, he spent his nights working on a novel, *When the Lion Feeds.* The story of an early European pioneer in Southern Africa who fights off the native Zulus and rival Europeans as he searches for gold, the novel proved an enormous success. Smith first gained international success in 1964 with the novel *When the Lion Feeds,* according to a writer for *Geographical.* "His name has since become synonymous with adventure blockbuster writing."

Smith's three related novels—*A Falcon Flies, Men of Men,* and *The Angels Weep*—are concerned with the European conquest of what is now Zimbabwe. In this trilogy, the Ballantynes, a fictional family, challenge the historical figure Cecil Rhodes, who amassed a fortune in South Africa and after whom both the nation of Rhodesia and the Rhodes scholarships were named. The essayist for *Contemporary Popular Writers* explained that "in this series, the novels' plots are intertwined with the tumultuous history of Rhodesia, including the slave trade, diamond mining, and tribal warfare." The *Washington Post*'s Richard Harwood, reviewing *Men of Men,* compared Smith favorably to other historical thriller writers: "Wilbur Smith is more artful than John Jakes and less pedantic than James Michener." Roger Manvell, who reviewed *A Falcon Flies* for *British Book News,* praised Smith for the detail of this work; he observed: "The author, who seems to possess an unrivalled knowledge of his subject, writes with an impressive authenticity, as if he had himself taken part in these varied actions a century and more ago." Cliff Glaviano of *Library Journal* found *A Falcon Flies* to be "full of adventure, romance, sex, blood, and gore and set in central and southern Africa and on the surrounding high seas about 1860."

In *Monsoon* Hal Courtney leaves his African estate to hunt down pirates preying on British shipping off the East African coast in the late 1700s. Taking his three sons into the battle with him, Courtney soon finds that the pirate hunt is only part of his mission; keeping his scheming and ambitious sons alive is also a challenge. Writing in *Booklist,* Vanessa Bush found that "readers who love swashbucklers will enjoy"*Monsoon,* while Kathy Piehl in the *Library Journal* noted: "Smith offers plenty of battles and harrowing escapes for adventure fans." A critic for *Publishers Weekly* concluded: "Once again the veteran author creates a masterful tale of action and suspense set on the high seas, arid deserts and steaming jungles."

Smith explored new historical territory in his three books set in ancient Egypt, *River God, The Seventh Scroll,* and *Warlock.* In these books, set some 4,000 years ago, he weaves a complex tale of royal intrigue, betrayal, and assassination. A tale of fictional pharaohs and eunuchs, *River God* concerns the warrior Tanus and a young woman who loves him, Lostris, whose father conspires to have her married off to the pharaoh instead. Complete with battles involving thousands of soldiers, descriptions of resplendent palaces, and crowds of hundreds of thousands of people on the banks of the Nile greeting their pharaoh, the book was hailed as "compulsively readable" by a *Publishers Weekly* reviewer. Similarly, Brian Jacomb of the *Washington Post Book World* declared it a "majestic novel, one filled to overflowing with passion, rage, treachery, barbarism, prolonged excitement and endless passages of sheer, exquisite color."

Smith followed *River God* with a sequel, *The Seventh Scroll.* Set in the present, the novel is the story of an adventurous search for the tomb of the Pharaoh Mamose, husband of Lostris. At the story's opening, Egyptologist Royan Al Simma and her husband, Duraid, have discovered a scroll from the tomb of Lostris that purports to tell the location of Mamose's tomb. However, Duraid is murdered by a rival. Royan then teams up with Sir Nicholas Quenton-Harper, a wealthy collector mourning the deaths of his wife and child. The two battle villainous rivals, booby traps, and other dangerous events in a race to find the tomb. A *Publishers Weekly* reviewer called the novel "intoxicating."

In *Warlock,* Smith's third novel about ancient Egypt, Taita, lover of the deceased queen Lostris, goes into the desert to live as a hermit. Studying magic, he becomes a mighty warlock with remarkable powers. Because of his power, Taita becomes tutor to young Prince Nefer, heir to the Egyptian throne. He finds that his magical skills are tested when rivals plot to kill the young prince. According to Kathleen Hughes in *Booklist,* in her review of *Warlock,* "Smith is an excellent storyteller, and the fast-moving action and the exciting plot will hook even those who normally don't appreciate historical fiction." Speaking of the same novel, the critic for *Publishers Weekly* noted that "though timorous readers may wish to steer clear, those willing to brave the blood and gore will be carried away by the sweep and pace of Smith's tale." "This most recent novel by a master storyteller," Jane Baird wrote of *Warlock* in *Library Journal,* "is resplendent with all the power and pageantry of Egypt, the center of civilization of the ancient world."

Some critics have faulted Smith's novels for their politics. Rob Nixon, writing in the *Village Voice Literary Supplement,* for example, criticized Smith for championing colonialism: "At a time when anti-apartheid literature crowds the shelves, *A Time To Die* serves as a reminder that a considerable audience remains for writing that glamorizes South African racism." But many other critics praise Smith for his masterful storytelling. Writing in the *Washington Post Book World,* Bruce Van-Wyngarden, in his review of *Power of the Sword,* noted that "the book's principal strengths lie in the author's considerable storytelling talents and his compelling way with action sequences. Smith writes with real panache about fighting and riding and shooting and bleeding."

Simon Ritchie of the *This Is York* Web site claimed: "Smith must surely be the world's greatest living storyteller."

BIOGRAPHICAL AND CRITICAL SOURCES:

BOOKS

Contemporary Literary Criticism, Volume 33, Thomson Gale (Detroit, MI), 1985.

Contemporary Popular Writers, St. James Press (Detroit, MI), 1997.

PERIODICALS

Booklist, March 1, 2001, Kathleen Hughes, review of *Warlock,* p. 1189; March 15, 2003, Margaret Flanagan, review of *The Blue Horizon,* p. 1254.

British Book News, August, 1980.

Geographical, April, 2001, "The Write Stuff," p. 114.

Guardian Weekly, August 19, 1990.

Kirkus Reviews, March 15, 2003, review of *The Blue Horizon,* p. 426.

Library Journal, May 15, 1999, Kathy Piehl, review of *Monsoon,* p. 128; April 15, 2001, Jane Baird, review of *Warlock,* p. 134; December, 2001, Cliff Glaviano, review of audiocassette edition of *Warlock,* p. 199; July, 2002, Cliff Glaviano, reviews of audiocassette editions of *The Angels Weep, The Leopard Hunts in Darkness,* and *Wild Justice,* p. 141; May 15, 2003, Robert Conroy, review of *The Blue Horizon,* p. 127; October 1, 2003, Cliff Glaviano, audiobook review of the audiobook version of *The Blue Horizon,* p. 132.

Listener, April 4, 1974.

Los Angeles Times Book Review, November 22, 1987; April 8, 1990.

M2 Best Books, February 19, 2002, "Best-Selling Author in Trust Fund Legal Battle."

New Statesman, October 20, 1972.

New York Times Book Review, October 25, 1970; April 23, 1972; July 29, 1973; May 30, 1976; September 4, 1977; February 24, 1980; April 26, 1981.

Publishers Weekly, December 6, 1993; March 20, 1995, p. 42; May 1, 1995, p. 38; April 26, 1999, review of *Monsoon,* p. 55; April 9, 2001, review of *Warlock,* p. 49; June 3, 2002, review of audiocassette edition of *Cry Wolf,* p. 32; April 28, 2003, review of *The Blue Horizon,* p. 426.

Spectator, July 6, 1991.

Times (London, England), April 30, 1981; June 16, 1990.

Tribune Books (Chicago, IL), April 21, 1991; February 16, 1992.

Village Voice Literary Supplement, July-August, 1990.

Virginia Quarterly Review, winter, 1978; summer, 1992.

Washington Post, August 3, 1983; August 4, 1984; October 7, 1985; September 20, 1986; October 9, 1987.

Washington Post Book World, September 20, 1986; February 24, 1994.

ONLINE

Liquid Review Web site, http://users.chariot.net.au/˜rastous/wilbur.htm/ (April 10, 2003), Stuart Beaton, interview with Wilbur Smith and Danielle Thomas.

Out There Web site, http://www.outthere.co.za/ (October, 1997), Jonah Hull, interview with Wilbur Smith.

This Is York Web site, http://www.thisisyork.co.uk/ (March 19, 2003), Simon Ritchie, "Licence to Thrill."

Wilbur Smith Books Web site, http://www.wilbursmithbooks.com/ (April 10, 2003).

* * *

SMITH, Wilbur Addison
See SMITH, Wilbur

* * *

SMITH, Zadie 1976-

PERSONAL: Born 1976, in England; daughter of an advertising executive and a child psychologist. *Education:* Cambridge University, B.A., 1998; attended Harvard University's Radcliffe Institute for Advanced Study.

ADDRESSES: Home—London, England. *Office*—c/o Author Mail, Random House, 299 Park Ave., New York, NY 10171- 0002.

CAREER: Novelist.

AWARDS, HONORS: Whitbread Award, 2000, for *White Teeth;* named one of the Granta Best of Young British Novelists, 2003; Orange Prize for Fiction nomination, and Jewish Quarterly Wingate Prize, both 2003, both for *The Autograph Man;* Man Booker Prize shortlist, 2005, and Commonwealth Writers' Prize (Eurasia region), both for *On Beauty.*

WRITINGS:

White Teeth: A Novel, Random House (New York, NY), 2000.

The Autograph Man, Random House (New York, NY), 2002.

On Beauty, Hamish Hamilton (New York, NY), 2005.

ADAPTATIONS: White Teeth was adapted into a British Broadcast Corporation four-part television mini-series, 2002.

SIDELIGHTS: British novelist Zadie Smith burst into the international fiction scene with the publication of her debut novel *White Teeth* in 2000, and was immediately hailed as a new voice in British literature. The half-Jamaican Smith has since been lauded for her multicultural exploration in *White Teeth,* which was written during her years as an undergraduate at Cambridge University. As Askhari Hodari commented in a review of *White Teeth* for *Black Issues Book Review,* Smith "has produced something few would expect from a twenty-something first-time novelist. Golf has Tiger Woods, basketball has Kobe Bryant, and now literature has Zadie Smith. What is this generation coming to?"

White Teeth is the story of the "lifelong friendship between Archie, a white, working-class Londoner, and Samad, a Muslim from Bangladesh, with issues of race, religion, generational conflict and genetically modified mice thrown spicily in to the pot," summarized Sarah Lyall in an interview with Smith in the *New York Times Book Review.* "Theirs is a relationship born of World War II, forged on a lie and nourished on the greasy eggs served at O'Connell's Pool House, which, by the way, is neither Irish nor a pool hall. In fact, nothing in their lives has turned out as it seemed it would," noted Susan Horsburgh in *Time.*

Critics were enthusiastic in their response to the book. "When Zadie Smith published her first book in Britain earlier this year, the press and literati agreed: the novel and the novelist were 'drop-dead cool,'" commented Jeff Giles in *Newsweek.* A *Publishers Weekly* critic called the book a "stunning, polymathic debut . . . . Smith's novel recalls the hyper-contemporary yet history-infused work of Rushdie, sharp-edged, fluorescent and many-faceted." A critic for *Economist* found the work clever, continuing: "But lots of novels are clever, and what makes this one true and original is the way the comedy fizzes up through the characters. Dickens, not Salman Rushdie, comes to mind, with all his theatricality and exuberance."

Though Giles felt that the plot was "tortured" and the work as a whole had too many characters, he lauded Smith as an "astonishing intellect. She writes sharp dialogue for every age and race—and she's funny as hell." Anthony Quinn in the *New York Times Book Review,* wondering if Smith has taken on a task beyond her reach with *White Teeth,* found that "aside from a rather wobbly final quarter, Smith holds it all together with a raucous energy and confidence that couldn't be a fluke." "Imagine Charlie Parker with a typewriter, Coltrane with a laptop," wrote Greg Tate in *Village Voice.* "Incredibly enough, Smith just might be even smarter than her smackdown writing declares her to be."

Although Smith's second novel, *The Autograph Man,* was met with decidedly mixed reviews, her third novel, *On Beauty,* earned international acclaim. The novel confirmed that Smith is certainly the prominent contemporary writer critics have declared her to be. *On Beauty* takes place in England and New England, and it follows the rivalry of two professors and the interminglings of the members of their respective families. The novel is concerned with race, politics, and love; each issue plays itself out in the conflicts that occur between the characters' intellectual ideals and their baser desires. *Library Journal* reviewer Barbara Hoffert also noted that a prominent theme in the book focuses on love and even stated that the book should have been titled "On Love" because "it is the ties binding this family—and those coming apart—that really matter." Additionally, a *Publishers Weekly* contributor commended Smith's "insightful probing of what makes life complicated (and beautiful)." And of the several characters in the story, *Time International* writer Lillian Kennett stated: "You are not simply entertained by the writer's versatility and brilliant characters; you really care about these people." Kennett also commented that *On Beauty* "is striking for the maturity of its sensibility and suggests that Smith is, indeed, a talent to watch over the long haul."

BIOGRAPHICAL AND CRITICAL SOURCES:

PERIODICALS

Black Issues Book Review, September, 2000, Askhari Hodari, "The Mystique of Zadie Smith," p. 26.

Booklist, April 1, 2000, Danise Hoover, review of *White Teeth,* p. 1436; August, 2005, Barbara Hoffert, review of *On Beauty,* p. 73.

Commonweal, August 11, 2000, Anita Mathias, review of *White Teeth,* p. 27.

Economist, February 19, 2000, review of *White Teeth,* p. 5.

Hudson Review, winter, 2001, Tom Wilhelmus, review of *White Teeth,* p. 694.

Library Journal, April 1, 2000, Rebecca A. Stuhr, review of *White Teeth,* p. 132.

New Republic, July 24, 2000, James Wood, "Human, All Too Inhuman: The Smallness of the 'Big' Novel," p. 41.

New Statesman & Society, January 29, 2001, Jason Cowley, "The Tiger Woods of Literature?," p. 57.

Newsweek, May 1, 2000, Jeff Giles, review of *White Teeth,* p. 73.

New York Review of Books, February 8, 2001, John Lanchester, review of *White Teeth,* p. 28.

New York Times Book Review, April 30, 2000, Anthony Quinn, review of *White Teeth,* pp. 7-8; April 30, 2000, Sarah Lyall, "A Good Start" (interview), p. 8;; October 6, 2002, Daniel Zalewski, review of *The Autograph Man,* p. 13.

Publishers Weekly, March 13, 2000, review of *White Teeth,* p. 60; August 1, 2005, review of *On Beauty,* p. 44.

Time, May 8, 2000, "Of Roots and Family Trees," p. 94; September 30, 2002, James Poniewozik, review of *The Autograph Man,* p. 92.

Time International, September 19, 2005, Lillian Kennett, review of *On Beauty,* p. 54.

Times Literary Supplement, January 21, 2000, Sukhdev Sandhu, "Excremental Children," p. 21.

Village Voice, May 16, 2000, Greg Tate, review of *White Teeth,* p. 75.

World & I, September, 2000, Merritt Mosley, review of *White Teeth,* p. 220.

World Literature Today, winter, 2001, Bruce King, review of *White Teeth,* p. 116.

Yale Review, July, 2000, Meghan O'Rourke, review of *White Teeth,* p. 159.

* * *

SNICKET, Lemony 1970-
[A pseudonym]
(Daniel Handler)

PERSONAL: Born Daniel Handler, 1970, in San Francisco, CA; married Lisa Brown. *Education:* Wesleyan University.

ADDRESSES: *Home*—San Francisco, CA. *Office*—c/o Author Mail, HarperCollins, 10 East 53rd St., New York, NY 10022. *E-mail*—lsnicket@harpercollins.com.

CAREER: Author, poet, and self-styled "studied expert in rhetorical analysis." Comedy writer, "The House of Blues Radio Hour," San Francisco, CA; freelance book, music, and movie reviewer.

AWARDS, HONORS: Academy of American Poets Prize, 1990; Olin Fellowship, 1992.

WRITINGS:

ADULT FICTION; AS DANIEL HANDLER

The Basic Eight, St. Martin's Press (New York, NY), 1999.

Watch Your Mouth, St. Martin's Press (New York, NY), 2000.

JUVENILE FICTION; AS LEMONY SNICKET; "A SERIES OF UNFORTUNATE EVENTS" SERIES

The Bad Beginning, illustrated by Bret Helquist, HarperTrophy (New York, NY), 1999.

The Reptile Room, illustrated by Bret Helquist, HarperTrophy (New York, NY), 1999.

The Wide Window, illustrated by Bret Helquist, HarperTrophy (New York, NY), 2000.

The Miserable Mill, illustrated by Bret Helquist, HarperTrophy (New York, NY), 2000.

The Austere Academy, illustrated by Bret Helquist, HarperTrophy (New York, NY), 2000.

The Ersatz Elevator, illustrated by Bret Helquist, HarperTrophy (New York, NY), 2001.

The Vile Village, illustrated by Bret Helquist, HarperTrophy (New York, NY), 2001.

The Hostile Hospital, illustrated by Bret Helquist, HarperTrophy (New York, NY), 2001.

A Series of Unfortunate Events (omnibus; contains *The Bad Beginning, The Reptile Room,* and *The Wide Window*), HarperTrophy (New York, NY), 2001.

Lemony Snicket: The Unauthorized Autobiography, HarperTrophy (New York, NY), 2002.

The Grim Grotto, HarperCollins (New York, NY), 2004.

The Penultimate Peril, Egmont Books, 2005.

Handler has also written for the *Voice Literary Supplement, Newsday, Salon,* and the *New York Times.* "A Series of Unfortunate Events" has been published in England, Canada, Germany, Italy, Norway, Israel, Japan, and Denmark. Handler also wrote the screenplay for *Rick,* an independent film, 2004.

ADAPTATIONS: The Basic Eight was optioned for a film by New Regency, a division of Warner Brothers; Dreamworks and Paramount Pictures plan to film *Lemony Snicket's Series of Unfortunate Events.* The movie will be directed by Brad Silberling.

WORK IN PROGRESS: Writing as Daniel Handler, a third novel, about pirates. Writing as Lemony Snicket, more volumes in the "A Series of Unfortunate Events." Adaptation of a movie for the Independent Film Channel from Joel Rose's novel, *Kill the Poor,* and a movie script with songwriter Stephin Merritt of the band The Magnetic Fields.

SIDELIGHTS: Daniel Handler has a fine sense of timing. As a writer for adults, he has produced two popular novels which have had an eerie prescience to them: his 1999 *The Basic Eight* deals, partly in a tongue-in-cheek manner, with a teenage murder, and hit the shelves just a month before the tragic events at Colorado's Columbine High School focused the nation's attention on teen violence; his second novel, a "mock-operatic incest comedy" as Amy Benfer of *Salon* described *Watch Your Mouth,*came out in time to benefit from a similar theme broached at the Oscar awards ceremony of 2000.

However, it is his juvenile writings, penned under the pseudonym of Lemony Snicket, that have most benefitted from chronological serendipity: "A Series of Unfortunate Events" has ridden the tsunami created by J.K. Rowling's "Harry Potter" books, tapping into a youthful readership eager to deal with irony, intelligent silliness, and Goth-like depressing situations in their fiction. When the *New York Times Book Review,* influenced by the huge sales of the "Harry Potter" books, initiated a children's bestseller list, Mr. Snicket weighed in at number fifteen; within a year, all five of the books written by the illusive and mysterious Mr. Snicket had made the top twenty-five, and the series had been optioned by Nickelodeon for a film treatment.

Handler was born and raised in San Francisco, the son of an accountant and a college dean. Growing up, Handler was "a bright and obvious person," as he characterized himself for Sally Lodge in *Publishers Weekly.* However, the incipient novelist "always wanted to be a dark, mysterious person."In books, he preferred stories "in which mysterious and creepy things happen," he told Lodge, hating books "where everyone joined the softball team and had a grand time or found true love on a picnic." The youthful Handler sought out stories à la Roald Dahl or Edward Gorey, and indeed his fiction for juveniles has often been compared to that duo. Snicket enjoyed reading the sort of things "set in an eerie castle that was invaded by a snake that strangled the residents." The first book Handler bought with his own money was Gorey's *The Blue Aspic.*

A student of San Francisco's prestigious and demanding Lowell High School, Handler graduated in 1988, tying for Best Personality of his graduating class. Eleven years later, Handler set his first novel at a barely concealed stand-in for this school, Roewer High with students "pushed to the limit academically, socially and athletically," as Handler wrote. After high school graduation, Handler attended Wesleyan University, winning a Poets Prize from the Academy of American Poets in 1990. His love for poetry soon developed into a passion for novels. "My poems were getting longer and longer, and more proselike," Handler commented to Greg Toppo in an Associated Press story carried on *CNNfyi.com.* Upon graduation, he received an Olin Fellowship which provided him with the financial support to work on his first novel. Publication of that book, however, would come several years later. Meanwhile, there was a living to be earned. Handler spent a couple of years in the mid-1990s writing comedy sketches for a nationally syndicated radio show based in San Francisco, "The House of Blues Radio Hour."

Things began looking up for Handler when he moved to New York City and began his literary career as a free-lance movie and book critic. By 1999, his first novel, *The Basic Eight,* was finally published and earned respectful if not praiseworthy reviews in major media. *The Basic Eight,* though written for adults, caused some reviewers and booksellers to label it YA as it focused on a cast of high school students in a clique called The Basic Eight. The school in question, Roewer High, was plainly a thinly disguised Lowell High in San Francisco. As Handler told Philana Woo in his alma mater's paper, *The Lowell,* "When I was at Lowell, it was called Roewer. . . . Lowell then was predominantly Asian, . . . and Roewer was the name people of all races referred to it. It was sort of the kids' joke about the fact that most of the school was Asian. I guess Roewer could be an offensive way of making a pun on an Asian accent."

Essentially beginning at the end of the action, *The Basic Eight* is narrated by Flannery Culp, who depicts the events of her senior year at Roewer High from her journal written in prison where she is serving time for the murder of a teacher and fellow student. Flan is, as a reviewer for *Publishers Weekly* observed, "precocious" and "pretentious," and now means to set the record straight. Reviled in the press as a leader of a Satanic cult, Flan has kept her journal to tell the real truth of the tragicomic events that have landed her in prison instead of in some Ivy League school.

At school, Flan, editor of the student paper but having trouble in calculus, relies on her seven friends—the "Queen Bee" Kate, lovely Natasha whom Flan admires, Gabriel, a black student and chef in the making who has a crush on Flan, Douglas, who has access to absinthe, V, whose name has been changed to provide anonymity to her wealthy family, Lily, and Jennifer Rose Milton. These eight form the elitist clique in question. Childhood games turn serious when the group begins experimenting with absinthe; Natasha comes to Flan's rescue by poisoning a biology teacher who has been plaguing her. There is also Adam State, love interest of Flan's, and it is her jealousy that ultimately leads to his murder—by croquet mallet—as well. The talk show circuit quickly picks up on the story, calling these privileged kids a Satanic cult.

Handler's characters are all coming of age and aping the adult world of their parents by throwing dinner parties and toting around hip flasks. "The links between teen social life, tabloid culture and serious violence have been explored below and exploited before," noted the reviewer for *Publishers Weekly,* "but Handler, and Flannery, know that. If they're not the first to use such material, they may well be the coolest." This same reviewer concluded, "Handler's confident satire is not only cheeky but packed with downright lovable characters whose youthful misadventures keep the novel neatly balanced between absurdity and poignancy." *Booklist*'s Stephanie Zvirin called the book "Part horror story, part black comedy," noting that *The Basic Eight* shows what can happen to "smart, privileged, cynical teens with too few rules, too much to drink, too little supervision, and boundless imagination." Zvirin felt that *The Basic Eight* "will leave readers on the brink of both laughter and despair." *Library Journal*'s Rebecca Kelm found Handler's writing to be "witty and perceptive, especially as schools and society are parodied," and the reviewer also noted his "clever use of vocabulary and study questions" that poke fun at the conventions of literary criticism in high schools. Kelm's admiration for the book, however, was tempered with the brutal murder at its center.

Other reviewers also had mixed praise. A writer for the *New Yorker* commented, "Handler is a charming writer with a lovely mastery of voice, but the book is weakened by his attempt to turn a clever idea into a social satire." Brian Howard, writing in *Citypaper.net,* felt that Handler "beautifully captures the ennui and distorted perspectives of a suburban upbringing, where dinner parties are the biggest concern." Howard also pointed to "a lot of excellent suspense writing" in the book, but concluded that "the oh-my-gosh plot twist, which ultimately ruins Culp's credibility, also does much to undo Handler's otherwise fine debut."

Handler told Woo in *The Lowell* that his theme with his first novel "is that young people are oftentimes full of great ideas and creativity and that those things are often stifled." For his second novel, *Watch Your Mouth,* Handler chose another coming of age crucible, the college years. Joseph is just finishing his junior year at prestigious Mather College. There he has met luscious and lascivious Cynthia Glass, whom he delights in calling Cyn with its intended double meaning. A surfeit of sex has caused Joseph to fall behind in his studies and earn an incomplete in one class. When Cyn recommends that Joseph spend the summer with her and her family in Pittsburgh, he leaps at the chance to stay close to his lover. There the two will work days as Jewish day-camp counselors, Joseph will finish his incomplete, and their nights will be their own.

Once settled in the Glass's home, however, Joseph is filled with a sort of foreboding. "Perhaps it's the summer heat in his attic room,"noted Ted Leventhal in a *Booklist* review of *Watch Your Mouth,* "or the overly erotic environment, but Joseph begins to imagine that there is something unhealthy about the family's intimacy." It seems father Ben pines for his daughter, Cyn; that mother Mimi yearns for her son, Stephen, and that Stephen may return the favor. Is this a product of Joseph's warped imagination, or is there any truth in it?

Joseph soon discovers or uncovers a triad of fascinations for the family: science, Kabbalah, and, well, incest. And in the basement, is that a golem Mrs. Glass is constructing? Written in the form of an opera, the novel employs realism and surrealism side by side, references to Judaism and modern literature share the same page. Billed as an "incest comedy," the novel steps perilously close to the bounds of good taste. "Did I hear you right, Mr. Reviewer, did you say 'incest comedy'?" wrote Jonathan Shipley in a *BookBrowser* review. "That's 'comedy'? It can be if you write it right. And who writes it right. Daniel Handler. Handler, the author of the critically-acclaimed *The Basic Eight,* comes back with a very odd, quirky, unusual story." A *Publishers Weekly* reviewer felt that Handler's second novel is so "twisted that even its protagonist can't keep up with the perverse turns of plot," and further observed that "this melodramatic satire of family life trembles between virtuosity and utter collapse." *Library Journal*'s Kelm called the book "quirky" and "offbeat," while *Salon*'s Edward Neuert noted that Handler "is more than ready to pick up the torch [of Kurt Vonnegut] and write the kind of deftly funny absurdist story that both horrifies with its subject matter and hooks you with its humor." Leventhal concluded his review noting that there are "plays within plays and puns within puns. . . . *Mouth* is clever, witty, and unpredictable."

If Handler has a way of getting away with the quirky novel or two, his alter ego, Lemony Snicket has perfected the gambit. "Try pitching this as a series of children's novels," wrote Toppo. "Three young siblings—handsome, clever and rich—lose their loving parents in a fire that destroys their mansion. Too gloomy? It gets worse." And indeed it does, in the ongoing adventures of "A Series of Unfortunate Events," siblings Violet, Klaus, and Sunny Baudelaire not only lose their parents, but are then set upon by the vile Count Olaf, whose one goal in life, it seems, is to bilk the children out of their fortune. After a close encounter with this dastardly villain in the opening novel of the series, *The Bad Beginning,* the children make their painful way from one relative to the next, each more hideous than the last. The Count, of course, makes reprise appearances in each successive volume, much to the delight of the legion of young readers these books have attracted. The trio of kids is led by inventive fourteen-year-old Violet, her rather bookish brother, twelve-year-old Klaus, and baby Sunny who has incredibly sharp teeth for an infant and employs a baby argot that speaks volumes. Eschewing the magic of Harry Potter, Snicket/Handler has imbued these children with survival skills of a more practical nature, enabling them to defend themselves from a cornucopia of hurled knives, falling lamps, storms, snakes, leeches, and just plain rotten folks. And all of this is related in a deadpan, sophisticated text that has its tongue firmly planted in cheek.

The birth of Lemony Snicket was actually influenced by Handler's debut novel, *The Basic Eight.* Susan Rich, editor at HarperTrophy and a fan of Handler's first novel, decided to try and woo him over to children's books. "I knew we shared a similar sensibility about children's books," Rich told Lodge in *Publishers Weekly,* "which I'd define as a resistance to fall into overly trodden paths of traditional stories, and a resistance to anything that is too sweet or patronizing or moralistic." Handler was at first resistant, but offered the chance to pen books he might have enjoyed reading himself when he was ten, he set to reworking the hundred or so pages of a mock-Gothic novel for adults that he had long ago abandoned. Handler, writing as Snicket—a name he had once devised to avoid getting on unwanted mail lists—was delighted to revamp the entire notion of what constitutes an appropriate novel for juveniles, repealing the old sports or fantasy categories that were available to him as a youth. The result was *The Bad Beginning,* the first of what Handler/Snicket see as a thirteen-volume set chronicling the adventures of the Baudelaire orphans. "If you are interested in stories with happy endings," the author wrote on the first page of that novel, "you would be better off reading some other book. In this book, not only is there no happy ending, there is no happy beginning and very few happy things in the middle. . . . I'm sorry to tell you this, but that's how the story goes."

When the three Baudelaire children lose their parents in a fire, they become—through the oversight of the ineffectual banker, Mr. Poe—wards of Count Olaf, a distant cousin. He sets them to labor in his house, meanwhile devising schemes with his theatrical troupe to deprive the orphans of their inheritance. The three survive the Count's attacks with spunk, initiative, and, in the case of Sunny, a set of sharp teeth. "The author uses formal, Latinate language and intrusive commentary to hilarious effect," noted a review for *Publishers Weekly* of this first title in the series. The same reviewer felt that the author "paints the satire with such broad strokes that most readers will view it from a safe distance." In the second book of the series, *The Reptile Room,* it seems the orphans will have a chance for happiness when they go to live with Dr. Montgomery Montgomery, a "very fun, but fatally naïve herpetologist," according to Ron Charles in the *Christian Science Monitor.* Unfortunately, their safe haven is short-lived, spoiled once again by the arrival of the oafish Count Olaf. Susan Dove Lempke, reviewing the first two titles in *Booklist,*thought that the "droll humor, reminiscent of Edward Gorey's, will be lost on some children; others may not enjoy the old-fashioned storytelling style that frequently addresses the reader directly and includes definitions of terms." Lempke went on, however, to conclude: "But plenty of children will laugh at the over-the-top satire; hiss at the creepy nefarious villains; and root for the intelligent, courageous, unfortunate Baudelaire orphans."Linda Bindner, writing in *School Library Journal,* noted that "While the misfortunes hover on the edge of being ridiculous, Snicket's energetic blend of humor, dramatic irony, and literary flair makes it all perfectly believable." Bindner also found that the use of sophisticated vocabulary and inclusion of author definitions make "these books challenging to older readers and excellent for reading aloud."

The third book in the series, *The Wide Window,* finds the orphans with elderly Aunt Josephine who lives on a house on stilts which overlooks Lake Lachrymose. Josephine is a widow as well as a frightful grammarian, and when Olaf finally tracks down the Baudelaires, he fools the aunt for a while into believing he is a sailboat captain. When she finally stumbles onto his true identity, he gets rid of her by pushing the good woman into leech-infested waters and the peripatetic children must find a new protector. *Booklist*'s Lempke noted that Snicket writes in "an old-fashioned tone," offering "plenty advice to readers in asides." "The effect is often hilarious as well as edifying," Lempke observed. Most importantly, as Lempke concluded, "readers never truly worry that [the Baudelaire orphans] will be defeated in this or their next adventure."

The fourth in the series, *The Miserable Mill,* begins with the three children on their way to Paltryville and yet another guardian, this time the owner of the Lucky Smells Lumbermill. Here they must work in the mill, survive on gum for lunch and casserole for dinner. Count Olaf, is of course, just off-stage ready to pounce. "The story is deliciously mock-Victorian and self-mockingly melodramatic," noted *Booklist* 's Carolyn Phelan, who also commented on the artwork and "the author's many asides to the reader" which both "underscore the droll humor. . . ." Phelan concluded, "Another plum for the orphans' fans." "This is for readers who appreciate this particular type of humor," observed Sharon R. Pearce in *School Library Journal.* Pearce noted that such humor "exaggerates the sour and makes anyone's real life seem sweet in comparison." The adventures continue in *The Austere Academy* and *The Ersatz Elevator.* In the former title, the Baudelaire children are consigned to a shack at the Prufrock Preparatory School where they will face snapping crabs, strict punishments, dripping fungus and the evils of the metric system. In the latter book, they must contend with new guardians Jerome and Esme Squalor, while trying to save two friends from the clutches of Count Olaf.

The Grim Grotto, the next chapter in the Baudelaire children's story, is as "cheerful" as "death, alopecia, and crabgrass," according to Alynda Wheat of *Entertainment Weekly.* This time the orphans team up with Captain Widdershins, commander of the submarine *Queequeg,* and his stepdaughter Fiona, in their quest to find a magical sugar bowl while evading the ever-present Count Olaf and a patch of poisonous mushrooms. Their underwater adventure is augmented by mechanical monsters and the tap-dancing Carmelita Spats. In an interview with Malcolm Jones in *Newsweek,* Snicket said that part of the reason the Baudelaire children have become so popular is because they are "heroes in which every reader could imagine themselves. . . . Working from a tradition of Gothic storytelling, I find that the external drama and melodrama are just more interesting than interior landscape." Additionally, Jones told Snicket he appreciated how "you really go out of your way to give both parents and kids a break . . . in your effort to avoid teaching moral lessons."

"The Snicket novels are morality tales, albeit twisted ones," observed Benfer in *Salon.* "Among other things, Snicket tells children that one should never stay up late on a school night, except to finish a very good book; he insists that there is nothing worse than someone who can't play the violin but insists upon doing so anyway." He employs continual authorial intrusions, providing definitions, giving stage directions. "I was mostly just knocking the heavy-handedness that I remembered from kid's books that I didn't like as a child," Handler reported to Benfer. "That sort of mockery seems to really appeal to kids." Another Handler trademark is the use of names in the Snicket books which come from literature: the Baudelaire orphans themselves are but the most obvious example of a long list including Mr. Poe and Prufrock Prep. "There's plenty of literary names and the like," Handler told Benfer, "but there's not so many outright jokes. And the literary names are there mostly because I look forward to kids growing up and finding Baudelaire in the poetry anthology and having that be something else to be excited about."

The formula has worked quite well, sending the Handler/Snicket books onto the best-seller charts and establishing a devoted fan base. More than 125,000 of the books in "A Series of Unfortunate Events" are in print, the Snicket Web site is a popular venue in cyberspace, and the elusive Mr. Snicket himself has become a popular speaker at schools. Correction. Mr. Snicket's representative, Mr. Handler, performs stand-ins for his friend, who has variously been injured or delayed or unaccountably held hostage somewhere while Mr. Handler entertains the youthful audience with his accordion and tales of the Snicket family tree. According to the official Snicket Web site, "Lemony Snicket was born before you were and is likely to die before you as well."

Lodge wrote in *Publishers Weekly* that obviously "the author's knack for combining the dark with the droll has hit a nerve just about everywhere," and word-of-mouth has greatly contributed to the success of the series. With Nickelodeon working on the film and Handler/Snicket collaborating on an expected thirteen volumes, the future looks surprisingly bright for the Baudelaire orphans.

BIOGRAPHICAL AND CRITICAL SOURCES:

PERIODICALS

ALAN Review, winter, 2001, Linda Broughton, review of *The Miserable Mill,* p. 35.

Book, July, 2001, *Kathleen Odean,* review of The Ersatz Elevator, p. 81.

Booklist, March 15, 1999, Stephanie Zvirin, review of *The Basic Eight,* p. 1289; December 1, 1999, Susan Dove Lempke, review of *The Bad Beginning,* p. 707; February 1, 2000, Susan Dove Lempke, review of *The Wide Window,* p. 1024; May 1, 2000, Carolyn Phelan, review of *The Miserable Mill,* p. 1670; June 1, 2000, Ted Leventhal, review of *Watch Your Mouth,* p. 1857; October 15, 2000, Susan Dove Lempke, review of *The Austere Academy,* p. 439.

Boys' Life, December, 2000, Stephen G. Michaud, review of "A Series of Unfortunate Events" titles, p. 61.

Christian Science Monitor, August 12, 1999, Ron Charles, review of *The Bad Beginning* and *The Reptile Room,* p. 21.

Entertainment Weekly, September 24, 2004, Alynda Wheat, a review of *The Grim Grotto,* p. 112.

Horn Book, March, 2001, Christine Heppermann, "Angel Wings and Hard Knocks," p. 239.

Library Journal, March 15, 1999, Rebecca Kelm, review of *The Basic Eight,* p. 108; June 1, 2000, Rebecca Kelm, review of *Watch Your Mouth,* p. 196.

Newsweek, September 27, 2004, Malcolm Jones, "Fame and Misfortune," p. 84.

New Yorker, June 21, 1999, review of *The Basic Eight.*

New York Times Magazine, April 29, 2001, Daphne Merkin, "Lemony Snicket Says, 'Don't Read My Books!'".

Publishers Weekly, March 1, 1999, review of *The Basic Eight,* p. 59; September 6, 1999, review of *The Bad Beginning,* p. 104; January 17, 2000, p. 58; May 29, 2000, Sally Lodge, "Oh, Sweet Misery," p. 42; June 19, 2000, review of *Watch Your Mouth,* p. 60.

School Library Journal, November, 1999, Linda Bindner, review of *The Bad Beginning,* p. 165; January, 2000, p. 136; July, 2000, Sharon R. Pearce, review of *The Miserable Mill,* p. 110; October, 2000, Ann Cook, review of *The Austere Academy,* p. 171; August, 2001, Farida S. Dowler, reviews of *The Ersatz Elevator* and *The Vile Village,* pp. 188-189.

Time for Kids, April 27, 2001, "He Tells Terrible Tales," p. 7.

ONLINE

*A Series of Unfortunate Events Web site,*http://www.lemonysnicket.com/ (March 26, 2001).

BookBrowser Review, http://www.bookbroswer.com/ (July 15, 2000), Jonathan Shipley, review of *Watch Your Mouth.*

Citypaper.net, http://www.cpcn.com/ (June 17-24, 1999), Brian Howard, review of *The Basic Eight.*

CNNfyi.com, http://www.cnn.cm/200/fyi/news/ (May 12, 2000), Greg Toppo, "Wry 'Series of Unfortunate Events' Books Earn Fans, Praise."

Lowell, http://www.thelowell.org/ (February 15, 1999), Philana Woo, "Author Reflects on High School Life."

Nancy Matson's Web site, http://www.nancymatson.com/ (March, 2000).

Salon.com, http://www.salon.com/ (July 24, 2000), Edward Neuert, "What to Read: July Fiction;" (August 17, 2000) Amy Benfer, "The Mysterious Mr. Snicket."

* * *

SNODGRASS, W.D. 1926-
(S.S. Gardons, William De Witt Snodgrass)

PERSONAL: Born January 5, 1926, in Wilkinsburg, PA; son of Bruce DeWitt (an accountant) and Jesse Helen (Murchie) Snodgrass; married Lila Jean Hank, June 6, 1946 (divorced, December, 1953); married Janice Marie Ferguson Wilson, March 19, 1954 (divorced, August, 1966); married Camille Rykowski, September 13, 1967 (divorced, 1978); married Kathleen Ann Brown, June 20, 1985; children: (first marriage) Cynthia Jean; (second marriage) Kathy Ann Wilson (stepdaughter), Russell Bruce. *Education:* Attended Geneva College, 1943-44, 1946-47; University of Iowa, B.A., 1949, M.A., 1951, M.F.A., 1953. *Hobbies and other interests:* "My wife and I spend roughly half our year in San Miguel de Allende, Mexico."

ADDRESSES: Home—RD 1 Box 51, Erieville, NY 13061-9801; c/o Border Crossings, 5912 San Bernardo, Laredo, TX 78014.

CAREER: Worked as hotel clerk and hospital aide in Iowa; Cornell University, Ithaca, NY, instructor in English, 1955-57; University of Rochester, Rochester, NY, instructor, 1957-58; Wayne State University, Detroit, MI, assistant professor of English, 1959-68; Syracuse University, Syracuse, NY, professor of English and speech, 1968-77; Old Dominion University, Norfolk, VA, visiting professor, 1978-79; University of Delaware, Newark, distinguished visiting professor, 1979-80, distinguished professor of creative writing and contemporary poetry, 1980-94; distinguished professor emeritus, 1994—. Leader of poetry workshop, Morehead Writers' Conference, 1955, Antioch Writers' Conference, 1958, 1959, and Narrative Poetry Workshop, State University of New York at Binghamton, 1977. Lectures and gives poetry readings. *Military service:* U.S. Navy, 1944-46.

MEMBER: National Institute of Arts and Letters, Academy of American Poets (fellow), PEN.

AWARDS, HONORS: Ingram Merrill Foundation Award, 1958; *Hudson Review* fellowship in poetry, 1958-59; Longview Foundation Literary Award, 1959; Poetry Society of America citation, 1960; National Institute of Arts and Letters grant, 1960; Pulitzer Prize for poetry, 1960, British Guinness Award, 1961, both for *Heart's Needle;* Yaddo resident award, 1960, 1961, 1965; Ford Foundation grant, 1963-64; Miles Poetry Award, 1966; National Endowment for the Arts grant, 1966-67; Guggenheim fellowship, 1972; Bicentennial medal from College of William and Mary, 1976; centennial medal from government of Romania, 1977; honorary doctorate of letters, Allegheny College, 1991; first prize for translations of Romanian letters, Colloquium of Translators and Editors, Siaia, Romania, 1995; nominee for National Book Critics Circle Award in criticism category, 2001, for *De/Compositions: 101 Good Poems Gone Wrong.*

WRITINGS:

Heart's Needle (poetry), Knopf, 1959.

(Translator, with Lore Segal) Christian Morgenstern, *Gallows Songs,* University of Michigan, 1967.

After Experience (poetry), Harper, 1967.

(Under pseudonym S.S. Gardons) *Remains: A Sequence of Poems,* Perishable Press, 1970, revised edition published as W.D. Snodgrass, BOA Editions, 1985.

In Radical Pursuit (critical essays), Harper, 1975.

(Translator) *Six Troubadour Songs,* Burning Deck Press, 1977.

The Fuehrer Bunker: A Cycle of Poems in Progress (poetry; also see below), BOA Editions, 1977, revised edition published as *The Fuehrer Bunker: The Complete Cycle: Poems,* BOA Editions, 1995.

(Translator from the Hungarian) *Traditional Hungarian Songs,* Seluzicki Fine Books, 1978.

If Birds Build with Your Hair (poetry), Nadja Press, 1979.

The Boy Made of Meat (poetry), William B. Ewert, 1982.

Six Minnesinger Songs, Burning Deck, 1983.

D.D. Byrde Calling Jennie Wrenne, William B. Ewert, 1984.

Heinrich Himmler: Platoons and Files, Pterodactyl Press, 1985.

A Colored Poem (poetry), Brighton Press, 1986.

The House the Poet Built (poetry), Brighton Press, 1986.

A Locked House (poetry), William B. Ewert, 1986.

Selected Poems, 1957-1987, Soho Press, 1987.

(With DeLoss McGraw) *W. D.'s Midnight Carnival,* Artra, 1988.

The Death of Cock Robin, University of Delaware Press, 1989.

To Shape a Song (poetry), Nadja Press, 1989.

Snow Songs (poetry), Nadja Press, 1992.

Each in His Season (poetry), BOA Editions, 1993.

Spring Suite (poetry), Nadja Press, 1994.

Selected Translations, BOA Editions, 1998.

After-Images: Autobiographical Sketches, BOA Editions, 1999.

(Translator) *Five Folk Ballads,* Romanian Cultural Foundation Publishing House, 1999.

De/Compositions: 101 Good Poems Gone Wrong, Graywolf Press, 2001.

Also author, sometimes under pseudonym S.S. Gardons, of fourteen limited fine press editions, including *These Trees Stand,* Carol Joyce, 1981, *Autumn Variations,* Nadja Press, 1990, and the translations *Antonio Vivaldi: The Four Seasons,* Tarq, 1984 (also published in *Syracuse Scholar*), and *Star and Other Poems,* by Mihai Eminescu, W.B. Ewert, 1990.

PLAYS

(Translator) Max Frisch, *Biederman and the Firebugs,* produced at the Regent Theater, Syracuse University, Syracuse, NY, 1966.

The Fuehrer Bunker (play; adaptation of book of his poetry of the same title), produced at River Playhouse, Old Dominion University, Norfolk, VA, 1978, then off-Broadway at American Place Theatre, 1981.

Dr. Joseph Goebbels, 22 April 1945, produced at West Gate Theatre, New York, 1981.

AUTHOR OF INTRODUCTION

Tom Marotta, *For They Are My Friends,* Art Reflections, 1976.

Barton Sutter, *Cedarhome* (poetry), BOA Editions, 1977.

Rainer Maria Rilke, *The Roses and the Windows,* translated by A. Poulin, Graywolf, 1979.

Michael Jennings, *The Hardeman Country Poems* (based on photographs by Dorothea Lange), Heliographics, 1980.

Jonathan Holden, *Leverage,* University of Virginia Press, 1983.

Alice Fulton, *Dance Script for Electric Ballerina,* University of Pennsylvania Press, 1983.

Jane E. Glasser, *Naming the Darkness,* Road Publishers, 1991.

William Dickey, *The Education of Desire,* Wesleyan, 1996.

Kay Murphy, *Belief Blues,* Portals, 1998.

CONTRIBUTOR

From the Iowa Poetry Workshop, Prairie Press, 1951.

Reading Modern Poetry, Scott, 1955.

New Poets of England and America, Meridian, 1957.

New World Writing, New American Library, 1957.

Theodore Roethke: Essays on the Poetry, University of Washington Press, 1965.

Also contributor to *Syracuse Scholar.* Contributor of poems, poetry translations (from the German, Romanian, French, Provencal, Italian, Hungarian, Dutch, and Danish), literary criticism, essays, and reviews to magazines, journals, and newspapers.

ADAPTATIONS: Several of Snodgrass's song translations have been performed by early music groups, including the Waverley Consort, Columbia Collegium (New York City), Persis Ensor (Boston), and the Antiqua Players (Pittsburgh).

WORK IN PROGRESS: "A book of critical essays on the craft of poetry."

SIDELIGHTS: W.D. Snodgrass is often credited with being one of the founding members of the "confessional" school of poetry, even though he dislikes the term confessional and does not regard his work as such. Nevertheless, his Pulitzer Prize-winning first collection, *Heart's Needle,* has had a tremendous impact on that particular facet of contemporary poetry. "Like other confessional poets, Snodgrass is at pains to reveal the repressed, violent feelings that often lurk beneath the seemingly placid surface of everyday life," David McDuff observes in *Stand.* The style was imitated and, in some cases, surpassed by other poets. This fact leads *Yale Review*'s Laurence Lieberman to comment that a later book, *After Experience,* reveals "an artist trapped in a style which . . . has reached a dead end," because the group style had taken a different direction than Snodgrass's own. However, later works by Snodgrass show him widening his vision to apply the lessons of self-examination to the problems of twentieth-century Western culture. His poems also present, beyond the direct-statement and sentimentality common to confessional poetry, an inclusiveness of detail and variety of technique aimed to impact the reader's subconscious as well as conscious mind.

The combination of the traditional and the confessional in Snodgrass's writing prompts Thomas Lask of the *New York Times* to write, "In *Heart's Needle,* . . . Snodgrass spoke in a distinctive voice. It was one that was jaunty and assertive on the surface but somber and hurt beneath. . . . It is one of the few books that successfully bridged the directness of contemporary free verse with the demands of the academy." Peter Porter echoes this opinion when he writes in *London Magazine:* "Snodgrass is a virtuoso, not just of versification but of his feelings. He sends them round the loops of self analysis with the same skill he uses to corset them into his poetry." The impact of Snodgrass's self-analytical approach is clearly felt in Stanley Moss's statement in the *New Republic* that the poet "has found a place for emotions felt, but previously left without words and out of consciousness. He has identified himself with exquisite suffering and guilt and with all those who barely manage to exist on the edge of life."

Regarding Snodgrass's translation (with Lore Segal) of Christian Morgenstern's *Gallows Songs,* Louise Bogan writes in *New Yorker:* "German . . . here takes on a demonic life of its own. . . . To translate Morgenstern is a very nearly impossible task, to which the present translators have faced up bravely and well." Even though some critics may not agree with Bogan—Hayden Carruth of *Poetry* calls the translation "dreadful"—*Books Abroad*'s Sidney Rosenfeld finds that in spite of its possible shortcomings, *Gallows Songs* opens "a door onto the world of Christian Morgenstern and impart[s] to the English reader some sense of the playfully profound genius that enlivens it."

Paul Gaston points out that Snodgrass's critical essays and translations help develop his talents and prevent him from reaching the complete dead end of Lieberman's prediction. "These endeavors," writes Gaston in his book *W.D. Snodgrass,* "reveal a poet intent on carefully establishing his creative priorities and perfecting his language." He continues, "Snodgrass's criticism gives the impressions of a mind reaching beyond the pleasures of cleverness to the hard-won satisfactions of wisdom." And finally, "[His] work with translations . . . has encouraged the increasing linguistic, metrical, and structural diversity of his own work."

This diversity is apparent in Snodgrass's third volume of original poetry, *The Fuehrer Bunker,* which uses dramatic monologues to recreate what was said by the men and women who shared Hitler's bunker from April 1 to May 1, 1945. "In these poems," writes Gertrude M. White in *Odyssey: A Journal of the Humanities,* "we are overhearing people talking to themselves, each character speaking in a verse form expressive of his or her personality, revealing who and what they are with a dramatic power that carries conviction almost against our will." Robert Peters, writing in the *American Book Review,* believes that the volume is "a rare example of ambitious, on-going verse sculpture. . . . It will be around for a long time to inspire writers who've come to realize the sad limitations of the locked-in, private, first lesson, obsessional poem."

However, the subject matter of the poems troubles critic Laurence Goldstein, who fears that the writer's choice of subject overwhelms the artistry of the writing. Goldstein, writing for the *Southern Review,* believes that writing about Nazism in the way that Snodgrass does in *The Fuehrer Bunker* violates the poetic aesthetic. "When a poet as skilled in sweet rhetoric as Snodgrass," Goldstein declares, "who can charm and disarm his audience at will, presents twenty-two dramatic monologues spoken by the most despised Nazis, nothing less than ultimate questions about the enterprise of contemporary poetry loom before us." "Is there a shameless sensationalism involved in trying to change belief on *that* dreadful subject?" the critic asks. "Shouldn't the poet pass by the Medusa head of *that* modern horror lest he petrify, or worse entertain, himself and his readers by staring at vipers?" *The Fuehrer Bunker,* which was first published as a work in progress in 1977, was finally released as a completed cycle of poems in 1995. Critics who reviewed the revised edition recognized its power, but their conclusions differed from Goldstein's fears. Frank Allen writes in *Library Journal* that "to hear these voices imaginatively re-created is purgative," while *Booklist* contributor Elizabeth Gunderson calls it "an astonishing work that lets us see with clarity the fall of the Third Reich—and wonder."

Snodgrass's collection *Each in His Season* also raised questions among critics. *New York Times Book Review* contributor Bruce Bennett calls the work "a large-scale, free-wheeling roller coaster of a book," adding that the poet "displays his life and art in often contradictory guises." A *Publishers Weekly* reviewer dismisses the volume, declaring that it "is almost completely stripped of content, with a few notable exceptions." William Pratt, writing in *World Literature Today,* declares that "*Each in His Season* does no credit to W.D. Snodgrass or to any of his models." A reviewer for *Poetry* magazine offers a different assessment, asserting that "among the major poets of his generation it would be difficult to find a wittier or more exuberant writer—or one more committed to the making of verbal music." "If Snodgrass is not always convincing as plaintiff or prosecutor," the critic concludes, "he is both pleasing and persuasive in his role as lyric poet, the 'robin with green face,' singing exquisitely of 'all things vile and ugly.'"

Snodgrass once told *CA* that "These Trees Stand . . . ," a poem which originally appeared in *Heart's Needle,* has been made into a volume "bound in exquisite leather in an edition of ten copies and two artist's proofs." The volume is illustrated with photographs by Robert Mahon. A number of his other books, he says, "have been issued only in small or fine press editions—often beautifully printed on fine papers for collectors who can afford to pay horrifying prices," ranging from $300 to $3,000.

BIOGRAPHICAL AND CRITICAL SOURCES:

BOOKS

Boyers, Robert, editor, *Contemporary Poetry in America,* Schocken Books, 1974.

Carroll, Paul, *The Poem in Its Skin,* Follett, 1968.

Contemporary Literary Criticism, Thomson Gale, Volume 2, 1974, Volume 6, 1976, Volume 10, 1979, Volume 18, 1981, Volume 68, 1991.

Gaston, Paul, *W.D. Snodgrass,* Twayne, 1978.
Haven, Steven, editor, *The Poetry of W.D. Snodgrass: Everything Human,* University of Michigan Press, 1993.
Howard, Richard, *Alone with America,* Thames and Hudson, 1970, pp. 471-484.
Hungerford, Edward, editor, *Poets in Progress,* revised edition, Northwestern University Press, 1967.
Mazzaro, Jerome, editor, *Modern American Poetry: Essays in Criticism,* McKay, 1970.
Phillips, Robert, *The Confessional Poets,* Southern Illinois University Press, 1973, pp. 45-72.
Raisor, Philip, *Tuned and Under Tension: The Recent Poetry of W.D. Snodgrass,* University of Delaware Press, 1998.
Rosenthal, M. L., *The New Poets,* Oxford University Press, 1967.
Spiller, Robert E., editor, *A Time of Harvest,* Hill & Wang, 1962.
White, William, compiler, *W.D. Snodgrass, A Bibliography,* Wayne State University Press, 1960.

PERIODICALS

American Book Review, December, 1977.
American Poetry Review, July-August, 1990, pp. 38-46.
Booklist, March 15, 1995, p. 1303.
Book World, April 14, 1968.
Detroit Free Press, Sunday supplement, June 6, 1965.
Kenyon Review, summer, 1959.
Library Journal, April 1, 1995, p. 99.
Literary Times, April, 1965.
London Magazine, March, 1969.
Los Angeles Times Book Review, August 2, 1987; November 1, 1987; January 3, 1988.
Massachusetts Review, spring, 1975.
Nation, September 16, 1968.
New Republic, June 15, 1968; February 15, 1975.
New Yorker, October 24, 1959.
New York Times, March 30, 1968; June 3, 1981.
New York Times Book Review, April 28, 1968; September 13, 1987, p. 52; April 17, 1994, pp. 20-21.
Observer Review, December 15, 1968.
Odyssey: A Journal of the Humanities, April, 1979.
Papers on Language & Literature, summer, 1977; fall, 1977, pp. 401-412.
Poetry, November, 1959; September, 1968; November, 1994, pp. 97-101.
Publishers Weekly, June 12, 1987, p. 79; August 9, 1993, p. 471.
Salmagundi, spring, 1972; spring, 1973; summer, 1973; spring/summer, 1988, pp. 176-204.
Shenandoah, summer, 1968.
Southern Review, winter, 1988, pp. 100-114; January, 1990, pp. 65-80.
Southwest Review, summer, 1975.
Stand, autumn, 1988.
Tri-Quarterly, spring, 1960.
Western Humanities Review, winter, 1970.
World Literature Today, spring, 1994, p. 375.
Yale Review, autumn, 1968.

* * *

SNODGRASS, William De Witt
See SNODGRASS, W.D.

* * *

SNYDER, Gary 1930-
(Gary Sherman Snyder)

PERSONAL: Born May 8, 1930, in San Francisco CA; son of Harold Alton and Lois (Wilkie) Snyder; married Alison Gass, 1950 (divorced, 1951); married Joanne Kyger (a poet), 1960 (divorced, 1964); married Masa Uehara, August 6, 1967 (divorced); married Carole Koda, April 28, 1991; children: (third marriage) Kai, Gen. *Education:* Reed College, B.A. (in anthropology and literature), 1951; attended Indiana University, 1951; University of California, Berkeley, graduate study in Oriental languages, 1953-56. *Politics:* Radical. *Religion:* Buddhist of the Mahayana-Vajrayana line.

ADDRESSES: Home—Kitkitdizze, NV. *Office*—c/o North Point Press, 850 Talbot Ave., Berkeley, CA 94706.

CAREER: Poet and translator, 1959—. Worked as seaman, logger, trail crew member, and forest lookout, 1948-56; lecturer at University of California, Berkeley, 1964-65; professor at University of California, Davis, 1985—. Visiting lecturer at numerous universities and writing workshops. Member of United Nations Conference on the Human Environment, 1972; former chair of California Arts Council.

MEMBER: American Academy and Institute of Arts and Letters.

AWARDS, HONORS: Scholarship from First Zen Institute of America, 1956, for study in Japan; National Institute and American Academy poetry award, 1966;

Bollingen Foundation grant, 1966-67; Frank O'Hara Prize, 1967; Levinson Prize from *Poetry* magazine, 1968; Guggenheim fellowship, 1968-69; Pulitzer Prize in poetry, 1975, for *Turtle Island;* American Book Award, Before Columbus Foundation, 1984, for *Axe Handles;* National Book Critics Circle Award nomination, 2004, for *Danger on Peaks: Poems*; American Academy of Arts and Letters award; Bess Hokin Prize; Robert Kirsch Lifetime Achievement Award, *Los Angeles Times;* Shelley Memorial Award.

WRITINGS:

POETRY

Riprap (also see below), Origin Press (San Francisco, CA), 1959.

Myths & Texts, Totem Press (New York, NY), 1960, reprinted, New Directions (New York, NY), 1978.

Riprap & Cold Mountain Poems (the *Cold Mountain* poems are Snyder's translations of poems by Han-Shan), Four Seasons Foundation (San Francisco, CA), 1965, reprinted, Shoemaker & Hoard (Washington, DC), 2004.

Six Sections from Mountains and Rivers without End, Four Seasons Foundation (San Francisco, CA), 1965, revised edition published as *Six Sections from Mountains and Rivers without End, Plus One,* 1970.

A Range of Poems (includes translations of the modern Japanese poet Miyazawa Kenji), Fulcrum (London, England), 1966.

Three Worlds, Three Realms, Six Roads, Griffin Press (Marlboro, VT), 1966.

The Back Country, Fulcrum (London, England), 1967, New Directions (New York, NY), 1968.

The Blue Sky, Phoenix Book Shop (New York, NY), 1969.

Regarding Wave, New Directions (New York, NY), 1970.

Manzanita, Kent State University Libraries (Kent, OH), 1971.

Piute Creek, State University College at Brockport (Brockport, NY), 1972.

The Fudo Trilogy: Spell against Demons, Smokey the Bear Sutra, The California Water Plan (also see below), illustrated by Michael Corr, Shaman Drum (Berkeley, CA), 1973.

Turtle Island, New Directions (New York, NY), 1974.

All in the Family, University of California Library, c. 1975.

Smokey the Bear Sutra (chapbook), 1976.

Songs for Gaia, illustrated by Corr, Copper Canyon (Port Townsend, WA), 1979.

Axe Handles, North Point Press (San Francisco, CA), 1983.

Good Wild Scared, Five Seasons Press (Madley, Hereford, England), 1984.

Left Out in the Rain: New Poems 1947- 1986, North Point Press (San Francisco, CA), 1986, reprinted, Shoemaker & Hoard (Washington, DC), 2005.

The Fates of Rocks & Trees, James Linden (San Francisco, CA), 1986.

No Nature: New and Selected Poems, Pantheon (New York, NY), 1992.

North Pacific Lands & Waters, Brooding Heron Press (Waldron Island, WA), 1993.

Mountains and Rivers without End, Counterpoint (Washington, DC), 1996.

Danger on Peaks: Poems, Shoemaker & Hoard (Washington, DC), 2004.

PROSE

Earth House Hold: Technical Notes and Queries to Fellow Dharma Revolutionaries (essays), New Directions (New York, NY), 1969.

(Contributor) *Ecology: Me,* Moving On, 1970.

The Old Ways: Six Essays, City Lights (San Francisco, CA), 1977.

On Bread & Poetry: A Panel Discussion between Gary Snyder, Lew Welch and Philip Whalen, edited by Donald M. Allen, Grey Fox (Bolinas, CA), 1977.

He Who Hunted Birds in His Father's Village (undergraduate thesis), preface by Nathaniel Tarn, Grey Fox (Bolinas, CA), 1979.

The Real Work: Interviews & Talks, 1964-1979, edited with introduction by Scott McLean, New Directions (New York, NY), 1980.

Passage through India (autobiography), Grey Fox (San Francisco, CA), 1983.

The Practice of the Wild, Farrar, Straus (New York, NY), 1990, reprinted, Shoemaker & Hoard (Washington, DC), 2004.

A Place in Space: Ethics, Aesthetics, and Watersheds (new and selected prose), Counterpoint (Washington, DC), 1995.

The Gary Snyder Reader: Prose, Poetry, and Translations, 1952-1998, Counterpoint (Washington, DC), 1999.

Look Out: A Selection of Writings, New Directions (New York, NY), 2002.

OTHER

The New Religion (sound recording), Big Sur Recordings, 1967.

Gary Snyder Reading His Poems in the Montpelier Room, Oct. 24, 1996, (sound recording) 1996.

A Place for Wayfaring: The Poetry and Prose of Gary Snyder / Patrick D. Murphy Oregon State University Press (Corvallis, OR), 2000.

(With Tom Killion and John Muir) *The High Sierra of California,* Heyday Books, 2002.

Contributor to anthologies, including *Contemporary American Poetry,* edited by Donald Hall, Penguin Books (New York, NY), 1962; *A Controversy of Poets,* edited by Paris Leary and Robert Kelly, Doubleday (New York, NY), 1965; and *Sustainable Poetry: Four American Ecopoets,* edited by Leonard M. Scigaj, University Press of Kentucky (Lexington, KY), 1999. Contributor to numerous periodicals, including *Janus, Evergreen Review, Black Mountain Review, Yugen, Chicago Review, Jabberwock, San Francisco Review, Big Table, Origin, Kulchur, Journal for the Protection of All Beings, Nation, City Lights Journal, Yale Literary Magazine, Beloit Poetry Journal,* and *Poetry.* The University of California, Davis, holds a collection of Snyder's manuscripts.

SIDELIGHTS: Gary Snyder is one of the rare modern poets who has bridged the gap between popular appeal and serious academic criticism. Snyder began his career in the 1950s as a noted member of the "Beat Generation," and since then he has explored a wide range of social and spiritual matters in both poetry and prose. Snyder's work blends physical reality—precise observations of nature—with inner insight received primarily through the practice of Zen Buddhism. *Southwest Review* essayist Abraham Rothberg noted that the poet "celebrates nature, the simple, the animal, the sexual, the tribal, the self . . . . He sees man as an indissoluble part of the natural environment, flourishing when he accepts and adapts to that natural heritage, creating a hell on earth and within himself when he is separated from it by his intellect and its technological and societal creations." While Snyder has gained the attention of readers as a spokesman for the preservation of the natural world and its earth-conscious cultures, he is not simply a "back-to-nature" poet with a facile message. In *American Poetry in the Twentieth Century,* Kenneth Rexroth observed that although Snyder proposes "a new ethic, a new esthetic, [and] a new life style," he is also "an accomplished technician who has learned from the poetry of several languages and who has developed a sure and flexible style capable of handling any material he wishes." According to Charles Altieri in *Enlarging the Temple: New Directions in American Poetry during the 1960s,* Snyder's achievement "is a considerable one. Judged simply in aesthetic terms, according to norms of precision, intelligence, imaginative play, and moments of deep resonance, he easily ranks among the best poets of his generation. Moreover, he manages to provide a fresh perspective on metaphysical themes, which he makes relevant and compelling."

Snyder's emphasis on metaphysics and his celebration of the natural order remove his work from the general tenor of Beat writing. *Dictionary of Literary Biography* contributor Dan McLeod explained that while authors such as Allen Ginsberg and Neal Cassady "represented in their different ways rather destructive responses to the alienation inherent in modern American technocracy, the example of Snyder's life and values offered a constructive, albeit underground, alternative to mainstream American culture." No less searing in his indictments of Western values than the other Beat writers, Snyder has proposed "a morality that is unharmful, that tends toward wholeness. An ethics not of the trigger or fist, but of the heart," to quote *New Republic* reviewer Timothy Baland. Snyder has looked to the Orient and to the beliefs of American Indians for positive responses to the world, and he has tempered his studies with stints of hard physical labor as a logger and trail builder. In the *Southwest Review,* Roger Jones called Snyder "one of the century's *healthiest* writers," a poet who "perceives man as completely situated within the schemes of natural order, and sees as a necessity man's awareness that he is as real and as whole as the world—a perception muddled by the metaphysical notion of the world as a mere stage for the enactment of our eternal destinies." Charles Molesworth elaborated on this premise in his work *Gary Snyder's Vision: Poetry and the Real Work.* Molesworth saw Snyder as "a moral visionary who is neither a scourge nor a satirist; . . . he has spoken as a prophet whose 'tribe' is without definite national or cultural boundaries."

Altieri believed that Snyder's "articulation of a possible religious faith" independent of Western culture has greatly enhanced his popularity, especially among younger readers. If that is so, Snyder's themes have also been served by an accessible style, drawn from the examples of Japanese haiku and Chinese verse. In a book entitled *Gary Snyder,* Bob Steuding remarked that Snyder "has created a new kind of poetry that is direct, concrete, non-Romantic, and ecological . . . . Snyder's work will be remembered in its own right as the example of a new direction taken in American literature." *Nation* contributor Richard Tillinghast wrote: "In Snyder the stuff of the world 'content'—has always shone with a wonderful sense of earthiness and health. He has always had things to tell us, experiences to relate, a set of values to expound . . . . He has influenced a generation." McLeod found Snyder's "poetic fusion of Buddhist and tribal world views with ecological science" a "remarkable cross-cultural achievement—an utterly appropriate postmodernist expression of a post-industrial sensibility." Robert Mezey put it more simply in the *Western Humanities Review* when he concluded: "This missionary is really a joyful poet, and the gratitude and celebration at the heart of his view of life often overwhelm the necessity to teach and explain. So the teaching is done silently, which is the best way to do it."

Born and raised in the American West, Snyder lived close to nature from earliest childhood. Even at a very young age he was distressed by the wanton destruction of the Pacific Northwestern forests, and he began to study and respect the Indian cultures that "seemed to have some sense of how a life harmonious with nature might be lived," according to Rothberg. Snyder went to public schools in Seattle and Portland, and he augmented his education by reading about Indian lore and pioneer adventures. Wild regions continued to fascinate him as he matured; he became an expert mountain climber and learned back-country survival techniques. A visit to the Seattle Art Museum introduced him to Chinese landscape painting, and he developed an interest in the Orient as an example of a high civilization that had maintained its bonds to nature. After high school Snyder divided his time between studies at the prestigious Reed College—and later Indiana University and the University of California, Berkeley—and work as a lumberjack, trail maker, and firewatcher in the deep woods. The balance between physical labor and intellectual pursuits informs his earliest writing; McLeod felt that the unlikely juxtaposition makes Snyder either "the last of an old breed or the beginning of a new breed of backwoodsmen figures in American literature." In *Alone with America: Essays on the Art of Poetry in the United States since 1950,* Richard Howard described Snyder's youth as "the rapturous life of a cosmic bum."

In the autumn of 1952 Snyder moved to the San Francisco Bay area in order to study Oriental languages at Berkeley. He was already immersed in Zen Buddhism and had begun to write poetry about his work in the wilderness. McLeod contended that the four years Snyder spent in San Francisco "were of enormous importance to his . . . growth as a poet." He became part of a community of writers, including Philip Whalen, Allen Ginsberg, and Jack Kerouac, who would come to be known as the Beat Generation and who would be heralded as the forerunners of a counterculture revolution in literature. The literary fame of the Beat Generation was launched with a single event: a poetry reading in October of 1955 at San Francisco's Six Gallery. While it is Ginsberg's poem "Howl" that is best remembered from that evening, Snyder also participated, reading his poem "The Berry Feast."

If Snyder was influenced by his antisocial contemporaries, he also exerted an influence on them. Kerouac modeled his character Japhy Ryder in *The Dharma Bums* on Snyder, and the poet encouraged his friends to take an interest in Eastern philosophy as an antidote to the ills of the West. McLeod noted, however, that although "he is clearly one of its major figures, Snyder was out of town when the Beat movement was most alive on the American scene." Having been awarded a scholarship by the First Zen Institute of America, Snyder moved to Japan in 1956 and stayed abroad almost continuously for the next twelve years. Part of that time he lived in an ashram and devoted himself to strenuous Zen study and meditation. He also travelled extensively, visiting India and Indonesia, and even venturing as far as Istanbul on an oil tanker, the *Sappa Creek.* His first two poetry collections, *Riprap* and *Myths & Texts,* were published in 1959 and 1960. After returning to the United States, Snyder built his own house— along the Yuba River in the northern Sierra Nevada mountains— where he has lived since.

Snyder's early poems represent a vigorous attempt to achieve freedom from the "establishment" mores of urban America. *Sagetrieb* contributor Thomas Parkinson described the works as moments in which "action and contemplation become identical states of being, and both states of secular grace. From this fusion wisdom emerges, and it is not useless but timed to the event. The result is a terrible sanity, a literal clairvoyance, an innate decorum." The poems in *Riprap* and *Myths & Texts* are miniature narratives captured from the active working life of the author; Rothberg contended that in them Snyder wants "to be considered a poet of ordinary men, writing in a language shaped in their idiom." Audiences responded to Snyder's portrayals of the vigorous backwoods visionary whose joy flows from physical pursuits and contemplation of the wild world. In the *Los Angeles Times Book Review,* Schuyler Ingle wrote: "I could sense [Snyder] in his lines, all long-haired and denim-clad, laced-up high-top logger boots. He was an educated, curious man comfortable with his own sexuality." Rothberg too detects the education underlying the hardier roles. According to the critic, Snyder "cannot quite conceal the intellect or learning in his work, which everywhere reveals his considerable knowledge of anthropology, linguistics, Zen Buddhism, history, and other arcane lore."

Unquestionably, Snyder's involvement with Buddhism has been important to his poetry from the outset. As Julian Gitzen noted in *Critical Quarterly,* Snyder "was attracted to Buddhism because its teachings conformed to and re-enforced his native personality, interests and beliefs." Much of the poet's work "manifests a . . . movement out to an awareness of self in cosmos complemented by the perception of cosmos contained within the self," to quote Altieri. In *American Poetry since 1960: Some Critical Perspectives,* Alan Williamson also stated that Snyder's canon "suggests a process of meditation or spiritual exercise, clearing the path from temporal life to the moment of Enlightenment—the sudden dropping-away of the phenomenal world in the contemplation of the infinite and eternal, All and Nothingness." The aim, according to Parkinson, is "not to achieve harmony with nature but to create an inner harmony that equals to the natural external harmony." *Criticism* essayist Robert Kern declared that the resulting poems "are almost celebrations of those moments when the mind's resistances have been overcome and the difficult transition has been made from ordinary consciousness to a state in which the mind has dropped its symbolic burden of words, books, abstractions, even personal history and identity—whatever might stand in the way of a direct, unhampered perception of things."

The structure of Snyder's poetry is influenced by the intellectual dilemma of using language—the medium of rational discourse—to disclose deeper, extra-rational states of being. *Dictionary of Literary Biography* essayist Alex Batman observed that Snyder realizes mere words may be inadequate for the articulation of his discoveries. The poet overcomes this problem by producing verse "based on the Oriental haiku—sharp, uncomplicated images that, like many Oriental paintings, form sketches that the reader's imagination must fill in." Gitzen wrote: "Snyder's poems in general possess [an] air of spontaneity, almost as though they were hastily written notes for poems, rather than finished constructions. Such unpolished form harmonizes with the Zen aesthetic." The critic added, however, that spontaneous and simple though the works may seem, they are in fact "the result of conscious and painstaking effort." Batman likewise found Snyder's pieces "deceptively simple rather than superficially simplistic." Altieri commented that for the skeptic or half-believer, "the real miracle is the skill with which Snyder uses the aesthetic devices of lyrical poetry to sustain his religious claims. His basic achievement is his power to make his readers reflect on the ontological core of the lyrical vision by calling attention to the way it can be things or processes themselves, and not merely the elements of a poem, which mutually create one another's significance and suggest a unifying power producing, sustaining, and giving meaning to these relationships." Steuding concluded that the "Buddhist perception of oneness . . . creates a poetry of immediacy and startling originality."

Buddhism is by no means the sole departure point for Snyder's work, however. Well-versed in anthropology and the lore of so-called "primitive" cultures, the author reveres myth and ritual as essential demonstrations of man-in-nature and nature-in-man. In *The American West,* Thomas W. Pew, Jr. wrote: "Snyder, like a handful of other writers since Carl Jung, has discovered the similarities of myth, religion, and his own personal dream content as well as the product of his meditations and has fashioned that collective material into words that set off little explosions in our thought process and our own deeper memory." Harking back to the Stone Age, Snyder sees the poet as a shaman who acts as a medium for songs and chants springing from the earth. McLeod explained: "The poet-shaman draws his songs from the [Earth] Mother Goddess and through the magic power of image, metaphor, music, and myth creates the artistic patterns that express the most deeply held knowledge and values of the community. Embodied in literary form, this knowledge and these values may survive and evolve, sustaining the group generation after generation." McLeod stated further that myth and ritual are for Snyder "far more than reflections of experience . . . . They are also a means whereby we can shape and control experience through the sympathetic magic inherent in the metaphysical connections that link myth and ritual to the quotidian world."

It is not surprising, therefore, that Snyder draws on the traditions of oral literature—chants, incantations, and songs—to communicate his experiences. *Denver Quarterly* contributor Kevin Oderman observed that the poet "writes out of a tradition of self-effacement, and his yearnings are for a communal poetry rooted in place." Scott McLean also addressed this idea in his introduction to Snyder's *The Real Work: Interviews & Talks, 1964-1979.* "All of Gary Snyder's study and work has been directed toward a poetry that would approach phenomena with a disciplined clarity that would then use the 'archaic' and the 'primitive' as models to once again see this poetry as woven through all the parts of our lives," McLean wrote. "Thus it draws its substance and forms from the broadest range of a people's day-to-day lives, enmeshed in the facts of work, the real trembling in joy and grief, thankfulness for good crops, the health of a child, the warmth of the lover's touch. Further, Snyder seeks to recover a poetry that could sing and thus relate us to: magpie, beaver, a mountain range, binding us to all these other lives, seeing our spiritual lives as bound up in the rounds of nature." McLean concluded that in terms of the human race's future, "Snyder's look toward the primitive may vouchsafe one of the only real alternative directions available." Addressing specifically the poetry, Jones admitted in *Southwest Review* that Snyder's shamanistic role is an important one for modern letters "as poetry seems to base itself less in sound than in the medium of print."

Many of Snyder's poems aim specifically at instilling an ecological consciousness in his audience. Jones observed that the poet advocates "peaceful stewardship, economy, responsibility with the world's resources, and, most importantly, sanity—all still within the capabilities of modern societies, and bound up in the perception of the world and its life-sources as a glorious whole." This theme pervades Snyder's 1974 Pulitzer Prize-winning volume, *Turtle Island,* a work in which the poet manages "to locate the self ecologically in its actions and interactions with its environment, to keep it anchored to its minute-by-minute manifestations in (and as a part of) the physical world," to quote Robert Kern in *Contemporary Literature.* According to Gitzen, Snyder assumes that "while man neither individually nor as a species is essential to nature . . . nature is essential to the existence of all men. Consideration for our own welfare demands that we abandon efforts to dominate nature and assume instead an awareness of our subjection to natural law . . . . Snyder repeatedly seeks to impress upon his readers the awesome immensity of space, time, energy, and matter working together to generate a destiny beyond the reach of human will." Some critics, such as *Partisan Review* contributor Robert Boyers, found Snyder's commitment "programmistic and facile," a simplistic evocation of the "noble savage" as hero. Others, including *New York Times Book Review* correspondent Herbert Leibowitz, applauded the poet's world view. "Snyder's sane housekeeping principles desperately need to become Government and corporate policy," Leibowitz wrote. "He is on the side of the gods."

"The curve of Snyder's career has been from the fact-like density of perceptual intensity to the harmonious patternmaking of the immanently mythic imagination," Molesworth stated. "Such a course of development has taken Snyder deeper and deeper into the workings of the political imagination as well." Snyder's more recent works reflect a growing concern for the environment and the plight of the American Indian as well as the new insights engendered by his domestic responsibilities. McLeod noted that a "shift from the examination of the self to the exercise of social responsibility is clearly reflected in the development of Snyder's writing which has moved from the still, almost purely meditative lyrics in *Riprap,* to the celebration of the human family as a vital part of a broad network of relationships linking all forms of life in *Regarding Wave,* to the eco- political poems and essays in *Turtle Island.*" *Axe Handles,* Snyder's 1983 collection, returns to the domestic environment—especially the relationship between father and sons—as a central motif. *Poetry* magazine reviewer Bruce Bawer contended that the work "conveys a luminous, poignant vision of a life afforded joy and strength by a recognition of the essential things which give it meaning. It is, to my tastes, Snyder's finest book."

Not all reviewers felt that Snyder's more recent poetry scales the heights he reached with *Turtle Island.* Reviewing *No Nature,* a collection of old and new poems published in 1992, David Barber commented in *Poetry* that "the vigor and output of Snyder's poetry has clearly been on the wane over the last twenty years . . . . The poet who was formerly adept at elucidating intimations now seems to be content with simply espousing positions." However, Richard Tillinghast, writing in the *New York Times Book Review,* claimed that Snyder possesses "a command of geology, anthropology and evolutionary biology unmatched among contemporary poets," adding that "there is an understated majesty about the ease with which Mr. Snyder puts the present into perspective." Both Tillinghast and Barber in particular commended Snyder's evocation of the subject of work. Noted Barber, "Few contemporary poets have written with such authentic incisiveness about the particulars of work and the rhythms of subsistence, and done so without succumbing to class-rooted righteousness or rural nostalgia."

One project that spanned much of the poet's career—a long poem, *Mountains and Rivers without End,* titled after a Chinese sideways scroll painting—was finally published in 1996 to glowing praise from critics. As Steuding claimed, "One finds directness and simplicity of statement, clarity and brilliance of mind, and profundity and depth of emotional range. In these instances, Snyder's is a poetry of incredible power and beauty." Similarly, a *Publishers Weekly* reviewer commented that *Mountains and Rivers without End* "is a major work by a venerable master of post-[World War II] American poetry." The poem is a conscious effort to recreate the social function of ancient epics: to tell a good story, while offering instruction in life by way of myth and history. Snyder's narrative is "less heroic in tone than Homer's," found Tom Clark in his *San Francisco Chronicle* review, but like classic works such as the *Odyssey, Mountains and Rivers without End* is "a universalizing, picaresque spiritual journey, the story not only of one man, but also of the human event on this planet," explained Clark. Ancient values are evoked and celebrated: fertility, the magic of animals, the power of dance, and the importance of tribal work. Snyder evokes an ancient civilization blessed by self-awareness, thriving in an unpolluted world. The narrative is "continually teetering perilously on the great divide between human and nonhuman worlds, demonstrating all over again the curiously ambivalent evenhandedness that has always created an interesting tension in his work," commented Clark. Conflicting desires to escape and redeem civilization form another part of the work, which show the poet in concrete landscapes of freeway and megalopolis. Taken as a whole, the poem celebrates "not only nature's exquisite delicacy and fragility but also its immense ruggedness, resilience and durability." Snyder's personal journey of several decades is reflected in the verses that took him so long to complete, and he commented to Jesse Hamlin in an interview for *San Francisco Chronicle* that those years were "a time of tremendous change, and yet I can see that the initial impulses with which I opened the work—which were curiosity and affection and respect for the whole natural world—naive in some ways as they were, were basically going in the right direction." He concluded: "I'm pleased with the poem," but he added: "I don't think in terms of masterpieces . . . . You do the work you do and you leave it for the world to judge where it fits. I did what I was impelled to do. It got me to the point where I could let go of it."

In addition to his many volumes of verse, Snyder has published books of prose essays and interviews that can be read "not only as partial explanation of the poetry but as the record of an evolving mind with extreme good sense in treating the problems of the world," according to Parkinson. Snyder's prose expands his sense of social purpose and reveals the series of interests and concerns that have sparked his creative writing. In *The Practice of the Wild,* published in 1990, Snyder muses on familiar topics such as environmental concerns, Native American culture, ecofeminism, language, and mythology. Praising the author's "exquisite craftsmanship and new maturity in style," Michael Strickland in the *Georgia Review* noted, "Any serious consideration of Snyder's work, whether critical text or classroom study, must now include *The Practice of the Wild.* " Environmental writer Bill McKibben expressed a similar view in the *New York Review of Books,* stating that the collection represents Snyder's "best prose work so far." Remarking on the author's wide-ranging skill, Parkinson suggested that Snyder is distinguished "not only as a poet but as a prose expositor—he has a gift for quiet, untroubled, accurate observation with occasional leaps to genuine eloquence. He has taken to himself a subject matter, complex, vast, and permanently interesting, a subject so compelling that it is not unreasonable to assert that he has become a center for a new set of cultural possibilities."

The Gary Snyder Reader: Prose, Poetry, and Translations, 1952-1988 was published in 1999, offering a rich selection of Snyder's work in one volume. Discussing the book in the *Seattle Times,* Richard Wallace remarked that many consider Snyder "one of the best poets to write about nature and wilderness since the early Chinese." The *Reader* presents poems, travel writings, letters, interviews, and portions from Snyder's prose works *Earth Household, The Practice of the Wild,* and *A Place in Space.* The prose selections clearly show "how fluid and original a thinker Snyder is," advised Wallace. He is not a "cranky wilderness freak" who believes man should keep nature completely pristine. He is in fact "much more revolutionary than that," looking for ways to deepen personal involvement in community, family, and nature. His philosophy is marked by repeated emphasis of the "witty and irritating idea that we are no smarter, and maybe less skilled, than our Paleolithic ancestors." But it is in his poetry that the writer truly shines, according to Wallace, as he lends his voice "to the ferocious energy of nonhuman beings. He has done it with a direct, masculine, and beautiful talent for more than four decades."

The collection *Danger on Peaks: Poems,* published in 2004, was released eight years after *Mountains and Rivers without End.* The book is Snyder's first collection of entirely new poems, however, to be published in more than twenty years. Although some of the closing poems in the volume address historically current events, including September 11, the bulk of the poems in the volume are set in the past. "As Snyder himself admits, 'most of my work/ such as it is/is done,'" reported *Library Journal* contributor Rochelle Ratner. In addition, many of the poems discuss human relationships. This is of note since Snyder is predominantly known as a nature and wilderness poet. While Carol Volk, writing in *Reviewers Bookwatch,* commented that the collection highlights Snyder's "unique voice," a *Publishers Weekly* reviewer observed that the book "seeks a kind of fraught peace."

Critics and general readers alike have responded to Snyder's "new set of cultural possibilities." Steuding proposed that the writer's work "truly influences one who reads him thoroughly to 'see' in a startling new way. Presenting the vision of an integrated and unified world, this heroic poetic effort cannot but help to create a much needed change of consciousness." Robert Mezey noted that Snyder "has a compelling vision of our relationship with this living nature, which is our nature, what it is and what it must be if we/nature survive on this planet, and his art serves that vision unwaveringly." According to Halvard Johnson in the *Minnesota Review,* the "unique power and value of Snyder's poetry lies not simply in clearly articulated images or in complex patterns of sound and rhythm, but rather in the freedom, the openness of spirit that permits the poems simply to be what they are, what they can be . . . . They respond to the rhythms of the world." Molesworth offered perhaps the most succinct appraisal of Gary Snyder's poetic vision. "Snyder has built a place for the mind to stay and to imagine more far- reaching harmonies while preserving all the wealth of the past," Molesworth concluded. "This, of course, is the world of his books where he is willing and even eager to give us another world both more ideal and more real than our own. The rest of the work is ours."

In an essay published in *A Controversy of Poets,* Snyder offered his own assessment of his art. "As a poet," he wrote, "I hold the most archaic values on earth. They go back to the late Paleolithic: the fertility of the soil, the magic of animals, the power-vision in solitude, the terrifying initiation and rebirth; the love and ecstasy of the dance, the common work of the tribe. I try to hold both history and wilderness in mind, that my poems may approach the true measure of things and stand against the unbalance and ignorance of our times."

BIOGRAPHICAL AND CRITICAL SOURCES:

BOOKS

Allen, Donald M., editor, *The New American Poetry,* Grove (New York, NY), 1960.

Almon, Bert, *Gary Snyder,* Boise State University Press (Boise, ID), 1979.

Altieri, Charles, *Enlarging the Temple: New Directions in American Poetry during the 1960s,* Bucknell University Press (Lewisburg, PA), 1979.

American Nature Writers, Volume 2, Scribner (New York, NY), 1996.

Charters, Samuel, *Some Poems/ Poets: Studies in American Underground Poetry since 1945,* Oyez, 1971.

Contemporary Literary Criticism, Gale (Detroit, MI), Volume 1, 1973, Volume 2, 1974, Volume 5, 1976, Volume 9, 1978, Volume 32, 1985.

Contemporary Poets, 7th edition, St. James Press (Detroit, MI), 2001.

Cook, Bruce, *The Beat Generation,* Scribner (New York, NY), 1971.

Dictionary of Literary Biography, Gale (Detroit, MI), Volume 5: *American Poets since World War II,* 1980; Volume 16: *The Beats: Literary Bohemians in Postwar America,* 1983; Volume 165: *American Poets since World War II,* second series, 1996; Volume 212: *Twentieth-Century American Western Writers,* Second Series, 1999; Volume 275: *Twentieth- Century American Nature Writers: Prose,* 2003.

Faas, Ekbert, editor, *Towards a New American Poetics: Essays & Interviews,* Black Sparrow Press, 1978.

Howard, Richard, *Alone with America: Essays on the Art of Poetry in the United States since 1950,* Atheneum, 1969.

Kherdian, David, *A Biographical Sketch and Descriptive Checklist of Gary Snyder,* Oyez, 1965.

Leary, Paris and Robert Kelly, editors, *A Controversy of Poets,* Doubleday (New York, NY), 1965.

McCord, Howard, *Some Notes to Gary Snyder's "Myths & Texts,"* Sand Dollar, 1971.

McNeill, Katherine, *Gary Snyder,* Phoenix (New York, NY), 1980.

Molesworth, Charles, *Gary Snyder's Vision: Poetry and the Real Work,* University of Missouri Press, 1983.

Rexroth, Kenneth, *Assays,* New Directions (New York, NY), 1961.

Rexroth, Kenneth, *American Poetry in the Twentieth Century,* Herder & Herder, 1971.

Schuler, Robert Jordan, *Journeys toward the Original Mind: The Long Poems of Gary Snyder,* Lang (New York, NY), 1994.

Shaw, Robert B., editor, *American Poetry since 1960: Some Critical Perspectives,* Dufour (Chester Springs, PA), 1974.

Sherman, Paul, *Repossessing and Renewing,* Louisiana State University Press (Baton Rouge, LA), 1976.

Snyder, Gary, *The Real Work: Interviews & Talks, 1964-1979,* edited and with introduction by Scott McLean, New Directions (New York, NY), 1980.

Steuding, Bob, *Gary Snyder,* Twayne (Boston, MA), 1976.

PERIODICALS

Alcheringa, autumn, 1972.

American Poetry Review, November, 1983.

American West, January-February, 1981; Volume 25; August, 1988, p. 30.

Austin American- Statesman, October 11, 2001, Mary Alice Davis, "The Gentle Message of a Poet," p. A17.

Beloit Poetry Journal, fall- winter, 1971-72.

Booklist, September 15, 1996, Ray Olson, review of *Mountains and Rivers without End,* p. 205; June 1, 1999, Ray Olson, review of *The Gary Snyder Reader: Prose, Poetry, and Translations, 1952-1998.*

Boundary II, Volume 4, 1976.

Colorado Quarterly, summer, 1968.

Contemporary Literature, spring, 1977; winter, 1998, Timothy G. Gray, "Semiotic Shepherds: Gary Snyder, Frank O'Hara, and the Embodiment of an Urban Pastoral," p. 523.

Critical Quarterly, winter, 1973.

Criticism, spring, 1977.

Denver Quarterly, fall, 1980.

Environment, December, 1996, Kenneth A. Ollif, review of *A Place in Space: Ethics, Aesthetics, and Watersheds,* p. 25.

Epoch: A Magazine of Contemporary Literature, fall, 1965.

Explicator, fall, 2001, M. Bennet Smith, review of *The Call of the Wild,* p. 47.

Far Point, Volume 4, 1970.

Georgia Review, summer, 1992, p. 382.

Holiday, March, 1966.

Iowa Review, summer, 1970.

Journal of Modern Literature, Volume 2, 1971-72; summer, 1999, Anthony Hunt, "Singing the Dyads: The Chinese Landscape Scroll and Gary Snyder's *Mountains and Rivers without End,*" p. 7.

Kansas Quarterly, spring, 1970.

Library Journal, July, 1999, Cynde Bloom Lahey, review of *The Gary Snyder Reader, 1952-1998,* p. 91; November 15, 2004, Rochelle Ratner, review of *Danger on Peaks: Poems,* p. 64.

Los Angeles Times, November 28, 1986.

Los Angeles Times Book Review, July 1, 1979; November 23, 1980; November 13, 1983; December 28, 1986.

Minnesota Review, fall, 1971.

Nation, September 1, 1969; November 19, 1983.

New Republic, April 4, 1970; March 24, 1997, Christopher Benfey, review of *Mountains and Rivers without End,* p. 38.

New Statesman, November 4, 1966.

New York Review of Books, January 22, 1976; April 11, 1991, p. 29.

New York Times Book Review, May 11, 1969; June 8, 1969; March 23, 1975; December 27, 1992, p. 2.

New York Times Magazine, October 6, 1996, p. 62.

Partisan Review, summer, 1969; winter, 1971-72.

Poetry, June, 197; June, 1972; September, 1984; June, 1994, p. 167.

Prairie Schooner, winter, 1960- 61.

Progressive, November, 1995, p. 28.

Publishers Weekly, August 17, 1990, p. 62; August 10, 1992, p. 58; July 31, 1995, p. 62; August 26, 1996, p. 94; May 31, 1999, review of *The Gary Snyder Reader,* p. 87; October 18, 2004, review of *Danger on Peaks,* p. 61.

Reviewer's Bookwatch, October, 2005, Carol Volk, review of *Danger on Peaks.*

Sagetrieb, spring, 1984.

San Francisco Chronicle, September 1, 1996, Tom Clark, review of *Mountains and Rivers without End,* p. 1; Jesse Hamlin, interview with Gary Snyder, p. 30.

Saturday Review, October 11, 1969; April 3, 1971.

Seattle Times, July 11, 1999, Richard Wallace, review of *The Gary Snyder Reader, 1952- 1998,* p. M9.

Sierra, March-April, 1997, Scott McLean, review of *Mountains and Rivers without End* and *A Place in Space,* p. 112.

Sixties, spring, 1962; spring, 1972.

Southern Review, summer, 1968.

Southwest Review, spring, 1971; winter, 1976; spring, 1982.

Spectator, December 25, 1971.

Sulfur 10, Volume 4, number 1, 1984.

Tamkang Review, spring, 1980.

Times Literary Supplement, December 24, 1971; May 30, 1980.

Village Voice, November 17, 1966; May 1, 1984.

Washington Post Book World, December 25, 1983.

Western American Literature, fall, 1968; spring, 1980; fall, 1980; spring, 1981.

Western Humanities Review, spring, 1975.

Whole Earth Review, winter, 1988, p. 22; spring, 1991, p. 80; spring, 1996, p. 7; summer, 1997, Rick Fields, review of *Mountains and Rivers without End,* p. 91; winter, 1997, review of *Turtle Island, A Place in Space,* and *The Practice of the Wild,* p. 59; fall, 2000, William Pitt Root, review of *The Gary Snyder Reader,* p. 98.

World Literature Today, summer, 1984; spring, 1997, Bernard F. Dick, review of *Mountains and Rivers without End,* p. 392.

Yale Review, July, 1997, Stephen Burt, review of *Mountains and Rivers without End,* p. 150.

* * *

SNYDER, Gary Sherman
See SNYDER, Gary

SOLO, Jay
See ELLISON, Harlan

* * *

SOLWOSKA, Mara
See FRENCH, Marilyn

* * *

SOLZHENITSYN, Aleksandr I. 1918-
(Aleksandr Isayevich Solzhenitsyn)

PERSONAL: Surname is pronounced "sohl-zhe-*neet*-sin"; first name sometimes transliterated as "Alexander" or "Alexandr"; born December 11, 1918, in Kislovodsk, Russia; immigrated to United States, 1976; returned to Russia, 1994; son of Isaaki (a military officer) and Taissia (a typist and stenographer; maiden name, Shcherbak) Solzhenitsyn; married Natalya Reshetovskaya (a professor and research chemist), April 27, 1940 (divorced), remarried, 1956 (divorced, 1972); married Natalya Svetlova (a mathematics teacher), April, 1973; children: (third marriage) Yermolai, Ignat, Stephan, Dmitri Turni (stepson). *Education:* Attended Moscow Institute of History, Philosophy, and Literature, 1939-41; University of Rostov, degree, 1941. *Hobbies and other interests:* Photography, bicycling, hiking, gardening.

ADDRESSES: Home—Ul Tverskaya 12 kv 169, Moscow 119 121, Russia. *Agent*—c/o Farrar, Straus, & Giroux, 19 Union Square West, New York, NY 10003.

CAREER: Writer. First Secondary School, Morozovka, Rostov, USSR (now Russia), physics teacher, 1941; arrested and imprisoned at Greater Lubyanka Prison, Moscow, 1945, Butyrki Prison, Moscow, 1946, Marfino Prison, 1947-50, and Ekibastuz labor camp, Kazakhstan, USSR, 1950-53; mathematics teacher in exile, Kok-Terek, Kazakhstan, mid-1950s; teacher of mathematics and physics in Ryazan, USSR, until early 1960s; banned from teaching and exiled from Moscow; arrested and imprisoned at Lefortovo Prison, 1974; exiled from USSR, 1974. Lecturer; moderator of *A Meeting with Solzhenitsyn* (talk show), No. 1 (Russian state television channel), 1994-95. *Military service:* Soviet Army, 1941-45; became captain of artillery unit; decorated twice (stripped of rank and decorations, 1945).

MEMBER: American Academy of Arts and Sciences, Hoover Institute on War, Revolution and Peace (honorary), Russian Academy of Sciences.

AWARDS, HONORS: Nominated for Lenin Prize, 1964; Prix du Meilleur Livre Etranger (France), 1969, for *The First Circle* and *Cancer Ward;* Nobel Prize for Literature, 1970; Freedoms Foundation Award, Stanford University, 1976; Templeton Foundation prize for "progress in religion," 1983; Medal of Honor for Literature, National Arts Club, 1993. Honorary degrees from various institutions, including Harvard University, 1978, and Holy Cross, 1984.

WRITINGS:

Odin den' Ivana Denisovicha (novella; first published in *Novy Mir,* 1962), Flegon Press (London, England), 1962, translation by Ralph Parker published as *One Day in the Life of Ivan Denisovich,* Dutton (New York, NY), 1963.

Dlya polzy'dela (novella; first published in *Novy Mir,* 1963), Russian Language Specialties, 1963, translation by David Floyd and Max Hayward published as *For the Good of the Cause,* Praeger (Westport, CT), 1964.

Sluchay na stantsii Krechetovka [and] Matrenin dvor (novellas; titles mean "An Incident at Krechetovka Station" and "Matryona's House"; first published in *Novy Mir,* 1963), Flegon Press (London, England), 1963, translation by Paul W. Blackstock published as *We Never Make Mistakes,* University of South Carolina Press (Columbia, SC), 1963.

Sochininiia (selected works), Posev (Frankfurt, Germany), 1966.

V kruge pervom (novel), Harper (New York, NY), 1968, translation by Thomas P. Whitney published as *The First Circle,* Harper (New York, NY), 1968.

Rakovyl korpus (novel), Bodley Head (London, England), 1968, translation by Nicholas Bethell and David Burg published in two volumes as *Cancer Ward,* Bodley Head (London, England), 1968–69, published as *The Cancer Ward,* Farrar, Straus (New York, NY), 1969.

Olen'i shalashovka (play), Flegon Press (London, England), 1968, translation by Nicholas Bethell and David Burg published as *The Love Girl and the Innocent,* Farrar, Straus (New York, NY), 1969.

Svecha na vetru (play), Flegon Press (London, England), 1968, translation by Keith Armes and Arthur Hudgins published as *Candle in the Wind,* University of Minnesota Press (Minneapolis, MN), 1973.

Les droits de l'ecrivain (title means "The Rights of the Writer"), Éditions du Seuil (Paris, France), 1969.

Krokhotnye Rasskazy, Librarie des Cinq Continents (Paris, France), 1970.

Krasnoe koleso (novel; title means "The Red Wheel"), Volume 1: *Avgust chetyrnadtsatogo,* Flegon Press (London, England), 1971, translation by Michael Glenny published as *August 1914,* Farrar, Straus (New York, NY), 1972, revised edition, YMCA Press (Paris, France), 1983, translation by Harry Willetts, Farrar, Straus (New York, NY), 1989, Volume 2: *Oktyabr' shestnadtsatogo,* YMCA Press (Paris, France), 1984, translation by Willetts published as *November 1916: The Red Wheel, Knot II,* Farrar, Straus (New York, NY), 1999, Volume 3: *Mart semnadtsatogo,* YMCA Press (London, England), 1986, Volume 4: *Aprel' semnadtsatogo,* YMCA Press (Paris, France), 1991.

Stories and Prose Poems by Aleksandr Solzhenitsyn, translated by Michael Glenny, Farrar, Straus (New York, NY), 1971.

Six Etudes by Aleksandr Solzhenitsyn, translated by James G. Walker, College City Press, 1971.

Nobelevskara lektsira po literature, YMCA Press (Paris, France), 1972, translation by F.D. Reeve published as *Nobel Lecture by Aleksandr Solzhenitsyn,* Farrar, Straus (New York, NY), 1972.

A Lenten Letter to Pimen, Patriarch of All Russia, translated by Theofanis G. Staurou, Burgess, 1972.

Arkhipelag Gulag, 1918-1956: Op 'bit khudozhestvennopo issledovaniia, YMCA Press (Paris, France), 1973, translation published as *The Gulag Archipelago, 1918-1956: An Experiment in Literary Investigation,* Harper (New York, NY), Volume 1, translated by Thomas P. Whitney, 1974, Volume 2, translated by Whitney, 1976, Volume 3, translated by Harry Willetts, 1979.

Mir i nasilie (title means "Peace and Violence"), [Frankfurt, Germany], 1974.

Prusskie nochi: pozma napisappaja v lagere v 1950 (title means "Prussian Nights: Epic Poems Written at the Forced Labor Camp, 1950"), YMCA Press (Paris, France), 1974.

Pis'mo vozhdram Sovetskogo Soruza, YMCA Press (Paris, France), 1974, translation by Hilary Sternberg published as *Letter to the Soviet Leaders,* Harper (New York, NY), 1974.

(And photographer with others) *Solzhenitsyn: A Pictorial Autobiography,* Farrar, Straus (New York, NY), 1974.

Bodalsra telenok s dubom, YMCA Press (Paris, France), 1975, translation published as *The Oak and the Calf,* Association Press, 1975, translation by Harry Willetts published as *The Oak and the Calf: Sketches of Literary Life in the Soviet Union,* Harper (New York, NY), 1980.

Lenin v Tsiurikhe, YMCA Press (Paris, France), 1975, translation by Harry Willetts published as *Lenin in Zurich,* Farrar, Straus (New York, NY), 1976.

Amerikanskie rechi (title means "American Speeches"), YMCA Press (Paris, France), 1975.

(With others) *From under the Rubble,* translated by Michael Scammell, Little, Brown (Boston, MA), 1975, published as *From under the Ruins,* Association Press, 1975.

(With others) *Detente: Prospects for Democracy and Dictatorship,* Transaction Books, 1975.

Warning to the West, Farrar, Straus (New York, NY), 1976.

Rasskazy (short stories), Posev (Frankfurt, Germany), 1976.

A World Split Apart (commencement address), Harper (New York, NY), 1979.

The Mortal Danger, Harper (New York, NY), 1981.

P'esy I kinostsenarii, YMCA Press (Paris, France), 1981.

Publitsistika: Stat'i i rechi, YMCA Press (Paris, France), 1981.

Victory Celebrations: A Comedy in Four Acts [and] *Prisoners: A Tragedy* (plays), translated by Helen Rapp and Nancy Thomas, Bodley Head (London, England), 1983.

(Editor) *Russkii slovar' iazykovogo rasshireniia,* [Russia], 1990.

Kak nam obustroit' Rossiiu, YMCA Press, 1990, translation published as *Rebuilding Russia: Reflections and Tentative Proposals,* Farrar, Straus (New York, NY), 1991.

Les Invisibles, Fayard, 1992, translation published as *Invisible Allies,* Counterpoint, 1995.

The Russian Question toward the End of the Century, Farrar, Straus (New York, NY), 1995.

Po minute v den', Argumenty i Fakty (Moscow, Russia), 1995.

Russia Is Falling, 1998.

Rossiia v obvale, Russkii Put' (Moscow, Russia), 1998.

Proterevshi glaza, Nash Dom (Moscow, Russia), 1999.

Sobranie sochinenii: v deviati tomakh, Terra (Moscow, Russia), 1999.

Dvesti let vmeste (1795-1995) (history), Russkii put' (Moscow, Russia), 2001.

Also author of unpublished works, including plays.

Contributor to periodicals, including *New Leader.*

ADAPTATIONS: The Love Girl and the Innocent was adapted for the stage by Paul Avila Mayer as *A Play by Aleksandr Solzhenitsyn,* 1970.

SIDELIGHTS: Aleksandr I. Solzhenitsyn is a notable Russian writer who first drew worldwide attention in 1962 with *One Day in the Life of Ivan Denisovich,* his novella recounting the arduous existence of prisoners in the system of concentration camps devised under Soviet dictator Josef Stalin. According to Ludmilla Koehler, writing in *Russian Review,* Solzhenitsyn's literary debut "swept into the world like a gust of fresh wind." In the ensuing twelve years Solzhenitsyn continued to produce esteemed works, including an ambitious study, *The Gulag Archipelago, 1918-1956: An Experiment in Literary Investigation,* and two novels, *The First Circle* and *Cancer Ward.* Such writings, while winning acclaim in the west, further aggravated his notoriety in the USSR, and in 1974, four years after receiving the Nobel Prize for literature, Solzhenitsyn was summarily expelled from his homeland.

Solzhenitsyn first ran afoul of communist authorities in 1945 while serving in the Soviet Army. Accused of transmitting questionable correspondence to a fellow officer, Solzhenitysn was sent to a Moscow prison, where he became a regular patron of the prison library and absorbed the works of writers ranging from Yevgeny Zamyatin, a Soviet master of the 1920s, to John Dos Passos, the celebrated American novelist. After being transferred to a research prison populated by scientists and technicians, Solzhenitsyn regularly occupied himself by imagining poems and committing them to memory. "Solzhenitsyn had done some writing during both World War II and his imprisonment thereafter," confirmed Edward E. Ericson, Jr., in *Solzhenitsyn: The Moral Vision.* "We cannot be sure how much of this work . . . he committed to memory before he felt it necessary, for safety's sake, to destroy the manuscripts." Solzhenitsyn continued to produce poetry in this unlikely manner after transferring to a concentration camp in 1950. Three years later, after receiving his release from the prison system, Solzhenitsyn was banished to central Asia, where he taught mathematics and science and began writing plays.

After his exile ended in 1956, Solzhenitsyn moved to Ryazan, where he continued to work as a teacher. He eventually shared his writings with friends, who proved sufficiently impressed to recommend their submission to *Novy Mir* editor Aleksandr Tvardovsky. Solzhenitsyn initially resisted the temptation to publish, but he eventually sent a short story, "Shch-854," which impressed Tvardovsky as a compelling portrait of a prisoner in the Soviet camps. Solzhenitsyn ultimately developed the tale into *One Day in the Life of Ivan Denisovich,* his understated novella—rendered in spare, plain prose—of one prisoner's typical activities. "Ivan Denisovich," affirmed Shirley J. Paolini in *Reference Guide to Short Fiction,* "represents the common individual incarcerated in a Soviet camp for an insignificant crime; his energies are devoted entirely to survival under brutal conditions." Lauren Livingston, writing in the *English Review,* summarized *One Day in the Life of Ivan Denisovich* as a "haunting read," and Gleb Zekulin, writing in *Soviet Studies,* recommended it as "a mine of information." Still another enthusiast, Vladimir J. Rus, wrote in *Canadian Slavonic Papers* that "Solzhenitsyn has given the world a moving picture of . . . a genuine joy in one's own existence, even when so limited in time, space, and one's own consciousness." Abraham Rothberg, meanwhile, acknowledged in *Aleksandr Solzhenitsyn: The Major Novels,* that in *One Day in the Life of Ivan Denisovich* Solzhenitsyn "explored new terrain in the use of language, exploiting a combination of prison slang, peasant and pornographic slang," and Christopher Moody, in *Solzhenitsyn,* deemed the story an "eloquent protest." Similarly, Robert L. Yarup observed in the *Explicator* that *One Day in the Life of Ivan Denisovich* concerns "man's irrepressible instinct for freedom."

One Day in the Life of Ivan Denisovich proved an immense success with Soviet readers, and Solzhenitsyn readily followed it in *Novy Mir* with short stories, including "Matryona's House," in which a former prisoner befriends an aging peasant woman who serves as his landlady. Andrej Kodjak, in his study *Alexander Solzhenitsyn,* noted that "Solzhenitsyn draws on his own experience to create the narrator, Ignatich." John Clardy, in a *Cimarron Review* essay, expressed particular praise for Solzhenitsyn's handling of characterization in "Matryona's House," declaring that "Matryona, like Tolstoy's Anna Karenina, stands out in our minds as a real personality." Leonid Rzhevsky, meanwhile, quoted another reader, in *Solzhenitsyn: Creator and Heroic Deed,* who considered Matryona "'the most brilliant image of the peasant woman in all of the Russian literature I have read.'" Still another critic, Stephen S. Lottridge, wrote in *Russian Literature Triquarterly* that "Matryona's House" relates "the trials and loss endured by an innocent and righteous person," while Robert Louis Jackson, in a piece featured in *Solzhenitsyn: A Collection of Critical Essays,* summarized the tale as "significant art." Sheryl A. Spitz, meanwhile, described the short work in a *Russian Review* essay as "the story of one individual's moral maturation."

The year 1968 saw the western publication of *The First Circle,* a lengthy novel—described by an essayist in *Encyclopedia of World Biography* as "harshly satiric"—about life in the Soviet prison system. Here an idealistic diplomat suddenly finds himself arrested and consigned to prison, where he soon meets an ardent communist, an engineer, and a scientist who longs to produce literature. In the novel—according to David M. Halperin, in an essay included in *Solzhenitsyn in Exile: Critical Essays and Documentary Materials*—Solzhenitsyn "examines both the omnipresence of lying as a demonstrable feature of Soviet society and as a metaphysical, demonic device." Furthermore, Solzhenitsyn, in his characterization of Stalin, emphasized that the dictator, however monstrous, however powerful, was nonetheless human. "In his portrait of Stalin in *The First Circle,*" wrote Paul N. Siegel in *Clio,* "Solzhenitsyn, in cutting the towering figure of the Stalin of Stalinist myth-making down to size, showed him to be a human being at ironic variance with the image."

Like *The First Circle, Cancer Ward*—which also appeared in the west in 1968—takes place in an isolated community. But unlike either *One Day in the Life of Ivan Denisovich* or *The First Circle,* which both occur in a prison, *Cancer Ward* unfolds in a hospital and charts the experiences of two patients: a bureaucrat who anticipates preferential treatment and a former prisoner with no tolerance for elitism. Jeffrey Meyers, writing in *Twentieth-Century Literature,* noted Solzhenitsyn's use of cancer as a metaphor for Stalinism. "There is no escape from cancer, despite periods of remission," declared Meyers, "just as there is no escape from the legacy of Stalinism, despite the political thaw."

While writing his ambitious novels, Solzhenitsyn also generated various literary sketches, some of which arrived in the west. John B. Dunlop, writing in *Solzhenitsyn in Exile: Critical Essays and Documentary Materials,* described these works as "prose poems of a powerful lyric intensity," and he added that "they are primarily concerned with the spiritual inadequacy of modern life."

In 1970, amid increasing recognition as the USSR's foremost writer, Solzhenitsyn received the Nobel Prize for literature. Unfortunately, communist authorities, having confiscated his papers three years earlier, refused to let him attend the awards ceremony in Stockholm.

Solzhenitsyn's reputation, meanwhile, continued to grow, particularly with the appearance of *The Gulag Archipelago, 1918-1956: An Experiment in Literary Investigation,* a formidable history of the Soviet prison system. This diverse work, which numbers three volumes, includes autobiographical material, straightforward history, and details on specific methods of interrogation and confinement. Writing in *Month,* Alla Braithwaite declared that *The Gulag Archipelago* "is not only a report, a record for history" but a volume in which the writer's "mood is one of reflection . . . but also of confession."

In 1974, one year after *The Gulag Archipelago* appeared in the West, Soviet authorities, who had previously denied Solzhenitsyn permission to leave the country, decided that he could no longer remain there, and after briefly imprisoning him, they sent him into an exile that would last until 1994. Solzhenitsyn settled in Vermont and continued to write, meanwhile condemning the West for its materialism and dearth of spirituality. Notable among his projects from this period of exile is *The Red Wheel,* a multi-volume saga that recalls Leo Tolstoy's *War and Peace* in both its scope and its plethora of both fictional and real characters. In 1972 the first volume of *The Red Wheel* appeared in English translation as *August 1914.* Geoffrey A. Hosking, in a *Times Literary Supplement* analysis, described *August 1914* as Solzhenitsyn's attempt to illustrate "why [the Soviet Union's] economic growth took place in a lopsided and debilitating manner, why Siberia remained underdeveloped, and . . . why Russians started disemboweling each other in great numbers." Irving Howe, though, came to regard *August 1914,* in the *New York Times Book Review,* as a "swollen and misshapen book."

Perhaps Solzhenitsyn agreed with Howe's appraisal, for in 1983 he produced a revision of *August 1914.* The next year he published a sequel, *November 1916,* which features over 2,000 pages delineating the activities of historical figures in St. Petersburg—then known as Petrograd. Philippe D. Radley, writing in *World Literature Today,* contended that "the tremendous size is . . . off-putting," and he cast it in "that curious genre . . . of fictionalized history." Michael Spinella, however, acknowledged *November 1916,* in his *Booklist* assessment, as a "distinguished tome," and M. Anna Falbo described it in *Library Journal* as Solzhenitsyn's "magnum opus." In 1986 Solzhenitsyn issued, in Russian, a third volume, *Mart semnadtsatogo,* and in 1991 he continued *The Red Wheel* with a fourth part, *Aprel' semnadtsatogo.*

In 1994, following the fall of the communist regime in the Soviet Union, Solzhenitsyn left the United States and settled in Moscow. The next year he issued *The Russian Question toward the End of the Century,* wherein he proposes a reaffirmation of compassion and peculiarly Russian fatalism. In addition, he calls for the reunification of Russia, the Ukraine, and Belarus. Tatyana Tolstaya, writing in the *New York Review of*

Books, dismissed Solzhenitsyn's political views as outdated and denounced his writing as egoistic. "Solzhenitsyn's fundamental approach to [Western civilization's] clumsy, myriad lords is that they are bad, improvident imperialists," Tolstaya declared. "And he himself is provident, that's the whole difference." Hugh Ragsdale, however, reported in the *Virginia Quarterly Review* that "a recent poll in Petersburg found far more sympathy for [Solzhenitsyn] than for anyone in Russia's present leadership," adding: "we cannot say of him—as of the Bourbons returned from exile—that he has learned nothing and forgotten nothing."

Solzhenitsyn's publications since his return to Russia include *Dvesti let vmeste (1795-1995),* a history of the Jewish experience in Russia in the nineteenth and twentieth centuries. Geoffrey A. Hosking, in a *Times Literary Supplement* review, lauded *Dvesti let vmeste* as a noteworthy volume and described it as a "vigorous" account.

BIOGRAPHICAL AND CRITICAL SOURCES:

BOOKS

Allaback, Steven, *Alexander Solzhenitsyn,* Taplinger (New York, NY), 1978.

Barker, Francis, *Solzhenitsyn: Politics and Form,* Barnes & Noble (Lanham, MD), 1977.

Carter, Stephen, *The Politics of Solzhenitsyn,* Macmillan (New York, NY), 1977.

Contemporary Literary Criticism, Thomson Gale (Detroit, MI), Volume 1, 1973, Volume 2, 1974, Volume 4, 1975, Volume 7, 1977, Volume 9, 1978, Volume 10, 1979, Volume 18, 1981, Volume 26, 1983, Volume 34, 1985, Volume 78, 1994.

Curtis, James M., *Solzhenitsyn's Traditional Imagination,* University of Georgia Press (Athens, GA), 1984.

Dunlop, John B., and others, editors, *Solzhenitsyn in Exile: Critical Essays and Documentary Materials,* Collier (New York, NY), 1973.

Encyclopedia of World Biography, Thomson Gale (Detroit, MI), 1998.

Ericson, Edward E., Jr., *Solzhenitsyn: The Moral Vision,* Eerdmans (Grand Rapids, MI), 1982.

Feuer, Kathryn, editor, *Solzhenitsyn: A Collection of Critical Essays,* Prentice-Hall (Englewood Cliffs, NJ), 1976.

Fiene, Donald M., *Alexander Solzhenitsyn: An International Bibliography of Writings by and about Him, 1962-1973,* Ardis (Ann Arbor, MI), 1973.

Flegon, A., *Alexander Solzhenitsyn: Myth and Reality,* Flegon Press (London, England), 1986.

Kelly, Donald R., *The Solzhenitsyn-Sakharov Dialogue: Politics, Society, and the Future,* Greenwood Press (Westport, CT), 1982.

Kodjak, Andrej, *Alexander Solzhenitsyn,* Twayne (Boston, MA), 1978.

Labedz, Leopold, *Solzhenitsyn: A Documentary Record,* Indiana University Press (Bloomington, IN), 1973.

Lukas, George, *Alexander Solzhenitsyn,* M.I.T. Press (Cambridge, MA), 1971.

Medvedev, Zhores, *Ten Years after "Ivan Denisovich,"* Knopf (New York, NY), 1973.

Moody, Christopher, *Solzhenitsyn,* Oliver & Boyd, 1973.

Pontuso, James F., *Solzhenitsyn's Political Thought,* University Press of Virginia (Charlottesville, VA), 1990.

Reference Guide to Short Fiction, 2nd edition, St. James Press (Detroit, MI), 1999, pp. 593-595.

Rothberg, Abraham, *Aleksandr Solzhenitsyn: The Major Novels,* Cornell University Press (Ithaca, NY), 1971.

Rzhevsky, Leonid, *Solzhenitsyn: Creator and Heroic Deed,* translated by Sonja Miller, University of Alabama Press (Tuscaloosa, AL), 1978.

Scammell, Michael, *Solzhenitsyn: A Biography,* Norton (New York, NY), 1984.

Short Story Criticism, Volume 32, Thomson Gale (Detroit, MI), 1999, pp. 328-412.

PERIODICALS

Booklist, September 1, 1998, Michael Spinella, review of *November 1916: The Red Wheel, Knot II,* p. 7.

Canadian Slavonic Papers, summer-fall, 1971, Vladimir J. Rus, "*One Day in the Life of Ivan Denisovich:* A Point-of-View Analysis," pp. 165-178.

Cimarron Review, October, 1970, John Clardy, "Alexander Solzhenitsyn and the Impending Event: An Added Dimension to Solve an Old Problem," pp. 16-23.

Clio, spring, 1983, pp. 211-232; fall, 1984, Paul N. Siegel, "Solzhenitsyn's Portrait of Lenin," pp. 1-13.

English Review, September, 1999, Lauren Livingston, review of *A Day in the Life of Ivan Denisovich,* p. 19.

Explicator, spring, 1982, Robert L. Yarup, "Solzhenitsyn's *One Day in the Life of Ivan Denisovich,*" pp. 61-63.

Independent (London, England), April 10, 1997, p. 18.

Library Journal, September 1, 1998, M. Anna Falbo, review of *November 1916: The Red Wheel, Knot II,* p. 217.

Modern Age, spring/summer, 1984, pp. 215-221; fall, 1989, pp. 294-310; spring, 1995, pp. 233-240.

Month, May, 1990, pp. 179-185.

New York Review of Books, December 19, 1968; December 21, 1989, pp. 11-13; November 24, 1991; February 7, 1993; October 19, 1995, p. 7.

New York Times Book Review, September 15, 1968; September 10, 1972; March 3, 1974; July 2, 1989, pp. 1, 17-18; January 7, 1996, p. 14.

Russian Literature Triquarterly, spring, 1973, Stephen S. Lottridge, "Solzhenitsyn and Leskov," pp. 478-489.

Russian Review, April, 1962, Ludmilla Koehler, "Alexander Solzhenitsyn and Russian Literary Tradition," pp. 176-184; April, 1997, Sheryl A. Spitz, "The Impact of Structure in Solzhenitsyn's 'Matryona's Home,'" pp. 167-183.

Soviet Studies, July, 1964, Gleb Zekulin, "Solzhenitsyn's Four Stories," pp. 45-62; October, 1982, pp. 601-615.

Times Literary Supplement, February 3, 1984, pp. 99-100; March 1, 2002, pp. 3-4.

Twentieth-Century Literature, December, 1977, pp. 498-517; spring, 1983, pp. 54-68.

Virginia Quarterly Review, autumn, 1995, Hugh Ragsdale, "The Solzhenitsyn That Nobody Knows," pp. 634-641.

Washington Post Book World, February 16, 1992, p. 7; December 31, 1995, pp. 1, 10.

World Literature Today, winter, 2000, Philippe D. Radley, review of *November 1916,* p. 190.

OTHER

BBC Books, http://www.bbc.co.uk/arts/books/ (January 30, 2003), "Alexandr Solzhenitsyn."

Nobel E-Museum, http://www.nobel.se/literature/ (October 29, 2002), "Alexander Solzhenitsyn—Autobiography."

* * *

SOLZHENITSYN, Aleksandr Isayevich
See SOLZHENITSYN, Aleksandr I.

* * *

SOMERS, Jane
See LESSING, Doris

SONTAG, Susan 1933-2004

PERSONAL: Born January 16, 1933, in New York, NY; died of leukemia December 28, 2004, in New York, NY; married Philip Rieff (a professor of sociology), 1950 (divorced, 1958); children: David. *Education:* Attended University of California, Berkeley, 1948-49; University of Chicago, B.A., 1951; Harvard University, M.A. (English), 1954, M.A. (philosophy), 1955, Ph.D. candidate, 1955-57; St. Anne's College, Oxford, graduate study, 1957.

CAREER: Novelist, short-story writer, critic, and essayist. University of Connecticut, Storrs, instructor in English, 1953-54; *Commentary,* New York City, editor, 1959; lecturer in philosophy, City College (now City College of the City University of New York), New York City, and Sarah Lawrence College, Bronxville, NY, 1959-60; Columbia University, New York City, instructor in department of religion, 1960-64; Rutgers University, New Brunswick, NJ, writer-in-residence, 1964-65. Director of motion pictures *Duet for Cannibals,* 1969, *Brother Carl: A Filmscript,* 1971, and *Promised Lands,* 1974; director of stage play *Waiting for Godot,* 1993.

MEMBER: PEN American Center (president, 1987-89), American Academy of Arts and Letters, American Academy of Arts and Sciences (elected 1993).

AWARDS, HONORS: Fellowships from American Association of University Women, 1957, Rockefeller Foundation, 1966, 1974, Guggenheim Memorial Foundation, 1966, 1975, and MacArthur Foundation, 1990-95; George Polk Memorial Award, 1966, for contributions toward better appreciation of theater, motion pictures, and literature; National Book Award nomination, 1966, for *Against Interpretation, and Other Essays;* Brandeis University Creative Arts Award, 1975; National Institute and American Academy award for literature, 1976; National Book Critics Circle prize for criticism, 1978, for *On Photography;* named Officier de l'Ordre des Arts et des Lettres, France, 1984; Malaparte Prize, 1992; National Book Award, 2000, for *In America*; Jerusalem Prize, Jerusalem International Book Fair, 2001; nominated for National Book Critics Circle award for criticism, 2003, for *Regarding the Pain of Others*; Peace Prize, German Publishers and Booksellers Association, 2003.

WRITINGS:

NONFICTION

Against Interpretation, and Other Essays, Farrar, Straus, 1966.

Styles of Radical Will, Farrar, Straus, 1969.
Trip to Hanoi, Farrar, Straus, 1968.
(Author of introduction) Dugald Stermer, compiler, *The Art of Revolution,* McGraw-Hill, 1970.
(Author of introduction) E.M. Cioran, *The Temptation to Exist,* translated by Richard Howard, Quadrangle, 1970.
(Editor and author of introduction) *Antonin Artaud: Selected Writings,* Farrar, Straus, 1976.
On Photography, Farrar, Straus, 1977.
Illness as Metaphor, Farrar, Straus, 1978.
Under the Sign of Saturn, Farrar, Straus, 1980.
(Editor and author of introduction) *A Barthes Reader,* Farrar, Straus, 1982.
A Susan Sontag Reader, introduction by Elizabeth Hardwick, Farrar, Straus, 1982.
(With Cesare Colombo) *Italy: One Hundred Years of Photography,* Alinari, 1988.
AIDS and Its Metaphors, Farrar, Straus, 1989.
Cage-Cunningham-Johns: Dancers on a Plane, Knopf, 1990.
(Author of introduction) Danilo Kis, editor, *Homo Poeticus: Essays and Interviews,* Farrar, Straus, 1995.
(Contributor) Michael Auping and others, *Howard Hodgkin Paintings,* Harry N. Abrams, 1995.
(Author of introduction) *Photographs from Storyville, the Red-Light District of New Orleans,* J. Cape (London), 1996.
(With Robert Wilson and Vittorio Santoro) *Rwwm: On Robert Wilson's Production Site Watermill,* Distributed Art, 1997.
(With Mikhail Lemkhin and Czeslaw Milosz) *Fragments: Joseph Brodsky, Leningrad,* Farrar, Straus, 1998.
Where the Stress Falls (essays), Farrar Straus & Giroux, 2001.
Regarding the Pain of Others, Farrar, Straus, 2003.

FICTION

The Benefactor (novel), Farrar, Straus, 1963.
Death Kit (novel), Farrar, Straus, 1967.
I, etcetera (short stories), Farrar, Straus, 1978.
The Way We Live Now (short story), Farrar, Straus, 1991.
The Volcano Lover: A Romance (novel), Farrar, Straus, 1992.
In America: A Novel, Farrar, Straus, 2000.

SCREENPLAYS

Duet for Cannibals (produced by Sandrew Film & Teater AB [Sweden], 1969), Farrar, Straus, 1970.
Brother Carl: A Filmscript (produced by Sandrew Film & Teater AB and Svenska Filminstitutet [Sweden], 1971), Farrar, Straus, 1974.

OTHER

(Author of fiction) Richard Misrach, *Violent Legacies: Three Cantos* (photography), Aperture (New York, NY), 1992.
Alice in Bed: A Play in Eight Scenes (play), Farrar, Straus, 1993.
Conversations with Susan Sontag, edited by Leland A. Poague, University Press of Mississippi (Jackson), 1995.
Lady from the Sea (play; adapted from the novel *The Lady from the Sea,* by Henri Ibsen; first produced in Ferrara, Italy, 1998), published in *Theater,* Vol. 29, no. 1, 1999.
(Contributor) Annie Leibovitz, *Women,* Random House (New York, NY), 1999.
(Contributor) Polly Borland, *The Babies,* PowerHouse Books (New York, NY), 2000.

Also author of *Literature* (monograph), 1966; and the screenplays *Promised Lands,* 1974 and *Unguided Tour,* 1983. Contributor to *Great Ideas Today,* 1966; also contributor of short stories, reviews, essays, and articles to numerous periodicals, including *Atlantic Monthly, American Review, Playboy, Partisan Review, Nation, Commentary, Harper's, New York Times,* and *New York Review of Books.*

WORK IN PROGRESS: Sontag's journals and letters will be edited for publication by her son, David Rieff. No release date has been set.

SIDELIGHTS: Susan Sontag was an American critic who penned controversial essays on topics ranging from "camp" to cancer, encompassing her views on literature, plays, film, photography, and politics. Though best known for her nonfiction, the author also has written novels and short stories and has written and directed several films; in an introduction to *A Susan Sontag Reader,* Elizabeth Hardwick called Sontag a "foraging pluralist" who is attracted to "waywardness," "outrageousness," and "the unpredictable, along with extremity." *New York Times Book Review* correspondent David Bromwich noted that her "subjects bear witness to Miss Sontag's range as well as her diligence. She keeps up—appears, at times, to do the keeping-up for a whole generation. . . . From ground to summit, from oblivion to oblivion, she covers the big movements and ideas and then sends out her report, not without qualms. For the art she most admires, an inward and recalcitrant art, exists in tension with her own role as its advocate." According to Susan Walker in the *Dictionary of Literary Biography,* Sontag's career as a writer "has been marked by a seriousness of pursuit and a relentless intelligence that analyzes modern culture on almost every possible level: artistic, philosophical, literary, political, and moral. . . . Sontag has produced a stimulating and varied body of work which entertains the issues of art while satisfying the rigors of her own intellect."

Sontag has been a shaper of contemporary criticism through her call for a new formal aestheticism. Michiko Kakutani observed in the *New York Times* that Sontag argues "that art and morality have no common ground, that it is style, not content, that matters most of all." Likewise, *Saturday Review* contributor Edward Grossman suggested that Sontag takes "distinctions between art and science, between high and low, to be largely, though not entirely, false and irrelevant," and she also dismisses the "old, mainly literary notion that art is the criticism of life." According to Stanley Aronowitz in the *Voice Literary Supplement,* Sontag's reactions "against the dessication of literature by sociology," seen especially in her works *Against Interpretation, and Other Essays* and *Styles of Radical Will,* have offered "a liberating vision." Although her ideas have evolved over the more than thirty-five years she has been writing, Sontag is still deeply involved in aesthetic awareness and is an advocate of sensuous perception of the arts. *Commentary* essayist Alicia Ostriker noted, however, that as an author, Sontag "is distinguished less by a decided or passionate point of view . . . than by an eagerness to explore anything new." Ostriker concludes: "Sensitive people are a dime a dozen. The rarer gift Miss Sontag has to offer is brains."

As a young critic writing for *Partisan Review, Harper's,* the *Nation* and the *New York Review of Books,* Sontag became known as a champion of European artists and thinkers. Chicago *Tribune Books* contributor Seymour Krim wrote: "Although she was reared in Arizona and California, . . . Sontag has been much more at home with modern Europe than with this country. She made this plain . . . when she gave us fresh studies of such people as Simone Weil, Camus, Sartre, Marxist critic Georg Lukacs, Nathalie Sarraute, Eugene Ionesco, etc. In Sontag's hands the distant and blurred became sharp and immediate, and [she] . . . is a trailblazer of what might be called America's new cultural internationalism." In a *New Republic* review, Leo Braudy stated that Sontag's particular polemic has been "to celebrate the leopards in the temple of literature, not those cool and calm consciousnesses . . . who abided all questions and saw life whole, but those whose own derangement allowed them to explode the lies of order so that better forms might be discovered. In her criticism she labors to turn even the most self-isolating, uncompromising, and personally outrageous of such figures . . . into humane teachers, whose flame, all the brighter for being trimmed, she will pass on to future generations." With a tone of "eminent rationality," to quote Wendy Lesser in *Threepenny Review,* Sontag has acquainted readers with "the artist as exemplary sufferer" and with "the fragmentation, exaggeration, morbidity, and lunacy with which art has responded to the modern world."

From case studies of neglected artists, Sontag moved to theoretical essays on the aims of modern art and the relationship between art and criticism. Her works "encourage, in art and criticism, . . . respect for sensuous surfaces, for feeling, for form, for style," according to Ostriker. A *Times Literary Supplement* reviewer observes that in *Against Interpretation, and Other Essays,* Sontag "is tired of interpretive criticism and mimetic art. . . . She proposes instead an art which is joyously itself and a criticism which enthusiastically dwells on the fact." John S. Peterson elaborated in the *Los Angeles Times:* "Sontag has argued that critical interpretation tends to be stifling and reactionary, and that the job of the critic is not to assign 'meanings' but to show how a work of art is what it is. Her own writings [are] not to be regarded as criticism, strictly speaking, but as case studies for an aesthetic, a theory of her own sensibility." *Nation* essayist Robert Sklar suggested that Sontag makes this aesthetic criticism a form of philosophical inquiry: "Art, particularly the language arts, are themselves caught in the trap of consciousness. When consciousness as we know it is destroyed, art as we know it will also come to an end—art as expression or representation, art as truth and beauty. The 'minimal art' of our own time, in painting, sculpture, the new novel, already aims, in this sense, at the abolition of art." Sklar concluded that Sontag's "form of prophecy and critical insight, this mode of radical will, can be extremely clarifying and stimulating for the willing reader."

Against Interpretation, and Other Essays and *Styles of Radical Will,* both published in the 1960s, assured Sontag a wide and controversial reputation. In the *Atlantic Monthly,* Hilton Kramer describes how the American intellectual community reacted to her works: "Sontag seemed to have an unfailing faculty for dividing intellectual opinion and inspiring a sense of outrage, consternation, and betrayal among the many readers—

especially older readers—who disagreed with her. And it was just this faculty for offending respectable opinion that, from the outset, was an important part of her appeal for those who welcomed her pronouncements. She was admired not only for what she said but for the pain, shock, and disarray she caused in saying it. Sontag thus succeeded in doing something that is given to very few critics to achieve. She made criticism a medium of intellectual scandal, and this won her instant celebrity in the world where ideas are absorbed into fashions and fashions combine to create a new cultural atmosphere." William Phillips in *Partisan Review* contended that since Sontag was taken as a spokesperson for "The New," she was perceived "as someone to take a stand for or against. Hence, as with so many of the younger writers, the reactions to her have fallen into the stereotypes of polarization. But because she is so articulate and takes all questions as her theoretical province, because her writing has political as well as literary implications, the polarization is both sharper and more distorting. Susan Sontag is both an exponent and a victim of the new polarization; an exponent in that she doesn't go in for modulation and adjustment, a victim because her concern with speculative and literary problems often falls outside the prevailing left-right fashions."

A near-fatal case of cancer interrupted Sontag's career in the mid-1970s, but as she recovered she wrote two of her best-known works, *On Photography* and *Illness as Metaphor.* In the *Washington Post Book World,* William McPherson described *On Photography* as "a brilliant analysis of the profound changes photographic images have made in our way of looking at the world, and at ourselves over the last 140 years. . . . *On Photography* merely describes a phenomenon we take as much for granted as water from the tap, and how that phenomenon has changed us—a remarkable enough achievement, when you think about it." William H. Gass offers even stronger praise for the National Book Critics Circle prize-winning work in the *New York Times Book Review.* Every page of *On Photography,* wrote Gass, "raises important and exciting questions about its subject and raises them in the best way. In a context of clarity, skepticism and passionate concern, with an energy that never weakens but never blusters, and with an admirable pungency of thought and directness of expression that sacrifices nothing of subtlety or refinement, Sontag encourages the reader's cooperation in her enterprise. . . . The book understands exactly the locale and the level of its argument." *Time* columnist Robert Hughes expressed a similar opinion. "It is hard to imagine any photographer's agreeing point for point with Sontag's polemic," Hughes concluded. "But it is a brilliant, irritating performance, and it opens window after window on one of the great *faits accomplis* of our culture. Not many photographers are worth a thousand of her words."

Illness as Metaphor is not an autobiographical account of Sontag's own experience with cancer, but rather an examination of the cultural myths that have developed around certain diseases, investing them with meaning beyond mere human debilitation. *New Republic* contributor Edwin J. Kenney, Jr. called the book "a critical analysis of our habitual, unconscious, and even pathological ways of conceptualizing illness and of using the vocabulary of illness to articulate our feelings about other crises, economic, political, and military. Sontag is seeking to go behind the language of the mind to expose and clarify the assumptions and fears the language masks; she wants to liberate us from the terrors that issue not from disease itself, but from our ways of imagining it." Braudy wrote: "In *Illness as Metaphor* [Sontag] condemns the way we have used metaphoric language to obscure and mystify the physical and material world, turning diseases into imagery, metamorphosing the final reality of bodily decay and death into the shrouded fantasies of moral pollution and staining sin." Writing in the *Atlantic Monthly,* Benjamin DeMott claimed that the work "isn't conceived as an act of conversion. It presents itself as an attack on some corrupt uses of language. In a series of ten meditations on the human failure to grasp that sickness is not a metaphor, not a sign standing in for something else, not a symbol of a moral or cultural condition, Miss Sontag develops the thesis that it is therefore wrong to use sickness as a means of interpreting the character of either individuals or nations."

Sontag's novels, *The Benefactor* and *Death Kit,* have received mixed reviews. Both works "emphasize fiction as a construct of words rather than as a mimesis," to quote Leon S. Roudiez's appraisal in *World Literature Today.* In a *New Republic* piece, Stanley Kauffmann called *The Benefactor* "a skillful amalgam of a number of continental sources in fiction and thought" and adds that it contains "a good deal of well fashioned writing." Kauffmann maintained, however, that the book "remains a neat knowledgeable construct, reclining on the laboratory table." Conversely, Alfred Kazin felt that the novel "works because its author really sees the world as a series of propositions *about* the world. Her theoreticalness consists of a loyalty not to certain ideas but to life as the improvisation of ideas. She is positive only about moving on from those ideas, and this makes her an interesting fantasist about a world conceived as nothing but someone thinking up new angles to it." *New*

York Review of Books essayist Denis Donoghue found *Death Kit* "an extremely ambitious book," but notes that it is "undermined by the fact that its ideas never become its experience: the ideas remain external, like the enforced correlation of dream and act in *The Benefactor.*" Maureen Howard, on the other hand, praised *Death Kit* in a *Saturday Review* column. "The writing is vigorous, the plot highly imaginative," Howard claims. "*Death Kit* . . . is about the endless and insane demands put upon us to choose coherence and life over chaos and death."

Sontag's 2000 novel, National Book Award-winning, *In America* is "a novel of ideas in which real figures from the past enact their lives against an assiduously researched, almost cinematically vivid background," noted a critic for *Publishers Weekly.* The novel revolves around an actress from the latter-nineteenth century named Maryna Zalezowska, based on the renowned Polish actress Helena Modrzejewska. In her mid-thirties, Maryna has become disenchanted with her life and, feeling a spiritual emptiness, decides to seek a more simple rural life which eventually finds her living for a time on a ranch in Anaheim, California—an experimental commune.

Reaction to *In America* was mixed. Donna Seaman in *Booklist* argued "Maryna's evolution as a woman and an artist is a tremendously compelling story by virtue not only of Sontag's consummate narrative skills but also by its embodiment of her passionate commitment to creativity as a path to freedom." Carl Rollyson in *New Criterion* did not agree, commenting that "much of *In America* reads like a diligently researched report, replete with quaint passages about what America was like in nineteenth-century New York and the Western United States. . . . Without a driving plot, the historical background only makes a static novel more static." James Wood in the *New Republic,* on the other hand, found that "it is striking how little historical detail seems to clog the surface of this novel; it has been smoothed into underground discretion. The book is not a disquisition on the America of the 1870s." Michiko Kakutani in the *New York Times Book Review* noted that a "theme of transcendence—of overcoming cultural and personal history . . . runs through" Sontag's oeuvre, but finds that "Sontag has said what she has to say in this novel more persuasively and with far more nuance and subtlety many times before." Wood, however, concluded: "[*In America*] is both Romantically expressive and artfully sly; it is unconscious and self-conscious in equal measure. If this is the only possible way to write historical fiction in a postmodern time, then Sontag has magnificently managed to make it look like freedom rather than determination. It is certainly an achievement."

Some critics express reservations about Sontag's work, most notably about her critical stance and her highly erudite presentations. For instance, writing in the *Nation,* Walter Kendrick claimed that the author's "eminence in American letters is disproportionate to the quality of her thought" because "she perpetuates a tradition of philosophical naivete that has always kept America subservient to Europe and that surely should have run its course by now." *Saturday Review* correspondent James Sloan Allen called Sontag "a virtuoso of the essay, the Paganini of criticism," who "has often overwhelmed her subjects and intimidated her readers with intellectual pyrotechniques, pretentious erudition, and cliquish hauteur. Lacking has been the quality of mind that deals in modern but sure understanding rather than bravura." Donoghue offered a similar opinion in the *New York Times Book Review:* "Her mind is powerful rather than subtle; it is impatient with nuances that ask to be heard, with minute discriminations that, if entertained, would impede the march of her argument." In his book *The Confusion of Realms,* Richard Gilman stated that while Sontag's essays are "true extensions of our awareness," they nevertheless reveal that beneath the "clean-functioning, superbly armed processes of her thought exists a confused, importunate, scarcely acknowledged desire that culture, the culture she knows so much about, be other than it is in order for her to be other than she is."

"Thinking about Susan Sontag in the middle of her career is to feel the happiness of more, more, nothing ended," wrote Hardwick. Indeed, although a compendium of her work was published in 1982 as *A Susan Sontag Reader,* the author continues to write, especially fiction. In the *Village Voice,* Kendrick suggests that Sontag is engaged in the lifetime project of "making a multifaceted creative and critical presence of herself." She undertakes this task with very exacting standards, as she told the *New York Times Book Review:* "Of course, I want readers, and I want my work to matter. Above all I don't just want the work to be good enough to last, I want it to *deserve* survival. That's a very great ambition because one knows that 99.9 percent of everything that's written at any given time is not going to last." Sontag remains a prominent figure in the American literary community; her presence in the intellectual world is felt through speeches as well as writings. Reflecting on her accomplishments in the *Threepenny Review,* Sontag once said, "What readers do with it, whether I am (as I hope) making work which will last—my part ends with my doing the best I can."

BIOGRAPHICAL AND CRITICAL SOURCES:

BOOKS

Contemporary Literary Criticism, Thomson Gale (Detroit), Volume 1, 1973, Volume 2, 1974, Volume 10, 1979, Volume 13, 1980, Volume 31, 1985, Volume 105, 1998.

Dictionary of Literary Biography, Thomson Gale, Volume 2: *American Novelists since World War II,* 1978, Volume 67: *Modern American Critics since 1955,* 1988.

Encyclopedia of World Literature in the Twentieth Century, St. James Press (Detroit, MI), 1999.

Gilman, Richard, *The Confusion of Realms,* Random House, 1970.

Kazin, Alfred, *Bright Book of Life: American Novelists and Storytellers from Hemingway to Mailer,* Little, Brown, 1973.

Kennedy, Liam, *Susan Sontag: Mind as Passion,* Manchester University Press (Manchester, England), 1995.

Poague, Leland, editor, *Conversations with Susan Sontag,* University Press of Mississippi (Jackson), 1995.

Sayres, Sohnya, *Susan Sontag: The Elegaic Modernist,* Routledge, 1990.

Smith, Sharon, *Women Who Make Movies,* Hopkinson & Blake, 1975.

Solotaroff, Theodore, *The Red Hot Vacuum,* Atheneum, 1970.

Vidal, Gore, *Reflections upon a Sinking Ship,* Little, Brown, 1969.

PERIODICALS

Antioch Review, spring, 1978.

Atlantic Monthly, September, 1966; November, 1978; September, 1982; November, 1992, p. 162.

Best Sellers, April, 1979.

Booklist, February 1, 2000, Donna Seaman, review of *In America,* p. 997.

College English, February, 1986.

Commentary, June, 1966.

Commonweal, February 3, 1978.

Detroit News, January 15, 1967.

Encounter, November, 1978.

Esquire, July, 1968; February, 1978.

Harper's, January, 1979; February, 1983.

Hudson Review, autumn, 1969; summer, 1983; spring, 1993, pp. 247-55.

Library Journal, July, 1993, p. 82; November 15, 1999, Rebecca Miller, review of *Women,* p. 65.

Los Angeles Times, December 22, 1980.

Los Angeles Times Book Review, November 19, 1978; December 12, 1982.

Ms., March, 1979.

Nation, October 2, 1967; March 24, 1969; June 2, 1969; October 23, 1982; May 1, 1989, p. 598; October 5, 1992, pp. 365-68.

New Criterion, April, 2000, Carl Rollyson, "Susan Sontag *In America:* A Novel," p. 80.

New Republic, September 21, 1963; February 19, 1966; September 2, 1967; May 3, 1969; January 21, 1978; July 8, 1978; November 25, 1978; November 29, 1980; December 26, 1988, pp. 28-33; March 27, 2000, James Wood, "The Palpable Past-Intimate," p. 29.

New Statesman, March 24, 1967.

Newsweek, December 5, 1977; June 12, 1978; October 11, 1982.

New Yorker, May 31, 1993, pp. 142-49.

New York Review of Books, June 9, 1966; September 28, 1967; March 13, 1969; July 20, 1978; January 25, 1979; November 6, 1980.

New York Times, August 18, 1967; February 4, 1969; May 2, 1969; October 3, 1969; November 14, 1977; January 30, 1978; June 1, 1978; November 11, 1978; October 13, 1980; November 11, 1980.

New York Times Book Review, September 8, 1963; January 23, 1966; August 27, 1967; July 13, 1969; February 13, 1972; December 18, 1977; July 16, 1978; November 26, 1978; November 23, 1980; September 12, 1982; October 24, 1982; January 22, 1989, p. 11; March 1, 1992, p. 20; February 29, 2000, Michiko Kakutani, review of *In America;* March 12, 2000, Sarah Kerr, review of *In America,* p. 6.

Partisan Review, summer, 1968; Volume 36, number 3, 1969.

Psychology Today, July, 1978.

Publishers Weekly, October 22, 1982; January 31, 2000, review of *In America,* p. 80.

Salmagundi, fall, 1975.

Saturday Review, February 12, 1966; August 26, 1967; May 3, 1969; December 10, 1977; October 28, 1978; October, 1980.

Sewanee Review, summer, 1974.

Spectator, March 17, 1979.

Threepenny Review, fall, 1981.

Time, August 18, 1967; December 26, 1977; January 27, 1986; March 13, 2000, Paul Gray, review of *In America,* p. 88.

Times Literary Supplement, March 16, 1967; April 25, 1967; January 8, 1970; March 17, 1978; November 23, 1979; December 10, 1982.

Tribune Books (Chicago), December 10, 1978; October 19, 1980; January 9, 1983.
Tri-Quarterly, fall, 1966.
Variety, April 29, 1996, p. 150.
Village Voice, August 31, 1967; October 15-21, 1980.
Voice Literary Supplement, November, 1982.
Washington Post, March 16, 1982.
Washington Post Book World, February 5, 1978; June 25, 1978; December 17, 1978; October 26, 1980.
World Literature Today, spring, 1983; autumn, 1992, p. 723.

* * *

SOTO, Gary 1952-

PERSONAL: Born April 12, 1952, in Fresno, CA; son of Manuel and Angie (Trevino) Soto; married Carolyn Sadako Oda, May 24, 1975; children: Mariko Heidi. *Education:* California State University, Fresno, B.A., 1974; University of California—Irvine, M.F.A., 1976.

ADDRESSES: Home—43 The Crescent, Berkeley, CA 94708.

CAREER: University of California—Berkeley, CA, assistant professor 1979-85; associate professor of English and ethnic studies, 1985-91, part-time senior lecturer in English department, 1991-93; full-time writer, 1992—; University of California, Riverside, CA, Distinguished Professor of Creative Writing. University of Cincinnati, Cincinnati, OH, Elliston Poet, 1988; Wayne State University, Detroit, MI, Martin Luther King/Cesar Chavez/Rosa Parks Visiting Professor of English, 1990. Serves as Young People's Ambassador for the California Rural Legal Assistance and United Farm Workers of America.

AWARDS, HONORS: Discovery-Nation prize, 1975; United States Award, International Poetry Forum, 1976, for *The Elements of San Joaquin;* Bess Hokin Prize from *Poetry,* 1978; Guggenheim fellowship, 1979-80; National Endowment for the Arts fellowships, 1981 and 1991; Levinson Award, *Poetry,* 1984; American Book Award, Before Columbus Foundation, 1985, for *Living up the Street;* California Arts Council fellowship, 1989; Beatty Award, California Library Association, 1991, and Reading Magic Award, *Parenting* magazine, all for *Baseball in April, and Other Stories;* George G. Stone Center Recognition of Merit, Claremont Graduate School, 1993, for *Baseball in April, and Other Stories;* Carnegie Medal, 1993, for *The Pool Party;* National Book Award, and *Los Angeles Times* Book Prize finalist, both 1995, both for *New and Selected Poems;* Literature Award, Hispanic Heritage Foundation, 1999; Author-Illustrator Civil Rights Award, National Education Association, 1999; Book Award, PEN Center West, 1999, for *Petty Crimes;* Silver Medal, Commonwealth Club of California, and Tomás Rivera Prize.

WRITINGS:

(With Michael Peich) *Heaven,* Aralia Press, 1970.
The Level at Which the Sky Begins, University of California (Irvine, CA), 1976.
The Elements of San Joaquin (poems), University of Pittsburgh Press (Pittsburgh, PA), 1977.
The Tale of Sunlight (poems), University of Pittsburgh Press (Pittsburgh, PA), 1978.
(With Ernesto Trejo) *Como Arbustos de Niebla,* Editorial Latitudes (Mexico City, Mexico), 1980.
Where Sparrows Work Hard (poems), University of Pittsburgh Press (Pittsburgh, PA), 1981.
Father is a Pillow Tied to a Broom, (Pittsburgh, PA), 1980.
Black Hair (poems), University of Pittsburgh Press (Pittsburgh, PA), 1985.
Living up the Street: Narrative Recollections (prose memoirs), Strawberry Hill (San Francisco, CA), 1985.
Small Faces (prose memoirs), Arte Publico (Houston, TX), 1986.
The Cat's Meow, illustrated by Carolyn Soto, Strawberry Hill (San Francisco, CA), 1987.
Lesser Evils: Ten Quartets (memoirs and essays), Arte Publico (Houston, TX), 1988.
(Editor) *California Childhood: Recollections and Stories of the Golden State,* Creative Arts Book Company (Berkeley, CA), 1988.
A Fire in My Hands (poems), Scholastic (New York, NY), 1990.
A Summer Life (autobiography), University Press of New England (Hanover, NH), 1990.
Baseball in April and Other Stories (short stories), Harcourt (San Diego, CA), 1990.
Who Will Know Us? (poems), Chronicle Books (San Francisco, CA), 1990.
Home Course in Religion (poems), Chronicle Books (San Francisco, CA), 1991.
Taking Sides, Harcourt (San Diego, CA), 1991.
Neighborhood Odes, Harcourt (San Diego, CA), 1992.
Pacific Crossing, Harcourt (San Diego, CA), 1992.
The Skirt, Delacorte (New York, NY), 1992.
Too Many Tamales (picture book), Putnam (New York, NY), 992.

(Editor) *Pieces of the Heart: New Chicano Fiction,* Chronicle Books (San Francisco, CA), 1993.
Local News (short stories), Harcourt (San Diego, CA), 1993.
The Pool Party, Delacorte (New York, NY), 1993 (also see below).
Pieces of the Heart: New Chicano Fiction, Chronicle Books (San Francisco, CA), 1993.
Crazy Weekend, Scholastic Inc. (New York, NY), 1994.
Jesse, Harcourt (San Diego, CA), 1994.
Afternoon Memory, Lagniappe Press (Tuscaloosa, AL), 1994.
Boys at Work, Delacorte (New York, NY), 1995.
Canto Familiar/Familiar Song (poetry), Harcourt (San Diego, CA), 1995.
The Cat's Meow, Scholastic Inc. (New York, NY), 1995.
Chato's Kitchen, Putnam (New York, NY), 1995.
(Editor) *Everyday Seductions,* Ploughshare Press (Sea Bright, NJ), 1995.
New and Selected Poems, Chronicle Books (San Francisco, CA), 1995.
Summer on Wheels, Scholastic Inc. (New York, NY), 1995.
The Sparrows Move South: Early Poems, Bancroft Library Press, 1995.
(With Celina Hinojosa) *The Mustache,* Putnam (New York, NY), 1995.
The Old Man and His Door, Putnam (New York, NY), 1996.
Snapshots of the Wedding, Putnam (New York, NY), 1996.
Tomando partido, Fondo de Cultura Economica, 1996.
(With John Digby) *Super-Eight Movies: Poems,* Lagniappe Press (Tuscaloosa, AL), 1996.
Off and Running (juvenile), illustrated by Eric Velasquez, Delacorte (New York, NY), 1996.
Buried Onions, Harcourt (San Diego, CA), 1997.
Novio Boy (play), Harcourt (San Diego, CA), 1997.
Junior College: Poems, Chronicle Books (San Francisco, CA), 1997.
Petty Crimes, Harcourt (San Diego, CA), 1998.
Big Bushy Mustache, Knopf (New York, NY), 1998.
Chato and the Party Animals, illustrated by Susan Guevara, Putnam (New York, NY), 1999.
Nerdlandia: A Play, Putnam (New York, NY), 1999.
A Natural Man, Chronicle Books (San Francisco, CA), 1999.
Nickel and Dime, University of New Mexico Press (Albuquerque, NM), 2000.
(With Linda Dalal Sawaya) *My Little Car (Mi carrito),* Putnam (New York, NY), 2000.
The Effects of Knut Hamsun on a Fresno Boy: Recollections and Short Essays, Persea (New York, NY), 2000.
Jessie de la Cruz: Profile of a United Farm Worker, Persea (New York, NY), 2000.
(With Molly Fisk) *100 Parades,* California Poets in the Schools, 2000.
(With Mildred D. Taylor and Others) *Scholastic Read XL, Grade 7,* Scholastic Inc. (New York, NY), 2001.
Poetry Lover, University of New Mexico Press (Albuquerque, NM), 2001.
If the Shoe Fits, illustrated by Terry Widener, Putnam (New York, NY), 2002.
Fernie and Me, Putnam (New York, NY), 2002.
Shadow of the Plum: Poems, Cedar Hill Publications (San Diego, CA), 2002.
Amnesia in a Republican County, University of New Mexico Press (Albuquerque, NM), 2003.
The Afterlife, Harcourt (New York, NY), 2003.
Cesar Chavez: A Hero for Everyone, illustrated by Lori Lohstoeter, Simon & Schuster (New York, NY), 2003.

Contributor of poems to *Nation, Ploughshares, Iowa Review, Ontario Review,* and *Poetry.*

SHORT FILMS

The Bike, Gary Soto Productions, 1991.
The Pool Party, Gary Soto Productions, 1993.
Novio Boy, Gary Soto Productions, 1994.

SIDELIGHTS: Gary Soto, born in Fresno, California, is an American poet and prose writer whose work has been strongly influenced by his working-class Mexican-American background. In his writing, as Raymund Paredes noted in the *Rocky Mountain Review,* "Soto establishes his acute sense of ethnicity and, simultaneously, his belief that certain emotions, values, and experiences transcend ethnic boundaries and allegiances." Many critics have echoed the assessment of Patricia de la Fuente in *Revista Chicano-Requeña* that Soto displays an "exceptionally high level of linguistic sophistication."

In his first volume of poetry, *The Elements of San Joaquin,* Soto offers a grim portrait of Mexican-American life. His poems depict the violence of urban life, the exhausting labor of rural life, and the futility of trying to recapture the innocence of childhood. In *Chicano Poetry,* Juan Bruce-Novoa likened Soto's poetic vision to T.S. Eliot's bleak portrait of the modern world in *The Waste Land.* Soto uses wind-swept dust as a dominant image, and he also introduces such elements as rape, unflushed toilets, a drowned baby and, as Bruce-Novoa quoted him, "men / Whose arms / Were bracelets / Of burns." Soto's skill with the figurative language of poetry has been noted by reviewers throughout his career, and in *Western American Literature* Jerry Bradley praised the metaphors in *The Elements of San Joaquin* as "evocative, enlightening, and haunting." Though unsettled by the negativism of the collection, Bruce-Novoa felt the work "convinces because of its well-wrought structure, the craft, the coherence of its totality." Moreover, he thought, because it brings such a vivid portrait of poverty to the reading public, *The Elements of San Joaquin* is "a social as well as a literary achievement."

Many critics have also observed that Soto's writing transcends social commentary. Bruce-Novoa said that one reason why the author's work has "great significance within Chicano literature" is because it represents "a definite shift toward a more personal, less politically motivated poetry." As Alan Williamson suggested in *Poetry,* Soto avoids either idealizing the poor for their oppression or encouraging their violent defiance. Instead, he focuses on the human suffering that poverty engenders. When Peter Cooley reviewed Soto's second volume of poetry, *The Tale of Sunlight,* in *Parnassus,* he praised the author's ability to temper the bleakness of *San Joaquin* with "imaginative expansiveness." The poems in *The Tale of Sunlight,* many of which focus on a child named Molina or on the owner of a Hispanic bar, display both the frustrations of poverty and what Williamson called "a vein of consolatory fantasy which passes beyond escapism into a pure imaginative generosity toward life." Williamson cited as an example "the poem in which an uncle's gray hair is seen as a visitation of magical butterflies."

In the poems in *Black Hair,* Soto focuses on his friends and family. He portrays fondly the times he shared with his friends as an adolescent and the more recent moments he has spent with his young daughter. Some critics, such as David Wojahn in *Poetry,* maintained that Soto was moving away from his strengths as a writer. While acknowledging that "by limiting his responses to a naive aplomb, Soto enables himself to write with a freshness that is at times arresting." Wojahn considered the work "a disappointment." He praised *San Joaquin* and *The Tale of Sunlight* as "thematically urgent . . . and ambitious in their scope" and said that "compared to them, *Black Hair* is a distinctly minor achievement." Others, such as Ellen Lesser in *Voice Literary Supplement,* were charmed by Soto's poetic tone, "the quality of the voice, the immediate, human presence that breathes through the lines." Lesser claimed that Soto's celebration of innocence and sentiment is shaded with a knowledge of "the larger, often threatening world." In the *Christian Science Monitor,* Tom D'Evelyn hailed Soto's ability to go beyond the circumstances of his own life and write of "something higher," concluding, "Somehow Gary Soto has become not an important Chicano poet but an important American poet. More power to him."

When Soto discusses American racial tensions in the prose collections *Living up the Street: Narrative Recollections* and *Small Faces,* he uses vignettes drawn from his childhood. One vignette shows the anger the author felt upon realizing that his brown-skinned brother would never be considered an attractive child by conventional American standards. Another shows Soto's surprise at discovering that, contrary to his family's advice to marry a Mexican, he was falling in love with a woman of Japanese ancestry. In these deliberately small-scale recollections, as Paredes noted, "it is a measure of Soto's skill that he so effectively invigorates and sharpens our understanding of the commonplace." With these volumes Soto acquired a solid reputation as a prose writer as well as a poet; *Living up the Street* earned him an American Book Award.

Soto's autobiographical prose continued with *Lesser Evils: Ten Quartets* and *A Summer Life.* The first of these, as Soto explained in an unpublished 1988 interview, reflects the author's experience with Catholicism—in the same interview Soto declared himself a reconciled Catholic. *A Summer Life* consists of thirty-nine short essays. According to Ernesto Trejo in the *Los Angeles Times Book Review,* these pieces "make up a compelling biography" of Soto's youth. As he had done in previous works, Soto here "holds the past up to memory's probing flashlight, turns it around ever so carefully, and finds in the smallest of incidents the occasion for literature." Writing in the *Americas Review,* Hector Torres compared *A Summer Life* with Soto's earlier autobiographical texts and asserted that the later book "moves with greater stylistic elegance and richer thematic coherence."

During the early 1990s Soto turned his attentions in a new direction: children's literature. A first volume of short stories for young readers, *Baseball in April and Other Stories,* was published in 1990. The eleven tales depict Mexican-American boys and girls as they enter adolescence in Hispanic California neighborhoods. In the *New York Times Book Review,* Roberto Gonzalez Echevarria called the stories "sensitive and economical." Echevarria praised Soto: "Because he stays within the teenagers' universe . . . he manages to convey all the social change and stress without bathos or didacticism. In fact, his stories are moving, yet humorous and entertaining." In the *Americas Review,* Torres suggested that *Baseball in April and Other Stories* was "the kind of work that could be used to teach high school and junior high school English classes."

One of Soto's juvenile characters, a boy named Lincoln Mendoza, appears as a protagonist in two works: *Taking Sides* and *Pacific Crossing.* As a Mexican-American eighth-grader in *Taking Sides,* Lincoln is confronted with challenges and insecurities when he and his mother move from San Francisco's Mission District to a predominantly Anglo suburb, and he must work to keep his heritage intact in his new environment. *Pacific Crossing* finds Lincoln and one of his friends facing cultural challenges in another context: they embark on a voyage to Japan as exchange students. Writing in the *Multicultural Review,* Osbelia Juarez Rocha called *Pacific Crossing* "cleverly crafted" and "entertaining."

Soto has also written poetry for younger readers, most notably the volumes *A Fire in My Hands* and *Neighborhood Odes,* both of which focus on growing up in the Mexican neighborhoods of California's Central Valley. Soto has ventured as well into the arena of children's picture books. *Too Many Tamales* depicts the story of Maria, a young girl who misplaces her mother's wedding ring in tamale dough while helping to prepare a Christmastime feast. Maria—with her cousins' help—embarks on a futile effort to recover the ring by consuming vast quantities of tamales. *Chato's Kitchen* introduces a cat whose efforts to entice the local "ratoncitos"—little mice—lead him to prepare abundant portions of fajitas, frijoles, enchiladas, and other foods.

Soto continued the adventures of the indomitable feline in *Chato's Surprise Pachanga* and *Chato and the Party Animals.* In the latter work, Chato learns that his pal Novio Boy has never had his own birthday party. The fellow feline doesn't even know when he was born, because he came from the pound. Chato decides to throw him a party—but then forgets to invite the guest of honor. The assembled party becomes a search operation, and when they cannot find Novio Boy, the guests turn mournful. The missing Novio Boy turns up with new adventures to tell, and the party becomes celebratory once again. "Rollicking language—a completely integrated and poetic combination of barrio slang, Spanish, and colloquial English—carries the story along," remarked *School Library Journal* reviewer Ann Welton, while *Booklist*'s Gillian Engberg praised the book's "startlingly expressive animals, symbols of Latino culture, and winged-cat angels [that] form dynamic, wild compositions."

In *Booklist* Hazel Rochman commended Soto's biography of a well-known Latina union activist in California, *Jessie de la Cruz: Profile of a United Farm Worker,* which joins his *Cesar Chavez: A Hero for Everyone* in his body of work for younger readers. Rochman termed it "stirring American history," and predicted that "teens will be caught by the facts of her hardship and struggle." As Soto noted on his Web site, he met de la Cruz and felt immediately drawn to tell her story. The longtime union activist had become an agricultural laborer as a very young child, and was intensely involved in the industry's struggles in California during the 1950s and 1960s. Soto himself once worked in the San Joaquin Valley as a fruit picker when he was younger, and was familiar with the backbreaking nature of the work. He interviewed those who knew de la Cruz and sought to infuse her story with a certain sense of drama. As he said in an interview published on his Web site, the most difficult part of writing the non-fiction work was "making it exciting for young people . . . I felt I had to make Jessie's story visual, otherwise I would lose the reader." He added, "Of course, we'll get some reactions such as, 'Oh, this is boring,' and my reaction will be to take that child into the fields to cut grapes for a season. Then he or she will know boredom."

While his children's books continue to find success, Soto's fictional exploration of Latino-American culture has also continued in a series of novels for older readers. *Nickel and Dime* recounts the lives of three adult men: Roberto and Gus, who are security guards at a bank, and Silver, a poet. One of the guards loses his job and finds himself plummeting into an economic free fall; another character also becomes homeless. Silver reminds his audience at an open-mike poetry night that poetry should not concern itself with mundane, self-absorbed matters; it should be about "people who suffer," he rails. Through the plight of the men, Soto attempts to show that even the best intentions cannot help those on the lower rungs of the economic ladder make it past "working poor" status, even in good times. A *Publishers Weekly* review of *Nickel and Dime* called its author "a versatile, unsentimental and clear storyteller, and his range of talents converge to illuminate the lives of these three Chicano men living in the shadows."

In another adult-themed novel, *The Afterlife,* Soto introduces readers to Chuy, a seventeen year old who, after being murdered at a dance in his native Fresno, narrates his experiences as a disembodied spirit overseeing the response by family and friends to his death. While criticizing the novel for its disjointed plot, *School Library Journal* reviewer Francesca Goldsmith nonetheless praised "Soto's simple and poetic language," citing as well the book's dreamlike quality. Noting, with other critics, the parallels with Thorton Wilder's classic American play *Our Town, Booklist* reviewer Ilene Cooper commented that in *The Afterlife* Soto "not only paints the scenery brilliantly but also captures the pain that follows an early death." Praising the novel for its sense of "hope and elegance," a *Publishers Weekly* reviewer added that Soto "counterbalances difficult ideas with moments of genuine tenderness," and concludes his fiction with "a provocative lesson about the importance of savoring every moment." Despite the novel's somber theme, the author "uses a light touch" and employs "his usual humor," added *Kliatt* critic Michele Winship, who also praised Soto for his likeable protagonist.

Soto's works have also been collected in books such as *The Effects of Knut Hamsun on a Fresno Boy: Recollections and Short Essays.* Some of the selections were previously published, while five new essays find Soto reflecting on his life as a writer. *Booklist*'s Hazel Rochman stated that Soto's lyrical style emerges even when recounting incidents from his childhood. "The poet is always here, not portentous, but in the cadences of how we talk," Rochman wrote.

In the *Dictionary of Literary Biography,* Hector Torres declared: "Soto's consistent attention to the craft of writing and his sensitivity to his subject matter have earned him an indisputable place in American and Chicano literature." Torres noted that critical response to Soto's work has been "overwhelmingly positive." He attributed that respect and admiration to Soto's ability to represent his experience "in a manner that shows his talent at creating poetry and prose that, through simple and direct diction, expresses the particulars of everyday life and simultaneously contains glimpses of the universal."

BIOGRAPHICAL AND CRITICAL SOURCES:

BOOKS

Bruce-Novoa, Juan, *Chicano Poetry: A Response to Chaos,* University of Texas Press (Austin, TX), 1982.

Children's Literature Review, Volume 38, Thomson Gale (Detroit, MI), 1996.

Contemporary Literary Criticism, Thomson Gale (Detroit, MI), Volume 32, 1985, Volume 80, 1994.

Dictionary of Literary Biography, Volume 82: *Chicano Writers,* Thomson Gale (Detroit, MI), 1989.

Hispanic Literature Criticism, Thomson Gale (Detroit, MI), 1994.

PERIODICALS

American Book Review, July-August, 1982.

Americas Review, spring, 1991, Hector Torres, review of *A Summer Life,* pp. 111-115.

Bloomsbury Review, January-February, 1987, Alicia Fields, "Small but Telling Moments," p. 10.

Booklist, April 1, 1992, Hazel Rochman, review of *A Fire in My Hands,* pp. 1437-1438; September 15, 1993, Hazel Rochman, review of *Too Many Tamales,* p. 151; June 1, 1995, review of *Boys at Work,* p. 1773; October 1, 1995, Hazel Rochman, review of *Canto Familiar,* p. 312; March 15, 1998, Hazel Rochman, review of *Petty Crimes,* p. 1245; October 1, 1999, Annie Ayres, review of *Nerdlandia: A Play,* p. 349; November 1, 1999, Karen Harris, review of *Pacific Crossing,* p. 549; February 15, 2000, James O'Laughlin, review of *Nickel and Dime,* p. 1085; August, 2000, Gillian Engberg, review of *Chato and the Party Animals,* p. 2150; November 1, 2000, Hazel Rochman, review of *The Effects of Knut Hamsun on a Fresno Boy: Recollections and Short Essays,* p. 512; November 15, 2000, Hazel Rochman, review of *Jessie de la Cruz: Profile of a United Farm Worker,* p. 633; August, 2003, Ilene Cooper, review of *The Afterlife,* p. 1981; December 15, 2003, Carolyn Phelan, review of *Cesar Chavez: A Hero for Everyone,* p. 748.

Bulletin of the Center for Children's Books, April, 1990, Roger Sutton, review of *Baseball in April and Other Stories,* p. 199.

Christian Science Monitor, March 6, 1985, Tom D'Evelyn, review of *Black Hair.*

Denver Quarterly, summer, 1982.

Horn Book, November-December, 1992, Ellen Fader, review of *Pacific Crossing,* pp. 725-726; November-December, 2003, Lauren Adams, review of *The Afterlife,* p. 755.

Kirkus Reviews, April 1, 1993, review of *Local News,* p. 464; June 15, 1993, review of *The Pool Party,* p. 792; April 1, 1997, review of *Buried Onions,* p. 1229; March 1, 1998, review of *Petty Crimes,*

p. 345; October 15, 2000, review of *The Effects of Knut Hamsun on a Fresno Boy,* pp. 1469-1470; September, 2003, review of *The Afterlife,* p. 1183.

Kliatt, September, 2003, Michele Winship, *The Afterlife,* p. 13.

Library Journal, December, 1999, Harold Augenbraum, review of *Nickel and Dime,* p. 190.

Los Angeles Times Book Review, August 5, 1990, Ernesto Trejo, "Memories of a Fresno Boyhood," pp. 1, 9; August 15, 1993, Suzanne Curley, "A Better Place to Live," p. 8.

Multicultural Review, June, 1993, Osbelia Juarez Rocha, review of *Pacific Crossing,* pp. 76, 78.

Nation, June 7, 1993, pp. 772-774.

NEA Today, November, 1992, p. 9.

New York Times Book Review, October 11, 1981, Alan Cheuse, "The Voices of Chicano," pp. 15, 36-37; August 20, 1990, Roberto Gonzalez Echevarria, "Growing up North of the Border," p. 45.

Parnassus, fall-winter, 1979, Peter Cooley, review of *The Tale of Sunlight.*

Poetry, March, 1980, Alan Williamson, "In a Middle Style," pp. 348-354; June, 1985.

Publishers Weekly, march 4, 1988, review of *Lesser Evils,* p. 102; March 23, 1992, review of *Neighborhood Odes,* p. 74; April 12, 1993, review of *Local News,* p. 64; August 16, 1993, p. 103; January 31, 1994, review of *Crazy Weekend,* p. 90; August 24, 1992, review of *The Skirt,* p. 80; February 6, 1995, review of *Chato's Kitchen,* pp. 84-85; January 20, 1997, review of *Snapshots from the Wedding,* p. 401; December 8, 1997, review of *Off and Running,* p. 74; April 26, 1999, Joanne M. Hammond, review of *Pacific Crossing,* p. 55; February 14, 2000, review of *Nickel and Dime,* p. 175; August 25, 2003, review of *The Afterlife,* p. 65.

Revista Chicano-Riqueña, summer, 1983.

Rocky Mountain Review, Volume 41, numbers 1-2, 1987, Raymund Paredes, "Recent Chicano Fiction," pp. 126-128.

San Francisco Review of Books, summer, 1986, Geoffrey Dunn, review of *Living up the Street,* p. 11.

School Library Journal, November, 1991, Bruce Anne Shook, review of *Taking Sides,* p. 124; March, 1992, Barbara Chatton, review of *A Fire in My Hands,* p. 264; May, 1992, Renee Steinberg, review of *Neighborhood Odes,* p. 128; June, 1995, Rosie Peasley, review of *Boys at Work,* p. 113; July, 1995, review of *Chato's Kitchen,* p. 69; July, 2000, Ann Welton, review of *Chato and the Party Animals,* p. 88; November, 2003, Francisca Goldsmith, review of *The Afterlife,* p. 148; January, 2004, John Sigwald, review of *Cesar Chavez,* p. 123.

Voice Literary Supplement, September, 1985, Ellen Lesser, reivew of *Black Hair.*

Voice of Youth Advocates, April, 1995, Maura Bresnahan, reivew of *Summer on Wheels,* pp. 27-28.

Western American Literature, spring, 1979, Jerry Bradley, review of *The Elements of San Joaquin;* May, 1989, Gerald Haslam, review of *Lesser Evils,* pp. 92-93.

ONLINE

Gary Soto Web site, http://www.garysoto.com/ (August 23, 2004).

* * *

SOYINKA, Wole 1934-

PERSONAL: Name is pronounced "*Woh-* leh Shaw-*yin*-ka"; given name, Akinwande Oluwole; born July 13, 1934, in Isara, Nigeria; son of Ayo (a headmaster) and Eniola Soyinka; married; children: four. *Education:* Attended University of Ibadan; University of Leeds, B.A. (with honors), 1959. *Religion:* "Human liberty."

ADDRESSES: *Office*—P.O. Box 935, Abeokuta, Ogun, Nigeria. *Agent*—Greenbaum, Wolff & Ernst, 437 Madison Ave., New York, NY 10022.

CAREER: Playwright, poet, and novelist. University of Ibadan, Nigeria, research fellow in drama, 1960-61, chairman of department of theatre arts, 1967-71; University of Ife, professor of drama, 1972; Cambridge University, Cambridge, England, fellow of Churchill College, 1973-74; University of Ife, chairman of department of dramatic arts, 1975-85. Director of own theatre groups, Orisun Players and 1960 Masks, in Lagos and Ibadan, Nigeria, and Unife Guerilla theatre, Ife-Ife, 1978. Visiting professor at University of Sheffield, 1974, University of Ghana, 1975, Yale University, 1979-80, and Cornell University, 1986. Goldwin Smith professor for African Studies and Theatre Arts, Cornell University, 1988-91; Robert W. Woodruff Professor of the Arts, Emory University. Director of plays and actor on stage, film, and radio.

MEMBER: International Theatre Institute (president), Union of Writers of the African Peoples (secretary-general), AAAL, African Academy of Sciences.

AWARDS, HONORS: Rockefeller Foundation grant, 1960; John Whiting Drama Prize, 1966; Dakar Negro Arts Festival award, 1966; Jock Campbell Award, *New*

Statesman, 1968, for *The Interpreters;* Nobel Prize in Literature, 1986; Leopold Sedan Senghor Award, 1986; Enrico Mattei Award for Humanities, 1986; named Commander of the Federal Republic of Nigeria by General Ibrahim Babangida, 1986; named Commander of the French Legion of Honor, 1989; named Commander of Order of the Italian Republic, 1990; D.Litt., Yale University, University of Leeds, 1973, University of Montpellier, France, and University of Lagos; Prisoner of Conscience Prize, Amnesty International.

WRITINGS:

POETRY

Idanre and Other Poems, Methuen (London, England), 1967, Hill & Wang (New York, NY), 1969.

Poems from Prison, Rex Collings (London, England), 1969, expanded edition published as *A Shuttle in the Crypt,* Hill & Wang (New York, NY), 1972.

(Editor and author of introduction) *Poems of Black Africa,* Hill & Wang (New York, NY), 1975.

Ogun Abibiman, Rex Collings (London, England), 1976.

Mandela's Earth and Other Poems, Random House (New York, NY), 1988.

Early Poems, Oxford University Press (New York, NY), 1997.

PLAYS

The Invention, first produced in London, England, at Royal Court Theatre, 1955.

A Dance of the Forests (also see below; first produced in London, England, 1960), Oxford University Press (London, England), 1962.

The Lion and the Jewel (also see below; first produced in London, England, at Royal Court Theatre, 1966), Oxford University Press (London, England), 1962.

Three Plays (includes *The Trials of Brother Jero* [also see below], one-act, produced Off-Broadway at Greenwich Mews Playhouse, November 9, 1967; *The Strong Breed* [also see below], one-act, produced at Greenwich Mews Playhouse, November 9, 1967; and *The Swamp Dwellers* [also see below]), Mbari Publications (Ibadan, Nigeria), 1962, Northwestern University Press (Evanston, IL), 1963.

Five Plays: A Dance of the Forests, The Lion and the Jewel, The Swamp Dwellers, The Trials of Brother Jero, The Strong Breed, Oxford University Press (London, England), 1964.

The Road (produced in Stratford, England, at Theatre Royal, 1965), Oxford University Press (London, England), 1965.

Kongi's Harvest (also see below; produced Off-Broadway at St. Mark's Playhouse, April 14, 1968), Oxford University Press (London, England), 1966.

Rites of the Harmattan Solstice, produced in Lagos, 1966.

Three Short Plays, Oxford University Press (London, England), 1969.

The Trials of Brother Jero, Oxford University Press (London, England), 1969, published with *The Strong Breed* as *The Trials of Brother Jero and The Strong Breed: Two Plays,* Dramatists Play Service (New York, NY), 1969.

Kongi's Harvest (screenplay), produced by Calpenny-Nigerian Films, 1970.

Madmen and Specialists (two-act; produced in Waterford, CT, at Eugene O'Neill Memorial Theatre, August 1, 1970), Methuen (London, England), 1971, Hill & Wang (New York, NY), 1972.

(Contributor) *Palaver: Three Dramatic Discussion Starters* (includes *The Lion and the Jewel*), Friendship Press (New York, NY), 1971.

Before the Blackout (revue sketches; also see below), Orisun Acting Editions (Ibadan, Nigeria), 1971.

(Editor) *Plays from the Third World: An Anthology,* Doubleday (New York, NY), 1971.

The Jero Plays: The Trials of Brother Jero and *Jero's Metamorphosis,* Methuen (London, England), 1973.

(Contributor) *African Theatre: Eight Prize-Winning Plays for Radio,* Heinemann (London, England), 1973.

Camwood on the Leaves, Methuen (London, England), 1973, published with *Before the Blackout* as *Camwood on the Leaves and Before the Blackout: Two Short Plays,* Third Press (New York, NY), 1974.

(Adapter) *The Bacchae of Euripides: A Communion Rite* (first produced in London, England, at Old Vic Theatre, August 2, 1973), Methuen (London, England), 1973, Norton (New York, NY), 1974.

Collected Plays, Oxford University Press (London, England), Volume 1: *A Dance of the Forests, The Swamp Dwellers, The Strong Breed, The Road, The Bacchae,* 1973, Volume 2: *The Lion and the Jewel, Kongi's Harvest, The Trials of Brother Jero, Jero's Metamorphosis, Madmen and Specialists,* 1974.

Death and the King's Horseman (produced at University of Ife, 1976; produced in Chicago, IL, at Goodman Theatre, 1979; produced in New York, NY, at Vivian Beaumont Theatre, March, 1987), Norton (New York, NY), 1975, new edition, Methuen Drama (London, England), 2002.

Opera Wonyosi (light opera; produced in Ife-Ife, Nigeria, 1977), Indiana University Press (Bloomington, IN), 1981.

Priority Projects, revue; produced on Nigeria tour, 1982.

Requiem for a Futurologist (produced in Ife-Ife, Nigeria, 1983), Rex Collings (London, England), 1985.

A Play of Giants (produced in New Haven, CT, 1984), Methuen (London, England), 1984.

Six Plays, Methuen (London, England), 1984.

The Beatification of Area Boy, first produced in Leeds, England, 1996.

Also author of television script, "Culture in Transition."

OTHER

The Interpreters (novel), Deutsch (London, England), 1965.

(Translator) D.O. Fagunwa, *The Forest of a Thousand Daemons: A Hunter's Saga* (novel), Nelson (London, England), 1967, Humanities Press (Atlantic Highlands, NJ), 1969.

(Contributor) D.W. Jefferson, editor, *The Morality of Art,* Routledge & Kegan Paul (London, England), 1969.

(Contributor) O.R. Dathorne and Wilfried Feuser, editors, *Africa in Prose,* Penguin (New York, NY), 1969.

The Man Died: Prison Notes of Wole Soyinka, Harper & Row (New York, NY), 1972; Noonday Press (New York, NY), 1988.

Season of Anomy (novel), Rex Collings (London, England), 1973.

Myth, Literature and the African World (essays), Cambridge University Press (New York, NY), 1976.

Ake: The Years of Childhood (autobiography), Random House (New York, NY), 1981.

Art, Dialogue, and Outrage (essays), New Horn Press (Oxford, England), 1988.

Isara: A Voyage around "Essay," (biography of the author's father), Random House (New York, NY), 1989.

Ibadan: The Penkelemes Years: A Memoir, Spectrum Books (Ibadan, Nigeria), 1994.

The Open Sore of a Continent: A Personal Narrative of the Nigerian Crisis, Oxford University Press (London, England), 1996.

The Burden of Memory, the Muse of Forgiveness (nonfiction), Oxford University Press (London, England), 1998.

Arms and the Arts—A Continent's Unequal Dialogue, University of Cape Town (Cape Town, South Africa), 1999.

(With Tania León) *Scourge of Hyacinths: An Opera in Twelve Scenes,* Peermusic Classical (New York, NY), 1999.

Conversations with Wole Soyinka, edited by Biodun Jeyifo, University Press of Mississippi (Jackson, MS), 2001.

Nigeria's Transition to Democracy: Illustrations and Realities, Centre for Advanced Social Science (CASS), (Port Harcourt, Nigeria), 2002.

Salutation to the Gut, (Ibadan, Nigeria), 2002.

Climate of Fear: The Quest for Dignity in a Dehumanized World (collected lectures), Random House (New York, NY), 2005.

You Must Set Forth at Dawn: A Memoir, Random House (New York, NY), 2006.

Coeditor, *Black Orpheus,* 1961-64; editor, *Transition* (now *Ch'Indaba*), 1974-76.

SIDELIGHTS: Many critics consider Wole Soyinka Africa's finest writer. The Nigerian playwright's unique style blends traditional Yoruban folk-drama with European dramatic form to provide both spectacle and penetrating satire. Soyinka told *New York Times Magazine* writer Jason Berry that in the African cultural tradition, the artist "has always functioned as the record of the mores and experience of his society." His plays, novels, and poetry all reflect that philosophy, serving as a record of twentieth- century Africa's political turmoil and its struggle to reconcile tradition with modernization. As a young child, Soyinka was comfortable with the conflicting cultures in his world, but as he grew older, he became increasingly aware of the pull between African tradition and Western modernization. Eldred Jones stated in his book *Wole Soyinka* that the author's work touches on universal themes as well as addressing specifically African concerns: "The essential ideas which emerge from a reading of Soyinka's work are not specially African ideas, although his characters and their mannerisms are African. His concern is with man on earth. Man is dressed for the nonce in African dress and lives in the sun and tropical forest, but he represents the whole race."

Ake, Soyinka's village, was mainly populated with people from the Yoruba tribe and was presided over by the *ogboni,* or tribal elders. Soyinka's grandfather introduced him to the pantheon of Yoruba gods and to other tribal folklore. His parents were key representatives of colonial influences, however: his mother was a devout

Christian convert and his father acted as headmaster for the village school established by the British. When Soyinka's father began urging Wole to leave Ake to attend the government school in Ibadan, the boy was spirited away by his grandfather, who administered a scarification rite of manhood. Soyinka was also consecrated to the god Ogun, ruler of metal, roads, and both the creative and destructive essence. Ogun is a recurring figure in Soyinka's work and has been named by the author as his muse.

Ake: The Years of Childhood, Soyinka's account of his first ten years, stands as "a classic of childhood memoirs wherever and whenever produced," stated *New York Times Book Review* contributor James Olney. Numerous critics have singled out Soyinka's ability to recapture the changing perspective of a child as the book's outstanding feature; it begins in a light tone but grows increasingly serious as the boy matures and becomes aware of the problems faced by the adults around him. The book concludes with an account of a tax revolt organized by Soyinka's mother and the beginnings of Nigerian independence. "Most of 'Ake' charms; that was Mr. Soyinka's intention," wrote John Leonard of the *New York Times.* "The last fifty pages, however, inspire and confound; they are transcendent." Olney was of a similar opinion, writing that "the lyricism, grace, humor and charm of 'Ake' . . . are in the service of a profoundly serious viewpoint . . . . Mr. Soyinka, however, does this dramatically, not discursively. Through recollection, restoration and re- creation, he conveys a personal vision that was formed by the childhood world that he now returns to evoke and exalt in his autobiography. This is the ideal circle of autobiography at its best. It is what makes 'Ake' in addition to its other great virtues, the best introduction available to the work of one of the liveliest, most exciting writers in the world today."

Soyinka published some poems and short stories in *Black Orpheus,* a highly regarded Nigerian literary magazine, before leaving Africa to attend the University of Leeds in England. There his first play was produced. *The Invention* is a comic satire based on a sudden loss of pigment by South Africa's black population. Unable to distinguish blacks from whites and thus enforce its apartheid policies, the government is thrown into chaos. "The play is Soyinka's sole direct treatment of the political situation in Africa," noted Thomas Hayes in the *Dictionary of Literary Biography Yearbook: 1986.*

Soyinka returned to Nigeria in 1960 shortly after the country's independence from colonial rule had been declared. He began to research Yoruba folklore and drama in depth and incorporated elements of both into his play *A Dance of the Forests,* which was commissioned as part of Nigeria's independence celebrations. In his play, Soyinka warned the newly independent Nigerians that the end of colonial rule did not mean an end to their country's problems. It shows a bickering group of mortals who summon up the *egungun* (spirits of the dead, revered by the Yoruba people) for a festival. They have presumed the *egungun* to be noble and wise, but they discover that their ancestors are as petty and spiteful as any living people. "The whole concept ridicules the African viewpoint that glorifies the past at the expense of the present," suggested John F. Povey in *Tri-Quarterly.* "The sentimentalized glamour of the past is exposed so that the same absurdities may not be reenacted in the future. This constitutes a bold assertion to an audience awaiting an easy appeal to racial heroics." Povey also praised Soyinka's skill in using dancing, drumming, and singing to reinforce his theme: "The dramatic power of the surging forest dance [in the play] carries its own visual conviction. It is this that shows Soyinka to be a man of the theatre, not simply a writer."

After warning against living in nostalgia for Africa's past in *A Dance of the Forests,* Soyinka lampooned the indiscriminate embrace of Western modernization in *The Lion and the Jewel.* A *Times Literary Supplement* reviewer called this play a "richly ribald comedy," which combines poetry and prose "with a marvellous lightness in the treatment of both." The plot revolves around Sidi, the village beauty, and the rivalry between her two suitors. Baroka is the village chief, an old man with many wives; Lakunle is the enthusiastically Westernized schoolteacher who dreams of molding Sidi into a "civilized" woman.

In *Introduction to Nigerian Literature,* Eldred Jones commented that *The Lion and the Jewel* represents "a clash between the genuine and the false; between the well-done and the half-baked. Lakunle the school teacher would have been a poor symbol of any desirable kind of progress . . . . He is a man of totally confused values. [Baroka's worth lies in] the traditional values of which he is so confident and in which he so completely outmaneouvres Lakunle who really has no values at all." Bruce King, editor of *Introduction to Nigerian Literature,* named *The Lion and the Jewel* "the best literary work to come out of Africa."

Soyinka was well established as Nigeria's premier playwright when, in 1965, he published his first novel, *The Interpreters.* The novel allowed him to expand on themes already expressed in his stage dramas and to present a sweeping view of Nigerian life in the years immediately following independence. Essentially plotless, *The Interpreters* is loosely structured around informal discussions among five young Nigerian intellectuals. Each one has been educated in a foreign country and returned, hoping to shape Nigeria's destiny. They are hampered by their own confused values, however, as well as the corruption they encounter everywhere. Some reviewers likened Soyinka's writing style in *The Interpreters* to that of James Joyce and William Faulkner. Others took exception to the formless quality of the novel, but Eustace Palmer asserted in *The Growth of the African Novel:* "If there are reservations about the novel's structure, there can be none about the thoroughness of the satire at society's expense. Soyinka's wide- ranging wit takes in all sections of a corrupt society . . . . He is careful to expose [the interpreters'] selfishness, egoism, cynicism and aimlessness. Indeed the conduct of the intellectuals both in and out of the university is a major preoccupation of Soyinka's in this novel. The aimlessness and superficiality of the lives of most of the interpreters is patent."

Neil McEwan pointed out in *Africa and the Novel* that for all its seriousness, *The Interpreters* is also "among the liveliest of recent novels in English. It is bright satire full of good sense and good humour which are African and contemporary: the highest spirits of its author's early work . . . . Behind the jokes of his novel is a theme that he has developed angrily elsewhere: that whatever progress may mean for Africa it is not a lesson to be learned from outside, however much of 'modernity' Africans may share with others." McEwan further observed that although *The Interpreters* does not have a rigidly structured plot, "there is unity in the warmth and sharpness of its comic vision. There are moments which sadden or anger; but they do not diminish the fun." Palmer noted that *The Interpreters* notably influenced the African fiction that followed it, shifting the focus "from historical, cultural and sociological analysis to penetrating social comment and social satire."

The year *The Interpreters* was published, 1965, also marked Soyinka's first arrest by the Nigerian police. He was accused of using a gun to force a radio announcer to broadcast incorrect election results. No evidence was ever produced, however, and the PEN writers' organization launched a protest campaign, headed by William Styron and Norman Mailer. Soyinka was released after three months. He was next arrested two years later, during Nigeria's civil war. Soyinka was completely opposed to the conflict and especially to the Nigerian government's brutal policies toward the Ibo people who were attempting to form their own country, Biafra. He traveled to Biafra to establish a peace commission composed of leading intellectuals from both sides; when he returned, the Nigerian police accused him of helping the Biafrans to buy jet fighters. Once again he was imprisoned, this time held for more than two years although never formally charged with any crime. Most of that time, he was kept in solitary confinement. When all of his fellow prisoners were vaccinated against meningitis, Soyinka was passed by; when he developed serious vision problems, they were ignored by his jailers. He was denied reading and writing materials, but he manufactured his own ink and began to keep a prison diary, written on toilet paper, cigarette packages and in between the lines of the few books he secretly obtained. Each poem or fragment of journal he managed to smuggle to the outside world became a literary event and a reassurance to his supporters that he still lived, despite rumors to the contrary. He was released in 1969 and left Nigeria soon after, not returning until a change of power took place in 1975.

Published as *The Man Died: Prison Notes of Wole Soyinka,* the author's diary constitutes "the most important work ever written about the Biafran war," believed Charles R. Larson, contributor to *Nation.* "'The Man Died' is not so much the story of Wole Soyinka's own temporary death during the Nigerian Civil War but a personified account of Nigeria's fall from sanity documented by one of the country's leading intellectuals." Gerald Weales's *New York Times Book Review* article suggested that the political content of *The Man Died* is less fascinating than "the notes that deal with prison life, the observation of everything from a warder's catarrh to the predatory life of insects after a rain. Of course, these are not simply reportorial. They are vehicles to carry the author's shifting states of mind, to convey the real subject matter of the book; the author's attempt to survive as a man, and as a mind. The notes are both a means to that survival and a record to it." Larson underlined the book's political impact, however, noting that ironically, "while other Nigerian writers were emotionally castrated by the war, Soyinka, who was placed in solitary confinement so that he wouldn't embarrass the government, was writing work after work, books that will no doubt embarrass the Nigerian Government more than anything the Ibo writers may ever publish." A *Times Literary Supplement* reviewer expressed similar sentiment, characterizing *The Man Died* as "a damning indictment of what Mr. Soyinka sees as the iniquities of wartime Nigeria and the criminal tyranny of its administration in peacetime." Many literary commentators felt that Soyinka's work changed profoundly after his prison term, darkening in tone and focusing on the war and its aftermath.

In the *Dictionary of Literary Biography Yearbook: 1986,* Hayes quoted Soyinka on his concerns after the war: "I have one abiding religion—human liberty . . . . conditioned to the truth that life is meaningless, insulting, without this fullest liberty, and in spite of the despairing knowledge that words alone seem unable to guarantee its possession, my writing grows more and more preoccupied with the theme of the oppressive boot, the irrelevance of the color of the foot that wears it and the struggle for individuality." In spite of its satire, most critics found *The Interpreters* to be ultimately an optimistic book. In contrast, Soyinka's second novel *Season of Anomy,* expresses almost no hope for Africa's future, wrote John Mellors in *London Magazine,* commenting that the author seemed to write the book "in a blazing fury, angry beyond complete control of words at the abuses of power and the outbreaks of both considered and spontaneous violence . . . . The plot charges along, dragging the reader (not because he doesn't want to go, but because he finds it hard to keep up) through forest, mortuary and prison camp in nightmare visions of tyranny, torture, slaughter and putrefaction . . . . [M]urder and mutilation, while sickeningly explicit, are justified by . . . the author's anger and compassion and insistence that bad will not become better by our refusal to examine it."

Like *Season of Anomy,* Soyinka's postwar plays are considered more brooding than his earlier work. *Madmen and Specialists* was described as "grim" by Martin Banham and Clive Wake in *African Theatre Today.* In the play, a doctor returns from the war trained as a specialist in torture and uses his new skills on his father. The play's major themes are "the loss of faith and rituals" and "the break-up of the family unit which traditionally in Africa has been the foundation of society," according to Charles Larson in the *New York Times Book Review.* Names and events in the play are fictionalized to avoid censorship, but Soyinka has clearly "leveled a wholesale criticism of life in Nigeria since the Civil War: a police state in which only madmen and spies can survive, in which the losers are mad and the winners are paranoid about the possibility of another rebellion. The prewar corruption and crime have returned, supported by the more sophisticated acts of terrorism and espionage introduced during the war." Larson believed that, in large part, the play was a product of the time Soyinka spent in prison as a political prisoner. "It is, not surprisingly, the most brutal piece of social criticism he has published," Larson commented.

In a similar tone, *A Play of Giants* presents four African leaders—thinly disguised versions of Jean Bedel Bokassa, Sese Seko Mobutu, Macias Ngeuma, and Idi Amin—meeting at the United Nations building, where "their conversation reflects the corruption and cruelty of their regimes and the casual, brutal flavor of their rule," commented Hayes, in whose opinion the play demonstrates that, "as Soyinka has matured he has hardened his criticism of all that restricts the individual's ability to choose, think, and act free from external oppression . . . . [It is] his harshest attack against modern Africa, a blunt, venomous assault on . . . African leaders and the powers who support them."

In *Isara: A Voyage around "Essay,"* Soyinka provides a portrait of his father, Akinyode Soditan, as well as "vivid sketches of characters and culturally intriguing events that cover a period of fifteen years," Charles Johnson related in the *Washington Post.* The narrative follows S.A., or "Essay," and his classmates through his years at St. Simeon's Teacher Training Seminary in Ilesa. Aided by documents left to him in a tin box, Soyinka dramatizes the changes that profoundly affected his father's life. The Great Depression that brought the Western world to its knees during the early 1930s was a time of economic opportunity for Africans. The quest for financial gain transformed African culture, as did Mussolini's invasion of Ethiopia and the onset of World War II. More threatening was the violent civil war for the throne following the death of their king. An aged peacemaker named Agunrin resolved the conflict by an appeal to the people's common past. "As each side presents its case, Agunrin, half listening, sinks into memories that unfold his people's collective history, and finally he speaks, finding his voice in a scene so masterfully rendered it alone is worth the price of the book," Johnson claimed. The book is neither a strict biography nor a straight historical account. However, "in his effort to expose Western readers to a unique, African perspective on the war years, Soyinka succeeds brilliantly," Johnson commented. *New York Times* reviewer Michiko Kakutani wrote that, in addition, "Essay emerges as a high-minded teacher, a mentor and companion, blessed with dignity and strong ideals, a father who inspired his son to achievement."

In his 1996 work, *The Open Sore of a Continent: A Personal Narrative of the Nigerian Crisis,* Soyinka takes an expansive and unrestrained look at Nigeria's dictatorship. A collection of essays originally delivered as lectures at Harvard, *The Open Sore* questions the corrupt government, the ideas of nationalism, and international intervention. The book begins with the execution of Ken Saro- Wiwa. For Soyinka, his death, along with the annulment of the elections in 1993, signaled the disintegration of the state. According to Robert D. Kaplan in the *New York Times Book Review,* Soyinka "uses these harsh facts to dissect, then reinvent not just Nigeria but the concept of nationhood itself."

In 1998 Soyinka ended a self-imposed exile from Nigeria that began in 1993 when a democratically elected government was to have assumed power. Instead, General Ibrahim Babangida, who had ruled the nation for eight years, prohibited the publication of the voting results and installed his deputy, General Sani Abacha, as head of the Nigerian state. Soyinka, along with other pro-democracy activists, was charged with treason for his criticism of the military regime. Faced with a death sentence, Soyinka went into exile in 1994, during which time he traveled and lectured in Europe and the United States. Following the death of Abacha, who held control for five years, the new government, led by General Abdulsalem Abubakar, released numerous political prisoners and promised to hold civilian elections. Soyinka's return to his homeland renewed hope for a democratic Nigerian state. When confronted following a series of lectures at Emory University in early 2004 with questions about why he continues to struggle against almost overwhelming political odds, Soyinka was quoted by Richard Halicks in the *Atlanta Journal-Constitution* as commenting: "My conviction simply is that power must always be defeated, that the struggle must always continue to defeat power. I don't go looking for fights. People don't believe this, I'm really a very lazy person. I enjoy my peace and quiet. There's nothing I love better than just to sit quietly somewhere, you know, have a glass of wine, read a book, listen to music, that really is my ideal existence." However, just months after that comment, Soyinka was tear gassed and again arrested, albeit briefly, while protesting the government of President Olusegun Obasanjo for what he and other human rights activists called, according to Andrew Meldrum of the *Guardian,* "a civilian dictatorship." Following his release, the almost- seventy-year-old Soyinka vowed to launch new antigovernment protests, which simply confirmed a statement he made several months before the arrest, quoted by Halicks, that seems to sum up his undaunted commitment to human liberty: "In prison I had lots of time to ponder, 'Why do I do things that get me into trouble?' I didn't find an answer. I also, to my surprise, didn't incur any internal suggestion that, when I get out of this one, I will stop. It has never occurred to me to stop."

Soyinka's work is frequently described as demanding but rewarding reading. Although his plays are widely praised, they are seldom performed, especially outside Africa. The dancing and choric speech often found in them are unfamiliar and difficult for non-African actors to master, a problem Holly Hill noted in her London *Times* review of the Lincoln Center Theatre production of *Death and the King's Horseman.* She awarded high praise to the play, however, saying it "has the stateliness and mystery of Greek tragedy." When the Swedish Academy awarded Soyinka the Nobel Prize in Literature in 1986, its members singled out *Death and the King's Horseman* and *A Dance of the Forests* as "evidence that Soyinka is 'one of the finest poetical playwrights that have written in English,'" reported Stanley Meisler of the *Los Angeles Times.*

In 2005 Soyinka published *Climate of Fear: The Quest for Dignity in a Dehumanized World,* a series of lectures that were initially presented at London's Royal Institution. The lectures discuss all of the current political and environmental forces that create a 'climate of fear' and posit that the true function of fear is to rob of dignity, and that the function of robbing of dignity is to dehumanize. Although Derek Hook, writing in *Theoria,* called the lectures "important critical contributions," he also noted that they are "frequently offset by an unfortunate mode of psychologism." Hook was perhaps more laudatory when he stated "insofar as Soyinka's discussion retains a balance . . . it holds something of promise." A *Kirkus Reviews* critic was more positive, commenting that the "gracefully stated" volume "wanders the boundary between memoir and political essay." Interestingly, Soyinka's *You Must Set Forth at Dawn: A Memoir,* was released shortly after the publication of *Climate of Fear.*

Soyinka has continued to publish valuable work throughout his forty-year career. Hayes, in a summary of Soyinka's literary importance, once stated: "His drama and fiction have challenged the West to broaden its aesthetic and accept African standards of art and literature. His personal and political life have challenged Africa to embrace the truly democratic values of the African tribe and reject the tyranny of power practiced on the continent by its colonizers and by many of its modern rulers."

BIOGRAPHICAL AND CRITICAL SOURCES:

BOOKS

Adelugba, Dapo, *Wole Soyinka: A Birthday Letter, and Other Essays,* University of Ibadan (Ibadan, Nigeria), 1984.

Adelugba, Dapo, editor, *Before Our Very Eyes: Tribute to Wole Soyinka,* Spectrum Books (Ibadan, Nigeria), 1987.

Agetua, John, *When the Man Died: Views, Reviews and Interview on Wole Soyinka's Controversial Book,* Agetua (Benin City, Nigeria), 1972.

Bamikunle, Aderemi, *Introduction to Soyinka's Poetry: Analysis of A Shuttle in the Crypt,* Ahmadu Bello University Press (Zaria, Nigeria), 1991.

Banham, Martin and Clive Wake, *African Theatre Today,* Pitman Publishing (New York, NY), 1976.

Banham, Martin, *Wole Soyinka's "The Lion and the Jewel,"* Rex Collings (London, England), 1981.

Black Literature Criticism, Gale (Detroit, MI), 1992.

Chinweizu, Onwuchekwa Jemie, and others, *Toward the Decolonization of African Literature,* Routledge (New York, NY), 1985, pp. 163-238.

Contemporary Literary Criticism, Gale (Detroit, MI), Volume 3, 1975, Volume 5, 1976, Volume 14, 1980, Volume 36, 1986, Volume 44, 1987.

Dictionary of Literary Biography, Volume 125: *Twentieth-Century Caribbean and Black African Writers, Second Series,* Gale (Detroit, MI), 1993.

Dictionary of Literary Biography Yearbook: 1986, Gale (Detroit, MI), 1987.

Drama Criticism, Volume 2, Gale (Detroit, MI), 1992.

Duerden, Dennis, and Cosmo Pieterse, editors, *African Writiers Talking: A Collection of Radio Interviews,* Heinemann (London, England), 1972.

Egudu, Romanus N., *Modern African Poetry and the African Predicament,* Barnes & Noble (New York, NY), 1978, pp. 104-124.

Etherton, Michael, *The Development of African Drama,* Hutchinson, 1982.

Fraser, Robert, *West African Poetry: A Critical History,* Cambridge University Press (New York, NY), 1986.

Gakwandi, Shatto Arthur, *The Novel and Contemporary Experience in America,* Heinemann (London, England), 1977.

Gibbs, James, editor, *Study Aid to "Kongi's Harvest,"* Rex Collings (London, England), 1973.

Gibbs, James, editor, *Critical Perspectives on Wole Soyinka,* Three Continents (Colorado Spring, CO), 1980.

Gibbs, James, *Wole Soyinka,* Macmillan (New York, NY), 1986.

Goodwin, K.L., *Understanding African Poetry: A Study of Ten African Poets,* Heinemann (London, England), 1982.

Graham-White, Anthony, *The Drama of Black Africa,* French, 1974.

Herdeck, Donald E., *Three Dynamite Authors: Derek Walcott (Nobel 1992), Naguib Mahfouz (Nobel 1988), Wole Soyinka (Nobel 1986): Ten Bio-Critical Essays from Their Works As Published by Three Continents Press,* Three Continents Press (Colorado Springs, CO), 1995.

Irele, Abiola, *The African Experience in Literature and Ideology,* Heinemann (London, England), 1981.

Jeyifo, Biodun, *The Truthful Lie: Essays in the Sociology of African Literature,* New Beacon, 1985, pp. 11-45.

Jones, Eldred, editor, *African Literature Today, Number 5: The Novel in Africa,* Heinemann (London, England), 1971.

Jones, Eldred, editor, *African Literature Today,* number 6: *Poetry in Africa,* Heinemann (London, England), 1973.

Jones, Eldred, *Wole Soyinka,* Twayne (Boston, MA), 1973, published in England as *The Writings of Wole Soyinka,* Heinemann (London, England), 1973, revised, Currey, 1988.

King, Bruce, editor, *Introduction to Nigerian Literature,* Africana Publishing (New York, NY), 1972.

Larson, Charles R., *The Emergence of African Fiction,* revised edition, Indiana University Press (Bloomington, IN), 1972.

Lindfors, Bernth, and James Gibbs, editors, *Research on Wole Soyinka,* Africa World Press (Trenton, NJ), 1992.

McEwan, Neil, *Africa and the Novel,* Humanities Press (Atlantic Highlands, NJ), 1983.

Moore, Gerald, *Wole Soyinka,* Africana Publishing (New York, NY), 1971.

Morell, Karen L., editor, *In Person—Achebe, Awoonor, and Soyinka at the University of Washington,* African Studies Program, Institute for Comparative and Foreign Area Studies, University of Washington (Seattle, WA), 1975.

Ogunba, Oyin, *The Movement of Transition: A Study of the Plays of Wole Soyinka,* Ibadan University Press (Ibadan, Nigeria), 1975.

Ogunba, Oyin and others, editors, *Theatre in Africa,* Ibadan University Press (Ibadan, Nigeria), 1978.

Okpu, B., *Wole Soyinka: A Bibliography,* Libriservice (Lagos, Nigeria), 1984.

Olaniyan, Tejumola, *Scars of Conquest/Masks of Resistance: The Invention of Cultural Identities in African, African-American, and Carribbean Drama,* Oxford University Press (London, England), 1995.

Omotoso, Kole, *Achebe or Soyinka: A Study in Contrasts,* Zell (London, England), 1996.

Palmer, Eustace, *The Growth of the African Novel,* Heinemann (London, England), 1979.

Parsons, E.M., editor, *Notes on Wole Soyinka's "The Jero Plays,"* Methuen (London, England), 1982.

Pieterse, Cosmo, and Dennis Duerden, editors, *African Writers Talking: A Collection of Radio Interviews,* Africana Publishing (New York, NY), 1972.

Quayson, Ato, *Strategic Transformations in Nigerian Writing: Orality and History in the Work of Rev.*

Samuel Johnson, Amos Tutuola, Wole Soyinka, and Ben Okri, Indiana University Press (Bloomington, IN), 1997.

Ricard, Alain, *Theatre et Nationalisme: Wole Soyinka et LeRoi Jones,* Presence Africaine (Paris, France), 1972.

Roscoe, Adrian A., *Mother Is Gold: A Study in West African Literature,* Cambridge University Press (Cambridge, England), 1971.

Soyinka, Wole, *The Man Died: Prison Notes of Wole Soyinka,* Harper & Row (New York, NY), 1972.

Soyinka, Wole, *Myth, Literature and the African World,* Cambridge University Press (Cambridge, England), 1976.

Soyinka, Wole, *Ake: The Years of Childhood,* Random House (New York, NY), 1981.

Soyinka, Wole, *Climate of Fear: The Quest for Dignity in a Dehumanized World* Random House (New York, NY), 2005.

Tucker, Martin, *Africa in Modern Literature: A Survey of Contemporary Writing in English,* Ungar (New York, NY), 1967.

Wilkinson, Jane, *Talking with African Writers,* J. Currey (Portsmouth, NH), 1992.

World Literature Criticism, Gale (Detroit, MI), 1992.

Wright, Derek, *Wole Soyinka Revisited,* Twayne (Boston, MA), 1993.

PERIODICALS

African American Review, spring, 1996, p. 99.

America, February 12, 1983.

American Theatre, January, 1997, p. 26.

Ariel, July, 1981.

Atlanta-Journal Constitution, April 4, 2004, Richard Halicks, "Q&A/Wole Soyinka: 'Power Must Always Be Defeated,'" section D, p. 1.

Black Orpheus, March, 1966.

Black World, August, 1975, pp. 20-48.

Book Forum, Volume 3, number 1, 1977.

Books Abroad, summer, 1972; spring, 1973.

British Book News, December, 1984; April, 1986.

Christian Science Monitor, July 31, 1970; August 15, 1970.

Commonweal, February 8, 1985.

Commonwealth Essays and Studies, spring, 1991, special on Wole Soyinka.

Contemporary Review, April, 1997, p. 211.

Detroit Free Press, March 20, 1983; October 17, 1986.

Detroit News, November 21, 1982.

Free Inquiry, fall, 1997, p. 48.

Globe and Mail (Toronto, Ontario, Canada), June 7, 1986; January 6, 1990.

Jet, July 18, 1994, p. 27.

Kirkus Reviews, December 15, 2004, review of *Climate of Fear: the Quest for Dignity in a Dehumanized World,* p. 1193.

London Magazine, April-May, 1974, John Mellors, review of *Season of Anomy.*

Los Angeles Times, October 17, 1986.

Los Angeles Times Book Review, October 15, 1989.

Nation, October 11, 1965; April 29, 1968; September 15, 1969; November 10, 1969; October 2, 1972; November 5, 1973; May 27, 1996, Charles R. Larson, review of *The Beatification of Area Boy,* p. 31.

New Perspectives, summer, 1994, p. 61.

New Republic, October 12, 1974; May 9, 1983; December 18, 1995, p. 12; June 16, 1997, p. 33.

New Statesman, December 20, 1968.

Newsweek, November 1, 1982.

New Yorker, May 16, 1977.

New York Review of Books, July 31, 1969; October 21, 1982.

New York Times, November 11, 1965; April 19, 1970; August 11, 1972; September 23, 1982, John Leonard, "Ake," section C, p. 18; May 29, 1986; May 31, 1986; June 15, 1986; October 17, 1986; November 9, 1986; March 1, 1987; March 2, 1987; November 3, 1989, Michiko Kakutani, review of *Isara: A Voyage Around "Essay,"* section C, p. 31; August 26, 1996, p. 26.

New York Times Book Review, July 29, 1973; December 24, 1973; October 10, 1982, James Olney, "Ake," p. 7; January 15, 1984; November 12, 1989; May 15, 1994, p. 24; August 11, 1996, Robert D. Kaplan, review of *The Open Sore of a Continent: A Personal Narrative of the Nigerian Crisis,* p. 79.

New York Times Magazine, September 18, 1983, Jason Berry, "A Voice Out of Africa," p. 92.

Progressive, August, 1997, p. 36.

Publishers Weekly, June 3, 1996.

Research in African Literatures, spring, 1983.

Saturday Review/World, October 19, 1974.

Spectator, November 6, 1959; December 15, 1973; November 24, 1981.

Theoria, April, 2005, Derek Hook, review of *Climate of Fear,* p. 141.

Time, October 27, 1986; December 5, 1994, p. 29.

Times (London, England), October 17, 1986; April 6, 1987; March 15, 1990.

Times Literary Supplement, April 1, 1965; June 10, 1965; January 18, 1968; December 31, 1971; March 2, 1973; December 14, 1973; February 8, 1974; March 1, 1974; October 17, 1975; August 5, 1977; February 26, 1982; September 23, 1988; March 22-29, 1990; February 24, 1995, Adewale

Maja-Pearce, review of *Ibadan: The Penkelemes Years: A Memoir;* June 13, 1997, Landeg White, "Walking a Step with Soyinka," p. 27.

Tribune Books (Chicago, IL), October 7, 1979; November 19, 1989; July 31, 1994.

Tri-Quarterly, fall, 1966, John F. Povey, review of *A Dance of the Forests.*

Village Voice, August 31, 1982.

Washington Post, October 30, 1979; October 17, 1986; November 10, 1989, Charles Johnson, review of *Isara,* section D, p. 3.

Washington Post Book World, November 10, 1996, p. 4.

World, February 13, 1973.

World Literature Today, winter, 1977; autumn, 1981; summer, 1982; summer, 2000, James Gibbs, review of *The Burden of Memory, the Muse of Forgiveness,* p. 573.

ONLINE

University of California—Berkeley, Institute of International Studies Web site, http://globetrotter.berkeley.edu/ (April 16, 1998), "Conversation with Nobel Laureate Wole Soyinka."

* * *

SPARK, Muriel 1918-
(Evelyn Cavallo, Muriel Sarah Spark)

PERSONAL: Born February 1, 1918, in Edinburgh, Scotland; daughter of Bernard and Sarah Elizabeth Maud (Uezzell) Camberg; married Sydney O. Spark, 1937 (divorced); children: Robin (son). *Education:* Attended James Gillespie's High School for Girls, Edinburgh, 1923-35; Heriot Watt College, 1935-37. *Religion:* Roman Catholic. *Hobbies and other interests:* Reading, travel.

ADDRESSES: *Home*—Italy. *Agent*—c/o Georges Borchardt, Inc., 136 East 57th St., New York, NY 10022; c/o David Higham Associates Ltd., 5-8 Lower John Street, Golden Square, London W1F 9HA, England.

CAREER: Writer. Employed in the Political Intelligence Department of the British government's Foreign Office, 1944-45; editorial assistant, *Argentor* (jewelry trade art magazine), 1946-47; general secretary, Poetry Society, 1947-49; editor of *Poetry Review,* 1947-49; editorial assistant, *European Affairs,* 1949-50; founder, *Forum* (literary magazine); part-time editor, Peter Owen Ltd. (publishing company).

MEMBER: PEN (honorary member), American Academy and Institute of Arts and Letters (honorary member), Society of Authors, Authors Guild, Royal Society of Edinburgh (honorary fellow).

AWARDS, HONORS: *Observer* short story prize, 1951, for "The Seraph and the Zambesi"; Prix Italia, 1962, for radio play adaptation of *The Ballad of Peckham Rye;* Yorkshire Post Book of the Year award, 1965, and James Tait Black Memorial Prize, 1966, both for *The Mandelbaum Gate;* Order of the British Empire, 1967; Scottish Book of the Year award, 1987, for *The Stories of Muriel Spark;* First Prize, F.N.A.C. La Meilleur Recueil des Nouvelles Etrangeres, 1987, for the Editions Fayard translation of *The Stories of Muriel Spark;* Officier de l'Ordre des Arts et des Lettres, France, 1988, Commandeur, 1996; Bram Stoker Award, 1988, for *Mary Shelley;* Ingersoll T.S. Eliot Award, 1992; Dame, Order of the British Empire, 1993; David Cohen British Literature Prize, 1997; PEN International Gold Pen Award, 1998; Campion Award, Catholic Book Club, 2001.Honorary degrees, University of Strathclyde, 1971, University of Edinburgh, 1989, University of Aberdeen, 1995, Watt University, 1995, University of St. Andrews, 1998, and Oxford University, 1999.

WRITINGS:

FICTION

The Comforters (also see below), Lippincott (Philadelphia, PA), 1957.

Robinson, Lippincott (Philadelphia, PA), 1958.

The Go-Away Bird and Other Stories (short stories), Macmillan (London, England), 1958, Lippincott (Philadelphia, PA), 1960.

Memento Mori (also see below), Lippincott (Philadelphia, PA), 1959.

The Ballad of Peckham Rye (also see below), Lippincott (Philadelphia, PA), 1960.

The Bachelors, Macmillan (London, England), 1960, Lippincott (Philadelphia, PA), 1961.

Voices at Play (short stories and radio plays), Macmillan (London, England), 1961, Lippincott (Philadelphia, PA), 1962.

The Prime of Miss Jean Brodie (also see below), Macmillan (London, England), 1961, Lippincott (Philadelphia, PA), 1962.

A Muriel Spark Trio (contains *The Comforters, Memento Mori,* and *The Ballad of Peckham Rye*), Lippincott (Philadelphia, PA), 1962.

The Girls of Slender Means (also see below), Knopf (New York, NY), 1963.

The Mandelbaum Gate, Knopf (New York, NY), 1965.

Collected Stories 1, Macmillan (London, England), 1967, Knopf (New York, NY), 1968.

The Public Image, Knopf (New York, NY), 1968.

The Very Fine Clock (juvenile), Knopf (New York, NY), 1968.

The Driver's Seat, Knopf (New York, NY), 1970.

Not to Disturb, Macmillan (London, England), 1971, Viking (New York, NY), 1972.

The Hothouse by the East River, Viking (New York, NY), 1973.

The Abbess of Crewe (also see below), Viking (New York, NY), 1973.

The Takeover, Viking (New York, NY), 1976.

Territorial Rights, Coward (New York, NY), 1979.

Loitering with Intent, Coward (New York, NY), 1981.

Bang-Bang You're Dead and Other Stories, Granada (New York, NY), 1982.

The Only Problem, Coward (New York, NY), 1984, Franklin Library (Franklin Center, PA), 1984.

The Stories of Muriel Spark, Dutton (New York, NY), 1985.

A Far Cry from Kensington, Houghton Mifflin (Boston, MA), 1988.

Symposium, Houghton Mifflin (Boston, MA), 1990.

The Novels of Muriel Spark (selections), Houghton Mifflin (Boston, MA), 1995.

Reality and Dreams, Constable (London, England), 1996.

Open to the Public: New and Collected Stories, New Directions (New York, NY), 1997.

Aiding and Abetting (novel), Viking (New York, NY), 2000.

A Hundred and Eleven Years without a Chauffeur (limited edition of 26 copies; story previously appeared in the *New Yorker*), Colophon Press (London, England), 2001.

The Complete Short Stories, Viking (New York, NY), 2001.

All the Stories of Muriel Spark, New Directions (New York, NY), 2001.

The Ghost Stories of Muriel Spark, New Directions (New York, NY), 2003.

Also author of *The Small Telephone* (juvenile), 1993.

POETRY

The Fanfarlo and Other Verse, Hand and Flower Press (Kent, England), 1952.

Collected Poems 1, Macmillan (London, England), 1967, Knopf (New York, NY), 1968,

Going Up to Sotheby's and Other Poems, Granada (New York, NY), 1982.

NONFICTION

*Child of Light: A Reassessment of Mary Wollstonecraft Shelley,*Tower Bridge Publications, 1951, revised edition published as *Mary Shelley,* Dutton (New York, NY), 1987.

Emily Bronte: Her Life and Work, P. Owen (London, England), 1953.

John Masefield, Nevill (London, England), 1953, revised edition, Hutchinson (London, England), 1992.

The Essence of the Brontes, P. Owen (London, England), 1993.

EDITOR

(And author of introduction) *A Selection of Poems by Emily Bronte,* Grey Walls Press (London, England), 1952.

The Letters of Mary Shelley, Wingate (London, England), 1953.

The Letters of the Brontes: A Selection, University of Oklahoma Press (Norman, OK), 1954, published as *The Bronte Letters,* Nevill (London, England), 1954.

(Coeditor) *Letters of John Henry Newman,* P. Owen (London, England), 1957.

OTHER

Doctors of Philosophy (play; produced in London, 1962), Macmillan (London, England), 1963, Knopf (New York, NY), 1966.

Curriculum Vitae: An Autobiography, Houghton Mifflin (Boston, MA), 1993.

Also author of radio plays *The Party through the Wall,* 1957, *The Interview,* 1958, *The Dry River Bed,* 1959, *The Ballad of Peckham Rye,* 1960, and *The Danger Zone,* 1961. Contributor of short stories and poems to the *New Yorker,* and of poems, articles, and reviews to magazines and newspapers. Some writings appear under the pseudonym Evelyn Cavallo.

ADAPTATIONS: Several of Muriel Spark's novels have been adapted for the stage, film, and television. A dramatization of *Memento Mori* was produced on stage in

1964 and a version was televised by British Broadcasting Corporation (BBC) in 1992. Jay Presson Allen's dramatization of *The Prime of Miss Jean Brodie,* published by Samuel French in 1969, was first produced in Torquay, England, at the Princess Theatre beginning April 5, 1966, then in Boston at the Colonial Theatre from December 26, 1967, to January 6, 1968, and finally on Broadway at the Helen Hayes Theatre beginning January 9, 1968. Allen also wrote the screenplay for the 1969 film version of the same novel, a Twentieth Century-Fox production starring Maggie Smith. John Wood's dramatization of *The Prime of Miss Jean Brodie* was produced in London at Wyndham's Theatre in 1967, and on Broadway in 1968; a six-part adaptation of the novel appeared on public television in England in 1978 and in the United States in 1979. *The Driver's Seat* was filmed in 1972, and in 1974 *The Girls of Slender Means* was adapted for BBC television. *The Abbess of Crewe* was filmed and released in 1976 under the title *Nasty Habits.*

SIDELIGHTS: In a career spanning more than half a century, Scottish writer Muriel Spark has enlightened and entertained with her poetry, critical works, biographies, and editorial contributions, but most of all with her score of novels. These include such popular works as *The Prime of Miss Jean Brodie, Memento Mori, The Girls of Slender Means, The Ballad of Peckham Rye, Territorial Rights, Loitering with Intent, The Abbess of Crewe, Symposium, Reality and Dreams,* and *Aiding and Abetting,* many of which have been adapted for radio, the stage, television, or film. Often described as one of the best, yet one of the least appreciated, of today's novelists, Spark confounds those readers and critics who have an affinity for labels and categories. In granting her the 2001 Campion Award, the Catholic Book Club—as quoted on the author's Web site—praised Spark's singular achievement: "Themes universal to the human condition—good and evil, honor and duplicity, self-aggrandizement and self-pity and courage amid poverty—are incarnate in her writing with a sometime eerily familiar face. For good or bad, hers are characters that endure in our memory."

Spark had already achieved some recognition as a critic and poet when she entered what was virtually her first attempt at fiction, the short story "The Seraph and the Zambesi," in a 1951 Christmas writing contest sponsored by the London *Observer.* The fanciful tale of a troublesome angel who bursts in on an acting troupe staging a holiday pageant on the banks of Africa's Zambesi River, "The Seraph and the Zambesi" won top honors in the competition and attracted a great deal of attention for its unconventional treatment of the Christmas theme. Several other stories set in Africa and England followed; soon Spark's successes in fiction began to overshadow those in criticism and poetry.

With financial and moral support from author Graham Greene, Spark struggled for nearly three years to sort out the aesthetic, psychological, and religious questions raised by her conversion to Catholicism and her attempt at writing longer fiction. Drawing on the tenets of her new faith, which she believes is especially "conducive to individuality, to finding one's own individual point of view," the young writer formulated her own theory of the novel. According to Frank Kermode in his book *Continuities,* this theory suggests that "a genuine relation exists between the forms of fiction and the forms of the world, between the novelist's creation and God'-s." In essence, Spark sees the novelist as very God-like—omniscient and omnipotent, able to manipulate plot, character, and dialogue at will. Viewed in this light, Kermode and others contended, Spark's first novel, *The Comforters,* is obviously "an experiment designed to discover whether . . . the novelist, pushing people and things around and giving 'disjointed happenings a shape,' is in any way like Providence."

Because Spark's Catholicism figures so prominently in *The Comforters* and subsequent works, it is "much more than an item of biographical interest," in the opinion of Victor Kelleher, who commented in *Critical Review:* "Spark does not stop short at simply bringing the question of Catholicism into her work; she has chosen to place the traditionally Christian outlook at the very heart of everything she writes. . . . [Her tales proclaim] the most basic of Christian truths: that all man's blessings emanate from God; that, in the absence of God, man is nothing more than a savage." Catharine Hughes makes a similar assessment of Spark's religious sentiment in an article in the *Catholic World.* The critic observed: "[Spark satirizes] humanity's foibles and incongruities from a decidedly Catholic orientation. One is conscious that she is a writer working within the framework of some of Christianity's greatest truths; that her perspective, which takes full cognizance of eternal values, is never burdened by a painful attempt to inflict them upon others."

At first glance, however, Spark's novels do not seem to reflect her strong religious and moral preoccupations. In terms of setting, for example, the author usually chooses to locate her modern morality tales in upper-class urban areas of England or Italy. Her "fun-house plots, full of trapdoors, abrupt apparitions, and smartly clicking secret panels," as novelist John Updike described them in a *New Yorker* article, focus on the often bizarre behavior of people belonging to a small, select group: elderly men and women linked by long-standing personal relationships in *Memento Mori;* unmarried male and female residents of the same London district in *The Bachelors;* students and teachers at a Scottish girls' school in *The Prime of Miss Jean Brodie;* servants on a Swiss estate in *Not to Disturb;* guests at a pair of neighboring Venetian hotels in *Territorial Rights.* The "action" in these stories springs from the elaborate ties Spark concocts between the members of each group—ties of blood, marriage, friendship, and other kinds of relationships. Commenting in her study of the author titled *Muriel Spark,* critic Patricia Stubbs observed that the use of such a technique reflects Spark's fascination with "the way in which the individual varies in different settings, or different company." "By taking this restricted group of protagonists," explained Stubbs, "[Spark] is able to create multiple ironies, arising from their connecting and conflicting destinies: by her selection of such a restricted canvas, she can display the many facets of her creatures' personalities, and the different roles which they, or society, decree they should play."

In the tradition of the intellectual novelist, Spark avoids florid descriptions of the physical world, preferring instead to concentrate on dialogue, on "the play of ideas and experiences upon the mind, and the interplay of minds upon each other," according to Joseph Hynes in his *Critical Essays on Muriel Spark.* Her characterizations are quick, sharp, and concise, and she teams her technical virtuosity with an elegant, acerbic wit and condescending attitude that most readers find highly entertaining. As Melvin Maddocks declared in *Life:* "Reading a Muriel Spark novel remains one of the minor pleasures of life. Like a perfect hostess, she caters to our small needs. In the manner available to only the best British novelists, she ordains a civilized atmosphere—two parts what Evelyn Waugh called creamy English charm, one part acid wit. She peoples her scene discriminatingly, showing a taste for interesting but not overpowering guests. . . . As the evening moves along, she has the good sense to lower the drawing-room lights and introduce a pleasantly chilling bit of tension—even violence—just to save us all, bless her, from the overexquisite sensibilities of the lady novelist."

The 1990 best-seller *Symposium* demonstrates the qualities to which Maddocks refers. It centers on Margaret Demien, a character whose wealthy mother-in-law dies while Margaret is away at a dinner party. Appearing to all as virtuous at first, Margaret openly expresses a more sinister intent. She is also connected to other mysterious deaths, so that when the guests receive news of the older woman's death, Margaret is a suspect. Peter Parker commented in the *Listener,* "This is a marvelous premise for a novel, and, as one would expect, Spark makes the most of opportunities for dark comedy. Against Margaret's willful attempt to become an instrument of evil is set an example of casual wickedness that unwittingly leads to mortal sin and provides the novel with a terrific final chapter. The book's epigraphs, taken from *Symposia* of Lucian and Plato, supply hints both of the book's resolution and of Spark's fictional method." The epigraphs also provide clues about the five couples at the dinner party, who in some ways represent the varieties of love Plato defined. "But the real philosophical dialogue in *Symposium* is not about love nor is it explicitly argued. Rather, it takes place almost between the lines and concerns the mysteries of evil and suffering, destiny and predestination, guilt and intention," Nina King related in a *Washington Post Book World* review. A *Publishers Weekly* reviewer also remarked, "Spark's exquisitely balanced tone proves that the richest comedy is that which explores the darkest themes."

Yet, as Barbara Grizzuti Harrison reminded readers in a *New York Times Book Review* article, Spark is at heart "a profoundly serious comic writer whose wit advances, never undermines or diminishes, her ideas." Spark once explained to *Contemporary Authors* that the intent behind her "mischief" is to make a lasting impression on her readers: "Satire is far more important, it has a more lasting effect, than a straight portrayal of what is wrong. I think that a lot of the world's problems should be ridiculed, but ridiculed properly rather than, well, wailed over. People go to the theater, for instance, to see a play about some outrage or other, and then they come away feeling that they've done something about it, which they haven't. But if these things are ridiculed, it sticks and the perpetrators stop doing it. . . . I do believe in satire as a very, very potent art form."

Despite all that has been written about her and her fiction, Spark remains an enigma to most critics. Described as an artist, a serious and accomplished writer, a moralist engaged with the human predicament, wildly entertaining, and a joy to read, Spark has nevertheless, in Stubbs's opinion, "succeeded triumphantly in evading classification." Updike, too, contends that Spark possesses a truly exceptional talent—a talent that without a doubt makes her an unclassifiable "original." In fact, he declared in the *New Yorker,* Spark "is one of the few writers of the language on either side of the Atlantic with enough resources, daring, and stamina to be altering, as well as feeding, the fiction machine."

Spark produced *Curriculum Vitae: An Autobiography* in 1993, at the age of seventy-five, partly to correct critical misunderstandings and inaccuracies about her life, and partly to put together the facts about her life and her fiction. "So many strange and erroneous accounts of parts of my life have been written since I became well known," *New Leader* contributor Hope Hale Davis quoted the author as saying, "that I felt it time to put the record straight." *Curriculum Vitae* covers the first thirty-nine years of Spark's life, up to the publication of her debut novel, *The Comforters.* It tells of her childhood in Edinburgh, daughter of a Jewish father and a Protestant English mother (whose accent mortified her daughter on more than one occasion). Spark also tells of her years at Gillespie's, where she studied under Christina Kay, who later served as the model for the title character in *The Prime of Miss Jean Brodie.* Unlike the fictional Brodie, however, Spark declares, Kay would never have manipulated her charges in an attempt to seduce a fellow teacher. *Curriculum Vitae* also covers Spark's time spent caring for her bedridden English grandmother; her unhappy marriage to and seven years in southern Rhodesia with the mentally disturbed Sydney O. Spark, who fathered her son, Robin; her war years in the propaganda wing of the British government; and her emergence as a powerful writer of fiction. "In her own fashion, reticent when she chooses but always free of invention," stated Helen Bevington in the *New York Times Book Review,* "Muriel Spark succeeds in her mission: she puts the record straight. With nearly half her life yet to consider, she will, I hope, tell us the rest of it."

Spark returned to the novel form in 1997 with *Reality and Dreams,* and again in 2000 with *Aiding and Abetting.* The former title features aging Tom Richards, a movie director recovering from a fall from a crane. His life is further set into a whirl by the disappearance of his younger daughter, plain-looking Miranda; this misfortune brings him and his wandering wife, Claire, together with Cora, his daughter by an earlier marriage, to try and find the second daughter, whom none of them has ever really accepted. Miranda turns up on a beach where Tom has earlier fantasized about a young girl, the subject of his last movie. Meanwhile, England is in the midst of economic crisis and redundancy. "The novel's awash with love, lust, disillusion, and banality," according to Dierdre Neilen, writing in *World Literature Today.* Neilen further commented that Spark's "writing compels the story forward, and the reader laughingly follows." Similarly, Francine Prose, writing in *People,* found the novel "witty [and] surprising," and advised readers to take this opportunity to sample Spark's voice: "elegant, wise, sympathetic, satiric—at once darkly sinister and brightly chipper." Gerda Oldham, writing in the *Antioch Review,* also thought Spark's "wit and irony" were the ingredients that make "her protagonist and his extended family tick." Lynda Obst, writing in the *Los Angeles Times Book Review,* described as "masterful" the plot twist in which Marigold lures her father and mother to look for her. And for Lucy Ferriss, writing in the *St. Louis Post-Dispatch,* "the more we chortle at the absurdity of Tom's dreams and the sordidness of his reality, the more we recognize our own absurdity and sordidness, our own reality and dreams."

Aiding and Abetting deals with the actual case of Lord Lucan, a British peer who, while apparently attempting to kill his estranged wife, managed to kill the family nanny instead. When he finally attacked his wife, he botched that job as well, and he went missing. The first murder warrant for a peer was issued, but Lucan has never been found. "The Lucan story seems ready-made for Spark's enchanter's powers," wrote Robert E. Hosmer, Jr. in the *Chicago Tribune.* Hosmer went on to note that Spark "presents an imaginative reconstruction of Lucan's life after that ghastly night," and that she tells a "terrifying human story that cuts across boundaries of gender, race and class to reveal unsettling truths about who we are and how we can behave."

Spark's novel posits two fictional Lucans who visit a psychotherapist in Paris, eventually forming a dangerous and threatening trio when secrets are revealed about all three. *Booklist*'s Brad Hooper thought that this twenty-first novel "shows no diminishment of [Spark's] still-abiding qualities." According to Hooper, Spark created an "intelligent but, above all, entertaining novel of deception." A contributor for *Publishers Weekly* also noted Spark's strengths as a writer: "terse, astringent and blessed with a wicked satiric wit." For this same reviewer, the reader becomes "immersed in a puzzling maze" with the three main characters. Thomas Mallon, writing in the *Atlantic Monthly,* similarly praised Spark's "brilliant, addled novels—deceptive, dark little comedies that eventually veer off into bizarre supernaturalness." Mallon found these powers still at work in *Aiding and Abetting:* "The typical Spark novel has always been stimulatingly off its rocker, and on the strength of *Aiding and Abetting,* there's yet no need to start persuading Dame Muriel into hers." *Newsweek*'s Jeff Giles had mixed praise for the novel, calling it a "sly, intriguing—if not entirely nourishing—book," while *Time*'s Paul Gray dubbed it an "engaging game of rat and louse [that] concludes with a bit of poetic justice that is ghastly and richly appropriate." Sandra Cookson, writing in *World Literature Today,* had unconditional praise for *Aiding and Abetting,* noting that in it

"Spark's prose is more tart, quirky, and spare than ever, her irony more relentless than in earlier novels."

In 2001 a limited edition of twenty-six copies of *A Hundred and Eleven Years without a Chauffeur* was published by Colophon Press. Each copy is signed and inscribed with a passage and a letter of the alphabet by Spark. The story previously appeared in the *New Yorker.* Further collections by Spark have appeared in the new millennium. *The Complete Short Stories* collects forty-one tales, many of them ghost tales, arranged according to theme rather than chronology. For Gabrielle Annan, reviewing the collection in the *Spectator,* the "neatest, wittiest, shortest, cleverest" of the ghost tales is "The Pearly Shadow," about a hallucination that is passed along like a cold. Religious stories as well as crime stories, ones set in Africa, and ones featuring a plucky female protagonist also find a place in the collection, which, in fact, is a mirror of Spark's artistic proclivities over the full span of her writing life. Reviewing the same collection in the *New Statesman,* Rebecca Abrams concluded that the "trademark" of all Spark's fiction, both novels and short stories, "is its lightness, the way it seems almost to shrug its shoulders at the people and lives it so piercingly brings to life."

BIOGRAPHICAL AND CRITICAL SOURCES:

BOOKS

Contemporary Literary Criticism, Thomson Gale (Detroit, MI), Volume 2, 1974, Volume 3, 1975, Volume 5, 1976, Volume 8, 1978, Volume 13, 1980, Volume 18, 1981, Volume 40, 1987, Volume 94, 1997.

Dictionary of Literary Biography, Thomson Gale (Detroit, MI), Volume 15: *British Novelists, 1930-1959,* 1983, Volume 139: *British Short-Fiction Writers, 1945-1980,* 1994.

Edgecombe, Rodney Stenning, *Vocation and Identity in the Fiction of Muriel Spark,* University of Missouri Press (Columbia, MO), 1990.

Enright, D. J., *Man Is an Onion: Reviews and Essays,* Chatto & Windus (London, England), 1972.

Hynes, Joseph, editor, *Critical Essays on Muriel Spark,* G.K. Hall (New York, NY), 1992.

Kemp, Peter, *Muriel Spark,* Elek, 1974, Barnes & Noble (New York, NY), 1975.

Kermode, Frank, *Continuities,* Random House (New York, NY), 1968.

Malkoff, Karl, *Muriel Spark,* Columbia University Press (New York, NY), 1968.

Page, Norman, *Muriel Spark,* St. Martin's Press (New York, NY), 1990.

Pearlman, Mickey, *Re-inventing Reality: Patterns and Characteristics in the Novels of Muriel Spark,* P. Lang (New York, NY), 1996.

Randisi, Jennifer Lynn, *On Her Way Rejoicing: The Fiction of Muriel Spark,* Catholic University of America Press (Washington, DC), 1991.

Short Story Criticism, Volume 10, Thomson Gale (Detroit, MI), 1992.

Sproxton, Judy, *The Women of Muriel Spark,* St. Martin's Press (New York, NY), 1992.

Sproxton, Judy, *Muriel Spark,* St. Martin's Press (New York, NY), 1994.

Stubbs, Patricia, *Muriel Spark,* Longman (London, England), 1973.

Whittaker, Ruth, *The Faith and Fiction of Muriel Spark,* Macmillan (London, England), 1978.

PERIODICALS

Antioch Review, winter, 1998, Gerda Oldham, review of *Reality and Dreams,* p. 116; spring, 2002, Barbara Beckerman Davis, review of *Aiding and Abetting,* p. 340.

Atlantic Monthly, February, 2001, Thomas Mallon, review of *Aiding and Abetting,* pp. 124-125.

Booklist, October 1, 2000, Brad Hooper, review of *Aiding and Abetting,* p. 292.

Catholic World, August, 1961, Catharine Hughes.

Chicago Tribune, June 19, 1997, Cassandra West, review of *Reality and Dreams,* p. 3; March 4, 2001, Robert E. Hosmer, Jr., review of *Aiding and Abetting,* p. 6; March 14, 2002, Sandy Bauers, review of *Aiding and Abetting,* p. B8.

Critical Review, number 18, 1976, article by Victor Kelleher.

Entertainment Weekly, March 30, 2001, Rebecca Ascher-Walsh, review of *Aiding and Abetting,* p. 64.

Library Journal, October 15, 2000, Barbara Love, review of *Aiding and Abetting,* p. 105.

Life, October 11, 1968, article by Melvin Maddocks.

Listener, September 20, 1990, Peter Parker, review of *Symposium.*

Los Angeles Times Book Review, June 8, 1997, Lynda Obst, review of *Reality and Dreams,* p. 10:2.

New Leader, May 17, 1993, Hope Hale Davis, review of *Curriculum Vitae,* p. 29.

New Statesman, October 1, 2001, Lisa Allardice, review of *Aiding and Abetting,* p. 80; October 15, 2001, Rebecca Abrams, review of *The Complete Short Stories,* pp. 56-57.

Newsweek, February 26, 2001, Jeff Giles, review of *Aiding and Abetting,* p. 71.

New Yorker, June 8, 1981, John Updike, review of *Loitering with Intent,* p. 148.

New York Times Book Review, May 31, 1981, Barbara Grizzuti Harrison, review of *Loitering with Intent,* p. 11; May 16, 1993, Helen Bevington, review of *Curriculum Vitae: An Autobiography;* March 11, 2001, Richard Eder, review of *Aiding and Abetting,* pp. 14-15.

People, August 25, 1997, Francine Prose, review of *Reality and Dreams,* p. 41; March 5, 2001, Joanne Kaufman, review of *Aiding and Abetting,* p. 51.

Publishers Weekly, October 26, 1990, review of *Symposium;* November 20, 2000, review of *Aiding and Abetting,* p. 44.

St. Louis Post-Dispatch, July 6, 1997, Lucy Ferriss, review of *Reality and Dreams,* p. F5.

Spectator, October 20, 2001, Gabrielle Annan, review of *The Complete Short Stories,* p. 53.

Time, March 12, 2001, Paul Gray, review of *Aiding and Abetting,* p. 90.

Village Voice, March 20, 2001, Charles McNulty, review of *Aiding and Abetting,* p. 66.

Virginia Quarterly Review, autumn, 1997, review of *Reality and Dreams,* p. 130.

Washington Post Book World, November 25, 1990, Nina King, review of *Symposium.*

World Literature Today, spring, 1997, Deirdre Neilen, review of *Reality and Dreams,* p. 373; summer, 2001, Sandra Cookson, review of *Aiding and Abetting,* p. 150.

ONLINE

David Higham Associates, http://www.davidhigham.co.uk/ (November 14, 2003).

Official Muriel Spark Web site, http://murielspark.com/ (November 14, 2003).

Penguin UK Web site, http://www.penguin.co.uk/ (November 14, 2003), Toby Litt, "Interview with Muriel Spark."

* * *

SPARK, Muriel Sarah
See SPARK, Muriel

* * *

SPARKS, Nicholas 1965-

PERSONAL: Born December 31, 1965, in Omaha, NE; son of Patrick Michael (a professor) and Jill Emma Marie (a homemaker and optometrist's assistant; maiden name, Thoene) Sparks; married, July, 1989; wife's name Catherine; children: Miles Andrew, Ryan Cody, Landon, Lexie Danielle and Savannah Marin (twins). *Education:* University of Notre Dame, B.B.A., 1988. *Politics:* Independent. *Religion:* Roman Catholic.

ADDRESSES: Home—New Bern, NC. *Agent*—c/o Author Mail, Warner Books, 1271 Avenue of the Americas, New York, NY 10020.

CAREER: Writer and novelist. Also worked as a real-estate appraiser, waiter, buyer and restorer of homes, business owner, and pharmaceutical company representative. Active contributor to the M.F.A./Creative Writing Program of the University of Notre Dame, providing internships, scholarships, and an annual fellowship.

AWARDS, HONORS: Book of the year nomination, American Booksellers Association, 1997, for *The Notebook.*

WRITINGS:

NOVELS

(With Billy Mills) *Wokini: A Lakota Journey to Happiness and Self-Understanding,* Orion Books (New York, NY), 1990.

The Notebook, Warner Books (New York, NY), 1996.

Message in a Bottle, Warner Books (New York, NY), 1998.

A Walk to Remember, Warner Books (New York, NY), 1999.

The Rescue, Warner Books (New York, NY), 2000.

A Bend in the Road, Warner Books (New York, NY), 2001.

Nights in Rodanthe, Warner Books (New York, NY), 2002.

The Guardian, Warner Books (New York, NY), 2003.

The Wedding, Warner Books (New York, NY), 2003.

(With Micah Sparks) *Three Weeks with My Brother,* Warner Books (New York, NY), 2004.

True Believer, Warner Books (New York, NY), 2005.

At First Sight, Warner Books (New York, NY), 2005.

Sparks's novels have been translated into over thirty-five languages.

ADAPTATIONS: Message in a Bottle was made into a 1999 film of the same title starring Kevin Costner, Robin Wright Penn, and Paul Newman and directed by

Luis Mandoki; *A Walk to Remember* was made by Warner Bros. into a 2002 film of the same title starring Mandy Moore and Shane West; an adaptation of *The Rescue* was planned as a television series; *A Bend in the Road* was adapted for audiobook, 2002; *Nights in Rodanthe* was adapted for audiobook, 2003; *The Notebook* was made into a film of the same title starring James Garner and Gena Rowlands, 2004; film rights for *Nights in Rodanthe, True Believer,* and *At First Sight* have been sold.

SIDELIGHTS: Nicholas Sparks's romance-heavy novels have spent weeks on the bestseller lists and have earned him a reputation as one of the few men to write successful love stories for a popular audience. His second foray, *Message in a Bottle,* became a 1999 motion picture starring Kevin Costner, while others have been optioned for the big screen as well. A film adaptation of Sparks's *A Walk to Remember* was released in 2002.

Sparks was born on the last day of 1965 and grew up in Minnesota and California. He was the valedictorian of his high-school class, and his prowess in track and field won him a full scholarship to the University of Notre Dame. There he broke a school record in the relay during his freshman year, but an injury sidelined him. Frustrated during his summer break, Sparks heeded his mother's advice and began writing to pass the time, penning a horror novel he titled *The Passing,* which was never published. On spring break in 1988, he met a University of New Hampshire student with whom he promptly fell in love, and who prompted his writing career to begin in earnest; Sparks wrote Catherine, who would eventually become his wife, a remarkable 150 letters in a two-month span.

Sparks's second novel, "The Royal Murders," also went unpublished. His law school applications were also rejected, and so Sparks became a real-estate appraiser, waited tables, then bought and restored old homes. He began his own business, and then sold it to embark upon a career as a pharmaceutical sales representative. Minor publishing success came after he teamed with Billy Mills, the father of one of Sparks's ex-girlfriends, on the 1990 book *Wokini: A Lakota Journey to Happiness and Self-Understanding*. Mills had won a gold medal in track in the 1964 Olympics and was the inspiration for the film *Running Brave.* The novel centers upon a young Lakota Indian, David, who comes of age after the tragic loss of his sister.

In 1993, Sparks and his wife relocated to New Bern, North Carolina. The following year the final episode of the long-running television situation comedy *Cheers* spurred him once again to try his hand at a novel. "I didn't want another eleven years to go by without chasing my dreams," he told *People* writer Kim Hubbard. "I decided I'd give myself three more chances at writing." The result was his 1996 novel *The Notebook,* which Sparks based on the romance between his wife's maternal grandparents. They had been married for sixty years and were too infirm to attend Sparks's 1989 wedding. The writer and his wife visited them the day after, and as Sparks recalled to Hubbard, "I realized they were flirting with each other. There was still a hint of passion after sixty-two years of marriage. That stayed with me."

The plot of *The Notebook* is framed by two chapters set in the present day inside a nursing home, where an elderly man reads to a weeping woman. Flashing back to 1946 and rural North Carolina, the novel introduces a young war veteran named Noah, who recalls a thwarted teen romance in a riverfront town during the summer of 1932. He still thinks about Allie, whose wealthy parents disapproved of him, and how he wrote her letters she never answered. Allie is now engaged to an attorney, and one day she reads about Noah's recent purchase of an old plantation home in town with the intention of renovating it. She tells her fiancé that she is taking an antiques-hunting jaunt by herself, but instead visits Noah and tells him that she never received his letters. Allie returns again the next day, and when the pair are caught in a storm out on the water their passion is rekindled. Meanwhile, Allie's mother arrives at Noah's home carrying a bundle of unopened letters and tells her daughter to "follow your heart." The final chapter finds Noah concluding his notebook story to Allie, who suffers from a severe case of Alzheimer's disease, on their forty-ninth wedding anniversary.

When Sparks sent the manuscript to an agent, it was sold within two days for a million dollars, and a movie deal was signed that same week as well. Sparks and his debut became an overnight sensation, and many reviewers noted that the novel seemed to replicate the success of Robert James Waller's best-selling *The Bridges of Madison County.* Though critical assessments were sometimes less than kind, *The Notebook* spent 115 weeks on hardcover and paperback bestseller lists. *Booklist*'s Joanne Wilkinson called it "an upscale Harlequin romance with great crossover appeal," but *Christian Century* writer Martha Whitmore Hickman asked: "Is it possible that, despite the medical prognosis, love can redeem some hours for those afflicted with Alzheimer's?"

Sparks kept his sales job for a time, surprised by the success of *The Notebook.* "I thought the book was pretty good when I wrote it," he told Hubbard in a *People* interview, "but I've gotten letters saying it was unforgettable. People—men, women, ministers—love this book." A film featuring James Garner, Ryan Gosley, Rachel McAdams, and Gena Rowlands was adapted from *The Notebook,* and Sparks himself went on to pen a sequel, *The Wedding,* in which Allie's daughter Jane experiences trouble in her thirty-year marriage with neglectful, work-consumed attorney Wilson Lewis. In *Booklist* Patty Engelmann dubbed *The Wedding* a "tender love story about a flawed hero trying to right his wrongs," while a *Publishers Weekly* reviewer praised Sparks for relating "a sweet story competently, without sinking too deeply into the mire of sentiment."

Sparks's next novel, *Message in a Bottle,* also spent months on the bestseller lists, including four weeks at the top. Inspired by the 1989 death of his mother in a horseback-riding accident, the 1998 work revolves around jaded Boston newspaper columnist and divorcee Theresa Osborne, who finds a letter in the sand of a Cape Cod beach one day. Its author is a man named Garrett, and the letter recounts a dream in which his lost love reappears. Theresa has spent the past three years trying to recover from her own failed marriage, and the letter ignites hope in her. She becomes obsessed with finding the writer and prints his letter in her column; she soon learns that it is one of many such missives found. Garrett turns out to be Garrett Blake, a diving instructor living in North Carolina. Theresa seeks Garrett out and learns that the woman to whom he is writing is his late wife, Catherine. "There are few surprises here as we watch the couple learn to love in Catherine's slowly waning shadow," a *Publishers Weekly* reviewer observed. Engelmann, writing in *Booklist,* termed the book "a deeply moving, beautifully written, and extremely romantic love story." *Message in a Bottle* was made into a film starring Kevin Costner, Robin Wright Penn, and Paul Newman.

First love is the theme of Sparks's third bestseller, *A Walk to Remember,* which the author penned as a way to deal with the premature death of a younger sister. The narrator of the 1999 novel is aging Landon Carter, who recalls his senior year of high school in Beaufort, North Carolina, in the late 1950s. Carter, the hedonistic son of a congressman, is senior class president and thus compelled to attend his homecoming dance. Scrambling to find a date, he asks drab Jamie Sullivan, the daughter of a Baptist minister. She agrees, but asks him to reciprocate and join her in a Christmas play scripted by her stern minister father. The two become unlikely friends, and Carter is moved by the play's theme; the elder Sullivan's love for his wife, Jamie's mother; and by Mrs. Sullivan's early death. Carter falls in love with Jamie, but learns of a tragic secret she harbors and is forced to make a life-altering decision. "Sparks," noted *Booklist* reviewer Engelmann, "proves once again that he is a master at pulling heartstrings," while a *Publishers Weekly* reviewer noted that *A Walk to Remember* is "sure to wring yet more tears from willing readers' eyes." The novel was adapted as a film in 2002.

Sparks continued his success with *The Rescue,* published in 2000. Its focus is on the unlikely romance that develops between Denise Holton, a single mother in a small North Carolina town, and the rugged Taylor McAden. Once a teacher, Denise has fallen on hard times and must live with her mother in order to devote enough time to her son, Kyle, who has a language-processing disability. One night her car veers off the road, and McAden, a contractor who also serves as a volunteer fireman, rescues Denise and her son. A bond develops between the hero and the little boy, and Denise finds herself attracted to McAden romantically. However, the brooding hero is also hiding some deep psychic wounds and seems unable to forge a relationship. "The story here is mostly a pretext for the emotional assault that Sparks delivers, but when he manages to link affect to action, the result is cunningly crafted melodrama," remarked a *Publishers Weekly* reviewer. Engelmann, writing in *Booklist,* asserted that "all of Sparks's trademark elements—love, loss, and small-town life—are present in this terrific summer read."

Sparks's fifth novel, *A Bend in the Road,* is filled with the writer's characteristic elements. Teacher Sarah Andrews meets Miles Ryan when Miles's second-grade son, Jonah, develops a learning disability stemming from the child's grief over his mother's death. Miles, too, has been wounded by the hit-and-run accident that killed his high school sweetheart and wife, Missy. When Sarah enters their lives, she has already experienced a divorce from a husband who could not live with Sarah's inability to bear children. Miles and Sarah eventually fall in love, but their future is clouded by a secret connected with Missy's death.

Nights in Rodanthe, which appeared in 2002, quickly became a bestseller, heading the lists in the *Wall Street Journal, Publishers Weekly,* and *New York Times.* It tells the story of two middle-aged people who have experienced failure in love. Adrienne Willis, a forty-five year old, is the divorced mother of three children whose husband abandoned her for a younger, more attractive woman. Paul Flanner, a divorced workaholic surgeon, was unable to devote enough time to his wife and children to sustain either a successful marriage or family life. Adrienne and Paul meet in a bed-and-breakfast in the town of Rodanthe, North Carolina. A romance is kindled over the next several days, and the two separate with the intention to continue an exploration of their love. Adrienne tells the story of their meeting—after a fourteen-year silence—to her daughter, Amanda, who is overcome with grief over the death of her own husband to the point that she is unable to properly attend to her young children's needs. As her mother's tale unfolds, so does the reason why Adrienne and Paul never married.

Nights in Rodanthe is "filled with a healthy dose of romance and emotion," commented Carol Fitzgerald in a *BookReporter* review. In *Kirkus Reviews* a critic felt that *Nights in Rodanthe* is a "harshly mechanical story" with a predictable plot, while in *Publishers Weekly* a reviewer remarked that "even fans may be irked" by the obvious twist in Sparks's characters' fates. Mary Frances Wilkens wrote in *Booklist,* however, that the novel encapsulates a "beautiful love story." On his Web site, Sparks explained that he used middle-aged protagonists in the book "because so many family elements can come to play" between more mature men and women.

In 2003 Sparks departed from his typical romantic stories with *The Guardian,* a novel that also incorporates elements of a thriller. Young widow Julie Barenson finds herself romantically involved with two men. Richard Franklin, a smooth-talking, wealthy gentleman, treats Julie in a lavish fashion. She breaks off their relationship after a few dates, however, and begins to see her late husband's best friend, Mike Harris. Franklin, unhappy about her rejection of his attention, begins to interfere in Julie's personal life in sinister ways. In an interview with a *BookReporter* contributor, Sparks revealed that he added a dark character like Franklin to his traditional romantic mix because "I wanted to write the type of novel that I hadn't written before . . . because I think it's important for my readers that they don't read the same book over and over."

Booklist writer Engelmann called *The Guardian* a "tricky tale of romantic suspense" with a nail-biting conclusion. Although "the writing is lax at best . . . . this one will be another bestseller," predicted a *Publishers Weekly* critic. Calling *The Guardian* "undoubtedly his finest work," David Exum commented of Sparks's work in *BookReporter,* "It is pulse-pounding, breathtaking, suspenseful and intriguing."

Three Weeks with My Brother tells the story of Sparks's "life-affirming round-the-world trip" with his brother, Micah, noted a reviewer in *Bookseller.* Stressed by his writing and promotional schedule as well as day-to-day life with his wife and five children, Sparks decided to accept an offer of a three-week, around-the-world trip. Since his wife was unable to commit to the trip, he asked his brother instead, who readily agreed. The book tells of the brothers' personal and professional successes and tragedies such as the death of their parents and younger sister, while also sharing the story of the Sparks family and how the close-knit clan helped and supported each other. In the book, the brothers recount their visits to spectacular and mysterious places such as Angkor Wat, the Taj Mahal, Australia's Ayers Rock, and the Arctic Circle, all the while strengthening their own fraternal ties. *Library Journal* reviewer Nann Blaine Hilyard commented, "This is a heartwarming story."

With *True Believer,* Sparks "has turned out another reliable romance, this time with a paranormal premise," noted *People* reviewer Moira Bailey. Protagonist Jeremy Marsh is a science journalist and columnist who relishes debunking occult phenomena and exposing paranormal frauds. After revealing the fakery of a popular but sleazy spirit guide, he heads to Boone Creek, North Carolina, at the request of Doris McClellan to investigate a mystery involving lights in the local cemetery. Jeremy is intrigued by Doris's orphaned granddaughter, Lexie Darnell, the inscrutable and stubborn thirty-year-old librarian with movie-star good looks but no beau. As he investigates the phenomena in the cemetery, and ratchets up his interest in Lexie, Jeremy discovers that Doris is a diviner. As his skepticism faces the challenge of strong evidence, Jeremy and Lexie work to overcome wounds in their past and embark on a new life of love. The novel's "mysteries and conflicts are resolved in largely predictable ways that will still satisfy Sparks's many fans," observed Rebecca Sturm Kelm in *Library Journal.*

Sparks resumes Jeremy and Lexie's story in *At First Sight.* The couple's relationship has progressed to the point of marriage, and Jeremy and the pregnant Lexie are planning for their nuptials. However, a well-meaning friend of Jeremy's plants a tiny but forceful doubt in his mind when he asks if Jeremy really loves her. A spate of mysterious e-mail messages, which suggest that Jeremy may not be the father of Lexie's baby, place their relationship in a negative light. Facing writer's block and the stress of adjusting to a rural environment, Jeremy begins to wonder if marrying Lexie is a good idea, after all. A selection of friends and family—including Lexie's psychic grandmother, her cranky and sullen ex, and an assortment of jealous friends—adds to the cracks in Jeremy and Lexie's relationship, and leaves the pair with serious decisions to make about themselves and about each other. Sparks explores the inner details of romance and "considers the sacrifices that each partner has to make in order to have a successful marriage," commented *Booklist* contributor Engelman. The story is "majorly manipulative and totally effective," commented a *Publishers Weekly* reviewer, who warned tear-prone readers to "Have plenty of tissues on hand."

BIOGRAPHICAL AND CRITICAL SOURCES:

PERIODICALS

Booklist, April 1, 1994, Pat Monaghan, review of *Wokini: A Lakota Journey to Happiness and Self-Understanding,* p. 1407; August, 1996, Joanne Wilkinson, review of *The Notebook,* p. 1856; October 15, 1997, Karen Harris, review of *The Notebook,* p. 424; February 15, 1998, Patty Engelmann, review of *Message in a Bottle,* p. 949; August, 1999, Patty Engelmann, review of *A Walk to Remember,* p. 1989; May 15, 2000, Nancy Paul, review of *A Walk to Remember,* p. 144; July, 2000, Patty Engelmann, review of *The Rescue,* p. 1976; January 1, 2002, review of audiobook version of *A Bend in the Road,* p. 875; January 1, 2003, Mary Frances Wilkens, review of audiobook version of *Nights in Rodanthe,* p. 920; March 1, 2003, Patty Engelmann, review of *The Guardian,* p. 1108; September 1, 2003, Patty Engelmann, review of *The Wedding,* p. 8; October 1, 2005, Patty Engelman, review of *At First Sight,* p. 5.

Bookseller, February 4, 2005, review of *Three Weeks with My Brother,* p. 34.

Christian Century, December 17, 1997, Martha Whitmore Hickman, review of *The Notebook,* p. 1201.

Entertainment Weekly, April 24, 1998, Daneet Steffens, review of *Message in a Bottle,* p. 75; October 15, 1999, Clarissa Cruz, review of *A Walk to Remember,* p. 74; November 10, 2000, review of *The Rescue,* p. 82.

Good Housekeeping, February, 2001, Nicholas Sparks, excerpt from *The Rescue,* p. 157.

Kirkus Reviews, August 1, 2002, review of *Nights in Rodanthe,* p. 1072; March 1, 2003, review of *The Guardian,* p. 343.

Kliatt, January, 2002, review of audiobook version of *A Bend in the Road,* p. 39.

Library Journal, October 1, 1997, Nancy Paul, review of *The Notebook,* p. 147; September 1, 2000, Rebecca Sturm Kelm, review of *The Rescue,* p. 253; February 15, 2005, Nann Blaine Hilyard, audiobook review of *Three Weeks with My Brother,* p. 170; April 15, 2005, Rebecca Sturm Kelm, review of *True Believer,* p. 79.

New York Times Book Review, June 14, 1998, Sarah Harrison Smith, review of *Message in a Bottle,* p. 21.

People, November 25, 1996, Kim Hubbard, "Sentimental Journal," p. 165; March 24, 1997, Lan N. Nguyen, "Most Sappy Fella," p. 35; April 20, 1998, Cynthia Sanz, review of *Message in a Bottle,* p. 47; March 1, 1999, p. 126; November 29, 1999, review of *A Walk to Remember,* p. 63; October 23, 2000, review of *The Rescue,* p. 57; November 13, 2000, "Nicholas Sparks: Sexiest Author," p. 97; September 22, 2003, Daisy Maryles, review of *The Wedding,* p. 31; October 6, 2003, Allison Adato, "Writing through the Pain," p. 141; May 2, 2005, Moira Bailey, review of *True Believer,* p. 47.

Publishers Weekly, July 22, 1996, review of *The Notebook,* p. 224; November 4, 1996, review of *The Notebook,* p. 45; March 3, 1997, Paul Nathan, "Dream Deal," p. 22; February 16, 1998, review of *Message in a Bottle,* p. 201; June 1, 1998, review of *Message in a Bottle,* p. 34; August 23, 1999, review of *A Walk to Remember,* p. 42; October 18, 1999, "Making Sparks Fly," p. 22; January 10, 2000, John F. Baker, "The Ongoing Saga of Sparks," p. 16; August 14, 2000, review of *The Rescue,* p. 331; August 26, 2002, review of *Nights in Rodanthe,* p. 44; March 17, 2003, review of *The Guardian,* p. 52; August 11, 2003, review of *The Wedding,* p. 255; April 25, 2005, Daisy Maryles, "Sparks Sparkles," p. 19; September 12, 2005, review of *At First Sight,* p. 41.

ONLINE

BookReporter, http://www.bookreporter.com/ (June 2, 2003), Carol Fitzgerald, review of *Nights in Rodanthe;* "Author Talk: April, 2003," interview with Sparks; David Exum, review of *The Guardian.*

Nicholas Sparks Home Page, http://www.nicholassparks.com/ (January 10, 2006).

* * *

SPAULDING, Douglas
See BRADBURY, Ray

* * *

SPAULDING, Leonard
See BRADBURY, Ray

SPENCER, Leonard G.
See SILVERBERG, Robert

* * *

SPENDER, Stephen 1909-1995
(Stephen Harold Spender)

PERSONAL: Born February 28, 1909, in London, England; died July 16, 1995, in London; son of Edward Harold (a journalist and lecturer) and Violet Hilda (Schuster) Spender; married Agnes Marie Pearn, 1936 (divorced); married Natasha Litvin (a pianist), 1941; children: (second marriage) Matthew Francis, Elizabeth. *Education:* Attended University College, Oxford, 1928-30.

CAREER: Writer. Elliston Chair of Poetry, University of Cincinnati, 1953; Beckman Professor, University of California, 1959; visiting lecturer, Northwestern University, 1963; Clark lecturer, Cambridge University, 1966; Mellon lecturer, Washington, DC, 1968; Northcliffe lecturer, University of London, 1969; visiting professor at University of Connecticut, 1968-70, University of Florida, 1976, Vanderbilt University, 1979, and University of South Carolina, 1981; University of London, University College, London, England, professor of English, 1970-77, professor emeritus, 1977-95.

Counselor in Section of Letters, UNESCO, 1947. Fellow of Institute of Advanced Studies, Wesleyan University, 1967. Consultant on poetry in English, Library of Congress, Washington, DC, 1965. *Military service:* National Fire Service, fireman, 1941-44.

MEMBER: PEN International (president, English Centre, beginning in 1975); American Academy of Arts and Letters and National Institute for Arts and Letters (honorary), Phi Beta Kappa, Beefsteak Club.

AWARDS, HONORS: Commander of the British Empire, 1962; Queen's Gold Medal for Poetry, 1971; named Companion of Literature, 1977; knighted by Queen Elizabeth II, 1983; *Los Angeles Times* Book Award in poetry nomination for *Collected Poems, 1928-1985,* 1986; honorary fellow, University College, Oxford; D.Litt. from University of Montpelier, Cornell University, and Loyola University.

WRITINGS:

POETRY

Nine Experiments: Being Poems Written at the Age of Eighteen, privately printed, 1928.

Twenty Poems, Basil Blackwell (Oxford, England), 1930.

Poems, Faber (London), 1933, Random House (New York, NY), 1934.

Perhaps (limited edition), privately printed, 1933.

Poem (limited edition), privately printed, 1934.

Vienna, Faber, 1934.

At Night, privately printed, 1935.

The Still Centre, Faber, 1939.

Selected Poems, Random House, 1940.

I Sit by the Window, Linden Press (New York, NY), c. 1940.

Ruins and Visions: Poems, 1934-1942, Random House, 1942.

Poems of Dedication, Random House, 1947.

Returning to Vienna, 1947: Nine Sketches, Banyan Press (Chicago), 1947.

The Edge of Being, Random House, 1949.

Sirmione Peninsula, Faber, 1954.

Collected Poems, 1928-1953, Random House, 1955, revised edition published as *Collected Poems, 1928-1985,* Faber, 1985.

Inscriptions, Poetry Book Society (London), 1958.

Selected Poems, Random House, 1964.

The Generous Days: Ten Poems, David Godine (Boston), 1969, enlarged edition published as *The Generous Days,* Faber, 1971.

Descartes, Steam Press (London), 1970.

Art Student, Poem-of-the-Month Club (London), 1970.

Recent Poems, Anvil Press Poetry (London), 1978.

Dolphins, St. Martin's (New York, NY), 1994.

PLAYS

Trial of a Judge: A Tragedy in Five Acts (first produced in London at Rupert Doone's Group Theatre on March 18, 1938), Random House, 1938.

(Translator and adapter with Goronwy Rees) *Danton's Death* (first produced in London, 1939; adaptation of a play by Georg Buechner), Faber, 1939.

To the Island, first produced at Oxford University, 1951.

(Adapter) *Lulu* (adaptation from plays by Frank Wedekind; also see below), produced in New York, 1958.

(Translator and adapter) *Mary Stuart* (adaptation of a play by Johann Christoph Friedrich von Schiller; produced on the West End at Old Vic, 1961; produced on Broadway at Vivian Beaumont Theatre, November 11, 1971), Faber, 1959, reprinted, Ticknor Fields, 1980.

(Translator and adapter) *The Oedipus Trilogy—King Oedipus, Oedipus at Colonos, Antigone: A Version by Stephen Spender* (three-act play; revision of play produced at Oxford Playhouse, 1983), Faber, 1985.

ESSAYS

The Destructive Element: A Study of Modern Writers and Beliefs, J. Cape (London), 1935, Houghton (Boston), 1936, reprinted, Folcroft (Folcroft, PA), 1970.

Forward from Liberalism, Random House, 1937.

The New Realism: A Discussion, Hogarth (London), 1939, Folcroft, 1977.

Life and the Poet, Secker Warburg (London), 1942, Folcroft, 1974.

European Witness, Reynal, 1946.

(Contributor) Richard H. Crossman, editor, *The God That Failed: Six Studies in Communism,* Harper, 1950.

Learning Laughter, Weidenfeld Nicolson (London), 1952, Harcourt, 1953.

The Creative Element: A Study of Vision, Despair, and Orthodoxy among Some Modern Writers, Hamish Hamilton (London), 1953, Folcroft, 1973.

The Making of a Poem, Hamish Hamilton, 1955, Norton, 1962.

The Imagination in the Modern World: Three Lectures, Library of Congress (Washington, DC), 1962.

The Struggle of the Modern, University of California Press (Berkeley, CA), 1963.

Chaos and Control in Poetry, Library of Congress, 1966.

The Year of the Young Rebels, Random House, 1969.

Love-Hate Relations: A Study of Anglo-American Sensibilities, Random House, 1974.

Eliot, Fontana, 1975, published as *T.S. Eliot,* Viking, 1976.

Henry Moore: Sculptures in Landscape, Studio Vista (London), 1978, C.N. Potter, 1979.

The Thirties and After: Poetry, Politics, People, 1933-1970, Random House, 1978.

(Contributor) *America Observed,* C.N. Potter, 1979.

(With David Hockney) *China Diary* (travel guide), with illustrations by Hockney, Thames Hudson, 1982.

In Irina's Garden with Henry Moore's Sculpture, Thames & Hudson, 1986.

EDITOR

W.H. Auden, *Poems,* privately printed, 1928.

(With Louis MacNeice) *Oxford Poetry 1929,* Basil Blackwell, 1929.

(With Bernard Spencer) *Oxford Poetry 1930,* Basil Blackwell, 1930.

(With John Lehmann and Christopher Isherwood) *New Writing, New Series I,* Hogarth, 1938.

(With Lehmann and Isherwood) *New Writing, New Series II,* Hogarth, 1939.

(With Lehmann and author of introduction) *Poems for Spain,* Hogarth, 1939.

Spiritual Exercises: To Cecil Day Lewis (poems), privately printed, 1943.

(And author of introduction) *A Choice of English Romantic Poetry,* Dial, 1947.

(And author of introduction) Walt Whitman, *Selected Poems,* Grey Walls Press (London), 1950.

Martin Huerlimann, *Europe in Photographs,* Thames Hudson, 1951.

(With Elizabeth Jennings and Dannie Abse) *New Poems 1956: An Anthology,* M. Joseph (London), 1956.

(And author of introduction) *Great Writings of Goethe,* New American Library, 1958.

(And author of introduction) *Great German Short Stories,* Dell, 1960.

(And author of introduction) *The Writer's Dilemma,* Oxford University Press, 1961.

(With Irving Kristol and Melvin J. Lasky) *Encounters: An Anthology from the First Ten Years of "Encounter" Magazine,* Basic Books, 1963.

(With Donald Hall) *The Concise Encyclopedia of English and American Poets and Poetry,* Hawthorn, 1963, revised edition, Hutchinson, 1970.

(And author of introduction) *A Choice of Shelley's Verse,* Faber, 1971.

(And author of introduction) *Selected Poems of Abba Kovne* [and] *Selected Poems of Nelly Sachs,* Penguin, 1971.

The Poems of Percy Bysshe Shelley, Limited Editions Club (Cambridge), 1971.

D.H. Lawrence: Novelist, Poet, Prophet, Harper, 1973.

W.H. Auden: A Tribute, Macmillan, 1975.

Herbert List: Junge Maenner, Twin Palms, 1988.

Hockney's Alphabet, Random House/American Friends of AIDS Crisis Trust, 1991.

TRANSLATOR

(And author of introduction and, with J.B. Leishman, commentary) Rainer Maria Rilke, *Duino Elegies* (bilingual edition), Norton, 1939, 4th edition, revised, Hogarth, 1963.

(With Hugh Hunt) Ernst Toller, *Pastor Hall* (three-act play), John Lane, 1939; also bound with *Blind Man's Buff* by Toller and Denis Johnson, Random House, 1939.

(With J.L. Gili) Federico Garcia Lorca, *Poems,* Oxford University Press, 1939.
(With Gili) *Selected Poems of Federico Garcia Lorca,* Hogarth, 1943.
(With Frances Cornford) Paul Eluard, *Le Dur desir de Durer,* Grey Falcon Press, 1950.
(And author of introduction) Rilke, *The Life of the Virgin Mary (Das Marien-Leben)* (bilingual edition), Philosophical Library, 1951.
(With Frances Fawcett) Wedekind, *Five Tragedies of Sex,* Theatre Arts, 1952.
(With Nikos Stangos) C.P. Cavafy, *Fourteen Poems,* Editions Electo, 1977.
Wedekind, *Lulu Plays and Other Sex Tragedies,* Riverrun, 1979.
The Burning Cactus (short stories), Random House, 1936, reprinted, Books for Libraries Press, 1971.

OTHER

The Backward Son (novel), Hogarth, 1940.
(With William Sansom and James Gordon) *Jim Braidy: The Story of Britain's Firemen,* Lindsay Drummond, 1943.
(Author of introduction and notes) *Botticelli,* Faber, 1945, Pitman (London), 1948.
(Author of introduction) Patrice de la Tour du Pin, *The Dedicated Life in Poetry* [and] *The Correspondence of Laurent de Cayeux,* Harvill Press, 1948.
World within World: The Autobiography of Stephen Spender, Harcourt, 1951, reprinted with an introduction by the author, St. Martin's, 1994.
Engaged in Writing, and The Fool and the Princess (short stories), Farrar, Straus (New York, NY), 1958.
(With Nicholas Nabokov) *Rasputin's End* (opera), Ricordi (Milan), 1963.
(Contributor with Patrick Leigh Fermor) *Ghika: Paintings, Drawings, Sculpture,* Lund, Humphries, 1964, Boston Book and Art Shop, 1965.
(Reteller) *The Magic Flute: Retold* (juvenile; based on the opera by Mozart), Putnam, 1966.
(Author of introduction) *Venice,* Vendome, 1979.
Letters to Christopher: Stephen Spender's Letters to Christopher Isherwood, 1929-1939, with "The Line of the Branch"—Two Thirties Journals, Black Sparrow (Santa Barbara, CA), 1980.
(Author of introduction) *Herbert List: Photographs, 1930-1970,* Thames Hudson, 1981.
(Contributor) Martin Friedman, *Hockney Paints the Stage,* Abbeville Press, 1983.
The Journals of Stephen Spender, 1939-1983, Random House, 1986.
The Temple (novel), Grove, 1988.
(Author of preface) David Finn, *Evocations of "Four Quartets,"* Black Swan, 1991.
(Translator, with others) *Selected Poems by Rilke,* Knopf (New York, NY), 1996.

Editor, with Cyril Connolly, of *Horizon,* 1939-41; co-editor, with Melvin J. Lasky, 1953-66, and corresponding editor, 1966-67, *Encounter;* cofounder of *Index on Censorship* (bimonthly magazine). Contributor to numerous anthologies.

SIDELIGHTS: Stephen Spender was a member of the generation of British poets who came to prominence in the 1930s, a group—sometimes referred to as the Oxford Poets—that included W.H. Auden, Christopher Isherwood, C. Day Lewis, and Louis MacNeice. In *World within World: The Autobiography of Stephen Spender* the author speculated that the names of the members of the group became irreversibly linked in the minds of critics for no other reason other than having their poems included in the same important poetic anthologies of the early thirties. However, in *The Angry Young Men of the Thirties* Elton Edward Smith found that the poets had much more in common and stated that they shared a "similarity of theme, image, and diction." According to Smith, the poets also all rejected the writing of the immediately preceding generation. Gerald Nicosia reached the same conclusion in his *Chicago Tribune Book World* essay on Spender's work. "While preserving a reverence for traditional values and a high standard of craftsmanship," Nicosia wrote, "they turned away from the esotericism of T.S. Eliot, insisting that the writer stay in touch with the urgent political issues of the day and that he speak in a voice whose clarity can be understood by all." Comparing the older and younger generations of writers, Smith noted that while the poets of the 1920s focused on themes removed from reality, "the poets of the 1930s represented a return to the objective world outside and the recognition of the importance of the things men do together in groups: political action, social structure, cultural development."

Spender's name was most frequently associated with that of W.H. Auden, perhaps the most famous poet of the thirties; yet some critics, including Alfred Kazin and Helen Vendler, found the two poets dissimilar in many ways. In the *New Yorker,* for example, Vendler observed that "at first [Spender] imitated Auden's self-possessed ironies, his determined use of technological objects. . . . But no two poets can have been more different. Auden's rigid, brilliant, peremptory, categorizing, allegorical mind demanded forms altogether different from Spender's dreamy, liquid, guilty, hovering sensibility. Auden is a poet of firmly historical time, Spender of timeless nostalgic space." In the *New York Times Book Review* Kazin similarly concluded that Spender "was mistakenly identified with Auden. Although they were virtual opposites in personality and in the direction of their talents, they became famous at the same time as 'pylon poets'—among the first to put England's gritty industrial landscape of the 1930's into poetry."

The term "pylon poets" refers to "The Pylons," a poem by Spender which many critics described as typical of the Auden generation. The much-anthologized work, included in one of Spender's earliest collections, *Poems,* as well as in his compilation of a lifetime's accomplishments, *Collected Poems, 1928-1985,* is characteristic of the group's imagery and also reflects the political and social concerns of its members. Smith recognized that in such a poem "the poet, instead of closing his eyes to the hideous steel towers of a rural electrification system and concentrating on the soft green fields, glorifies the pylons and grants to them the future. And the nonhuman structure proves to be of the very highest social value, for rural electrification programs help create a new world of human equality."

The decade of the thirties was marked by turbulent events that would shape the course of history: the worldwide economic depression, the Spanish Civil War, and the beginnings of the Second World War. Seeing the established world crumbling around them, the writers of the period sought to create a new reality to replace the old, which in their minds had become obsolete. According to D.E.S. Maxwell, commenting in his *Poets of the Thirties,* "the imaginative writing of the thirties created an unusual *milieu* of urban squalor and political intrigue. This kind of statement—a suggestion of decay producing violence and leading to change—as much as any absolute and unanimous political partisanship gave this poetry its marxist reputation. Communism and 'the communist' (a poster-type stock figure) were frequently invoked." For a time Spender, like many young intellectuals of the era, was a member of the Communist party. "Spender believed," Smith noted, "that communism offered the only workable analysis and solution of complex world problems, that it was sure eventually to win, and that for significance and relevance the artist must somehow link his art to the Communist diagnosis." Smith described Spender's poem, "The Funeral" (included in *Collected Poems: 1928-1953* but omitted from the 1985 revision of the same work), as "a Communist elegy" and observes that much of Spender's other works from the same early period as "The Funeral," including his play, *Trial of a Judge: A Tragedy in Five Acts,* his poems from *Vienna,* and his essays in *The Destructive Element: A Study of Modern Writers and Beliefs* and *Forward from Liberalism* deal with the Communist question.

Washington Post Book World contributor Monroe K. Spears considered "The Funeral," one of Spender's least successful poems, but nevertheless acknowledged that it reveals some of the same characteristics of the poet as his better work: "an ardent idealism, an earnest dedication that leaves him vulnerable in his sympathy for the deprived and exploited, his hopes for a better world, [and] his reverence for greatness and heroism, especially in art." Critics noted that Spender's attitudes, developed in the thirties, continued to influence the poet throughout his life. As Peter Stansky pointed out in the *New Republic:* "The 1930s were a shaping time for Spender, casting a long shadow over all that came after. . . . It would seem that the rest of his life, even more than he may realize, has been a matter of coming to terms with the 1930s, and the conflicting claims of literature and politics as he knew them in that decade of achievement, fame, and disillusion."

Spender continued to write poetry throughout his life, but it came to consume less of his literary output in later years than it did in the 1930s and 1940s. The last collection of poems published before his death was *Dolphins.* "To find him still reaching out at 85—the same age as [English novelist and poet Thomas] Hardy was when he published his last poems—is confirmation of the old truism that feeling is not an optional extra of humans but bred in the bone," commented William Scammell in the *Spectator.* In the title piece, Spender turns his attention to those creatures of the sea which have captivated poets for centuries. "For him, their movements constitute a kind of scripture, communicating at an ontological level beyond merely human speech," observed Peter Firchow in *World Literature Today.* "Their message is utterly simple, the simplest and most basic of all: 'I AM.'" For several critics, these two words spoke volumes about Spender's poetry. In a *Times Literary Supplement* review, Julian Symons explained, "If Stephen Spender ever intended to create a poetry of 'direct social function,' the idea was long ago abandoned in favour of a concern to express in verse his own true beliefs and attitudes, about which he remains permanently uncertain."

Firchow found that most of the poems in *Dolphins* did not live up to the high standards that Spender had set in his previous work, but the reviewer did admit that "two long autobiographical poems, 'A First War Childhood' and 'Wordsworth,' come close." Symons praised Spender's long poem about the life of Arthur Rimbaud. "The sequence is successful in part because Spender can have found no difficulty in imagining himself both Rimbaud and [Paul] Verlaine, in part because of his strong dramatic sense," wrote the reviewer. "Yet the most striking poem here records not the insight of the witness, but the anguish of the absentee," observed Boyd Tonkin in the *New Statesman and Society.* "'History and Reality' pays homage to the Jewish, Catholic and quasi-Marxist thinker Simone Weil, who starved herself in solidarity with Hitler's victims."

Despite Spender's status as one of the leading poets of the twentieth century, a number of critics have noted his value beyond his poetry. Symons maintained, "As one looks back, Spender's principal achievement seems to have been less his poems or any particular piece of prose than the candor of the ceaseless critical self-examination he has conducted for more than half a century in autobiography, journals, criticism, poems." Peter Stansky also observed that Spender was at his best when he was writing autobiography. The poet himself seemed to have pointed out this fact when he wrote in the postscript to *Thirties and After: Poetry, Politics, People, 1933-1970:* "I myself am, it is only too clear, an autobiographer. Autobiography provides the line of continuity in my work. I am not someone who can shed or disclaim his past."

The past often became the subject of Spender's writing in the eighties. Particularly *The Journals of Stephen Spender, 1939-1983, Collected Poems, 1928-1985,* and *Letters to Christopher: Stephen Spender's Letters to Christopher Isherwood, 1929-1939, with "The Line of the Branch"—Two Thirties Journals* placed a special emphasis on autobiographical material that reviewers found revealed Spender as both an admirable personality and a notable writer. In a *New York Times Book Review* commentary by Samuel Hynes on the collection of Spender's letters, for instance, the critic expressed his belief that "the person who emerges from these letters is neither a madman nor a fool, but an honest, intelligent, troubled young man, groping toward maturity in a troubled time. And the author of the journals is something more; he is a writer of sensitivity and power." Discussing the same volume in the *Times Literary Supplement* Philip Gardener noted, "If, since the war, Spender's creative engine has run at less than full power, one remains grateful for his best work, the context of which is fascinatingly provided by these letters and journals."

One of Spender's earliest published works of autobiography, *World within World,* came to be emblematic of the author's candor, commitment to honesty, and longevity. First published in 1951, the book created a stir for Spender's frank disclosure of a homosexual relationship he had had at around the time of the Spanish Civil War. The relationship ended when Spender married. Spender's ex-lover then ran off to fight in Spain; Spender ended up going after him to try to get him out of the country. The book earned a second life when it became the subject of another controversy in the 1990s. In 1993, American writer David Leavitt published his novel *While England Sleeps,* in which a writer has a homosexual affair that follows many of the events of Spender's life but adds more explicit sexual detail. Feeling his integrity and his literary license threatened, Spender accused Leavitt of plagiarism. He also filed a lawsuit in British courts to stop the British publication of the book, charging the American novelist with copyright infringement and violation of a British law that assures authors the right to control adaptations of their work. In 1994, Leavitt and his publisher, Viking Penguin, agreed to a settlement that would withdraw the book from publication; Leavitt made changes to *While England Sleeps* for a revised edition.

During this period of intense attention focused on *World within World,* St. Martin's reprinted the autobiography with a new introduction by Spender. As a result, many readers were afforded the opportunity to discover or rediscover Spender's work. "With the passage of time," commented Eric Pace in a *New York Times* obituary, "'World within World' has proved to be in many ways Sir Stephen's most enduring prose work because it gives the reader revealing glimpses of its author, Auden and Mr. Isherwood and of what it was like to be a British poet in the 1930's."

In the final analysis, "Some of Spender's poems, criticism, memoirs, translations have contributed to the formation of a period, which to some extent, they now represent . . . ," Robert Craft observed in his *New York Review of Books* critique of *The Journals of Stephen Spender, 1939-1983.* "Yet Spender himself stands taller than his work. The leastinsular writer of his generation and the most generous, he is a kinder man—*hypocrite lecteur!*—than most of us deserve."

BIOGRAPHICAL AND CRITICAL SOURCES:

BOOKS

Sutherland, John, *Stephen Spender: A Literary Life,* Oxford University Press (New York, NY), 2005.

PERIODICALS

American Scholar, Winter, 1988, p. 148.
Boston Globe, November 12, 1993, p. 45.
Chicago Tribune Book World, January 12, 1986.
New Republic, September 23, 1978; August 1, 1988, p. 52.
New Statesman and Society, February 26, 1988, p. 22; February 25, 1994, p. 41.
New Yorker, November 10, 1986; February 28, 1994, p. 72; January 8, 1996, p. 58.
New York Review of Books, January 25, 1979; April 24, 1986.
New York Times, February 17, 1994, p. C24; February 20, 1994, sec. 4, p. 14.
New York Times Book Review, February 1, 1981, January 26, 1986; September 11, 1988, p. 20; September 4, 1994, p. 10.
New York Times Magazine, April 3, 1994, p. 36.
People, December 25, 1995, p. 166.
Publishers Weekly, February 21, 1994, p. 10; March 20, 1995, p. 16.
Spectator, February 26, 1994, p. 37.
Times Literary Supplement, April 17, 1981; February 18, 1994, p. 10.
Washington Post, February 17, 1994, p. A1; October 26, 1993, p. F1.
Washington Post Book World, January 12, 1986.
World Literature Today, spring, 1995, p. 367.

* * *

SPENDER, Stephen Harold
See SPENDER, Stephen

* * *

SPIEGELMAN, Art 1948-
(Joe Cutrate, Al Flooglebuckle, Skeeter Grant)

PERSONAL: Born February 15, 1948, in Stockholm, Sweden; immigrated to United States; naturalized citizen; son of Vladek (in sales) and Anja (Zylberberg) Spiegelman; married Françoise Mouly (a publisher), July 12, 1977; children: Nadja Rachel, Dashiell Alan. *Education:* Attended Harpur College (now State University of New York at Binghamton), 1965-68.

ADDRESSES: Agent—Deborah Karl, 52 West Clinton Ave., Irvington, NY 10533; Steven Barclay Agency, 12 Western Avenue, Petaluma, CA 94952.

CAREER: Freelance artist and writer. Topps Chewing Gum, Inc., Brooklyn, NY, creative consultant, artist, designer, editor, and writer for novelty packaging and bubble gum cards and stickers, including Wacky Packages and Garbage Pail Kids, 1966-89; *New Yorker,* staff artist and writer, 1991-2003. Instructor in studio class on comics, San Francisco Academy of Art, 1974-75; instructor in history and aesthetics of comics at New York School of Visual Arts, 1979-87.

MEMBER: PEN.

AWARDS, HONORS: Playboy Editorial Award for best comic strip, and Yellow Kid Award (Italy) for best comic strip author, both 1982; Regional Design Award, *Print* magazine, 1983, 1984, and 1985; Joel M. Cavior Award for Jewish Writing, and National Book Critics Circle nomination, both 1986, both for *Maus: A Survivors Tale, My Father Bleeds History;* Inkpot Award, San Diego Comics Convention, and Stripschappenning Award (Netherlands) for best foreign comics album, both 1987; Special Pulitzer Prize, for both *Maus: A Survivors Tale, My Father Bleeds History* and *Maus: A Survivors Tale II, and Here My Troubles Began;* National Book Critics Circle Award, *Los Angeles Times* award, and American Book Award, Before Columbus Foundation Award, both 1992, both for *Maus: A Survivors Tale II, and Here My Troubles Began;* Guggenheim fellowship, 1990; National Book Critics Circle nomination, 1991; two nominations for Harvey Awards for *Jack Cole and Plastic Man: Forms Stretched to Their Limits.*

WRITINGS:

COMICS

The Complete Mr. Infinity, S.F. Book Co. (New York, NY), 1970.
The Viper Vicar of Vice, Villainy, and Vickedness, privately printed, 1972.
Zip-a-Tune and More Melodies, S.F. Book Co. (New York, NY), 1972.
(Compiling editor, with Bob Schneider) *Whole Grains: A Book of Quotations,* D. Links (New York, NY), 1972.
Ace Hole, Midget Detective, Apex Novelties (New York, NY), 1974.
Language of Comics, State University of New York at Binghamton, 1974.

Breakdowns: From Maus to Now: An Anthology of Strips, Belier Press (New York, NY), 1977.

Work and Turn, Raw Books (New York, NY), 1979.

Every Day Has Its Dog, Raw Books (New York, NY), 1979.

Two-fisted Painters Action Adventure, Raw Books (New York, NY), 1980.

(Contributor) Nicole Hollander, Skip Morrow, and Ron Wolin, editors, *Drawn Together: Relationships Lampooned, Harpooned, and Cartooned,* Crown (New York, NY), 1983.

Maus: A Survivors Tale, Pantheon (New York, NY), Volume I: *My Father Bleeds History,* 1986, Volume II: *And Here My Troubles Began,* 1991.

(Editor) Françoise Mouly, *Raw: The Graphic Aspirin for War Fever,* Raw Books & Graphics (New York, NY), 1986.

(Editor, with Françoise Mouly, and contributor) *Read Yourself Raw: Comix Anthology for Damned Intellectuals,* Pantheon (New York, NY), 1987.

(Editor, with Françoise Mouly, and contributor) Mark Beyer, *Agony, Raw,* Pantheon (New York, NY), 1987.

(Editor, with Françoise Mouly, and contributor), Gary Panter, *Jimbo: Adventures in Paradise,* Pantheon (New York, NY), 1988.

Raw: Open Wounds from the Cutting Edge of Commix, No. 1, Penguin (New York, NY), 1989.

Raw, No. 2, edited by Françoise Mouly, Penguin (New York, NY), 1990.

(Editor, with Françoise Mouly and R. Sikoryak) *Warts and All/Drew Friedman and Josh Alan Friedman,* Penguin (New York, NY), 1990.

Raw 3: High Culture for Lowbrows, Viking (New York, NY), 1991.

(Editor, with R. Sikoryak) Charles Burns, *Skin Deep: Tales of Doomed Romance,* Penguin (New York, NY), 1992.

The Complete Maus (CD-ROM), Voyager (New York, NY), 1994.

(Illustrator) Joseph Moncura March, *The Wild Party: The Lost Classic,* Pantheon (New York, NY), 1994.

(Editor, with R. Sikoryak) *The Narrative Corpse,* Raw Books & Gates of Heck (Richmond, VA), 1995.

I'm a Dog! (children's book), HarperCollins (New York, NY), 1997.

(Author of introduction) Bob Adelman, editor, *Tijuana Bibles: Art and Wit in America's Forbidden Funnies, 1930s-1950s,* Simon & Schuster (New York, NY), 1997.

(Editor, with Françoise Mouly) *Little Lit: Folklore and Fairy Tale Funnies,* HarperCollins (New York, NY), 2000.

(Editor, with Françoise Mouly) *Little Lit 2: Strange Stories for Strange Kids,* Joana Cotler Books/RAW (New York, NY), 2001.

(With Chip Kidd) *Jack Cole and Plastic Man: Forms Stretched to Their Limits,* Chronicle Books (San Francisco, CA), 2001.

(Editor, with Françoise Mouly) *It Was a Dark and Silly Night . . . ,* HarperCollins (New York, NY), 2003.

Contributor to books, including *The Apex Treasury of Underground Comics,* edited by Don Donahue and Susan Goodrich, D. Links (New York, NY), 1974; and *The Complete Color Polly and Her Pals,* Volume 1: *The Surrealist Period, 1926-1927,* Remco Worldservice (New York, NY), 1990. Also contributor to numerous underground comics. Editor of *Douglas Comix,* 1972, and (with Bill Griffith; and contributor) *Arcade, the Comics Revue,* 1975-76; founding coeditor and contributor, *Raw,* 1980—. Some works appear under the pseudonyms Joe Cutrate, Al Flooglebuckle, and Skeeter Grant.

WORK IN PROGRESS: Drawn to Death: A Three-Panel Opera with composer Phillip Johnston; the comic series *In the Shadow of No Towers.*

SIDELIGHTS: The two-volume graphic-novel saga *Maus: A Survivors Tale* has been cited as "among the remarkable achievements in comics" by Dale Luciano in *Comics Journal.* The comic, an epic parable of the Holocaust that substitutes mice and cats for human Jews and Nazis, marks a zenith in the artistic career of writer and illustrator Art Spiegelman. Prior to the creation of *Maus* Spiegelman made a name for himself on the underground comics scene, and was a significant presence in graphic art beginning in his teen years when he wrote, printed, and distributed his own comics magazine. In the early 1980s Spiegelman and his wife, Françoise Mouly, produced the first issue of *Raw,* an underground comics—or as Spiegelman and Mouly refer to them, "comix"—anthology that grew into a highly respected alternative press by the middle of its first decade. It was not until the publication of the volume of *Maus* in 1986, however, that a wide range of readers became aware of Spiegelman's visionary talent and his considerable impact on the realm of comics. In an interview with Joey Cavalieri for *Comics Journal,* Spiegelman called *Maus* "the point where my work starts. . . . Up to that point, I feel like I'd been floundering. . . . All of a sudden, I found my own voice, my own needs, things that I wanted to do in comics."

The first volume of *Maus: A Survivor's Tale,* subtitled *My Father Bleeds History,* starts with Spiegelman, representing himself as a humanoid mouse, going to his father, Vladek, for information about the Holocaust. As Vladek's tale begins, he and his wife, Anja, are living in Poland with their young child, Richieu, at the outset of World War II. The Nazis, portrayed as cats, have overrun much of Eastern Europe, and their oppression is felt by everyone, especially the Jews/mice. The story recounts Vladek's service in the Polish army and subsequent incarceration in a German war prison. When he finally returns to Anja and his son, the Nazi "Final Solution"—to exterminate the entire Jewish race—is well underway. There is talk of Jews being rounded up and shipped off to camps where they are either put to strenuous work or put to death. Vladek and Anja's attempt to flee is thwarted and they are sent to Auschwitz, Poland, the site of one of the most notorious camps. As the first section of *Maus: A Survivor's Tale* concludes, Richieu has been taken from his parents by the Nazis—never to be seen again—and Vladek and Anja are separated and put in crowded train cars for shipment to Auschwitz.

As the second *Maus* volume, *And Here My Troubles Began,* opens, Art and his wife, Françoise, are visiting Vladek at his summer home in the Catskills. During the visit Art and his father resume their discussion. Vladek recounts how he and Anja were put in separate camps, he in the Auschwitz facility, she in the neighboring Birkenau. The horrors and inhumanity of concentration-camp life are related in graphic detail. Vladek recalls the discomfort of cramming three or four men into a bunk that is only a few feet wide and the ignominy of scrounging for any scrap of food to sate his unending hunger. His existence at Auschwitz is marked by agonizing physical labor, severe abuse at the hands of the Nazis, and the ever-present fear that he—or Anja—may be among the next Jews sent to the gas chambers. Despite these overwhelming incentives to abandon hope, Vladek is bolstered by his clandestine meetings with Anja and the discovery of supportive allies among his fellow prisoners. In an encounter with a former priest, Vladek is told that the numerals in his serial identification, which the Nazis tattooed upon their victims, add up to eighteen, a number signifying life.

Vladek manages to hold on through several harrowing incidents, including a bout with typhus. As the war ends and the Allied troops make their way toward Auschwitz, Vladek and some fellow prisoners flee the camp and eventually make their way to safety. In the haste of his escape, however, Vladek loses contact with Anja and does not know if she is alive. Their reunion marks a happy point in Vladek's tale. As the book continues Vladek and Anja desperately search orphanages in Europe for Richieu, to no avail. They eventually immigrate to Sweden, where Art is born, and from there the family moves to America. However, the horrors of the war have scarred Anja permanently, and in 1968 she commits suicide. The book concludes with Art visiting Vladek just before Vladek's death in 1982.

Although *Maus* is essentially the story of Vladek and Anja's ordeal, Spiegelman has stated that *Maus* is also, in part, "a meditation on my own awareness of myself as a Jew." There are deeply personal passages depicting conversations between Art and his psychiatrist, Pavel, who, like Vladek, survived the Nazi's attempted purge. Their conversation ranges from Anja's suicide to the guilt Art feels for being successful in light of his father's tribulation. As much as *Maus* serves as a piece of edifying literature, it also provided its creator with an opportunity to confront his personal demons. As Spiegelman wrote in *Village Voice, Maus* was motivated "by an impulse to look dead-on at the root cause of my own deepest fears and nightmares."

Not surprisingly, *Maus* sparked much critical discussion, much of it regarding Spiegelman's use of animals in the place of humans. When he began the book, Spiegelman made no mention of Jews or Nazis. The protagonists were mice, persecuted because they are "Maus." Likewise, the antagonists were cats, or "Die Katzen," and they chase mice, although "chasing" the mice means rounding them up in camps for work, torture, and extermination. The closest the strip came to an outright identification with the Holocaust was in naming the concentration camp "Mauschwitz." As Spiegelman began the expanded version of *Maus* however, he found it necessary to write in terms of "Jews" and "Nazis" when going into detail. He decided to maintain his characters as animals, however, citing a fear that using human characters would turn the work into a "corny" plea for sympathy. He explained to Joey Cavalieri in *Comics Journal,* "To use these ciphers, the cats and mice, is actually a way to allow you past the cipher at the people who are experiencing it. So it's really a much more direct way of dealing with the material."

Luciano agreed with Spiegelman's reasoning in his description of *Maus:* "By making the characters cats and mice, the result is that the characters 'human' qualities are highlighted all the more, to an inexplicably poignant effect." "By relating a story of hideous inhumanity in non-human terms," declared *Los Angeles Times Book Review* contributor James Colbert, "*Maus* and *Maus II* allow us as readers to go outside ourselves and to look objectively at ourselves and at otherwise unspeakable events." Luciano continued, "The situations recalled and acted-out in *Maus* place the characters in a variety of delicate situations: they express themselves with a simplicity and candor that is unsettling because it is so accurately *human.*" "And while the presentation is enormously effective (and while the events Mr. Spiegelman relates are factually accurate, in most ways a memoir)," Colbert concluded, "the fact is, too that these events did not take place among mice, cats and dogs. That is fiction—and it is fiction of the very highest order."

Full recognition of *Maus*'s influence came in 1992, when Spiegelman received a special Pulitzer Prize for the work. The event marked a change in his status as a writer—he joined the prestigious *New Yorker* magazine as a contributing editor and artist the same year—and launched another round of *Maus* commentary from critics. A special exhibition, "Art Spiegelman: The Road to Maus," featuring the artist's sketches and stories used in the composition of the work, opened at the Galerie St. Etienne late the same year. The exhibition—as well as the related CD-ROM that appeared in 1994—shows how the work evolved both out of the author's relationship with his father and his own need to understand himself. *Maus* goes "further than many Holocaust memoirs," wrote April Austin in *Christian Science Monitor,* "because they portray the difficulties of *living with* a Holocaust survivor. Spiegelman achieves this by writing himself . . . into the stories, breaking into his mouse-father's narrative with descriptions of their present-day conversations."

Spiegelman's appointment as contributing artist at *New Yorker* sparked a new wave of controversy, as many were taken aback by the graphic content of his interior and cover illustrations. The artist, working with newly appointed editor-in-chief Tina Brown, helped create a new style for the magazine as Brown worked to change the magazine's content and image. "In case you hadn't noticed or are one of *New Yorker* traditionalists who refuse to pick up the magazine these days," declared Sean Mitchell in *Los Angeles Times,*"it now contains comic strips by Spiegelman, Edward Sorel and other artists who once toiled mainly in the pages of the nation's 'underground' and alternative media. The truth is, they are—many of them, anyway—comic strips of a high order." Spiegelman kindled intense controversy for cover illustrations, one being a Valentine's Day cover showing a Hasidic Jewish man embracing a black woman. Mitchell noted of these covers that they are "meant not just to be plainly understood but also to reach up and tattoo your eyeballs with images once unimaginable in the magazine of old moneyed taste." Other covers included depictions of a naked press corps reviewing a fashion show model in spiked heels. Spiegelman viewed his appointment not as an escape from *New Yorker* tradition, but as a return to it. He told Mitchell that during the "Pre-Tina" era "it was a kind of live wire—like Peter Arno's cartoons were pretty hot for their moment. Charles Addams was considered rather morbid. It wasn't all those cartoons about businessmen in suits talking to each other over martinis." He continued to relish the creative freedom given him at the magazine until the events of September 11, 2001, changed the creative climate of the nation. Spiegelman resigned from *New Yorker* in February of 2003. His reasons, as explained to an interviewer for the Italian *Corriere della Sera* and posted in translation on *Electronic Iraq:* "From the time that the Twin Towers fell, it seems as if I've been living in internal exile, or like a political dissident confined to an island. I no longer feel in harmony with American culture, especially now that the entire media has become conservative and tremendously timid. . . . On the contrary, I am more and more inclined to provocation."

In addition to his own cartoon work, beginning in 2000 Spiegelman has collaborated with his wife, Françoise Mouly, on the "Little Lit" comic book series, which collects pieces by noted cartoonists and illustrators of children's books such as Ian Falconer, Jules Feiffer, Walt Kelly, Barbara McClintock, and Maurice Sendak, as well as by Spiegelman. *Folklore and Fairy Tale Funnies,* the first book in the series, begins with Spiegelman's story of "Prince Rooster." Also included in this volume are renditions of "Princess and the Pea" and "Jack and the Beanstalk" along with a Japanese folktale called "The Fisherman and the Sea Princess." Artists Bruce McCall, Charles Burns, and Chris Ware contributed brainteasers, scratchboard hide-and-seek games, and a board game.

"Little Lit" raised the controversy characteristic of most Spiegelman enterprises. Appraising *Folklore and Fairy Tale Funnies,* a *Horn Book* review stated that "Many of the stories are illustrated with an affectionately retro flair." Claude Lalumiere wrote in *January Magazine* that the work is "a pretentious collection of misplaced nostalgia" that seems written more for adults than for children, even though it is advertised and recommended for the latter. "Spiegelman and Mouly's sophisticated collection . . . lingers at the crossroad between kids and adults, classics and parodies," commented a more appreciative *Publishers Weekly* critic. In a *Booksense* interview with Christopher Monte Smith, Spiegelman stated the reasons for focusing on fairy tales: "The tales are kinetic, filled with transformations. There's a lot to draw and see. Fairy tales and folklore . . . offer archetypal themes and memorable situations. We wanted to do a book for all ages, that could hold the interest of very young children and grown-ups."

Maurice Sendak and Jules Feiffer are among the cartoonists represented in the second "Little Lit" installment, *Strange Stories for Strange Kids.* One of the comics is based upon David Sedaris's story "Pretty Ugly." This volume also contains the original 1942 episode of the classic comic strip "Barnaby," produced by the late Crockett Johnson, as well as activity pages and jokes. The volume makes up "an exceptionally strong set of stories and games for kids that will also be appealing to teens and adults," noted a writer for *Rational Magic.* Grace Oliff of *School Library Journal* stated, "The stories all possess a sharp intelligence and unique imagination," while in a *Horn Book* review, Roger Sutton found the cartoons and stories "purposeful . . . even when absurd." *Booklist*'s Gillian Engberg felt that *Strange Stories for Strange Kids* "will excite readers of many ages," and Andrew D. Arnold in a *Time* review called the book "a delightful album of sophisticated, G-rated comix." Arnold concluded: "Thanks to the intelligence of editors Spiegelman and Mouly, you can't be too old to appreciate *Little Lit: Strange Stories for Strange Kids.*"

Jack Cole and Plastic Man: Forms Stretched to Their Limits is a memorial by Spiegelman and Chip Kidd to an early cartoonist and his quirky superhero. Trained via a mail-order illustration course prior to beginning his career as a professional cartoonist in 1936, Jack Cole originally worked in the crime and horror comic-book genre until becoming a cartoonist for *Playboy.* His most notable creation was Plastic Man, a criminal who becomes a stretchable superhero as the result of a chemical accident. *Jack Cole and Plastic Man* includes a 1999 *New Yorker* essay about Cole's life which was written by Spiegelman. Kidd, a book designer, arranged to reprint Cole's cartoons in paper stocks that imitate the original work.

Jack Cole and Plastic Man "is an excellent memorial to an innovative American cartoonist," remarked a *Publishers Weekly* reviewer, while a writer for *DC Comics* online called the book "a fascinating back story [with] a colorful cast of characters." "Spiegelman and Kidd have assembled an attractive and innovative package," said Noel Murray in an *Onion A.V. Club* article, adding that because of its nostalgic feel, the work should "be held, smelled, and felt as much as read."

BIOGRAPHICAL AND CRITICAL SOURCES:

BOOKS

Contemporary Literary Criticism, Volume 76, Thomson Gale (Detroit, MI), 1993.

Witek, Joseph, *Comic Books As History: The Narrative Art of Jack Jackson, Art Spiegelman, and Harvey Pekar,* University Press of Mississippi (Jackson, MS), 1989.

PERIODICALS

Booklist, December 15, 2001, Gillian Engberg, review of *Little Lit: Strange Stories for Strange Kids,* p. 726.

Boston Globe, November 23, 1994, p. 25.

Bulletin of the Center for Children's Books, January, 2002, review of *Little Lit,* p. 185.

Christian Science Monitor, December 14, 1992, p. 14.

Comics Journal, August, 1981, Joey Cavalieri, "An Interview with Art Spiegelman and Françoise Mouly," pp. 98-125; December, 1986, pp. 43-45; April, 1989, pp. 110-1117.

Commonweal, December 5, 1997, p. 20; April 6, 2001, review of *Little Lit,* p. 22.

Entertainment Weekly, October 14, 2001, review of *Jack Cole and Plastic Man: Forms Stretched to Their Limit,* p. 12; November 2, 2001, review of *Little Lit,* p. 70.

Globe and Mail (Toronto, Ontario, Canada), December 15, 2001, review of *Little Lit,* p. D19.

Horn Book, September, 2000, Roger Sutton, review of *Little Lit,* p. 590; January-February, 2002, Roger Sutton, review of *Little Lit 2: Strange Stories for Strange Kids,* p. 73.

Library Journal, February 1, 2002, review of *Jack Cole and Plastic Man,* p. 57.

Los Angeles Times, December 18, 1994, p. 7.

Los Angeles Times Book Review, November 8, 1992, p. 2.

New Yorker, December 10, 2001, review of *Jack Cole and Plastic Man,* p. 107.

New York Times, February 11, 1994, p. D17.

New York Times Book Review, November 3, 1991, pp. 1, 35-36; January 20, 2002, review of *Little Lit 2,* p. 14.

Publishers Weekly, April 26, 1991; January 31, 1994, pp. 26-27; October 10, 1994, p. 61; September 4, 2000, review of *Little Lit,* p. 106; September 3, 2001, review of *Jack Cole and Plastic Man,* p. 67; November 19, 2001, review of *Little Lit 2,* p. 66.

Rolling Stone, November 20, 1986, pp. 103-106, 146-148.

School Library Journal, March, 2002, Grace Oliff, review of *Little Lit 2,* p. 221.

Times Educational Supplement, December 2, 1994, p. 7.

Village Voice, June 6, 1989, pp. 21-22.

Voice of Youth Advocates, October, 2001, review of *Little Lit,* p. 271.

ONLINE

Art and Culture Network, http://www.artandculture.com/ (June 2, 2003).

Booksense, http://www.booksense.com/ (June 2, 2003), Christopher Monte Smith, interview with Art Spiegelman.

DC Comics, http://dccomics.com/beyond_comics/ (January 2, 2004), review of *Jack Cole and Plastic Man.*

Electronic Iraq, http://www.electroniciraq.net /(February 11, 2003), interview with Spiegelman from *Corriere della Sera.*

January Magazine, http://www.januarymagazine.com/ (June 2, 2003), Claude Lalumiere, review of *Little Lit: Folklore and Fairy Tale Funnies.*

Onion A.V. Club, http://www.theonionavclub.com/ (June 2, 2003), Noel Murray, review of *Jack Cole and Plastic Man.*

Rational Magic, http://www.rationalmagic.com/ (June 2, 2003), review of *Little Lit 2: Strange Stories for Strange Kids.*

Steven Barclay Agency Web site, http://www.barclayagency.com/ (November 16, 2003).

* * *

SPILLANE, Frank Morrison
See SPILLANE, Mickey

* * *

SPILLANE, Mickey 1918-
(Frank Morrison Spillane)

PERSONAL: Born March 9, 1918, in Brooklyn, NY; son of John Joseph (a bartender) and Catherine Anne Spillane; married Mary Ann Pearce, 1945 (divorced); married Sherri Malinou, November, 1965 (divorced); married Jane Rodgers Johnson, October, 1983; children: (first marriage) Kathy, Mark, Mike, Carolyn; (third marriage; stepdaughters) Britt, Lisa. *Education:* Attended Kansas State College (now University). *Religion:* Jehovah Witness.

ADDRESSES: Home—Murrells Inlet, Myrtle Beach, SC. *Office*—c/o Author Mail, Simon & Schuster, 1230 Avenue of the Americas, New York, NY 10020.

CAREER: Writer of mystery and detective novels, short stories, books for children, comic books, and scripts for television and films. With producer Robert Fellows, formed an independent film company in Nashville, TN, called Spillane-Fellows Productions, which filmed features and television productions, 1969. Creator of television series *Mike Hammer,* 1984-87. Actor; has appeared in more than 110 commercials for Miller Lite Beer. *Military service:* U.S. Army Air Forces; taught cadets and flew fighter missions during World War II; became captain.

AWARDS, HONORS: Junior Literary Guild Award, 1979, for *The Day the Sea Rolled Back;* Lifetime Achievement Award, 1983, and short story award, 1990, both from Private Eye Writers of America; Grand Master Award, Mystery Writers of America, 1995.

WRITINGS:

CRIME NOVELS

I, the Jury (also see below), Dutton (New York, NY), 1947, reprinted, New American Library (New York, NY), 1973.

Vengeance Is Mine! (also see below), Dutton (New York, NY), 1950.

My Gun Is Quick (also see below), Dutton (New York, NY), 1950, reprinted, Signet (New York, NY), 1988.

The Big Kill (also see below), Dutton (New York, NY), 1951, reprinted, New English Library (London, England), 1984.

One Lonely Night, Dutton (New York, NY), 1951.

The Long Wait, Dutton (New York, NY), 1951, reprinted, New American Library (New York, NY), 1972.

Kiss Me, Deadly (also see below), Dutton (New York, NY), 1952.

The Deep, Dutton (New York, NY), 1961.

The Girl Hunters (also see below), Dutton (New York, NY), 1962.

Me, Hood!, Corgi (London), 1963, New American Library (New York, NY), 1969.

Day of the Guns, Dutton, 1964, reprinted, New American Library (New York, NY), 1981.

The Snake, Dutton (New York, NY), 1964.

The Flier, Corgi, 1964.

Bloody Sunrise, Dutton (New York, NY), 1965.

The Death Dealers, Dutton (New York, NY), 1965, reprinted, New American Library, 1981.

Killer Mine, Corgi, 1965.

The Twisted Thing, Dutton (New York, NY), 1966, published as *For Whom the Gods Would Destroy,* New American Library (New York, NY), 1971.

The By-Pass Control, Dutton (New York, NY), 1967.

The Delta Factor, Dutton (New York, NY), 1967.

Body Lovers, New American Library (New York, NY), 1967.

Killer Mine, New American Library (New York, NY), 1968.

Survival: Zero, Dutton (New York, NY), 1970.

Tough Guys, New American Library (New York, NY), 1970.

The Erection Set, Dutton (New York, NY), 1972.

The Last Cop Out, New American Library (New York, NY), 1973.

Mickey Spillane: Five Complete Mike Hammer Novels (contains *I, the Jury, Vengeance Is Mine!, My Gun Is Quick, The Big Kill,* and *Kiss Me, Deadly*), Avenel Books (New York, NY), 1987.

The Hammer Strikes Again: Five Complete Mike Hammer Novels (contains *One Lonely Night, The Snake, The Twisted Thing, The Body Lovers,* and *Survival: Zero*), Avenel Books (New York, NY), 1989.

The Killing Man, Dutton (New York, NY), 1989.

(Author of text) *Mikey Spillane's Mike Danger* (comic book series), Tekno Comics (Boca Raton, FL), 1995.

Black Alley, Dutton (New York, NY), 1996.

Together We Kill: The Uncollected Stories of Mickey Spillane, edited and with an introduction by Max Allan Collins, Five Star (Waterville, ME), 2001.

Something's Down There, Simon & Schuster (New York, NY), 2003.

Also author of *Return of the Hood.*

OTHER

(With Robert Fellows and Roy Rowland) *The Girl Hunters* (screenplay; based on Spillane's novel of the same title and starring Spillane in role of Mike Hammer), Colorama Features, 1963.

Vintage Spillane: A New Omnibus (short stories), W.H. Allen (London, England), 1974.

The Day the Sea Rolled Back (children's book), Windmill Books (New York, NY), 1979.

The Ship That Never Was (children's book), Bantam (New York, NY), 1982.

Tomorrow I Die (short stories), Mysterious Press, 1984.

(Editor, with Max Allan Collins) *Murder Is My Business,* Dutton (New York, NY), 1994.

(Editor, with Max Allan Collins) *A Century of Noir: Thirty-two Classic Crime Stories,* New American Library (New York, NY), 2002.

Also author of *The Shrinking Island.* Creator and writer of comic books, including *Mike Danger.* Author of several television and movie screenplays. Contributor of short stories to magazines.

ADAPTATIONS: I, the Jury was adapted to film in 1953 by United Artists; a remake of *I, the Jury* was filmed in 1981 by Twentieth Century-Fox; *The Long Wait* was filmed in 1954, *Kiss Me, Deadly* in 1955, and *My Gun Is Quick* in 1957, all by United Artists; *The Delta Factor* was filmed in 1970 by Colorama Features. *Mickey Spillane's Mike Hammer,* a television series based on Spillane's mystery novels and his character Mike Hammer, was produced by Revue Productions, distributed by MCA-TV, and premiered in 1958; another television series based on Spillane's writings, *Mike Hammer,* starring Stacy Keach, was produced and broadcast from 1984 to 1987. "That Hammer Guy" was produced on radio, 1953. Abridged recordings of *The Big Kill* and *My Gun Is Quick,* each read by Stacy Keach, were released as audio-cassettes by Simon & Schuster Audioworks (New York, NY), 1990.

SIDELIGHTS: Mickey Spillane, who was born Frank Morrison Spillane, started his writing career in the early 1940s scripting comic books for Funnies, Inc. Spillane made the switch from comic books to novels in 1946 when, needing $1,000 to buy a parcel of land, he decided the easiest and quickest way to earn the money was to write a novel. Three weeks later, he sent the finished manuscript of *I, the Jury* to Dutton. Although the editorial committee questioned its good taste and literary merit, they felt the book would sell. *I, the Jury* did indeed sell—well over eight million copies have been sold to date. In addition to buying the property, Spillane was able to construct a house on the site as well. This book would be the start of a long and prolific career during which, as Julie Baumgold pointed out in *Esquire,* Spillane "sold two hundred million books and became the most widely read and fifth most translated writer in the world." All those books have made Spillane famous, wealthy, and a personality in his own right.

Spillane has no illusions about what he has accomplished through his books. As he explained to Baumgold, "I'm not an author, I'm a writer. . . . I can write a book in a few weeks, never rewrite, never read galleys. Bad reviews don't matter."

I, the Jury did sell, because it pleased the public, not because it won critical acclaim. Critics generally blasted the book's dark and seamy subject matter. These responses reflected the time in which the book was published, 1947, and the belief that the world depicted in the book was only a small, dirty fringe on mainstream America, a fringe that Spillane was exploiting for its shock effect. Yet, as Frederic D. Schwarz, writing in *American Heritage,* noted, *I, the Jury* may represent one of the first signs of recognition of "the darker side of postwar America." Schwarz paired the July, 1947, publication of Spillane's first novel with an event that occurred on July 4 of that year. Hundreds of motorcyclists and their followers overwhelmed the town of Hollister, California, trashing it in a weekend of biker wildness. As Schwarz pointed out, "The incident formed the basis for a 1954 movie, *The Wild One,*" starring Marlon Brando. Both the bikers' rampage and *I, the Jury,* according to Schwarz, "reflect a violent nature of the era." Spillane, who, Baumgold observed, lives under the motto "A Wild Man Proper," has always dismissed the charges of sensationalizing. As Schwarz quoted him, "I don't really go for sex and violence unless it's necessary."

Not only did *I, the Jury* introduce Spillane to the book-buying public, but it also gave birth to the character, Mike Hammer, a 6-foot, 190-pound, rough and tough private investigator. Spillane's next several novels recorded the action-packed adventures of Hammer as he drank, fought, and killed his way through solving mystery after mystery. While Hammer is not featured in all of Spillane's mysteries, he is undoubtedly the most popular of Spillane's leading men.

"Spillane is like eating takeout fried chicken: so much fun to consume, but you can feel those lowlife grease-induced zits rising before you've finished the first drumstick," noted Sally Eckhoff in the *Voice Literary Supplement.* "*My Gun Is Quick* is just the book to have with you on a Hamptons weekend or a stint at an exclusive art colony where everybody else is reading Huysmans. Guaranteed they leave you alone. But don't try to slide into *Me, Hood!* unless you want to permanently transform yourself into a snarling closet crimebuster. Any more of those seamed stockings, pawnshops, and stereotypical Irish gumshoes, and you'll be screaming for a Bergman movie to break your trance." In his 1951 review of *The Big Kill, New York Times* writer Anthony Boucher commented: "As rife with sexuality and sadism as any of his novels, based on a complete misunderstanding of law and on the wildest coincidence in detective fiction, it still can boast the absence of the hypocritical 'crusading' sentiments of Mike Hammer. For that reason, and for some slight ingenuity in its denouement, it may rank as the best Spillane—which is the faintest praise this department has ever bestowed."

In 1952 Spillane began a nine-year break from writing mystery novels. Some people have attributed this hiatus to his religious conversion to the sect of Jehovah's Witnesses, while others feel that Spillane earned enough money from his writings and by selling the film rights to several of his books to live comfortably, enjoying life in his new beach home on Murrells Inlet, located in Myrtle Beach, South Carolina. Although he stopped writing mysteries, Spillane wrote short stories for magazines and scripts for television and films. He also appeared on a number of television programs, often performing in parodies of his tough detective characters.

Spillane reappeared on the publishing scene in 1961 with his murder mystery *The Deep,* and in the following year Mike Hammer returned to fight crime in *The Girl Hunter.* The public was ecstatic—buying copies of the novel as soon as they were placed on the shelf, and reviewers seemed to soften their criticism somewhat at Hammer's return. Many of Spillane's later books also were somewhat praised by critics. For example, a reviewer for the *Times Literary Supplement* remarked: "Nasty as much of it is, [*The Deep*] has a genuine narrative grip; and there is a certain sociological conscience at work in the presentation of the street which has bred so much crime and an unusual perception in the portrait of an old Irish patrol officer." And Newgate Callendar commented in the *New York Times Book Review* that "editorials were written condemning [Spillane's novels], and preachers took to the pulpit. But things have changed, and one reads Spillane's . . . *The Erection Set* with almost a feeling of sentimental *deja vu.* The sex, sadism and assorted violence remain. Basically, what the Spillane books are about is the all-conquering hero myth. We all like to escape into a fantasy world to identify with the figure who is all-knowing, all-powerful, infinitely virile, sending off auras of threat in solar pulsations."

Spillane followed *The Erection Set* with *The Last Cop Out,* and then came another hiatus in his publication of crime novels. During this time, Spillane's publisher dared him to write a children's book. A number of editors at the company felt he could never change his style of writing in order to appeal or be acceptable to a much younger, more impressionable audience. Not one to back down from a challenge, Spillane produced *The Day the Sea Rolled Back* in 1979 and, three years later, *The Ship That Never Was.* In general, reviewers have praised the books for their suspense and clean-cut high adventure.

In 1989 Spillane published his first Mike Hammer novel since 1970. In this return of Mike Hammer, *The Killing Man,* the detective returns to his office to find his secretary (and the unrecognized love of his life), Velda, unconscious on the floor and a dead man at his desk. True to form, Hammer sets out to bring the perpetrator to his own special brand of justice. Mickey Friedman, writing in the *New York Times Book Review,* maintained that "the book is a limp performance; the author makes no attempt to revitalize ingredients that are shopworn by now, and the book seems more like a ritual than a novel."

The year 1996 saw the publication of Spillane's thirteenth Mike Hammer novel, *Black Alley.* Hammer has just emerged from a coma, having been shot and put at the brink of death by gangsters. As with his first novel, *I, the Jury,* this book begins with the death of one of Hammer's military buddies. He sets off in search of his friend's murderer and billions in dirty mob money. The plot is familiar, but as a *Publishers Weekly* contributor wrote, "Spillane's hard-boiled hero has softened with time; he finally tells Velda how he really feels about her—but, on doctor's orders, he refrains from consummation." *Forbes* magazine's Steve Forbes found much to reward the reader in *Black Alley.* He observed, "The action never lets up as the tough, street-smart Hammer grapples with intense physical pain, revenue-hungry federal agents, cold-blooded gangsters, a recovering-alcoholic physician and a determined get-him-to-the-alter secretary."

Spillane's short fiction is showcased in *Together We Kill: The Uncollected Stories of Mickey Spillane.* Included in the collection are "The Night I Died," the only 1950s Mike Hammer story; "Together We Kill," a love story set in World War II; and "The Veiled Woman," a rare science fiction tale. The novella "Hot Cat" makes its first U.S. appearance in this volume. Wes Lukowsky, writing in *Booklist,* noted that collections such as this one often consist of "curiosities and rejects," but *Together We Kill* is not one of them. "Spillane's superviolent, no-frills approach to the genre is out of fashion today, but he remains a solid storyteller," Lukowsky remarked.

Spillane lends his first-hand knowledge of hard-boiled detective stories to *A Century of Noir: Thirty-two Classic Crime Stories,* edited with noted mystery writer Max Allan Collins. Described by Dick Adler in the *Chicago Tribune* as "a terrific collection of thirty-two hard-boiled crime stories," the book contains tales by genre luminaries such as John D. MacDonald, Evan Hunter, Lawrence Block, Sarah Paretsky, and Ross Macdonald. Also included is a tale by coeditor Collins and a Spillane story, "Tomorrow I Die," a "mordant novelette with a surprise ending," wrote Dick Lochte in the *Los Angeles Times.*

A new Spillane novel appeared in 2003. In *Something's Down There,* retired government spook Mako Hooker lives a leisurely retired life on Peolle Island in the Caribbean, fishing and boating with his fishing partner, Billy Bright. When a mysterious underwater creature begins attacking fishing boats, and functional World War II-era mines begin surfacing in the local troubled waters, Hooker finds himself reactivated by the government and charged with investigating the problems. Complicating matters is ex-mobster Anthony Pell, intent on gathering video evidence of the sea monster, and government agent Chana, a virulently hated old enemy of Hooker. A *Kirkus Reviews* critic declared that the book "ends with an unforgivably muffled finale that will leave an awful lot of readers wondering just what was down there." A *Publishers Weekly* reviewer, however, called the book an "entertaining island adventure" and "classic Spillane."

Neither a heavy drinker or smoker, Spillane doesn't manifest the stereotypical characteristics of his detective hero—he "even hates the city he sets the Hammer books in, New York," reported Peter Lennon in a profile of Spillane in the Manchester *Guardian.* Spillane even prefers mild oaths to dedicated swearing. "The final shock was that he has got religion in a big way. He is an active Jehovah's Witness who does house-to-house visits," Lennon wrote.

Spillane's work has often been savaged as being simplistic and lacking in literary merit. At the height of his career in the 1950s and 1960s, "Spillane was considered the lowest of lowbrows," wrote Terry Teachout in *National Review,* "though he had some unlikely admirers, among them Kingsley Amis, who thought [Spillane] was a better writer than Dashiell Hammett or Raymond Chandler, and Ayn Rand, who said he was her favorite novelist since Victor Hugo." There are hints, however, that Rand was interested in more than Spillane's writing. Her letters to Spillane, reprinted in *Letters of Ayn Rand,* suggest that at the very least, she was an unlikely ally who may have had romance in mind, observed John Meroney in the *Washington Post.* "When asked whether Ayn Rand had a crush on him, Spillane just smiles," Meroney wrote. "'I really liked her,' he says, noting that much of their camaraderie came from an 'us against them' view of the critics. 'They hate us, don't they?,' Spillane would say to her."

Critics notwithstanding, Spillane's audience has been very loyal to his Mike Hammer character and his other mystery novels. This loyalty and Spillane's ability to give his readers what they want accounts for hundreds of millions of books sold. It also accounts for the fact that seven of his books are still listed among the top fifteen all-time fiction best sellers published in the last fifty years. In 1984 Spillane shared these thoughts with the *Washington Post:* "I'm sixty-six. . . . If you're a singer, you lose your voice. A baseball player loses his arm. A writer gets more knowledge, and if he's good, the older he gets, the better he writes. They can't kill me. I still got potential." Or as Baumgold commented in *Esquire,* "Mickey Spillane still has a few good surprise endings left."

BIOGRAPHICAL AND CRITICAL SOURCES:

BOOKS

Collins, Max Allan, and James L. Traylor, *One Lonely Knight: Mickey Spillane's Mike Hammer,* Popular Press (Bowling Green, OH), 1984.

Contemporary Literary Criticism, Thomson Gale (Detroit), Volume 3, 1975, Volume 13, 1980.

St. James Guide to Crime and Mystery Writers, 4th edition, St. James Press (Detroit), 1996.

Van Dover, J. Kenneth, *Murder in the Millions: Erle Stanley Gardner, Mickey Spillane, and Ian Fleming,* Ungar (New York, NY), 1984.

PERIODICALS

American Heritage, July-August, 1997, Frederic D Schwarz, "Sex, Violence, and Motorcycles," p. 98.

Book, July-August, 2002, Allison Block, "Comfortable As an Old Gumshoe," p. 23.

Booklist, January 1, 2002, Wes Lukowsky, review of *Together We Kill: The Uncollected Stories of Mickey Spillane,* p. 820.

Chicago Sun-Times, Hillel Italie, "Mickey Spillane: Still Alive—and Writing," p. 7.

Chicago Tribune, May 5, 2002, Dick Adler, "Crimes, Questions, and Sleuths Old and New," p. 2.

Esquire, August, 1995, Julie Baumgold, "A Wild Man Proper," p. 132.

Forbes, December 16, 1996, Steve Forbes, review of *Black Alley,* p. 26.

Guardian (Manchester, England), July 23, 1999, Peter Lennon, profile of Mickey Spillane, p. 2.

Kirkus Reviews, February 1, 2002, review of *A Century of Noir: Thirty-two Classic Crime Stories,* p. 147; October 1, 2003, review of *Something's Down There,* p. 1198.

Los Angeles Times, May 8, 2002, Dick Lochte, "Mysteries: Guilt, Vengeance Come into Play for a Thrilling Read," p. E2.

National Review, October 1, 2001, Terry Teachout, "A Guy's Guy," pp. 50-52.

New York Times, November 11, 1951, Anthony Boucher, review of *The Big Kill.*

New York Times Book Review, February 27, 1972, Newgate Callendar, review of *The Erection Set*; October 15, 1989, Mickey Friedman, review of *The Killing Man,* p. 43.

Publishers Weekly, September 2, 1996, review of *Black Alley,* p. 11; October 6, 2003, review of *Something's Down There,* pp. 56-57.

Times Literary Supplement, November 10, 1961, review of *The Deep*; September 19, 1980.

Voice Literary Supplement, July, 1988, Sally Eckhoff, "Mysterious Pleasures: Sleaze Please," p. S13.

Washington Post, October 24, 1984 (interview); August 22, 2001, John Meroney, "Man of Mysteries: It'd Been Years since Spillane Pulled a Job. Could We Find Him? Yeah, It Was Easy," p. C1.

ONLINE

Pegasos Web site, http://www.kirjasto.sci.fi/ (November 14, 2003), profile of Mickey Spillane.

Unofficial Mickey Spillane Mike Hammer Web site, http://www.interlog.com/˜roco/hammer.html/ (November 14, 2003).

* * *

STACK, Andy
See RULE, Ann

* * *

STACY, Donald
See POHL, Frederik

* * *

STANCYKOWNA
See SZYMBORSKA, Wislawa

* * *

STARK, Richard
See WESTLAKE, Donald E.

STEEL, Danielle 1947-
(Danielle Fernande Steel)

PERSONAL: Born August 14, 1947, in New York, NY; daughter of John and Norma (Stone) Schuelein-Steel; married Thomas Perkins, 1998; children: (first marriage) one daughter; (third marriage) two stepsons, four daughters, two sons. *Education:* Educated in France; attended Parsons School of Design, 1963, and New York University, 1963-67. *Religion:* Catholic.

ADDRESSES: *Home*—P.O. Box 1637, New York, NY 10156-1637. *Agent*—Janklow & Nesbit Associates, Inc., 445 Park Ave., New York, NY 10022.

CAREER: Writer. Supergirls, Ltd. (public relations firm), New York, NY, vice president of public relations, 1968-71; Grey Advertising, San Francisco, CA, copywriter, 1973-74; has worked at other positions in public relations and advertising; taught creative writing in English, 1975-76. National chair of the American Library Association. Founder of Nick Traina Foundation to benefit mental health.

AWARDS, HONORS: Order of Arts and Letters, the French government, 2002.

WRITINGS:

NOVELS

Going Home, Pocket Books (New York, NY), 1973.
Passion's Promise, Dell (New York, NY), 1977.
The Promise (based on a screenplay by Garry Michael White), Dell (New York, NY), 1978.
Now and Forever, Dell (New York, NY), 1978.
Season of Passion, Dell (New York, NY), 1979.
Summer's End, Dell (New York, NY), 1979.
The Ring, Delacorte (New York, NY), 1980.
Loving, Dell (New York, NY), 1980.
Remembrance, Delacorte (New York, NY), 1981.
Palomino, Dell (New York, NY), 1981.
To Love Again, Dell (New York, NY), 1981.
Crossings, Delacorte (New York, NY), 1982.
Once in a Lifetime, Dell (New York, NY), 1982.
A Perfect Stranger, Dell (New York, NY), 1982.
Changes, Delacorte (New York, NY), 1983.
Thurston House, Dell (New York, NY), 1983.
Full Circle, Delacorte (New York, NY), 1984.
Secrets, Delacorte (New York, NY), 1985.
Family Album, Delacorte (New York, NY), 1985.
Wanderlust, Delacorte (New York, NY), 1986.
Fine Things, Delacorte (New York, NY), 1987.
Kaleidoscope, Delacorte (New York, NY), 1987.
Zoya, Delacorte (New York, NY), 1988.
Star, Delacorte (New York, NY), 1989.
Daddy, Delacorte (New York, NY), 1989.
Message from 'Nam, Delacorte (New York, NY), 1990.
Heartbeat, Delacorte (New York, NY), 1991.
No Greater Love, Delacorte (New York, NY), 1991.
Mixed Blessings, Delacorte (New York, NY), 1992.
Jewels, Delacorte (New York, NY), 1992.
Vanished, Delacorte (New York, NY), 1993.
The Gift, Delacorte (New York, NY), 1994, Spanish-language version with Maria Jose Rodellar published as *El Regalo,* 1994.
Accident, Delacorte (New York, NY), 1994.
Wings, Delacorte (New York, NY), 1994.
Five Days in Paris, Delacorte (New York, NY), 1995.
Lightning, Delacorte (New York, NY), 1995.
Malice, Delacorte (New York, NY), 1996.
Silent Honor, Delacorte (New York, NY), 1996.
The Ranch, Delacorte (New York, NY), 1997.
Special Delivery, Delacorte (New York, NY), 1997.
The Ghost, Delacorte (New York, NY), 1997.
The Long Road Home, Delacorte (New York, NY), 1998.
The Klone and I: A High-Tech Love Story, Delacorte (New York, NY), 1998.
Mirror Image, Delacorte (New York, NY), 1998.
Now and Forever, Delacorte (New York, NY), 1998.
Bittersweet, Delacorte (New York, NY), 1999.
Granny Dan, Delacorte (New York, NY), 1999.
Irresistible Forces, Delacorte (New York, NY), 1999.
The House on Hope Street, Delacorte (New York, NY), 2000.
The Wedding, Delacorte (New York, NY), 2000.
Journey, Delacorte (New York, NY), 2000.
Leap of Faith, Delacorte (New York, NY), 2001.
Lone Eagle, Delacorte (New York, NY), 2001.
The Kiss, Delacorte (New York, NY), 2001.
The Cottage, Dell (New York, NY), 2002.
Answered Prayers, Delacorte (New York, NY), 2002.
Sunset in St. Tropez, Delacorte (New York, NY), 2002.
Dating Game, Delacorte (New York, NY), 2003.
Johnny Angel, Delacorte (New York, NY), 2003.
Safe Harbour, Delacorte (New York, NY), 2003.
Echoes, Delacorte (New York, NY), 2004.
Miracle, Delacorte (New York, NY), 2004.
Second Chance, Delacorte (New York, NY), 2004.
Ransom, Dell (New York, NY), 2004.
Impossible, Delacorte (New York, NY), 2005.
Toxic Bachelors, Delacorte (New York, NY), 2005.
The House, Delacorte (New York, NY), 2005.

HRH, Delacorte (New York, NY), 2006.
First Sight, Delacorte (New York, NY), 2006.
Coming Out, Delacorte (New York, NY), 2006.

FOR CHILDREN

Amando, Lectorum Publications, 1985.
Martha's Best Friend, Delacorte (New York, NY), 1989.
Martha's New Daddy, Delacorte (New York, NY), 1989.
Martha's New School, Delacorte (New York, NY), 1989.
Max and the Baby-Sitter, Delacorte (New York, NY), 1989.
Max's Daddy Goes to the Hospital, Delacorte (New York, NY), 1989.
Max's New Baby, Delacorte (New York, NY), 1989.
Martha's New Puppy, Delacorte (New York, NY), 1990.
Max Runs Away, Delacorte (New York, NY), 1990.
Max and Grandma and Grandpa Winky, Delacorte (New York, NY), 1991.
Martha and Hilary and the Stranger, Delacorte (New York, NY), 1991.
Freddie's Trip, Dell (New York, NY), 1992.
Freddie's First Night Away, Dell (New York, NY), 1992.
Freddie's Accident, Dell (New York, NY), 1992.
Freddie and the Doctor, Dell (New York, NY), 1992.

OTHER

Love Poems: Danielle Steel (poetry), Dell (New York, NY), 1981, abridged edition, Delacorte (New York, NY), 1984.
(Coauthor) *Having a Baby* (nonfiction), Dell (New York, NY), 1984.
His Bright Light: The Story of Nick Traina (biography/memoir), Delacorte (New York, NY), 1998.

Contributor to *The Fabergé Case: From the Private Collection of Traina,* by John Traina. Contributor of articles and poetry to numerous periodicals, including *Good Housekeeping, McCall's, Ladies' Home Journal,* and *Cosmopolitan.* Many of Steel's titles have been translated into Spanish.

ADAPTATIONS: Numerous works have been adapted for film or television: *Now and Forever,* adapted into a movie and released by Inter Planetary Pictures, 1983; *Crossings,* made into an ABC-TV miniseries, 1986; *Kaleidoscope* and *Fine Things,* made into NBC television movies, 1990; *Changes, Daddy,* and *Palomino,* aired by NBC, 1991; *Jewels,* adapted as a four-hour miniseries, 1992; *Secrets,* 1992; *Heartbeat, Star,* and *Message from Nam,* 1993; *Once in a Lifetime, A Perfect Stranger,* and *Family Album,* 1994; *Mixed Blessings,* 1995; *Danielle Steel's "Zoya,"* made into a miniseries, 1996; and *No Greater Love, The Ring, Full Circle,* and *Remembrance,* 1996. Several of Steel's other novels, including *Wanderlust* and *Thurston House,* have also been optioned for television films and miniseries. New Line Home Entertainment has optioned nearly forty of Steel's bestselling novels for DVD-movie production. Audio adaptations include *The Ranch,* Bantam Books Audio, 1997; *Echoes, Five Days in Paris, The Ranch, Second Chance,* and *The Gift,* all Random House Audio, 2004; *The Ghost, The Long Road Home, Malice,* and *Silent Honor,* all Random House Audio, 2005.

SIDELIGHTS: After producing a score of bestselling novels, Danielle Steel has distinguished herself as nothing less than "a publishing phenomenon," Jacqueline Briskin reported in the *Los Angeles Times Book Review.* Since the publication of her first hardcover in 1980, Steel has consistently hit both hardback and paperback bestseller lists; there are reportedly over 450 million of her books in print. Her popularity has also spilled over into television, where twenty-one film versions of her books have been produced and garnered good ratings.

Steel's fiction is peopled by women in powerful or glamorous positions; often they are forced to choose the priorities in their lives. Thus, in *Changes* a New York anchorwoman who weds a Beverly Hills surgeon must decide whether her career means more to her than her long-distance marriage does. *Jewels* tells of the struggles of an American-born noblewoman, the Duchess of Whitfield, to find peace and raise her children in pre-World War II Europe. And while reviewers seldom express admiration for the style of romantic novelists in general—*Chicago Tribune Book World* critic L.J. Davis claimed that *Changes* is written in "the sort of basilisk prose that makes it impossible to tear your eyes from the page even as your brain is slowly [turning] to stone"—some reviewers, such as a *Detroit News* writer, found that the author's "flair for spinning colorful and textured plots out of raw material . . . is fun reading. The topic [of *Changes*] is timely and socially relevant." Toronto *Globe & Mail* contributor Peggy Hill similarly concluded about 1988's *Zoya:* "Steel has the ability to give such formula writing enough strength to not collapse into an exhausted state of cliché. *Zoya* is a fine example of that achievement."

In addition to her contemporary fiction, Steel also confronts serious issues in her books. *Mixed Blessings* looks at issues of infertility in a work that a *Rapport* reviewer called "not only well written but extremely well researched." "On the whole," the reviewer concluded, "*Mixed Blessings* is definitely one of Steel's all-time best books." *Vanished* confronts the problem of kidnapped children in a story "set mainly in 1930's Manhattan," declared a *Kirkus Reviews* contributor. "The questions Steel raises about the tug-of-wars between guilt and responsibility . . . are anything but simple," stated Stuart Whitwell in *Booklist.* "The author of *Mixed Blessings* keeps her secrets well," stated a *Publishers Weekly* reviewer, "and . . . presents a strong portrait of a tormented young woman moving toward stability."

In *Accident* Steel offers a story about the stresses placed on a family after a serious car accident puts a couple's teenaged daughter in the hospital for a brain injury. Romance reenters protagonist Page Clark's life when she falls for the Norwegian divorced father of her daughter's friend—this after having learned that her husband has been having an affair with another woman. "Steel's good intentions—to show the resilience of the human spirit in the face of insurmountable odds—are obscured by her prose," stated Joyce R. Slater in the *Chicago Tribune.* "The ending is predictable but pleasant," declared a *Publishers Weekly* contributor, "bound to delight Steel's fans."

Malice is the story of Grace Adams's attempts to deal with her self-defense murder of her abusive father, while *The Gift* tells how a 1950s family slowly comes to accept the death of their youngest daughter and welcomes an unmarried expectant mother into their fold. "The narrative," stated a critic in a *Publishers Weekly* review of *The Gift,* has "well-meaning characters, uplifting sentiments and a few moments that could make a stone weep." A *Rapport* reviewer asserted that the most significant part of the story is "the affirmation of the grand design of tragedy and its transcendent message of purpose."

In 1998 Steel produced *The Klone and I: A High- Tech Love Story.* "While sticking to the typical Steel plot . . . this time around, she throws a bit of humor and weird sexual fantasy into the mix," commented Kathleen Hughes in *Booklist.* The story revolves around Stephanie, who, having been left by her husband, meets a new man, Peter, on a trip to Paris. Stephanie soon learns that Peter has cloned himself and Stephanie must decide between the two of them. Critics were largely positive in their assessment of *The Klone and I.* "Give Steel points for turning from her usual tearjerkers . . . and trying her hand at a playful romantic comedy with a twist," wrote a critic for *Kirkus Reviews.* A *Publishers Weekly* critic argued that although "the SF element is minimal (approximately one part Ray Bradbury to thirty-five parts Steel), Steel's speculative whimsy spices her romantic concoction to produce a light but charming read."

In 2000, the prolific Steel published three new novels, *House on Hope Street, The Wedding,* and *Journey.* Critics generally felt these novels gave Steel's fans exactly what they were looking for. In a *Booklist* review of *The Wedding,* for example, Patty Engelmann wrote, "All the key elements are here: a glamorous Hollywood setting along with the beautiful people and all their insecurities." Engelmann called the work "a good old- fashioned love story," claiming Steel is in "peak form." Engelmann felt similarly about *The House on Hope Street:* "Standard Steel fare and an excellent beach book, this will definitely please her readers." *Journey* received a similar reaction from critics. "Steel has her formula down pat, and she executes her story with her usual smooth pacing," concluded a critic for *Publishers Weekly.*

In the 2004 novel *Second Chance,* Steel features a high-roller fashion editor who falls for a conservative businessman. Hughes, writing again in *Booklist,* remarked, "Steel's fans will enjoy the detailed descriptions of privileged lifestyles and the ultimate happy resolution." A *Publishers Weekly* reviewer noted that although some readers will dislike the fact that the heroine gives up her career, "others will enjoy the usual Steel frills: plenty of gorgeous outfits, fine dining and exquisite real estate."

Ransom was also released in 2004, amidst promises that it would be different from most of Steel's prior fiction. The story involves a kidnapping, and its characters include an ex- drug dealer, a widow, a shady businessman, and a police officer. In *Brandweek,* Ginger Danto suggested that the edgier flavor of the novel was a sign of the times. Danto wrote, " *Ransom* deals with crime, and apparently more violence than either writer or devoted reader are accustomed. As such, it is a deft reflection of the times, as movies and TV shore up more violence in the name of entertainment than ever before, perhaps to remain relevant alongside searing coverage of current events." In terms of the novel itself, a *Publishers Weekly* reviewer found the book disappointing: "The novel begins slowly . . . and never picks up speed, with Steel narrating as if from a distance, glossing over critical scenes and skimping on dialogue." Patty Engelmann of *Booklist* reached a similar conclusion: "This lackluster suspense novel and its plastic characters will have automatic appeal for Steel fans, but other readers may find it wanting."

The next year Steel published *Impossible* and *Toxic Bachelors.* Both novels are love stories, but while *Impossible* features a couple who are socially and temperamentally ill-suited to one another, *Toxic Bachelors* tells of three different men who find themselves falling in love despite their promiscuous lifestyles. Reviewers of both novels felt fans would be pleased to find that each book contains Steel's signature style, subject matter, and plot mechanisms. In a *Booklist* review of *Impossible* Hughes wrote: "Steel knows what her fans want." Of *Toxic Bachelors, Booklist* critic Hughes stated that the story concludes with the "happy endings that will keep her fans reading and waiting for more." In another review of the same novel, a *Kirkus Reviews* critic agreed by stating: "Steel's massive fan base is unlikely to quibble."

In addition to her novels, children's fiction, and poetry, Steel ventured into biographical memoir in 1998 with *His Bright Light: The Story of Nick Traina.* The intensely personal memoir recounts the nineteen turbulent years of Steel's son's life—a life of manic depression, drugs, and ultimately suicide. Susan McCaffrey wrote in *Library Journal* that while Steel "is at times melodramatic and the pace is sometimes hampered by the inclusion of lengthy letters and poems, this is a compelling and surprisingly objective portrait of the devastating effects of mental illness." Steel founded the Nick Traina Foundation after her son's death to benefit mental health and other children's causes. Proceeds from *His Bright Light* went directly to the foundation.

Steel once told *CA:* "I want to give [readers] entertainment and something to think about."

BIOGRAPHICAL AND CRITICAL SOURCES:

BOOKS

Almanac of Famous People, 6th edition, Gale (Detroit, MI), 1998.

Bane, Vickie L. (with Lorenzo Benet), *The Lives of Danielle Steel: The Unauthorized Biography of America's Number One Best-Selling Author,* St. Martin's Press (New York, NY), 1994.

Bestsellers 89, Issue 1, Gale (Detroit, MI), 1989.

Bestsellers 90, Issue 4, Gale (Detroit, MI), 1991.

Contemporary Popular Writers, St. James Press (Detroit, MI), 1997.

Encyclopedia of World Biography, second edition, seventeen volumes, Gale (Detroit, MI), 1998.

Newsmakers, issue two, Gale (Detroit, MI), 1999.

Twentieth-Century Romance and Historical Writers, 3rd edition, St. James Press (Detroit, MI), 1994.

PERIODICALS

Booklist, April 1, 1992, p. 1413; October 15, 1992, p. 380; June 1 & 15, 1993, p. 1735; October 15, 1994, pp. 372-373; April 15, 1995, p. 1453; October 15, 1995, p. 364; March 1, 1996, p. 1077; February 1, 1998, Kathleen Hughes, review of *The Long Road Home,* p. 877; April, 1998, Kathleen Hughes, review of *The Klone and I: A High-Tech Love Story,* p. 1278; October 15, 1998, Kathleen Hughes, review of *Mirror Image,* p. 371; March 1, 1999, Melanie Duncan, review of *Bittersweet,* p. 1104; February 1, 2000, Patty Engelmann, review of *The Wedding,* p. 997; March 15, 2000, Patty Engelmann, review of *The House on Hope Street,* p. 1294; August, 2000, Whitney Scott, review of *Journey,* p. 2076; January 1, 2004, Patty Engelmann, review of *Ransom,* p. 790; June 1, 2004, Kathleen Hughes, review of *Second Chance,* p. 1671; February 1, 2005, Kathleen Hughes, review of *Impossible,* p. 918; September 1, 2005, Kathleen Hughes, review of *Toxic Bachelors,* p. 7.

Books, July, 1992, p. 18.

Brandweek, March 15, 2004, Ginger Danto, "A Literary Bandwagon," p. 25.

Chicago Tribune, September 26, 1993, pp. 6-7; March 27, 1994, p. 4.

Chicago Tribune Book World, August 28, 1983, L.J. Davis, review of *Changes.*

Detroit Free Press, December 1, 1989.

Detroit News, September 11, 1983, review of *Changes.*

Globe & Mail (Toronto, Ontario, Canada), July 9, 1988, Peggy Hill, review of *Zoya.*

Kirkus Reviews, October 1, 1992, p. 1212; June 1, 1993, p. 685; January 1, 1994, p. 16; April 15, 1994, p. 504; September 15, 1994, p. 1225; April 1, 1995, p. 422; October 1, 1995, pp. 1377- 1378; March 1, 1996, pp. 328-329; April 1, 1998, review of *The Klone and I;* August 15, 2000, review of *Journey,* p. 1141; October 1, 2004, review of *Echoes,* p. 936; September 1, 2005, review of *Toxic Bachelors,* p. 941.

Library Journal, September 1, 1993; October 15, 1993; October 15, 1994, p. 89; June 1, 1998, Kathy Ingels Helmond, review of *The Klone and I,* p. 161; December, 1998, Susan McCaffrey, review of *His Bright Light,* p. 172; March 1, 2005, Carol J. Bissett, review of *Impossible,* p. 80.

Los Angeles Times, January 6, 1988.

Los Angeles Times Book Review, April 14, 1985.

New York Times Book Review, September 11, 1983; August 19, 1984; March 3, 1985; July 9, 1995, p. 21.

People, October 3, 1994, p. 43.

Publishers Weekly, March 30, 1992, p. 88; October 26, 1992, pp. 55-56; June 7, 1993, p. 52; January 10, 1994, p. 41; May 23, 1994, p. 76; October 10, 1994, p. 60; December 12, 1994, p. 17; February 13, 1995, p. 21; May 1, 1995, p. 41; October 16, 1995, p. 44; March 25, 1996, p. 63; February 2, 1998, review of *The Long Road Home,* p. 78; April 20, 1998, review of *The Klone and I,* p. 44; June 1, 1998, review of *The Klone and I,* p. 34; October 26, 1998, review of *Mirror Image,* p. 45; March 15, 1999, review of *Bittersweet,* p. 46; May 24, 1999, review of *Granny Dan,* p. 65; February 14, 2000, review of *The Wedding,* p. 171; April 17, 2000, review of *The House on Hope Street,* p. 46; August 28, 2000, review of *Journey,* p. 50; March 5, 2001, review of *Lone Eagle,* p. 61; May 21, 2001, review of *Leap of Faith,* p. 82; January 12, 2004, review of *Ransom,* p. 36; May 31, 2004, review of *Second Chance,* p. 53; October 4, 2004, review of *Echoes,* p. 68.

Rapport, Volume 17, number 3, 1993, p. 23; Volume 18, number 1, 1994, p. 26; Volume 18, number 3, 1994, p. 23.

Saturday Evening Post, January, 1999, Patrick Perry, review of *His Bright Light,* p. 65.

Time, November 25, 1985.

Washington Post Book World, July 3, 1983; March 3, 1985.

ONLINE

Danielle Steel Home Page, http://www.randomhouse.com/features/steel/ (June 27, 2001).

* * *

STEEL, Danielle Fernande
See STEEL, Danielle

STEIG, William 1907-2003
(William H. Steig)

PERSONAL: Born November 14, 1907, in New York, NY; died October 3, 2003, in Boston, MA; son of Joseph (a housepainter) and Laura (a seamstress; maiden name, Ebel) Steig; married Elizabeth Mead, January 2, 1936 (divorced); married Kari Homestead, 1950 (divorced, 1963); married Stephanie Healey, December 12, 1964 (divorced, December, 1966); married Jeanne Doron, 1969; children: (first marriage) Lucy, Jeremy; (second marriage) Margit Laura. *Education:* Attended City College (now City College of the City University of New York), 1923-25; National Academy of Design, New York, NY, 1925-29.

CAREER: Freelance cartoonist contributing mainly to the *New Yorker,* 1930—; author and illustrator of children's books, 1968—. Worked for various advertising agencies. Sculptor. *Exhibitions:* Artwork has been exhibited at Downtown Gallery, New York City, 1939, Smith College, 1940, and has been included in collections at the Rhode Island Museum, Smith College Museum, and Brooklyn Museum.

AWARDS, HONORS: Children's Book of the Year nomination, Spring Book Festival picture book honor, National Book Award, and *Boston Globe-Horn Book* honor, all 1969, American Library Association (ALA) Notable Book designation and Caldecott Medal, both 1970, and Lewis Carroll Shelf Award, 1978, all for *Sylvester and the Magic Pebble;* National Book Award, *New York Times* Best Illustrated Children's Book of the Year, *New York Times* Outstanding Book, and ALA Notable Book designation, all 1971, and Children's Book Showcase title, 1972, all for *Amos and Boris;* Christopher Award, 1972, National Book Award, 1973, *Boston Globe-Horn Book* honor, ALA Notable Book designation, and William Allen White Children's Book Award, Kansas State College, all 1975, all for *Dominic; New York Times* Outstanding Book of the Year and ALA Notable Book designation, both 1973, for *The Real Thief;* Children's Book of the Year nomination and ALA Notable Book designation, both 1974, for *Farmer Palmer's Wagon Ride; New York Times* Outstanding Book of the Year, 1976, Newbery Honor Book, Children's Book Showcase title, ALA Notable Book designation, Lewis Carroll Shelf Award, and *Boston Globe-Horn Book* honor, all 1977, for *Abel's Island;* Caldecott Honor Book, Children's Book Showcase title,

ALA Notable Book designation, and *Boston Globe-Horn Book* honor, all 1977, and Art Books for Children Award, 1978, all for *The Amazing Bone;* Irma Simonton Black Award for best children's book, *New York Times* Best Illustrated Children's Book, *New York Times* Outstanding Book, all 1980, for *Gorky Rises;* Hans Christian Andersen Medal nomination, 1982; *New York Times* Outstanding Book, 1982, American Book Award, Parents' Choice illustration award, *Boston Globe-Horn Book* honor, and Newbery Honor Book, all 1983, and International Board on Books for Young People Honor Book, 1984, all for *Doctor De Soto;* Children's Picture Book Award, *Redbook,* 1984, for *Yellow and Pink,* 1985, for *Solomon the Rusty Nail,* and 1986, for *Brave Irene; New York Times* Best Illustrated Book, 1986, for *Brave Irene;* nomination, Hans Christian Andersen Medal, 1988; Children's Picture Book Award, *Redbook,* 1988, for *Spinky Sulks;* Parents' Choice Picture Book Award, and Reading Magic Award, both 1990, both for *Shrek!;* New England Book Award, 1993.

WRITINGS:

CARTOONS

Man about Town, Long & Smith (New York, NY), 1932.

About People: A Book of Symbolical Drawings, Random House (New York, NY), 1939.

The Lonely Ones, preface by Wolcott Gibbs, Duell, Sloan (New York, NY), 1942.

All Embarrassed, Duell, Sloan (New York, NY), 1944.

Small Fry (collection of *New Yorker* cartoons), Duell, Sloan (New York, NY), 1944.

Persistent Faces, Duell, Sloan (New York, NY), 1945.

Till Death Do Us Part: Some Ballet Notes on Marriage, Duell, Sloan (New York, NY), 1947.

The Agony in the Kindergarten, Duell, Sloan (New York, NY), 1950.

The Rejected Lovers, Knopf (New York, NY), 1951.

The Steig Album: Seven Complete Books, Duell, Sloan (New York, NY), 1953.

Dreams of Glory, and Other Drawings, Knopf (New York, NY), 1953.

Continuous Performances, Duell, Sloan (New York, NY), 1963.

Male/Female, Farrar, Straus (New York, NY), 1971.

William Steig: Drawings (collection of *New Yorker* cartoons), Farrar, Straus (New York, NY), 1979.

Ruminations, Farrar, Straus (New York, NY), 1984.

Spinky Sulks, Farrar, Straus (New York, NY), 1988.

Our Miserable Life, Farrar, Straus (New York, NY), 1990.

SELF-ILLUSTRATED BOOKS FOR CHILDREN

C D B! (word games), Windmill Books (New York, NY), 1968, revised edition, Simon & Schuster Books for Young Readers (New York, NY), 2000.

Roland the Minstrel Pig, Windmill Books (New York, NY), 1968.

Sylvester and the Magic Pebble, Windmill Books (New York, NY), 1969, Little Simon (New York, NY), 1995.

The Bad Island, Windmill Books (New York, NY), 1969, revised edition published as *Rotten Island,* David Godine (Boston, MA), 1984.

An Eye for Elephants (limericks), Windmill Books (New York, NY), 1970.

The Bad Speller (reader), Windmill Books (New York, NY), 1970.

Amos and Boris, Farrar, Straus (New York, NY), 1971, reprinted, Sunburst, 1992.

Dominic, Farrar, Straus (New York, NY), 1972.

The Real Thief, Farrar, Straus (New York, NY), 1973.

Farmer Palmer's Wagon Ride, Farrar, Straus (New York, NY), 1974.

The Amazing Bone, Farrar, Straus (New York, NY), 1976.

Abel's Island, Farrar, Straus (New York, NY), 1976.

Caleb and Kate, Farrar, Straus (New York, NY), 1977.

Tiffky Doofky, Farrar, Straus (New York, NY), 1978.

Gorky Rises, Farrar, Straus (New York, NY), 1980.

Doctor De Soto, Farrar, Straus (New York, NY), 1982.

Yellow and Pink, Farrar, Straus (New York, NY), 1984, reprinted, 2003.

C D C? (word games), Farrar, Straus (New York, NY), 1984, reprinted, 2003.

Solomon the Rusty Nail, Farrar, Straus (New York, NY), 1984.

Brave Irene, Farrar, Straus (New York, NY), 1986.

The Zabajaba Jungle, Farrar, Straus (New York, NY), 1987.

Alpha Beta Chowder, HarperCollins (New York, NY), 1992.

Doctor De Soto Goes to Africa, HarperCollins (New York, NY), 1992.

Shrek!, Farrar, Straus (New York, NY), 1993.

Pete's a Pizza, HarperCollins (New York, NY), 1998, published as a board book, 2003.

OTHER

Zeke Pippin, HarperCollins (New York, NY), 1994.

Collected Drawings, Moyer Bell (Wakefield, RI), 1994.

Grown-Ups Get to Do All the Driving, HarperCollins (New York, NY), 1995.
The Toy Brother, HarperCollins (New York, NY), 1996.
Toby, Where Are You?, pictures By Teryl Euvremer, HarperCollins (New York, NY), 1997.
(Illustrator) *A Handful of Beans: Six Fairy Tales,* by Jeanne Steig, HarperCollins (New York, NY), 1998.
(Illustrator) *Arthur Yorink's The Flying Latke,* Simon & Schuster Books for Young Readers (New York, NY), 1999.
Wizzil (children's book), illustrated by Quentin Blake, Farrar, Straus (New York, NY), 2000.
Made for Each Other, Joanna Cotler Books (New York, NY), 2000.
(Illustrator) *A Gift from Zeus: Sixteen Favorite Myths,* by Jeanne Steig, Joanna Cotler Books (New York, NY), 2001.
Potch & Polly, Farrar, Straus (New York, NY), 2001.
Sick of Each Other, HarperCollins (New York, NY), 2001.
Which Would You Rather Be?, Joanna Cotler Books (New York, NY), 2002.
When Everybody Wore a Hat, Joanna Cotler Books (New York, NY), 2003.

Illustrator of numerous books, including Will Cuppy's *How to Become Extinct,* Garden City Books, 1941; Wilhelm Reich's *Listen, Little Man!,* translation by Theodore P. Wolfe, Orgone Institute Press, 1948, reprinted, Octagon Books, 1971; and Irwin Steig's *Poker for Fun and Profit,* Astor-Honor, 1959. Contributor of cartoons to periodicals, including *Collier's, Judge, Life,* and *Vanity Fair.*

Steig's manuscripts are included in the Kerlan Collection at the University of Minnesota, Minneapolis.

ADAPTATIONS: Many of Steig's books have been adapted as filmstrips, including *Amos and Boris,* Miller-Brody, 1975; *Farmer Palmer's Wagon Ride,* Miller-Brody, 1976; and *Brave Irene,* Weston Woods, 1988. Many of Steig's children's books have also been adapted for film, including *Doctor De Soto,* Weston Woods, 1985; *The Amazing Bone,* Weston Woods, 1985; *Abel's Island,* Lucerne Media, 1988; and *Brave Irene,* Weston Woods, 1989. *Doctor De Soto and Other Stories* was adapted for read-along cassette, Caedmon, 1985. *Shrek!* was adapted as an animated feature film, titled *Shrek,* released in 2001 by DreamWorks SKG, and directed by Andrew Adamson and Vicky Jenson.

SIDELIGHTS: William Steig, wrote a *New York Times* reporter in 1997, "is not quite a household name, but his 67-year ink trail is instantly recognizable." As the artist who established himself as one of the twentieth century's most penetratingly observant cartoonists, Steig is perhaps best known as the creator of the acerbic green ogre Shrek, whose adventures were adapted into an Academy Award-winning film in 2001.

Steig's drawings have appeared regularly in the *New Yorker* since 1930. When he decided to try his hand at writing and illustrating children's books in 1968, he began a second career in which he found equal success, eventually winning the prestigious Caldecott Award and an American Book Award. Growing up in the Bronx, New York, Steig was the son of a house painter and a seamstress, both of whom were Socialists. That led to some discussion in the household concerning career paths: "My parents didn't want their sons to become laborers, because we'd be exploited by businessmen, and they didn't want us to become businessmen, because then we'd exploit the laborers," he told Anita Silvey for *Children's Books and Their Creators.* The arts seemed to be the path of choice. Among the four Steig brothers, Irwin became a journalist and painter; Henry played saxophone; Arthur had a gift for drawing and reading; and William began developing his cartooning style.

During the pre-Depression jazz age, Steig attended City College (now part of the City University of New York) and the National Academy of Design. He explained in an interview with Michael Patrick Hearn for the *Washington Post Book World:* "I went to art school because I was given my choice whether to get to work or go to school. What I had in mind at the time was to go to sea when I got the chance—at least for a while. But my father went broke in the crash of '29. . . . So it devolved on me to find some way to support my family."

That need for quick income led to his first cartoon sale to the *New Yorker.* He told Hearn, "It showed two guys in prison and one was complaining that his kid was incorrigible and that he couldn't keep him in line." Since that June, 1930, offering, almost every issue of the *New Yorker* has been "enriched . . . with [Steig's] drawings and cartoons, varied in style and subject, but always comic in their perception, fluent and delicate in their execution," declared a *Times Literary Supplement* contributor. His cartoons most often illustrate the psychopathology of everyday strife, showing characters that are "'fantastic but recognizable,' as anyone will agree who glances up from them to look around at the occupants of a subway car or of the office where he works," noted a *Books* reviewer. "That is why they are so cruel and so frightening and so funny."

Collections of Steig's drawings have proven extremely popular, and they indicate the variety of his work. In

The Lonely Ones, Steig sketched "impressions of people . . . set off from the rest of the world by certain private obsessions," explained Wolcott Gibbs in the book's preface. *All Embarrassed* focuses on bewildered adults caught in humiliating situations. *Small Fry* consists of one hundred drawings, rendered in delicate washes, of children. Whatever his subject or style, critics have consistently cited Steig's work for its piercing insights. A *Weekly Book Review* critic wrote of *All Embarrassed:* "As in all the best comic or satiric art, these Steig pictures have a caustic, sobering, and philosophic quality: they call upon introspection and self-judgment. And while they make us laugh or shudder, or see in some hippopotamus-like face or lax torso the fearful likeness of a neighbor, they also do a pretty thorough job of slapping the stuffing out of our own unreasonably cocky little selves. . . . Steig is . . . a master-hand at x-raying human beings." "I tend to criticize people for caring too much about what they are," Steig once remarked to *Hartford Courant* interviewer Alison Wyrley Birch.

After almost forty years as "one of our most original and influential cartoonists," in the words of Karla Kuskin in the *New York Times Book Review,* Steig responded to the urging of a children's book publisher and produced *Roland the Minstrel Pig,* his first juvenile work. Since then Steig has produced a new children's book almost every year. *C D B!, Roland the Minstrel Pig, Amos and Boris, Dominic, Doctor De Soto* and the rest of Steig's juveniles have consistently won praise for their rich language, imaginative stories, and delightful illustrations. And in spite of the sardonicism that infuses his adult work, "there is a sweet, gook humor that runs through all his [children's] books," stated Kuskin. "The author of 'People are no damn good,' one of the most famous cartoons of the 1940's, doesn't complain to kids. Giving despair the slip he becomes a benign evangelist for justice, youth and joy."

"Like Isaac Bashevis Singer, E.B. White and a select company of others, Steig is a writer of children's books whose work reaches beyond the specific confines of a child audience," noted James E. Higgins in *Children's Literature in Education.* "[He] has the unusual childlike capacity to present incidents of wonder and marvel as if they are but everyday occurrences. He writes not out of a remembrance of childhood, but out of the essence of childhood which no adult can afford to give up or to deny." The power of luck, the capacity of nature for transformation and rebirth, the existence of beneficial magic; all are a part of this "childhood essence" and are ever-present in Steig's books. Wishes, even unspoken ones, are granted in the author's vision of how the world should be. In *The Amazing Bone,* the daydreaming Pearl the Pig dawdles on her walk home from school. She discovers a magic bone, lost by a witch who "ate snails cooked in garlic at every meal and was always complaining about her rheumatism and asking nosy questions." That the bone talks is not surprising to our heroine, or even to her parent, and is accepted as a matter of course by the reader.

When the animated blockbuster *Shrek* was nominated for an Academy Award for "best adapted screenplay" many moviegoers were moved to wonder whence the script was adapted. *Shrek* the film was based on Steig's 1990 picture book of the same title (though with an exclamation point added). The author/artist reportedly approved of the screen adaptation of the tale of the titular ogre (his name means "fear" in Yiddish) whose nightmares include images of flowery fields and happy children: "some of the children kept hugging and kissing him, and there was nothing he could do to make them stop." In Steig's original telling, the "ugliest guy in town," as *Publishers Weekly* reviewer Diane Roback called him, hears the prophecy of a witch that he will marry a princess even uglier than he. The ogre's adventures in finding his mate make up the bulk of the tale. Accordingly, Shrek's big love scene with his princess is a wild affair: "Shrek snapped at her nose. She nipped at his ear. They clawed their way into each other's arms. Like fire and smoke, these two belonged together."

As evinced by *Shrek!* and his other books, positive themes reoccur throughout Steig's works: the abundant world of nature, the security of home and family, the importance of friendship, the strength that comes from self-reliance. Many of the animal characters inhabiting Steig's sunlit world also possess "heroic" qualities; quests, whether in the form of a search for a loved one or for adventure's sake alone, are frequently undertaken. Higgins remarked, "In his works for children . . . [Steig] sets his lens to capture that which is good in life. He shares with children what can happen to humans when we are at our best."

In the opinion of Anita Moss, "Many of Steig's picture books incorporate wish-fulfillment childhood fantasies." Writing for *St. James Guide to Children's Writers,* Moss elaborated: "An adventurous frog in *Gorky Rises* concocts a magical potion that enables him to soar to the stars, break free of adult constraints, and yet return home safely with concrete and indisputable proof that his adventures have actually happened. In *Doctor De Soto* a mouse dentist outwits the crafty fox who poses as a patient. In *Solomon the Rusty Nail* Steig again features the theme of transformation and the child's concern with identity." In this book Solomon the rabbit makes a hasty wish, turning into a nail to escape the jaws of a hungry cat. But Solomon's plan backfires when the cat nails him to a house; after the house catches fire the rusty nail escapes and turns back into a rabbit, who returns home to his grateful parents. "Change, though terrifying, Steig seems to imply, is finally a good and beneficial thing," Moss commented.

Following the success of the film version of his *Shrek!*, Steig continued to write and draw. Even into his nineties, the author/artist produced such picture books as *Which Would You Rather Be?* and *Potch and Polly.* In the former title, a wand-wielding rabbit entices a girl and boy to decide what they would rather be: a mouse or an elephant, a stick or a stone, lightning or thunder. Every choice comes with its advantages and consequences, reinforcing the theme of choice to young readers.

Steig avoids interjecting political or social overtones to make his books "mean" anything. Human concerns over existence, self-discovery, and death are dealt with indirectly. "I feel this way: I have a position—a point of view," Steig told *CA*. "But I don't have to think about it to express it. I can write about anything and my point of view will come out. So when I am at work my conscious intention is to tell a story to the reader."

The artist had a brief sojourn into the corporate world working as an advertising illustrator during the 1960s. But he reacted to such artistic restriction, as *People* reporter Joshua Hammer revealed, "with severe psychosomatic muscle cramps." "Doing advertising was something I couldn't stand to do," the artist told Hammer. "I just hate to follow someone else's impulse." But being his own boss is no less easy. Steig finds writing and illustrating children's books to be much different than drawing cartoons, as he explained to Sally Lodge in *Publishers Weekly:* "Working for kids is not the same as working for adults. Kids' books take a lot longer. I can do a drawing in 15 minutes. Once my editor, Michael di Capua, approves an idea for a children's book, it takes me about a week to write it and a month to do the illustrations." Steig has always found illustrating to be the most difficult part of his job, and confided to Higgins: "I love to draw, and I love to write—but I hate to illustrate. . . . When you draw, you draw anything that wants to come out, but when you illustrate you have to draw someone who has on a polka-dot dress. It has to be the same as the previous picture. You have to remember what it says in the story. It's not the way I want to draw at all."

BIOGRAPHICAL AND CRITICAL SOURCES:

BOOKS

Children's Literature Review, Thomson Gale (Detroit, MI), Volume 2, 1976, pp. 158-161; Volume 15, 1988, pp. 175-202.

Dictionary of Literary Biography, Volume 61: *American Writers for Children since 1960: Poets, Illustrators, and Nonfiction Authors,* Thomson Gale (Detroit, MI), 1987, pp. 297-305.

Kingman, Lee, editor, *Newbery and Caldecott Medal Books: 1966-1975,* Horn Book (New York, NY), 1975.

Lanes, Selma G., *Down the Rabbit Hole: Adventures and Misadventures in the Realm of Children's Literature,* Atheneum (New York, NY), 1971.

Lorenz, Lee, *The World of William Steig,* Artisan, 1998.

Silvey, Anita, *Children's Books and Their Creators,* Houghton Mifflin (New York, NY), 1995.

Steig, William, *The Amazing Bone,* Farrar, Straus (New York, NY), 1976.

Townsend, John Rowe, *Written for Children: An Outline of English-Language Children's Literature,* revised edition, Lippincott (New York, NY), 1974.

PERIODICALS

Booklist, January 1, 1975, November 1, 1994, Lauren Peterson, review of *Zeke Pippin,* p. 510; April 1, 1995, Hazel Rochman, review of *Grown-Ups Get to Do All the Driving,* p. 1393; February 15, 1996, Susan Dove Lempke, review of *The Toy Brother,* p. 1027; November 15, 1998, Rochman, review of *A Handful of Beans: Six Fairy Tales,* p. 589; October 15, 1999, Elaine Hanson, review of *Shrek!,* p. 466; October 1, 2000, Michael Cart, review of *Wizzil,* p. 337; May 1, 2001, Gillian Engberg, review of *Toby, Where Are You?,* p. 1693; July, 2001, Lolly Gepson, review of *Pete's a Pizza,* p. 2027; August, 2002, Michael Cart, review of *Which Would You Rather Be?,* p. 1977.

Books, January 17, 1943.

Children's Book Review, June, 1973; summer, 1975.

Children's Books, July-August, 1968; December, 1968; November, 1970; April, 1975.

Children's Literature in Education, spring, 1978, pp. 3-16.

Christian Science Monitor, November 11, 1971.

Hartford Courant, September 8, 1974.

Horn Book, August, 1968; August, 1970, pp. 359-363; February, 1972; October, 1972; April, 1975; August, 1975; October, 1975; August, 1976; December, 1976; April, 1977; June, 1977; January-February, 1995, Anna Flowers, review of *Zeke Pippin,* p. 55; May-June, 1996, Maria Salvadore, review of *The Toy Brother,* p. 329; November, 1998, Kristi Beavin, review of *Sylvester and the Magic Pebble,* p. 769; January, 1999, review of *A Handful of Beans,* p. 78; November, 2000, Leonard Marcus, review of *Sylvester and the Magic Pebble,* p. 652; May, 2001, Joanna Rudge Long, review of *A Gift from Zeus: Sixteen Favorite Myths,* p. 300.

Junior Bookshelf, February, 1972; February, 1973; April, 1973; August, 1973; June, 1975.

Kirkus Reviews, May 1, 2002, review of *Which Would You Rather Be?,* p. 668/

Life, December 17, 1971.

Los Angeles Times Book Review, December 5, 1982.

Newsweek, May 15, 1995, Malcolm Jones, Jr., review of *Grown-Ups Get to Do All the Driving,* p. 60.

New York, December 16, 1974.

New Yorker, December 2, 1974.

New York Times, November 29, 1997, Sarah Boxer, "Wry Child of the Unconscious."

New York Times Book Review, April 21, 1968; February 16, 1969; October 19, 1969; October 17, 1971; July 9, 1972; September 2, 1973; November 10, 1974; July 18, 1976; November 14, 1976; November 13, 1977; November 25, 1979; December 12, 1982; August 12, 1984; November 9, 1986; June 28, 1987, p. 26.

People, December 3, 1984, Joshua Hammer, "With Pen, Ink and the Eye of an Innocent, a Brilliantly Off-Center Writer/Cartoonist Refuses to Surrender to Age," pp. 87-98.

Publishers Weekly, October 15, 1979, pp. 6-7; July 24, 1987, pp. 116-18; September 14, 1990, Diane Roback, review of *Shrek!,* p. 124; February 20, 1995, review of *Grown-Ups Get to Do All the Driving,* p. 204; January 15, 1996, review of *The Toy Brother,* p. 461; July 6, 1998, review of *Pete's a Pizza,* p. 58; October 5, 1998, review of *A Handful of Beans,* p. 88; July 3, 2000, review of *Wizzil,* p. 70; June 25, 2001, review of *A Gift from Zeus,* p. 73; May 20, 2002, review of *Which Would You Rather Be?,* p. 64; June 24, 2002, review of *Potch and Polly,* p. 56.

Saturday Review/World, December 4, 1973.

School Library Journal, September, 1968; May, 1969; September, 1972; November, 1973; August, 2000, Rosalyn Pierini, review of *Wizzil,* p. 165; February, 2001, Lee Bock, review of *Sick of Each Other,* p. 140; June, 2001, Patricia Lothrop-Green, review of *A Gift from Zeus,* p. 181; June, 2002, Carol MacKay, review of *Which Would You Rather Be?,* p. 110; August, 2002, Joy Fleischhacker, review of *Potch and Polly,* p. 170.

Time, December 27, 1971; December 17, 1984, Stefan Kanfer, review of *CDC?,* p. 84.

Times Literary Supplement, September 12, 1980.

Washington Post Book World, May 11, 1980.

Weekly Book Review, July 23, 1944.

ONLINE

Boston Globe, http://www.boston.com/globe/ (June 22, 1997), John Koch, author interview.

William Steig Web site, http://www.williamsteig.com/ (October 9, 2002).

* * *

STEIG, William H.
See STEIG, William

* * *

STEINEM, Gloria 1934-

PERSONAL: Born March 25, 1934, in Toledo, OH; daughter of Leo and Ruth (Nuneviller) Steinem. *Education:* Smith College, B.A. (magna cum laude), 1956; University of Delhi and University of Calcutta (India), graduate study, 1957-58.

ADDRESSES: *Office*—Ms. Magazine, 230 Park Ave., New York, NY 10136.

CAREER: Editor, writer, lecturer. Independent Research Service, Cambridge, MA, and New York, NY, director, 1959-60; *Glamour* magazine, New York, NY, contributing editor, 1962-69; *New York* magazine, New York, NY, cofounder and contributing editor, 1968-72; *Ms.* magazine, New York, NY, cofounder and editor, 1972-87, columnist, 1980-87, consulting editor, 1988—. Contributing correspondent to *Today* show, National Broadcasting Company, Inc. (NBC). Active in civil rights and peace campaigns, including those of United Farm Workers, Vietnam War, Tax Protest, and Committee for the Legal Defense of Angela Davis. Editorial consultant to Conde Nast Publications, 1962-69, Curtis Publishing, 1964-65, Random House Publishing, 1988—, and McCall Publishing.

MEMBER: PEN, National Press Club, Society of Magazine Writers, Authors Guild, Authors League of America, American Federation of Television and Radio Artists, National Organization for Women, Women's Action Alliance (cofounder; chairperson, 1970—), National Women's Political Caucus (founding member; member of national advisory committee, 1971—), *Ms.* Foundation for Women (cofounder; member of board, 1972—), Coalition of Labor Union Women (founding member, 1974), Phi Beta Kappa.

AWARDS, HONORS: Chester Bowles Asian fellow in India, 1957-58; Penney-Missouri journalism award, 1970, for *New York* article "After Black Power, Women's Liberation"; Ohio Governor's journalism award, 1972; named Woman of the Year, *McCall's* magazine, 1972; Doctorate of Human Justice from Simmons College, 1973; Bill of Rights award, American Civil Liberties Union of Southern California, 1975; Woodrow Wilson International Center for Scholars fellow, 1977; Ceres Medal from United Nations; Front Page Award; Clarion Award; nine citations from *World Almanac* as one of the twenty-five most influential women in America; PEN Center West Literary Award of Honor, 2002.

WRITINGS:

The Thousand Indias, Government of India, 1957.

The Beach Book, Viking (New York, NY), 1963.

(With G. Chester) *Wonder Woman,* Holt (New York, NY), 1972.

Outrageous Acts and Everyday Rebellions, Holt (New York, NY), 1983.

Marilyn: Norma Jeane, Holt (New York, NY), 1986.

Bedside Book of Self-Esteem, Little, Brown (Boston, MA), 1989.

Revolution from Within: A Book of Self-Esteem, Little, Brown (Boston, MA), 1992.

Moving beyond Words, Simon & Schuster (New York, NY), 1993.

(Editor, with others) *The Reader's Companion to U.S. Women's History,* Houghton Mifflin (Boston, MA), 1998.

AUTHOR OF INTRODUCTION OR FOREWORD

Marlo Thomas and others, *Free to Be . . . You and Me,* McGraw (New York, NY), 1974.

Lois Beachy Underhill, *The Woman Who Ran for President: The Many Lives of Victoria Woodhull,* Bridge Works Publishing Company (Bridgehampton, NY), 1995.

Bonnie Watkins, editor, *In the Company of Women: Voices from the Women's Movement,* Minnesota Historical Society Press (Saint Paul, MN), 1996.

Gail Hanlon, editor, *Voicing Power: Conversations with Visionary Women,* Westview Press (Boulder, CO), 1997.

Marilyn Waring, *Counting for Nothing: What Men Value and What Women Are Worth,* University of Toronto Press (Toronto, Ontario, Canada), 1999.

Eve Ensler, *The Vagina Monologues,* Dramatists Play Service (New York, NY), 2000.

Angela Bonavoglia, editor, *Choices We Made: Twenty-five Women and Men Speak Out about Abortion,* Avalon Publishing Group (New York, NY), 2001.

Steve Neal, editor, *Eleanor and Harry: The Correspondence of Eleanor Roosevelt and Harry S. Truman,* Simon & Schuster (New York, NY), 2003.

Helen Hunt, *Faith and Feminism: A Holy Alliance,* Atria Books (New York, NY), 2004.

OTHER

Contributor to *Running against the Machine,* edited by Peter Manso, Doubleday (New York, NY), 1969. Writer for television, including series "That Was the Week that Was," NBC, 1964-65. Author of films and political campaign material. Former author of column, "The City Politic," in *New York.* Contributor to periodicals, including *Cosmopolitan, Esquire, Family Circle, Life, Show,* and *Vogue.* Editorial consultant, *Seventeen,* 1969-70, and *Show.*

ADAPTATIONS: "I Was a Playboy Bunny" was produced as an American Broadcasting Companies, Inc. (ABC) television movie, *A Bunny's Tale,* 1985.

SIDELIGHTS: Gloria Steinem is recognized as one of the foremost organizers of the modern women's movement. Her major contribution, according to Maureen Corrigan in the *New York Times Book Review,* is "her ability to popularize feminist issues to a wide and often wary audience." Her grandmother, Pauline Steinem, was the president of a turn-of-the-century women's suffrage group and was a representative to the 1908 International Council of Women, but Gloria was not substantially influenced by her while growing up in Toledo, Ohio. Her mother and father divorced when she was young, and at the age of ten Gloria was left alone to care for both herself and her mentally ill mother.

Steinem left home when she was seventeen to attend Smith College on a scholarship. Like many women of the era, she was engaged by her senior year but broke her engagement to continue her political science studies in India, where she had adjusted quickly, adopting native dress and ways. Because English served as the common language, she was "able to really talk, and tell jokes, and understand political arguments," she told Miriam Berkley in an interview for *Publishers Weekly.* Steinem was also able to freelance for Indian newspapers. She supplemented her university studies by seeking out the company of the activists who were then working for an independent India. As a member of a group called the Radical Humanists, she traveled to southern India at the time of the terrible caste riots there, working as a member of a peacemaking team. Steinem's experiences gave her a deep sympathy for the underclasses as well as an enduring love of India.

When the time came for her to return to the United States, Steinem did so filled with an "enormous sense of urgency about the contrast between wealth and poverty," she told Berkley. Because she "rarely met people who had shared this experience," Steinem related, it became "like a dream. It had no relation to my real, everyday life. . . . I couldn't write about it." Instead, Steinem established a successful freelance career, writing articles about celebrities, fashions, and tropical vacations, while devoting her spare time to work for the civil rights movement. Berkley described Steinem's life in the early 1960s as "schizophrenically split between career and conscience." "I was . . . divided up into pieces as a person," the author told Elisabeth Bumiller in the *Washington Post.* "I was working on one thing, and caring about another, which I think is the way a lot of us have to live our lives. I'm lucky it came together."

Steinem's best-known article from her early career is "I Was a Playboy Bunny." Assigned to cover the 1963 opening of the New York City Playboy Club for *Show* magazine, she went undercover to work as a "Bunny," or waitress, for two weeks. The resulting article is an "excellent, ironic, illuminating bit of reporting," claimed Angela Carter in the *Washington Post Book Review.* Steinem was instructed by the "Bunny Mother" in techniques for stuffing her bodice and bending over to serve drinks, cautioned against sneezing, which would split the seams of her Bunny costume, presented with a copy of the "Bunny Bible," the lengthy code of conduct for Playboy waitresses, and informed that all new Bunnies were required to have a pelvic examination performed by the club's specially appointed doctor. "I Was a Playboy Bunny" is "hysterically funny," according to Ann Marie Lapinski in the *Chicago Tribune.* It is also as "full of feminist consciousness as some of [Steinem's] later reportage," argued Carter, who commented: "If it is implicit rather than explicit, it is no less powerful for that." Of her experiences in the club, Steinem remarked to *Los Angeles Times* interviewer Elenita Ravicz, "Being a Bunny was more humiliating than I thought it would be. True, it was never the kind of job I would have considered under ordinary circumstances, but I expected it to be more glamorous and better paid than it was. . . . Customers there seemed to be there because they could be treated as superiors. . . . There is a real power difference when one group is semi-nude and the other is fully-clothed."

By the mid-sixties Steinem was getting more substantial writing assignments and earning respect for her pieces on political figures. In 1968 she and Clay Felker founded *New York* magazine, to which Steinem supplied the monthly column "The City Politic" and articles such as "Ho Chi Minh in New York." She was still seen as something of a trendy celebrity by many in the male-dominated world of journalism, however. Bumiller quoted a 1969 *Time* article describing Steinem as "one of the best dates to take to a New York party these days. . . . Writers, politicians, editors, publishers and tuned-in businessmen are all intensely curious about her. Gloria is not only a successful freelance writer and contributing editor of *New York* magazine; she is also a trim, undeniably female, blonde-streaked brunette. . . . She does something for her soft suits and clinging dresses, has legs worthy of her miniskirts, and a brain that keeps conversation lively without getting tricky." Steinem's popularity in such social circles soon waned, however, because of her growing interest in controversial women's issues.

Colleague reaction to a 1969 article she wrote about a New York abortion hearing shocked Steinem. At the hearing Steinem heard testimony from women who had endured illegal abortions, risking injury, possibly ending in sterilization, and sometimes being forced to have sex with the abortionist. She told Ravicz, "I wrote an article about the hearing and my male colleagues, really nice men I got along well with, took me aside one by one and said, 'don't get involved with these crazy women. You've taken so much trouble to establish your reputation as a serious journalist, don't throw it all away.' That was when I realized men valued me only to the extent I imitated them." Instead of abandoning the "crazy women" of the abortion hearing, Steinem followed up her coverage with an extensively researched article on reproductivity and other feminist issues. Her article "After Black Power, Women's Liberation" won her the Penney-Missouri journalism award, but also "unleashed a storm of negative reactions . . . from male colleagues. The response from the publishing establishment, and its reluctance to publish other work on the subject, opened her eyes. She began to pursue not only writing but also speaking engagements and became an active part of the women's movement she had once only observed," related Berkley.

Steinem came to believe that a magazine controlled by women was necessary if a truly open forum on women's issues was to exist. Accordingly, she and others began working toward that goal. Felker offered to subsidize a sample issue and to include a thirty-page excerpt of the new publication in *New York* magazine. Steinem and the rest of the staff worked without pay and produced the first issue of *Ms.* in January, 1972. "We called it the spring issue," Steinem recalled to Berkley. "We were really afraid that if it didn't sell it would embarrass the women's movement. So we called it Spring so that it could lie there on the newsstands for a long time." Such worries were unfounded—the entire 300,000-copy run of *Ms.* sold out in eight days.

Steinem was suddenly the editor of a very successful monthly magazine, but was somewhat ambivalent about the position: "I backed into [starting *Ms.*]," she admitted to Beth Austin in an interview for the *Chicago Tribune.* "I felt very strongly there should be a feminist magazine. But I didn't want to start it myself. I wanted to be a freelance writer. I'd never had a job, never worked in an office, never worked with a group before. It just happened." Steinem believed that she would turn the editorship of *Ms.* over to someone else as soon as the magazine was squarely on its feet. "I said, 'I'm going to do this two years, that's it.' I kept on saying that until . . . I'd already been doing it for almost seven years. Then I took a fellowship at the Woodrow Wilson Center, which is part of the Smithsonian Institution in Washington [D.C.]. So I was away from the office for the first time for substantial periods of time. . . . I just missed it terribly. And I suddenly realized that, where I thought I'd been delaying life, there *was* life."

As a spokesperson for the women's movement, Steinem has been criticized as subversive and strident by some and as overly tolerant and conservative by others. An overview of the opinions that made her a figurehead of the Woman's Movement during the 1980s is published as *Outrageous Acts and Everyday Rebellions,* a collection representing twenty years of Steinem's writing on a variety of subjects, including politics, pornography, her mother, and Marilyn Monroe. Carter criticized the book, complaining that Steinem presents only "the acceptable face of feminism" and that she is "straightjacketed by her own ideology." Diane Johnson offered a more favorable appraisal in the *New York Times Book Review:* "Reading Miss Steinem's essays . . . one is struck by their intelligence, restraint and common sense, as well as by the energetic and involved life they reflect. . . . This is a consciousness-raising book. . . . Her views, like her writing itself, are characterized by engaging qualities of unpretentious clarity and forceful expression." Douglas Hill wrote in the Toronto *Globe & Mail:* "Honesty, fairness and consistency gleam in these pages. And Steinem writes superbly. . . . It's her special strength to write as cleanly and affectingly about her mother's mental illness as about the practice of genital mutilation endured by 75 million women worldwide or the inadequacies of William Styron's fiction."

Steinem's next book grew from an essay in *Outrageous Acts* concerning Marilyn Monroe, the actress who became internationally famous as a "sex goddess" in the 1950s and apparently committed suicide in 1962. When photojournalist George Barris decided to publish a series of photographs taken of Monroe shortly before her death, Steinem was asked to contribute the text. While researching *Marilyn: Norma Jeane,* she became aware that although over forty books had already been published about the late film star, only a few were written by women. Most of the biographies focused on the scandalous aspects of Monroe's death and personal relationships, or reinforced her image as the ultimate pin-up. Steinem explained to *Washington Post* interviewer Chip Brown: "I tried to take away the fantasy of Marilyn and replace it with reality. . . . The book doesn't have a thesis so much as an emphasis—an emphasis on Norma Jeane, on the private, real, internal person. I hadn't read a book about Marilyn that made me feel I knew her. My purpose was to try to get to know or to portray the real person inside the public image." Commenting on the ironic fact that Monroe derived little pleasure from her physical relationships, Steinem suggested to Brown that "it's hard for men to admit that a sex goddess didn't enjoy sex. . . . It's part of the desire to believe she was murdered—the same cultural impulse that says if she's a sex goddess she had to have enjoyed sex doesn't want to believe she killed herself, doesn't want to accept her unhappiness."

Brown saw Steinem's *Marilyn* as a feminist rebuttal to Norman Mailer's biography of Monroe: "His book is an extravagant concerto for the 'Stradivarius of sex.' Monroe is the supreme object. . . . [Steinem] stresses the limited choices women had then—and underscores Monroe's struggle for independence, her desire to be taken seriously." London *Times* reviewer Fiona MacCarthy found fault with Steinem's "passionate involvement with the helpless child in Marilyn," believing that it is an example of "the new phenomenon of women letting women off too lightly. . . . Her sentimental vision of the real Marilyn entrapped in the sex-goddess body sometimes makes one wonder where is now the Gloria Steinem who worked on the campaign trail in the 1960s both as a reporter and an aide to George McGovern. Has she lost all astuteness?" But Diana Trilling argued that *Marilyn: Norma Jeane* is "thoughtful and absorbing." Her *New York Times Book Review* evaluation called the biography "a quiet book; it has none of the sensationalism that has colored other purportedly serious books about the film star, Norman Mailer's in particular. . . . In writing about Marilyn Monroe, Gloria Steinem for the most part admirably avoids the ideological excess that we have come to associate with the women's movement—Monroe emerges from her book a far more dimensional figure than she would have been if she had been presented as simply the victim of a male-dominated society."

Bumiller summarized Steinem's view of the woman's movement in an interview in the *Washington Post:* "it's not dead or even sick, but has instead spread out from the middle class to be integrated into issues like unemployment and the gender gap. [Steinem] sees four enormous goals ahead: 'reproductive freedom, democratic families, a depoliticized culture and work redefined. . . . We are talking about overthrowing, or humanizing—pick your verb, depending on how patient you feel—the sex and race caste systems.'" As the task of meeting these goals was engaged by a new generation of feminists, Steinem turned her energies, and her focus, inward. "I've lived my first 50 years externally, reacting more than acting," she told Molly O'Neill in an interview for the *New York Times* in the year she turned sixty. "I've been much too nice." Steinem's study of her own life became the subject of 1992's *Revolution from Within,* an introspective, circular exploration of the ways in which self-esteem affects everything: handwriting, body language, family relationships, the American system of public education, and world economic policies. Basing her comments on insights drawn from her personal self-exploration as well as her own belief in learning from nature, Steinem provides readers with a "Meditation Guide," suggests means for them to discover and understand their own "inner child," and includes an appendix of self-help books under the heading "Bibliotherapy."

Revolution from Within received a reaction from feminist circles. "How can it be," questioned Carol Sternhell in *Women's Review of Books,* "after so many years of trying to change the world, that one of our best-known feminists is suddenly advising women to change ourselves instead?" Steinem's focus on self-esteem appeared to many mainstream reviewers to be an attempt to jump aboard the pop-psychology bandwagon, and *Revolution from Within*'s rapid climb to the top of the best-seller lists seemed to bear them out. Feminist critics, however, feared that the book was much more: a sign that this figurehead of the woman's movement had "sold out." Critic Joseph Adelson assured readers that Steinem's "old externalizing mentality is still there, powerful as ever," in his review of *Revolution from Within* for *Commentary.* But, he later noted, "anyone expecting coherent discourse may find much of this book unreadable. It rambles from topic to topic, a mishmash of pseudo-profundities, dubious information, and half-baked opinions." Mary Beard was similarly critical of the work in the *Times Literary Supplement:* "Following in all the worst traditions of popular psychology and self-help manuals, [Steinem] identifies the malaise at the heart of the modern human condition as childhood injury . . . a claim that is so obviously true that it hardly requires the three-hundred page demonstration that she gives it."

Critics viewed Steinem's next book, *Moving beyond Words,* in a more positive light. Published in 1993, *Moving beyond Words* is a collection of essays—three previously published and three new—that, as Maureen Corrigan contended in the *New York Times Book Review,* demonstrate "that what appears to be 'natural' is, in fact, socially constructed." In one of the book's examples, "What If Freud Were Phyllis?," Steinem performs a fictional sex-change operation on the noted psychotherapist that results in theories of "womb envy" and the like, dramatizing her contention that the basis of many of the late doctor's assumptions lies couched in male superiority. "More than any other brief text I have read, this essay simply revokes, cancels and terminates the reader's ability to take gender inequity for granted," concluded Patricia Limerick in her review for the *Washington Post.* The essay "Sex, Lies and Advertising" takes to task the manipulative practices of magazine advertising, a concern of Steinem's that resulted in *Ms.* magazine's decision to eliminate advertising from its pages in 1990. "Doing Sixty" draws its insights from Steinem's personal exploration of self—similarly recounted in *Revolution from Within*—in its celebration of age as a time to give oneself permission to take risks with fewer worries about social repercussions. In "The Masculinization of Wealth," Steinem contends that wealthy women—who are resented by society and abused by members of their own families to such a point that, even with great financial resources, they are powerless in society—are as much victims of patriarchy as their poorer female counterparts. While also praising the work as a whole, Limerick found that Steinem fails to adequately address the inequities involved when racial discrimination is coupled with gender discrimination. Limerick declared: "I wanted a chapter on feminism, race and poverty that equalled in power and persuasion the essay on feminism and wealth." Limerick ultimately concluded: "The pleasures and satisfactions of 'being who we really are' prove to be as unequally distributed as income and opportunity. . . . I cannot read [these closing remarks] without thinking that this book, at its end, takes an unexpected turn back to a protected world of white, middle-class privilege and choice." *Moving beyond Words,* found Susan Cheever in the *Los Angeles Times Book Review,* "is a book that spells out, over and over, the many different direct and subtle ways in which women are reduced to powerlessness in our world."

As the women's movement moves into what many call its second wave, marked by dissent among its ranks and what fellow feminist and author Susan Faludi has termed a social "backlash" in her 1991 book of the same name, Steinem remains positive about the future of feminism. "The first wave was about women gaining a legal identity," she told O'Neill, "and it took 150 years. The second wave of feminism is about social equality. We've come a long way, but it's only been 25 years. . . . Women used to say, 'I am not a feminist, but. . . .' Now they say, 'I am a feminist, but. . . .'"

BIOGRAPHICAL AND CRITICAL SOURCES:

BOOKS

Heilbrun, Carolyn, *The Education of a Woman: The Life of Gloria Steinem,* Dial (New York, NY), 1995.

Lazo, Caroline Evensen, *Gloria Steinem: Feminist Extraordinaire,* Lerner Publications (Minneapolis, MN), 1998.

Stern, Sydney Ladensohn, *Gloria Steinem: Her Passions, Politics, and Mystique,* Carol Publishing Group (New York, NY), 1997.

PERIODICALS

Belles Lettres, summer, 1992, p. 26.

Chicago Tribune, October 2, 1983; January 11, 1987.

Commentary, May, 1992, pp. 54-55.

Detroit News, August 28, 1983.

Esquire, June, 1984.

Globe & Mail (Toronto, Ontario, Canada), February 8, 1986.

London Review of Books, April 23, 1992, p. 17.

Los Angeles Times, December 11, 1984; December 10, 1986; May 6, 1987.

Los Angeles Times Book Review, June 19, 1994, p. 2.

National Review, March 2, 1992, pp. 47-48.

New Republic, July 11, 1994, pp. 32-36.

New Statesmen, February 20, 1987, pp. 19-20.

New York Times, April 4, 1987; May 10, 1988; February 9, 1995, pp. C1, 10.

New York Times Book Review, September 4, 1983; December 21, 1986, p. 1; May 22, 1994, p. 37.

People, June 11, 1984; February 25, 1985.

Publishers Weekly, August 12, 1983.

Times (London, England), February 19, 1987.

Times Literary Supplement, April 24, 1992, p. 11.

Washington Post, October 12, 1983; December 7, 1986.

Washington Post Book World, October 9, 1983; June 26, 1994, p. 1.

Women's Review of Books, June, 1992, pp. 5-6.

* * *

STEINER, George 1929-

PERSONAL: Born April 23, 1929, in Paris, France; immigrated to the United States in 1940, naturalized citizen, 1944; son of Frederick George (a banker) and Elsie (Franzos) Steiner; married Zara Alice Shakow (a university professor), July 7, 1955; children: David Milton, Deborah Tarn. *Education:* University of Chicago, B.A., 1948; Harvard University, M.A., 1950; Oxford University, Ph.D., 1955. *Hobbies and other interests:* Mountain walking, music, chess.

ADDRESSES: Home—32 Barrow Rd., Cambridge CB2 2AS, England. *Office*—Churchill College, Cambridge, England.

CAREER: Economist, London, England, member of editorial staff, 1952-56; Princeton University, Princeton, NJ, fellow of Institute for Advanced Study, 1956-58, Gauss Lecturer, 1959-60; Cambridge University, Cambridge, England, fellow of Churchill College, 1961-69, Extraordinary Fellow, 1969—; University of Geneva, Geneva, Switzerland, professor of English and comparative literature, 1974—. Visiting professor at New York University, 1966-67, University of California, 1973-74, and at Harvard University, Yale University, Princeton University, College of France, and Stanford University; University of London, Maurice Lecturer,

1984; Cambridge University, Leslie Stephen Lecturer, 1985; University of Glasgow, W.P. Ker Lecturer, 1986, Gifford Lecturer, 1990; visiting professor College of France, 1992; Oxford University, First Lord Weidenfeld professor of comparative literature, 1994—.

MEMBER: English Association (president, 1975), Royal Society of Literature (fellow), British Academy (fellow), German Academy of Literature (corresponding member), Athenaeum Club (London), Savile Club (London), Harvard Club (New York, NY), American Academy of Arts and Sciences (honorary member).

AWARDS, HONORS: Bell Prize, 1950; Rhodes scholar, 1955; Fulbright professorship, 1958-59; O. Henry Short Story Prize, 1959; Morton Dauwen Zabel Award from National Institute of Arts and Letters, 1970; Guggenheim fellowship, 1971-72; Cortina Ulisse Prize, 1972; Remembrance Award, 1974, for *The Language of Silence;* PEN-Faulkner Award nomination, 1983, for *The Portage to San Cristobal of A. H.;* named Chevalier de la Legion d'Honneur, 1984; Macmillan Silver Pen Award, 1992, for *Proofs and Three Parables;* PEN International Fiction Prize, 1993; Truman Capote Lifetime Award for Literature, 1999. Honorary degrees from colleges and universities, including D.Litt. degrees from Louvain University, 1980, Mount Holyoke College, 1983, University of Glasgow, 1990, University of Liege, 1990, University of Ulster, 1993, Durham University, 1995, Kenyon College, 1996, Trinity College, Dublin, 1996, University of Rome, 1998, and the Sorbonne, 1998.

WRITINGS:

Tolstoy or Dostoevsky: An Essay in the Old Criticism, Penguin (Harmondsworth, England), 1958, Dutton (New York, NY), 1971.

The Death of Tragedy, Hill & Wang (London, England), 1960, Knopf (New York, NY), 1961.

(Editor, with Robert Fagles) *Homer: A Collection of Critical Essays,* Prentice-Hall (Englewood Cliffs, NJ), 1962.

Anno Domini: Three Stories, Atheneum (New York, NY), 1964.

(Editor and author of introduction) *The Penguin Book of Modern Verse Translation,* Penguin (Harmondsworth, England), 1966, published as *Poem into Poem: World Poetry in Modern Verse Translation,* 1970.

Language and Silence: Essays on Language, Literature, and the Inhuman, Atheneum (New York, NY), 1967.

Extraterritorial: Papers on Literature and the Language Revolution, Atheneum (New York, NY), 1971.

In Bluebeard's Castle: Some Notes toward the Redefinition of Culture, Yale University Press (New Haven, CT), 1971.

Fields of Force: Fischer and Spassky in Reykjavik, Viking (New York, NY), 1973, published as *The Sporting Scene: White Knights in Reykjavik,* Faber (London, England), 1973.

Nostalgia for the Absolute, CBC Enterprises, 1974.

After Babel: Aspects of Language and Translation, Oxford University Press (Oxford, England), 1975, 3rd edition, Oxford University Press (New York, NY), 1998.

The Uncommon Reader, Bennington College Press (Bennington, VT), 1978.

On Difficulty and Other Essays, Oxford University Press (Oxford, England), 1978.

Martin Heidegger, Viking (New York, NY), 1978, published as *Heidegger,* Fontana (London, England), 1978.

The Portage to San Cristobal of A. H. (novel; also see below), Simon & Schuster (New York, NY), 1981, published with new afterword, University of Chicago Press (Chicago, IL), 1999.

George Steiner: A Reader, Oxford University Press (New York, NY), 1984.

Antigones: How the Antigone Legend Has Endured in Western Literature, Art, and Thought, Oxford University Press (New York, NY), 1984.

Real Presences: Is There Anything in What We Say?, University of Chicago Press (Chicago, IL), 1989.

Proofs and Three Parables (fiction), Viking (New York, NY), 1992.

What Is Comparative Literature?: An Inaugural Lecture Delivered before the University of Oxford on 11 October 1994, Oxford University Press (New York, NY), 1995.

No Passion Spent: Essays 1978-1995, Yale University Press (New Haven, CT), 1996.

The Deeps of the Sea (fiction; contains *The Portage to San Cristobal of A. H.*), Faber (London, England), 1996.

(Editor and author of introduction and notes) *Homer in English,* Penguin (New York, NY), 1996.

(With Antoine Spire and others) *Barbarie de l ignorance: Juste l ombre d un certain ennui,* Bord de l'eau (Latresne, France), 1998.

Errata: An Examined Life, Yale University Press (New Haven, CT), 1998.

(With Antoine Spire and others) *Ce qui me hante,* Bord de l'eau (Latresne, France), 1999.

Grammars of Creation: Originating in the Gifford Lectures for 1990, Yale University Press (New Haven, CT), 2001.

Lessons of the Masters, Harvard University Press (Cambridge, MA), 2003.

Author of introduction to *The Trial,* by Franz Kafka, translated by Willa and Edwin Muir, Schocken Books (New York, NY), 1995. Columnist and book reviewer for the *New Yorker;* contributor of essays, reviews, and articles to numerous periodicals, including *Commentary, Harper's,* and *Nation.* Author of works produced on audio cassette, including *A Necessary Treason: The Poet and the Translator,* J. Norton, 1970; and *The Poet as Translator: To Traduce or Transfigure,* J. Norton, 1970.

ADAPTATIONS: After Babel was adapted for television as *The Tongues of Men,* 1977. *The Portage to San Cristobal of A. H.* was adapted for the stage under the same title by Christopher Hampton, first produced in America at Hartford Stage, Hartford, CT, January 7, 1983.

SIDELIGHTS: "George Steiner is the most brilliant cultural journalist at present writing in English, or perhaps in any language," a *Times Literary Supplement* reviewer wrote. Steiner is known on two continents for his literary criticism and far-ranging essays on linguistics, ethics, translation, the fine arts, and science. According to Pearl K. Bell in the *New Leader,* few present-day literary critics "can match George Steiner in erudition and sweep. Actually, he resists confinement within the fields of literature, preferring more venturesome forays into the history of ideas. . . . Steiner has proceeded on the confident assumption that no activity of the human mind is in any way alien or inaccessible to his own." Steiner writes for the educated general reader rather than for the academic specialist; London *Times* contributor Philip Howard called the author "an intellectual who bestrides the boundaries of cultures and disciplines." In addition to his numerous books, including *Language and Silence: Essays on Language, Literature, and the Inhuman* and *After Babel: Aspects of Language and Translation,* Steiner produces regular columns for *New Yorker* magazine, where he serves primarily as a book reviewer. Almost always controversial for his bold assertions and assessments of highly specialized theories, Steiner "has been called both a mellifluous genius and an oversimplifying intellectual exhibitionist," to quote Curt Suplee in the *Washington Post. National Review* correspondent Scott Lahti claimed, however, that most readers appreciate Steiner's "provocative manner of expression . . . by turns richly allusive, metaphoric, intensely concerned, prophetic, apocalyptic—and almost always captivating."

Much of Steiner's criticism reflects his own sensitivity to the shaping events of modern history. "One way or another," noted a *Times Literary Supplement* reviewer, "in his view, the word has been pushed into a corner; non-verbal forms of discourse have taken over so many fields where writing once reigned supreme. . . . There is also the terrible cloud that has been cast over language and literature by the actions of a thoroughly literate and cultured people between 1933 and 1945," provoking a need for the critic "to expose all such dehumanization of the word." In the *New Republic* Theodore Solotaroff proposed that Steiner, himself a Jew who escaped France just before the Nazi atrocities descended, regards himself as heir to a European intellectual community that was annihilated by the Holocaust. Solotaroff suggested that Steiner stands "in a deep sense for the whole generation of his peers—these children who did not survive, who left this great tradition bereft of its natural proteges, who make such a haunting absence today in the life of the European mind. . . . There is a driving, obsessive quality to Steiner's acquisitiveness, a fever in his point of view which goes beyond curiosity and self-assertion." Indeed, one of Steiner's central preoccupations, discussed in both his fiction and his nonfiction, is the relation between high culture and barbarism—how, for instance, a concentration camp guard could enjoy a novel or a symphony after sending people to the gas chambers. *Punch* contributor Melvyn Bragg wrote: "The drive, the necessity, the fate which kept Sisyphus going has been, with Steiner, the Holocaust. In that blaze, he has written, not only did a people burn, but words turned to ashes, meaning and value were powdered to be ground into dirt by the heels of vacant inheritors." Steiner himself told the *New York Times Book Review* that central to everything he is and believes and has written "is my astonishment, naive as it seems to people, that you can use human speech both to bless, to love, to build, to forgive and also to torture, to hate, to destroy and to annihilate."

Rootlessness—or, as he puts it, extraterritoriality, also serves as a foundation for Steiner's essays on language and literature. *Dictionary of Literary Biography* contributor Bruce Robbins saw in Steiner "the willed trace of a radical homelessness that he has made a personal motif for almost thirty years." Steiner was born in Paris to Viennese parents; he was only eleven when his family fled to the United States in 1940. Thus he grew up with a full command of three languages—English, French, and German—and his adult life has included extensive work on the nature and limitations of human communication. "The recent preoccupation of all thoughtful practitioners of the humanities with language is [Steiner's] preoccupation," observed David H. Stewart in the *Western Humanities Review.* "Semantics, semiotics, psycho-linguistics, structuralist literary criticism: these are his concerns. These he orchestrates into his continuing effort to explain how human beings communicate and what their *manner* of communication does to the content and style of their minds." In *Book World,* Richard Freedman contended that Steiner's interests have led him to investigate "the very roots of communication . . . how the special patterns of the some 4,000 languages now spoken in the world determine not only the course of the literature, but of the psychology, philosophy, and even the physiology of the people who speak and write them." As Malcolm Bradbury put it in the London *Times,* part of Steiner's appeal is that he "celebrates, and *is,* the great scholar-reader for whom endless reinterpretation of major ideas and myths is fundamental to existence. He becomes himself the case in point: native in three languages, read in many more, learned over a massive range, requiring of those who study or debate with him an unremitting dedication. All this is expressed with a charismatic power which makes even difficulty seem easy, and invites rebellion against low educational standards, intellectual simplifications, and false prophesy."

Steiner was educated on two continents, having studied at the University of Chicago, Harvard, and Oxford University on a Rhodes scholarship. His first book, published the year he turned thirty, concerns not English literature but the works of two great Russian writers, Tolstoy and Dostoevsky. Titled *Tolstoy or Dostoevsky: An Essay in the Old Criticism,* the book "announces the particular place Steiner has assigned himself," wrote Robbins. "Neither Europe nor America, his Russia is a no-man's-land that permits him to remain, to use his term, unhoused." In addition to offering an analysis of the two writers' lives, thoughts, and historical milieu, the work challenges the *au courant* "New Criticism" by assigning moral, philosophical, and historical worth to the texts. A *Times Literary Supplement* correspondent observed that Steiner "is concerned not with a catalogue of casual, incidental parallels between life and fiction but with the overmastering ideas which so preoccupied the two men that they could not help finding parallel expression in their lives and their works." Another *Times Literary Supplement* reviewer likewise declared that Steiner "feels he is addressing not professional scholars merely, safely shut in the confines of one particular discipline, but all thinking men who are aware of the larger world of social and political realities about them. Dr. Steiner's style derives part of its force from his seeing intellectual questions against the background of historical crises and catastrophes."

In 1967 Steiner published *Language and Silence,* a collection of essays that establish the author's "philosophy of language." The book explores in depth the vision of the humanely educated Nazi and the diminution of the word's vitality in an audio-visual era. Solotaroff maintained that *Language and Silence* "casts a bright and searching light into the murky disarray of current letters and literacy: it looks back to a darkness and disruption of Western culture that continues to plague and challenge the moral purpose of literature, among other fields, and it looks forward to possibilities of art and thought that may carry us beyond our broken heritage. It provides an articulate and comprehensive discussion of the impact of science and mass communications on the ability of language to describe the realities of the earth and the world." Steiner's conclusion—that silence and the refusal to write is the last-resort moral act in the face of bestiality—aroused conflicting opinions among his critics. In the *New York Times Book Review,* Robert Gorham Davis suggested that the author "displaces onto language many of his feelings about history and religion. He makes it an independent living organism which can be poisoned or killed." The critic added, however, that throughout the volume, "thoughts are expressed with such a fine and knowledgeable specificity that when we are forced to disagree with Steiner, we always know exactly upon what grounds. He teaches and enlightens even where he does not convince." *New York Times* contributor Eliot Fremont-Smith concluded that *Language and Silence* "will confirm, if confirmation is necessary, [Steiner's] reputation as one of the most erudite, resourceful and unrelentingly serious critics working today."

Many observers have argued that *After Babel* is Steiner's monumental work, a "deeply ambivalent hymn to language," as Geoffrey H. Hartman put it in the *New York Times Book Review.* The book offers a wide-ranging inquiry into the fields of linguistics and translation, with commentary on the vagaries of communication both inside and between languages. *Washington Post Book World* reviewer Peter Brunette explained that in *After Babel* Steiner proposes "the radical notion that the world's many diverse languages (4,000 plus, at last count) were created to disguise and hide things from outsiders, rather than to assist communication, as we often assume. A corollary is that the vast majority of our day-to-day language production is internal, and is not meant to communicate at all." In *Listener,* Hyam Maccoby contended that Steiner's predilection is for a view "that a language is the soul of a particular culture, and affects by its very syntax what can be said or thought in that culture; and that the differences between languages are more important than their similarities (which he calls 'deep but trivial')." The book brought Steiner into a debate with linguists such as Noam Chomsky, who are searching for the key to a "universal grammar" that all human beings share. Many critics felt that in *After Babel* Steiner presents a forceful challenge to the notion of an innate, universal grammar. According to Raymond Oliver in the *Southern Review,* the book "is dense but lucid and often graceful; its erudition is balanced by sharpness of insights, its theoretical intelligence by critical finesse; and it pleads the cause of poetry, language, and translation with impassioned eloquence. . . . We are ready to be sustained and delighted by the sumptuous literary feast [Steiner] has prepared us." *New Yorker* columnist Naomi Bliven likewise pointed out that Steiner's subject "is extravagantly rich, and he ponders it on the most generous scale, discussing how we use and misuse, understand and misunderstand words, and so, without always being aware of what we are doing, create art, history, nationality, and our sense of belonging to a civilization. . . . He is frequently ironic and witty, but for the most part his language and his ideas display even-handedness, seriousness without heaviness, learning without pedantry, and sober charm."

"Steiner's performance is mindful of a larger public," wrote Robbins. Not surprisingly, therefore, the author does not shy from forceful communication or controversial conclusions. For instance, in his novel *The Portage to San Cristobal of A. H.,* Steiner gives readers an opportunity to ponder world history from Adolf Hitler's eloquent point of view. Some critics found the novel morally outrageous, while others cited it for its stimulating—if not necessarily laudable—ideas. Steiner's essays have also had their detractors. Bradbury suggested that his nonfiction has "a quality of onward-driving personal history, and it is not surprising that they have left many arguments in their wake." Bradbury added that Steiner's impact "in provoking British scholars to a much more internationalist and comparative viewpoint has been great, but not always gratefully received." Lahti, for one, found Steiner's conclusions "often fragmentary, and his frequent resort to extravagant assertions and perverse generalizations lessens the force of his arguments." Similarly, *New York Review of Books* contributor D.J. Enright faulted Steiner for "a histrionic habit, an overheated tone, a melodramatization of what (God knows) is often dramatic enough, a proclivity to fly to extreme positions. The effect is to antagonize the reader on the brink of assent."

Steiner's *Proofs and Three Parables,* a slim collection of short fiction, received Britain's MacMillan Silver Pen Award. Reviewers praised the book, noting its function as an engagingly readable introduction to some of Steiner's philosophical ideas. The short story "Proofs," for example, features "a sustained and often hilarious debate between [a proof-reader who is a former member of the Italian Communist party] and his old friend, Father Carlo Tessone, on the meaning of life in a post-communist world," summarized David Lohrey in *Los Angeles Times Book Review.* Lohrey concluded that Steiner articulates "the superfluousness of the individual in our time and one's increasing belief that this world no longer cares for the distinction between things done well and those merely completed." The volume also contains three parables, "Desert Island Disks," "Noel, Noel," and "Conversation Piece," all of which use unusual symbolism and playful dialogue to articulate Steiner's philosophical ruminations concerning culture, history, and philosophy.

In *Real Presences: Is There Anything in What We Say?,* Steiner "offers a dark picture of contemporary Western culture," according to Michael F. Suarez in *Review of English Studies.* Steiner argues in the volume for a return to the "transcendent" potential of art which, he believes, has been undermined by the post-modern concern with deconstruction of artistic "texts" and constant awareness of the "intertextuality" of all art forms. In other words, he deems the postmodern view of art as a series of "signs," a destructive force that has contributed to the essential irrelevance of art in the modern world. "A [method of] criticism, then, that does not assume that it can transcend itself—let alone its object—is not real, and deconstruction is, *par excellence,* such a criticism," commented Richard Cavell in *Canadian Literature.* "Only art, for Steiner, can answer to art."

In *No Passion Spent* Steiner presents a volume of essays on a variety of religious, philosophical, linguistic, and literary subjects. He explores the decline of literacy and serious reading in western civilization and searches for the source of philosophical divisions in human thought that have contributed to destructive tendencies throughout history. Central to several of his essays is the history of Judaism and the adversarial relationship between the Jewish faith and Christianity. "In *No Passion Spent,* Steiner faces his divine source and drinks from the Bible, Homer and Socrates, Jesus, Freud and Shakespeare, as well as Kafka, Kierkegaard, Husserl and Simone Weil," noted Guymannes-Abbott in *New Statesman & Society. Spectator* contributor Tony Connor found Steiner's rhetoric "exhilarating," but complained that "too much of [Steiner's writing] is only interesting if one is interested in Steiner; too much of his commentary on writers serves only to direct the reader back to the authoritative and grandly dispensing figure of the critic."

Critics praised Steiner's collection of short fiction, *The Deeps of the Sea,* also published in 1996. The volume includes Steiner's acclaimed novel, *The Portage to San Cristobal of A. H.,* along with several shorter works. Connor found Steiner's stories "better, on the whole, when they come closer to parables, and when they are interesting it is because of the ideas they contain."

Errata: An Examined Life is a series of essays, "primarily a tour of ideas, not of places or people," to quote Anthony Gottlieb in the *New York Times Book Review.* While drawing anecdotes from his own life, Steiner primarily searches for "occasions for reflection on the intellectual world and his position in it," Gottlieb remarked. Among the other topics upon which he touches are the current status of so-called "classic" art and literature, the Jewish diaspora, Judeo-Christian morality and its impact on the twentieth century, and the pitfalls of computer translation. In *Review of Contemporary Fiction* Thomas Hove concluded that few of Steiner's peers in the critical canon "can match the bravado of his evaluative and impressionistic formulations, and even fewer can convey . . . so many dimensions of response to linguistic and artistic expression." A *Publishers Weekly* contributor praised *Errata* as "an intimate and captivating glimpse into Steiner's mind and thought."

A great deal of debate attended the publication of *Grammars of Creation,* a book based on Steiner's Gifford Lectures at the University of Glasgow. The work defies easy summarization, but it studies in depth the evolution of grammar and language in an era of atheism and postmodernism. Once again he focuses on the Holocaust and its moral and intellectual effects upon language, and he debates the future of artistic creativity in an era of rising narcissism and admiration of scientific progress. According to a critic for the online *Independent,* Steiner seeks "to discover how to shape the legacy of language so that it is capable of yielding fresh meaning. In *Grammars of Creation,* he argues that what is required is nothing less than a new 'grammar' of creativity, a new set of rules, to articulate the riches of language in freshly constructive ways that match the ethos and beliefs of our complex, anxious, information-overloaded world."

National Review correspondent Michael Potemra called *Grammars of Creation* "an intellectual tour de force," and Jeffrey Snowbarger in *Booklist* likewise deemed it "the high point of a lengthy and productive career." In the *Times Literary Supplement,* Peter D. Smith commented: "Steiner's account of artistic creation in *Grammars of Creation* . . . is deeply felt and powerful. The description of how writers create characters by breathing 'a dynamic, intrusive and unforgettable *élan vital* into a constellation of words and action' is one among many memorable insights. His perceptive readings of Dante and the Shoah poet, Paul Celan, are typical of a work in which the author's erudition is matched only by his eloquence." A *Publishers Weekly* reviewer contended that readers of the work would be "dazzled by a learning and an elegance that, in the minds of others less fatalistic, may yet prove redemptive." And John Kennedy in the *Antioch Review* declared: "In this essential text, Steiner is a virtuoso, a fully armed witness to past and present ideas of creation in Western culture."

Reviewers have commonly observed that Steiner intends to challenge his audience, deliberately provoking strong opinions. In the *New Republic,* Robert Boyers wrote: "Readers will sense, on every page, an invitation to respond, to argue, to resist. But so nimble and alert to possibility is the critic's articulating voice that one will rather pay careful attention than resist. Ultimately, no doubt, 'collaborative disagreement' may seem possible, but few will feel dismissive or ungrateful. . . . No reader will fail to feel Steiner's encouragement as he moves out on his own." According to Edward W. Said in *Nation,* Steiner "is that rare thing, a critic propelled by diverse enthusiasms, a man able to understand the implications of trends in different fields, an autodidact for whom no subject is too arcane. Yet Steiner is to be read for his quirks, rather than in spite of them. He does not peddle a system nor a set of norms by which all things can be managed, every text decoded. He writes to be understood by nonspecialists, and his terms of reference come from his experience—which is trilingual, eccentric and highly urbane—not from something as stable as doctrine or authority." Bradbury stated that what can always be said of Steiner "is that what he questions and quarrels with, he reads and knows. And, whatever the quarrels, Steiner is a major figure, who has sustained a profoundly enquiring philosophy of literature." Fremont-Smith expressed a similar opinion. "Whether or not one agrees with Mr. Steiner's analyses," the reviewer concluded, "he does set one thinking, and thinking, moreover, about issues that are paramount."

BIOGRAPHICAL AND CRITICAL SOURCES:

BOOKS

Contemporary Literary Criticism, Volume 24, Thomson Gale (Detroit, MI), 1983.

Dictionary of Literary Biography, Volume 67: *American Critics since 1955,* Thomson Gale (Detroit, MI), 1988.

Scott, Nathan A., and Ronald A. Sharp, editors, *Reading George Steiner,* Johns Hopkins University (Baltimore, MD), 1994.

PERIODICALS

Antioch Review, winter, 2002, John Kennedy, review of *Grammars of Creation,* p. 161.
Booklist, April 1, 2001, Jeffrey Snowbarger, review of *Grammars of Creation,* p. 1430.
Book World, January 2, 1972.
Canadian Literature, spring, 1995, p. 193.
Christian Science Monitor, May 25, 1975.
Commentary, October, 1968; November, 1975.
Commonweal, May 12, 1961; October 27, 1967.
Contemporary Review, January, 2002, Geoffrey Heptonstall, "George Steiner's Passionate Reason," p. 54.
Detroit News, April 25, 1982.
Library Journal, September 15, 2003, William D. Walsh, review of *Lessons of the Masters,* p. 59.
Listener, April 27, 1972; January 30, 1975; March 22, 1979; July 3, 1980.
London Magazine, December, 1967.
Los Angeles Times, October 23, 1980; June 6, 1993, p. 8.
Los Angeles Times Book Review, April 11, 1982; November 18, 1984.
Modern Language Review, January, 1987, p. 158.
Nation, March 2, 1985.
National Review, December 31, 1971; August 31, 1979; June 11, 1982; July 26, 1985; May 28, 2001, Michael Potemra, "Shelf Life."
New Leader, June 23, 1975.
New Republic, May 13, 1967; January 27, 1979; May 12, 1979; April 21, 1982; November 19, 1984.
New Statesman, November 17, 1961; October 20, 1967; October 22, 1971; January 31, 1975; December 1, 1978; June 27, 1980; January 5, 1996, p. 37; March 1, 1996, p. 36.
Newsweek, April 26, 1982; January 5, 1996, p. 37.
New Yorker, January 30, 1965; May 5, 1975.
New York Review of Books, October 12, 1967; November 18, 1971; October 30, 1975; April 19, 1979; August 12, 1982; December 6, 1984.
New York Times, March 20, 1967; June 22, 1971; July 1, 1974; May 7, 1975; April 16, 1982; January 7, 1983; April 1, 1993, p. C21; June 27, 1996, p. B5.
New York Times Book Review, May 28, 1967; August 1, 1971; October 13, 1974; June 8, 1975; January 21, 1979; May 2, 1982; December 16, 1984; June 30, 1996, p. 16; April 12, 1998, Anthony Gottlieb, "Idea Man," p. 18; September 2, 2001, Roger Kimball, "Is the Future Just a Tense?," p. 12.
Observer, December 17, 1978; March 28, 1993, p. 7; June 30, 1996, p. 16.
Publishers Weekly, January 19, 1998, review of *Errata: An Examined Life,* p. 360; March 19, 2001, review of *Grammars of Creation,* p. 86.
Punch, June 17, 1981.
Review of Contemporary Fiction, spring, 1998, Thomas Hove, review of *Errata,* p. 206.
Southern Review, winter, 1978.
Spectator, April, 1960; December 2, 1978; July 19, 1980; January 13, 1996, p. 29.
Time, July 26, 1971; March 29, 1982.
Times (London, England), March 20, 1982; June 23, 1984; June 28, 1984.
Times Literary Supplement, March 11, 1960; September 28, 1967; December 17, 1971; May 19, 1972; May 18, 1973; January 31, 1975; November 17, 1978; June 12, 1981; April 6, 2001, Peter D. Smith, "The Wingbeat of the Unknown," p. 13.
Voice Literary Supplement, April, 1982; December, 1984.
Washington Post, May 13, 1982.
Washington Post Book World, January 14, 1979; May 2, 1982; December 30, 1984; January 19, 1986; June 23, 1996, p. 11.
Western Humanities Review, autumn, 1979.
Yale Review, autumn, 1967.

ONLINE

Complete Review, http://www.complete-review.com/ (September 30, 2001), review of *Grammars of Creation.*
Independent Online, http://www.independent.co.uk/ (March 17, 2001), "When Words Have Failed Us."
San Francisco Chronicle, http://www.sfgate.com/ (April 22, 2001), Kenneth Baker, "Are We in the Twilight of Western Art and Thought?"

* * *

STEINER, K. Leslie
See DeLANY, Samuel R.

* * *

STEPHENSON, Neal 1959-

PERSONAL: Born October 31, 1959, in Fort Meade, MD; son of David Town (a professor) and Janet (a laboratory technician; maiden name, Jewsbury) Stephenson; married Ellen Marie Lackermann (a physician), June 28, 1985. *Education:* Boston University, B.A., 1981.

ADDRESSES: Agent—Liz Darhansoff, 1220 Park Ave., New York, NY 10128.

CAREER: Ames Laboratory, U.S. Department of Energy, Ames, IA, research assistant, 1978-79; Boston University, Boston, MA, teaching assistant in physics department, 1979; Corporation for a Cleaner Commonwealth (environmental group), Boston, researcher, 1980; University of Iowa, Iowa City, clerk in library, 1981-83; writer.

AWARDS, HONORS: Hugo Award for Best Novel, Mystery Writers of America, 1996, for *The Diamond Age;* Arthur C. Clarke Award, 2004, for *Quicksilver.*

WRITINGS:

NOVELS

The Big U, Vintage Trade (New York, NY), 1984.
Zodiac: The Eco-Thriller, Atlantic Monthly Press (New York, NY), 1988.
Snow Crash, Bantam (New York, NY), 1992.
The Diamond Age; or, A Young Lady's Illustrated Primer, Bantam (New York, NY), 1995.
Cryptonomicon, Avon (New York, NY), 1999.
In the Beginning . . . Was the Command Line, Perennial (New York, NY), 1999.

"BAROQUE CYCLE"; NOVELS

Quicksilver, Morrow (New York, NY), 2003.
The Confusion, Morrow (New York, NY), 2004.
The System of the World, Morrow (New York, NY), 2004.

Contributor to the *Akron Beacon Journal.*

SIDELIGHTS: Neal Stephenson's first novel, *The Big U,* revolves around the American Megaversity, a huge, modern university, funded by a radioactive waste dump, and whose students arm themselves with machine guns. The satirical book, loaded with student pranks reminiscent of those in the 1978 film *National Lampoon's Animal House,* was deemed "a lot of fun" by Alan Cheuse in the *New York Times Book Review,* the critic noting that Stephenson's novel would appeal greatly to "alert and inquisitive students with a taste for campus comedy." Despite such positive reviews, however, *The Big U* did not find a large readership. Stephenson's second outing, *Zodiac: The Eco-Thriller,* was described by Steve Levy of *Newsweek* as "a tale of ecoactivism that won the hearts of tree huggers but didn't sell, either."

Stephenson's third novel, the widely acclaimed *Snow Crash,* proved to be the author's breakthrough book, bringing him cult status as one of the major cyberpunk novelists of his generation. According to *Entertainment Weekly* writer Chris Hashawaty, "The young and wired have turned . . . *Snow Crash* . . . into their dog-eared bible." Nadine Kolowrat, also writing in *Entertainment Weekly,* observed that 1992's *Snow Crash* "proved to be the pass-along favorite of sci-fi heads, hackers, and regular joes alike."

Snow Crash takes place partly in the Metaverse, a complex virtual-reality creation, and partly in the world that spawned it, a high-tech future dominated by corporations that are in turn opposed by renegade computer hackers. A similar setting was first made popular in William Gibson's seminal 1984 cyberpunk novel *Neuromancer* and has become the sine qua non of the genre. However, most reviewers find that Stephenson manages his own original and compelling take on what has become a cliché in the science-fiction field. John Leonard wrote in the *Nation* that no other cyberpunk writer has depicted virtual reality "so lyrically" as Stephenson, while Levy believed that, "when it comes to depicting the nerd mind-set, no one tops Stephenson." The "snow crash" of the book's title refers to a street drug/computer virus that has invaded the Metaverse, causing not only computer crashes in the virtual world but the physical collapse in the real world of those who encounter it. The central character of the novel, Hiro Protagonist—who has chosen his own name—employs information both from the Bible and ancient Summerian culture to track down the origins of snow crash. In the process he discovers a plot to take over and transform civilization. A writer for the *New York Times Book Review* noted that "Hiro's adventures . . . are brilliantly realized," and praised Stephenson as "an engaging guide to an onrushing tomorrow that is as farcical as it is horrific."

An *Entertainment Weekly* reviewer described Stephenson's follow-up to *Snow Crash, The Diamond Age; or, A Young Lady's Illustrated Primer,* as "equal parts Victorian novel, fairy tale, and sci-fi; a tantalizing peak into the twenty-first century that bogs down in its various subplots." Whereas virtual reality serves as the technological background for *Snow Crash, The Diamond Age* explores nanotechnology, the manipulation of atomic particles both to transform matter and to create submicroscopic machines. Though traversing several continents in the course of its action, the novel is set for the most part in a future Shanghai at a time when the nations of the world have been replaced by enclaves of individuals who share common cultural identities and beliefs. Computer engineer John Hackworth is hired by a rich and powerful neo-Victorian to write a primer to help educate his granddaughter. The plot of the book turns on the complications that arise when a stolen copy of the primer falls into the hands of a working-class girl who uses it for her own education.

"Building steadily to a wholly earned and intriguing climax," stated a reviewer for *Publishers Weekly, The Diamond Age* "presents its sometimes difficult technical concepts in accessible ways." Noting that the book is a somewhat lengthy read, the reviewer nonetheless maintained that the science-fiction novel would also "appeal to readers other than habitual SF users." Kolowrat took a more critical stance, commenting that "reading about someone reading a book is about as riveting as watching an actor think." The critic also found Stephenson's use of a Victorian vocabulary in a science-fictional environment to be jarring, but granted that *The Diamond Age* "does have great riffs on a futuristic world and some mindbending settings."

Stephenson followed *The Diamond Age* with his fifth novel, the highly successful *Cryptonomicon.* The most mainstream of Stephenson's works, the 928-page *Cryptonomicon* centers on two major characters, mathematician Lawrence Waterhouse and his programmer grandson, Randy. The book moves back and forth in time between World War II, when Lawrence is employed deciphering German and Japanese military codes, and the present, when Randy is involved in the technological development of Southeast Asia. A hidden treasure in Japanese gold ties the two story lines together, as does their examination of the birth and development of information technology.

Lev Grossman, reviewing *Cryptonomicon* for *Entertainment Weekly,* cautioned: "don't write off Stephenson's novel as just another fast-paced, find-the-MacGuffin techno-thriller. It's an engrossing look at the way the flow of information shapes history—as well as a rare glimpse in the soul of a hardcore geek." Jackie Cassada, in *Library Journal,* called *Cryptonomicon* "a story of epic proportions," and concluded: "Stephenson's freewheeling prose and ironic voice lend a sense of familiarity to a story that transcends the genre and demands a wide readership among fans of techno thrillers as well as a general audience." Reviewing *Cryptonomicon* for the *New York Times Book Review,* Dwight Gardner made a general observation about Stephenson's novels: "Despite all the high-tech frippery, there's something old-fashioned about Stephenson's work. He cares as much about telling good stories as he does about farming out cool ideas. There's a strong whiff of moralism in his books, too. The bay guys in his fiction—that is, anyone who stands in a well-intentioned hacker's way—meet bad ends."

Readers of *Cryptonomicon* were also pleased with the publication of Stephenson's genre-defying and often unwieldy historical trilogy the "Baroque Cycle," which features as a major character the ancestor of *Cryptonomicon*'s Waterhouses. The first installation of the trilogy, the almost 1,000-page *Quicksilver,* chronicles the adventures of a group of alchemists and vagabonds in the seventeenth and eighteenth century—some fictional, some not—including Daniel Waterhouse, Isaac Newton, and Samuel Pepys. A *Kirkus Reviews* critic commented on the book's "meandering, dense narrative," but called such a caveat "a trifle compared to [Stephenson's] awe-inspiring ambition and cheeky sense of humor." Grossman, writing for *Time,* noted that *Quicksilver* "will defy any category, genre, precedent or label," and praised Stephenson's ability to bring history to life: "he makes complex ideas clear, and he makes them funny, heartbreaking and thrilling."

The "Baroque Cycle" continues in the second volume, *The Confusion,* and the final installment, *The System of the World.* In the second book, Stephenson follows two parallel storylines that feature Jack Shaftoe and Eliza, characters from *Quicksilver.* A *Publishers Weekly* reviewer called *The Confusion* a "vast, splendid, and absorbing sequel," and while the reviewer noted that "one can't call anything about the Baroque Cycle 'brisk,'" the book's "richness of detail and language" received praise. A *Kirkus Reviews* critic summarized: "Packed with more derring-do than a dozen pirate films and with smarter, sparklier dialogue than a handful of Pulitzer winners, this is run-and-gun adventure fiction of the most literate kind."

BIOGRAPHICAL AND CRITICAL SOURCES:

PERIODICALS

Booklist, April 1, 1999, p. 1366.

Entertainment Weekly, January 27, 1995, p. 43; June 23, 1995, p. 60; March 15, 1996, p. 59; May 21, 1999, p. 24.

Kirkus Reviews, July 15, 2003, review of *Quicksilver,* p. 935; February 1, 2004, review of *The Confusion,* p. 107.
Library Journal, May 15, 1999, p. 130.
Los Angeles Times, September 7, 1984.
Nation, November 15, 1993, p. 580.
Newsweek, May 10, 1999, p. 90.
New York Times Book Review, September 30, 1984; December 14, 1992; March 12, 1995; May 23, 1999.
Publishers Weekly, March 16, 1992, p. 74; December 19, 1994, p. 49; March 22, 1999, p. 67; May 12, 1999, p. 24; August 25, 2003, review of *Quicksilver,* p. 39; March 29, 2004, review of *The Confusion,* p. 38.
Time, September 8, 2003, Lev Grossman, "Isaac Newton, Action Hero," p. 91.

ONLINE

Neal Stephenson Web site, http://www.nealstephenson.com/ (August 17, 2004).

* * *

STERLING, Brett
See BRADBURY, Ray

* * *

STERLING, Bruce 1954-

PERSONAL: Born April 14, 1954, in Brownsville, TX; son of M.B. (an engineer) and Gloria (a registered nurse; maiden name, Vela) Sterling; married Nancy Adell Baxter, November 20, 1979. *Education:* Attended University of Texas at Austin, 1972-76. *Politics:* "Green."

ADDRESSES: *Agent*—Writers House, Inc., 21 West 26th St., New York, NY 10010.

CAREER: Texas Legislative Council, Austin, proofreader, 1977-83; writer, 1983—.

MEMBER: American Association for the Advancement of Science, Science Fiction Writers of America, Electronic Frontier Foundation.

AWARDS, HONORS: Hugo Award for Best Novelette, Mystery Writers of America, 1997, for *Bicycle Repairman,* and 1999, for *Taklamakan;* three stories, "Swarm," "Spider Rose," and "Cicada Queen," have been nominated for Hugo and/or Nebula awards.

WRITINGS:

SCIENCE FICTION

Involution Ocean (novel), Berkley Publishing (New York, NY), 1977.
The Artificial Kid (novel), Harper (New York, NY), 1980.
Schismatrix (novel), Arbor House, 1985.
(Editor and contributor) *Mirrorshades: The Cyberpunk Anthology,* Arbor House, 1986.
Islands in the Net (novel), Arbor House, 1988.
Crystal Express (story collection; includes "Swarm," "Spider Rose," and "Cicada Queen"), illustrated by Rick Lieder, Arkham House, 1989.
(With William Gibson) *The Difference Engine* (novel), Bantam (New York, NY), 1990.
Globalhead (story collection), Ziesing (Shingletown, CA), 1992.
Distraction: A Novel, Bantam Books (New York, NY), 1998.
Zeitgeist, Bantam Books (New York, NY), 2000.
The Zenith Angle, Del Rey (New York, NY), 2004.

Also author of the novelettes *Bicycle Repairman* and *Taklamakan.*

NONFICTION

The Hacker Crackdown: Law and Disorder on the Electronic Frontier (nonfiction), Bantam (New York, NY), 1992.
(With Hans Moravec and David Brin) *Thinking Robots, an Aware Internet, and Cyberpunk Librarians: The LITA President's Program* (collected essays), edited by R. Bruce Miller and Milton T. Wolf, Library and Information Technology Association, 1992.
Globalhead: Stories, Mark V. Ziesing (Shingletown, CA), 1992.
Heavy Weather, Bantam (New York, NY), 1994.
Schismatrix Plus, Ace Books (New York, NY), 1996.
Holy Fire: A Novel, Bantam (New York, NY), 1996.
The Artificial Kid, HardWired (San Francisco, CA), 1997.
Tomorrow Now: Envisioning the Next Fifty Years, Random House (New York, NY), 2002.
(Author of introduction) Jules Verne, *The Mysterious Island,* Signet (New York, NY), 2004.

Work represented in anthologies, including *Universe 13,* edited by Terry Carr, 1983; *Heatseeker,* edited by John Shirley, compiled and with a foreword by Stephen

P. Brown, Scream/Press, 1989; *Semiotext(e) SF,* edited by Rudy Rucker, Peter Lambourne Wilson, and Robert Anton Wilson, Autonomedia, 1990; *Universe 1,* edited by Robert Silverberg and Karen Haber, Doubleday, 1990; *When the Music's Over,* edited by Lewis Shiner, Bantam Spectra, 1991. Has written extensively online, including blogs and articles. Also contributor of numerous speculative fiction stories to periodicals, including *Omni, Isaac Asimov's Science Fiction Magazine, The Magazine of Fantasy and Science Fiction,* and *Interzone.*

SIDELIGHTS: Bruce Sterling is "the standard bearer of the cyberpunks, a loosely grouped cadre of science-fiction hotshots who have taken the genre by storm during the past few years," according to *Village Voice* critic Richard Gehr. The "cyberpunk" movement, described by Sterling as "an unholy alliance of the technical world of pop culture, visionary fluidity, and street-level anarchy" in his work *Mirrorshades: The Cyberpunk Anthology,* seeks to examine the benefits, as well as pose the troubling questions, that result when scientific discoveries push the boundaries of human knowledge.

Mirrorshades, edited by Sterling, collects twelve stories, including works by William Gibson, Rudy Rucker, and John Shirley, among others. "Gaze into a pair of mirrorshades and what do you see?" asks Gehr. "Yourself, and the world you live in. Slip a pair on and what happens? Instant anonymity, outlaws, police, and thieves. This metaphor is something a culture addict can get behind, and no one has gotten further behind it than Bruce Sterling." Though Gehr praised Sterling's introduction, calling it "a dazzling, eye-opening ride through the modern world," he later cautioned: "The remainder of the book barely justifies its claims." Referring to the final story, "Mozart in Mirrorshades," written by Sterling and Lewis Shiner, Gehr declared that it "drags history's major youth icon kicking and screaming (for joy) into the present, summing up the cyberpunk aesthetic in a torrent of wild action and virtuoso speculation." Gerald Jonas, writing in *New York Times Book Review,* summarized: "What we find [in the stories] is a science fiction that takes the runaway power of science and technology for granted, that plays paranoia straight and finds comic relief in anarchy, and gives center stage to characters who ask of the future not, 'What's new under the sun?' but 'What's in it for me?'"

Sterling's next work, *Islands in the Net,* pits protagonist Laura Webster, a resort manager, against a complex web of conspiracy when she discovers her corporate employer's collusion with information pirates in this novel of intrigue set in the near future. In *Analog Science Fiction/Science Fact,* Tom Easton explained that "the world is growing ever more tightly linked by computerized data exchanges, summing up to the 'Net ' of the title, but there are a few places—islands—that parasitize the Net as data pirates (e.g., Grenada, Singapore). There is also Africa, so beset by ecological and political disaster that it is a metaphorical island totally surrounded by the Net, but not part of it."

Roz Kaveney, reviewing *Islands in the Net* in the *Washington Post Book World,* stated: "Sterling has a real gift for turning ideas from the science pages of newspapers into entertaining science-fictional conceits." Kaveney further noted: "There is nothing cold or heartless about Sterling's hip portrayal of the early twenty-first century" and terms the novel "a series of gaudy but information-packed tourist maps of a future." Gerald Jonas, in the *New York Times Book Review,* remarked that Sterling "reveals himself . . . to be a serious and insightful futurist" and added that although "the always surprising plot jumps around the world," the author "remains in firm control throughout." In the *Nation,* Erik Davis wrote: "Bruce Sterling does not have Gibson's visual imagination nor his infectious style, but he fleshes out his cyberpunk imaginings with more concentrated thought." "Sterling himself is steeped in cutting-edge technologies," Davis continued, "and the knowledge shows itself." He concluded that the book "is like an intelligent computer simulation of global politics."

Crystal Express comprises twelve stories, including the Nebula and Hugo Award-nominees "Swarm," "Spider Rose," and "Cicada Queen." Gregory Feeley, in the *Washington Post Book World,* commented that Sterling's writings are "characterized by intellectual playfulness, a careful, almost mannered style and a flamboyant virtuosity in matters of formal invention." Dan Chow, reviewing the collection in *Locus,* judged, "If anything is repetitive in *Crystal Express,* it is the author's remarkable knowledge of his characters and settings, no matter how diverse they might be. . . . Taken as a whole, they form a meditation greater than the sum of the stories themselves." Chow declared that "the cyberpunk label is far too restrictive for this author" and deemed Sterling a writer "of dazzling range and insight."

The Difference Engine, written with Gibson, is a novel falling into the "alternative history" subgenre of science fiction. The book, observed Paul Delaney in the *London Review of Books,* "belongs to the thriving Post-modern genre of historical pastiche" and "shuffles the cards of history in order to prove by example the 'Wiener thesis' of recent years: that Britain's ambivalent response to the Industrial Revolution has led to its relative economic backwardness today." The "difference engines" are steam-driven computers, threatened by the Modus, a terrorist-wielded computer virus. Delaney summarized the political scenario: "The Industrial Radicals have made Britain a richer and more egalitarian country; but they have also turned their information system into a political weapon. . . . Herein lies a favourite theme of Gibson and Sterling: the official institutions of a society always work on yesterday's agenda, while the future is being made by an underground of anarchists, criminals and fanatics."

The onset of a new century found Sterling, like many people, pondering what the future could bring. Using the seven ages of humanity outlined in Shakespeare's *As You Like It,* he explored this topic in *Tomorrow Now: Envisioning the Next Fifty Years,* with thoughtful essays that do not try to scare readers to death with horrific predictions. The book was well received. *Booklist* reviewer Margaret Flanagan wrote, "Often surprising, always humorous, Sterling's individual slant on what may evolve serves as a visionary overview of the twenty-first century."

Sterling's novel *The Zenith Angle* uses fiction to look at life in a post-9/11 world. The novel's protagonist, Derek Vandeveer, leaves the private sector to work for the government, trying to keep cyberspace secure. It is a frustrating job as Vandeveer tries to find out who has attacked a top secret satellite. A *Library Journal* reviewer hailed the book as "highly recommendable" because it incorporates "up-to-the-minute technology with engaging characters and a clear vision of tomorrow."

Sterling once commented that his writing is concerned with "technological literacy, imaginative concentration, visionary intensity, and a global, twenty-first-century point of view. I want to bridge the gap between the two cultures, or at least shout loudly from the bottom of the gulf."

BIOGRAPHICAL AND CRITICAL SOURCES:

BOOKS

Contemporary Literary Criticism, Volume 72, Thomson Gale (Detroit, MI), 1992.

McCaffrey, Larry, editor, *Across the Wounded Galaxies: Interviews with Contemporary American Science Fiction Writers,* University of Illinois Press (Bloomington, IL), 1990.

Spinrad, Norman *Science Fiction in the Real World,* Southern Illinois University Press (Carbondale, IL), 1990.

PERIODICALS

Analog Science Fiction/Science Fact, December, 1988, pp. 163-165.

Booklist, October 15, 1996, p. 408; November 15, 1998, p. 574; November 1, 2002, p. 456.

Entertainment Weekly, January 31, 1992, p. 54; April 23, 2004, p. 86.

Fortune, October 9, 2000, p. 323.

Kirkus Reviews, September 15, 2002, p. 1373; April 1, 2004 p. 304.

Library Journal, October 15, 2000, p. 108; May 15, 2004, p. 118

Locus, September, 1989, p. 27.

London Review of Books, August 29, 1991, p. 22.

Nation, May 8, 1989, p. 636.

New York Times Book Review, January 18, 1987, p. 33; October 2, 1988, p. 30; December 20, 1992, p. 18; December 27, 1992, p. 22.

PC Magazine, May 25, 1993, p. 85.

Popular Science, June 1, 2004, p. 116.

Publishers Weekly, September 7, 1992, p. 87; September 5, 1994, p. 97; August 5, 1996. p. 435; November 9, 1998, p. 60; September 23, 2002, p. 62-63; April 5, 2004, p. 46.

Reason, January, 2004, pp. 42-50.

Texas Monthly, December, 1992, pp. 98-100; December, 1995, p. 28.

Time, December 21, 1998, p. 66.

Village Voice, February 3, 1987, p. 50; January 17, 1989, p. 58.

Village Voice Literary Supplement, December, 1992, p. 5.

Washington Post Book World, June 30, 1985, p. 6; June 26, 1988, p. 10; February 26, 1989, p. 12; August 27, 1989, p. 11.

Whole Earth Review, summer, 1993, p. 27.

ONLINE

Edge Foundation Web site, http://www.edge/org/ (August 20, 2004), biography of Bruce Sterling.

GORP Web site, http://away.com/ (August 20, 2004), "Bruce Sterling: The Future of the Outdoors: End of the Trail."

Reason Online, http://www.reason.com/ (August 20, 2004), Mike Godwin, "Cybergreen: Bruce Sterling on Media, Design, Fiction, and the Future."

Rice University Web Site, http://www.rice.edu/ (August 20, 2004), "Bruce Sterling."

* * *

STINE, Jovial Bob
See STINE, R.L.

* * *

STINE, R.L. 1943-

(Eric Affabee, Zachary Blue, Jovial Bob Stine, Robert Lawrence Stine)

PERSONAL: Born October 8, 1943 in Columbus, OH; son of Lewis (a shipping manager) and Anne (Feinstein) Stine; married Jane Waldhorn (owner/managing director of Parachute Press), June 22, 1969; children: Matthew Daniel. *Education:* Ohio State University, B.A. 1965; graduate study at New York University, 1966-67. *Religion:* Jewish. *Hobbies and other interests:* Swimming, watching old movie classics from the 1930s and 1940s, reading (especially P.G. Wodehouse novels).

ADDRESSES: Office—c/o Parachute Press, 156 Fifth Avenue, New York, NY 10010.

CAREER: Author of books for children and adults, 1980—. Social studies teacher at a junior high school in Columbus, OH, 1965-66; writer for several magazines in New York, NY, 1966-68; Scholastic, Inc., New York, NY, assistant editor, *Junior Scholastic* magazine, 1968-71, editor, *Search* magazine, 1972-75, editor/creator, *Bananas* magazine, 1975-84, editor/creator, *Maniac* magazine, 1984-85; head writer for *Eureeka's Castle,* Nickelodeon cable television network, 1986-87.

MEMBER: Writers Guild of America, Mystery Writers of America.

AWARDS, HONORS: Children's Choice Award, American Library Association, for several novels; Lifetime Achievement Award, Ohioanna Library Association; *Guinness World Records* listing for best-selling children's series in history, 2000, for the "Goosebumps" series; three time winner of Nickelodeon Kid's Choice Award.

WRITINGS:

YOUNG ADULT NOVELS

Blind Date, Scholastic (New York, NY), 1986.
Twisted, Scholastic (New York, NY), 1987.
Broken Date ("Crosswinds" series), Simon & Schuster (New York, NY), 1988.
The Baby-Sitter, Scholastic (New York, NY), 1989.
Phone Calls, Archway (New York, NY), 1990.
How I Broke up with Ernie, Archway (New York, NY), 1990.
Curtains, Archway (New York, NY), 1990.
The Boyfriend, Scholastic (New York, NY), 1990.
Beach Party, Scholastic (New York, NY), 1990.
Snowman, Scholastic (New York, NY), 1991.
The Girlfriend, Scholastic (New York, NY), 1991.
Baby-Sitter II, Scholastic (New York, NY), 1991.
Beach House, Scholastic (New York, NY), 1992.
Hit and Run, Scholastic (New York, NY), 1992.
Hitchhiker, Scholastic (New York, NY), 1993.
Baby-sitter III, Scholastic (New York, NY), 1993.
The Dead Girl Friend, Scholastic (New York, NY), 1993.
Halloween Night, Scholastic (New York, NY), 1993.
Call Waiting, Scholastic (New York, NY), 1994.
Halloween Night 2, Scholastic (New York, NY), 1994.

"FEAR STREET" SERIES

The New Girl, Archway (New York, NY), 1989.
The Surprise Party, Archway (New York, NY), 1990.
The Stepsister, Archway (New York, NY), 1990.
Missing, Archway (New York, NY), 1990.
Halloween Party, Archway (New York, NY), 1990.
The Wrong Number, Archway (New York, NY), 1990.
The Sleepwalker, Archway (New York, NY) 1991.
Ski Weekend, Archway (New York, NY), 1991.
Silent Night, Archway (New York, NY), 1991.
The Secret Bedroom, Archway (New York, NY), 1991.
The Overnight, Archway (New York, NY), 1991.
Lights Out, Archway (New York, NY), 1991.
Haunted, Archway (New York, NY), 1991.
The Fire Game, Archway (New York, NY), 1991.
The Knife, Archway (New York, NY), 1992.
Prom Queen, Archway (New York, NY), 1992.

First Date, Archway (New York, NY), 1992, 2005.
The Best Friend, Archway (New York, NY), 1992.
Sunburn, Archway (New York, NY), 1993.
The Cheater, Archway (New York, NY), 1993.
The New Boy, Archway (New York, NY), 1994.
Bad Dreams, Archway (New York, NY), 1994.
The Dare, Archway (New York, NY), 1994.
Double Date, Archway (New York, NY), 1994.
The First Horror, Archway (New York, NY), 1994.
The Mind Reader, Archway (New York, NY), 1994.
One Evil Summer, Archway (New York, NY), 1994.
The Second Horror, Archway (New York, NY), 1994.
The Third Horror, Archway (New York, NY), 1994.
The Thrill Club, Archway (New York, NY), 1994.
College Weekend, Archway (New York, NY), 1995.
Final Grade, Archway (New York, NY), 1995.
The Stepsister 2, Archway (New York, NY), 1995.
Switched, Archway (New York, NY), 1995.
Truth or Dare, Archway (New York, NY), 1995.
Wrong Number 2, Archway (New York, NY), 1995.
What Holly Heard, Pocket Books (New York, NY), 1996.
The Face, Pocket Books (New York, NY), 1996.
Secret Admirer, Pocket Books (New York, NY), 1996.
The Perfect Date, Pocket Books (New York, NY), 1996.
The Boy Next Door, Simon & Schuster (New York, NY), 1996.
Night Games, Pocket Books (New York, NY), 1996.
Runaway, Archway (New York, NY), 1997.
Killer's Kiss, Archway (New York, NY), 1997.
All-Night Party, Archway (New York, NY), 1997.
The Rich Girl, Archway (New York, NY), 1997.
Cat, Archway (New York, NY), 1997.
Fear Hall: The Beginning, Archway (New York, NY), 1997.
Fear Hall: The Conclusion, Archway (New York, NY), 1997.

"FEAR STREET SUPER CHILLER" SERIES

Party Summer, Archway (New York, NY), 1991.
Goodnight Kiss, Archway (New York, NY), 1992.
Silent Night, Archway (New York, NY), 1992.
Broken Hearts, Archway (New York, NY), 1993.
Silent Night II, Archway (New York, NY), 1993.
The Dead Lifeguard, Archway (New York, NY), 1994.
Bad Moonlight, Archway (New York, NY), 1995.
Dead End, Archway (New York, NY), 1995.
High Tide, Archway (New York, NY), 1997.

"FEAR STREET CHEERLEADERS" SERIES

The First Evil, Archway (New York, NY), 1992.
The Second Evil, Archway (New York, NY), 1992.
The Third Evil, Archway (New York, NY), 1992.
The New Evil, Archway (New York, NY), 1994.

"FEAR STREET SAGA" SERIES

The Betrayal, Archway (New York, NY), 1993.
The Secret, Archway (New York, NY), 1993.
The Burning, Archway (New York, NY), 1993.
A New Fear, Pocket Books (New York, NY), 1996.
House of Whispers, Simon & Schuster (New York, NY), 1996.
The Hidden Evil, Archway (New York, NY), 1997.
Daughters of Silence, Archway (New York, NY), 1997.
Children of Fear, Archway (New York, NY), 1997.

"GHOSTS OF FEAR STREET" SERIES

Nightmare in 3-D, Pocket Books (New York, NY), 1996.
Stay away from the Treehouse, Pocket Books (New York, NY), 1996.
Eye of the Fortuneteller, Pocket Books (New York, NY), 1996.
Fright Knight, Pocket Books (New York, NY), 1996.
Revenge of the Shadow People, Pocket Books (New York, NY), 1996.
The Bugman Lives, Pocket Books (New York, NY), 1996.
The Boy Who Ate Fear Street, Pocket Books (New York, NY), 1996.
Night of the Werecat, Pocket Books (New York, NY), 1996.
Body Switchers from Outer Space, Pocket Books (New York, NY), 1996.
Fright Christmas, Pocket Books (New York, NY), 1996.
Don't Ever Get Sick at Granny's, Pocket Books (New York, NY), 1997.

"GOOSEBUMPS" SERIES

Welcome to Dead House, Scholastic (New York, NY), 1992.
Stay out of the Basement, Scholastic (New York, NY), 1992.

Monster Blood, Scholastic (New York, NY), 1992.
Say Cheese and Die, Scholastic (New York, NY), 1992.
The Curse of the Mummy's Tomb, Scholastic (New York, NY), 1993.
Let's Get Invisible, Scholastic (New York, NY), 1993.
Night of the Living Dummy, Scholastic (New York, NY), 1993.
The Girl Who Cried Monster, Scholastic (New York, NY), 1993.
Welcome to Camp Nightmare, Scholastic (New York, NY), 1993.
The Ghost Next Door, Scholastic (New York, NY), 1993.
The Haunted Mask, Scholastic (New York, NY), 1993.
Be Careful What You Wish For, Scholastic (New York, NY), 1993.
Piano Lessons Can Be Murder, Scholastic (New York, NY), 1993.
The Werewolf of Fever Swamp, Scholastic (New York, NY), 1993.
You Can't Scare Me, Scholastic (New York, NY), 1993.
One Day at Horrorland, Scholastic (New York, NY), 1994.
Why I'm Afraid of Bees, Scholastic (New York, NY), 1994.
Monster Blood 2, Scholastic (New York, NY), 1994.
Deep Trouble, Scholastic (New York, NY), 1994.
The Scarecrow Walks at Midnight, Scholastic (New York, NY), 1994.
Go Eat Worms!, Scholastic (New York, NY), 1994.
Ghost Beach, Scholastic (New York, NY), 1994.
Return of the Mummy, Scholastic (New York, NY), 1994.
Phantom of the Auditorium, Scholastic (New York, NY), 1994.
Attack of the Mutant, Scholastic (New York, NY), 1994.
My Hairiest Adventure, Scholastic (New York, NY), 1994.
A Night in Terror Tower, Scholastic (New York, NY), 1995.
The Cuckoo Clock of Doom, Scholastic (New York, NY), 1995.
Monster Blood 3, Scholastic (New York, NY), 1995.
It Came from beneath the Sink, Scholastic (New York, NY), 1995.
The Night of the Living Dummy 2, Scholastic (New York, NY), 1995.
The Barking Ghost, Scholastic (New York, NY), 1995.
The Horror at Camp Jellyjam, Scholastic (New York, NY), 1995.
Revenge of the Lawn Gnomes, Scholastic (New York, NY), 1995.
A Shocker on Shock Street, Scholastic (New York, NY), 1995.
The Haunted Mask 2, Scholastic (New York, NY), 1995.
The Headless Ghost, Scholastic (New York, NY), 1995.
The Abominable Snowman of Pasadena, Scholastic (New York, NY), 1995.
How I Got My Shrunken Head, Scholastic (New York, NY), 1996.
Night of the Living Dummy 3, Scholastic (New York, NY), 1996.
Bad Hare Day, Scholastic (New York, NY), 1996.
Egg Monsters from Mars, Scholastic (New York, NY), 1996.
The Beast from the East, Scholastic (New York, NY), 1996.
Say Cheese and Die—Again!, Scholastic (New York, NY), 1996.
Ghost Camp, Scholastic (New York, NY), 1996.
How to Kill a Monster, Scholastic (New York, NY), 1996.
Legend of the Lost Legend, Scholastic (New York, NY), 1996.
Attack of the Jack-o'-Lanterns, Scholastic (New York, NY), 1996.
Vampire Breath, Scholastic (New York, NY), 1996.
Calling All Creeps!, Scholastic (New York, NY), 1996.
Beware the Snowman, Scholastic (New York, NY), 1997.
How I Learned to Fly, Scholastic (New York, NY), 1997.
Chicken, Chicken, Scholastic (New York, NY), 1997.
Don't Go to Sleep!, Scholastic (New York, NY), 1997.
The Blob That Ate Everyone, Scholastic (New York, NY), 1997.
The Curse of Camp Cold Lake, Scholastic (New York, NY), 1997.
My Best Friend Is Invisible, Scholastic (New York, NY), 1997.
Deep Trouble II, Scholastic (New York, NY), 1997.
The Haunted School, Scholastic (New York, NY), 1997.
Werewolf Skin, Scholastic (New York, NY), 1997.
I Live in Your Basement!, Scholastic (New York, NY), 1997.
Monster Blood IV, Scholastic (New York, NY), 1997.

Also author of "Goosebumps Presents" books based on the television series, including *The Girl Who Cried Monster,* 1996, and *Welcome to Camp Nightmare,* 1996.

"GIVE YOURSELF GOOSEBUMPS" SERIES

Escape from the Carnival of Horrors, Scholastic (New York, NY), 1995.

Tick Tock, You're Dead, Scholastic (New York, NY), 1995.
Trapped in Bat Wing Hall, Scholastic (New York, NY), 1995.
The Deadly Experiments of Dr. Eeek, Scholastic (New York, NY), 1996.
Night in Werewolf Woods, Scholastic (New York, NY), 1996.
Beware of the Purple Peanut Butter, Scholastic (New York, NY), 1996.
Under the Magician's Spell, Scholastic (New York, NY), 1996.
The Curse of the Creeping Coffin, Scholastic (New York, NY), 1996.
The Knight in Screaming Armor, Scholastic (New York, NY), 1996.
Diary of a Mad Mummy, Scholastic (New York, NY), 1996.
Deep in the Jungle of Doom, Scholastic (New York, NY), 1996.
Welcome to the Wicked Wax Museum, Scholastic (New York, NY), 1996.
Scream of the Evil Genie, Scholastic (New York, NY), 1997.
The Creepy Creations of Professor Shock, Scholastic (New York, NY), 1997.
Please Don't Feed the Vampire, Scholastic (New York, NY), 1997.
Secret Agent Grandma, Scholastic (New York, NY), 1997.
The Little Comic Shop of Horrors, Scholastic (New York, NY), 1997.
Attack of the Beastly Babysitter, Scholastic (New York, NY), 1997.
Escape from Camp Run for Your Life, Scholastic (New York, NY), 1997.
Toy Terror: Batteries Included, Scholastic (New York, NY), 1997.
The Twisted Tale of Tiki Island, Scholastic (New York, NY), 1997.
Return to the Carnival of Horrors, Scholastic (New York, NY), 1998.
Zapped in Space, Scholastic (New York, NY), 1998.
Lost In Stinkeye Swamp, Scholastic (New York, NY), 1998.
Shop Till You Drop . . . Dead, Scholastic (New York, NY), 1998.
Alone in Snakebite Canyon, Scholastic (New York, NY), 1998.
Checkout Time at the Dead-End Hotel, Scholastic (New York, NY), 1998.
Night of a Thousand Claws, Scholastic (New York, NY), 1998.
You're Plant Food!, Scholastic (New York, NY), 1998.
Werewolf of Twisted Tree Lodge, Scholastic (New York, NY), 1998.
It's Only a Nightmare!, Scholastic (New York, NY), 1998.
It Came from the Internet, Scholastic (New York, NY), 1999.
Elevator to Nowhere, Scholastic (New York, NY), 1999.
Hocus-Pocus Horror, Scholastic (New York, NY), 1999.
Ship of Ghouls, Scholastic (New York, NY), 1999.
Escape from Horror House, Scholastic (New York, NY), 1999.
Into the Twister of Terror, Scholastic (New York, NY), 1999.
Scary Birthday to You!, Scholastic (New York, NY), 1999.
Zombie School, Scholastic (New York, NY), 1999.
Danger Time, Scholastic (New York, NY), 2000.
All-Day Nightmare, Scholastic (New York, NY), 2000.

"GIVE YOURSELF GOOSEBUMPS SPECIAL EDITION" SERIES

Into the Jaws of Doom, Scholastic (New York, NY), 1998.
Return to Terror Tower, Scholastic (New York, NY), 1998.
Trapped in the Circus of Fear, Scholastic (New York, NY), 1998.
One Night in Payne House, Scholastic (New York, NY), 1998.
The Curse of the Cave Creatures, Scholastic (New York, NY), 1999.
Revenge of the Body Squeezers, Scholastic (New York, NY), 1999.
Trick or . . . Trapped, Scholastic (New York, NY), 1999.
Weekend at Poison Lake, Scholastic (New York, NY), 1999.

"GOOSEBUMPS 2000" SERIES

Cry of the Cat, Scholastic (New York, NY), 1998.
Bride of the Living Dummy, Scholastic (New York, NY), 1998.
Creature Teacher, Scholastic (New York, NY), 1998.
Invasion of the Body Squeezers Part 1, Scholastic (New York, NY), 1998.
Invasion of the Body Squeezers Part 2, Scholastic (New York, NY), 1998.
I Am Your Evil Twin, Scholastic (New York, NY), 1998.
Revenge R Us, Scholastic (New York, NY), 1998.

Fright Camp, Scholastic (New York, NY), 1998.
Are You Terrified Yet?, Scholastic (New York, NY), 1998.
Headless Halloween, Scholastic (New York, NY), 1999.
Attack of the Graveyard Ghouls, Scholastic (New York, NY), 1999.
Brain Juice, Scholastic (New York, NY), 1999.
Return to Horrorland, Scholastic (New York, NY), 1999.
Jekyll and Heidi, Scholastic (New York, NY), 1999.
Scream School, Scholastic (New York, NY), 1999.
The Mummy Walks, Scholastic (New York, NY), 1999.
The Werewolf in the Living Room, Scholastic (New York, NY), 1999.
Horrors of the Black Ring, Scholastic (New York, NY), 1999.
Return to Ghost Camp, Scholastic (New York, NY), 1999.
Be Afraid—Be Very Afraid!, Scholastic (New York, NY), 1999.
The Haunted Car!, Scholastic (New York, NY), 1999.
Full Moon Fever, Scholastic (New York, NY), 1999.
Slappy's Nightmare, Scholastic (New York, NY), 1999.
Earth Geeks Must Go!, Scholastic (New York, NY), 1999.
Ghost in the Mirror, Scholastic (New York, NY), 2000.

Also author of *Tales to Give You Goosebumps,* and *More Tales to Give You Goosebumps.*

"NIGHTMARE ROOM" SERIES

Liar, Liar, HarperCollins (New York, NY), 2000.
Don't Forget Me!, Avon (New York, NY), 2000.
Dear Diary, I'm Dead, HarperCollins (New York, NY), 2000.
Shadow Girl, Avon (New York, NY), 2001.
The Howler, Avon (New York, NY), 2001.
Camp Nowhere, HarperCollins (New York, NY), 2001.
They Call Me Creature, HarperCollins (New York, NY), 2001.

JUVENILE

The Time Raider, illustrations by David Febland, Scholastic (New York, NY), 1982.
The Golden Sword of Dragonwalk, illustrations by Febland, Scholastic (New York, NY), 1983.
Horrors of the Haunted Museum, Scholastic (New York, NY), 1984.
Instant Millionaire, illustrations by Jowill Woodman, Scholastic (New York, NY), 1984.
Through the Forest of Twisted Dreams, Avon (New York, NY), 1984.
The Badlands of Hark, illustrations by Bob Roper, Scholastic (New York, NY), 1985.
The Invaders of Hark, Scholastic (New York, NY), 1985.
Demons of the Deep, illustrations by Fred Carrillo, Golden Books (New York, NY), 1985.
Challenge of the Wolf Knight (*"Wizards, Warriors, and You"* Series), Avon (New York, NY), 1985.
James Bond in Win, Place, or Die, Ballantine (New York, NY), 1985.
Conquest of the Time Master, Avon (New York, NY), 1985.
Cavern of the Phantoms, Avon (New York, NY), 1986.
Mystery of the Imposter, Avon (New York, NY), 1986.
Golden Girl and the Vanishing Unicorn (*"Golden Girl"* series), Ballantine (New York, NY), 1986.
The Beast, Minstrel (New York, NY), 1994.
I Saw You That Night!, Scholastic (New York, NY), 1994.
The Beast 2, Minstrel (New York, NY), 1995.
When Good Ghouls Go Bad, Avon (New York, NY), 2001.

JUVENILE: "INDIANA JONES" SERIES

Indiana Jones and the Curse of Horror Island, Ballantine (New York, NY), 1984.
Indiana Jones and the Giants of the Silver Tower, Ballantine (New York, NY), 1984.
Indiana Jones and the Cult of the Mummy's Crypt, Ballantine (New York, NY), 1985.
Indiana Jones and the Ape Slaves of Howling Island, Ballantine (New York, NY), 1987.

JUVENILE: "G.I. JOE" SERIES

Operation: Deadly Decoy, Ballantine (New York, NY), 1986.
Operation: Mindbender, Ballantine (New York, NY), 1986.
Serpentor and the Mummy Warrior, 1987.
Jungle Raid, Ballantine (New York, NY), 1988.
Siege of Serpentor, Ballantine (New York, NY), 1988.

JUVENILE; UNDER NAME JOVIAL BOB STINE

The Absurdly Silly Encyclopedia and Flyswatter, illustrations by Bob Taylor, Scholastic (New York, NY), 1978.

How to Be Funny: An Extremely Silly Guidebook, illustrations by Carol Nicklaus, Dutton (New York, NY), 1978.

The Complete Book of Nerds, illustrations by Sam Viviano, Scholastic (New York, NY), 1979.

The Dynamite Do-It-Yourself Pen Pal Kit, illustrations by Jared Lee, Scholastic (New York, NY), 1980.

Dynamite's Funny Book of the Sad Facts of Life, illustrations by Jared Lee, Scholastic (New York, NY), 1980.

Going Out! Going Steady! Going Bananas!, photographs by Dan Nelken, Scholastic (New York, NY), 1980.

The Pig's Book of World Records, illustrations by Peter Lippman, Random House (New York, NY), 1980.

(With wife, Jane Stine) *The Sick of Being Sick Book,* edited by Ann Durrell, illustrations by Carol Nicklaus, Dutton (New York, NY), 1980.

Bananas Looks at TV, Scholastic (New York, NY), 1981.

The Beast Handbook, illustrations by Bob Taylor, Scholastic (New York, NY), 1981.

(With J. Stine) *The Cool Kids' Guide to Summer Camp,* illustrations by Jerry Zimmerman, Scholastic (New York, NY), 1981.

Gnasty Gnomes, illustrations by Peter Lippman, Random House (New York, NY), 1981.

Don't Stand in the Soup, illustrations by Carol Nicklaus, Bantam (New York, NY), 1982.

(With J. Stine) *Bored with Being Bored!: How to Beat the Boredom Blahs,* illustrations by Jerry Zimmerman, Four Winds (New York, NY), 1982.

Blips!: The First Book of Video Game Funnies, illustrations by Bryan Hendrix, Scholastic (New York, NY), 1983.

(With J. Stine) *Everything You Need to Survive: Brothers and Sisters,* illustrated by Sal Murdocca, Random House (New York, NY), 1983.

(With J. Stine) *Everything You Need to Survive: First Dates,* illustrated by Sal Murdocca, Random House (New York, NY), 1983.

(With J. Stine) *Everything You Need to Survive: Homework,* illustrated by Sal Murdocca, Random House (New York, NY), 1983.

(With J. Stine) *Everything You Need to Survive: Money Problems,* illustrated by Sal Murdocca, Random House (New York, NY), 1983.

Jovial Bob's Computer Joke Book, Scholastic (New York, NY), 1985

Miami Mice, illustrations by Eric Gurney, Scholastic (New York, NY), 1986.

One Hundred and One Silly Monster Jokes, Scholastic (New York, NY), 1986.

The Doggone Dog Joke Book, Parachute Press, 1986.

Pork & Beans: Play Date, illustrations by José Aruego and Ariane Dewey, Scholastic (New York, NY), 1989.

Ghostbusters II Storybook, Scholastic (New York, NY), 1989.

One Hundred and One Vacation Jokes, illustrated by Rick Majica, Scholastic (New York, NY), 1990.

The Amazing Adventures of Me, Myself and I, Bantam (New York, NY), 1991.

OTHER

Superstitious (adult horror), Warner Books (New York, NY), 1995.

It Came from Ohio: My Life as a Writer, (autobiography), Scholastic (New York, NY), 1997.

Nightmare Hour (short stories), HarperCollins (New York, NY), 1999.

The Haunting Hour (short stories), HarperCollins (New York, NY), 2001.

Beware! R.L. Stine Picks His Favorite Scary Stories, HarperCollins (New York, NY), 2002.

Also author of several "Twistaplot" books for Scholastic and "You Choose the Storyline" books for Ballantine and Avon.

ADAPTATIONS: The "Goosebumps" series was produced by Scholastic Inc. as a live-action television series for the Fox Television Network beginning in 1995; *When Good Ghouls Go Bad* was adapted for video by Fox, 2001; *The Nightmare Room* series was adapted for a television show by Kids WB (Warner Brothers) network, 2001.

SIDELIGHTS: "As she gazed at the plate, the eggs shimmered, then transformed themselves. Corky's mouth dropped open as she now stared at two enormous wet eyeballs. 'No!' The eyeballs stared back at her. Their color darkened to gray. Then the gray became a sickening green, the green of decay, and a foul odor rose up from the plate." Where does R.L. Stine, the author of over two hundred books for children and teenagers, get ideas for scenes like this one? "That's the question people ask me most often, but to this date I don't really have a good answer," Stine once commented. "I get ideas from all kinds of places. People know how desperate I am for ideas, because I'm doing so many books, so they try to help me. Just recently I was on vacation, lying on the beach, talking to a guy I'd just met. I told him I wrote horror books, and he said, 'You should do one on earwigs. Earwigs are really scary.' Everybody has an idea . . . sometimes people send me things like newspaper clippings of stories they found. I actually did a 'Fear Street' based on a true story, about a girl who planned to murder her teacher. I've never dreamed an idea—kids always ask me if I have—and I've never woken up in the morning with one. It's a shame . . . I'm still waiting for that. Mostly, I spend a lot of time just thinking about it. My son always asks me, 'Dad, how do you get an idea?' And I have to say, 'You sit down and think until you have one.' He hates that answer, but I have no choice—I have to have the ideas."

With several best-selling series going full speed, Stine *really* didn't have a choice. For his popular "Fear Street" series and his "Goosebumps" series, Stine wrote twenty-four horror novels a year. His newest series, "Nightmare Room," required an equally gargantuan effort of wordsmithing. As if that weren't enough to keep him almost perpetually chained to his computer, Stine also does the occasional "special" title.

Stine claims he never planned to write horror novels in the first place. For many years, Stine was known as "Jovial Bob Stine," and his specialty was making younger kids laugh, not giving teens the shivers. He began his career in children's publishing at Scholastic, where he spent sixteen years working on four different magazines, two of which he created. These two periodicals, *Bananas* and *Maniac,* focused on humor, and eventually led Stine to his career as an author of children's books. Ellen Rudin, an editor at Dutton, was impressed with *Bananas,* and asked Stine to consider writing a humorous book for younger readers. Since starting his magazine career, Stine hadn't thought seriously about writing a book, but he readily agreed to work up an idea anyway. The result was *How to Be Funny* by Jovial Bob Stine, published in 1978. Many more funny books followed during the late seventies and well into the eighties. Most of these titles were published by several different publishing houses, and some were coauthored by Stine's wife, Jane (who at that time was the editor of *Dynamite,* another children's magazine published by Scholastic).

During the eighties, Stine also began writing "Twistaplot" books for Scholastic, as well as other "You Choose the Storyline" books for Ballantine and Avon, some under the pseudonyms Eric Affabee and Zachary Blue. These books, which featured as many as thirty endings and many plot twists, proved to be great training for future novel writing.

When Scholastic began having financial trouble in the mid-1980s, Stine was let go in a reorganization. Far from a personal disaster, however, being fired provided Stine with the opportunity to devote more time to writing books. It was around this time that Jean Feiwel, editorial director of Scholastic Books, suggested that the author try his hand at a horror novel. The result was *Blind Date,* which features a teenage boy with a memory lapse, the mysterious teenage girl who wants to date him, and plenty of twists and turns in the plot.

Like several of Stine's horror novels that have been written in the interim, *Blind Date* had a title long before it had characters or a storyline. Feiwel suggested the title, and Stine went home to build a novel around it. Since then, titles often come to him before the stories themselves. "If I can get a title first, then I start getting ideas for it. Like *The Baby-sitter.* You start to think, what's scary about being a baby-sitter? Or *The Stepsister* . . . what would be scary about getting a new stepsister? Usually the title will lead me to ideas about what the book should be," Stine once commented.

This same process worked for Stine's "Fear Street" series. With the success of *Blind Date* and two Scholastic novels that followed, *Twisted* and *The Baby-sitter,* it occurred to the author and his wife that a series of novels that came out on a regular basis might sell well. By this time, Jane had also left Scholastic to open her own book packaging company, Parachute Press. Jane suggested that Stine come up with a concept for a series that she could sell through Parachute Press. "So I sat down and thought," Stine once remarked. "When the words 'Fear Street' sort of magically appeared, I wrote them down, and then came up with the concept."

The "Fear Street" series, which now has one hundred titles and millions of copies in print, is a collection of novels connected primarily by their setting. The main characters usually reside on Fear Street, a place "where your worst nightmares live," according to the cover copy on early titles. All the series' characters attend Shadyside High, a school where the death rate must be horrific, since nearly every book features at least one murder.

As Paul Gray noted in *Time* magazine, "Fear Street" stories, like other "teen tinglers," subscribe to "a fairly consistent set of formulas." The teenage heroes or heroines are normal (although not always nice) kids who suddenly find their lives fraught with danger. Sometimes the menace comes from supernatural forces, as in the "Cheerleaders" trilogy. The first book of this series introduces Bobbi and Corky Corcoran, sisters who join the cheerleading squad at their new school, Shadyside High. After Bobbi dies in a bizarre "accident," Corky realizes there may have been some truth to her sister's ravings about the strange things she had seen and experienced recently. Investigating her sister's death, Corky discovers the "evil," a century-old force that has risen from the grave. Although she seemingly outwits the evil by the end of the book, it returns to terrorize the cheerleading squad through two more books, until Corky is finally able to permanently destroy it.

Sometimes the villains in the "Fear Street" novels are mere mortals with murderous tendencies, as in *Silent Night* and *Broken Hearts. Silent Night* is the story of Reva Dalby, a beautiful but cold rich girl who finds herself on the receiving end of some cruel practical jokes. When two people are murdered, it appears that Reva may be the killer's next target. *Broken Hearts* features another entirely human killer. This murderer announces his intentions by sending future victims valentines with nasty messages inside ("Who's sending these cards?/ Don't bother to wonder/ On Valentine's Day/ You'll be six feet under.") Whatever the source of the menace, these kids don't turn to adults for salvation. They consult friends and do their best to find their own way out of their predicaments. Or sometimes, like Bobbi in *The First Evil* and Josie in *Broken Hearts,* they never find a way out, but simply die trying.

Other important components of the "Fear Street" formula are an emphasis on plot over characterization, and a hair-raising pace. One way Stine keeps his stories moving is to end every chapter with a cliff-hanger, a feature the author says his readers find particularly appealing. It doesn't seem to matter that the suspense sometimes dissolves instantly when the reader turns the page, such as when the "hideous, bloated head of a corpse" in Corky's bed turns out to be Halloween mask, or when the man who tries to accost Reva in a dimly lit department store turns out to be a mannequin she's brushed against. As Stine once commented, his fans "like the fact that there is some kind of jolt at the end of every chapter. They know that if they read to the end of the chapter they're going to have some kind of funny surprise, something scary, something that's going to happen . . . and force them to keep reading."

While Stine's fans don't seem to mind the formulaic nature of his books, the critics are sometimes less generous. In a review of *Twisted,* a *Publishers Weekly* reviewer said that "For shock value, this book adds up to a lot of cheap tricks." A *Publishers Weekly* review of *Ski Weekend* was similarly critical, noting that "the contrived plot barely manages to hold together a series of bland cliffhangers." In a review of *The Second Evil* for *Voice of Youth Advocates,* Caroline S. McKinney declared that "these formula stories are very predictable and require very little thought on the part of the reader." Nevertheless, many reviewers have recognized—sometimes begrudgingly—Stine's talent for hooking his readers and keeping them entertained. Alice Cronin, in a review of *The Sleepwalker* for *School Library Journal,* stated that "Stine writes a good story. Teens will love the action." In a review of *Curtains,* a *Publishers Weekly* columnist noted that although "the book . . . will never be mistaken for serious literature, it is sure to engross Stine's considerable following." And in a review of *Silent Night* in *Voice of Youth Advocates,* Sylvia C. Mitchell declared that "If all series books were this good, I'd begin to drop my . . . prejudices against them."

Stine agrees that the merit of his work lies in the books' entertainment value, not their literary significance, but he sees nothing wrong with that. "I believe that kids as well as adults are entitled to books of no socially redeeming value," he once noted. And although his books may be frightening, the scares are "safe scares," as he told Gray. "You're home in your room and reading. The books are not half as scary as the real world."

In fact, Stine makes a point of ensuring that the horror in his books retains an element of the unreal. "I don't put in anything that would be too close to their lives," he once commented, when asked what would be going too far for his readers. "I wouldn't do child abuse, or AIDS, or suicide, or anything that could really touch someone's life like that. The books are supposed to be just entertainment, that's all they are."

To work, though, the teens in his books must seem real, even if the horror elements stay in the realm of the fantastic. Stine works hard at making his characters talk like real kids, dress like real kids, and have the concerns of real kids. Though they may be worried about some unseen evil or a mysterious killer, they still care about whether or not they have a date for Saturday night. When it comes to the way his characters look, sound and behave, "I don't want to sound like some middle-aged guy who doesn't know what he's doing," Stine commented.

Luckily, Stine has a son, Matt, who provided him with plenty of first-hand experience with teens. "He had lots of friends," Stine said in his interview, "and I listened to them." Stine does his homework, too, by reading teen magazines and watching MTV. "It's very important in these books," he says, "that the kids sound and look like real kids, suddenly trapped in something horrible."

One thing Stine does not do, however, is try to keep up with the latest in teen slang. "I don't have them saying things like 'gnarly,' and other stuff people accuse me of putting in," Stine once remarked. "I'd like these books to be read five years from now, and that kind of slang really dates them fast. Besides," he added, "most kids talk normal."

An indication of the degree of admiration Stine engenders in his readers is the amount of fan mail he receives. Stine commented the letters are the "best part" of his success, and he reads every one. Most of the kids who write tell Stine how much they enjoy his books, and some say that his novels are the only ones they read. Stine gets letters from teachers and librarians too, sometimes telling about students who would never read a book before, but now can't wait for the next Stine thriller.

On one occasion, though, the mail brought a strange letter that baffled and disturbed Stine. A girl from Florida wrote, "I loved your book *The Baby-sitter.* You made it all seem so real. The same thing happened to me, only it was my uncle who tried to kill me. Keep up the good work. Thanks a lot." Stine didn't quite know what to make of it. "I didn't know if she was putting me on, or if it was a plea for help, or what," he says. Fortunately, the letter came in a group from a class, and Stine had the teacher's name and address: "I wrote to her and said, 'Maybe you should look into this.'" Stine never got a response from the teacher, though, and he still wonders what the real story behind that letter was.

At times, teen writer-wannabes ask Stine for his advice on becoming successful. He tells them not to do what he did, which was spend a good portion of his teen years sending his work to publishers, hoping to make a sale. All he accomplished, Stine once commented, was to waste people's time and collect a lot of rejection letters, which was "horrible." Instead, Stine tells them to read, read—and read some more. That way "you pick up all these different styles, almost by osmosis," he said, "and you'll be a better writer for it."

Aspiring writers might also want to take a tip from Stine's method of crafting his horror stories. These days he always begins with a chapter-by-chapter outline that details the action. This wasn't the case with his first novels. "I started doing it this way kicking and screaming," Stine once recalled. "I didn't want any part of these outlines, because sometimes you end up revising the outline, and revising it again until (the editor) approves it, and it's an arduous process. But that's the whole work. An outline helps me see whether or not the books make sense. I always start with the ending—that's the first thing I know. Then I can go back and figure out how to fool the reader, how to keep them from guessing the ending. By the time I sit down to write the book, I really know everything that's going to happen. I can just have fun and write it."

With over 300 million copies of his books in print, Stine has become a household word in children's books, enshrined in the *Guinness World Records 2000: Millennium Edition* as author of the world's top-selling children's stories. The success of "Fear Street" and "Goosebumps" series did not slow him down; in 2000 he began the "Nightmare Room" series with a new publisher, HarperCollins, aimed at the eight-to twelve-year-olds market. Stine told Andrea Sachs in *Time* magazine that he saw the new series "more like a fun house" than the "roller coaster ride" which "Goosebumps" was intended to be. "You step inside this place, and everything seems normal at first. And then you look and see, ah, the floor is tilted. And then it looks like the walls are closing in on you. . . . You're not in your old reality." Sachs felt that two early titles in the series, *Don't Forget Me!* and *Locker 13,* "read like slightly more sophisticated installments of 'Goosebumps.'" Stine's prose is, according to Sachs, "as usual, simple, his dialogue attuned to the speech of the young. . . . The plots of both involve Stine's trademark: teenagers being frightened witless in a context assuring readers that nothing truly dangerous will occur." This safety in the midst of terror is Stine's signature. As he admitted to Sachs, "There's more teasing than horror in my books."

BIOGRAPHICAL AND CRITICAL SOURCES:

BOOKS

Authors and Artists for Young Adults, Volume 13, Thomson Gale (Detroit, MI), 1994.

Children's Literature Review, Volume 37, Thomson Gale (Detroit, MI), 1996, pp. 101-123.

Jones, Patrick, *What's So Scary about R.L. Stine?,* Scarecrow Press (Metuchen, NJ), 1998.

Roginski, Jim, *Behind the Covers,* Libraries Unlimited, 1985, pp. 206-13.

Stine, R. L., *The Third Evil,* Archway (New York, NY), 1992.
Stine, R. L., *Broken Hearts,* Archway (New York, NY), 1993.
St. James Guide to Young Adult Writers, 2nd edition, St. James Press, 1999.

PERIODICALS

Booklist, October 15, 1999, p. 446.
Language Arts, November, 1998, pp. 115-122.
Los Angeles Times, June 29, 1997, p. 1.
Newsweek, January 24, 2001, p. 8.
New York Times, April 2, 1997, p. A16.
Publishers Weekly, July 10, 1987, review of *Twisted,* p. 87; September 28, 1990, review of *Curtains,* p. 104; December 7, 1990, review of *Fear Street: Ski Weekend,* p. 830; May 11, 1998, p. 20; August 30, 1999, p. 85; September 25, 2000, p. 118; September 10, 2001, p. 29; September 24, 2001, p. 94.
School Library Journal, September, 1990, Alice Cronin, review of *The Sleepwalker;* December, 1997, p. 70; December, 1999, p. 142; April, 2001, p. 149.
Storyworks, January, 2001, p. 7.
Time, August 2, 1992, Paul Gray, "Carnage: An Open Book," p. 54; August 28, 2000, Andrea Sachs, "Another Stab at Chills," pp. 56-57.
Voice of Youth Advocates, April, 1992, Sylvia C. Mitchell, review of *Silent Night,* pp. 36-37; February, 1993, Caroline S. McKinney, review of *Cheerleaders: The Second Evil,* p. 360.
Washington Post, May 5, 1996, p. X13; January 19, 1997, p. C7.

* * *

STINE, Robert Lawrence
See STINE, R.L.

* * *

STONE, Robert 1937-
(Robert Anthony Stone)

PERSONAL: Born August 21, 1937, in New York, NY; son of C. Homer and Gladys Catherine (a teacher; maiden name, Grant) Stone; married Janice G. Burr, December 11, 1959; children: Deidre M., Ian A. *Education:* Attended New York University, 1958-60, and Stanford University, 1962-64. *Hobbies and other interests:* Scuba diving, acting.

ADDRESSES: *Agent*—Neal Olson, Donadio & Olson, 121 West 27th Street, New York, NY 10001.

CAREER: Novelist and screenwriter. *New York Daily News,* New York, NY, copyboy and caption writer, 1958-60; worked at various jobs, 1960-62, in a coffee factory and as an actor in New Orleans, LA, and as an advertising copywriter in New York; *National Mirror,* New York, writer, 1965-67; freelance writer in London, Hollywood, and Saigon, South Vietnam (now Ho Chi Minh City, Vietnam), 1967-71; Princeton University, Princeton, NJ, writer-in-residence, 1971-72, faculty member, 1985 and 1986; Amherst College, Amherst, MA, associate professor of English, 1972-75, writer-in-residence, 1977-78; faculty member at Stanford University, 1979, University of Hawaii at Manoa, 1979-80, Harvard University, 1981, University of California—Irvine, 1982, New York University, 1983-84, University of California—San Diego, 1985 Johns Hopkins University, 1993 and Yale University, 1994. *Military service:* U.S. Navy, 1955-58; served in amphibious force of the Atlantic Fleet and as senior enlisted journalist on Operation Deep Freeze Three in Antarctica; became petty officer third class.

MEMBER: PEN (member of executive board), Authors League of America, Authors Guild, Writers Guild of America, West.

AWARDS, HONORS: Wallace Stegner fellowship, Stanford University, 1962-64; Houghton Mifflin literary fellowship, 1967, and William Faulkner Foundation Award for notable first novel, 1968, both for *A Hall of Mirrors;* Guggenheim fellowship, 1971; National Book Award, 1975, for *Dog Soldiers;* nomination for best script adapted from another medium, Writers Guild of America, 1979, for "Who'll Stop the Rain"; *Los Angeles Times* Book Prize, 1982, for *A Flag for Sunrise;* nominations for American Book Award, National Book Critics Circle Award, and PEN/Faulkner Award, all 1982, all for *A Flag for Sunrise;* runner-up for Pulitzer Prize in fiction, 1982, for *A Flag for Sunrise;* American Academy and Institute of Arts and Letters Award, 1982; John Dos Passos Prize for literature, 1982; National Endowment for the Arts fellowship, 1983; co-recipient of Harold and Mildred Strauss Livings award, 1988; grant from National Institute of Arts and Letters.

WRITINGS:

NOVELS

A Hall of Mirrors, Houghton Mifflin (Boston, MA), 1967.

Dog Soldiers, Houghton Mifflin (Boston, MA), 1974.
A Flag for Sunrise, Knopf (New York, NY), 1981.
Children of Light, Knopf (New York, NY), 1986.
Outerbridge Reach, Weidenfeld & Nicolson (London, England), 1989.
Damascus Gate, Houghton Mifflin (Boston, MA), 1998.
Bay of Souls, Houghton Mifflin (Boston, MA), 2003.

SCREENPLAYS

WUSA (based on his novel *A Hall of Mirrors*), Paramount, 1970.
(With Judith Roscoe) *Who'll Stop the Rain* (based on his novel *Dog Soldiers*), United Artists, 1978.

OTHER

(Photographs, author of introduction) *Deeds of War* Thames and Hudson (New York, NY), 1989.
Day Hikes in Aspen, Colorado (photographs), Day Hike Books (Red Lodge, MT), 1996.
Bear and His Daughter: Stories (short stories), Houghton Mifflin (Boston, MA), 1997.
(Author of introduction) *The Stories of Paul Bowles,* Ecco (New York, NY), 2001.

Contributor to books, including Richard Scowcroft and Wallace Stegner, editors, *Twenty Years of Stanford Short Stories,* Stanford University Press, 1966; *New American Review 6,* New American Library, 1969; David Burnett and Martha Foley, editors, *Best American Short Stories, 1970,* Houghton Mifflin, 1970; James B. Hall and Elizabeth Hall, editors, *The Realm of Fiction: Seventy-four Short Stories,* McGraw, 1977; Theodore Solotaroff, editor, *American Review 26,* Bantam, 1977; William O'Rourke, editor, *On the Job: Fiction about Work by Contemporary American Writers,* Vintage, 1977; Rust Hills and Tom Jenks, editors, *Esquire Fiction Reader,* Volume I, Wampeter, 1985; *Images of War* (nonfiction), Boston Publishing, 1986; and *Who We Are.* Contributor of articles and reviews to periodicals, including *Atlantic, Harper's, Life, New York Times Book Review, Manchester Guardian,* and *TriQuarterly.*

SIDELIGHTS: With his first four novels, Robert Stone established himself as one of America's most stringent political voices and an artist of considerable caliber. His books, many critics acknowledge, are not for everyone. A typical Stone protagonist is a down-and-out, cynical drifter engrossed in the drug culture or otherwise at odds with the law. Stone's stories have taken readers to the bowels of society, from the underbelly of New Orleans to the jungles of Vietnam, from the brutality of war-torn Central America to the artificial glamour of Hollywood. In this way the author is often compared to Graham Greene, Joseph Conrad, John Dos Passos, and Nathanael West, but Stone's individuality ultimately distinguishes him as "the apostle of strung out," as *New York Times Book Review* critic Jean Strouse saw him.

Stone has earned that epithet. A native of Brooklyn, New York, a product of Catholic school upbringing, the young man started his career in the 1950s as a newspaper copyboy, but soon Stone and his wife dropped their conventional life to see America. "They got as far as New Orleans, where they both worked at a variety of menial jobs that never lifted them above the poverty level," reported Sybil Steinberg in *Publishers Weekly.* Finally, the Stones, joined by a daughter born in a charity hospital, returned to New York City. There the author joined the emerging bohemian scene, counting Jack Kerouac among his confederates, and the group's dedication to discovery took them to northern California and to Ken Kesey.

Stone's days in Louisiana undoubtedly provided him with the background material for his first novel, *A Hall of Mirrors.* While this story of a young man's encounter with class politics is set in New Orleans, the book is really about all of America, as several reviewers suggested. "The unspoken theme of *A Hall of Mirrors* is the relation between the prosperous official society and its necessary underworld of drop-outs and cast-offs," noted *Commonweal* critic Emile Capouya. "These parallel systems meet in the persons of two characters. One is the millionaire demagogue, who wants to get more power than he already has by exploiting the fears of the poor white trash. The other is Rheinhardt, the pattern of the available 'intellectual,' the disabused journeyman liar of the communications industries." The communications industry in question is WSA, a right-wing propagandist radio station that Rheinhardt infiltrates. The author's "breadth of mind and . . . seriousness [set] him apart from any number of merely talented writers, for he instinctively makes the connection between the accidents of his fable and the world of his readers' experience," wrote Capouya, adding that Rheinhardt is "[Albert] Camus' *Stranger* in a less abstract, less absolute form."

"Stone's language is a joy," declared Ivan Gold in his *New York Times Book Review* piece on *A Hall of Mirrors.* "Rich yet unobtrusive, self-effacing but in complete control—here is a growing sense of awe, once one has finished the book, at what the effort must have cost him. When so accomplished a style is joined to an ear which encompasses the dictions of hippies, and senators, and a good portion of the worlds in between; which seems incapable of producing or reproducing a line of dialogue which does not ring true, it takes an act of willfulness on the part of the reader not to be drawn in, and moved, and altered."

The serious scholarly attention accorded Stone's first novel was summed up in the words of L. Hugh Moore, who noted in *Critique: Studies in Modern Fiction:* "Stone's vision of the modern world and society is a profoundly pessimistic one. The implications of his main, related metaphors—the undersea world and evolution—are, indeed, disturbing. To see the world as an environment, an ecological system, that is as cold, hostile, and brutal as the sea floor is hardly new. Nor is his view of his characters as denizens of the deep profoundly original. What disturbs and what makes the novel contemporarily relevant is the fact that Stone offers no melioristic possibility. To survive in the new ice age is immoral; neither work, bitter humor, nor withdrawal is humanly possible. 'Despair and die' is the final message of the novel."

Suspenseful, convincing, cruel, funny and frightening are just some of the words critics used to describe Stone's next novel, the 1975 National Book award-winning *Dog Soldiers.* Like *A Hall of Mirrors,* this book exposes corruption and greed, this time in settings ranging from Saigon to California. During the waning days of the Vietnam war, journalist John Converse, stationed in Saigon, gets an offer he cannot refuse: If he smuggles three kilograms of pure heroin back to the States, he will earn $40,000. Engaging an accomplice, Ray Hicks, into the scheme, Converse manages to get the package to California and to leave it in possession of his wife, Marge. "The stark evil in this plan quickly flows into nightmare," *Time*'s Paul Gray wrote, as agents for a corrupt federal officer pursue Converse and his cohorts.

Dog Soldiers "is more than a white-knuckled plot; it is a harrowing allegory," continued Gray. "The novice smugglers evade a sense of their own villainy through sophistry or indifference. Converse rationalizes that in a world capable of producing the horrors of war, 'people are just naturally going to want to get high'" *New York Review of Books* critic Roger Sale took a different view. "The more seriously Stone takes his characters, the more carefully he brings their aimlessness to a decision, the more he eventually either jettisons the aimlessness or falsifies the decisiveness and its importance. I'm not sure how he could better have pondered his materials and his wonderful first half, but the remainder is good writing that seems divorced from a wider purpose than its own existence, and so seems just like writing."

Despite his reservations, however, Sale concluded that *Dog Soldiers* ultimately shows the author's "clear eye for detail and clear-eyed determination to see these lives through to some end without sentimentalizing them. Throughout, thus, his integrity gives us a sense of learning at first hand what most of us have known only as hearsay or freakout. He brings the news, as novelists are supposed to do; he makes one think we have only begun to understand our immediate past." And a *Washington Post Book World* reviewer, labeling *Dog Soldiers* the most important novel of the year, adding that "Stone writes like a Graham Greene whose God is utterly dead, and he favors the same sort of setting, the same juxtaposition of the exotic and the banal."

Stone's third novel, *A Flag for Sunrise,* "is about Catholics—a nun, a priest, an anthropologist, a drifter—caught up among spies, gun runners, murderers, maniacs, and revolutionaries in a poor Central American country ruled by American business interests and the CIA through a local military regime," summarized Leonard Michaels in the *Saturday Review.* "The plot is complicated and built upon short scenes, some of them so intensely dramatic they could be published independently. What holds them together is suspenseful action, an atmosphere of neurasthenic menace, and Stone's prose style. Lean, tough, quick, and smart, it is perfect for violent action, yet lyrical enough for Stone's nun as she contemplates her own mind, her 'inward place.'"

To *Los Angeles Times Book Review* writer Carolyn See, Stone "does American imperialism so well it is possible to read his third novel as a purely aesthetic experience. The decay is so attractive, so muted, so 'literary,' that reading it is . . . like curling up with Graham Greene in Africa or Joseph Conrad in the deep Pacific." William Logan found distinct ties between the author's first and third books. *A Flag for Sunrise,* he noted in Chicago's *Tribune Books,* "so carefully duplicates the structure of *A Hall of Mirrors,* even to the rhythm of its title. In each, the narration emanated from three characters whose careless intertwinings led to a cataclysm only one escaped alive."

Jonathan Yardley had criticism for the author's style. While Stone "writes very well, [creating] plausible characters [with] a deft hand for dramatic incident," the critic commented in the *Washington Post Book World,* the author "is a preacher masquerading in novelist's clothing, indulging himself in rhetoric right out of SDS or the IWW. It is the politics of his novels rather than the craft of them that seems ultimately to interest him the most; the problem is that there is nothing interesting about his politics." Elaborating, Yardley pointed out that the nun character, Sister Justin, "is clearly intended to be the novel's moral center, but she is simply too good to be true." Also, Stone "trivializes what he hopes to glorify. The stock roles that his characters play and the stock rhetoric that they utter are nothing more than safe, comfortable responses to a situation that is considerably more complex and ambiguous than Stone appears to realize." However, Yardley remarked, when the author "gets off his soapbox and pays attention to the craft of fiction, he is very good."

On the other hand, *Commonweal* critic Frank McConnell called *A Flag for Sunrise* "an important political novel precisely because it is such a perceptive religious novel." Further, Stone offers "an indication of a new trend in the American sensibility. For Conrad, Greene, and [John] le Carré can be considered the elegists of Britain's dreams of empire and the explorers of that vaster, richer territory of the spirit that lies beyond the hope of triumph over history. Robert Stone is the first American writer I know of who shares that melancholy, that maturity, and that bitter sanity. And if his novel is fierce in its despair, it is even fiercer in its unvoiced suggestion of a sensibility that renders despair itself mute before the absurd, unending possibility of love." "*Flag* is a disturbing book in many ways, some of them not intended," in Richard Poirier's opinion. Poirier, in the *New York Review of Books,* added that he was "not referring to Stone's politics as such but to the degree to which they may reveal more about his opportunism as a novelist than about his anxieties as a citizen."

Stone's first two novels were made into feature films. While he contributed to both screenplays, *WSA,* based on *A Hall of Mirrors,* and *Who'll Stop the Rain,* based on *Dog Soldiers,* are remarkable for the unfavorable responses both received from film critics and audiences. Many factors go into the fate of a film, however—the work of the director, cast, crew and production company included—and Stone has stated in interviews that the finished products were never even close to the screen treatments he had originally conceived. Still, his experiences in film provided the author with the impetus for his fourth novel, *Children of Light.* Set on the location of a film, it chronicles the wasted days of a washed-up screenwriter and a schizophrenic actress; the novel offers "a fine, complex, often funny tale, full of lights and shadows, with great dialogue and a sharp sense of character and place," according to Jean Strouse in the *New York Times Book Review.*

The book "is jam-packed with people pretending to be other than they are, people with masks, people who have become their lies. Even the film location, Mexico pretending to be Louisiana, is schizoid. The only sane person is the mad one, [the actress] Lee Verger," noted *Washington Post Book World* critic Stephen Dobyns. The author "has taken some spectacular risks, particularly with his climax," observed Christopher Lehmann-Haupt. "His drama plays, and one's sense of dread builds up like a bank of storm clouds."

Lehmann-Haupt, commented in a *New York Times* article, that while *Children of Light* is Stone's "most dramatically coherent performance to date," nevertheless "there is a mechanical quality about the way [he] manipulates his characters that keeps the reader's mind divided. Part of one's reaction is to be amazed at the effects he is pulling off, but another part is to wonder why his characters are so remorselessly condemned to their respective fates. Why is [main character] Gordon Walker a drunk and a coke addict? Why is Lee Verger schizophrenic? Why are all the film types so wiseacre, heartless and nasty? What do all the drugs and alcohol mean? Are they no more than God's way of telling Hollywood that it has too much money? Not that this reader was able to figure out."

Again, Stone's dialogue won wide praise. Not only does the author's language "snap like a bullwhip," felt Toronto *Globe and Mail* reviewer Norman Snider, but the author, "having paid hard dues in Hollywood, has an acute sense of how the patois of the film biz equally encompasses relationships as well as professional arrangements. [A character's] husband, for instance, 'takes a walk' out of the marriage in exactly the same way performers or directors would walk off a film they suspect will damage their career."

Children of Light "seems far more slanted than anything Stone has written before," in A. Alvarez's opinion. "He has always kept apart from the current fashion that confuses fiction with the art of the self and is suspicious of anyone with a strong gift for narrative. Stone, who has a strong imaginative grip on the contemporary American scene and writes like an angel—a fallen, hard-driving angel—is also a marvelous storyteller. He does not take sides and is as much at one with Pablo, the murderous speed freak, as he is with Holliwell, the liberal intellectual," wrote Alvarez in the *New York Review of Books.* The critic sums up that in order for the author to reach his own level of truth, "he has sacrificed the intricate, gallows-humor detachment that has made him, in his previous books, one of the most impressive novelists of his generation."

Vietnam echoes in Stone's novel *Outerbridge Reach.* It is the tale of a Vietnam veteran, Owen Browne, who works for a yacht brokerage. When his boss is forced to withdraw from a solo around-the-world yacht race due to financial problems, Browne volunteers to take his place. Also figuring in the plot are Browne's wife Anne and a filmmaker, Ron. The book is based on an actual event in which an Englishman, Donald Crowhurst, faked an around-the-world voyage, went insane, and likely committed suicide. Several critics found the story and Stone's writing compelling. *New York Times* reviewer Christopher Lehmann-Haupt wrote, "the true appeal of reading *Outerbridge Reach* lies in the texture of its prose and the harsh realism of its characters." Commenting on Stone's "fascination" with pain, John Casey wrote in the Chicago *Tribune Books,* Stone "has a fascinated, almost Mayan, relation to it." He continued, "That characteristic made me recoil from the end of *A Flag for Sunrise* and, to a lesser extent, from a part of *Outerbridge Reach.* I don't know whether I recoil because I see life more hopefully than Stone does or because I can't help admiring the style, design and allure of his version of how powerful the vortex is, both outside us and in us."

Stone's 1997 *Bear and His Daughter* is a collection of short stories, many of which were previously published in periodicals including *New Yorker, Harper's* and *American Review.* "The older stories are in no way inferior," argued Margot Livesey in the *Boston Book Review* online. Livesey compared the collection to those of such literary luminaries as James Joyce and Flannery O'Connor. Christopher Lehmann-Haupt argued in the *New York Times Book Review* that, compared with novel-length works, Stone's "dark vision is better suited to short fiction. In thrall to this dark vision, the reader wishes only that Mr. Stone's characters will survive with some small fragment of hope." Livesey concluded: "*Bear and His Daughter* is a beautiful and necessary book. To read it could save your life."

Stone returned to the novel form with the 1998 publication *Damascus Gate.* "*Damascus Gate* has a number of elements which will be familiar to Robert Stone's readers: drugs, alcohol, the threat of violence, death, and characters searching desperately for a meaning that eludes them," commented John Garvey in *Commonweal.* Set in Jerusalem, the novel follows journalist Christopher Lucas who is writing about the "Jerusalem Syndrome," a reportedly delusion breakdown that certain individuals suffer upon visiting the city. "What follows is a religious thriller," summarized Hillel Halkin in the *New Republic.* "Stone's characters . . . all become inexorably tangled in the obsessive journey of Adam De Kuff, a manic-depressive from New Orleans who believes he is the Messiah," wrote J.D. Reed in *People.*

Critical reaction to the novel was largely positive. "Stone's fascination with moral collisions and pirouettes shines through *Damascus Gate,* and the rewards, sentence by sentence, are frequent," found Todd Gitlin in the *Nation.* "All seekers of Revelation and jihad will be equally offended—no small tribute." Halkin, who compared Stone's style to those of Hemingway, Conrad, and Joyce, disagreed, calling the work "really a rip-off of a country and a tradition that deserve better at his hands." James Gardner, in the *National Review,* had an opposing view: "Stone reveals himself to be both learned and shrewd. Whether his subject is the syncretic kabbalism of Pico della Mirandola, the music of Fats Waller, or cigarette consumption in an Israeli bar, he always gets it right, knowing just enough more than his reader to have something worth telling him, but incorporating this knowledge so seamlessly into the fabric of his work that is never irksome." Garvey concluded: "Stone shows how close and at the same time how far apart are the worlds of the nihilist and the genuine believer. And if you feel uncomfortable with the ideas that crop up here, read the book as a great thriller. It works wonderfully at both levels."

In a 1981 *Washington Post* interview, Stone explained his reasons for telling the stories he does: He believes that by exposing readers to the darker side of society, he is abetting "the awareness of ironies and continuities, showing people that being decent is really hard and that we carry within ourselves our own worst enemy."

Stone once commented that the combination of teaching college English courses at various universities and writing books "works rather well. It tends to give the week a certain kind of shape, and it doesn't hurt to talk about writing, because it helps me find out what I believe about writing. The great thing about writing courses is that even if you can't teach anybody to write—which you certainly can't—you get to talk about everything. Writing courses are really more the philosophy of composition than they are anything else. You can't teach people how to write, but you can talk about life, about how it is, how people are. That's not a bad way to pass a couple of hours."

BIOGRAPHICAL AND CRITICAL SOURCES:

BOOKS

Contemporary Literary Criticism, Thomson Gale (Detroit, MI), Volume 5, 1976, Volume 23, 1983, Volume 42, 1987.

Dictionary of Literary Biography, Volume 152: *American Novelists since World War II, Fourth Series,* Thomson Gale (Detroit, MI), 1995.

Lopez, Ken, with Bev Chaney, *Robert Stone: A Bibliography,* Numinous Press (Hadley, MA), 1992.

Solotaroff, Robert, *Robert Stone,* Twayne (New York, NY), 1994.

PERIODICALS

Atlantic, November, 1981.

Booklist, February 15, 1998, Bill Ott, review of *Demascus Gate,* p. 949; January 1, 1999, review of *Damascus Gate,* p. 780.

Boston Globe, May 3, 1998.

Commentary, March, 1982.

Commonweal, April 5, 1968; March 12, 1982; May 23, 1986; June 5, 1998, John Garvey, review of *Damascus Gate,* p. 24.

Critique: Studies in Modern Fiction, Volume 15, number 3, 1969.

Encounter, September, 1975.

Esquire, August, 1985.

Globe and Mail (Toronto, Ontario, Canada), April 26, 1986.

Harper's, April 28, 1975.

Library Journal, March 15, 1998, Lawrence Rungren, review of *Damascus Gate,* p. 96.

London Review of Books, May 28, 1992, p. 20.

Los Angeles Times Book Review, November 8, 1981; March 23, 1986.

Maclean's, April 13, 1992, p. 74.

Modern Fiction Studies, spring, 1984.

Nation, April 13, 1992, p. 489; November 16, 1992, p. 588; May 11, 1998, Todd Gitlin, review of *Damascus Gate,* p. 50.

National Catholic Reporter, September 25, 1992, p. 12.

National Review, April 27, 1992, p. 49; June 2, 1998, James Gardner, review of *Damascus Gate,* p. 53.

New Boston Review, February, 1982.

New Republic, January 4, 1975; November 18, 1981; April 28, 1986; April 20, 1992, p. 42; May 25, 1998, Hillel Halkin, review of *Damascus Gate,* p. 29.

Newsweek, November 11, 1974; October 26, 1981; March 17, 1986; February 24, 1992, p. 69.

New Yorker, May 4, 1992, p. 93.

New York Review of Books, April 3, 1975; December 3, 1981; April 10, 1986; March 26, 1992, p. 29.

New York Times, October 31, 1974; October 16, 1981; March 13, 1986; February 17, 1992, p. C18.

New York Times Book Review, September 24, 1967; November 3, 1974; October 18, 1981; April 15, 1984; March 16, 1986; February 23, 1992, p. 1; April 3, 1997, Christopher Lehmann-Haupt, review of *Bear and His Daughter.*

New York Times Magazine, January 19, 1992, p. 18.

People, May 18, 1998, J.D. Reed, review of *Damascus Gate,* p. 45.

Publishers Weekly, March 21, 1986; October 5, 1992, p. 67; February 16, 1998, review of *Damascus Gate,* p. 200.

Saturday Review, November, 1981.

Seattle Times, May 3, 1998.

Sunday Times (London, England), October 15, 1998.

Tikkun, September-October, 1998, John Leonard, review of *Damascus Gate,* p. 71.

Time, November 11, 1974; October 26, 1981; March 10, 1986; February 17, 1992, p. F8.

Times Literary Supplement, May 30, 1975; December 4, 1981; March 21, 1986.

Tribune Books (Chicago, IL), October 25, 1981; March 9, 1986; March 1, 1992, p. 1.

TriQuarterly, winter, 1982.

Washington Post, November 15, 1981; April 11, 1997, p. B02.

Washington Post Book World, December 8, 1974; November 1, 1981; March 23, 1986.

ONLINE

Aljadid: A Review & Record of Arab Culture and Arts, http://www.aljadid.com/ (winter, 1999).

Boston Book Review, http://www.bookwire.bowker.com/ (July 11, 2000).

Denver Post Online, http://www.denverpost.com/ (July 11, 2000).

Post-Gazette, http://www.post-gazette.com/ (July 11, 2000).

* * *

STONE, Robert Anthony

See STONE, Robert

STONE, Rosetta
See GEISEL, Theodor Seuss

* * *

STOPPARD, Tom 1937-
(William Boot, Tomas Straussler)

PERSONAL: Born Tomas Straussler, July 3, 1937, in Zlin (now Gottwaldov), Czechoslovakia; naturalized British citizen; son of Eugene Straussler (a physician) and Martha Stoppard; married Jose Ingle, 1965 (divorced, 1972); married Miriam Moore-Robinson (a physician), 1972 (divorced, 1992); children: (first marriage) Oliver, Barnaby; (second marriage) two sons. *Education:* Pocklington School, Yorkshire, A-levels, 1954.

ADDRESSES: *Home*—Chelsea Harbor, London, England. *Agent*—Peters, Fraser & Dunlop, The Chambers, 5th Floor, Chelsea Harbor, Lots Road, London SW10 0XF, England.

CAREER: Playwright, novelist, and radio and television script writer. *Western Daily Press,* Bristol, England, reporter and critic, 1958-60; *Evening World,* Bristol, reporter, 1958-60; freelance reporter, 1960-63. Director of play *Born Yesterday,* London, England, 1973; director of film *Rosencrantz and Guildenstern Are Dead,* 1991. Member of Royal National Theatre Board, 1989—.

MEMBER: Royal Society of Literature (fellow).

AWARDS, HONORS: Ford Foundation grant, 1964; John Whiting Award, Arts Council of Great Britain, 1967; London *Evening Standard* Drama Awards, 1967, for most promising playwright for *Rosencrantz and Guildenstern Are Dead,* 1972, for best play for *Jumpers,* 1974, for best comedy for *Travesties,* and 1983, for best play for *The Real Thing;* Prix Italia, 1968, for *Albert's Bridge*; Antoinette Perry Awards for best play, 1968, for *Rosencrantz and Guildenstern Are Dead,* 1976, for *Travesties,* and 1984, for *The Real Thing,* and nomination, 1995, for *Arcadia;* New York Drama Critics Circle Awards, 1968, for best play for *Rosencrantz and Guildenstern Are Dead,* 1976, for best play *Travesties,* and 1984, for best foreign play *The Real Thing;* M.Lit., University of Bristol, 1976, Brunel University, 1979, University of Sussex, 1980; Commander, Order of the British Empire, 1978; Shakespeare Prize (Hamburg, Germany), 1979; Academy Award nomination, and Los Angeles Critics Circle Award for best original screenplay (with Terry Gilliam and Charles McKeown), both 1985, both for *Brazil;* Grand Prize, Venice Film Festival, 1990, for *Rosencrantz and Guildenstern Are Dead;* knighted by Queen Elizabeth II, 1997; Academy Award for best screenplay written directly for the screen, 1998, for *Shakespeare in Love;* inducted into Order of the Merit, 2000.

WRITINGS:

PLAYS

The Gamblers, produced in Bristol, England, 1965.

Tango (based on the play by Slawomir Mrozek; produced in London, England, 1966; produced on the West End, 1968), J. Cape (London, England), 1968.

Rosencrantz and Guildenstern Are Dead (three-act; also see below; first produced at Edinburgh Festival, 1966; produced on the West End, 1967; produced on Broadway, 1967), Samuel French (New York, NY), 1967.

Enter a Free Man (based on his teleplay *A Walk on the Water;* also see below; first produced on the West End, 1968; produced off-Broadway, 1974), Faber (London, England), 1968.

The Real Inspector Hound (one-act; first produced on the West End, 1968; produced off-Broadway with *After Magritte,* 1972), Samuel French (New York, NY), 1968.

Albert's Bridge [and] *If You're Glad I'll Be Frank* (based on his radio plays; also see below), produced in Edinburgh, 1969, produced in New York, NY, 1987.

After Magritte (one-act; first produced in London, England, 1970; produced off-Broadway with *The Real Inspector Hound,* 1972), Faber (London, England), 1971.

Dogg's Our Pet (also see below; produced in London, England, 1971), published in *Six of the Best,* Inter-Action Imprint, 1976.

Jumpers (first produced on the West End, 1972; produced in Washington, DC, 1974; produced on Broadway, 1974; revived in London, England (2003); produced in New York, NY, 2004); Grove (New York, NY), 1972, revised edition, Faber (London, England), 1986.

The House of Bernarda Alba (based on the play by Federico García Lorca), produced in London, England, 1973.

Travesties (produced on the West End, 1974; produced on Broadway, 1974), Grove (New York, NY), 1975.

Dirty Linen and New-Found-Land (produced in London, England, 1976; produced on Broadway, 1977), Grove (New York, NY), 1976.

Every Good Boy Deserves Favor, music by Andre Previn, first produced in London, England, 1977, produced on the West End, 1978, produced in New York, NY, 1979.

Night and Day (produced on the West End, 1978; produced on Broadway, 1979), Grove (New York, NY), 1979, revised edition, Samuel French (New York, NY), 1980.

Dogg's Hamlet, Cahoot's Macbeth (double-bill of one-act plays; *Dogg's Hamlet* based on his play *Dogg's Our Pet;* produced in New York, NY, 1979), Faber (London, England), 1979.

Undiscovered Country (adapted from Arthur Schnitzler's *Das Weite Land;* produced on the West End, 1979; produced in Hartford, CT, 1981), Faber (London, England), 1980.

On the Razzle (adapted from Johann Nestroy's *Einen Jux will er sich Machen;* produced on the West End, 1981; produced in Los Angeles, CA, 1985), Faber (London, England), 1981.

The Real Thing (produced on the West End, 1982; produced on Broadway, 1984), Faber (London, England), 1982, revised edition, 1983.

Rough Crossing (adaptation of Ferenc Molnar's *The Play's the Thing;* produced in London, England, 1984; produced in New York, NY, 1990), Faber (London, England), 1985.

Dalliance (adapted from Arthur Schnitzler's *Liebelei*), produced in London, England, 1986.

(Translator) Vaclav Havel, *Largo Desolato,* Faber (London, England), 1987.

Hapgood (produced in New York, NY, 1988), Faber (London, England), 1988.

Artist Descending a Staircase (based on his radio play [also see below]; produced on the West End, 1988; produced on Broadway, 1989), Faber, 1990.

Arcadia, produced in London, England, 1994; produced on Broadway, 1995.

The Coast of Utopia (trilogy of plays), produced at the Royal National Theater, London, England, 2002.

Salvage: The Coast of Utopia Trilogy, Grove (New York, NY), 2003.

Shipwreck: The Coast of Utopia Trilogy, Grove (New York, NY), 2003.

Voyage: The Coast of Utopia Trilogy, Grove (New York, NY), 2003.

Also author of *Home and Dry* and *Riley.*

SCREENPLAYS

(With Thomas Wiseman) *The Romantic Englishwoman,* New World Pictures, 1975.

Despair (adapted from the novel by Vladimir Nabokov), New Line Cinema, 1978.

The Human Factor (adapted from the novel by Graham Greene), Metro-Goldwyn-Mayer (MGM), 1980.

(With Terry Gilliam and Charles McKeown) *Brazil,* Universal, 1985.

Empire of the Sun (adapted from the novel by J.G. Ballard), Warner Bros., 1987.

The Russia House (adapted from the novel by John le Carre), MGM/United Artists, 1989.

(And director) *Rosencrantz and Guildenstern Are Dead* (adapted from his play), Cinecom, 1991, published as *Rosencrantz and Guildenstern Are Dead: The Film,* Faber (London, England), 1991.

Billy Bathgate (adapted from the novel by E.L. Doctorow), Touchstone Pictures, 1991.

(With Marc Norman) *Shakespeare in Love,* Miramax, 1998.

FOR TELEVISION

A Walk on the Water, ITV Television, 1963, broadcast as *The Preservation of George Riley,* British Broadcasting Corporation (BBC-TV), 1964.

A Separate Peace (BBC-TV, 1966), Samuel French (New York, NY), 1977.

Teeth, BBC-TV, 1967.

Another Moon Called Earth, BBC-TV, 1967.

Neutral Ground, Thames Television, 1968.

The Engagement (based on his radio play *The Dissolution of Dominic Boot;* also see below), NBC-TV, 1970.

One Pair of Eyes, BBC-TV, 1972.

(With Clive Exton) *Eleventh House,* BBC-TV, 1975.

(With Clive Exton) *Boundaries,* BBC-TV, 1975.

Three Men in a Boat (based on the novel by Jerome K. Jerome), BBC-TV, 1975.

Professional Foul, BBC-TV, 1977, Public Broadcasting Service (PBS-TV), 1978.

Squaring the Circle: Poland, 1980-81 (BBC-TV, 1985), Faber (London, England), 1985.

RADIO PLAYS

The Dissolution of Dominic Boot, BBC-Radio, 1964.

"M" Is for Moon among Other Things, BBC-Radio, 1964.

If You're Glad I'll Be Frank (BBC-Radio, 1966), Faber (London, England), 1969.

Albert's Bridge, BBC-Radio, 1967.

Albert's Bridge [and] If You're Glad I'll Be Frank: Two Plays for Radio, Faber (London, England), 1969.

The Real Inspector Hound [and] After Magritte, Grove (New York, NY), 1970.
Where Are They Now?, BBC-Radio, 1970.
Artist Descending a Staircase, BBC-Radio, 1972.
Artist Descending a Staircase [and] Where Are They Now?: Two Plays for Radio, Faber (London, England), 1973.
Albert's Bridge, and Other Plays, Grove (New York, NY), 1977.
Every Good Boy Deserves Favor [and] Professional Foul, Grove (New York, NY), 1978.
The Dog It Was That Died, BBC-Radio, 1982.
The Dog It Was That Died, and Other Plays (contains *Teeth, Another Moon Called Earth, Neutral Ground, A Separate Peace, "M" Is for Moon among Other Things,* and *The Dissolution of Dominic Boot*), Faber (London, England), 1983.
Four Plays for Radio, Faber (London, England), 1984.
Dalliance [and] Undiscovered Country, Faber (London, England), 1986.
Stoppard: The Radio Plays 1964-1983, Faber (London, England), 1991.
In the Native State (BBC-Radio, 1991), revised edition published as *Indian Ink,* Faber (Boston, MA), 1995.

Also author of episodes of radio serials *The Dales,* 1964, and *A Student's Diary,* 1965.

OTHER

Lord Malquist and Mr. Moon (novel), Anthony Blond, 1966, Knopf (New York, NY), 1968.
(With Paul Delaney), *Tom Stoppard in Conversation,* University of Michigan Press (Ann Arbor, MI), 1994.
(With Mel Gussow) *Conversations with Stoppard,* Limelight (New York, NY), 1995.
(With Charles Rosen, Jonathan Miller, Garry Wills, and Geoffrey O'Brien) *Doing It: Five Performing Arts,* New York Review of Books (New York, NY), 2001.
(Translator from the Russian), Anton Chekhov, *The Seagull,* Faber (London, England), 2001.

Contributor of short stories to *Introduction 2,* 1964. Reviewer, sometimes under pseudonym William Boot, for *Scene,* 1962.

WORK IN PROGRESS: An original screenplay; negotiating to adapt Philip Pullman's award-winning trilogy *His Dark Materials* for New Line Cinema.

SIDELIGHTS: Tom Stoppard's plays revolutionized modern theatre with their uniquely comic combinations of verbal intricacy, complex structure, and philosophical themes. With such award-winning works as *Rosencrantz and Guildenstern Are Dead, Jumpers, Travesties,* and *The Real Thing* to his credit, Stoppard compares with "the masters of the comic tradition," Joan Fitzpatrick Dean wrote in *Tom Stoppard: Comedy As a Moral Matrix.* "Like the best comic dramatists, his gift for language and physical comedy fuses with an active perception of the excesses, eccentricities, and foibles of man." "Stoppard is that peculiar anomaly—a serious comic writer born in an age of tragicomedy and a renewed interest in theatrical realism," Enoch Brater summarized in *Essays on Contemporary British Drama.* "Such deviation from dramatic norms . . . marks his original signature on the contemporary English stage," the critic continued, for his "'high comedy of ideas' is a refreshing exception to the rule. Offering us 'a funny play,' Stoppard's world 'makes coherent, in terms of theatre, a fairly complicated intellectual argument.' That the argument is worth making, that it is constantly developing and sharpening its focus, and that it always seeks to engage an audience in a continuing dialogue, are the special characteristics of Stoppard's dramatic achievement. They are also the features which dignify and ultimately transform the comic tradition to which his work belongs."

"Stoppard's virtuosity was immediately apparent" in his first major dramatic work, *Rosencrantz and Guildenstern Are Dead,* Mel Gussow of the *New York Times* asserted. The play revisits Shakespeare's *Hamlet* through the eyes of the two players whose task of delivering Hamlet's death sentence prompts their own execution instead. Vaguely aware of the scheming at Elsinore and their own irrelevance to it, Rosencrantz and Guildenstern meander through the drama playing games of language and chance until, circumscribed by Shakespeare's script, they cease to exist. "In focusing on Shakespeare's minor characters Stoppard does not fill out their lives but rather extends their thinness," Anne Wright observed in her *Dictionary of Literary Biography* essay. By turning *Hamlet* "inside out" in this way, the play is "simultaneously frivolous in conception but dead serious in execution," Brater stated, and it addressed issues of existentialism reminiscent of Samuel Beckett's drama *Waiting for Godot.* The result, the critic added, "is not only a relaxed view of *Hamlet,* but a new kind of comic writing halfway between parody and travesty."

Also notable is the play's innovative use of language and Shakespeare's actual text. *Rosencrantz and Guildenstern Are Dead* is interwoven with references to

Hamlet as well as containing actual lines of the bard's verse; in addition, Stoppard packs the drama with "intricate word plays, colliding contradictions and verbal and visual puns," as Gussow described it. This "stylistic counterpoint of Shakespeare's poetry and rhetoric with the colloquial idiom of the linguistic games and music-hall patter" proves very effective, Wright commented. "Stoppard's lines pant with inner panic," a *Time* reviewer noted, as the title characters, according to *Village Voice*'s Michael Smith, ultimately "talk themselves out of existence." The play became one of Stoppard's most popular and acclaimed works; twenty years after its premiere, Gussow concluded, *Rosencrantz and Guildenstern* "remains an acrobatic display of linguistic pyrotechnics as well as a provocative existential comedy about life in limbo."

"With its dazzling feel for the duplicities and delights of language and its sense that modern consciousness is a gummed-up kaleidoscope that needs to be given a severe shake," Jack Kroll of *Newsweek* contended, *Rosencrantz and Guildenstern* established "the characteristic Stoppard effect." Stoppard's 1972 play *Jumpers* is a similar "montage of themes and techniques," said Wright, "by turns a whodunit, a farce of marital infidelity, and a philosophical inquiry." The inquiry is performed by George Moore, a professor of moral philosophy whose wife, Dottie, is suspected of both adultery and murder. The play is among Stoppard's most visually elaborate works, with a troupe of gymnastic philosophers, two lunar astronauts fighting over the only return berth to Earth, and sight gags such as an unfortunate accident involving George's pet hare and tortoise. The play also alternates between George's intellectual lectures and Dottie's music-hall numbers, creating further uncertainties. "The play ends with the murder unsolved, both the adultery and the existence of God unproved, one of the astronauts killed by the other, and another gymnast—the Archbishop of Canterbury—shot," Wright outlined.

"In *Jumpers,* much of the action and humor hinges on linguistic ambiguities and confusions," G.B. Crump wrote in *Contemporary Literature.* "These confusions mirror larger ambiguities present in the reality represented in the drama." As Brater elaborated, the play "never fixes moral philosophy and musical comedy in any stable order, hierarchy, or progression." The consequence, C.W.E. Bigsby related in *Contemporary Dramatists,* is that "the relativity of truth, man's apparent need to divert himself from painful realities, the failure of language to do more than parody conviction, the inability of the rational mind to adequately explain man to himself—all these coalesce in a play which unites the very best of Stoppard's characteristics as a playwright—a mastery of language, a clear sense of style and rhythm, and a wit which has both a verbal and visual dimension."

A *Times Literary Supplement* reviewer, however, believed that in *Jumpers* Stoppard's complex language overwhelms the drama: "Good intentions are swamped by words that get nowhere. No actor speaking this highly intellectual and convoluted jargon can talk and move at the same time. To be heard and understood, the actor must stand still and the stage around him must freeze." Thus, the critic continued, "the stage loses its scenic power, the word its resonance, and therefore, the playfulness of the 'play' is muted." In contrast, other critics found the playwright's linguistic intricacies suited to his sophisticated humor and ideas. Victor L. Cahn, for instance, stated in his *Beyond Absurdity: The Plays of Tom Stoppard* that Stoppard's "emphasis on variety of language" demonstrated his "belief in man's ability to communicate. He manages at the same time to make his language amusing, yet richly woven with ideas." "Stoppard is one of those rare writers who can move easily between treating language as an object in itself and making it totally transparent to meaning," Kroll likewise reported. In addition, this verbal ability allows Stoppard to successfully draw from and merge with the work of other writers; as Susan Rusinko claimed in *World Literature Today,* "His inventive puns, parodies, and pastiches brilliantly serve the cause of theatricality to the point that the original disappears with the wave of the word magician's wand."

Stoppard makes use of another dramatic adaptation in his second Tony Award-winner, *Travesties.* The play takes as its starting point the historical fact that Zurich in 1917 was inhabited by three revolutionaries: the communist leader Lenin, modernist writer James Joyce, and dadaist poet-critic Tristan Tzara. Their interactions are related through the recollections of Henry Carr, a minor British official who meets Lenin at the local library and the others during a production of Oscar Wilde's *The Importance of Being Earnest.* In a manner similar to that of *Rosencrantz and Guildenstern Are Dead,* Stoppard used plot line and characterization from Wilde's play to parallel and emphasize events and characters in his own work; the play "races forward on Mr. Stoppard's verbal roller coaster, leaving one dizzy yet exhilarated by its sudden semantic twists, turns, dips, and loops," Wilborn Hampton remarked in the *New York Times.* The result, Wright asserted, is "a virtuoso piece, a 'travesty' of the style of each of its masters, including Joycean narrative and dadaist verse as well as Wildean wit. The parody extends to the discourse appropriate to Lenin, as the play incorporates lectures and polemical sequences."

"Multilayered, complex, intellectually astringent," Alan Rich declared in *New York,* "Stoppard's play bats about a remarkable number of important ideas," especially those concerning art, revolutionary politics, and the relationship between the two. Brater explained that "in terms of dramatic form [the play] is the culmination of Stoppard's attempt to 'marry' the play of ideas to comedy and farce. But in terms of theme the play demonstrates the author's increasing political consciousness." The critic continued: "In questioning the compatibility of the revolutionary and artistic temperaments, Stoppard for the first time makes politics a central issue in his work." But the playwright was able to deepen his examinations of more "serious" issues without sacrificing entertainment value or humor, as Alan Rich concluded: "The external brilliances in *Travesties,* its manic virtuosity of language, its diabolical manipulation of time and notion, cannot elude any visitor to Tom Stoppard's verbal prank. . . . It is thinking-man's theater that makes it a privilege to think."

Stoppard's political concerns come to the fore in *Every Good Boy Deserves Favor,* a piece for actors and orchestra set to the music of Andre Previn. Set in a prison hospital inhabited by lunatics and dissidents, *Every Good Boy Deserves Favor* "has the witty dialogue and clever plot that we associate with Stoppard's plays, and a sense of social concern that we didn't," *Los Angeles Times* critic Dan Sullivan recounted. Stoppard brings the musicians into the action of the play through the character of a madman who believes he conducts an imaginary orchestra; not only does the group respond to his direction, but one of the violinists doubles as his psychiatrist. The play's use of "irony, mixed identities, outrageous conceits (not to mention a full-scale symphony orchestra)," observed *Washington Post* contributor Michael Billington, distinguished it as "the work of a dazzling high-wire performer." In addition, the critic noted, *Every Good Boy* is "a profoundly moral play about the brainwashing of political dissidents in Soviet mental hospitals."

John Simon, writing in *New York,* faulted the play for being "too clever by half," and added that the concept of a play for full orchestra seems forced and contrived. But Gussow posited that "the full orchestra and the enormous stage give the play a richness and even an opulence that embellishes the author's comic point of view." He continued: "So much of the comedy comes from the contrast between the small reality—two men in a tiny cell—and the enormity of the delusion." "Nothing if not imaginative, Stoppard's plot makes the orchestra an active, provocative participant in the story," Richard Christiansen wrote in the *Chicago Tribune.* Nevertheless, the critic advised, the play also stands "on its own as a moving and eloquent work, an occasional piece of quick wit and deep thoughtfulness."

With *Night and Day* Stoppard broaches another "public issue: the role of the press in what is commonly called the Western World," as James Lardner described it in the *Washington Post.* Set in an African nation beset by revolution, *Night and Day* looks at issues of censorship, politics, colonialism, and journalistic ethics through the character of a young, idealistic reporter. "There are theatergoers who will not sit still for a play that encompasses an intellectual debate, no matter how gracefully rendered," Lardner theorized. Indeed, some observers criticized the play for emphasizing ideas over characters; *New York Times* reviewer Walter Kerr, for instance, said that "virtually no effort is made during the evening to link up thought and events, arguments and action. The debate really takes place in a void." In contrast, Judith Martin believed that in *Night and Day* "it even seems as if the good lines were written for the play, rather than the play's having been written to display unrelated good cracks," as she wrote in the *Washington Post Weekend.* "This is a taut drama, dealing intelligently and with a degree of moral passion with a range of difficult issues," Wright concluded. "Moreover, despite its clear plea for freedom of speech and action, the play does not oversimplify the issues: *Night and Day* presents a genuine dramatic debate which confronts divergent and often contradictory attitudes."

Indeed, Stoppard's plays frequently demonstrated a "delight in contradiction and paradox," according to *New York Times* contributor Benedict Nightingale, with "rebuttal constantly following argument, counter rebuttal following rebuttal, and no conclusion." Gussow explained in the *New York Times:* Stoppard "has always taken pride in his ability to refute himself endlessly, a practice especially well suited to dialogue. His interest is less in offering a judgment than in making light of other people's pretensions." A play such as *Jumpers,* for instance, takes various alternatives, "brings them together and lets them fight it out," London *Times* critic Irving Wardle summarized. The purpose of this war, stated Brater, is to confront the audience "with the recognizable dilemma of the man who, having read much, can't be sure of anything. The more possibilities Stoppard's marginal man allows for, the less he understands." Stoppard commented on the lack of firm conclusions in his work to Samuel G. Freedman in the *New York Times:* "If one had arrived at a definite answer, there wouldn't be a play to write about. . . . Most interesting questions . . . cannot be simply resolved." "Only a writer who cares deeply about convictions would dare to write plays to call his own convictions and those of others to account," Carl E. Rollyson, Jr. suggested in the *Dictionary of Literary Biography Yearbook.* Throughout his career, the critic continued, Stoppard "has been willing to test his principles and his lack of principles more directly and personally even as he has taken on profoundly difficult historical and political subjects that many artists of his stature would shy away from."

In the double-bill *Dogg's Hamlet, Cahoot's Macbeth,* for example, Stoppard "brilliantly harnessed his linguistic ingenuity to his passion for the cause of artistic freedom," Gerald M. Berkowitz noted in *Theatre Journal.* In the first half, *Dogg's Hamlet,* a group of schoolboys contort the English language by giving entirely new meanings to familiar words; their interactions with puzzled outsiders culminate in an abbreviated performance of *Hamlet.* The second play, *Cahoot's Macbeth,* presents an underground performance of Shakespeare that is interrupted by government censors; only by switching to "Dogg," the language of the first play, do the actors avoid arrest. Critics were split over the effectiveness of this double-bill; *Chicago Tribune* writer Sid Smith, for instance, found that the second play "promises more than it delivers, certainly more than a rehash of the first play's comedy." Berkowitz, however, thought that "Stoppard knows what he's doing," for instead of reducing "this serious play to the farcical level of the first," the switch to Dogg reinforced his message, which "strikes us with tremendous power: repressive societies fear artistic expression because it is a 'language' they don't share and thus can't control." As a result, the critic concluded, *Dogg's Hamlet, Cahoot's Macbeth* "may well be . . . [Stoppard's] most important play so far, and a harbinger of major works to come."

Berkowitz's words were prophetic, for in 1982 Stoppard premiered one of his most highly acclaimed dramas, *The Real Thing.* While the playwright returned to a favorite form, that of the play-within-a-play, his subject—"an imaginatively and uniquely theatrical exploration of the pain and the power of love," as Christiansen characterized it—surprised many critics. The opening reveals a man confronting his wife with evidence of her adultery; it soon becomes clear, however, that this encounter is only a scene in a play. "Reality" is much more complex, for the actors in the first scene are being betrayed by their spouses—the playwright and his mistress Annie, another actress. Henry is the successful author of witty, cerebral dramas of infidelity, but his own struggles with love, especially those in his sometimes-troubled marriage to Annie, prove more difficult and painful. Annie's romantic involvement with a young actor and professional involvement with the young revolutionary Brodie cause Henry to not only question his assumptions about love, but his opinions about the significance of writing. While the meaning of the "real thing" might seem a commonplace theme for Stoppard to examine, "home truths can be banal," Sullivan observed. "All that an author can do is to write a non-banal play around them, and this Stoppard has done."

Augmenting Stoppard's examination of romance and writing is a structure which scatters scenes from Henry's play throughout the show, thus forcing the audience to decide what is "real" and what is "drama." "The ingenious patterning helps to put the real thing into the same perspective as the artificial thing," Ronald Hayman suggested in the *Times Literary Supplement,* explaining that the playwright is clever in selecting "theatre people as his subject and to perch the action so spectacularly between their theatrical lives and their private lives." Thus "some of the play's intricacies defy full appreciation on a single viewing," *Washington Post* writer David Richards maintained, for the text is "intrinsically playful even as it deals with the delicate and obscure covenants that link men and women." But Frank Rich regarded the interchanges between "reality" and "drama" as "mannered digressions designed mainly to add literary gilding to a conventional story." "But it's not cleverness for cleverness' sake," Richards countered. "Indeed, Stoppard is asking where theater leaves off and reality begins." Rollyson likewise asserted that this blurring of reality is Stoppard's intent: "Gradually their 'real' lives come to resemble their stage roles, but the point is that the theatricality of human lives is as 'real' as anything else about the nature of their existence."

The Real Thing "is an integrally designed piece whose content and form are inseparable," Frank Rich proposed. "The play is not only about how Henry learns to feel love, but also about how he learns to write about love." "Henry agonizes about being unable to write love scenes and complains that his credibility is hanging by a thread," Hayman elaborated, and the resulting dialogue "bristles wittily." Henry also learns, however, that the same words which provide him with his livelihood are insufficient to completely resolve real-life problems. Consequently, *The Real Thing* had a dramatic power created by "that tension between its glittering verbal surface and those dark, confused emotions beyond the reach of words," Richards wrote in another review. While the play "is every bit as clever as *Travesties* or *Jumpers,*" the critic remarked in his first article, it also "recognizes the impotence of the intellect when confronted with the ambiguities of love." "Without blunting his wit," Catharine Hughes concluded in *America,* "Stoppard hints not of a new beginning—he does not require one—but a deepening of the talent that has been in evidence since New York audiences first encountered him in *Rosencrantz and Guildenstern Are Dead.*"

Stoppard's *Arcadia* juxtaposes three different time periods on one stage—the years 1809 and 1812 as well as present day—and combines such topics as mathematics and chaos theory, landscape gardening, and Lord Byron. In addition, noted Anne Barton in the *New York Review of Books,* "*Arcadia* constantly engages the imaginary in a dialogue with the historically true." Several reviewers noted the need for playgoers to review the printed text before seeing the play, seeing the play twice, or utilizing both methods to yield a better understanding of the complex story. In terms of staging and theatrics, however, "*Arcadia* is muted by comparison with most of Stoppard's previous work," found Barton. Barton praised the effort, hailing it as "wonderfully inventive and funny, full of the epigrams, puns and verbal pyrotechnics characteristic of this dramatist." Joseph Hynes, commenting in the *Virginia Quarterly Review,* praised Stoppard's effort as "the wittiest, most movingly paradoxical, English dramatic language of this half-century."

Produced in 2002, Stoppard's anticipated *The Coast of Utopia* is a nine-hour look at the lives of some of Russia's revolutionary and liberal minds from the nineteenth century. Though not particularly impressed by the plays as a whole, an *American Theater* critic wrote that *Voyage* can possibly stand on its own and "can be seen to possess the emotional and physical sweep of Chekhov and Gorky." The reviewer considered *The Coast of Utopia* a grand undertaking and wrote that Stoppard and the trilogy are "brave enough to hint the fact that we may never reach the promised land [Utopia]." Herb Greer, a theater critic for *World and I,* acknowledged that Stoppard's work usually contains "wonderfully civilized humor." Ultimately however, Stoppard over-researched and over-thought his characters in *Voyage, Shipwreck,* and *Salvage.*

Stoppard's personal insights into his work were captured in *Conversations with Stoppard.* Spanning a twenty-year period, these conversations are the result of interviews Stoppard had with theatre critic Mel Gussow and focus primarily on the development of and influences on his work. Bevya Rosten in the *New York Times Book Review* remarked, "Gussow offers a chance to engage with the witty and quirky mind of a unique artist." Susan Rushinko, commenting in *World Literature Today,* noted that "Stoppard's remarks about his writing habits and sources of ideas for his plays are as free-wheeling and as fascinating as the debates in his plays." Rushinko also remarked on Stoppard's confession of his "early admiration for Margaret Thatcher and Rupert Murdoch" as well as his sources of names for his characters. However, Jane Montgomery, in the *Times Literary Supplement,* found Gussow somewhat lax in his interviewing methods. "Gussow's interrogation is not probing . . . nor is his search for Stoppard's inner balance particularly contingent. His prepared questions often appear stilted in context, and he seems to rely chiefly on Stoppard's own graceful loquacity to steer the conversation." "On one level," Montgomery continued, "this is informative and interesting. . . . But just how many of [Stoppard's] 'apparent impromptus' were 'worked out beforehand' is the kind of interesting question Gussow will not, or cannot, address."

Stoppard's talents extend beyond writing for the stage; he is also noted for several highly literate screenplay adaptations, such as *Empire of the Sun, The Russia House,* and his own *Rosencrantz and Guildenstern Are Dead.* He has also distinguished himself as the creator of original works for radio, and he is "one of the writers who use the medium most imaginatively," Hayman stated in the *Times Literary Supplement,* for Stoppard "enjoys doing what can't be done on any other medium." The playwright makes the most of the exclusively aural medium, for in works such as *Albert's Bridge* and *If You're Glad I'll Be Frank* "what is left to the imagination gives the comedy its impetus," Gussow observed. As Rollyson explained, this strategy worked well because Stoppard "is under no constraint to hew to the facts or to balance his facility with words against the action or visualization for the stage and screen." In addition, Stoppard told Paul Donovan of the *Sunday Times Review,* "If you are dependent only on what people can hear, you can jerk things around in time and space, draw parallels and spin loops." The result, Rollyson concluded, is that "Stoppard has always worked well in radio and has produced for it some of his most innovative probings of human psychology."

Stoppard's use of various dramatic techniques, intricately worked into innovative forms, contributes greatly to the vitality of his plays. "He is a skilled craftsman," Wright said, "handling with great dexterity and precision plots of extreme ingenuity and intricacy. The plays are steeped in theatrical convention and stock comic situations, with mistaken identity, verbal misunderstandings, innuendo, and farcical incongruity." The playwright's use of traditional dramatic elements, contended

Dean, reveals his "penchant for and skill in parodying popular dramatic genres. Like most contemporary playwrights, he has not contented himself with the confines of representational drama but has broken out of those constraints by revivifying the soliloquy, aside, song, and interior monologue." Despite his "free" use of various dramatic forms, Stoppard is able to superimpose an overall structure on his plays, Cahn declared: "Amid all the clutter and episodic action, a structure emerges, a tribute to the organizing powers of the playwright's rationality and his expectations of the audience's ability to grasp that structure." As the author related to Kroll, "Theater is an event, not a text. I respond to spectacle. Ambushing the audience is what theater is all about."

Part of Stoppard's "ambush" involves the way he shrewdly infuses his plays with sophisticated concepts. As Billington described, Stoppard "can take a complex idea, deck it out in fancy dress and send it skipping and gambolling in front of large numbers of people," for the playwright has "a matchless ability to weave into a serious debate boffo laughs and knockdown zingers." This combination has led some critics to attempt to classify his works as either humorous or philosophical. Stoppard himself, however, believes that questions concerning the comic intent of his works are superfluous. "All along I thought of myself as writing entertainments, like *The Real Inspector Hound,* and plays of ideas like *Jumpers,*" he told Gussow. "The confusion arises because I treat plays of ideas in just about the same knockabout way as I treat the entertainments." He further explained to *Washington Post* interviewer Joseph McLellan: "The stuff I write tends to work itself out in comedy terms most of the time." But whatever degree of comedy or seriousness in Stoppard's approach, Nightingale concluded in the *New York Times,* he is consistent in the themes he examines: "All along he's confronted dauntingly large subjects, all along he's asked dauntingly intricate questions about them, and all along he's sought to touch the laugh glands as well as the intellect."

Various reviewers have attempted to analyze and define Stoppard's thematic concerns as he presents them within his plays. His ideas are often considered from an existentialist perspective and encompass such concepts as "the nature of perception, art, illusion and reality, the relativity of meaning, and the problematic status of truth," Wright declared. "Recurring themes include chance, choice, freedom, identity, memory, time, and death." Stoppard provided Tom Prideaux of *Look* with a simpler interpretation of his concerns: "One writes about human beings under stress—whether it is about losing one's trousers or being nailed to the cross." Cahn suggested, however, that Stoppard's works contains a "unifying element" by consistently demonstrating the playwright's "faith in man's mind." The critic elaborated: "He rejects the irrational, the reliance on emotion instead of intellect, the retreat from independent thought."

Stoppard's focus on human intellect and ideas has led some critics to fault his work as one-dimensional. Roger Scruton, for example, maintained in *Encounter* that "Stoppard is not a dramatist—he does not portray characters, who develop in relation to each other, and generate dialogue from their mutual constraints." "Stoppard has never been known for powerful characterizations," DeVries similarly conceded. "People in his plays have usually taken a back seat to the ideas they articulate." However, the critic added, this "simple trade-off . . . has worked because of the compelling intelligence of the ideas." The playwright himself admitted to Gussow in the *New York Times:* "I'm a playwright interested in ideas and forced to invent characters to express those ideas." Other observers, however, refute the notion that Stoppard's work is wanting in depth. "I, for one, have never been disturbed by a lack of feeling or emotion in his plays," Wilson noted, "though it is true that he has often pursued a philosophical conundrum or turn of phrase at the expense of his characters." And still others believe Stoppard's philosophical investigations are a means of exploring the humanity of his characters. As Nightingale noted in the *New Statesman:* "What other dramatist worries so earnestly yet entertainingly about the moral nature both of ourselves and of the dark bewildering universe we glumly inhabit?"

Because Stoppard's wit "can hold its own with Oscar Wilde, G.B. Shaw and Noel Coward," Edwin Wilson commented in the *Wall Street Journal,* he is able to take his "fascination with ideas . . . and make them exciting." "Stoppard's special distinction is his linguistic and conceptual virtuosity," Gussow asserted in the *New York Times Magazine.* "One has to look back to Shaw and Wilde to find an English playwright who could so enlist the language as his companion in creativity. Others might finish ahead in terms of tragic vision or emotional commitment, but as a wordsmith Stoppard is supreme." Dean, who allies Stoppard with "the wittiest if not greatest writers of the English language," explained that "Stoppard indulges himself as well as his audience in the sheer pleasure of experiencing the density and richness of which the language is capable. Moreover, his attention to language results not only in humor but also in precision. As a means of considering the difficulty of communication as well as a comic vehicle, language is assiduously explored and exploited by Stoppard."

"There is plenty to indicate that if Stoppard had done no more than employ the drama as a vehicle for moral messages he would still have been a force in the theatre," Clive James suggested in *Encounter.* But, the critic continued, "Stoppard's heady dramatic designs impress us not as deliberately sophisticated variations on the reality we know but as simplified models of a greater reality—the inhuman cosmos which contains the human world. . . . If his speculative scope recalls modern physics, his linguistic rigour recalls modern philosophy. It is a potent combination whatever its validity." "If his plays endure," Dean claimed, "Stoppard's unique accomplishment may prove to be the theatrical treatment of the intellectual and artistic follies of our age." "In the past Stoppard has given us a new kind of comedy to capture the drama of contemporary ideas," Brater similarly stated. "Judging from the quality of his new work, there is no reason to suspect that this serious writer masquerading as a comedian has run out of ammunition. For style in Stoppard has always been a question of substance as well as technique. What he has found in his theater," the critic concluded, "is not only a special way of saying something, but something, at least, that needed very much to be said."

BIOGRAPHICAL AND CRITICAL SOURCES:

BOOKS

Bigsby, Christopher, and William Edgar, editors, *Writers and Their Work,* Longman (London, England), 1976.

Bock, Hedwig, and Albert Wertheim, editors, *Essays on Contemporary British Drama,* Hüber (Munich, Germany), 1981.

Brustein, Robert, *The Third Theatre,* Knopf (New York, NY), 1969.

Cahn, Victor L., *Beyond Absurdity: The Plays of Tom Stoppard,* Fairleigh Dickinson University Presses (Rutherford, NJ), 1979.

Contemporary Dramatists, St. James Press (London, England), 1982.

Contemporary Literary Criticism, Thomson Gale (Detroit, MI), Volume 1, 1973, Volume 3, 1975, Volume 4, 1975, Volume 5, 1976, Volume 8, 1978, Volume 15, 1980, Volume 29, 1984, Volume 34, 1985, Volume 63, 1991, Volume 91, 1996.

Dean, Joan Fitzpatrick, *Tom Stoppard: Comedy As a Moral Matrix,* University of Missouri Press (Columbia, MO), 1981.

Dictionary of Literary Biography, Volume 13: *British Dramatists since World War II,* Thomson Gale (Detroit, MI), 1982.

Dictionary of Literary Biography Yearbook: 1985, Thomson Gale (Detroit, MI), 1985.

Nadel, Ira, *Double Act: A Life of Tom Stoppard,* Methuen (London, England), 2002.

Schlueter, June, *Dramatic Closure: Reading the End,* Fairleigh Dickinson University Press (Rutherford, NJ), 1995.

Taylor, John Russell, *The Second Wave: British Drama for the Seventies,* Methuen (London, England), 1971.

PERIODICALS

America, February 18, 1984; January 29, 1994, p. 23.

American Theater, November, 2002, review of *The Coast of Utopia,* p. 40.

Atlantic, May, 1968.

Chicago Tribune, April 24, 1985; June 3, 1985; September 20, 1985; March 17, 1991.

Christian Science Monitor, April 25, 1974; November 6, 1975; December 6, 1982; January 11, 1984.

Commentary, December, 1967; June, 1974.

Commonweal, November 10, 1967.

Contemporary Literature, summer, 1979.

Drama, summer, 1968; fall, 1969; summer, 1972; winter, 1973; autumn, 1974.

Encounter, September, 1974; November, 1975; February, 1983.

Harper's Bazaar, March, 1995, p. 126.

Hudson Review, winter, 1967-68; summer, 1968.

Life, February 9, 1968.

Listener, April 11, 1968; April 18, 1968; June 20, 1974.

London, August, 1968; August-September, 1976.

Look, December 26, 1967; February 9, 1968.

Los Angeles Times, June 6, 1986; December 20, 1986; February 20, 1991.

Nation, November 6, 1967; May 11, 1974; May 18, 1974.

National Observer, October 23, 1967.

National Review, December 12, 1967; November 29, 1993, p. 71.

New Leader, September 21, 1992, p. 21.

New Republic, June 15, 1968; May 18, 1974; November 22, 1975; January 30, 1984.

New Statesman, June 14, 1974.

Newsweek, August 7, 1967; August 31, 1970; March 4, 1974; January 8, 1975; November 10, 1975; January 16, 1984; April 3, 1995, p. 64.

New York, March 11, 1974; May 13, 1974; August 26, 1974; November 17, 1975; August 13-20, 1979; July 26, 1993, p. 51; January 9, 1995, p. 36.

New Yorker, May 6, 1967; October 28, 1967; May 4, 1968; May 6, 1972; March 4, 1974; May 6, 1974; January 6, 1975; January 24, 1977.
New York Post, April 23, 1974; January 6, 1984.
New York Review of Books, June 8, 1995, p. 28.
New York Times, October 18, 1967; October 29, 1967; March 24, 1968; May 8, 1968; June 19, 1968; July 8, 1968; October 15, 1968; April 23, 1974; July 29, 1979; August 1, 1979; October 4, 1979; November 25, 1979; November 28, 1979; June 23, 1983; November 22, 1983; January 6, 1984; January 15, 1984; February 20, 1984; August 1, 1984; May 17, 1987; May 18, 1987; November 22, 1987; November 3, 1989; November 26, 1989; December 26, 1989; February 8, 1991.
New York Times Book Review, August 25, 1968; March 3, 1996, p. 19.
New York Times Magazine, January 1, 1984.
Observer (London, England), August 1, 1993.
Observer Review, April 16, 1967; December 17, 1967; June 23, 1968.
Playboy, May, 1968.
Plays and Players, July, 1970.
Publishers Weekly, February 12, 1996, p. 24.
Punch, April 19, 1967.
Reporter, November 16, 1967.
Saturday Review, August 26, 1972; January 8, 1977.
Show Business, April 25, 1974.
Spectator, June 22, 1974.
Stage, February 10, 1972.
Sunday Times Review, April 21, 1991.
Theatre Journal, March, 1980.
Time, October 27, 1967; August 9, 1968; March 11, 1974; May 6, 1974; June 20, 1983; August 24, 1992, p. 69; July 19, 1993, p. 60.
Times (London, England), November 18, 1982; April 3, 1985.
Times Literary Supplement, March 21, 1968; December 29, 1972; November 26, 1982; December 24, 1982; September 29, 1995, p. 23.
Times Saturday Review (London, England), June 29, 1991.
Transatlantic Review, summer, 1968.
Variety, November 22, p. 36.
Village Voice, May 4, 1967; October 26, 1967; May 2, 1974.
Virginia Quarterly Review, autumn, 1995, p. 642.
Vogue, November 15, 1967; April 15, 1968; December, 1994, p. 180.
Wall Street Journal, March 11, 1974; November 3, 1975; January 6, 1984.
Washington Post, May 11, 1969; June 25, 1969; July 9, 1969; August 29, 1978; November 26, 1978; January 12, 1984; May 23, 1985.
World and I, May, 2003, Herb Greer, review of *The Coast of Utopia,,* p. 228.
World Literature Today, winter, 1978; summer, 1986; spring, 1995, p. 369; winter, 1996, p. 193.

* * *

STRAUB, Peter 1943-
(Peter Francis Straub)

PERSONAL: Born March 2, 1943, in Milwaukee, WI; son of Gordon Anthony and Elvena (Nilsestuen) Straub; married Susan Bitker (a counselor), August 22, 1966; children: Benjamin Bitker, Emma Sydney Valli. *Education:* University of Wisconsin—Madison, B.A., 1965; Columbia University, M.A., 1966; attended University College, Dublin, 1969-72. *Hobbies and other interests:* Jazz, opera.

ADDRESSES: Home—53 West 85th St., New York, NY 10024.

CAREER: University School, Milwaukee, WI, English teacher, 1966-69; writer, 1969—.

MEMBER: International PEN, Mystery Writers of America, Horror Writers Association.

AWARDS, HONORS: "Best Novel" nomination, World Fantasy Awards, 1981, for *Shadowland;* British Fantasy Award and August Derleth Award, both 1983, both for *Floating Dragon;* World Fantasy Award for Best Novel, World Fantasy Convention, 1989, for *Koko;* World Fantasy Award for Best Novella, World Fantasy Convention, 1993, for *The Ghost Village;* Bram Stoker Award for Best Novel, Horror Writers Association, 1994, for *The Throat,* and 2000, for *Mister X;* Bram Stoker Award for Best Fiction Collection, Horror Writers Association, 2000, for *Magic Terror;* World Fantasy Award nomination, best anthology category, 2003, for *Conjunctions 39: The New Wave Fabulists;* Bram Stoker Award for Best Novel, 2003, for *Lost Boy, Lost Girl,* and 2004, for *In the Night Room.*

WRITINGS:

Ishmael (poetry), Turret Books (London, England), 1972, Underwood/Miller, 1973.

Open Air (poetry), Irish University Press (Shannon, Ireland), 1972.

Marriages (novel), Coward (New York, NY), 1973.

Julia (novel; also see below), Coward (New York, NY), 1975, published as *Full Circle,* Corgi (London, England), 1977.

If You Could See Me Now (novel; also see below), Coward (New York, NY), 1977.

Ghost Story (novel), Coward (New York, NY), 1979.

Shadowland (novel), Coward (New York), 1980.

The General's Wife (story), D.M. Grant (West Kingston, RI), 1982.

Floating Dragon (novel), Putnam (New York, NY), 1983.

Leeson Park and Belsize Square: Poems 1970-1975, Underwood/Miller, 1983.

(With Stephen King) *The Talisman* (novel), Viking (New York, NY), 1984, reprinted, Random House (New York, NY), 2001.

Wild Animals: Three Novels (contains *Julia, If You Could See Me Now,* and *Under Venus* [also see below]), Putnam (New York, NY), 1984.

Blue Rose (novella), Underwood/Miller, 1985.

Under Venus, Berkley (New York, NY), 1985.

Koko (first novel in the *"Blue Rose"* trilogy), Dutton (New York, NY), 1988.

Mystery (second novel in the *"Blue Rose"* trilogy), Dutton (New York, NY), 1990.

Mrs. God, paintings by Rick Berry, Donald Grant (Hampton Falls, NH), 1990.

Houses without Doors (short stories), Dutton (New York, NY), 1990.

The Throat (third novel in the *"Blue Rose"* trilogy), Dutton (New York, NY), 1993.

The Hellfire Club (novel), Random House (New York, NY), 1996.

Mister X, Random House (New York, NY), 1999.

Magic Terror: Seven Tales, Random House (New York, NY), 2000.

(With Stephen King) *Black House,* Random House (New York, NY), 2001.

Lost Boy, Lost Girl (novel), Random House (New York, NY), 2003.

In the Night Room (novel), Random House (New York, NY), 2004.

(Editor) *H.P. Lovecraft: Tales*, Library of America (New York, NY), 2005.

Also author of the novella *The Ghost Village* and editor of anthology *Conjunctions 39: The New Wave Fabulists,* Bard College, 2003. Straub's novels have been translated into a number of foreign languages.

ADAPTATIONS: Julia was adapted for the 1981 Peter Fetterman film, *The Haunting of Julia* (titled *Full Circle* in England); *Ghost Story* was adapted for the 1981 Universal Pictures film of the same title. *Floating Dragon* was adapted for cassette by Listen for Pleasure Cassettes in 1987; *Koko* was adapted for cassette by Simon & Schuster Audioworks in 1989.

SIDELIGHTS: One of the most popular practitioners of horror and suspense fiction, American writer Peter Straub is the author of such well-known titles as *Ghost Story, Shadowland, Floating Dragon, The Talisman* (with Stephen King), and *Koko.* More than ten million copies of his novels have been sold. Straub employs an array of ghastly elements, including hauntings, vengeful agents of murder, gruesome deaths, and fantastical happenings. He is especially good at, as *Maclean's* Barbara Matthews noted, "stark cold horror—the kind worshippers of the genre love to spirit away and read quickly, inhaling fright and holding it in their lungs until it becomes brittle enough to shatter if so much as a telephone rings." More than spine-tingling thrillers, however, Straub's novels are also imaginative explorations into the realistic, often personal, roots of the unreal. Patricia L. Skarda observed in *Dictionary of Literary Biography Yearbook* that Straub's "best work . . . focuses on private experiences on the margin where nature and supernature meet, where reality converges with dream, where writing leaves off and the imagination takes over." Straub commented to Joseph Barbato in *Publishers Weekly* on the effects he wishes to elicit: "I want readers to feel as if they've left the real world behind just a little bit, but are still buoyed up and confident, as if dreaming. I want them left standing in midair with a lot of peculiar visions in their heads."

Straub decided to become a novelist—though not a horror novelist—in the early 1970s, after abandoning an academic career. A former high school English teacher who left the United States for Dublin's University College, Straub was at work on a doctorate when he became disenchanted. "The plan was to get a Ph.D. and come back to get a better job," he told Joseph McLellan in the *Washington Post.* "Then, in Ireland, I suddenly realized what the trouble really was: I had always thought of myself as a novelist although I had not written a novel. I could feel fiction growing inside me, characters and situations forming themselves in my mind as I walked down the street." Already a published poet, Straub began work in 1972 on his first novel, *Marriages,* about the extramarital affair of an American businessman in Europe. Published a year later, *Marriages* received favorable reviews. Ronald Bryden in the *Listener* called it "the other side of the Jamesian tradition: an American chronicle of the quest for European richness, complexity and depth," while a *Times Literary Supplement* critic characterized Straub as a "poetic novelist," adding that "it may be this skill which enables him to place so securely the sense of gesture, and the texture of atmosphere, which characterizes *Marriages.* "

Straub was at work on a second novel, *Under Venus,* when financial pressures prompted a change to his writing efforts. "*Marriages* had not done very well," he told Barbato, explaining that it was released at "just about the time that publishers were beginning to cut back on midlist—and bottom-list—authors. And I was one of those guys coming along with more of the same. It unnerved me. I knew I could never hold a real job—that I'd be an impossible employee anywhere. I had to save my life by writing a book that could get published." Despite numerous revisions, *Under Venus* failed to attract a publisher (later it appeared in the three-novel collection *Wild Animals*). Straub's agent stepped in and suggested he try writing a Gothic. "I found that I had a natural bent toward this kind of thing," he told Barbato. "Later, I had to deal with that, because I had never seen myself as that type of writer. I dealt with it by trying to see just how much I could do with that peculiar stock of imagery and leaden conventions that you're given as a horror novelist."

Straub's horror debut occurred in 1975 with *Julia,* the harrowing tale of an American woman in England haunted by the tortured ghost of a murdered child—and the emerging knowledge of responsibility in the death of her own daughter (the victim of an emergency tracheotomy). While some reviewers noted inconsistent plotting and characterization, many acknowledged Straub's flair for the gothic. "In the last resort, *Julia* . . . succeeds in the brutal business of delivering supernatural thrills," wrote Michael Mason in the *Times Literary Supplement;* Straub "has thought of a nasty kind of haunting, and he presses it upon the reader to a satisfying point of discomfort." Valentine Cunningham in *New Statesman* called the book "an extraordinarily gripping and tantalising read. . . . Every dubious solution and ambivalent pattern is possible, for almost anything becomes believable under the novelist's stunningly gothic manipulations."

After *Julia* Straub wrote *If You Could See Me Now,* a tale set in the U.S. Midwest, about the vengeful spirit of a murdered girl who returns to inflict horrors upon the community where she died. Critics particularly praised the novel's narrative timing, structure, and the authenticity of local settings. "Straub is good at slick manipulation of pace," wrote Jonathan Keates in *New Statesman,* adding that "he has an equally nifty way with rustic grotesques." Keates called the book "crisp, classy buggaboo . . . full of neatly managed understatements and chillingly calculated surprises." Peter Ackroyd in *Spectator* singled out the book's "filmic" qualities: "*If You Could See Me Now* makes great play, for example, with contrasts of speech and silence, of crowd scenes and empty landscapes, and of the ways in which a written 'close-up' can be employed to suggest deep 'emotion.' Some of the book's scenes, in fact, can only be understood in visual terms."

Following these ventures, Straub embarked upon the novel that would become his breakthrough, the bestselling *Ghost Story.* Drawing upon various horror story motifs and conventions, *Ghost Story* is the tale of a rural New England community terrorized by a young woman, killed years earlier, who returns to exact retribution from the four elderly townsmen (The Chowder Society) responsible for her death. The Chowder Society's members, who regularly meet to exchange ghost stories, become involved in a frantic race to save themselves and the town from the gruesome revenge of the "shapeshifter" Eva Galli. "What's interesting about *Ghost Story* is that Mr. Straub . . . seems to have decided to write a summarizing American tale of the supernatural, and to throw into it every scrap of horror-cliche and campfire trash that he can muster," commented Christopher Lehmann-Haupt in the *New York Times.* "Still, because Mr. Straub is so good at writing eerie set-pieces and because the very complexity of his story keeps it baffling to the end, I look back on the time spent reading *Ghost Story* as on an interval distorted by fever."

Straub's aim in *Ghost Story,* as Jennifer Dunning quoted the author in the *New York Times,* was to "take the genre and pull it upstairs a little bit. . . . Not exactly transcend the genre, but make a little more of the material than has been made of it in the recent past." *Ghost Story* draws from early masters in the field, including Nathaniel Hawthorne, Henry James, Edgar Allan Poe, and Sheridan Le Fanu. Some reviewers objected to the novel's overt deference to these influences. "Although Straub's 'affection' for the proven devices of his betters is estimable, many of these allusions seem rather pedantic and pointless," wrote Jack Sullivan in the *Washington Post Book World.* Douglas Hill commented in *Maclean's* that "at times the book stumbles over its structure: all the epigraphs and cute chapter titles are merely pretentious." Straub admitted to Thomas Lask in the *New York Times,* "There was a certain amount of audacity in the overt references to the great writers, but today the form is debased, and it is a messianic thing to me to elevate it and make it honorable." A number of reviewers were impressed with Straub's creation. Gene Lyons in the *New York Times Book Review* called *Ghost Story* "a quite sophisticated literary entertainment," while Valerie Lloyd remarked in *Newsweek* that "with considerable technical skill, Peter Straub has constructed an extravagant entertainment which, though flawed, achieves in its second half some awesome effects." She concluded: "It is, I think, the best thing of its kind since Shirley Jackson's 'The Haunting of Hill House.'"

Straub moved back to the United States after the success of *Ghost Story* and embarked upon a period that produced some of his best-known and bestselling titles. However, his next novel, *Shadowland,* received mixed reviews and, according to Skarda, "confused an audience expecting ghoulish ghosts." The story of two boys who become involved in a world of magic where anything happens, *Shadowland* 's "prophecy and telepathy, use and misuse of sleights of hand and mind convert a strange Arizona prep school and a Vermont home into a platonic inversion where every shadow seems substance." Lehmann-Haupt noted that in *Shadowland* Straub "appears to be taking the classic elements of the Grimms' fairy tale as far as they can go." Some critics remarked that the fantastical events in the novel appeared too much at random, thereby diminishing the suspense. "*Shadowland* ultimately has neither the gnomic simplicity of the fairy-tale nor the eerie sense of a grossly interrupted reality, which [Straub] caught more successfully in *Ghost Story,*" commented Thomas Sutcliffe in the *Times Literary Supplement.*

Straub's bestselling novel *Floating Dragon,* however, seemed to meet the expectations generated by *Ghost Story.* In the sweeping story of a malevolent spirit which periodically visits an affluent Connecticut suburb with death and destruction, Straub creates "a compendium of horrors designed to punish the shallow housewives, adulterers, corporate tycoons, and even the children in a commuter community," noted Skarda. "*Floating Dragon,* beneath its remarkable repertoire of horrific details, is a simple moral tale of the confrontation between good and evil," wrote Alan Bold in the *Times Literary Supplement.* "Nevertheless, it represents a new level of sophistication in the Gothic novel. Straub plays games with the structure, rapidly switching from third-person to first-person narrative, and teases the reader with biblical symbols and red herrings. The novel is sustained with great skill as the battle between good and evil is impressively, if agonizingly, stretched over the disturbingly supernatural plot." Alan Ryan commented in the *Washington Post Book World:* "If *Floating Dragon* is sometimes baffling, flawed in some structural elements, and perhaps a little too long for its own good, it is at the same time both ruthlessly contemporary and steeped in tradition, gruesomely chilling, and told with a narrative strength and a lively colloquial style that readers should welcome."

In his next novel Straub teamed up with friend and fellow horror writer Stephen King—via word processors connected by telephone—to produce the blockbuster *The Talisman.* Drawing upon both writers' immense popularity, the book was an instant bestseller; critics, however, felt that it was a bit overstocked with mad capers and special effects. The fantasy/adventure story of a boy who goes in search of a magic object to cure his dying mother, *The Talisman* outlines a power struggle between good and evil in a strange world. "There's a dizzying amount of flipping in this book," maintained Peter Gorner in the *Chicago Tribune,* "and often the point is elusive." Lehmann-Haupt suggested that *The Talisman* "suffers from a surfeit of monstrosity. It takes forever to develop its smallest plot complications. It telegraphs its clues with the subtlety of falling telephone poles. It stoops to outrageous sentimentality over its boy hero. . . . It repeats and repeats unto silliness." These elements, however, are also part of the book's appeal, according to Frank Herbert in the *Washington Post Book World:* " *The Talisman* is exactly what it sets out to be—a fine variation on suspense and horror filled with many surprises, a ground King and Straub have plowed before with great success, together and individually. Together, they demonstrate once more that they are the Minnesota Fats of the novel-into-film. When they say six ball in the side pocket, that's where the six ball goes."

Straub's subsequent bestseller, *Koko,* is a notable departure from his past supernatural novels, and the first in the loosely defined "Blue Rose" trilogy, which also consists of the subsequent novels *Mystery* and *The Throat.* A psychological suspense thriller, *Koko* is the story of four Vietnam War veterans who travel to the Far East to track down a former platoon member they believe has become a deranged killer. Straub remarked to *Bestsellers '89* on his change of direction: "By the time I began *Koko,* I had pretty much done everything I could think to do with supernatural fiction. . . . Whether I knew it or not, I was saying goodbye to imagery and situations involving hallucination versus reality with which I had been involved for years. . . . What I wanted to do next was to work with the set of feelings that lay behind horror—to move in closer to the world, to work more strictly within the realistic tradition."

Straub's venture was well received. A reviewer for *Publishers Weekly* called *Koko* "a dizzying spin through those eerie psychic badlands where nightmare and insanity seem to fuse with reality." Emily Tennyson added in the *Detroit Free Press:* "Like the war that Straub seeks to analyze and explain, *Koko* wrenches the spirits of those who took part and were taken apart by Vietnam. Much more than a tale of escape and murder, *Koko* is an examination of fear in the human soul." While *Koko* affirmed Straub's ability to create terror, it was also a positive sign of a new scope to his fiction. Lucius Shepard remarked in the *Washington Post Book World:* "Judged as a thriller, *Koko* deserves to be compared with the best of the genre, to novels such as *Gorky Park* and *The Honorable Schoolboy*. . . . *Koko* is vastly entertaining, often brilliantly written, full of finely realized moments and miniatures of characterization. . . . What all this most hearteningly signals is that Peter Straub is aspiring toward a writerly range which may cause his future novels to face more discriminating judgments yet."

Set in the mid-1950s and early 1960s, Straub's novel *Mystery* focuses on Tom Pasmore, who survives a near—or perhaps actual—death experience at age ten when he is hit by a car. As Tom recuperates from his trauma, he befriends a neighbor, Lamont von Heilitz, who gradually involves him in investigating two murders—one having occurred many years ago, the other a recent event. "The story has more twists, turns, and blind alleys than most mysteries," commented Clarence Petersen in the Chicago *Tribune Books.* Also offering praise for the novel, Geoffrey Stokes in *Voice Literary Supplement* asserted that "it is the story of a secret that is trying to emerge."

The Throat is the concluding novel of Straub's trilogy of psychological horror fiction. Set in the town of Millhaven, the plot centers on the mysterious reemergence of the "Blue Rose" serial murders, which were thought to have been solved long ago. The main character, crime writer and sleuth Tim Underhill, "is forced to explore regions of his psyche and his past that are, to say the least, disturbing," observed Frank Wilson of the *New York Times Book Review.* Critics have emphasized the novel's defiance of many of the conventions of the genres it draws upon—horror and crime fiction being the most overt. Douglas E. Winter of the *Washington Post Book World,* for example, deemed the book "a masterpiece of concealment and revelation, the most intelligent novel of suspense to come along in years."

The Hellfire Club introduces Dick Dart, a serial killer who has been preying on women in a small Connecticut town. Much of the plot concerns the events that follow his kidnapping of Nora Chancel, who happens to be the publisher of a notoriously volatile and influential horror novel titled "Night Journey." As the plot of *The Hellfire Club* progresses, Nora's experience begins to resemble that of the thriller her company published. Critics have emphasized the meta-fictional, multilayered qualities of *The Hellfire Club,* admiring its complexity. "What remains impressive . . . is the way Mr. Straub has worked the fantastic elements of his story into a largely realistic plot, thereby allowing him to avoid a literal descent into the hellfire of his title," asserted Christopher Lehmann-Haupt in the *New York Times.* "This technique is promising, and one hopes he will exploit it even more successfully in future works."

In addition to his numerous novels, Straub has also written shorter narrative pieces. His short fiction appears in the collections *Houses without Doors,* which contains two novellas and five short stories, and *Magic Terror: Seven Tales,* which won a Bram Stoker Award. *Houses without Doors* received warm reviews, with critics praising in particular "Blue Rose," the story of a sadistic young man who murders his younger brother, and "The Juniper Tree," about a boy who experiences child abuse inside a movie theater. *Magic Terror* provides stories that reveal psychopathic sadists, serial killers, and—of course—ghosts. "Horror stories do not come any juicier than these arsenic-laced literary cordials," concluded Ray Olson in *Booklist.*

The Gothic novel *Mister X* pays tribute to H.P. Lovecraft with a story of terror based on familial ties. On a trip home to Edgerton, Illinois, to visit his mother's deathbed, Ned Dunstan learns of deep family secrets and of the very real danger that his father, known only as Mr. X, will murder him. Ned must discover his father's whereabouts, a task made more difficult by the killer's supernatural ability to elude pursuit. A *Publishers Weekly* reviewer called *Mister X.* "an ingenious whodunit with an intoxicating shot of the supernatural . . . one of the most invigorating horror reads of the year." In *Entertainment Weekly,* Straub admitted that the novel reflects a return to the horror/fantasy genre. "I felt free to indulge in the supernatural . . . into a territory where more or less anything goes," he said.

In 2001 Straub and Stephen King collaborated on a second novel featuring Jack Sawyer, titled *Black House.* Where Sawyer was a child in *The Talisman,* he is now an adult, a retired cop called to Wisconsin to help find a vicious serial killer of children. Sawyer's uncomfortable memories of a supernatural realm called The Territories leads him to a mysterious black house in the woods that turns out to be a portal to the other world. The story includes "dark wit, sly literary references, suspense and heartache," to quote Mary Elizabeth Williams in the *New York Times Book Review.* Several reviewers applauded the ability shown by Straub and King to keep their collaboration seamless. "Writing fiction is generally a solo exercise, and collaborations often smack of gimmickry," observed Bruce Fretts in *Entertainment Weekly.* "Yet this partnership brings out both authors' strengths—King's down-and-dirty storytelling and Straub's more sweeping literary style." *Washington Post Book World* contributor Neil Gaiman likewise concluded: "*Black House* allows us to see two master-craftsmen, each at the top of his game, collaborating with every evidence of enormous enjoyment on a summery heartland gothic. The book is hugely pleasurable, and repays a reader in search of horror, adventure or of any of the other joys, both light and dark, one can get from the best work of either of these two scribbling fellows."

BIOGRAPHICAL AND CRITICAL SOURCES:

BOOKS

Bestsellers '89, issue 1, Thomson Gale (Detroit, MI), 1989.

Contemporary Literary Criticism, Volume 28, Thomson Gale (Detroit, MI), 1984.

St. James Guide to Horror, Ghost & Gothic Writers, St. James (Detroit, MI), 1998.

PERIODICALS

Book, September, 2001, Stephanie Foote, review of *Black House,* p. 80.

Booklist, April 15, 2000, Ray Olson, review of *Magic Terror,* p. 1499.

Chicago Tribune, May 16, 1979; December 16, 1981; November 8, 1984.

Detroit Free Press, November 13, 1988.

Entertainment Weekly, February 9, 1996, p. 46; August 20, 1999, Clarissa Cruz, "The Other Fright Knight," p. 120; September 21, 2001, Bruce Fretts, "Back in 'Black': Stephen King and Peter Straub Return to the Shadows with the Delightfully Creepy Black House," p. 76.

Kirkus Reviews, August 15, 1990, p. 1126.

Library Journal, November 15, 1995, p. 101; July, 1999, Alicia Graybill, review of *Mister X,* p. 137; April 1, 2000, Alicia Graybill, review of *Magic Terror: Seven Tales,* p. 134; January 1, 2001, Michael Rogers, review of *Under Venus,* p. 164.

Listener, March 15, 1973.

Locus, September, 1991, p. 23.

Los Angeles Times Book Review, January 30, 1983; March 20, 1983; September 18, 1988; November 18, 1990.

Maclean's, May 21, 1979; January 12, 1981; March 14, 1983.

New Statesman, February 27, 1976; June 24, 1977.

Newsweek, March 26, 1979; December 24, 1984.

New York Times, April 3, 1979; April 27, 1979; May 20, 1979; October 24, 1980; December 16, 1981; January 26, 1983; November 8, 1984; February 1, 1996, p. B4; August 7, 2000, Christopher Lehmann-Haupt, "The Monster under the Bed (or Teaching the Class)."

New York Times Book Review, April 8, 1979; March 6, 1983; March 24, 1985; October 9, 1988; June 27, 1993, p. 24; February 25, 1996, p. 9; August 6, 2000, Bill Kent, review of *Magic Terror,* p. 17; November 4, 2001, Mary Elizabeth Williams, review of *Black House,* p. 32.

People, January 28, 1985.

Publishers Weekly, January 28, 1983; May 11, 1984; August 12, 1988; April 10, 1995, p. 17; November 27, 1995, p. 49; July 12, 1999, review of *Mister X,* p. 77; November 1, 1999, review of *Mister X,* p. 49; November 22, 1999, John F. Baker, "King & Straub Back Together," p. 14; September 4, 2000, review of *Magic Terror,* p. 42; September 24, 2001, Daisy Maryles, "And So Do King/Straub," p. 20; October 8, 2001, Scott Nybakken, review of *Black House,* p. 59.

Spectator, July 9, 1977.

Times Literary Supplement, March 23, 1973; February 27, 1976; April 17, 1981; March 11, 1983.

Tribune Books (Chicago), October 2, 1988; January 20, 1991, p. 12; February 18, 1996, p. 6.

Voice Literary Supplement, May, 1993, p. 25.

Washington Post, October 31, 1980; February 6, 1981; February 16, 1981; November 27, 1984.

Washington Post Book World, April 8, 1979; October 14, 1984; August 21, 1988; April 28, 1991; May 16, 1993, p. 5.

OTHER

Post Review of Black House, http://www.net-site.com/ September 30, 2001), Neil Gaiman, review of *Black House.*

Peter Straub Web site, http://www.net-site.com/straub/ (September 30, 2001).

* * *

STRAUB, Peter Francis
See STRAUB, Peter

STRAUSSLER, Tomas
See STOPPARD, Tom

See STOPPARD, Tom

* * *

STYRON, William 1925-

PERSONAL: Born June 11, 1925, in Newport News, VA; son of William Clark (a shipyard engineer) and Pauline (Abraham) Styron; married Rose Burgunder, May 4, 1953; children: Susanna, Paola, Thomas, Alexandra. *Education:* Attended Christchurch School, Middlesex County, VA, and Davidson College, NC, 1942-43; Duke University, B.A., 1947; studied writing at New School for Social Research, 1947. *Politics:* Democrat.

ADDRESSES: Home—12 Rucum Road, Roxbury, CT 06783, and Vineyard Haven, MA (summer).

CAREER: Writer. McGraw-Hill Book Co. (publishers), New York, NY, associate editor, 1947. Fellow of Silliman College, Yale University, 1964—. Honorary consultant in American Letters to the Library of Congress. Cannes Film Festival, jury president, 1983. *American Scholar,* member of editorial board, 1970-76; advisory editor of *Paris Review. Military service:* U.S. Marine Corps, World War II, 1944-45; became first lieutenant; recalled briefly in 1951.

MEMBER: National Institute of Arts and Letters, American Academy of Arts and Sciences, American Academy of Arts and Letters (inducted, 1988), Society of American Historians, Signet Society of Harvard (honorary), Academie Goncourt, Phi Beta Kappa.

AWARDS, HONORS: American Academy of Arts and Letters Prix de Rome, 1952, for *Lie down in Darkness;* Litt.D., Duke University, 1968, and Davidson College (Davidson, NC), 1986; Pulitzer Prize, 1968, and Howells Medal of the American Academy of Arts and Letters, 1970, both for *The Confessions of Nat Turner;* American Book Award, and National Book Critics Circle Award nominee, both 1980, both for *Sophie's Choice;* Connecticut Arts Award, 1984; Cino del Duca prize, 1985; Commandeur, Ordre des Arts et des Lettres (France), 1987; Edward MacDowell Medal, 1988; Bobst Award, 1989; National Magazine award, 1990; National Medal of Arts, 1993; Medal of Honor, National Arts Club, 1995; Commonwealth Award, 1995.

WRITINGS:

Lie Down in Darkness, Bobbs-Merrill (Indianapolis, IN), 1951.
The Long March, Vintage (New York, NY), 1957.
Set This House on Fire, Random House (New York, NY), 1960.
The Confessions of Nat Turner, Random House (New York, NY), 1967.
Sophie's Choice, Random House (New York, NY), 1979.

PLAYS

In the Clap Shack (three-act play; first produced at Yale Repertory Theatre, 1972), Random House (New York, NY), 1973.

OTHER

The Four Seasons, illustrated by Harold Altman, Pennsylvania State University Press (University Park, PA), 1965.
Admiral Robert Penn Warren and the Snows of Winter: A Tribute, Palaemon Press (Winston-Salem, NC), 1978.
The Message of Auschwitz, Press de la Warr (Blacksburg, VA), 1979.
Against Fear, Palaemon Press (Winston-Salem, NC), 1981.
The Achievement of William Styron (autobiography), edited by Robert K. Morris with Irving Malin, University of Georgia Press (Athens, GA), 1981.
This Quiet Dust, and Other Writings (essays), Random House (New York, NY), 1982.
(Author of introduction) Robert Satter, *Doing Justice: A Trial Judge at Work,* American Lawyer Books/ Simon & Schuster (New York, NY), 1990.
Darkness Visible: A Memoir of Madness, Random House (New York, NY), 1990.
A Tidewater Morning: Three Tales from Youth, Random House (New York, NY), 1993.
(With Mariana Ruth Cook) *Fathers and Daughters: In Their Own Words,* Chronicle Books (San Francisco, CA), 1994.
(With James L.W. West III) *William Styron, a Life,* Random House (New York, NY), 1998.
(With others) *Dead Run: The Untold Story of Dennis Stockton and America's Only Mass Escape from Death Row,* Times Books (New York, NY), 1999.

Also author of *Inheritance of the Night: Early Drafts of "Lie Down in Darkness,"* Duke University Press (Durham, NC), 1993. Editor of *Paris Review: Best Short Stories,* Dutton (New York, NY), 1959. Contributor to *Esquire, New York Review of Books,* and other publications.

Manuscript collections of Styron's work are held by the Library of Congress, Washington, DC, and Duke University, Durham, NC.

ADAPTATIONS: *Sophie's Choice* was adapted for film, Universal Pictures, 1982; it featured Meryl Streep in the title role.

SIDELIGHTS: William Styron's novels have brought him major literary awards, broad critical notice, and a reputation for raising controversial issues. Writtten in the style of the Southern Gothic tradition made familiar by author William Faulkner, Styron's work has been described as both reckless and poetic, and his subject matter has been the focus of debate. In *The Confessions of Nat Turner* and *Sophie's Choice,* he wrote about victims of oppression: a slave and a concentration camp survivor. Although some critics have questioned his approach and his ability to enter the mind of a black slave or a mother in the Holocaust, most have praised Styron for probing into difficult subjects. Reviewers often consider Styron's timing a positive factor in the success of these two books; *Sophie's Choice,* published during renewed concern about the Holocaust, and *The Confessions of Nat Turner,* published during the racially explosive late 1960s, each found large audiences. George Steiner commented in the *New Yorker:* "The crisis of civil rights, the new relationships to each other and to their own individual sensibilities that this crisis has forced on both whites and Negroes . . . give Mr. Styron's fable [*The Confessions of Nat Turner*] a special relevance."

Styron based *The Confessions of Nat Turner* on the transcript of testimony given by a slave, Nat Turner, who had led a brief revolt against slave owners in Virginia's Tidewater district. Styron considered his book a "meditation on history" rather than a strict retelling of events. He explained in a letter to the *Nation* that "in writing *The Confessions of Nat Turner* I at no time pretended that my narrative was an exact transcription of historical events; had perfect accuracy been my aim I would have written a work of history rather than a novel." Philip Rahv asserted that Styron's viewpoint was more valuable than a historical perspective. Rahv wrote in the *New York Review of Books:* "This narrative is something more than a novelistic counterpart of scholarly studies of slavery in America; it incarnates its theme, bringing home to us the monstrous reality of slavery in a psychodynamic manner that at the same time does not in the least neglect social or economic aspects."

Styron's subjective approach drew ire from critics who felt that his portrait of Nat is based on white stereotypes. A *Negro Digest* critic took particular issue with Styron's depiction of Nat's sexuality: "In the name of fiction, Mr. Styron can do whatever he likes with History. When his interpretation, however, duplicates what is white America's favorite fantasy (i.e., every black male—especially the leader—is motivated by a latent [?] desire to sleep with the Great White Woman), he is obligated to explain . . . this coincidental duplication—or to be criticized accordingly. Since there is no such explanation in the technique of the novel and since it offers no vision or new perspective, but rather reaffirms an old stale, shameful fantasy . . . it is at best a good commercial novel." Albert Murray concurred in the *New Leader:* "Alas, what Negroes will find in Styron's 'confessions' is much the same old failure of sensibility that plagues most other fiction about black people. That is to say, they will all find a Nat Turner whom many white people may accept at a safe distance, but hardly one with whom Negroes will easily identify."

Styron wrote about human suffering in a more contemporary setting—post-World War II Brooklyn—in *Sophie's Choice.* Sophie is a beautiful Polish gentile who survived Auschwitz but lost two of her children and much of her self-esteem there. Her lover, Nathan—mad, brilliant, and Jewish—is haunted by the atrocities of the Holocaust, although he personally escaped them, and he torments Sophie with reminders. Stingo, a young writer who lives downstairs from Sophie and Nathan, narrates. According to Geoffrey Wolff in *Esquire,* "Stingo is in the tradition of *The Great Gatsby*'s Nick Carraway. Like Nick, he bears witness to the passion of characters he chances upon and tries modestly to judge and pardon. Like Nick, he is a refugee from settled values—Virginia's Tidewater country—back from a great war to make his way in the great world."

David Caute in the *New Statesman* heard additional voices. For Caute, in Styron's prose the "neo-Biblical cadences of Southern prose, of Wolfe and Faulkner, jostle . . . with the cosmopolitan sensibility of an F. Scott Fitzgerald." Other critics agreed that the influence of other writers sometimes muffles Styron's own voice. Jack Beatty wrote in the *New Republic* that *Sophie's Choice* "is written in an unvaryingly mannered style—High Southern—that draws constant spell-destroying attention to itself." The High Southern style associated with Faulkner and Thomas Wolfe is characterized by elaborate, even Gothic descriptions, and although Styron is "a novelist hard to categorise," he shows his "allegiance to that style . . . in all . . . [his] writing," according to Caute, with "a reluctance to leave any noun uncaressed by an adjective." Paul Gray, reviewing *Sophie's Choice* in *Time,* agreed, noting that Styron "often let Stingo pile up adjectives in the manner of Thomas Wolfe: 'Brooklyn's greenly beautiful, homely, teeming, begrimed and incomprehensible vastness'. . . . True, Stingo is pictured as a beginning writer, heavily in debt to Faulkner, Wolfe and the Southern literary tradition, but Styron may have preserved more redundant oratory than the effect of Stingo's youth strictly required."

Robert Towers, writing in the *New York Review of Books,* also faulted Styron for verbosity. "'All my life, I have retained a strain of uncontrolled didacticism,' says Stingo at one point," Towers noted, "and *Sophie's Choice* bears him out. The novel is made to drag along an enormous burden of commentary, ranging all the way from the meaning of the Holocaust, the ineluctable nature of evil, the corrosive effects of guilt, the horrors of slavery, and the frailty of goodness and hope to such topics as the misunderstanding of the South by Northern liberals, Southern manners as opposed to those of New York taxi drivers, and the existence of prejudice and cruelty in even the best of us." But Wolff defended Styron, observing that "the book's narrative flow is suspenseful if languid, if sometimes even glacial," and that *Sophie's Choice* "achieved an almost palpable evocation of its place and time—Poland before and during the war, Brooklyn and Coney Island immediately after." Caute, despite his criticisms, contended that Styron's prose is "marked also by clarity, honesty and accessibility."

In response to critics who questioned the validity of *Confessions* and *Sophie's Choice* on the grounds of Styron's personal background, Towers argued that "it should not be necessary to defend the right of Styron—a non-Jew, a Southern Protestant in background—to this subject matter—any more than his right to assume, in the first person, the 'identity' of the leader of a slave rebellion in Virginia in 1831." Gray agreed. "The question," he wrote in *Time,* "is not whether Styron has a right to use alien experiences but whether his novel proves that he knows what he is writing about. In this instance, the overriding answer is yes."

It cannot be said of Styron's 1990 work *Darkness Visible: A Memoir of Madness* that the author was writing of "alien experiences," as he had first-hand knowledge of the book's focus. *Darkness Visible* is Styron's account of his slow fall into depression in 1985. Leading up to his experience was the loss of his mother when he was thirteen, his father's own battle with depression, and Styron's forty-year dependency on alcohol. According to an interview with Laurel Graeber in the *New York Times Book Review,* the catalyst for Styron's account of his depression was his defense of the writer Primo Levi, who committed suicide in 1987. "Styron found himself defending Levi . . . from statements that seemed to attribute his action to moral weakness," wrote Graeber. Following an essay he published on the subject, Styron spoke on it, wrote a longer article, and then produced *Darkness Visible.*

Styron was compelled, "in romantic confessional style, that he had to write it, and it is good to have it," stated Karl Miller in his review of *Darkness Visible* for the *London Review of Books.* Noting that the book contains "some tremendous writing," Victoria Glendinning added that "The rhythmic beat of some sentences demands that they be read aloud," in a review for the *New York Times Book Review.* Miller noted that "There are passages in the book which might have been written in the nineteenth century—some of them, give or take a word or two, by Poe. . . . Styron writes of the dungeons 'of his spirit,' of a 'long-beshrouded metaphysical truth'—language that belongs to the Gothic strain of certain of his fictions."

A Tidewater Morning: Three Tales from Youth was Styron's first work following his depression and recovery. The three stories are autobiographical in nature and are narrated by a man in his fifties. The title novella takes place in 1938, the year Styron's own mother died, and focuses on a thirteen-year-old boy who watches his mother die of cancer. In the story "Love Day" the narrator recalls his experience in the U.S. Marines as a young man of twenty. The third story tells of a ten-year-old's friendship with neighbors who are descended from a prominent Southern family but have fallen onto harder times. The story "Shadrach" portrays a ninety-year-old former slave who returns to the family's land to die. James L.W. West III in *Sewanee Review* compared the collection to Faulkner's *Go down, Moses* and Hemingway's *In Our Time,* due to the connectedness of the stories "in ways obvious and subtle: this arrangement gives them a cumulative weight and thematic resonance that they would not possess if read separately." According to West, "The strongest cords binding these stories together are thematic. Styron is working through familiar territory for him, contemplating the fearful mysteries of grief, remorse, memory, guilt, rebellion, warfare, and death. . . . At crucial points . . . [the narrator] lifts himself above his doubt or pain, and fashions an imaginative rendering of the moment. This, Styron seems to be telling us, is the only way finally to address some of the almost intolerable ambiguities and injustices of our time."

BIOGRAPHICAL AND CRITICAL SOURCES:

BOOKS

Bryer, Jackson R., and Mary B. Hatem, *William Styron: A Reference Guide,* G.K. Hall (Boston, MA), 1978.

Casciato, Arthur D., and James L.W. West III, editors, *Critical Essays on William Styron,* G.K. Hall (Boston, MA), 1982.

Cologne-Brookes, Gavin, *The Novels of William Styron: From Harmony to History,* Louisiana State University (Baton Rouge, LA), 1995.

Concise Dictionary of American Literary Biography: Broadening Views, 1968-1988, Thomson Gale (Detroit, MI), 1989.

Contemporary Literary Criticism, Thomson Gale (Detroit, MI), Volume 1, 1973, Volume 3, 1975, Volume 11, 1979, Volume 15, 1980, Volume 60, 1990.

Cowley, Malcolm, *Writers at Work: The "Paris Review" Interviews, First Series,* Viking (New York, NY), 1958.

Crane, John K., *The Root of All Evil: The Thematic Unity of William Styron's Fiction,* University of South Carolina Press (Columbia, SC), 1985.

Dictionary of Literary Biography, Volume 143: *American Novelists since World War II, Third Series,* Thomson Gale (Detroit, MI), 1994.

Dictionary of Literary Biography Yearbook: 1980, Thomson Gale (Detroit, MI), 1981.

Friedman, Melvin J., *William Styron,* Bowling Green University (Bowling Green, OH), 1974.

Geismar, Maxwell, *American Moderns,* Hill & Wang (New York, NY), 1958.

Hadaller, David, *Gynicide: Women in the Novels of William Styron,* Fairleigh Dickinson University Press (Madison, NJ), 1996.

Kostelanetz, Richard, editor, *On Contemporary Literature,* Avon (New York, NY), 1964.

Leon, Philip W., *William Styron: An Annotated Bibliography of Criticism,* Greenwood Press (Westport, CT), 1978.

Mackin, Cooper R., *William Styron,* Steck Vaughn (Austin, TX), 1969.

Malin, Irving, and Robert K. Morris, editors, *The Achievement of William Styron,* University of Georgia Press (Athens, GA), 1975, revised edition, 1981.

Pearce, Richard, *William Styron* ("Pamphlets on American Writers" series), University of Minnesota Press (Minneapolis, MN), 1971.

Ratner, Marc L., *William Styron,* Twayne (New York, NY), 1972.

Ross, Daniel William, *The Critical Response to William Styron,* Greenwood Press (Westport, CT), 1995.

Ruderman, Judith, *William Styron,* Ungar (New York, NY), 1989.

Short Story Criticism, Volume 25, Thomson Gale (Detroit, MI), 1997.

Waldmeir, Joseph J., editor, *Recent American Fiction,* Michigan State University Press (Lansing, MI), 1963.

West, James L. W., III, *William Styron: A Descriptive Bibliography,* G.K. Hall (Boston, MA), 1977.

West, James L. W., III, *William Styron: A Life,* Random House (New York, NY), 1998.

PERIODICALS

Chicago Tribune, July 3, 1989.

Chicago Tribune Book World, May 27, 1979; January 16, 1983.

College Literature, number 1, 1987, pp. 1-16.

Commonweal, December 22, 1967.

Critique, number 2, 1985, pp. 57-65.

Detroit News, June 24, 1979.

English Journal, April, 1996, p. 87.

Esquire, July 3, 1979; December 1, 1985.

Harper's, July, 1967.

Journal of the American Medical Association, March 6, 1991, pp. 1184-1185.

London Review of Books, March 21, 1991, p. 6.

Los Angeles Times, December 14, 1983.

Los Angeles Times Book Review, January 16, 1983.

Mississippi Quarterly, number 2, 1989, pp. 129-145.

Nation, October 16, 1967; April 22, 1968; July 7, 1979.

New Leader, December 4, 1967.

New Republic, June 30, 1979.

New Statesman, May 7, 1979; November 19, 1993, pp. 47-48.

New Statesman & Society, March 8, 1991, pp. 37-38.

Newsweek, October 16, 1967; May 28, 1979.

New Yorker, November 25, 1967; June 18, 1979.

New York Review of Books, October 26, 1967; September 12, 1968; July 19, 1979.

New York Times, August 5, 1967; October 3, 1967; May 29, 1979; November 27, 1982.

New York Times Book Review, October 8, 1967; August 11, 1968; May 27, 1979; June 6, 1982; November 21, 1982; December 12, 1982; August 19, 1990.

Observer Review, May 5, 1968.

Partisan Review, winter, 1968; summer, 1968.

Sewanee Review, spring, 1994.

Southern Literary Journal, fall, 2001, p. 56.

Southern Quarterly, winter, 2002, Edwin T. Arnold, "The William Styron-Donald Harington Letters," pp. 98-141.

Southern Review, autumn, 2001, Michael Mewshaw, "A Writer's Account," p. 790.

Spectator, October 13, 1979.

Time, October 13, 1967; June 11, 1979.

Times Literary Supplement, May 19, 1968; November 30, 1979; June 10, 1983; December 10, 1993, p. 19.

Twentieth Century Literature, fall, 2000, Abigail Cheever, "Prozac Americans: Depression, Identity, and Selfhood," p. 346; fall, 2001, Lis Carstens, "Sexual Politics and Confessional Testimony in *Sophie's Choice,*" p. 293.

Village Voice, December 14, 1967.

Voice of Youth Advocates, February, 1994, p. 374.

Washington Post, May 18, 1979; January 4, 1983.

Washington Post Book World, May 29, 1979; December 5, 1982.

Whole Earth Review, fall, 1995, p. 41.

Yale Review, winter, 1968.

* * *

SWENSON, May 1919-1989

PERSONAL: Born May 28, 1919, in Logan, UT; died December 4, 1989, in Ocean View, DE (some sources say Bethany Beach, DE, or Salisbury, MD); daughter of Dan Arthur (a teacher) and Anna M. (Helberg) Swenson. *Education:* Utah State University, B.A., 1939.

CAREER: Poet, 1949-89. New Directions, New York, NY, editor, 1959-66; writer in residence at Purdue University, West Lafayette, IN, 1966-67, University of North Carolina, 1968-69 and 1974, Lothbridge University, Alberta, Canada, 1970, and University of California—Riverside, 1976; taught poetry at several universities, including Bryn Mawr and Utah State University; lectured and gave readings at more than fifty American universities and colleges, as well as at the New York YM-YWHA Poetry Center, and San Francisco Poetry Center. Conductor of workshops at University of Indiana Writers Conference and Bread Loaf Writers Conference, Vermont. Participant at the Yaddo and MacDowell colonies for writers.

MEMBER: Academy of American Poets (chancellor, 1980-89), American Academy and Institute of Arts and Letters.

AWARDS, HONORS: Poetry Introductions Prize, 1955; Robert Frost Poetry Fellowship for Bread Loaf Writers' Conference, 1957; Guggenheim fellowship, 1959; William Rose Benet Prize, Poetry Society of America, 1959; Longview Foundation award, 1959; National Institute of Arts and Letters award, 1960; Amy Lowell Travelling Scholarship, 1960; Ford Foundation grant, 1964; Brandeis University Creative Arts Award, 1967; Rockefeller Writing fellowship, 1967; Distinguished Service Medal, Utah State University, 1967; Lucy Martin Donnelly Award, Bryn Mawr College, 1968; Shelley Poetry Award, 1968; National Endowment for the Arts Grant, 1977; National Book Award nomination, 1978, for *New and Selected Things Taking Place;* Academy of American Poets fellowship, 1979; Bollingen Poetry Award, 1981; MacArthur Award, 1987; National Book Critics Circle award nomination (poetry), 1987, for *In Other Words;* honorary degrees from Utah State University, 1987; Utah State University Press created the May Swenson Poetry Award in Swenson's honor.

WRITINGS:

POETRY

Another Animal, Scribner (New York, NY), 1954.

A Cage of Spines, Rinehart (New York, NY), 1958.

To Mix With Time: New and Selected Poems, Scribner (New York, NY), 1963.

Poems to Solve (for children "14-up"), illustrated by Christy Hale, Scribner (New York, NY), 1966.

Half Sun Half Sleep (new poems and her translations of six Swedish poets), Scribner (New York, NY), 1967.

Iconographs (includes "Feel Me"), Scribner (New York, NY), 1970.

More Poems to Solve, Scribner (New York, NY), 1971.

(Translator, with Leif Sjoberg) *Windows and Stones, Selected Poems of Tomas Transtromer* (translated from Swedish), University of Pittsburgh Press (Pittsburgh, PA), 1972.

New and Selected Things Taking Place (includes "Ending"), Little, Brown (Boston, MA), 1978.

In Other Words, Knopf (New York, NY), 1988.

The Centaur, illustrated by Barry Moser, Macmillan (New York, NY), 1994.

Nature: Poems Old And New, Houghton Mifflin (Boston, MA), 1994.

May Out West, Utah State University Press (Logan, UT), 1996.

Dear Elizabeth: Five Poems and Three Letters to Elizabeth Bishop, Utah State University Press (Logan, UT), 2000.

The Complete Love Poems of May Swenson, Houghton Mifflin (Boston, MA), 2003.

OTHER

The Floor (one-act play), first produced under the program title *Doubles and Opposites* at American Place Theater, New York, May 11, 1966, on a triple bill with "23 Pat O'Brien Movies," by Bruce Jay Friedman, and "Miss Pete," by Andrew Glaze.

Made with Words, University of Michigan Press (Ann Arbor, MI), 1997.

Contributor of poems to anthologies, including *A Treasury of Great Poems,* edited by Louis Untermeyer, Simon & Schuster, 1955; *New Poets 2,* Ballantine, 1957; *New Poets of England America,* edited by Donald Hall, Robert Pack, and Louis Simpson, Meridian, 1957; *A Country in the Mind,* edited by Ray B. West, Angel Island Publications, 1962; *Twentieth-Century American Poetry,* edited by Conrad Aiken, Modern Library, 1963; *100 American Poems of the Twentieth Century,* Harcourt, 1963; *The Modern Poets,* edited by John Malcolm Brinnin and Bill Read, McGraw, 1963; and *The New Modern Poetry,* edited by M.L. Rosenthal, Macmillan, 1967; poems also included in translation in anthologies published in Italy and Germany.

Contributor of poetry, stories, and criticism to *Poetry, Nation, Saturday Review, Atlantic Monthly, Harper's, New Yorker, Southern Review, Hudson Review, Parnassus, Antaeus,* and other periodicals. Swenson's work is included in the sound recording *Today's Poets: Their Poems, Their Voices,* Volume 2, Scholastic Records, 1968, and recordings for the Library of Congress, Spoken Arts Records, Folkways Records, and others. Her poems have been set to music by Otto Leuning, Howard Swanson, Emerson Meyers, Joyce McKeel, Claudio Spies, Lester Trimble, and Warren Benson.

SIDELIGHTS: During her prolific career, May Swenson received numerous literary-award prizes and nominations for her poetry. Often experimental in both form and appearance, her poems earned her widespread critical acclaim. As Priscilla Long commented in *The Women's Review of Books,* "Swenson was a visionary poet, a prodigious observer of the fragile and miraculous natural world."

Swenson's poetry has been praised for its imagery, which is alternately precise and beguiling, and for the quality of her personal and imaginative observations. In addition, her poetry "exhibits . . . her continuing alertness to the liveliness of nature. Correspondences among all life forms pour from her work, confirming that nothing is meaningless. The universe's basic beauty and balance is the stuff and soul of her poems," Eloise Klein Healy observed in the *Los Angeles Times.*

Richard Howard emphasized in a *Tri-Quarterly* review that Swenson's enterprise is "to get out of herself and into those larger, warmer energies of earth, and to do so by liturgical means." Howard wrote: "When May Swenson, speaking in her thaumaturgical fashion of poetry, says that 'attention to the silence in between is the amulet that makes it work,' we are reminded, while on other occasions in her work we are reassured, that there is a kind of poetry, as there used to be a kind of love, which dares not speak its name." Thus Swenson's "orphic cadences," her "siren-songs, with their obsessive reliance on the devices of incantation," are the means by which she seeks to "discover runes, the conjurations by which she can not only apostrophize the hand, the cat and the cloud in their innominate otherness, but by which she can, in some essential and relieving way, become them, leave her own impinging selfhood in the paralyzed region where names are assigned, and assume instead the energies of natural process."

In *Book Week,* Chad Walsh noted: "In most of Miss Swenson's poems the sheer thingness of things is joyfully celebrated." Walsh called her "the poet par excellence of sights and colors." Stephen Stepanchev, author of *American Poetry since 1945,* agreed that Swenson's "distinction is that she is able to make . . . her reader see clearly what he has merely looked at before." Stepanchev, however, was one of the few critics to find her poems less than completely effective. "Miss Swenson," he wrote, "works in a free verse that is supple but rather prosaic, despite her picturemaking efforts."

Howard, writing of Swenson's development as a poet, stated that "from the first . . . Swenson has practiced, in riddles, chants, hex-signs and a whole panoply of invented sortilege unwonted in Western poetry since the

Witch of Endor brought up Samuel, the ways not only of summoning Being into her grasp, but of getting herself out of that grasp and into alien shapes, into those emblems of power most often identified with the sexual." Of the more recent poems, Howard wrote: "They are the witty, resigned poems of a woman . . . eager still to manipulate the phenomenal world by magic, but so possessed, now, of the means of her identity that the ritual, spellbinding, litaneutical elements of her art, have grown consistent with her temporal, conditioned, suffering experience and seem—to pay her the highest compliment she could care to receive—no more than natural."

Reviewing *Half Sun Half Sleep, New York Times Book Review* contributor Karl Shapiro wrote: "[Swenson's] concentration on the verbal equivalent of experience is so true, so often brilliant, that one watches her with hope and pleasure, praying for victory all the way." In a *Poetry* review of *Half Sun Half Sleep,* William Stafford said of this collection: "No one today is more deft and lucky in discovering a poem than May Swenson. Her work often appears to be proceeding calmly, just descriptive and accurate; but then suddenly it opens into something that looms beyond the material, something that impends and implies. . . . So graceful is the progression in her poems that they launch confidently into any form, carrying through it to easy, apt variations. Often her way is to define things, but the definitions have a stealthy trend; what she chooses and the way she progresses heap upon the reader a consistent, incremental effect." And Shapiro offered this analysis of Swenson's achievement in this book: "The whole volume is an album of experiments . . . that pay off. It is strange to see the once-radical *carmen figuratum,* the calligraphic poem, spatial forms, imagist and surreal forms—all the heritage of the early years of the century—being used with such ease and unselfconsciousness."

Swenson herself wrote that the experience of poetry is "based in a craving to get through the curtains of things as they *appear,* to things as they are, and then into the larger, wilder space of things as they *are becoming.* This ambition involves a paradox: an instinctive belief in the senses as exquisite tools for this investigation and, at the same time, a suspicion about their crudeness." Swenson also noted: "The poet, tracing the edge of a great shadow whose outline shifts and varies, proving there is an invisible moving source of light behind, hopes (naively, in view of his ephemerality) to reach and touch the foot of that solid whatever-it-is that casts the shadow. If sometimes it seems he does touch it, it is only to be faced with a more distant, even less accessible mystery. Because all is movement—all is breathing change."

Among the "strategies and devices, the shamanism and sorcery this poet deploys," as Howard admiringly described them, is Swenson's use of the riddle in *Poems to Solve.* The book may be enjoyed by both children and adults; the poems here are another serious attempt to accommodate "the mystery that only when a thing is apprehended as something else can it be known as itself." Swenson wrote of these poems: "It is essential, of course, with a device such as this to make not a riddle-pretending-to-be-a-poem but a poem that is also, and as if incidentally, a riddle—a solvable one. The aim is not to mystify or mislead but to clarify and make recognizable through the reader's own uncontaminated perceptions."

Nature: Poems Old and New, published four years after Swenson's death, emphasizes Swenson's sympathy for and identification with the outdoors. "Swenson was an unrelentingly lyrical poet," Priscilla Long wrote in the *Women's Review of Books,* "a master of the poetic line in which similar sounds accumulate and resonate so that the poem exists, beyond its meanings, as a rattle or a music box, or, in moments of greatness, a symphony." Her collection *Nature* is "so inward, independent, and intense, so intimate and impersonal at once," declared critic Langdon Hammer in the *Yale Review,* that "it has been difficult to place in the field of contemporary poetry." Several other critics, however, identified the work as an appreciation of Swenson's profound talent, collecting the best of her work between two covers. "The poetry thinks, feels, examines," explained a *Publishers Weekly* contributor; "it's patiently, meticulously sensuous, and adventurously varied in form, much as nature is." "These poems, harvested from her life's work and arranged in this delightful format," Rochelle Natt wrote in the *American Book Review,* "promote a lasting vision of Swenson's valuable contribution to American poetry."

BIOGRAPHICAL AND CRITICAL SOURCES:

BOOKS

Brinnin, John Malcolm, and Bill Read, editors, *The Modern Poets: An American-British Anthology,* McGraw (New York, NY), 1963.

Contemporary Literary Criticism, Thomson Gale (Detroit, MI), Volume 4, 1975; Volume 14, 1980, Volume 61, 1990.

Contemporary Poets, St. Martin's Press (New York, NY), 1980.

Deutsch, Babette, editor, *Poetry in Our Time,* 2nd edition, Doubleday (New York, NY), 1963.

Dictionary of Literary Biography, Volume 5: *American Poets since World War II,* Thomson Gale (Detroit, MI), 1980.

Hoffman, Daniel, editor, *The Harvard Guide to American Writing,* Belknap Press (Cambridge, MA), 1977.

Nemerov, Howard, editor, *Poets on Poetry,* Basic Books (New York, NY), 1966.

Poems for Young Readers: Selections from Their Own Writing by Poets Attending the Houston Festival of Contemporary Poetry, National Council of Teachers of English (Urbana, IL), 1966.

Stepanchev, Stephen, *American Poetry Since 1945,* Harper (New York, NY), 1965.

Untermeyer, Louis, editor, *A Treasury of Great Poems, English and American,* Simon & Schuster (New York, NY), 1955.

PERIODICALS

American Book Review, September, 1995, Rochelle Natt, review of *Nature: Poems Old and New,* p. 14.

Atlantic, February, 1968.

Booklist, June 1, 1993; June 1, 1994, Donna Seaman, review of *Nature,* p. 1763.

Book Week, June 4, 1967, Chad Walsh.

Christian Science Monitor, February 12, 1979.

Horn Book, May-June, 1993, Nancy Vasilakis, review of *The Complete Poems to Solve,* p. 341.

Los Angeles Times, March 22, 1979.

New Republic, March 7, 1988, Mary Jo Salter, review of *In Other Words,* pp. 40-41.

New York Times, March 19, 1979; June 16, 1987.

New York Times Book Review, September 1, 1963; May 7, 1967, Karl Shapiro, review of *Half Sun Half Sleep;* February 11, 1979; June 12, 1988, Michael Heller, review of *In Other Words: New Poems,* p. 15; January 19, 1992, Edward Hirsch, review of *The Love Poems of May Swenson,* p. 12.

Poetry, December, 1967, William Stafford, review of *Half Sun Half Sleep;* February, 1979; July, 1989, Linda Gregerson, review of *In Other Words,* pp. 233-238; February, 1993, Alfred Corn, review of *The Love Poems of May Swenson,* pp. 295-298; November, 2001, Christian Wiman, review of *Nature,* pp. 97-100.

Prairie Schooner, spring, 1968.

Publishers Weekly, May 30, 1994, review of *Nature,* pp. 46-47.

Tri-Quarterly, fall, 1966, Richard Howard.

Wilson Quarterly, winter, 1997, Anthony Hecht, "May Swenson: Selected and Introduced by Anthony Hecht," pp. 105-112.

Women's Review of Books, January, 1995, Priscilla Long, review of *Nature,* pp. 8-9.

Yale Review, January, 1995, Langdon Hammer, review of *Nature,* pp. 121-41.

ONLINE

American Academy of Poets Web Site, http://www.poets.org/ (February 15, 2001), "May Swenson."

Utah State University Press Web Site, http://www.usu.edu/ (September 8, 2004).

* * *

SWIFT, Graham 1949-
(Graham Colin Swift)

PERSONAL: Born May 4, 1949, in London, England; son of Allan Stanley (a civil servant) and Sheila Irene (Bourne) Swift. *Education:* Attended Dulwich College, 1960-67; Queen's College, Cambridge, B.A., 1970, M.A., 1975; attended York University, 1970-73. *Hobbies and other interests:* Fishing.

ADDRESSES: *Home*—London, England. *Office*—c/o Author Mail, A.P. Watt Ltd., 20 John St., London WC1N 2DR, England.

CAREER: Writer. Worked as part-time teacher of English at colleges in London, England, 1974-83.

MEMBER: PEN, Society of Authors, Royal Society of Literature (fellow).

AWARDS, HONORS: Geoffrey Faber Memorial Award, 1983, for *Shuttlecock; Guardian* Fiction Prize and nomination for Booker McConnell Prize, both 1983, Winifred Holtby Prize from Royal Society of Literature, 1984, and Premio Grinzane Cavour (Italy), 1987, all for *Waterland;* Prix du Meilleur Livre Étranger (France), 1994, for *Ever After;* Booker McConnell Prize, and James Tait Black Memorial Prize for Best Novel, both 1996, both for *Last Orders;* D.Litt. from University of East Anglia and University of York, 1998.

WRITINGS:

NOVELS

The Sweet-Shop Owner, Allen Lane (London, England), 1980, Washington Square Press (New York, NY), 1985.

Shuttlecock, Allen Lane (London, England), 1981, Washington Square Press (New York, NY), 1984.
Waterland, Poseidon Press (New York, NY), 1984.
Out of This World, Poseidon Press (New York, NY), 1988.
Ever After, Knopf (New York, NY), 1992.
Last Orders, Knopf (New York, NY), 1996.
The Light of Day, Knopf (New York, NY), 2003.

OTHER

Learning to Swim and Other Stories, London Magazine Editions (London, England), 1982, Poseidon Press (New York, NY), 1985.
(Editor, with David Profumo) *The Magic Wheel: An Anthology of Fishing in Literature,* Picador (London, England), 1986.

ADAPTATIONS: *Waterland* was adapted for film by Peter Prince and released by Palace Pictures, 1992; *Last Orders* was adapted for Sony Pictures Classics, 2002.

SIDELIGHTS: Some enthusiastic devotees of British novelist Graham Swift believe that he was brought up in the Fens region of eastern England, the setting for his acclaimed novel *Waterland,* according to *Maclean's* contributor John Bemrose. Swift, however, is a native of urban London and the son of a civil servant. "For Swift," wrote Bemrose, "the misconceptions about his origins only prove that he has done his job as a maker of fiction. 'I have enormous faith in the imagination,'" Swift told Bemrose. "'If your imagination cannot transport you mentally from where you are to somewhere quite different, then don't be a novelist, be something else.'"

Swift's reputation—particularly in the United States—rests largely on the merits of *Waterland,* which was nominated for Great Britain's prestigious Booker McConnell Prize in 1983. The novel is a complex, first-person account by history teacher Tom Crick, who relates his early romance, marital problems, and career difficulties all in obsessively analytical detail. *Waterland* begins with Crick recounting the discovery of a corpse in the Fens, a flat waterland where Crick's father works as a lock-keeper. After this episode the narrative shifts to an apparent classroom where Crick is discussing his dismissal from his teaching post. He reveals that his largely autobiographical lectures have prompted distress from school administrators who urge him to resign. Crick also discloses that his life has been unsettled by his wife's arrest—and subsequent commitment in a mental institution—for having kidnaped a child.

Waterland shifts back and forth between Crick's recollection of discovering the corpse and his account of his present private and professional difficulties. Interspersed among these autobiographical episodes are historical and philosophical analyses. Crick provides extensive background on the Fens and its inhabitants—past and present—while consistently debating the worth of this history. He acknowledges the possibly dubious nature of such history, yet he constantly returns to it as a means of explaining or understanding the present. The validity of history as a means of understanding the present is a major point of debate in *Waterland,* and one that provides much of the novel's philosophical tension.

Equally compelling, however, is the mystery of the corpse. As an adolescent, Crick discovers that a murder has been committed and that he and his family have been implicated. His detective work in identifying the killer—and his depiction of the sexual activities that prompted the murder—constitute what some critics consider the novel's most dramatic aspects.

Upon its publication in 1983, *Waterland* was greeted enthusiastically by British critics and was considered among the year's finest novels. The following spring, when *Waterland* was published in the United States, more reviewers hailed it as a wide-ranging, enlightening work. "Its textured descriptions of the English fens," explained Linda Gray Sexton in the *New York Times Book Review,* "invited comparisons with Thomas Hardy." Michiko Kakutani wrote in the *New York Times Book Review* that Swift's novel is "highly ambitious . . . a book that reads at once as a gothic family saga, a detective story and as a philosophical meditation on the nature and uses of history." Michael Wood noted in the *New York Review of Books* that *Waterland* is "formidably intelligent," and Charles Champlin declared in an appraisal for the *Los Angeles Times Book Review* that the novel "carries with all else a profound knowledge of a people, a place and their interweaving." Champlin called *Waterland* "a fine and original work."

Following the success of *Waterland* Swift's two earlier novels were published in the United States. His debut work, *The Sweet-Shop Owner,* concerns the memories and opinions of an industrious shopkeeper named Willy Chapman as he lives his final hours. Victimized by his marriage to "an insistently assertive shrew, a frigid near-hysteric who retreats into illness and invalidism," according to Frank Rudman in the *Spectator,* and by an ungrateful daughter who refuses to visit him even long enough to collect her inheritance, Chapman finally closes his shop and heads home to die, reflecting on forty years of unhappiness and lack of fulfillment. Writing in the *New Statesman,* Alan Hollinghurst called *The Sweet-Shop Owner* a "marvelous first novel," and American critics seconded that opinion. Michael Gorra, for instance, wrote in the *New York Times Book Review* that the work establishes Swift "as one of the brightest promises the English novel has now to offer." Like other reviewers, Gorra noted similarities between *The Sweet-Shop Owner* and the writings of early twentieth-century Irish novelist James Joyce. "There is a touch of Joyce," Gorra declared, "in . . . Swift's revelation of the hidden poetry of small men's lives."

Shuttlecock, Swift's second novel, is also an analytical tale about the past. The work's protagonist is a police department archivist who scans records to discover possible connections between various crimes. Like all Swift's protagonists, the archivist is obsessed with the past, particularly the life of his father, a former war hero in the French Resistance, once captured by the Gestapo and now confined in a mental hospital following his breakdown. Tension mounts when the archivist discovers evidence linking his father's past activities with information missing from police files—information that suggests, according to John Mellors in *London,* "that Dad's first breakdown had been in wartime, that he had betrayed other agents in the network, that his 'escape' had been set up for him by his captors as a quid pro quo." The narrator destroys the file that might have answered this question without reading it first, so the mystery remains unresolved at the novel's end. A reviewer for the *Washington Post Book World,* in assessing both *Shuttlecock* and *The Sweet-Shop Owner,* stated that "Swift's narratives twist and turn, knotting together inexorably the past with the present, sweeping us along steadily."

Swift's fiction collection *Learning to Swim and Other Stories* was published in the United States in 1985, but its American reception failed to match that accorded *Waterland.* While more than one U.S. critic found certain of the tales too studied and uncompelling, in Britain reviewers praised *Learning to Swim* as insightful and provocative. Hollinghurst, for instance, wrote in the *Times Literary Supplement* that Swift's "concentrated, enigmatic stories address their subjects with such intelligent conviction and clarity that their ambiguities are . . . challengingly displayed." Hollinghurst was especially impressed with "The Watch," a tale about a family whose males are assured longevity by a magical watch, and "The Hypochondriac," the story of a patient's seemingly imagined—but ultimately real, and fatal—pains. "Swift's ideas are large," Hollinghurst observed, "but his manner is meticulous, orderly and attentive."

Out of This World, Swift's next novel after *Waterland,* again closely examines the interplay between history and the present. The book consists of two interlocking monologues, those of former photojournalist Harry Beech and of his estranged daughter, Sophie. Harry's dedication to photography—his photos of violence in war zones and elsewhere in the world are famous—contributes to the alienation of his daughter. At the beginning of the novel, explained *Times Literary Supplement* contributor Anne Duchene, "there has been no communication between them for ten years, since Harry's father was blown up by a car-bomb and Sophie saw Harry taking photographs a moment later." Now in his sixties, Harry works as an aerial photographer, trying to understand the acts of violence he has witnessed. Sophie, now married with two healthy children, lives in New York City, where she consults a psychiatrist in order to resolve her feelings about her father and herself. Eventually Harry writes to Sophie, asking her blessing on his remarriage, and she flies to England for a reunion with him.

The success of *Waterland* inevitably prompted critical comparisons with *Out of This World.* J.L. Carr, writing in the *Spectator,* called *Waterland* "innovatory, moving, memorable"; but, the critic said, "although I read [*Out of This World*] with ringing ears, I was not unsettled by its protagonists' disasters. . . . Now and then, as the [father and daughter] pair tried to unload their little burdens of guilt upon me, I resentfully felt sorry for myself. What have they to complain about?" Duchene stated, "The writing . . . lacks the resonance of *Waterland* and the manic Kafkaesque energies of *Shuttlecock.*" Readers, she continued, "might have wished to get more lift-off . . . from what we know to be the author's powerful, annealing imagination. We ask a great deal of him only because of his past flights." Sexton, writing in the *New York Times Book Review,* was more complimentary. "Swift's achievement is that the important story of [Harry's and Sophie's] self-education has been told with such simple, startling beauty," Sexton declared. "Not a book the reader is likely to forget, *Out of This World* deserves to be ranked at the forefront of contemporary literature."

Ever After, Swift's 1992 novel, is reminiscent of its predecessors in its examination of the effects of history and ancestry on people living in modern times. It is the story of Bill Unwin, an erstwhile university professor who has just gone through a traumatic period: within the past eighteen months he has lost his mother, his stepfather, and his beloved actress-wife. Seriously depressed, he attempts suicide, and it is while he convalesces that he begins to tell his tale. It turns out that Unwin's academic career was created for him—for many years he had been his wife's manager, and his seat at the university exists only because his rich American stepfather established it with the provision that Unwin was to have it. Unwin occupies his time at the university by editing the papers of a Victorian ancestor named Matthew Pearce, whose faith was shattered by the death of his son, his reading of Darwin's theories of natural selection, and his encounter with the fossil of an ichthyosaur on a beach in Dorset. Unwin is just as helpless to answer questions about Pearce's life as he is to answer questions about his own: why did his father, Colonel Unwin, commit suicide? Was Colonel Unwin really his father, and did news of his wife's supposed infidelity drive him to shoot himself? "A latter-day Hamlet," stated Pico Iyer in *Time,* "Unwin is driven mad by the sense that all of us are playacting, adrift in a world of 'suppose,'"

Like *Out of This World, Ever After* tempted comparisons with *Waterland.* "It seems to be a convention that when you are writing about Graham Swift, somewhere in the first paragraph or two you refer to *Waterland,*" explained Hilary Mantel in the *New York Review of Books.* "It would be a great thing to kick over the traces and declare *Waterland* a mere bagatelle beside Swift's new novel; unfortunately, that is impossible." "How could any comment more sharply irritate Graham Swift," asked Michael Levenson in the *New Republic,* "than the cruelly recurrent, dully obvious opinion that neither his two novels written before *Waterland* nor the two written since even belong on the same shelf as that strong book?"

As was the case with *Out of This World,* reviews of *Ever After* were mixed. Iyer, for instance, referred to the novel as "a dense, literary text that race[s] ahead with the compulsive fury of a page turner." Ursula K. Le Guin wrote in the *Washington Post Book World,* "The multiple plot covers 150 years in 276 pages quite effortlessly, and though full of references, characters, events and second thoughts, it turns and doubles without confusion in time and space. It is masterfully done. Only it all seems, despite its dense, charged texture, a bit thin and arbitrary." "The prose is rich, lush and unhurried," declared *New York Times Book Review* contributor MacDonald Harris; "this is a modern British novel for the reader who is getting bored with the contemporary American mode of fiction and turns back, now and then, to [Anthony] Trollope, [Thomas] Hardy, or George Eliot." Lorna Sage, writing in the *Times Literary Supplement,* also compared Swift to Hardy "in his insistence that the naive questions about extinction matter." "*Ever After,*" concluded Mantel, "may have deeply advanced Swift as a thinker, but sadly it has not advanced him as a novelist."

Critical consensus changed with Swift's 1996 novel, *Last Orders.* This work, which took Britain's most prestigious literary honor, the Booker McConnell Prize, confirmed in many critics' minds that the author had at last produced a worthy successor to *Waterland. Last Orders,* which takes place in the 1980s England of Thatcher and rising unemployment, follows four aging men as they journey from London to the seaside resort of Margate to deliver a fifth friend—recently deceased and now cremated—to that man's requested resting place: scattered to the winds off the Margate pier. For these working-class characters, memories of glory days during World War II and the conflicts of wives and children in the present dog them even as they recall the life of their lost comrade. "Little by little, a portrait of the man and his life emerges—petty, sad, frustrating," as an *Economist* critic stated. To *Spectator* writer Caroline Moore, "*Last Orders* contains many of the devices, the themes and concerns we have met before. There is the interweaving of past and present, of people and places—a web of lives shaped by ordinary guilts, warped by small but painful betrayals."

Noting that *Last Orders* includes a characteristic Swift plot twist whereby sons come into conflict with their fathers over career choices, Moore admitted that one "longs to know what [Swift's] own father did, and what he felt about his son becoming a writer." This psychology aside, Moore praised *Last Orders* as the work of "an intelligently subtle writer" who has created a story which "evokes a luminously complete and complex world."

Calling *Last Orders* nothing less than Swift's finest book to date, Oliver Reynolds in the *Times Literary Supplement* risked incurring the wrath of others who would accord that honor to *Waterland.* To Reynolds, this "emotionally charged and technically superb" story "is a wonderful example of the novel's power to resolve the wavering meanings of the life we all share into a definite focus, one where the clarity with which things are seen renders them precious." Both Jay Parini in the *New York Times Book Review* and John Casey of the *Los Angeles Times* lauded Swift for his use of the rich

British idiom in *Last Orders.* This "slangy, scrappy" vernacular, in fact, caught Casey by surprise: "I may have not caught every nuance with my American ear. I wish I could hear it aloud; this novel would be a wonderful book on tape with each character played by a different actor."

Although the Booker judges recognized Swift's novel with the $44,000 first prize, controversy arose on the publication of *Last Orders* when reviewers compared the book's plot and theme to *As I Lay Dying,* a William Faulkner work of the 1930s. An Australian academic accused Swift of plagiarizing Faulkner's work, which charge infuriated Swift. Swift said that while he acknowledges authors are naturally influenced by each other, the idea of stealing was out of the question. Swift's assertion was backed by the Booker judges, who agreed that no plagiarism took place.

Swift's next novel, *The Light of Day,* concerns a murder and a love story. The narrative begins on the second anniversary of the crime; Sarah, the guilty woman, is being visited in jail by George, the man who loves her and who was acting as her private investigator when she killed her adulterous husband. While the storyline may conjure up a conventional detective story, *The Light of Day* is a unique book. "Swift has always combined narrative complexity—interwoven story lines and cunning shifts of perspective—with a perfect instinct for the moral and emotional plights that define us," wrote Sven Birkerts in *Books.* Birkerts felt that *The Light of Day* follows this pattern, and "comes at us with the puncturing clarity of a siren in the night." The real mystery to be solved is the motivations of the characters; as the book progresses, readers learn of George's disgraceful dismissal from the police force and his own corruption. The book is "at once perfectly balanced and eerily incisive. It is also unexpectedly redemptive. By the end of the novel we have seen deep into the soul of George Webb. We may have visited a place of fear and terrible vengeance but we come away feeling that a searching beam has been thrown in another direction—toward the hidden sources of love and faith," maintained Birkerts.

The Light of Day offers the hope that "even in the course of a single day, we are capable of remaking ourselves," observed Bill Ott in *Booklist,* going on to describe the book as "a remarkable feat of storytelling by one of our most accomplished novelists." Swift himself told Benedicte Page in *Bookseller* that he considers *The Light of Day* his most optimistic work. He explained: "George is a man who has found a new reason for living, and I think that's important. for us all to believe in, as life goes on, and as we all feel disappointments. For George it is a marvellous thing, and he knows it, and he is not wasting it."

BIOGRAPHICAL AND CRITICAL SOURCES:

BOOKS

Contemporary Literary Criticism, Volume 41, Thomson Gale (Detroit, MI), 1987.

Contemporary Novelists, 7th edition, Thomson Gale (Detroit, MI), 2001.

PERIODICALS

Booklist, March 15, 2003, Bill Ott, review of *The Light of Day,* p. 1254.

Books, January, 1993, p. 18; May, 2003, Sven Birkerts, review of *The Light of Day,* p. 73.

Bookseller, December 6, 2002, Benedicte Page, review of *The Light of Day,* p. 35.

Buffalo News, June 8, 2003, Michael D. Langan, review of *The Light of Day,* p. F5.

Detroit News, May 19, 1985.

Economist, March 16, 1996, p. 14.

Globe and Mail (Toronto, Ontario, Canada), September 1, 1984; February 8, 1986.

Guardian (London, England), March 1, 2003, John O'Mahony, "Graham Swift: Triumph of the Common Man," p. 20; March 8, 2003, review of *The Light of Day,* p. 9; April 5, 2003, John Mullan, "*Last Orders:* Week 1, Dialogue," p. 32; April 12, 2003, John Mullan, "*Last Orders:* Week 2, Clichés," p. 32; April 19, 2003, John Mullan, "*Last Orders:* Week 3, Interior Monologue," p. 32.

Library Journal, January, 2002, Nancy Pearl, review of *Last Orders,* p. 188; March 1, 2003, Barbara Hoffert, review of *The Light of Day,* p. 120.

Listener, January 6, 1983.

London, November, 1981, pp. 88-90.

London Review of Books, February 8, 1996, pp. 20-21.

Los Angeles Times, July 7, 1996, p. 6; May 21, 2003, Scott Martelle, review of *The Light of Day,* p. E9.

Los Angeles Times Book Review, April 1, 1984.

Maclean's, May 6, 1996, p. 61; November 11, 1996, p. 16.

Mirror (London, England), March 1, 2003, review of *The Light of Day,* p. 56.

Nation, March 31, 1980.

National Review, March 10, 1997, p. 58.

New Republic, June 22, 1992, pp. 38-40.
New Statesman and Society, April 25, 1980; March 18, 1983; October 7, 1983; January 19, 1996, p. 37.
Newsweek, April 30, 1984.
New York Review of Books, August 16, 1984; June 11, 1992, p. 23; April 4, 1996, pp. 8, 10.
New York Times, March 20, 1984; May 4, 2003, Anthony Quinn, review of *The Light of Day,* p. 6.
New York Times Book Review, March 25, 1984; June 23, 1985, pp. 11-12; September 11, 1988, p. 14; October 22, 1989, p. 38; March 29, 1992, p. 21; May 16, 1993, p. 40; May 5, 1996, p. 13; May 4, 2003, Anthony Quinn, review of *The Light of Day,* p. 6.
Observer (London, England), March 2, 2003, Adam Mars-Jones, review of *The Light of Day,* p. 17.
Publishers Weekly, February 22, 1993, p. 91; March 31, 2003, review of *The Light of Day,* p. 39.
St. Louis Post-Dispatch, June 1, 2003, G.E. Murray, review of *The Light of Day,* p. F12.
San Francisco Chronicle, May 18, 2003, David Kipen, review of *The Light of Day,* p. M1.
Spectator, April 26, 1980, p. 23; October 8, 1983; March 12, 1988, p. 28; November 28, 1992, p. 40; January 27, 1996, pp. 33-34.
Time, April 13, 1992, p. 78.
Times (London, England), March 10, 1997, p. 1.
Times Literary Supplement, July 27, 1982; October 7, 1983; March 11, 1988, p. 275; February 21, 1992, p. 6; April 16, 1993, p. 22; January 19, 1996, p. 25.
Village Voice, July 2, 1985; September, 1993, p. 29.
Washington Post Book World, March 18, 1984; April 14, 1985; June 9, 1985; March 22, 1992, p. 6.
Writer, February, 1998, Lewis Burke Frumkes, interview with Swift, p. 19.

ONLINE

BookPage, http://www.bookpage.com/ (April, 1992), Adam Begley, interview with Swift.

* * *

SWIFT, Graham Colin
See SWIFT, Graham

* * *

SWITHEN, John
See KING, Stephen

* * *

SYMMES, Robert
See DUNCAN, Robert

* * *

SYRUC, J.
See MILOSZ, Czeslaw

* * *

SZYMBORSKA, Wislawa 1923- (Stancykowna)

PERSONAL: Born July 2, 1923, in Prowent-Bnin, Poland; married (husband deceased). *Education:* Attended Jagellonian University, 1945-48.

ADDRESSES: Home—Ul. Krolewska 82/89, 30-079, Cracow, Poland.

CAREER: Poet and critic; Poetry editor and columnist, *Zycie literackie* (literary weekly magazine), 1953-81.

MEMBER: Polish Writers' Association (member of general board, 1978-83).

AWARDS, HONORS: Cracow literary prize, 1954; Gold Cross of Merit, 1955; Ministry of Culture prize, 1963; Knight's Cross, Order of Polonia Resituta, 1974; Goethe Prize, 1991; Herder Prize, 1995; Polish PEN Club prize, 1996; Nobel Prize for Literature, Swedish Academy, 1996.

WRITINGS:

POETRY

Dlatego zyjemy (title means "That's Why We Are Alive"), [Warsaw, Poland], 1952.
Pytania zadawane sobie (title means "Questions Put to Myself"), [Warsaw, Poland], 1954.
Wolanie do Yeti (title means "Calling out to Yeti"), [Warsaw, Poland], 1957.
Sol (title means "Salt"), Panstwowy Instytut Wydawniczy (Warsaw, Poland), 1962.
Wiersze wybrane (collection), Panstwowy Instytut Wydawniczy (Warsaw, Poland), 1964, reprinted 2000.

Sto pociech (title means "A Hundred Joys"), Panstwowy Instytut Wydawniczy (Warsaw, Poland), 1967.

Poezje wybrane (title means "Selected Poems"), Ludowa Spoldzielnia Wydawnicza (Warsaw, Poland), 1967.

Poezje (title means "Poems"), Przedmowa Jerzego Kwiatkowskiego (Warsaw, Poland), 1970.

Wybor poezje (collection), Czytelnik (Warsaw, Poland), 1970.

Wszelki wypadek (title means "There but for the Grace"), Czytelnik (Warsaw, Poland), 1972.

Wybor wierszy (collection), Panstwowy Instytut Wydawniczy (Warsaw, Poland), 1973.

Tarsjusz i inne wiersze (title means "Tarsius and Other Poems"), Krajowa Agencja Wydawnicza (Warsaw, Poland), 1976.

Wielka liczba (title means "A Great Number"), Czytelnik (Warsaw, Poland), 1976.

Sounds, Feelings, Thoughts: Seventy Poems, translated by Magnus J. Krynski and Robert A. Maguire, Princeton University Press (Princeton, NJ), 1981.

Poezje wybrane (II), (title means "Selected Poems II"), Ludowa Spoldzielnia Wydawnicza (Warsaw, Poland), 1983.

Ludzie na moscie, Czytelnik (Warsaw, Poland), 1986, translation by Adam Czerniawski published as *People on a Bridge: Poems,* Forest (Boston, MA), 1990.

Poezje = Poems (bilingual edition), translated by Krynski and Maguire, Wydawnictwo Literackie (Cracow, Poland), 1989.

Wieczor autorski: wiersze (title means "Authors' Evening: Poems"), Anagram (Warsaw, Poland), 1992.

Koniec i poczatek (title means "The End and the Beginning"), Wydawnictwo Literackie (Cracow, Poland), 1993.

View with a Grain of Sand: Selected Poems, translated by Stanislaw Baranczak and Clare Cavanagh, Harcourt (New York, NY), 1995.

Widok z ziarnkiem piasku: 102 Wiersze, Wydawnictwo Literacki (Cracow, Poland), 1996.

Nothing Twice: Selected Poems, selected and translated by Stanislaw Baranczak and Clare Cavanagh, Wydawnictwo Literackie (Cracow, Poland), 1997.

Hundert Gedichte, Hundert Freuden, Wydawnictwo Literackie (Cracow, Poland), 1997.

O asmierci bez przesady = de la mort sans exagerer, Wydawnictwo Literackie (Cracow, Poland), 1997.

Nulla e in regalo, Wydawnictwo Literackie (Cracow, Poland), 1998.

Poems, New and Collected, 1957-1997, translated from the Polish by Stanislaw Baranczak and Clare Cavanagh, Harcourt Brace (New York, NY), 1998.

Nic darowane = Keyn shum masoneh = Nothing's a gift = Nichts ist geschenkt = Me'um lo nitan bematanah, Amerykansko-Polsko-Izraelska Fundacja Shalom (Warsaw, Poland), 1999.

Poczta literacka, czyli, Jak zostac (lub nie zostac) pisarzem, Wydawnictwo Literackie (Cracow, Poland), 2000.

Miracle Fair: Selected Poems, Norton (New York, NY), 2001.

Nowe lektury nadobowiazkowe: 1997-2002, Wydawnictwo Literackie (Cracow, Poland), 2002.

Nonrequired Reading: Prose Pieces, Harcourt (New York, NY), 2002.

Chwila (title means "Moment"), Wydawnictwo Literackie (Cracow, Poland), 2002, published in bilingual edition as *Chwila/Moment,* translations by Clare Cavanagh and Stanislaw Baranczak, 2003.

Wierze, BOSZ (Olszanica, Poland), 2003.

Rymowanki dla duzych dzieci: z wyklejankami autorki, Wydawnictwo Literackie (Cracow, Poland), 2003.

OTHER

Lektury nadobowiazkowe (collected book reviews; title means "Non-Compulsory Reading"), Wydawnictwo Literackie (Cracow, Poland), 1973.

Zycie na poczekaniu: Lekcja literatury z Jerzym Kwiatowskim i Marianem Stala, Wydawnictwo Literackie (Cracow, Poland), 1996.

Contributor to anthologies, including *Polish Writing Today,* Penguin (New York, NY), 1967; *The New Polish Poetry,* University of Pittsburgh Press (Pittsburgh, PA), 1978; and *Anthologie de la poesie polonaise: 1400-1980,* revised edition, Age d'homme, 1981. Also contributor, under pseudonym Stancykowna, to *Arka* (underground publication) and *Kultura* (exile magazine; published in Paris).

SIDELIGHTS: Polish author Wislawa Szymborska was thrust into the international spotlight in 1996 after receiving the Nobel Prize for Literature. Although she is one of her country's most popular female writers and is valued as a national treasure, Szymborska remains little known to English-speaking readers, although by the late twentieth century several of her books—including her poetry—were available in English translation, among them; *People on a Bridge, View with a Grain of Sand,* and *Nonrequired Reading: Prose Pieces.* The reclusive and private Szymborska was cited by the Swedish Academy for "poetry that with ironic precision allows the historical and biological context to come to light in fragments of human reality." Her poetry, described by *Los Angeles Times* critic Dean E. Murphy, is "seductively simple verse . . . [which has] captured the wit and wisdom of everyday life" in Poland during much of the twentieth century.

Explaining Szymborska's work, translator Stanislaw Baranczak noted in *New York Times Book Review:* "The typical lyrical situation on which a Szymborska poem is founded is the confrontation between the directly stated or implied opinion on an issue and the question that raises doubt about its validity. The opinion not only reflects some widely shared belief or is representative of some widespread mind-set," Baranczak added, "but also, as a rule, has a certain doctrinaire ring to it: the philosophy behind it is usually speculative, anti-empirical, prone to hasty generalizations, collectivist, dogmatic and intolerant."

Szymborska received critical acclaim for the first collection of her work to appear in English translation, *Sounds, Feelings, Thoughts: Seventy Poems.* "Of the poetic voices to come out of Poland after 1945 Wislawa Szymborska's is probably the most elusive as well as the most distinctive," wrote Jaroslaw Anders in *New York Review of Books.* Anders commented: "*Sounds, Feelings, Thoughts* contains poems from [Szymborska's] five books written since 1957, comprising more or less half of what the poet herself considers her canon. Its publication is of interest not only because of Szymborska's importance as a poet, but also because her work demonstrates that the diversity of poetic modes in Poland is much greater than is usually perceived." Alice-Catherine Carls, in a review of *Sounds, Feelings, Thoughts* in *Library Journal,* called the work "one of those rare books which put one in a state of 'grace,'" while Robert Hudzik, also in *Library Journal,* maintained that the collection "reveals a poet of startling originality and deep sympathy."

The 1995 collection *Views with a Grain of Sand: Selected Poems* was also praised by many critics who lauded Szymborska's directness and distinctive voice. Stephen Dobyns in *Washington Post Book World* praised both the humor of Szymborska's work as well as the translation by Baranczak and Clare Cavanagh. Edward Hirsch in a *New York Review of Books* review concurred, arguing that the volume reveals "the full force of [Szymborska's] fierce and unexpected wit." Louis McKee, in a *Library Journal* review, also praised the "wonderfully wicked" wit of Szymborska. Dobyns concluded: "The poems are surprising, funny and deeply moving. Szymborska is a world-class poet, and this book will go far to make her known in the United States."

Publication of *Poems New and Collected, 1957-1997* inspired further critical acclaim. "It may seem superfluous to praise a Nobel Laureate in literature, but Szymborska is a splendid writer richly deserving of her recent renown," affirmed Graham Christian in *Library Journal.* Noting the poet's "unflinching examination of torture and other wrongs inflicted by repressive regimes," Christian went on to say that Szymborska's verse contains "the exhilarating power of a kind of serious laughter." Despite the poems' frequently grim subject matter, "Syzmborska's tough naturalism does allow rays of light to penetrate its bleak landscapes, leaving lasting, sustaining impressions," declared a reviewer for *Publishers Weekly.*

Szymborska's 2002 collection, *Nonrequired Reading: Prose Pieces,* is a collection of short book reviews she wrote while working as a columnist. Nancy R. Ives in *Library Journal* stated, "The skillful simplicity and lyric quality of these essays make them distinctive. With her poet's gift for compression, Szymborska captures large concepts and brilliantly reduces them to pithy, two-page essays." A reviewer for *Publishers Weekly* forecasted, "While the conceit of a commonplace book of reader responses may be a little quirky," reviews would assist the general reader in understanding and appreciating Szymborska's works. "This may very well be the season's sleeper hit among literati," the reviewer added, "particularly among non-regular readers of poetry who nevertheless recognize Szymborska's name."

Many commentators have remarked on the deceptively simple quality of Syzmborska's work. In simple language, she speaks of ordinary things, only to reveal extraordinary truths. In a *Publishers Weekly* article about the poet, Joanna Trzeciak praised "the wit and clarity of Szymborska's turns of phrase. Under her pen, simple language becomes striking. Ever the gentle subversive, she stubbornly refuses to see anything in the world as ordinary. The result is a poetry of elegance and irony, full of surprising turns." And Denise Wiloch, a contributor to *Contemporary Women Poets,* pointed out that "the seemingly casual musings she captures in her poems are deceptive and full of irony. Her work reverberates long after it is read."

Syzmborska "knows philosophy, literature, and history, but mostly she knows common human experience," concludes *Booklist* writer Ray Olson. "Her work is ultimately wisdom literature, written in a first person that expresses a universal humanity that American poets—lockstep individualists all—haven't dared essay since early in this century. She is like Brecht without hatred, Sandburg without socialist posturing, Dickinson without hermetism, Whitman without illusory optimism: a great poet."

Szymborska's works have been translated into Arabic, Hebrew, Japanese, Chinese, and other languages.

BIOGRAPHICAL AND CRITICAL SOURCES:

BOOKS

Balbus, Stanislaw, *Swiat ze wszystkich stron swiata: O Wislawie Szymborski,* Wydawnictwo Literackie (Cracow, Poland), 1996.

Baranczak, Stanislaw, *Breathing under Water and Other East European Essays,* Harvard University Press (Cambridge, MA), 1990.

Contemporary Women Poets, St. James Press (Detroit, MI), 1998.

Levine, Madeline, *Contemporary Polish Poetry: 1925-1975,* Twayne (Boston, MA), 1981.

PERIODICALS

Booklist, April 15, 1998, Ray Olson, review of *Poems New and Collected, 1957-1997;* March 15, 1999, Ray Olson, review of *Poems New and Collected 1957-1997,* p. 1276.

Choice, January, 1992, review of *People on a Bridge,* p. 752.

Humanities Review, spring, 1982, p. 141.

Library Journal, September 1, 1981, p. 1636; July, 1995, p. 85; April 1, 1998, Graham Christian, review of *Poems New and Collected, 1957-1997,* p. 92; November 1, 2002, Nancy R. Ives, review of *Nonrequired Reading: Prose Pieces,* p. 91.

Los Angeles Times, October 4, 1996; October 13, 1996.

Maclean's, October 14, 1996, p. 11.

New Republic, January 1, 1996, p. 36; December 30, 1996, p. 27.

New Yorker, December 14, 1992, p. 94; March 1, 1993, p. 86.

New York Review of Books, October 21, 1982, p. 47; November 14, 1996, p. 17; October 21, 1993, p. 42; April 18, 1996, p. 35; October 8, 1998, p. 37.

New York Times, October 4, 1996, p. C13.

New York Times Book Review, October 27, 1996, Stanislaw Baraczak, "The Reluctant Poet," p. 51.

New York Times Magazine, December 1, 1996, p. 46.

Observer (London, England), August 18, 1991, p. 51.

People, May 5, 1997, review of *View with a Grain of Sand,* p. 41.

Publishers Weekly, April 7, 1997, Joanna Trzeciak, "Wislawa Szymborska: The Enchantment of Everyday Objects," p. 68; March 30, 1998, review of *Poems New and Collected, 1957-1997,* p. 77; September 23, 2002, review of *Nonrequired Reading,* p. 69.

Time, October 14, 1996, p. 33.

Times Literary Supplement, September 17, 1999, Clair Wills, "How Real Is Reality?," p. 25.

U.S. News and World Report, October 14, 1996, p. 32.

Wall Street Journal, October 4, 1996.

Washington Post Book World, July 30, 1995, p. 8.

World Literature Today, spring, 1982, p. 368; winter, 1992, Bogdana Carpenter, review of *People on a Bridge,* pp. 163-164; winter, 1997; summer, 1991, Alice-Catherine Carls, review of *Poezje = Poems,* p. 519.

T

TALENT FAMILY, The
See SEDARIS, David

* * *

TALESE, Gay 1932-

PERSONAL: Given name originally Gaetano; born February 7, 1932, in Ocean City, NJ; son of Joseph Francis and Catherine (DePaolo) Talese; married Nan Ahearn (a publishing executive), June 10, 1959; children: Pamela, Catherine. *Education:* University of Alabama, B.A., 1953.

ADDRESSES: *Home*—109 E. 61st St., New York, NY 10021-8101; and 154 E. Atlantic Blvd., Ocean City, NJ 08226-4511 (summer).

CAREER: *New York Times,* New York, NY, 1953-65, began as copy boy, became reporter; full-time writer, 1965—. *Military service:* U.S. Army, 1953-55; became first lieutenant.

MEMBER: PEN (vice president, 1984-87; member of board of directors, beginning 1980), Authors League of America, Sigma Delta Chi, Phi Sigma Kappa.

AWARDS, HONORS: Best Sports Stories Award for Magazine Story, E.P. Dutton, 1967, for "The Silent Season of a Hero"; Christopher Book Award, 1970, for *The Kingdom and the Power.*

WRITINGS:

NONFICTION

New York: A Serendipiter's Journey, Harper (New York, NY), 1961.

The Bridge, Harper (New York, NY), 1964; Walker (New York, NY), 2003.

The Overreachers, Harper (New York, NY), 1965.

The Kingdom and the Power, World Publishing (Cleveland, OH), 1969.

Fame and Obscurity, World Publishing (Cleveland, OH), 1970.

Honor Thy Father, World Publishing (Cleveland, OH), 1971.

Thy Neighbor's Wife, Doubleday (New York, NY), 1980.

(Editor, with Robert Atwan) *The Best American Essays 1987,* Ticknor & Fields (New York, NY), 1987.

Unto the Sons, Knopf (New York, NY), 1992.

(With Barbara Lounsberry) *Writing Creative Nonfiction: The Literature of Reality,* HarperCollins (New York, NY), 1995.

The Gay Talese Reader: Portraits and Encounters, Walker (New York, NY), 2003.

Contributor of articles to magazines, including *Reader's Digest, New York Times Magazine,* and *Saturday Evening Post.* Contributing editor, *Esquire,* beginning 1966.

ADAPTATIONS: *Honor Thy Father* was filmed as a made-for-television movie by Columbia Broadcasting System, 1973.

SIDELIGHTS: As a pioneer of the new journalism, Gay Talese was one of the first writers to apply the techniques of fiction to nonfiction. In a *Writer's Digest* interview with Leonard Wallace Robinson, Talese described how and why he began writing in this style while reporting for the *New York Times:* "I found I was leaving the assignment each day, unable with the techniques available to me or permissible to the *New York Times,* to really tell, to report, all that I saw, to communicate through the techniques that were permitted by the archaic copy desk. . . . [So] I started . . . to use the techniques of the short story writer in some of the *Esquire* pieces I did in the early Sixties. . . . It may read like fiction, it may give the impression that it was made up, over-dramatizing incidents for the effect those incidents may cause in the writing, but without question . . . there is reporting. There is reporting that fortifies the whole structure. Fact reporting, leg work."

Now considered classics of the genre, Talese's *Esquire* articles probed the private lives of celebrities such as Frank Sinatra, Joe DiMaggio, and Floyd Patterson. The success of these stories prompted Talese to apply this new technique to larger subjects, and, in 1969, he produced his first best-seller, *The Kingdom and the Power,* a nonfiction work about the *New York Times* written in novelistic style. Since then Talese has explored such controversial topics as the Mafia in 1971's *Honor Thy Father* and sexuality in America in 1980's *Thy Neighbor's Wife.* Widely respected as a master of his craft, Talese thought of writing fiction, but, as he explained to the *Los Angeles Times*'s Wayne Warga, nonfiction has challenged him more: "I suggest there is art in journalism. I don't want to resort to changing names, to fictionalizing. The reality is more fascinating. My mission is to get deep into the heart and soul of the people in this country."

Talese grew up in Ocean City, a resort town in New Jersey that he describes as "festive and bright in the summertime" and "depressing" the rest of the year. As the son of an Italian immigrant, young Talese was "actually a minority within a minority," according to *Time* magazine's R.Z. Sheppard. He was Catholic in a Protestant community and Italian in a predominately Irish parish. A repressed, unhappy child, Talese remembers himself as a loner who failed most of the classes at his conservative parochial school. Then, when he was thirteen, he made a discovery. "I became involved with the school newspaper," he told Francis Coppola in an *Esquire Film Quarterly* interview, and realized that "you can be shy, as I was, but you can still approach strangers and ask them questions." Throughout high school and college, Talese continued his writing, majoring in journalism at the University of Alabama, contributing sports columns to the campus newspaper, and hoping to work someday for the *New York Herald Tribune,* where his literary idol, Red Smith, had a column of his own. After graduation, Talese made the rounds of the major New York newspapers, applying for a job and finally being offered one by the paper where he thought his chances were least promising—the *New York Times.* Hired as a copy boy, he was promoted to reporter in just two years.

In 1961, Talese published his first book, *New York: A Serendipiter's Journey.* Composed largely of material from his *New York Times* articles, the book was a critical success and sold about 12,000 copies, mostly in New York. His next venture was *The Bridge,* a book in which, according to a *Playboy* magazine contributor, "he took the plunge into the book-length nonfiction novel style." To prepare for this story, Talese spent over a year observing the workers who built the Verrazano-Narrows Bridge connecting Brooklyn and Staten Island. In the *New York Times Book Review,* Herbert Mitgang called the book "a vivid document," noting that Talese "imparts drama and romance to this bridge-building story by concentrating on the boomers, the iron workers who stitch steel and live high in more ways than one." While the publication was not a best-seller, it was critically well received, and set the scene for the three larger works that would follow in the next sixteen years.

The first of these, *The Kingdom and the Power,* is an intimate portrait of the *New York Times* where Talese worked as a reporter for ten years. Published four years after he left the paper, the book is "rich in intimate detail, personal insights and characterizations," according to Ben H. Bagdikian in the *New York Times Book Review.* "In this book," Bagdikian continued, "the men of The Times emerge not as godlike models of intrepid journalism, but as unique individuals who, in addition to other human traits, have trouble with ambitions, alcohol, wives and analysts." In his author's note, Talese describes the book as "a human history of an institution in transition." Specifically, he relates the infighting between James "Scotty" Reston, a respected columnist and head of the *New York Times* Washington bureau, and E. Clifton Daniel, managing editor of the paper, for control of the Washington bureau, which had maintained independent status for years. In the end, Reston wins and is appointed executive editor. "That outcome, of great moment inside the *Times,* is of less than secondary interest to the rest of the world," explained a *Time* critic, who added that "to curry reader excitement, Talese has had to transform the newsroom on the third floor of the *Times* building into a fortress of Machiavellian maneuver. (One wonders, sometimes, how the paper ever got put out at all.)"

Talese's decision to dramatize the story and to relate the process of change at an American institution from the human perspective has been more praised than criticized. Detractors of *The Kingdom and the Power* argue that the *New York Times* owners and employees are ultimately unworthy of such elaborate attention, that their petty squabbling diminishes the institution they represent. Supporters argue that Talese's approach is the best way to reveal the inside story and is an example of new journalism at its best. Among critics, John Leo wrote in *Commonweal:* "The new journalist in Talese is forever trying to capture the real *Times* by a telling scene of explaining what everyone felt at a critical moment. But the effort doesn't amount to much. . . . It is often spectacularly effective in delineating a person, a small group of people or a social event. But for an institution, and a ponderous non-dramatic one at that, well, maybe only the boring old journalism will do." Because his focus is on personality rather than issues, some critics found the book's perspective skewed. As Harold E. Fey noted in the *Christian Century,* Talese "seems unable to understand or to formulate adequately the *Times*'s high purpose, its worthy conceptions of public responsibility, its firm identification of personal with journalistic integrity. These also have something to do with power. And they have much to do with the *New York Times.* They help to explain, as Talese does not, why the *Times,* in his own words, 'influences the world.'"

Fred Powledge, reviewing *The Kingdom and the Power* in the *Nation,* found merit in Talese's approach, noting that the journalist "does not attempt to resolve questions [about journalistic procedure and social responsibility,] and some may consider this a fault. I do not think so. If he had entered this vast and relatively unexplored territory the book would have lost some of its timeless, surgically clean quality." And, writing in *Life,* Murray Kempton noted that "by talking about their lives [Talese] has done something for his subjects which they could not do for themselves with their product, and done it superlatively well." "There are surely criticisms to be made [of the great power the *New York Times* wields over public opinion]," David Bernstein noted in the *New Leader,* "but they are meaningless without an understanding of the private worlds of individual reporters, editors, and publishers and of how these worlds interact. Gay Talese is quite right to place his emphasis upon all this when he describes the kingdom that is the *Times.* What might appear at first glance to be a frivolous book is in fact a serious and important account of one of the few genuinely powerful institutions in our society." Powledge remarked, "The inner conflicts and passions of these men are beautifully documented in *The Kingdom and the Power.* It is no less than a landmark in the field of writing about journalism."

In 1971, Talese produced what many consider to be another landmark—*Honor Thy Father,* an inside look at the life of mafioso Bill Bonanno and a book so popular that it sold more than 300,000 copies within four months of its publication. Like all of Talese's efforts, the story was extensively researched and written in the intimate style of the new journalism. Almost six years elapsed between the day in 1965 when Talese first met Bonanno outside a New York courtroom and the publication of the book. During that time Talese actually lived with the Bonanno family and persuaded them to talk about their business and personal lives, becoming, to use his words, "a source of communication within a family that had long been repressed by a tradition of silence."

While the tone of the book is nonjudgmental, Talese's compassionate portrayal of underworld figures—including Bill and his father, New York boss Joseph Bonanno—incited charges that Talese was giving gangsters moral sanction. Writing in the *New York Times Book Review,* Colin McInnes argued that "Talese has become so seduced by his subject and its 'hero,' that he conveys the impression that being a mobster is much the same as being a sportsman, film star or any other kind of public personality." But others, such as a *Times Literary Supplement* critic, defended Talese's treatment, noting that the author's "insight will do more to help us understand the criminal than any amount of moral recrimination." Writing in the *New York Review of Books,* Wilfrid Sheed expressed a similar view: "Talese has been criticized for writing what amounts to promotional material for the Bonanno family, but his book is an invaluable document and I don't know how such books can be obtained without some compromise. It is a lot to ask of an author that he betray the confidence of a Mafia family. As with a tapped phone call, one must interpret the message. . . . Talese signals occasionally to his educated audience—dull, aren't they? Almost pathetic. But that's all he can do."

Furthermore, Sheed argued, the technique of new journalism, "an unfortunate strategy for most subjects, is weirdly right" here: "The prose matches the stiff watchful façade of the Mafia. One is reminded of a touched-up country wedding photo, with the cheeks identically rouged and the eyes glazed, of the kind the Bonanno family might have ordered for themselves back in Sicily."

After the success of *Honor Thy Father,* Doubleday offered Talese a $1.2 million contract for two books. "I was interested in sexual changes and how . . . morality was being defined," Talese told a *Media People* interviewer. To gather material for a chronicle of the

American sexual revolution, he submerged himself in the subculture of massage parlors, pornographic publishing, blue movies, and, ultimately, Sandstone, a California sexual retreat. He also studied First Amendment decisions in the Supreme Court and law libraries, tracing the effect of Puritanism on Americans' rights. As his research stretched from months into years, however, Talese realized that what began as a professional exploration had become a personal odyssey. And because he was asking others to reveal their most intimate sexual proclivities, he felt it would be hypocritical not to reveal his own. Thus, before he had written a word of his book, Talese became the subject of two revealing profiles in *Esquire* and *New York* magazines, the latter titled "An Evening in the Nude with Gay Talese." The public was titillated, and the resulting publicity virtually guaranteed the book's financial success. In October of 1979, months before the publication reached bookstores, United Artists bid a record-breaking $2.5 million for film rights to the book Talese titled *Thy Neighbor's Wife.* Published in 1980, the book was number one on the *New York Times* best-seller list for three consecutive months.

Despite its popularity, *Thy Neighbor's Wife* received negative reviews from many literary critics. Virginia Johnson-Masters, a respected sex researcher, foresaw the ensuing controversy when she wrote an early *Vogue* review saying that Talese "shows us many things about ourselves and the social environment in which we live. Some of them we may not appreciate or want any part of. However, Talese, the author, is fair. Read carefully and perceive that he really does not proselytize, he informs." Johnson-Masters added: *Thy Neighbor's Wife* "is a scholarly, readable and thoroughly entertaining book. . . . It is a meticulously researched context of people, events, and circumstances through which a reader can identify the process of breakdown in repressive sexual myths dominating our society until quite recently."

Writing in the *New York Times Book Review,* psychiatrist Robert Coles noted that Talese "has a serious interest in watching his fellow human beings, in listening to them, and in presenting honestly what he has seen and heard. He writes clear unpretentious prose. He has a gift, through a phrase here, a sentence there, of making important narrative and historical connections. We are given, really, a number of well-told stories, their social message cumulative: A drastically transformed American sexuality has emerged during this past couple of decades." Despite such praise from sociologists and psychologists, many reviewers criticized the book. Objections ranged from Ernest van den Haag's charge in the *National Review* that *Thy Neighbor's Wife* is "remarkably shallow" to Robert Sherrill's allegation in the *Washington Post* that it is "constructed mostly of the sort of intellectual plywood you find in most neighborhood bars: part voyeurism, part amateur psychoanalysis, part sixpack philosophy." The most common objections included Talese's apparent lack of analysis, his omission of homosexuality, and his supposed anti-female attitude.

In his *Playboy* review of the book, critic John Leonard articulated each of these objections: "Since Talese parajournalizes so promiscuously—reaching into [his subjects'] minds, reading their thoughts, scratching their itches—one would expect at the very least to emerge from his book, as if from a novel, with some improved comprehension of what they stand for and a different angle on the culture that produced them. One emerges instead, as if from a soft-porn movie in the middle of the afternoon, reproached by sunlight and feeling peripheral to the main business of the universe. If Talese expects us to take his revolutionaries as seriously as he himself takes them, he has to put them in a social context and make them sound interesting. He doesn't." Furthermore, Leonard continued, "Talese almost totally ignores feminism. Gay liberation doesn't interest him. Children, conveniently, do not exist; if they did exist, they would make group sex—Tinkertoys! Erector Sets!—an unseemly hassle. . . . Missing from *Thy Neighbor's Wife* are history and stamina and celebration and mystery, along with birth, blood, death and beauty, not to mention earth, fire, water, politics, and everything else that isn't our urgent plumbing, that refuses to swim in our libidinal pool."

Returning to large-scale nonfiction after over a decade, in his 1992 work *Unto the Sons* Talese "recreates the transformation of hundreds of thousands of immigrants and their descendants from Italians into Americans by tracing his own family" history, explained Joseph A. Califano in the *Washington Post Book World.* The product of more than a decade of research in the small southern Italian town of Maida, the book, as Talese told Jerry Adler in *Newsweek,* was a conscious change from writing about other famous figures. "After a lot of writing about people I didn't know," the author added, "I wanted to write about my private province." Califano compared *Unto the Sons* to Alex Haley's *Roots,* and declared that the author "has constructed from fact, scraps of memories and perceptive fancy a yeasty blend of public and family history that will ring true to anyone whose parents or grandparents migrated from Italy around the turn of the century." In some ways, the story Talese presents is a metaphor for the American immigrant experience. "In accepting and coming to terms with his own father," stated reviewer William Broyles, Jr. in the *Los Angeles Times Book Review,* "Talese discovers how much of his father lives in him, and lets us see how much the Old World still lives in us."

In 2003 Talese published *The Gay Talese Reader: Portraits and Encounters,* which draws from his journalistic works published between 1961 and 1997. Terren Ilana Wein, in a review for *Library Journal,* considered the book a "beautifully written collection of essays" that "truly represents the best of this still highly prolific author's work." David Pitt, reviewing the collection in *Booklist,* called *The Gay Talese Reader* "a sterling introduction to the multitalented Talese."

BIOGRAPHICAL AND CRITICAL SOURCES:

BOOKS

Authors in the News, Volume 1, Thomson Gale (Detroit, MI), 1976.

Contemporary Issues Criticism, Volume 1, Thomson Gale (Detroit, MI), 1982.

Contemporary Literary Criticism, Volume 37, Thomson Gale (Detroit, MI), 1986.

PERIODICALS

Booklist, October 15, 2003, David Pitt, review of *The Gay Talese Reader: Portraits and Encounters,* p. 360.

Chicago Tribune, June 8, 1980, review of *Thy Neighbor's Wife;* October 2, 1987.

Christian Century, October 8, 1969.

Commonweal, October 17, 1969, review of *The Kingdom and the Power.*

Entertainment Weekly, February 21, 1992, p. 46; April 3, 1992, p. 26; March 26, 1993, p. 74; December 19, 2003, review of *The Gay Talese Reader,* p. 80.

Esquire Film Quarterly, July, 1981.

Library Journal, November 15, 2003, p. 68.

Life, June 27, 1969.

Los Angeles Times, May 23, 1980.

Los Angeles Times Book Review, April 27, 1980; February 23, 1992, William Broyles, Jr., review of *Unto the Sons,* pp. 2, 9.

Media People, May, 1980.

MELUS, fall, 2003, review of *The Gay Talese Reader,* p. 149.

Nation, September 15, 1969.

National Review, August 12, 1969; March 6, 1981.

New Leader, May 26, 1969.

Newsweek, July 21, 1969, review of *The Kingdom and the Power;* April 28, 1980, review of *Thy Neighbor's Wife;* February 10, 1992, review of *Unto the Sons,* p. 62.

New York Review of Books, July 20, 1972.

New York Times, May 21, 1969, review of *The Kingdom and the Power;* October 5, 1971, review of *Honor Thy Father;* April 30, 1980.

New York Times Book Review, January 17, 1965; June 8, 1969; August 2, 1970; October 31, 1971; May 4, 1980; February 9, 1992, p. 3; March 21, 1993, p. 32.

New York Times Magazine, April 20, 1980.

Nieman Reports, fall, 1999, p. 44.

People, April 14, 1980, review of *Thy Neighbor's Wife;* March 2, 1992, p. 25; March 9, 1992, review of *Unto the Sons,* p. 96.

Playboy, May, 1980.

PR Week (U.S.), September 15, 2003, p. 12.

Publishers Weekly, January 7, 1983; July 25, 1991, p. 16; January 1, 1992, p. 42; October 20, 2003, pp. 46-47.

San Francisco Review of Books, May-June, 1993, pp. 27-28.

Sports Illustrated, October 13, 1997, p. 20.

Time, July 4, 1969, review of *The Kingdom and the Power;* October 4, 1971, review of *Honor Thy Father;* February 10, 1992, p. 72.

Times Literary Supplement, May 14, 1971; April 4, 1972; July 4, 1980.

Vogue, June, 1980, Virginia Masters-Johnson, review of *Thy Neighbor's Wife;* February, 1992, review of *Unto the Sons,* p. 120.

Washington Post, October 18, 1979; April 27, 1980, review of *Thy Neighbor's Wife;* May 7, 1980; May 15, 1980.

Washington Post Book World, November 15, 1987; February 16, 1992, Joseph A. Califano, review of *Unto the Sons,* pp. 1-2.

Writer's Digest, January, 1970.

ONLINE

Gay Talese Home Page, http://www.gaytalese.com/ (August 23, 2004).

* * *

TAN, Amy 1952-
(Amy Ruth Tan)

PERSONAL: Born February 19, 1952, in Oakland, CA; daughter of John Yuehhan (a minister and electrical engineer) and Daisy (a vocational nurse and member of a

Joy Luck Club; maiden name, Li Bing Zi) Tan; married Louis M. DeMattei (a tax attorney), April 6, 1974. *Education:* San Jose State University, B.A., 1973, M.A., 1974; postgraduate study at University of California, Berkeley, 1974- 76. *Hobbies and other interests:* Billiards, skiing, drawing, piano playing.

ADDRESSES: Agent—Sandra Dijkstra, 1155 Camino del Mar, PMB 515, Del Mar, CA 92014- 2605.

CAREER: Writer. Alameda County Association for Mentally Retarded, Oakland, CA, language consultant to programs for disabled children, 1976-81; MORE Project, San Francisco, CA, project director, 1980-81; worked as reporter, managing editor, and associate publisher for *Emergency Room Reports* (now *Emergency Medicine Reports),* 1981-83; freelance technical writer, 1983-87; *Los Angeles Times* Los Angeles, CA, literary editor of *West,* 2006—.

AWARDS, HONORS: Commonwealth Club gold award for fiction, Bay Area Book Reviewers award for best fiction, American Library Association's best book for young adults award, nomination for National Book Critics Circle award for best novel, and nomination for *Los Angeles Times* book award, all 1989, all for *The Joy Luck Club; The Kitchen God's Wife* was a 1991 *Booklist* editor's choice; Best American Essays award, 1991; honorary L.H.D., Dominican College, 1991; Barnes & Noble Writers for Writers Award, sponsored by *Poets & Writers* magazine, 2003; 2005 Editor's Choice selection, *Booklist,* for *Saving Fish from Drowning.*

WRITINGS:

The Joy Luck Club (novel), Putnam (New York, NY), 1989.

The Kitchen God's Wife (novel), Putnam (New York, NY), 1991.

The Moon Lady (juvenile), illustrated by Gretchen Schield, Macmillan (New York, NY), 1992.

(With Ronald Bass) *The Joy Luck Club* (screenplay), Hollywood Pictures, 1993.

The Chinese Siamese Cat (juvenile), illustrated by Gretchen Schield, Macmillan (New York, NY), 1994.

The Hundred Secret Senses (novel), Putnam (New York, NY), 1995.

(Guest editor) *The Best American Short Stories, 1999,* Houghton Mifflin (Boston, MA), 1999.

The Bonesetter's Daughter (novel), Putnam (New York, NY), 2001.

The Opposite of Fate: A Book of Musings (nonfiction), Putnam (New York, NY), 2003.

Saving Fish from Drowning (novel), Putnam (New York, NY), 2005.

Also author of short stories, including "The Rules of the Game." Work represented in *State of the Language,* edited by Christopher Ricks and Leonard Michaels, 2nd edition, University of California Press, 1989; and *Best American Essays, 1991,* edited by Joyce Carol Oates, Ticknor & Fields, 1991. Contributor to *Big City Cool: Short Stories about Urban Youth,* edited by M. Jerry Weiss and Helen S. Weiss, Viking (New York, NY), 2002. Also contributor to periodicals, including *Atlantic, McCall's, Threepenny Review, Grand Street,* and *Seventeen.*

ADAPTATIONS: The Joy Luck Club was released on audiocassette by Dove, as was *The Kitchen God's Wife,* 1991. *The Joy Luck Club* was adapted for the stage by Susan Kim and produced in China, 1993; and adapted into a feature film, written by Tan and Ronald Bass, directed by Wayne Wang, and released in 1993.

SIDELIGHTS: Amy Tan's novels concerning the bonds between Chinese-American mothers and daughters have earned her a worldwide audience. Although immersed in the rich lore of Chinese myth and history, Tan's works transcend the particular and become testaments to the universal themes of love and forgiveness. Tan introduces characters who are ambivalent, as she once was, about their Chinese background, but who move to a deeper understanding of themselves as they confront their ancestors' struggles in China and America. According to Susan Balée in a *Philadelphia Inquirer* review, all of Tan's novels "explore the same subject—mother/ daughter relationships, with a side focus on the problems of sisterhood—but they don't grow stale with repetition. In this, Tan is perhaps like Jane Austen . . . . After all, [Austen's] details vary from novel to novel; she found new ways to approach and explicate her subject. Tan does the same thing with another archetypal subject, and . . . like Austen, she will enjoy a secure place in the literary canon 200 years after the ink dries on the last page of her last book."

Tan was born in 1952 in Oakland, California, the daughter of Chinese immigrants. Her father was a Baptist minister. Her mother had fled a disastrous marriage in China and only slowly revealed the truth about the children she left behind. When Amy was a teenager, both her older brother and her father died of brain tumors within months of each other. Understandably concerned about the safety of the home they lived in, Amy's mother took the remaining two children and moved to Montreaux, Switzerland. There, the already tenuous relationship between mother and daughter worsened. In the *Philadelphia Inquirer Sunday Magazine,* Nita Lelyveld observed: "By the time Tan headed to college back in the States, she and her mother were barely speaking. But separated from her mother, hopping from college to college, unsure what to do, she found an unexpected anchor: her own heritage . . . . Still she and her mother fought constantly."

Tan's literary career was not planned. Her mother wanted her to be a neurosurgeon and a concert pianist, and in college she studied literature and linguistics. She first began writing fiction as a form of therapy. Considered a workaholic by her friends, Tan had been working ninety hours a week as a freelance technical writer. She became dissatisfied with her work life, however, and hoped to eradicate her workaholic tendencies through psychological counseling. But when her therapist fell asleep several times during her counseling sessions, Tan quit and decided to curb her working hours by delving into jazz piano lessons and writing fiction instead. Tan's first literary efforts were short stories, one of which secured her a position in the Squaw Valley Community of Writers, a fiction writers' workshop. Tan's hobby soon developed into a new career when her first novel, *The Joy Luck Club,* was published.

Set in the late 1980s, *The Joy Luck Club* details the generational and cultural differences between a young woman, June, and her late Chinese mother's three Chinese friends. June's mother and the three older women had formed the Joy Luck Club, a social group, in San Francisco in 1949. Nearly forty years later, June's mother has died. The surviving members, the "aunties," recruit June to replace her mother in their mah-jongg games, then send her to China to meet her stepsisters and to inform them of her mother's death. When June expresses reservations about her ability to execute this assignment, the older women respond with disappointment. June then realizes that the women rightly suspect that she, and their own daughters, know little of the older women's lives or of the strength and hope they hope to give the next generation. Throughout the novel, the various mothers and daughters attempt to articulate their own concerns about the past and the present and about themselves and their relations.

The Joy Luck Club has been praised as a thought-provoking, engaging novel. In *Quill & Quire,* Denise Chong declared, "These moving and powerful stories share the irony, pain, and sorrow of the imperfect ways in which mothers and daughters love each other. Tan's vision is courageous and insightful." In her review in the Toronto *Globe and Mail,* Nancy Wigston maintained that Tan's literary debut "is that rare find, a first novel that you keep thinking about, keep telling your friends about long after you've finished reading it." *Time* reviewer John Skow found the work "bright, sharp-flavored," adding that it "rings clearly, like a fine porcelain bowl." Some critics were particularly impressed with Tan's ear for authentic dialogue. Carolyn See, for instance, wrote in the *Los Angeles Times Book Review* that Tan ranks among the "magicians of language." Dorris placed the book within the realm of true literature, which "is writing that makes a difference, that alters the way we understand the world and ourselves, that transcends topicality, and by those criteria, *The Joy Luck Club* is the real thing." The novel spent nine months on the *New York Times* best-seller list.

Tan followed *The Joy Luck Club* with *The Kitchen God's Wife,* in which a young woman in California realizes a greater understanding of her mother's Chinese background. A generation gap exists between the two heroines: Mother Winnie has only awkwardly adapted to the relatively free-wheeling ways of American, particularly Californian, life. Daughter Pearl, on the other hand, is more comfortable in a world of sports and fast food than she is when listening, at least initially, to her mother's recollections of her own arduous life in China. As Winnie continues to recount the secrets of her past, including her own mother's mysterious disappearance, her marriage to a psychotic and brutal man, the deaths of her first three children, and her journey to America in 1949, Pearl is able to view her mother in a new light and gathers the courage to reveal a secret of her own.

Critics hailed *The Kitchen God's Wife,* admiring its poignancy and bittersweet humor. Sabine Durrant, writing in the London *Times,* called the book "gripping" and "enchanting." Charles Foran, in his review for the Toronto *Globe and Mail,* proclaimed Tan's work "a fine novel" of "exuberant storytelling and rich drama." In a *Washington Post Book World* review, Wendy Law-Yone asserted that Tan exceeded the expectations raised by her first book, declaring that *The Kitchen God's Wife* "is bigger, bolder and, I have to say, better." Referring to *The Kitchen God's Wife* in a *Time* review, Pico Iyer affirmed, "Tan has transcended herself again."

In her third novel Tan shifts her focus from the mother-daughter bond to the relationship between sisters. The main characters in *The Hundred Secret Senses* are half-sisters Olivia and Kwan. Olivia is the daughter of an American mother and a Chinese father who died before Olivia's fourth birthday. In adulthood, she is a pragmatic, somewhat priggish yuppie. Kwan, her Chinese half-sister, arrives in her life when she is six. Twelve years older than Olivia, clumsy, and barely able to speak English, Kwan is an immediate source of resentment and embarrassment to Olivia. Kwan's belief that she can speak with spirits is another source of humiliation, one that leads her stepfather to commit his stepdaughter for electroshock therapy. Through the years, Olivia treats Kwan rudely and dismissively, yet her older sister remains devoted to her and is determined to awaken Olivia to the reality of the spirit world. To this end, the two travel to China, where Kwan believes they lived another life together in an earlier century.

For some reviewers Tan's use of the supernatural poses a problem. Claire Messud, for example, wrote in the *New York Times Book Review* that Tan's evocation of the spirit world is unconvincing. The critic noted: "To accept the novel as anything more than a mildly entertaining and slightly ridiculous ghost story, the reader must also make [a] demanding leap of faith, turning a blind eye to rash improbabilities and a host of loose ends. For this reader, at least, that leap was not possible." Messud added, however, that Kwan is "a memorable creation" who "gently forces Olivia to face the worst in herself and, in so doing, to find her strengths. We could all do with such a sister."

New York Times reviewer Michiko Kakutani also expressed a mixed opinion of Tan's third novel. Kakutani praised it as "a contemporary tale of familial love and resentment, nimbly evoked in Ms. Tan's guileless prose," but mused that the main story in *The Hundred Secret Senses* is "unfortunately overlaid by another, more sensational tale of reincarnation that undermines the reader's trust." The critic went on: "Of course, there's nothing inherently implausible about ghosts. Maxine Hong Kingston handled similar material with consummate ardor and grace in *The Woman Warrior,* but Ms. Tan doesn't seem to know how to make Kwan's beliefs in the spirit world palpable or engaging." She affirmed, however, that "Tan is able to create enormously sympathetic people who inhabit some middle ground between real life and the more primary-colored world of fable. In doing so, she draws the reader into these characters' lives, and into the minutiae of their daily concerns."

Other commentators have been unreserved in their enthusiasm for *The Hundred Secret Senses.* Chicago *Tribune Books* contributor Penelope Mesic stated that the book contains "three qualities almost never found together: popularity, authenticity and excellence." Mesic concluded that the work is an "effortless mix of invention and reliance on reality that makes Tan's fiction so engrossing—a kind of consistency of action that suggests one could ask anything about a character and Tan could answer. She provides what is most irresistible in popular fiction: a feeling of abundance, an account so circumstantial, powerful and ingenious that it seems the story could go on forever." Gail Caldwell declared in the *Boston Globe* that *The Hundred Secret Senses* is simply "the wisest and most captivating novel Tan has written."

Real life has continued to inspire Tan with new novels, and *The Bonesetter's Daughter* is no exception. Tragically, Tan's mother was diagnosed with Alzheimer's disease in the mid- 1990s and died from the condition in 1999. In *The Bonesetter's Daughter* both the ailing mother and her Americanized daughter work together to recover not only the mother's life history, but also the tragic story of Precious Auntie, the mother's nursemaid. Having discovered a manuscript her mother wrote in Mandarin Chinese, the protagonist, Ruth, becomes acquainted with a series of dramatic events in rural China that paved the way for her mother's immigration to America. Ruth also begins to understand that Precious Auntie has long been a ghostly presence in both women's lives. As her mother's memory unravels, Ruth—ironically a ghostwriter by profession—becomes the bearer of the family history, and more self-aware for the knowledge.

"Tan's splendid new novel abounds not only with tellers and listeners but with people who truly understand stories and people who preserve them," observed Nancy Willard in her *New York Times Book Review* appraisal of *The Bonesetter's Daughter. Christian Science Monitor* contributor Yvonne Zipp noted, "Finding emotional healing in the face of disease has launched a thousand Movies of the Week, but in the hands of a writer as generous as Tan, it's a subject that still resonates as an antidote to grief." Reviewer Nicole Mones wrote in the *Washington Post Book World* that Tan's loyal readers "will find their pleasure in this new book magnified by a sense of mature succession from Tan's first novel." "In the end," Mones concluded, "it's the novel's depth of feeling that resonates and lingers. Tan writes with real soul. Her three generations of women are animated by the sort of understanding and empathy that can't be faked. In an age when few novels truly compel the emotions—and when too few even try— *The Bonesetter's Daughter* moves beyond its flaws to deliver a cleansing ray of light to the heart."

In her next book, *The Opposite of Fate: A Book of Musings,* Tan presents her first effort at nonfiction as she explores her past and her current life through a series of essays. In the book, Tan discusses the complicated relationship she had with her mother, Daisy. Writing in *Time International,* Bryan Walsh commented, "The formidable Daisy, who appears frequently in this collection of essays, had a distinct voice of her own, typified by this Talibanic pronouncement on the mortal perils of dating: 'Don't ever let boy kiss you. You do, you can't stop. Then you have baby. You put baby in garbage can. Police find you, put you in jail, then you life over, better just kill yourself.'" Tan also discusses her ongoing battle with Lyme disease, which caused her to battle depression and pain and have strange hallucinations. Other essays focus on literary fame and its impact and even about playing in a rock-and-roll band with Stephen King. Jessica Shaw of *Entertainment Weekly* found the essays to be "self-indulgent" and concluded that the reader may "wish fate had led her to write another novel." A *Publishers Weekly* contributor, however, noted, "As she reflects on how things have happened in fifty-odd years, Tan's writing winds from poetic to prosaic." Joyce Sparrow, writing in *Library Journal,* called the essays "sometimes humorous and occasionally wrenching" and an "excellent selection of pieces."

While *Saving Fish from Drowning* is a novel, it differs in tone, theme, and subject matter from Tan's previous works of fiction. Rather than focus on Chinese-Americans and their relationships, the book focuses instead on Americans visiting Burma, and takes on a decidedly more political tone. When a tour bus full of Americans is kidnapped by a tribe so friendly that the Americans are unaware of the fact of their own kidnapping, a comedy of local cultural farces and international political clashes ensues. While critics praised several aspects of the novel, they also felt that the farcical tone was not as successful as Tan's usual approach. "Amy Tan is wonderful at old fictions of ancient lands," commented Andrew Solomon in the *New York Times Book Review,* "let us hope she will return to that territory in the future." Solomon also noted, however, that the novel is "well paced" and that Tan's "lovely and evocative images add charm . . . in passages that might be dull in lesser hands." Jennifer Reese, writing in Entertainment Weekly, also stated of Tan: "she's a top-notch observer of the upper-class American abroad."

Tan once remarked in a *Bestsellers* interview that at an earlier age she tried to distance herself from her Chinese background. Her fiction writing, she said, helped her to discover "how very Chinese I was. And how much had stayed with me that I had tried to deny." She remains particularly grateful for her mother's influence. As she told the *Seattle Times,* "My books have amounted to taking her stories—a gift to me—and giving them back to her. To me, it was the ultimate thing I ever could have done for myself and my mother."

BIOGRAPHICAL AND CRITICAL SOURCES:

BOOKS

Bestsellers 1989, Issue 3, Gale (Detroit, MI), 1989.

Concise Dictionary of American Literary Biography Supplement: Modern Writers, 1900-1998, Gale (Detroit, MI), 1998.

Contemporary Literary Criticism, Volume 59, Gale (Detroit, MI), 1990.

Dictionary of Literary Biography, Volume 173: *American Novelists since World War II, Fifth Series,* Gale (Detroit, MI), 1996.

Encyclopedia of World Biography, 2nd edition, Gale (Detroit, MI), 1998.

Ling, Amy, *Between Worlds: Women Writers of Chinese Ancestry,* Pergamon (New York, NY), 1990.

Newsmakers 1998, Issue 3, Gale (Detroit, MI), 1998.

Palumbo-Liu, David, editor, *The Ethnic Canon: Histories, Institutions, and Interventions,* University of Minnesota Press (Minneapolis, MN), pp. 174-210.

Sau-ling Cynthia Wong, *Reading Asian American Literatures: From Necessity to Extravagance,* Princeton University Press (Princeton, NJ), 1993.

PERIODICALS

America, May 4, 1996, p. 27.

Atlanta Journal and Constitution, November 26, 1995, p. K11.

Boston Globe, November 10, 1992, p. 69; May 21, 1993, p. 23; September 19, 1993, p. 77; October 22, 1995, p. B37.

Canadian Literature, summer, 1992, p. 196.

Chicago Tribune, August 6, 1989; March 17, 1991; September 26, 1993, section 13, p. 20; November 9, 1995, section 2C, p. 16.

Christian Science Monitor, September 16, 1993, p. 11; February 15, 2001, Yvonne Zipp, "A Life Recalled from China: A Daughter Struggles for Assimilation, while Mother Clings to Their Culture," p. 20.

Critique, spring, 1993, p. 193.

Detroit News, March 26, 1989, p. 2D.

Economist, December 12, 1992, p. 101.

Entertainment Weekly, November 7, 2003, Jessica Shaw, review of *The Opposite of Fate: A Book of Musings* p. 76;; October 21, 2005, Jennifer Reese, review of *Saving Fish from Drowning,* p. 78.

Fortune, August 26, 1991, p. 116; December 28, 1992, p. 105.

Globe and Mail (Toronto, Ontario, Canada), April 29, 1989; June 29, 1991, p. C8.

Kirkus, September 1, 1992, p. 1135.

Library Journal, November 15, 2003, Joyce Sparrow, review of *The Opposite of Fate,* p. 68.

Life, April, 1994, p. 108.

London Review of Books, July 11, 1991, p. 19.

Los Angeles Times, March 12, 1989; May 28, 1992, p. E7; September 5, 1993, "California" section, p. 8; September 8, 1993, p. F1; October 30, 1995, p. E4.

Los Angeles Times Book Review, March 12, 1989, p. 1; July 5, 1992, p. 10; December 6, 1992, p. 10.

Ms., November, 1991; November- December, 1995, p. 88.

New Statesman, February 16, 1996, p. 38.

New Statesman and Society, July 12, 1991, pp. 37-38.

Newsweek, April 17, 1989, pp. 68- 69; June 24, 1991, p. 63; November 6, 1995, p. 91.

New York, March 20, 1989, p. 82; June 17, 1991, p. 83.

New York Times, July 5, 1989; September 8, 1993, p. C15; November 17, 1995, p. C29.

New York Times Book Review, March 19, 1989, pp. 3, 28; June 16, 1991, p. 9; November 8, 1992, p. 31; October 29, 1995, p. 11; February 18, 2001, Nancy Willard, "Talking to Ghosts," p. 9; October 16, 2005, Andrew Solomon, review of *Saving Fish from Drowning,* p. 22.

People, April 10, 1989, pp. 149- 150; November 3, 2003, p. 89.

Philadelphia Inquirer, February 18, 2001, Susan Balée, "True to Form."

Philadelphia Inquirer Sunday Magazine, February 18, 2001, Nita Lelyveld, "Mother As Muse: Amy Tan Had to Unravel the Mystery of Li Bingzi, Who Had Become the Voice of Her Novels."

Publishers Weekly, July 7, 1989, pp. 24-26; April 5, 1991, pp. 4-7; July 20, 1992, pp. 249-250; August 9, 1993, pp. 32-34; July 11, 1994, p. 78; September 11, 1995, p. 73; September 15, 2003, review of *The Opposite of Fate,* p. 51.

School Library Journal, September, 1992, p. 255.

Seattle Times, July 7, 1991, Donn Fry, "The Joy and Luck of Amy Tan."

Time, March 27, 1989, p. 98; June 3, 1991, p. 67; February 19, 2001, Andrea Sachs, "The Joys and Sorrows of Amy Tan," p. 72.

Time International, December 15, 2003; December 5, 2005, Donald Morrison, review of *Saving Fish from Drowning,* p. 6.

Times (London, England), July 11, 1991, p. 16.

Times Educational Supplement, August 4, 1989, p. 19; August 2, 1991, p. 18; February 5, 1993, p. 10; January 16, 1995, p. 16.

Times Literary Supplement, December 29, 1989, p. 1447; July 5, 1991, p. 20.

Tribune Books (Chicago, IL), March 12, 1989, pp. 1, 11; November 5, 1995, pp. 1, 11.

USA Today, October 5, 1993, p. D12.

Wall Street Journal, September 1, 1992, p. A12; August 19, 1993, p. A8; September 9, 1993, p. A18; December 6, 1994, p. B1.

Washington Post, October 8, 1989; May 21, 1993, p. WW16; May 27, 1993, p. D9; September 21, 1993, pp. D1, D10; September 24, 1993, p. WW47; October 23, 1995, p. D1.

Washington Post Book World, March 5, 1989, p. 7; June 16, 1991, pp. 1-2; February 11, 2001, Nicole Mones, "China Syndrome," p. 4.

ONLINE

Voices from the Gaps: Women Writers of Color, http://www.voices.cla.umn.edu/ (March 6, 2004), "Amy Tan."

* * *

TAN, Amy Ruth
See TAN, Amy

* * *

TANNER, William
See AMIS, Kingsley

* * *

TARTT, Donna 1964(?)-

PERSONAL: Born c. 1964, in Greenwood, MS. *Education:* Attended University of Mississippi and Bennington College.

ADDRESSES: *Home*—New York, NY; upstate New York; Grenada, MS. *Agent*—Amanda Urban, International Creative Management, 40 West 57th St., New York, NY 10019.

CAREER: Novelist.

AWARDS, HONORS: W.H. Smith Literary Award, 2003, for *The Little Friend;* Orange Prize for Fiction nomination, 2003, for *The Little Friend.*

WRITINGS:

The Secret History (novel), Knopf (New York, NY), 1992.
The Little Friend, Knopf (New York, NY), 2002.

ADAPTATIONS: An abridged version of *The Secret History,* read by Robert Sean Leonard, was released on audiocassette by Random House.

SIDELIGHTS: The splash of publicity surrounding Donna Tartt's $450,000 advance for *The Secret History*—the author's first novel—threatened to overshadow the work itself. The story concerns a group of college students who, under the influence of an eccentric professor of Greek, assemble themselves into an exclusive clique, eschewing the common activities of college life. A collective attitude of moral superiority and an interest in classics bind the group together, but ultimately their beliefs erode the group-members' values to the point where murder becomes an acceptable notion. *The Secret History,* Patricia Holtz summed up in the Toronto *Globe and Mail,* is the story "of would-be intellectuals devoid . . . of traditional moral character" and "of criminal acts committed by amateurs . . . and the resulting repercussions."

The setting of the novel, Hampden College, bears a strong resemblance to Tartt's Vermont alma mater, Bennington College. She had attended the University of Mississippi as a freshman, but found the campus too confining and restrictive. Moving to the more liberal campus of Bennington for her second year, Tartt attended writing classes with fellow-student and writer Bret Easton Ellis (author of *Less Than Zero* and *American Psycho*). Tartt started writing the book which would become *The Secret History* at Bennington, but it took her eight years to finish it. Ellis, who had read the manuscript, eventually introduced Tartt to agent Amanda Urban, "a name synonymous with hot young authors," according to Daniel Max in *Elle.* Tartt's phenomenal publishing deal for *The Secret History* generated a vast amount of publicity (in addition to her large advance on the novel, movie rights, and foreign contracts for eleven countries, Tartt received $500,000 for the paperback rights). The author was also profiled in a number of major magazines, including *Vanity Fair, Elle, Esquire,* and *Mirabella.*

The Secret History is less a mystery—the killers are revealed on the first page—than "an exploration of evil, both banal and bizarre," in the words of Martha Duffy in *Time.* The story is narrated by Richard Papen, a transfer student who disavows his own middle-class upbringing to gain entrance into an elitist circle of students. "The gradual moral seduction of Richard is all the more cleverly revealed by its depiction in his own voice," commented Andrew Rosenheim in the *New York Times Book Review.* As Richard becomes accepted by the group, he learns that four out of the five other members had participated in the bloody murder of a farmer who interrupted their late-night "bacchanal." When one among the small coterie threatens to betray this dark secret, that person, too, is killed. "Tartt shows a superior sense of pace, playing off her red herrings and foreshadowings like an old hand at the suspense game," Duffy stated in *Time.* In the *New York Times Book Review,* Rosenheim praised Tartt's "skillful investigation of the chasm between academe's supposed ideals and the vagaries of its actual behavior" and further commented that her prose was "at once lush and precise." Nancy Wood, reviewing *The Secret History* in *Maclean's,* believed that Tartt "is strongest when she finds poetry in everyday events: the sights and smells of a campus, the familiarity of certain television shows." *The Secret History,* Wood concluded, "stands out as well written and original."

The buzz surrounding Tartt's second novel, *The Little Friend,* was just as strong as the speculation about her first one. This time her second work came after a ten-year absence from the literary scene, and this long waiting period heightened the expectations for her new work. *The Little Friend* also dealt with murder, but this time the murder remains unsolved. The main character, Harriet, is twelve years old and determined to find out who killed her brother, Robin, when she was just a baby. Robin's murder all but destroyed Harriet's family and her parents basically leave Harriet and her sister in the care of their grandmother, who raises them along with her own sisters and a maid. The book is also a portrait of the South in the 1970s, and some critics recognized echoes of Faulkner and other well-known Southern writers in the tale. With the long wait and the phenomenal success of her previous work in the shadows, critical reaction covered the entire spectrum, between contempt and unabashed praise. In *Entertainment Weekly,* Troy Patterson commented, "*The Little Friend. . .* wipes out. It is an extended prose catastrophe." In contrast, a *Booklist* reviewer described it as "exceptionally suspenseful" and "flawlessly written."

BIOGRAPHICAL AND CRITICAL SOURCES:

BOOKS

Hargreaves, Tracy, *Donna Tartt's "Secret History": A Reader's Guide,* Continuum (New York, NY), 2001.

PERIODICALS

Book, November-December 2002, pp. 80-81.
Booklist, September 1, 2002, p. 8; January 1, 2003, p. 793.
Bookseller, June 28, 2002, pp. 30-31.
Economist, October 26, 2002.
Elle, September 1992, pp. 172-176.
Entertainment Weekly, October 15, 2003, p. 70; November 1, 2002, p.72.
Globe and Mail (Toronto, Ontario, Canada), September 26, 1992, p. C8.
Kirkus Reviews, September 1, 2002, p. 1262.
Kliatt, January, 2004, p. 19.
Library Journal, October 15, 2002, p. 96.
Los Angeles Times Book Review, September 13, 1992, pp. 1, 13.
Maclean's, October 12, 1992, p. 85.
New Republic, December 30, 2002, p. 38.
New Statesman, October 28, 2002, pp. 48-49.
Newsweek, September 7, 1992, pp. 54-55; October 21, 2002, p. 66.
New Yorker, October 28, 2002.
New York Times Book Review, September 13, 1992, p. 3.
O, November, 2002, p. 176.
Publishers Weekly, September 7, 1992, p. 29; September 9, 2002, p. 40; November 4, 2002, p. 18.
Spectator, October 26, 2002, pp. 54-55.
Time, August 31, 1992, p. 69; October 21, 2002, p. 74.
World and I, March, 2003, p. 40.

ONLINE

BBC Web Site, http://www.bbc.co.uk/ (August 19, 2004), profile of Donna Tartt.
Donna Tartt Shrine, http://www.purpleglitter.com/ (August 19, 2004).
Guardian Unlimited Web Site, http://books.guardian.co.uk/ (August 19, 2004), Katharine Viner, "A Talent to Tantalise."
University of Mississippi Web Site, http://www.olemiss.edu/ (April 27, 2003), "Donna Tartt."

* * *

TAYLOR, Kamala Purnaiya
See MARKANDAYA, Kamala

* * *

TAYLOR, Mildred D. 1943-
(Mildred Delois Taylor)

PERSONAL: Born September 13, 1943, in Jackson, MS; daughter of Wilbert Lee and Deletha Marie (Davis) Taylor; married Errol Zea-Daly, August, 1972 (divorced, 1975). *Education:* University of Toledo, B.Ed., 1965; University of Colorado, M.A., 1969.

ADDRESSES: Home—Boulder, CO. *Agent*—c/o Author Mail, Random House, 1745 Broadway, New York, NY 10019.

CAREER: Writer. United States Peace Corps, English and history teacher in Tuba City, AZ, 1965, and in Yirgalem, Ethiopia, 1965-67, recruiter, 1967-68, instructor in Maine, 1968; University of Colorado, study skills coordinator, 1969-71; proofreader and editor in Los Angeles, CA, 1971-73.

AWARDS, HONORS: First prize in African-American category, Council on Interracial Books for Children, 1973, and outstanding book of the year citation, *New York Times,* 1975, both for *Song of the Trees;* American Library Association Notable Book citation, 1976, National Book Award finalist, *Boston Globe-Horn Book* Honor Book citation, and Newbery Medal, all 1977, and Buxtehuder Bulle Award, 1985, all for *Roll of Thunder, Hear My Cry;* outstanding book of the year citation, *New York Times,* 1981, Jane Addams honor, 1982, American Book Award nomination, 1982, and Coretta Scott King Award, 1982, all for *Let the Circle Be Unbroken; New York Times* notable book citation, 1987, and Christopher Award, 1988, both for *The Gold Cadillac;* Coretta Scott King Book Award, 1988, for *The Friendship,* 1990, for *The Road to Memphis,* and 2002, for *The Land;* Christopher Award, 1991, for *Mississippi Bridge;* ALAN Award for Significant Contribution to Young Adult Literature, National Council of Teachers of English, 1997; Jason Award, 1997, for *The Well: David's Story;* Scott O'Dell Historical Fiction Award, 2002, for *The Land;* NSK Neustadt Prize for Children's Literature, 2004, for body of work.

WRITINGS:

Song of the Trees, illustrated by Jerry Pinkney, Dial (New York, NY), 1975.
Roll of Thunder, Hear My Cry, Dial (New York, NY), 1976, reprinted (twenty-fifth anniversary edition), Phyllis Fogelman Books (New York, NY), 2001.
Let the Circle Be Unbroken, Dial (New York, NY), 1981.
The Friendship, illustrated by Max Ginsburg, Dial (New York, NY), 1987.
The Gold Cadillac, illustrated by Michael Hays, Dial (New York, NY), 1987.
The Road to Memphis, Dial (New York, NY), 1990.
Mississippi Bridge, Dial (New York, NY), 1990.
The Well: David's Story, Dial (New York, NY), 1995.
The Land, Phyllis Fogelman Books (New York, NY), 2001.

ADAPTATIONS: Roll of Thunder, Hear My Cry was recorded by Newbery Awards Records in 1978, and as a three-part television miniseries of the same title by American Broadcasting Companies, Inc. (ABC), 1978. *Let the Circle Be Unbroken* was made into an audio book by Recorded Books, Incorporated, 1998. *Roll of Thunder, Hear My Cry,* and *The Land* were made into audio books by Listening Library, both 2001.

SIDELIGHTS: With her writings, award-winning author Mildred D. Taylor shares pride in her racial heritage and provides historical fiction about life for black Americans. As a child, Taylor was regaled with stories of proud, dignified ancestors, but she received a different version of history from white, mainstream America. Believing that school history texts diminished the contributions of blacks and glossed over the injustices to which they had been subjected, Taylor vowed to write stories offering a truer vision of black families and their racial struggles. Taylor draws upon family narratives, using a first-person voice that mirrors her relatives' rendition of such tales, and she has been praised for the authentic ring of her characters' ordeals. Taylor invented the chronicle of the Logan family, and her series of books follows the group's activities and experiences throughout the mid-twentieth century. Taylor uses this period because she wishes to emphasize how this generation's reactions to segregation helped to pave the way for the reforms of the civil rights movement and an improvement of interracial relations in the United States.

Taylor brings a unique vantage point to her fiction. Born in 1943, she was part of a transitional generation that witnessed both blatant discrimination against black Americans and the legislative reform to amend historical transgressions. Taylor also experienced the differing racial climates of the North and South. Although born in Jackson, Mississippi, Taylor moved north with her family when she was only three months old. In an essay for *Something about the Author Autobiography Series* (*SAAS*), she recounted that her father, infuriated by repeated racial incidents, decided to leave the South in the mid-1940s because "he refused to allow my older sister, Wilma, and me to live our lives as he had to live his, in a segregated, racist society that allowed little or no opportunity to blacks." Although racism was persistent throughout the country, the North was perceived as an area offering greater freedom and job opportunities. Despite their relocation, the family did not abandon their Southern roots; they made an annual trek to visit relatives. Reminiscing about such trips in her Newbery Award acceptance speech, printed in *Horn Book,* Taylor remarked, "As a small child, I loved the South. . . . In my early years, the trip was a marvelous adventure; a twenty hour picnic that took us into another time, another world." At that time Taylor did not understand that the nature of these trips was a direct result of the racist policies of the South; the family packed food because they were not allowed in Southern restaurants and hotels, and they traveled back roads out of fear of harassment from bigoted police officers. Yet Taylor soon realized that she was expected to act—and was treated—differently in the South merely because of the color of her skin. She continued, "one summer I suddenly felt a climbing nausea as we crossed the Ohio River into Kentucky" because of the blatant discrimination in the South and the fear it inspired. Despite the uneasiness these vacations involved, Taylor's father insisted that his daughters be aware of these injustices commonly invoked in the United States. His reasoning, as she explained in her essay for *SAAS,* was "that without understanding the loss of liberty in the South, we couldn't appreciate the liberty of the North."

Yet, for the author, the South also held pleasant memories as the home of her ancestors. In an article for *Horn Book* she remarked, "I also remember the other South—the South of family and community, the South filled with warmth and love—and how it opened to me a sense of history and filled me with pride." This vision of the South was passed down in an oral tradition; when Taylor's extended family gathered, relatives would recreate the family's history with stories acted out on porches and around bonfires. Her father was a noted storyteller, engaging family members with fascinating tales of colorful, proud ancestors who retained dignity even when faced with the inhumanity and degradation of slavery. In an article for *Books for Schools and Libraries,* Taylor disclosed the effect such tales had on her: "I began to imagine myself as a storyteller. . . . But I was a shy and quiet child, so I turned to creating stories for myself instead, carving elaborate daydreams in my mind."

When the author was ten years old, her family moved into a newly integrated Ohio town, and she was the only black child in her class. This was a scene repeated throughout her formative years, and Taylor felt burdened by the realization that her actions would be judged—by whites unfamiliar with blacks—as representative of her entire race. In school, when the subject was history, Taylor was uncomfortable because her understanding of black heritage contrasted sharply with that presented in textbooks. In *Horn Book,* she commented that such publications contained only a "lackluster history of Black people . . . a history of a docile, subservient people happy with their fate who did little or nothing to shatter the chains that bound them, both before and after slavery." Knowing this to be false, Taylor tried to think of ways to repudiate the information in those books. In her *SAAS* essay she recalled, "I remember once trying to explain those family stories in class, about the way things really were. . . . Most of the students thought I was making the stories up. Some even laughed at me. I couldn't explain things to them. Even the teacher seemed not to believe me. They all believed what was in the history book."

The bias of such accounts had a motivating effect on Taylor. In *Horn Book* she explained, "By the time I entered high school, I had a driving compulsion to paint a truer picture of Black people. I wanted to show the endurance of the Black World, with strong fathers and concerned mothers; I wanted to show happy, loved children. . . . I wanted to show a Black family united in love and pride, of which the reader would like to be a part."

However, it was not until 1973 that Taylor wrote her first book. Spurred on by a contest deadline, she produced the manuscript for *Song of the Trees* in only four days. Three months later she received a telegram naming her the winner in the African-American category of the Council on Interracial Books for Children contest. *Song of the Trees* introduced the Logan clan: Big Ma, Papa, Mama, Uncle Hammer, Stacey, Christopher-John, Cassie, and Little Man. This book, based on an actual incident, is told through the voice of the Logan daughter, Cassie. Jobs are scarce in 1930s Mississippi because of the Depression, and Cassie's father is away in Louisiana trying to earn enough money to pay the taxes on the family's land. In his absence, white men threaten to cut down trees on the Logan's property. However Papa returns in time to take a stand against the white men. Ruby Martin, in a *Journal of Reading* review, praised *Song of the Trees* as "so beautifully told, the prose rings poetry."

Taylor's next book, *Roll of Thunder, Hear My Cry,* which earned the prestigious Newbery medal in 1977, continues the story of the Logan family and the author "creates a remarkable family portrait," according David A. Wright in *Dictionary of Literary Biography.* Using a limited time frame, the book examines the family's life and demonstrates how discrimination is an everyday occurrence. Stacey, Christopher-John, Cassie, and Little Man all attend school, suffering humiliations such as being splashed by the school bus that only picks up white children and receiving school texts in poor condition only because the white school no longer had need for them. Mama loses her teaching job because she defies school district officials by including a discussion of slavery in a history lesson even though it is not in the book. After a horrifying racial incident in which several black men are set on fire, the Logans help orchestrate a boycott of a crooked white merchant's store, a suspected ringleader in the burnings. This act sets off a series of events, including the threat of foreclosure on the Logan's land, the near lynching of the Logan children's classmate, and a suspicious fire.

Stuart Hannabuss, writing in *Junior Bookshelf,* commented that *Roll of Thunder, Hear My Cry* is "full of episodes of emotional power." Noting the effect of such scenes, David Rees, in his work *The Marble in the Water: Essays on Contemporary Writers of Fiction for Children and Young Adults,* remarked that "it's impossible not to feel anger and a sense of burning in reading this book." And *Interracial Books for Children Bulletin* contributor Emily R. Moore concluded, "*Roll of Thunder, Hear My Cry* deserves to become a classic in children's literature."

In the next addition to the Logan chronicle, *Let the Circle Be Unbroken,* "Taylor's recurrent theme of family unity has its strongest appearance," according to

Wright. Cassie recounts the hardships of the Depression for both white and black sharecroppers and shows how sometimes people of the same economic status work together regardless of race. Yet, the author also presents more situations of racial struggle. The Logan children's classmate is unfairly convicted for his part in a robbery that took place in *Roll of Thunder, Hear My Cry.* Cassie helps an elderly black woman memorize the state constitution so that she can register to vote, but nonetheless the woman is refused this basic civil right. *New York Times Book Review* contributor June Jordan praised the book for its "dramatic tension and virtuoso characterization." In a review of *Let the Circle Be Unbroken* for the *Christian Science Monitor,* Christine McDonnell observed, "Though many of Cassie and Stacey's experiences happen because they are black, their growing pains and self-discovery are universal." McDonnell added, "The Logans' story will strengthen and satisfy all who read it."

The Friendship, written in 1987, presents a racial confrontation between two men in 1930s Mississippi. Tom Bee, a black man, had saved the life of John Wallace, a white storekeeper, when the two were young men. In gratitude, John insisted that the two would always remain friends, evidenced by their using first names to address each other. However, years later, John reneges on this promise and shoots Tom for addressing him by his first name in public—an act considered insubordination because blacks were supposed to refer to white men or women as "mister" and "misses." Frances Bradburn, writing in *Wilson Library Bulletin* stated, "This is a story that children will experience rather than simply read. . . . The humiliation, the injustice, but above all the quiet determination, courage, and pride of Mr. Tom Bee will speak to all children."

Taylor's next work, *The Gold Cadillac,* is set in the 1950s and chronicles a black family's car trip to the South to visit relatives. Much like the family vacations of Taylor's youth, the family is confronted with "whites only" signs and suffers harassment from white police officers who are both jealous and suspicious of the family's car and the prosperity it represents. Such incidents help the two young sisters appreciate the greater freedom and opportunity they enjoy in their Ohio hometown.

In the fourth book of the Logan saga, *The Road to Memphis,* Cassie is a high school senior dreaming of becoming a lawyer. She attends school in Jackson, Mississippi, and is for the first time without the protection of her parents and grandmother. Her brother Stacey and a friend are also in Jackson working in factories. There the trio face more racial incidents and also must contend with the outbreak of World War II. After Stacey's friend is forced to flee the city because he defended himself against a white attack, even though he realized he would be punished, Cassie grapples with her decision to pursue a career in the white-controlled legal system.

Another of Taylor's works, *Mississippi Bridge,* is told from the point of view of Jeremy Simms, a white character who has been present in the Logan books. In these works Jeremy was distinguished from the racist townsfolk in that he continually made offers of friendship to the Logan children. *Mississippi Bridge* chronicles another racist incident in which, during stormy weather, black bus passengers are forced to get off of the bus to make room for white riders. This story concludes in an incident that some critics perceived as judgment for the white's discriminatory actions.

The Well: David's Story, which Taylor published in 1995, revisits the Logan family, this time focusing on ten-year-old David Logan (father of Cassie in *Roll of Thunder, Hear My Cry*) and his family, who share their well water with both black and white neighbors in Mississippi in the early 1900s. Despite their kindness, the Logans are still treated with disrespect by the white neighbors. A reviewer writing for *Publishers Weekly* noted, "Taylor, obviously in tune with these fully developed characters, creates for them an intense and compelling situation and skillfully delivers powerful messages about racism and moral fortitude."

Taylor's next book, *The Land,* also a prequel to *Roll of Thunder, Hear My Cry,* deals with Paul-Edward Logan, Cassie's grandfather, during the period right after the Civil War. Writing in *Publishers Weekly,* a reviewer commented, "Like any good historian, Taylor extracts truth from past events without sugarcoating issues." Noting that Taylor's tone "is more uplifting than the bitter," the reviewer added, "Rather than dismissing hypocrisies, she digs beneath the surface of Paul-Edward's friends and foes, showing how their values have been shaped by the social norms." A reviewer for *Horn Book* noted Taylor's masterful use of the realities of racism "to frame a powerful coming-of-age story of a bewildered boy becoming a man beholden to no one." Finally, Hazel Rochman, writing for *Booklist,* pointed out, "The novel will make a great discussion book in American history classes dealing with black history; pioneer life; and the Reconstruction period, about which little has been written for this age group."

With each of her books, Taylor has provided a glimpse into the history of black Americans. Even though her characters face repeated racial indignities, they show courage and resourcefulness in overcoming their problems. Taylor has earned esteem and recognition for her writing, but she gives her father credit for much of her success. Both the stories he told and the example he set in fighting against discrimination helped her form the basis of her books. The author accepted her Newbery Medal for *Roll of Thunder, Hear My Cry* on behalf of her father and remarked that "without his teachings, without his words, my words would not have been." Taylor added in *Horn Book* that she hopes her books about the Logan family "will one day be instrumental in teaching children of all colors the tremendous influence that Cassie's generation . . . had in bringing about the great Civil Rights movement of the fifties and sixties." In her acceptance speech for the 1997 ALAN Award, Taylor also pointed out, "In the writing of my books I have tried to present not only a history of my family, but the effects of racism, not only to the victims of racism but also to racists themselves." Taylor has said that she still has a final book to write about the Logans and will be returning to Cassie's voice to tell the story.

In 2004, Taylor was honored as the first winner of the NSK Neustadt Prize for Childrens' Literature. Commenting on Taylor's career in light of this award, Dianne Johnson of *World Literature Today* remarked that the author "respects her readers of every age and background, and she respects her characters by showing them in their fullness as individuals and as knowing or unknowing players in big social movements. The plots are full of the suspense and drama of the real lives of real people." In nominating Taylor for the award, Johnson applauded Taylor's African-American characters: "Her black characters, full of integrity, contradictions, intelligence, confusions, and passions, help to eradicate the 'all-white world of children's books' and the many stereotypes of black people that once predominated this world." Another contributor to *World Literature Today,* Robert Con Davis-Undiano, also commented on Taylor's important contributions to literature for young readers: "Taylor has been a signal writer in America. By signal writer, I mean that she is a writer whose work has marked a huge cultural shift in the lives of many American families who have suffered the indignities of poverty and racial discrimination. . . . There are literally tens of thousands of young adults in America, and many more young people still in school, who attribute their strong sense of the meaning of social inequity and the need for social change to their reading of Taylor's work."

BIOGRAPHICAL AND CRITICAL SOURCES:

BOOKS

Authors and Artists for Young Adults, Volume 10, Thomson Gale (Detroit, MI), 1993.

Beacham's Guide to Literature for Young Adults, Beacham Publishing (Osprey, FL), Volume 3, 1990, pp. 1135-1143, Volume 8, 1994, pp. 3890-3897.

Children's Literature Review, Volume 9, Thomson Gale (Detroit, MI), 1985.

Contemporary Black Biography, Volume 26, Thomson Gale (Detroit, MI), 2000.

Contemporary Literary Criticism, Volume 21, Thomson Gale (Detroit, MI), 1982.

Crowe, Chris, *Presenting Mildred D. Taylor,* Twayne (New York, NY), 1999.

Dictionary of Literary Biography, Volume 52: *American Writers for Children since 1960: Fiction,* Thomson Gale (Detroit, MI), 1986, pp. 365-367.

Rees, David, *The Marble in the Water: Essays on Contemporary Writers of Fiction for Children and Young Adults,* "The Color of Skin: Mildred Taylor," pp. 108-109.

Something about the Author Autobiography Series, Volume 5, Thomson Gale (Detroit, MI), 1988, pp. 267-286.

PERIODICALS

ALAN Review, spring, 1995, Barbara T. Bontempo, "Exploring Prejudice in Young Adult Literature through Drama and Role Play"; spring, 1998, Mildred D. Taylor, "Acceptance Speech for the 1997 ALAN Award."

Booklist, December 1, 1990, p. 740; May 15, 1997, Karen Harris, review of *The Road to Memphis,* p. 1596; August, 2001, Hazel Rochman, review of *The Land,* p. 2108.

Books for Schools and Libraries, 1985, Mildred D. Taylor, autobiographical article.

Christian Science Monitor, October 14, 1981, Christine McDonnell, "Powerful Lesson of Family Love," pp. B1, B11.

Horn Book, August, 1977, Mildred D. Taylor, Newbery Award Acceptance Speech, pp. 401-409; September, 2001, review of *The Land,* p. 596.

Interracial Books for Children Bulletin, Volume 7, 1976, Emily R. Moore, "The Bookshelf: *Roll of Thunder, Hear My Cry,*" p. 18.

Journal of Reading, February, 1977, Ruby Martin, "Books for Young People," pp. 432-435.

Junior Bookshelf, October, 1982, Stuart Hannabuss, "Beyond the Formula: Part II," p. 175.

New York Times Book Review, November 15, 1981, June Jordan, "Mississippi in the Thirties," pp. 55, 58; May 20, 1990.

Publishers Weekly, April 13, 1990, review of *The Road to Memphis,* p. 67; July 17, 1990, review of *Mississippi Bridge,* p. 234; January 2, 1995, review of *The Well: David's Story,* p. 77; August 13, 2001, review of *The Land,* p. 313; October 22, 2001, Jennifer M. Brown, "Stories behind the Book," p. 24.

School Library Journal, Bruce Anne Shook, review of *The Land,* p. 190.

Times Literary Supplement, March 26, 1982.

Wilson Library Bulletin, March, 1988, Frances Bradburn, "Middle Readers' Right to Read," p. 42.

World Literature Today, May-August, 2004, Dianne Johnson, "A Tribute to Mildred D. Taylor," p. 3, 4, and Robert Con Davis-Undiano, "Mildred D. Taylor and the Art of Making a Difference," p. 11.

* * *

TAYLOR, Mildred Delois
See TAYLOR, Mildred D.

* * *

TENNESHAW, S.M.
See SILVERBERG, Robert

* * *

TERKEL, Louis
See TERKEL, Studs

* * *

TERKEL, Studs 1912-
[A pseudonym]
(Louis Terkel)

PERSONAL: Born May 16, 1912, in New York, NY; son of Samuel and Anna (Finkel) Terkel; married Ida Goldberg, July 2, 1939 (deceased, 1999); children: Paul. *Education:* University of Chicago, Ph.B., 1932, J.D., 1934.

ADDRESSES: Home—850 West Castlewood Ter., Chicago, IL 60640. *Office*—WFMT Radio, 5400 North St. Louis Ave., Chicago, IL 60625.

CAREER: Worked as a civil service employee in Washington, DC, and as a stage actor and movie house manager during the 1930s and 1940s; host of interview show *Wax Museum* on radio station WFMT, Chicago, IL, beginning 1945. Moderator of television program *Studs' Place,* Chicago, 1950-53. Actor in stage plays, including *Detective Story,* 1950, *A View from the Bridge,* 1958, *Light up the Sky,* 1959, and *The Cave Dwellers,* 1960. Master of ceremonies at Newport Folk Festival, 1959 and 1960, Ravinia Music Festival, Highland Park, IL, 1959, University of Chicago Folk Festival, 1961, and others. Also columnist and narrator of films.

AWARDS, HONORS: Ohio State University award, 1959, and UNESCO Prix Italia award, 1962, both for *Wax Museum*; University of Chicago Alumni Association Communicator of the Year award, 1969; National Book Award nominee, 1975; George Foster Peabody Broadcasting Award, 1980; Society of Midland Authors Award, 1982, for *American Dreams: Lost and Found,* and 1983, for best writer; Eugene V. Debs Award, 1983, for public service; Pulitzer Prize in nonfiction, 1985, for *"The Good War": An Oral History of World War II*; Hugh M. Hefner First Amendment Award for Lifetime Achievement, 1990; Mind Book of the Year award, 2003, for *Will the Circle Be Unbroken?;* Ivan Sandrof Lifetime Achievement Award, National Book Critics Circle, 2003.

WRITINGS:

(With Milly Hawk Daniel) *Giants of Jazz,* Crowell (New York, NY), 1957, revised edition, 1975.

Division Street: America, Pantheon (New York, NY), 1967, 2nd edition, New Press (New York, NY), 1993.

Hard Times: An Oral History of the Great Depression, Pantheon (New York, NY), 1970.

Working: People Talk about What They Do All Day and How They Feel about What They Do, Pantheon (New York, NY), 1974.

Envelopes of Sound: Six Practitioners Discuss the Method, Theory, and Practice of Oral History and Oral Testimony, Precedent Publishing, 1975, second edition published as *Envelopes of Sound: The Art of Oral History,* 1985.

Talking to Myself: A Memoir of My Times, Pantheon (New York, NY), 1977.

American Dreams: Lost and Found, Pantheon (New York, NY), 1980.

"The Good War": An Oral History of World War II, Pantheon (New York, NY), 1984.

(Author of foreword) Hollinger F. Barnard, editor, *Outside the Magic Circle: Autobiography of Virginia Foster Durr,* University of Alabama Press (Tuscaloosa, AL), 1985.

(With Nelson Algren) *The Neon Wilderness,* Writers and Readers, 1986.

Chicago, Pantheon (New York, NY), 1986.

The Great Divide: Second Thoughts on the American Dream, Pantheon (New York, NY), 1988.

(Author of introduction) John Steinbeck, *The Grapes of Wrath,* Viking (New York, NY), 1989.

RACE: How Blacks and Whites Think and Feel about the American Obsession, New Press (New York, NY), 1992.

Coming of Age: The Story of Our Century by Those Who've Lived It, St. Martin's Press (New York, NY), 1995.

My American Century, Norton (New York, NY), 1997.

The Spectator: Talk about Movies and Plays with the People Who Make Them, New Press (New York, NY), 1999.

Will the Circle Be Unbroken?: Reflections on Death, Rebirth, and Hunger for a Faith, New Press (New York, NY), 2001.

Hope Dies Last: Keeping the Faith in Difficult Times, New Press (New York, NY), 2003.

Also author of play *Amazing Grace,* first produced in Ann Arbor, MI, 1967. Featured on sound recordings, including *Television: The First Fifty Years,* Center for Cassette Studies, 1975.

ADAPTATIONS: Working was adapted as a musical by Stephen Schwartz and produced on Broadway, 1978; *American Dreams: Lost and Found* was adapted for the stage by Peter Frisch, Dramatists Play Service, 1987; *Talking to Myself* was adapted as a play by Paul Sills and produced in Evanston, IL, 1988; *The American Clock: A Vaudeville,* a play by Arthur Miller, was based in part on Terkel's *Hard Times,* Dramatists Play Service, 1992; *RACE* was adapted as a play by David Schwimmer and produced in Chicago, 2003.

SIDELIGHTS: Making a career out of collecting the voice of America for much of the twentieth century, Chicago-based writer Studs Terkel, who was born Louis Terkel, has provided a sympathetic ear to the American people, devoting several of his books to their intimate, revealing, first-person narratives. Armed with his tape machine, Terkel has cris-crossed the country to get his interviews, and his subjects speak candidly on topics as distinct as the Great Depression, World War II, and their jobs, their fears, and their faith in—or frustration with—the American Dream. Some of Terkel's interviews have been with celebrities, but his most remembered—and many say his best—have been with "real people." "I celebrate the non-celebrated," the author once told *Philadelphia Bulletin* contributor Lewis Beale. "I've found that average people want to talk about themselves, their hopes, dreams, aspirations, provided they sense that you're interested in what they're saying." And, as Terkel once explained in a talk before the Friends of Libraries U.S.A., he has also discovered that "the average American has an indigenous intelligence, a native wit. It's only a question of piquing that intelligence."

Born in New York City, the writer is closely associated with his years living and working in Chicago; he adopted the name Studs from another colorful Chicago character, the fictional Studs Lonigan. Trained in law, Terkel became a successful actor and broadcaster. He was also an enthusiastic liberal whose fall from favor with the House Un-American Activities Committee during the 1950s led to the early cancellation of his television talk show, *Studs' Place.* As Terkel explained to Lee Michael Katz in a *Washington Post* interview, he was never a Communist, but he "belonged to a left-wing theatre group. Basically my name appeared on many petitions. Rent control. Ending Jim Crow. Abolishing the poll tax. You know, as subversive issues as that. Coming out in favor of Social Security prematurely. You think I'm kidding? These were very controversial issues, considered commie issues." But Terkel also maintained that the blacklisting helped his career: "If it weren't for the blacklist I might have been emceeing [today] on these network TV shows and have been literally dead because . . . I'd have said something that would have knocked me off [the air], obviously. But I would never have done these books, I would never have gone on to the little FM station playing classical music. So, long live the blacklist!"

After his early successes *Division Street: America* and *Hard Times: An Oral History of the Great Depression,* Terkel produced possibly his best-known book of interviews, *Working: People Talk about What They Do All Day and How They Feel about What They Do.* His interviews are threaded through with the recurring theme of disillusionment; many of his subjects told Terkel of the lack of emotional, spiritual, and, of course, monetary fulfillment in their jobs. A compendium of several dozen interviews from Americans in all walks of life, *Working* was described by *Washington Post Book World* reviewer Bernard Weisberger as "earthy, passionate, honest, sometimes tender, sometimes crisp, juicy as reality, seasoned with experience. It is tempting to say that people are naturally interesting talkers, but that would be untrue to our memories of boredom past and ungenerous to Terkel's skill. . . . He has a formidable gift for evoking and recognizing articulateness in a variety of people and coaxing it from private shelters." Although Anatole Broyard in *New York Times* contended, "Most people gripe better than they sing, and 'Working' sometimes sounds like the Book of Job," Peter S. Prescott, reviewing the book for *Newsweek,* dubbed *Working* "an impressive achievement. . . . Terkel understands that what people need—more than sex, almost as much as food—and what they perhaps will never find, is a sympathetic ear. . . . This is, I think, a very valuable document, a book that would be of use to writers and sociologists if only for the vast amount of technical information it contains."

Following the success of *Working,* Terkel in 1977 turned his tape recorder on himself to create *Talking to Myself: A Memoir of My Times.* "This is not a personal book in the usual sense," warned Nora Ephron in *New York Times Book Review.* "There is nothing about Terkel's father, next to nothing about his mother, a bare smidgen about his brother, a couple of stories about his wife. What you see is what you get: Terkel's voice. Talking to himself." Indeed, the author acknowledges "an inhibition" in writing about his family; as Terkel told Katz in a *Washington Post* interview, "I shy away from personal stuff, I really do. In [*Talking to Myself*] there's stuff I haven't revealed, and it's not worth revealing." Terkel's autobiography is "a marvelous and maddening book," according to *New York Times* critic John Leonard. "Marvelous, because we get to know the stout-hearted Terkel; maddening, because having gotten to know him, we want more, and he won't give."

Terkel's next work, *American Dreams: Lost and Found,* used the same approach as *Working,* each book containing some one hundred interviews with an assortment of Americans. Michael Leapman in the London *Times* noted that Terkel "does not tell us the questions he used to provoke what streams of articulate observations from his one hundred subjects. The evidence suggests that one question to them all was 'What is the American Dream?'" In a *Newsweek* article, Prescott stated, "Because it is not confined to a single city, or time, or particular part of the human condition, Terkel's *American Dreams: Lost and Found* is his most diverse." Robert Sherrill in *New York Times Book Review* noted in particular Terkel's interviews with people such as the grandson of a slave remembering the day he registered to vote, and a former leader in the Ku Klux Klan who became a union organizer to consolidate workers of all colors, and concluded: *American Dreams* "offers us an apple on every one of these pages."

In the Pulitzer Prize-winning *"The Good War": An Oral History of World War II* Terkel confines his interviews to those who experienced the war firsthand, providing a kind of informal history of that time. The author says that the quotation marks in the title are deliberate in order to drive home the irony of any war being "good." "As in Terkel's previous oral histories," Jonathan Yardley noted in *Washington Post Book World* that "*'The Good War'* is a clangorous but carefully orchestrated jumble of voices." Loudon Wainwright in *New York Times Book Review* found that the book "gives the American experience in World War II great immediacy. Reading it, I felt a renewed connection with that slice of my own past and a surprisingly powerful kinship with the voices from it." Wainwright also wrote, "It is hard to see how any reader now or then can fail to benefit from its 600 pages. For Mr. Terkel, who in six books over the past 15 years has turned an oral history into a popular literary form, has captured an especially broad and impressive chorus of voices on his tape recorder this time."

"The Good War" drew significant critical attention due to Terkel's interviews with African-American veterans of the era who remembered segregationist rules which applied on and off the base. One interviewee describes how African-American soldiers had to ride in the back of a streetcar while German prisoners of war rode up front. "Another explains why black pilots were so good," Prescott explained. "'We had extensive training,'" Prescott quoted veteran as saying. "'In the beginning, they didn't know what to do with us, so they just kept on training and training and training us. When we went overseas, most of our fliers had three times the flying training that white pilots had.'" On the other hand, as Turkel interviewee Dempsey Travis recalls in the book, the war for many African Americans represented "a step on the first rung of the ladder." During the war, Dempsey was the manager of the first integrated post exchange or military store in Maryland.

Terkel takes a contemporary look at class inequity in *The Great Divide: Second Thoughts on the American Dream,* which follows his formula of interviewing and compiling anecdotes from some one hundred people. This work, however, deals with economics rather than ideology, commenting on standards of living and the way society's definitions of the poor have shifted. "Once, the poor were 'victims'; now, they are 'losers,'" related Richard Eder in *Los Angeles Times Book Review.* "The dimensions of our social problems, the gulf between those who are making it and those who aren't, is as wide as ever, [Terkel] writes." However, "not everyone speaks of failed visions," such as the successful stockbroker Terkel interviewed, Stefan Kanfer commented in *Time.* Yet, "Americans should weep, for this is a book about the moral effects" the economic prosperity of the 1980s, "the loss of memory and community, the dumbing and numbing of America," insisted *Nation* contributor Bharati Mukherjee.

Harking back to the issue of race addressed in *"The Good War,"* Terkel compiled an entire work on the subject in 1992. *RACE: How Blacks and Whites Think and Feel about the American Obsession* is, like his other volumes, a collection of voices from nearly one hundred people of varying ethnicity, some famous, most not. This time they are speaking with Terkel on the subject of racial relations in America. Juan Williams, writing for *Washington Post Book World* maintained, "The strength of Terkel's book is its documentation of how race obsesses the national mind." In *Village Voice,* Michael Tomasky observed, "Terkel reminds us that race is not just a debate about a set of policies, but a web of contradictory feelings and impulses inside all of us, and any mill worker or teacher or cop is capable of both meanness and generosity of spirit, often at the same time."

At the age of eighty-three, Terkel turned his interviewer's eye to a subject close to home. *Coming of Age: The Story of Our Century by Those Who've Lived It* is a compilation of his conversations with around seventy men and women, ages seventy and older. While he includes several famous seniors, such as John Kenneth Galbraith, Katherine Dunham, and Uta Hagen, the majority of Terkel's interviewees are plain folks. John Espey drily noted in *Washington Post Book World,* "Most of them are unreconstructed Old Lefties, followed in number by enlightened moderates, the mix leavened with an occasional innocent." Despite the somewhat slanted view that results from this distribution, Espey explained, "What becomes clear as one reads on is the importance of the individual conviction of rightness, of carrying on." Rebecca Pepper Sinkler, writing for *New York Times Book Review,* commented that while the author "aims higher than the old-codger interview . . . Terkel's interviews don't soar. He seems to have asked all his subjects a series of unimaginative questions . . . [that] elicit banal answers." However, Sinkler added, "the language and imagery in other interviews is inspired." Judith Dunford in Chicago's *Tribune Books* reported, "For all its appeal, *Coming of Age* has real problems. One is the steady, nearly unvarying voice of the replies, which have been edited half to death." The other, she asserted, is "the uneasy sense . . . that Terkel believes the '30s were the decade that matters, that . . . nothing else is." Dunford concluded that the book is "best read as a remarkable storybook. . . . It's like sitting at the feet of dozens of engaging elders."

Political and community activism and civic involvement is the subject of *Hope Dies Last: Keeping the Faith in Difficult Times,* which Terkel published in 2003. In a work that *Book* contributor Eric Wargo dubbed "refreshing" and "uplifting" Terkel tracks down a host of what Donna Seaman in *Booklist* referred to as "objectors, dissenters, observers, protestors, and do-gooders," some well known—Pete Seeger, John Kenneth Galbraith, Tom Hayden, Dennis Kucinich—and some from the grassroots, to hear their opinions about how one finds hope in pessimistic times. Hayden speaks for many when he tells Terkel: "I live now with one goal: to try to learn to be the kind of elder who was missing when I was a kid." Praising Terkel as a "master oral historian, indefatigable humanist, and charming raconteur," Seaman praised the collection, joining other reviewers who roundly praised *Hope Dies Last* as inspiring.

"Terkel is an impassioned, humane, and remarkably energetic . . . Chicago broadcaster and writer who owes his status as a living legend and national treasure to his skill at what he calls 'prowling and stalking,'" Jane Howard quipped in a *Washington Post Book World* piece. "He prowls and stalks with a tape recorder, tracking down the ideas of his fellow Americans, and he sure is good at what he does." "Terkel can be justly charged with employing a formula," according to Kanfer in *Time.* "Still, it is *his* formula, sedulously aped but never accurately reproduced." *Tribune Books* contributor Willie Morris asserted, "Terkel's books have touched profoundly upon our lives."

In 2002 Terkel endowed the Studs and Ida Terkel Author Fund to support "promising authors in a range of fields who share Terkel's fascination with everyday life in America." Terkel's publisher, the New Press, agreed to commission three to five new books a year through the fund.

BIOGRAPHICAL AND CRITICAL SOURCES:

BOOKS

Authors in the News, Volume 1, Thomson Gale (Detroit, MI), 1976.

Contemporary Literary Criticism, Volume 38, Thomson Gale (Detroit, MI), 1986.

Parker, Tony, *A Life in Words,* Holt (New York, NY), 1996.

Terkel, Studs, *Talking to Myself: A Memoir of My Times,* Pantheon (New York, NY), 1977.

Terkel, Studs, *Hope Dies Last: Keeping the Faith in Difficult Times,* New Press (New York, NY), 2003.

PERIODICALS

America, September 16, 1995, p. 31.

Atlantic, July, 1977; November, 1980; February, 1995, p. 99.

Book, November-December, 2003, Eric Wargo, review of *Hope Dies Last: Keeping the Faith in Difficult Times,* p. 86.

Booklist, September 1, 2003, Donna Seaman, review of *Hope Dies Last,* p. 4.

Chicago Tribune Book World, September 14, 1980.

Detroit News, September 21, 1980.

Detroit News Magazine, May 10, 1981.

Library Journal, March 15, 1993, p. 127; September 1, 1995, p. 190; September 1, 2003, Stephen L. Hupp, review of *Hope Dies Last,* p. 188.

Los Angeles Times, December 12, 1980.

Los Angeles Times Book Review, September 28, 1980; October 14, 1984; October 10, 1988, p. 3; September 24, 1989, p. 14; May 3, 1992, p. 4.

Milwaukee Journal, April 23, 1974.

Modern Maturity, April-May, 1993, p. 72.

Mother Jones, September-October, 1995, p. 22.

Nation, March 30, 1970; April 6, 1974; June 4, 1977; December 8, 1984; December 5, 1988, p. 622; August 17, 1992, p. 178; June 10, 2002, p. 8; December 15, 2003, p. 35; February 24, 2004, p. 22.

National Catholic Reporter, August 1, 2003, p. 6.

New Republic, April 6, 1974; November 15, 1980; November 28, 1988, p. 38; April 13, 1992, p. 30.

New Statesman, March 4, 2002, Matthew Dodd, "The Common Man," p. 38.

Newsweek, April 1, 1974; April 18, 1977; October 13, 1980; October 15, 1984.

New York, September 11, 1995, p. 88.

New York Review of Books, August 13, 1970.

New York Times, April 30, 1970; March 21, 1974; March 22, 1974; April 11, 1977; May 14, 1978; September 24, 1980; September 26, 1984.

New York Times Book Review, April 19, 1970; March 21, 1974; March 22, 1974; April 11, 1977; May 14, 1978; September 24, 1980; September 26, 1984; October 5, 1986, p. 58; October 9, 1988, p. 10; May 3, 1992, p. 13; September 24, 1995, p. 7; December 19, 1996, p. 15.

People, December 4, 1995, p. 36.

Philadelphia Bulletin, April 17, 1974, Lewis Beale, interview with Terkel.

Progressive, November, 1995, p. 40.

Publishers Weekly, July 6, 1984; March 27, 1995, p. 23; September 15, 2003, review of *Hope Dies Last,* p. 53.

Saturday Review, April 18, 1970; April 20, 1974; April 30, 1977; September, 1980.

Scholastic Update, December 8, 1995, p. 8.

Spectator, March 15, 1986, p. 28; April 13, 2002, p. 55.

Time, May 13, 1974; April 18, 1977; September 29, 1980; October 8, 1984; October 3, 1988, p. 88; March 30, 1992, p. 69.

Times (London, England), May 12, 1981; March 28, 1985.

Times Literary Supplement, December 16, 1977; June 26, 1981; March 7, 1986, p. 243; February 17, 1989, p. 157.

Tribune Books (Chicago, IL), September 11, 1988, p. 1; September 10, 1995, p. 1.

Village Voice, May 23, 1977; October 2, 1984; March 31, 1992, p. 90.

Washington Post, May 5, 1974; April 24, 1977; October 5, 1980; September 30, 1984.

Washington Post Book World, May 5, 1974; April 24, 1977; October 5, 1980; September 30, 1984; December 22, 1985; September 11, 1988, p. 1; May 17, 1992, p. 1; August 27, 1995, p. 1.

Yale Review, January, 1993, p. 131.

* * *

THEROUX, Paul 1941-
(Paul Edward Theroux)

PERSONAL: Surname rhymes with "skiddoo"; born April 10, 1941, in Medford, MA; son of Albert Eugene (a salesman) and Anne (Dittami) Theroux; married Anne Castle (a broadcaster), December 4, 1967 (divorced, 1993); married Sheila Donnely, November 18, 1995; children (first marriage): Marcel Raymond, Louis Sebastian. *Education:* Attended University of Maine, 1959-60; University of Massachusetts, B.A., 1963; Syracuse University, further study, 1963. *Hobbies and other interests:* Rowing.

ADDRESSES: Home—35 Elsynge Rd., London SW18 2HR, England. *Office*—c/o Author Mail, Hamish Hamilton Ltd, 27 Wrights Lane, London W8 5TZ, England.

CAREER: Soche Hill College, Limbe, Malawi, lecturer in English, 1963-65; Makerere University, Kampala, Uganda, lecturer in English, 1965-68; University of

Singapore, lecturer in English, 1968-71; professional writer, 1971—. Visiting lecturer, University of Virginia, 1972-73. Has given numerous lectures on literature in the United States and abroad.

MEMBER: American Academy and Institute of Arts and Letters, Royal Geography Society, Royal Society of Literature.

AWARDS, HONORS: Robert Hamlet one-act play award, 1960; *Playboy* Editorial Award, 1971, 1976; *New York Times Book Review* Editors' Choice citation, 1975, for *The Great Railway Bazaar: By Train through Asia;* American Academy and Institute of Arts and Letters award for literature, 1977; Whitbread Prize for Best Novel, 1978, for *Picture Palace;* American Book Award nominations, 1981, for *The Old Patagonian Express: By Train through the Americas,* and 1983, for *The Mosquito Coast;* James Tait Black Memorial Prize for Best Novel, 1981, for *The Mosquito Coast;* Thomas Cook Travel Book Prize, 1989. Honorary degrees from Trinity College and Tufts University, both in 1980, and University of Massachusetts—Amherst, 1988.

WRITINGS:

NOVELS

Waldo, Houghton (Boston, MA), 1967.
Fong and the Indians, Houghton (Boston, MA), 1968.
Girls at Play, Houghton (Boston, MA), 1969.
Murder in Mount Holly, Alan Ross, 1969.
Jungle Lovers, Houghton (Boston, MA), 1971.
Saint Jack (also see below), Houghton (Boston, MA), 1973, reprinted, Penguin Books (New York, NY) 1997.
The Black House, Houghton (Boston, MA), 1974.
The Family Arsenal, Houghton (Boston, MA), 1976.
Picture Palace, Houghton (Boston, MA), 1978, reprinted, Penguin Books (New York, NY), 1999.
(With Peter Bogdanovich and Howard Sackler) *Saint Jack* (screenplay; based on Theroux's novel), New World/Shoals Creek/Playboy/Copa de Oro, 1979.
The Mosquito Coast, with woodcuts by David Frampton, Houghton (Boston, MA), 1982.
Doctor Slaughter (also see below), Hamish Hamilton (London, England), 1984.
Half Moon Street: Two Short Novels (contains *Doctor Slaughter* and *Doctor DeMarr*), Houghton (Boston, MA), 1984.
O-Zone, Putnam (New York, NY), 1986.
My Secret History, Putnam (New York, NY), 1989.
Doctor DeMarr (also see above), illustrations by Marshall Arisman, Hutchinson (London, England), 1990.
Chicago Loop, Random House (New York, NY), 1991.
Millroy the Magician, Random House (New York, NY), 1994.
My Other Life, Houghton (Boston, MA), 1996.
On the Edge of the Great Rift: Three Novels of Africa (contains *Fong and the Indians, Girls at Play,* and *Jungle Lovers*) Penguin (London, England), 1996.
Kowloon Tong, Houghton (Boston, MA), 1997.
The Collected Short Novels, Penguin Books (London, England), 1999.

SHORT STORIES

Sinning with Annie and Other Stories, Houghton (Boston, MA), 1972.
The Consul's File, Houghton (Boston, MA), 1977.
World's End and Other Stories, Houghton (Boston, MA), 1980.
The London Embassy, Houghton (Boston, MA), 1982.
The Collected Stories, Viking Press (New York, NY), 1997.
Hotel Honolulu, Houghton (Boston, MA), 2001.
The Stranger at the Palazzo d'Oro and Other Stories, Houghton (Boston, MA), 2004.
Blinding Light, (novel), Houghton (Boston, MA), 2005.

NONFICTION

V.S. Naipaul: An Introduction to His Works, Deutsch (London, England), 1972.
The Great Railway Bazaar: By Train through Asia, Houghton (Boston, MA), 1975.
The Old Patagonian Express: By Train through the Americas, Houghton (Boston, MA), 1979, reprinted, 1997.
Sailing through China, illustrated by Patrick Procktor, Houghton (Boston, MA), 1984, published as *Down the Yangtze,* Penguin Books (London, England), 1995.
The Kingdom by the Sea: A Journey around Great Britain, Houghton (Boston, MA), 1985.
(With Steve McCurry) *The Imperial Way: By Rail from Peshawar to Chittagong,* Houghton (Boston, MA), 1985.
Sunrise with Seamonsters: Travels and Discoveries 1964-1984, Houghton (Boston, MA), 1985.
(With Bruce Chatwin) *Patagonia Revisited,* illustrated by Kyffin Williams, Houghton (Boston, MA), 1986.

Riding the Iron Rooster: By Train through China, Putnam (New York, NY), 1989.

To the Ends of the Earth: The Selected Travels of Paul Theroux, Random House, (New York, NY), 1990.

Travelling the World: The Illustrated Travels of Paul Theroux, Random House (New York, NY), 1990.

The Happy Isles of Oceania: Paddling the Pacific, Fawcett (New York, NY), 1992.

The Pillars of Hercules: A Grand Tour of the Mediterranean, Putnam (New York, NY), 1995.

Sir Vidia's Shadow: A Friendship across Five Continents, Houghton (Boston, MA), 1998, with a new afterword by the author, 2000.

Fresh Air Fiend: Travel Writings, 1985-2000, Houghton (Boston, MA), 2000.

Nurse Wolf and Doctor Sacks, Short Books (London, England), 2001.

Dark Star Safari: Overland from Cairo to Cape Town, Houghton (Boston, MA), 2003.

Vineyard Days, Vineyard Nights, photographs by Nancy Ellison, Stewart, Tabori & Chang (New York, NY), 2004.

OTHER

A Christmas Card (for juveniles) illustrated by John Lawrence, Houghton (Boston, MA), 1978.

London Snow: A Christmas Story (for juveniles) illustrated by John Lawrence, Houghton (Boston, MA), 1979.

The White Man's Burden: A Play in Two Acts, Hamish Hamilton (London, England), 1987.

ADAPTATIONS: The Mosquito Coast was adapted for film by Paul Schrader, directed by Peter Weir, and starred Harrison Ford, Warner Bros., 1986; *Doctor Slaughter* was adapted for film by Edward Behr and Bob Swain as *Half Moon Street,* directed by Swain, starring Sigourney Weaver and Michael Caine, RKO/Fox, 1986; *London Embassy* was adapted as a British television mini-series by T.R. Bowen and Ian Kennedy Martin, directed by David Giles III, and Ronald Wilson, 1987; *Chinese Box* is a screenplay adaptation by Jean-Claude Carriere and Larry Gross of a story by Gross, Wayne Wang, and Theroux, directed by Wang, starring Jeremy Irons, WW/Trimark, 1997.

SIDELIGHTS: In a career spanning the last four decades of the twentieth century, author Paul Theroux has established a reputation as one of modern literature's most respected chroniclers of the expatriate experience. His novels find themes in the anomalies of post-imperial life, and are set such exotic locales as Malawi, Singapore, and Honduras, as well as in the economic and social decay besetting Great Britain in the late twentieth century. As Samuel Coale noted in *Critique:* "Drastic change indeed stalks the world of [Theroux's] fiction, that precisely rendered realm where cultures clash and characters encounter each other as society's pawns in a larger pattern." An American citizen who lives in London most of the year, Theroux has gained equal renown for his nonfiction travel books, some of which feature continent-crossing railway journeys of months' duration. By traveling, suggested *New Yorker* contributor Susan Lardner, "Theroux has tested a belief in the continuing strangeness of the world, and discovered openings for melodrama and romantic gestures that other writers have given up for lost." Helen Dudar wrote in *Chicago Tribune Book World* that Theroux has become "our foremost fictional specialist in the outsized outsider, the ravenous wanderer who sees or knows or wants more than most of us allow ourselves to hope for."

Theroux's family background and upbringing in the "prim suburbs of Boston" hardly seem adequate preparation for his adult role as an award-winning novelist, essayist, and world traveler. He was born in Medford, Massachusetts, in 1941, to working-class parents who had, he related in *New York Times,* "no place, no influence, no money nor power." They did, however, have numerous children. In his essay collection *Sunrise with Seamonsters: Travels and Discoveries 1964-1984,* Theroux writes: "It was part of my luck to have been born in a populous family of nine unexampled wits." Included in this roster of six siblings are two elder brothers—Eugene, a Washington, DC-based lawyer and expert in Sino-American trade, and Alexander, a novelist whose critical reception has rivaled Paul's. *New York Times* contributor James Atlas characterized the three oldest Theroux brothers as "collective tutors in the acquisition of culture" who "shared their various talents among themselves and passed them down to their younger brothers."

As a sophomore at the University of Massachusetts, Theroux declared himself to be a pacifist and insisted on receiving an exemption from the then-mandatory R.O.T.C. program. Though "neither a brilliant nor inspired student," according to Atlas, Theroux called further attention to himself in 1962 by being arrested for leading an antiwar demonstration—"when demonstrations were rare and actually bothered people," Theroux noted in *Sunrise with Seamonsters.* Upon graduation from the University of Massachusetts in 1963, Theroux joined the Peace Corps, an organization he describes as "a sort of Howard Johnson's on the main drag to maturity." He was sent to Limbe, Malawi, in South Central Africa to teach English.

For a time Theroux supplemented his Peace Corps stipend by writing articles for *Christian Science Monitor* and several African periodicals. In the course of his stay in Malawi, he found himself on friendly terms with a group of political leaders who eventually fell from favor with the unstable Hastings Banda regime. This association, as well as a duplicitous use of some of Theroux's articles by the German equivalent of the C.I.A., led to Theroux's deportation from Malawi in 1965, under the charge of spying. Several years later, Theroux described the incident in an essay that was reprinted in *Sunrise with Seamonsters.* "My readiness to say yes to favors may suggest a simplicity of mind, a fatal gullibility," he wrote, "but I was bored, and the daily annoyance of living in a dictatorship, which is like suffering an unhappy family in a locked house, had softened my temper to the point where anything different, lunch with a stranger, the request for an article, the challenge of a difficult task, changed that day and revived my mind." Theroux was expelled from the Peace Corps and fined for "six months' unsatisfactory service," but no further government action ensued based on the events in Malawi.

Immediately following his expulsion from the Peace Corps, Theroux returned to Africa, where he became a lecturer in English at Makerere University in Kampala, Uganda. He remained in Uganda until 1968, when he and his wife, Anne Castle, were attacked during a political demonstration against the policies of white-controlled Rhodesia. The violent end to his stay in Uganda notwithstanding, Theroux found much-needed intellectual stimulation at the university, as well as the time to work on his writing. In 1966 author V.S. Naipaul visited Makerere University and struck up an amiable but exacting working relationship with the young writer. Theroux recalls the period in *Sunrise with Seamonsters:* "It was like private tuition—as if, at this crucial time in my life, . . . he had come all the way to Africa to remind me of what writing really was and to make me aware of what a difficult path I was setting out on. . . . With me he was a generous, rational teacher." It was Naipaul, Theroux said, who suggested that he write fiction about Africa, with attention to the comic and the tragic aspects of life there. Theroux, in turn, published a critical appraisal of Naipaul's work, titled *V.S. Naipaul: An Introduction to His Works,* in 1972, and more recently penned *Sir Vidia's Shadow: A Friendship across Five Continents.*

Waldo, Theroux's first novel, was published in 1967, while the author was still living in Uganda. Timothy J. Evans noted in *Dictionary of Literary Biography* that the work "deals with the theme of a man trying to find or create order in his life" and that the book is the first expression of themes Theroux has continued to use. "Order is not discovered by the characters" in *Waldo,* Evans remarked, "and it is not imposed by the writer on the novel." Evans related that critical reaction to *Waldo* falls in extremes of praise and disparagement but that the book's quality falls rather midpoint between the two poles. "The novel does have a point," Evans concluded, "and it has some humorous, satiric passages which make it worth reading, but it is very episodic, with vignettes of uneven quality." A *Times Literary Supplement* reviewer offered a similar assessment: "Most of the time, *Waldo* seems to wander along, quite amiably and quite readably, but without much sense of direction."

In 1968 Theroux left Uganda and took a teaching position at the University of Singapore. While there he published three novels set in Africa: *Fong and the Indians, Girls at Play,* and *Jungle Lovers.* As a group, these novels explore the frustrating and potentially tragic difficulties of social interaction in postcolonial Africa. In *New York Review of Books* Robert Towers wrote of Theroux: "Unafraid of ethnic generalizations, he spares no one—African, Englishman, Chinaman, Indian, American—in his wildly absurd confrontations between the old and the new exploiters and the poor bastards caught in the middle; recklessly he juxtaposes the crumbling institutions of colonialism with some of the more bizarre outgrowths of the Third World." In *Fong and the Indians,* for instance, Theroux describes the misadventures of a Chinese Catholic grocer in an imaginary African state. According to *Saturday Review* contributor Constance Wagner, the novel depicts "Africans, Asians, whites, cheating, despising, mistrusting one another. . . . With a smile Theroux lays bare the myopic self-serving not of Africa but of man. . . . Laugh as you will, you realize in the end that this short novel contains more of sanity and truth than a dozen fat morality plays on ugly Americanism."

Critics have found elements of satire and hopelessness in Theroux's novels about Africa. A *Times Literary Supplement* reviewer stated of *Jungle Lovers* that "Increasingly a more wryly observed Africa emerges from the condescension or primitivism of expatriate fiction. . . . [Theroux's] fable, with roots in satiric caricature and documentary terror, uses the linguistic complexity to underscore the wavering relationships between lingering British, Africans, and the two American protagonists." Writing in *Spectator,* Auberon Waugh called *Jungle Lovers* "the most vivid account of the sheer hopelessness of independent Black Africa" and "a serious and excellent novel, welcome above all for its refreshing pessimism." Evans suggested that a "repeated assertion of empathy for the blacks does not convincingly cover an attitude of paternalism" on the author's part in *Jungle Lovers.* Evans nevertheless added that in the book, "The British and American settlers are also viewed with ridicule, and Theroux seems content to leave the Americans' plans for change open to question." The destructive implications of one particularly naive American's plans for change form the violent climax of *Girls at Play,* a work one *Times Literary Supplement* critic characterized as "unremittingly depressing." *New Yorker*'s Lardner felt that Theroux's novels set in Africa reveal him to be "a connoisseur of the conflict of ideals and illusions with things as they turn out to be." Irony, she concluded, "is his natural style."

While teaching in Singapore, Theroux was made to promise that he would not write any fiction about that island. The informal constraint was removed when he relocated in London, and he published *Saint Jack,* a novel set in Singapore. *Atlantic* reviewer Edward Weeks called the work "a highly professional, often amusing, withering account of prostitution in the once glamorous East." A low-key first person narrative by a middle-aged, expatriate American pimp, *Saint Jack* received substantial praise from critics. "There has never been any question about the quality of Theroux's prose or the bite of his satire," wrote Jonathan Yardley in *Washington Post Book World.* "In *Saint Jack,* more than in any of his previous fiction, the sardonic is balanced with compassion, and in Jack Flowers we are given a character whose yearnings touch upon our own." Evans thought the protagonist "could never change, because he represents life in Singapore. . . . Jack may dream of an ideal existence and wish that he could write the novel which would depict it, but he cannot. . . . Life will be a treadmill for him." Though Weeks suggested that under the surface humor "one is aware of the author's scorn for this disheveled, corrupt memento of colonialism," other reviewers cited Theroux for a sympathetic portrayal of a quixotic hero. "Jack Flowers is funny, endearing, outrageous, poignant, noble—and utterly believable," commented Yardley. "He is Paul Theroux's finest accomplishment." In 1979 Peter Bogdanovich directed the movie version of *Saint Jack,* based on a screenplay Theroux helped to write.

Theroux's commercial and critical success was still to a certain extent dependent upon his British readership when he published *The Black House* in 1974. The novel, a gothic tale with psychological dimensions set in a rural part of England, has garnered mixed reviews. *New York Times Book Review* contributor Michael Mewshaw felt that while "it is a tribute to [Theroux's] integrity and ambition that he is not content to keep repeating himself," *The Black House* is "an abrupt departure from the comic vision of his earlier work" and "does a serious disservice to his talent." Claire Tomalin offered a contrasting viewpoint in *New Statesman.* "The book is about a man panicked by doubts about just where he and other creatures do belong," Tomalin wrote. "The degree of skill with which Theroux handles these various themes, and the level of mastery of his writing, have produced a novel of unusual scope and promise still more for the future."

The Mosquito Coast, a novel published in 1982, is among Theroux's best-known works of fiction. Told from the point of view of a thirteen-year-old narrator, the story explores a family's exodus from Massachusetts to the jungles of Honduras under the domination of a manic and eccentric father. *Times Literary Supplement* contributor Valentine Cunningham termed the father, Allie Fox, "a truly amazing and unforgettable figure, an American titan whose actions unlock the essences of oppressive Americanism, revealing evils we're to take as intrinsic to the rationality and mechanization that helped make his country what it is." Towers likewise cited the theme of "Yankee-ingenuity-gone-berserk" in his piece for *New York Review of Books,* adding that Theroux handles the concept "with commendable skill." Towers explained, "Though Allie Fox is an archetypal character whose career follows an emblematic line," "Theroux has avoided the sterility of much quasi-allegorical writing by endowing his main character with a lively and dense specificity." Jonathan Raban, meanwhile, commented in *Saturday Review* that "in Allie Fox, Theroux has created his first epic hero. If one can imagine an American tradition that takes in Benjamin Franklin, Captain Ahab, Huey Long, and the Reverend Jim Jones, then Allie Fox is its latest, most complete incarnation."

The Mosquito Coast garnered an American Book Award nomination along with favorable reviews. Raban termed the work "not just [Theroux's] finest novel so far. It is—in a characteristically hooded way—a novelist's act of self-definition, a midterm appraisal of his own resources. It is a wonderful book, with so many levels to it that it feels bottomless." Some critics, though, were not so impressed. *Los Angeles Times Book Review* contributor Edward M. White remarked that *The Mosquito Coast* is "an abstract and witty book, embodying Theroux's usual themes about the conflict of cultures. The abstraction is particularly damaging, here, however, where it becomes authorial manipulation of characters and plotting in the interests of theoretical design." In

Chicago Tribune Book World, William Logan voiced the opinion that because Theroux "cannot create a human referent for his characters, the narrative is labored and overlong, the irony clumsy, and the end congested with symbolism." In his *New York Times Book Review* article, Thomas R. Edwards offered an opposite view. "Theroux's book . . . is, characteristically, a fine entertainment, a gripping adventure story, a remarkable comic portrait of minds and cultures at cross-purposes. But under its unintimidating surface, . . . 'The Mosquito Coast' shows a cosmopolitan expatriate novelist pondering his imaginative sources as an American writer, and the relation of those sources to the world as it now seems to be. This excellent story . . . is also an impressively serious act of imagination."

Theroux extended his ruminations on America fifty years into the future in his next work, the lengthy *O-Zone.* The novel, observed Yardley in the *Washington Post Book World,* "is on several counts a striking departure for its author. . . . It is his first genuinely 'American' novel . . . and it deals more directly with questions of American national identity and character than any of his other books, either fiction or nonfiction." The O-Zone of the title is a vast area located in the U.S. heartland that is evacuated after a supposedly disastrous nuclear accident, The inhabitants of an overpopulated and overpoliced New York City, the O-Zone represents both the terror of the unknown and a potential escape from a dreadful reality. The O-Zone, noted Yardley, "is a foreign place within a nation that has become foreign to itself." Eight New Yorkers travel to the O-Zone and are surprised to find themselves in a paradise that allows them to reclaim their common humanity. Their leader is a fifteen-year-old math whiz named Fizzy who, in the words of *New York Times Book Review* contributor Susan Fromberg Schaeffer, is "the kind of man who can lead humanity out of the double wilderness of emotional alienation and dehumanizing science to achieve, in himself, a desperately needed symbiosis between the two."

Some reviewers saw Theroux's next effort, *My Secret History,* as an account of the author's own life, for the story of Andre Parent bears close resemblance to that of his creator. Parent was born in Massachusetts, travels to Africa, marries a British woman, lives in London, and writes popular travel books. He is also a deeply troubled man leading a double life, and certain critics found in Parent's troubles clues to understanding Paul Theroux, despite Theroux's warning in a prefatory note: "Although some of the events and places depicted in the novel bear a similarity to those in my own life, the characters all strolled out of my imagination." The book, commented Yardley in *Washington Post Book World,* "is the story of a man so haunted by guilt and so driven by sexual greed that he is capable only in rare moments of seeing women as anything except agents for the appeasement of his lust." Thus Parent's secret history consists of hidden sexual pleasures and lies and it is not surprising when that history blows up in the character's face, shaking his surface life to its very core. Parent survives the clash of his public and his secret life largely because his wife allows him to transcend it. Thus, related *New York Times Book Review* contributor Wendy Lesser, *My Secret History* becomes a book "about the permanence of marriage in the face of mistrust and infidelity; it's about the wisdom of women and the foolishness of men; and it's about mature love as the necessary and sometimes successful antidote to youthful selfishness."

Theroux followed *My Secret History* with *My Other Life* in 1996. "This is a life I could have lived had things been different," the author noted in prefacing the work, a disclaimer similar to that which appeared in Theroux's previous novel. Characterizing the work as a collection of short stories rather than a novel, Piers Paul Read observed in *Spectator* that "the Theroux of this fiction, if not the real-life Theroux, clearly dislikes his life in London. . . . in [some] stories there are . . . stinging comments on English life, accurate enough when it comes to the literary world but verging on the absurd when it comes, for example, to the royal family. A bitchiness creeps in." In the London *Observer* Kate Kellaway speculated, "Perhaps Theroux's travel writing habits affect his attitude here," "He makes a grand tour of himself observantly but uncritically as if looking through a train window." Much of the book revolves around its protagonist questioning what his life would have been like had it been of the traditional sort—at one point he visits the former husband of an ex-lover, "because whoever he might be he was the man I would have become." Noting particularly the author's "rendering of women as two-dimensional objects" and his "sourness about ex-wives," Rhoda Koenig commented in *Wall Street Journal* that "Theroux offhandedly tells us that things changed after he began spending so much time away writing his travel books. But isn't the real cause whatever it was that took him away?"

Parker Jagoda, the main character in Theroux's disturbing novel *Chicago Loop,* finds his own "other" life encroaching on his public life, but here the results are disastrous. Jagoda is a wealthy and fastidious Chicago businessman who lives with his beautiful wife in a ritzy North Shore neighborhood. He has begun placing personal ads in the Chicago newspapers, and when a pathetic blonde named Sharon responds, Jagoda leads her back to her apartment and brutally kills her, all the while telling himself that she has made him do it. Although Jagoda tries to suppress memories of the murder, the event keeps bubbling up in his consciousness and he decides that the only way to atone for his deed is to reenter Sharon's world—as Sharon. Thus begins an odyssey in which the successful urban professional dresses like the woman he has killed, seeks out situations where he will be sexually abused, and eventually commits a spectacularly appropriate suicide.

Theroux's 1994 novel *Millroy the Magician* also deals with a dual life, but one with overtones far less dark. The satiric tale revolves around narrator Jilly Farina, a fourteen-year-old girl who runs away from an abusive alcoholic father and becomes enthralled by Millroy, a carnival magician who serves as the book's hero. Millroy eventually becomes widely hailed on supermarket tabloids and talk shows for his skills as an evangelist of the American diet; he stars on a children's television show and begins opening up a chain of restaurants run by his dietary converts and featuring his own biblically sanctioned recipes. Jilly, disguised as Millroy's son, Alex, handles the business side of Millroy's career. Noting that the book depends on the technique of magic realism for its believability, Chicago *Tribune Books* critic Nicholas Delbanco thought that the development of the relationship between Jilly and Millroy "is never credible and takes too long. We feel as if we're getting every detail of Millroy's meteoric rise and fall, overhearing every conversation and meeting every visitor to trailer or diner or television studio or hut." Also feeling that the novel loses its effect as a parable due to the same matter-of-factness, Sven Birkerts wrote in *Washington Post Book World,* "The thing about Millroy and his narration through Jilly's eyes is that we are never, not even at the last, sure whether there is genuine goodness in him or whether he is but another power-seeker awed by his own self-myth." Calling the book an "unusual, often funny, dark satire of America's obsession with trim bodies and religious television," *New York Times Book Review* critic Charles Johnson added that *Millroy the Magician* "may strike some readers as maddeningly predictable and aswim in stereotypes of Middle America, gay people, troubled children and people of color. . . . One can only hope that . . . those who reach the end of Mr. Theroux's three-ring circus of a novel see its final act as worth the price of admission."

Kowloon Tong is a timely political thriller in the Graham Greene vein: "Bunt" Mullard and his mother Betty, British expatriates in Hong Kong, live in a world of teas, horse races, and Macao casinos, until the impending takeover by the People's Republic of China throws them into a world of dangerous intrigue. A Chinese gangster is determined to gain control of their textile factory, and he won't take no for an answer. Theroux wryly observes that Hong Kong, originally taken from the Chinese by military force, is on the way to being taken back in a similarly brutal way. Thomas Kenneally, writing in *New York Times,* found Bunt's character excessively passive, but noted that "Theroux's astringent misanthropy and narrative momentum are powerful propellants." In *New York Times Book Review,* Richard Bernstein, deemed *Kowloon Tong* not one of Theroux's more ambitious works, "but one that is recognizably his, full of faulty, off-kilter characters and furnished with a graphic sense of place."

In *Sunrise with Seamonsters* Theroux writes: "Travel is a creative act—not simply loafing and inviting your soul, but feeding the imagination, accounting for each fresh wonder, memorizing and moving on. The discoveries the traveler makes in broad daylight—the curious problems of the eye he solves—resemble those that thrill and sustain a novelist in his solitude." Boarding a train at Victoria Station in London after dropping off his manuscript for *The Black House* with his publisher, Theroux then set off on a four-month odyssey through Asia, the Far East, and the former Soviet Union, eventually returning to his point of departure with "four thick notebooks" on his lap. The edited notebooks became *The Great Railway Bazaar: By Train through Asia.*

Though travel accounts are not generally known for their commercial appeal, *The Great Railway Bazaar* was an enormous success. In *Publishers Weekly,* John F. Baker called Theroux's accomplishment an "amazing first." As Baker explained, the author "made his way onto the best seller list . . . with nothing more than a travel book, . . . thereby becoming probably the first writer since Mark Twain whose travels made a more than fleeting impression in booksellers' accounts." The work also garnered critical praise. *Washington Post Book World* contributor David Roberts thought the account "represents travel writing at its very best—almost the best, one is tempted to say, that it can attain. Paul Theroux . . . here transforms what was clearly a long, ultimately tedious journey by train . . . into a singularly entertaining book." "Though it is a travel book and not a novel," Towers commented, *The Great Railway Bazaar* "incorporates many of the qualities of Theroux's fiction: it is funny, sardonic, wonderfully sensuous and evocative in its descriptions, casually horrifying in its impact."

The success of *The Great Railway Bazaar,* combined with an admitted wanderlust, led Theroux to pen several more travel memoirs. Best known among these are *The Old Patagonian Express: By Train through the Americas, The Kingdom by the Sea: A Journey around Great Britain,* and *The Pillars of Hercules: A Grand Tour of the Mediterranean.* Employing the same elements of rail travel, walking excursion, and personal rumination, these works explore Central and South America and the coastline regions of the British Isles, respectively, although none enjoyed the critical reception that attended publication of *The Great Railway Bazaar.* Some reviewers found the works scornful and repetitive; as Patrick Breslin noted of *The Old Patagonian Express* in *Washington Post Book World,* "Theroux so loses himself in the mechanics of how he got to Patagonia, and the people who irritated him along the way, that there is little room in the book for anything else. And since not very much out of the ordinary happened to him, one's interest flags." In *New York Times,* John Leonard commented that Theroux's traveling style "tends to be contentious; at the drop of an offhand remark in a bar or a dining car, he will opinionize." Leonard added, however, that "One forgives him because one tends to agree with his opinions."

The Pillars of Hercules is Theroux's account of his journey through the Mediterranean realm. Calling the book "a marketing department's dream," Graham Coster added in *London Review of Books* that the book is "designed with travel-brochure simplicity and accessibility" in mind. *Washington Post Book World* reviewer John Ash questioned many of Theroux's references to location—"Clearly, he travels intuitively, disdaining maps and guidebooks. . . . I'm a little surprised he made it home"—and felt that the author was arrogant and contemptuous toward his location. Regarding Theroux's dismissal of Greece—"The whole of Greece seemed to me to be a cut-price theme park of broken marble, a place where you were harangued in a high-minded way about Ancient Greek culture, while some swarthy little person picked your pocket"—Ash responded, "Theroux is famous for his curmudgeonly verve, but this is not that. It is fatuous and ugly." Stephen Greenblatt, however, wrote in *New York Times Book Review* that the many brief exchanges between Theroux and the people he meets on his journey "disclose a redeeming quality that lies behind Mr. Theroux's grumpiness and cynicism and helps to account for his improvisational energy: he is driven by an intense, insatiable curiosity."

Theroux has continued to produce fiction and travel chronicles into the twenty-first century. *The Stranger at the Palazzo d'Oro and Other Stories* is a collection of tales about sexual desire and its sometimes dangerous complications: One story deals with a Boston boy abused by a Roman Catholic priest, another with interracial love in South Africa. Theroux, "one of our foremost chroniclers of the expatriate experience," in the words of *Library Journal* contributor David W. Henderson, "once again proves his adeptness at exploring otherness." Theroux, noted Rebecca Donner in *People,* handles "the complexities of matters of the heart with subtlety and grace." In the nonfiction work *Dark Star Safari: Overland from Cairo to Cape Town* Theroux revisits some of the African locales where he served with the Peace Corps, gets into arguments with Christian missionaries, and observes the political and social problems that affect much of Africa. "His cogent insights are well integrated," reported a *Publishers Weekly* reviewer, adding that "as a travel guide, Theroux can both rankle and beguile," but overall he has produced a "marvelous report."

Theroux has long labored outside of the realm of academia, and he has occasionally expressed mild contempt for university creative-writing programs and patronage in the form of fellowships, endowments, and grants. Succinctly stating his position in *Sunrise with Seamonsters,* he commented: "The writer doesn't want a patron half so badly as he wants a paying public." The takeover of creative writing by the universities in the United States has, he said, "changed the profession out of all recognition. It has made it narrower, more rarified, more neurotic; it has altered the way literature is taught and it has diminished our pleasure in reading." Theroux's own writing, highly successful commercially, has not gained a great deal of attention within the academic community. As Theroux told *Publishers Weekly,* however, "No serious writer writes for money alone, but it's equally a mistake to think that if your writing makes money you're not serious." He remains greatly concerned, he admitted in a *Chicago Tribune Book World* interview, that his writing should continue to entertain readers. "My fear is that I'll be boring," he said. "You never actually run out of ideas, but you might run out of ideas that are intelligent, amusing, original. I don't want to be a bore. I would rather open a beauty parlor—I swear."

BIOGRAPHICAL AND CRITICAL SOURCES:

BOOKS

Coale, Samuel, *Paul Theroux,* Twayne (New York, NY), 1987.

Contemporary Literary Criticism, Thomson Gale (Detroit, MI), Volume 5, 1976, Volume 8, 1978, Volume 11, 1979, Volume 15, 1980, Volume 28, 1984, Volume 46, 1988.

Dictionary of Literary Biography, Thomson Gale (Detroit, MI), Volume 2: *American Novelists since World War II, First Series,* 1978, Volume 218: *American Short-Story Writers Since World War II, Second Series,* 1999.

PERIODICALS

Antioch Review, winter, 1977.

Atlantic, October, 1973; April, 1976; October, 1983.

Booklist, July 19, 1997.

Chicago Tribune Book World, September 16, 1979; February 21, 1982; August 15, 1982; March 27, 1983; November 13, 1983; June 30, 1985; February 9, 1986.

Critique, March, 1981.

Detroit News, June 4, 1978; September 9, 1979; November 13, 1983; February 16, 1986.

Economist, July 23, 1988, p. 77; October 24, 1992, p. 102; November 20, 1993, p. 111.

Esquire, December, 1971; April, 1983.

Globe and Mail (Toronto, Ontario, Canada), October 19, 1985.

Kirkus Reviews, April 1, 1997.

Library Journal, March 1, 1994, p. 138; March 15, 1995, p. 102; April 1, 1995, p. 142; September 15, 1995, p. 85; February 1, 1996, p. 90; December, 2003, David W. Henderson, review of *The Stranger at the Palazzo d'Oro and Other Stories,* p. 170.

London Review of Books, February 8, 1996, Graham Coster, review of *The Pillars of Hercules: A Grand Tour of the Mediterranean,* p. 18.

Los Angeles Times, November 13, 1983; October 25, 1984; September 26, 1986.

Los Angeles Times Book Review, October 7, 1979; September 21, 1980; April 18, 1982; March 13, 1983; September 21, 1986.

Maclean's, August 15, 1988, p. 50; August 14, 1989, p. 55.

National Review, June 29, 1971; November 10, 1972; June 2, 1989, p. 58.

New Republic, November 29, 1969; September 25, 1976; November 27, 1976; September 22, 1979; February 24, 1982; April 11, 1983; July 17, 1989, p. 40; March 2, 1992, p. 29.

New Statesman, June 11, 1971; October 4, 1974; October 17, 1975; March 26, 1976; September 1, 1978; October 24, 1980.

New Statesman & Society, September 16, 1988, p. 40; June 30, 1989, p. 33; April 6, 1990, p. 38; November 6, 1992, p. 49; October 8, 1993, p. 38.

Newsweek, September 24, 1973; November 11, 1974; September 8, 1975; June 19, 1976; August 15, 1977; September 10, 1979; March 1, 1982; April 25, 1983; October 24, 1983; October 22, 1984; August 12, 1985.

New York, February 28, 1994, p. 127.

New Yorker, November 11, 1967; November 8, 1969; December 29, 1975; January 7, 1985; February 16, 1987, p. 108; August 10, 1992, p. 80; March 14, 1994, p. 92; June 26, 1995, p. 144.

New York Review of Books, September 23, 1971; September 30, 1976; November 10, 1977; August 17, 1978; April 15, 1982; June 2, 1983.

New York Times, May 29, 1971; July 22, 1976; August 23, 1977; April 30, 1978; May 31, 1978; April 27, 1979; August 28, 1979; February 11, 1982; February 28, 1983; October 13, 1983; October 1, 1984; June 5, 1985; September 15, 1996; September 23, 1996, p. B2; June 8, 1997.

New York Times Book Review, November 3, 1968; September 28, 1969; August 8, 1971; November 5, 1972; September 9, 1973; September 8, 1974; August 24, 1975; December 28, 1975; July 11, 1976; August 21, 1977; June 18, 1978; July 22, 1979; August 26, 1979; August 24, 1980; February 14, 1982; March 20, 1983; October 23, 1983; April 22, 1984; October 28, 1984; June 2, 1985; November 10, 1985; September 14, 1986; May 10, 1987, p. 34; July 19, 1988, p. 17; June 4, 1989, p. 1; March 17, 1991, p. 7; December 1, 1991, p. 20; June 14, 1992, p. 7; December 6, 1992, p. 52; March 6, 1994, p. 9; November 5, 1995, p. 11; June, 1997.

Observer (London, England), June 30, 1996, p. 15.

People, February 9, 2004, Rebecca Donner, review of *The Stranger at the Palazzo d'Oro and Other Stories,* p. 44.

Publishers Weekly, July 26, 1976; June 24, 1996, p. 43; January 6, 2003, review of *Dark Star Safari: Overland from Cairo to Cape Town,* p. 49.

Saturday Review, September 28, 1968; July 24, 1976; September 3, 1977; July 8, 1978, October 27, 1979; February, 1982; November-December, 1983.

Spectator, June 12, 1971; October 12, 1974; March 15, 1975; October 18, 1975; March 27, 1976; June 4, 1977; September 16, 1978; October 17, 1981; June 30, 1984; June 29, 1985; July 6, 1996, p. 32.

Time, August 23, 1968; August 25, 1975; August 2, 1976; September 5, 1977; June 5, 1978; February 22, 1982; October 31, 1983; July 1, 1985; May 16, 1988, p. 95; May 22, 1989, p. 112; March 25,

1991, p. 71; June 15, 1992, p. 73; March 7, 1994, p. 69; November 6, 1995, p. 83.
Times Literary Supplement, April 11, 1968; June 12, 1969; June 25, 1971; November 17, 1972; April 27, 1973; October 4, 1974; March 14, 1975; March 26, 1976; June 3, 1977; October 31, 1980; November 21, 1980; October 16, 1981; October 8, 1982; October 28, 1983; June 8, 1984; August 2, 1985; October 31, 1986; July 5, 1996.
Tribune Books (Chicago, IL), March 27, 1994, Nicholas Delbanco, review of *Millroy the Magician,* p. 4.
Wall Street Journal, September 13, 1996, Rhoda Koenig, p. A10.
Washington Post Book World, September 14, 1973; September 15, 1974; September 7, 1975; May 30, 1976; July 11, 1976; August 21, 1977; June 25, 1978; September 2, 1979; August 17, 1980; March 6, 1983; October 16, 1983; December 9, 1984; July 7, 1985; February 27, 1994, p. 2; October 8, 1995, p. 5.
Yale Review, spring, 1979.

* * *

THEROUX, Paul Edward
See THEROUX, Paul

* * *

THOMAS, D.M. 1935-
(Donald Michael Thomas)

PERSONAL: Born January 27, 1935, in Redruth, Cornwall, England; son of Harold Redvers (a builder) and Amy (a homemaker; maiden name, Moyle) Thomas; children: Caitlin, Sean, Ross. *Education:* New College, Oxford, B.A. (with first-class honors), 1958, M.A., 1961. *Hobbies and other interests:* "Besides sex and death, I am interested in Russian literature, music, most sports, and my Celtic homeland, Cornwall."

ADDRESSES: Home—The Coach House, Rashleigh Vale, Truro, Cornwall TR1 1TJ, England. *Agent*—John Johnson, Clerkenwell Green, London ECR 0HT, England.

CAREER: Poet, novelist, biographer, and translator. Grammar school English teacher in Teignmouth, Devonshire, England, 1960-64; Hereford College of Education, Hereford, England, lecturer, 1964-66, senior lecturer in English, 1966-79, head of department, 1977-79. Visiting lecturer in English, Hamline University, 1967; visiting professor of literature, American University, spring, 1982. *Military service:* British Army, two years.

MEMBER: Bard of the Cornish Gorseth.

AWARDS, HONORS: Richard Hilary Award, 1960; Translators Award from British Arts Council, 1975, for translations of works by Anna Akhmatova; Cholmondeley Award, 1978, for poetry; *Guardian*/Gollancz Fantasy Novel Award, 1979, for *The Flute-Player;* Cheltenham Prize, *Los Angeles Times* Book Award, and Booker McConnell Prize nomination, all 1981, all for *The White Hotel;* Orwell Prize for Biography, 1998, for *Solzhenitsyn.*

WRITINGS:

POETRY

Personal and Possessive, Outposts, 1964.
(With Peter Redgrove and D.M. Black) *Modern Poets 11,* Penguin, 1968.
Two Voices, Grossman, 1968.
Lover's Horoscope: Kinetic Poet, Purple Sage, 1970.
Logan Stone, Grossman, 1971.
The Shaft, Arc, 1973.
Symphony in Moscow, Keepsake Press, 1974.
Lilith-Prints, Second Aeon Publications, 1974.
Love and Other Deaths, Merrimack Book Service, 1975.
The Honeymoon Voyage, Secker & Warburg (London, England), 1978.
Protest: A Poem after a Medieval Armenian Poem by Frik, privately printed, 1980.
Dreaming in Bronze, Secker & Warburg (London, England), 1981.
Selected Poems, Viking (New York, NY), 1983.
(With Sylvia Kantaris) *News from the Front,* Arc, 1983.
The Puberty Tree: New and Selected Poems, Bloodaxe (Newcastle upon Tyne, England), 1992.
Dear Shadows, Fal Publications (Truro, England), 2004.

FICTION; NOVELS, EXCEPT WHERE INDICATED

The Devil and the Floral Dance (juvenile), Robson, 1978.
The Flute-Player, Dutton (New York, NY), 1979.
Birthstone, Gollancz (London, England), 1980.

The White Hotel, Gollancz (London, England), 1980, Viking (New York, NY), 1981.
Flying in to Love, Bloomsbury (London, England), 1992.
Pictures at an Exhibition, Bloomsbury (London, England), 1993.
Eating Pavlova, Bloomsbury (London, England), 1994.
Lady with a Laptop, Carroll & Graf (New York, NY), 1996.
Charlotte: The Final Journey of Jane Eyre, Duck Editions, 2000.

"RUSSIAN NIGHTS" SERIES; NOVELS

Ararat, Viking (New York, NY), 1983.
Swallow, Viking (New York, NY), 1984.
Sphinx, Gollancz (London, England), 1986, Viking (New York, NY), 1987.
Summit, Gollancz (London, England), 1987, Viking (New York, NY), 1988.
Lying Together, Viking (New York, NY), 1990.

EDITOR

The Granite Kingdom: Poems of Cornwall, Barton, 1970.
Poetry in Crosslight (textbook), Longman (London, England), 1975.
Songs from the Earth: Selected Poems of John Harris, Cornish Miner 1829-84, Lodenek Press, 1977.

TRANSLATOR

Anna Akhmatova, *Requiem and Poem without a Hero,* Ohio University Press (Athen, OH), 1976.
Anna Akhmatova, *Way of All the Earth,* Ohio University Press (Athen, OH), 1979.
Yevgeny Yevtushenko, *Invisible Threads,* Macmillan (London, England), 1981.
Alexander Pushkin, *The Bronze Horseman,* Viking (New York, NY), 1982.
Yevgeny Yevtushenko, *A Dove in Santiago,* Viking (New York, NY), 1983.
Alexander Pushkin, *Boris Godunov,* Sixth Chamber Press, 1985.
Anna Akhmatova, *You Will Hear Thunder: Poems,* Ohio University Press (Athen, OH), 1985.
Anna Akhmatova, *Selected Poems,* Penguin (New York, NY), 1989.

OTHER

Memories and Hallucinations: A Memoir, Viking (New York, NY), 1988.
Alexander Solzhenitsyn: A Century in His Life, St. Martin's Press (New York, NY), 1998.
Hell Fire Corner (play), first produced in Truro, England, 2004.

Some of Thomas's translations have been adapted as radio plays, including *You Will Hear Thunder,* 1981, and *Boris Godunov,* 1984. Work represented in anthologies, including *Best SF: 1969,* edited by Harry Harrison and Brian Aldiss, Putnam, 1970; *Inside Outer Space,* edited by Robert Vas Dias, Anchor Books, 1970; and *Twenty-three Modern British Poets,* edited by John Matthias, Swallow Press, 1971. Contributor to literary journals in England and the United States.

SIDELIGHTS: In 1980, after spending nearly a year closeted in a small study at Oxford University, D.M. Thomas emerged with the manuscript for his third novel. Known until that time primarily as a poet and translator of Russian verse, Thomas first branched out into adult fiction with the 1979 book *The Flute-Player,* a fantasy-like meditation on art and its struggle to endure and even flourish in a totalitarian regime. A second fantasy novel, *Birthstone,* followed soon after; it tells the story of a woman trying to create a single, stable identity out of the fragmented parts of her personality. Both works—especially *The Flute-Player,* which won a contest for best fantasy novel—received praise for their imaginative, poetic treatments of familiar themes, but neither sold more than a few hundred copies.

Upon its publication in late 1980, Thomas's *The White Hotel,* seemed destined for the same fate. A complex blend of the real and the surreal and of the apparent dichotomy between the Freudian concepts of the pleasure instinct and the death instinct, the work generated relatively little interest among British critics and readers; what reaction there was, the author later recalled in a *New York Times Magazine* article, could best be summed up as "restrained approval." Within just a few months, however, it became clear that on the other side of the Atlantic, at least, that would not be the case. Published in the United States in the spring of 1981, *The White Hotel* met with what William Borders referred to in *New York Times* as a "thunderclap of critical praise" that sparked sales and made Thomas an instant celebrity. Already into its second printing before the official publication date, *The White Hotel* eventually sold more than 95,000 copies in its hardcover edition and almost 1.5 million copies in the paperback reprint—making it without a doubt "the sleeper novel of the season," to quote a *Publishers Weekly* writer. While Thomas's more recent work has been viewed as uneven by critics, his imaginative approach to fiction has gained him a place as a significant practitioner of postmodernist technique.

Divided into seven distinct sections, *The White Hotel* begins with a prologue that consists of a series of letters to, from, or about psychoanalyst Sigmund Freud and several of his colleagues in which the doctor discusses the case of one of his female patients, "Frau Anna G.," who is suffering from a severe hysterical illness. Her psychic distress manifests itself physically as asthma, anorexia, pains in the left breast and ovary, and a general feeling of anxiety that conventional treatments have not alleviated. In his letters, Freud speculates that the case of "Frau Anna G." will substantiate his theory of a death instinct that coexists with the erotic one.

Following the prologue are two sections devoted to writings by the mysterious "Frau Anna G." herself. The first sample is a long poem in which "Anna" describes an erotic fantasy she has concerning an affair with Freud's son. The affair begins in a train compartment and continues at a lakeside "white hotel," where a series of explicit and unusual love scenes is played out against a backdrop of horrible death and destruction involving other guests at the hotel; none of the violence, however, interferes with or diminishes the lovers' passion and self-absorbed pursuit of physical pleasure. The second writing sample, ostensibly written at Freud's request, is an expanded prose version of "Anna"'s fantasy, "a wild, lyrical, irrational embroidery upon her original," remarked Thomas Flanagan in *Nation.* According to *Village Voice* critic Laurie Stone, it is this prose version that serves as "a key to [Anna's] fears, imaginative transformations, and clairvoyant projections."

The fourth section of *The White Hotel* is comprised of Freud's long analysis of the case of "Frau Anna G.," now revealed to be Lisa Erdman, an opera singer of Russian-Jewish descent. A pastiche of actual case histories written by Freud, the section connects Lisa's fantasies to events in her real life and concludes with the doctor's observation that "she was cured of everything but life, so to speak. . . . She took away with her a reasonable prospect of survival, in an existence that would doubtless never be less than difficult." Sections five and six chronicle the course of Lisa's life after she is treated and "cured" by Freud, the conventional narrative ending with a chilling account of her execution in 1941 at Babi Yar along with thousands of other Russian Jews. At this point the reader discovers what Lisa's fantasies mean, both in terms of her own life and death and, in a broader sense, European society in the twentieth century.

The White Hotel's seventh and final section is a surreal epilogue in which Lisa, now in a purgatory-like land that is unmistakably Palestine, is reunited with people who had figured prominently in her life, including her mother and Freud. There, too, in this strange place are thousands of other souls awaiting forgiveness, love, and understanding; Lisa is last seen agreeing to help the latest wave of "immigrants" settle in: "No one could, or would, be turned away; for they had nowhere else to go."

The initial reaction to *The White Hotel* among British critics was "bafflingly contradictory," as Thomas himself reported in *New York Times Magazine.* Among the few major periodicals that published reviews, the discussions often highlighted the novel's pornographic content, especially the two chapters containing Lisa's poetic and prose versions of her fantasy. *Punch* reviewers Mary Anne Bonney and Susan Jeffreys, for example, dismissed the entire book as "humorlessly insubstantial" and singled out Lisa's poem in particular as "a sexual fantasy of some crudity and little literary worth." Commenting in *Times Literary Supplement,* Anne Duchene agreed that the early sections of the book "are not for the squeamish," but conceded that "they have to be undergone, by committed readers, as part of the raw material for the later, much more interesting sections."

Even the most gracious British reviews were, at best, reluctant in their praise. Though *London Review of Books* critic Robert Taubman also found the sexual scenes "not real or erotic," with an "unconvincing look of pornography," he nevertheless went on to declare: "The analysis that follows sounds an authentic note. . . . At the same time, it provides the reader with an absorbing Chinese box narrative of hidden memories, reversals of meaning and deceptions uncovered." A reviewer for *Encounter* compared reading *The White Hotel* to watching an Ingmar Bergman film: "You are battered with symbolism, in perpetual pursuit of images, of references, of bizarre surrealist objects. . . . I'm not sure that I enjoyed it, but I am certainly respectful."

U.S. critics were far less inclined than the British to make an issue out of *The White Hotel*'s sexual content.

The few who even raised the possibility described Thomas's poem and its prose rendition as highly erotic rather than pornographic; several reviewers mentioned that the decision to use such a technique is an unusual and very effective way of revealing the soul of Lisa Erdman. Though George Levine commented in *New York Review of Books* that the author's language is occasionally "merely vulgar or banal," he went on to note that it often achieves "a lush, romantic intensity, with a remarkable precision of imagery. [The] writing is full of dislocation and surprise; it is seductive, frightening, and beautifully alive. . . . Such language immediately established the mysterious 'Anna G.' as a powerful presence." Leslie Epstein expressed a similar opinion, declaring in *New York Times Book Review* that "the poem seems to speak directly from the unconscious." In short, wrote *Time* reviewer Paul Gray, *The White Hotel* "easily transcends titillation. Those who come to the novel with prurient interests alone will quickly grow baffled and bored."

Susan Fromberg Schaeffer stated in Chicago's *Tribune Books* that "the bones of a wonderful story are here [in *The White Hotel*], but Lisa Erdman and her world do not come alive. . . . Thomas loses sight of his own characters, his own obligation to breathe life and power into his fictional world." Epstein agreed, pointing out that Lisa "seems to float through the various crises that afflict her," and she has "no intellectual life" despite the complex political, social, and cultural forces that swirl around her. She is, in essence, no more that a "casualty at first of her psyche and then of history," in Taubman's opinion. In addition, Epstein contended, "The notion of the death instinct is shaky enough in Freud's own theory, and the application of a 'struggle between the life instinct and the death instinct' to this poor patient strikes me as nothing more that a bald assertion, unsupported by the evidence."

Following *The White Hotel,* Thomas turned his novelist energies to *Ararat,* the first book in what became a trilogy and then stretched further into the "Russian Nights" quintet, dedicated to the Russian poet Alexander Pushkin. In *Ararat* the author sets up the beginning of an intricately woven mesh of deceptions that continues and grows through most of the quintet. As *Ararat* opens, the Russian poet Rozanov goes to Gorki to sleep with a blind woman who is writing a thesis on his poetry. Finding her unappealing as a sexual partner, he agrees to invent and tell a story on a subject she chooses, which turns out to be improvisation. In the story he improvises, there are three other storytellers—all writers attending a conference in Russian Armenia—who vie with each other in an improvisation contest. One of the tales offered in the contest includes a fragment of an unfinished Pushkin story novelist Thomas had actually translated, and that work is presented by the storyteller, the poet Surkov, as still being in progress, with himself as composer. In this story of Pushkin's—or Surkov's—there is an Italian storyteller who gives an inspired improvisation on a subject proposed for him by a St. Petersburg audience. Thus in Rozanov's telling, which involves on a second level the storytelling of the three others, stories and storytellers multiply within and around each other. As they do so, it becomes increasingly unclear who is the improviser and where the line is to be drawn between truth and fiction.

Ararat, like *The White Hotel* before it, met with a mixed critical reception, though not divided so dramatically along British and American lines as before. Galen Strawson, writing for *Times Literary Supplement,* admired both the complexity and the disarray of the novel's construction and praised Thomas's portrayal of the "unwaveringly egotistical and calculatingly promiscuous" author. Strawson remarked, however, that "there are some very self-indulgent passages in this book . . . and some very slack ones too." He commented further that "a puzzle does not make a work of literature; even if responses elicited by the former, as it works its illusion of depth and significance, can easily be mistaken for responses elicited by the latter." Isabel Raphael, reviewing *Ararat* for the London *Times,* found the structure "extraordinarily unpleasant," comparing it to "one of those Russian dolls, with its tantalizingly identical layers leading to an ultimately impenetrable heart." Further, she noted, "Whereas *The White Hotel* was a triumphant hymn to the power of sexuality," in *Ararat* "every act of love [is] a violation couched in obscene language and calculated to sicken and revolt." Anthony Burgess expressed the view in *Punch* that Thomas "is to be watched, but with great suspicion."

Comparisons between *Ararat* and *The White Hotel* were inevitable, both because of the former's success and because of the unusual structures of each. In *New Republic,* Ann Tyler pointed out that *Ararat* "takes its title from its preoccupation with the Armenian diaspora of 1915." The depiction of Nazi atrocities in *The White Hotel,* the critic recalled, "appeared to have some point; everything led up to it. . . . [*Ararat*] was disturbing to read, but one felt it was necessarily disturbing. . . . The Armenian tragedy is merely one more quirky scene in a book that's full of quirky scenes." She also reasoned, "Books are meant to carry us to other lives. . . . When a book drives its readers to diagramming the plot, you know it's not going to carry you very far." Diane Johnson made a more positive comparison in *New*

York Times Book Review, arguing that *Ararat,* like *The White Hotel,* "provides an abundant display of the author's astonishing virtuosity in poetry, in prose, in translating—a writer combining an impassioned European soul with the formal instincts of a spider weaving an immensely complex, elegant and sophisticated web."

In *Swallow* and *Sphinx,* Thomas carries his *Ararat* characters into more stories within stories and through narrative constructions that, like those in *Ararat* and *The White Hotel,* call into play not only prose but poetry and dreams. In *Swallow* Rozanov becomes a fiction, a creation of the Italian storyteller Corinna, who was introduced in *Ararat* and who is now participating in an Olympiad, an international poetic improvisation contest. Corinna improvises not only Rozanov but also tells the story of *Ararat,* which elicits two opposite critical responses from the judges—much as Thomas's actual novel did from critics.

An insight provided by *Swallow,* as noted by Richard Eder in the *Los Angeles Times Book Review,* is that both the apparently "real" storytellers and the storytellers they create in their improvisations "are all variations of the same figure: the Soviet artist who navigates between libertarian impulses and the need to be officially supported. They travel, they prosper, they agonize and womanize and conduct a nicely calculated battle between speaking out and selling out." Eder found *Swallow* to be, "despite occasional indulgences, . . . an often-captivating book. Some flights are aborted, but most catch some flash of unsuspected light." John Leggett, on the other hand, felt that "while it is surely an unkindness to an author to give away the ending of his story, the resolution of Mr. Thomas's Olympiad strikes me as such a cop-out that I feel obliged to do just that"—whereupon he did, in *New York Times Book Review.* Though he liked the "attractive architectural plan" of the book, Leggett believed that it raises expectations it fails to meet. "Alongside *The White Hotel,* which dealt so beguilingly with erotic fantasy and Freudian analysis," the critic concluded, "*Swallow* seems a bird of tawdry feather."

In a *New York Times* review of the third "Russian Nights" novel, Walter Goodman perceived that the sphinx of the title "may be Russia itself." *Sphinx* brings back some of the series' earlier characters and introduces two new ones: Soviet Jewish storyteller Shimon Barash, and a Welsh journalist named Lloyd George. Goodman dubbed *Sphinx* "a virtuoso performance," though he believed it did not "glisten quite as brightly as *Ararat* or provide the belly laughs of *Swallow.*" George Stade explained *Sphinx* in *New York Times Book Review* as "a kind of trilogy" in itself, "a continuation that recapitulates the whole as we have it. Part One is an expressionist play, Part Two a prose narrative, Part Three a narrative poem." Though he acknowledged that the first three novels in the "Russian Nights" series could be enjoyed on their own, he added that there is "no doubt that, from volume to volume, Mr. Thomas's meanings, especially those he grafts onto the concept of improvisation, sprout, grow, exfoliate in all directions."

"Thomas clearly had a lot of fun writing *Summit,*" surmised William French in the Toronto *Globe and Mail* of the series' fourth book. "But beneath his japery," French continued, "we can glimpse several serious themes. Perhaps the strongest one is the difficulty of communicating, one human being to another, and being understood." This is part of what *Summit* demonstrates through its plot, involving a meeting in Geneva between superpower leaders Grobichov and "Tiger" O'Reilly, the U.S. president who was formerly a movie star and is accompanied by his vice president, Shrub. Anthony Olcott in *Washington Post Book World* faulted *Summit*'s attempt at farce and satire, citing Thomas's failure to "take the wholly unimaginable and persuade us that indeed, perhaps, these men, these leaders are capable of such grotesqueries" as they commit at the summit. On a more positive note, recalling that Thomas tells the reader that the entire story is "the dream of a woman about to die in an air crash," Olcott concluded that the "Russian Nights" series "also slams into the ground with [*Summit,*] . . . but that only enhances Thomas's point in the whole quartet, that life's beauty lies in the dreaming, as his art so well conveys." Michiko Kakutani, writing in *New York Times,* described the novel as "a clever and often hilarious entertainment that opens a small window on the absurdities and perils of modern history."

The title of Thomas's 1992 novel, *Flying in to Love,* refers to the Dallas, Texas airfield John F. Kennedy flew into in 1963, shortly before his assassination, and the novel focuses on the late president and the figures who were near him, both physically and professionally, at the time of his death. In the words of T.J. Binyon in *Times Literary Supplement,* "Characters carom against each other like billiard balls, touching but not communicating, and each break takes us back to Kennedy himself to explore further aspects of his character." Binyon ultimately judged *Flying in to Love* to be, "despite its narrative pretensions . . . just another fictionalized investigation into the circumstances surrounding Kennedy's death."

In a *Concise Dictionary of British Literary Biography* essay, Karen Dorn quoted Thomas as reporting that, after he had finished the first draft of *Flying in to Love,* he had a dream that revealed a link between his compelling interest in Kennedy and his grief over his father's death, and that connected Kennedy's Camelot with the Cornish castle associated with the history and mythology of King Arthur. "Readers familiar with Thomas's interests," Dorn wrote in closing, "will remember the 1982 BBC radio talk in which he recalled Boris Pasternak's remark in *Doctor Zhivago* . . . that the artist is always meditating on death and thus always creating new life."

Thomas's 1993 novel, *Pictures at an Exhibition,* returns to the same territory of *The White Hotel. Pictures* shares many elements with Thomas's earlier novel: it comprises several distinct sections; it mixes actual historical events and persons with fictional ones; and it deals heavily with the Holocaust. In the novel's first section, a doctor working at the Auschwitz concentration camp seeks treatment for terrible headaches from a Jewish prisoner of the camp. The second section jumps to present-day London, and features many of the characters introduced in the first section. Subsequent sections include a collection of Nazi documents, reproduced verbatim, that describe the mass killing of ninety Jewish children. Thomas features several unsettling paintings by Norwegian artist Edvard Munch as a backdrop to his story.

Critics were mixed in their assessment of *Pictures at an Exhibition.* Frederick Busch, writing in *New York Times Book Review,* praised the manner in which the novelist sets up his plot, calling "Thomas's construction of a narrative puzzle that we become eager to unlock . . . masterly." However, Busch concluded, Thomas fails to pull all of the novel's pieces together into an effective whole: "The book proves alternately horrifying and annoying. . . . its plot is tied together in an unconvincing Freudian bundle." Chicago's *Tribune Books* contributor Andy Solomon, while admitting that Thomas's novel is disturbing, avers that "By the end, the plot has become a swirl of anguish, guilt and loss."

Returning to Freud for inspiration, *Eating Pavlova* is a fictional account of the psychoanalyst's final days. Thomas features a Freud who has vivid sexual fantasies as he is dying of cancer and who struggles to define his relationship with his daughter, Anna. "This is a Freud designed to pep up any party," remarked David Buckley in the London *Observer.* While noting the author's loose interpretation of the facts of Freud's life, *New Statesman* reviewer David Cohen called the book "strange and often moving" and declared that "Thomas is so outrageous that no one should complain of his fact-mangling."

Thomas departs from the terrain of psychoanalysis and Holocaust themes in his 1996 novel *Lady with a Laptop,* deemed "perfectly pleasant but inconsequential picture of a group of would-be writers at a creative writing course" held on the Greek island of Skagathos, by a *Publishers Weekly* contributor. The protagonist, the mildly successful British author leading the class, experiences bad luck and angst, but "as adventure becomes misadventure, the authorial tongue remains lodged in authorial cheek," commented Chicago's *Tribune Books* reviewer Nicholas Delbanco. Also set in the present day is *Charlotte: The Final Journey of Jane Eyre,* and his protagonist is also attending a writer's event on a remote island. This time the protagonist is a woman, Miranda, and her story is woven into Charlotte Brontë's classic story of Jane Eyre. Noting that Thomas's "postmodern tale within a tale about a tale proliferates" throughout *Charlotte, New Statesman* reviewer Patricia Duncker found the novel's intertwining plot threads—Miranda's abusive past, lackluster marriage, and sexual experimentation and Jane's short and equally lackluster marriage to Rochester—seductive but "uneven." While noting that the novel ill-serves Brontë's novel as a fitting conclusion, a *Publishers Weekly* contributor explained that *Charlotte* is "a variation of Thomas's exploration of the 'landscape of hysteria,'" as set forth in *The White Hotel.*

Alexander Solzhenitsyn: A Century in His Life marks Thomas's first foray into biography. Solzhenitsyn, the uncompromising Russian writer and former political prisoner best known for *One Day in the Life of Ivan Denisovich, The Gulag Archipelago,* and *Oak and Calf,* is sympathetically portrayed by Thomas, who admires his subject's literary artistry, his adherence to principle, and his determination to be his own man. Despite such adulation, Solzhenitsyn, who for his part never granted Thomas an interview, was displeased with the work, which draws upon interviews with his first wife and speculates rather than relying on fact. While noting that *Alexander Solzhenitsyn* resembles "a highly charged, over-sentimental novel" rather than a work of scholarship, *New Statesman* contributor Jan Dalley nonetheless maintained that Thomas's book is valuable due to the fact that Communism, the cold war, and the Russian dissident's role in standing up against communism's evils "is becoming obscure with extraordinary speed. Even well-educated 20 year olds today hardly know what the Iron Curtain was, and fell no tiny shudder at the letters K, G and B." Lesley Chamberlain, writing in *Los Angles Times Book Review,* praised the work, writing that Thomas "deserves our thanks for writing a marvelously readable, indispensable book about an impossibly complex man." In *Booklist* Ray Olson noted that, taking into account Thomas's perspective as "utterly anti-Communist," his biography of Solzhenitsyn "is more excitingly, artfully readable than most good biographies."

BIOGRAPHICAL AND CRITICAL SOURCES:

BOOKS

Concise Dictionary of British Literary Biography, Volume 8: *Contemporary Writers, 1960 to the Present,* Thomson Gale (Detroit, MI), 1992.

Contemporary Authors Autobiography Series, Volume 11, Thomson Gale (Detroit, MI), 1990.

Contemporary Literary Criticism, Thomson Gale (Detroit, MI), Volume 13, 1980, Volume 22, 1982, Volume 31, 1985.

Dictionary of Literary Biography, Volume 40: *Poets of Great Britain and Ireland since 1960,* Thomson Gale (Detroit, MI), 1985.

Dictionary of Literary Biography Yearbook: 1982, Thomson Gale (Detroit, MI), 1983.

Weibel, Paul, *Reconstruction the Past: G. and The White Hotel, Two Contemporary "Historical" Novels,* P. Lang (New York, NY), 1989.

PERIODICALS

Booklist, December 15, 1997, Ray Olson, review of *Alexander Solzhenitsyn: A Century in His Life,* p. 666.

Choice, June, 1999, V.D. Barooshian, review of *Alexander Solzhenitsyn,* p. 1794.

Christian Century, June 17, 1998, Eric E. Erickson, Jr., "Solzhenitsyn's Century," p. 12.

Contemporary Review, August, 1998, Virginia Rounding, review of *Alexander Solzhenitsyn,* p. 105.

Critique, fall, 2001, p. 63.

Detroit News, March 22, 1981; November 17, 1982.

Encounter, August, 1981; July-August, 1983.

Globe and Mail (Toronto, Ontario, Canada), March 10, 1984; July 21, 1984; February 27, 1988; August 4, 1990.

Journal of Modern Literature, fall, 1995, p. 328.

Library Journal, October 15, 1993, p. 91; September 1, 1994, p. 217; May 1, 1996, David W. Henderson, review of *Lady with a Laptop,* p. 135.

London Review of Books, February 5, 1981; April 1, 1983.

Los Angeles Times, March 17, 1981; October 11, 1988.

Los Angeles Times Book Review, October 31, 1982; April 3, 1983; November 18, 1984; January 2, 1994, p. 6; February 15, 1998, p. 8.

Nation, May 2, 1981; April 23, 1983.

New Leader, April 20, 1981; May 30, 1983.

New Republic, March 28, 1981; April 4, 1983.

New Statesman, June 22, 1979; March 21, 1980; January 16, 1981; March 4, 1983; June 29, 1984; May 13, 1994, p. 40; March 13, 1998, Jan Dalley, review of *Alexander Solzhenitsyn,* p. 52; May 22, 2000, Patricia Duncker, review of *Charlotte,* p. 55.

Newsweek, March 16, 1981; March 15, 1982; April 4, 1983.

New Yorker, March 30, 1981.

New York Review of Books, May 28, 1981; June 16, 1983; November 22, 1984; December 3, 1998, p. 36.

New York Times, March 13, 1981; March 24, 1981; September 21, 1982; March 29, 1983; October 31, 1984; January 21, 1987; July 24, 1990.

New York Times Book Review, March 15, 1981; June 28, 1981; September 26, 1982; March 27, 1983; November 4, 1984; January 18, 1987; October 2, 1988; July 8, 1990; October 31, 1993, p. 13; October 23, 1994, p. 28; March 1, 1998, p. 9.

New York Times Magazine, June 13, 1982.

Observer (London, England), June 24, 1979; February 27, 1983; July 1, 1984; April 17, 1994, p. 22.

People, June 29, 1981.

Publishers Weekly, March 27, 1981; April 17, 1981; January 8, 1982; August 22, 1994; April 15, 1996, review of *Lady with a Laptop,* p. 48; December 1, 1997, p. 37; May 14, 2001, review of *Charlotte,* p. 55.

Punch, October 14, 1981; March 2, 1983.

School Library Journal, March, 1993, p. 236.

Spectator, February 21, 1998, Raymond Carr, review of *Alexander Solzhenitsyn,* p. 28.

Time, March 16, 1981; April 25, 1983.

Times (London, England), January 15, 1981; March 3, 1983; June 9, 1983; March 10, 1984; June 28, 1984; October 15, 1988.

Times Higher Education Supplement, December 25, 1998, p. 24.

Times Literary Supplement, November 30, 1979; March 14, 1980; January 16, 1981; January 22, 1982; February 25, 1983; June 29, 1983; June 29, 1984; July 1-7, 1988; February 7, 1992.

Tribune Books (Chicago, IL), March 22, 1981; June 12, 1983; November 7, 1993, p. 3; June 9, 1996, p. 9.

Voice Literary Supplement, October, 1982.

Wall Street Journal, May 20, 1996, p. A12.

Washington Post, December 15, 1979; January 27, 1982.

Washington Post Book World, March 15, 1981; May 16, 1982; March 27, 1983; September 9, 1984; January 24, 1988; October 2, 1988.

ONLINE

D.M. Thomas Web site, http://www.dmthomasonline.com/ (June 28, 2004).

* * *

THOMAS, Donald Michael
See THOMAS, D.M.

* * *

THOMAS, Joyce Carol 1938-

PERSONAL: Born May 25, 1938, in Ponca City, OK; daughter of Floyd David (a bricklayer) and Leona (a housekeeper and hair stylist; maiden name, Thompson) Haynes; married Gettis L. Withers (a chemist), May 31, 1959 (divorced, 1968); married Roy T. Thomas, Jr., (a professor), September 7, 1968 (divorced, 1979); children: Monica Pecot, Gregory Withers, Michael Withers, Roy T. Thomas III. *Education:* Attended San Francisco City College, 1957-58, and University of San Francisco, 1957-58; College of San Mateo, A.A., 1964; San Jose State College (now University), B.A., 1966; Stanford University, M.A., 1967.

ADDRESSES: Home—2422 Cedar St., Berkeley, CA 94708. *Agent*—Anna Ghosh, Scovil-Chichak-Galen Literary Agency, Inc., 381 Park Ave. S., Ste. 1020, New York, NY 10016. *E-mail*—author@joycecarolthomas.com.

CAREER: Worked as a telephone operator in San Francisco, CA, 1957-58; Ravenwood School District, East Palo Alto, CA, teacher of French and Spanish, 1968-70; San Jose State College (now University), San Jose, CA, assistant professor of black studies, 1969-72; Contra Costa College, San Pablo, CA, teacher of drama and English, 1973-75; St. Mary's College, Moraga, CA, professor of English, 1975-77; San Jose State University, San Jose, reading program director, 1979-82, associate professor of English, 1982-83; University of Tennessee, Knoxville, associate professor, 1989-92, professor of English, 1992-95. Visiting associate professor of English at Purdue University, spring, 1983.

MEMBER: Dramatists Guild, Authors Guild, Authors League of America.

AWARDS, HONORS: Danforth graduate fellow, University of California at Berkeley, 1973-75; Stanford University scholar, 1979-80, and Djerassi fellow, 1982 and 1983; *New York Times* outstanding book of the year citation, American Library Association (ALA) best book citation, and American Book Award, Before Columbus Foundation, all 1982, and National Book Award for children's fiction, Association of American Publishers, 1983, all for *Marked by Fire;* Coretta Scott King Award, ALA, 1984, for *Bright Shadow;* named Outstanding Woman of the Twentieth Century, Sigma Gamma Rho, 1986; Pick of the Lists, American Booksellers, 1986, and Oklahoma Sequoyah Young Adult Book Award Masterlist, 1988-89, both for *The Golden Pasture;* Arkansas Traveler Award, 1987; Oklahoma Senate and House of Representatives citations, 1989; Chancellor's Award for Research and Creativity, University of Tennessee, and Selected Title for Children and Young Adults, National Conference of Christians and Jews, both 1991, both for *A Gathering of Flowers;* Proclamation, City of Berkeley, 1992, and Kentucky Blue Grass Award masterlist, 1995, both for *When the Nightingale Sings;* 100 Children's Books list, New York Public Library, 1993, Coretta Scott King Honor Book, ALA, Notable Children's Books, National Council of Teachers of English, and Mirrors and Windows: Seeing the Human Family Award, National Conference of Christians and Jews, all 1994, all for *Brown Honey in Broomwheat Tea;* Poet Laureate Award, Oklahoma State University Center for Poets and Writers, 1996-2000; Oklahoma Governor's Award, 1998; Celebrated Storyteller Award, *People* magazine, 1999, for *Gingerbread Days;* Notable Children's Book Award, ALA, Notable Children's Trade Book in Social Studies Award, National Council for the Social Studies/Children's Book Council, Teacher's Choice Award, International Reading Association, and Coretta Scott King Illustrator Honor Book, all 1999, all for *I Have Heard of a Land;* Parents' Choice Award, 2000, and Oklahoma Book Award, 2001, both for *Hush Songs;* Arrell Gibson Lifetime Achievement Award, Oklahoma Center for the Book, 2001, for body of work; Parents' Choice Award, 2004, for *What's the Hurry, Fox?*

WRITINGS:

YOUNG ADULT NOVELS

Marked by Fire, Avon (New York, NY), 1982.

Bright Shadow, (sequel to *Marked by Fire*), Avon (New York, NY), 1983.

Water Girl, Avon (New York, NY), 1986.
The Golden Pasture, Scholastic (New York, NY), 1986.
Journey, Scholastic (New York, NY), 1988.
When the Nightingale Sings, HarperCollins (New York, NY), 1992.
House of Light (sequel to *Marked by Fire* and *Bright Shadow*), Hyperion (New York, NY), 2001.
Abide with Me, Hyperion (New York, NY), 2001.

FOR CHILDREN

Cherish Me (picture book), illustrated by Nneka Bennett, HarperCollins (New York, NY), 1998.
You Are My Perfect Baby (board book), illustrated by Nneka Bennett, HarperCollins (New York, NY), 1999.
The Gospel Cinderella (picture book), illustrated by David Diaz, HarperCollins (New York, NY), 2000.
The Bowlegged Rooster and Other Tales That Signify (short stories), HarperCollins (New York, NY), 2000.
Hush Songs: African American Lullabies (picture book), illustrated by Brenda Joysmith, Hyperion (New York, NY), 2000.
Joy! (board book), illustrated by Pamela Johnson, Hyperion (New York, NY), 2001.
Angel's Lullaby (board book), illustrated by Pamela Johnson, Hyperion (New York, NY), 2001.
(Adapter) Zora Neale Hurston, *What's the Hurry, Fox?: And Other Animal Stories,* illustrated by Bryan Collier, HarperCollins (New York, NY), 2004.
(Adapter) Zora Neale Hurston, *The Skull Talks Back and Other Haunting Tales,* illustrated by Leonard Jenkins, HarperCollins (New York, NY), 2004.

POETRY

Bittersweet, Firesign Press (San Jose, CA), 1973.
Crystal Breezes, Firesign Press (San Jose, CA), 1974.
Blessing, Jocato Press (Berkeley, CA), 1975.
Black Child, illustrated by Tom Feelings, Zamani Productions (New York, NY), 1981.
Inside the Rainbow, Zikawana Press (Palo Alto, CA), 1982.
Brown Honey in Broomwheat Tea, illustrated by Floyd Cooper, HarperCollins (New York, NY), 1993.
Gingerbread Days, illustrated by Floyd Cooper, HarperCollins (New York, NY), 1995.
The Blacker the Berry, illustrated by Brenda Joysmith, HarperCollins (New York, NY), 1997.
I Have Heard of a Land, illustrated by Floyd Cooper, HarperCollins (New York, NY), 1998.
A Mother's Heart, a Daughter's Love, HarperCollins (New York, NY), 2001.
Crowning Glory, illustrated by Brenda Joysmith, HarperCollins (New York, NY), 2002.

PLAYS

(And producer) *A Song in the Sky* (two-act), produced in San Francisco, CA, at Montgomery Theater, 1976.
Look! What a Wonder! (two-act), produced in Berkeley, CA, at Berkeley Community Theatre, 1976.
(And producer) *Magnolia* (two-act), produced in San Francisco, CA, at Old San Francisco Opera House, 1977.
(And producer) *Ambrosia* (two-act), produced in San Francisco, CA, at Little Fox Theatre, 1978.
Gospel Roots (two-act), produced in Carson, CA, at California State University, 1981.
I Have Heard of a Land, produced in Oklahoma City, OK, at Claussen Theatre, 1989.
When the Nightingale Sings, produced in Knoxville, TN, at Clarence Brown Theatre, 1991.
(And director) *A Mother's Heart* (two-act), produced in San Francisco, CA, at Marsh Theater, 2001.

OTHER

(Editor and contributor) *A Gathering of Flowers: Stories about Being Young in America* (includes Thomas's short story "Young Reverend Zelma Lee Moses"), HarperCollins (New York, NY), 1990.
(Editor and contributor) *Linda Brown, You Are Not Alone: The Brown v. Board of Education Decision,* Jump at the Sun (New York, NY), 2003.

Contributor of short story, "Handling Snakes," to *I Believe in Water,* edited by Marilyn Singer, HarperCollins (New York, NY), 2000. Contributor to periodicals, including *American Poetry Review, Black Scholar, Calafia, Drum Voices, Giant Talk,* and *Yardbird Reader.* Editor of *Ambrosia* (women's newsletter), 1980.

ADAPTATIONS: Thomas's novel *Marked by Fire* was adapted as a stage musical by James Racheff and Ted Kociolek.

SIDELIGHTS: Joyce Carol Thomas is a celebrated author of young adult novels, poetry, and picture books, as well as fiction and poetry for adults. The winner of the 1983 National Book Award for her first novel, *Marked by Fire,* and the Coretta Scott King Award for her second, *Bright Shadow,* Thomas hit the ground running with her writing career and has never looked back. Using her own unique rural background of Oklahoma and California, she has created a lyrical world of childhood—portraying not only its joys but also its gross injustices—that resonates across racial lines. In both her poetry and fiction, Thomas conjures stories of African-American heritage, family history, and universal truths. Thomas's background as a migrant farm worker in rural Oklahoma and California supplies her with the prolific stock of characters and situations that fill her novels, while her love affair with language began with the words and songs she heard in church.

Thomas grew up in Ponca City, Oklahoma, a small, dusty town where she lived across from the school. This place has found a permanent home in Thomas's mind. "Although now I live half a continent away from my hometown," Thomas related in *Something about the Author Autobiography Series* (*SAAS*), "when it comes to my writing I find that I am often still there." She has set several of her novels in her hometown, including *Marked by Fire, Bright Shadow, The Golden Pasture,* and *House of Light.* Thomas loved school as a child and became anxious whenever it appeared she might be late—she didn't want to miss anything. However, she usually missed the first month of school in order to finish up work on her family's farm. Times were lean for Thomas's family, but they always made do. This she attributes partly to her mother's genius at making healthy foods that weren't expensive; she has memories of huge spreads being laid out for Sunday dinners. These scenes of food have stuck with Thomas, for she finds food is one of the focuses in her novels. "Because in such a home food was another language for love, my books are redolent of sugar and spice, kale and collards," Thomas commented in *SAAS.*

When Thomas was ten years old, the family moved to rural Tracy, California. There Thomas learned to milk cows, fish for minnows, and harvest tomatoes and grapes. She also became intimately acquainted with black widow spiders—there was a nest of them under her bed. She was later to use this experience in her novel *Journey.* Likewise, she had a similar experience with wasps when her brother locked her in a closet containing a nest of them; *Marked by Fire* contains some frightening scenes with these insects. In Tracy, California, Thomas continued spending long summers harvesting crops. She worked beside many Mexicans and began a long-lasting fascination with their language. "When the Spanish speakers talked they seemed to sing," Thomas remarked in *SAAS.* When she went to college, she majored in Spanish and French. "From this base of languages I taught myself much that I know about writing," she related in *SAAS.* She went on to earn a master's degree from Stanford University, and then taught foreign languages in public school.

From 1973 to 1978, Thomas wrote poetry and plays for adults, taught in various colleges and universities, and traveled to conferences and festivals all over the world, including Lagos, Nigeria. In 1982, Thomas's career took a turn when she published *Marked by Fire,* a novel for a young adult audience. Steeped in the setting and traditions of her hometown, the novel focused on Abyssinia Jackson, a girl who was born in a cotton field during harvest time. The title refers to the fact that she received a burn on her face from a brush fire during her birth. This leaves her "marked for unbearable pain and unspeakable joy," according to the local healer. The child shows a remarkable talent for singing until she is raped by a member of the church. The story of how she heals from this tragedy fills the rest of the novel.

The book was critically acclaimed and placed on required reading lists at many high schools and universities. Writing in *Black Scholar,* critic Dorothy Randall-Tsuruta noted that Thomas's "poetic tone gives this work what scents give the roses already so pleasing in color." Reviewing this debut novel in *School Library Journal,* Hazel Rochman felt that while the "lack of a fast-paced narrative line and the mythical overtones may present obstacles to some readers, many will be moved" by the story of Abyssinia. *Best Sellers* reviewer Wendell Wray noted that Thomas "captures the flavor of black folk life in Oklahoma." Wray further observed that though she "has set for herself a challenging task . . . Thomas's book works." Commenting about her stormy novel, Thomas once stated that "as a writer I work to create books filled with conflict. . . . I address this quest in part by matching the pitiful absurdities and heady contradictions of life itself, in part by leading the heroine to twin fountains of magic and the macabre, and evoking the holy and the horrible in the same breath. Nor is it ever enough to match these. Through the character of Abyssinia, I strive for what is beyond these, seeking to find newer worlds."

Bright Shadow, a sequel to *Marked by Fire,* was published in 1983. In this work, Abyssinia goes to college and ends up falling in love with Carl Lee Jefferson. The couple work through many problems in order to find their own kind of love. The winner of the Coretta Scott King Award, *Bright Shadow* was called "appealing" by

Zena Sutherland, writing in the *Bulletin of the Center for Children's Books.* However, as with many of Thomas's books, some critics faulted her for the use of overly epic language. Sutherland, for one, felt that "the often-ornate phraseology" sometimes weakens the story.

Several of Thomas's subsequent books also feature these popular characters from her first two books, including *The Golden Pasture,* which journeys back to Carl Lee's earlier life on his grandfather's ranch, and *Water Girl,* which tells the story of Abyssinia's teenage daughter, Amber, who was given up for adoption. Amber only learns of her biological mother when, after an earthquake, she finds an old letter that speaks of the adoption. Reviewing *The Golden Pasture* in *Publishers Weekly,* a contributor called the book "a spirited, lyrical tale with a memorable cast of characters."

With *Journey,* her fifth novel, Thomas broke new literary ground for herself, mixing fantasy and mystery to come up with a story of crime and family history. Meggie Alexander, "blessed" at birth by a tarantula, has uncommon powers. As an adolescent she investigates the disappearance of several of her friends in the woods, and discovers that some of them have been murdered. Meggie herself is soon kidnapped and thrust into horrible danger. Less well received than many of her other novels, *Journey* did earn accolades from a writer for *Kirkus Reviews* who felt that Thomas "dramatically juxtaposes her story's horror with the joy of existence." Other reviewers, such as Starr LaTronica of *School Library Journal,* were less enthusiastic. "This discordant mixture of fantasy and mystery . . . never blend[s] successfully," LaTronica wrote.

With *When the Nightingale Sings,* Thomas creates a sort of Cinderella story about young Marigold, who is discovered in a swamp and lives with her foster mother, Ruby, and twin stepsisters. As in the fairy tale, this family treats the young girl as a servant rather than a relative. Finally, Marigold turns her attentions away from this abusive foster family and to the local Baptist Church. It is there she finds real salvation, discovering the gift of music in gospel songs. Reviewing this and other books by Thomas in the *St. James Guide to Young Adult Writers,* a contributor noted that Thomas's use of language "is exquisite; this craftsmanship provides words that are of music, voice, and song. Her characters are often musical, and the church—the gospel music, rhythm, movement, and harmony—provides not only a backdrop, but a language that expresses the spirit of the community." The same critic went on to observe, "Proverbs, folk wisdom, scripture, and prophecy are liberally scattered among the voices of the characters."

Thomas tells a similar story in *The Gospel Cinderella,* illustrated by David Diaz. Queen Mother Rhythm's baby was lost in a hurricane, and now, many years later, she holds a Great Gospel Convention to find a new lead singer—a Daughter of Rhythm—for the Great Gospel Choir. The lost baby survived, and was found by Crooked Foster Mother and named Cinderella—"seein' how you're as dirty as a cinder pile." Crooked Foster Mother's twin daughters, Hennie and Minnie, decide to go audition, despite the fact that they are horrible singers. Cinderella has an amazing voice, but, as an overworked servant, she is not allowed to go. She sneaks out anyway and, of course, sings beautifully. "The ending is predictable and follows the basic folkloric story structure," commented a *Kirkus Reviews* contributor, but, as Ilene Cooper wrote in *Booklist,* "there's certain freshness in having the women in the forefront."

Thomas's first adult novel, *House of Light,* furthers the story of Abyssinia Jackson begun in *Marked by Fire* and continued in *Bright Shadow.* Now a doctor and healer, Abby Jackson-Jefferson is the main narrator of these tales, which relate the lives of a myriad of patients in Ponca City, Oklahoma. Reviewing the title in *Booklist,* Hazel Rochman felt that this title "is sure to be popular for the lively dialogue, the sense of community, and yes, the hopeful message." A *Publishers Weekly* contributor called the book "moving" and "marred only by unsubtle repetition, a rhetorical device Thomas relies on too frequently." However, a *Kirkus Reviews* critic offered a different opinion, writing that "lyrical, earthy prose gives this deceptively simple story depth and richness."

Much of Thomas's talent, energy, and output has been focused on poetry for young readers and on picture books for the very young. In partnership with illustrator Floyd Cooper, Thomas has created a trio of poetry books aimed at the five-to-nine-year-old reading audience. In the award-winning *Brown Honey in Broomwheat Tea,* Thomas gathers a dozen poems dealing with the family, home, and the African-American experience in a "highly readable and attractive picture book," according to a reviewer for *Booklist.* A *Publishers Weekly* contributor called the poems "lyrical" evocations of the African-American heritage. The title poem recalls Thomas's own childhood, when broomwheat tea was used as an elixir for anything that ailed the young girl. Thomas and Cooper again teamed up for *Gingerbread Days,* a picture book, containing a dozen poems, that "celebrates the passage of a year within the circle of an extended African-American family," as Meg Stackpole noted in a *School Library Journal* review. "Like food stored away for winter, this rich harvest of poems contains enough sustenance to last throughout the year," wrote a *Publishers Weekly* reviewer of the same book. "Thomas's simple but touching language describes a hopeful world . . . where love is as wonderful as gingerbread, warm and spicy from the oven," the same reviewer concluded. *Horn Book*'s Martha V. Parravano observed that *Gingerbread Days* was a "worthy companion" to *Brown Honey in Broomwheat Tea,* "made even stronger by Floyd Cooper's glowing, golden illustrations." *I Have Heard of a Land,* which continues the Thomas-Cooper collaboration, is an illustrated book of poems that celebrate the role of African-American women pioneers in the nineteenth-century frontier, largely in Oklahoma. A writer for *Publishers Weekly* called the book a "moving poetic account of a brave black woman," while *Booklist*'s Ilene Cooper dubbed it a "lyrical tribute to the pioneer spirit."

Another book of poetry by Thomas, *Crowning Glory,* was illustrated by Brenda Joysmith. In the poems contained in *Crowning Glory,* "Thomas lovingly extols the virtues and beauty of braids[,] cornrows[, and] dreadlocks," Barbara Buckley explained in *School Library Journal.* The poems are written from the point of view of a young girl, who observes and participates in her extended family's hair-care rituals. Great Grandma shows the girl how to wrap black twine through her hair to make it stronger; the girl's mother braids her hair; and she has a relaxing experience having her hair washed at Glory's Beauty Shop. "These poems are as much about the love among all the women of her family, as they tenderly share secrets and wisdom, as it is about hairstyles," commented a *Kirkus Reviews* contributor.

Thomas has also worked with illustrator Nneka Bennett on two books for very young children, *Cherish Me* and *You Are My Perfect Baby.* Reviewing the first title in *Booklist,* Kathy Broderick called Thomas's poem "compelling" and described the book as a "winning offering." Another title for the very young is *Hush Songs: African American Lullabies,* a book designed for adults to sing to babies and preschoolers which collects ten African-American lullabies, including three written by Thomas, under one cover. Claiming that "the songs themselves are timeless," *Booklist* reviewer Rochman wrote that the lullabies "touch all of us." With *A Mother's Heart, a Daughter's Love,* Thomas honors the bond between those two family member with poems from the point of view of each. In the *Bowlegged Rooster and Other Tales That Signify,* she serves up five short stories for young readers featuring Papa Rooster and his chick, all set in Possum Neck, Mississippi. "Although the plots are not always terrifically involving," wrote Steven Engelfried in *School Library Journal,* "the animals' personalities and the bustling atmosphere of the barnyard make these tales appealing." Shelley Townsend-Hudson, writing in *Booklist,* felt these tales are "a joy to hear as well as to read."

More recently, Thomas adapted for children some of the many traditional African-American folktales collected by Zora Neale Hurston in the 1930s in *Every Tongue Got to Confess.* In *What's the Hurry, Fox?: And Other Animal Stories,* Thomas's first collection of these adaptations, she "us[es] humor, wit, and a colloquial style true to the spirit of the originals," Hazel Rochman wrote in *Booklist.* The tales were originally transcribed in a thick Southern dialect that would be inaccessible to many modern children; in Thomas's versions "their regional flavor has been toned down, but not completely erased," noted a *Kirkus Reviews* contributor, but other than that few changes were made to the stories.

Thomas is also the editor of the collection *Linda Brown, You are Not Alone: The Brown v. Board of Education Decision.* The book features essays and poems by several well-known children's book authors, both African-American (Ishmael Reed, Quincy Troupe) and white (Lois Lowry, Katherine Paterson), who look back at the end of educational segregation fifty years after the landmark Brown v. Board of Education ruling. "Their personal reminiscences capture a spectrum of powerfully expressed emotions," wrote a *Publishers Weekly* reviewer. Several critics noted that the target audience of the pieces varied widely; some essays discussed such concepts as "white flight" and "model minorities" at a level that would be above most elementary school children, while the illustrations by Curtis James and other selections seemed to indicate just such an audience. However, "all the passages will bring children up close to the complex realities of segregated society," Gillian Engberg wrote in *Booklist.*

With her imagination and ability to bring authenticity to her novels, Thomas has been highly praised and often compared to other noted black women authors, including Maya Angelou, Toni Morrison, and Alice Walker. "If I had to give advice to young people," Thomas commented in her *SAAS* essay, "it would be that whatever your career choice, prepare yourself to do it well. Quality takes talent and time. Believe in your dreams. Have faith in yourself. Keep working and enjoying today even as you reach for tomorrow. If you choose to write, value your experiences. And color them in the indelible ink of your own background."

"I work for authenticity of voice," Thomas commented in *SAAS,* "fidelity to detail, and naturalness of developments." It is this authenticity that critics say sings out in all of Thomas's work, and that allows her fiction and poetry to transcend race, gender, and geography. "I treasure and value the experiences that include us all as people," Thomas concluded in *SAAS*. "I don't pay any attention to boundaries."

Thomas once commented: "I am happiest around sunlight, flowers, and trees. I like quiet, comfortable places to think. I especially like to encourage my children, my grandchildren and all young people. I enjoy the process of writing. It starts within the imagination. What a wonderful place is the mind. So welcoming! . . . I hope you [readers] will be happy in whatever direction you choose to take your life. And if you come across a book of mine, I wish you happy reading."

BIOGRAPHICAL AND CRITICAL SOURCES:

BOOKS

Authors and Artists for Young Adults, Volume 12, Thomson Gale (Detroit, MI), 1994.

Children's Literature Review, Volume 19, Thomson Gale (Detroit, MI), 1990.

Contemporary Literary Criticism, Volume 35, Thomson Gale (Detroit, MI), 1985.

Dictionary of Literary Biography, Volume 33: *Afro-American Fiction Writers after 1955,* Thomson Gale (Detroit, MI), 1984.

St. James Guide to Young Adult Writers, 2nd edition, St. James Press (Detroit, MI), 1999.

Something about the Author Autobiography Series, Volume 7, Thomson Gale (Detroit, MI), 1989.

Thomas, Joyce Carol, *Marked by Fire,* Avon (New York, NY), 1982.

Thomas, Joyce Carol, *The Gospel Cinderella* (picture book), illustrated by David Diaz, HarperCollins (New York, NY), 2000.

PERIODICALS

African American Review, spring, 1998, Darwin L. Henderson and Anthony L. Manna, "Evoking the 'Holy and the Horrible': Conversations with Joyce Carol Thomas," pp. 139-147.

Best Sellers, June, 1982, Wendell Wray, review of *Marked by Fire,* pp. 123-124.

Black Issues Review, May, 2001, Althea Gamble, review of *House of Light,* p. 23; July-August, 2004, Suzanne Rust, review of *What's the Hurry, Fox?: And Other Animal Stories,* p. 60.

Black Scholar, summer, 1982, Dorothy Randall-Tsuruta, review of *Marked by Fire,* p. 48.

Booklist, February 15, 1986, pp. 861-862; February 15, 1994, review of *Brown Honey in Broomwheat Tea,* p. 1081; September 15, 1995, Susan Dove Lempke, review of *Gingerbread Days,* p. 176; March 15, 1997, Sue-Ellen Beauregard, review of *Brown Honey in Broomwheat Tea* (video), p. 1249; February 15, 1998, Ilene Cooper, review of *I Have Heard of a Land,* p. 1009; January 1, 1999, Kathy Broderick, review of *Cherish Me,* p. 891; October 1, 2000, Shelley Townsend-Hudson, review of *The Bowlegged Rooster and Other Tales That Signify,* p. 342; December 15, 2000, Hazel Rochman, review of *Hush Songs: African American Lullabies,* p. 823; February 15, 2001, Hazel Rochman, review of *House of Light,* p. 1101; March 15, 2001, Gillian Engberg, review of *A Mother's Heart, a Daughter's Love,* p. 1392; September 15, 2002, Cynthia Turnquest, review of *Crowning Glory,* p. 238; December 1, 2003, Gillian Engberg, review of *Linda Brown, You Are Not Alone: The Brown v. Board of Education Decision,* p. 658; February 14, 2004, Ilene Cooper, review of *The Gospel Cinderella,* p. 1078; May 15, 2004, Hazel Rochman, review of *What's the Hurry, Fox?,* p. 1622.

Bulletin of the Center for Children's Books, February, 1984, Zena Sutherland, review of *Bright Shadow,* p. 119; June, 1998, pp. 376-377.

Ebony, February, 2004, review of *Linda Brown, You Are Not Alone,* p. 24.

English Journal, April, 1991, Elizabeth A. Belden and Judith M. Beckman, review of *A Gathering of Flowers: Stories about Being Young in America,* p. 83; October, 1993, John H. Bushman and Kay Parks Bushman, review of *When the Nightingale Sings,* p. 81.

Horn Book, March-April, 1996, Martha V. Parravano, review of *Gingerbread Days,* pp. 219-220.

Kirkus Reviews, September 15, 1988, review of *Journey,* p. 1410; February 1, 2001, review of *House of Light;* May 15, 2002, review of *Crowning Glory,* p. 742; November 15, 2003, review of *Linda Brown, You Are Not Alone,* p. 1364; April 1, 2004, review of *What's the Hurry, Fox?,* p. 331; April 15, 2004, review of *The Gospel Cinderella,* p. 402.

Publishers Weekly, July 25, 1986, review of *The Golden Pasture,* p. 191; September 9, 1988, Kimberly Olson Fakih and Diane Roback, review of *Journey,* p. 140; October 11, 1993, review of *Brown Honey in Broomwheat Tea,* p. 87; September 25, 1995, review of *Gingerbread Days,* p. 57; January 8, 1996, review of *Brown Honey in Broomwheat Tea,* p. 70; April 6, 1998, review of *I Have Heard of a Land,* p. 77; October 19, 1998, p. 83; February 19, 2001, review of *House of Light,* p. 69; May 6, 2002, review of *Crowning Glory,* pp. 57-58; December 8, 2003, review of *Linda Brown, You Are Not Alone,* pp. 62-63; April 19, 2004, review of *What's the Hurry, Fox?,* pp. 63-64; May 24, 2004, review of *The Gospel Cinderella,* p. 62.

School Library Journal, March, 1982, Hazel Rochman, review of *Marked by Fire,* p. 162; January, 1984, pp. 89-90; August, 1986, David A. Lindsey, review of *The Golden Pasture,* p. 107; October, 1988, Starr LaTronica, review of *Journey,* p. 165; October, 1990, Marjorie Lewis, review of *A Gathering of Flowers,* p. 145; February, 1993, Amy Healey, review of *When the Nightingale Sings,* pp. 106-107; November, 1993, Lyn Miller-Lachmann, review of *Brown Honey in Broomwheat Tea,* p. 103; January, 1996, Meg Stackpole, review of *Gingerbread Days,* p. 107; December, 1998, Martha Topol, review of *Cherish Me!,* p. 116; August, 1999, p. 132; November, 2000, Steven Engelfried, review of *The Bowlegged Rooster and Other Tales That Signify,* p. 135; February, 2002, Bina Williams, review of *Joy!,* p. 114; June, 2002, Barbara Buckley, review of *Crowning Glory,* pp. 126-127; January, 2004, Kelly Czarnecki, review of *Linda Brown, You Are Not Alone,* p. 161; April, 2004, Mary N. Oluonye, review of *What's the Hurry, Fox?,* p. 144; May, 2004, Mary N. Oluonye, review of *The Gospel Cinderella,* pp. 136-137.

Variety, September 9, 1987, p. 75.

ONLINE

Joyce Carol Thomas Web Site, http://www.joycecarolthomas.com/ (August 14, 2004).

Tennessee Authors Web Site, http://www.lib.utk.edu/ (August 15, 2004), Jennifer Duke-Sylvester, "Joyce Carol Thomas."

* * *

THOMPSON, Hunter S. 1937(?)-2005

(Raoul Duke, Sebastian Owl, Hunter Stockton Thompson)

PERSONAL: Born July 18, 1937 (some sources say 1939), in Louisville, KY; died of a self-inflicted gunshot wound, February 20, 2005, in Woody Creek, CO; son of Jack R. (an insurance agent) and Virginia (Ray) Thompson; married Sandra Dawn, May 19, 1963 (divorced); married Anita Beymuk, April 24, 2003; children: Juan. *Education:* Studied journalism at Columbia University. *Politics:* "Anarchist." *Hobbies and other interests:* Collecting guns.

CAREER: Writer and journalist. Began as a sports writer in Florida; *Time,* Caribbean correspondent, 1959; *New York Herald Tribune,* Caribbean correspondent, 1959-60; *National Observer,* South American correspondent, 1961-63; *Nation,* West Coast correspondent, 1964-66; *Ramparts,* columnist, 1967-68; *Scanlan's Monthly,* columnist, 1969-70; *Rolling Stone,* national affairs editor, 1970-84; *High Times,* global affairs correspondent, 1977-82; *San Francisco Examiner,* media critic, 1985-90; *Smart,* editor-at-large, beginning in 1988. Freelance political analyst for various European magazines, beginning in 1988;. Candidate for sheriff of Pitkin County, CO, 1968; member, sheriff's advisory committee, Pitkin County, 1976-81; executive director, Woody Creek Rod and Gun Club. *Military service:* U.S. Air Force, 1956-58; journalist for base magazine.

WRITINGS:

Hell's Angels: A Strange and Terrible Saga, Random House (New York, NY), 1966, reprinted, Modern Library (New York, NY), 1999.

Fear and Loathing in Las Vegas: A Savage Journey to the Heart of the American Dream, illustrated by Ralph Steadman, Random House (New York, NY), 1972, published with an introduction by P.J. O'Rourke as *Fear and Loathing in Las Vegas and Other American Stories,* Modern Library (New York, NY), 1996.

Fear and Loathing on the Campaign Trail '72, illustrated by Ralph Steadman, Straight Arrow Books (San Francisco, CA), 1973.

The Great Shark Hunt: Strange Tales from a Strange Time; Gonzo Papers, Volume One, Summit Books (New York, NY), 1979.

(With Ralph Steadman) *The Curse of Lono,* Bantam (New York, NY), 1983.

Generation of Swine: Tales of Shame and Degradation in the '80s; Gonzo Papers, Volume Two, Summit Books (New York, NY), 1988.

(Author of introduction) Ralph Steadman, *America,* Fantagraphics Books (Seattle, WA), 1989.

Songs of the Doomed: More Notes on the Death of the American Dream; Gonzo Papers, Volume Three, Summit Books (New York, NY), 1990.

Silk Road: Thirty-three Years in the Passing Lane, Simon & Schuster (New York, NY), 1990.

Untitled Novel, David McKay (New York, NY), 1992.

Better than Sex: Confessions of a Political Junkie; Gonzo Papers, Volume Four, Random House (New York, NY), 1993.

The Proud Highway: The Saga of a Desperate Southern Gentleman, 1955-1967, edited by Douglas Brinkley, foreword by William J. Kennedy, Villard (New York, NY), 1997.

(Author of introduction) Ralph Steadman, *Gonzo: The Art,* Harcourt (New York, NY), 1998.

The Rum Diary: The Long Lost Novel, Simon & Schuster (New York, NY), 1998.

Screwjack and Other Stories, Simon & Schuster (New York, NY), 2000.

Fear and Loathing in America: Brutal Odyssey of an Outlaw Journalist, 1968-1976 (correspondence), Simon & Schuster (New York, NY), 2000.

The Kingdom of Fear: Loathsome Secrets of a Star-crossed Child in the Final Days of the American Century, Simon & Schuster (New York, NY), 2003.

Hey Rube, Simon & Schuster (New York, NY), 2004.

Author of the novel *Prince Jellyfish,* 1960. Contributor to *Russell Chatham,* by Etel Adnan, Winn Books, 1984. Contributor of articles and essays, sometimes under pseudonym Raoul Duke, to *Esquire, London Observer, New York Times Magazine, Reporter, Harper's,* and other publications.

ADAPTATIONS: The motion picture *Where the Buffalo Roam* is based on the life and writings of Thompson, written by John Kaye, directed by Art Linson, starring Bill Murray as Thompson, Universal, 1980; *Fear and Loathing in Las Vegas* was adapted as a motion picture, written by Terry Gilliam with Tony Garisoni, Tod Davies, and Alex Cox, directed by Gilliam, starring Johnny Depp and Benicio del Toro, Universal, 1998. An audio version of *Fear and Loathing in Las Vegas* was released by Margaritaville Records, 1996 and features music by Todd Snider and voices of Harry Dean Stanton and Jim Jarmusch. *The Rum Diary* is being made into a motion picture starring Johnny Depp and Benicio del Toro.

SIDELIGHTS: Hunter S. Thompson ranks among the first and foremost practitioners of New Journalism, a genre that evolved in the 1960s to reflect the particular mood of those times. Thompson, who has called his brand of reportage "Gonzo Journalism," was perhaps the most visible and most vituperative of the New Journalism correspondents, a group whose ranks included Tom Wolfe and Gay Talese, among others. As national affairs editor for *Rolling Stone* and author of such widely read books as *Hell's Angels: A Strange and Terrible Saga, Fear and Loathing in Las Vegas,* and *Fear and Loathing on the Campaign Trail '72,* Thompson recorded both the disillusionment and the delirium of a volatile era. According to Morris Dickstein in *Gates of Eden: American Culture in the Sixties,* Thompson "paraded one of the few original prose styles of recent years," a style that indulged in insult and stream-of-invective to an unparalleled degree. He pioneered a new approach to reporting, allowing the story of covering an event to become the central story itself, while never disguising the fact that he was "a half-cranked geek journalist caught in the center of the action," to quote Jerome Klinkowitz in *The Life of Fiction.*

Thompson was considered a seasoned journalist while still in his twenties. His early journalism was conventional, but as the tenor of the nation began to change (and as his own experiments with drugs increased), he embraced the nascent New Journalism style. *New York Times Book Review* contributor Crawford Woods explained that New Journalism's roots lay in "the particular sense of the 1960s that a new voice was demanded by the way people's public and private lives were coming together in a sensual panic stew, with murder its meat and potatoes, grass and acid its spice. How to tell the story of a time when all fiction was science fiction, all facts lies? The New Journalism was born." It was a style that "put the pseudo-objective soporifics of the broadsheets to shame by applying to journalism the techniques of the realistic novel," explained Richard Vigilante in the *National Review,* adding, "But, at the same time, it required a romance with reality that undermined the ideologues' lust for self-deceit. For all the literary liberties of the most famous New Journalists, their stories, when done right, were more true than traditional journalism."

Riding and drinking with the Hell's Angels motorcycle gang, taking massive quantities of hallucinogenic drugs, and careening to assignments on little food and less sleep, Thompson became the "professional wildman" of the New Journalists, to quote *Village Voice* contributor Vivian Gornick. He also became a nationally known figure whose work "in particular caused currents of envy in the world of the straight journalists, who coveted his freedom from restraint," according to an *Atlantic* essayist. "He became a cult figure," Peter O. Whitmer wrote in *Saturday Review,* "the outlaw who could drink excessively, drug indulgently, shout abusively, *and* write insightfully."

In *Critique,* John Hellmann wrote: "By conceiving his journalism as a form of fiction, Thompson has been able to shape actual events into meaningful works of literary art." Thompson's "Gonzo Journalism" narratives are first-person accounts in which the author appears as a persona, sometimes Raoul Duke, but more commonly Dr. Hunter S. Thompson, a specialist variously in divinity, pharmaceuticals, or reporting.

To research *Hell's Angels: A Strange and Terrible Saga,* Thompson's 1966 account of the infamous California motorcycle gang, the young author rode with the Angels for almost a year, recording their road rallies, their home lives, and their sexual adventures. The book strives to present the gang objectively while exposing the fact that its brutal reputation was primarily the creation of the scandal-mongering media. *New Republic* contributor Richard M. Elman observed that in *Hell's Angels* Thompson has "managed to correct many popular misconceptions about [the Angels], and in the process, provided his readers with a tendentious but informative participant-observer study of those who are doomed to lose." In *Nation,* Elmer Bendiner likewise noted that throughout the book, "Thompson's point of view remains eminently sane and honest. He does not weep for the Angels or romanticize them or glorify them. Neither does he despise them. Instead, he views them as creatures of an irresponsible society, given their image by an irresponsible press, embodying the nation's puerile fantasy life. He sees the menace not so much in the Hell's Angels themselves, as in the poverty of spirit and perennial adolescence that spawned them." *Hell's Angels* garnered a mixture of critical reactions. *Atlantic* correspondent Oscar Handlin contended that Thompson's "lurid narrative, despite its sympathy for his subjects, reveals the threat they pose." William Hogan in *Saturday Review* called the work "a jarring piece of contemporary Californiana, as well as an examination of a weird branch of present-day show business." According to Elman, Thompson's "fascinating invocation to, evocation *of,* and reportage *about* the Hell's Angels . . . is certainly the most informative, thorough, and vividly written account of this phenomenon yet to appear."

Fear and Loathing in Las Vegas is an all-out display of Gonzo Journalism that remains Thompson's best-known work. As Hellmann described the book in *Fables of Fact: The New Journalism as New Fiction, Fear and Loathing in Las Vegas* "is, in barest outline, the author's purported autobiographical confession of his failure to fulfill the magazine's assignment to 'cover' two events in Las Vegas, the Fourth Annual 'Mint 400' motorcycle desert race and the National Conference of District Attorneys Seminar on Narcotics and Dangerous Drugs. It is more exactly the author's (or 'Raoul Duke'-s') tale of his hallucinations and adventures. . . . The book is, then, even in its most general subject and presentation, either a report of an actual experience which was largely fantasy or an actual fantasy which is disguised as report."

In the guise of Raoul Duke, Thompson relates a series of episodic adventures revolving around drug use and *carte blanche* access to Las Vegas's finest hotels, accompanied by a three-hundred-pound Samoan attorney named Dr. Gonzo (based on Thompson's friend Oscar Zeta Acosta), who "serves as a parody of noble savage 'sidekicks' from Chingachgook to Tonto," according to Hellmann. *National Observer* contributor Michael Putney called the book "a trip, literally and figuratively, all the way to bad craziness and back again. It is also the most brilliant piece of writing about the dope subculture since Tom Wolfe's *Electric Kool-Aid Acid Test* and, at the same time, an acid, wrenchingly funny portrait of straight America's most celebrated and mean-spirited pleasure-dome, Las Vegas."

Thompson continues to explore "the politics of unreason" in *Fear and Loathing on the Campaign Trail '72,* a collection of articles that first appeared in *Rolling Stone* magazine. *Nation* correspondent Steven d'Arazien called the work "a New Journalism account of the 1972 presidential campaign from before New Hampshire to Miami and beyond. . . . It will be regarded as a classic in the genre." As national affairs editor for *Rolling Stone,* Thompson traveled with the press corps that followed candidate George McGovern; according to Dickstein he "recorded the nuts and bolts of a presidential campaign with all the contempt and incredulity that other reporters must feel but censor out." According to Jules Witcover in *Progressive* magazine, the book, though "heavily personalized writing-on-the-run, riddled here and there by the clear eye of hindsight, does convey an honest picture of a political writer picking his way through all the hoopla, propaganda, tedium, and exhaustion of a campaign." Critics' opinions of the book depended on their assessment of Thompson's reporting style. *Columbia Journalism Review* essayist Wayne C. Booth characterized the work as "an inflated footnote on how Thompson used the campaign to achieve a 'very special kind of High.'" He concluded, "Cleverness, energy and brashness cannot, finally, make up for ignorance and lack of critical training." On the other hand, *Saturday Review* contributor Joseph Kanon found *Fear and Loathing on the Campaign Trail '72* to contain "the best political reporting in some time," and concluded that the book "manages to give politics, after years of televised lobotomy, some flesh." *New York Times* columnist Christopher Lehmann-Haupt admitted that while Thompson "doesn't exactly see America as

Grandma Moses depicted it, or the way they painted it for us in civics class, he does in his own mad way betray a profound democratic concern for the polity. And in its own mad way, it's damned refreshing."

Thompson's subsequent books, *The Great Shark Hunt: Strange Tales from a Strange Time*—in which many of his essays on Watergate are collected—*The Curse of Lono, Generation of Swine: Tales of Shame and Degradation in the '80s,* and *Songs of the Doomed: More Notes on the Death of the American Dream,* have continued to mine his vein of personal, high-energy reporting. *Los Angeles Times Book Review* correspondent Peter S. Greenburg noted that *The Great Shark Hunt* "is not so much an attack on America as it is a frightfully perceptive autopsy of our culture. . . . Thompson is the master of the cosmic metaphor and combines this talent with all the subtlety of a run at someone's jugular with a red-hot rail spike." In *The Curse of Lono* Thompson recounts his antics during a visit to Hawaii with his longtime friend and illustrator, Ralph Steadman. Once again the author demonstrates his "very nearly unrelieved distemper," an attribute William F. Buckley, Jr., described as "the Sign of Thompson" in *New York Times Book Review. Washington Post Book World* reviewer Michael Dirda claimed of the work, "No one writes like Hunter Thompson, though many have tried, and *The Curse of Lono* dispenses pages rabid with his hilarious, frenzied rantings, gusts of '60s madness for the stuffy '80s."

In 1990 Thompson became the subject of media attention when a woman—described variously as an actress, a reporter, and an ex-pornographic film producer—accused him of sexual assault, claiming Thompson had grabbed her when she refused his invitation to join him in his hot tub. Local police conducted an eleven-hour search of Thompson's home, uncovering small quantities of marijuana, cocaine, and LSD, a number of Valium-like pills, an antique Gatling gun, and four sticks of dynamite. Thompson was charged with five felonies and three misdemeanors and faced up to fifty years in prison if found guilty on all counts. Soon, however, the case against Thompson began to erode and, after a preliminary hearing, the charges were dismissed. A number of people suggested that the entire case had simply been an attempt to rid the exclusive Aspen community of someone many of its newer residents considered a nuisance.

These events and others are described in *Songs of the Doomed: More Notes on the Death of the American Dream.* A *Washington Post Book World* contributor suspected that at times, "'Dr.' Thompson has, after years of pursuing the complete derangement of his senses, finally made the journey to real madness, to a place where the parameters of truth and fantasy have blended into each other, and the result of this loss of perspective is often more disconcerting than it is enlightening."

More of Thompson's political writings are collected in *Better than Sex: Confessions of a Political Junkie,* which includes his thoughts on George Bush's presidency and Bill Clinton's campaign and first years in office. While the collection was not rated as highly as Thompson's earlier political ruminations, Thomas Gaughan maintained in *Booklist* that *Better than Sex* "quite shrewdly" asserts that "Bush is so guilty he makes Nixon look innocent . . . and Clinton is a swine, but he's our swine." In contrast, L.S. Klepp of *Entertainment Weekly* felt that the book "reads as if Thompson had emptied the contents of several files and wastebaskets into a large envelope addressed to his indulgent publisher and let it go at that."

Thompson's early years in journalism are documented in *The Proud Highway: Saga of a Desperate Southern Gentleman.* A compilation of some three hundred letters—just a fraction of his output—to friends and editors, famous writers, and anyone else to whom he wanted to express his opinion, the book reflects Thompson's early thirst for fame and penchant for bombast, according to reviewers. With an eye toward creating a literary persona, Thompson sent thousands of letters in his early years, asking Lyndon Johnson, for example, to appoint him governor of American Samoa, and imploring novelist William Faulkner—whom he had never met—to send him weekly checks. "Like all great wits, from Oscar Wilde to Gore Vidal," wrote Pico Iyer in *Time,* "Thompson saw that a pose was more compelling than a personality, not least because it was more consistent." Iyer concluded that "the pleasure of these letters is that they have all the rude vitality of the man who was not yet a myth."

According to David Gates in *Newsweek, The Proud Highway* illustrates several things about Thompson: "First, though Thompson casts himself as a wild man, he's also a precisionist. Second, he has ungodly energy: these letters are just the warm-up and spillover from his fiction, journalistic pieces and his first book. . . . Third, funny as he is, he's dead serious about his art and his reputation: he made carbons of all these letters. Just in case." Other reviewers duly praised the volume as well. "By turns exasperating and entertaining," wrote a reviewer for *Publishers Weekly,* the book "is also a devastating portrait of the writer as an incorrigible outsider." And Bonnie Smothers in *Booklist* wrote that "letters like Hunter's are a reminder of what a letter can be—our own personal literature that is, indeed, a testament to our life and times."

In 1999 Thompson published his first novel, *The Rum Diary,* written while he was a neophyte reporter in the Caribbean at the dawn of the 1960s. True to the style he developed in his journalism, the novel is mostly autobiographical, recounting the adventures of a young journalist, Paul Kemp, who writes for a Puerto Rican newspaper and lives dangerously, swilling alcohol and pugnaciously tempting fate. The novel received mixed reviews. Vanessa V. Friedman, writing in *Entertainment Weekly,* called it "little more than a fervent first novel by a young man in thrall to both Hemingway and Kerouac." In contrast, Mike Benediktsson, in *Library Journal,* appreciated "the narrative's tight, urgent prose" that "exposes the twisted roots of Thompson's gonzo journalism." Similarly, a *Publishers Weekly* reviewer acknowledged that the novel lays the groundwork for Thompson's later style, but that "the best parts of the book are its occasional, almost grudging, acknowledgments of natural beauty."

Originally published in a limited edition in 1991, Thompson's *Screwjack and Other Stories* was released by Simon & Schuster in 2000. The book contains three stories that "offer the sustained flashes of the brilliance that characterized Thompson's early classics," according to one *Publishers Weekly* contributor. Stories such as "Death of a Poet" contain a mixture of violence, sex, and drugs set in the late 1960s. A *Publishers Weekly* critic considered this a "slight" addition to the author's ouevre, but still worth a look from loyal Thompson fans. The year 2000 also saw the publication of a collection of Thompson's letters titled *Fear and Loathing in America: Brutal Odyssey of an Outlaw Journalist, 1968-1976.* Many of the missives in this book are addressed to publishers and concern books he was working on at the time; critics found them interesting for Thompson's observations of famous politicians, authors, and other renowned figures, such as President Jimmy Carter and Tom Wolfe. "What may surprise readers," commented a *Publishers Weekly* reviewer, "is the sweetness of much of the writing." However, the critic added, "Thompson's strong suit is still invective, of which he remains the unsurpassed master."

In 2003 Thompson's memoir, titled *The Kingdom of Fear: Loathsome Secrets of a Star-crossed Child in the Final Days of the American Century,* was published. A *Publishers Weekly* contributor called the book "an autobiography that is typically unorthodox in style but still revealing previously unknown facts about its subject." The memoir covers everything from Thompson's first brush with the law in 1946 to his run in with Clarence Thomas before he was elected to the Supreme Court to his latest take on the American political scene. "The book makes a strong case for Thompson as both a social prophet (his day-after analysis of the 9/11 tragedy proves particularly prescient) and a patriot," wrote a reviewer in *Book.* Ulrich Baer, writing in *Library Journal,* called Thompson's writing "lazy" but also noted, "There are some canny observations on the difference between outlaws and lawbreakers, insights into the corruption of politics by politicians' lust for power, and instructive pieces on voter rebellion." *Booklist* contributor Ray Olsen commented that "Thompson remains, in this hodgepodge of pieces spanning most of his life . . . a larger-than-life middle-American humorist whose only peers are Mark Twain and William Burroughs."

Although Thompson's style and his personality have led to conflicting opinions about his writing, more critics have praised Thompson than disparaged him. As Jerome Klinkowitz wrote, "For all of the charges against him, Hunter S. Thompson is an amazingly insightful writer. His 'journalism' is not in the least irresponsible. On the contrary, in each of his books he's pointed out the lies and gross distortions of conventional journalism. . . . Moreover, his books are richly intelligent." According to Gornick, Thompson's talent "lies in his ability to describe his own manic plunge into drink, drugs, and madness through a use of controlled exaggeration that is truly marvelous." John Leonard expressed a similar opinion in *New York Times.* Thompson "became, in the late 1960's, our point guard, our official crazy, patrolling the edge," Leonard wrote. "He reported back that the paranoids were right, and they were. The cool inwardness . . . the hugging of the self to keep from cracking up, is not for him. He inhabits his nerve endings; they are on the outside, like the skin of a baby. . . . He is also, as if this needs to be said, hilarious."

Thompson fatally shot himself on February 20, 2005, in Colorado. Thompson's will called for "The Gonzo Trust," a group of three people, lawyers Hal Haddon and George Tobia, along with historian Douglas Brinkley, to manage Thompson's archives and literary estate.

BIOGRAPHICAL AND CRITICAL SOURCES:

BOOKS

Adnan, Etel, *Russell Chatham,* Clark City Press (Livingston, MT), 1987.

Carroll, E. Jean, *Hunter: The Strange and Savage Life of Hunter S. Thompson,* Dutton (New York, NY), 1993.

Contemporary Literary Criticism, Thomson Gale (Detroit, MI), Volume 9, 1978, Volume 17, 1981, Volume 40, 1986, Volume 104, 1998.

Contemporary Popular Writers, St. James Press (Detroit, MI), 1997.

Dickstein, Morris, *Gates of Eden: American Culture in the Sixties,* Basic Books (New York, NY), 1977.

Dictionary of Literary Biography, Volume 185: *American Literary Journalists, 1945-1995, First Series,* Thomson Gale (Detroit, MI), 1998.

Hellman, John, *Fables of Fact: The New Journalism as New Fiction,* University of Illinois Press (Urbana, IL), 1981.

Klinkowitz, Jerome, *The Life of Fiction,* University of Illinois Press (Urbana, IL), 1977.

McKeen, William, *Hunter S. Thompson,* Twayne (Boston, MA), 1991.

Vonnegut, Kurt, Jr.,*Wampeters Foma & Granfalloons,* Delacorte (New York, NY), 1974.

Whitmer, Peter O., *When the Going Gets Weird: The Twisted Life and Times of Hunter S. Thompson: A Very Unauthorized Biography,* Hyperion (New York, NY), 1993.

PERIODICALS

American Spectator, December, 1990, p. 42.

Atlantic, February, 1967, Oscar Handlin, review of *Hell's Angels*; July, 1973.

Book, March-April 2003, review of *Kingdom of Fear: Loathsome Secrets of a Star-crossed Child in the Final Days of the American Century,* p. 80.

Booklist, October 1, 1994, Thomas Gaughan, review of *Better than Sex: Confessions of a Political Junkie,* p. 187; April 15, 1997, Bonnie Smothers, review of *The Proud Highway,* p. 1364; December 15, 2002, Ray Olson, review of *Kingdom of Fear,* p. 706.

Columbia Journalism Review, November-December, 1973, Wayne C. Booth, review of *Fear and Loathing on the Campaign Trail '72*; September-October, 1979; March, 2001, James Boylan, review of *Fear and Loathing in America: The Brutal Odyssey of an Outlaw Journalist, 1968-1976,* p. 70.

Commonweal, April 7, 1967.

Critique, Volume 21, number 1, 1979, John Hellman.

Detroit News, August 26, 1979; November 27, 1983.

Entertainment Weekly, September 9, 1994, L.S. Klepp, review of *Better than Sex,* p. 73; October 16, 1998, Vanessa V. Friedman, review of *The Rum Diary,* p. 82; January 12, 2001, Glenn Gaslin, "Fear and Loathing on the Net: Hunter Thompson Goes Cyber," p. 87; March 23, 2001, Rebecca Ascher-Walsh, "Real World: News from Hollywood," p. 74.

Esquire, April, 1991, p. 152; February, 1993, p. 61.

Harper's, July, 1973.

Kirkus Reviews, June 15, 2004, review of *Hey Rube,* p. 572.

Library Journal, October 15, 1998, Mike Benediktsson, review of *The Rum Diary,* p. 101; February 15, 1999, Theresa Connors, review of *The Rum Diary,* p. 38; November 1, 2000, Michael Rogers, review of *Screwjack and Other Stories,* p. 143; February 1, 2003, Ulrich Baer, review of *Kingdom of Fear,* p. 99.

London Magazine, June-July, 1973.

Los Angeles Times Book Review, August 12, 1979, Peter S. Greenburgy, review of *The Great Shark Hunt: Strange Tales from a Strange Time.*

Nation, April 3, 1967; August 13, 1973; October 13, 1979; June 4, 1990, p. 765.

National Observer, August 5, 1972, Michael Putney, review of *Fear and Loathing in Las Vegas.*

National Review, September 16, 1988, p. 52.

New Leader, November 28, 1988, p. 21.

New Republic, February 25, 1967; October 14, 1972; October 13, 1973; August 25, 1979; January 7, 1991, p. 38.

New Statesman, November 11, 1988, p. 33.

Newsweek, March 6, 1987; May 19, 1997, David Gates, review of *The Proud Highway,* p. 85.

New York, September 26, 1994, p. 102.

New Yorker, March 4, 1967.

New York Review of Books, October 4, 1973.

New York Times, February 23, 1967; June 22, 1972; May 18, 1973; August 10, 1979.

New York Times Book Review, January 29, 1967; March 5, 1967; July 23, 1972; July 15, 1973; December 2, 1973; August 5, 1979; October 14, 1979; January 15, 1984; August 14, 1988, p. 17; November 25, 1990, pp. 7-8; October 23, 1994, p. 18; February 23, 2003, Jack Shafer, review of *Kingdom of Fear,* p. 5.

People, February 10, 2003, review of *Kingdom of Fear,* p. 49.

Progressive, July, 1973, Jules Witcover, review of *Fear and Loathing on the Campaign Trail '72.*

Publishers Weekly, April 21, 1997, review of *The Proud Highway,* p. 49; September 21, 1998, review of *The Rum Diary,* p. 71; October 23, 2000, review of *Screwjack,* p. 38; October 30, 2000, review of *Fear and Loathing in America,* p. 54; January 13, 2003, review of *Kingdom of Fear,* p. 51; January 13, 2003, Lynn Andrian, interview with Thompson, p. 53.

Rolling Stone, June 28, 1990, pp. 64-68; July 12, 1990, pp. 21-22; May 30, 1991, pp. 38-39; January 23, 1992, pp. 22-32; June 16, 1994, pp. 42-44.
Saturday Night, March, 1991, pp. 62-63.
Saturday Review, February 18, 1967, William Hogan, review of *Hell's Angels*; April 21, 1973, Joseph Kanon, review of *Fear and Loathing on the Campaign Trail '72.*
Time, June 16, 1997, Pico Iyer, review of *The Proud Highway,* p. 80.
Times (London, England), May 12, 1982.
Times Literary Supplement, January 11, 1968; November 3, 1972.
Village Voice, November 19, 1979, Vivian Gornick.
Washington Monthly, April, 1981.
Washington Post Book World, August 19, 1979, review of *The Great Shark Hunt*; December 18, 1983, review of *Songs of the Doomed: More Notes on the Death of the American Dream.*

ONLINE

The Great Thompson Hunt, http://www.gonzo.org/ (April 2, 2002).

OBITUARIES:

Chicago Tribune, February 21, 2005, pp. 1, 6.
Los Angeles Times, February 22, 2005, pp. A1, A18.
New York Times, February 22, 2005, p. A17.
Times (London, England), February 22, 2005, p. 55.

* * *

THOMPSON, Hunter Stockton
See THOMPSON, Hunter S.

* * *

THORNTON, Hall
See SILVERBERG, Robert

* * *

TIGER, Derry
See ELLISON, Harlan

* * *

TORNIMPARTE, Alessandra
See GINZBURG, Natalia

TREMBLAY, Michel 1942-

PERSONAL: Born June 25, 1942, in Montreal, Quebec, Canada; son of Armand (a linotype operator) and Rheauna Tremblay; *Education:* Attended Institut des Arts Graphiques.

ADDRESSES: Agent—Agence Goodwin, 839 Sherbrooke E., Suite 2, Montreal, Quebec H2L 1K6, Canada.

CAREER: Writer. Radio-Canada television, linotype operator, costume department, 1963-66.

MEMBER: Union of Quebec Writers, Centre des Auteurs Dramatiques (CEAD), Playwrights Union.

AWARDS, HONORS: First prize in Radio Canada's Young Author's Competition, 1964, for unpublished play *Le Train;* Meritas Trophy, 1970, 1972; Canada Council Award, 1971; Floyd S. Chalmers Canadian Play awards, Ontario Arts Council, 1972-75, 1978, 1986, and 1989, for *Le Vrai Monde?;* Prix Victor-Morin, Societe Saint-Jean-Baptiste de Montreal, 1974; Canadian Film Festival Award for best scenario, 1975, for *Françoise Durocher, Waitress;* Ontario Lieutenant-Governor's Medal, 1976 and 1977; Prix France-Quebec, Quebec Ministere des Relations Internationales, 1981, for novel *Therese et Pierrette a l'ecole des Saints-Anges,* and 1985, for novel *La Duchesse et le Roturier;* Premiere Selection, Prix Medicis, 1983; L'Ordre des arts et des lettres (France), chevalier, 1984, officier, 1991; Best Play award at Le Festival du theatre des Ameriques, 1985, for *Albertine, en cinq temps;* Montreal's Prix de la Critique, 1986, for *Albertine, en cinq temps;* Athanase-David, 1988; Prix du public au Festival de Bruxelles, 1990, for *Le Coeur decouvert: Roman d'amours;* Grand Prix du Public, 1990; Doctorat Honoris Causa from Concordia University, 1990, McGill University, 1991, Stirling University, Scotland, 1992, and Windsor University, Ontario, 1993; Mclean's Honor Role, 1991; Prix Jacques-Cartier Lyon, 1991; Banff National Center Award, 1993; six Canadian Arts Council grants; Governor-General's Literary Award for Translation, 1998, for *Bambi and Me;* Governor-General's Award for Performing Arts, 1999.

WRITINGS:

PLAYS

Le Train (originally broadcast by Radio Canada, 1964; first produced in Montreal, 1965), Lemeac (Montreal, Quebec, Canada), 1990.
Cinq (one-act plays; includes *Berthe, Johnny Mangano and His Astonishing Dogs,* and *Gloria Star*), first produced in Montreal, 1966, revised version published as *En pieces detachees* (first produced in

Montreal, 1969), Lemeac (Montreal, Quebec, Canada), 1972, translation by Allan Van Meer published as *Like Death Warmed Over,* (produced in Winnipeg, 1973), Playwrights Co-op (Toronto, Ontario, Canada), 1973, translation published as *Montreal Smoked Meat* (produced in Toronto, 1974), Talon Books (Vancouver, British Columbia, Canada), 1975, translation also produced in Vancouver as *Broken Pieces,* 1974.

Les Belles-Soeurs (title means "The Sisters-In-Law"; two-act play; first produced in Montreal, 1968), Holt (Montreal, Quebec, Canada), 1968, translation by John Van Burek and Bill Glassco, Talon Books (Vancouver, British Columbia, Canada), 1974, published as *The Guid Sisters* (first produced in Toronto and Glasgow, 1987), Exile (Toronto, Ontario, Canada), 1988.

La Duchesse de Langeais (two-act play), first produced in Montreal, 1970.

En pieces detachees [and] *La Duchesse de Langeais,* Lemeac (Montreal, Quebec, Canada), 1970.

Les Paons (one-act fantasy; first produced in Ottawa, 1971), Centre des Auteurs Dramatiques (Quebec, Canada), 1969.

Trois Petit Tours (includes television adaptations of *Berthe, Johnny Mangano and His Astonishing Dogs,* and *Gloria Star;* broadcast in 1969), Lemeac (Montreal, Quebec, Canada), 1971.

A toi, pour toujours, ta Marie-Lou (one-act play; first produced in Montreal, 1971), introduction by Michel Belair, Lemeac (Montreal, Quebec, Canada), 1971, translation by John Van Burek and Bill Glassco published as *Forever Yours, Marie-Lou,* Talon Books (Vancouver, British Columbia, Canada), 1975.

Demain matin, Montreal m'attend (title means "Tomorrow Morning, Montreal Wait for Me"; first produced in Montreal, 1972), Lemeac (Montreal, Quebec, Canada), 1972.

Hosanna (two-act; first produced in Montreal, 1973, produced on Broadway, 1981), translation by John Van Burek and Bill Glassco, Talon Books (Vancouver, British Columbia, Canada), 1974.

Hosanna [and] *La Duchesse de Langeais,* Lemeac (Montreal, Quebec, Canada), 1973.

Bonjour, la, bonjour (title means "Hello, There, Hello"; first produced in Ottawa, 1974), Lemeac (Montreal, Quebec, Canada), 1974, translation by John Van Burek and Bill Glassco published as *Bonjour, la, bonjour* (produced in 1975), Talon Books (Vancouver, British Columbia, Canada), 1975.

Les Heros de mon enfance (musical comedy; title means "My Childhood Heroes"; first produced in Eastman, Quebec, 1975), Lemeac (Montreal, Quebec, Canada), 1976.

Surprise! Surprise! (one-act play), first produced in Montreal, 1975.

Sainte-Carmen de la Main (two-act play; first produced in Montreal, 1976), Lemeac (Montreal, Quebec, Canada), 1976, translation by John Van Burek published as *Sainte-Carmen of the Main* (broadcast on BBC-Radio, 1987), Talon Books (Vancouver, British Columbia, Canada), 1981.

La Duchesse de Langeais and Other Plays (includes *Trois Petit Tours* and *Surprise! Surprise!*), translations by John Van Burek, Talon Books (Vancouver, British Columbia, Canada), 1976.

Damnée Manon, sacrée Sandra (one-act; first produced in Montreal, 1977; produced as *Sandra/Manon* in Edinburgh and London, 1984), translation by John Van Burek published as *Damnée Manon, sacrée Sandra* (produced in United States, 1981), Talon Books (Vancouver, British Columbia, Canada), 1981.

Damnée Manon, sacrée Sandra [and] *Surprise! Surprise!,* Lemeac (Montreal, Quebec, Canada), 1977.

L'Impromptu d'Outremont (two-act play; first produced in Montreal, 1980), Lemeac (Montreal, Quebec, Canada), 1980, translation by John Van Burek published as *The Impromptu of Outremont* (produced, 1981), Talon Books (Vancouver, British Columbia, Canada), 1981.

Les Anciennes Odeurs (first produced in Montreal, 1981), Lemeac (Montreal, Quebec, Canada), 1981, translation by John Stowe published as *Remember Me,* Talon Books (Vancouver, British Columbia, Canada), 1984.

Les Grandes Vacances, first produced in Montreal, 1981.

Albertine, en cinq temps (first produced in Ottawa, 1984), Lemeac (Montreal, Quebec, Canada), 1984, translation by John Van Burek and Bill Glassco published as *Albertine in Five Times* (produced in Toronto, Edinburgh, and London, 1986), Talon Books (Vancouver, British Columbia, Canada), 1987.

Le Vrai Monde? (first produced concurrently in Ottawa and Montreal, 1987), Lemeac (Montreal, Quebec, Canada), 1987, translation published as *The Real World?* (produced in London, 1990), Talon Books (Vancouver, British Columbia, Canada), 1988.

La Maison suspendue (first produced in Montreal and Toronto, 1990), Lemeac (Montreal, Quebec, Canada), 1990, translation by John Van Burek, Talon Books (Vancouver, British Columbia, Canada), 1991.

Marcel poursuivi par les chiens (first produced in Montreal, 1992), Lemeac (Montreal, Quebec, Canada), 1992, translation by John Van Burek and Bill

Glassco, Talon Books (Vancouver, British Columbia, Canada), 1993.

Theatre I (includes ten plays), Actes Sud (Arles, France), 1991.

Encore une fois, si vous permettez: comedie en un acte, Lemeac (Montreal, Quebec, Canada), 1998, translated by Linda Gaboriau as *For the Pleasure of Seeing Her Again,*1998.

RADIO PLAYS

Six heures au plus tard, Lemeac (Montreal, Quebec, Canada), 1986.

FICTION

Contes pour buveurs attardes (stories), Editions du Jour (Montreal, Quebec, Canada), 1966, translation by Michael Bullock published as *Stories for Late Night Drinkers,* Intermedia Press (Vancouver, British Columbia, Canada), 1977.

La Cite dans l'oeuf (fantasy novel; title means "The City inside the Egg"), Editions du Jour (Montreal, Quebec, Canada), 1969.

C't'a ton tour, Laura Cadieux (title means "It's Your Turn, Laura Cadieux"), Editions du Jour (Montreal, Quebec, Canada), 1973.

La Grosse Femme d'a côte est enceinte (first novel in "Chroniques du plateau Mont-Royal" tetralogy), Lemeac (Montreal, Quebec, Canada), 1978, translation by Sheila Fischman published as *The Fat Woman Next Door Is Pregnant,* Talon Books Vancouver, British Columbia, Canada), 1981.

Therese et Pierrette a l'ecole des Saints-Anges (second in tetralogy), Lemeac (Montreal, Quebec, Canada), 1980, translation by Sheila Fischman published as *Therese and Pierrette and the Little Hanging Angel,* McClelland & Stewart (Toronto, Ontario, Canada), 1984.

La Duchesse et le roturier (third in tetralogy), Lemeac (Montreal, Quebec, Canada), 1982.

Des Nouvelles d'Edouard (fourth in tetralogy), Lemeac (Montreal, Quebec, Canada), 1984.

Le Coeur decouvert: Roman d'amours, Lemeac (Montreal, Quebec, Canada), 1986, translation by Sheila Fischman published as *The Heart Laid Bare,* McClelland & Stewart (Toronto, Ontario, Canada), 1989, published as *Making Room,* Serpent's Tail (London, England), 1990.

Le Premier Quartier de la lune, Lemeac (Montreal, Quebec, Canada), 1989.

Douze Coups de Theatre, Lemeac (Montreal, Quebec, Canada), 1992.

Le Coeur Eclate, Lemeac (Montreal, Quebec, Canada), 1993.

En Circuit Ferme, Lemeac (Montreal, Quebec, Canada), 1994.

Quarante-quatre Minutes, Quarante-quatre Secondes, Lemeac (Montreal, Quebec, Canada), 1997.

Objet de Beaute, Talon Books (Vancouver, British Columbia, Canada), 1998, translated by Sheila Fischman as *A Thing of Beauty,* 1998.

Hotel Bristol, New York, NY, Lemeac (Montreal, Quebec, Canada), 1999.

Duchesse et le Routier, Talon Books (Vancouver, British Columbia, Canada), 1999, translated by Sheila Fischman as *The Duchess and the Commoner,* 1999.

Messe Solennelle pour une Pleine Lune d'Ete, Nick Hern Books (London, England), 2000, translated by Martin Bowman and Bill Findlay as *Solemn Mass for a Full Moon in Summer,* 2000.

Des Nouvelles d'Edouard, Talon Books (Vancouver, British Columbia, Canada), 2000, translated by Sheila Fischman as *News from Edouard,* 2000.

L'Homme Qui Entendait Siffler une Bouilloire, Lemeac (Vancouver, British Columbia, Canada), 2001.

Douze Coups de Theatre, Talon Books (Vancouver, British Columbia, Canada), 2002, translated by Sheila Fischman as *Twelve Opening Acts,* 2002.

Etat des Lieux, Talon Books (Vancouver, British Columbia, Canada), 2002, translated by Linda Gaboriau as *Impromptu on Nun's Island,* 2002.

Bonbons Assortis, Lemeac (Montreal, Quebec, Canada), 2002.

Le Passe Anterieur: Piece en un Act, Lemeac (Montreal, Quebec, Canada), 2003, translated by Linda Gaboriau as *Past Perfect,* 2004.

L'Imperatif Present, Lemeac (Montreal, Quebec, Canada), 2003.

Le Cahier Noir, Lemeac (Montreal, Quebec, Canada), 2003.

Ange Cornu avec des Ailes de Tole, Talon Books (Montreal, Quebec, Canada), 2003.

Some Night My Prince Will Come, Talon Books (Montreal, Quebec, Canada), 2004.

Passe Anterieur, Talon Books (Montreal, Quebec, Canada), in press.

SCREENPLAYS

(And dialogue, with Andre Brassard) *Françoise Durocher, Waitress,* National Film Board of Canada, 1972.

(And dialogue, with Andre Brassard) *Il etait une fois dans l'est* (title means "Once Upon a Time in the East"), Cine Art, 1974.
(Author of scenario and dialogue) *Parlez-nous d'amour* (title means "Speak to Us of Love"), Films 16, 1976.
(Author of scenario and dialogue) *Le Soleil se leve en retard,* Films 16, 1977.

Also author of *Le Coeur decouvert,* 1986, *Le Grand Jour,* 1988, and *Le Vrai Monde?,* 1991.

DRAMATIC ADAPTATIONS

Messe noir (adapted from selected stories in *Contes pour buveurs attardes*), first produced in Montreal, 1965.
(With Andre Brassard) *Lysistrata* (translated and adapted from Aristophanes's play of the same title; first produced in Ottawa, 1969), Lemeac (Montreal, Quebec, Canada), 1969.
L'Effet des rayons gamma sur les vieux-garcons (translated and adapted from Paul Zindel's *The Effect of Gamma Rays on Man-in-the-Moon Marigolds;* first produced in Montreal, 1970), Lemeac (Montreal, Quebec, Canada), 1970.
". . . *Et Mademoiselle Roberge boit un peu. . .* " (three-act; translated and adapted from Paul Zindel's play *And Miss Reardon Drinks a Little;* first produced in Montreal, 1972), Lemeac (Montreal, Quebec, Canada), 1971.
Le Pays du Dragon (translated and adapted from four of Tennessee Williams's one-act plays), first produced in Montreal, 1971.
Mistero buffo (translated and adapted from Dario Fo's play of the same name), first produced in Montreal, 1973.
Mademoiselle Marguerite (translated and adapted from Roberto Athayde's *Aparaceu a Margarida;* first produced in Ottawa, 1976), Lemeac (Montreal, Quebec, Canada), 1975.
(With Kim Yaroshevskaya) *Oncle Vania* (translated and adapted from Anton Chekhov's play of the same name), Lemeac (Montreal, Quebec, Canada), 1983.
Le Gars de Quebec (adapted from Nikolay Gogol's *Le Revizov;* first produced in Montreal, 1985), Lemeac (Montreal, Quebec, Canada), 1985.
Six heures au plus tard (adapted from a work by Marc Perrier; first produced in Montreal, 1986), Lemeac (Montreal, Quebec, Canada), 1986.
Que a peur de Virginia Woolf (translated and adapted from Edward Albee's *Who's Afraid of Virginia Woolf*), first produced in Montreal, 1988.
Les Trompettes de la Mort (adapted from a work by Nicolas de Koning Tilly), first produced in Montreal, 1991.
Premiere de classe (adapted from a work by Casey Kurtti), first produced in Montreal, 1992.

OTHER

(With Claude Paulette and Luc Noppen) *Quebec, trois siecles d'architecture,* Libre Expression, 1979.
Nelligan (opera libretto; produced in Montreal, 1990), Lemeac (Montreal, Quebec, Canada), 1990.
Les Vues Animées, Lemeac (Montreal, Quebec, Canada), 1990, translation by Sheila Fischman published as *Bambi and Me,* Talon Books (Vancouver, British Columbia, Canada), 1998.
Pieces a Conviction: Entretiens avec Michel Tremblay/ Luc Boulanger, Lemeac (Montreal, Quebec, Canada), 2001.

Also author of *Bonheur d'occasion,* an adaptation of a novel by Gabrielle Roy, 1977. Contributor to anthologies, including *Heroines,* edited by Joyce Doolittle, Players Press (Studio City, CA), 1992. Also contributor to periodicals, including *La Barre de Jour.* A collection of Tremblay's manuscripts is held at the Bibliotheque National du Canada, Ottawa.

ADAPTATIONS: Sainte-Carmen of the Main was adapted as a two-act opera with music by Sydney Hodkinson, libretto by Lee Devin, and published by Associated Music Publishers, 1986.

SIDELIGHTS: Michel Tremblay is "the most important Quebeçois artist of his generation," declared Salem Alaton in a Toronto *Globe and Mail* review. Beginning his career in the mid-1960s, the French-Canadian playwright, fiction writer, and screenwriter has become best known for dramatic works that challenge traditional myths of French-Canadian life. Indeed, for years critics have contended that Tremblay's concentration on the social and cultural problems of Quebec earned him local acclaim at the expense of more universal recognition. In the 1980s, however, Tremblay began to command an international audience. Alaton theorized that it is the "edgy, Quebeçois specificity" of Tremblay's work, once considered a liability, that has ultimately been responsible for the playwright's success. With his work widely translated and produced, Tremblay is now regarded as a world-class dramatist who, in the words of *Quill and Quire* reviewer Mark

Czarnecki, provides a persuasive example "of the much-debated cultural proposition that the more local the reference, the more universal the truth."

Tremblay grew up in the east end of Montreal, in the working-class neighborhood of the rue Fabre. The oppressive conditions of life in this impoverished area, along with the glitzy nightlife of the Main district, later provided the backdrop for much of Tremblay's work. Despite the inauspicious environment of his youth, Tremblay began writing when quite young and was a promising student who at age thirteen received a scholarship to a classical college. Unable to endure the elitist attitudes fostered at the school, however, Tremblay left after several months to study graphic arts and become a linotype operator. He nevertheless continued to write during those years and by the time he was eighteen had completed his first play, *Le Train.* Several years later, in 1964, it won first prize in Radio Canada's Young Author Competition.

Shortly thereafter, Tremblay made Quebec theater history. Eschewing the classical French typically used in works for the stage, Tremblay wrote a play, *Les Belles-Soeurs,* in *joual,* the language of the people. Though Tremblay had not intended to create a political work, his use of *joual*—regarded by many as a debased form of the French language—signaled to his detractors and supporters alike the desire to supplant the province's traditional French culture with an independent Quebec culture. His critics decried the play while his admirers lauded it as a contribution to what is known in Quebec as the "theatre of liberation."

Written in 1965 but denied production until 1968, *Les Belles-Soeurs* catapulted the young dramatist to fame. The play was not radical, however, for its language alone. *Les Belles-Soeurs* was also controversial for its naturalistic view of French-Canadian life. Its plot is straightforward: after winning one million trading stamps, Gabriel Lauzon, an average east-end Montreal homemaker invites her women friends to a stamp-pasting gathering; by play's end, the women have turned on one another in a battle for the stamps. *Les Belles-Soeurs,* averred John Ripley in a critique for *Canadian Literature,* "explodes two centuries of popular belief, ecclesiastical teaching, and literary myth about Quebeçois women. Far from being the traditional guardians of religious and moral values, happy progenitors of large families, and good-humored housekeepers, they stand revealed as malevolent misfits, consumed with hatred of life and of themselves."

Les Belles-Soeurs is the first in what became an eleven-play cycle which, in its entirety, many critics regarded as Tremblay's finest achievement. Ripley suggested that Quebec's "recent past, characterized by a desperate struggle to replace authoritarianism, negative identity, and destructiveness with self-respect, love, and transcendence, is nowhere better encapsulated than in the *Les Belles-Soeurs* cycle." Ripley's sentiments were echoed by critic Renate Usmiani, who in his *Studies in Canadian Literature: Michel Tremblay* stated: "The most general underlying theme of all [Tremblay's] works is the universal desire of the human being to transcend his finite condition." More specifically, Usmiani proposed that the typical Tremblay character is either trying to escape from family life as represented by the rue Fabre, from the false world of the Main, or from the limitations of self into a transcendent ecstasy.

One picture of life along the rue Fabre is offered by *A toi, pour toujours, ta Marie-Lou.* Deemed "a devastating psycho-social analysis of the traditional working-class Quebeçois family" by Ripley, the play presents four characters juxtaposed in two different time periods. Marie-Louise is a homemaker whose problems manifest themselves as sexual frigidity and religious fanaticism; Leopold, her husband, is a factory worker who becomes an alcoholic. Their marriage, according to Ripley, "is a sado-masochistic battle with no prospect of victory for either side," and thus Leopold ends their lives in a suicidal car crash. The drama progresses as, ten years later, their daughters discuss the tragedy and its impact on their lives. Manon, still living in the family home, has remained loyal to her mother and taken refuge in a similar fanaticism, seemingly unable to save herself. For Carmen, who has managed to make a life for herself as a singer in the Main district, there appears to be some hope. Both characters return in subsequent plays.

Although Leopold and Marie-Louise die to escape the rue Fabre, Tremblay's pen finds others searching for alternatives in the world of the Main. For them, "the Main stands for glamour, freedom, life itself," asserted Usmiani. Typified by prostitutes and transvestites, however, the Main, in Usmiani's opinion, "turns out to be ultimately as inbred, frustrating and limiting, in its own kinky way, as the petty household world around rue Fabre." *La Duchesse de Langeais* and *Hosanna,* whose title characters seek escape from reality in homosexuality, provide two examples. The former is a dramatic monologue delivered by the Duchess, an aging transvestite prostitute who has been rejected by a younger lover. Ripley theorized that the Duchess has chosen to "escape from male impotence" by "the adoption of a role precisely the opposite of the one normally expected." Cast aside by his young partner, however, the Duchess fails to find satisfaction and remains an essentially pathetic character. More optimistically, *Hosanna* finds lovers Hosanna (Claude), who is forever role-playing, and Cuirette (Raymond) beginning to communicate after a particularly humiliating crisis. They are eventually able to discard their female personas and accept themselves as male homosexuals, freely admitting their love for one another. In so doing, according to Ripley, the two realize that although they are different, they still have a place in the world.

In *Damnée Manon, sacrée Sandra,* the final play of the cycle, Tremblay moves away from the nightmare of family life and illusions of the Main to explore the possibility of fulfillment through mysticism. The drama unfolds through the monologues of two characters. Manon, from the earlier *A toi, pour toujours, ta Marie-Lou,* represents an attempt at transcendence through religious mysticism. Sandra, who also appeared previously in Tremblay's work, is a transvestite who seeks transcendence through sex. Both now live on the rue Fabre, as they did in childhood, and during the course of the play each comes to appreciate that the other has chosen a different path toward the same goal. Usmiani described the two characters as "physical incarnations, exteriorizations, of the two paths toward ecstasy conceived by the author," adding that on one level their world "is not a physical reality on the rue Fabre, but the psychological reality of the poet's own mind." The critic concluded that in Tremblay's work "there is no transcendence beyond that which the self can provide."

By the time Tremblay finished the *Belles-Soeurs* cycle in 1977, the political climate in Quebec had improved, and he gave permission, previously withheld, for his plays to be produced in English in Quebec. At this juncture he also switched genres, beginning work on a series of semi-autobiographical novels. The playwright's venture into fiction has been successful, and thus far, at least two of the volumes in his "Chroniques du plateau Mont-Royal" tetralogy have been translated into English. The first volume in the series, *La Grosse Femme d'a côte est enceinte,* was translated as *The Fat Woman Next Door Is Pregnant.* Not only are the characters of this novel residents of the rue Fabre, as in so many of Tremblay's dramas, but the fat woman of the title is Tremblay's mother, and the story is based on the author's recollections of life in the apartment of his birth. *Quill and Quire* reviewer Czarnecki contended that *The Fat Woman*'s one-day time frame achieves "a similar effect" to that of James Joyce's famed *Ulysses.* Reviewing for the same publication, Philip Stratford called *The Fat Woman* "a generous, good-natured fresco teeming with life and invention." Regarded as both funny and sentimental, the book became a best-seller in Quebec. Its sequel, *Therese et Pierrette a l'ecole des Saints-Anges,* translated as *Therese and Pierrette and the Little Hanging Angel,* also fared well, winning the prestigious Prix France-Quebec in 1981. Set during a four-day time period, the volume concentrates on three eleven-year-old students at the École des Saints-Anges, a Roman Catholic girls' school. In this novel censuring the religious education system, Tremblay exhibits "epic gifts," in Czarnecki's opinion, that "extend to capturing life in its smallest details, creating an imaginative world complete in itself, ready to immerse and rebaptize the reader."

Tremblay concluded his tetralogy with *La Duchesse et le Roturier* in 1982 and *Des Nouvelles d'Edouard* in 1984. During the 1980s, however, Tremblay also returned to writing plays. Although some critics regard his dramas of the eighties as unequal to his earlier work, many of them appraise the 1987 *Le Vrai Monde?* as his best.

In this play Tremblay looks back to 1965, to his own beginning as an artist, and questions what right he had to use the lives of family and friends in service to his art. Calling it both "an expression of guilt" and "an eloquent statement about the relationship between art and life," *Globe and Mail* critic Matthew Fraser found *Le Vrai Monde?* "a masterful piece of drama." Another reviewer for the *Globe and Mail,* Ray Conlogue, contended that it is "a formidable play" in which Tremblay tries "to defend his art." In his interview for the Toronto paper with Alaton, Tremblay offered a slightly different perspective, telling the critic: "It is almost a condemnation of what an artist does to real life." And when Alaton asked him why he wrote, the dramatist responded: "Maybe I am an artist because artists give purpose to a thing which has not purpose, which is life. . . . You put [a play] before 500 people every night and you say, 'Sometimes, this is what life might mean.' And people who live the same nonsense life as you understand this."

Tremblay's 1990 play *La Maison Suspendue* departs from other Tremblay plays in that it is set in rural Quebec rather than in Montreal. In the play, three generations of a family endure life in a big house in the country. The generations are bound together by an eleven-year-old boy, who appears as the same person in each generation. "*La Maison Suspendue* is about the ways in which a family creates and recreates itself through stories," remarked *Books in Canada* contributor Ann Jansen. Writing in *Canadian Literature,* Neal Carson noted, "The play can be read as a story of family conflict and reconciliation, or even as an expression of the author's own regrets and apprehensions as he reaches late middle age."

In *Les Vues animées,* Tremblay presents a dozen autobiographical narratives, each centered around a particular movie. "With this charming collection of short, autobiographical narratives, Tremblay affirms his double debt to the cinema as spiritual mother of his creative awakening and catalyst of the initiatory phases of his early years," commented Constantina Mitchell in *Canadian Literature.* Discussing the work with David Homel of *Books in Canada,* Tremblay explained, "I wanted to write a coming-of-age book using the movies. Each chapter was like a step forward for the character, a discovery—of fear, of sexuality, of art—and that thematic aspect saved me from nostalgia."

Commenting on Tremblay's contribution to French-Canadian literature, Marie Claire Blais noted in *Time International* that "sensitivity and compassion are precisely the qualities that make Michel Tremblay's work so universal, humane and understanding. . . . He has the gift of speaking to us all, giving voice to our truest feelings with the greatest simplicity and directness. He sees through our eyes and speaks with our words, however distinct we are from one another."

BIOGRAPHICAL AND CRITICAL SOURCES:

BOOKS

Anthony, Geraldine, *Stage Voices: Twelve Canadian Playwrights Talk about Their Lives and Work,* Doubleday (New York, NY), 1978, pp. 275-91.

Belair, Michel, *Michel Tremblay,* Press de L'Universite du Quebec, 1972.

Contemporary Literary Criticism, Volume 29, Thomson Gale (Detroit, MI), 1984.

Contemporary World Writers, 2nd edition, St. James Press (Detroit, MI), 1993.

Dargnat, Mathilde, *Michel Tremblay,* Harmattan (Paris, France), 2002.

Dictionary of Literary Biography, Volume 60: *Canadian Writers since 1960, Second Series,* Thomson Gale (Detroit, MI), 1987.

Gay and Lesbian Literature, St. James Press (Detroit, MI), 1994.

Godin, Jean-Cleo, and Laurent Mailhot, *Le Theatre quebeçois,* HMH (Montreal, Quebec, Canada), 1970, pp. 191-202.

International Dictionary of Theatre, Volume 2: *Playwrights,* St. James Press (Detroit, MI), 1994.

Massey, Irving, *Identity And Community: Reflections on English, Yiddish, and French Literature in Canada,* Wayne State University Press (Detroit, MI), 1994.

Usmiani, Renate, *Michel Tremblay: A Critical Study,* Douglas & McIntyre (Vancouver, British Columbia, Canada), 1981.

Usmiani, Renate, *Studies in Canadian Literature: Michel Tremblay,* Douglas & McIntyre (Vancouver, British Columbia, Canada), 1982.

PERIODICALS

Americas, September-October 1995, Barbara Mujica, review of *Un Ange Corneau avec Ailes de Tole* p.62.

Books in Canada, January-February, 1986; February, 1992, pp. 16, 28; March, 1995, p. 38.

Canadian Drama, number 2, 1976, pp. 206-218.

Canadian Literature, summer, 1980; autumn, 1992, p. 171; spring, 1993, p. 134.

Canadian Theatre Review, fall, 1979, pp. 12-37.

Chicago Tribune, March 8, 1980.

Essays on Canadian Writing, number 11, 1978.

Globe and Mail, November 16, 1986; April 25, 1987; October 3, 1987.

Maclean's, April 30, 1984; April 22, 1985; March 19, 1990, p. 56; December 30, 1991, pp. 36-37; December 30, 1991, p. 36.

New York Times, December 11, 1983.

Perspectives, February 17, 1973, pp. 6-9.

Quebec Studies, number 4, 1986.

Quill and Quire, February, 1982; April, 1982; June, 1984; January, 1995, p. 38.

Studies in Canadian Literature, Volume 14, number 2, 1989.

Time International, December 6, 2002, Marie Clair Blais, "Passionate Humanist: Michel Tremblay," p. 53.

Variety, January 24, 1994, p. 76.

Washington Post, June 22, 1978.

* * *

TREVOR, William 1928-
(William Trevor Cox)

PERSONAL: Born May 24, 1928, in Mitchelstown, County Cork, Ireland; son of James William (a bank official) and Gertrude (Davison) Cox; married Jane Ryan, August 26, 1952; children: Patrick, Dominic. *Educa-*

tion: Attended St. Columba's College (Dublin, Ireland), 1941-46; Trinity College (Dublin, Ireland), B.A., 1950. *Politics:* Liberal.

ADDRESSES: Office—c/o Sterling Lord Literistic Ltd., 1 Madison Ave, New York, NY 10010; c/o Peters, Fraser & Dunlop Group, 503-504 The Chambers, Chelsea Harbour, Lots Road, London SW10 0FX, England.

CAREER: Teacher in County Armagh, Northern Ireland, 1952-53; art teacher at prep school near Rugby, England, 1953-55, and in Somerset, England, 1956-59; while teaching, worked as a church sculptor; advertising copywriter for Notley's, London, England, 1960-65; writer, 1965—. *Exhibitions:* One-man exhibitions in Dublin, Ireland, and Bath, England.

MEMBER: Irish Academy of Letters.

AWARDS, HONORS: Winner of Irish section, "Unknown Political Prisoner" sculpture competition, 1953; second prize, *Transatlantic Review* short story competition, 1964; Hawthornden Prize, Royal Society of Literature, 1965, for *The Old Boys;* Society of Authors' traveling scholarship, 1972; Benson Medal, Royal Society of Literature, 1975, for *Angels at the Ritz, and Other Stories;* Allied Irish Bank Prize for literature, 1976; Heinemann Award for fiction, 1976; Whitbread Prize, 1978, for *The Children of Dynmouth,* and 1983, for *Fools of Fortune;* Commander, Order of the British Empire, 1979; Irish Community Prize, 1979; Giles Cooper Award for radio play, 1980, for *Beyond the Pale,* and 1982, for *Autumn Sunshine;* Jacob Award for television play, 1983; D.Litt., University of Exeter, 1984, Trinity College, Dublin, 1986, University of Belfast, 1989, and National University of Ireland, Cork, 1990; *Sunday Express* Book of the Year Award, and Whitbread Prize, both 1994, both for *Felicia's Journey;* Lannan Literary Award for Fiction, 1996; David Cohen British Literature Prize, 1999; Macmillan Silver Pen Award, and *Irish Times* Literary Award for Fiction, 2001, both for *The Hill Bachelors;* shortlisted for Booker Prize, 2002, for *The Story of Lucy Gault;* received honorary knighthood for services to literature, presented by Ireland's Culture Secretary Tessa Jowell; shortlisted for Whitbread Prize for best novel and James Tait Black Memorial Prize for fiction, both 2002, for *The Story of Lucy Gault;* Knighted, Queen Elizabeth II of Great Britain, 2002, for his service to literature.

WRITINGS:

NOVELS

A Standard of Behavior, Hutchinson (London, England), 1958.

The Old Boys (also see below), Viking (New York, NY), 1964.

The Boarding-House, Viking (New York, NY), 1965.

The Love Department, Bodley Head (London, England), 1966, Viking (New York, NY), 1967.

Mrs. Eckdorf in O'Neill's Hotel, Bodley Head (London, England), 1969, Viking (New York, NY), 1970.

Miss Gomez and the Brethren, Bodley Head (London, England), 1971.

Elizabeth Alone, Bodley Head (London, England), 1973, Viking (New York, NY), 1974.

The Children of Dynmouth, Bodley Head (London, England), 1976, Viking (New York, NY), 1977.

Other People's Worlds, Bodley Head (London, England), 1980, Viking (New York, NY), 1981.

Fools of Fortune, Viking (New York, NY), 1983.

Nights at the Alexandra, Harper (New York, NY), 1987.

The Silence in the Garden, Viking (New York, NY), 1988.

Two Lives (contains the novels *Reading Turgenev* and *My House in Umbria*), Viking (New York, NY), 1991.

Felicia's Journey, Viking (New York, NY), 1994.

Juliet's Story, Simon & Schuster (New York, NY), 1994.

The Silence in the Garden, Penguin (New York, NY), 1996.

Death in Summer, Viking (New York, NY), 1998.

The Story of Lucy Gault, Viking (New York, NY), 2002.

My House in Umbria (see *Two Lives* above), Penguin Books (New York, NY), 2003.

STORIES

The Day We Got Drunk on Cake, and Other Stories, Bodley Head (London, England), 1967, Viking (New York, NY), 1968.

The Ballroom of Romance, and Other Stories (includes "The Mark-2 Wife," "The Grass Widows," and "O Fat White Woman"; also see below), Viking (New York, NY), 1972.

Angels at the Ritz, and Other Stories, Bodley Head (London, England), 1975, Viking (New York, NY), 1976.

Lovers of Their Time, and Other Stories (includes "Matilda's England" and "Attracta"), Viking (New York, NY), 1978.

The Distant Past, and Other Stories, Poolbeg Press (Dublin Ireland), 1979.

Beyond the Pale, and Other Stories, Bodley Head (London, England), 1981, Viking (New York, NY), 1982.

The Stories of William Trevor (includes "The Penthouse Apartment," "Broken Homes," "A Complicated Nature," and "In at the Birth"), Penguin (England), 1983.

The News from Ireland, and Other Stories, Viking (New York, NY), 1986.

Family Sins, and Other Stories (includes "Kathleen's Field," "Events at Drimaghleen," "Coffee with Oliver," and "The Third Party"), Viking (New York, NY), 1989.

William Trevor: Collected Stories, Viking (New York, NY), 1992.

Outside Ireland: Selected Stories, Penguin (New York, NY), 1995.

Cocktails at Doney's and Other Stories, Bloomsbury, 1996.

After Rain: Stories, Viking (New York, NY), 1996.

Ireland: Selected Stories, Penguin (New York, NY), 1998.

The Hill Bachelors, Viking (New York, NY), 2000.

A Bit on the Side, Viking (New York, NY), 2004.

Also author of other stories, including "The Wedding in the Garden," "Mulvihill's Memorial," "Miss Smith," "The Bedroom Eyes of Mrs. Vansittart," and "The Time of Year." Stories anthologized in numerous collections, including *The Bedside Guardian,* edited by W.L. Webb, Collins, 1969, *The Bodley Head Book of Longer Short Stories,* edited by James Michie, Bodley Head (London, England), 1974, *Best for Winter,* edited by A.D. Maclean, Macmillan, 1979, *The Bodley Head Book of Irish Short Stories,* edited by Marcus, Bodley Head (London, England), 1980, and *Seven Deadly Sins,* Severn House, 1983.

PLAYS

The Elephant's Foot, produced in Nottingham, England, 1966.

The Girl, S. French (London, England), 1968.

The Old Boys (adapted from his novel; produced in the West End, 1971), Davis-Poynter, 1971.

Going Home (one-act; produced in London, England, at King's Head Islington, February 29, 1972), S. French (London, England), 1972.

A Night with Mrs. da Tanka (one-act; produced in London, England, 1972), S. French (London, England), 1972.

A Perfect Relationship (one-act), produced in London, England, 1973.

The 57th Saturday (one-act), produced in London, England, 1973.

Marriages (one-act; produced in London, England, 1973), S. French (London, England), 1974.

Beyond the Pale (radio play), broadcast in England, 1980, televised, 1989.

Scenes from an Album, produced in Dublin, Ireland, at the Abbey Theatre, 1981.

Also author of television and radio plays for British Broadcasting Corporation, Inc. (BBC) and ITV, some adapted from his stories, including *The Mark-2 Wife, O Fat White Woman, The Grass Widows,The General's Day, Love Affair, Last Wishes, Matilda's England, Secret Orchards, Autumn Sunshine,The Penthouse Apartment, Travellers,* and *Events at Drimaghleen.*

OTHER

Old School Ties (memoir), Lemon Tree Press (London, England), 1976.

A Writer's Ireland: Landscape in Literature (nonfiction), Viking (New York, NY), 1984.

(Editor) *The Oxford Book of Irish Short Stories,* Oxford University Press (New York, NY), 1989.

Excursions in the Real World: Autobiographical Essays, Knopf (New York, NY), 1994.

A collection of Trevor's manuscripts is housed at the University of Tulsa.

ADAPTATIONS: *The Old Boys* was adapted as a BBC television play, 1965; *The Ballroom of Romance* was broadcast on BBC-TV, 1982; *The Children of Dynmouth* was aired on BBC-TV, 1987; a screenplay by Michael Hirst was based on *Fools of Fortune* and directed by Pat O'Connor, 1990; *Elizabeth Alone* was also produced for BBC-TV; *Felicia's Journey* was adapted as a film by Atom Egoyan, 1999; *My House in Umbria* was adapted for film by Hugh Whitemore, directed by Richard Loncraine, and premiered on HBO, May 25, 2003.

SIDELIGHTS: Short story writer, novelist, and playwright William Trevor is an Irish-born English writer. Considered by many critics to be one of the finest living short story writers in English, Trevor is equally renowned as a novelist, and is widely known in England for the television adaptations of his novels. Having lived in both Ireland and England, Trevor has written about people in both countries, often focusing on ordinary people who lead tragic, lonely lives. "I don't really have any heroes or heroines," Trevor remarked in a

Publishers Weekly interview with Amanda Smith. "I don't seem to go in for them. I think I am interested in people who are not necessarily the victims of other people, but simply the victims of circumstances. . . . I'm very interested in the sadness of fate, the things that just happen to people." Originally working as a sculptor, Trevor became displeased with the increasingly abstract turn his art was taking, and so he took up writing as a means of better expressing his concern for the human condition. "I think the humanity that isn't in abstract art began to go into [my] short stories," Trevor told Smith.

Trevor's ability to empathize with a broad array of characters is among the qualities that critics most admire in his fiction. A contributor to the *Economist* praised Trevor as "piercingly sympathetic with the most socially negligible passer-by," while *Commonweal*'s Suzanne Berne hailed his blend of "microscopically precise detail and cosmic insights into the human heart." A *Publishers Weekly* reviewer observed that Trevor "is equally able to inhabit the worlds of priests, restless American expatriates and quarrelsome academics, always with an acute sense of their wide range of voices and habits of mind."

In much of Trevor's fiction, the events or situations that most affect his characters occur offstage and often years in the past. Sometimes these are personal, as in *The Old Boys,* in which the public school reunion of eight octogenarians causes them to revert back to childish competitive behavior by reminding them of old grudges and rivalries. In other cases these events are historical, as in the "The Mourning," from *The Hill Bachelors,* in which a naïve young man is almost persuaded to plant a bomb for the IRA. His realization that, before him, another young man had died in this attempt gives him the strength to reject the job.

Satire is also prominent in such early Trevor books as *The Boarding-House* and *The Love Department,* although the situations in which his characters find themselves are often lamentable. However, *New York Times Book Review* critic Robert Towers wrote, since "the mid-1970's there has been . . . a subtle change of tone in the stories. The harsh comedy—the gleeful misanthropy—is less in evidence, as is the stance of impartiality; in the later work one can guess rather clearly where the author's sympathies lie."

In what one *Times Literary Supplement* reviewer declared to be "a collection that is never disappointing," *The Ballroom of Romance, and Other Stories* portrays a series of characters who are caught in dreary, barren lives, but lack the necessary confidence to change. Instead, they can only reflect upon what might have been, their memories and dreams leaving them isolated and alone. The reviewer noted, "The stories may be sad, but they have about them the unmistakable ring of truth." It is with these sad stories of ordinary people that the author finds himself repeatedly concerned. They may live unhappy lives because of their unwillingness or inability to give up the past or their illusions of reality, or, as with Trevor's *Elizabeth Alone,* because they are simply victims of fate.

In *Elizabeth Alone* Trevor first proposes a possible reason for human suffering. Set in a hospital, the book presents a series of ostensibly comic situations while simultaneously probing deeper issues through its sympathetic character portrayals. The title character, Elizabeth Aidallbery, has in one way or another lost everyone who was important in her life and has even begun to lose her sense of identity. She finds the strength to overcome her loneliness and carry on through one of her hospital mates, Miss Samson, whose religious faith has recently been shaken. Miss Samson convinces Elizabeth that the importance of caring for others, even—or perhaps especially—if the world has no God, gives people a purpose in life. A *Times Literary Supplement* reviewer complimented Trevor on his ability to execute this conclusion convincingly in a seriocomic novel, attributing this success to "the authority he has built up, as a writer, out of the sheer, detailed understanding of the characters he creates. . . . The stance of compassion which is adopted finally in *Elizabeth Alone* can now be seen to be implicit in all Mr. Trevor's best work. It gives him a place as a writer capable of handling the human comedy instead of merely manipulating comic human beings."

Collections such as *Angels at the Ritz, and Other Stories* and *Lovers of Their Time, and Other Stories* continue to illustrate Trevor's concern for average people and the importance of the effects of time. "Trevor is especially adept at making the presence of the past, the presence of people offstage, lean upon his characters," said Peter S. Prescott in a *Newsweek* review of *Angels at the Ritz.* Similarly, *New York Times Book Review* contributor Victoria Glendinning commented on the stories in *Lovers of Their Time,* "Nothing very extraordinary happens to [Trevor's] teachers, tradesmen, farmers and shop-assistants; the action is all off-stage, and they are caught and thrown off course by the wash of great and passionate events that happened in another time, another place."

With *The Children of Dynmouth,* Trevor's first Whitbread Prize-winning book, the author focuses on an unsympathetic boy named Timothy Gedge. Abandoned by his father and ignored by the rest of his family, Timothy has become a despicable character who has a crude sense of humor and is fascinated by death. Desperate for attention, he becomes convinced that he can find fame by doing an act for the variety television show, "Opportunity Knocks." But to get the props he needs, Timothy blackmails several of the respectable citizens of Dynmouth and "by the novel's end he has come close to destroying several people," wrote Joyce Carol Oates in the *New York Times Book Review.* "Timothy's malice arises from his chronic aloneness, so that it isn't possible, as the [character of] the vicar recognizes, to see the boy as evil."

Some critics saw Timothy's rescue by the vicar at the novel's conclusion to be a weak solution to an otherwise excellent book. "To imply that sooner or later the shrinks and the socialists will put an end to evil is to drag out an old chestnut indeed," wrote *Sewanee Review* contributor Walter Sullivan. Sullivan found that this flaw negates "the fine performance which leads up to this foolishness." Thomas R. Edwards commented in the *New York Review of Books* that *The Children of Dynmouth* "succeeds in being funny, frightening, and morally poised and intelligent at once." Oates similarly concluded that it is "a skillfully written novel, a small masterpiece of understatement."

In another Whitbread Prize-winning novel, *Fools of Fortune,* Trevor chronicles the years of lonely isolation of two lovers separated by a tragic turn of fate. *Washington Post Book World* critic Charles Champlin called the book a "benchmark novel against which other contemporary novels will have to be measured," one which reflects the "last seven decades of English-Irish history." The novel relates how British soldiers misguidedly destroy Willie Quinton's family and home in the year 1918, and how Willie's revenge on a British officer leads to his exile from Ireland. Forced to leave his beloved English cousin, Marianne, he is denied the chance to see her or their daughter, Imelda, for years to come. The Quintons, remarked Jonathan Yardley in the *Washington Post Book World,* "are all good, honorable people, but they—like poor Ireland—are victims of mere chance, arbitrary and random."

With other tales, such as the central story of *The News from Ireland, and Other Stories* and the novel *The Silence in the Garden,* Trevor relates the struggles in Ireland to the misfortunes of his characters and, as Richard Eder of the *Los Angeles Times* put it, "the passing of a kind of civility that Yeats celebrated." In the case of *The Silence in the Garden,* the story of how war and terrorism ruin a once-happy and prosperous Anglo-Irish family, *Washington Post Book World* critic Gregory A. Schirmer noted that Trevor "has much to say about the attitudes and patterns that lie behind the [British-Irish] violence, and about the ways in which the present is inevitably—and, in Ireland, often tragically—shaped by the past."

Although Trevor's stories and novels often involve dramatic events, he is mainly concerned with how these events preoccupy and obsess his characters. This inner tension is subtly portrayed through the author's quiet, understated writing style. Michiko Kakutani of the *New York Times* described this style in a review of *Fools of Fortune* as "spare, lilting prose . . . delineat[ing] these melodramatic events with economy and precision." For some critics, however, Trevor's use of understatement is a drawback in his writing. Anatole Broyard, for one, wrote in a *New York Times* review of *Beyond the Pale and Other Stories,* "Though everyone regards [Trevor] as a master of understatement, I wonder whether it isn't conceited in a way to insist on writing such carefully removed stories, so breathlessly poised on the edge of nonexistence."

In 1992 sixty of Trevor's short stories were published in *William Trevor: Collected Stories.* Reviewers were generally enthusiastic about the quality of the collection. Joseph Coates wrote in the Chicago *Tribune Books,* "The stories of this modern master often hinge on a slightness and subtlety that are the last thing we think of hefting a volume of this size." Coates went on to say that "despite this massive output, the salient characteristic of his work is the careful craftsmanship that produces its deceptively transparent surfaces. . . . What gives Trevor's stories their paradoxical sparkle . . . is his fascination with the endless variety and sheer unaccountability of human life, the infinite inventiveness with which people make their odd, pathetic but always somehow dignified arrangements for getting through their days and nights, with or without satisfaction, with or without the slimmest of memories to sustain them."

Trevor's sympathy for outcasts is at the core of his 1994 novel, *Felicia's Journey.* The plot concerns a young Irish girl, Felicia, who travels to the gloomy industrial districts of England in search of the young man who seduced and then abandoned her. She is preyed upon by Mr. Hilditch, a huge, lonely man with hidden sociopathic tendencies. Cunningly he weaves his web around her, engineering "chance" meetings and making innocent-sounding offers of help to her. Felicia stays with him for a time, and then, sensing evil, turns to Mrs. Calligary, a door-to-door evangelist. But when the missionary-like retreat Mrs. Calligary offers becomes unbearable, Felicia returns to her doom at Mr. Hilditch's residence. Reviewers differed sharply in their assessment of *Felicia's Journey.* Some, such as *Spectator* contributor Peregrine Hodson, found the book's many references to brand names and other details to be pointless and tedious. "Having finished *Felicia's Journey,* I felt I had read an extremely long short story," remarked Hodson. "Some may find, in the author's descriptions of minutiae, evidence of the artist's eye, which misses nothing. Others may feel the accumulation of trivia—'Marlboro, it said on the packet on the table'—clogs the narrative."

Richard Eder expressed a more serious objection to the book in the *Los Angeles Times Book Review.* He praised the author's rendering of Felicia, stating that "William Trevor, who is good at a great deal, is particularly good with the meek; and most particularly with the rural Irish meek. He finds the passion in them and he finds the ruses they devise to preserve . . . their lives." But Eder dismissed Mr. Hilditch as an unconvincing authorial device, one which unfortunately dominated the book: "True, [Trevor] can do splendid bullies, tricksters and arrogant bastards; but in each case he builds on their humanity and warps it just enough. . . . A monster, on the other hand, is a kind of void. . . . A writer can portray a man with a hole—an absence—in him, but a writer needs to be a special kind of metaphysician . . . to make the hole the character. . . . Hilditch is not enough of a character to generate a moral or significant action; he is a device through which the author acts."

Trevor's collection of stories, *After Rain,* is set in the familiar setting of Irish villages; more stories of failed relationships are displayed as Trevor describes a huge range of human emotions. Kakutani remarked that Trevor writes "with such assurance that he's able to collapse entire lives into a few brief pages, showing us how a character's past connects to his future, how his fate, in short, has been constructed." Some critics thought the collection lacks humor, and Kakutani believed there is a decided "mood of resignation" that permeates the stories.

The Hill Bachelors, Trevor's tenth volume of short stories, drew consistent praise. Finding some of the weaker stories marked by too much authorial manipulation, Kakutani nevertheless noted that Trevor "always manages to give the reader a sense of the entire arc of their lives," and hailed the volume for its "masterful variations on . . . familiar melodies, demonstrating once again [Trevor's] authority and poise as a storyteller, his Chekhovian understanding of missed connections and misplaced hopes." Suggesting that the book reveals more generosity toward its characters than is evident in Trevor's earlier work, *New York Times Book Review* contributor William H. Pritchard found the collection wise and moving. "No story here," claimed Brad Hooper in *Booklist,* "is anything less than a bravura performance." Among the stories that critics singled out for special praise were "Death of a Professor," in which a university don guesses what his colleagues really think of him after his fake obituary is published as a prank; "Against the Odds," in which an enterprising older woman lures a susceptible widower into "lending" her his life savings and then disappears; and the title story, concerning a young farmer's return to the land where no young woman is inclined to follow him.

The setting for Trevor's novel *The Story of Lucy Gault* is 1920s Ireland in the throes of violent upheaval. The privileged Gault family is considering moving to England, Mrs. Gault's home, but their daughter Lucy wants to stay in the country she loves and runs away. "By the middle of the second paragraph of *The Story of Lucy Gault,* everything that is going to happen . . . has been set in motion by a single act of violence, a night of terrifying but (given the novel's setting, Ireland during the 1920s) unexceptional, even quotidian, mayhem and menace," wrote Francine Prose in *Harper's.* The fateful event is Captain Gault's wounding of one of three young men who have come to set fire to their family home. This event makes the Gaults ultimately realize that they will never be safe in Ireland again. When Lucy runs away and becomes injured in a fall, the Gaults come to the mistaken conclusion that she has drowned and leave Ireland. Lucy is eventually found but her parents have virtually disappeared and their whereabouts remain unknown for the next thirty years. Writing in the *Atlantic Monthly,* a reviewer noted, "Exile, guilt, the peculiar (peculiarly Irish) fatalism that guilt engenders, and the ordinary antidotes for these griefs—religion, art, an orderly life . . . are the subjects and themes of *The Story of Lucy Gault,* but they are hardly the sum of its effect. For in his stately depiction of a tragic tale that might, in other hands, seem overwrought, perhaps even overdetermined, Trevor has once again captured the terrible beauty of Ireland's fate, and the fate of us all—at the mercy of history, circumstance, and the vicissitudes of time." *New Statesman* contributor Geordie Greig commented, "It is rare to read a novel where not a single word seems out of place. William Trevor's new novel is such a book." Diana

McRae, writing in *Library Journal,* said that "Trevor's smooth, spare prose captures the quirky workings of the heart, and compassion for the human condition mitigates the harsh blows that fate often deals his characters."

Trevor has been compared to such luminaries as Muriel Spark, Anton Chekov, and Andre Malraux, but most often to his Irish predecessor, James Joyce. *New York Times Book Review* critic Ted Solotaroff compared Joyce and Trevor this way: "Both Trevor and the early Joyce are geniuses at presenting a seemingly ordinary life as it is, socially, psychologically, morally, and then revealing the force of these conditions in the threatened individual's moment of resistance to them. This is the deeper realism: accurate observation turning into moral vision." "Yet like Joyce before him," concluded *Washington Post Book World* contributor Howard Frank Mosher, "Trevor is entirely his own writer, with his own uncompromised vision of human limitations made accessible by a rare generosity toward his characters and their blighted lives."

While Trevor may be compared by many to Joyce, an *Economist* contributor reviewing Trevor's 2004 book of short stories, *A Bit on the Side,* noted, "Joyce was the supreme example of the writer's writer. His fellow countryman firmly belongs with his readers." The reviewer went on to comment, "With his writing, the reader never pauses to admire literary elegance for its own sake. There are no verbal flourishes . . . and no self-conscious Joycean obscurities. Each and every sentence is as long and plain as it needs to be, crafted in a very particular way to engage and draw the reader into the small human drama which is under scrutiny." The collection of twelve stories include tales about a man revealing to his wife that he once led a life of crime, a woman whose experience of a tragedy leads her to recount her parents' unstable marriage, and the outcome of a schoolgirl who gossips about a cuckolded man who is tutoring her. Hermione Lee, writing in the *Guardian,* commented, "I think this latest collection of William Trevor's stories—his 11th, as good as ever and as recognisable as ever—has the wrong title. He's chosen it from a story of muted London adultery, in which the inconclusive lovers part for no very good reason, sad, but sustained by how well they've behaved and by 'the delicacy of their reticence.' Though not the strongest story in the collection, it displays all the 'delicacy' and wisdom we've come to expect from Trevor, and to praise in him, over many years."

BIOGRAPHICAL AND CRITICAL SOURCES:

BOOKS

Contemporary Dramatists, St. James Press (Detroit, MI), 1993.

Contemporary Literary Criticism, Thomson Gale (Detroit, MI), Volume 7, 1977, Volume 9, 1978, Volume 14, 1980, Volume 25, 1983, Volume 71, 1992.

Contemporary Novelists, St. James Press (Detroit, MI), 1991.

Dictionary of Literary Biography, Thomson Gale (Detroit, MI), Volume 14: *British Novelists since 1960,* 1983, Volume 139: *British Short-Fiction Writers, 1945-1980,* 1994.

Schirmer, Gregory A., *William Trevor: A Study of His Fiction,* Routledge, 1990.

PERIODICALS

Atlantic Monthly, August, 1986; October, 2002, review of *The Story of Lucy Gault,* pp. 157-158.

Booklist, September 1, 2000, Brad Hooper, review of *The Hill Bachelors,* p. 8; August, 2002, Brad Hooper, review of *The Story of Lucy Gault,* p. 1887.

Boston Book Review, 1998.

Boston Globe, November 15, 1992, p. 91; February 6, 1994, p. 89; February 13, 1994, p. A15; January 8, 1995, p. 47.

Chicago Tribune, November 13, 1987; September 30, 1988; April 6, 1994, section 5, p. 3; January 15, 1995, section 14, p. 3.

Chicago Tribune Book World, July 29, 1979; March 15, 1981; February 14, 1982; October 30, 1983.

Christian Science Monitor, February 26, 1970; March 10, 1994, p. 14; January 10, 1995, p. 13.

Commonweal, December 3, 1999, Jon Nilson, review of *The Collected Stories,* p. 29; June 16, 2000, Suzanne Berne, "Summer Reading," p. 20.

Economist (U.S.), November 11, 2000, review of *The Hill Bachelors,* p. 108; June 12, 2004, review of *A Bit on the Side,* p. 82.

Encounter, January, 1979.

Globe and Mail (Toronto, Ontario, Canada), December 31, 1983; October 24, 1987; September 17, 1988.

Guardian (Manchester, England), Hermione Lee, review of *A Bit on the Side,* p. 26.

Harper's, October, 1983, pp. 74-75; December, 2002, Francine Prose, "Comfort Cult: On the Honest Unloveliness of William Trevor's World," p. 76.

Hudson Review, winter, 1991, pp. 686-690.

Irish Literary Supplement, spring, 1991, p. 20.

Irish Times, May 22, 1988.

Kansas City Star (via Knight-Ridder/Tribune News Service), January 21, 2004, John Mark Eberhart, "'Lucy Gault' Author Styles His Prose with Concision" (interview with author).

Library Journal, September 1, 2002, Diana McRae, review of *The Story of Lucy Gault,* p. 216.
Listener, July 21, 1988, pp. 25-26.
London Magazine, August, 1968.
London Review of Books, June 23, 1988, p. 22; December 16, 1993, pp. 22-23.
Los Angeles Times, October 2, 1983; September 29, 1988; February 10, 1994, Richard Eder, review of "Excursions in the Real World: Memoirs," p. E10.
Los Angeles Times Book Review, January 11, 1981; March 11, 1984, p. 4; May 4, 1986, p. 3; August 6, 1989; May 20, 1990, p. 3; September 5, 1993, p. 6; February 13, 1994, p. 6; January 8, 1995, p. 3.
Nation, December 3, 1983, pp. 574-577; November 18, 2002, Patrick Smith, review of *The Story of Lucy Gault,* p. 40.
New Republic, February 4, 1967; November 28, 1983, pp. 37-39; June 9, 1986, pp. 28-30; February 6, 1989, pp. 37-40; October 1, 1990, pp. 40-41.
New Statesman, October 15, 1971; July 9, 1976; September 22, 1978; September 9, 2002, Geordie Greig, review of *The Story of Lucy Gault,* p. 53.
New Statesman & Society, August 27, 1993, pp. 40-41.
Newsweek, June 14, 1976; February 22, 1982; October 10, 1983.
New Yorker, July 12, 1976.
New York Review of Books, April 19, 1979; March 19, 1981; December 22, 1983, pp. 53-54; June 26, 1986, pp. 32-33, 35; May 17, 1990; September 26, 1991, pp. 29-30.
New York Times, September 31, 1972; March 31, 1979; January 17, 1981; February 3, 1982; September 26, 1983; May 14, 1986; August 27, 1988; May 11, 1990, p. C33; January 3, 1995, p. B27; November 12, 1996; October 17, 2000, Michiko Kakutani, review of *The Hill Bachelors,* p. B7.
New York Times Book Review, February 11, 1968; July 11, 1976; April 8, 1979; February 1, 1981; February 21, 1982; October 2, 1983, pp. 1, 22, 24; June 8, 1986, p. 14; January 17, 1988, p. 24; October 9, 1988, p. 12; June 3, 1990, p. 9; September 8, 1991, p. 3; February 3, 1993, p. 1; February 28, 1993, pp. 1, 25-27; February 13, 1994, p. 7; January 8, 1995, pp. 1, 22; October 22, 2000, William H. Pritchard, review of *The Hill Bachelors,* p. 11.
Observer, June 11, 1980; April 6, 1986, p. 27; June 5, 1988; November 1, 1987; February 4, 1990; May 26, 1991.
Plays and Players, September, 1971.
Publishers Weekly, October 28, 1983, Amanda Smith, interview with Trevor; September 11, 2000, review of *The Hill Bachelors,* p. 65; August 5, 2002, review of *The Story of Lucy Gault,* p. 52.
San Francisco Review of Books, Volume 16, number 3, 1991, pp. 47-48.
Saturday Review, May 12, 1970, pp. 44-45.
Sewanee Review, spring, 1978, Walter Sullivan, review of *The Children of Dynmouth,* pp. 320-325.
Spectator, October 11, 1969; May 13, 1972; November 29, 1986, p. 25; June 1, 1991, p. 28; October 17, 1992, pp. 25-26; August 28, 1993, p. 32; August 20, 1994, p. 34.
Sunday Times, May 29, 1988, pp. 68-69; May 26, 1991, pp. 6-7.
Time, January 26, 1970; October 10, 1983.
Times (London, England), June 18, 1980; October 15, 1981; April 28, 1983; March 20, 1986; May 30, 1991, p. 12.
Times Literary Supplement, October 26, 1973, review of *Elizabeth Alone;* June 20, 1980; October 16, 1981; April 29, 1983; August 31, 1984; April 11, 1986; November 5, 1987; June 10, 1988; January 26, 1990, p. 87; May 31, 1991, p. 21; September 17, 1993, p. 24; August 19, 1994, p. 20.
Tribune Books (Chicago, IL), September 10, 1989; November 22, 1992, p. 1.
Variety, May 24, 1999, Emanuel Levy, review of *Felicia's Journey* (film), p. 65.
Vogue, February 1, 1968.
Wall Street Journal, March 2, 1994, p. A9; January 26, 1995, p. A12.
Washington Post, March 11, 1995, p. A17.
Washington Post Book World, April 8, 1979; February 1, 1981; February 21, 1982; September 25, 1983, p. 3; March 4, 1984; May 25, 1986, p. 6; August 28, 1988; May 27, 1990; August 18, 1991; January 22, 1995, pp. 1, 10.
Writer, October, 1990.

* * *

TRILLIN, Calvin 1935-
(Calvin Marshall Trillin)

PERSONAL: Born December 5, 1935, in Kansas City, MO; son of Abe and Edyth (Weitzman) Trillin; married Alice Stewart (an English teacher and consultant), August 13, 1965 (died, 2001); children: Abigail, Sarah. *Education:* Yale University, B.A., 1957.

ADDRESSES: *Office*—c/o New Yorker, 4 Times Square, New York, NY 10036-6522.

CAREER: *Time* magazine, New York, NY, 1960-63, began as reporter in Atlanta, GA, and New York, NY, became writer in New York, NY; *New Yorker,* New York,

NY, staff writer, 1963—; *Nation,* columnist, 1978-85; King Features, syndicated columnist, 1986-1995; *Time,* columnist, 1996—.

AWARDS, HONORS: National Book Award nomination (paperback), 1980, for *Alice, Let's Eat: Further Adventures of a Happy Eater;* Books-across-the-Sea Ambassador of Honor citation, English-Speaking Union, 1985, for *Third Helpings.* Honorary degrees from Beloit College, 1987, Albertus Magnus College, 1990, State University of New York (SUNY), 1996, University of North Carolina, 1998, and Susquehanna University, 1999.

WRITINGS:

NONFICTION

An Education in Georgia: Charlayne Hunter, Hamilton Holmes, and the Integration of the University of Georgia, Viking (New York, NY), 1964.
U.S. Journal, Dutton (New York, NY), 1971.
American Fried: Adventures of a Happy Eater, Doubleday (New York, NY), 1974.
Alice, Let's Eat: Further Adventures of a Happy Eater, Random House (New York, NY), 1978.
Uncivil Liberties (collected columns), Ticknor & Fields (New York, NY), 1982.
Third Helpings, Ticknor & Fields (New York, NY), 1983.
Killings, Ticknor & Fields (New York, NY), 1984.
With All Disrespect: More Uncivil Liberties (collected columns), Ticknor & Fields (New York, NY), 1985.
If You Can't Say Something Nice (collected columns), Ticknor & Fields (New York, NY), 1987.
Travels with Alice, Ticknor & Fields (New York, NY), 1989.
Enough's Enough (and Other Rules of Life) (collected columns), Ticknor & Fields (New York, NY), 1990.
Remembering Denny, Farrar, Straus (New York, NY), 1993.
The Tummy Trilogy (contains *American Fried, Alice, Let's Eat,* and *Third Helpings*), Farrar, Straus (New York, NY), 1994.
Feeding a Yen; Savoring Local Specialities, from Kansas City to Cuzco, Random House (New York, NY), 2003.

FICTION

Barnett Frummer Is an Unbloomed Flower and Other Adventures of Barnett Frummer, Rosalie Mondle, Roland Magruder, and Their Friends (short stories), Viking (New York, NY), 1969.
Runestruck (novel), Little, Brown (Boston, MA), 1977.
Floater (novel), Ticknor & Fields (New York, NY), 1980.
American Stories (short stories), Ticknor & Fields (New York, NY), 1991.
Tepper Isn't Going Out: A Novel, Random House (New York, NY), 2002.

OTHER

(And performer) *Calvin Trillin's Uncle Sam* (one-man show), produced at American Place Theatre (New York, NY), 1988.
(And performer) *Calvin Trillin's Words, No Music* (one-man show), produced at American Place Theatre (New York, NY), 1990.
Deadline Poet; or, My Life As a Doggerelist, Farrar, Straus (New York, NY), 1994.
Too Soon to Tell, Farrar, Straus (New York, NY), 1995.
Messages from My Father, Farrar, Straus (New York, NY), 1996.
Family Man (essays), Farrar, Straus (New York, NY), 1998.
Obliviously On He Sails: The Bush Administration in Rhyme, Random House (New York, NY), 2004.

Author of the column "Uncivil Liberties," *Nation,* 1978-85, King Features Syndicate, 1986—. Contributor to periodicals, including *Atlantic, Harper's, Life, Esquire,* and *New York Times Magazine.*

ADAPTATIONS: The Tummy Trilogy has been made into an audio recording.

SIDELIGHTS: Calvin Trillin is a journalist, critic, and novelist who has won acclaim "partly because of his wayward scrambles across [America] in search of regional food . . . and partly because he has mastered a television manner that communicates his understated, tongue-in-cheek humor," according to Barry Siegel in a *Los Angeles Times* article. But in some ways, continued Siegel, "it is regrettable that Trillin is so funny, because this quality tends to obscure the fact that in his 'U.S. Journal' [a continuing series in the *New Yorker*] he may be offering some of the most valuable and unique reporting in the country today."

Trillin's early career saw him working at *Time,* where as a journalistic "floater" he migrated from one department to the next. As the author told *Publishers Weekly* interviewer John F. Baker, he spent some time in the

"Medicine" section: "I didn't care for that—it seemed to tend toward the intestinal whenever I was there, with weekly breakthroughs in spleen research"; and also in the "Religion" section, which ill-suited Trillin. "I finally got out of that by prefacing everything with 'alleged'; I'd write about 'the alleged parting of the Red Sea,' even 'the alleged Crucifixion,' and eventually they let me go."

Apparently, Trillin gained enough insight from his career at *Time* to produce, years later, a comic novel titled *Floater.* The fictional newsweekly through which protagonist Fred Becker floats is populated with trend-obsessed editors, egomaniacal writers, and eccentrics of every description. Becker enjoys his unfettered career until a rumor provided to him by a remarkably unreliable source threatens his future. The rumor—that the President's wife is pregnant—could cause Becker to be promoted to an odious bureau chief position if he is the first to report it truthfully. While Becker ponders what to do with his scoop, he accidentally leaks the rumor, only to find that the scoop is phony, "part of an elaborate, internecine power struggle at the magazine that is as unlikely as it is hilarious," according to Dan Wakefield in the *Nation.*

Some critics found *Floater* too thin. *Los Angeles Times Book Review* contributor Stuart Schoffman thought "the chief flaw . . . is that the characters are so bloodless and inactive, pounded into two-dimensionality like paper-thin slices of veal." John D. Callaway noted in the *Chicago Tribune Book World* that, while *Floater*'s humor often appealed to him, the characters "are less memorably drawn than the actors who star in 30-second commercials." Wakefield found Trillin's satire "sure and sharp but never mean-spirited. A kind of affection for the magazine comes through, and when Becker considers leaving it, he thinks how much he would miss the camaraderie, the gossip and stories and daily routines." Wakefield concluded that "Trillin is one of those rare writers who possess grace as well as wit."

Trillin's nonfiction, gleaned from his magazine pieces, covers a wide range. There are humor collections (*Uncivil Liberties* and *With All Disrespect: More Uncivil Liberties*), political and social commentary (*U.S. Journal* and *Too Soon to Tell*), a study of homicide (*Killings*), and a book devoted to his father, the subject of several of Trillin's columns over the years, titled *Messages from My Father.*

With *U.S. Journal* the author recalls his travels across America, finding stories in everyday events in which there may be no apparent "news value." These subjects befit Trillin, who grew up in Kansas City, Missouri, and has always considered himself a Midwesterner, despite his years of living in New York City. He sees his subjects as worthy of examination, even if they are not famous or important. "Upwardly mobile reporters tend to gauge themselves by the importance of the people they interview," Trillin told Siegel.

"I don't think like that. Most of the people I talk to have never spoken to a reporter before. I began the 'U.S. Journal' series partly because I wanted to stay in touch with the country. I like regional stories. The fact is, government and politics are important, but they aren't the country."

Writing about *U.S. Journal* in the *New York Times Book Review,* Evan S. Connell stated: "Trillin's scales usually are balanced; he is a judicious journalist and has presented an agreeable collection. More important, several passages show compelling depth. As cautious as he is, he can create a wave of emotion in the reader—usually a wave of rage at the bigots, paralytic bureaucrats and myopic hucksters who infest [the book]. His account of desperate people in South Carolina is guaranteed to spoil your lunch."

In 1978, Trillin began to write "Uncivil Liberties," a humor column for the *Nation.* More recently published in syndication throughout the country, the column has been both a popular and critical success. *Uncivil Liberties* and *With All Disrespect: More Uncivil Liberties,* which present that work in collected form, are likewise praised for the author's slightly skewed views of contemporary culture. "At the outset, Trillin defined the column as 'a thousand words every three weeks for saying whatever's on my mind, particularly if what's on my mind is marginally ignoble,'" as Jonathan Yardley reported in a *Washington Post* review. "Even in his less-inspired efforts," wrote Yardley, "he is perceptive, funny and iconoclastic." Trillin is "consistently sharp and imaginative" in *Uncivil Liberties,* according to a *Detroit News* critic, "but don't expect a banquet of belly laughs from these fifty easy pieces. They're more likely to elicit appreciative smiles at the author's capacity for setting up and delivering clever dissections of his chosen prey."

More of Trillin's columns appear in the collections *If You Can't Say Something Nice, Enough's Enough (and Other Rules of Life),* and *Too Soon to Tell.* The columnist even conformed his comic view of U.S. politics to tropes and iambs in *Deadline Poet; or, My Life As a*

Doggerelist. In this collection, which contains three years' worth of verse Trillin penned with regularity for the *Nation,* readers will enjoy one of the few known versifications of U.S. economic fluctuations: "Statistics now show where the boom dough went. / The middle classes hardly gained a nickel. / Two-thirds went to the richest one percent. / A breakthrough: we produced an upward trickle." As political satirist Mark Russell wrote in the *New York Times Book Review:* "Calvin Trillin is the name to lob into those fashionable hand-wringing laments about what has happened to the state of American humor and how the schlock is the message. Mark Twain, Robert Benchley and [S. J.] Perelman are dead but Calvin Trillin is right there with the post-funeral cocktail to assure us that life goes on."

Essays in each of Trillin's collections range in subject from the disappearance of chicken à la king (Trillin suggests that it is being stored by the government in huge silos) to the legality of miming—"At one point," Russell continued, "his wife must remind him that he has no legal standing for making a citizen's arrest of someone for performing mime in public." "It's to be hoped," declared Ross Thomas in the *Washington Post Book World,* "that Trillin will receive at least a footnote in the history of politics for having thought up the general purpose, fits-one, fits-all slogan, which is, of course, 'Never Been Indicted.'" "It is Trillin's eye for spotting raging silliness among those who take themselves very, very seriously," explained Wes Smith in the *Chicago Tribune,* "that has made him an enormously popular wag."

In 1990's *Too Soon to Tell,* ninety columns mix the author's characteristic humor with pointed commentary on modern culture. From monkfish to the poseur lip-synching rock duo Milli Vanilli, Trillin uses newsworthy events as stepping stones toward each of his well-reasoned and pointed observations, opinions, or recollections. Noting that the author's "deadpan timing" keeps his essays from becoming dated, Michael Dirda commented in the *Washington Post Book World* that "Trillin can write well about anything: murder, Washington politics, Kansas City barbecue, the death of a gay friend, out-of-the-way places, growing up. What seems common to his diverse productiveness," the critic continued, "is a kind of old-fashioned patriotism: Trillin loves and celebrates American life even as he grouses about it."

More focused in subject matter was Trillin's 1984 collection, *Killings.* Based on several *New Yorker* articles, the book examines the kinds of murder that don't ordinarily make national headlines—those occurring in small towns, their victims uncelebrated individuals. "Trillin's interest—and ours—lies not in how some of us die but in how we live," noted *Nation* reviewer Ann Jones. The author, continued Jones, finds that the motivation for some of the murders should be viewed within the context of the social tensions in the cities and towns where the killings took place. "He describes what sociologists would call a conflict of cultures," wrote Jones. "A hillbilly guns down a trespassing filmmaker. A frustrated Navajo abducts a New Mexico mayor. . . . Sometimes the conflict is more intimate [as in the case of] Lawrence Hartman, an exemplary Iowa farmer who in middle age, bedazzled by the big city and a young cocktail waitress, beat his wife to death." "In several cases the killing seems inadvertent, as if the killer didn't actually want to do it, but couldn't think of any other way to pass through the situation. Lack of imagination may be a motive," Anatole Broyard pointed out in a *New York Times* piece.

In *Killings,* Trillin "fashions suspense by starting with ordinary, day-to-day details; the violence grows imperceptibly," as Richard Eder explained in the *Los Angeles Times.* "He roots his pieces in some particular community and set of circumstances and makes them so real that the death becomes not an extraordinary event but a natural process that has failed. Some of the most vivid reflections are those of neighbors who ask themselves what went wrong," Eder concluded. To Yardley, the author "is a practitioner of hit-and-run journalism in the sense that he pounces on a locality, tells its story, and then moves on to the next. But he rises well above the genre for two reasons: His unusually deep interest in people . . . and his desire to find meaning in what at first seems meaningless. *Killings* is more than just another collection of magazine pieces; its internal coherence, unusual in such volumes, derives from the empathy and intelligence of its author."

If empathy and intelligence characterize Trillin's attitude toward people, most critics agree that passion and poignancy describe his attitude toward food. The author has made his true love known in three volumes, each celebrating the variety of American cuisine. Indeed, Trillin's eloquence on such matters as fried chicken and Chicago-style pizza has caused him to be labeled "the Walt Whitman of American eats" by Craig Claiborne in the *New York Times Book Review* and a "food pornographer" by Nelson W. Polsby in *Harper's. American Fried: Adventures of a Happy Eater* is the first of Trillin's books on food and travel, and is "composed of a blend of waspish sociology and a sensuality so explicit as to border on the prurient," warned a *Saturday Review* critic. In his review, Polsby appreciated the author's dilemma as a roving gourmand. When Trillin arrives in town, explained Polsby, the gentry "refuse to tell him where [the good] restaurants are. Instead, they are forever touting him onto big-priced fake 'Continental' eateries, places with lots of decor, long-winded menus, revolving views of the surrounding wasteland, and terrible food. When hunger strikes in a strange town, he despairs of interviewing local informants, and he has taken to rummaging through the restaurant section of the Yellow Pages, looking for restaurants having no display ads or those called by only the first name of the proprietor." "Some will say [that, in *American Fried,* Trillin] has written a nasty satire on gourmets, but they err who think so," claimed *Washington Post Book World* writer Henry Mitchell. "Trillin genuinely loves all the stuff he writes about, no doubt of that. Love transforms all. As Proust took the simple madeleine and with genius made it a glory of his book, so Trillin takes the hamburger, takes the chili-dog, takes the pizza, and does as much or more."

An entreaty to his wife comprises the title of Trillin's second food-appreciation book, *Alice, Let's Eat: Further Adventures of a Happy Eater.* Alice Trillin, it seems, did not quite share her husband's enthusiasm for barbecue and burgers, and the couple's conflicts figure as a dramatic element in the volume. While Trillin has some fun at his wife's expense in *Alice, Let's Eat,* Alice once told her side of the story in a *Nation* review of her husband's book. "I am not against quests for the perfect ham hock or the perfect barbecue or even, for that matter, for the perfect roast polecat haunch," she explained. "But I think that anyone starting out on such a quest should be aware that his guide is someone who will travel all the way to a place called Horse Cave, Kentucky, because he likes the way the name Horse Cave, Kentucky sounds when he drops it to me over the phone. . . . This is offered as a warning by someone who has been assigned the role of heavy in her husband's book just because she likes to say fettuccine with white truffles and cream occasionally—a dish considered by some to represent the elitist Eastern Establishment."

New Republic reviewer Ben Yagoda regretted that there is some "bad news" about *Alice, Let's Eat:* the book "is not quite as consistently delightful as *American Fried.* I blame this in part on the fact that in the new book Trillin is disappointed a number of times—by the Kentucky mutton, by a Vermont wildgame supper where he can't tell the beaver from the buffalo. . . . Also, he ventures away from the U.S. too often: there's a trip to Martinique, one to France, and two to England." Outside of America, claimed Yagoda, "Trillin seems somehow out of place, like a hamburger stand on the Champs Elysées. But read *Alice, Let's Eat,*" concluded the critic, who called Trillin "a worthy celebrant of one of the few authentic triumphs of American culture. His book will bring a smile to your lips and a growl to your stomach."

Third Helpings differs from Trillin's first two food books because it contains a campaign "to have the national Thanksgiving dish changed from turkey to spaghetti carbonara." The author defends his stance with a retelling of the First Thanksgiving legend. In Trillin's version the Indians joined the Pilgrims for a Thanksgiving feast, taking the precaution "of [bringing] along one dish of their own. They brought a dish their ancestors had been taught earlier by Christopher Columbus, discoverer of the New World. The dish was spaghetti carbonara." As in the earlier works, American patriotism figures into *Third Helpings.* After sampling the food at a Mediterranean resort, Trillin declares that the fancy fare is no better "than the Italian sausage sandwiches he dotes upon on Mulberry Street in lower Manhattan," as *Newsweek*'s Gene Lyons related. "Neither, for that matter, does the Italian cuisine surpass the roast duck and dirty rice at Didee's in Baton Rouge or Opelousas, Louisiana." In pieces such as the account of the Crawford County, Kansas, fried chicken war between Chicken Annie and Chicken Mary, Trillin proves to Beryl Lieff Benderly that "under cover of a mania for dim sum, spaghetti carbonara, and pit barbecue, [the author] is actually a superlative prose stylist, an inimitable humorist, and an absolutely first-rate people writer." In a *Washington Post Book World* article, Benderly added that Trillin's articles "concern not only comestibles by characters; they concentrate on talented devotees who take what they eat and serve every bit as seriously as Trillin does."

Trillin's fourth contribution to his ongoing saga of food and travel is *Travels with Alice.* In this volume, Trillin wanders through France, Italy, and other places around the globe, ostensibly to take in the culture, but really to take in the native eatables. "Even when the itinerary is the standard tour of museums, monuments and monasteries," stated *Chicago Tribune* contributor James Idems, "his nose is atwitch and his eye peeled for the out-of-the-way market or café that specializes in the local cuisine." "This late-twentieth-century autocrat of the breakfast table takes these setbacks in stride, ever confident that if he just keeps hanging around, keeping one eye on the scenery and the other on the menu, sooner or later a meal worth eating will make its presence known," declared Yardley in the *Washington Post.* "So far he's been right, with the happy result that he's well-fed and his readers are well-read."

From love of food and all things American, Trillin turned to love of family in 1996's *Messages from My Father: A Memoir.* Writing about his father—a dreamer who wanted greatness for his children, a proud American, and a loving, idealistic man with a subtle sense of humor—Trillin recalls his own childhood memories of his Russian-born father Abe Trillin, a grocery store owner who was determined that Calvin graduate from Yale and become president of the United States. "In *Messages from My Father,* Mr. Trillin reveals the elusive source of his gifts," maintained Christopher Lehmann-Haupt in his *New York Times* review, "and he demonstrates how well he learned the subtle lessons conveyed to him." On a more somber note, Trillin recounts the death of a homosexual friend he had known since his days at Yale in the best-selling 1993 work *Remembering Denny,* which Michael Dorris lauded as "an eloquent, heartfelt protest against disappointment and stunted opportunity" in the *New York Times Book Review.*

In 1988, following in the footsteps of Mark Twain, Trillin took his humor on the stage—he had previously performed on the Johnny Carson show and on radio—with the opening of his one-man show *Calvin Trillin's Uncle Sam,* which featured geography. He succeeded it in 1990 with another, *Calvin Trillin's Words, No Music,* which features "language . . . politics, certainly some mention of a few presidents," as he told fellow humorist Jackie Mason in a conversation published in the *New York Times.* "Calvin Trillin is the Buster Keaton of performance humorists," declared Mel Gussow in a *New York Times* review of the second show. "As droll as he is deadpan, he never once suggests that he thinks he is as funny as we know he is. He lets the audience do the laughing. . . . His ease and professionalism in facing his public should be an inspiration to writers who hide behind hard covers."

In his book *Family Man,* Trillin ruminates on the family and parenthood. A.J. Anderson in the *Library Journal* wrote, "He demonstrates once again that he thoroughly understands the difficult technique of clever light writing."

Although Trillin had a collection of short stories called *American Stories* published in 1995, more than twenty years passed between his novel *Floater* and his next novel, *Tepper Isn't Going Out,* published in 2002. In this comic novel of New York, Trillin tells the story of Murray Tepper who searches out parking spaces so he can sit in his car and read the newspaper in peace. Since finding parking on the streets in New York is difficult, Tepper's predilection for snatching parking spaces raises the ire of many, including the city's mayor, who tries to stop Tepper. On the other hand, other New Yorkers become intrigued with Tepper after an article about him appears in the *East Village Rag,* and they begin to line up outside his car to talk with a man they have come to believe has some special kind of wisdom. "Readers feeling the need to relax with a book that's very funny, humane, and not too taxing to read will enjoy this clever tale of urban life at the time of the millennium," wrote Mary Ellen Quinn in *Booklist.* A reviewer writing in *Publishers Weekly* noted that "Trillin captures dozens of pitch-perfect New York moments." In a review in the *Los Angeles Times,* Brigitte Frase called the book, "A much-needed addition to automotive literature, it certainly hits the spot. Trillin is at his charmingly funny best in this good-humored satire of urban politics and media spin."

Like many political commentators, Trillin found a great subject in President George W. Bush. His collection *Obliviously On He Sails: The Bush Administration in Rhyme,* covers the Bush Administration in verse. Ray Olson of *Booklist* wrote, "There's nothing for improving a satirist's form like having a good target. . . . The present presidential administration, led as it is by the least articulate politician in living memory (as Trillin notes, 'W' is no Dan Quayle), seems heaven-sent for satire, however, and Trillin rises to its benison."

A reporter, novelist, and essayist, Trillin has shown that he can tackle almost any type of writing. "I've never known exactly which hat I was wearing," Trillin is quoted as saying in the *Columbia Journalism Review.* "The reporter fedora with the press badge in the hatband, or the jester with the pompom bouncing in my eyes."

BIOGRAPHICAL AND CRITICAL SOURCES:

BOOKS

Authors in the News, Volume 1, Thomson Gale (Detroit, MI), 1976.

Dictionary of Literary Biography, Volume 185: *American Literary Journalists, 1945-1955, First Series,* Thomson Gale (Detroit, MI), 1997, pp. 324-327

Trillin, Calvin, *Third Helpings,* Ticknor & Fields (New York, NY), 1983.

Trillin, Calvin, *Deadline Poet; or, My Life As a Doggerelist,* Farrar, Straus (New York, NY), 1994.

Trillin, Calvin, *Messages from My Father: A Memoir,* Farrar, Straus (New York, NY), 1996.

PERIODICALS

America, April 16, 1994, p. 2.

American Journalism Review, December, 1985, Scott Kraft, "The Chronicles of Calvin Trillin," pp. 43-47.

Booklist, March 15, 1998, review of *Family Man,* p. 1178; July, 1999, review of *The Tummy Trilogy,* p. 1909; November 1, 2001, Mary Ellen Quinn, review of *Tepper Isn't Going Out: A Novel,* p. 444.

Chicago Tribune, February 26, 1984; December 15, 1988; November 23, 1989.

Chicago Tribune Book World, November 30, 1980; March 18, 1984.

Columbia Journalism Review, November-December, 2001, "Funny Guys," p. 92.

Commentary, August, 1971.

Detroit News, May 30, 1982.

Entertainment Weekly, June 2, 1995, p. 53.

Harper's, August, 1974.

Kansas City Magazine, November, 1974.

Kirkus Reviews, April 15, 1998, review of *Family Man,* p. 570.

Knight-Ridder/Tribune News Service, March 20, 2002, Jean Blish Siers, review of *Tepper Isn't Going Out,* p. K2221.

Library Journal; April 15, 1994, p. 82; May 1, 1995, p. 97; April 15, 1996, p. 144; May 1, 1996, p. 104; September 15, 1998, A.J. Anderson, review of *Family Man,* p. 81; November 1, 2001, A.J. Anderson, review of *Tepper Isn't Going Out,* p. 134.

Life, November 7, 1969.

Los Angeles Times, November 18, 1980; March 11, 1984; March 23, 1984; February 10, 2002, Brigitte Frase, "A Space of One's Own: *Tepper Isn't Going Out: A Novel,*" p. R-4.

Los Angeles Times Book Review, December 7, 1980; April 24, 1984; November 11, 1990, p. 9; March 8, 1992, p. 10; April 19, 1994, p. 6; June 16, 1996.

Nation, October 21, 1978; October 11, 1980; March 3, 1984; December 22, 1984; February 4, 2002, review of *Tepper Isn't Going Out,* p. 32.

New Leader, November-December, 2001, Walter Goodman, review of *Tepper Isn't Going Out,* p. 36.

New Republic, April 17, 1971; October 7, 1978.

Newsweek, October 27, 1980; April 4, 1983; February 13, 1984.

New York Review of Books, July 16, 1998, review of *Family Man,* p. 15.

New York Times, November 7, 1969; July 2, 1971; May 12, 1977; October 14, 1980; May 26, 1982; April 14, 1983; January 28, 1984; October 7, 1990; October 15, 1990; June 6, 1996, p. C17; June 25, 1998, review of *Family Man,* p. E9; February 12, 2002, Mel Gussow, review of *Tepper Isn't Going Out,* p. B1.

New York Times Book Review, November 8, 1987, p. 11; October 22, 1989, p. 10; October 28, 1990, p. 9; December 9, 1990, p. 38; October 13, 1991, p. 22; January 12, 1992, p. 24; April 24, 1994, p. 16; June 25, 1995, p. 20; June 30, 1996, p. 15; June 20, 1999, review of *Family Man,* p. 24; June 2, 2002, review of *Tepper Isn't Going Out,* p. 24.

People, November 2, 1987.

Publishers Weekly, November 21, 1980; April 3, 1995, p. 50; March 25, 1996, p. 70; March 23, 1998, review of *Family Man,* p. 84; October 22, 2001, review of *Tepper Isn't Going Out,* p. 41.

Readings: A Journal of Reviews and Commentary in Mental Health, September, 1998, review of *Family Man,* p. 6.

Saturday Review, May 8, 1971; May 18, 1974.

Time, March 22, 1971; December 22, 1980; July 5, 1982; March 5, 1984; February 12, 1996, p. 17; June 15, 1998, review of *Family Man,* p. 81.

Times Literary Supplement, January 17, 1992, p. 24.

Tribune Books (Chicago, IL), October 21, 1990, p. 8; October 13, 1991, p. 6; February 9, 1992, p. 8; February 23, 1992, p. 8.

Village Voice, September 25, 1978.

Voice Literary Supplement, October, 1989.

Washington Post, October 23, 1980; December 4, 1980; May 19, 1982; February 8, 1984; April 16, 1985; October 11, 1989.

Washington Post Book World, October 26, 1969; June 2, 1974; April 10, 1983; April 10, 1987; October 18, 1987; March 29, 1992, p. 12; June 20, 1999, review of *Family Man,* p. 10.

ONLINE

Salon.com, http://www.salon.com/ (September, 4, 2002), Laura Miller, "The Food Writer and Humorist Gets Serious about Fathers and Sons," interview with Calvin Trillin.

* * *

TRILLIN, Calvin Marshall
See TRILLIN, Calvin

TROUT, Kilgore
See FARMER, Philip José

* * *

TUROW, Scott 1949-

PERSONAL: Born April 12, 1949, in Chicago, IL; son of David D. (a physician) and Rita (a writer; maiden name, Pastron) Turow; married Annette Weisberg (an artist), April 4, 1971; children: Rachel, Gabriel, Eve. *Education:* Amherst College, B.A., 1970; Stanford University, M.A., 1974; Harvard University, J.D., 1978. *Religion:* Jewish.

ADDRESSES: *Office*—Sonnenschein, Carlin, Nath & Rosenthal, Sears Tower, Suite 8000, Chicago, IL 60606. *E-mail*—SFT@Sonnenschein.com.

CAREER: Attorney and novelist. Stanford University, Stanford, CA, E.H. Jones Lecturer in Creative Writing, 1972-75; Suffolk County District Attorney's Office, Boston, MA, clerk, 1977-78; U.S. Court of Appeals for the Seventh District, Chicago, IL, assistant U.S. district attorney, 1978-86; Sonnenschein, Carlin, Nath, & Rosenthal (law firm), Chicago, partner, beginning 1986. Writer, 1972—.

AWARDS, HONORS: Writing award, College English Association/Book- of-the-Month Club, 1970; Edith Mirrielees fellow, 1972; Silver Dagger Award, Crime Writers Association, 1988, for *Presumed Innocent;* Writer for Writers award, 2001.

WRITINGS:

One L: An Inside Account of Life in the First Year at Harvard Law School (nonfiction), Putnam (New York, NY), 1977.

Presumed Innocent (novel), Farrar, Straus (New York, NY), 1987.

The Burden of Proof (novel), Farrar, Straus (New York, NY), 1990.

Pleading Guilty (novel), Farrar, Straus (New York, NY), 1993.

The Laws of Our Fathers (novel), Farrar, Straus (New York, NY), 1996.

Personal Injuries (novel), Farrar, Straus (New York, NY), 1999.

(Editor) *Guilty As Charged: A Mystery Writers of America Anthology,* Compass Press (Thorndike, ME), 2001.

Reversible Errors, Farrar, Straus (New York, NY), 2002.

Ultimate Punishment: A Lawyer's Reflections on Dealing with the Death Penalty (nonfiction), Farrar, Straus (New York, NY), 2003.

Ordinary Heroes (novel), Farrar, Straus (New York, NY), 2005.

Also author of unpublished novel *The Way Things Are.* Work anthologized in *Best American Short Stories,* 1971, 1972. Contributor of stories, articles, and reviews to literary journals, including *Transatlantic Review, Ploughshares, Harvard, New England,* and *Place,* and contributor to newspapers.

ADAPTATIONS: *Presumed Innocent,* a film based on Turow's novel of the same title, was released by Warner Bros., written by Frank Pierson and Alan J. Pakula, directed by Pakula, starring Harrison Ford, Bonnie Bedelia, Brian Dennehy, and Raul Julia, 1990; *The Burden of Proof,* a two-part television film based on the novel, was adapted by John Gay and starred Hector Elizondo, Brian Dennehy, and Adrienne Barbeau, 1992; *Reversible Errors* was adapted as a television miniseries in 2004.

SIDELIGHTS: Scott Turow uses his insider's knowledge of the American legal system to form the basis for best-selling suspense novels. A practicing attorney who has also studied creative writing, Turow explores the murky terrain of urban justice through highly plotted fiction. "No one on the contemporary scene writes better mystery-suspense novels than Chicago attorney Scott Turow," noted Bill Blum in the *Los Angeles Times Book Review.* "In a genre overcrowded with transparent plots and one-dimensional super-sleuths, Turow's first novel, *Presumed Innocent,* was a work of serious fiction as well as a gripping tale of murder and courtroom drama." *New York Times Magazine* correspondent Jeff Shear praised Turow for the "brash, backroom sensibility that informs his work as a novelist." Noting the range of legal thrillers available to readers, *Trial* reviewer Rebecca Porter noted that Turrow's 2003 novel *Reversible Errors* is exceptional due to the author's "refusal to paint the issue in black and white." Turow's "characters are challenged morally, ethically, and emotionally," Porter added—"and respond with a depth lacking in most legal potboilers. Add an intricate plot, in which Good and Evil are both clothed in gray, and the reader can't plow through without paying attention."

It is a rare writer indeed who collects millions of dollars from a first novel. Even more rare is the author who crafts a novel while holding a full- time, high-profile job. Turow did both, writing drafts of *Presumed Innocent* in his spare moments on the commuter train while working as an assistant U.S. district attorney in Chicago. *Washington Post* contributor Steve Coll wrote that through his determination to write fiction without sacrificing his profession, Turow "has fulfilled every literate working stiff's fantasy."

For his part, Turow maintains that his background in the legal system has provided him with subject matter for fiction as well as practical experience in crafting a narrative. He told a *Publishers Weekly* writer, "As a lawyer, I never decided I didn't want to be a writer. I decided it would have to be a private passion, rather than something I could use . . . . My idea was to stay *alive* as a writer, just to continue to nurture that part of my soul." Turow not only "stayed alive" as a writer, he prospered. His novels have topped the best-seller lists and have found favor with many of the nation's book critics. *Time* reviewer Paul Gray contended that the author's works "revolve around a nexus of old-fashioned values: honesty, loyalty, trust. When those values are violated—sometimes salaciously, always entertainingly—lawyers and the legal system rush in to try to set things right again. But the central quest in Turow's fiction is not for favorable verdicts but for the redemption of souls, the healing of society. Best-sellers seldom get more serious than that."

Turow was born and raised in the Chicago area, the son of an obstetrician. In his early years the family lived in the city. Later they moved to an affluent suburb, Winnetka, Illinois, where Turow attended New Trier High School. As the author told a *Washington Post* contributor, he inherited his own driving ambition from his father, who was "out delivering babies at all hours of the day and night and wasn't around very much." The author added, "I suppose that's the embedded mental image of the hard-working male that I have become." Both of Turow's parents helped to nurture that spirit of hard work, because they wanted their son to become a physician too. Turow had other ideas, however. Even though he flunked freshman English at New Trier High, he grew to love writing, eventually becoming the editor of the school newspaper. He decided he wanted to be a writer, so enrolled in Amherst College in Massachusetts as an English major.

At Amherst Turow began to write short stories and novels, and a few of his short pieces were printed in literary magazines such as the *Transatlantic Review,* a rare feat for an undergraduate. After earning his bachelor's degree in 1970, Turow won a fellowship to the Stanford University creative-writing program. There he taught while working on a novel about Chicago called *The Way Things Are.* He began to question the direction of his career when he received twenty-five rejections for his completed manuscript; only one publisher, Farrar, Straus & Giroux, offered even the slightest encouragement. Turow told a *New York Times Magazine* writer that the cool reception his novel earned "made me realize that I wasn't one-tenth the writer I hoped to be . . . . I could not sustain the vision of myself as a writer only." In a *Los Angeles Times* interview he said, "I became convinced that one could not make a living in the U.S. writing serious fiction. I was never terribly bitter about that. I didn't see why the world had an obligation to support novelists."

Even while writing *The Way Things Are* Turow was becoming interested in the law, and in 1975, he entered Harvard Law School. Even then he put his writing talents to work. When his literary agent secured him a contract for a personal, nonfiction account of the first year in the law school, Turow took notes during his hectic class schedule and finished the book during summer recess. In 1977 Putnam published Turow's *One L: An Inside Account of Life in the First Year at Harvard Law School.* The work sold modestly at first, but it eventually became "required reading for anyone contemplating a career in law," noted Justin Blewitt in *Best Sellers. New York Times* critic P.M. Stern called *One L* "a compelling and important book. It is compelling in its vivid portrayal of the high-tension competitiveness of Harvard Law School and of the group madness it seems to induce in the student body. It is important because it offers an inside look at what law students do and don't learn and who they are and are not equipped to represent when they graduate."

After receiving his law degree in 1978, Turow returned to Chicago to work with the U.S. District Attorney's office there. As a prosecutor, he was assigned to the infamous "Operation Greylord," a series of trials that exposed judicial corruption in the city's courts. Little by little, the intrigues of corruption and legal wrangling began to work their way into the notebooks Turow kept for his fiction. He set aside a novel he was drafting and began to tinker with a story about an attorney. "I was learning a lot about bribery and I wanted to write about that," he told the *Washington Post.*

For several years Turow did his writing in the little spare time left him after meeting the demands of Operation Greylord and his growing family in the suburbs.

He edited chapters of his new novel during his commute to and from work on the train and rose early in the morning to work on his fiction before he left for the office. Finally, his wife convinced him to quit his job and finish the novel. He accepted a partnership at the downtown Chicago firm of Sonnenschein, Carlin, Nath & Rosenthal and then took a three-month hiatus from the firm in order to write. His finished manuscript was mailed to a New York agent just two weeks before he was due to start his new job.

Turow was confident that his novel would be published, but he was astonished by the level of interest shown by New York's biggest publishing houses. A bidding war ensued over the rights to publish the work, and the sums soon exceeded 200,000 dollars. Ultimately, Turow did not choose the high bidder but instead took an offer from Farrar, Straus because of the firm's literary reputation—and because of the encouragement he had received from its editors during his student days. The payment Farrar, Straus offered Turow was the largest sum that company had ever paid for a first novel.

Presumed Innocent tells the story of a troubled deputy prosecutor in a big city who is assigned to investigate the murder of a female colleague. As the nightmare case unfolds, the prosecutor, Rusty Sabich, finds himself on trial for murdering the woman with whom he once had an adulterous affair. Gray wrote that in *Presumed Innocent* Turow "uses [a] grotesque death as a means of exposing the trail of municipal corruption that has spread through [fictitious] Kindle County. The issue is not merely whether a murderer will be brought to justice but whether public institutions and their guardians are any longer capable of finding the truth." Turow told *Publishers Weekly* that his book is "a comment on the different kinds of truth we recognize. If the criminal-justice system is supposed to be a truth-finding device, it's an awkward one at best. There are all kinds of playing around in the book that illuminate that, and yet by the same token, the results in the end are just. And that's not accidental . . . . Absolutely everybody in the novel is guilty of something. That's a truth of life that I learned as a prosecutor. We all do things we wish we hadn't done and that we're not necessarily proud of."

Fellow attorney-turned-author George V. Higgins noted in the *Chicago Tribune* that *Presumed Innocent* is a "beautifully crafted tale . . . . Packed with data, rich in incident, painstakingly imagined, it snags both of your lapels and presses you down in your chair until you've finished it." Toronto *Globe & Mail* correspondent H. J. Kirchhoff called the novel "surprisingly assured," adding, "The prose is crisp and polished, every character is distinct and fully realized, and the dialogue is authentic. Turow has blended his experience in the rough-and-tumble of the criminal courts with a sympathetic eye for the vagaries of the human condition and an intimate understanding of the dark side of the human soul." Shear concluded that the criminal-justice system *Presumed Innocent* portrays, "without tears or pretense, has seldom appeared in literature quite like this."

"*Presumed Innocent* won the literary lottery," observed Mei-Mei Chan in *USA Weekend.* The novel spent more than forty-three weeks on the best- seller lists, went through sixteen hardcover printings, and sold four million paperback copies. Turow reaped three million dollars for the paperback rights and another one million dollars for the movie rights. A film adaptation of the work, released in 1990, was one of the ten top-grossing movies of that year. When Turow published his second novel—almost simultaneously with the debut of the movie version of *Presumed Innocent*—he joined the ranks of Ernest Hemingway, J. D. Salinger, and Alex Haley by becoming the ninety-second writer to appear on the cover of *Time* magazine.

By the time *The Burden of Proof* appeared in the summer of 1990, Turow had established a routine that included several hours a day for his writing. He still practiced law, but he spent his mornings at home, in contact with the downtown firm by telephone and fax machine. His schedule remained daunting, however, as his celebrity status made him a sought-after interview subject in the various media. But, as Turow told *New York Times Magazine,* he does his best work under such pressure. "I run on a combination of fear, anxiety, and compulsion," he said. "I have to control my habit to work all the time."

The Burden of Proof takes its hero from among the characters in *Presumed Innocent.* Sandy Stern is a middle-aged defense attorney who returns home from a business trip to find his wife dead in an apparent suicide. As he confronts the loss and the circumstances behind it, he becomes enmeshed in a web of family intrigues, insider stock trading schemes, and unanswered questions about his wife's private life. Toronto *Globe & Mail* reviewer Margaret Cannon wrote that in *The Burden of Proof* Turow "has let his imagination loose and, while courtroom derring-do is still a hefty part of the plot, it doesn't subsume the tragic story about some very damaged people." In the *Washington Post Book World,* Jonathan Yardley wrote that "Turow's second novel proves beyond any reasonable doubt that his hugely successful first was no fluke . . . . It's that rare book, a popular novel that is also serious, if not 'literary' fiction. *The Burden of Proof* means to entertain, and does so with immense skill, so if all you want is intelligent amusement it will serve you handily: but it is also a complex, multilayered meditation on 'the heartsore arithmetic of human events,' and as such rises far above the norm of what is generally categorized as 'commercial' fiction."

Turow's third novel, *Pleading Guilty,* broke new ground for the author. "Although fully peopled with lawyers," explained Charles Champlin in the *Los Angeles Times Book Review,* "the story hardly peeps into a courtroom." A high-placed partner in a prestigious Midwestern law firm has suddenly gone missing, along with about five and a half million dollars of the firm's funds. Instead of calling in the police (which would raise a scandal and cost the firm business), the partners turn to one of their employees, Mack Malloy, a former policeman, to find the missing partner and the missing money. In the process, Malloy encounters a body in a refrigerator, an old nemesis, and, eventually, the missing man and money. " *Pleading Guilty,* written as Mack's diary of the . . . events, demonstrates that Mr. Turow, at his best descriptive form, is worthy to be ranked with Dashiell Hammett or Raymond Chandler," said Champlin. "Scott Turow writes as well as ever," declared *Washington Post Book World* contributor Ross Thomas, "and is skilled enough not only to entertain his readers but also convince them they are acquiring vital inside stuff about the legal profession."

Although *The Laws of Our Fathers* reintroduces Turow's famous court scenes, it also moves in different directions compared to the author's previous work. The shooting death of the wife of a state senator reunites a group of 1960s radicals who had been friends but had gone their separate ways at the end of the decade. "The novel is less a legal thriller than a meditative examination of the hold that time past exerts over time present," said Michiko Kakutani in the *New York Times Book Review.* "Beneath the layers of a deep legal deviousness," stated a *Kirkus Reviews* contributor, "Turow never lets you forget that his characters lived and loved before they ever got dragged into court." "The resulting story is by turns moving and manipulative, compelling and contrived," Kakutani concluded. "Though deeply flawed, it stands as Mr. Turow's most ambitious novel yet."

Robbie Feaver is the failed actor and corrupt personal injury lawyer of *Personal Injuries,* a novel based on elements of Turow's experiences with Operation Greylord. "Without knowing anything about the Greylord case, I can attest that this novel has the ring of authenticity," wrote Dennis Drabelle in the *Washington Post Book World.* "It blends widespread graft, a spidery villain insulated at the heart of a complex web, suffering, murder, suicide, and also a measure of humor into a narrative that proceeds with the inevitability—and the surprises—of real life." The story is narrated by Feaver's lawyer, George Mason, called "a colorless fellow who readily admits that he did not witness most of the events he is describing," said Kakutani.

Feaver pays off judges from a secret bank account which is discovered by the F.B.I. while the agency is setting up a sting to nail those judges. Feaver is offered an ultimatum—wear a wire and turn informant or face prosecution. Feaver, a womanizer, but devoted to his wife dying of Lou Gehrig's disease, is assigned an F.B.I. agent, Evon Miller, who, because she is a lesbian, resists Feaver's charm. Gary Krist wrote in the *New York Times Book Review* that "to watch the two of them gradually probing the multiple veils, curtains, and trapdoors of each other's personalities, penetrating a little deeper each time, is to experience the kind of reading pleasure that only the best novelists—genre or otherwise—can provide . . . . And Robbie Feaver may be [Turow's] most inspired creation yet—a slick, mercurial, bighearted con artist, as flawed yet somehow as noble as those tragic figures he never got to play onstage."

Reviewing the novel for *Salon.com,* Jonathan Groner wrote that "the book doesn't pack much mystery . . . . Once the main action is under way and Feaver, wired for sight and sound, has set out among the judges and the courtroom lackeys, there are few surprises. But *Personal Injuries* succeeds as a long look at a world where greed, sloth, and lust holds sway despite the efforts of some good men and women." Drabelle concluded by saying that "lawyers like to differentiate between substance, the content of the law, and procedure, the steps by which you make the system work. In Turow's first novel, *Presumed Innocent,* substance dominated, in the form of a magnificently surprising answer to the whodunit question. *Personal Injuries* holds no similar shock, but the loving attentiveness to procedure—the nuts and bolts of that sting—makes it an absorbing crime novel, perhaps Turow's best."

In *Ultimate Punishment: A Lawyer's Reflections on Dealing with the Death Penalty,* Turow tackles the controversial issue of capital punishment. He first lays the groundwork by providing a history of the death penalty in America, along with overviews of the differing positions on its use. Laurie Selwyn of *Library Journal* praised the book for its even-handed approach to the issue, adding that it is "useful for law, debate, political science, and ethics students." A reviewer for *Publishers Weekly* found the book to be "a sober and elegantly concise examination" containing "useful insights into this fiercely debated subject." William Vance Trollinger, Jr. of the *Christian Century* found Turow's book compelling. In his review, he wrote, "Those who carefully follow his reasoning will not be surprised when, at the end, he declares that he is now opposed to capital punishment. But his compelling logic leaves us with a crucial question: Why do so many Americans and American politicians continue to support the death penalty?"

Turow returned to fiction with the publication of *Ordinary Heroes.* The novel, however, is not a legal thriller, but a World War II story. In it, journalist Stewart Dubinsky discovers documents indicating that his deceased father, David (a former World War II soldier), was court-martialed for allegedly aiding a suspected spy's escape from prison. Stewart later discovers his father's memoirs and much of the narrative in *Ordinary Heroes* is devoted to passages from them. Although Jeffrey Miller, writing in the Toronto *Globe & Mail,* felt that some of the soldiers' dialogue was "stilted," most critics felt that Turow's effort was quite successful. As *Booklist* contributor Allison Block noted, "the author's action sequences . . . do plenty to quicken the pulse." In addition, a *Kirkus Reviews* writer stated, "Without diminishing his page-turning narrative momentum, Turow extends his literary range."

Turow has said repeatedly that he does not intend to retire from his law practice, even though the profits from his writing career give him that option. The author told the *Chicago Tribune* that he spent many years defining himself as a writer before he became a lawyer. "I really didn't have any sense of identity as a lawyer. I really felt I was faking it," he said. "Somewhere along the way that changed; somewhere along the line I went through this kind of shift of identity. People ask me what I do. I certainly answer I am a lawyer. I don't say I'm a writer. I find that kind of a grandiose claim for somebody who spends sixty hours a week doing something else." Turow told *Publishers Weekly* that he is grateful for the level of success he has achieved with his books but that his perspective on writing has not changed. "Making money was not my intention," he said. "I wrote out of the same impulse that everyone else writes out of—I wrote because there were parts of my experience that I could best deal with that way." He concluded, "Obviously it was enormously fulfilling."

BIOGRAPHICAL AND CRITICAL SOURCES:

BOOKS

Bestsellers 90, issue 3, Thomson Gale (Detroit, MI), 1991.

Contemporary Popular Writers, St. James Press (Detroit, MI), 1997.

Lundy, Derek, *Scott Turow: Meeting the Enemy,* ECW Press, 1995.

St. James Guide to Crime and Mystery Writers, 4th edition, St. James Press (Detroit, MI), 1996.

PERIODICALS

Best Sellers, November, 1977, Justin Blewitt, review of *One L: An Inside Account of Life in the First Year at Harvard Law School.*

Booklist, July, 1999, review of *Personal Injuries,* p. 1896; September 1, 2002, Kristine Huntley, review of *Reversible Errors,* p. 8; September 1, 2005, Allison Block, review of *Ordinary Heroes,* p. 8.

Books, autumn, 1999, review of *Personal Injuries,* p. 19.

Chicago Tribune, June 7, 1987; June 10, 1987; February 16, 1990.

Christian Century, February 10, 2004, William Vance Trollinger, Jr., "No More Death Row," p. 24.

Christian Science Monitor, October 24, 2000, "*One L*—a Survivor's Tale," p. 13.

Esquire, October, 1999, review of *Personal Injuries,* p. 84.

Globe & Mail (Toronto, Ontario, Canada), July 11, 1987; August 8, 1987; June 16, 1990; October 9, 1999, review of *Personal Injuries,* p. D15; November 27, 1999, review of *Personal Injuries,* p. D50; November 5, 2005, Jeffrey Miller, review of *Ordinary Heroes,* p. D16.

Harper's Bazaar, June, 1990.

Interview, June, 1990, p. 170.

Kirkus Reviews, August 1, 1996, review of *The Laws of Our Fathers,* p. 1090; July 1, 1999, review of *Personal Injuries,* p. 997; September 1, 2005, review of *Ordinary Heroes,* p. 942.

Kliatt, November, 1998, review of *The Laws of Our Fathers,* p. 49; May, 2003, Sue Rosenzweig, review of *Reversible Errors,* p. 63.

Ladies' Home Journal, July, 1996, p. 124.

Library Journal, August, 1996, p. 115; August, 1999, review of *Personal Injuries,* p. 143; March 1, 2004, Laurie Selwyn, review of *Ultimate Punishment: A Lawyer's Reflections on Dealing with the Death Penalty,* p. 127.

Los Angeles Times, July 24, 1987; October 12, 1989; June 11, 1990; July 27, 1990; September 9, 1990.

Los Angeles Times Book Review, June 3, 1990; June 13, 1993, Charles Champlin, review of *Pleading Guilty,* p. 11; October 10, 1999, review of *Personal Injuries,* p. 10; September 15, 2003, Stephen L. Hupp, review of *Reversible Errors,* p. 106.

New Republic, March 14, 1994, pp. 32-38.

Newsweek, October 17, 1977; June 29, 1987; June 4, 1990; July 5, 1993; July 26, 1993; September 27, 1999, review of *Personal Injuries,* p. 66.

New York Times, September 15, 1977; February 8, 1987; June 15, 1987; August 6, 1987; December 1, 1987; April 19, 1988; May 31, 1990.

New York Times Book Review, September 25, 1977; June 28, 1987, pp. 1, 29; June 3, 1990; June 6, 1993, p. 7; October 8, 1996, Michiko Kakutani, review of *The Laws of Our Fathers,* p. 4; October 5, 1999, Michiko Kakutani, "The Case of a Lawyer and His Judicial Sting," p. 6; October 24, 1999, Gary Krist, "When in Doubt, Lie," p. 7.

New York Times Magazine, June 7, 1987, Jeff Shear, review of *Presumed Innocent.*

Publishers Weekly, July 10, 1987; September 15, 1989; April 1, 1996, p. 22; August 2, 1999, review of *Personal Injuries,* p. 69; November 1, 1999, review of *Personal Injuries,* p. 47; August 19, 2002, review of *Reversible Errors,* p. 64; August 25, 2003, review of *Ultimate Punishment,* p. 48.

Time, July 20, 1987, Paul Gray, review of *Presumed Innocent;* June 11, 1990; October 18, 1999, review of *Personal Injuries,* p. 114; September 6, 1999, review of *Personal Injuries,* p. 76; December 20, 1999, review of *Personal Injuries,* p. 104.

Times Literary Supplement, November 5, 1999, review of *Personal Injuries,* p. 24.

Trial, March, 2003, Rebecca Porter, review of *Reversible Errors,* p. 68.

USA Weekend, June 1, 1990, Mei-Mei Chan, review of *Presumed Innocent.*

Wall Street Journal, October 1, 1999, Nicholas Kulish, review of *Personal Injuries,* p. 6.

Washington Post, October 2, 1977; August 30, 1987; June 9, 1990; June 12, 1990; July 27, 1990.

Washington Post Book World, June 3, 1990; December 2, 1990; June 27, 1993, Ross Thomas, review of *Pleading Guilty,* pp. 1, 8; October 3, 1999, Dennis Drabelle, "Legal Lies," p. 5.

ONLINE

BookPage.com, http://www.bookpage.com/ (October 1, 2001), James Buckley, Jr., "Going Undercover in Life and Law: A Talk with Scott Turow."

Salon.com, http://www.salon.com/ (October 5, 1999), Jonathan Groner, review of *Personal Injuries.*

Scott Turow Home Page, http://www.scottturow.com/ (September 10, 2004).

* * *

TYLER, Anne 1941-

PERSONAL: Born October 25, 1941, in Minneapolis, MN; daughter of Lloyd Parry (a chemist) and Phyllis (Mahon) Tyler; married Taghi Modarressi (a psychiatrist and writer), May 3, 1963 (died, 1997); children: Tezh, Mitra. *Education:* Duke University, B.A., 1961; graduate study at Columbia University, 1961-62. *Religion:* Quaker.

ADDRESSES: *Home*—222 Tunbridge Rd., Baltimore, MD 21212. *Agent*—Russell and Volkening, Inc., 50 West 29th St., New York, NY 10001.

CAREER: Writer. Duke University Library, Durham, NC, Russian bibliographer, 1962-63; McGill University Law Library, Montreal, Quebec, Canada, assistant to librarian, 1964-65.

MEMBER: PEN, American Academy and Institute of Arts and Letters, Authors Guild, Phi Beta Kappa, American Academy of Arts and Sciences.

AWARDS, HONORS: *Mademoiselle* award for writing, 1966; Award for Literature, American Academy and Institute of Arts and Letters, 1977; National Book Critics Circle fiction award nomination, 1980, Janet Heidinger Kafka prize, 1981, and American Book Award nomination in paperback fiction, 1982, all for *Morgan's Passing;* National Book Critics Circle fiction award nomination, 1982, American Book Award nomination in fiction, PEN/Faulkner Award for fiction, and Pulitzer Prize nomination for fiction, all 1983, all for *Dinner at the Homesick Restaurant;* National Book Critics Circle fiction award and Pulitzer Prize nomination for fiction, both 1985, both for *The Accidental Tourist;* Pulitzer Prize, 1988, for *Breathing Lessons.*

WRITINGS:

If Morning Ever Comes, Alfred A. Knopf (New York, NY), 1964.

The Tin Can Tree, Alfred A. Knopf (New York, NY), 1965, reprinted, Fawcett Columbine (New York, NY), 1996.

A Slipping-down Life, Alfred A. Knopf (New York, NY), 1970.

The Clock Winder, Alfred A. Knopf (New York, NY), 1972.

Celestial Navigation, Alfred A. Knopf (New York, NY), 1974.

Searching for Caleb, Alfred A. Knopf (New York, NY), 1976.

Earthly Possessions, Alfred A. Knopf (New York, NY), 1977, reprinted, Fawcett Columbine (New York, NY), 1996.

Morgan's Passing, Alfred A. Knopf (New York, NY), 1980, reprinted, Fawcett Columbine (New York, NY), 1996.

Dinner at the Homesick Restaurant (also see below), Alfred A. Knopf (New York, NY), 1982.

(Editor, with Shannon Ravenel, and author of introduction) *Best American Short Stories 1983,* Houghton Mifflin (Boston, MA), 1983.

The Accidental Tourist (also see below), Alfred A. Knopf (New York, NY), 1985, reprinted, ImPress (New York, NY) 1999.

Breathing Lessons (also see below), Alfred A. Knopf (New York, NY), 1988.

Anne Tyler: Four Complete Novels (contains *Dinner at the Homesick Restaurant, Morgan's Passing, The Tin Can Tree,* and *If Morning Ever Comes*), Avenel Books (New York, NY), 1990.

Anne Tyler: A New Collection (omnibus volume; contains *The Accidental Tourist, Breathing Lessons,* and *Searching for Caleb*), Wings Books (New York, NY), 1991.

Saint Maybe (also see below), Alfred A. Knopf (New York, NY), 1991.

Tumble Tower (juvenile), illustrated by daughter Mitra Modarressi, Orchard Books (New York, NY), 1993.

(With Robert W. Lenski) *Breathing Lessons* (screenplay; based on her novel), Republic Pictures, 1994.

Ladder of Years (also see below), Alfred A. Knopf (New York, NY), 1995.

(Editor, with Shannon Ravenel) *Best of the South: From Ten Years of New Stories from the South,* Algonquin Books (Chapel Hill, NC), 1996.

A Patchwork Planet (also see below), Alfred A. Knopf (New York, NY), 1998.

A Patchwork Planet, Ladder of Years, Saint Maybe: Three Complete Novels, Bright Sky Press (Albany, TX), 2001.

The Amateur Marriage, Alfred A. Knopf (New York, NY), 2004.

Contributor of short stories, poetry, and articles to many periodicals, including *Saturday Evening Post, New Yorker, Seventeen, Critic, Antioch Review,* and *Southern Review.*

ADAPTATIONS: A film adaptation of *The Accidental Tourist,* starring Kathleen Turner and William Hurt, was released by Warner Brothers, 1988; it was also recorded as a book on tape by Recorded Books, 1991.

SIDELIGHTS: Despite her status as a best-selling novelist, Anne Tyler remains a private person who rarely lets public demands interfere with her family life. She shuns most interviews, avoids talk show appearances, and prefers her home in Baltimore, Maryland to New York City. As the author explained in an e-mail correspondence with Alden Mudge for *Bookpage* online, Tyler explained: "I'm too shy for personal appearances, and I've found out that anytime I talk about my writing, I can't do any writing for many weeks afterward." In a body of work that spans over four decades, Tyler has earned what former *Detroit News* reporter Bruce Cook called "a solid *literary* reputation . . . that is based solely on the quality of her books."

Tyler's work has always been critically well received, but reviews of her early novels were generally relegated to the back pages of book review sections. Not until the publication of *Celestial Navigation,* when she captured the attention of novelist Gail Godwin, and *Searching for Caleb,* when John Updike recommended her to readers, did she gain widespread acclaim. "Now," said Cook, "her books are reviewed in the front of the literary journals and that means she is somebody to reckon with. No longer one of America's best unknown writers, she is now recognized as one of America's best writers. Period."

Born in Minnesota, Tyler lived in various Quaker communes throughout the Midwest and South before settling in the mountains of North Carolina for five years. She attended high school in Raleigh and at sixteen entered Duke University where she fell under the influence of Reynolds Price, then a promising young novelist who had attended her high school. It was Price who encouraged the young Russian major to pursue her writing, and she did—but it remained a secondary pursuit until 1967, the year she and her husband settled in Baltimore.

In an interview with Bruce Cook published in *Saturday Review,* Tyler described Baltimore as "wonderful territory for a writer—so many different things to poke around in." And the longer she stayed there, the more prominently Baltimore figured in her books, lending them an ambiance both citified and southern, and leading Price to proclaim her "the nearest thing we have to an urban Southern novelist." Writing in *New Yorker,* John Updike compared her to Flannery O'Connor, Carson McCullers, and Eudora Welty: "Anne Tyler, in her gifts both of dreaming and of realizing, evokes comparison with these writers, and in her tone and subject matter seems deliberately to seek association with the Southern ambiance that, in less cosmopolitan times, they naturally and inevitably breathed. Even their aura of regional isolation is imitated by Miss Tyler as she holds fast, in her imagination and in her person, to a Baltimore with only Southern exits; her characters when they flee, never flee north."

Other reviewers, such as Katha Pollitt, found Tyler's novels more difficult to classify. "They are Southern in their sure sense of family and place," Pollitt wrote in *New York Times Book Review,* "but [they] lack the taste for violence and the Gothic that often characterizes self-consciously Southern literature. They are modern in their fictional techniques, yet utterly unconcerned with the contemporary moment as a subject, so that, with only minor dislocations, her stories could just as well have taken place in the twenties or thirties. The current school of feminist-influenced novels seems to have passed her by completely: her women are strong, often stronger than the men in their lives, but solidly grounded in traditional roles."

The key to Tyler's writing may well lie in the homage she pays to Eudora Welty, her favorite writer and one to whom she has been repeatedly compared. "Reading her taught me there were stories to be written about the mundane life around me," Tyler told Cook. Or as she phrased it to Marguerite Michaels in *New York Times Book Review,* "Reading Eudora Welty when I was growing up showed me that very small things are often really larger than the large things." Thomas M. Disch is one of several critics who believes that Tyler's insight into the lives of ordinary people is her special gift. Writing in *Washington Post Book World,* he called it an "uncommon accomplishment that she can make such characters interesting and amusing without violating their limitations." Despite their resemblances to people we meet in real life, Tyler's characters are totally fictitious. "None of the people I write about are people I know," she told Michaels. "That would be no fun. And it would be very boring to write about me. Even if I led an exciting life, why live it again on paper? I want to live other lives. I've never quite believed that one chance is all I get. Writing is my way of making other chances."

Tyler's major theme, according to Mary Ellen Brooks in *Dictionary of Literary Biography,* "is the obstinate endurance of the human spirit, reflected in every character's acceptance or rejection of his fate and in how that attitude affects his day to day life. She uses the family unit as a vehicle for portraying 'how people manage to endure together—how they grate against each other, adjust, intrude and protect themselves from intrusions, give up, and start all over again in the morning.'" Frequently her characters respond to stress by running away, but their flight, Brooks explained, "proves to be only a temporary and ineffectual means of dealing with reality."

Because the action of her novels is so often circular—ending exactly where it begins—Tyler's fiction has been criticized for lack of development. This was especially true of her early novels where the narratives are straightforward and the pacing slow. In fact, what impressed reviewers most about Tyler's first book, *If Morning Ever Comes,* was not the story itself but the promise it seemed to hold for future works of fiction. "The trouble with this competently put-together book is that the hero is hardly better defined at the end than he is at the beginning," observed Julian Gloag in *Saturday Review.* "Writing about a dull and totally humorless character, Miss Tyler has inevitably produced a totally humorless and mainly dull novel. Anne Tyler is only twenty-two, and in the light of this her refusal to take risks is a bit puzzling. I'd like to see what she could do if she stopped narrowing her own eyes and let herself go. It might be very good."

For her part, Tyler reportedly came to dislike her first book as well as her second, which received similar criticism. *The Tin Can Tree* was written largely to pass the time while she was looking for a job. As Millicent Bell wrote in *New York Times Book Review:* "Life, this young writer seems to be saying, achieves its once-and-for-all shape and then the camera clicks. This view, which brings her characters back on the last page to where they started, does not make for that sense of development which is the true novel's motive force. Because of it, I think, her book remains a sketch, a description, a snapshot. But as such, it still has a certain dry clarity. And the hand that has clicked its shutter has selected a moment of truth."

Perhaps the most salient feature of Tyler's next novel, *A Slipping-down Life*—which was misclassified as young adult literature and thus not widely reviewed—is its genesis. In discussing her craft with Michaels, Tyler explained: "Sometimes a book will start with a picture that pops into my mind and I ask myself questions about it and if I put all the answers together, I've got a novel. A real picture would be the old newspaper clipping about the Texas girl who slashed 'Elvis' in her forehead." In the novel, this incident is transformed into an episode in the life of Evie Decker, a fictional teenager grappling for her identity. "I believe this is the best thing I've ever done," Evie says of her self-mutilation. "Something out of character. Definite." In *Dictionary of Literary Biography,* Brooks described the novel as "an accurate description of loneliness, failure to communicate, and regrets over decisions that are irreversible—problems with which any age group can identify. Tyler, who described *A Slipping-down Life* as one of her most bizarre works, believes that the novel 'is flawed, but represents, for me, a certain brave stepping forth.'"

So, too, does Tyler's fifth novel, *Celestial Navigation,* a book that the author wrote while "fighting the urge to remain in retreat even though the children had started school." Told from the viewpoints of six different characters, *Celestial Navigation* is far more intricate than Tyler's earlier novels, and most critics considered it a breakthrough. Katha Pollitt found the work "extraordinarily moving and beautiful," while Doris Grumbach praised Tyler's "ability to enmesh the reader in what is a simple, uneventful story a notable achievement." In her *New York Times Book Review* article, Gail Godwin explained how "Tyler is especially gifted at the art of freeing her characters and then keeping track of them as they move in their unique and often solitary orbits. Her fiction is filled with displaced persons who persist stubbornly in their own destinies. They are 'oddballs,' visionaries, lonely souls, but she has a way of transcribing their peculiarities with such loving wholeness that when we examine them we keep finding more and more pieces of ourselves."

In *Morgan's Passing* Tyler turns from an exploration of the "oddball" as introvert to the "oddball" as extrovert in the creation of Morgan Gower, a forty-two-year-old hardware store manager with a knack for assuming other roles. Simply put, Morgan is an imposter, a man who changes identities every time he changes clothes. Though *Morgan's Passing* was nominated for a National Book Critics Circle award and an American Book Award, critics have been sharply divided in their assessment of the work. Those who liked it praised Tyler's handling of the characters and her artful mingling of comedy and seriousness. "Though she allows her tale to veer toward farce, Tyler always checks it in time with the tug of an emotion, a twitch of regret," wrote *Time*'s Paul Gray, concluding that *Morgan's Passing* "is not another novel about a mid-life crisis, it is a buoyant story about a struggle unto death." Tyler acknowledged in a *Detroit News* interview with Bruce Cook that her "big worry in doing the book was that people would be morally offended by [Morgan]." However, critic Marilyn Murray Willison sang her questionably protagonist's praises. "In spite of his inability to restore order to his life, his nicotine-stained hands and teeth, his silly wardrobe, his refusal to accept reality, Morgan emerges from Tyler's book a true hero," Willison wrote in *Los Angeles Times Book Review.*

Several critics, however, found Morgan to be problematic and considered *Morgan's Passing* a disappointment. "For all its many felicities of observation and incident, *Morgan's Passing* does not come up to the high standard of Anne Tyler's other recent work. There is a self-indulgence in the portraiture of Morgan himself, whose numerous identity assumptions became for me merely tiresome," Paul Binding wrote in *New Statesman.* And *New York Review of Books* contributing critic James Wolcott dismissed *Morgan's Passing* as "a book of small compass, pent-up energy. . . . there's no suspense, no surprise. Instead, the book is stuffed with accounts of weddings, crowded dinners, cute squabbles, and symbolic-as-all-get-out puppet shows. Sentence by sentence, the book is engaging, but there's nothing beneath the jokes and tussles to propel the reader through these cluttered lives. It's a book with an idle motor." Writing in *New Yorker,* John Updike explained his disappointment: "Tyler continues to look close, and to fabricate, out of the cardboard and Magic Markers available to the festive imagination, images of the illusory lives we lead. More than that it would be unkind to ask, did we not imagine, for the scope of the gift displayed, that something of that gift is still being withheld."

With *Dinner at the Homesick Restaurant,* her ninth and, some say, finest novel, Tyler redeemed herself in many critics' eyes. Updike, for instance, maintained that this book achieves "a new level of power and gives us a lucid and delightful yet complex and sombre improvisation on her favorite theme, family life." Writing in *Chicago Tribune Book World,* Larry McMurtry echoed these sentiments, writing that Tyler "recognizes and conveys beautifully the alternations of tragedy and farce in family life, and never more beautifully than in *Dinner at the Homesick Restaurant.*" Benjamin Demott was even more impressed. "Funny, heart-hammering, wise, [the novel] edges deep into truth that's simultaneously (and interdependently) psychological, moral and formal—deeper than many living novelists of serious reputation have penetrated, deeper than Miss Tyler herself has gone before. It is a border crossing," Demott wrote in *New York Times Book Review.* McMurtry believed that *Dinner at the Homesick Restaurant* "amply demonstrates the tenacity of familial involvement," while *Los Angeles Times* reporter Carolyn See maintained that Tyler shows how a family "is alive with needs of its own; it never relaxes its hold. Even when you are far away (especially when you're far away), it immobilizes you in its grip, which can—in another way—be looked at as a caress."

Dinner at the Homesick Restaurant unfolds in a series of self-contained chapters, each, in Updike's words, "rounded like a short story," and each reflecting a different family member's point of view. This narrative technique, as Sarah English noted, "allows [Tyler] to juxtapose past and present and thus to convey the vision—that she has always had—of the past not as a continuum but as layers of still, vivid memories. The wealth of points of view also allows Tyler to show more fully than ever the essential subjectivity of the past. . . . Every character's vision of the past is different." This portrait of family entanglements was too somber for some critics' tastes, however, including Cynthia Propper Seton's. "What may be the trouble with *Dinner at the Homesick Restaurant,*" she wrote in *Washington Post Book World,* "is that the . . . family is not marginal enough, its members are too grave a proposition for a mind so full of mischief as Anne Tyler's. They depressed her." In her *Detroit News* review, however, Cynthia King maintained that "despite the joyless atmosphere, the author's humor bubbles through." Demott concluded, "What one wants to do on finishing such a work as *Dinner at the Homesick Restaurant* is maintain balance, keep things intact for a stretch, stay under the spell as long as possible. The before and after are immaterial; nothing counts except the knowledge, solid and serene, that's all at once breathing in the room. We're speaking obviously, about an extremely beautiful book."

The Accidental Tourist, Tyler's tenth novel, again combines the author's subtle, understated probing into human nature and her eye for comic detail. The title serves both as a reference to the protagonist's occupation and as a metaphor for his life. Macon Leary writes travel guides for people who dislike traveling and who would prefer to stay in the comfort and familiarity of their own homes. The guide books—the series is titled *The Accidental Tourist*—advise reluctant travelers on how to visit foreign places without experiencing the annoyances and jarring peculiarities that each new city offers. Thus, Macon counsels his readers on where they can find American-style hamburgers in Amsterdam, for instance, or on the type of reading material to carry on the plane so as to ward off chatty passengers. As with her previous novels, reviewers praised the gently ironic humor and sympathetic, likable characters that Tyler created in *The Accidental Tourist.* Richard Eder of *Los Angeles Times Book Review* noted that the character of Macon Leary "is an oddity of the first water, and yet we grow so close to him that there is not the slightest warp in the lucid, touching and very funny story of an inhibited man moving out into life." Other critics observed that Tyler fuses the mix of tragedy and comedy that appears in most of her previous books. McMurtry, writing in *New York Times Book Review* about "the mingling of misery and contentment in the daily lives of her families" that Tyler constructs, commented that "these themes, some of which she has been sifting for more than twenty years, cohere with high definition in the muted . . . personality of Macon Leary." Some reviewers criticized Tyler for her tendency to draw sympathetic characters and to infuse humor into so many of her scenes. *Chicago Tribune Book World* critic John Blades wondered whether "Tyler, with her sedative resolutions to life's most grievous and perplexing problems, can be taken seriously as a writer." Most reviewers, though, praised the book and its author. Eder noted, "I don't know if there is a better American writer going."

In her Pulitzer Prize-winning eleventh novel, *Breathing Lessons,* Tyler examines the themes of marriage, love, and regret. The story concerns Maggie and Ira Moran, married for twenty-eight years, and a journey they make to the funeral of an old friend. During the trip they both reflect on their years together—some happy, some sad. Maggie is gregarious and curious, while Ira is practical and withdrawn. Both at times regret their decision to marry, but they also recognize the strength of the bond between them. Critics again remarked on Tyler's ability to evoke sympathy for her characters and her talent for constructing humorous scenes. Eder, writing in *Los Angeles Times Book Review,* generally summed up critical reaction by noting that "there are moments when the struggle among Maggie, Ira, and the melancholy of time passing forms a fiery triangle more powerful and moving . . . than anything she has done."

"Tyler's twelfth novel, *Saint Maybe,*" wrote *Dictionary of Literary Biography* contributor Caren J. Town, "addresses most directly another important Tyler concern: religion." The protagonist of *Saint Maybe* is Ian Bedloe, a well-adjusted teenager. Ian's family life changes drastically when his older brother Danny marries a divorcee named Lucy, who has two children of her own. Danny commits suicide after the birth of his daughter Daphne and Lucy dies of an overdose of sleeping pills soon after. Ian is overcome with guilt; he seeks guidance from a fundamentalist sect known as the Church of the Second Chance, led by the charismatic Brother Emmett. Emmett charges Ian to care for his brother's children as a penance for his connection with Danny's death. "Tyler has a well-known skepticism about the premise of most religions," declared Town: "'It's not that I have anything against ministers,' she . . . [said] in a discussion about *Earthly Possessions,* 'but that I'm particularly concerned with how much right anyone has to change someone, and ministers are people who feel they have that right.'" Brad Leithauser in *New York Review of Books* remarked, "*Saint Maybe* winds up being something of a curious creation: a secular tale of holy redemption."

Tyler uses her characters in *Saint Maybe* to examine the role of modern American family life. "Is the family an anchor in the storm?" asked Marilyn Gardner of *Christian Science Monitor.* "Or is it a shackle? Do duty and devotion hold together the members who make up a family as well as the family itself? Or do families become, not support systems, but burdens of guilt, leading to damaging sacrifices of personal freedom?" *New York Times Book Review* contributor Jay Parini wrote, "In many ways it is Anne Tyler's most sophisticated work, a realistic chronicle that celebrates family life without erasing the pain and boredom that families almost necessarily inflict upon their members."

Tyler moved in a different direction with her next book, *Tumble Tower*—which features illustrations by her daughter Mitra Modarressi—and creates "a kid-pleasing story about Princess Molly the Messy and her royal family of neatnicks," according to *Christian Science Monitor* contributor Karen Williams. Unlike her obsessed parents and siblings, including Prince Thomas the Tidy, Molly lives a comfortably unkempt life. "The moral of Tyler's tale," declared Suzanne Curley in *Los Angeles Times Book Review,* "is that a princess unfazed by half-eaten candy bars left under her chair cushions, kittens nesting among fluffy slippers on the closet floor or a bed 'all lumpy and knobby with half-finished books' probably has her priorities straight, and may have much to teach about the way clutter often goes hand-in-hand with coziness."

In Tyler's *Ladder of Years,* stated *New York Times Book Review* contributor Cathleen Schine, "the story that appears to unfold of its own accord is a fairy tale of sorts, a fairy tale with echoes of both the tragedy of *King Lear* and the absurdity of the modern romance novel." Suzanne L. MacLachlan in *Christian Science Monitor* explained that the novel "is written from the viewpoint of a woman approaching middle age who feels she is losing her family." One day Delia Grinstead simply walks out on her obnoxious husband and her uncaring teenaged children and starts a new life in a Maryland town some miles away. She becomes self-supporting, taking a job as a lawyer's secretary. "Just as she subverts the domestic with fantasy—her situations are earthbound until you notice that they are gliding along two inches above the earth—she subverts fantasy with the domestic," explained a *Los Angeles Times Book Review* contributor. Delia's old patterns of behavior begin to reassert themselves and she returns home for her oldest daughter's wedding. "Her eventual journey back to her home and family are, in many ways," MacLachlan stated, "the universal search for self. She finds, in the end, that the people she has left behind have traveled further than she." Declared *New York Times* reviewer Christopher Lehmann-Haupt in his review of *Ladder of Years,* "As always, Ms. Tyler writes with a clarity that makes the commonplace seem fresh and the pathetic touching."

The hero of Tyler's novel *A Patchwork Planet* is an likeable ne'er-do-well. As a teenager, Barnaby Gaitlin disappointed his rich Baltimore parents by breaking into other people's houses, not so much as a thief but to go through family mementos and pry into others' lives. Unlike most of Tyler's fiction, *A Patchwork Planet* is written in the first person; Barnaby tells his own story. "One of Tyler's major strengths," observed Jonelle Bonta in *Metroactive Books,* "has always been her uncanny ability to depict children, describing their simplistic reactions to life's complex situations with unsentimental understanding. In *A Patchwork Planet,* a similar rich talent is revealed: an empathy with the elderly." Linda Simon, reviewing the novel for *World and I,* commented that by the end of *A Patchwork Blanket* "Nothing changes in Barnaby except his own self-perception. And yet, Tyler shows us, this change in perception may allow us to see the world as a bit less haphazard and incoherent, and to celebrate our place, however modest, on our own makeshift patch of the planet." Gill Hornby, writing for *Literary Review* online, noted that "Barnaby's life is so engrossing, there is such a clatter of subplots—family squabbles, car purchases, domestic wrangles—that it is only when you get to the last, perfect cadence that you realize how carefully, minutely plotted a novel this is. . . . probably Tyler's finest novel yet."

Reviewing Tyler's *Back When We Were Grownups,* a *Kirkus Reviews* critic described the book as "packed with life in all its humdrum complexity—and funny, so funny, the kind that compels reading aloud." Beth Kephart of *Book* noted: "In her deeply moving and perfectly syncopated new novel . . . Tyler presents a stunning portrait of fifty-three-year-old Rebecca Davitch, a 'wide and soft and dimpled' woman whose style of dress edges 'dangerously close to Bag Lady,' whose hair naturally assumes a 'pup tent' shape and whose compulsive goodness has become the source . . . of much eloquent soul-searching." L. Gregory Jones of *Christian Century* found similarities between Rebecca and the character of Delia Grinstead in Tyler's *Ladder of Years.* According to Jones, the two women "present contrasting ways of trying to escape their present lives. One woman concludes that she has been an impostor in her own life, and so needs to assume a different character; the other wants to assume a different character by becoming an impostor." Rebecca's life is revealed to the reader in flashbacks as she reminisces and reflects on what has brought her to this point. Despite a brief and tentative dalliance with the college sweetheart to whom she was once engaged, Rebecca comes to realize while watching old family movies that she has enjoyed her life immensely and ended up right where she belongs. In a review critical of *Back When We Were Grownups,* Michiko Kakutani of *New York Times* noted that Tyler's "fiction has always hovered perilously close to the line between heartfelt emotion and cloying sentimentality," and went on to conclude: "In showing how family traits are passed down generation to generation, in showing how shared rituals, celebrations and crises create a communal history, she [Tyler] demonstrates the talents that galvanized so many of her earlier books and that help redeem this very flawed novel." Linnea Lannon of *People* expressed an opinion more in accordance with that of other reviewers: "A wonderful life makes for a wonderful novel."

In his *Bookpage* article, Mudge wrote, "What Tyler herself has always been particularly good at is depicting the fullness of life lived on a human scale. Her characters are not—and do not aspire to become—members of the glitterati or the literati. . . . Their dramas are the commonplace dramas of family and community life. Tyler's great art has been to illuminate her characters' lives with wry wit and insight, not to exalt them to some larger, brighter stage." Such talents are fully realized in *The Amateur Marriage,* which Mudge concluded, "Quite simply, . . . ranks among Tyler's best to date." *The Amateur Marriage* is the story of Michael Anton and Pauline Barclay, whose accidental meeting in Baltimore just after the attack on Pearl Harbor that pulled the United States into World War II culminates in a hasty—and ultimately unhappy—marriage. Tyler traces their lives as they raise their family, into old age, and through the 9/11 terrorist attack on the United States. As Tyler told Mudge, *The Amateur Marriage* "grew out of the reflection that of all the opportunities to show differences in character, surely an unhappy marriage must be the richest. I didn't want a good-person-bad-person marriage, but a marriage in which solely the two styles of character provide the friction." Reviewing *The Amateur Marriage* for *Bookreporter.-com,* Barbara Lipkien Gershenbaum called it one of Tyler's best works. "The old cliché that 'time heals all wounds' lurks beneath the surface of *The Amateur Marriage,* but Tyler doesn't really dig down to it in any obvious ways. Rather, as in real life, her fictional world continues to turn, and one at a time each character moves on with his/her wounds, bound at some time to heal."

Writing in *New York Times Book Review,* Carol Shields stated that Tyler "has always been a warmly compassionate recorder of middle-class America, yet one who is wide open to the riffs, the reverberations, the trajectories of the dislocated." According to Alice McDermott of *Washington Post:* "Surprise is not the point in an Anne Tyler novel, nor is plot, or even connectedness. The charm of an Anne Tyler novel lies in the clarity of her prose and the wisdom of her observations, in her fine ear for the 'clamor' of family. While the world of each of her novels resembles nothing so much as the world of all her other novels, her stories remain stubbornly like life."

BIOGRAPHICAL AND CRITICAL SOURCES:

PERIODICALS

Antioch Review, winter, 1999, Gerda Oldham, review of *A Patchwork Planet,* p. 112.

Book, May, 2001, Beth Kephart, review of *Back When We Were Grownups,* p. 63.

Chicago Tribune Book World, March 23, 1980; March 21, 1982; July 20, 1986.

Christian Century, July 4, 2001, L. Gregory Jones, "Living into Our Histories," p. 29.

Christian Science Monitor, September 25, 1991, Marilyn Gardner, review of *Saint Maybe,* p. 13; December 17, 1993, Karen Williams, review of *Tumble Tower,* p. 12; May 18, 1995, Suzanne MacLachlan, review of *Ladder of Years,* p. 13; May 3, 2001, Ron Charles, "Grandma Wonders If It's Ever Too Late," p. 21.

Detroit News, April 6, 1980; April 18, 1982.

Kirkus Reviews, February 15, 1995, p. 180; March 15, 2001, review of *Back When We Were Grownups,* p. 361.

Los Angeles Times, March 30, 1982; September 14, 1983.

Los Angeles Times Book Review, March 30, 1980; September 15, 1985; September 11, 1988; September 5, 1993, p. 9; May 7, 1995, p. 3.

New Statesman, April 4, 1975; December 5, 1980, Paul Binding, review of *Morgan's Passing.*

New Yorker, March 29, 1976; June 6, 1977; June 23, 1980, John Updike, review of *Morgan's Passing,* p. 95; April 5, 1982, John Updike, review of *Dinner at the Homesick Restaurant,* p. 193; May 8, 1995, Tom Shone, review of *Ladder of Years,* pp. 89-90.

New York Review of Books, April 3, 1980, James Wolcott, review of *Morgan's Passing,* p. 34; January 16, 1992, Brad Leithauser, review of *Saint Maybe,* pp. 53-55.

New York Times, May 3, 1977; March 17, 1980, John Leonard, review of *Morgan's Passing,* p. C17; March 22, 1982, Christopher Lehmann-Haupt, review of *Dinner at the Homesick Restaurant,* p. 21; September 3, 1988, Michiko Kakutani, review of *Breathing Lessons,* p. 13; April 27, 1995, Christopher Lehmann-Haupt, review of *Ladder of Years,* p. B2; May 18, 2001, Michiko Kakutani, review of *Back When We Were Grownups,* p. B3.

New York Times Book Review, November 22, 1964; November 21, 1965; March 15, 1970; May 21, 1972; April 28, 1974; January 18, 1976; May 8, 1977; March 14, 1982, Benjamin DeMott, review of *Dinner at the Homesick Restaurant,* p. 1; September 8, 1985, Larry McMurtry, review of *The Accidental Tourist,* p. 1; August 25, 1991, Jay Parini, review of *Saint Maybe,* pp. 1, 26; May 7, 1995, Cathleen Schine, review of *Ladder of Years,* p. 12; April 19, 1998, Carol Shields, review of *A Patchwork Planet,* p. 12; May 20, 2001, John Leonard, review of *Back When We Were Grownups,* p. 14.

People, May 21, 2001, Linnea Lannon, review of *Back When We Were Grownups,* p. 51.

Saturday Review, December 26, 1964; November 20, 1965; June 17, 1972; March 6, 1976; September 4, 1976; March 15, 1980, Eva Hoffman, review of *Morgan's Passing,* p. 38.

School Library Journal, December, 1991, Katherine Fitch, review of *Saint Maybe,* pp. 149-150.

Time, May 9, 1977; March 17, 1980; April 5, 1982, R.Z. Shephard, review of *Dinner at the Homesick Restaurant,* p. 77; September 16, 1985, R.Z. Shephard, review of *The Accidental Tourist,* p. 78.

Times Literary Supplement, July 15, 1965; May 23, 1975; December 9, 1977; October 31, 1980; October 29, 1982; October 4, 1985; January 20, 1989.

Washington Post, May 20, 2001, Alice McDermott, review of *Back When We Were Grownups,* p. T03.

Washington Post Book World, March 16, 1980; April 4, 1982; September 4, 1988.

World and I, August, 1998, Linda Simon, review of *A Patchwork Planet,* p. 274.

ONLINE

BookPage, http://www.bookpage.com/ (April 25, 2004), Allen Mudge, "Mismatched Mates, Anne Tyler Explores the Dramas of Everyday Family Life" (interview).

Bookreporter.com,, http://www.bookreporter.com/ (April 25, 2004), Barbara Lipkien Gershenbaum, review of *The Amateur Marriage.*

Literary Review Online, http://www.litrev.dircon.co.uk/ (August 5, 2001), Gill Hornby, "A Man You Can Trust."

Metroactive Books Online, http://www.metroactive.com/ (June 25, 1998), Jonelle Bonta, "Screwball."

* * *

TYREE, Omar
(Omar Rashad Tyree, Urban Griot)

PERSONAL: Born in Philadelphia, PA; married; children: Ameer, one other son. *Education:* Attended University of Pittsburgh; Howard University, B.S. (with honors), 1991.

ADDRESSES: *Home*—New Castle, DE. *Agent*—c/o Author Mail, Simon & Schuster, 1230 Avenue of the Americas, New York, NY 10020.

CAREER: Author, publisher, lecturer, and performance poet. *Capital Spotlight* (weekly newspaper), Washington, DC, reporter, assistant editor, and advertising salesperson; *News Dimensions* (weekly newspaper), chief reporter; freelance writer; founder of MARS Productions, beginning 1993. Has lectured to organizations, at colleges, high schools and community events; has appeared on television programs, including *For Black Men Only* and *America's Black Forum.*

WRITINGS:

Colored, on White Campus: The Education of a Racial World (novel), MARS Productions (Washington, DC), 1992, published as *Battlezone: The Struggle to Survive the American Institution,* MARS Productions (Washington, DC), 1994.

Flyy-Girl (novel), MARS Productions (Washington, DC), 1993.

Capital City: The Chronicles of a D.C. Underworld, MARS Productions (Washington, DC), 1994.

A Do-Right Man (novel), Simon & Schuster (New York, NY), 1997.

Single Mom (novel), Simon & Schuster (New York, NY), 1998.

For the Love of Money (sequel to *Flyy Girl*), Simon & Schuster (New York, NY), 2000.

Just Say No!, Simon & Schuster (New York, NY), 2001.

Leslie, Simon & Schuster (New York, NY), 2002.

(Under pseudonym Urban Griot) *College Boy,* Pocket Books (New York, NY), 2003.

Diary of a Groupie, Simon & Schuster (New York, NY), 2003.

(Under pseudonym Urban Griot) *Cold Blooded: A Hardcore Novel,* Simon & Schuster (New York, NY), 2004.

Contributor to periodicals, including *Washington View Magazine* and *Washington Post;* contributor to *Testimony: Young African-Americans on Self-Discovery and Black Identity,* Beacon Press, 1995.

ADAPTATIONS: Several of Tyree's books have been adapted as audiobooks.

SIDELIGHTS: Omar Tyree has been persistent, and successful, in his efforts to become a published author and messenger for the experience of black America. He has lectured to organizations, at colleges, high schools, and community events; in addition, his commentaries have occasionally been televised. His writings have appeared in periodicals such as *Washington View Magazine* and the *Washington Post,* as well as in works of fiction. Tyree's focus is on sharing his beliefs and the realties associated with being a black person in the United States. Through Tyree's own publishing company, MARS Productions, the author was able to release some of his first books. He has self-published several novels, among them *Flyy-Girl,* which has since been released by New York-based Simon & Schuster.

As *Library Journal* contributor Shirley Gibson Coleman explained, Tyree's novel *A Do-Right Man* "gives an honest if tiring interpretation of a black man struggling to do right" and provides readers with a "rare view of the true-to-life emotions of black males." The "hip-to-the-punch" and "feel-good" novel is saved from sinking to "fairy tale" status, concluded a *Publishers Weekly* reviewer, by "Tyree's good humor and ear for dialogue."

Another of Tyree's early novels, *Single Mom,* "reads mostly like an impassioned essay or sociology textbook," according to Nancy Pearl in *Library Journal.* Of *Single Mom,* a *Publishers Weekly* writer declared: "In one way or another, each of the figures is a mouthpiece for responsible fatherhood or the difficulties of single motherhood."

Tyree's breakthrough novel, *Flyy-Girl,* earned its author a loyal readership but received mixed reviews from critics. The novel follows Tracy Ellison Grant, a middle-class Philadelphian, through her adolescence. In *Publishers Weekly* a reviewer described the novel as an "unremarkable African American coming-of-age story" that suffers from "a crucial lack of depth." According to the critic, "teenage chatter" overwhelms Tyree's message, rendering the novel ultimately "trite and superficial." Despite a "mildly rushed ending," Shirley Gibson Coleman found more to like, writing in her *Library Journal* review that *Flyy-Girl* is "entertaining" and displays dialogue that is "true to life." In stark contrast to the *Publishers Weekly* critic's contention that Tyree's novel is "unremarkable," Coleman ranked *Flyy-Girl* among "the best" black coming-of-age stories the critic had "read in a long time." However, a *Kirkus Reviews* contributor echoed some of the same criticisms as had the *Publishers Weekly* reviewer, citing *Flyy-Girl* as a "morality tale" and a "shapeless docudrama," and indicating that it contains "some silly Afrocentric theorizing."

Enhanced by what Coleman described as Tyree's "skillful use of dialog," *For the Love of Money* continues the story started in *Flyy-Girl,* and finds Tracy, now age twenty-eight and an up-and-coming actress and successful script writer, clearly on her way to material success. With her love life in a current state of disrepair, she returns to Germantown, Philadelphia, but finds herself out of step with old friends. Ultimately, a relationship is rekindled with an old boyfriend in a novel that a *Publishers Weekly* dubbed "rowdy and predictable." Still, the reviewer added, Tracy's "adventures provide cool commentary on ambition, love, friendship, and the price of fame." Praising *For the Love of Money* as a "cogent and deftly constructed tale," Glenn Townes noted in *Black Issues Book Review* that Tyree's savvy protagonist "maintains her go-on girl attitude" despite personal setbacks.

Other novels from Tyree, who has averaged about a book per year, include 2002's *Leslie,* which focuses on a nineteen-year-old New Orleans college student whose interest in the voodoo traditions of her Haitian father ultimately lead her to disaster. "Tyree has woven complex characters that overcome seemlingly hopeless circumstances," noted *Booklist* contributor Lillian Lewis, describing the three friends who manage to improve their lot in life while Leslie, with all her advantages, travels her doomed downward spiral. In *Ebony,* a contributor described *Leslie* as "a modern horror story with social commentary on the effects of poverty." *Diary of a Groupie,* released in 2003, focuses, in characteristic Tyree fashion, on attractive, sexy, and ambitious Tabitha Night, whose social connections are channeled by a private investigator hoping to reveal the lewd practices of a well-known actor. Noting that in the novel "nothing is what it seems," *Black Issues Book Review* critic Curtis Stephens praised *Diary of a Groupie* as "absorbing and spellbinding."

BIOGRAPHICAL AND CRITICAL SOURCES:

PERIODICALS

Black Issues Book Review, September, 2000, Glenn Townes, review of *For the Love of Money,* p. 22; September, 2001, p. 15; July-August, 2002, pp. 40-44; July-August, 2003, Curtis Stephen, review of *Diary of a Groupie,* p. 55.

Book, July-August, 2002, Chris Barsanti, review of *Leslie,* p. 82.

Booklist, October 1, 1996, p. 309; June 1, 2000, Lillian Lewis, review of *Leslie,* p. 1862; February 15, 2000, p. 1082; June 1, 2001, Lillian Lewis, review of *Just Say No!,* p. 1850; July, 2002, p. 1824.

Ebony, October 1, 1997, pp. 1481-1482; November, 2002, review of *Leslie,* pp. 18-19.

Essence, August, 2001, p. 64.

Kirkus Reviews, August 1, 1996, pp. 1090-1091; October 1, 1997, pp. 1481-1482; June 1, 2002, p. 767; May 1, 2003, review of *Diary of a Groupie,* pp. 640-641.

Library Journal, September 15, 1996, p. 98; November 15, 1997, p. 78; September 15, 1998, pp. 114-115; October 15, 1999, p. 108; July 3, 2000, review of *For the Love of Money,* p. 49; August, 2000, p. 163.

Publishers Weekly, August 26, 1996, p. 76; October 6, 1997, p. 74; August 17, 1998, p. 46; September 20, 1999, p. 73; July 3, 2000, review of *For the Love of Money,* p. 49; August 6, 2001, p. 62; July 29, 2002, pp. 53-54; May 12, 2003, review of *Diary of a Groupie,* p. 43.

ONLINE

African-American Literature Book Club Web Site, http://www.aalbc.com/ (August 20, 2004), "Omar Tyree."

Awareness Magazine Online, http://www.awarenessmagazine.net/ (August 20, 2004), Rebecca Shepherd, interview with Tyree.

Omar Tyree Home Page, http://www.omartyree.com/ (August 20, 2004).

* * *

TYREE, Omar Rashad
See TYREE, Omar

U

UCHIDA, Yoshiko 1921-1992

PERSONAL: Surname is pronounced "Oo-*chee*-dah"; born November 24, 1921, in Alameda, CA; died after a stroke, June 21, 1992, in Berkeley, CA; daughter of Dwight Takashi (a businessman) and Iku (Umegaki) Uchida. *Education:* University of California—Berkeley, A.B. (cum laude), 1942; Smith College, M.Ed., 1944. *Politics:* Democrat. *Religion:* Protestant. *Hobbies and other interests:* Fine arts, folk crafts.

CAREER: Elementary school teacher in Japanese relocation center in Utah, 1942-43; Frankford Friends' School, Philadelphia, PA, teacher, 1944-45; Institute of Pacific Relations, membership secretary, 1946-47; United Student Christian Council, secretary, 1947-52; full-time writer, 1952-57; University of California—Berkeley, secretary, 1957-62; full-time writer, 1962-92.

AWARDS, HONORS: Ford Foundation research fellow in Japan, 1952; Children's Spring Book Festival honor award, *New York Herald Tribune,* 1955, for *The Magic Listening Cap;* Notable Book citation, American Library Association, 1972, for *Journey to Topaz;* medal for best juvenile book by a California author, Commonwealth Club of California, 1972, for *Samurai of Gold Hill;* Award of Merit, California Association of Teachers of English, 1973; citation, Contra Costa chapter of Japanese American Citizens League, 1976, for outstanding contribution to the cultural development of society; Morris S. Rosenblatt Award, Utah State Historical Society, 1981, for article, "Topaz, City of Dust"; Distinguished Service Award, University of Oregon, 1981; Commonwealth Club of California medal, 1982, for *A Jar of Dreams;* award from Berkeley Chapter of Japanese American Citizens League, 1983; *School Library Journal,* Best Book of the Year citation, 1983, for *The Best Bad Thing;* New York Public Library, Best Book of the Year citation, 1983, for *The Best Bad Thing;* Best Book of 1985 citation, Bay Area Book Reviewers, 1985, for *The Happiest Ending;* Child Study Association of America, Children's Book of the Year citation, 1985, for *The Happiest Ending;* San Mateo and San Francisco Reading Associations, Young Authors' Hall of Fame award, 1985, for *The Happiest Ending;* Friends of Children and Literature award, 1987, for *A Jar of Dreams;* Japanese American of the Biennium award, Japanese American Citizens Leagues, 1988, for outstanding achievement.

WRITINGS:

JUVENILES

The Dancing Kettle and Other Japanese Folk Tales, illustrations by Richard C. Jones, Harcourt (New York, NY), 1949, reprinted, Creative Arts Book Co., 1986.

New Friends for Susan, illustrations by Henry Sugimoto, Scribner (New York, NY), 1951.

(Self-illustrated) *The Magic Listening Cap—More Folk Tales from Japan,* Harcourt (New York, NY), 1955, reprinted, Creative Arts Book Co., 1987.

(Self-illustrated) *The Full Circle* (junior high school study book), Friendship, 1957.

Takao and Grandfather's Sword, illustrations by William M. Hutchinson, Harcourt (New York, NY), 1958.

The Promised Year, illustrations by William M. Hutchinson, Harcourt (New York, NY), 1959.

Mik and the Prowler, illustrations by William M. Hutchinson, Harcourt (New York, NY), 1960.

Rokubei and the Thousand Rice Bowls, illustrations by Kazue Mizumura, Scribner (New York, NY), 1962.

The Forever Christmas Tree, illustrations by Kazue Mizumura, Scribner (New York, NY), 1963.

Sumi's Prize, illustrations by Kazue Mizumura, Scribner (New York, NY), 1964.

The Sea of Gold, and Other Tales from Japan, illustrations by Marianne Yamaguchi, Scribner (New York, NY), 1965.

Sumi's Special Happening, illustrations by Kazue Mizumura, Scribner (New York, NY), 1966.

In-Between Miya, illustrations by Susan Bennett, Scribner (New York, NY), 1967.

Hisako's Mysteries, illustrations by Susan Bennett, Scribner (New York, NY), 1969.

Sumi and the Goat and the Tokyo Express, illustrations by Kazue Mizumura, Scribner (New York, NY), 1969.

Makoto, the Smallest Boy: A Story of Japan, illustrations by Akihito Shirawaka, Crowell (New York, NY), 1970.

Journey to Topaz: A Story of the Japanese-American Evacuation, illustrations by Donald Carrick, Scribner (New York, NY), 1971.

Samurai of Gold Hill, illustrations by Ati Forberg, Scribner (New York, NY), 1972.

The Old Man with the Bump (cassette based on story from *The Dancing Kettle*), Houghton Mifflin (Boston, MA), 1973.

The Birthday Visitor, illustrations by Charles Robinson, Scribner (New York, NY), 1975.

The Rooster Who Understood Japanese, illustrations by Charles Robinson, Scribner (New York, NY), 1976.

The Two Foolish Cats (filmstrip with cassette based on a story from *The Sea of Gold*), Encyclopaedia Britannica Educational, 1977.

Journey Home (sequel to *Journey to Topaz*), illustrations by Charles Robinson, McElderry Books (New York, NY), 1978.

The Fox and the Bear (cassette based on a story from *The Magic Listening Cap*), Science Research Associates, 1979.

A Jar of Dreams, McElderry Books (New York, NY), 1981.

The Best Bad Thing (sequel to *A Jar of Dreams*), McElderry Books (New York, NY), 1983.

Tabi: Journey through Time, Stories of the Japanese in America, United Methodist Publishing House, 1984.

The Happiest Ending (sequel to *The Best Bad Thing*), McElderry Books (New York, NY), 1985.

The Two Foolish Cats, illustrations by Margot Zemach, McElderry Books (New York, NY), 1987.

The Terrible Leak, Creative Education (Mankato, MN), 1990.

The Invisible Thread (autobiography), J. Messner (New York, NY), 1991.

The Magic Purse, illustrations by Keiko Narahashi, McElderry Books (New York, NY), 1993.

The Bracelet, illustrations by Joanna Yardley, Philomel (New York, NY), 1993.

The Wise Old Woman, illustrations by Martin Springett, McElderry Books (New York, NY), 1994.

FOR ADULTS

We Do Not Work Alone: The Thoughts of Kanjiro Kawai, Folk Art Society (Japan), 1953.

(Translator of English portions) Soetsu Yanagi, editor, *Shoji Hamada,* Asahi Shimbun Publishing, 1961.

The History of Sycamore Church, Sycamore Congregational Church, 1974.

Desert Exile: The Uprooting of a Japanese-American Family, University of Washington Press (Seattle, WA), 1982.

Picture Bride (novel), Northland Press, 1987.

Contributor to books, including *Flight Near and Far,* Holt, 1970; *Scribner Anthology for Young People,* Scribner, 1976; *Literature and Life,* Scott, Foresman, 1979; *Fairy Tales of the Sea,* Harper, 1981; *Anthology of Children's Literature,* Scott, Foresman, 1984; and *Explorations,* Houghton Mifflin, 1986. Author of regular column, "Letter from San Francisco," in *Craft Horizons,* 1958-61. Contributor to exhibit catalogue of Oakland Museum, 1976. Contributor of stories and articles to newspapers and periodicals, including *Woman's Day, Gourmet, Utah Historical Quarterly, Far East,* and *California Monthly.*

Uchida's manuscripts are housed at the Kerlan Collection, University of Oregon Library, Eugene, and Bancroft Library, University of California—Berkeley.

SIDELIGHTS: Yoshiko Uchida's appreciation for her Japanese heritage inspired her to become the author of many books on Japanese culture for readers of all ages. "In fiction, the graceful and lively books of Yoshiko Uchida have drawn upon the author's own childhood to document the Japanese-American experience for middle-grade readers," Patty Campbell commented in the *New York Times Book Review.* Among Uchida's nonfiction works for adults are studies of Japanese folk artists such as *We Do Not Work Alone: The Thoughts of*

Kanjiro Kawai, as well as a memoir of wartime imprisonment, *Desert Exile: The Uprooting of a Japanese-American Family.*

After the bombing of Pearl Harbor, Americans of Japanese descent were incarcerated by order of the U.S. government. Uchida was a senior at the University of California—Berkeley, when her family was sent to Tanforan Racetracks, where thousands of Japanese-Americans lived in stables and barracks. After five months at Tanforan, they were moved to Topaz, a guarded camp in the Utah desert. Uchida taught in the elementary schools there until the spring of 1943, when she was released to accept a fellowship for graduate study at Smith College. Her parents were also released that year.

Uchida earned a master's degree in education, but because teaching limited her time for writing, she found a secretarial job that allowed her to write in the evenings. As she once explained in her contribution to *Something about the Author Autobiography Series,* "I was writing short stories at the time, sending them to the *New Yorker, Atlantic Monthly,* and *Harper's*—and routinely receiving printed rejection slips. After a time, however, the slips contained encouraging penciled notes and a *New Yorker* editor even met with me to suggest that I write about my concentration camp experiences. . . . And many of the short stories I wrote during those days were published eventually in literature anthologies for young people."

By the time *Woman's Day* accepted one of her stories, Uchida had discovered that writing for children promised more success. Her first book, *The Dancing Kettle and Other Japanese Folk Tales,* was well received, and when a Ford Foundation grant enabled Uchida to visit Japan, she collected more traditional tales. In addition, she became fascinated with Japanese arts and crafts, and learned more about them from philosopher Soetsu Yanagi and other founders of the Folk Art Movement in Japan. But her most important gain from the visit, she later explained, was the awareness "of a new dimension of myself as a Japanese-American and [a] deepened . . . respect and admiration for the culture that had made my parents what they were."

The final children's books Uchida wrote before her death in 1992 reflect her interests not only in Japan but also in her Japanese-American heritage. *The Magic Purse,* for instance, offers a tale with many mythical Japanese elements. In the book, a poor farmer journeying through a swamp encounters a beautiful maiden held captive by the lord of the swamp. She persuades him to carry a letter for her to her parents in another swamp, giving him a magic purse as a reward for his efforts. The purse contains gold coins that forever multiply, and the coins make the farmer a rich man, even as he returns year after year to the swamp to make peace with the swamp lord and to remember the maiden. *The Bracelet,* meanwhile, is set in California during World War II and features a seven-year-old Japanese-American girl, Emi, who is being shipped off to an internment camp with her mother and sister; her father has already been taken to another camp. Once at the camp (Tanforan Racetracks, the same camp that the author lived in as a girl), Emi realizes that she has lost the gold bracelet that her best friend Laurie gave to her as a parting gift. Despite being despondent over the loss of the bracelet, Emi comes to understand that her memory of Laurie is something more precious than the bracelet, because the memory will stay with her forever. In *The Wise Old Woman,* Uchida's final children's book, the author tells the story of a small village in medieval Japan in which the cruel young village lord has decreed that any person reaching seventy years of age must be taken into the mountains and left to die. A young farmer, unable to bear the thought of taking his mother away and letting her die, instead builds a secret room where she can hide. Later, a neighboring ruler comes to the village and declares that the village will be destroyed unless its citizens can carry out three seemingly impossible tasks. When the farmer's mother proves to be the only one capable of figuring out how to complete the tasks, the cruel young lord realizes the error of his age decree and revokes it, leaving the old woman—and others like her—free to remain with their families.

The death of the author's mother in 1966 prompted Uchida to write a book for her parents "and the other first-generation Japanese (the Issei), who had endured so much." The result was *Journey to Topaz: A Story of the Japanese-American Evacuation.* Based on her own experiences in the camps during the war, the book marks the author's shift in emphasis from Japanese culture to the Japanese-American experience in the United States. Every book Uchida wrote following *Journey to Topaz* responded to the growing need for identity among third generation Japanese Americans. As Uchida once explained, "Through my books I hope to give young Asian-Americans a sense of their past and to reinforce their self-esteem and self-knowledge. At the same time, I want to dispel the stereotypic image still held by many non-Asians about the Japanese and write about them as real people. I hope to convey the strength of spirit and the sense of hope and purpose I have observed in many first-generation Japanese. Beyond that, I write to celebrate our common humanity, for the basic elements of humanity are present in all our strivings."

BIOGRAPHICAL AND CRITICAL SOURCES:

BOOKS

Children's Literature Review, Volume 6, Thomson Gale (Detroit, MI), 1984.

Something about the Author Autobiography Series, Volume 1, Thomson Gale (Detroit, MI), 1986.

Twentieth-Century Children's Writers, 3rd edition, St. James Press (Detroit, MI), 1989.

PERIODICALS

Children's Book World, November 5, 1967.

Five Owls, January-February, 1994.

New York Times Book Review, February 9, 1986; November 14, 1993, p. 21.

Publishers Weekly, October 24, 1994, p. 61.

School Library Journal, November, 1993, p. 103; December, 1993, p. 95; July, 1995, p. 75.

Young Readers' Review, January, 1967.

* * *

UHRY, Alfred 1936-

PERSONAL: Born 1936, in Atlanta, GA; son of Ralph K. (a furniture designer and artist) and Alene (a social worker; maiden name, Fox) Uhry; married Joanna Kellogg (a teacher), June 13, 1959; children: Emily, Elizabeth, Kate, Nell. *Education:* Brown University, B.A., 1958.

ADDRESSES: *Office*—c/o Playwrights Horizons, 416 West 42nd St., New York, NY 10036. *Agent*—Flora Roberts Agency, 157 West 57th St., Penthouse A, New York, NY 10019.

CAREER: Playwright and lyricist. Worked with composer Frank Loesser, 1960-63; Calhoun High School (private school), New York, NY, instructor in English and drama, until 1980; affiliated with Goodspeed Opera House, 1980-84; New York University, New York, NY, instructor in lyric writing, 1985-88; worked on comedy scripts for television.

MEMBER: Academy of Motion Picture Arts and Sciences, Dramatists Guild.

AWARDS, HONORS: Drama Desk Award nominations, 1975, for *The Robber Bridegroom,* and 1987, for *Driving Miss Daisy;* Antoinette Perry ("Tony") Award nomination, American Theater Wing and League of American Theaters, 1976, for *The Robber Bridegroom;* Pulitzer Prize for drama, 1988, for *Driving Miss Daisy;* Academy Award for best screenplay adaptation, Academy of Motion Picture Arts and Sciences, 1989, for *Driving Miss Daisy;* American Theater Critics Association Best Play, Outer Critics Circle Award and Tony Award for best play, 1997, all for *The Last Night of Ballyhoo;* Tony Award for book of a musical, 1999, for *Parade.*

WRITINGS:

(Lyricist; book by Terrence McNally; music by Robert Waldman) *Here's Where I Belong* (musical; based on John Steinbeck's novel *East of Eden*), produced in New York, NY, 1968.

(Lyricist and librettist; music by Robert Waldman) *The Robber Bridegroom* (two-act musical; based on Eudora Welty's novella of the same title; produced Off-Off Broadway, 1975, produced on Broadway, 1975), Drama Book Specialists, 1978.

Chapeau (musical; based on a French farce, *An Italian Straw Hat*), produced at Saratoga Performing Arts Center, 1977.

(Lyricist; book by Conn Fleming; music by Robert Waldman) *Swing* (musical), produced in Wilmington, DE, 1980, produced at John F. Kennedy Center for the Performing Arts, 1980.

(Adaptor) George M. Cohan, *Little Johnny Jones* (two-act musical), produced on Broadway, 1982.

(Lyricist and librettist) *America's Sweetheart* (musical; based on John Kobler's book of the same title), produced in Hartford, CT, 1985.

Driving Miss Daisy (play; produced Off-Broadway, 1987), Theater Communications Group, 1988.

(With Amy Jones, Perry Howze, and Randy Howze) *Mystic Pizza* (screenplay), Metro-Goldwyn-Mayer, 1988.

Driving Miss Daisy (screenplay), Warner Bros., 1989.

Rich in Love, Metro-Goldwyn-Mayer, 1993.

The Last Night of Ballyhoo, Theater Communications Group (New York, NY), 1997.

Parade, music and lyrics by Jason Robert Brown, produced at Lincoln Center Theater, 1999.

Also author of screenplay, *Blondie,* Walt Disney Co., and worked on script for *Paradise Road,* 1997. Adapted musical comedies for revivals, including *Funny Face.*

ADAPTATIONS: The Robber Bridegroom was adapted for a sound recording, Columbia Special Products, 1978.

WORK IN PROGRESS: A screenplay, *Charm.*

SIDELIGHTS: After years of working in the wings as a lyricist and librettist, Alfred Uhry burst into the limelight with his first original play, the Off-Broadway hit *Driving Miss Daisy,* in 1987. He had had some success in the mid-1970s with the Broadway musical *The Robber Bridegroom,* receiving a Tony Award nomination for his work, but subsequent projects had fizzled. Uhry was considering leaving the theater altogether when the idea for *Driving Miss Daisy*—about an elderly Jewish woman and the black chauffeur foisted on her by her son—finally struck him as viable. The finished play garnered him a Pulitzer Prize and box-office success; his film adaptation won an Academy Award.

Uhry's first well-known work, *The Robber Bridegroom,* is a rustic musical based on a novella by Mississippi writer Eudora Welty; Uhry wrote the "book," or script, and the song lyrics. The story concerns a gentleman thief in backwoods Mississippi who decides to steal not only money but love. First produced in small venues, the play became a surprise hit on New York's Off-Broadway circuit in 1975 and ran on Broadway for nearly one hundred fifty performances during the 1976-1977 season. In a 1976 *New York Times* review, Clive Barnes characterized the work as "unpretentious . . . but extremely stylish" and commended Uhry for being "very fair to the original." Barnes felt that Uhry succeeded in retaining "not only Miss Welty's strange command of fantasy but also something of the original's underlying menace." Barry Bostwick, who starred in the 1976 production, won a Tony Award for his performance.

After *The Robber Bridegroom* Uhry's fortunes waned somewhat. He turned to teaching, and he worked on other musicals, including a revival of George M. Cohan's *Little Johnny Jones* starring teen idol Donny Osmond. Some of the musicals closed on opening night or soon after; others never opened. By 1984 Uhry was struggling to get a workshop production of a musical about gangster Al Capone off the ground—*America's Sweetheart*—and thinking about leaving theater for good. In an interview with *Chicago Tribune* entertainment editor Richard Christiansen, Uhry commented: "Here I was, . . . working without pay, and doing something that was very, very hard. Something whispered in my ear that it was time to sit down and write a play."

Uhry had always known his family's legend about his grandmother, a cantankerous former schoolteacher who continued to drive long after she could do so safely and who was finally forced to relinquish the driver's seat to a black chauffeur. The tale hadn't seemed worth mining for drama at first. "I can't tell you how uninteresting it all seemed to me when I was a young man," Uhry told Leslie Bennetts in a *New York Times* interview. While he contemplated trading theater for teaching, however, he decided he could write the story of his grandmother, if only for himself. Such a play could counter misperceptions about race relations in the South. The chauffeur was neither a cowed servant nor a fiery revolutionary; the grandmother was not openly hostile toward blacks and even insisted she was not prejudiced. "Being rude is frowned upon in the South," Uhry observed. "Probably the same things are going on under the surface as everywhere else, but in the South everyone's sugary and sweet and polite." The relationship's twenty-five-year span covered the civil rights struggles from the 1950s to early 1970s, allowing Uhry to reflect some of the changes of that era in his play. And the changes in the relationship itself provided ample material—two very different people, suspicious of each other and resolutely formal in their relations, nonetheless become friends.

When *Driving Miss Daisy* begins, seventy-two-year-old Daisy has just wrecked her new car, and her son, Boolie, decides she needs a driver. Over her strong objections, Boolie hires Hoke, a black man ten years her junior, to drive for her. At first Daisy refuses to use his services; grudgingly, she finally consents. She finds fault with Hoke at every opportunity, but over the years she takes a more positive interest in him and even teaches him to read. Years pass before she will admit any kind of fondness for him, however. Daisy is in her nineties when she finally admits Hoke is her best friend. "This odd love story, though it never underestimates the difficulty of intimacy between the races, could easily grow mawkish," noted Robert Brustein in a *New Republic* review. "It is a tribute to Uhry's discreet understatement that the sentiment does not grow into corn." Such understatement turned out to be inherent in Uhry's subject—as he told Bennetts: "Sentiment was never going to get in [my grandmother's] way. When I was a little boy and wrote her letters, she would send them back to me—corrected."

Other critics joined in praising the restraint, humor, and humanity of *Driving Miss Daisy.* In the *New York Times,* Mel Gussow observed that Uhry "wisely refrains from melodramatic confrontation. The play remains quiet, and it becomes disarming, as it delineates the characters with almost offhanded glimpses." A quick trip to the store, a visit to the synagogue, a day at the cemetery become occasions to examine Daisy and Hoke's backgrounds, attitudes, and misperceptions. Daisy learns that Hoke is illiterate, for example, only because when they visit the cemetery he can't find the headstone she asked him to put flowers on for a friend. Daisy's conviction that blacks are thieves stands revealed when she prematurely accuses Hoke of stealing a can of salmon from her pantry. "*Driving Miss Daisy* is all of a piece," assessed Brustein, "combining elements of sense and sensibility, not to mention generous portions of pride and prejudice. It is the work of decent people, working against odds to show how humans still manage to reach out to each other in a divided world." Describing it as "sparely written, powerfully felt," Christiansen concluded his *Chicago Tribune* review by calling the work "a little play to treasure for the rest of our lives."

Critics were similarly receptive to the film version, starring veteran actress Jessica Tandy as Daisy and Morgan Freeman recreating his stage role as Hoke. The adaptation, written by playwright Uhry himself, "aspires more to complex observation of human behavior than to simple moralism about it," remarked Richard Schickel in *Time.* "Precisely because it has its priorities straight, it succeeds superbly on both levels." Vincent Canby of the *New York Times* deemed it "the most successful stage-to-screen translation" since Academy Award-winner *Dangerous Liaisons.* Canby commended both Uhry and director Bruce Beresford, who, "working in concert, see to it that the essential spirit of *Driving Miss Daisy* shines through."

The adaptation of *Driving Miss Daisy* was not quite Uhry's first experience with writing for the screen: earlier he had helped finish the script for the 1988 film *Mystic Pizza,* about three young women working in a pizza parlor in Mystic, Connecticut. Already credited to three screenwriters, the script came to the playwright with some problems and a story that interested Uhry, the father of four daughters. All three characters are working-class Portuguese-American girls making their way through various romantic entanglements on their way to maturity. Jojo is in love but afraid to get married; gorgeous Daisy is involved with a blue-blood recently expelled from Yale University; Daisy's sister Kat, set on attending Yale herself, falls in love with a married man. The finished film received mixed reviews. In a *Washington Post* review, Hal Hinson found the conflicts "at best, formulaic," the film itself "old-fashioned" and clichéd. *New York Times* critic Janet Maslin, however, stated that although the situations might be predictable, the film "manages to seem fresh anyhow." Suggesting that all its elements "are presented in an entirely winning way," Maslin asserted that *Mystic Pizza* "offers warm, inviting and funny glimpses into the lives and loves of three appealing young women."

With *Driving Miss Daisy* a hit with stage and screen audiences, Uhry became recognized as an artistic representative of his home town, Atlanta. In that spirit, he was commissioned for the 1996 Cultural Olympiad in Atlanta, an arts festival that accompanied the Summer Olympic Games. Uhry wrote the comedy-drama *Last Night of Ballyhoo* for the festival; the play takes place in 1939 at the eve of the world premiere of *Gone with the Wind*—the last time prior to the Olympics that the city had been in the international spotlight, according to the author. This play explores the Jewish experience in the South as seen through a family preparing for Ballyhoo, a cotillion for young Jewish belles of the pre-World War II era. Debutante Lala Levy, tragically dateless for the ball, is the object of obsession by her mother, Boo. "Preparations for and attendance of the gala ball parallel the gala Atlanta premiere of *Gone with the Wind* as well as the gala events that occur in the film prior to the outbreak of the Civil War," as Mel Koler described it in *Contemporary Southern Writers.* When *Last Night of Ballyhoo* was taken to Broadway in February 1997, Dana Ivey, who created the character of Daisy on Broadway, returned to play Boo Levy in what proved to be a popular production. "Uhry's dialogue is packed with laughs," declared Greg Evans of *Variety,* "and the byplay between Ivey and [co-star Celia Weston] is wonderfully performed." *Ballyhoo* went on to win a spate of awards, including a Tony for best play.

As an established voice for the Jewish South, Uhry was a natural choice to provide the book for the new 1999 musical, *Parade.* Based on a true story, *Parade* deals with the trial of Leo Frank, an Atlanta pencil factory manager indicted for the rape and murder of a thirteen-year-old employee, Mary Phagan, in 1913. Though the evidence against Frank was flimsy and his defense inadequate, "Georgians were satisfied with the result," noted *New Leader* contributor Stefan Kanfer. "As soon as they learned Frank's name and background they thought the worst of him. He was, after all, a Jew. Moreover, he was a Jew from New York." Through the relentless intervention of Frank's wife, Lucille, his sentence was commuted to life imprisonment. This infuriated a vigilante mob, who kidnapped Frank and offered him one more chance to "confess" to the murder. When he refused, they lynched him.

While generally well received, *Parade* was the focus of some critics who found the subject matter somewhat heavy-handed for a musical. Kanfer wondered why the drama was in this format at all: "Granted, [the musicals] *Rent* and *Titanic* have recently demonstrated that grief can inspire Broadway melodies. The sad fact, though, is that Frank was not nearly as compelling in life as he was in death. He appeared to have very little personality then, and seems even more remote today." Kanfer also noted that the depiction of Southern bigots and kangaroo courts has been explored, to greater effect, in works like *To Kill a Mockingbird* and *Inherit the Wind. Parade*'s characterization of small-minded Atlantans, remarked *Variety* writer Charles Isherwood, "makes for less than nuanced drama." Still, *Parade* netted Uhry a Tony award for his book.

Addressing the issue of critics, Uhry had this to say: "Critics are a necessary evil as far as I'm concerned. I don't think they write their reviews for me, but I suppose we need them in society. I put no store by good reviews or bad reviews. Bad ones hurt my feelings, sure. But they don't change my opinion of things I like or don't like."

BIOGRAPHICAL AND CRITICAL SOURCES:

BOOKS

Contemporary Dramatists, St. James Press (Detroit, MI), 1999.

Contemporary Southern Writers, St. James Press (Detroit, MI), 1999.

PERIODICALS

Atlanta Constitution, April 25, 1990, Keith Graham, "Alfred Uhry Driven by His Craft."

Back Stage West, December 13, 2001, Terri Roberts, review of *The Last Night of Ballyhoo,* p. 13.

Chicago Tribune, April 3, 1988; April 24, 1988.

Daily Variety, November 4, 2002, Markland Taylor, review of *Edgardo Mine,* p. 8.

Entertainment Weekly, June 20, 1997, Mark Harris, review of *The Last Night of Ballyhoo,* p. 31.

Explicator, Spring, 2003, Brian Sutton, "Williams's The Glass Menagerie and Uhty's Last Night of Ballyhoo," pp. 172-174.

Los Angeles Times, April 2, 1988.

National Review, April 12, 1993, John Simon, review of *Rich in Love,* p. 64.

New Leader, January 11, 1999, Stefan Kanfer, review of *Murder in the Present Tense,* p. 22.

New Republic, September 28, 1987, Robert Brustein, review of *Driving Miss Daisy.*

New Yorker, April 27, 1987.

New York Times, October 19, 1975; October 11, 1976, Clive Barnes, review of *The Robber Bridegroom;* April 16, 1987; October 11, 1987; December 23, 1987; October 23, 1988, Janet Maslin, review of *Mystic Pizza;* June 4, 1989; December 13, 1989; February 23, 1997, Alex Witchel, "Remembering Prejudice, of a Different Sort."

People, May 23, 1988; March 8, 1993, Leah Rozen, review of *Rich in Love,* p. 15.

Time, December 18, 1989, Richard Schickel, review of *Driving Miss Daisy;* March 8, 1993, review of *Rich in Love,* p. 73.

Variety, February 21, 1994, p. 169; March 3, 1997, Greg Evans, review of *The Last Night of Ballyhoo,* p. 77; December 21, 1998, Charles Isherwood, review of *Parade,* p. 85.

Washington Post, October 22, 1988, Hal Hinson, review of *Mystic Pizza.*

ONLINE

Chelsea Forum, Inc. Web Site, http://www.chelseaforum.com/ (August 20, 2004), "Alfred Uhry."

* * *

UNCLE SHELBY
See SILVERSTEIN, Shel

* * *

UPDIKE, John 1932-
(John Hoyer Updike)

PERSONAL: Born March 18, 1932, in Shillington, PA; son of Wesley Russell (a teacher) and Linda Grace (an author; maiden name, Hoyer) Updike; married Mary Entwistle Pennington, June 26, 1953 (divorced, 1977); married Martha Ruggles Bernhard, September 30, 1977;

children: (first marriage) Elizabeth Pennington, David Hoyer, Michael John, Miranda Margaret; (second marriage) three stepchildren. *Education:* Harvard University, A.B. (summa cum laude), 1954; attended Ruskin School of Drawing and Fine Art, Oxford, 1954-55. *Politics:* Democrat. *Religion:* Christian.

ADDRESSES: Home—Beverly Farms, MA. *Agent*—c/o Author Mail, Alfred A. Knopf, 201 E. 50th St., New York, NY 10022.

CAREER: Novelist, critic, short story writer, poet, essayist, and dramatist. *New Yorker* magazine, reporter, 1955-57. Visited USSR as part of a cultural exchange program of the U.S. Department of State, 1964.

MEMBER: American Academy and Institute of Arts and Letters (secretary, chancellor), American Academy of Arts and Sciences.

AWARDS, HONORS: Guggenheim fellowship in poetry, 1959; American Academy and National Institute of Arts and Letters Richard and Hilda Rosenthal Foundation Award, 1960, for *The Poorhouse Fair;* National Book Award in fiction, 1964, and Prix Medicis Etranger (France), 1966, both for *The Centaur;* O. Henry Award for fiction, 1966, for short story, "The Bulgarian Poetess;" Fulbright fellow in Africa, 1972; American Book Award nomination, 1980, for *Too Far to Go: The Maples Stories;* Edward MacDowell Medal for Literature, MacDowell Colony, 1981; Pulitzer Prize for fiction, 1981, and National Book award for fiction, 1982, both for *Rabbit Is Rich;* National Book Critics Circle award for criticism, 1984, for *Hugging the Shore: Essays and Criticism;* Medal of Honor for Literature, National Arts Club (New York, NY), 1984; National Book Critics Circle award in fiction nomination, 1986, for *Roger's Version;* PEN/ Malamud Memorial Prize, PEN/ Faulkner Award Foundation, 1988, for "excellence in short story writing;" National Medal of Arts, 1989; National Book Critics Award and Pulitzer Prize, both 1990, and Howells medal, American Academy of Arts and Letters, 1995, all for *Rabbit at Rest;* Premio Scanno, 1991; named Commandeur de l'Ordre des Arts et des Lettres, 1995; Ambassador Book Award, English-speaking Union, 1996, for *In the Beauty of the Lilies;* Campion Award, *America* magazine, 1997; Harvard Arts First Medal, 1997; National Book Foundation Medal for distinguished contribution to American letters, 1998; Los Angeles Public Library literary award, 1999; Caldecott Medal, 2000, for *A Child's Calendar,* illustrated by Trina Schart Hyman; PEN/Faulkner Award for Fiction, 2004, for *The Early Stories: 1953-1975;* recipient of numerous honorary doctoral degrees, including Ursinsus College, 1962, Moravian College, 1967, Lafayette College, 1974, Albright College, 1982, and Harvard University, 1992.

WRITINGS:

NOVELS

The Poorhouse Fair (also see below), Knopf (New York, NY), 1959, with an introduction by Updike, Ballantine (New York, NY), 2004.

Rabbit, Run (also see below), Knopf (New York, NY), 1960.

The Centaur, Knopf (New York, NY), 1963.

Of the Farm, Knopf (New York, NY), 1965, reprinted, Ballantine (New York, NY), 2004.

The Poorhouse Fair [and] *Rabbit, Run,* Modern Library (New York, NY), 1965.

Couples, Knopf (New York, NY), 1968.

The Indian, Blue Cloud Abbey (Marvin, SD), 1971.

Rabbit Redux (also see below), Knopf (New York, NY), 1971.

A Month of Sundays, Knopf (New York, NY), 1975.

Marry Me: A Romance, Knopf (New York, NY), 1976.

The Coup, Knopf, (New York, NY) 1978.

Rabbit Is Rich (also see below), Knopf (New York, NY), 1981.

Rabbit Is Rich/Rabbit Redux/Rabbit, Run (also see below), Quality Paperback Book Club, 1981.

The Witches of Eastwick, Knopf (New York, NY), 1984.

Roger's Version, Knopf (New York, NY), 1986.

S., Knopf (New York, NY), 1988.

Rabbit at Rest, Knopf (New York, NY), 1990.

Memories of the Ford Administration, Knopf (New York, NY), 1992.

Brazil, Knopf (New York, NY), 1994.

Rabbit Angstrom: The Four Novels (contains *Rabbit Is Rich, Rabbit Redux, Rabbit, Run,* and *Rabbit at Rest*), Knopf/Everymans (New York, NY), 1995, published as *The Rabbit Novels,* Ballantine (New York, NY), 2003.

In the Beauty of the Lilies, Knopf (New York, NY), 1996.

Toward the End of Time, Knopf (New York, NY), 1997.

Gertrude and Claudius, Knopf (New York, NY), 2000.

Seek My Face, Knopf (New York, NY), 2002.

Villages, Knopf (New York, NY), 2004.

Terrorist, Knopf (New York, NY), 2006.

POETRY

The Carpentered Hen and Other Tame Creatures (also see below), Harper (New York, NY), 1958, published as *Hoping for a Hoopoe,* Gollancz (London, England), 1959.
Telephone Poles and Other Poems (also see below), Knopf (New York, NY), 1963.
Verse: The Carpentered Hen and Other Tame Creatures/Telephone Poles and Other Poems, Fawcett (New York, NY), 1965.
The Angels (poem; limited edition), King and Queen Press (Pensacola, FL), 1968.
Bath after Sailing (poem; limited edition), Pendulum Press (Monroe, CT), 1968.
Midpoint and Other Poems, Knopf (New York, NY), 1969.
Seventy Poems, Penguin (New York, NY), 1972.
Six Poems (limited edition), Oliphant Press, 1973.
Cunts (poem; limited edition), Frank Hallman, 1974.
Tossing and Turning, Knopf (New York, NY), 1977.
Sixteen Sonnets (limited edition), Halty Ferguson (Cambridge, MA), 1979.
Five Poems (limited edition), Bits Press (Cleveland, OH), 1980.
Spring Trio (limited edition), Palaemon Press (Winston-Salem, NC), 1982.
Jester's Dozen (limited edition), Lord John (Northridge, CA), 1984.
Facing Nature: Poems, Knopf (New York, NY), 1985.
Collected Poems: 1953- 1993, Knopf (New York, NY), 1993.
Americana and Other Poems, Knopf (New York, NY), 2001.

SHORT STORIES

The Same Door, Knopf (New York, NY), 1959.
Pigeon Feathers and Other Stories, Knopf (New York, NY), 1962.
Olinger Stories: A Selection, Vintage (New York, NY), 1964.
The Music School, Knopf (New York, NY), 1966.
Bech: A Book, Knopf (New York, NY), 1970.
Museums and Women and Other Stories, Knopf (New York, NY), 1972.
Warm Wine: An Idyll, Albondocani Press (New York, NY), 1973.
Couples: A Short Story, Halty Ferguson (Cambridge, MA), 1976.
From the Journal of a Leper, Lord John (Northridge, CA), 1978.
Too Far to Go: The Maples Stories, Fawcett (New York, NY), 1979.
Three Illuminations in the Life of an American Author (short story), Targ (New York, NY), 1979.
Problems and Other Stories, Knopf (New York, NY), 1979.
Your Lover Just Called: Stories of Joan and Richard Maple, Penguin Books (New York, NY), 1980.
The Chaste Planet, Metacom (Worcester, MA), 1980.
People One Knows: Interviews with Insufficiently Famous Americans, Lord John (Northridge, CA), 1980.
Invasion of the Book Envelopes, Ewert (Concord, MA), 1981.
Bech Is Back, Knopf (New York, NY), 1982.
The Beloved (short story), Lord John (Northridge, CA), 1982.
Confessions of a Wild Bore, Tamazunchale Press, 1984.
More Stately Mansions, Nouveau Press (Jackson, MS), 1987.
Trust Me: Short Stories, Knopf (New York, NY), 1987.
The Afterlife and Other Stories, Knopf (New York, NY), 1994.
Bech at Bay: A Quasi- Novel, Knopf (New York, NY), 1998.
A & P, Harcourt (Fort Worth, TX), 1998.
Licks of Love: Short Stories and a Sequel, "Rabbit Remembered," Knopf (New York, NY), 2000.
The Complete Henry Bech: Twenty Stories, with an introduction by Malcolm Bradbury, Knopf (New York, NY), 2001.
The Early Stories: 1953- 1975, Knopf (New York, NY), 2004.

ESSAYS

Assorted Prose, Knopf (New York, NY), 1965.
On Meeting Authors, Wickford (Newburyport, MA), 1968.
A Good Place, Aloe (Atlanta, GA), 1973.
Picked-up Pieces, Knopf (New York, NY), 1975.
Hub Fans Bid Kid Adieu, Lord John (Northridge, CA), 1977.
Talk from the Fifties,, Lord John (Northridge, CA), 1979.
Ego and Art in Walt Whitman, Targ (New York, NY), 1980.
Hawthorne's Creed, Targ (New York, NY), 1981.
Hugging the Shore: Essays and Criticism, Knopf (New York, NY), 1983.
Emersonianism, Bits Press, 1984.
Just Looking: Essays on Art, Knopf (New York, NY), 1989.

Odd Jobs: Essays and Criticism, Knopf (New York, NY), 1991.

Concerts at Castle Hill (music criticism), Lord John (Northridge, CA), 1993.

Golf Dreams: Writings on Golf, Knopf (New York, NY), 1996.

More Matter: Essays and Criticism, Knopf (New York, NY), 1999.

More Matter: Essays and Criticism, Knopf (New York, NY), 1999.

Still Looking, Knopf (New York, NY), 2005.

OTHER

(Adapter, with Warren Chappell) *The Magic Flute* (juvenile fiction; adapted from libretto of same title by Wolfgang Amadeus Mozart), Knopf (New York, NY), 1962.

(Adapter, with Warren Chappell) *The Ring* (juvenile fiction; adapted from libretto by Richard Wagner), Knopf (New York, NY), 1964.

A Child's Calendar (juvenile poetry), Knopf (New York, NY), 1965, new edition with illustrations by Trina Schart Hyman, Holiday House (New York, NY), 1999.

Three Texts from Early Ipswich (historical pageant; produced in Ipswich, MA, 1968), Seventeenth Century Day Committee of the Town of Ipswich, 1968.

(Adapter) *Bottom's Dream* (juvenile fiction; adapted from William Shakespeare's play *A Midsummer Night's Dream*), Knopf (New York, NY), 1969.

(Editor) David Levine, *Pens and Needles: Literary Caricatures,* Gambit (Ipswich, MA), 1970.

A Good Place: Being a Personal Account of Ipswich, Massachusetts, Aloe Editions (New York, NY), 1973.

Buchanan Dying (play; produced in Lancaster, MA, 1976), Knopf (New York, NY), 1974.

(Author of introduction) Henry Green, *Loving, Living, Party Going,* Penguin Books, 1978.

(Author of introduction) Bruno Schulz, *Sanatorium under the Sign of the Hourglass,* Penguin Books, 1979.

(Author of afterword) Edmund Wilson, *Memoirs of Hecate County,* Nonpareil (Boston, MA), 1980.

(Editor, with Shannon Ravenel and author of introduction) *The Best American Short Stories: 1984,* Houghton (Boston, MA), 1984.

Self-Consciousness: Memoirs, Knopf (New York, NY), 1989.

The Alligators (children's fiction), Creative Education (Mankato, IL), 1990.

(With Mary Steichen Calderone and Edward Steichen) *The First Picture Book: Everyday Things for Babies,* Fotofolio/Whitney Museum of American Art, 1991.

(Author of introduction) *The Art of Mickey Mouse,* edited by Craig Yoe and Janet Morra-Yoe, Hyperion (New York, NY), 1991.

(Author of introduction) *Heroes and Anti-Heroes,* Random House (New York, NY), 1991.

(Author of introduction) Henry Green, *Surviving,* Viking (New York, NY), 1993.

A Helpful Alphabet of Friendly Objects (juvenile poetry; photographs by David Updike), Knopf (New York, NY), 1994.

(Author of introduction) Edith Wharton, *The Age of Innocence,* Ballantine (New York, NY), 1996.

(Author of introduction) Herman Melville, *The Complete Shorter Fiction,* Knopf (New York, NY), 1997.

(Author of introduction) Jill Krementz, *The Writer's Desk,* Random House (New York, NY), 1997.

(Editor) *A Century of Arts and Letters: The History of the National Institute of Arts and Letters as Told, Decade by Decade, by Eleven Members,* Columbia University Press (New York, NY), 1998.

(Editor, with Katrina Kenison, also selector and author of introduction) *The Best American Short Stories of the Century,* Houghton (Boston, MA), 1999, expanded edition, 2000.

(Author of introduction) Max Beerbohm, *Seven Men,* New York Review Books (New York, NY), 2000.

(Editor) Karl Schapiro, *Selected Poems,* Library of America (New York, NY), 2003.

Also author with Günther Schuller of words and music for *The Fisherman and His Wife,* performed in Boston, MA, 1970. "Talk of the Town" reporter, *New Yorker,* 1955-57. Contributor to books, including Martin Levin, editor, *Five Boyhoods,* Doubleday (New York, NY), 1962; contributor of translations to Jorge Luis Borges, *Selected Poems: 1923-1967,* edited by Norman Thomas di Giovanni, Delacorte (New York, NY), 1972. Contributor of short stories, book reviews, and poems to *New Yorker* and other periodicals.

Updike's papers are housed in the Houghton Library, Harvard University.

ADAPTATIONS: Couples was purchased by United Artists in 1969; *Rabbit, Run* was filmed by Warner Bros. in 1970; *Bech: A Book* was adapted as the play *Bech Takes Pot Luck,* produced in New York, NY, 1970; *The Music School* was broadcast by Public Broadcasting

System, 1976; *Two Far to Go* was made into a television movie by National Broadcasting Co. in March, 1979, later revised and released for theater distribution by Sea Cliff Productions, 1982; director George Miller's movie *The Witches of Eastwick,* 1987, was loosely based on Updike's novel of the same title; "The Christian Roommates," a short story, was made into a ninety-minute movie for television; the novel *S.* was adapted as *S.: An Opera in Two Acts,* music by Ronald Perera, libretto by Constance Congdon, conception and artistic collaboration by Mark Harrison (Boston, MA), E.C. Schirmer, 2004.

SIDELIGHTS: John Updike "has earned an . . . imposing stance on the literary landscape," wrote *Los Angeles Times* contributor Katherine Stephen, "earning virtually every American literary award, repeated best-sellerdom and the near-royal status of the American author-celebrity." Hailed by critics and readers as one of the great American novelists of his generation, Updike has been hailed as a premiere chronicler of middle America in all its mundane glory. "A reader would be hard pressed to name a contemporary author other than John Updike who is more in tune with the way most Americans live," wrote Donald J. Greiner in a *Dictionary of Literary Biography* essay. "Man, wife, home, children, job—these . . . concerns have rested at the heart of his art since he published his first book . . . and they have continued to help him dissect, lovingly and clearly, the daily routine of middle America in small town and suburb."

Most critics familiar with Updike have strong opinions about the author's work. As Joseph Kanon explained in *Saturday Review:* "The debate . . . has long since divided itself into two pretty firmly entrenched camps: those who admire the work consider him one of the keepers of the language; those who don't say he writes beautifully about nothing very much." Updike acknowledges this charge but believes the complaint lacks validity. "There is a great deal to be said about almost anything," he explained to Jane Howard in a *Life* magazine interview. "Everything can be as interesting as every other thing. An old milk carton is worth a rose . . . . The idea of a hero is aristocratic. Now either nobody is a hero or everyone is. I vote for everyone. My subject is the American Protestant small town middle class. I like middles. It is in middles that extremes clash, where ambiguity restlessly rules."

Debate about the effectiveness of Updike's writing began in 1957 with publication of *The Poorhouse Fair,* his first novel. As Curt Suplee noted in his *Washington Post* profile of the author: "Updike's fiction is not overburdened by action, and his spare story lines are embellished with a lush and elegantly wrought style that some readers find majestic (John Barth calls him the Andrew Wyeth of American writers) and others intolerable. Norman Podhoretz described his prose in 'The Poorhouse Fair' as 'overly lyrical, bloated like a child who has eaten too much candy.'" Other critics differed: *New York Times* reviewer Donald Barr called *The Poorhouse Fair* "a work of art," and *Chicago Sunday Tribune*'s Fanny Butcher cited the work for "the author's brilliant use of words and . . . subtle observations."

"There is one point on which his critics all agree," observed Rachael C. Burchard in *John Updike: Yea Sayings.* "His style is superb. His work is worth reading if for no reason other than to enjoy the piquant phrase, the lyric vision, the fluent rhetoric." In a cover story on Updike, *Time* magazine's Paul Gray claimed: "No one else using the English language over the past two and a half decades has written so well in so many ways as he." A reviewer for *Books Abroad* noted that "Critics continually comment on the technical virtuosity of Updike," while in *John Updike* Suzanne Henning Uphaus declared: "In the midst of diversity there are certain elements common to all of Updike's writing. Most important, there is Updike's remarkable mastery of language."

Other commentators fail to see Updike's work in such a favorable light. For example, in her *Partisan Review* commentary on *Couples* Elizabeth Dalton asserted: "In its delicacy and fullness Updike's style seems to register a flow of fragments almost perfectly toned. And yet, after pages and pages of his minutely detailed impressions, the accumulated effect is one of waste." John W. Aldridge wrote in *Time to Murder and Create: The Contemporary Novel in Crisis* that the novelist "has none of the attributes we conventionally associate with major literary talent. He does not have an interesting mind. He does not possess remarkable narrative gifts or a distinguished style. He does not create dynamic or colorful or deeply meaningful characters . . . . In fact, one of the problems he poses for the critic is that he engages the imagination so little that one has real difficulty remembering his work long enough to think clearly about it." Updike "has difficulty in reining in his superfluous facility with words," Edward Hoagland complained in *New York Times Book Review.* "He is too fluent."

Many of the most disparaging reviews of Updike's work have come from critics who object not only to his writing style, but also to the author's subject matter. Commenting on the frenzy of criticism from reviewers that met the 1968 publication of *Couples,* Updike's explicit look at sexual freedom in a small New England town, Robert Detweiler noted in *John Updike:* "As frequently happens, the furor accompanying the depiction of sexual amorality increased the difficulty of judging the novel's artistic quality. Most of the reviews appeared to be impulsive reactions to the subject matter rather than measured assessments." In the case of this novel, negative critical response did little to tone down public enthusiasm for the work; it was on *Publishers Weekly* bestseller list for thirty-six weeks.

Couples was not the first Updike novel to deal with the sexual habits of middle-class America or to receive disapproving reviews from commentators upset by the author's frank language. "Looking back," wrote Eliot Fremont-Smith in *Village Voice,* "it must have been the sexuality that so upset the respectable critics of *Rabbit, Run* in 1960. Their consternation had to do with what seemed a great divide between John Updike's exquisite command of prose . . . and the apparent no-good vulgar nothing he expended it on." *Rabbit, Run* is the first installment in Updike's continuing saga of Harry "Rabbit" Angstrom that has expanded to include *Rabbit Redux,* the highly celebrated *Rabbit Is Rich,* and *Rabbit at Rest.* Published at ten-year intervals, the novels follow the life of "Rabbit" as he tries to leave his marriage, discovers his wife has been unfaithful, finds himself laid off from his blue-collar job, and as he confronts middle-age, ill health, and death. Greiner noted that in the Rabbit tetralogy, Updike "takes a common American experience—the graduation from high school of a star athlete who has no life to lead once the applause diminishes and the headlines fade—and turns it into a subtle expose of the frailty of the American dream . . . . It is now clear that he has written a saga of middle-class America in the second half of the twentieth century."

Both celebrated and vilified for its sexual focus and its deeply ambivalent central character, the "Rabbit" tetralogy has garnered a number of significant awards. The third volume in the series, *Rabbit Is Rich,* received the Pulitzer Prize, and the National Book Award. The final volume also earned a Pulitzer and a National Book Critics Award. Anthony Quinton in a London *Times* review argued that the "Rabbit novels are John Updike's best since they give the fullest scope to his remarkable gifts as observer and describer. What they amount to is a social and, so to speak, emotional history of the United States over the last twenty years or more, the period of Rabbit's and his creator's conscious life." Greiner wrote: "Like James Fenimore Cooper's Leatherstocking, Hawthorne's Hester, and Mark Twain's Huck, Harry is one of the immortal characters who first absorb and then define a national culture . . . . Personal limitation mirrors national malaise." Greiner concludes: "It is sad to think of death setting its snare for Rabbit Angstrom because, after four decades and four long novels, he has joined the pantheon of American literary heroes. Yet a glimpse of final defeat is the price to be paid for membership in that exclusive club." All four of Updike's Rabbit novels were published together as *The Rabbit Novels,* released in 2003.

In *John Updike and the Three Great Secret Things* George Hunt suggested that sex, religion, and art "characterize the predominant subject matter, thematic concerns, and central questions found throughout [Updike's] adult fiction." According to Greiner, Updike criticism has shifted since the 1960s from a consideration of the novelist's style to a focus on his themes and how they interrelate. "Later commentators," Greiner asserted, "are concerned with his intellectually rigorous union of theology and fiction and with his suggestion that sex is a kind of emerging religion in the suburban enclaves of the middle class."

Exploring the interrelatedness of sex and religion in Updike's fiction, Jean Strouse observed in a *Newsweek* review, "Readers and critics have accused Updike of being obsessed with sex. Maybe—but I think he is using Harry Angstrom and Piet Hanema in 'Couples,' and Richard Maple in 'Too Far to Go,' to explore that modern search for 'something behind all this . . . that wants me to find it.' Melville—and many others—may have announced the demise of God, but nobody has managed to excise the desire for something beyond death and daily life, a desire that has in the twentieth century shifted its focus from God to sex." *New York Times* reviewer Michiko Kakutani offered a similar explanation of the development of what she called Updike's "favorite preoccupations:" "His heroes, over the years, have all suffered from 'the tension and guilt of being human.' Torn between vestigial spiritual yearnings and the new imperatives of self-fulfillment, they hunger for salvation even as they submit to the importunate demands of the flesh."

Updike's 1992 novel, *Memories of the Ford Administration,* centers around a history professor, Alf Clayton, and his contribution to an historical journal concerning the Ford administration. Alf ruminates upon his past and discovers, as Charles Johnson in *New York Times Book Review* noted, he "can only remember two things—his knot of extramarital affairs and his never-completed opus on the life of President James Buchanan." As Richard Eder commented in *Los Angeles Times Book Review,* "Alf's struggles with his formless life and time are intercut with his stabs at portraying Buchanan's hapless struggles with his." Nicholas von Hoffman in a Chicago *Tribune Books* review found the layered plots of *Memories* something "only a writer of great technical accomplishment can bring off . . . . While one of the plots pulls us through the sex, the dissolving marital unions, the saturnalian nights of the Ford years, another works its sinuous way into the past and finds an American male unrecognizable to us moderns." Bruce Bawer in *Washington Post Book World* compared *Memories of the Ford Administration* to Updike's *Rabbit at Rest,* arguing that there "is the same sad sense of life winding down, of the aging eagle stretching his wings; the same fixation on orgasms and grace." Bawer concluded that despite the juxtaposition of Alf and Buchanan offering at times "a touching sense of the isolation and helplessness of the human condition," at other times it "seems sheer contrivance." Hoffman, however, concluded that Updike "has the ability to evoke the microepochs that fascinate us." Despite differing appraisals, most critics agree that, as Johnson commented, *Memories* is "quintessential Updike, an exploration of a modern American terrain of desire, guilt and moral ambiguity that he has made distinctly his own."

Breaking with this familiar terrain in 1994, the prolific Updike published his sixteenth novel, *Brazil.* As Tom Shone explained in *Times Literary Supplement, Brazil*'s genre, magic realism, makes for "the most bizarrely uncharacteristic novel Updike has yet written." *Brazil* is the story of two lovers: the poor, black Tristao, and the well-to-do white Isabel living in Rio de Janeiro. The plot, as Caroline Moore summarized it in *Spectator,* is uninhibited: "Isabel invited Tristao to deflower her at their first encounter; they steal from her uncle and flee on the proceeds to a hotel . . . . They are pursued, recaptured, re-elope, and undergo severe yet picaresque sufferings in the wilds of western Brazil, including starvation and slavery." Both Isabel and Tristao "survive a transformation of identity," as Alexander Theroux commented in Chicago's *Tribune Books,* "for at one crucial point in the novel there takes place an astonishing role reversal in which she turns black, he white—a piece of fantasy born as much of the ongoing requirements of Updike's parable as of the young lovers' passion."

Brazil received mixed reviews from many critics. Michael Dirda in a *Washington Post Book World* review found aspects of *Brazil* "that irritate, like the nips of tropical insects," but argues that these are "compensated for by the novel's zesty readability." Michiko Kakutani argued in *New York Times* that though "there are occasional passages [in *Brazil*] that sparkle with Mr. Updike's patented gift for the lyrical metaphor, his descriptions of Tristao and Isabel's adventures often feel forced and contrived." Rhoda Koenig gave *Brazil* a similarly mixed review in *New York:* "The main characters themselves are not credible, with their mythic passions, expressed in diction more formal and flowery than would ever issue from a boy of the slums and a girl from the world of pampered inanity." Koenig concluded, however, that Updike's *Brazil* "is a novel of endless and astonishing fertility," and is "the most absorbing and unsettling novel, apart from the Rabbit books, that [Updike] has written in some time." Barbara Kingsolver in a review of *Brazil* for *New York Times Book Review* found that Updike's "prose is measured, layered, insightful, smooth, as addictive a verbal drug as exists on the modern market. For every tiresome appearance of Tristao's yam, there is also an image or observation that seems, against all odds, to mark the arrival of something new in the English language."

Updike returns to more familiar thematic territory in 1996's *In the Beauty of the Lilies,* a four- generation saga of the spiritual emptiness of modern American life. The novel begins, as Julian Barnes of *New York Times Book Review* noted, with "a sly misdirection. D.W. Griffith is filming 'A Call to Arms' . . . in the spring of 1910. Mary Pickford, short of sleep and overcostumed for a hot day, faints." Updike then introduces the Reverend Clarence Arthur Wilmot, and never returns to Griffith and Pickford. The novel follows Clarence's loss of faith, his switch from clergyman to encyclopedia salesman, his death, and then follows his family three further generations. When film is mentioned again in the text, Barnes argues, the connection is made by the reader: "religion and the movies: two great illusionary forces, two worlds in which the primal image is of darkness conquered by light." Sybil S. Steinberg in a *Publishers Weekly* interview with Updike paraphrased: "The four generations that *Lilies* depicts . . . are meant to allude to the biblical line from Abraham to Isaac to Joseph and his brothers." Updike told Steinberg that his Sunday school education left him "haunted by that particular [biblical] saga, and the notion that we are members of our ancestors. I wanted to give an American version of that sense." Barnes concluded that *Lilies* is "a novel of accumulated wisdom, with . . . Updike in full control of his subtle, crafty and incessantly observing art." Steinberg also noted Updike's control, finding that his "gift for exact, metaphorical observation binds matters of the soul to the ephemera of daily life."

Toward the End of Time is unlike typical Updike fare in that it is set in the future. The setting is the year 2020 after a war between the United States and China that has toppled the government and turned the Great Plains into "a radioactive dustbowl and left the management of local affairs to thugs who demand protection money," summarized a *Publishers Weekly* critic. Updike's protagonist, Ben Turnbull, has kept a journal depicting a year in his life. In his journal, Ben reveals his "basic Updikean traits" similar to other Updike characters, including his "importunate sexual urges combined with vague spiritual yearnings, an inclination toward melancholy introspection and a love of golf," noted Michiko Kakutani in *New York Times Book Review.* But, argued Kakutani, Turnbull is less like Rabbit Angstrom and more a "narcissistic and dirty minded old man." "As Ben confronts the looming certainty that time is running out for him and the universe, the narrative sweeps to a bittersweet conclusion," found a critic for *Publishers Weekly.*

Critics of *Toward the End of Time* were typically mixed in their assessment. Kakutani asked: "How could this veteran novelist, who just this year published the magisterial and masterly *In the Beauty of the Lilies,* follow that dazzling performance with this callous and perfunctory book? . . . Updike's usual sympathy for—and insight into—his characters gives way to cartoonish caricature, while his fascination with the intricacies of marriage, adultery and male-female relations devolves into the clumsy string-pulling of a chauvinistic puppeteer." James Wood, reviewing the novel for *New Republic,* commented that "too much of this novel advances into serenity when it should retreat into anguish, and too much of it finds what already exists rather than creates what does not." Woods criticized "the novel's reliance on a narrative that is already familiar to us," noting that this "sucks interest away from its fictionalized telling;" still, the critic did have praise for the "gorgeousness in the book" and its "fine words."

Updike's *Gertrude and Claudius* is a fictional exploration of the lives of Hamlet's parents and the relationship between Hamlet's mother and uncle. "Updike has appropriated the old Scandinavian legend about a prince who avenges his father's murder," wrote Ron Charles in *Christian Science Monitor.* "But in this version, Updike wonders if Hamlet's mom and dad were such bad parents after all." In the work, Updike creates the fictional lives of Gertrude, King Hamlet (her first husband), and Claudius, the king's brother who, as in Shakespeare's famous play, murders Claudius and soon after marries Gertrude. "This is a new perspective," found Adam Begley in *People,* citing Updike's plot about "a middle-aged queen falling for her husband's darkly mysterious younger brother."

Critics were again mixed. "Ultimately . . . one wonders what Updike hoped to achieve by deflating this Danish colossus into a soap opera befitting an age in which half of all marriages end in divorce," opined Norah Vincent in her appraisal of *Gertrude and Claudius* for *National Review.* "Turning Hamlet into a spoiled suburban brat may be amusing, but in the end it's a bit like portraying Macbeth as a hen-pecked Walter Mitty . . . . For all its pleasures, *Gertrude and Claudius* can't help being a disappointment to those who still find dignity and meaning in the tragic view of life." "Most likely, Updike's just having fun," countered Rex Roberts in *Insight on the News.* " *Gertrude and Claudius* allowed him to indulge his considerable talents, to writ a bit of Shakespearean rag . . . . Readers will enjoy *Gertrude and Claudius* best by giving themselves over to the book's playful spirit." Richard Eder in *New York Times Book Review* was even more laudatory: "Just as Shakespeare used older chronicles to construct his anguished balance between imagination and action, Updike has used Shakespeare to write a free-standing, pleasurable and wonderfully dexterous novel about three figures in complex interplay with their public state, their private longings and one another."

In *Villages* Updike writes of seventy-something Owen Mackenzie, a retired computer programmer who lives with his second wife. Most of the book is occupied by Owen's recollections of his erotic encounters with his wives and numerous lovers. The book is really a sort of history of sex in twentieth-century America, as Owen's burgeoning sexual awareness coincides with the American sexual revolution. Owen's sex life is indeed shaped, from his first encounter to the present-day, by the changing trends of, and attitudes toward, American sexuality.

Updike, as usual, does not shy away from the more graphic aspects of sex, and, as usual, his work has been met with mixed reviews. *New Statesman* critic Stephen Amidon noted that the author's "grinning disregard for the grammar of political correctness is a welcome tonic." Yet, Amidon went on to note, "there is something vaguely monstrous about . . . an utterly eroticised space where everything . . . is filtered through the prism of . . . sexual needs." In addition, an *Economist* contributor felt the descriptive passages fell short, stating that parts "could only have been written by an author who has described a few too many thighs," and concluding that the "point, too, is reductive." On the other hand, Stephen Abell, writing in the *Spectator,* was directly contradictory. He stated, Updike's "mind's eye has the quality of compound vision, separating the world into essential parts that make up the whole."

Like his novels, Updike's short stories and poetry also illustrate his command of language and his deep affection for everyday life in all its banality. "Read as a whole, [Updike's] short-story volumes offer a social commentary on American domesticity since midcentury, and, while the prose is always lyrical and the observations always sharp, a tone of sadness—wistfulness—prevails," wrote Greiner in *Dictionary of Literary Biography.* Reviewing *The Afterlife and Other Stories,* Peter Kemp in the London *Sunday Times* found nearly the entire volume of stories "masterpieces of stead delineation, in which psychological and emotional nuance are traced with as much lucid finesse as the wealth of visual detail." Noting that poetry is not Updike's "primary medium," Mark Ford in *Times Literary Supplement* nonetheless found that Updike's verse "evokes with the clarity and precision of his fiction the contours of particular moments and places." Greiner maintained that the "happy union of lyrical prose and intellectual probing that is the highlight of [Updike's] fiction shows itself everywhere in his nonfiction."

Particularly praised by critics has been the author's collected work *The Early Stories: 1953- 1975,* which won the PEN/Faulkner award in 2003. As Scott Shibuya Brown commented in *Atlantic,* reading through this 864-page volume "is a testament to many things, not least Updike's prodigious work habits (reputedly three pages a day, six days a week)." Beginning with 1953's "Ace in the Hole" and extending to his more experimental work, such as "Love Song, for a Moog Synthesizer," the 103-story collection demonstrates the author's "masterful ability to find beauty in the mundane and foreshadows the emotional complexity of his later novels," according to *Entertainment Weekly* reviewer Michelle Kung. Updike's work "is as prolific and valuable and given to experimentation as it was in those early years," noted Kyle Minor in appraising *The Early Stories* for *Antioch Review,* Minor adding that this comprehensive collection of Updike's formative short fiction "can be considered a good gift to the emerging writer" due to the author's skills as a stylist.

Updike is also a prolific author of prose nonfiction, including "book reviews, essays, addresses, comic feuilletons and random, autobiographical jottings," according to Michiko Kakutani in a review of *More Matter: Essays and Criticism* for *New York Times Book Review.* His other collections include *Hugging the Shore, Odd Jobs, Golf Dreams,* and the 2005 critical essays *Still Looking.* "In his strongest pieces," wrote Kakutani, "Updike's awesome pictorial powers of description combine with a rigorous, searching intelligence to produce essays of enormous tactile power and conviction. . . . His best pieces manage both to edify and to beguile."

Updike's skill in portraying the anxieties and frustrations of middle-America is considered the outstanding feature of his works. "He is our unchallenged master at evoking the heroic void of ordinary life," Suplee maintained, "where small braveries contend in vain against the nagging entropy of things, where the fear of death drips from a faulty faucet and supermarket daydreams turn to God. With heart-clutching clarity, he transmutes the stubborn banality of middle-class existence into tableaux that shiver with the hint of spiritual meaning." According to Kakutani, Updike's work "has not only lyrically defined the joys and sorrows of the American middle class, but also gives—as he once wrote of another author—'the happy impression of an oeuvre, of a continuous task carried forward variously, of a solid personality, of a plenitude of gifts explored, knowingly.'" A *Publishers Weekly* reviewer maintained that "one looks forward to the changing perspective (though not changing themes) that each decade brings to this masterful writer's work."

BIOGRAPHICAL AND CRITICAL SOURCES:

BOOKS

Aldridge, John W.,*Time to Murder and Create: The Contemporary Novel in Crisis,* McKay (New York, NY), 1966.

Baker, Nicholas, *U and I: A True Story,* Vintage (New York, NY), 1995.

Bloom, Harold, editor, *John Updike: Modern Critical Views,* Chelsea House (New York, NY), 1987.

Boswell, Marshall, *John Updike's Rabbit Tetralogy: Mastered Irony In Motion,* University of Missouri Press (Columbia, MO), 2000.

Broer, Lawrence R., editor, *Rabbit Tales: Poetry and Politics in John Updike's Rabbit Novels,* University of Alabama Press (Tuscaloosa, AL), 1998.

Burchard, Rachael C., *John Updike: Yea Sayings,* Southern Illinois University Press (Carbondale, IL), 1971.

Concise Dictionary of American Literary Biography: Broadening Views, 1968-1988, Gale (Detroit, MI), 1989.

Contemporary Authors Bibliographical Series, Volume 1, Gale (Detroit, MI), 1986.

Contemporary Literary Criticism, Gale (Detroit, MI), Volume 1, 1973, Volume 2, 1974, Volume 3, 1975, Volume 5, 1976, Volume 7, 1977, Volume 9, 1978, Volume 13, 1980, Volume 15, 1980, Volume 23, 1983, Volume 34, 1985, Volume 43, 1987, Volume 70, 1991.

De Bellis, Jack, *John Updike: A Bibliography, 1967-1993,* foreword by Updike, Greenwood Press (Westport, CT), 1994.

De Bellis, Jack, editor, *The Critical Response to John Updike's "Rabbit" Angstrom Saga,* Praeger (Westport, CT), 2004.

Detweiler, Robert, *John Updike,* Twayne (Boston, MA), 1972, revised edition, 1984.

Dictionary of Literary Biography, Gale (Detroit, MI), Volume 2: *American Novelists since World War II,* 1978, Volume 5: *American Poets since World War II,* 1980, Volume 143: *American Novelists since World War II, Third Series,* 1994.

Dictionary of Literary Biography Documentary Series, Volume 3, Gale (Detroit, MI), 1983.

Dictionary of Literary Biography Yearbook, Gale (Detroit, MI), *1980,* 1981, *1982,* 1983.

Greiner, Donald J., *John Updike's Novels,* Ohio University Press (Athens, OH), 1984.

Greiner, Donald J., *Adultery in the American Novel: Updike, James, Hawthorne,* University of South Carolina Press (Columbia, SC), 1985.

Hunt, George, *John Updike and the Three Great Secret Things,* Eerdmans (Grand Rapids, MI), 1980.

Kamm, Antony, *Biographical Companion to Literature in English,* Scarecrow Press (Metuchen, NJ), 1997.

Luscher, Robert M., *John Updike: A Study of the Short Fiction,* Twayne (New York, NY), 1993.

Miller, D. Quentin, *John Updike and the Cold War: Drawing the Iron Curtain,* University of Missouri Press (Columbia, MO), 2001.

Neary, John, *Something and Nothingness: The Fiction of John Updike and John Fowles,* Southern Illinois University Press (Carbondale, IL), 1992.

Newman, Judie, *John Updike,* St. Martin's Press (New York, NY), 1988.

Plath, James, editor, *Conversations with John Updike,* University Press of Mississippi (Jackson, MS), 1994.

Ristoff, Dilvo I., *John Updike's Rabbit at Rest: Appropriating History,* P. Lang (New York, NY), 1998.

Schiff, James A., *Updike's Version: Rewriting the Scarlet Letter,* University of Missouri Press (Columbia, MO), 1992.

Schiff, James A., *John Updike Revisited,* Twayne (New York, NY), 1998.

Short Story Criticism, Volume 13, Gale (Detroit, MI), 1993.

Singh, Sukhbir,*The Survivor in Contemporary American Fiction: Saul Bellow, Bernard Malamud, John Updike, Kurt Vonnegut, Jr.,* B. R. Publishing (Delhi, India), 1991.

Tallent, Elizabeth, *Married Men and Magic Tricks: John Updike's Erotic Heroes,* Creative Arts (Berkeley, CA), 1981.

Thorburn, David, and Howard Eiland, editors, *John Updike: A Collection of Critical Essays,* G. K. Hall (Boston, MA), 1982.

Trachtenberg, Stanley, editor, *New Essays on Rabbit, Run,* Cambridge University Press (Cambridge, England), 1993.

Updike, John, *Self-Consciousness: Memoirs,* Knopf (New York, NY), 1989.

Uphaus, Suzanne Henning, *John Updike,* Ungar (New York, NY), 1980.

Yerkes, James, editor, *John Updike and Religion: The Sense of the Sacred and the Motions of Grace,* Eerdmans (Grand Rapids, MI), 1999.

PERIODICALS

America, November 30, 1996, Daniel T. Wackerman, review of *Golf Dreams,* p. 5; October 4, 1997, George W. Hunt, "Of Many Things," p. 2; January 17, 1998, James J. Miracky, review of *Toward the End of Time,* p. 25; March 27, 1999, Diane Fortuna, review of *Bech at Bay,* p. 22.

Antioch Review, spring, 2004, Kyle Minor, review of *The Early Stories: 1953- 1975,* p. 367.

Atlantic, December, 2002, review of *Seek My Face,* p. 147; November, 2003, Scott Shibuya Brown, review of *The Early Stories,* p. 160.

Book, November- December, 2000, D.T. Max, "Noticers in Chief: John Updike and Rabbit," p. 33; November-December, 2003, James Schiff, review of *The Early Stories,* p. 84.

Booklist, August, 1997, Brad Hooper, review of *Toward the End of Time,* p. 1849; August, 1998, Brad Hooper, review of *Bech at Bay,* p. 1925; September 1, 1999, Carolyn Phelan, review of *A Child's Calendar,* p. 130; September 1, 1999, Brad Hooper, review of *More Matter,* p. 58; January 1, 2000, Brad Hooper, review of *Gertrude and Claudius,* p. 835; June 1, 2002, Candace Smith, review of *A Childhood in the U.S.A.,* p. 1746; August, 2002, Brad Hooper, review of *Seek My Face,* p. 1888; January 1, 2003, review of *Seek My Face,* p. 793; September 15, 2005, Donna Seaman, review of *Still Looking,* p. 18.

Books Abroad, winter, 1967.

Books and Culture, January-February, 2004, p. 32.

Chicago Sunday Tribune, January 11, 1959, Fanny Butcher, review of *The Poorhouse Fair.*

Christian Century, July 17, 1996, p. 730; November 19, 1997, James Yerkes, review of *Toward the End of Time,* p. 1079; November 17, 1999, James Yerkes, review of *More Matter,* p. 1132; February 23, 2000, James Yerkes, review of *Gertrude and Claudius,* p. 220.

Christian Science Monitor, February 14, 1994; February 3, 2000, Ron Charles, review of *Gertrude and Claudius,* p. 21.
Commentary, January, 1999, John Gross, review of *Bech at Bay,* p. 63.
Economist, February, 12, 2005, review of *Villages,* p. 83.
Entertainment Weekly, October 17, 1997, L.S. Klepp, review of *Toward the End of Time,* p. 66; November 6, 1998, review of *Bech at Bay,* p. 82; November 7, 2003, Michelle Kung, review of *The Early Stories,* p. 76.
Insight on the News, November 8, 1999, Rex Roberts, review of *More Matter,* p. 28; March 13, 2000, Rex Roberts, review of *Gertrude and Claudius,* p. 26.
Kenyon Review, spring, 1992.
Kirkus Reviews, September 1, 1994, p. 1162.
Library Journal, September 15, 1997, Edward B. St. John, review of *Toward the End of Time,* p. 103; February 15, 1999, Michael Rogers, "The Gospel of the Book: LJ Talks to John Updike," p. 114; February 15, 2000, David W. Henderson, review of *Gertrude and Claudius,* p. 200; November 15, 2002, Barbara Hoffert, review of *Seek My Face,* p. 104; November 1, 2005, Wesley A. Mills, review of *Still Looking,* p. 76.
Life, November 4, 1966.
London Review of Books, March 11, 1993, p. 9.
Los Angeles Times, January 4, 1987, Katherin Stephen.
Los Angeles Times Book Review, November 1, 1992, p. 3.
Modern Fiction Studies, spring, 1974 (devoted to Updike); autumn, 1975; spring, 1991 (devoted to Updike).
Nation, November 3, 1997, Tom LeClair, review of *Toward the End of Time,* p. 62.
National Review, March 20, 2000, Norah Vincent, review of *Gertrude and Claudius,* p. 57.
New Criterion, November, 1998, Brooke Allen, review of *Bech at Bay,* p. 60.
New Republic, May 27, 1996, James Wood, review of *In the Beauty of the Lilies,* p. 29.; November 17, 1997, Robert Boyers, review of *Toward the End of Time,* p. 38; October 11, 1999, James Wood, review of *More Matter,* p. 41; February 21, 2000, Stephen Greenblatt, review of *Gertrude and Claudius,* p. 32.
New Statesmen, January, 24, 2005, Stephen Amidon, review of *Villages,* p. 51.
Newsweek, November 15, 1971; September 28, 1981; October 18, 1982; October 13, 1997, Jeff Giles, review of *Toward the End of Time,* p. 78.
New York, January 31, 1994, p. 62.
New Yorker, December 1, 2003, Louis Menand, review of *The Early Stories,* p. 104.
New York Review of Books, April 11, 1968; August 8, 1974; April 3, 1975; November 19, 1981; November 18, 1982; November 24, 1983; June 14, 1984; December 4, 1986; February 29, 1996, p. 4.
New York Times, January 11, 1959; October 7, 1982; August 27, 1986; January 25, 1994, p. C19; March 27, 2003, John Russell, review of *Seek My Face,* p. 37.
New York Times Book Review, March 18, 1962; April 7, 1963; April 7, 1968; June 21, 1970; November 14, 1971; September 27, 1981; October 17, 1982; September 18, 1983; May 13, 1984; August 31, 1986; April 26, 1987; November 1, 1992, p. 11; February 6, 1994, p. 1; January 28, 1996, p. 9; September 19, 1996, Christopher Lehmann-Haupt, review of *Golf Dreams;* November 10, 1996, David Owen, review of *Golf Dreams,* p. 57; September 30, 1997, Michiko Kakutani, review of *Toward the End of Time;* October 13, 1998, Michiko Kakutani, review of *Bech at Bay;* September 21, 1999, Michiko Kakutani, review of *More Matter;* February 27, 2000, Richard Eder, review of *Gertrude and Claudius,* p. 9.
New York Times Sunday Magazine, December 10, 1978.
Partisan Review, winter, 1969, Elizabeth Dalton, review of *Couples.*
People, September 23, 1996, Alex Tresniowski, review of *Golf Dreams,* p. 29; December 1, 1997, David Lehman, review of *Toward the End of Time,* p. 56; April 10, 2000, Adam Begley, review of *Gertrude and Claudius,* p. 49.
Publishers Weekly, September 5, 1994, p. 88; January 8, 1996; p. 47; July 29, 1996, review of *Golf Dreams,* p. 79; August 4, 1997, review of *Toward the End of Time,* p. 62; July 20, 1998, review of *Bech at Bay,* p. 204; August 30, 1999, review of *A Child's Calendar,* p. 82; August 30, 1999, review of *More Matter,* p. 66; January 3, 2000, review of *Gertrude and Claudius,* p. 57; September 9, 2002, review of *Seek My Face,* p. 39.
Saturday Review, March 17, 1962; September 30, 1972.
Sewanee Review, spring, 2002, Sanford Pinsker, "Why Updike's Fiction Continues to Matter," p. 332.
Southern Review, spring, 2002, James Schiff, interview with Updike, p. 420.
Spectator, April 9, 1994, Caroline Moore, review of *Brazil,* p. 25; February 12, 2005, Stephen Abell, review of *Villages,* p. 37.
Sports Illustrated, September 9, 1996, Michael Bamberger, review of *Golf Dreams,* p. 12.
Theology Today, January, 2003, John McTavish, "Myth, Gospel, and John Updike's *Centaur,*" pp. 596- 606.
Time, April 26, 1968; October 18, 1982; August 25, 1986; November 18, 2002, Richard Lacayo, review of *Seek My Face,* p. 134.

Times (London, England), January 14, 1982; February 5, 1995.
Times Literary Supplement, January 15, 1982; January 20, 1984; September 28, 1984; October 24, 1986; February 25, 1994, p. 21; April 1, 1994, p. 21.
Tribune Books (Chicago, IL), September 30, 1990, p. 4; November 1, 1992, p. 9; January 30, 1994, p. 9.
Twentieth Century Literature, April, 1966; July, 1967; October, 1971; winter, 1978.
Village Voice, September 30, 1981, Eliot Fremont-Smith.
Washington Post, September 27, 1981; April 26, 1982.
Washington Post Book World, November 1, 1992, p. 9; February 13, 1994, p. 14; February 4, 1996, p. 10.
World Literature Today, winter, 1994, p. 128; October-December, 2003, Daniel Garrett, review of *Seek My Face,* p. 96.

ONLINE

New York Times Online, http://www.nytimes.com/ (May 2, 2004) "Life and Times: John Updike."
Salon.com, http://www.salon.com/ (May 4, 2004), Dwight Garner, interview with Updike.

OTHER

John Updike: In His Own Words (video recording), Films for the Humanities and Sciences, 1997.

* * *

UPDIKE, John Hoyer
See UPDIKE, John

* * *

URBAN GRIOT
See TYREE, Omar

* * *

URIS, Leon 1924-2003
(Leon Marcus Uris)

PERSONAL: Born August 3, 1924, in Baltimore, MA; died of renal failure, June 21, 2003, in Shelter Island, NY; son of Wolf William (a shopkeeper) and Anna (Blumberg) Uris; married Betty Katherine Beck, 1945 (divorced, January, 1968); married Margery Edwards, September 8, 1968 (committed suicide, February 20, 1969); married Jill Peabody (a photographer), February 15, 1970; children: (first marriage) Karen Lynn, Mark Jay, Michael Cady; (third marriage) Rachael Jackson, one other child. *Education:* Attended public schools in Baltimore, MD. *Hobbies and other interests:* Skiing, bowling, trail-biking, and tennis.

CAREER: Novelist. Worked previously as a circulation district manager for *San Francisco Call-Bulletin. Military service:* U.S. Marine Corps, 1942-45; served in the Pacific at Guadalcanal and Tarawa.

MEMBER: Writers League, Screenwriters Guild.

AWARDS, HONORS: Daroff Memorial Award, 1959; National Institute of Arts and Letters grant, 1959; California Literature Silver Medal award, 1962, for *Mila 18,* and Gold Medal award, 1965, for *Armageddon*; honorary doctorates, University of Colorado, 1976, Santa Clara University, 1977, Wittenberg University, 1980, and Lincoln College, 1985; John F. Kennedy Medal, Irish/American Society of New York, 1977; gold medal, Eire Society of Boston, 1978; Jobotinsky Medal, State of Israel, 1980; Hall Fellowship (with wife, Jill Uris), Concord Academy, 1980; Scopus Award, Hebrew University of Jerusalem, 1981; Books for the Teen Age designation, New York Public Library, 1980-82, for *Exodus.*

WRITINGS:

NOVELS

Battle Cry (also see below), Putnam (New York, NY), 1953, bound with *Tales of the South Pacific,* by James A. Michener, and *Mister Roberts,* by Thomas Heggen, Wings Books (New York, NY), 1996.
The Angry Hills, Random House (New York, NY), 1955.
Exodus (also see below), Doubleday (New York, NY), 1957, reprinted, Gramercy Books (New York, NY), 2000.
Mila 18, Doubleday (New York, NY), 1960.
Armageddon: A Novel of Berlin, Doubleday (New York, NY), 1964.
Topaz, McGraw (New York, NY), 1967.
QB VII, Doubleday (New York, NY), 1970.
Trinity, Doubleday (New York, NY), 1976.
The Haj, Doubleday (New York, NY), 1984.

Mitla Pass, Doubleday (New York, NY), 1988.
Redemption (sequel to *Trinity*), HarperCollins (New York, NY), 1995.
A God in Ruins: A Novel, HarperCollins (New York, NY), 1999.
O'Hara's Choice, HarperCollins (New York, NY), 2003.

SCREENPLAYS

Battle Cry, Warner Brothers, 1954.
Gunfight at the O.K. Corral (also see below), Paramount, 1957.

OTHER

(Author of commentary) *Exodus Revisited,* photographs by Dimitrios Harissiadis, Doubleday (New York, NY), 1959, published as *In the Steps of Exodus,* Heinemann (London, England), 1962.
The Third Temple (essay), bound with *Strike Zion,* by William Stevenson, Bantam (New York, NY), 1967.
Ari (book and lyrics; based on his novel, *Exodus*; also known as *Exodus, the Musical*), music by Walt Smith, produced on Broadway, 1971.
(Author of commentary) *Ireland: A Terrible Beauty: The Story of Ireland Today,* photographs by wife, Jill Uris, Doubleday (New York, NY), 1975.
(With Jill Uris) *Jerusalem, Song of Songs,* photographs by Jill Uris, Doubleday (New York, NY), 1981.

Contributor to anthologies, including *Fabulous Yesterdays,* Harper (New York, NY), 1961; *American Men at Arms,* compiled by F. Van Wyck Mason, Little, Brown (Boston, MA), 1965; *A Treasury of Jewish Sea Stories,* edited by Samuel Sobel, Jonathan David, 1965; and *Great Spy Stories from Fiction,* by Allan Dulles, Harper (New York, NY), 1969. Also contributor to periodicals, including *Esquire, Coronet, Ladies' Home Journal,* and *TWA Ambassador.*

Uris's work has been translated into other languages, including Spanish, Italian, and Portuguese.

ADAPTATIONS: Gunfight at the O.K. Corral was novelized by Nelson C. Nye, Norden Publications, 1956; *The Angry Hills* was adapted for film and released by Metro-Goldwyn-Mayer, 1959; *Exodus* was adapted for a film directed by Otto Preminger, United Artists (UA), 1960; *Topaz* was adapted for a film directed by Alfred Hitchcock, UA, 1969; *QB VII* was adapted into a television movie, ABC-TV, 1974.

SIDELIGHTS: American writer Leon Uris is the author of several bestselling novels based upon details and events drawn from contemporary history. He received acclaim early in his career as the author of such popular books as *Exodus,* a landmark novelization of the history of the Jewish settlement of modern Israel, and the espionage thriller *Topaz.* Uris's later works included *QB VII,* a semi-autobiographical account of the trial of an author charged with libel by a German physician and former Nazi, *Trinity,* a novel set amid Ireland's political and religious turmoil, and his final novel, *O'Hara's Choice,* a saga of the Marines who fought during the U.S. Civil War published posthumously in 2003. Panoramic historical fiction that proved to be commercially successful, Uris's fast-paced novels earned him a dedicated readership. Yet, throughout his career critical opinion on his work was mixed. While critics praised his storytelling abilities—the appeal of his novels has been described as cinematic in nature—his works have sometimes been cited for problems with grammar, for his occasionally cardboard characters and stiff dialogue, and his tendency to take liberties with historical facts. Sharon D. Downey and Richard A. Kallan, noting both Uris's immense popular appeal and what they perceived as flaws in regards to traditional literary standards, asserted in *Communications Monographs* that, "in short, Uris remains a reader's writer and a critic's nightmare."

Uris was born in Baltimore, Maryland. His father, William Uris, was a Polish immigrant who worked as a paperhanger and later a storekeeper; his mother, Anna Blumberg Uris, was a homemaker. Uris went to school in Norfolk, Virginia, failed English three times, and never graduated from high school. When he was seventeen he joined the U.S. Marine Corps and began writing in the early 1950s, inspired by his four-year tour of duty during World War II. He wrote for years without selling anything, but finally sold an article on football to *Esquire* in 1950.

His first novel, *Battle Cry,* was published by G.P. Putnam in 1953 after making the rounds of several publishing houses. The novel was based on Uris's experiences in the Marines during training and combat. "There were those who thought I was crazy, others who gave me encouragement," Uris once told Bernard Kalb in *Saturday Review.* "My guiding thought throughout was that the real Marine story had not been told. We were a different breed of men who looked at war in a different way." *Battle Cry* was praised by reviewers for its realistic depiction of the dedicated men who risked their lives in the front lines of battle. Commenting on the author's unique approach to the subject of war, critic Merle Miller noted in the *Saturday Review* that *Battle Cry* "may have started a whole new and healthy trend in war literature." The book proved to be as popular with readers as it was with critics, and Uris went on to write the screenplay for the film version of his novel, which was released by Warner Brothers in 1954.

The success of *Battle Cry* encouraged Uris to continue writing and he was soon at work on his second novel, *The Angry Hills.* Loosely based on the diary of an uncle who had fought in Greece with a Jewish unit of the British armed forces, the work was published in 1955. Although the response from critics was that as an adventure story, the book is too fast-paced, *The Angry Hills* is significant in that it focused Uris's interest in the Middle East, the Palestinian issue, and the history of Israel, home to many of his relatives. Although his preoccupation with these subjects would stay out of his major work for the next few years—after publication of his second novel Uris was soon at work on a screenplay for the classic western drama *Gunfight at the O.K. Corral*—it would figure prominently in several of his later novels, most notably *Exodus,* ultimately one of the largest-selling books in twentieth-century publishing history.

Exodus is the history of European Jews and their efforts to establish the state of Israel as a Jewish homeland. Although faulting Uris for what was perceived as a tendency toward lengthy and partisan passages, critics hailed *Exodus* as a gripping human drama and a novel of heroic proportions. A descriptive account of the Warsaw Ghetto included in this novel provided the seed for Uris's next book, *Mila 18,* which continued his fascination with the predicament of Jews in the twentieth century. From there he worked with noted Greek photographer Dimitrios Harissiadis on the photo-essay *Exodus Revisited,* a complement to the research he did for *Mila 18.* The author's lifelong passion for the Jewish people and for Israel was also the motivation behind several other books, including *The Haj,* an account of the birth of Israel told from the point of view of a Palestinian Arab, and *Mitla Pass,* a novel about an Israeli soldier during the Sinai War that was published in 1988 to mixed reviews but immediate bestseller status.

Some critics accept flaws of a technical nature as an acceptable tradeoff for a well-wrought story when reviewing Uris's novels. Pete Hamill explained in the *New York Times Book Review:* "Uris is a storyteller, in a direct line from those men who sat around fires in the days before history and made the tribe more human. The subject is man, not words; story is all, the form it takes is secondary." Although not unaware of the problematic aspects of the novel genre, Hamill stated: "It is a simple thing to point out that Uris often writes crudely, that his dialogue can be wooden, that his structure occasionally groans under the excess baggage of exposition and information. Simple, but irrelevant. None of that matters as you are swept along in the narrative." Critic Dan Wakefield agreed, noting in a review of *Exodus* for the *Nation:* "The plot is so exciting that the characters become exciting too; not because of their individuality or depth, but because of the historic drama they are involved in." Wakefield added: "The real achievement . . . lies not so much in its virtues as a novel as in its skillful rendering of the furiously complex history of modern Israel in a palatable, popular form that is usually faithful to the spirit of the complicated realities."

In researching *Exodus* Uris read almost 300 books, traveled 12,000 miles within Israel's boundaries, and interviewed more than 1,200 individuals. Similar efforts went into his other books, including *Trinity,* which arose out of the people and places Uris and his third wife, photographer Jill Peabody Uris, encountered on a trip to document modern Ireland. The wealth of historical background in his novels caused Uris's books to be alternately called "nonfiction novels," "propaganda" novels, or just plain "journalism" by critics. A reviewer for the *Christian Science Monitor* addressed the danger in mixing fact and fiction: "Few readers are expert enough to be 100 percent certain where Mr. Uris's imagination has taken over the record." Nevertheless, as Maxwell Geismar pointed out in *Saturday Review:* "If Mr. Uris sometimes lacks tone as a novelist, if his central figures are social types rather than individual portraits, there is also a kind of 'underground power' in his writing. No other novel I have read recently has had the same capacity [as *Exodus*] to refresh our memory, inform our intelligence, and to stir the heart." In the same vein, Hamill wrote of *Trinity:* "The novel sprawls, occasionally bores, meanders like a river. . . . But when the story is finished the reader has been to places where he or she has never been before. The news items . . . will never seem quite the same again."

Uris revisited the Ireland of *Trinity* after almost twenty years in *Redemption.* The earlier volume looked at the nineteenth-century Irish struggle for independence; *Redemption* continues the story through the years of World War I. "The conflict between two of the three dominant families of *Trinity,* the tempestuous Larkins and their staid British counterparts, the Hubbles, is the focus here," explained a *Publishers Weekly* reviewer. The story, in which young Rory Larkin makes an attempt to assist Irish rebels in the Catholic Easter Uprising of 1916, describes how Rory's commanding officer is assassinated and how Rory himself is implicated. "With its contrivances, digressions and shifting time lines," Malachy Duffy stated in the *New York Times Book Review,* "the novel often resembles the Irish countryside—full of twists and turns, replete with bogs and quagmires."

In *A God in Ruins,* Uris penned an account of a U.S. presidential race using flashbacks from the lives of his two fictional candidates. Quinn Patrick O'Connell was adopted as a child by Colorado ranchers and became a Marine hero and governor before running for the presidency. However, a week before the election he discovers that his birth heritage is Jewish, thus sparking a wave of anti-Semitism. The plot then turns to the issue of gun control, an issue O'Connell emphasizes. His campaign rival is Republican incumbent Thornton Tomtree, who is implicated in violent national tragedies involving guns and militia groups. In a *Library Journal* review of *A God in Ruins* Lisa Bier commented that the characters are flat and that the plot remains unresolved. A *Publishers Weekly* reviewer also wrote that the issues of anti-Semitism and gun control vie for readers' attention, leading to a "stylistically scattered" story.

After a prolific career, Uris died in June of 2003, at his home on Shelter Island, New York. Webster Scott offered his assessment of Uris's work in the *Washington Post Book World,* comparing the novelist to such popular writers as James A. Michener and James Clavell. Such writers, Scott noted, "may tell us relatively little about our inner weather, but they report on storms and setting suns outside. They read the environment we must function in. Occasionally they replicate our social structures. They sift the history that brought us to the present. They give us the briefing papers necessary to convert news stories into human stories. All of which serve our emotional need to make order out of confusion, to explain the inexplicable." Recalling Uris's body of work, *Guardian* writer Eric Homberger noted of the novelist's passing: "He was, in truth, an educator of the American public in the Zionist interpretation of modern Jewish history. The deep tradition of non-violence in Jewish tradition was swept aside in his muscular reinterpretation of the modern Jewish identity. Many other cultural stereotypes—the learned Jew, the pious Jew, and the streetwise Jew as entrepreneur—were similarly dismissed." As quoted in a *Washington Post* obituary by Adam Bernstein, Uris's advice to writers was simple. "Apply the seat of one's pants to the seat of the chair and write," he once said. "There is no other way."

BIOGRAPHICAL AND CRITICAL SOURCES:

BOOKS

Authors in the News, Thomson Gale (Detroit, MI), Volume 1, 1976, Volume 2, 1976.

Bestsellers 89, Issue 2, Thomson Gale (Detroit, MI), 1989.

Contemporary Literary Criticism, Thomson Gale (Detroit, MI), Volume 7, 1977, Volume 32, 1985.

Contemporary Novelists, 6th edition, St. James Press (Detroit, MI), 1996.

PERIODICALS

Atlantic Monthly, July, 1964.

Book, July, 1999, p. 75.

Booklist, April 15, 1995, Ray Olson, review of *Redemption,* p. 1453; May 1, 1999, p. 1559.

Chicago Tribune, November 24, 1988.

Chicago Tribune Book World, April 29, 1984, p. 33.

Christian Science Monitor, December 4, 1958; November 16, 1967; July 10, 2001, p. 20.

Commentary, October, 1961.

Communication Monographs, September, 1982.

Economist, June 19, 1999, review of *A God in Ruins,* p. 3.

Globe and Mail (Toronto, Ontario, Canada), January 7, 1989; June 12, 1999, p. D12.

Inside Books, November, 1988, pp. 25-26.

Journal of American Culture, spring, 1999, p. 9.

Kirkus Reviews, April 1, 1995, p. 422; May 15, 1999, p. 754; August 15, 2003, review of *O'Hara's Choice,* p. 1043.

Library Journal, June 15, 1999, Lisa Bier, review of *A God in Ruins,* p. 110; January, 2000, p. 188.

Los Angeles Times Book Review, September 27, 1984, p. 8; October 30, 1988, p. 12.

Nation, April 11, 1959.

Newsweek, May 21, 1984, p. 84.

New York Herald Tribune Book Review, September 28, 1958.

New York Review of Books, April 16, 1964.

New York Times, October 12, 1958; April 27, 1984.

New York Times Book Review, June 4, 1961; June 28, 1964; October 15, 1967; March 14, 1976, p. 5; April 22, 1984, p. 7; January 1, 1989, p. 14; July 2, 1995, p. 11.

Philadelphia Bulletin, March 31, 1976.

Publishers Weekly, March 29, 1976, pp. 6-7; September 23, 1988, p. 59; April 24, 1995, review of *Redemp-*

tion, p. 58; May 24, 1999, review of *A God in Ruins,* p. 64; July, 1999, p. 64.
Saturday Review, April 25, 1953, pp. 16-17; September 27, 1958.
Time, December 8, 1958; June 2, 1961.
Times Literary Supplement, October 27, 1961.
Washington Post Book World, April 1, 1984, pp. 1-2; October 30, 1988.

URIS, Leon Marcus
See URIS, Leon

* * *

URMUZ
See CODRESCU, Andrei

V

VANCE, Gerald
See SILVERBERG, Robert

* * *

VAN DUYN, Mona 1921-2004
(Mona Jane Van Duyn)

PERSONAL: Surname is pronounced "van dine"; born May 9, 1921, in Waterloo, IA; died of bone cancer December 2, 2004, in University City, MO; daughter of Earl George (in business) and Lora G. (Kramer) Van Duyn; married Jarvis A. Thurston (a professor of English), August 31, 1943. *Education:* Iowa State Teachers College (now University of Northern Iowa), B.A., 1942; State University of Iowa, M.A., 1943. *Politics:* Independent. *Hobbies and other interests:* Gardening, sewing, reading.

CAREER: Poet and educator. State University of Iowa, Iowa City, instructor in English, 1943-46; University of Louisville, Louisville, KY, instructor in English, 1946-50; Washington University, St. Louis, MO, lecturer in English, 1950-67; writer. Poet-in-residence, Breadloaf Writing Conference, 1974 and 1976; lecturer, Salzburg Seminar in American Studies, 1973, and Sewanee Writing Conference, 1990 and 1991. Adjunct professor, Washington University, 1983; Visiting Hurst Professor, 1987. Poetry consultant, Olin Library Modern Literature Collection.

MEMBER: National Academy of Arts and Letters, Academy of American Poets (chancellor, 1985), American Academy of Arts and Sciences.

AWARDS, HONORS: Eunice Tietjens Memorial Prize, *Poetry,* 1956, for *Three Valentines to the Wide World;* Helen Bullis Prize, *Poetry Northwest,* 1964; National Endowment for the Arts grant, 1966-67, 1985; Harriet Monroe Memorial Prize, *Poetry,* 1968; Hart Crane Memorial Award, American Weave Press, 1968; first prize, Borestone Mountain Awards, 1968; Bollingen Prize, Yale University Library, 1970; National Book Award for Poetry, 1971, for *To See, to Take;* Guggenheim fellowship, 1972-73; Loines Prize, National Institute of Arts and Letters, 1976; Academy of American Poets fellowship, 1981; Sandburg Prize, Cornell College, 1982; Shelley Memorial Award, Poetry Society of America, 1987, for body of work; Ruth Lilly Poetry Prize, Modern Poetry Association, 1989; Missouri Arts award, 1990; Pulitzer Prize for poetry, 1991, for *Near Changes;* Golden Plate award, American Academy of Achievement, 1992; St. Louis Award, Arts and Education Council, 1994; named U.S. Poet Laureate, 1992-93. Honorary D.Litt., Washington University, 1971, Cornell College, 1972, University of Northern Iowa, 1991, University of the South, 1993, George Washington University, 1993, and Georgetown University, 1993.

WRITINGS:

Valentines to the Wide World (also see below), Cummington Publishing (New Rochelle, NY), 1959.

A Time of Bees (also see below), University of North Carolina Press (Chapel Hill, NC), 1964.

To See, to Take (also see below), Atheneum (New York, NY), 1970.

Bedtime Stories (also see below), Ceres Press (Woodstock, NY), 1972.

Merciful Disguises: Poems Published and Unpublished (includes *Valentines to the Wide World, A Time of Bees, To See, to Take,* and *Bedtime Stories*), Atheneum (New York, NY), 1973.

Letters from a Father, and Other Poems, Atheneum (New York, NY), 1982.

Near Changes, Knopf (New York, NY), 1990.

Lives and Deaths of the Poets and Non-Poets, privately published, 1991.

If It Be Not I: Collected Poems (includes *Valentines to the World, A Time of Bees, To See, to Take, Bedtime Stories, Merciful Disguises,* and *Letters from a Father and Other Poems*), Knopf (New York, NY), 1992.

Firefall, Knopf (New York, NY), 1992.

Matters of Poetry, Library of Congress (Washington, DC), 1993.

(Author of introduction) Donna Masini, *That Kind of Danger,* Beacon Press (Boston, MA), 1994.

Selected Poems, Knopf (New York, NY), 2002.

Poems represented in anthologies, including *The New Pocket Anthology of American Verse,* edited by Oscar Williams, Pocket Books (New York, NY), 1957; *Midland,* edited by Paul Engle, Random House (New York, NY), 1961; and *The Honey and the Gall,* edited by Chad Walsh, Macmillan (New York, NY), 1967.

Contributor to periodicals, including *Kenyon Review, Poetry, Western Review, Atlantic, New Republic, Poetry, Yale Review,* and *New Yorker.* Founder and editor with husband, Jarvis Thurston, *Perspective,* 1947-67; poetry advisor, *College English,* 1955-57.

SIDELIGHTS: Mona Van Duyn was a distinguished writer whose honors include a Bollingen Prize, a National Book Award, and a term as the United States' official poet laureate. "She is a poet of great wisdom, skill, and versatility," affirmed a contributor to *Virginia Quarterly Review.* Elizabeth Frank, meanwhile, described Van Duyn in a *Nation* appraisal as "a poet who usually tries harder than any of her contemporaries to coax affirmation out of the waste and exhaustion of modern life." Another enthusiast, Susan Ludvigson, wrote in the *Dictionary of Literary Biography* that "Van Duyn's poems are about people—people whose ordinary lives include sickness and death, disappointment and despair, as well as faith and humor and love." Ludvigson added, however, that "the commonness of [Van Duyn's] subjects is misleading, for the poetry encompasses far more than such a catalogue suggests." To Ludvigson, Van Duyn's poetry constitutes "a generous mixture of the ordinary and the unusual, the natural and the sophisticated." Another writer, Doris Earnshaw, noted in *World Literature Today* that "we feel in [Van Duyn's] poetry the joy of the lighted water and the air," and Jane Augustine commented in *Contemporary Poets* that Van Duyn's poems "get 'down to the bone' of human experience."

Van Duyn published her first poetry collection, *Valentines to the Wide World,* in 1958, and readily established herself as an authoritative presence. "Her voice is already assured," noted Ludvigson, "her manner confident." John Woods, meanwhile, wrote in *Poetry* that Van Duyn "appears to be a fully-engaged poet" and contended that she assumes "several attitudes, several voices." Another reviewer, W.D. Snodgrass, wrote in *Hudson Review* of Van Duyn's "quiet and eccentric music," and he deemed her poems "peculiar and gracious."

Valentines to the Wide World includes "Toward a Definition of Marriage," in which Van Duyn compares married love to a novel, a circus, and a collection of old papers. "When the poem ends," observed Ludvigson in the *Dictionary of Literary Biography,* "the conclusion of the poet is that . . . love remains the foundation of the marriage." Ludvigson acknowledged "Toward a Definition of Marriage" as "perhaps the finest piece" in *Valentines to the Wide World.*

In her next book of poems, *A Time of Bees,* Van Duyn addresses a range of subjects, including gardens, friendship, and life in a mental institution. "Using her characteristic halfrhymes, sometimes in quatrains, sometimes in couplets, Van Duyn creates poems impressive for their intelligence and their determined attempts to find reason in an unreasonable world," maintained Ludvigson in the *Dictionary of Literary Biography.* The essayist expressed particular praise for the title poem, wherein a married couple endeavors to rid their porch of bees. Ludvigson noted that a concluding episode, in which the female narrator expresses revulsion for the extermination of newborn bees, draws parallels with both "the mystery of love and . . . the differences between men an women." She deemed the poem "excellent."

In 1970 Van Duyn received the National Book Award for her third poetry collection, *To See, to Take,* which was described in *American Women Writers: A Critical Reference Guide from Colonial Times to the Present* as a volume "concentrating on observations of middle-class suburban life." Notable among the poems in this collection is "Marriage, with Beasts," "in which a couple's tour of a zoo prompts a consideration of love." David Kalstone, writing in the *New York Times Book Review,* contended that *To See, to Take* "has a special rhythm, swinging out, exploring, detaching itself," and he hailed "Marriage, with Beasts" as "funniest and eeriest of all." In addition, Kalstone acknowledged the entire volume for its "sustained skill and wisdom," and he praised it as a collection that generates "large, painful, powerful connections, and one in which we sense a whole life grasped, in the most urgent and rewarding senses of the word." Equally impressed, Arthur Oberg summarized *To See, to Take,* in a *Southern Review* critique, as "one of the finest books to appear in American poetry in recent years."

Van Duyn's *Bedtime Stories* marks a departure from previous poetry collections, for it presents recollections from the perspective of the author's grandmother and relates them in the narrator's Germanic dialect. Writing in *Ploughshares,* Lorrie Goldensohn observed that the poems in *Bedtime Stories* serve as further representations of Van Duyn's affinity for "agrarian domesticity," and she noted "a necessary event in the larger life of these poems: the subversion of their maturities and finish into new vitalities."

Van Duyn followed *Bedtime Stories* with *Merciful Disguises: Poems Published and Unpublished,* which includes verse from her earlier collections. In a *New York Times* review, Harvey Shapiro contended, "The early poems [in *Merciful Disguises*] sometimes wobble unsteadily," but he noted that later poems prove "essayistic, discursive but powerful in their wisdom." *New Republic* reviewer Louis Coxe, meanwhile, saw the book as "a written-out diary of the poet as one of us: humorous, observant and lively."

Letters from a Father, and Other Poems, which Van Duyn published in 1982, includes a series of six poems structured as missives from father to daughter. In the initial poems, the father dwells on his ailments and those of his wife, but in later poems he comes to report increasingly on the birds gathering at the feeder provided by the daughter. "By the end of the poem," wrote Robert Hass in the *Washington Post Book World,* "there is very little information about physical debility, the note of self-pity is gone, and there are long reports about birds." Hass stated that the poem "gets at an area of human experience that literature—outside of Samuel Beckett—has hardly touched." Another reviewer, M.L. Rosenthal, wrote in the *New York Times Book Review* that the title poem is "so endearing, so unusual in its plain humanity, that one is tempted to take it at sentimental face-value and ignore the death obsession with which it begins." Richard Lattimore, meanwhile, wrote in *Hudson Review* that "it may be couplets, rhymed stanzas, even a sonnet—but whatever it is, [Van Duyn] dishes it out with practiced casual skill," and he called Van Duyn "a good poet to be writing, these days."

Van Duyn continues to consider life's more mundane aspects in *Near Changes,* a 1990 publication that Constance Hunting, writing in *Parnassus,* called "a consolidation and an advance of her talent." Notable among the poems in the collection are "Condemned Site," where she recalls five friends who have died, and "Late Loving," in which she reflects on a marriage nearing its fiftieth year. Alfred Corn, in his *Poetry* review, stated that "'Late Loving' must be the most moving (and honest) poem ever written about marriage approaching the golden anniversary." Likewise enthused, Edward Hirsch wrote in the *New York Times Book Review* that Van Duyn "has a gift for making the ordinary appear strange and for turning a common situation into a metaphysical exploration." He concluded that in *Near Changes* Van Duyn "has 'fixed' her world with pathos and wit." For this collection, Van Duyn received the Pulitzer Prize for poetry.

In 1992 Van Duyn became the official poet laureate of the United States, thus prompting Judith Hall, writing in the *Antioch Review,* to acknowledge her as "a poet of relationships recollected in tranquillity." That same year, the poet published *If It Be Not I: Collected Poems,* a formidable volume amassing her previously published verse. Reviewing *If It Be Not I,* Doris Earnshaw stated in *World Literature Today* that Van Duyn "can write a poem on canning pears that delights you, all the more as you realize by the last line that you have read a perfect sonnet."

Van Duyn commemorated her appointment as poet laureate by issuing a collection of new poems, *Firefly,* which includes verse she describes as "minimalist sonnets." Some critics expressed displeasure with the new collection. William Logan, for example, contended in *Parnassus* that "many of . . . [Van Duyn's] late poems have been driven by the moment rather than coming to embody it," and Liz Rosenberg claimed in Chicago's *Tribune Books* that "*Firefall* feels hastily put together." Rosenberg added, "Irony is Van Duyn's least becoming attire, and she wears it too often here." A more favorably assessment came from Robyn Selman, who wrote in the *Village Voice* that "*Firefall* contains some especially delightful shorter pieces." Another reviewer, Rachel Hadas, observed in the *New York Times Book Review* that *Firefall* "varies the pace . . . with skinny 'minimalist sonnets' that capture large themes . . . with aphoristic slimness." Ben Howard, meanwhile, wrote in *Poetry* that though Van Duyn's book "breaks no new ground," it nonetheless "speaks a human, forgiving spirit, rich in warmth and moral wisdom." Another critic, Robert B. Shaw, perceived *Firefly,* in a *Shenandoah* essay, as evidence that Van Duyn "has grown more venturesome as a craftsman."

Van Duyn's more recent publications include *Selected Poems,* a 2002 collection that led *Book* reviewer Stephen Whited to note the poet's "devotion to accessible, domestic subjects." Similarly impressed, a *Publishers Weekly* critic summarized Van Duyn's art as "acutely emotional poems about deceptively ordinary domestic experiences." Another reviewer, Richard Wakefield, concluded his *Seattle Times* appraisal by affirming that *Selected Poems* "illuminates many brave new world and shows us that they are beautiful not in spite of but, often, because of their imperfections."

BIOGRAPHICAL AND CRITICAL SOURCES:

BOOKS

American Women Writers: A Critical Reference Guide from Colonial Times to the Present, 2nd edition, St. James Press (Detroit, MI), 1999.

Burns, Michael, editor, *Discovery and Reminiscence: Essays on the Poetry of Mona Van Duyn* University of Arkansas Press (Fayetteville, AR), 1998.

Contemporary Literary Criticism, Thomson Gale (Detroit, MI), Volume 3, 1975, Volume 7, 1977, Volume 116.

Contemporary Poets, 7th edition, St. James Press (Detroit, MI), 2001.

Dictionary of Literary Biography, Volume 5: *American Poets since World War II,* Thomson Gale (Detroit, MI), 1980, pp. 334-340.

Modern American Literature, St. James Press (Detroit, MI), 1999, pp. 315-317.

PERIODICALS

Antioch Review, winter, 1994, Judith Hall, "Strangers May Run: The Nation's First Poet Laureate," pp. 141-146.

Books, July-August, 2002, Stephen Whited, review of *Selected Poems,* p. 79.

Hudson Review, spring, 1960, W.D. Snodgrass, "Four Gentlemen, Two Ladies," pp. 120-131; spring, 1983, Richard Lattimore, "Poetry Chronicle," pp. 210-211.

Nation, May 4, 1970; November 27, 1982, Elizabeth Frank, review of *Letters from a Father, and Other Poems,* pp. 563, 565.

New Republic, October 6, 1973, Louise Coxe, review of *Merciful Disguises,* pp. 26-28; December 31, 1990, Cynthia Zarin, article on Mona Van Duyn, pp. 36-40.

New York Times, January 11, 1971; September 22, 1973, Harvey Shapiro, "As Three Poets See Reality," p. 22.

New York Times Book Review, November 21, 1965; August 2, 1970, David Kalstone, "Charms to Stave off the Executioner," pp. 5, 22; December 9, 1973; March 13, 1983, M.L. Rosenthal, "A Common Sadness," p. 6; November 18, 1990, Edward Hirsch, "Violent Desires," p. 24; July 18, 1993, Rachel Hadas, "Serious Poets," p. 18.

Parnassus, spring/ summer, 1974; Volume 16, number 2, 1991, Constance Hunting, "Methods of Transport," pp. 377-389; February, 1992, William Logan, "Late Callings," pp. 317-327.

Poetry, April, 1960, John Woods, "The Teeming Catalogue," pp. 47-51; June, 1965; June, 1971; October, 1990, Alfred Corn, review of *Near Changes,* pp. 47-50; December, 1993, Ben Howard, "Masters of Transience," pp. 158-170.

Ploughshares, March, 1978, Lorrie Goldensohn, "Mona Van Duyn and the Politics of Love," pp. 31-44.

Publishers Weekly, April 29, 2002, review of *Selected Poems,* p. 65.

Seattle Times, June 30, 2002, Richard Wakefield, "Celebrating the Best of Mona Van Duyn."

Shenandoah, spring, 1994, Robert Shaw, "Life Work," pp. 38-48.

Southern Review, winter, 1973, Arthur Oberg, "Deer, Doors, Dark," pp. 243-256.

Tribune Books (Chicago, IL), April 11, 1993, Liz Rosenberg, "The Collected Mona Van Duyn," p. 6.

Village Voice, July 1, 1993, Robyn Selman, "Housekeeping," pp. 60-61.

Virginia Quarterly Review, spring, 1965; winter, 1974.

Washington Post Book World, January 6, 1974; September 5, 1982, Robert Hass, review of *Letters from a Father, and Other Poems,* pp. 6-7.

World Literature Today, spring, 1994, Doris Earnshaw, review of *If It Be Not I: Collected Poems, 1959-1982,* p. 135, and review of *Firefall,* p. 376.

OTHER

Poetry Daily, http://www.poems.com/ (August 13, 2002).

VAN DUYN, Mona Jane
See VAN DUYN, Mona

* * *

VARGAS LLOSA, Jorge Mario Pedro
See VARGAS LLOSA, Mario

* * *

VARGAS LLOSA, Mario 1936-
(Jorge Mario Pedro Vargas Llosa)

PERSONAL: Born March 28, 1936, in Arequipa, Peru; became Spanish citizen, 1994; son of Ernesto Vargas Maldonaldo and Dora Llosa Ureta; married Julia Urquidi, 1955 (divorced); married Patricia Llosa, 1965; children: (second marriage) Alvaro, Gonzalo, Morgana. *Education:* Attended University of San Marcos; University of Madrid, Ph.D., 1959. *Politics:* Liberal. *Religion:* Agnostic. *Hobbies and other interests:* Films, jogging, football.

ADDRESSES: *Home*—Spain. *Agent*—Agencia Carmen Balcells, Diagonal 580, 08021 Barcelona, Spain.

CAREER: Writer. Journalist with *La Industria,* Piura, Peru, and with Radio Panamericana and *La Cronica,* both in Lima, Peru, c. 1950s; worked in Paris, France, as a journalist with Agence France-Presse, as a broadcaster with the radio-television network ORTF, and as a language teacher; Queen Mary College and Kings College, London, England, faculty member, 1966-68; Washington State University, Seattle, writer-in-residence, 1968; University of Puerto Rico, visiting professor, 1969; *Libre,* Paris, France, cofounder, 1971; Columbia University, New York, NY, Edward Laroque Tinker Visiting Professor, 1975; former fellow, Woodrow Wilson Center, Washington, DC; former host of Peruvian television program *The Tower of Babel;* Peruvian presidential candidate, Liberty Movement, 1990.

MEMBER: PEN (president 1976-79), Academy Peruana de la Lengua.

AWARDS, HONORS: Premio Leopoldo Alas, 1959, for *Los jefes;* Premio Biblioteca Breve, 1962, for *La ciudad y los perros;* Premio de la Critica Española, 1963, for *La ciudad y los perros,* and 1967, for *La casa verde;* Premio Nacional de la Novela, and Premio Internacional Literatura Romulo Gallegos, both 1967, both for *La casa verde;* annual prize for theater (Argentina), 1981; Congressional Medal of Honour (Peru), 1981; Instituo Italo Latinoamericano Iila prize (Italy), 1982; Ritz Paris Hemingway Award, 1985, for *The War of the End of the World;* Legion d'honneur (France), 1985; Principe de Asturias Prize for Letters, 1986; named Chevalier de l'Ordre des Arts et des Lettres (France), 1993; Cervantes prize for literature, 1994; Jerusalem prize, 1995; National Book Critics Circle Award for Criticism, 1997, for *Making Waves.*

WRITINGS:

FICTION

Los jefes (story collection; title means "The Leaders"; also see below), Rocas (Barcelona, Spain), 1959, translation by Ronald Christ and Gregory Kolovakos published in *The Cubs and Other Stories,* Harper (New York, NY), 1979.

La ciudad y los perros (novel), Seix Barral (Barcelona, Spain), 1963, translation by Lysander Kemp published as *The Time of the Hero,* Grove (New York, NY), 1966, 2nd edition, Alfaguara (Madrid, Spain), 1999.

La casa verde (novel), Seix Barral (Barcelona, Spain), 1966, translation by Gregory Rabassa published as *The Green House,* Harper (New York, NY), 1968.

Los cachorros (novella; title means "The Cubs"; also see below), Lumen (Barcelona, Spain), 1967.

Conversacion en la catedral (novel), two volumes, Seix Barral (Barcelona, Spain), 1969, translation by Gregory Rabassa published as *Conversation in the Cathedral,* Harper (New York, NY), 1975.

Los cachorros; Los jefes, Peisa (Lima, Peru), 1973.

Pantaleon y las visitadoras (novel), Seix Barral (Barcelona, Spain), 1973, translation by Ronald Christ and Gregory Kolovakos published as *Captain Pantoja and the Special Service,* Harper (New York, NY), 1978.

La tia Julia y el escribidor (novel), Seix Barral (Barcelona, Spain), 1977, translation by Helen Lane published as *Aunt Julia and the Scriptwriter,* Farrar, Straus (New York, NY), 1982.

The Cubs and Other Stories, translations by Ronald Christ and Gregory Kolovakos, Harper (New York, NY), 1979.

La guerra del fin del mundo (novel), Seix Barral (Barcelona, Spain), 1981, translation by Helen Lane published as *The War of the End of the World,* Farrar, Straus (New York, NY), 1984.

Historia de Mayta (novel), Seix Barral (Barcelona, Spain), 1985, translation by Alfred MacAdam published as *The Real Life of Alejandro Mayta,* Farrar, Straus (New York, NY), 1986.

Quien mato a Palomino Molero? (novel), Seix Barral (Barcelona, Spain), 1986, translation by Alfred MacAdam published as *Who Killed Palomino Molero?,* Farrar, Straus (New York, NY), 1987.

El hablador (novel), Seix Barral (Barcelona, Spain), 1987, translation by Helen Lane published as *The Storyteller,* Farrar, Straus (New York, NY), 1989.

Elogio de la madrastra (novel), Tusquets (Barcelona, Spain), 1988, translation by Helen Lane published as *In Praise of the Stepmother,* Farrar, Straus (New York, NY), 1990.

Lituma en los Andes (novel), Planeta (Barcelona, Spain), 1993, translation by Edith Grossman published as *Death in the Andes,* Farrar, Straus (New York, NY), 1996.

Los cuadernos de don Rigoberto, Alfaguara (Madrid, Spain), 1997, translation by Edith Grossman published as *The Notebooks of Don Rigoberto,* Farrar, Straus (New York, NY), 1998.

La fiesta del chivo, Alfaguara (Madrid, Spain), 2000, translation by Edith Grossman published as *The Feast of the Goat,* Farrar, Straus (New York, NY), 2002.

El paraíso en la otra esquina, Alfaguara (Lima, Peru), 2003, translation by Natasha Wimmer published as *The Way to Paradise*, Farrar, Straus (New York, NY), 2003.

PLAYS

La senorita de Tacna (produced as *Senorita from Tacna* in New York, NY, 1983; produced as *The Young Lady from Tacna* in Los Angeles, 1985), Seix Barral (Barcelona, Spain), 1981, translation by David Graham-Young published as *The Young Lady from Tacna* in *Mario Vargas Llosa: Three Plays* (also see below), 1990.

Kathie y el hipopotamo: Comedia en dos actos (translation by Kerry McKenny and Anthony Oliver-Smith produced as *Kathie and the Hippopotamus* in Edinburgh, Scotland, 1986), Seix Barral (Barcelona, Spain), 1983, translation by David Graham-Young published in *Mario Vargas Llosa: Three Plays* (also see below), 1990.

La chunga (translation by Joanne Pottlitzer first produced in New York, NY, 1986), Seix Barral (Barcelona, Spain), 1986, translation by David Graham-Young published in *Mario Vargas Llosa: Three Plays* (also see below), 1990.

Mario Vargas Llosa: Three Plays (contains *The Young Lady from Tacna, Kathie and the Hippopotamus,* and *La chunga*), Hill & Wang (New York, NY), 1990.

El señor de los balcones (title means "Lord of the Balconies"), Seix Barral (Barcelona, Spain), 1993.

Also author of *Le Huida* (title means "The Escape"), produced in Piura, Peru.

OTHER

La novela, Fundacion de Cultura Universitaria (Montevideo, Uruguay), 1968.

(With Gabriel García Márquez) *La novela en America Latina,* Milla Batres (Lima, Peru), 1968.

(Editor, with G. Brotherston) *Seven Stories from Spanish America,* Elsevier Science, 1968.

Antologia minima de M. Vargas Llosa, Tiempo Contemporaneo (Buenos Aires, Argentina), 1969.

Letra de batalla per "Tirant lo Blanc," Edicions 62, 1969, published as *Carta de batalla por Tirant lo Blanc,* Seix Barral (Barcelona, Spain), 1991.

(With Oscar Collazos and Julio Cortazar) *Literatura en la revolucion y revolucion en la literatura,* Siglo Veintiuno (Mexico City, Mexico), 1970.

Los cachorros; El desafio; Dia domingo, Salvat (Barcelona, Spain), 1970, *Dia domingo* published separately, Amadis (Buenos Aires, Argentina), 1971.

García Márquez: Historia de un deicidio (title means "García Márquez: The Story of a Deicide"), Seix Barral (Barcelona, Spain), 1971.

La historia secreta de una novela, Tusquets (Madrid, Spain), 1971.

(With Martin de Riquer) *El combate imaginario: Las cartas de batalla de Joanot Martorell,* Seix Barral (Barcelona, Spain), 1972.

(With Angel Rama) *García Márquez y la problematica de la novela,* Corregidor-Marcha (Buenos Aires, Argentina), 1973.

Obras escogidas: novelas y cuentos, Aguilar (Madrid, Spain), 1973.

La orgia perpetua: Flaubert y "Madame Bovary," Taurus (Madrid, Spain), 1975, translation by Helen Lane published as *The Perpetual Orgy: Flaubert and "Madame Bovary,"* Farrar, Straus (New York, NY), 1986.

Conversacion en la catedral; La orgia perpetua; Pantaleon y las visitadoras, Aguilar (Madrid, Spain), 1978.

Jose Maria Arguedas, entre sapos y halcones, Ediciones Cultura Hispanica del Centro Iberoamericano de Cooperacion (Madrid, Spain), 1978.

La utopia arcaica, Centre of Latin American Studies, University of Cambridge (Cambridge, England), 1978.

The Genesis and Evolution of "Pantaleon y las visitadoras," City College (New York, NY), 1979.

Art, Authenticity, and Latin-American Culture, Wilson Center (Washington, DC), 1981.

Entre Sartre y Camus, Huracan (Rio Piedras, Puerto Rico), 1981.

Contra viento y marea (journalism; title means "Against All Odds"), three volumes, Seix Barral (Barcelona, Spain), 1983–1990.

La cultura de la libertad, la libertad de la cultura, Fundacion Eduardo Frei (Santiago, Chile), 1985.

El debate, Universidad del Pacifico, Centro de Investigacion (Lima, Peru), 1990.

La verdad de las mentiras (essays; title means "The Truth of Lies"), Seix Barral (Barcelona, Spain), 1990.

A Writer's Reality, Syracuse University Press (Syracuse, NY), 1991.

El pez en el agua: Memorias, Seix Barral (Barcelona, Spain), 1993, translation by Helen Lane published as *A Fish in the Water: A Memoir,* Farrar, Straus (New York, NY), 1994.

Desafios a la libertad, Aguilar (Madrid, Spain), 1994.

Ojos bonitos, cuadros feos, Peisa (Lima, Peru), 1996.

Making Waves, edited and translated by John King, Farrar, Straus (New York, NY), 1997.

Una historia no oficial, Espasa Calpe (Madrid, Spain), 1997.

(With Paul Bowles) *Claudio Bravo: Paintings and Drawings,* Abbeville Press (New York, NY), 1997.

Cartas a un joven novelista (title means "Letters to a Young Novelist"), Ariel/Planeta (Barcelona, Spain), 1997.

Obra reunida. Narrativa breve (short stories), Alfaguara (Madrid, Spain), 1999.

(With others) *Los desafios a la socieda abierta: A fines del siglo XX* (title means "Challenges to the Open Society: At the End of the Twentieth Century"), Ameghino (Buenos Aires, Argentina), 1999.

(Author of introduction) Plinio Apuleyo Mendoza, and Carlos Alberto Montaner, *Guide to the Perfect Latin-American Idiot,* translation by Michaela Lajda Ames, Madison Books, distributed by National Book Network (Lanham, MD), 2000.

El lenguaje de la pasion, El Pais (Madrid, Spain), 2001, translation by Natasha Wimmer published as *The Language of Passion,* Farrar, Straus (New York, NY), 2003.

(Author of text) *Andes,* photographs by Pablo Corral Vega, National Geographic Society (Washington, DC), 2001.

Literatura y politica (transcription of conferences), Technical School of Monterrey (Monterrey, Mexico), 2001.

Palma, Valor nacional (speech given October 6, 1956), Universidad Ricardo Palma (Lima, Peru), 2003.

(Author of text) *Diario de Irak,* photographs by daughter, Morgana Vargas Llosa, Aguilar (Buenos Aires, Argentina), 2003.

Contributor to *The Eye of the Heart,* 1973; contributor to periodicals, including *Commentary, Harper's, National Review, New Perspectives Quarterly, New York Times Book Review, New York Times Magazine, UNESCO Courier,* and *World Press Review.* Selected works have been recorded by the Library of Congress Archive of Recorded Poetry and Literature.

ADAPTATIONS: The Cubs was filmed in 1971; *Captain Pantoja and the Special Service* was filmed in 1976 (Vargas Llosa directed the film, which was banned in Peru); *Aunt Julia and the Scriptwriter* was adapted as a television series in Peru, as a screenplay written by William Boyd and directed by Jon Amiel in 1989, and as a motion picture titled *Tune in Tomorrow,* c. 1990; *The Feast of the Goat* was adapted for the stage by Veronia Triana and Jorge Ali Triana and directed by Jorge Ali Triana at the Gramercy Arts Theater in New York in 2003.

SIDELIGHTS: Peruvian-born writer Mario Vargas Llosa often draws from his personal experiences to write of the injustices and corruption of contemporary Latin America. At one time an admirer of communist Cuba, since the early 1970s Vargas Llosa has been opposed to tyrannies of both the political left and right. He advocates democracy, a free market, and individual liberty and cautions against extreme or violent political action, instead calling for peaceful democratic reforms. In 1989 Vargas Llosa was chosen to be the presidential candidate of Fredemo, a political coalition in Peru; though at one point he held a large lead in election polls, in the end he lost the election to Alberto Fujimori. Through his novels—marked by complex structures and an innovative merging of dialogue and description in an attempt to recreate the actual feeling of life—Vargas Llosa has established himself as one of the most important of contemporary writers in the Spanish language.

As a young man, Vargas Llosa spent two years at the Leoncio Prado Military Academy. Sent there by his father, who had discovered that his son wrote poetry and was therefore fearful for the boy's masculinity, Vargas

Llosa found the school, with its "restrictions, the military discipline and the brutal, bullying atmosphere, unbearable," he later recalled in the *New York Times Magazine*. His years at the school inspired his first novel, *The Time of the Hero,* first published in Spanish as *La ciudad y los perros.* The book is, R.Z. Sheppard stated in *Time,* "a brutal slab of naturalism about life and violent death." The novel's success was ensured when the school's officials objected to Vargas Llosa's portrayal of their institution. "One thousand copies were ceremoniously burned in the patio of the school and several generals attacked it bitterly. One of them said that the book was the work of a 'degenerate mind,' and another, who was more imaginative, claimed that I had undoubtedly been paid by Ecuador to undermine the prestige of the Peruvian Army," Vargas Llosa recalled in his *New York Times Magazine* article.

Vargas Llosa wrote *The Time of the Hero* after leaving Peru for Europe in 1958, when he was twenty-two. In embracing Europe and entering into self-imposed exile from his native land, Vargas Llosa was following in the footsteps of numerous Latin-American writers, including Jorge Luis Borges, Julio Cortazar, and Carlos Fuentes. Vargas Llosa was to stay in Europe for thirty years, not returning to Peru until the late 1980s after the country had slipped into political chaos and economic impoverishment. These conditions prompted Vargas Llosa's decision to seek the presidency of Peru. During his three decades in Europe, Vargas Llosa became an internationally celebrated author.

Though Vargas Llosa had attracted widespread attention with his first novel, it was his second novel that cemented his status as a major novelist. In the award-winning *La casa verde* (*The Green House*), Vargas Llosa draws upon another period from his childhood for inspiration. For several years his family lived in the Peruvian jungle town of Piura, and his memories of the gaudy local brothel, known to everyone as the Green House, form the basis of his novel. The book's several stories are interwoven in a nonlinear narrative revolving around the brothel and the family that owns it, the military that runs the town, a dealer in stolen rubber in the nearby jungle, and a prostitute who was raised in a convent. "Scenes overlap, different times and places overrun each other . . . echoes precede voices, and disembodied consciences dissolve almost before they can be identified," Luis Harss and Barbara Dohmann wrote in *Into the Mainstream: Conversations with Latin-American Writers.* Gregory Rabassa, writing in *World Literature Today,* noted that the novel's title "is the connective theme that links the primitive world of the jungle to the primal lusts of 'civilization' which are enclosed by the green walls of the whorehouse." Rabassa saw, too, that Vargas Llosa's narrative style "has not reduced time to a device of measurement or location, a practical tool, but has conjoined it with space, so that the characters carry their space with them too . . . inseparable from their time." Harss and Dohmann found that *The Green House* "is probably the most accomplished work of fiction ever to come out of Latin America. It has sweep, beauty, imaginative scope, and a sustained eruptive power that carries the reader from first page to last like a fish in a bloodstream."

With *Conversacion en la catedral,* translated as *Conversation in the Cathedral,* Vargas Llosa widened his scope. Whereas in previous novels he had sought to recreate the repression and corruption of a particular place, in *Conversation in the Cathedral* he attempts to provide a panoramic view of his native country. As John M. Kirk stated in the *International Fiction Review,* this novel "presents a wider, more encompassing view of Peruvian society. . . . [Vargas Llosa's] gaze extends further afield in a determined effort to incorporate as many representative regions of Peru as possible." Set during the dictatorship of Manuel Odria in the late 1940s and 1950s, the society depicted in the novel "is one of corruption in virtually all the shapes and spheres you can imagine," Wolfgang A. Luchting wrote in the *Review of the Center for Inter-American Relations.* Penny Leroux, in a review of the book for the *Nation,* called it "one of the most scathing denunciations ever written on the corruption and immorality of Latin America's ruling classes."

The nonlinear writing of *Conversation in the Cathedral* was seen by several critics to be the culmination of Vargas Llosa's narrative experimentation. Writing in the *Review of the Center for Inter-American Relations,* Ronald Christ called the novel "a masterpiece of montage" and "a massive assault on simultaneity." Christ argued that Vargas Llosa links fragments of prose together to achieve a montage effect that "promotes a linking of actions and words, speech and description, image and image, point of view and point of view." Kirk explained that in *Conversation in the Cathedral,* Vargas Llosa is "attempting the ambitious and obviously impossible plan of conveying to the reader all aspects of the reality of [Peruvian] society, of writing the 'total' novel." By interweaving five different narratives, Vargas Llosa forces the reader to study the text closely, making the reader an "accomplice of the writer [which] undoubtedly helps the reader to a more profound understanding of the work." Kirk concluded that *Conversation in the Cathedral* is "both a perfect showcase for all the structural techniques and thematic obsessions found in [Vargas Llosa's] . . . other work, as well as being the true culmination of his personal anguish for Peru."

Speaking of these early novels in *Modern Latin American Literature,* D.P. Gallagher argued that one effect of their complex nonlinear structures is to "re-enact the complexity of the situations described in them." By juxtaposing unrelated elements, cutting off dialogue at critical moments, and breaking the narration, Vargas Llosa suggests the disparate geological conditions of Peru, recreates the difficulties involved in living in that country, and re-enacts "the very nature of conversation and of communication in general, particularly in a society devoted to the concealment of truth and to the flaunting of deceptive images," Gallagher believed. Ronald de Feo pointed out in the *New Republic* that these early novels all explore "with a near-savage seriousness and single-mindedness themes of social and political corruption." But in *Captain Pantoja and the Special Service* "a new unexpected element entered Vargas Llosa's work: an unrestrained sense of humor," de Feo reported.

A farcical novel involving a military officer's assignment to provide prostitutes for troops in the Peruvian jungle, *Captain Pantoja and the Special Service* is "told through an artful combination of dry military dispatches, juicy personal letters, verbose radio rhetoric, and lurid sensationalist news reports," Gene Bell-Villada wrote in *Commonweal.* Vargas Llosa also mixes conversations from different places and times, as he did in previous novels. And like these earlier works, *Captain Pantoja and the Special Service* "sniffs out corruption in high places, but it also presents something of a break, Vargas Llosa here shedding his high seriousness and adopting a humorous ribald tone," Bell-Villada concluded. The novel's satirical attack is aimed not at the military, a *Times Literary Supplement* reviewer wrote, but at "any institution which channels instincts into a socially acceptable ritual. The humor of the narrative derives less from this serious underlying motive, however, than from the various linguistic codes into which people channel the darker forces."

The humorous tone of *Captain Pantoja and the Special Service* is also found in *Aunt Julia and the Scriptwriter.* The novel concerns two characters based on people in Vargas Llosa's own life: his first wife, Julia, who was his aunt by marriage, and a writer of radio soap opera whom Vargas Llosa names Pedro Camacho in the novel. The eighteen-year-old narrator, Mario, has a love affair with the thirty-two-year-old Julia. Their story is interrupted in alternate chapters by Camacho's wildly complicated soap opera scripts. As Camacho goes mad, his daily scripts for ten different soap operas become more and more entangled, with characters from one serial appearing in others and all of his plots converging into a single unlikely story. The scripts display "fissures through which are revealed secret obsessions, aversions and perversions that allow us to view his soap operas as the story of his disturbed mind," Jose Miguel Oviedo wrote in *World Literature Today.* "The result," explained Nicholas Shakespeare in the *Times Literary Supplement,* "is that Camacho ends up in an asylum, while Mario concludes his real-life soap opera by running off to marry Aunt Julia."

Although *Aunt Julia and the Scriptwriter* is as humorous as *Captain Pantoja and the Special Service,* "it has a thematic richness and density the other book lacked," de Feo believed. This richness is found in the novel's exploration of the writer's life and of the relationship between a creative work and its inspiration. In the contrasting of soap opera plots with the real-life romance of Mario and Julia, the novel raises questions about the distinctions between fiction and fact. In a review for *New York,* Carolyn Clay called *Aunt Julia and the Scriptwriter* "a treatise on the art of writing, on the relationship of stimuli to imagination." It is, de Feo observed, "a multilayered, high-spirited, and in the end terribly affecting text about the interplay of fiction and reality, the transformation of life into art, and life seen and sometimes even lived as fiction."

In *The War of the End of the World,* Vargas Llosa for the first time sets his story outside of his native Peru. He turns instead to Brazil and bases his story on an apocalyptic religious movement that gained momentum toward the end of the nineteenth century. Convinced that the year 1900 marked the end of the world, these zealots, led by a man named the Counselor, set up the community of Canudos. Because of the Counselor's continued denunciations of the Brazilian government, which he called the "antichrist" for its legal separation of church and state, the national government sent in troops to break up this religious community. The first military assault was repulsed, as were the second and third, but the fourth expedition involved a force of some 4,000 soldiers. They laid waste to the entire area and killed nearly 40,000 people.

Vargas Llosa told Wendy Smith in *Publishers Weekly* that he was drawn to write of this bloody episode because he felt the fanaticism of both sides in this conflict is exemplary of late-twentieth-century Latin America. "Fanaticism is the root of violence in Latin America," he explained. In the Brazilian war, he believes, is a microcosm of Latin America. "Canudos presents a limited situation in which you can see clearly. Everything is there: a society in which on the one hand people are living a very old-fashioned life and have an archaic way of thinking, and on the other hand progressives want to impose modernism on society with guns. This creates a total lack of communication, of dialogue, and when there is no communication, war or repression or upheaval comes immediately," he told Smith. In an article for the *Washington Post,* Vargas Llosa explained to Curt Suplee that "in the history of the Canudos war you could really see something that has been happening in Latin American history over the nineteenth and twentieth centuries—the total lack of communication between two sections of a society which kill each other fighting *ghosts,* no? Fighting fictional enemies who are invented out of fanaticism. This kind of reciprocal incapacity of understanding is probably the main problem we have to overcome in Latin America."

Not only is *The War of the End of the World* set in the nineteenth century, but its length and approach are also of that time. A writer for the London *Times* called it "a massive novel in the nineteenth-century tradition: massive in content, in its ambitions, in its technical achievement." Gordon Brotherston of the *Times Literary Supplement* described the book as being "on the grand scale of the nineteenth century," while Salman Rushdie in the *New Republic* similarly defined the novel as "a modern tragedy on the grand scale." Richard Locke wrote in the *Washington Post Book World* that *The War of the End of the World* "overshadows the majority of novels published . . . in the past few years. Indeed, it makes most recent American fiction seem very small, very private, very gray, and very timid."

Vargas Llosa's political perspective in *The War of the End of the World* exhibited a marked change from his earlier works. He does not attack a corrupt society, instead treating both sides in the Canudos war ironically. The novel ends with a character from either side locked in a fight to the death. As Rushdie observed, "This image would seem to crystallize Vargas Llosa's political vision." This condemnation of both sides in the Canudos conflict reflects Vargas Llosa's view of the contemporary Latin-American scene, where rightist dictatorships often battle communist guerrillas. Suplee described Vargas Llosa as "a humanist who reviles with equal vigor tyrannies of the right or left (is there really a difference, he asks, between 'good tortures and bad tortures'?)."

Although his political views have changed during the course of his career, taking him from a leftist supporter of communist Cuba to a strong advocate of democracy, Vargas Llosa's abhorrence of dictatorship, violence, and corruption has remained constant. He sees Latin-American intellectuals as participants in a continuing cycle of "repression, chaos, and subversion," he told Philip Bennett in the *Washington Post.* Many of these intellectuals, Vargas Llosa explained further, "are seduced by rigidly dogmatic stands. Although they are not accustomed to pick up a rifle or throw bombs from their studies, they foment and defend the violence." Speaking of the late-twentieth-century conflict in Peru between the government and the Maoist guerrilla movement the Shining Path, Vargas Llosa clarified to Suplee that "the struggle between the guerrillas and the armed forces is really a settling of accounts between privileged sectors of society, and the peasant masses are used cynically and brutally by those who say they want to 'liberate' them."

Vargas Llosa believes that a Latin-American writer is obligated to speak out on political matters. "If you're a writer in a country like Peru," he told Suplee, "you're a privileged person because you know how to read and write, you have an audience, you are respected. It is a moral obligation of a writer in Latin America to be involved in civic activities." This belief led Vargas Llosa in 1987 to speak out when the Peruvian government proposed to nationalize the country's banks. His protest quickly led to a mass movement in opposition to the plan, and the government was forced to back down. Vargas Llosa's supporters went on to create Fredemo, a political party calling for democracy, a free market, and individual liberty. Together with two other political parties, Fredemo established a coalition group called the Liberty Movement. In June of 1989 Vargas Llosa was chosen to be the coalition's presidential candidate for Peru's 1990 elections. Visiting small rural towns, the urban strongholds of his Marxist opponents, and the jungle villages of the country's Indians, Vargas Llosa campaigned on what he believes is Peru's foremost problem: "We have to defend democracy against the military and against the extreme Left." Opinion polls in late summer of 1988 showed him to be the leading contender for the presidency, with a 44-to-19-percent lead over his nearest opponent. By the time of the election, however, Vargas Llosa's lead had eroded, and he ended up losing the election to Alberto Fujimori.

Vargas Llosa chronicles his experience as a presidential candidate in *A Fish in the Water.* In addition to discussing the campaign, however, the author also offers a memoir of his early years in Peru. Noted Rockwell Gray in Chicago's *Tribune Books,* "One string of alternating chapters in the book ends with the young writer's departure for France in 1958; the other recreates the exhausting and dangerous [presidential] campaign that carried him to every corner of Peru." Alan Riding in the *New York Times Book Review* added that the book "serves as [Vargas Llosa's] . . . mea culpa: he explains why the aspiring writer of the 1950's became a politician in the late 1980's and why, in the end, this was a terrible mistake." Vargas Llosa's account of his childhood and young adulthood includes his ambivalent relationship with his father, whom he met for the first time at age eleven and toward whom he had an intense dislike. Mark Falcoff, writing in the *Times Literary Supplement,* declared, "The pages of this book dealing with the father-son relationship are among the most violent and passionate Vargas Llosa has ever written." The author also covers his years at a military prep school and his university years in Lima.

In discussing his failed presidential campaign in *A Fish in the Water,* Vargas Llosa portrays the political backstabbing, unavoidable compromises, and character attacks that characterized the campaign against Fujimori. He also writes about his alienation from the majority of Peruvians: as a white, wealthy, educated, expatriate intellectual, he had little in common with poor Peruvians of Indian descent, many of whom do not speak Spanish. Commented Riding, "Tall, white and well dressed, he invariably looked out of place." Falcoff explained that "the chapters dealing with the presidential campaign suggest an impressive knowledge of Peruvian society at all levels and in the several regions, particularly the needs of its humblest groups." Gray, however, remarked, "Much of this book is engaging and informative, but it becomes at times slack, even gossipy, and assumes an interest in the nuances of Peruvian political and literary life shared by very few American readers."

After losing the campaign, Vargas Llosa returned to Europe—this time to Spain, where he assumed Spanish citizenship. His first novel after running for president, *Death in the Andes,* is set in his homeland amid the modern political and social strife evidenced by the rebellion of the Shining Path guerrilla movement. In part a murder mystery, the novel follows Corporal Lituma as he ventures from his home in Peru's coastal region to a mountain village to investigate the disappearance of three men. In addition to the story line of the missing men, Vargas Llosa intersperses tales of violence committed by the Shining Path as well as a romantic story involving Tomas Carreño, Lituma's guide and partner. Critics praised Vargas Llosa's skill in creating a technically ambitious novel, although some reviewers remarked that the author failed to integrate the various plot lines into a coherent story line. *New York Times Book Review* contributor Madison Smartt Bell, for instance, commented that "amid this multiplicity of plot potential, the reader may share Lituma's difficulty in finding any central focus, or even in identifying a single continuous thread." Similarly, Rockwell Gray, again writing in Chicago's *Tribune Books,* averred that "for all the author's adroit weaving of shifts in viewpoint, voice and time—his attempt to grasp Peru's dilemma from many angles—this technically interesting novel is not on a par with his best work." In contrast, *Washington Post Book World* contributor Marie Arana-Ward wrote, "This is well-knit social criticism as trenchant as any by [Honore] Balzac or [Gustave] Flaubert—an ingenious patchwork of the conflicting mythologies that have shaped the New World psyche since the big bang of Columbus's first step on shore." And Bell admitted, "The individual vignettes are often brilliant."

Vargas Llosa's next novel, *The Notebooks of Don Rigoberto,* is also set in Peru. In this dream-like narrative, Don Rigoberto has separated from his beautiful wife, Doña Lucrecia, because of a sexual encounter between her and her stepson, Fonchito, a precocious boy who has yet to reach puberty. Don Rigoberto misses his wife terribly, and to appease his loneliness he imagines, and writes about, Lucrecia's erotic life—with him as well as with other lovers. It is unclear how much of the narrative is meant to be true and how much is a fantasy. This book lacks the political overtones of much of Vargas Llosa's work, but it does provide "grand, sexy reading for sophisticated audiences," reflected Barbara Hoffert in *Library Journal.* A *Publishers Weekly* writer remarked, "As in much of his writing, Vargas Llosa creates a certain timelessness, a dream-like play on the present. The more he leaves sex to the imagination, the more erotic and beautifully suggestive it becomes."

The author mixes fiction and fact in his novel *The Feast of the Goat,* concerning Dominican dictator Rafael Trujillo. Trujillo was assassinated in 1961, and his death remains a cause for celebration in the Dominican Republic. Despite his cruelty and perversions, Trujillo was supported by the U.S. government since he was seen as being strongly against communism. Vargas Llosa tells the story of Urania Cabral, a successful New York City lawyer who was victimized by her father and Trujillo shortly before the dictator's death. Moving forward and back in time, in the author's trademark style, the novel gives a detailed portrait of Trujillo and his frustration with the one enemy he could not conquer: his own advancing age. Obsessive about his habits and grooming, he is unable to do a thing about his increasing incontinence and sexual impotence. The methods he used to victimize individuals and, in fact, his entire country are laid out here, while the stories of Urania, her father, and the men who killed Trujillo are also presented with empathy. "This is an impressively crafted novel," commented Sebastian Shakespeare in the *New Statesman.* "The set pieces are magnificent . . . but it's the small details that you recall: the smell of cheap perfume sprayed on to electric chairs to conceal the stench of urine, excrement and charred flesh." Noting that the Trujillista era was noted for its vileness, Liliana Wendorff added in *Library Journal* that Vargas Llosa "skillfully uses language to demystify subjects that could easily offend." Concluded Jonathan Heawood in the *Guardian Unlimited,* "*The Feast of the Goat* is as dark and complicated as a Jacobean revenge tragedy; but it is also rich and humane."

"A major figure in contemporary Latin American letters," as Locke explained, and "the man whom many describe as the national conscience of his native Peru," as George de Lama wrote in the *Chicago Tribune,* Vargas Llosa is usually ranked with Jorgé Luis Borges, Gabriel García Márquez, and other writers in what has been called the Latin American "Boom" of the 1960s. His body of work set in his native Peru, Suzanne Jill Levine explained in the *New York Times Book Review,* is "one of the largest narrative efforts in contemporary Latin American letters. . . . [He] has begun a complete inventory of the political, social, economic and cultural reality of Peru. . . . Very deliberately, Vargas Llosa has chosen to be his country's conscience." But Vargas Llosa warns that a writer's role is limited. "Even great writers can be totally blind on political matters and can put their prestige and their imagination and fantasy at the service of a policy, which, if it materialized, would be destruction of what they do," Sheppard quoted Vargas Llosa as telling a PEN conference. "To be in the situation of Poland is no better than to be in the situation of Chile. I feel perplexed by these questions. I want to fight for societies where perplexity is still permitted."

BIOGRAPHICAL AND CRITICAL SOURCES:

BOOKS

Acosta, Oscar, and others, *Las honduras de Mario Vargas Llosa,* Universidad Pedagógica Nacional Francisco Morazán (Tegucigalpa, Honduras), 2003.

A Marxist Reading of Fuentes, Vargas Llosa, and Puig, University Press of America (Lanham, MD), 1994.

Booker, Keith M., *Vargas Llosa among the Postmodernists,* University Press of Florida (Gainesville, FL), 1994.

Cano Gaviria, Ricardo, *El buitre y el ave fenix: Conversaciones con Mario Vargas Llosa,* Anagrama (Barcelona, Spain), 1972.

Castro-Klarén, Sara, *Mario Vargas Llosa: análisis introductorio,* Latinoamericana Editores, 1988.

Contemporary Literary Criticism, Thomson Gale (Detroit, MI), Volume 3, 1975, Volume 6, 1976, Volume 9, 1978, Volume 10, 1979, Volume 15, 1980, Volume 31, 1985, Volume 42, 1987, Volume 85, 1995.

Dictionary of Literary Biography, Volume 145: *Modern Latin-American Fiction Writers, Second Series,* Thomson Gale (Detroit, MI), 1994.

El autor y su obra: Mario Vargas Llosa, Universidad Computense de Madrid (Madrid, Spain), 1990.

Encyclopedia of World Biography, 2nd edition, Thomson Gale (Detroit, MI), 1998.

Encyclopedia of World Literature in the Twentieth Century, St. James Press (Detroit, MI), 1999.

Establier Pérez, Helene, *Mario Vargas Llosa y el nuevo arte de hacer novelas,* Universidad de Alicante, 1998.

Feal, Rosemary Geisdorfer, *Novel Lives: The Fictional Autobiographies of Guillermo Cabrera Infante and Mario Vargas Llosa,* University of North Carolina Press (Chapel Hill, NC), 1986.

Gallagher, D. P., *Modern Latin-American Literature,* Oxford University Press (New York, NY), 1973.

Gerdes, Dick, *Mario Vargas Llosa,* Twayne (Boston, MA), 1985.

Gladieu, Marie-Madeleine, *Mario Vargas Llosa,* L'Harmattan (Paris, France), 1989.

Gnutzmann, Rita, *Cómo leer a Mario Vargas Llosa,* Ediciones Júcar, 1992.

Harss, Luis, and Barbara Dohmann, *Into the Mainstream: Conversations with Latin-American Writers,* Harper (New York, NY), 1967.

Hernández de López, Ana María, *Mario Vargas Llosa: opera omnia,* Editorial Pliegos (Madrid, Spain), 1994.

Hispanic Literature Criticism, Thomson Gale (Detroit, MI), 1994.

Köllman, Sabine, *Vargas Llosa's Fiction and the Demons of Politics,* P. Lang (New York, NY), 2002.

Kristal, Efrain, *Temptation of the Word: The Novels of Mario Vargas Llosa,* Vanderbilt University Press (Nashville, TN), 1998.

Lewis, Marvin A., *From Lime to Leticia: The Peruvian Novels of Mario Vargas Llosa,* University Press of America (Lanham, MD), 1983.

Moses, Michael Valdez, *The Novel and the Globalization of Culture,* Oxford University Press (New York, NY), 1995.

Muñoz, Braulio, *A Storyteller: Mario Vargas Llosa between Civilization and Barbarism,* Rowman & Littlefield Publishers (Lanham, MD), 2000.

Oviedo, Jose Miguel, editor, *Mario Vargas Llosa: el escritor y la critica,* Taurus (Madrid, Spain), 1981.

Oviedo, Jose Miguel, *Mario Vargas Llosa: La invencion de una realidad,* Seix Barral (Barcelona, Spain), 1982.

Pereira, Antonio, *La concepcion literaria de Mario Vargas Llosa,* Universidad Nacional Autonoma de Mexico (Mexico City, Mexico), 1981.

Reference Guide to World Literature, 2nd edition, Thomson Gale (Detroit, MI), 1995.

Requejo, Nestor Tenorio, editor, *Mario Vargas Llosa, el fuego de la literatura: textos básicos de aproximación a la narrativa vargasllosiana,* Arteidea Editores (Lima, Peru), 2001.

Rodriguez Elizondo, José, *Vargas Llosa: historia de un doble parricidio,* La Noria (Santiago, Chile), 1993.

Rodriguez Rea, Miguel Angel, *Tras las huellas de un crítico: Mario Vargas Llosa,* Fonda Editorial (Lima, Peru), 1998.

Rossmann, Charles, and Alan Warren Friedman, editors, *Mario Vargas Llosa: A Collection of Critical Essays,* University of Texas Press (Austin, TX), 1978.

Standish, Peter, *Vargas Llosa: La ciudad y los perros,* Grant & Cutler (London, England), 1983.

Williams, Raymond L., *Vargas Llosa: otra historia de un decidio,* Universidad Nacional Autónoma de México (Mexico, DF), 2001.

Williams, Raymond Leslie, *Mario Vargas Llosa,* Ungar (New York, NY), 1986.

PERIODICALS

Americas, March-April, 1989, p. 22; March-April, 1995, p. 62; January, 2001, p. 63.

Atlantic Monthly, March, 1936, pp. 122-124.

Book, November-December, 2003, pp. 9-10.

Bookletter, April 28, 1975.

Booklist, March 15, 1994, p. 1299; March 1, 1998, review of *The Notebooks of Don Rigoberto,* p. 1097; August, 1998, review of *Los cuadernos de Don Rigoberto,* p. 1980; September 1, 1998, review of *Los cuadernos de Don Rigoberto,* p. 74; January 1, 2002, review of *The Feast of the Goat,* p. 762; June 1, 2003, p. 1730; September 15, 2003, p. 181.

Bulletin of Bibliography, December, 1986.

Chicago Tribune, January 3, 1989; June 23, 1989; August 3, 1989.

Commonweal, June 8, 1979.

Esquire, April, 1990, p. 103.

Globe & Mail (Toronto, Ontario, Canada), July 17, 1999, review of *The Notebooks of Don Rigoberto,* p. D16.

Harper's, June, 1987, p. 15.

Hispamerica, Volume 63, 1992, pp. 33-41.

Hispania, March, 1976.

Hudson Review, winter, 1976.

International Fiction Review, January, 1977.

Interview, September, 1988, p. 86.

Kirkus Reviews, March 15, 1998, review of *The Notebooks of Don Rigoberto,* p. 363; March 1, 2003, p. 371; October 1, 2003, p. 1200.

Latin American Literary Review, Volume 11, number 22, 1983, pp. 15-25; January-June, 1987, pp. 121-131, 201-206.

Library Journal, March 15, 1994, p. 116; May 1, 1994, p. 114; April 15, 1997, pp. 82-83; April 1, 1998, Barbara Hoffert, review of *The Notebooks of Don Rigoberto,* p. 126; July, 1998, review of *Cartas a un novelista,* p. 77; January, 1999, review of *The Notebooks of Don Rigoberto,* p. 57; June 1, 2001, Liliana Wendorff, review of *The Feast of the Goat,* p. S31; January, 2002, review of *The Feast of the Goat,* p. 52; April 1, 2003, pp. 99-100; October 15, 2003, p. 100.

London Review of Books, September 17, 1998, review of *The Notebooks of Don Rigoberto,* p. 30.

Los Angeles Times, May 20, 1985; December 18, 1988.

Los Angeles Times Book Review, February 2, 1986.

Maclean's, April 9, 1990, p. 32.

Modern Language Notes, March, 1990, pp. 351-366.

Mother Jones, January, 1989, p. 22.

Nation, November 22, 1975; February 12, 1996, p. 28.

National Review, December 10, 1982; May 16, 1994, p. 65; April 17, 1995, p. 53.

New Leader, March 17, 1975; November 15, 1982; June 6, 1994, pp. 5-6.

New Perspectives Quarterly, fall, 1993, p. 53.

New Republic, August 16-23, 1982; October 8, 1984, pp. 25-27; June 8, 1987, p. 54; February 12, 1990, p. 20.

New Scientist, October 24, 1998, review of *Death in the Andes,* p. 50.

New Statesman, June 21, 1996, pp. 46-47; March 25, 2002, Sebastian Shakespeare, review of *The Feast of the Goat,* p. 57; November 24, 2003, Jonathan Heawood, review of *The Way to Paradise,* p. 55.

Newsweek, February 10, 1986; April 9, 1990, p. 33; October 1, 1990, p. 67.

New York, August 23, 1982.

New Yorker, February 24, 1986, pp. 98, 101-104; August 24, 1987, p. 83; December 25, 1989, p. 103; October 1, 1990, pp. 107-110; April 15, 1996, p. 84; June 17, 2002.

New York Review of Books, March 20, 1975; January 24, 1980; July 16, 1987, p. 35; October 11, 1990, p. 17; May 26, 1994, p. 19; May 9, 1996, p. 16;

July 16, 1998, review of *The Notebooks of Don Rigoberto,* p. 31; July 4, 1999, review of *The Notebooks of Don Rigoberto,* p. 20.
New York Times, March 30, 1985; January 8, 1986; February 9, 1986; February 12, 1986; September 10, 1989; December 6, 1998, review of *Making Waves,* p. 97.
New York Times Book Review, March 23, 1975; April 9, 1978; September 23, 1979; August 1, 1982; December 2, 1984; February 2, 1986; May 31, 1987, p. 13; October 29, 1989, p. 1; October 14, 1990, p. 11; March 10, 1991, p. 13; May 15, 1994, p. 10; February 18, 1996, p. 7; August 3, 1997, Jay Parini, review of *Making Waves,* p. 8; December 6, 1998, review of *The Notebooks of Don Rigoberto,* p. 71; September 13, 1998, review of *Making Waves, The Real Life of Alejandro Mayta,* and *Who Killed Palomino Molero?,* p. 44; June 28, 1998, review of *The Notebooks of Don Rigoberto,* p. 10; November 25, 2001, Walter Kirn, review of *The Feast of the Goat,* p. 10.
New York Times Magazine, November 20, 1983; November 5, 1989, p. 44.
Observer (London, England), June 28, 1998, review of *The Notebooks of Don Rigoberto,* p. 17; August 15, 1999, review of *The Notebooks of Don Rigoberto,* p. 14.
Paris Review, fall, 1990, pp. 47-72.
Partisan Review, Volume 46, number 4, 1979.
People, April 9, 1990, p. 71.
PMLA, Volume 106, number 1, 1991, pp. 46-59.
Publishers Weekly, October 5, 1984; April 11, 1994, p.49; November 20, 1995, p. 65; April 21, 1997 p. 49; March 23, 1998, review of *The Notebooks of Don Rigoberto,* p. 76; April 22, 2002. p. 57; September 29, 2003, p. 40.
Review of Contemporary Fiction, spring, 1997, pp. 15-24; spring, 1997, pp. 58-69; spring, 1997, pp. 70-75; spring, 1997 pp. 76-77; spring, 1998, pp. 231-232; spring 2003, p. 165.
Review of the Center for Inter-American Relations, spring, 1975.
Saturday Review, January 11, 1975.
School Library Journal, June, 2003, pp. 45-46.
Spectator, May 14, 1983; July 25, 1998, review of *The Notebooks of Don Rigoberto,* p. 32; November 15, 2003, Sebastian Smee, "Gaugin and His Gritty Granny," p. 54.
Time, February 17, 1975; August 9, 1982; January 27, 1986; March 10, 1986; July 27, 1987, p. 64; September 7, 1987; November 13, 1989, p. 110; April 9, 1990, p. 56; October 22, 1990, p. 89; June 13, 1994, p. 75; February 12, 1996, p. 75.
Times (London, England), May 13, 1985; August 5, 1986; June 29, 1998, review of *The Notebooks of Don Rigoberto,* p. 74.
Times Literary Supplement, October 12, 1973; May 20, 1983; March 8, 1985; May 17, 1985; July 1, 1988; June 17, 1994, p. 11; August 7, 1998, review of *The Notebooks of Don Rigoberto,* p. 7.
Tribune Books (Chicago, IL), October 7, 1979; January 12, 1986, October 29, 1989; September 11, 1994, p. 7; March 3, 1996, p. 6.
U.S. News and World Report, May 9, 1988, p. 69; November 5, 1990, p. 15.
Virginia Quarterly Review, autumn, 1998, review of *Making Waves,* p. 121.
Vital Speeches, October 1, 1992, p. 755.
Vogue, October, 1990, p. 254.
Wall Street Journal, June 12, 1998, review of *The Notebooks of Don Rigoberto,* p. W12.
Washington Post, August 29, 1983; October 1, 1984; March 26, 1989.
Washington Post Book World, August 26, 1984; February 9, 1986; May 22, 1994, p. 5; February 25, 1996, p. 1; July 26, 1998, review of *The Notebooks of Don Rigoberto,* p. 8.
Wilson Quarterly, summer, 2002, p. 105.
World Literature Today, winter, 1978 (special issue on Vargas Llosa); spring, 1978; winter, 1999, review of *Los cuadernos de Don Rigoberto,* p. 120; summer, 2000, review of *La fiesta del chivo,* p. 676; April-June, 2003, p. 79.

ONLINE

Guardian Unlimited, http://books.guardian.co.uk/ (May 1, 2002), review of *The Feast of the Goat.*
January Magazine Web Site, http://www.januarymagazine.com/ (August 16, 2004), Heidi Johnson-Wright, interview with Mario Vargas Llosa.
Mario Vargas Llosa Home Page, http://www.mvargasllosa.com/ (August 16, 2004).

OTHER

Sklodowska, Elzbieta, *An Interview with Mario Vargas Llosa,* American Audio Prose Library, 1994.

* * *

VERDU, Matilde
See CELA, Camilo José

* * *

VIDAL, Eugene Luther Gore
See VIDAL, Gore

VIDAL, Gore 1925-
(Edgar Box, Eugene Luther Gore Vidal)

PERSONAL: Born October 3, 1925, in West Point, NY; son of Eugene Luther (a U.S. government official) and Nina (Gore) Vidal. *Education:* Graduate of Phillips Exeter Academy, 1943. *Politics:* Democrat.

ADDRESSES: *Home*—La Rondinaia, 84010 Ravello, Salerno, Italy. *Agent*—Lynn Nesbit, 598 Madison Ave., New York, NY 10022-1614.

CAREER: Writer. E.P. Dutton, New York, NY, editor, 1946; Democratic Party candidate for Congress in the Twenty-ninth District of New York, 1960; member of President's Advisory Committee on the Arts, 1961-63; host of *Hot Line* (television program), 1964; cofounder of New Party, 1968-71; cochair of People's Party, 1970-72; ran for nomination as Democratic Party senatorial candidate in California, 1982. Lecturer; has appeared on television and radio talk shows. *Military service:* U.S. Army, Army Transportation Corps, 1943-46; became First Mate; served in Pacific Theater during World War II.

MEMBER: American Academy of Arts and Letters.

AWARDS, HONORS: Edgar Allan Poe Award, Mystery Writers of America, 1955, for television drama; Antoinette Perry Award nomination for best play, 1960, and for best play revival, 2001, and Drama Desk Award for outstanding revival of a play, 2001, all for *The Best Man;* Screen Writers Annual Award nomination, and Cannes Critics Prize, both 1964, both for screenplay *The Best Man;* National Book Critics Circle Award for criticism, 1982, for *The Second American Revolution and Other Essays;* named honorary citizen, Ravello, Italy, 1983; Prix Deauville, 1983, for *Creation;* National Book Award for nonfiction, 1993, for *United States: Essays, 1952-1992*; Chevalier, Ordre des Arts et des Lettres (France).

WRITINGS:

NOVELS

Williwaw (also see below), Dutton (New York, NY), 1946, reprinted, University of Chicago Press (Chicago, IL), 2003, published as *Dangerous Voyage,* Amereon, 1946.

In a Yellow Wood, Dutton (New York, NY), 1947.

The City and the Pillar, Dutton (New York, NY), 1948, revised edition published as *The City and the Pillar Revised,* 1965.

The Season of Comfort, Dutton (New York, NY), 1949.

A Search for the King: A Twelfth-Century Legend, Dutton (New York, NY), 1950.

Dark Green, Bright Red, Dutton (New York, NY), 1950.

The Judgment of Paris, Dutton (New York, NY), 1952, revised edition, Little, Brown (Boston, MA), 1965.

Messiah, Dutton (New York, NY), 1954, revised edition, Little, Brown (Boston, MA), 1965.

Julian (also see below; two chapters first published as *Julian the Apostate,* 1962), Little, Brown (Boston, MA), 1964, reprinted, Vintage (New York, NY), 2003.

Washington, D.C. (part one of series), Little, Brown (Boston, MA), 1967.

Myra Breckinridge (also see below), Little, Brown (Boston, MA), 1968.

Two Sisters: A Novel in the Form of a Memoir, Little, Brown (Boston, MA), 1970.

Burr (part two of series; also see below), Random House (New York, NY), 1973.

Myron (also see below), Random House (New York, NY), 1974.

1876 (part three of series), Random House (New York, NY), 1976.

Kalki (also see below), Random House (New York, NY), 1978.

Creation, Random House (New York, NY), 1981, reprinted, Doubleday (New York, NY), 2002.

Duluth, Random House (New York, NY), 1983.

Lincoln (part four of series), Random House (New York, NY), 1984.

Myra Breckinridge [and] *Myron,* Random House (New York, NY), 1986.

Empire (part five of series), Random House (New York, NY), 1987.

Hollywood (part six of series), Random House (New York, NY), 1990.

Live from Golgotha: The Gospel according to Gore Vidal, Random House (New York, NY), 1992.

The Smithsonian Institution, Random House (New York, NY), 1998.

The Golden Age (part seven of series), Doubleday (New York, NY), 2000.

UNDER PSEUDONYM EDGAR BOX; MYSTERIES

Death in the Fifth Position (also see below), Dutton (New York, NY), 1952.

Death before Bedtime. . . (also see below), Dutton (New York, NY), 1953.
Death Likes It Hot (also see below), Dutton (New York, NY), 1954.
Three by Box: The Complete Mysteries of Edgar Box (contains *Death in the Fifth Position, Death before Bedtime . . . ,* and *Death Likes It Hot*), Random House (New York, NY), 1978.

TELEPLAYS

Visit to a Small Planet and Other Television Plays (contains *Visit to a Small Planet* [also see below; aired on *Goodyear Playhouse,* 1955], *Barn Burning* [1954], *Dark Possession* [1954], *The Death of Billy the Kid* [1955], *A Sense of Justice* [1955], *Smoke* [1954], *Summer Pavilion* [1955], and *The Turn of the Screw* [1955]), Little, Brown (Boston, MA), 1956.
Dress Gray (based on the novel by Lucien Truscott), National Broadcasting Corporation (NBC-TV), 1986.
Gore Vidal's Billy the Kid, Turner Network Television, 1989.

Also author or adaptor of *Dr. Jekyll and Mr. Hyde,* 1955, *Stage Door,* 1955, *A Farewell to Arms,* 1955, *Honor* (also see below), 1956, *The Indestructible Mr. Gore,* 1959, and *Dear Arthur,* 1960. Author of teleplays for series *Philco-Goodyear Playhouse, Studio One,* and *Omnibus Theater.*

SCREENPLAYS

The Catered Affair, Metro-Goldwyn-Mayer (MGM), 1956.
I Accuse, MGM, 1958.
(With Robert Hamer) *The Scapegoat,* MGM, 1959.
(With Tennessee Williams) *Suddenly Last Summer,* Columbia, 1959.
The Best Man (adapted from Vidal's play of the same title; also see below; produced by United Artists, 1964), edited by George P. Garrett, Irvington, 1989.
(With Francis Ford Coppola) *Is Paris Burning?* (based on the novel by Dominique Lapierre), Paramount, 1966.
The Last of the Mobile Hotshots, Warner Bros., 1970.

Also author of screenplay adaptations of his novels *Kalki* and *Burr.*

STAGE PLAYS

Visit to a Small Planet: A Comedy Akin to a Vaudeville (also see below; adapted from his television play; produced on Broadway, 1957), Little, Brown (Boston, MA), 1957, revised edition, Dramatists Play Service (New York, NY), 1959.
The Best Man: A Play of Politics (also see below; produced on Broadway, 1960), Little, Brown (Boston, MA), 1960, revised edition, Dramatists Play Service (New York, NY), 1977.
On the March to the Sea: A Southron Comedy (also see below; adapted from the teleplay *Honor*), produced in Bonn, West Germany (now Germany), 1961.
Three Plays (contains *Visit to a Small Planet, The Best Man: A Play of Politics,* and *On the March to the Sea: A Southron Comedy*), Heinemann (London, England), 1962.
(Translator and editor) Friedrich Dürrenmatt, *Romulus: A New Comedy* (produced on Broadway, 1962), Dramatists Play Service (New York, NY), 1962.
Weekend (produced in New Haven, CT, 1968; produced on Broadway, 1968), Dramatists Play Service (New York, NY), 1968.
An Evening with Richard Nixon (produced in New York, NY, 1972), Random House (New York, NY), 1972.

Vidal's *Romulus: The Broadway Adaptation* was performed with Friedrich Dürrenmatt's *Romulus the Great* (translated by Gerhard Nelhaus), 1966.

ESSAYS

Rocking the Boat, Little, Brown (Boston, MA), 1962.
Sex, Death, and Money, Bantam (New York, NY), 1968.
Reflections upon a Sinking Ship, Little, Brown (Boston, MA), 1969.
Homage to Daniel Shays: Collected Essays, 1952-1972, Random House (New York, NY), 1972, published as *Collected Essays, 1952-1972,* Heinemann (London, England), 1974, published as *On Our Own Now,* Panther (London, England), 1976.
Matters of Fact and of Fiction: Essays, 1973-1976, Random House (New York, NY), 1977.
The Second American Revolution and Other Essays, Random House (New York, NY), 1982, published as *Pink Triangle and Yellow Star and Other Essays,* [London, England], 1982.
Armageddon? Essays, 1983- 1987, Andre Deutsch (New York, NY), 1987.

At Home: Essays, Random House (New York, NY), 1989.

A View from the Diner's Club: Essays, 1987-1991, Andre Deutsch (New York, NY), 1991.

Screening History, Harvard University Press (Cambridge, MA), 1992.

The Decline and Fall of the American Empire, Odonian Press, 1992.

United States: Essays, 1952-1992, Random House (New York, NY), 1992.

The Last Empire: Essays, 1992-2000, Doubleday (New York, NY), 2001.

Dreaming War: Blood for Oil and the Cheney-Bush Junta, Thunder's Mouth Press (New York, NY), 2002.

Perpetual War for Perpetual Peace: How We Got to Be So Hated, Thunder's Mouth Press (New York, NY), 2002.

Inventing a Nation: Washington, Adams, Jefferson, Yale University Press (New Haven, CT), 2003.

Imperial America: Reflections on the United States of Amnesia, Nation Books (New York, NY), 2004.

OTHER

A Thirsty Evil: Seven Short Stories (also see below), Zero Press, 1956.

Three: Williwaw, A Thirsty Evil: Seven Short Stories, [and] *Julian the Apostate,* New American Library (New York, NY), 1962.

(Editor) *Best Television Plays,* Ballantine (New York, NY), 1965.

An Evening with Richard Nixon (recording; based on Vidal's play of the same title), Ode Records, 1973.

(With others) *Great American Families,* Norton (New York, NY), 1977.

(Author of introduction) *Edith Wharton Omnibus,* Doubleday (New York, NY), 1978.

(With Robert J. Stanton) *Views from a Window: Conversations with Gore Vidal,* Lyle Stuart (Secaucus, NJ), 1980.

(Author of introduction) Paul Bowles, *The Collected Stories,* Black Sparrow Press (Santa Barbara, CA), 1983.

(Author of foreword) Logan Pearsall Smith, *All Trivia,* Ticknor & Fields (New York, NY), 1984.

(Author of introduction) Tennessee Williams, *The Collected Stories,* New Directions (Newton, NJ), 1985.

(Author of introduction) Fritz Peters, *Finistere,* Seeker Press, 1985.

(Editor) Henry James, *The Golden Bowl,* Penguin (New York, NY), 1985.

Vidal in Venice, Summit Books (New York, NY), 1987.

(Author of introduction) *Dawn Powell,* QPB, 1989.

(Author of foreword) Alfred Chester, *Head of a Sad Angel: Stories, 1953-1966,* edited by Edward Field, Black Sparrow Press, 1990.

(Author of foreword) Marion E. Rodgers, editor, *Impossible H.L. Mencken: A Selection of His Best Newspaper Stories,* Doubleday (New York, NY), 1991.

(Author of introduction) Don Bachardy and James P. White, editors, *Where Joy Resides: A Christopher Isherwood Reader,* Farrar, Straus (New York, NY), 1991.

(Author of foreword) Robert McAlmon, *Miss Knight and Others,* edited by Edward N. Lorusso, University of New Mexico Press (Albuquerque, NM), 1992.

Palimpsest: A Memoir, Random House (New York, NY), 1995.

The American Presidency, Odonian, 1998.

Sexually Speaking: Collected Sex Writings, Cleis (Pittsburgh, PA), 1999.

The Essential Gore Vidal (omnibus volume), Random House (New York, NY), 1999.

(With Richard Peabody and Lucinda Ebersole) *Conversations with Gore Vidal,* University Press of Mississippi (Jackson, MS), 2005.

Contributor to periodicals, including *New York Review of Books, Times Literary Supplement,* and *Nation.* Member of advisory board, *Partisan Review,* 1960-71.

ADAPTATIONS: The Death of Billy the Kid was the basis for the film *The Left-handed Gun,* filmed by Warner Bros., 1958; *Visit to a Small Planet* was filmed by Paramount, 1960; *Myra Breckinridge* was filmed by Twentieth Century-Fox, 1970.

SIDELIGHTS: In a career that has spanned much of the twentieth century, Gore Vidal has become one of America's literary giants. Familiar to the general public as a witty and wicked talk show guest, two-time political candidate, and creator of the outrageous fictional character Myra Breckinridge, Vidal has written numerous novels, plays, screenplays, essays, and reviews. Called "one of the more alert and favoured writers of our time" by a critic in the London *Observer,* Vidal remained the subject of critical and media attention for much of his career, particularly during and after the 1960s. His work is noted for its eloquence, intelligence, urbane humor, and biting satire, as well as for its attacks on cultural and political sacred cows. "Vidal's novels, plays, and essays can be divided roughly into three areas of animosity," explained *Time* correspondent R.Z. Sheppard. "The first is the author's belief that

Western civilization erred, when it abandoned pagan humanism for the stern, heterosexual authority of the Judaeo-Christian patriarchy . . . . The second area that draws Vidal's scorn is American politics, which he dramatizes as a circus of opportunism and hypocrisy." For the third area, Vidal's "most freewheeling disdain is directed at popular culture, macho sexuality and social pretensions."

Vidal's writings run the gamut from historical fiction to autobiographical essays to political commentary, and his styles range from witty and cultured to sarcastic and acidic. "Vidal is a difficult writer to categorize because he is a man of several voices," wrote Robert F. Kiernan in his book *Gore Vidal.* "He has brooded over ancient empires in several novels, as though he were possessed by the spirit of Gibbon, yet he has also written about the American *crise de virilite* and managed to sound a good deal like Hemingway. He has sent young Americans in search of old Europe, as a dutiful son of Henry James, but he has also written novels about the American political system and acknowledged a debt to Henry Adams. In his essays he often seems like Lord Macaulay, magisterial and urbane, while in the Breckinridge novels he evokes Ronald Firbank, irrepressible and playful." In the *Nation,* Patrick Smith observed: "Vidal has given us many gifts. His gathered essays are nonpareil in postwar American letters. With *Julian,* published in 1964, he began to exploit the historical novel to an extent no one I can think of approaches . . . . In the land of Updike and Jane Smiley, one does not stray . . . far from the nineteenth century without risking opprobrium. Some of Vidal's risks—too many, one could argue—have not come good. Praise be to him, though, for all the leaps he has attempted. In no artist's work can the failures be subtracted from the triumphs."

Greatly influenced by his maternal grandfather, Oklahoma senator Thomas P. Gore, Vidal developed a lifelong passion for politics. "I do nothing but think about my country," he once noted in a *Time* article. "The United States is my theme, and all that dwell in it." His interest has taken a variety of forms outside his writing. He has twice run for political office—for the U.S. House of Representatives in 1960 and the U.S. Senate in 1982—originated the idea for the Peace Corps, campaigned for presidential candidate Eugene McCarthy in 1968, and served as an organizer and secretary-of-state designate for the ultraliberal People's party. He also became quite well known as a political commentator and journalist. "The only thing I've ever really wanted in my life was to be President," he told a *Time* writer. His interest in the U.S. political system, as well as his intimate knowledge of politicians and powerbrokers, has informed many of Vidal's works, such as his political plays, *The Best Man, Weekend,* and *An Evening with Richard Nixon,* and his celebrated historical novels, *Washington, D.C., Burr, 1876, Lincoln, Empire, Hollywood,* and *The Golden Age.*

Vidal sees himself as a "correctionist," a word he has used to describe his political views many times since his 1960 congressional campaign. In his essay "Writing Plays for Television," reprinted in *Homage to Daniel Shays,* Vidal wrote: "I am at heart a propagandist, a tremendous hater, a tiresome nag, complacently positive that there is no human problem which could not be solved if people would simply do as I advise." Nothing is too large or small for his attention; at one moment he will rail against the U.S. military-industrial complex and the Chase Manhattan Bank; later he is outlining a plan to curb the earth's burgeoning population. "His tone is that of the seer scorned; yet he can hardly claim to be the prophet ignored," commented a *Time* writer. "For thirty years he has been a cinder in the public eye."

With the publication of *Williwaw* in 1946, Vidal joined the ranks of the literary *enfants terribles* who dominated the American cultural scene just after World War II. His name was often linked with other post-War prodigies such as Truman Capote, John Horn Burns, James Jones, and—several years later—Norman Mailer. Five years after the release of *Williwaw,* John W. Aldridge wrote in *After the Lost Generation: A Critical Study of the Writers of Two Wars* that "Vidal, at twenty-five, occupies an enviable position in American letters. Not only is he the youngest of the group of new writers whose first books began attracting attention right after the war, but he has already produced as large and varied a body of work as many of his contemporaries may be expected to produce comfortably in a lifetime." Although giving Vidal's fourth novel, *The Season of Comfort,* a lukewarm review in the *Saturday Review of Literature,* Aldridge remarked that "so far, of the handful of writers who are young enough to qualify as members of a new literary generation, only Gore Vidal has made more than a fledgling attempt to discover the sensibility of the Forties."

Begun while Vidal was recuperating from a bout of rheumatoid arthritis contracted during his U.S. Army Transportation Corps service in the Bering Sea during World War II, *Williwaw* describes the effect of an Arctic squall—called a "williwaw"—on the crew members of an army transport ship. The plotting is simple, the language concise, and a number of critics applauded Vidal's self-restraint. Aldridge, writing in *After the Lost Generation,* called *Williwaw* "a slight and unpretentious book," and Kiernan opined, "that nineteen-year-old Gore Vidal should have been capable of writing *Williwaw* is astonishing."

Vidal quickly followed up the success of *Williwaw* with another novel, *In a Yellow Wood,* published barely a year later. The book, which takes its title from Robert Frost's poem "The Road Not Taken"—"Two roads diverged in a yellow wood / . . . I took the one less travelled by / And that has made all the difference"—recounts a day in the life of Robert Holton, a rather dull young clerk at a brokerage house. Holton is a determinedly conventional man and when he again meets his exotic Italian wartime mistress and his happy-go-lucky army buddy, he is disturbed rather than excited by their invitations to experiment with a more fascinating life. He turns down their offers, choosing to continue his boring but safe existence.

The novel shows "a psychological astuteness," noted *New York Herald Tribune Weekly Book Review* contributor Stephan Stepanchev, who admired the way Vidal structures the book by reflecting Holton through the eyes of the various people with whom he comes in contact. *In a Yellow Wood,* Stepanchev continued, demonstrates "that the author has a good eye for metropolitan surfaces and an accurate ear for ordinary speech." Some critics, such as N. L. Rothman in the *Saturday Review of Literature,* praised *In a Yellow Wood* for its "controlled naturalism . . . concentrated workmanship . . . rigid and painstaking selection of details, plus . . . [a] delicacy of understatement that reaps its delicacy of overtone." Though the book received favorable reviews at the time of its publication, Vidal himself considers it a failure. Twenty-seven years after its release in 1947, he told a *Paris Review* interviewer that the novel is doomed to remain "in limbo forever. I can't rewrite it because it's so bad that I can't reread it."

With two fairly successful novels to his credit, Vidal wanted to try something different. "I was bored with playing it safe," he recalled in the foreword to the 1965 revision of his next novel, 1948's *The City and the Pillar.* "I wanted to take risks, to try something no American had done before." *The City and the Pillar* immediately appeared on best-seller lists and raised conflicts in the New York publishing world that would reverberate for years. The subject of the novel—homosexuality—was not a topic new to American literature; what was new, however, was the way in which Vidal treats his subject, presenting the novel's young gay protagonist as a perfectly average, athletic, handsome, boy-next-door type. Vidal "wrote what had never been published by a reputable American writer: an unreserved novel about the homosexual demimonde and the 'naturalness' of homosexual relations," observed Kiernan.

While an inquisitive public put *The City and the Pillar* on the best-seller lists, the more conservative press helped dampen the career of its author. A *New York Times* contributor gave the book a very negative review, refused to accept any advertising for it, and then either did not review or published extremely harsh reviews of Vidal's next five novels and story collections. (At one point Vidal resorted to publishing a series of mystery novels under the pseudonym Edgar Box in order to get them reviewed.) According to Vidal in his annotation to the revised version of *The City and the Pillar,* the *New York Times*' judgment continued "to haunt that book, and all my writing ever since."

Perhaps because of such backlash, the five novels Vidal published after *The City and the Pillar* were commercial failures. Searching for his authorial voice, Vidal discarded his naturalistic style and experimented with a number of techniques in *The Season of Comfort, A Search for the King,* and *Dark Green, Bright Red.* These books, generally judged to be inferior works, were followed up by *The Judgment of Paris* and *Messiah.* Largely ignored at the time of their publications, both have since been recognized as well-crafted novels written in what has become Vidal's mature style. However, critical recognition of these novels came too late to salvage Vidal's flagging career as a novelist. His financial resources dwindling, he embarked instead on what he termed his "five-year plan": he went to Hollywood to write screenplays for films and television, determined to earn enough money to last him the rest of his life.

Television was in its heyday in the mid-1950s when Vidal was writing scripts for such highly acclaimed programs as *Philco- Goodyear Playhouse, Studio One,* and *Omnibus Theater.* As a screenwriter for the movies, he made contributions to the scripts of *Ben Hur, I Accuse, Suddenly Last Summer, The Catered Affair, The Scapegoat,* and *The Left-handed Gun,* among others. A self- proclaimed "writer for hire," Vidal eventually met his goal of financial independence, although it took him closer to ten years than five.

During his Hollywood years Vidal also began to write plays. His first theater script, *Visit to a Small Planet,* grew out of a television play of the same title. The story of a visitor from another planet who comes to Earth to watch the U.S. Civil War battle at Manassas Junction but instead ends up in mid-twentieth-century Virginia, *Visit to a Small Planet* had a Broadway run of 338 performances and an extended national and international tour. It was later produced as a motion picture starring Jerry Lewis.

With the success of *Visit to a Small Planet,* Vidal continued to write plays. "As a playwright, I am a sport, whose only serious interest is the subversion of a society which bores and appalls me," Vidal wrote in an essay about this vocation. The rest of his plays have indeed been attacks on politics, politicians, and what he views as middle-class hypocrisy. A typical example is *The Best Man,* a political drama concerning two contenders for the presidential nomination and one of Vidal's most successful plays. Produced in 1959 in order to take advantage of the 1960 election fever, *The Best Man* had a respectable Broadway run and was later adapted into an award-winning film that is still often shown on television.

In 1964 Vidal published *Julian,* his first novel in ten years and his first historical novel written in the style that became his trademark. Presented as the journal of the eccentric fourth-century Roman emperor Julian, and framed by a commentary in the form of margin notes and letters by two of Julian's aging contemporaries, the novel is full of cutting remarks, catty asides, ribald jokes, fourth-century gossip, and references to the state of the commentators' health, careers, and sexual performance. It is this humorous interjection of the trivial and the personal into an impeccably researched historical novel which has made Vidal famous.

In writing historical fiction "the interpreter is everything," said Dudley Fitts in the *New York Times Book Review,* and "if, like Gore Vidal in this evocation of Julian the Apostate, he is able to penetrate to depths of human meaning . . . his vision may create a design not wholly remote from parable or allegory." Like Fitts, a number of other reviewers also appreciated the fact that Vidal "is attempting something other than the recreation of the past for its own sake," as Walter Allen put it in the *New York Review of Books.* "While it would be absurd to see the novel as a parable for our time or to look for any close parallels between Julian's situation and our own, it is impossible to escape the conclusion that Vidal intends the book to have some direct relevance to the world today. The brilliance of his portrayal of Julian persuades us that it has." Still, other critics found Vidal's Julian a less than compelling figure. *Saturday Review* essayist Granville Hicks, for instance, insisted that Julian "doesn't . . . really grasp the imagination. Looking at him simply as a character in a novel, one wonders whether he is worth writing about at such great length."

A string of best-selling novels followed. Like *Julian,* these works combined Vidal's gifts for mimicry and satire, his savage sense of humor, his passion for personal and political intrigue, and his jaundiced view of the ruling classes. "The fact is that Vidal Novelist had an unusually long apprenticeship," maintained Gerald Weale in the *Atlantic.* "The early books . . . are workmanlike enough, but they are curiously flat and undefined, without any of the zest and bitchy vitality Vidal shows in even the most ordinary conversations. But when he did return [from screenwriting] to the novel a decade later in *Julian,* he brought to it the flavor and energy of his own person. He is still an overly intellectual novelist, but now his subjects are more in keeping with his particular novelistic shtik."

In the *New York Times,* John Leonard pointed out that Vidal has a tendency to "twin" his novels, following one book sometime later with another one using either the same characters, subject, or milieu. Kiernan observed that " *Messiah* and *Kalki* are twin novels about the coming apocalypse, whereas *Burr* and *1876* are paired novels about American history. *Myra Breckinridge* and *Myron* are unmistakable twins, enjoying virtually Siamese attachment. The second novels in these pairs never seem to represent a rethinking or reworking of the material in the first."

Julian's twin is *Creation,* an epic of the ancient world as told by Cyrus Spitama. Contemptuous of the Greeks and their philosophical concepts, Cyrus is an avid defender of the Zoroastrian doctrine of dualism. Yet he also seeks to confirm his understanding of the world, and in his travels he speaks with the great prophets and philosophers of the East. "As a grandson and the last descendant in the male line of the prophet Zoroaster, Cyrus feels obliged to argue theology, to devise an acceptable theory for the creation of the universe and to account for the existence of evil within it," explained Paul Gray in *Time.* Though Cyrus often strays from this narrative path, Kanfer considered Cyrus's message about creation to be best revealed through the telling of his life's story, rather than stated explicitly. " *Julian* was wonderful," affirmed Leonard; " *Creation,* I am happy to report, is even better."

Creation's allure for many critics lies in its richness of fact and detail. "There isn't a page of *Creation* that doesn't inform," Leonard praised, "and very few pages that do not delight." Rex Warner, in the *Washington Post Book World,* also admired Vidal's facile handling of miscellaneous information and called Cyrus "the greatest name-dropper who ever lived." "What Cyrus Spitama is really good at is gossip-writing," noted Warner. "He can tell you of all the intrigues of the Persian court and knows most of the secrets of the harem." For other reviewers, however, Vidal's presentation of the ancient world was unnerving, and his attention to the minutiae of history rather than to its broader scope, tedious. Gray acknowledged the book's shortcomings, but added: "Whatever its flaws, *Creation* offers a leisurely guided stroll through a complex era. The book is encyclopedic enough to be short on intrinsic pattern; it is also filled with information, oddities and wonder."

After *Julian,* Vidal turned his eye toward American history, producing the interrelated volumes *Washington, D.C., Burr, 1876, Lincoln, Empire, Hollywood,* and *The Golden Age.* The first of these, *Washington, D.C.,* introduces to the reader Vidal's interest in exposing the seamier side of American politics. Peter Ackroyd, writing in the *Spectator,* called the novel "a lounge-lizard look" at Washington's power structure that is "giddily melodramatic [as well as] soberly historical." *Burr* is told as the memoirs of American founding father-turned-renegade Aaron Burr, and *1876* is an account of the United States' centennial year. Both are narrated by the character Charles Schemerhorn Schuyler, who first appears as the young, opportunistic illegitimate son of Aaron Burr, and in the second novel is seen forty years later, a jaded expatriate come home to recoup his lost fortunes. These novels are told in the style familiar to readers of *Julian* and *Creation;* as Gray remarked, Vidal "can make old facts look like contemporary gossip. And he takes wicked pleasure in turning accepted notions about the past upside down." Reviewing *Burr,* Christopher Lehmann-Haupt in the *New York Times* declared: "Vidal gives us an interpretation of our early history that says in effect that all the old verities were never much to begin with . . . . And how thoroughly enjoyable is the entire process of disillusionment!"

The novel *1876* also takes demythologizing the American past as its task and, as many critics pointed out, the events recounted in the novel were startlingly similar to those taking place near the time of the book's publication in 1976. Parallels abound: the corrupt Ulysses S. Grant with discredited President Richard Nixon, the Whiskey Ring scandal with Watergate, the Hayes-Tilden presidential race with the election of 1972 and the administration of Gerald Ford. The novel is, according to Paul Levy in *Books and Bookmen,* "an historical contribution of large importance . . . . What Vidal has done by investigating the scandals leading up to the 1876 election and the election itself is to show that nothing much has changed in America's last hundred years."

A major criticism of *1876* has been that, unlike *Burr,* it lacks a strong central character. Whereas Aaron Burr is extraordinarily compelling—for himself and as the rival and critic of Thomas Jefferson, Alexander Hamilton, and other Revolutionary heroes —*1876*'s protagonist, Charlie Schuyler, is not as interesting, serving merely as a mouthpiece for Vidal's observations. In order to compensate, *New Statesman*'s Philip French maintained, "all of Vidal's considerable craft, wit, political insight, elegance and irony is called into play. Unfortunately some of the material here is intractable and many readers will feel that he has overestimated their potential interest in American history of a century ago." Michael Wood called *1876* a "less vivid" book than its predecessor, but added that it "is in one sense a more serious book. It asks us to believe, not in a rogue hero like Burr, and not even in a man like [failed presidential candidate Samuel] Tilden . . . but in politics itself, that grimy and intricate activity we can't afford to give up."

Lincoln is also concerned with the history of the United States. Released in 1984 with an extraordinary 200,000-copy first printing and preview excerpts in the *Atlantic* and *Gentleman's Quarterly, Lincoln* was called "a momentous fictional biography" and a "masterpiece" by Stephen Rubin in the *Chicago Tribune Book World.* "The intelligence, the wit, the humor, the outrageousness are omnipresent," said the critic. "If Vidal is impatient with novelistic techniques such as transitions, he allows himself the luxury to marvelously plot a true political novel of breadth and rich texture. The pace he sets for himself is a noble andante that gives him the time for a spectacular array of detail work, the element that ultimately makes *Lincoln* unforgettable."

Lincoln became a tremendously popular novel, partly because its mature depiction of a popular historical figure appealed to a much wider audience than some of the author's earlier works. "In his historical reconstructions," Evans explained, Vidal "curbs his high spirits in the interest of narrative efficiency." He does so, the reviewer continued, without sacrificing entertainment: "His relish for political trickery, public sophistry and self-advertisement in government is given full piquancy. *Lincoln* abounds in portraits of subtle politicos."

Set in the late 1890s to early 1900s and covering the rise of American industry, *Empire,* according to *Newsweek* contributor David Gates, "reanimates the moribund genre of historical fiction with a few modernist jots—and still stays within the conventions of the Good Read." Gates added that even critics of the novel "won't be able to deny that they've been elegantly entertained." Lehmann-Haupt considered *Empire* the best of Vidal's series, stating that Vidal tells "a dramatically compelling story without sacrificing either his complex view of American history or his unusual ability to caricature its major players."

Hollywood takes up where *Empire* leaves off, with America's entrance into World War I, covering the presidencies of Woodrow Wilson and Warren Harding, in addition to the rise of the film industry of Hollywood. "Like the earlier books, the new novel is an imaginative re-creation, a heady mix of fact and fancy, wisdom and nonsense," stated Joel Conarroe in the *New York Times Book Review.* Conarroe commended Vidal's colorful portrayals of such figures as President Wilson and his wife, Edith, the actors Charlie Chaplin and Douglas Fairbanks, as well as the witty Alice Roosevelt Longworth. David Walton in the *Detroit News,* however, commented that while "there are a number of effective scenes and sharply rendered lines in this book . . . *Hollywood* is too sprawling, too diffused and uncentered, and in most ways too much concerned with what's behind the scenes ever to establish a consistent foreground."

The Golden Age, Vidal's final installment in the American historical fiction series, revisits some of the same characters and situations that the author pondered in *Washington, D.C.* A span of thirty-three years separate these two volumes, and the passage of time has altered both Vidal's focus and agenda in the latter title. "Vidal's interest this time is less concentrated on his characters' private vicissitudes," observed Janet Maslin in the *New York Times Book Review.* "Like Orson Welles, who of course turns up in a heavily name-dropping story that begins in 1939, he is interested in deep focus. So the series' familiar figures . . . are integrated into an ambitious historical tableau." As he was a young man at the time of the story—and a first-hand observer of Washington politics—Vidal includes himself as a character too. Beneath the surface banter, however, large issues loom: Roosevelt secretly plots to involve the United States in World War II, Harry S. Truman ushers in the Atomic Age and the cold war, and the military-industrial complex gears up for the Korean War. A *Time* reviewer declared that *The Golden Age* "coats its ethical inquiries with plenty of narrative sweeteners: the sweep of history, celebrity walk-ons, conspiracy theories and reams of conversation, much of it witty . . . . But the issue of power and who should hold it is never far from the surface."

Popular as Vidal's historical novels have been, the author's greatest coup, according to many critics, has been *Myra Breckinridge,* a campy, satiric look at modern America. An instant smash, *Myra Breckinridge* takes potshots at almost everything, from uptight heterosexuality to the burgeoning population, from the New American Novel to 1940s movie stars, and from American youth to the American dream. Above all, *Myra Breckinridge* is about breaking the barriers of sexuality, a theme in much of Vidal's fiction and nonfiction.

"To say Mr. Vidal's new novel is queer would be an understatement; it is a queer, queer book, a virtuoso exercise in kinkiness, a draught of fizzy hemlock, a strikingly intelligent attempt to go as far as possible in outrageousness," declared John Weightman in the *Observer Review.* "Literature about sex is so often soggy and embarrassing or clinical and sick-making. Mr. Vidal pitches his narrative in a key of slightly demented funniness, and sustains this note right to the end." Indeed, the irrepressible Myra is an odd character: a homosexual male turned female through a sex change operation, she goes to California to claim her share in a drama academy and to write a book about the films of the 1940s. Teaching empathy and posture at the academy, Myra expounds her views on every possible subject—yet in the end, according to her logic, it all leads back to sex and power. "Myra Breckinridge herself sees all life as a naming of parts, an equating of groins, a pleasing and/or painful forcing of orifices. Which is the essence, after all, of pornography," observed a *Times Literary Supplement* critic.

While *Myra Breckinridge* is sexually graphic, most reviewers recognized it as a satire on pornography. Nat Hentoff noted that Vidal, "walking on the waters of polymorphous perversity and sexual revolution . . . has written the first popular book of perverse pornography—a book for which one does not need even the slightest special taste." *Newsweek* correspondent Joseph Morgenstern referred to the book as "gleefully dirty, wittily dirty, gracefully and intricately dirty in its creation and development of a genuine film freak." *Myron,* a sequel to *Myra Breckenridge* in which Myra returns to her male form and is transported to the set of a 1940s B-movie, was described as "surprisingly colorless and lumpish" by James Boatright in the *New Republic.*

In 1992 Vidal penned the much-hyped novel *Live from Golgotha: The Gospel according to Gore Vidal,* a scathingly irreverent examination of the origins and subsequent perversion of Christianity. The novel's protagonist is Timothy, the confidant of Saint Paul, who will become Saint Timothy. Some sixty years after the crucifixion of Jesus Christ, Timothy is visited by the ghost of Saint Paul, who warns him that, in the distant future, a super-sophisticated computer hacker is deleting the Gospels from the files of Heaven and Earth alike, thereby erasing the memories of the faithful. Timothy's task, Paul explains, is to write the last, definitive account of the Gospels and hide it, so that it can be discovered by theologians two thousand years hence.

The problem, we soon discover, is that Timothy's recollections are vastly different from those of the New Testament's Matthew, Mark, Luke, and John: Saint Paul, for example, is depicted as an evangelical huckster and a pederast, and Jesus is a buffoon with a glandular problem. History is further obfuscated by the visitations, in the form of visions, of celebrities and network executives from the twentieth century. Having perfected the technology to both travel and broadcast through time, they plan to broadcast the crucifixion "live" on television, and they ask Timothy to act as emcee. When introduced to television—and, in particular, to CNN—Timothy's memories and accounts become increasingly unreliable, and he calls into question whether it was actually Jesus who died on the cross.

Clearly, with *Live from Golgotha* Vidal anticipated offending more than a few readers. "Very early on," noted *New Statesman*'s Douglas Kennedy, "Vidal lets it be known that he is gunning for the Rushdie prize for droll blasphemy." Andrew Greeley, writing in the *Washington Post Book World,* warned that "if Christians viewed blasphemy the way orthodox Moslems do, some Christian version of the Ayatollah might have put out a contract on Vidal." *Los Angeles Times Book Review* critic John Rechy, moreover, proclaimed: "If God exists and Jesus is His son, then Gore Vidal is going to hell."

Despite the caustic portrayal of Jesus and his followers, *Live from Golgotha* stirred up surprisingly little controversy. Alfred Kazin, writing in the *New Republic,* called the novel "nothing but bawdy entertainment for the bathhouse boys" that is "actually no dirtier than anything else these days." Thomas M. Disch opined in the *Nation* that Vidal's novel is less polemical than such works as Martin Scorcese's *The Last Temptation of Christ,* because "the Gospel according to Gore Vidal is not to be taken as serious fictional evocation of the (possible) history behind the myths . . . . Not even the most naive reader could approach *Live from Golgotha* as a serious challenger to the Gospel according to anyone else." "Some readers will find it sacrilegious," admitted *New York Times* critic Herbert Mitgang. "But it's too funny to be condemned simply as a blasphemous novel." Kennedy, too, found the novel "unapologetically giddy and gloriously excessive," full of "demented energy that you will either find bracing or just plain exasperating." John Calvin Batchelor, writing in Chicago's *Tribune Books,* claimed that, "despite every Rushdie-like blasphemy he can think of, what [Vidal] achieves is a serious argument about the birth and meaning of Christianity." *Commonweal*'s Irving Malin concurred: "Although Vidal offers a *fiendish* gospel—a counter-gospel—he must be taken seriously. He is, after all, asking basic epistemological questions . . . . I suggest that Vidal's provocative, distasteful novel is, perhaps, one of his most sustained meditations on the nature of things. It will be read for many years."

The Smithsonian Institution also experiments with time travel and unlikely campy pairings between characters from various eras in American history. The novel begins with a secret invitation to a thirteen-year-old mathematical genius named T.—he must go to the Smithsonian Institution after hours. Once inside the museum, T. discovers that the exhibits come to life. The first ladies roam about—one of them seduces T.—and the presidents argue about modern matters. The issue at hand is the onset of World War II, and T. has been recruited by a cartel of scientists who are trying to build a bomb that will kill people but leave buildings intact. Given the knowledge that he will be killed himself in the upcoming war, T. tries to go back in time to change history and avert U.S. involvement in the conflict.

In his *New York Times* review, Christopher Lehmann-Haupt wrote: "Despite its seeming zaniness, *The Smithsonian Institution* is appealing in several ways . . . . Despite a certain amount of mumbo-jumbo, you come to believe in the novel's world of intersecting realities, where all time collapses into a quantum present and individuals meet different versions of themselves along the space-time continuum." *New Criterion* contributor Brooke Allen considered the novel one of Vidal's weaker efforts. "Vidal has obviously been dabbling in the work of Stephen Hawking, and his slight, rather goofy plot nearly gets buried under a morass of amateurish scientific speculation on the nature of time and other mysteries," Allen suggested. "Science fiction is not really Vidal's thing, and the reader must simply plod on until the author turns to historical comedy, which he brings off with far more elan." Some critics, including Allen, noted the wealth of insider material based on Vidal's own experiences. A *Publishers Weekly* reviewer concluded: "If the tale of T. remains a mostly private, somewhat rueful joke, it will no doubt charm Vidal's most devoted readers."

In addition to well-reviewed novels, Vidal has also received critical acclaim for his essays and criticism. "It is not that Vidal's essays are better than his novels," explained Gerald Clarke in the *Atlantic.* "It is rather that his essays are more consistently good and that the qualities that limit him as a novelist are precisely those that a good essayist needs: a forceful intelligence, a cool detachment, an unpretentious, graceful style, and a sense of perspective that distinguishes the big from the little. If most of his fictional characters seem unbelievable, his judgments on real people are both original and irrefutable." Vidal's essays display the same incisive wit and characteristic elan that make him such a popular talk show guest and interview subject; his nonfiction is full of autobiographical asides, personal references to the famous and the infamous, allusions to ancient and modern history.

Dubbing Vidal's essays "the intellectual equivalent of the comics," Joseph Epstein added in a *Commentary* profile of Vidal: "Intellectual journals are not noted for providing many laughs, but laughter is Gore Vidal's specialty—what he plays for and what he is about. The chief play in a Vidal essay is to point out that the emperor has no clothes and then go a step further and remove the poor man's skin. The spectacle can be most amusing, assuming of course that it is not one's own carcass that is being stripped." According to Robert Plunket in the *Advocate,* Vidal's "marvelously bitchy commentary makes for delicious company. As he dispenses scandal, insight, and punch lines, all that's missing is the pitcher of martinis. But amid all the dish are some touching nuggets. . . . Most of all, one comes away awed by Vidal's career—not just his writing but also the people he has known."

Wit alone has not made Vidal the respected essayist he is; critics have noted that his essays and reviews reveal an erudition and knowledge that is impressive, and an insight that is often remarkable. Simon, reviewing the essay collection *Matters of Fact and of Fiction* in *Esquire,* wrote: "I think that Gore Vidal's greatest service to this society could be in the proper packaging of his style and language. I do not see fiction as being his true medium. . . . Vidal is an essayist of talent . . . [and *Matters of Fact and of Fiction*] contains some very good pieces, as weighty as anything in Oscar Wilde and easily as witty as the best of Matthew Arnold." In the volumes *United States: 1952-1992* and *The Last Empire: Essays 1992-2000,* Vidal draws together the best of over four decades of commentary, including literary criticism—he makes no bones about his contempt for the writing of John Updike—politics, and biography. Calling *The Last Empire* "vintage Vidal," Marvin J. LaHood noted in *World Literature Today* that "because Vidal's greatest talent may be as an essayist, this longish collection is good reading." A *Publishers Weekly* contributor agreed, noting that the selections reveal "the mandarinist populist to be at the height of his powers of both vituperation and sagacity."

After the events of September 11, 2001, and the U.S. government's War on Terror that followed in its wake, Vidal held no punches in expressing his views on the state of world politics, publishing widely in periodicals ranging from the *Nation* to the *Times Literary Supplement.* In the books *Perpetual War for Perpetual Peace: How We Got to Be So Hated,* and *Dreaming War: Blood for Oil and the Cheney-Bush Junta,* he collects some of these essays, and thus secures his place as "a prolific preacher against America's imperialist policies," according to a *Publishers Weekly* reviewer. *Perpetual War for Perpetual Peace* recalls the U.S. government's assaults on Ruby Ridge, Waco, and Operation Desert Storm while taking a particularly close look at the Oklahoma City bombings because of their retributive quality in light of U.S. aggressions around the world. Vidal's essay "September 11, 2001" is also included; rejected by several U.S. magazines, it posits the idea that the attacks were justified in much the same way Vidal sees the Oklahoma City bombings as justified. The three new essays in *Imperial America: Reflections on the United States of Amnesia* criticize the Bush administration, demonstrating, according to a *Publishers Weekly* contributor, that "Vidal's Jeffersonian anti- imperialism is fashionable again with the left wing" on the eve of the 2004 presidential elections. Among other topics, *Dreaming War* draws parallels between the September 11th attacks and the attack on Pearl Harbor during the presidency of Franklin Roosevelt, and Vidal argues that both Bush now and Roosevelt then knew in advance of the attacks and used these tragedies to fuel their own political ends. "That Vidal is fonder of sermonizing than logical argument, of assertion rather than cold data is no matter," noted a *Kirkus Reviews* contributor of *Dreaming War:* "This is trademark Goring and unforgiving: woe to its unfortunate target."

Although many critics inevitably take issue with Vidal's often radical points of view, few challenge the grace and elegance with which he expresses his opinions. "No one else in what he calls 'the land of the tin ear' can combine better sentences into more elegantly sustained demolition derbies than Vidal does in some of his best essays," observed Thomas Mallon in the *National Review.* McPherson suggested: "Technical virtuosity is what Vidal possesses to an extraordinary degree; and intelligence and erudition, irreverence, and an ability to cut through cant. I used to think of him as the brightest rhinestone around. I've revised my opinion though; he's the genuine article."

Throughout most of his fifty-odd-year career as a writer and public personality, Vidal vowed that he would never write an autobiography. However, the 1995 publication of *Palimpsest: A Memoir* proved him wrong. Covering Vidal's first four decades, the book focuses on what *Washington Post Book World* critic Jonathan Yardley termed "the most public period of his life," in which Vidal worked as a Hollywood scriptwriter, playwright, and sometime political candidate. Yardley added, "Vidal knows that private turmoil and public provocation make splendid stories, while laboring away in his office, [as Vidal did after age forty,] makes no story at all. Thus craftsmanship far more than reticence or coyness is surely the explanation for his decision to cut things off where he does." Feasting on the tumultuous saga of his dysfunctional family, high-profile friendships, numerous homosexual liaisons but only one great love, various forays into the political arena, and writings, *Palimpsest* is, "for all its tilts and malice and wonderful jokes, an oddly disinterested work," opined Michael Wood in the *New York Times Book Review.* "As I am supposed to be remembering myself, I am central to these memories," Vidal wrote. "I am, however, happier to be at the edge, as one is in an essay, studying someone else or what someone else has made art of." Widely praised by reviewers, *Palimpsest* prompted Karl Miller to write in the *Times Literary Supplement:* Vidal's "essays, and this memoir, with its repertoire of stories and sayings, are a dimension of his elegant and pointed speech, and there are admirers of his who think that he speaks better than he writes, and that his essays are better than his fictions."

Once asked by *Newsweek* interviewer Arthur Cooper if it is fun being Gore Vidal, the author's response was characteristic. "Gore Vidal isn't what I set out to be," he explained. "Early on I wanted to be Franklin Roosevelt, and then as I realized I had to make a choice I saw myself more in the great tradition, somebody like Thomas Mann, going on and on into my old age turning everything into literature like a bivalve collecting sea water. But I don't mind what I've become . . . . I do exactly what I want to do and I've made a living—which you're not supposed to do if you write the way you want to. I've had really great luck."

BIOGRAPHICAL AND CRITICAL SOURCES:

BOOKS

Aldridge, John W., *After the Lost Generation: A Critical Study of the Writers of Two Wars,* McGraw-Hill (New York, NY), 1951.

Authors in the News, Volume 1, Gale (Detroit, MI), 1976.

Bestsellers 90, Issue 2, Gale (Detroit, MI), 1990.

Bloom, Harold, *The Western Canon: The Books and School of the Ages,* Harcourt (New York, NY), 1994.

Brustein, Robert, *Season of Discontent: Dramatic Opinions, 1959-1965,* Simon & Schuster (New York, NY), 1965.

Burgess, Anthony, *Ninety-nine Novels: The Best in English since 1939,* Summit, 1984.

Contemporary Literary Criticism, Gale (Detroit, MI), Volume 2, 1974, Volume 4, 1975, Volume 6, 1976, Volume 8, 1978, Volume 10, 1979, Volume 22, 1982, Volume 33, 1985, Volume 72, 1992.

Dick, Bernard F., *The Apostate Angel: A Critical Study of Gore Vidal,* Random House (New York, NY), 1974.

Dictionary of Literary Biography, Volume 6: *American Novelists since World War II,* Gale (Detroit, MI), 1980, Volume 152: *American Novelists since World War II, Fourth Series,* Gale (Detroit, MI), 1995.

Kaplan, Fred, *Gore Vidal: A Biography,* Doubleday (New York, NY), 1999.

Kiernan, Robert F., *Gore Vidal,* Ungar (New York, NY), 1982.

McCrindle, Joseph F., editor, *Behind the Scenes: Theater and Film Interviews from the Transatlantic Review,* Holt (New York, NY), 1971.

Parini, Jay, editor, *Gore Vidal: Writer against the Grain,* Columbia University Press (New York, NY), 1992.

Stanton, Robert J., *Gore Vidal: A Primary and Secondary Bibliography,* G. K. Hall (Boston, MA), 1978.

Stanton, Robert J., and Gore Vidal, editors, *Views from a Window: Conversations with Gore Vidal,* Lyle Stuart (Secaucus, NJ), 1980.

Vidal, Gore, *Messiah,* Dutton (New York, NY), 1954.

Vidal, Gore, *Three: Williwaw, A Thirsty Evil: Seven Short Stories* [and] *Julian the Apostate,* New American Library (New York, NY), 1962.

Vidal, Gore, *The City and the Pillar Revised,* Dutton (New York, NY), 1965.

Vidal, Gore, *Palimpsest: A Memoir,* Random House (New York, NY), 1995.

Weightman, John, *The Concept of the Avant Garde: Explorations in Modernism,* Alcove, 1973.

White, Ray Lewis, *Gore Vidal,* Twayne (Boston, MA), 1968.

PERIODICALS

Advocate, March 30, 1999, Robert Plunket, "Vital Vidal," p. 76.

America, September 5, 1970; May 20, 1978; January 16, 1993.

American Film, November, 1987.

American Spectator, June, 1982.

Architectural Digest, January, 1994.

Atlantic, February, 1949; March, 1972; December, 1973; April, 1976; April, 1981; October, 1992.

Best Sellers, June 15, 1964; May 1, 1967; April 1, 1969; July, 1977.

Book Forum, summer, 1978.

Booklist, February 1, 2003, John Green, review of *Dreaming War,* p. 955; October 15, 2003, Gilbert Taylor, review of *Inventing a Nation: Washington, Adams, Jefferson,* p. 386.

Books, April, 1970.

Books and Bookmen, August, 1967; May, 1974; June, 1976; October, 1977; October, 1982.

Book Week, June 7, 1964; April 30, 1967; March 3, 1969; April 13, 1969.

Chicago Tribune, November 20, 1985; June 22, 1987; February 18, 1990.

Christian Science Monitor, June 18, 1964; May 11, 1967.

Commentary, March, 1974; June, 1977.

Commonweal, January 7, 1977; November 6, 1992.

Critic, June, 1968.

Critique, December, 1980.

Detroit News, May 31, 1981; June 19, 1983; June 17, 1984; January 24, 1990.

Economist, November 6, 1993.

Encounter, September, 1978; November, 1981.

Esquire, August, 1977; April, 1981.

Film Quarterly, fall, 1993.

Gay & Lesbian Review Worldwide, November/December, 2005, Thom Nickels, review of *Conversations with Gore Vidal,* p. 37.

Gentlemen's Quarterly, November, 1995, p. 72.

Globe and Mail (Toronto, Ontario, Canada), June 20, 1987; February 24, 1990.

Harper's, September, 1970; March, 1976; May, 1977.

Hudson Review, autumn, 1978.

Interview, June, 1987; June, 1988; January, 1996, p. 22.

Journal of American History, September, 1994, p. 806.

Kirkus Reviews, May 1, 1946; December 15, 2002, p. 1836.

Library Journal, December 1, 1947; January, 1994, p. 186; November 1, 1995, p. 76; August, 2000, David W. Henderson, review of *The Golden Age,* p. 163; May 15, 2001, Mary Jones, review of *The Last Empire,* p. 125; November 1, 2003, Grant A. Fredericksen, review of *Inventing a Nation,* p. 100.

Listener, May 23, 1968; September 26, 1968; March 21, 1974; March 25, 1976; September 22, 1977; April 30, 1981; September 2, 1982.

London Magazine, December, 1974; January, 1975.

Los Angeles Times, March 24, 1981; July 15, 1984; February 14, 1987; October 7, 1987; November 12, 1987; December 5, 1988; August 4, 1989.

Los Angeles Times Book Review, July 3, 1983; June 24, 1984; January 12, 1986; February 18, 1990; September 13, 1992; October 11, 1992.

Los Angeles Times Magazine, January 28, 1990.

Maclean's, October 13, 1986; May 2, 1994, p. 64.

Magazine of Fantasy and Science Fiction, April, 1979.

Miami Herald, November 25, 1973.

Modern Maturity, April-May, 1994.

Nation, April 1, 1968; May 25, 1974; April 17, 1976; March 21, 1981; June 16, 1984; November 16, 1992; July 5, 1993; December 13, 1999, Patrick Smith, "'Our' Gide?," p. 22.

National Catholic Reporter, November 20, 1992.

National Observer, March 11, 1968.

National Review, May 20, 1969; March 1, 1974; May 12, 1978; September 18, 1981; August 20, 1982; November 30, 1992; December 31, 1995, p. 41.

New Criterion, May, 1998, Brooke Allen, "Creating a Fuhrer," p. 55.

New Leader, September 21, 1970; December 10, 1973.

New Republic, February 25, 1957; July 18, 1970; May 27, 1972; April 24, 1976; May 12, 1978; April 25, 1981; October 5, 1992; August 1, 1994, p. 8.

New Statesman, July 14, 1967; September 20, 1968; August 23, 1968; July 4, 1969; March 22, 1974; March 19, 1976; August 19, 1977; April 14, 1978; April 6, 1979; May 8, 1981; August 20, 1982; May 6, 1983; November 3, 1989, p. 38; November 15, 1991; November 6, 1992; October 8, 1993; October 27, 1995, p. 44; March 24, 2003, p. 54.

Newsweek, June 15, 1964; February 26, 1968; March 31, 1969; July 6, 1970; November 5, 1973; November 18, 1974; March 8, 1976; May 9, 1977; April 20, 1981; June 11, 1984; June 15, 1987, p. 70; October 9, 1995, p. 82.

New York, May 15, 1972; October 21, 1974; May 31, 1993.

New Yorker, March 22, 1947; January 10, 1948; February 16, 1957; April 23, 1960; May 6, 1972; April 5, 1976; April 17, 1978; October 26, 1992.

New York Herald Tribune Weekly Book Review, March 16, 1947; January 18, 1949.

New York Review of Books, July 30, 1964; June 15, 1967; May 9, 1968; June 19, 1969; March 22, 1973; November 15, 1973; November 14, 1974; April 29, 1976; May 26, 1977; April 20, 1978; May 14, 1981; April 8, 1993.

New York Times, June 23, 1946; March 16, 1947; June 11, 1948; February 6, 1949; January 27, 1957; February 8, 1957; February 3, 1968; March 25, 1969;

July 7, 1970; April 28, 1972; May 1, 1972; October 25, 1973; March 2, 1976; April 20, 1977; March 30, 1978; March 10, 1981; April 27, 1982; May 30, 1984; March 23, 1986; May 22, 1987; June 11, 1987; November 14, 1988; May 10, 1989; January 18, 1990; September 9, 1990; September 23, 1992; May 7, 1996, p. A17; March 19, 1998, Christopher Lehmann-Haupt, "Think History's Dull? Not Mrs. Grover Cleveland"; September 26, 2000, Walter Goodman, "Where Are the Hardy-Har-Hars of Yesteryear?," p. B2; September 28, 2000, Janet Maslin, "The Washington Crowd, Graying Now, Is Revisited," p. B8.

New York Times Book Review, August 12, 1962; May 31, 1964; April 30, 1967; January 28, 1968; February 1, 1968; February 15, 1968; September 1, 1968; April 6, 1969; July 12, 1970; December 31, 1972; October 28, 1973; March 7, 1976; April 17, 1977; April 2, 1978; December 21, 1980; March 29, 1981; May 2, 1982; June 5, 1983; June 3, 1984; June 14, 1987; January 21, 1990; August 30, 1992; October 4, 1992; November 29, 1992; June 20, 1993; October 8, 1995, p. 7.

Observer (London, England), September 13, 1970; August 15, 1982.

Observer Review, September 15, 1968; July 6, 1969; February 7, 1971.

People, September 12, 1988; November 2, 1992.

Playbill, October, 1968.

Playboy, May, 1968; June, 1969.

Prairie Schooner, fall, 1976.

Publishers Weekly, October 29, 1973; July 13, 1984; April 1, 2002, p, 63; February 2, 1998, review of *The Smithsonian Institution,* p. 82; May 28, 2001, p. 78; January 27, 2003, review of *Dreaming War: Blood for Oil and the Cheney-Bush Junta,* p. 250; September 8, 2003, review of *Inventing a Nation,* p. 65; April 19, 2004, review of *Imperial America: Reflections on the United States of Amnesia,* p. 47.

Punch, August 9, 1967; September 18, 1968; May 27, 1981; April 27, 1983.

Reporter, June 29, 1967; April 4, 1968.

Saturday Review, February 23, 1957; August 4, 1962; June 6, 1964; June 24, 1967; May 20, 1972; December 16, 1972; February 8, 1975; March 6, 1976; April 29, 1978; March, 1981; May, 1982.

Saturday Review of Literature, July 6, 1946; May 31, 1947; January 10, 1948; January 15, 1949; October 14, 1950.

Saturday Review/World, December 18, 1973.

Spectator, October 4, 1968; August 2, 1969; March 23, 1974; August 24, 1974; March 27, 1976; September 3, 1977; April 22, 1978; May 2, 1981; August, 1982; November 16, 1991; October 10, 1992; December 7, 2002, Frederic Raphael, review of *Perpetual War for Perpetual Peace: How We Got to Be So Hated,* p. 43; November 29, 2003, Harry Mount, review of of *Inventing a Nation,* p. 58.

Time, July 27, 1962; June 12, 1964; March 28, 1969; August 22, 1969; July 13, 1970; December 11, 1972; October 21, 1974; March 1, 1976; March 27, 1978; March 30, 1981; June 13, 1983; June 22, 1987; September 28, 1992; November 29, 1993, p. 23; October 9, 1995, p. 76; September 25, 2000, "The World according to Gore: A New Novel Concludes the Old Provocateur's Rewrite of U.S. History, and a Revived Play Keeps His Political Thrusts Fresh," p. 92; September 8, 2001, p. 37; May 11, 2002, p. 41; December 7, 2002, p. 43.

Times (London, England), April 30, 1981; September 28, 1983; June 19, 1987; November 16, 1991.

Times Literary Supplement, November 12, 1964; July 27, 1967; October 10, 1968; July 24, 1969; September 18, 1970; February 21, 1975; March 26, 1976; September 30, 1977; April 14, 1978; May 29, 1981; August 27, 1982; May 13, 1983; November 10-16, 1989; December 6, 1991; October 2, 1992; October 20, 1995, p. 7.

Tribune Books (Chicago, IL), April 26, 1981; April 22, 1984; June 3, 1984; June 22, 1987; January 28, 1990; September 6, 1992; September 20, 1992.

TV Guide, March 21, 1970.

Vanity Fair, November, 1995, p. 60.

Variety, December 15, 1971; May 3, 1972; October 16, 1995, p. 8.

Village Voice, February 23, 1976; May 9, 1977.

Voice Literary Supplement, September, 1992.

Washington Post, July 4, 1984; June 21, 1987; October 24, 1987; November 3, 1987; January 14, 1990.

Washington Post Book World, October 28, 1973; May 1, 1977; April 16, 1978; January 18, 1981; March 22, 1981; April 25, 1982; May 15, 1983; June 10, 1984; January 14, 1990; September 20, 1992; October 8, 1995, p. 3.

Weekly Book Review, June 23, 1946.

World, December 19, 1972.

World Literature Today, spring, 2001, Marvin J. Ladd, review of *The Golden Age,* p. 335; spring, 2002, p. 160; April-June, 2003, p. 107.

* * *

VILE, Curt
See MOORE, Alan

* * *

VINE, Barbara
See RENDELL, Ruth

VIZENOR, Gerald Robert 1934-

PERSONAL: Born October 22, 1934, in Minneapolis, MN; son of Clement William and LaVerne Lydia (Peterson) Vizenor; married Judith Helen Horns, 1959, (some sources say September, 1960; divorced, 1968); married Laura Jane Hall, May, 1981; children: (first marriage) Robert Thomas. *Education:* Attended New York University, 1955-56; University of Minnesota, B.A., 1960, graduate study, 1962-65; additional graduate study at Harvard University.

ADDRESSES: Office—American Studies, 325 Campbell Hall, University of California, Berkeley, CA 94720. *E-mail*—vizenor@uclink4.berkeley.edu.

CAREER: Ramsey County Corrections Authority, St. Paul, MN, group worker, 1957-58; Capital Community Center, St. Paul, roving group worker, 1958; Minnesota Department of Corrections, Minnesota State Reformatory, St. Cloud, corrections agent, 1960-61; *Minneapolis Tribune,* Minneapolis, MN, staff writer, 1968-70; Park Rapids Public Schools, Park Rapids, MN, teacher trainer, 1971; instructor at Lake Forest College, Lake Forest, IL, and Bemidji State University, Bemidji, MN, 1971-73; University of California—Berkeley, lecturer, 1976-80, professor of Native American Studies, 1991—, Richard and Rhoda Goldman Distinguished Professor, division of undergraduate and interdisciplinary studies, 2000-2002; University of Minnesota, Minneapolis, professor of American Indian studies, 1980-87; University of California—Santa Cruz, professor of literature, 1987-90. Kresge College, acting provost, 1990; University of Oklahoma, David Burke Chair of Letters, 1991. *Military service:* Minnesota National Guard, 1950-51; U.S. Army, 1952-55, served in Japan.

AWARDS, HONORS: Research grants for writing from University of Minnesota Graduate School and University of California—Santa Cruz; Film-in-the-Cities national competition winner, Robert Redford Sundance Film Institute, 1983, and best film citation, San Francisco Film Festival for American Indian Films, both for *Harold of Orange;* Fiction Collective prize, 1986, and American Book Award, 1988, for *Griever: An American Monkey King in China;* Artists Fellowship in Literature, California Arts Council, 1989, for professional achievement in literature; Josephine Miles Award, PEN Oakland, 1990, for *Interior Landscapes: Autobiographical Myths and Metaphors,* and 1996, for *Native American Literature;*named one of "100 Visionaries," *Utne Reader,* 1995; Teachers Hall of Fame, University of Minnesota Alumni Association, 1995; Doctorate of Humane Letters, Macalester College, St. Paul, MN, 1999; Literary Laureate honorary literary award, San Francisco Public Library, 2000; Lifetime Literary Achievement Award, Native Writer's Circle of the Americas, University of Oklahoma, 2001.

WRITINGS:

POETRY

Born in the Wind, privately printed, 1960.
The Old Park Sleepers, Obercraft, 1961.
Two Wings the Butterfly (haiku), privately printed, 1962.
South of the Painted Stone, Obercraft, 1963.
Raising the Moon Vines (haiku), Callimachus (Minneapolis, MN), 1964, reprinted, Nodin (Minneapolis, MN), 1999.
Seventeen Chirps (haiku), Nodin (Minneapolis, MN), 1964.
Empty Swings (haiku), Nodin (Minneapolis, MN), 1967.
(Contributor) Kenneth Rosen, editor, *Voices of the Rainbow,* Viking (New York, NY), 1975.
Matsushima: Pine Islands (haiku), Nodin (Minneapolis, MN), 1984.
Cranes Arise (haiku), Nodin (Minneapolis, MN), 1999.

NOVELS

Darkness in Saint Louis Bearheart, Truck Press (St. Paul, MN), 1973, published as *Bearheart: The Heirship Chronicles,* University of Minnesota Press (Minneapolis, MN), 1990.
Griever: An American Monkey King in China, Fiction Collective (New York, NY), 1987.
The Trickster of Liberty: Tribal Heirs to a Wild Baronage, University of Minnesota Press (Minneapolis, MN), 1988.
The Heirs of Columbus, Wesleyan University Press (Hanover, NH), 1992.
Dead Voices: Natural Agonies in the New World, University of Oklahoma Press (Norman, OK), 1992.
Hotline Healers: An Almost Browne Novel, Wesleyan University Press (Hanover, NH), 1997.
Chancers: A Novel, University of Oklahoma Press (Norman, OK), 2000.
Hiroshima Bugi: Atomu 57, University of Nebraska Press, (Lincoln, NE), 2003.

SHORT STORY COLLECTIONS

Wordarrows: Indians and Whites in the New Fur Trade (stories), University of Minnesota Press (Minneapolis, MN), 1978, University of Nebraska Press (Lincoln, NE), 2003.

Earthdivers: Tribal Narratives on Mixed Descent (stories), University of Minnesota Press (Minneapolis, MN), 1981.

Landfill Meditation: Crossblood Stories (short stories), Wesleyan University Press (Hanover, NH), 1991.

EDITOR

Escorts to White Earth, 1868-1968: 100 Year Reservation, Four Winds (New York, NY), 1968.

Narrative Chance: Postmodern Discourse on Native American Literatures, University of Oklahoma Press (Norman, OK), 1989.

Native American Literature: A Brief Introduction and Anthology, HarperCollins (New York, NY), 1995.

OTHER

Summer in the Spring: Lyric Poems of the Ojibway, Interpreted and Reexpressed, Nodin (Minneapolis, MN), 1965, published as *Anishinabe Nagomon: Songs of the Ojibwa,* Nodin (Minneapolis, MN), 1974, revised edition published as *Summer in the Spring: Ojibwa Lyric Poems and Tribal Stories,* Nodin (Minneapolis, MN), 1981, published as *Summer in the Spring: Anishinaabe Lyric Poems and Stories, New Edition,* University of Oklahoma Press (Norman, OK), 1993.

Thomas James White Hawk, Four Winds (New York, NY), 1968.

The Everlasting Sky: New Voices from the People Named the Chippewa, Crowell (New York, NY), 1972, published as *The Everlasting Sky: Voices of the Anishinabe People,* Minnesota Historical Society Press (St. Paul, MN), 2001.

Anishinabe Adisokan: Stories of the Ojibwa, Nodin (Minneapolis, MN), 1974.

Tribal Scenes and Ceremonies (editorial articles), Nodin (Minneapolis, MN), 1976.

The People Named the Chippewa: Narrative Histories, University of Minnesota Press (Minneapolis, MN), 1984.

Harold of Orange (screenplay), Native American Public Broadcasting Consortium Video, 1984.

Crossbloods: Bone Courts, Bingo, and Other Reports (essays), University of Minnesota Press (Minneapolis, MN), 1990.

Interior Landscapes: Autobiographical Myths and Metaphors, University of Minnesota Press (Minneapolis, MN), 1990.

Manifest Manners: Postindian Warriors of Survivance (essays), Wesleyan University Press (Hanover, NH), 1994, published with a new preface as *Manifest Manners: Narratives of Postindian Survivance,* Wesleyan University Press (Hanover, NH), 1999.

Shadow Distance: Gerald Vizenor Reader (selected fiction and essays), Wesleyan University Press (Hanover, NH), 1994.

Fugitive Poses: Native American Indian Scenes of Absence and Presence, University of Nebraska Press (Lincoln, NE), 1998.

(With A. Robert Lee) *Postindian Conversations,* University of Nebraska Press (Lincoln, NE), 1999.

Member of editorial board for North American Indian Prose Award and *American Indian Lives* autobiography series, University of Nebraska Press; member of editorial advisory board, *Zeitschrift für Anglistik und Amerikanistik* quarterly journal.

Contributor to books, including *Growing up in Minnesota,* edited by Chester Anderson, University of Minnesota Press, 1976; *This Song Remembers,* edited by Jane Katz, Houghton Mifflin, 1980; *Stories Migrating Home*,edited by Kimberly Blaeser, Loonfeather Press, 1999; *Reverberations: Tactics of Resistance, Forms of Agency in Trans/Cultural Practices,* edited by Jean Fisher, Jan van Eyck Edition (Maastricht, the Netherlands), 2000; and *The Norton Anthology of Theory and Criticism,* edited by Vincent B. Leitch, Norton, 2001. Contributor to periodicals, including *Modern Haiku, Star Tribune, Native American Press, California Monthly, Third Text* (London), *Alaska Quarterly Review,* and *Cross Cultural Poetics.*

Vizenor's manuscripts, letters, and other literary material were collected for the American Literature Manuscripts Collection, Beinecke Library, Yale University.

SIDELIGHTS: Gerald Robert Vizenor is an acclaimed novelist, poet, and teacher. The themes and content of his works have arisen not only from his personal and cultural experiences, but also from the strong oral traditions of his Native American ancestors. *Dictionary of Literary Biography* contributor Alan R. Velie noted, "One of the most versatile, innovative, and productive

American writers, [Vizenor] is widely regarded as a leading American Indian writer and as a major presence in American letters." Kimberly M. Blaeser, in her essay for *Dictionary of Literary Biography,* commented, "Revolutionary in style and vision, Vizenor's works have broken new ground in the field of Native American literature."

Vizenor is of mixed-blood descent. His father, Clement William, was an Ojibwa Indian, originally from the White Earth Reservation in Minnesota, and his mother, LaVerne Peterson, lived in Minneapolis; the two met when Vizenor's father first came to the city. In 1950 Vizenor joined the Minnesota National Guard and from 1952 to 1955 and served with the U.S. Army in Japan. While serving in Japan, Vizenor became familiar with haiku, an unrhymed, seventeen syllable Japanese poetic form in which nature and human nature are linked in the poet's perception and representation of a single moment. "The Japanese and their literature were my liberation," he later wrote in the *Chicago Review.* "That presence of haiku, more than other literature, touched my imagination and brought me closer to a sense of tribal consciousness. . . . I would have to leave the nation of my birth to understand the wisdom and survivance of tribal literature." During the following decade, he produced several volumes of haiku, including *Raising the Moon Vines* and *Seventeen Chirps,* both published in 1964, and *Empty Swings,* published in 1967.

In the years following, Vizenor explored many different genres. In 1973 he published his first novel, *Darkness in Saint Louis Bearheart,* later published as *Bearheart: The Heirship Chronicles. Bearheart* is an almost apocalyptic novel in which Proude Ceadarfair and Rosina, his wife, are forced to leave their home in Minnesota. The United States has run out of petroleum-based fuel, and Proude's cedar trees are needed for fuel. The two travel south, accompanied by an odd collection of pilgrims, and face an assortment of strange villains: an evil gambler who will wager gasoline against the lives of those who choose to gamble with him, "food fascists," who carve witches up to use their flesh as food, and a group of people born crippled due to the pollution of the environment.

In the 1980s Vizenor forewent a tenured position at the University of Minnesota to explore a teaching opportunity in China. Originally planning to write essays during his stay, Vizenor's poetic outlook underwent a radical transformation after attending a theatrical production that included scenes from the Monkey King opera. The Monkey King is a mischievous figure from Chinese myth similar to the "trickster" character found in Native American legend. In an interview with Larry McCaffery and Tom Marshall for *Chicago Review,* Vizenor confided that this opera had altered his perspectiveand "changed everything" for him. Seeing a dynamic Chinese audience "so completely engaged in the production," led Vizenor to rethink his original, graduate school reading of the Monkey King. Experiencing the performance transformed the material from mere cultural documentation to a work beyond socio-political ramifications, encompassing the consciousness of the Chinese people as folk literature. Sensing he had a "powerful theme" for a book born of this experience, Vizenor then developed Griever, a trickster main character, for his award-winning novel *Griever: An American Monkey King in China,* published in 1987. *The Trickster of Liberty: Tribal Heirs to a Wild Baronage,* published in 1988, also explores the trickster theme and imagery.

In *Griever,* the title character is an English teacher at a Chinese university. As a trickster figure, Griever does his best to liberate people from authority, but most of his efforts fail. Velie explained, "In depicting Griever, Vizenor combines the Anishinaabe trickster Nanabozho with Monkey, the trickster hero of Chinese folktale and opera." In *The Trickster of Liberty,* Griever appears as a minor character, and readers learn that he received his name from the book *How to Be Sad and Downcast and Still Live in Better Health than People Who Pretend to Be So Happy,* a manual his father didn't take with him when he left Griever to grow up on White Earth Reservation. Most of the stories in *The Trickster of Liberty* focus on the Browne family. According to Velie, "Vizenor again uses fantasy as a vehicle for his trenchant social and political commentary."

In 1990 Vizenor published an autobiographical volume, *Interior Landscapes: Autobiographical Myths and Metaphors.* In addition to novels, he has also written several works concerning the economic, social, and political plight of Native Americans, specifically his own Ojibwa tribe. "George Raft was an inspiration to my mother and, in a sense, he was responsible for my conception," Vizenor wrote in *Interior Landscapes.* "She saw the thirties screen star, a dark social hero with moral courage, in the spirited manner of my father, a newcomer from the White Earth Reservation. 'The first time I saw your father he looked like George Raft, not the gangster but the dancer. He was handsome and he had nerve,' my mother told me. 'The first thing he said to me was, "I got lots of girls but I always like new ones." He came by in a car with one of his friends. Nobody would talk like that now, but that's how we got together.' I was conceived on a cold night in a kerosene heated tenement near downtown Minneapolis. President Franklin Delano Roosevelt had been inaugurated the year before, at the depth of the Great Depression. He told the nation, 'The only thing we have to fear is fear itself.' My mother, and millions of other women stranded in cold rooms, heard the new president, listened to their new men, and were roused to remember the movies; elected politicians turned economies, but the bright lights in the depression came from the romantic and glamorous screen stars."

Vizenor's *Landfill Meditation* is a collection of short fiction that demonstrates the author's concern with the theme of mixed racial heritage and his familiar narrative technique of combining autobiographical elements with fiction. The opening story, "Almost Browne," for example, is a semi-autobiographical story of a pregnant white woman and her Chippewa partner who run out of gas on their way to a reservation hospital. Commented Robert L. Berner in *World Literature Today,* Vizenor's "fictions are almost stories, almost fictional, almost real." The trickster character Almost Browne, a member of the Browne family first introduced in *The Trickster of Liberty,* reappears in the novel *Hotline Healers,* which tells eleven stories of the life and lineage of Almost Browne. These stories "combine [Vizenor's] Anishinaabe heritage as well as his cutting and clear social commentary on issues such as tribal sovereignty, American politics, and ethnic studies" according to Meredith James in a review for *World Literature Today.*

In *Dead Voices: Natural Agonies in the New World,* Vizenor explores the Native American myth of the trickster figure in the context of the modern world. Using the motif of a Native American card game called "wanaki" as the narrative structure, the novel's chapters each begin with the turn of a playing card accompanied by a different animal. Ritual, symbol, magic, transformation, and jokes all play a role in the narrative, which reviewers have alternately found highly inventive and confusing. "The attempt to resurrect traditional myths and set them loose in the modern world is a creditable one," observed Robert Crum in the *New York Times Book Review.* "Unfortunately, the characters in this book are less animals than puppets." Articulating the challenge Vizenor presents to readers of *Dead Voices,* David Mogen of *Western American Literature* asserted: "Because the very voice of the novel embodies a paradox of articulation, this is a difficult book to read, one in which meaning and narrative alike seem to hover just beyond the reach of written language."

As editor of *Narrative Chance: Postmodern Discourse on Native American Indian Literatures,* Vizenor selected diverse essays exploring the role of Native American writers in the context of the European literary tradition. "[*Narrative Chance* challenges] the reader to consider what it means when Native peoples apart from a European critical tradition must write within that tradition to preserve and maintain distinctly different world views," according to Alanna Kathleen Brown in *Modern Fiction Studies.* Among the noted essays included in the collection are Elaine Jahner's "Metalanguages," Louis Owens's "Gerald Vizenor's *Darkness in Saint Louis Bearheart,*" and Vizenor's introductory essay, "Trickster Discourse: Comic Holotropes and Languages Games."

The role of Native American writers, as well as the definition of who an Indian is, comes up in several of Vizenor's works, including *Fugitive Poses: Native American Indian Scenes of Absence and Presence* and *Postindian Conversations,* which he wrote with A. Robert Lee. In a review of *Fugitive Poses,* John Wilson of *Books & Culture* noted that "no one has thought longer, harder, and more trickily about this trick question [who is an 'Indian'?] than the prodigiously inventive . . . Vizenor." *Fugitive Poses* contains a series of essays by Vizenor which deconstruct the image of the "indian" (Vizenor leaves the term without capitalization). Shamoon Zamir of *Modern Language Quarterly* commented that the book "pursues Vizenor's career-long (and, as far as Native American writers are concerned, unique) attempt to align or bring into dialogue his own sense of meanings of Native American narratives and cultural insights and poststructuralist theory." James Stripes of *American Indian Quarterly* commented, "Vizenor's writing resists the grasp of reductive readings of texts to theses. Instead, his writing provokes attentive and imaginative reading." *Postindian Conversations* is a collection of interviews conducted by A. Robert Lee with Vizenor. Many of the interviews make references to Vizenor's previous work, which some reviewers thought might be confusing to readers less familiar with Vizenor's writings. The book also makes use of several terms of Vizenor's own invention. Michelle Herman Raheja of *American Indian Quarterly* wrote, "Through these interviews, the reader gets an intimate glimpse into Vizenor's thoughts on both his personal life and the experiences that influenced his literary career." Lara Merlin, in her review for *World Literature Today,* noted, "This series of interviews will fascinate Vizenor's fans and foes alike," and called Vizenor "one of the most provocative of Native American writers."

"In his fictions, Vizenor aims for nothing less than a change in the American image of the Indian as a savage on the verge of extinction," wrote Linda Lizut Helstern in an essay for *Studies in Short Fiction.* This is certainly the case in Vizenor's novels *The Heirs of Columbus* and *Chancers.* In *The Heirs of Columbus,* Vizenor posits that Columbus was actually of Mayan descent: the story he tells has the Mayans "discovering" Europe and the Old World long before the voyage of 1492. By recreating Columbus as a Native American, Vizenor flips the image of the victimized Indian on its head. "One cannot be an innocent and pitiable victim if one is also partially responsible for the atrocity committed," wrote Michael Hardin in his essay for *MELUS.* Hardin continued, "Giving the storytellers in *Heirs of Columbus* the power to heal works textually, but it also works self-referentially. As author/storyteller, Vizenor too can be, and clearly wants to be, one whose stories heal." But Christopher Columbus is only a marginal character in the novel; the main character is descendant Stone Columbus, a trickster storyteller. Stone and the other descendants of Columbus meet annually to share stories and envision the creation of a new tribal identity.

In *Chancers,* Vizenor tackles the issue of repatriation of Native American skeletal remains. In the novel, a group of University of California students calling themselves the Solar Dancers set out to resurrect native remains from the Phoebe Hearst Museum of Anthropology. To do this, they sacrifice members of the faculty and museum administration, use the skulls of the academics to replace the native bones; the resurrected spirits are called the Chancers. The Solar Dancers are opposed by a group of trickster figures known as the Round Dancers, and the two groups battle to a comic end. Budd Arthur of *Booklist* called the novel "a valuable and accessible look at Native American Issues." Ellen Flexman wrote for *Library Journal* that Vizenor "capture[s] the dilemmas of modern Native life without succumbing to rage or despair."

In discussing Vizenor's body of works, Blaeser concluded, "The subjects on which Vizenor has wielded his satire include historical and literary representations of Native Americans, contemporary identity politics, repatriation of tribal remains, reservation gaming, American Indian Movement leaders, and Christopher Columbus. His fearsome challenges to romantic Indian fallacies often situate the author and his literary works in the center of controversy, and he thrives there."

BIOGRAPHICAL AND CRITICAL SOURCES:

BOOKS

Blaeser, Kimberly M., *Gerald Vizenor: Writing in Oral Tradition,* University of Oklahoma Press (Norman, OK), 1996.

Bruchac, Joseph, *Survival This Way: Interviews with American Indian Poets,* Sun Tracks and The University of Arizona Press (Tucson, AZ), 1987, pp. 287-310.

Contemporary Literary Criticism, Volume 103, Thomson Gale (Detroit, MI), 1998.

Dictionary of Literary Biography, Thomson Gale (Detroit, MI), Volume 175: *Native American Writers of the United States,* 1997, pp. 295-307, Volume 227: *American Novelists since World War II, Sixth Series,* 2000, pp. 324-334.

Krupat, Arnold, *The Turn to the Native: Studies in Criticism and Culture,* University of Nebraska Press (Lincoln, NE), 1996.

Swann, Brian and Arnold Krupat, *I Tell You Now: Autobiographical Essays by Native American Writers,* University of Nebraska Press (Lincoln, NE), 1987, pp. 100-283.

Velie, Alan R., *Four American Indian Literary Masters: N. Scott Momaday, James Welch, Leslie Marmon Silko, and Gerald Vizenor,* University of Oklahoma Press (Norman, OK), 1982, pp. 123-48.

Vizenor, Gerald Robert, *Interior Landscapes: Autobiographical Myths and Metaphors,* University of Minnesota Press (Minneapolis, MN), 1990.

PERIODICALS

American Book Review, January-February, 1988, pp. 12-13, 20.

American Indian Quarterly, Special Issue, winter, 1985, pp. 1-78; summer, 1998, James Stripes, review of *Fugitive Poses: Native American Indian Scenes of Absence and Presence,* p. 393; winter, 1999, Zubeda Jalalzai, "Tricksters, Captives, and Conjurers: The 'Roots' of Liminality and Gerald Vizenor's *Bearheart,*" p. 20; spring, 2001, Michelle Hermann Raheja, review of *Postindian Conversations,* p. 324.

Bloomsbury Review, April-May, 1991, p. 5.

Booklist, September 15, 2000, Budd Arthur, review of *Chancers,* p. 220.

Books & Culture, July-August, 2002, John Wilson, "Mixedblood Trickster," p. 5.

Chicago Review, fall, 1993, "The Envoy to Haiku," pp. 55-62.

Chronicle of Higher Education, July 13, 1994, pp. A8, A12.

Ethnic and Racial Studies, September, 1999, Jay Miller, review of *Fugitive Poses,* p. 925.

Journal of American Studies, December, 1999, David Greenham, review of *Fugitive Poses,* p. 555.

Journal of Modern Language, Spring, 1999, Rodney Mader, review of *Fugitive Poses,* p. 538.

Library Journal, October 15, 1994, p. 73; January, 1995, p. 103; August, 2000, Ellen Flexman, review of *Chancers,* p. 163.

Los Angeles Times Book Review, September 8, 1991; October 11, 1992, p. 6.

MELUS, spring, 1991-92, pp. 75-85; winter, 1998, Michael Hardin, "The Trickster of History: *The Heirs of Columbus* and the Dehistorization of Narrative," p. 25.

Modern Fiction Studies, summer, 1994, Alanna Kathleen Brown, review of *Narrative Chance: Postmodern Discourse on Native American Indian Literatures,* p. 362.

Modern Language Quarterly, June, 2000, Shamoon Zamir, review of *Fugitive Poses,* p. 419.

Nation, October 21, 1991, pp. 465, 486-490.

New York Times Book Review, January 10, 1988, p. 18; November 8, 1992, Robert Crum, review of *Dead Voices: Natural Agonies in the New World,* p. 18.

Publishers Weekly, August 16, 1999, review of *Postindian Conversations,* p. 75.

Studies in Short Fiction, fall, 1999, Linda Lizut Helstern, "'Bad Breath': Gerald Vizenor's Lacanian Fable," p. 351.

Village Voice Literary Supplement, November, 1991, p. 29.

Western American Literature, August, 1988, p. 160; August, 1992, David Mogen, review of *Dead Voices,* pp. 180-81; winter, 1994, p. 361.

Wilson Library Bulletin, December, 1992, p. 33.

World Literature Today, summer, 1992, Robert L. Berner, review of *Landfall Meditation,* p. 561; spring, 1993, pp. 423-424; winter, 1999, Meredith James, review of *Hotline Healers: An Almost Browne Novel,* p. 189; autumn, 2000, Lara Merlin, review of *Postindian Conversations,* p. 901.

* * *

VOGEL, Paula A. 1951-
(Paula Anne Vogel)

PERSONAL: Born November 16, 1951, in Washington, DC; daughter of Donald S. (in advertising) and Phyllis (Bremerman) Vogel. *Education:* Catholic University of America, B.A., 1974; Cornell University, A.B.D., 1977.

ADDRESSES: Home—42 Grove St., No. 13, New York, NY 10014. *Agent*—c/o Peter Franklin, William Morris Agency, 1325 Avenue of the Americas, New York, NY 10019.

CAREER: American Place Theatre, New York, NY, member of staff, 1978-79; Cornell University, Ithaca, NY, member of faculty of theatre arts, 1979-82; Brown University, head of MFA writing program, 1985—. Executive member of Women's Studies, 1977-78. Playwrighting instructor, 1981, and consultant at Perseverance Theatre, Juneau, AK; consultant at Central Casting Theatre, Ithaca; board member, Saratoga International Theatre Institute. Conductor of playwrighting workshops at McGill University and at St. Elizabeth's Hospital; has taught at the Maximum Security Center for women at the Adult Corrections Institute in Rhode Island.

MEMBER: Bryn Mawr Drop-out Society (founder), Dramatists Guild, Circle Repertory, Writers Guild of America East.

AWARDS, HONORS: Heerbes-McCalmon Playwrighting Award, 1975 and 1976; American College Theatre Festival Award for best new play, 1977, for *Meg*; American National Theatre and Academy-West Award, 1978; playwrighting fellowship from National Endowment for the Arts, 1979-80; received commission from Actor's Theatre of Louisville; Pew/TCG senior residency award, 1995-97; Guggenheim Award, 1995; Fund for New American Plays Award, 1995, for *Hot 'n' Throbbing*; New York Drama Critics Award for best new play, Drama Desk Award for outstanding play, Lucille Lortel, and Obie Award, all 1997, and Pulitzer Prize for Drama, 1998, all for *How I Learned to Drive*; also recipient of a Bunting Fellowship, a McKnight Fellowship at the Playwright's Center, two National Endowment for the Arts fellowships, and a residency at the Rockefeller Foundation's Bellagio Center.

WRITINGS:

PLAYS

Meg (three-act; first produced in Washington, DC, at Kennedy Center, 1977), Samuel French (New York, NY), 1977.

Apple-Brown Betty (one-act), first produced in Louisville, KY, at Actor's Theatre of Louisville, February, 1979.

Desdemona: A Play about a Handkerchief (two-act; first produced in Binghamton, NY, at State University of New York at Binghamton, April, 1980), Dramatists Play Service (New York, NY), 1994.

The Oldest Profession (one-act), first produced in New York, NY, at Hudson Guild Theatre, December, 1981.

Bertha in Blue (one-act), first produced in New York, NY, at Hudson Guild Theatre, December, 1981.

The Last Pat Epstein Show before the Reruns (two-act), first produced in Ithaca, NY, at Central Casting Theatre, February, 1982.

The Baltimore Waltz, Dramatists Play Service (New York, NY), 1992.

And Baby Makes Seven, first produced in San Francisco, CA, 1992.

Hot 'n' Throbbing, produced in New York, NY, 1992; produced in New York, NY, at the Peter Norton Space, 2005.

The Baltimore Waltz and Other Plays, Theatre Communications Group, 1996.

The Mineola Twins, first produced in Juneau, AK, 1996.

How I Learned to Drive, Dramatists Play Service (New York, NY), 1997.

Also author of "Dribble." *Baltimore Waltz* has been produced in over sixty regional theatres in the United States, Canada, Brazil, and England, including Circle Repertory, Center Stage, Yale Repertory, Alley Theatre, and the Magic.

OTHER

(With Terrence McNally and Harvey Fierstein) *On Common Ground* (screenplay), Showtime, 2000.

WORK IN PROGRESS: The Castrato Play, a five-character play about castrati in seventeenth-century Italy; *Method Acting,* a novel about academia and the violation of acting.

SIDELIGHTS: Paula A. Vogel is not one to shy away from often highly politicized, commonly taboo topics . . . she faces them head on with eloquence and compassion. Throughout her career Vogel, an award-winning playwright, has delved into an assortment of topics from the nontraditional family to AIDS to domestic violence to pedophilia. As she explained to the Minneapolis *Star Tribune,* "I always feel that I'm writing the script and my audience is writing the play. The fact that 200 people can go in there and come out to have arguments in the car and lobby, and that everyone is always right: That makes it an ideal platform for democracy." Vogel had her first big success with *The Baltimore Waltz* in 1992, then won the Pulitzer Prize for drama in 1998 for *How I Learned to Drive.*

In 1986, Vogel's brother Carl, whom she was very close to, contracted HIV, the virus that causes AIDS. Eventually, Carl became very ill and Vogel cared for him. During this time she developed the idea for *The Baltimore Waltz.* "I wrote this play in my head while in the hospital, waiting for the doctors," Vogel remarked to Pamela Sommers in the *Washington Post.* The play concerns a woman, Anna, who comes down with Acquired Toilet Disease (ATD), an affliction of single, female elementary school teachers, and her brother, Carl, a gay library employee. Vogel uses the fictional ATD to force the audience to re-examine their views on AIDS, which is the real subject of the play. Her characters lament that no one is aggressively seeking a cure for the disease ATD because it afflicts a segment of the population that is relatively powerless. Later in the play, the audience discovers that the story is actually taking place in Anna's mind as she tends to her dying brother Carl in a Baltimore hospital.

How I Learned to Drive was inspired by one of Vogel's favorite novels, Vladimir Nabokov's *Lolita.* Dick Scanlan in the *Advocate* praised "Vogel's flair for poetic dialogue in an era when a television style of naturalism has seeped its way into the theater." Stefan Kanfer in the *New Leader* also applauded Vogel's writing, stating, "Neither her plot nor her people are predictable; in the middle of the saddest scene she evokes a laugh, and just when a moment seems to be edging on hilarity she introduces a wistful note that leaves the smiles frozen on the audience's faces." The play was an off-Broadway hit and earned the 1998 Pulitzer Prize for drama.

In conjunction with *How I Learned to Drive,* Vogel wrote *The Mineola Twins.* Vogel published *How I Learned to Drive* together with *The Mineola Twins* as *The Mammary Plays,* but Ben Brantley in the New York Times commented on [*The Mineola Twins,*] "Those who know this dramatist only from . . . *How I Learned to Drive* . . . may have difficulty recognizing her voice here." *The Mineola Twins* is a comedy about the political schism that divides people, as well as the confining roles prescribed for women.

Vogel once told *CA:* "A crucial influence on my future writing career was my dismissal from the theatre arts faculty of Cornell University. The playwright is in an unenviable position. On the one hand, as a practitioner interested in writing crafted, intelligent, forward-looking plays, she (or he) is at the same time unable to find permanent financial support from academic communities which espouse high theatrical standards. One can only bite the bullet, write, and live as a VISTA volunteer for the arts."

BIOGRAPHICAL AND CRITICAL SOURCES:

BOOKS

Newsmakers 1999, Issue 2, Thomson Gale (Detroit, MI), 1999.
Contemporary Dramatists, 6th edition, St. James Press (Detroit, MI), 1999.

PERIODICALS

Advocate, June 10, 1997, p. 61; January 20, 1998, p. 99; February 2, 1999, Dick Scanlan, review of *How I Learned to Drive,* p. 42.
American Theater, February 1997, p. 24.
Dallas Morning News, May 27, 1997, p. 21A; April 15, 1998, p. 33A; October 25, 1998, p. 1C.
Independent on Sunday, June 21, 1998, p. 7.
Jewish Exponent, July 17, 1997.
Los Angeles Times, April 15, 1998, p. A14.
Nation, July 28, 1997, p. 24.
New Leader, June 30, 1997, Stefan Kanfer, review of *How I Learned to Drive,* p. 21
New Republic, July 7, 1997, p. 28.
Newsday, July 29, 1993, p. 67; November 12, 1993, p. 73; March 17, 1997, p. B5.
New York, April 7, 1997, p. 46.
New York Times, May 7, 1993, p. C5; November 12, 1993, p. C20; March 16, 1997, sec, 2, p. 6; March 17, 1997, p. C11; Ben Brantley, February 19, 1999, Ben Brantley, review of *The Mammary Plays,* p. B1.
Reuters, April 14, 1998.
Star Tribune (Minneapolis, MN), May 15, 1998, p. 1E; May 19, 1998, p. 4E.
Variety, April 20, 1998, p. 57.
Washington Post, May 22, 1994, p. G14.

* * *

VOGEL, Paula Anne
See VOGEL, Paula A.

* * *

VOIGT, Cynthia 1942-

PERSONAL: Born February 25, 1942, in Boston, MA; daughter of Frederick C. (a corporate executive) and Elise (Keeney) Irving; married first husband September, 1964 (divorced, 1972); married Walter Voigt (a teacher), August 30, 1974; children: Jessica, Peter. *Education:* Smith College, B.A., 1963. *Politics:* Independent. *Hobbies and other interests:* "Reading, eating well (especially with friends), tennis, movies, hanging around with our children, and considering the weather."

ADDRESSES: Home—Deer Isle, ME. *Agent*—Merrilee Heifetz, Writers House, Inc., 21 W. 26th St., New York, NY 10010.

CAREER: J. Walter Thompson Advertising Agency, New York, NY, secretary, 1964; high school English teacher in Glen Burnie, MD, 1965-67; The Key School, Annapolis, MD, English teacher, 1968-69, department chair, 1971-79, part-time teacher and department chair, 1981-88; author of books for young readers, 1981—.

AWARDS, HONORS: Notable Children's Trade Book in the Field of Social Studies, National Council for Social Studies/Children's Book Council, and American Book Award nominee, both 1981, for *Homecoming;* American Library Association (ALA) Best Young Adult Books citation, 1982, for *Tell Me If the Lovers Are Losers;* ALA Best Children's Books citation, 1982, and Newbery Medal, ALA, 1983, both for *Dicey's Song;* ALA Best Young Adult Books citation, 1983, and Newbery Honor book, 1984, both for *A Solitary Blue;* Edgar Allan Poe Award for best juvenile mystery, Mystery Writers of America, 1984, for *The Callender Papers;* Silver Pencil Award (Dutch), 1988, and Deutscher Jugendliteratur Preis, 1989, both for *The Runner;* Alan Award for achievement in young adult literature, 1989; California Young Reader's Award, 1990, for *Izzy, Willy-Nilly.*

WRITINGS:

"TILLERMAN FAMILY" SERIES

Homecoming, Atheneum (New York, NY), 1981, reprinted, Simon Pulse (New York, NY), 2002.
Dicey's Song, Atheneum (New York, NY), 1982, reprinted, Simon Pulse (New York, NY), 2002.
A Solitary Blue, Atheneum (New York, NY), 1983, reprinted, Aladdin (New York, NY), 2003.
The Runner, Atheneum (New York, NY), 1985.
Come a Stranger, Atheneum (New York, NY), 1986.
Sons from Afar, Macmillan (New York, NY), 1987.
Seventeen against the Dealer, Macmillan (New York, NY), 1989.

YOUNG ADULT NOVELS

Tell Me If the Lovers Are Losers, Atheneum (New York, NY), 1982.
The Callender Papers, Atheneum (New York, NY), 1983, reprinted, Aladdin (New York, NY), 2000.
Building Blocks, Atheneum (New York, NY), 1984, reprinted, Aladdin (New York, NY), 2002.
Izzy, Willy-Nilly, Atheneum (New York, NY), 1986.
Tree by Leaf, Macmillan (New York, NY), 1988.
The Vandemark Mummy, Atheneum (New York, NY), 1991.
David and Jonathan, Scholastic (New York, NY), 1992.
Orfe, Macmillan (New York, NY), 1993.
When She Hollers, Scholastic (New York, NY), 1994.
When Bad Things Happen to Bad People, Atheneum (New York, NY), 2006.

"THE KINGDOM" SERIES

Jackaroo, Atheneum (New York, NY), 1985, reprinted, Simon Pulse (New York, NY), 2003.
On Fortune's Wheel, Macmillan (New York, NY), 1990.
The Wings of a Falcon, Scholastic (New York, NY), 1993.
Elske, Atheneum (New York, NY), 1999.

"BAD GIRLS" SERIES

The Bad Girls, Scholastic (New York, NY), 1996.
Bad, Badder, Baddest, Scholastic (New York, NY), 1997.
It's Not Easy Being Bad, Atheneum (New York, NY), 2000.
Bad Girls in Love, Atheneum (New York, NY), 2002.

OTHER

Stories about Rosie (picture book), illustrated by Dennis Kendrick, Macmillan (New York, NY), 1986.
(Compiler, with David Bergman) *Shore Writers' Sampler II* (stories and poetry), Friendly Harbor Press, 1988.
Glass Mountain (adult fiction), Harcourt (New York, NY), 1991.
The Rosie Stories (picture book), illustrated by Cat Bowman Smith, Holiday House (New York, NY), 2003.
Angus and Sadie (picture book), illustrated by Tom Leigh, HarperCollins (New York, NY), 2005.

ADAPTATIONS: Several of Voigt's titles have been recorded as audio books.

SIDELIGHTS: Cynthia Voigt is an accomplished storyteller noted for her well-developed characters, interesting plots, and authentic atmosphere. In her novels for children and young adults, she examines such serious topics as child abandonment, verbal abuse, racism, and coping with amputation. Reviewers have praised Voigt's fluent and skillfully executed writing style, compelling topics, and vividly detailed descriptions. Critics also have described Voigt's themes as universal and meaningful to young adults, particularly noting her expertise in fashioning convincing characters and rich relationships in which both adults and children grow in understanding. In a *Twentieth-Century Children's Writers* essay, Sylvia Patterson Iskander described the qualities that have made Voigt's writings appealing to readers: "Voigt's understanding of narrative techniques, power to create memorable characters, admirable but not goody-goody, knowledge of the problems of youth, and desire to teach by transporting readers into the characters' inner lives result in reversing unpromising, perhaps tragic, situations to positive, optimistic ones."

Voigt was born in Boston, Massachusetts, the second of five children, but her childhood was spent in small-town southern Connecticut. Voigt began to develop an interest in books early on, recalling: "My grandmother lived in northern Connecticut, in a house three stories high; its corridors lined with bookcases." Voigt noted that she had already become an avid reader, with books such as "*Nancy Drew, Cherry Ames, The Black Stallion,* and the Terhune book[s]," when one day at her grandmother's house she "pulled *The Secret Garden* off one of her shelves and read it. This was the first book I found entirely for myself, and I cherished it. There weren't any so-called 'young adult' books when I was growing up. If you were a good reader, once you hit fourth grade, things got a little thin. I started to read adult books, with my mother making sure what I had chosen was not 'too adult.' I read Tolstoy, Shakespeare, Camus, and many classics, except for *Moby Dick,* which I finally read in college. It knocked me out. I came to Dickens and Trollope later in life."

By the time Voigt began high school, she had set her sights on a career as a writer. She began writing short stories and poetry, and upon entering Smith College, a women's college in Massachusetts, she enrolled in creative writing courses. Her work, however, received little encouragement from her teachers. "Clearly what I was submitting didn't catch anyone's eye," she once remarked. "I never had a bad teacher like my character, Mr. Chappelle in *A Solitary Blue.*" On the other hand, she did find that some of her teachers at Smith "resented teaching women, feeling themselves too good for the position. We had very little patience with that attitude."

Following graduation from Smith College, Voigt moved to New York City, where she worked for the J. Walter Thompson Advertising Agency. "I married in 1964 and moved with my first husband to Santa Fe, New Mexico," she recalled. "I was to work as a secretary to help support us while he was in school. But even with my New York experience it was difficult to find a job. I drifted into the Department of Education one day and asked what I would have to do to qualify myself to teach school. They learned that I'd attended Smith College and signed me up for accrediting courses at a Christian Brothers college. Within six months I met the terms of certification. I vowed I would never teach when I left Smith, and yet, the minute I walked into a classroom, I loved it."

By the time of her divorce from her first husband, Voigt had settled in Annapolis, Maryland. "I had been writing throughout college, but during most of my first marriage, I didn't write much at all," Voigt once commented. Voigt had worked at the high school in Glen Burnie, Maryland. She then was hired by The Key School in Annapolis: "I was assigned to teach English in second, fifth and seventh grades. The second graders were a kick and a half. I assigned book reports to my fifth graders. I would go to the library and starting with the letter 'A' peruse books at the fifth, sixth, and seventh-grade age level. If a book looked interesting, I checked it out. I once went home with thirty books! It was then that I realized one could tell stories which had the shape of real books—novels—for kids the age of my students. I began to get ideas for young adult novels and juvenile books. That first year of teaching and *reading* really paid off in spades! I felt I had suddenly discovered and was exploring a new country."

In 1974, the author married Walter Voigt, a teacher of Latin and Greek at The Key School. "I was teaching full time, but was able to continue the writing I'd begun while I was living alone by sticking to my regime of one hour a day," the author recalled. When Voigt became pregnant, she switched to teaching part-time and dedicated more of her time to writing. "The summer I was pregnant I wrote the first draft of *The Callender Papers.* When my son, Peter, was an infant, I took him to school and taught with him in a 'Snuggli.' When he was a year old, I wrote *Tell Me If the Lovers Are Losers,* and the next year (he was in a playpen in the faculty lounge next to my classroom), I began *Homecoming.*

"One day while I was writing *Tell Me If the Lovers Are Losers,* I went to the market and saw a car full of kids left to wait alone in the parking lot. As the electric supermarket doors whooshed open, I asked myself 'What would happen if nobody ever came back for those kids?' I made some jottings in my notebook, and let them 'stew' for a year, the way most of my ideas do. When I sat down to write the story that grew from my question (and this is typical of my process) I made a list of character names. Then I tried them on to see if they fit. I knew Dicey was the main character, but was not sure precisely *who* she was. The more I wrote about her, the more real she became to me. I'd planned a book about half the size of *Homecoming.* But a few chapters into the novel, the grandmother became central and I began to see that there was a lot more going on than would fit in one book." *Homecoming* became Voigt's first published novel, appearing in 1981.

With *Homecoming,* the author begins the saga of the Tillermans, four fatherless children aged six through thirteen who are abandoned in a shopping mall parking lot by their mentally ill mother. Dicey, the eldest, takes it upon herself to care for all four, and they eventually move to their grandmother's home in distant Maryland. "The plot is well developed, fast paced, with some suspense. The book deals with the pain of losses—death, separation, poverty—but also with responsibility, friends, wisdom, happiness, survival," wrote *Christian Science Monitor* critic Joanna Shaw-Eagle. Although many critics questioned whether the length of the work and its often-negative portrayal of adults made it inappropriate for young adult readers, Kathleen Leverich of the *New York Times Book Review* took these elements into consideration when she concluded that "the accomplishments of this feisty band of complex and . . . sympathetically conceived kids makes for an enthralling journey to a gratifying end."

Dicey's Song continues the Tillermans' story, concentrating on young Dicey's emerging understanding of her new life in her grandmother's house in Maryland and her relationships with her siblings and grandmother. *Dicey's Song* was praised for its cohesive plot and the depth of its characterizations, particularly of Dicey and her eccentric grandmother. In her review in *Bulletin of the Center for Children's Books,* Zena Sutherland called *Dicey's Song* "a rich and perceptive book." In 1983, the book earned Voigt the prestigious Newbery Medal.

In *A Solitary Blue,* Voigt centers on Jeff, a friend of Dicey's introduced in the earlier Tillerman novels, whose mother abandons him to the care of his remote father while she goes off to help needy children. The story depicts the evolution of Jeff's understanding of his parents and of himself. According to Gloria P. Rohmann in her review in *School Library Journal,* the book "ultimately disappoints"; but other critics, while noting flaws, praised the depiction of the relationship between Jeff and his father. Jane Langton in her critique in the *New York Times Book Review* called *A Solitary Blue* "beautifully written," comparing it to Charles Dickens's *Bleak House. A Solitary Blue* was named a Newbery Honor book in 1984.

On the *Scholastic Web site,* readers asked Voigt how it felt to win the Newbery Medal. She answered, "It felt absolutely terrific. Part of the great thing was that I didn't expect it. I didn't expect it not because I didn't think I'd be considered, but because I thought the committee was meeting later in the month! I said to myself, 'Okay, you can get anxious about this at the end of January.' But the phone call came in the middle of January, which took me totally by surprise! It was like getting something you hoped for but didn't know if you were really going to get—like getting into college times ten. I think if my parents had given me the horse that I asked for when I was twelve, I might have felt the same way. It was like being queen for a day. It was terrific."

The Runner is a spin-off from the Tillerman novels which is set a generation before the others and centered on Samuel "Bullet" Tillerman, whose obsession is long-distance running and whose torment is his autocratic father. The plot turns on Bullet's prejudice against black people, which is eventually softened by his association with Tamer Shipp, a black runner. Although some critics found the plot contrived and the writing overdone, Alice Digilio of the *Washington Post Book World* concluded, "Voigt sails *The Runner* through some heavy seas, but always with a steady hand." In *Come a Stranger,* Voigt supplements the Tillerman series with another novel that takes racism as its focus. The plot centers on Mina Smiths, a character first introduced in *Dicey's Song,* whose experience of being the only black girl at ballet camp one summer impels her to try to identify with whites. Tamer Shipp appears as Mina's minister, to whom she goes for guidance. Though some critics faulted the author for stereotyping her black characters, others praised Voigt for the depth of her characterizations and smooth writing style.

Voigt completed her Tillerman series with the books *Sons from Afar* and *Seventeen against the Dealer.* She once commented on the writing process for the Tillerman books: "Bullet's story, which is what *The Runner* is, crossed my mind when I was writing *Homecoming* and put him in there. It had been in the back of my mind for that two-or three-year period. In the meantime I was writing two other Tillerman books, which had come naturally one out of the other. The ideas get in my head, and then there's a time when it's the right time to write them, I hope. And that's when I sit down to do them."

Tell Me If the Lovers Are Losers, Voigt's second published novel, focuses on three female college freshmen who become roommates, then teammates on the same volleyball team, and then friends. While some critics faulted the novel for what *New York Times Book Review* critic Kathleen Leverich called "exaggeration of character and the sacrifice of the theme to improbable theatrics," others, like Sally Estes of *Booklist,* dubbed *Tell Me If the Lovers Are Losers* "both provocative and rewarding for older, more perceptive high school age readers."

Voigt's next publication was *The Callender Papers,* a Gothic mystery set in late-nineteenth-century New England. Thirteen-year-old Jean Wainwright agrees to sort through the papers of Irene Callender, who died under mysterious circumstances and whose child then disappeared. Jean eventually finds the answer to the mystery, learning some lessons about life in the process. A number of critics observed that *The Callender Papers* was lighter fare than Voigt usually offers her readers, but most also found the mystery satisfying and well written.

Voigt created another novel for slightly younger adolescents in her 1984 work, *Building Blocks.* In what Zena Sutherland of *Bulletin of the Center for Children's Books* described as "an interesting time-travel story," Voigt depicts a strengthening relationship between a father and son through understanding gained when the son is transported from 1974 to the Depression. There he becomes friends with the ten-year-old boy who will become his father. *Building Blocks* was generally well-received, even by critics who did not admire the science-fiction element in the plot. *New Directions for Women* reviewer Elizabeth Sachs wrote: "Though the transition back in time is awkward, the scenes of Brann with his young boy father are beautiful."

Voigt also utilizes magical elements in *Jackaroo,* a book Karen P. Smith described in *School Library Journal* as "an intense and elegantly written historical adventure-romance." Set in a mythical place during the Middle Ages, *Jackaroo* features a strong teenage heroine who takes on the persona of the legendary Jackaroo in order to save her family and community. As Mary M. Burns remarked in *Horn Book:* "As in all of Cynthia Voigt's books, the style is fluid . . . the setting is evoked through skillfully crafted description; the situations speak directly to the human condition."

Voigt continued the story begun in *Jackaroo* with *On Fortune's Wheel,* and then resurrected the setting again in *The Wings of a Falcon,* a novel a *Kirkus Reviews* critic called "grand, thought-provoking entertainment." This work centers on Oriel and his friend Griff, who escape from an island of slavery to travel across unknown lands, only to be captured by Wolfers, a destructive band of barbarians, before escaping and settling on a farm in the north. Reviewers noted the book's length and mature themes in their generally positive reviews. In her review in *School Library Journal,* Susan L. Rogers compared Voigt's fantasy trilogy to her Tillerman series: "Each volume stands on its own, but together they create a tapestry more complex, meaningful, and compelling than its individual parts."

With the addition of a fourth title in the same setting, *Elske,* the quartet of books became known as "The Kingdom" series. Elske is only twelve when she flees her homeland in order to escape being sacrificed and buried with her people's dead leader. She takes on the role of a servant in a neighboring country, and because she is intelligent and honest, she eventually becomes the handmaiden to Beriel, the woman who should be on the throne of the kingdom. Beriel and Elske travel together, trying to find a way for Beriel to win back her kingdom. Shelle Rosenfeld of *Booklist* considered the character of Elske to be "a notable addition to Voigt's long line of strong female protagonists." According to a *Publishers Weekly* reviewer, "this spellbinding work continually challenges readers to keep up with its far-seeing, swift-thinking protagonist." Though commenting that the book might be beyond the reading level of some teen readers, Burns noted in *Horn Book* that, "for the right reader, it will be an engrossing experience." "This is not just another adventure featuring a warrior maiden," the critic continued; "it is challenging and thoughtful."

In *Izzy, Willy-Nilly,* Voigt depicts the trauma faced by an active teenager whose leg is amputated after a car accident. Through this incident, and with the help of Roseamunde, an awkward girl who embodies all that Izzy did not before her accident, Voigt's protagonist finds resources and wisdom within herself that she might otherwise never have known. Though some critics complained about the book's length and some unrealistic elements in the plot, Patty Campbell of *Wilson Library Bulletin* dubbed *Izzy, Willy-Nilly* the "best young adult novel of the season, and perhaps of the year."

The Vandemark Mummy was more warmly received. A mystery for younger adolescents, the plot centers on a brother and sister who go with their father when he is hired as the curator for an Egyptian collection at Vandemark College. When the collection's mummy is stolen and then found in a damaged condition, the sister disappears trying to uncover the thief. A reviewer for *Junior Bookshelf* wrote: "Serious issues are under debate, but the story is exciting and highly entertaining." In *David and Jonathan,* Voigt returns to more weighty matters for the older adolescent with a story that deals with the Holocaust, the Vietnam war, and homosexuality. A *Junior Bookshelf* contributor called *David and Jonathan* "highly serious," adding: "It is equally highly readable."

Voigt is also the author of picture books about dogs, two of which feature Rosie. *Stories about Rosie* features humorous stories focusing on the Voigt family dog and told from the dog's perspective. While some critics found the stories too long and complex for a picture-book audience, a *Publishers Weekly* reviewer concluded: "*Rosie* is a lightweight, just-right book for dog fans everywhere." Rosie returns in *The Rosie Stories,* and her escapades include wanting to eat her breakfast at the same time as her human family, knocking over a trash can, and practicing aerobics with the family's mother. "Voigt cleverly uses Rosie's repetition of words to create a feeling of success in new readers," praised Louise Brueggemann in her review for *Booklist.* A *Kirkus Reviews* contributor recommended the book "for dog lovers of all ages. Good dog, Rosie!"

Angus and Sadie introduces readers to two border collies who live on a farm in Maine. Though the two are siblings, they do not seem very alike at all. While the "Rosie" books focus on the relationship between Rosie and her family, *Angus and Sadie* looks more closely at the relationship between the two canine siblings.

In 1996, Voigt began a new series for middle-grade readers, introducing Mikey and Margolo in *The Bad Girls.* The series follows the two girls from fifth grade on into middle school as they rebel against authority, popular expectations, and ultimately begin to deal with issues of growing up, falling in love, and deciding whether or not it is worthwhile to fit in. In *Bad Girls,* Mikey and Margalo first encounter each other—Mikey is an obvious troublemaker who likes to act mean and dangerous, while Margalo is a quiet and manipulative girl who knows how to work behind the scenes to get her way. When they first meet, they are cautious and distrustful, but eventually they band together as outsiders. "Readers will recognize the fact that meanness can be about anger and misery as well as glorious mischief," explained Hazel Rochman in her *Booklist* review. As Lauren Adams wrote in *Horn Book,* "Voigt deftly portrays the dynamics of a fifth-grade classroom . . . [and] clearly takes wicked pleasure in her bad girls, as will the readers." The girls move on to sixth grade and the activity is on the homefront instead of in the classroom in *Bad, Badder, Baddest.* Mikey's parents may be getting a divorce, and Mikey and Margalo plot to keep them together so that the two girls will not have to be separated. "Rarely are heroines so charismatic," commented a reviewer for *Publishers Weekly.* Carolyn Phelan, writing in *Booklist,* called the title "a laugh-out-loud sitcom with outrageous dialogue and hilarious one-liners."

The adventures of Mikey and Margolo continue in *It's Not Easy Being Bad.* In this book, the girls are entering junior high, and they decide they want the respect of their classmates. Mikey charges head on with a plan doomed for failure, while Margalo plots to win them both respect by protesting the school's rule that seventh graders are not allowed to play on certain teams. Mikey's talent in tennis and Margalo's persistence in combating unfair rules help them to get the attention they desire. Debbie Carton, writing for *Booklist,* called *It's Not Easy Being Bad* "an on-target portrait of a segment of middle-school society." A *Publishers Weekly* critic felt that though the book is "more intelligent than most similarly themed middle-grade fiction," the third addition to the series "doesn't stand up to its predecessors." A *Horn Book* contributor, however, found the book to be "unburdened by the too-heavy issues of the second book," and noted that the story is "propelled by the daily conflict in the hallways and cafeteria."

Bad Girls in Love follows Mikey and Margalo into eighth grade and their first experiences with attraction to a member of the opposite sex. Mikey, who had always considered herself a tom boy, falls hard for the most popular boy in school. Though she tries subtle things like wearing skirts to school to try to gain the boy's attention, Mikey tackles the situation with as much bluntness and fervor as she has shown dealing with every other problem she encounters. Margalo, on the other hand, reveals nothing about her crush, keeping it secret that she is attracted to her teacher Mr. Schramm. "This may well be the Bad Girls' most delicious outing yet," applauded a contributor to *Kirkus Reviews.* Paul Rohrlick, writing in *Kliatt,* named it a "gossipy, true-to-life tale about first crushes." While *School Library Journal* reviewer Susan Oliver found the entry into the series to be "shallow and unsatisfying," Hazel Rochman wrote in *Booklist* that Voigt "gets the junior-high jungle exactly right." *Horn Book* critic Lauren Adams felt similarly: "Voigt realistically conveys the heartache of first infatuation with compassion and without bleakness," she concluded.

When asked by readers on the *Scholastic Web site* why she decided to write the "Bad Girls" series, Voigt explained: "I think the question of what makes someone bad is worth exploring. I think Mikey and Margolo are inconvenient. I think they're terrific. I wanted to see if I could have girls who would do bad things because they wanted to. Not criminal, not cruel, but just the kinds of things that would not sit well in a classroom. I get tired of writing about people who are supposed to be bad but are only misunderstood. I think all of us are egotistical and are interested in ourselves and our own well-being. We should have more fun with that."

Voigt's books have earned her acclaim from readers and critics for both their thoughtful themes and entertaining prose. While the products of her work have achieved success in the publishing world, Voigt once commented that the actual process of writing also has an important place in her life: "Awards are external, they happen after the real work has been done. They are presents, and while they are intensely satisfying they do not give me the same kind of pleasure as being in the middle of a work that is going well. . . . Writing is something I need to do to keep myself on an even keel. It's kept me quiet; it's kept me off the streets." Voigt's advice to aspiring writers reflects this ethic: "Do it, not for awards, but for the pleasure of writing."

BIOGRAPHICAL AND CRITICAL SOURCES:

BOOKS

Children's Literature Review, Volume 13, Thomson Gale (Detroit, MI), 1987.

Twentieth-Century Children's Writers, 3rd edition, St. James Press, 1989, pp. 1004-1005.

PERIODICALS

ALAN Review, spring, 1994, pp. 56-59.

Booklist, March 15, 1982, Sally Estes, review of *Tell Me If the Lovers Are Losers,* p. 950; April 1, 1996, Hazel Rochman, review of *Bad Girls,* p. 1366; November 1, 1997, Carolyn Phelan, review of *Bad, Badder, Baddest,* p. 472; September 1, 1999, Shelle Rosenfeld, review of *Elske,* p. 125; November 15, 2000, Debbie Carton, review of *It's Not Easy Being Bad,* p. 643; July, 2001, Lolly Gepson, review of *Izzy, Willy-Nilly,* p. 2029; August, 2002, Hazel Rochman, review of *Bad Girls in Love,* p. 1964; December 1, 2003, Louise Brueggemann, review of *The Rosie Stories,* p. 686.

Bulletin of the Center for Children's Books, October, 1982, Zena Sutherland, review of *Dicey's Song,* p. 38; April, 1984, Zena Sutherland, review of *Building Blocks,* p. 158; September, 1993, p. 25.

Christian Science Monitor, May 13, 1983, Joanna Shaw-Eagle, "Cynthia Voigt: Family Comes First," p. B2.

Horn Book, March-April, 1986, Mary M. Burns, review of *Jackaroo,* p. 210; August, 1993, pp. 410-413; July-August, 1996, Lauren Adams, review of *Bad Girls,* p. 465; January-February, 1998, Lauren Adams, review of *Bad, Badder, Baddest,* p. 82; January, 2000, Mary M. Burns., review of *Elske,* p. 85; January, 2001, Lauren Adams, review of *It's Not Easy Being Bad,* p. 97; September-October, 2002, Lauren Adams, review of *Bad Girls in Love,* p. 582.

Junior Bookshelf, February, 1992, review of *David and Jonathan,* p. 38; April, 1993, review of *The Vandemark Mummy,* pp. 79-80.

Kirkus Reviews, August 1, 1993, review of *The Wings of a Falcon,* p. 1009; June 1, 2002, review of *Bad Girls in Love,* p. 812; November 1, 2003, review of *The Rosie Stories,* p. 1314.

Kliatt, January, 1993, p. 13; July, 2002, Paul Rohrlick, review of *Bad Girls in Love,* p. 14.

New Directions for Women, spring, 1986, Elizabeth Sachs, review of *Building Blocks,* p. 13.

New York Times Book Review, May 10, 1981, Kathleen Leverich, review of *Homecoming,* p. 38; May 16, 1982, Kathleen Leverich, review of *Tell Me If the Lovers Are Losers,* p. 28; November 27, 1983, Jane Langton, review of *A Solitary Blue,* pp. 34-35.

Publishers Weekly, September 26, 1986, review of *Stories about Rosie,* p. 82; July 18, 1994, pp. 225-226; September 22, 1997, review of *Bad, Badder, Baddest,* p. 81; August 9, 1999, review of *Bad, Badder, Baddest,* p. 355; November 15, 1999, review of *Elske,* p. 67; July 9, 2001, review of *Elske,* p. 70.

School Library Journal, September, 1983, Gloria P. Rohmann, review of *A Solitary Blue,* pp. 139-140; December, 1985, Karen P. Smith, review of *Jackaroo,* p. 96; December, 1992, pp. 133-134; October, 1993, Susan L. Rogers, review of *The Wings of a Falcon,* p. 156; November, 2000, Ronni Krasnow, review of *It's Not Easy Being Bad,* p. 164; November 27, 2000, review of *It's Not Easy Being Bad,* p. 77; May, 2001, Darlene Ford, review of *Izzy, Willy-Nilly,* p. 75; July, 2002, Susan Oliver, review of *Bad Girls in Love,* p. 126; December, 2003, Laura Scott, review of *The Rosie Stories,* p. 129; May, 2004, Vicki Reutter, review of *Homecoming,* p. 64.

Voice of Youth Advocates, December, 1992, Beverly Youree, review of *Orfe,* p. 288.

Washington Post Book World, July 14, 1985, Alice Digilio, "What Makes Bullet Run?," p. 8.

Wilson Library Bulletin, November, 1986, Patty Campbell, review of *Izzy, Willy-Nilly,* p. 49.

ONLINE

Scholastic Web site, http://www2.scholastic.com/ (April 27, 2005), interview with Voigt.

* * *

VOLLMANN, William T. 1959-

PERSONAL: Born July 28, 1959, in Santa Monica, CA; son of Thomas E. (a professor) and Tanis (a homemaker) Vollmann. *Education:* Attended Deep Springs College, 1977-79; Cornell University, B.A. (summa cum laude), 1981; graduate study at University of California, Berkeley. 1982-83. *Politics:* "Environmentalist egalitarian." *Religion:* "Agnostic Plus." *Hobbies and other interests:* Bookmaking, sketching, wilderness travel, ladies, exotic weapons.

ADDRESSES: *Office*—c/o Viking Penguin, 375 Hudson St., New York, NY 10014.

CAREER: Writer. CoTangent Press, founder.

MEMBER: Center for Book Arts.

AWARDS, HONORS: Ella Lyman Cabot Trust fellowship grant, 1982; regent's fellow, University of California, Berkeley, 1982-83; Aid for Afghan Refugees grant-in-aid, 1983; Ludwig Vogelstein Award, 1987; corecipient of Maine Photographic Workshops grant, 1987; Whiting Writers' Award, 1988, for *You Bright and Risen Angels: A Cartoon;* Shiva Naipaul Memorial Prize, 1989, for an excerpt from *Seven Dreams: A Book of North American Landscapes*; nominated for National Book Critics Circle award for general nonfiction, 2003, for *Rising Up and Rising Down*; National Book Award for fiction, National Book Foundation, 2005, for *Europe Central.*

WRITINGS:

You Bright and Risen Angels: A Cartoon (novel), Atheneum (New York, NY), 1987.

The Rainbow Stories, Atheneum (New York, NY), 1989.

Seven Dreams: A Book of North American Landscapes (novels), Viking (New York, NY), Volume 1: *The Ice Shirt,* 1990, Volume 2: *Fathers and Crows,* 1992, Volume 6: *The Rifles,* 1994, Volume 3: *Argall: The True Story of Pocahontas and Captain John Smith,* 2001.

Whores for Gloria; or, Everything Was Beautiful until the Girls Got Anxious (documentary novel), Pantheon (New York, NY), 1991.

Thirteen Stories and Thirteen Epitaphs, Pantheon (New York, NY), 1991.

An Afghanistan Picture Show; or, How I Saved the World (memoir), Farrar, Straus (New York, NY), 1992.

Butterfly Stories: A Novel, Grove/Atlantic (New York, NY), 1993.

Open All Night, photographs by Ken Miller, Overlook Press, (Woodstock, NY), 1995.

The Atlas: People, Places, and Visions (stories), Viking (New York, NY), 1996.

The Royal Family (novel), Viking (New York, NY), 2000.

(Editor, with Michael Hemmingson and Larry McCaffery) *Expelled from Eden: A William T. Vollmann Reader,* Thunder's Mouth Press (New York, NY), 2003.

Rising Up and Rising Down (criticism), McSweeney's, 2003

Europe Central (short stories), Viking (New York, NY), 2005.

Uncentering the Earth: Copernicus and The Revolutions of the Heavenly Spheres, (nonfiction), Norton (New York, NY), 2006.

Contributor of text to *Ariel Ruiz i Altaba: Embryonic Landscapes,* Actar Editorial (Barcelona, Spain), 2003.

SIDELIGHTS: William T. Vollmann's body of work derives both from his experiences—such as participating in the Afghan-Soviet war and associating with prostitutes and drug abusers in San Francisco's Tenderloin district—and a literary imagination that has prompted some critics to compare him to the innovative American novelist Thomas Pynchon. His novels and short stories often have complicated plots and a variety of character types, and he frequently critiques past and present human behavior, offering his unusual interpretations of U.S. history in the series *Seven Dreams: A Book of North American Landscapes* and denouncing modern materialism and hypocrisy in works such as *The Royal Family.* "The oeuvre of Vollmann may be divided into two categories: his historical works and what might be best described as his 'extreme fiction,'" commented a contributor to *Contemporary Novelists,* who described the latter as "portraits of the marginalized" and "excursions into the sexual fringes of society." Indeed, Vollmann once told *CA* that he aims to produce "works that promote love and understanding for people whom others with my background may despise or fail to know."

Vollmann's first published novel, *You Bright and Risen Angels: A Cartoon,* examines the nature of political power struggles through the depiction of an inane war between insects and the inventors of electricity. At the beginning of the story the godlike narrator, referred to as "the author," creates each of the characters by means of a computer. The individuals are divided into ideological sects such as reactionaries and revolutionaries that, along with the insects, wage constant battles against one another in order to obtain dominion over all. The novel's vast number of characters and geographic locations drew criticism from *New York Times Book Review* contributor Gail Pool, who termed *You Bright and Risen Angels* "a large, sprawling, disorderly book . . . that operates on many levels and suggests many interpretations." Pool, however, concluded her review by praising the book's "ingenious creation of a universe whose bizarre characters and events illuminate our own."

Vollmann's second book, a collection of short narratives titled *The Rainbow Stories,* is a "domineering display of a rare talent," in the opinion of *Chicago Tribune* critic John Calvin Batchelor. Set mainly in the slums of San Francisco, the tales offer a candid and often disturbing insight into the lives of prostitutes, derelicts, and criminals. Each story's tone is to some extent determined by the color of the spectrum included in its title; the theme of death, for example, pervades "The Blue Yonder," an unsettling account of the death and autopsy of a bag lady. The stories abound with detailed description, and the narration is often in a journalistic style; Vollmann acknowledges in footnotes and in a section at the end of the book the information he obtained from people he met in San Francisco's Tenderloin neighborhood. *New York Times Book Review* contributor Caryn James called the book's authentic accounts "amazing in their power to attract and repel at once," but also thought Vollmann "merely hides behind the reporter's adherence to facts" and neglects to adequately develop his characters. James saw "touches of hard brilliance" in the work, however, and "huge ambition and talent" in its author. And Batchelor, in his review, praised *The Rainbow Stories* as "playful, wildly energetic low-life visions."

With *The Ice-Shirt,* the first volume of *Seven Dreams: A Book of North American Landscapes,* Vollmann begins what he terms a "symbolic history" of North America, as quoted by James Wood in the London *Times.* Drawing on a significant number of historical and mythological sources, listed at the end of the novel, Vollmann recounts the brief colonization of a portion of North America by Vikings, an event that is believed to have occurred long before Christopher Columbus's voyage to the West. The author's symbolic interpretation of the event asserts, in part, that winter was brought to the previously temperate environment of North America by the power-hungry Norse people who waged destructive wars against the natives before leaving a few years later. David Sacks, writing in the *New York Times Book Review,* observed, "without apparent strain, the story interweaves numerous characters, sea voyages, murders and supernatural horrors." Wood called *The Ice-Shirt* a "seriously adventurous modernist book" but complained, "it is impossible to recount the plot . . . because it is impossible to follow it." Although he also acknowledged some weaknesses in the novel with regard to plot, Sacks also remarked that "*The Ice-Shirt* impresses mightily in its scope, its scene-painting and its enciphered social message."

Fathers and Crows, the second volume in Vollmann's metahistorical "Seven Dreams" series, is an epic hybrid of history and fiction that recounts the missionary endeavors of French Jesuit priests in seventeenth-century Canada. Set some 500 years after the conclusion of *The Ice-Shirt,* the story finds Vollmann assuming the fictional identity of William the Blind to re-create the complex and brutal conflict between the French and native peoples, supported by numerous historical sources, maps, chronologies, and glossaries. In an interview with *Publishers Weekly,* Vollmann commented on *Fathers and Crows:* "In many ways I think this book is comparable to *War and Peace.* I'd like to see these books taught in history classes." In the *Los Angeles Times Book Review,* David Ulin wrote that " *Fathers and Crows* is a difficult book, minutely detailed and densely written, flowing lush and heavy . . . . But it is a . . . work of such elegant structure and uncompromising intelligence that it will change the way you think about the opening of the New World—indeed, the way you think about all of history, and what it means." Citing Vollmann's obvious sympathy with the Native Americans, Steven Moore observed in a *Washington Post Book World* review that " *Fathers and Crows* is neither a romantic evocation of the Noble Savage nor a politically correct idealization. The Native Americans could be as racist, sexist, and brutal as any European imperialist." Madison Smartt Bell, critiquing for the *Chicago Tribune,* commended Vollmann's effective juxtaposition of time in the novel and balanced treatment of the vastly complicated series of relationships. Related Bell: "Dozens of individual stories unfold in this book, and Vollmann has blended them so skillfully into his Stream of Time that the great flood of history itself is imbued with a human poignancy."

The Rifles, another installment in the "Seven Dreams" series (although the third to be published, it is numbered volume six, to reflect its place in the chronological order of the stories), centers on the tragic adventures of the British explorer Sir John Franklin, who perished on a naval expedition to discover a Northwest passage in the Canadian Arctic. Franklin's mid-nineteenth- century exploits are mirrored in a parallel plot involving a modern-day affair between a Native American woman and an American novelist who bears a resemblance to Vollmann, though he claims to be the reincarnation of John Franklin. As in previous volumes of the series, Vollmann draws heavily on historical sources to reinterpret the European domination of North America. In a *Time* review of *The Rifles,* John Skow summarized the recurring preoccupation of the *Seven Dreams* series: "Corruption of native inhabitants by Europeans is the broad theme of this enormously ambitious project." He added that Vollmann conjures "a vision of absolute evil: civilization, native cultures not excepted, is a pestilence, and mankind is a monstrous curse laid upon nature." Vollmann's proclivity for elaborate historical commentary and narrative digression received some criticism. For instance, *New York Times Book Review* commentator James McManus remarked that *The Rifles* "often has the feel of unrevised field notes hastily shuffled with printed source material—as though the moral urgency of the subject precluded much fuss about narrative integrity."

In *Whores for Gloria; or, Everything Was Beautiful until the Girls Got Anxious,* Vollmann returns to the locale of *The Rainbow Stories* to recount the hardships of Jimmy, an alcoholic Vietnam veteran who wanders among the derelicts of San Francisco's Tenderloin in search of a beloved prostitute named Gloria. Unable to locate the elusive or illusory Gloria, Jimmy reconstructs her through conversation with other prostitutes. In the *Voice Literary Supplement,* Eli Gottlieb observed that "Vollmann deftly strews the path of his narrative with vignettes, offering us sharp vérité glances into the lives of the half- dozen hookers, bums, and pimps who cross Jimmy's path." Gottlieb added: "The time [Vollmann] doubtless spent among his subjects, and the intricate sympathy he established with them as a result, are an essential part of his achievement." According to a *Kirkus Reviews* commentator, "Vollmann's fierce writing seems often more designed to shock than to elucidate, but poor Jimmy does have some credibility, even if at times strained." The novel includes a glossary of slang.

Thirteen Stories and Thirteen Epitaphs chronicles a series of fictitious travels in the United States and abroad. *New York Times Book Review* critic Catherine Bush remarked that the collection "can be read as a feverish contemporary travelogue—and as a tour of Mr. Vollmann's brain." She related, "It's a frontline bulletin from the world of those whom . . . Pico Iyer has called 'the Transit Loungers,' the new rootless wanderers who speed through cities and continents as if through revolving doors, torn between global familiarity and the loss of home." Jumping from San Francisco to Afghanistan, Thailand, Guatemala, the American Southwest, and an allegorical New York called Gun City, Vollmann portrays idiosyncratic extremity and depravity through the experiences of prostitutes, junkies, hobos, skinheads, and other marginalized people. In the *Times Literary Supplement,* Mary Hawthorne commented that "the fragmentary, sometimes chaotic nature of most of these stories, however—their illogic, their clutter of styles and digressions—renders them, like life, like dreams, elusive in the end." *New Republic* reviewer Sven Birkerts offered the opinion that "reading Vollmann's stories, we feel that the lower depths may be stranger and more disturbingly various than we had allowed."

Real-life travels form the basis of *An Afghanistan Picture Show; or, How I Saved the World,* which recounts Vollmann's post- college excursion to aid the Afghan guerrillas against Soviet invaders in the early 1980s. At age twenty-two, driven by a youthful and naive humanitarian desire to support the cause of freedom against oppression, Vollmann spent several months in Afghanistan, interviewing refugees and recording their experiences. However, Vollmann's weakened physical health and inexperience with weapons rendered him ineffective when finally summoned to accompany the guerrillas on a raid. As Annette Kobak related in the *New York Times Book Review,* Vollmann "tells us . . . that he wanted to be the man personally to give the guerrillas both nickels and shells: he would take photographs to exhibit back home to raise cash for the cause (the literal meaning of his 'Picture Show'); and he would go into Afghanistan with the mujahedeen and sock the Soviets." In the *Washington Post Book World,* Steven Moore commented that "the book succeeds not only in achieving its original goal—to bring attention to the plight of Afghan refugees . . . but also in dramatizing the limitations of altruism and activism, the difficulty of understanding the context of any culture other than your own." *Los Angeles Times Book Review* contributor William McGowan remarked that "despite its unevenness and unexplained assumptions, however, *An Afghanistan Picture Show* is a bold and original accomplishment, hardly the 'Failed Pilgrim's Progress' that Vollmann dejectedly calls it . . . . [In] his honest accounts of [the Afghanis'] plight, and his morally and emotionally complicated reactions to it, Vollmann . . . has written a powerful, searching addition to the literature of personal witness."

In *Butterfly Stories,* Vollmann chronicles the peregrinations of an unnamed narrator, variously referred to as "the butterfly boy," "the journalist," and "the husband," who survives schoolyard bullying to travel about North America, Europe, and Asia in search of love. Vollmann describes extensive indulgence in Far Eastern brothels; the protagonist eventually contracts AIDS, then falls in love with a Cambodian prostitute. A critic for the *Review of Contemporary Fiction* described the protagonist's journey thus: "The narrator flits like a butterfly: not a symbol of lighthearted caprice but of ceaseless wandering and searching . . . . The narrator's lack of shame and pride is almost ascetic in its self- abnegation, giving him a pure quality despite his incessant whoring." In a *New York Times Magazine* review, Madison Smartt Bell termed the work a "parable of suicide through sexual intercourse; the purpose of the act is to unite the journalist with his dead prostitute lover, but the story is still terrifying to read." *Hudson Review* commentator Gary Krist disliked what he saw as Vollmann's sensationalism and "artificial compassion." "In Vollmann's eyes," Krist wrote, "the world is teeming with prostitutes and consumers of prostitution, buying and selling, degrading and being degraded . . . as they look for a satisfaction they'll never find."

The Atlas: People, Places, and Visions, more overtly autobiographical than Vollmann's other volumes of short stories, relates his far-flung travels in the United

States, Canada, India, and Europe, including experiences in war-ravaged Bosnia. A *Publishers Weekly* reviewer observed that "although Vollmann's style is to play it coy with respect to what is fact and what is fiction, there is no mystery as to who is doing the talking here." As in many of his other writings, the central characters are prostitutes and various social misfits connected by their existential loneliness. Vollmann's assemblage of sketches and vignettes takes the form of a palindrome, with twenty-six numbered pieces followed by another twenty-six reverse numbered pieces, complemented by a prologue, title piece, and epilogue. Describing the book as somewhat fragmented and redundant, a *Library Journal* reviewer noted that Vollmann's essays vacillate between "stark reportage" and surreal depiction of "violence, lust, greed, and alienation."

Vollmann deals again with prostitutes, drug addicts, and others on society's fringes in *The Royal Family.* The primary characters are the Tyler brothers, both San Francisco residents but otherwise deeply different: John is a prosperous lawyer with a lavish lifestyle, while Henry is a private detective intimately familiar with the marginal world of the Tenderloin. While John carries on an affair with a yuppie-type woman named Celia, Henry falls in love with John's wife, Irene. After Irene commits suicide, Henry buries himself in his latest case, tracking down the so-called queen of the prostitutes for an outwardly respectable but genuinely shady client named Brady. Henry begins to suspect Brady's motives, and Brady then dismisses him, but Henry still pursues the Queen, finds her, and enters into a sexual relationship with her. Vollmann portrays most of the prostitutes and other Tenderloin denizens as being more honest and ethical than the people of the mainstream, bourgeois world, such as John, Celia, and Brady, the last who turns out to have plans for an ostensibly "virtual" sex club that actually will exploit, abuse, and even kill real women.

"Vollmann avoids simply glamorizing the outcasts but remains, deep down, a Blakean romantic; prostitution is for him not only the universal indictment of the human race but also, paradoxically, the only paradise we can actually visit," remarked a *Publishers Weekly* reviewer. Lee Siegel, writing in the *New Republic,* commented that Vollmann "wishes to show . . . that candor about the basest aspects of life removes the slur of baseness from them, and that the lack of candor about basic human desires lies at the core of the commercialism that is killing us." Siegel also noted that "in *The Royal Family,* a forbidden experience is always made to resemble a respectable experience, so that the former might teach the latter a lesson; the 'deviant' is always superior to the 'normal.'" Siegel found the novel's themes less than compelling, saying Vollmann "seems to assert the authenticity of debasement, yet the woman who administers degradation to [Henry] Tyler—the Queen—is a fine and generous person who possesses the middle-class qualities of decency and familial instinct that Vollmann seems to detest." *Review of Contemporary Fiction* critic Trey Strecker, however, deemed the novel "ambitious and powerful," although "slightly uneven," and praised its "brilliant set pieces" and "angry depiction of the wasted, commercialized American landscape." And while *Library Journal* contributor Edward B. St. John thought *The Royal Family* would be "highly offensive" to some readers, he granted that "others will be won over by the author's passion."

Vollmann returned to his "Seven Dreams" series with *Argall: The True Story of Pocahontas and Captain John Smith,* numbered volume three, for its place in the chronology, although published fourth. In his version of this story of the Jamestown colony in Virginia, a story that has often been sentimentalized and distorted, Vollmann devotes one portion of the book largely to the ambitious yet naive Smith, who becomes colonial governor, and the other to Pocahontas, the Indian princess who thwarts a plan to execute him. Pocahontas, though, goes on to lose her culture, as she is forced to adopt English ways after being abducted by Captain Argall, who succeeds Smith as governor and also introduces slavery to the colonies. The novel is "a heady, complex, linguistically dense and savagely cynical version of a story familiar in outline if not in detail," related William Tipper in the *Washington Post Book World.* As in *Fathers and Crows,* the narrator is William the Blind, who uses a highly idiosyncratic form of Elizabethan English, which "frequently teeters on the brink of absurdity," in the opinion of Chicago *Tribune Books* reviewer Adam Kirsch. But Donna Seaman commented in *Booklist* that Vollmann nevertheless manages to produce "playful but lancing prose." She added that his depictions of Smith, Pocahontas, and her father, Powhatan, are "fresh, ribald, and sympathetic," while Captain Argall is "pure evil." A *Publishers Weekly* critic found the portrayal of Pocahontas particularly "respectful and moving, much different from the author's usual mannered sexual outrageousness," although Seaman noted that "compelling women characters" have been a hallmark of the *Seven Dreams* series. Kirsch deemed the characters lacking, saying, "none of them . . . has a genuine interior life," but allowed that the book has virtues, in that Vollmann "strikes a good balance between history and symbol, fact and interpretation." Edward B. St. John, again reviewing for *Library Journal,* pronounced the novel "arguably the best installment in this magnificent series," while Seaman called it "the work of genius."

Since the publication of *Argall,* Vollmann has edited, with Michael Hemmingson and Larry McCaffery, a collection of his own work titled *Expelled from Eden: A William T. Vollmann Reader.* In addition to this volume, he has authored *Rising Up and Rising Down,* a social critique on human violence; *Europe Central,* a collection of short stories that won the National Book Award; and *Uncentering the Earth: Copernicus and The Revolutions of the Heavenly Spheres.* The latter volume is an examination of sixteenth-century astronomer Nicolaus Copernicus and his groundbreaking book *The Revolutions of the Heavenly Spheres.* It was one of the first publications to state that the sun, not the earth (as was commonly believed at the time), is located at the center of our solar system. Vollmann's *Uncentering the Earth* analyzes Copernicus's calculations and concludes that although they were faulty, the theories they posited were correct. *Booklist* critic Seaman noted that "Vollmann writes with vigor and poetic insight," and while a *Kirkus Reviews* contributor stated that the book "is not for the scientifically fainthearted," they also observed that it is "peppered with intrigue and conflict and even a little human interest."

BIOGRAPHICAL AND CRITICAL SOURCES:

BOOKS

Contemporary Literary Criticism, Volume 89, Gale (Detroit, MI), 1996.

Contemporary Novelists, 7th edition, St. James Press (Detroit, MI), 2001.

Contemporary Popular Writers, St. James Press (Detroit, MI), 1997.

PERIODICALS

Book, July/August 2000, Tom LeClair, review of *The Royal Family,* pp. 69- 70.

Booklist, March 15, 1993, p. 1299; January 1, 1994, p. 808; February 1, 1996, p. 899; August, 2001, Donna Seaman, review of *Argall: The True Story of Pocahontas and Captain John Smith,* p. 2053; October 15, 2004, Donna Seaman, review of *Rising Up and Rising Down,* p. 369; February 1, 2005, Donna Seaman, review of *Expelled from Eden: A William T. Vollmann Reader,* p. 931; January 1, 2006, Donna Seaman, review of *Uncentering the Earth: Copernicus and The Revolutions of the Heavenly Spheres,* p. 40.

Chicago Tribune, July 26, 1992, p. 3; September 30, 2001, Adam Kirsch, review of *Argall,* p. 2.

Entertainment Weekly, March 29, 1996, p. 59.

Hudson Review, summer, 1994, pp. 299-305.

Kirkus Reviews, November 15, 1991; March 1, 1993; September 1, 1993; December 15, 2005, review of *Uncentering the Earth,* p. 1315.

Library Journal, March 1, 1996, p. 95; July, 2000, Edward B. St. John, review of *The Royal Family,* p. 144; September 1, 2001, St. John, review of *Argall,* p. 236; January 1, 2006, Sarah Rutter, review of *Uncentering the Earth,* p. 150.

Los Angeles Times Book Review, July 19, 1992, p. 3; August 23, 1992, p. 2.

Nation, March 21, 1994, p. 384; May 6, 1996, pp. 72, 74-75.

New Republic, April 11, 1994, p. 40; January 22, 2001, Lee Siegel, "Rock Bottom," p. 38.

New York, September 11, 1995, p. 86; April 8, 1996, p. 58.

New York Review of Books, December 15, 2005, Michael Wood, review of *Expelled from Eden,* p. 64.

New York Times Book Review, April 21, 1987, p. 10; August 13, 1989, p. 6; October 14, 1990, p. 13; July 26, 1992, p. 10; September 6, 1992, p. 14; February 27, 1994, p. 6; October 23, 1994, p. 12; September 30, 2001, Jay Parini, review of *Argall,* p. 18.

New York Times Magazine, February 6, 1994, p. 18.

Publishers Weekly, May 18, 1992, pp. 51-52; July 13, 1992, p. 36-37; December 1993, review of *The Rifles,* p. 57; January 15, 1996, p. 441; June 5, 2000, review of *The Royal Family,* p. 69; September 3, 2001, review of *Argall,* p. TK; September 22, 2003, review of *Rising Up and Rising Down,* p. 98; February 7, 2005, review of *Europe Central,* p. 38.

Review of Contemporary Fiction, spring, 1994, pp. 212-213; fall, 2000, Trey Strecker, review of *The Royal Family,* p. 139.

Time, March 28, 1994, p. 68.

Times (London, England), May 31, 1990.

Times Literary Supplement, November 29, 1991.

Tribune Books (Chicago, IL), June 25, 1989; November 4, 1990, p. 5; September 30, 2001, Adam Kirsch, "American Promise Fulfilled and Betrayed: Historical Novel a Revisionist Look at the Legend of Pocahontas," p. 2.

Voice Literary Supplement, February 1992, p. 6.

Washington Post Book World, August 2, 1992, p. 1; February 13, 1994, p. 11; October 14, 2001, William Tipper, "On Native Ground," p. 7.

Yale Review, April 1994, p. 152.

ONLINE

ALTX, http://www.altx.com/ (January 6, 2002), "The Write Stuff" (interview).

Salon.com, http://www.salon.com/ (January 6, 2002), Cary Tennis, "Red-Light Fever."

* * *

VONNEGUT, Kurt, Jr. 1922-

PERSONAL: Born November 11, 1922, in Indianapolis, IN; son of Kurt (an architect) and Edith Sophia (Lieber) Vonnegut; married Jane Marie Cox, September 1, 1945 (divorced, 1979); married Jill Krementz (a photographer), November, 1979; children: (first marriage) Mark, Edith, Nanette; (adopted deceased sister's children) James, Steven, and Kurt Adams; (second marriage) Lili (adopted). *Education:* Attended Cornell University, 1940-42, and Carnegie Institute of Technology (now Carnegie-Mellon University), 1943; attended University of Chicago, 1945-47, M.A., 1971. *Hobbies and other interests:* Painting, wood carving, welded sculpture.

ADDRESSES: Home—Northampton, MA. *Agent*—Donald C. Farber, Esq., 460 Park Ave., 11th Floor, New York, NY 10022-1987.

CAREER: Cornell Daily Sun, Ithaca, NY, editor, 1941-42; Chicago City News Bureau, Chicago, IL, police reporter, 1947; General Electric Co., Schenectady, NY, employed in public relations, 1947-50; freelance writer, 1950—. Teacher at Hopefield School, Sandwich, MA, beginning 1965; lecturer at University of Iowa Writers Workshop, 1965-67, and at Harvard University, 1970-71; Distinguished Professor of English Prose, City College of the City University of New York, 1973-74; faculty member at Smith College, 2001—. Speaker, National Coalition against Censorship, 1986. Appeared in cameo film roles in *Back to School,* Orion, 1986, *Mother Night,* Fine Line, 1996, and *Breakfast of Champions,* Buena Vista, 1999. *Military service:* U.S. Army, Infantry, 1942-45; was POW; received Purple Heart.

MEMBER: Authors League of America, PEN (American Center; vice president, 1974—), National Institute of Arts and Letters, Delta Upsilon, Barnstable Yacht Club, Barnstable Comedy Club.

AWARDS, HONORS: Guggenheim fellow, 1967; National Institute of Arts and Letters grant, 1970; Litt.D., Hobart and William Smith Colleges, 1974; Literary Lion award, New York Public Library, 1981; Eugene V. Debs Award, Eugene V. Debs Foundation, 1981, for public service; Emmy Award for Outstanding Children's Program, National Academy of Television Arts and Sciences, 1985, for *Displaced Person;* Bronze Medallion, Guild Hall, 1986; named New York's State Author by the New York State Writers' Institute, 2001.

WRITINGS:

NOVELS

Player Piano, Scribner (New York, NY), 1952, published as *Utopia 14,* Bantam (New York, NY), 1954, published under original title with new preface, Holt (New York, NY), 1966.

The Sirens of Titan, Dell (New York, NY), 1959.

Mother Night, Gold Medal Books (New York, NY), 1961.

Cat's Cradle (also see below), Holt (New York, NY), 1963.

God Bless You, Mr. Rosewater; or, Pearls before Swine (also see below), Holt (New York, NY), 1965.

Slaughterhouse Five; or, The Children's Crusade: A Duty-Dance with Death, by Kurt Vonnegut Jr., a Fourth-Generation German-American Now Living in Easy Circumstances on Cape Cod (and Smoking Too Much) Who, as an American Infantry Scout Hors de Combat, as a Prisoner of War, Witnessed the Fire-bombing of Dresden, Germany, the Florence of the Elbe, a Long Time Ago, and Survived to Tell the Tale: This Is a Novel Somewhat in the Telegraphic Schizophrenic Manner of Tales of the Planet Tralfamadore, Where the Flying Saucers Come From, Seymour Lawrence/Delacorte (New York, NY), 1969, twenty-fifth anniversary edition, 1994.

Breakfast of Champions; or, Goodbye Blue Monday (also see below), Seymour Lawrence/Delacorte (New York, NY), 1973.

Slapstick; or, Lonesome No More, Seymour Lawrence/Delacorte (New York, NY), 1976.

Jailbird, Seymour Lawrence/Delacorte (New York, NY), 1979.

Deadeye Dick, Seymour Lawrence/Delacorte (New York, NY), 1982.

Galapagos, Seymour Lawrence/Delacorte (New York, NY), 1985.

Bluebeard, Delacorte (New York, NY), 1987.

Hocus Pocus, Putnam (New York, NY), 1990.

Three Complete Novels (contains *Breakfast of Champions,God Bless You, Mr. Rosewater,* and *Cat's Cradle*), Wings (New York, NY), 1995.

Timequake, Putnam (New York, NY), 1997.

SHORT FICTION

Canary in a Cathouse, Fawcett (New York, NY), 1961.
Welcome to the Monkey House: A Collection of Short Works, Seymour Lawrence/Delacorte (New York, NY), 1968.
Bagombo Snuff Box, Putnam (New York, NY), 1999.
God Bless You, Dr. Kevorkian, Seven Stories (New York, NY), 1999.

PLAYS

Penelope (produced on Cape Cod, MA, 1960), revised version published as *Happy Birthday, Wanda June* (produced off-Broadway, 1970; also see below), Seymour Lawrence/Delacorte (New York, NY), 1971, revised edition, Samuel French (New York, NY), 1971.
Happy Birthday, Wanda June (screenplay; based on Vonnegut's play), Columbia, 1971.
Between Time and Timbuktu; or, Prometheus Five: A Space Fantasy (television play; produced on National Educational Television Network, 1972), Seymour Lawrence/Delacorte (New York, NY), 1972.
Miss Temptation, edited by David Coperman, Dramatic Publishing Company (Woodstock, IL), 1993.

Also author of *Something Borrowed,* 1958; *The Very First Christmas Morning,* 1962; *EPICAC,* 1963; *My Name Is Everyone,* 1964; and *Fortitude,* 1968.

OTHER

Wampeters, Foma, and Grandfalloons (Opinions) (essays), Seymour Lawrence/Delacorte (New York, NY), 1974.
(With Ivan Chermayeff) *Sun, Moon, Star* (juvenile), Harper (New York, NY), 1980.
Palm Sunday: An Autobiographical Collage, Seymour Lawrence/Delacorte (New York, NY), 1981.
Nothing Is Lost Save Honor: Two Essays (contains "The Worst Addiction of Them All" and "Fates Worse than Death: Lecture at St. John the Divine, New York City, May 23, 1982"), Toothpaste Press (West Branch, IA), 1984.
Fates Worse than Death: An Autobiographical Collage of the 1980s (autobiography), Putnam (New York, NY), 1991.
(Author of foreword) Leeds, Marc, *The Vonnegut Encyclopedia: An Authorized Compendium,* Greenwood Press (Westport, CT), 1995.

Contributor to books, including *Bob and Ray: A Retrospective, June 15-July 10, 1982,* Museum of Broadcasting (New York, NY), 1982; W.E. Block, and M.A. Walker, editors, *Discrimination, Affirmative Action, and Equal Opportunity: An Economic and Social Perspective,* Fraser Institute (Vancouver, British Columbia, Canada), 1982; *Like Shaking Hands with God: A Conversation about Writing* (with Lee Stringer), Seven Stories Press (New York, NY), 1999; and *Modern Fiction and Art,* University of Kentucky Art Museum (Lexington, KT), 1999. Contributor of fiction to numerous publications, including *Cornell Daily Sun, Cosmopolitan, Ladies' Home Journal, McCall's, Playboy,* and *Saturday Evening Post.*

ADAPTATIONS: Slaughterhouse Five was adapted for film by Stephen Geller, Universal, 1972; "Who Am I This Time" (short story) was adapted for film, Rubicon Films, 1982; *God Bless You, Mr. Rosewater* was adapted for the stage by Howard Ashman and produced by Vonnegut's daughter, Edith, 1979; *Slapstick* was adapted for film as *Slapstick of Another Kind,* Paul-Serendipity, 1984; "D. P." (short story) was adapted for television as *Displaced Person,* Hemisphere, 1985; *Mother Night* was adapted for film by Robert B. Weide, Fine Line, 1996; *Breakfast of Champions* was adapted for film by director Alan Rudolph, Buena Vista, 1999. Several of Vonnegut's novels have been adapted as audio books.

SIDELIGHTS: Lauded as one of the most respected American novelists of the twentieth century, Kurt Vonnegut was virtually ignored by critics at the beginning of his writing career. In *Literary Disruptions: The Making of a Post-Contemporary Fiction,* Jerome Klinkowitz observed that "Vonnegut's rise to eminence coincides precisely with the shift in taste which brought a whole new reading public—and eventually critical appreciation—to the works of Richard Brautigan, Donald Barthelme, Jerzy Kosinski, and others. Ten years and several books their elder, Vonnegut . . . was well prepared to be the senior member of the new disruptive group, and the first of its numbers to be seriously considered for the Nobel Prize. By 1973, when *Breakfast of Champions* appeared, . . . there was little doubt that a fiction widely scorned only six years before was now a dominant mode in serious contemporary literature."

While such early works as *Player Piano* and *The Sirens of Titan* were at first categorized as science fiction, Vonnegut's books go far beyond the realm of most pure SF. As Ernest W. Ranly explained in *Commonweal:* "Vonnegut at times adds fantasy to his stories, whereas pure sci-fi permits only what is possible within a given scientific hypothesis. Vonnegut adds humor, a wild black humor, while most sci-fi is serious to the point of boredom. Vonnegut, generally, adds a distinctive sense and literary class. And, finally, Vonnegut seems pre-occupied with genuine human questions, about war, peace, technology, human happiness. He is even bitterly anti-machine, anti-technology, anti-science."

Mother Night, Vonnegut's third novel, is the story of an American playwright living in Germany at the outbreak of World War II who is persuaded by the Allies to remain in Germany as a spy while posing as a radio propagandist. After the war he fades into obscurity in the United States until, with his wartime cover still intact, he is kidnaped by Israeli agents to stand trial for his crime. Michael Wood remarked in *New York Review of Books,* "What is impressive about *Mother Night* is its extraordinary tone which allows Vonnegut to be very funny without being crass or unfeeling." *Mother Night,* the critic added, "is not an attempt to defeat an enemy by ridicule, but an attempt to contemplate horror by means of laughter, because laughter, of all our inappropriate responses to total, terminal horror, seems the least inappropriate, the least inhuman."

Mother Night is Vonnegut's first novel to employ a first-person narration, and is also the first in which technology and the future play no significant part. For this reason it is seen by many as a transitional novel between the author's early and more mature work. Perhaps most obvious, in comparison with Vonnegut's first two novels, *Mother Night* relies very little on time shifts, resulting in a more unified or "conventional" book. In his *Kurt Vonnegut Jr.,* Peter J. Reed described it as "Vonnegut's most traditional novel in form. Paradoxically, perhaps, that also accounts for the relative weaknesses of the book. For *Mother Night* lacks some of the excitement and verve of *The Sirens of Titan,* for example, and it is sometimes less likely to carry its reader along than that earlier, more wandering fantasy."

In 1963's *Cat's Cradle,* Vonnegut penned his most autobiographical work up to that point. The Hoenikker family of the novel closely parallels Vonnegut's own family, consisting of an elder son who is a scientist, a tall middle daughter, and a younger son who joins Delta Upsilon. The narrator is again a writer who, in this case, is working on a book called *The Day the World Ended,* about the bombing of Hiroshima. For decades after its publication *Cat's Cradle* consistently appeared on high school and college reading lists; Reed said that it might be the most widely read of Vonnegut's novels among young people. He explained that "to 'the counter-culture' it should appeal as a book which counters almost every aspect of the culture of our society. To a generation which delights in the 'put on,' parody and artifice, often as the most meaningful expressions of deeply held convictions in a world which they see as prone to distortion, *Cat's Cradle*'s play with language, symbol and artifice should find accord."

God Bless You, Mr. Rosewater; or, Pearls before Swine introduces a theme that crops up repeatedly in the later novels and which is often considered to be the essence of all of Vonnegut's writing. It is expressed by the main character, Eliot Rosewater, in the motto "Goddamn it, you've got to be kind." John R. May commented in a *Twentieth-Century Literature* review that it is the author's "most positive and humane work. . . . We may not be able, Vonnegut is saying, to undo the harm that has been done, but we can certainly love, simply because there are people, those who have been made useless by our past stupidity and greed, our previous crimes against our brothers. And if that seems insane, then the better the world for such folly." *Book Week* contributor Daniel Talbot wrote: "It's a tribute to Kurt Vonnegut Jr. that he has covered such a large territory of human follies in so short a book. . . . The net effect is at once explosively funny and agonizing."

In *Slaughterhouse Five; or, the Children's Crusade* Vonnegut delivers a complete treatise on the World War II bombing of Dresden. The main character, Billy Pilgrim, is a young infantry scout who is captured during the Battle of the Bulge and quartered in a Dresden slaughterhouse, where he and other prisoners are employed in the production of a vitamin supplement for pregnant women. During the February 13, 1945, firebombing by Allied aircraft, these prisoners take shelter in an underground meat locker. When they emerge, the city has been leveled and they are forced to dig corpses out of the rubble. The story of Billy Pilgrim is the story of Vonnegut, who was captured and survived the firestorm in which 135,000 German civilians perished—more than the number of deaths in the bombings of Hiroshima and Nagasaki combined. Robert Scholes summed up the theme of *Slaughterhouse Five* in *New York Times Book Review,* writing: "Be kind. Don't hurt. Death is coming for all of us anyway, and it is better to be Lot's wife looking back through salty eyes than the Deity that destroyed those cities of the plain in order to save them." The reviewer concluded that "*Slaughterhouse Five* is an extraordinary success. It is a book we need to read, and to reread."

The enduring popularity of *Slaughterhouse Five* is due, in part, to its timeliness; it deals with issues that have remained vital to Americans who came of age in the late 1960s: war, ecology, overpopulation, and consumerism. Klinkowitz, writing in *Literary Subversions: New American Fiction and the Practice of Criticism,* saw larger reasons for the book's success, noting that "Vonnegut was able to write and publish a novel, *Slaughterhouse Five,* which so perfectly caught America's transformative mood that its story and structure became best-selling metaphors for the new age."

After the publication of *Slaughterhouse Five* Vonnegut entered a period of depression during which he vowed, at one point, never to write another novel. He concentrated, instead, on lecturing, teaching, and finishing a play, *Happy Birthday, Wanda June,* that he had begun several years earlier. The play, which ran Off-Broadway from October, 1970 to March, 1971, received mixed reviews. *Newsweek*'s Jack Kroll wrote that "almost every time an American novelist writes a play he shows up most of our thumb-tongued playwrights, who lack the melody of mind, the wit, dash and accuracy of Saul Bellow and Bruce Jay Friedman. And the same thing must be said of the writing in *Happy Birthday, Wanda June* . . . Vonnegut's dialogue is not only fast and funny, with a palpable taste and crackle, but it also means something. And his comic sense is a superior one; *Wanda June* has as many laughs as anything by Neil Simon." On the other hand, in *New Republic* Stanley Kauffmann called the play "a disaster, full of callow wit, rheumatic invention, and dormitory profundity. . . . The height of its imagination is exemplified by a scene in Heaven between a golden-haired little girl and a Nazi Gauleiter in which they discuss the way Jesus plays shuffleboard." Despite some negative reviews, *Happy Birthday, Wanda June* was adapted as a feature film in 1971, with the screenplay by Vonnegut.

Breakfast of Champions marked the end of Vonnegut's depression and his return to the novel form; in honor of this event, he subtitles his work *Goodbye Blue Monday.* In *Breakfast of Champions,* as in most of Vonnegut's writing, there are very clear autobiographical tendencies. In this novel, however, the author seems to be even more wrapped up in his characters than usual. He appears as Philboyd Sludge, the author of a book which focuses on Dwayne Hoover, a Pontiac dealer (Vonnegut once ran a Saab dealership) who goes berserk after reading a novel by Kilgore Trout, who also represents Vonnegut. Toward the end of the book, Vonnegut arranges a meeting between himself and Trout, in which he cuts the character loose forever; by this time the previously unsuccessful Trout has become rich and famous and is finally able to stand on his own.

Catastrophe comes easily in 1982's *Deadeye Dick.* The title character's father saves the life of a starving artist, the young Adolph Hitler, when the two are in school together; the narrator, Rudy Waltz, gains his cruel nickname at age twelve when a shot he fires from his father's rifle accidentally kills a pregnant woman; and later, a neutron bomb detonates, either by accident, or by the government's covert design, in Waltz's home town, killing everyone, but leaving the machines and buildings unharmed. Interspersed with these horrors are recipes, provided by Rudy, who has gone on to become a chef and copartner with his brother in a restaurant in Haiti. Writing in *New York Times Book Review,* Benjamin De Mott noted that throughout "the grand old Vonnegutian comedy of causelessness still holds center stage. . . . Why does the child of a gun safety specialist, using a rifle from his father's collection, emerge as a double murderer? A tough question. Why do human beings take satisfaction in creating a neutron bomb that destroys 'only' human beings, not their accouterments? Another toughie. Why should grief-struck Rudy Waltz, headed for a presumably moving moment at his parents' graveside, allow his train of thought to light on a certain cookie, whereupon . . . instead of grief we're provided with a recipe for almond macaroons?"

If catastrophe comes more easily to man than courtesy and decency, man's large brain is to blame, Vonnegut asserts in his next novel. *Galapagos* "brings Vonnegut's lifelong belief in the imperfectibility of human nature to its logical conclusion," observed a London *Times* reviewer. The novel recounts the evolution of man over thousands of years. Narrated by the spectral remains of Vietnam vet Leon Trout, *Galapagos* follows the experiences of a group of tourists who are shipwrecked in the islands where nineteenth-century evolutionary biologist Charles Darwin formulated the notion of progressive adaptation; over time, their oversized brains diminish, sexual interests atrophy, and their hands become flippers, all to the benefit of the race and the ecosystem. "This will eliminate war, starvation, and nuclear terror—that is, many of the things Mr. Vonnegut likes to complain about in his novels," remarked *New York Times* reviewer Michiko Kakutani. But for all the seriousness of its message, the book contains sufficient humor to make it satisfying as "a well-crafted comic strip," Kakutani added.

Although it takes place in the near future, the text of 1990's *Hocus Pocus,* like many Vonnegut novels, ranges freely through the much of the twentieth century. As Vonnegut's protagonist Eugene Debs Hartke describes it, America in 2001 is "a thoroughly looted bankrupt nation whose assets had been sold off to foreigners, a nation swamped by unchecked plagues and superstition and illiteracy and hypnotic TV." Like the central characters in *Mother Night* and *Slaughterhouse-Five,* Hartke is a man incarcerated. His story ranges from West Point to Vietnam—he is the last American soldier to leave—from his job as physics instructor at a college for dyslexics—he is dismissed for his pessimism—to his job at a prison run for profit by the Japanese. Hartke is unjustly accused of masterminding a prison break and ends up in jail himself. Along the way some familiar Vonnegut standbys—the Tralfamadorians from *Sirens of Titan,* and the SF writer Kilgore Trout from *Breakfast of Champions*—turn up, and as in other novels, Vonnegut freely peppers the text with quotes from Bartlett's *Familiar Quotations.*

The novel *Timequake* appeared in 1997, though Vonnegut had completed it several years earlier. Having decided the newly completed novel was in fact "pointless," its author went back to the drawing board and reworked its best parts into a digressive stew, which he then declared as his final literary utterance. The germ of a plot remains: At the turn of the millennium, the world falls victim to a wrinkle in space-time that forces everyone on earth to relive the 1990s. This provides a jumping-off point for Vonnegut's ruminations about moral decay, mortality, and the state of Western culture at the close of the twentieth century. A few familiar devices do remain, such as the presence of Kilgore Trout and the employment of a Zen-like repetitive phrase. "Hi ho" and "So it goes" had been refrains in earlier novels; this time the refrain is "tingaling."

Reviews have split their verdict on *Timequake*'s significance, though few reserved comment on Vonnegut's claim that he was washed up. R.Z. Sheppard in a *Time* review derided Vonnegut for "seeking sympathy" from book reviewers by announcing *Timequake* as his final novel. "Having a novelist's free hand to write what you will does not mean you are entitled to a free ride," Sheppard observed, going on to express his annoyance at the novel's lack of story and Vonnegut's "familiar tone of weary bemusement." In *Newsweek,* Brad Stone called the author "notoriously skilled in this business of lowering reader expectations," but then went on to praise the novel lavishly. *Timequake,* Stone wrote, is Vonnegut's "funniest book since *Breakfast of Champions.*"

In 1999 a collection of Vonnegut's short fiction was released under the title *Bagombo Snuff Box.* The book contains twenty-three stories penned during the 1950s and 1960s and published in *Colliers* and *Saturday Evening Post.* A critic for *Publishers Weekly* wrote that the stories "will be of most interest to completists and scholars" since the finer of his stories from that period had already been published in the 1968 collection *Welcome to the Monkey House.* Early in 2000, another collection was released, *God Bless You, Dr. Kevorkian,* which is composed of rewritten pieces Vonnegut originally created for radio station WNYC. In the stories he visits with notable dead people, among them Mary Wollstonecraft Shelley, Eugene V. Debs, and John Brown. *Booklist* reviewer Donna Seaman called these pieces "warmhearted, caustic, and wise."

While Vonnegut's short and long fiction remains couchedly candid in its reflection of his personal views on many subjects, his essays and other works of nonfiction are even more so. He has published several collections of essays, interviews, and speeches, including *Palm Sunday: An Autobiographical Collage* in 1981 and *Fates Worse than Death: An Autobiographical Collage of the 1980s,* a similar mix to *Palm Sunday,* published a decade later. In *Fates Worse than Death* collected essays and speeches are interwoven with memoir and parenthetical commentary written especially for the volume. Subject matter ranges from the broadly political—Western imperialism and America's war-greed—to the painfully personal—Vonnegut's own prisoner-of-war experiences and bouts with mental illness. Douglas Anderson described the collection in *New York Times Book Review* as "scarily funny" and felt that "it offers a rare insight into an author who has customarily hidden his heart." In *Times Literary Supplement* James Woods concluded that the "more Vonnegut writes the more American he seems—a kind of de-solemnized Emerson, at once arguer, doubter, sermonizer and gossip."

Vonnegut's status as a master of contemporary fiction is built only partly on the strength of his themes. Writing in *Dictionary of Literary Biography,* Robert Group noted that the author "offers a mixture of wistful humanism and cynical existentialism that implies a way of dealing with modern realities completely different from that of most American writers. In the tradition of [Laurence] Sterne and [Henry] Fielding, he uses wit and wisdom to show that though man may live in a purposeless universe full of self-seeking manipulations, there is hope for something better. . . . Like Trout or Vonnegut one must cry out against absurdity, even if one is ignored. Vonnegut creates a vision so preposterous that indignation might provide the basis for change—while laughter allows one to cope with the moment."

Looking back on his career and synthesizing his views about writing, Vonnegut told Joel Bleifuss of *In These Times:* "Literature is by definition opinionated. It is bound to provoke the arguments in many quarters, not excluding the hometown or even the family of the author. Any ink-on-paper author can only hope at best to seem responsible to small groups or like-minded people somewhere."

BIOGRAPHICAL AND CRITICAL SOURCES:

BOOKS

American Writers, Scribner's (New York, NY), 1981.

Bloom, Harold, editor, *Kurt Vonnegut,* Chelsea House (Philadelphia, PA), 2000.

Broer, Lawrence R., editor, *Sanity Plea: Schizophrenia in the Novels of Kurt Vonnegut,* revised edition, University of Alabama Press (Tuscaloosa, AL), 1994.

Chernuchin, Michael, editor, *Vonnegut Talks!,* Pylon Press (Forest Hills, NY), 1977.

Contemporary Literary Criticism, Thomson Gale (Detroit, MI), Volume 1, 1973, Volume 2, 1974, Volume 3, 1975, Volume 4, 1975, Volume 5, 1976, Volume 8, 1978, Volume 12, 1980, Volume 22, 1982, Volume 60, 1986.

Dictionary of Literary Biography, Thomson Gale (Detroit, MI), Volume 2: *American Novelists since World War II,* 1978, Volume 8: *Twentieth-Century American Science Fiction Writers, Part 2,* 1981.

Dictionary of Literary Biography Documentary Series, Volume 3, Thomson Gale (Detroit, MI), 1983.

Dictionary of Literary Biography Yearbook, 1980, Thomson Gale (Detroit, MI), 1981.

Giannone, Richard, *Vonnegut: A Preface to His Novels,* Kennikat Press (Port Washington, NY), 1977.

Kazin, Alfred, *Bright Book of Life: American Novelists and Storytellers from Hemingway to Mailer,* Little, Brown (Boston, MA), 1973.

Klinkowitz, Jerome, and Donald L. Lawler, editors, *Vonnegut in America: An Introduction to the Life and Work of Kurt Vonnegut,* Delacorte (New York, NY), 1977.

Klinkowitz, Jerome, and John Somer, editors, *The Vonnegut Statement: Original Essays on the Life and Work of Kurt Vonnegut,* Delacorte (New York, NY), 1973.

Klinkowitz, Jerome, *Kurt Vonnegut,* Methuen (New York, NY), 1982.

Klinkowitz, Jerome, *Literary Disruptions: The Making of a Post-Contemporary American Fiction,* University of Illinois Press (Urbana, IL), 1975.

Klinkowitz, Jerome, *Literary Subversions: New American Fiction and the Practice of Criticism,* Southern Illinois University Press (Carbondale, IL), 1985.

Klinkowitz, Jerome, *The American 1960s: Imaginative Acts in a Decade of Change,* Iowa State University Press (Ames, IA), 1980.

Krementz, Jill, editor, *Happy Birthday, Kurt Vonnegut: A Festschrift for Kurt Vonnegut on His Sixtieth Birthday,* Delacorte (New York, NY), 1982.

Lundquist, James, *Kurt Vonnegut,* Ungar (New York, NY), 1977.

Morse, Donald E., *The Novels of Kurt Vonnegut: Imagining Being an American,* Praeger (Westport, CT), 2003.

Plimpton, George, editor, *Writers at Work: The "Paris Review" Interviews,* sixth series, Penguin (New York, NY), 1984.

Reed, Peter J., *Kurt Vonnegut, Jr.,* Warner Books (New York, NY), 1972.

Schatt, Stanley, *Kurt Vonnegut, Jr.,* Twayne (Boston, MA), 1976.

Tomedi, John, *Kurt Vonnegut,* Chelsea House (Philadelphia, PA), 2004.

Vonnegut, Kurt, *God Bless You, Mr. Rosewater; or, Pearls before Swine,* Holt (New York, NY), 1965.

Vonnegut, Kurt, *Hocus Pocus,* Putnam (New York, NY), 1990.

PERIODICALS

Booklist, August, 1999, Donna Seaman, review of *Bagombo Snuff Box,* p. 1989; December 1, 1999, Donna Seaman, review of *God Bless You, Dr. Kevorkian,* p. 661.

Book Week, April 11, 1965.

Commonweal, September 16, 1966; June 6, 1969; November 27, 1970; May 7, 1971; December 7, 1973.

Detroit News, June 18, 1972; September 16, 1979; October 3, 1982; November 10, 1985; January 5, 1986.

Film Comment, November-December, 1985.

Globe and Mail (Toronto, Ontario, Canada), March 17, 1984; February 8, 1986; October 17, 1987.

International Fiction Review, summer, 1980.

Library Journal, September 1, 1999, Joshua Cohen, review of *Bagombo Snuff Box,* p. 236.

Life, April 9, 1965; August 16, 1968; September 12, 1969; November 20, 1970.

Los Angeles Times, February 7, 1983.

Los Angeles Times Book Review, September 23, 1979; October 31, 1982; March 3, 1984; April 18, 1984; September 29, 1985; September 2, 1990, pp. 1, 10.

Modern Fiction Studies, spring, 1973; summer, 1975; winter, 1980-81.

Nation, September 23, 1968; June 9, 1969; September 15, 1979; March 21, 1981; November 13, 1982.

National Review, September 28, 1973; November 26, 1976; November 23, 1979; December 10, 1982.

New Republic, August 18, 1952; October 8, 1966; April 26, 1969; November 7, 1970; June 12, 1971; May 12, 1973; September 28, 1973; June 1, 1974; July 5, 1974; September 25, 1976; November 26, 1976.

Newsweek, August 19, 1968; March 3, 1969; April 14, 1969; October 19, 1970; December 20, 1971; May 14, 1973; October 1, 1979; September 29, 1997, Brad Stone, review of *Timequake,* p. 78.

New Yorker, August 16, 1952; May 15, 1965; May 17, 1969; October 17, 1970; October 25, 1976; November 8, 1982.

New York Review of Books, July 2, 1970; May 31, 1973; November 25, 1976; November 22, 1979.

New York Times, August 19, 1968; September 13, 1969; October 6, 1970; October 18, 1970; May 27, 1971; May 13, 1973; October 3, 1975; September 7, 1979; September 24, 1979; October 15, 1979; March 27, 1981; November 5, 1982; February 4, 1983; February 17, 1983; September 25, 1985, Michiko Kakutani, review of *Galagapos,,* p. 21; January 27, 1987; April 4, 1987.

New York Times Book Review, June 2, 1963; April 25, 1965; August 6, 1967; September 1, 1968; April 6, 1969; February 4, 1973; May 13, 1973; October 3, 1976; September 9, 1979; March 15, 1981; October 17, 1982, Benjamin De Mott, review of *Deadeye Dick,* p. 1; October 6, 1985; October 18, 1987, p. 12; September 9, 1990, p. 12; September 15, 1991, Douglas Anderson, review of *Fates Worse than Death,* p. 26; November 1, 1992, p. 32.

New York Times Magazine, January 24, 1971.

People, October 19, 1987.

Progressive, August, 1981.

Publishers Weekly, October 25, 1985; January 31, 1986; August 9, 1999, review of *Bagombo Snuff Box,* p. 342; October 4, 1999, review of audio version of *Bagombo Snuff Box,* p. 36; December 13, 1999, review of *God Bless You, Dr. Kevorkian,* p. 64.

South Atlantic Quarterly, winter, 1979.

Studies in Modern Fiction, Volume 12, number 3, 1971; Volume 14, number 3, 1973; Volume 15, number 2, 1973; Volume 17, number 1, 1975; Volume 18, number 3, 1977; Volume 26, number 2, 1985.

Time, August 30, 1968; April 11, 1969; June 29, 1970; June 3, 1974; October 25, 1976; September 10, 1979; October 25, 1982; October 21, 1985; September 28, 1987, p. 68; September 3, 1990, p. 73; September 29, 1997, R.Z. Sheppard, review of *Timequake,* p. 95; February 14, 2000, p. 25.

Times (London, England), July 8, 1981; February 17, 1983; May 17, 1986, review of *Galapagos;* May 30, 1987.

Times Literary Supplement, November 11, 1965; December 12, 1968; July 17, 1969; November 5, 1976; December 7, 1979; June 19, 1981; September 26, 1980; February 25, 1983; November 8, 1985, Thomas M. Disch, review of *Galapagos;* October 26, 1990, p. 1146; November 15, 1991, James Woods, review of *Fates Worse than Death,* p. 8; October 15, 1999, Michael Newton, review of *Bagombo Snuff Box,* p. 25.

Tribune Books (Chicago, IL), September 27, 1987, p. 1; August 19, 1990, p. 6; September 1, 1991, p. 4; November 24, 1991, p. 8; September 6, 1992, p. 2.

Twentieth-Century Literature, January, 1972, John R. May, review of *God Bless You, Mr. Rosewater; or, Pearls before Swine.*

U.S. News & World Report, February 14, 2000, "The Kindness of Strangers," p. 12.

Village Voice, February 22, 1983.

Virginia Quarterly Review, summer, 1981.

Washington Post, October 12, 1970; May 13, 1973; May 15, 1981; February 2, 1982.

Washington Post Book World, March 8, 1981; October 17, 1982; September 22, 1985; October 4, 1987; August 19, 1990, pp. 1-2; October 21, 1990, p. 15.

Western Humanities Review, summer, 1974.

World Literature Today, winter, 1981.

ONLINE

In These Times, http://www.inthesetimes.com/ (January 27, 2003), Joel Bliefuss, "Kurt Vonnegut vs. the!&#!@."

Kurt Vonnegut Home Page, http://www.vonnegut.com/ (April 15, 2004).

* * *

VOSCE, Trudie
See OZICK, Cynthia

W

WAKOSKI, Diane 1937-

PERSONAL: Born August 3, 1937, in Whittier, CA; daughter of John Joseph and Marie (Mengel) Wakoski; married S. Shepard Sherbell (a magazine editor), October 22, 1965 (divorced); married Michael Watterlond, February 22, 1973 (divorced, 1975); married Robert J. Turney, February 14, 1982. *Education:* University of California—Berkeley, B.A., 1960. *Hobbies and other interests:* Astrology, detective fiction, cooking, collecting American art pottery, growing orchids.

ADDRESSES: *Home*—607 Division, East Lansing, MI 48823. *Office*—Michigan State University, 207 Morrill Hall, East Lansing, MI 48824-1036. *E-mail*—wakoski@msu.edu.

CAREER: Poet and educator. British Book Centre, New York, NY, clerk, 1960-63; Junior High School 22, New York, NY, teacher, 1963-66; New School for Social Research, New York, NY, lecturer, 1969; writer-in-residence, California Institute of Technology, 1972, University of Virginia, 1972-73, Willamette University, 1974, University of California—Irvine, 1974, University of Wisconsin—Madison, 1975, Michigan State University, 1975, Whitman College, 1976, University of Washington, 1977, University of Hawaii, 1978, and Emory University, 1980, 1981; member of faculty at Michigan State University, 1976—.

MEMBER: PEN, Authors Guild, Authors League of America, Poetry Society of America.

AWARDS, HONORS: Robert Frost fellowship, Bread Loaf Writers Conference, 1966; Cassandra Foundation award, 1970; New York State Council on the Arts grant, 1971; Guggenheim Foundation grant, 1972; National Endowment for the Arts grant, 1973; Fulbright grant, 1984; Michigan Arts Council grant, 1988; Michigan Arts Foundation award recipient, 1989; distinguished faculty award, Michigan State University, 1989, William Carlos Williams Prize, 1989, for *Emerald Ice: Selected Poems, 1962-1987;* university distinguished professor award, Michigan State University, 1990; Author of the Year award, Michigan Library Association, 2003.

WRITINGS:

POETRY

Coins and Coffins (also see below), Hawk's Well Press (New York, NY), 1962.

(With Rochelle Owens, Barbara Moraff, and Carol Berge) *Four Young Lady Poets,* edited by LeRoi Jones, Totem-Corinth (New York, NY), 1962.

Dream Sheet, Software Press (New York, NY), 1965.

Discrepancies and Apparitions (also see below), Doubleday (New York, NY), 1966.

The George Washington Poems (also see below), Riverrun Press (New York, NY), 1967.

The Diamond Merchant, Sans Souci Press (Cambridge, MA), 1968.

Inside the Blood Factory, Doubleday (Garden City, NY), 1968.

(With Robert Kelly and Ron Loewinsohn) *The Well Wherein a Deer's Head Bleeds: A Play for Winter Solstice,* Black Sparrow Press (Los Angeles, CA), 1968.

Greed, Black Sparrow Press (Los Angeles, CA), Parts 1 and 2, 1968, Parts 3 and 4, 1969, Parts 5, 6, 7, 1971, Parts 8, 9, 11, 1973.

The Lament of the Lady Bank Dick, Sans Souci Press (Cambridge, MA), 1969.

The Moon Has a Complicated Geography, Odda Tala Press (Palo Alto, CA), 1969.

Poems, Key Printing Co., 1969.

Some Black Poems for the Buddha's Birthday, Pierripont Press, 1969.

Thanking My Mother for Piano Lessons, Perishable Press (Mount Horeb, WI), 1969.

Love, You Big Fat Snail, Tenth Muse (San Francisco, CA), 1970.

Black Dream Ditty for Billy "the Kid" M Seen in Dr. Generosity's Bar Recruiting for Hell's Angels and Black Mafia, Black Sparrow Press (Los Angeles, CA), 1970.

The Wise Men Drawn to Kneel in Wonder at the Fact So of Itself, Black Sparrow Press (Los Angeles, CA), 1970.

The Magellanic Clouds, Black Sparrow Press (Los Angeles, CA), 1970.

On Barbara's Shore, Black Sparrow Press (Los Angeles, CA), 1971.

(Contributor) *The Nest,* Black Sparrow Press (Los Angeles, CA), 1971.

The Motorcycle Betrayal Poems, Simon & Schuster (New York, NY), 1971.

This Water Baby: For Tony, Unicorn Press (Santa Barbara, CA), 1971.

Exorcism, My Dukes (Boston, MA), 1971.

The Purple Finch Song, Perishable Press (Mount Horeb, WI), 1972.

Sometimes a Poet Will Hijack the Moon, Burning Deck (Providence, RI), 1972.

Smudging, Black Sparrow Press (Los Angeles, CA), 1972.

The Pumpkin Pie: or, Reassurances Are Always False, Tho We Love Them, Only Physics Counts, Black Sparrow Press (Los Angeles, CA), 1972.

Winter Sequences, Black Sparrow Press (Los Angeles, CA), 1973.

Dancing on the Grave of a Son of a Bitch, Black Sparrow Press (Los Angeles, CA), 1973.

Stilllife: Michael, Silver Flute, and Violets, University of Connecticut Library (Storrs, CT), 1973.

The Owl and the Snake: A Fable, Perishable Press (Mount Horeb, WI), 1973.

(Contributor) Karl Malkoff, editor, *Crowell's Handbook of Contemporary American Poetry,* Crowell (New York, NY), 1973.

The Wandering Tatler, Perishable Press (Mount Horeb, WI), 1974.

Trilogy (includes *Coins and Coffins,Discrepancies and Apparitions,* and *The George Washington Poems*), Doubleday (Garden City, NY), 1974.

Looking for the King of Spain (also see below), Black Sparrow Press (Los Angeles, CA), 1974.

Abalone, Black Sparrow Press (Los Angeles, CA), 1974.

Virtuoso Literature for Two and Four Hands, Doubleday (Garden City, NY), 1975.

The Fable of the Lion and the Scorpion, Pentagram Press (Milwaukee, WI), 1975.

The Laguna Contract of Diane Wakoski, Crepuscular Press (Madison, WI), 1976.

George Washington's Camp Cups, Red Ozier Press (Madison, WI), 1976.

Waiting for the King of Spain, Black Sparrow Press (Santa Barbara, CA), 1976.

The Last Poem, Black Sparrow Press (Santa Barbara, CA), 1976.

The Ring, Black Sparrow Press (Santa Barbara, CA), 1977.

Spending Christmas with the Man from Receiving at Sears, Black Sparrow Press (Santa Barbara, CA), 1977.

Overnight Projects with Wood, Red Ozier Press (Madison, WI), 1977.

Pachelbel's Canon (also see below), Black Sparrow Press (Santa Barbara, CA) 1978.

The Man Who Shook Hands, Doubleday (Garden City, NY), 1978.

Trophies, Black Sparrow Press (Santa Barbara, CA), 1979.

Cap of Darkness (includes *Looking for the King of Spain* and *Pachelbel's Canon*), Black Sparrow Press (Santa Barbara, CA), 1980.

(With Ellen Lanyon) *Making a Sacher Torte: Nine Poems, Twelve Illustrations,* Perishable Press (Mount Horeb, WI), 1981.

Saturn's Rings, Targ Editions, (New York, NY), 1982.

Divers, Barbarian Press, 1982.

The Lady Who Drove Me to the Airport, Metacom Press (Worcester, MA), 1982.

The Magician's Feastletters, Black Sparrow Press (Santa Barbara, CA), 1982.

The Collected Greed, Parts 1-13, Black Sparrow Press (Santa Barbara, CA), 1984.

The Managed World, Red Ozier Press (New York, NY), 1985.

Why My Mother Likes Liberace: A Musical Selection, SUN/Gemini Press (Tucson, AZ), 1985.

Celebration of the Rose: For Norman on Christmas Day, Caliban Press (Montclair, NJ), 1987.

Roses, Caliban Press (Montclair, NJ), 1987.

Husks of Wheat, California State University, Northridge Library (Northridge, CA), 1987.

Emerald Ice: Selected Poems 1962-1987, Black Sparrow Press (Santa Rosa, CA), 1988.

Medea the Sorceress ("Archaeology of Movies and Books" series), Black Sparrow Press (Santa Rosa, CA), 1991.

Jason the Sailor ("Archaeology of Movies and Books" series), Black Sparrow Press (Santa Rosa, CA), 1993.

The Emerald City of Las Vegas ("Archaeology of Movies and Books" series), Black Sparrow Press (Santa Rosa, CA), 1995.

Argonaut Rose ("Archaeology of Movies and Books" series), Black Sparrow Press (Santa Rosa, CA), 1998.

The Butcher's Apron: New and Selected Poems, Including "Greed: Part 14," Black Sparrow Press (Santa Rosa, CA), 2000.

OTHER

Form Is an Extension of Content (essay), Black Sparrow Press (Los Angeles, CA), 1972.

Creating a Personal Mythology (essays), Black Sparrow Press (Los Angeles, CA), 1975.

Variations on a Theme (essay), Black Sparrow Press (Santa Barbara, CA), 1976.

(Author of introduction) Barbara Drake, *Love at the Egyptian Theatre,* Red Cedar Press (East Lansing, MI), 1978.

(Author of introduction) Lynne Savitt, *Lust in Twenty-eight Flavors,* Second Coming Press (San Francisco, CA), 1979.

Toward a New Poetry (essays), University of Michigan Press (Ann Arbor, MI), 1980.

Unveilings, photographs by Lynn Stern, Hudson Hill Press (New York, NY), 1989.

Contributor to "Burning Deck Post Cards: The Third Ten," Burning Deck Press, and to periodicals. *American Poetry Review,* columnist, 1972-74.

WORK IN PROGRESS: A sequence of poems titled *Noir.*

SIDELIGHTS: Diane Wakoski, described as an "important and moving poet" by Paul Zweig in the *New York Times Book Review,* is frequently named among the foremost twentieth-century American poets by virtue of her experiential vision and her unique voice. Wakoski's poems focus on intensely personal experiences—on her unhappy childhood, on the painful relationships she has had with men and, perhaps most frequently, on the subject of being Diane Wakoski. This is not to say, however, that her work is explicitly autobiographical. She has invented and incorporated personae from mythology and archetype as a liberation from what she has called the "obsessive muse," that spurs writers to face their personal terrors and turn them into art.

Occasionally some critics have found Wakoski's thematic concerns difficult to appreciate, especially the recurring "anti-male rage" theme noted by Peter Schjeldahl in the *New York Times Book Review.* Wakoski's poems, according to Schjeldahl, "are professionally supple and clear . . . but their pervasive unpleasantness makes her popularity rather surprising. One can only conclude that a number of people are angry enough at life to enjoy the sentimental and desolating resentment with which she writes about it."

Many other critics, however, believed that it is through this very rage and resentment that Wakoski makes a significant statement in her work. James F. Mersmann, for example, commented in *Margins* that Wakoski's poetry "gives us a moving vision of the terrible last stages of a disintegrating personality and a disintegrating society, and it painfully embodies the schizophrenia, alienation, and lovelessness of our time." Douglas Blazek concluded in *Poetry* that Wakoski's poems have the "substance necessary to qualify them notches above the works of creative 'geniuses,' 'stylists,' and 'cultural avatars' who have little to say." The stylistic and structural aspects of Wakoski's poetry are as unique as her poetic statement. Often described as prosy, her poems are usually written in the first person. Rosellen Brown wrote in *Parnassus* that Wakoski "is a marvelously abundant woman" who sounds in her poetry "like some friend of yours who's flung herself down in your kitchen to tell you something urgent and makes you laugh and respect her good old-fashioned guts at the same time."

"Diane's style of writing," wrote David Ignatow in *Margins,* "reminds me of the baroque style of dress . . . the huge flounces, furbelows, puffed sleeves, trailing skirts, tight waist, heaving bosoms and stylishly protruding buttocks, all carried off with great elegance of movement and poise." In *Mediterranean Review,* critic Robert DeMaria found that, "stylistically, [Wakoski] has a marvelous and distinctive voice. It lingers in one's mind after one has read her. . . . Her timing is excellent, so excellent that she can convert prose into poetry at times. And most of what she writes is really prose, only slightly transformed, not only because of its arrangement on the page, but because of this music she injects into it."

While the structure of Wakoski's poems appears to be informal and casually built, her artistic control is tight.

As Hayden Carruth suggested in the *Hudson Review*, "Wakoski has a way of beginning her poems with the most unpromising materials imaginable, then carrying them on, often on and on and on, talkily, until at the end they come into surprising focus, unified works. With her it is a question of thematic and imagistic control; I think her poems are deeply, rather than verbally, structured." In *Contemporary Literature*, Marjorie G. Perloff spoke of Wakoski's purpose in writing nontraditionally structured poems, saying that Wakoski "strives for a voice that is wholly natural, spontaneous, and direct. Accordingly, she avoids all fixed forms, definite rhythms, or organized image patterns in the drive to tell us the Whole Truth about herself, to be *sincere*."

"Although Wakoski's poems are not traditional structures," noted Debra Hulbert in *Prairie Schooner*, "she builds them solidly with words which feel chosen, with repetition of images throughout a poem." This repetition, an element that critics mention often, makes its own statement apart from the individual themes of the poems. "Repetition," remarked Gloria Bowles in *Margins*, "has become Wakoski's basic stylistic mode. And since form is an extension of content (et vice versa) Wakoski's poetic themes have become obsessive. Repetition is a formal fact of her poetry and, so she suggests, the basic structure of our lives."

Wakoski's poems often rely on digressions, on tangential wanderings through imagery and fantasy, to present ideas and themes. Blazek observed that "many of her poems sound as if they're constantly in trouble, falling into triteness, clumsiness, or indirection. She is constantly jumping into deep water to save a drowning stanza or into burning buildings to recover disintegrating meaning, always managing to pull these rescues off, sometimes with what appears to be a superhuman determination, drawing gasps from witnesses who never lose that initial impression of disaster." But, he said, these "imaginative excursions and side-journeys (she can get strung-out in just about any poem over a page long) are well-founded in her life—they're not just facile language cyclone-spinning itself to naught. They are doors into her psyche."

Toby Olson, writing in *Margins*, believed that "one of the central forces of . . . [Wakoski's] poems proceeds from a fundamentally serious playfulness, an evident desire to spin out and open the image rather than to close the structure. . . . One of their most compelling qualities is their obsessiveness: the need at every turn to digress, to let the magic of the words take her where they will, because they are so beautiful, because the ability to speak out is not to be taken for granted, is to be wondered at in its foreignness, is to be followed." As *Dictionary of Literary Biography* contributor Mark Harris observed: "In many of Wakoski's poems the obsessive muse focuses on the idea of beauty. Taken as a whole, her work may be regarded as a linguistic/poetic quest for beauty."

The "magic" of Wakoski's words is also wrought through her use of imagery and through her creation of a consistent personal mythology. Commenting on two of the poet's earliest works, *Coins and Coffins* and *Discrepancies and Apparitions*, Sheila Weller wrote in *Ms.* that the books "established [Wakoski] as a poet of fierce imagination. She was at once an eerie imagist (always the swooping gulls, deciduating hands, the hawk that 'pecks out my eyes like two cherries'); and a rapt parablist, reworking Wild West legend and cosmological symbols, transmuting fairy-tale scenes ('three children dancing around an orange tree') into macaberie ('o you see the round orange tree? . . . glinting through the leaves, / the hanged man'). These poems are vivid landscapes—as diabolic as Dali, as gauzy as Monet."

In *Poetry*, Sandra M. Gilbert described Wakoski as "a fabulist, a weaver of gorgeous webs of imagery and a teller of archetypically glamorous tales [who has] always attempted self-definition through self-mythologizing. 'The poems were a way of inventing myself into a new life,' she has said." "The myth of herself," observed H. Zinnes in *World Literature Today*, is of "one 'clothed in fat,' with an ugly face, without wit, brilliance or elegance, but having some 'obsession for truth and history.' This plain seeker after love . . . is of course a poet with a great deal of wit. . . . a poet who in her work and life is not merely searching for a lover," although many of her poems touch on this theme.

In Harris's opinion, "Wakoski's preference for single words and rhythms that mirror the patterns of speech can mislead the reader into reading her poems too literally. This mistake in turn leads the reader to consider her themes trivial, for by reading on only the literal level, one misses the substance and complexity provided by the emblematic level. . . . The strength of the poetry . . . is that both sides of a paradox can be presented together, equally and simultaneously, a situation that life cannot duplicate. At its best, Wakoski believes, poetry employs the objects, events and experiences of life in a way that allows the reader to experience their emotional substance. Her emblematic use of language is one of her methods for obtaining this result."

Wakoski's personal mythology embraces many archetypal figures as well, including George Washington, the king of Spain, the motorcycle mechanic, the "man in Receiving at Sears," Beethoven, the "man with the gold tooth," and the "man who shook hands." These characters, most of whom appear more than once in Wakoski's canon, serve as symbols, emblematic of emotional states, past experiences, fantasies, and, sometimes, of real people in the poet's life.

George Washington, for example, appears in *The George Washington Poems,* a collection Weller called "witty, caustic takes on the male mystique. In a voice by turns consciously absurdist and tremulously earnest, she takes the first President as her 'mythical father-lover,' romanticizes and barbs 'the militaristic, penalizing, fact-over-feeling male mind that I've always been afraid of and fascinated by.'" Wakoski speaks to George Washington in the poems with various voices—as Martha Washington, as a bitter child whose father has left home, as a lover left behind in the Revolutionary War. As Norman Martien explained in *Partisan Review,* "the George Washington myths serve to express the failure of a woman's relations to her men, but the myths also give her a means of talking about it. Partly *because* 'George' is so distant, he can be a safe listener. . . . [and] he can allow her a voice that can reaffirm human connection, impossible at closer ranges." This theme of the failure of relationships, of betrayal by others (especially men), is a central concern of Wakoski's, and many of her mythological figures embody one or more of the facets of human relations in which she sees the possibility of betrayal or loss.

The figure of the motorcycle mechanic in *The Motorcycle Betrayal Poems* symbolizes, as Wakoski says in her dedicatory statement, "all those men who betrayed me at one time or another." According to Zweig, the book is "haunted by a curious mythology composed of mustached lovers, 'mechanics' who do not understand the engine humming under [the narrator's] skin, the great-grandfatherly warmth of Beethoven and George Washington, to whom she turns with humor but also with a sort of desperation." In this book, noted Eric Mottram in *Parnassus,* Wakoski "operates in a world of women as adjuncts to men and the erotics of bikes; the poems are survival gestures." According to Weller, the book "made . . . women start at [Wakoski's] power to personalize the paradox" of male-female relationships—"their anger at the rejecting male archetype . . . yet their willing glorification of it . . . The book's theme is the mythology and confusions of . . . love, and the fury at betrayal by symbols, envy, lovers, and self."

The theme of betrayal, and its resulting pain, also appears in *Inside the Blood Factory.* Here, as Zweig observed, Wakoski writes "poems of loss. The loss of childhood; the loss of lovers and family; the perpetual loss a woman lives with when she thinks she is not beautiful. These losses [create] a scorched earth of isolation around her, which she [describes] harshly and precisely. . . . From this vulnerable retreat, a stream of liberating images [emerges] to grapple with the world and mythify it." Peter D. Zivkovic, writing in *Southwest Review,* believed that *Inside the Blood Factory* is "significantly more than a memorable reading experience. Perhaps the most remarkable thing about . . . [the book] is the consistent strength of the individual poems. There is not," Zivkovic concluded, "a single weak poem in the volume—an achievement worthy of Frost and other American giants."

Fourteen years after *Inside the Blood Factory,* Wakoski produced *Saturn's Rings* and *The Magician's Feastletters. Saturn's Rings* is a collection of surrealist poems loosely connected by the metaphorical theme of self-banishment and characteristic self-scrutiny. As Holly Prado noted in the *Los Angeles Times Book Review,* "Fearing decay, ignorance, and the inevitability of death, Wakoski writes with the intensity of someone fiercely alive, who still wants to unscramble failures, loneliness, the image of herself as the homely girl who was never acceptable." Noting the limitations of her shorter pieces in the collection, Paul Oppenheimer commented in the *American Book Review* on the concluding series of eleven poems from which the title of the collection derives: *Saturn's Rings* "is an often captivating, often self-pitying cry from the depths. . . . The cry is especially moving when uttered in the bright, chromic voice of Wakoski's most surrealistic lines. She is fine at depicting the possibility that 'the world / is flying out of control,' and that we may be living in 'a disintegrating time.'" In *The Magician's Feastletters,* arranged in four sections that parallel the four seasons, Wakoski uses food as a metaphor for love and deprivation. Though tending toward abstraction, Clayton Eshleman noted the concreteness of Wakoski's imagery and description of everyday items. As he wrote in the *Los Angeles Times Book Review,* "Wakoski [begins] to reverse a whole system of frozen values geared to affirm youth/sexuality/summer/product and to denigrate aging/impotence/winter/soul. Especially in the light of current fashions in American poetry (where empty description is as touted as pretentious nonsense), Wakoski's poetry is extremely valuable."

The Collected Greed, Parts 1-13 and *Emerald Ice: Selected Poems 1962-1987* bring together examples of Wakoski's finest writing over a twenty-five-year period. *The Collected Greed* is an assemblage of poetry from previous installments of *Greed* published between 1968 and 1973, with the addition of two previously unpublished parts. In the *Los Angeles Times Book Review* Kenneth Funsten offered high praise for "The Greed to Be Fulfilled," one of the new sections. Here Wakoski traces her personal quest for purpose and completion in a surreal glass house where she revisits George Washington and representations of Charles Bukowski and the king of Spain. Funsten wrote, "The confessional voice of the self-centered ego reaches a new plane of maturity when it decides that intellectual things, not emotional ones, are what matter." Throughout the collection Wakoski explores various manifestations of greed, defined by her as "an unwillingness to give up one thing / for another," as quoted in Funsten's review.

In the 1990s Wakoski produced *Jason the Sailor* and *The Emerald City of Las Vegas,* both belonging to the "Archaeology of Movies and Books" series that began with *Medea the Sorceress* in 1991. In *Jason the Sailor,* consisting of poems, letters, and excerpted texts by Camille Paglia, Nick Herbert, and Jeremy Bernstein, Wakoski explores archetypal love, betrayal, and the dynamics of male-female relationships, concluding, as quoted in a *Kliatt* review of the work, "Women need men, the other halves of ourselves." *The Emerald City of Las Vegas* similarly examines the mythology of modern America in casinos and through excerpts from L. Frank Baum's *The Wizard of Oz.* A *Publishers Weekly* reviewer concluded that the book represents Wakoski's "inner conversation about what it means to be a woman, to be no longer young, to be a poet." The fourth book in the series is *Argonaut Rose,* in which Wakoski writes of her own history and popular culture. *Library Journal* reviewer Graham Christian said that she "remains an interesting poet to watch."

The Butcher's Apron: New and Selected Poems, Including "Greed: Part 14" focuses on the purchase, preparation, and enjoyment of food. Some of the poems read as recipes, as in "Braised Short Ribs." Wakoski writes of food failures, such as a pumpkin pie that won't set, and food she ate as a child. *Library Journal* contributor Judy Clarence wrote that the volume is pervaded by Wakoski's "feminine gentility," and felt that it should not be read in one sitting, but should "be dipped into now and then, as if one were sticking a finger into a pot of honey." A *Publishers Weekly* reviewer commended the work for its "plainly spoken, autobiographically grounded line."

Wakoski lives and works in East Lansing, Michigan, and expressed plans to create another extensive sequence of poems, possibly running to multiple volumes. In her work "The Blue Swan: An Essay on Music in Poetry" she summed up the process of poetry writing: "first comes the story. Then comes the reaction to the story. Then comes the telling and retelling of the story. And finally . . . comes boredom with the story, so that finally we invent music, and the nature of music is that you must hear all the digressions."

BIOGRAPHICAL AND CRITICAL SOURCES:

BOOKS

Contemporary Literary Criticism, Thomson Gale (Detroit, MI), Volume 2, 1974, Volume 4, 1975, Volume 7, 1977, Volume 9, 1978, Volume 11, 1979, Volume 40, 1986.

Contemporary Poets, 6th edition, St. James Press (Detroit, MI), 1996.

Contemporary Women Poets, St. James Press (Detroit, MI), 1998.

Dictionary of Literary Biography, Volume 5: *American Poets after World War II, Part 2,* Thomson Gale (Detroit, MI), 1980.

Lauter, Estella, *Women as Mythmakers: Poetry and Visual Art by Twentieth-Century Women,* Indiana University Press (Bloomington, IN), 1984.

Roberts, Sheila, editor, *Still the Frame Holds,* Borgo Press (San Francisco, CA), 1993.

PERIODICALS

American Book Review, September-October, 1987, Paul Oppenheimer, review of *Saturn's Rings.*

Contemporary Literature, winter, 1975; winter, 1976, "An Interview with Diane Wakoski," pp. 1-19.

Far Point, spring-summer, 1970, Philip L. Gerber and Robert J. Gemmett, "A Terrible War: A Conversation with Diane Wakoski," pp. 44-54.

Gypsy Scholar, summer, 1979, "A Colloquy with Diane Wakoski," pp. 61-73.

Hudson Review, summer, 1974.

Journal of International Women's Studies, Nancy Bunge, "Using Imagination to Create New Rules: Diane Wakoski's Poetry," p. 191.

Kliatt, September, 1993, p. 26, review of *Jason the Sailor.*

Library Journal, June 1, 1982, p. 1100; November 15, 1986, p. 100; December, 1988; February 1, 1991; August, 1993, p. 109; August, 1995, p. 80; March 1, 1998, Graham Christian, review of *Argonaut*

Rose, p. 92; February 15, 2001, Judy Clarence, review of *The Butcher's Apron: New and Selected Poems, Including "Greed: Part 14,"* p. 172.

Los Angeles Times Book Review, July 18, 1982, p. 11; November 4, 1984, p. 4; October 26, 1986, p. 14.

Margins, January, 1976.

Mediterranean Review, spring, 1972.

Ms., March, 1976, Sheila Weller, reviews of *Coins and Coffins* and *Discrepancies and Apparitions.*

New York Times Book Review, December 12, 1971; August 13, 1978.

Parnassus, fall-winter, 1972; spring-summer, 1973.

Partisan Review, winter, 1971, Norman Martien, review of *The George Washington Poems.*

Poetry, June, 1974; August, 1976.

Prairie Schooner, spring, 1973.

Publishers Weekly, July 31, 1995, p. 74, review of *The Emerald City of Las Vegas;* February 23, 1998, review of *Argonaut Rose,* p. 71; December 4, 2000, review of *The Butcher's Apron,* p. 67.

Southwest Review, spring, 1975, Peter D. Zivkovic, review of *Inside the Blood Factory.*

Virginia Quarterly Review, autumn, 1972.

Women's Review of Books, April, 2001, Gertrude Reif Hughes, review of *The Butcher's Apron,* p. 14.

World Literature Today, autumn, 1978.

Writer's Digest, November, 1991.

ONLINE

Academy of American Poets Web site, http://www.onlinepoetryclassroom.org/poets/ (August 24, 2004).

* * *

WALCOTT, Derek 1930-
(Derek Alton Walcott)

PERSONAL: Born January 23, 1930, in Castries, St. Lucia, West Indies; son of Warwick (a civil servant, poet, and visual artist) and Alix (a teacher) Walcott; married Fay Moston, 1954 (divorced, 1959); married Margaret Ruth Maillard, 1962 (divorced); married Norline Metivier (an actress and dancer), 1982 (divorced); children: (first marriage) Peter, (second marriage) two daughters. *Education:* Attended St. Mary's College (St. Lucia); University of the West Indies (Kingston, Jamaica), B.A. 1953.

ADDRESSES: Home—(summer) 165 Duke of Edinburgh Ave., Diego Martin, Trinidad and Tobago; (winter) 71 St. Mary's, Boston, MA 02215. *Office*—Creative Writing Department, Boston University, 236 Bay State Rd., Boston, MA 02215. *Agent*—Bridget Aschenberg, International Famous Agency, 1301 Avenue of the Americas, New York, NY 10019.

CAREER: Poet and playwright. Teacher at St. Mary's College, Castries, St. Lucia, West Indies, 1947-50 and 1954, Grenada Boys' Secondary School, St. George's, Grenada, West Indies, 1953-54, and at Jamaica College, Kingston, 1955. Feature writer, 1960-62, and drama critic, 1963-68, for *Trinidad Guardian* (Port-of-Spain, Trinidad); feature writer for *Public Opinion* (Kingston), 1956-57. Cofounder of St. Lucia Arts Guild, 1950, and Basement Theatre, Port-of-Spain, Trinidad; founding director of Little Carib Theatre Workshop (later Trinidad Theatre Workshop), 1959-76; Boston University, assistant professor of creative writing, 1981, visiting professor, 1985, currently professor of English. Visiting professor at Columbia University, 1981, and Harvard University, 1982 and 1987. Also lecturer at Rutgers University and Yale University.

AWARDS, HONORS: Rockefeller grant, 1957, 1966, and fellowship, 1958; Jamaica Drama Festival prize, 1958, for *Drums and Colours: An Epic Drama;* Arts Advisory Council of Jamaica prize, 1960; Guinness Award, 1961, for "A Sea-Chantey"; Borestone Mountain poetry awards, 1964, for "Tarpon," and 1977, for "Midsummer, England"; Ingram Merrill Foundation grant, 1962; named fellow of the Royal Society of Literature, 1966; Heinemann Award, Royal Society of Literature, 1966, for *The Castaway,* and 1983, for *The Fortunate Traveller;* Cholmondeley Award, 1969, for *The Gulf;* Eugene O'Neill Foundation-Wesleyan University fellowship, 1969; Gold Hummingbird Medal, Order of the Hummingbird, Trinidad and Tobago, 1969 (one source says 1979); Obie Award, 1971, for *Dream on Monkey Mountain;* honorary doctorate of letters, University of the West Indies, Mona, Jamaica, 1972; O.B.E. (Officer, Order of British Empire), 1972; Jock Campbell/*New Statesman* Prize, 1974, for *Another Life;* Guggenheim fellowship, 1977; named honorary member of the American Academy and Institute of Arts and Letters, 1979; *American Poetry Review* Award, 1979; International Writer's Prize, Welsh Arts Council, 1980; John D. and Catherine T. MacArthur Foundation grant, 1981; Los Angeles *Times* Prize in poetry, 1986, for *Collected Poems, 1948-1984;* Queen Elizabeth II Gold Medal for Poetry, 1988; Nobel Prize for literature, 1992; St. Lucia Cross, 1993.

WRITINGS:

POETRY

25 Poems, Guardian Commercial Printery (Port-of-Spain, Trinidad), 1948.

Epitaph for the Young: XII Cantos, Barbados Advocate (Bridgetown, Barbados), 1949.

Poems, Kingston City Printery (Kingston, Jamaica), 1953.

In a Green Night: Poems, J. Cape (London, England), 1962, published as *In a Green Night: Poems, 1948-1960,* J. Cape (London, England), 1969.

Selected Poems, Farrar, Straus (New York, NY), 1964.

The Castaway, J. Cape (London, England), 1965.

The Gulf and Other Poems, J. Cape (London, England), 1969, published with selections from *The Castaway* as *The Gulf: Poems,* Farrar, Straus (New York, NY), 1970.

Another Life (long poem), Farrar, Straus (New York, NY), 1973, 2nd edition published with introduction, chronology and selected bibliography by Robert D. Hammer, Three Continents Press (Washington, DC), 1982.

Sea Grapes, Farrar, Straus (New York, NY), 1976.

Selected Verse, Heinemann (London, England), 1976.

The Star-Apple Kingdom, Farrar, Straus (New York, NY), 1979.

The Fortunate Traveller, Farrar, Straus (New York, NY), 1981.

Selected Poetry, selected, annotated, and introduced by Wayne Brown, Heinemann (London, England), 1981, revised edition, 1993.

The Caribbean Poetry of Derek Walcott and the Art of Romare Beardon, Limited Editions Club (New York, NY), 1983.

Midsummer, Farrar, Straus (New York, NY), 1984.

Collected Poems, 1948-1984, Farrar, Straus (New York, NY), 1986.

The Arkansas Testament, Farrar, Straus (New York, NY), 1987.

Omeros, Farrar, Straus (New York, NY), 1990.

Collected Poems, Faber (London, England), 1990.

Poems, 1965-1980, J. Cape (London, England), 1992.

Derek Walcott: Selected Poems, Longman (London, England), 1993.

The Bounty, Farrar, Straus (New York, NY), 1997.

Tiepolo's Hound, Farrar, Straus (New York, NY), 2000.

Contributor of poems to numerous periodicals, including *New Statesman, London Magazine, Encounter, Evergreen Review, Caribbean Quarterly, Tamarack Review,* and *Bim.*

PLAYS

Cry for a Leader, produced in St. Lucia, 1950.

Senza Alcum Sospetto (radio play), broadcast 1950, produced as *Paolo and Francesca,* in St. Lucia, 1951.

(And director) *Henri Christophe: A Chronicle in Seven Scenes* (first produced in Castries, West Indies, 1950; produced in London, England, 1952), Barbados Advocate (Bridgetown, Barbados), 1950.

Robin and Andrea, published in *Bim* (Christ Church, Barados), 1950.

Three Assassins, produced in St. Lucia, West Indies, 1951.

The Price of Mercy, produced in St. Lucia, West Indies, 1951.

(And director) *Harry Dernier: A Play for Radio Production* (produced in Mona, Jamaica, 1952; radio play broadcast as *Dernier,* 1952), Barbados Advocate (Bridgetown, Barbados), 1952.

(And director) *The Wine of the Country* (produced in Mona, Jamaica, 1956), University College of the West Indies (Mona, Jamaica), 1953.

The Sea at Dauphin: A Play in One Act (first produced in Mona, Jamaica, 1953; produced in Trinidad, 1954, London, England, 1960, New York, NY, 1978), Extra-Mural Department, University College of the West Indies (Mona, Jamaica), 1954, also included in *Dream on Monkey Mountain and Other Plays* (also see below).

Crossroads, produced in Jamaica, 1954.

(And director) *The Charlatan,* Walcott directed first production in Mona, Jamaica, 1954; revised version with music by Fred Hope and Rupert Dennison produced in Port-of-Spain, Trinidad, 1973; revised version with music by Galt MacDermot produced in Los Angeles, 1974; revised version produced in Port-of-Spain, Trinidad, 1977.

Ione: A Play with Music (first produced in Kingston, 1957), Extra-Mural Department, University College of the West Indies (Mona, Jamaica), 1957.

Drums and Colours: An Epic Drama (first produced in Port-of-Spain, Trinidad, 1958), published in *Caribbean Quarterly,* March-June, 1961.

(And director) *Ti-Jean and His Brothers* (first produced in Castries, St. Lucia, 1957; Walcott directed a revised version produced in Port-of-Spain, Trinidad, 1958; produced in Hanover, NH, 1971; Walcott directed a production Off-Broadway at Delacorte Theatre, 1972; produced in London, 1986), included in *Dream on Monkey Mountain and Other Plays* (also see below).

Malcauchon; or, The Six in the Rain (sometimes "Malcauchon" transliterated as "Malcochon"; one-act; first produced as *Malcauchon* in Castries, St. Lucia, 1959; produced as *Six in the Rain,* in London, England, 1960; produced Off-Broadway at St. Mark's Playhouse, 1969), Extra-Mural Department, University of West Indies (Port-of-Spain, Trinidad), 1966, also included in *Dream on Monkey Mountain and Other Plays* (also see below).

Jourmard; or, A Comedy till the Last Minute, first produced in St. Lucia, 1959; produced in New York, NY, 1962.

(And director) *Batai* (carnival show), produced in Port-of-Spain, Trinidad, 1965.

(And director) *Dream on Monkey Mountain* (first produced in Toronto, Ontario, Canada, 1967; produced in Waterford, CT, 1969; and Off-Broadway at St. Mark's Playhouse, 1970), included in *Dream on Monkey Mountain and Other Plays* (also see below).

(And director) *Franklin: A Tale of the Islands,* first produced in Georgetown, Guyana, 1969; Walcott directed a revised version produced in Port-of-Spain, Trinidad, 1973.

Dream on Monkey Mountain and Other Plays (contains *Dream on Monkey Mountain, The Sea at Dauphin, Malcauchon; or, The Six in the Rain, Ti-Jean and His Brothers,* and the essay "What the Twilight Says: An Overture"), Farrar, Straus (New York, NY), 1970.

(And director) *In a Fine Castle,* (Walcott directed first production in Mona, Jamaica, 1970; produced in Los Angeles, CA, 1972), excerpt as *Conscience of a Revolution* published in *Express* (Port-of-Spain, Trinidad), October 24, 1971.

The Joker of Seville (musical; music by Galt MacDermot; adaptation of the play by Tirso de Molina; first produced in Port-of-Spain, Trinidad, 1974), included in *The Joker of Seville and O Babylon!: Two Plays* (also see below).

(And director) *O Babylon!* (music by Galt MacDermot; Walcott directed first production in Port-of-Spain, Trinidad, 1976; produced in London, England, 1988), included in *The Joker of Seville and O Babylon!: Two Plays* (also see below).

(And director) *Remembrance* (three-act; Walcott directed first production in St. Croix, Virgin Islands, December, 1977; produced Off-Broadway at The Other Stage, 1979; and London, England, 1980), included in *Remembrance & Pantomime: Two Plays* (also see below).

The Snow Queen (television play), excerpt published in *People* (Port-of-Spain, Trinidad), April, 1977.

Pantomime (first produced in Port-of-Spain, Trinidad, 1978; produced London, England, 1979, Washington, DC, 1981, and Off-Broadway at the Hudson Guild Theater, 1986), included in *Remembrance & Pantomime: Two Plays* (also see below).

The Joker of Seville and O Babylon!: Two Plays, Farrar, Straus (New York, NY), 1978.

(And director) *Marie Laveau* (music by Galt MacDermot; first produced in St. Thomas, U.S. Virgin Islands, 1979), excerpts published in *Trinidad and Tobago Review* (Tunapuna), 1979.

Remembrance & Pantomime: Two Plays, Farrar, Straus (New York, NY), 1980.

Beef, No Chicken (Walcott directed first production in New Haven, CT, 1982; produced in London, England, 1989), included in *Three Plays* (also see below).

The Isle Is Full of Noises, first produced at the John W. Huntington Theater, Hartford, CT, 1982.

Three Plays (contains *The Last Carnival, Beef, No Chicken,* and *A Branch of the Blue Nile*), Farrar, Straus (New York, NY), 1986.

Steel, first produced at the American Repertory Theatre, Cambridge, MA, 1991.

The Odyssey: A Stage Version, Farrar, Straus (New York, NY), 1993.

(With Paul Simon) *The Capeman: A Musical* (produced on Broadway at the Marquis Theater, December, 1997), Farrar, Straus (New York, NY), 1998.

The Haitian Trilogy, Farrar, Straus and Giroux (New York, NY), 2002.

Also author of the play *To Die for Grenada.*

OTHER

Henri Christophe: A Chronicle in Seven Scenes, Barbados Advocate (Bridgetown, Barbados), 1950.

Another Life: Fully Annotated, Lynne Rienner Publishers (Boulder, CO), reprinted with a critical essay and comprehensive notes by Edward Baugh and Colbert Nepaulsingh, 2004.

The Poet in the Theatre, Poetry Book Society (London, England), 1990.

The Antilles: Fragments of Epic Memory: The Nobel Lecture, Farrar, Straus (New York, NY), 1993.

Conversations with Derek Walcott, edited by William Baer, University of Mississippi (Jackson, MS), 1996.

(With Joseph Brodsky and Seamus Heaney) *Homage to Robert Frost,* Farrar, Straus (New York, NY), 1996.

What the Twilight Says (essays), Farrar, Straus (New York, NY), 1998.

Tiepolo's Hound, Farrar, Strauss (New York, NY), 2000.

Walker and Ghost Dance, Farrar, Straus (New York, NY), 2002.

CONTRIBUTOR

John Figueroa, editor, *Caribbean Voices,* Evans (London, England), 1966.

Barbara Howes, editor, *From the Green Antilles,* Macmillan (New York, NY), 1966.

Howard Sergeant, editor, *Commonwealth Poems of Today,* Murray (London, England), 1967.

O.R. Dathorne, editor, *Caribbean Verse,* Heinemann (London, England), 1968.

Anne Walmsley, compiler, *The Sun's Eye: West Indian Writing for Young Readers,* Longmans, Green (London, England) 1968.

Orde Coombs, editor, *Is Massa Day Dead?,* Doubleday (New York, NY), 1974.

D.J. Enright, editor, *Oxford Book of Contemporary Verse, 1945-1980,* Oxford University Press (New York, NY), 1980.

Errol Hill, editor, *Plays for Today,* Longman (London, England), 1985.

(Author of introduction) George Plimpton, editor, *Latin American Writers at Work,* Modern Library (New York, NY), 2003.

Also contributor to *Caribbean Literature,* edited by George Robert Coulthard; *New Voices of the Commonwealth,* edited by Howard Sergeant; and *Young Commonwealth Poetry,* edited by Peter Ludwig Brent.

Some of Walcott's personal papers are housed at the University of the West Indies in Saint Augustine, Trinidad.

SIDELIGHTS: Upon awarding Derek Walcott the Nobel Prize for Literature in 1992, the Swedish Academy, as quoted in the *Detroit Free Press,* wrote: "In him, West Indian culture has found its great poet." Walcott was the first native Caribbean writer to win the prize. Although born of mixed racial and ethnic heritage on St. Lucia, a West Indian island where a French/English patois is spoken, poet and playwright Derek Walcott was educated as a British subject. Taught to speak English as a second language, he grew skilled in his adopted tongue. His use of the language drew praise from critics, including British poet and novelist Robert Graves who, according to *Times Literary Supplement* contributor Vicki Feaver, "has gone as far to state that [Walcott] handles English with a closer understanding of its inner magic than most (if not all) of his English-born contemporaries." "Walcott has had to contend with the charge that he is so deeply influenced by Western tradition that he has yet to achieve his own voice. Yet this scion of African and European heritage embodies the cultural matrix of the New World. Thus, inevitable questions of origins, identity, and the creation of meaningful order in a chaotic world lead Walcott to themes that transcend race, place, and time," remarked Robert D. Hamner in the *Dictionary of Literary Biography.* "In his literary works," noted the Swedish Academy in its citation, "Walcott has laid a course for his own cultural environment, but through them he speaks to each and every one of us." Among Walcott's "central concerns," delineated Bruce King in *Contemporary Poets,* "are the existence of evil, especially in the form of political tyranny and racial hatred . . . his relationship to time, death, and God. . . . and his [feelings of] estrangement."

The major theme of Walcott's writing is the dichotomy between black and white, subject and ruler, and the elements of both Caribbean and Western civilization present in his culture and ancestry. In "What the Twilight Says," the introduction to *Dream on Monkey Mountain and Other Plays,* Walcott refers to his "schizophrenic boyhood," in which he led "two lives: the interior life of poetry [and] the outward life of action and dialect." In his study *Derek Walcott,* Robert D. Hamner noted that this "schizophrenia" is common among West Indians and comments further that "since [Walcott] is descended from a white grandfather and a black grandmother on both paternal and maternal sides, he is living example of the divided loyalties and hatreds that keep his society suspended between two worlds."

"As a West Indian . . . writing in English, with Africa and England in his blood," Alan Shapiro wrote in the *Chicago Tribune Book World,* "Walcott is inescapably the victim and beneficiary of the colonial society in which he was reared. He is a kind of Caribbean Orestes . . . unable to satisfy his allegiance to one side of his nature without at the same time betraying the other." Caryl Phillips described Walcott's work in much the same way in a *Los Angeles Times Book Review* essay. The critic noted that Walcott's poetry was "steeped in an ambivalence toward the outside world and its relationship to his own native land of St. Lucia."

One often-quoted poem, "A Far Cry from Africa," from *In a Green Night: Poems, 1948-1960,* deals directly with Walcott's sense of cultural confusion. In another poem, "The Schooner Flight," from his collection *The Star-Apple Kingdom,* the poet used a Trinidadian sailor named Shabine to appraise his own place as a person of mixed blood in a world divided into whites and blacks. According to the mariner: "The first chain my hands and apologize, *History* the next said I wasn't black enough for their pride." Not white enough for whites, not black enough for blacks.

It was Walcott, of course, who spoke, and *New York Review of Books* contributor Thomas R. Edwards noted how the poet suffered the same fate as his poetic alter-ego, Shabine. Edwards wrote, "Walcott is a cultivated cosmopolitan poet who is black, and as such he risks irrelevant praise as well as blame, whites finding it clever of him to be able to sound so much like other sophisticated poets, blacks feeling that he's sold his soul by practicing white arts."

Although pained by the contrasts in his background, Walcott chose to embrace both his island and his colonial heritage. His love of both sides of his psyche was apparent in his work. As Hamner noted in his study *Derek Walcott:* "Nurtured on oral tales of gods, devils, and cunning tricksters passed down by generations of slaves, Walcott should retell folk stories; and he does. On the other hand, since he has an affinity for and is educated in Western classics, he should retell the traditional themes of European experience; and he does. As inheritor of two vitally rich cultures, he utilizes one, then the other, and finally creates out of the two his own personalized style."

"Many of [Walcott's] early poems attempt to see both sides of his racial heritage," noted King, informing: "Walcott's volumes after *The Castaway* note his increasing alienation from the actual society of Saint Lucia while presenting him as part of Caribbean history, whether representative of a group of artists, a generation discovering West Indianness, or the alienated, nonconforming 'red' (colored) among blacks and whites. He often later returns to the same story, adding disillusionments, divorces, exile, nostalgia, and a larger body of acquaintances and places, commenting on the continuing injustices of a world in which the powerful enslave and suppress the weak; he is aware too that he is aging and threatened by the approach of death."

Walcott seems closest to his island roots in his plays. For the most part, he reserves his native language—patois or creole—to them. They also feature Caribbean settings and themes. According to *Literary Review* contributor David Mason, through his plays Walcott hopes to create a "catalytic theater responsible for social change or at least social identity."

Although a volume of poems was his first published work, Walcott originally concentrated his efforts on the theater. In 1950, two years after Walcott used two-hundred borrowed dollars to print and self-distribute (via street corners) his poetry debut, *25 Poems,* he and his twin brother founded St. Lucia Arts Guild. The importance of this, according to Hamner in *the Dictionary of Literary Biography,* was that it was "the first time Derek could cast, direct, and produce plays as he wrote them." Hamner explained, "The event is fortuitous because Walcott's creativity is evolutionary. His normal practice is to improvise and revise material even while it is in the middle of a production run."

During the fifties, Walcott wrote a series of plays in verse, including *Henri Christophe: A Chronicle in Seven Scenes, The Sea at Dauphin: A Play in One Act,* and *Ione: A Play with Music.* The first play deals with an episode in Caribbean history: ex-slave Henri Christophe's rise to kingship of Haiti in the early 1800s. The second marks Walcott's first use of the mixed French/English language of his native island in a play. Dennis Jones noted in the *Dictionary of Literary Biography Yearbook: 1981* that while Walcott uses the folk idiom of the islands in the play, the speech of the characters is not strictly imitative. It is instead "made eloquent, as the common folk represented in the work are made noble, by the magic of the artist."

In "What the Twilight Says" Walcott describes his use of language in his plays. In particular, he expresses a desire to mold "a language that went beyond mimicry, . . . one which finally settled on its own mode of inflection, and which begins to create an oral culture, of chants, jokes, folk-songs, and fables." The presence of "chants, jokes, and fables" in Walcott's plays caused critics such as Jones and the *Los Angeles Times* critic Juana Duty Kennedy to use the term "folk dramas" to describe the playwright's best pieces for theater. In *Books and Bookmen* Romilly Cavan observed the numerous folk elements in Walcott's plays: "The laments of superstitious fishermen, charcoal-burners and prisoners are quickly counter-pointed by talking crickets, frogs, and birds. Demons are raised, dreams take actual shape, [and] supernatural voices mingle with the natural lilting elliptical speech rhythms of downtrodden natives." Animals who speak and a folk-representation of the devil, for example, were characters in the play *Ti-Jean and His Brothers.*

Walcott's most highly praised play, *Dream on Monkey Mountain,* is also a folk drama. It was awarded a 1971 Obie Award and called "a poem in dramatic form" by Edith Oliver in the *New Yorker.* The play's title is itself enough to immediately transport the viewer into the superstitious, legend-filled world of the Caribbean back country. In the play, Walcott draws a parallel between the hallucinations of an old charcoal vendor and the colonial reality of the Caribbean. Islanders subjected to the imposition of a colonial culture on their own eventually question the validity of both cultures. Ultimately, they may determine that their island culture—because it has no official status other than as an enticement for tourists—is nothing but a sterile hallucination. Conversely, as Jones noted, they may reach the conclusion at which Walcott wished his audience to reach: the charcoal vendor's "dreams connect to the past, and that it is in that past kept alive in the dreams of the folk that an element of freedom is maintained in the colonized world."

Reviews by some American critics have reflected their apparent unfamiliarity with the Caribbean reality which Walcott described in his plays. For example, while Walter Goodman wrote in the *New York Times* that Walcott's *Pantomime* "stays with you as a fresh and funny work filled with thoughtful insights and illuminated by bright performances," Frank Rich's comments on the play in the same newspaper were not as favorable. "Walcott's best writing has always been as a poet . . . ," Rich observed, "and that judgment remains unaltered by *Pantomime.* For some reason, [Walcott] refuses to bring the same esthetic rigor to his playwriting that he does to his powerfully dense verse."

In James Atlas's *New York Times Magazine* essay on Walcott, the critic confronted Rich's remarks head on, and explained that the poet would respond to Rich by commenting "that he doesn't conceive of his plays as finished works but as provisional effects to address his own people. 'The great challenge to me,' he says, 'was to write as powerfully as I could without writing down to the audience, so that the large emotions could be taken in by a fisherman or a guy on the street, even if he didn't understand every line.'"

If Walcott's plays reveal what is most Caribbean about him, his poetry reveals what is most English. If he hoped to reach the common person in his plays, the same cannot be said of his poetry. His poems are based on the traditional forms of English poetry, filled with classical allusions, elaborate metaphors, complex rhyme schemes, and other sophisticated poetic devices. In the *New York Times Book Review,* Selden Rodman called Walcott's poems "almost Elizabethan in their richness." The *New York Times* writer Michiko Kakutani also recognized British influences in Walcott's poetry, noting that "from England, [Walcott] appropriated an old-fashioned love of eloquence, an Elizabethan richness of words and a penchant for complicated, formal rhymes. In fact, in a day when more and more poets have adopted a grudging, minimalist style, [his] verse remains dense and elaborate, filled with dazzling complexities of style."

Some critics objected that Walcott's attention to style sometimes detracted from his poetry, either by being unsuitable for his Caribbean themes or by becoming more important than the poems' content. Denis Donoghue, for example, remarked in the *New York Times Book Review,* "It is my impression that his standard English style [is] dangerously high for nearly every purpose except that of Jacobean tragedy." In Steve Ratiner's *Christian Science Monitor* review of *Midsummer,* the critic observed that "after a time, we are so awash in sparkling language and intricate metaphor, the subject of the poem is all but obscured." *New York Review of Books* contributor Helen Vendleroks found an "unhappy disjunction between [Walcott's] explosive subject . . . and his harmonious pentameters, his lyrical allusions, his stately rhymes, [and] his Yeatsian meditations."

More criticism has come from those who thought that the influence of other poets on Walcott's work has drowned out his authentic voice. While Vendler, for instance, described Walcott as a "man of great sensibility and talent," she dismissed much of his poetry as "ventriloquism" and wrote that in Walcott's collection *The Fortunate Traveller* he seemed "at the mercy of influence, this time the influence of Robert Lowell." Poet J.D. McClatchy also noticed Lowell's influence in *The Fortunate Traveller* as well as two other Walcott poetry collections: *The Star-Apple Kingdom* and *Midsummer.* In his *New Republic* review, McClatchy not only found similarities in the two men's styles but also a similar pattern of development in their poetry. "Like Lowell," the critic noted, "Walcott's mode has . . . shifted from the mythological to the historical, from fictions to facts, and his voice has gotten more clipped and severe. There are times when the influence is almost too direct, as in 'Old New England,' [a poem from *The Fortunate Traveller*] where he paces off Lowell's own territory."

Both major criticisms of Walcott's poetry were answered in Sven Birkerts's *New Republic* essay. Birkerts observed: "Walcott writes a strongly accented, densely packed line that seldom slackens and yet never loses conversational intimacy. He works in form, but he is not formal. His agitated phonetic surfaces can at times recall Lowell's, but the two are quite different. In Lowell, one feels the torque of mind; in Walcott, the senses predominate. And Walcott's lines ring with a spontaneity that Lowell's often lack."

Other critics defended the integrity of Walcott's poems. Poet James Dickey noted in the *New York Times Book Review,* "Fortunately, for him and for us . . . Walcott has the energy and the exuberant strength to break through his literary influences into a highly colored, pulsating realm of his own." In his *Poetry* review of *Midsummer,* Paul Breslin wrote: "For the most part, . . . Walcott's voice remains as distinctive as ever, and the occasional echoes of Lowell register as homage rather than unwitting imitation."

Hamner wrote that when dealing with Walcott's poetry, the term *assimilation* rather than *imitation* should be used. The critic observed, "Walcott passed through his youthful apprenticeship phase wherein he consciously traced the models of established masters. He was humble enough to learn from example and honest enough to disclose his intention to appropriate whatever stores he found useful in the canon of world literature. . . . But Walcott does not stop with imitation. Assimilation means to ingest into the mind and thoroughly comprehend; it also means to merge into or become one with a cultural tradition."

In *Omeros,* whose title is the contemporary Greek word for Homer, Walcott paid homage to the ancient poet in an epic poem that replaced the Homeric Cyclades with the Antilles. Two of the main characters, the West Indian fishermen Achille and Philoctete, set out on a journey to the land of their ancestors on the West African coast. The characters are concerned not with the events of the Trojan War, but rather with the array of civilization, from African antiquity to frontier America and present-day Boston and London. Half-way through the book, the poet himself enters the narrative. *Los Angeles Times Book Review* critic Nick Owchar noted that "the message of *Omeros* grows with the poet's entrance." He wrote, "Walcott's philosophical intentions never come closer to being realized than when he turns . . . criticism on himself. Divestiture, as an artist, is Walcott's forte. He considers his own dangerous use of metaphors: 'When would I not hear the Trojan War / in two fishermen cursing?' he asked near the end. The poet's danger, like every person's, is to distance himself from human suffering by reinterpreting it."

Washington Post Book World reviewer Michael Heyward observed, "*Omeros* is not a translation or even a recreation of either of Homer's great epics. . . .The ancient work it resembles most . . . is Ovid's *Metamorphoses,* with its panoply of characters, its seamless episodic structure, and its panoramic treatment of a mythic world both actual and legendary." He concluded, "We are used to encountering the dynamic exploration of politics and history and folk legend in the contemporary novel, the domain—thanks to Rushdie, Marquez, Gaddis, and others—of modern epic. . . . *Omeros* is not a novel and it does not approximate the form of a novel, but it does rival the novel's mastery of a mythic, multidimensional narrative. Strenuous and thrilling, it swims against the tide."

The uniqueness of Walcott's work stems from his ability to interweave British and island influences, to express what McClatchy called "his mixed state" and do so "without indulging in either ethnic chic or imperial drag." His plays offer pictures of the common Caribbean folk and comment on the ills bred by colonialism. His poetry combines native patois and English rhetorical devices in a constant struggle to force an allegiance between the two halves of his split heritage. According to *Los Angeles Times Book Review* contributor Arthur Vogelsang, "These continuing polarities shoot an electricity to each other which is questioning and beautiful and which helps form a vision all together Caribbean and international, personal (him to you, you to him), independent, and essential for readers of contemporary literature on all the continents."

"Only a few poets at any given time are capable of distinctive style, much less a distinctive mature style; and Walcott's mature style, as evolved in *Midsummer* and further perfected [in *The Bounty*], is his best," wrote Adam Kirch in a *New Republic* review of *The Bounty,* a collection of poems which, once again, showed that Walcott "is urgently concerned with the past and his place in it." Kirch thought that "the subject of History never comes up in Walcott's poetry without a strong note of ambivalence and longing." "Walcott," explained Kirch, "has never tried to escape the fact that the islands are, in the most neutral sense of the term, lacking in History with a glamorous (and ominous) capital 'H'; they lie outside the grand progression of classical and renaissance Europe, their culture and language imported, not to say imposed. What has troubled him, for most of his career, is whether this deprivation is to be mourned or celebrated. For many years he seemed committed to celebration; but he was always too honest to conceal his desire to mourn."

Some of Walcott's perspectives and thoughts are compiled in *What the Twilight Says,*"an insightful book for those with serious poetic interests," wrote *Library Journal* reviewer Scott Hightower. A range of writers, "almost exclusively male and lofty" were addressed in the 1998 collection of essays that Walcott first published between the years of 1970 and 1997. This "first prose collection" was praised by a *Publishers Weekly* critic who commented: "[*What the Twilight Says*] engages with literature, politics and their intersection. . . . [with writing] so intense that it threatens to disintegrate into lyric." A critic for *Publishers Weekly* praised "the beaut[iful] . . . sound" of Walcott's writing. "Reading Derek Walcott can be like listening to some grand cathedral music that's all tangled up in its own echoes: it's lovely, most definitely, but," stated Christian Wiman in a *Poetry* review of *The Bounty,*"it can sometimes be tough to tell one note from the next."

Music is not a foreign element to Walcott. Even though the playwright claimed in a 1997 interview with *Interview* contributor Brendan Lemon that he "hardly listen[s] to [and] . . . never play[s] music," he interwove his dramatic writing with music in a number of theatrical productions. For example, in his musical, *The Capeman,* Walcott collaborated with Paul Simon. *The Capeman,* described Lemon, was "a musical about 1950s Puerto Rican-gang member Salvador Agron." According to Margaret Spillane in *Progressive,* both creators "wanted *Capeman* to do what no other Broadway show had done before: consider the fears and terrors and raptures of New York's urban poor at a human scale—not some giant icon of the downtrodden in the manner of *Les Miz,* and not the outsized exotics of *West Side Story.* They insisted that their depiction of New York Puerto Rican life would be recognizable to people who actually inhabit New York Puerto Rican lives."

Reviews of the eleven million dollar *Capeman,*"the most expensive Broadway musical of all times," reported Spillane, were harsh and the show closed quickly. "The criticisms went beyond murmurs about unorthodox rehearsal expenditures," stated Spillane. In Celia Wren's *Commonweal* review the production was said to contain a "tide of blunders" and its "[musical] score seem[ed] to have been written first, and the drama patched in afterwards [which resulted in calamity]." When summarizing other criticisms, Spillane mentioned "the show didn't offer any monumental characters" and noted that some groups feared that the story "would glorify crime." "Journalists stiffened at the prospect of reckoning with the difficult material of the story," thought Spillane, believing the criticisms to be unfounded and adamantly defending *Capeman.* Spillane felt that political-like motives were at work when "the New York show biz press corps crushed *The Capeman.*" "I saw *The Capeman* twice," wrote Spillane, "and both times I kept swiveling my head in search of what journalists had reported: fidgeting, dissatisfied audience members. . . . But all I could see was people riveted or rocking, sometimes weeping, usually transfixed. At the curtain calls, people yelled and whooped and stomped out their pleasure."

In *Tiepolo's Hound* Walcott focuses on the painter Camille Pissarro. Pissarro experienced cultural confusion, similiar to Walcott's, in that Pissarro was a French Sephardic Jew living in the West Indies. Pissarro eventually left the West Indies for Europe to search for himself. It was while abroad that he established himself as one of the fathers of French Impressionism. When Walcott was a young man he learned to paint from "an old master," but he left his painting in order to focus his energies on poetry. Walcott's poem was a "spiritual journey" for him too, according a *Yomiuri Shimbun* reviewer, who noted Walcott's description of "his constant amazement at the potential and realization of art in poetry, music, and painting. His poem is . . . a tribute to Pissarro." Walcott combined his love for the islands, poetry, and painting to create the work, and yet his "catalyst" for the entire work was Pissarro and Walcott's interest in French Impressionism. *World Literature Today* writer Jim Hannan praised Walcott for reaching "most deeply into his and the reader's heart when he reflects on the calm and devastating clarity on his residual doubts, failures, and longings for an art greater than poetry."

The Haitian Trilogy was an ambitious three-part play that Walcott wrote early in his career, and was published in 2002 long after he established himself as a great poet. *Library Journal* contributor Thomas E. Luddy commented that it came from "a powerful imagination" and that it was "stuffed with historical characters." The plays begin with Columbus's third voyage to the New World and ends in the nineteenth century. *Booklist* critic Jack Helbig noted that Walcott's "Haitian Earth is more Brechtian in scope" and praised Walcott for his use and understanding of dialect as "remarkable."

BIOGRAPHICAL AND CRITICAL SOURCES:

BOOKS

Baugh, Edward, *Derek Walcott: Memory As Vision: Another Life,* Longman (London, England), 1978.

Bloom, Harold, *Derek Walcott,* Chelsea House (New York, NY), 1988.

Brown, Stewart, editor, *The Art of Derek Walcott,* Dufour (Chester Springs, PA), 1991.

Contemporary Literary Criticism, Thomson Gale (Detroit, MI), Volume 2, 1974, Volume 4, 1975, Volume 9, 1978, Volume 14, 1980, Volume 25, 1983, Volume 42, 1987, Volume 67, 1992, Volume 76, 1993.

Contemporary Poets, 6th edition, St. James Press (Detroit, MI), 1996.

Dictionary of Literary Biography, Volume 117: *Twentieth-Century Caribbean and Black African Writers,* Thomson Gale (Detroit, MI), 1992.

Dictionary of Literary Biography Yearbook, Thomson Gale (Detroit, MI), *1981,* 1982, and *1992,* 1993.

Dictionary of Twentieth-Century Culture, Volume 5: *African-American Culture,* Thomson Gale (Detroit, MI), 1996.

Goldstraw, Irma, *Derek Walcott: An Annotated Bibliography of His Works,* Garland Publishing (New York, NY), 1984.

Hamner, Robert D., *Derek Walcott,* Twayne (Boston, MA), 1981.

Hamner, Robert D., compiler and editor, *Critical Perspectives on Derek Walcott,* Three Continents Press (Washington, DC), 1993.

Hamner, Robert D., *Epic of the Dispossessed: Derek Walcott's "Omeros,"* University of Missouri Press (Columbia, MO), 1997.

Harper, Michael S., and Robert B. Stepto, editors, *Chant of Saints,* University of Illinois Press (Urbana, IL), 1979.

Herdeck, Donald E., editor, *Three Dynamite Authors: Derek Walcott (Nobel 1992), Naguib Mahfouz (Nobel 1988), Wole Soyinka (Nobel 1986): Ten Bio-critical Essays from Their Works As Published by Three Continents Press,* Three Continents Press (Colorado Springs, CO), 1995.

King, Bruce Alvin, *Derek Walcott and West Indian Drama: Not Only a Playwright but a Company, the Trinidad Theatre Workshop, 1959-1993,* Oxford University (New York, NY), 1995.

Olaniyan, Tejumola, *Scars of Conquest/Masks of Resistance: The Invention of Cultural Identities in African, African-American, and Caribbean Drama,* Oxford University Press (New York, NY), 1995.

Parker, Michael, and Roger Starkey, editors, *Postcolonial Literatures: Achebe, Ngugi, Desai, Walcott,* St. Martin's Press (New York, NY), 1995.

Rodman, Selden, *Tongues of Fallen Angels,* New Directions (New York, NY), 1974.

Schomburg Center Guide to Black Literature, Thomson Gale (Detroit, MI), 1996.

Terada, Rei, *Derek Walcott's Poetry: American Mimicry,* Northeastern University Press (Boston, MA), 1992.

Thomas, Ned, *Derek Walcott, Poet of the Islands,* Welsh Arts Council (Cardiff, Wales), 1980.

Walcott, Derek, *In a Green Night: Poems, 1948-1960,* J. Cape (London, England), 1962.

Walcott, Derek, *Dream on Monkey Mountain and Other Plays,* Farrar, Straus (New York, NY), 1970.

Walcott, Derek, *The Star-Apple Kingdom,* Farrar, Straus (New York, NY), 1979.

Walcott, Derek, *Collected Poems, 1948-1984,* Farrar, Straus (New York, NY), 1986.

Wheatcroft, John, editor, *Our Other Voices: Nine Poets Speaking,* Bucknell University Press (Lewisberg, VA), 1991.

Wieland, James, *The Ensphering Mind: History, Myth, and Fictions in the Poetry of Allen Curnow, Nissim Ezekiel, A.D. Hope, A.M. Klein, Christopher Okigbo, and Derek Walcott,* Three Continents Press (Washington, DC), 1988.

PERIODICALS

African American Review, winter, 1999, "Conversations with Derek Walcott," p. 708.

American Poetry Review, May-June, 1978.

American Theatre, May-June, 1993, Patti Hartigan, "The Passions of Derek Walcott," p. 14.

Architectural Digest, January, 1997.

Art Journal, spring, 2001, review of *Tiepolo's Hound,* p. 107.

Atlanta Journal and Constitution, April 23, 1995.

Black Issues Book Review, May, 2001, Gregory A. Pardlo, review of *Tiepolo's Hound,* p. 34.

Booklist, April 15, 1997; December 1, 2001, Jack Helbig, review of *The Haitian Trilogy,* p. 625; August, 2002, Jack Helbig, review of *Walker and Ghost Dance,* p. 1912.

Books and Bookmen, April, 1972.

Book World, December 13, 1970; January 3, 1999, review of *What the Twilight Says,* p. 13.

Boston Globe, January 20, 1996; October 16, 1996; October 12, 1997; November 16, 1997.

Callaloo, spring, 1999, review of *Omeros,* p. 509; winter, 2001, review of *Omeros,* p. 276.

Caribbean Writer, Volume 13, 1999, review of *What the Twilight Says,* p. 234.

Chicago Tribune Book World, May 2, 1982; September 9, 1984; March 9, 1986.

Choice, March, 1995.

Christian Science Monitor, March 19, 1982; April 6, 1984.

Chronicle of Higher Education, April 19, 1996, p. A23.

Classical World, September, 1999, reviews of *Omeros,* p. 7, and *The Odyssey: A Stage Version,* p. 71.

Commonweal, April 10, 1998, review of *Capeman.*

Contemporary Literature, summer, 1979; winter, 1994, Graham Huggan, "A Tale of Two Parrots: Walcott, Rhys, and the Uses of Colonial Mimicry," p. 643.

Detroit Free Press, October 9, 1992.

Economist, September 6, 1997, review of *The Bounty.*

English Journal, March, 1994, p. 94.

Entertainment Weekly, February 13, 1998.

Georgia Review, summer, 1984.

Hudson Review, summer, 1984.

Interview, December, 1997, author interview.

Journal of Commonwealth Literature, December, 1976; August, 1981; August, 1986.

Library Journal, November 1, 1994, p. 127; June 1, 1996; April 15, 1997, review of *The Bounty;* October 15, 1998; May 15, 2000, Graham Christian, review of *Tiepolo's Hound,* p. 98; November 1, 2001, review of *The Haitian Trilogy,* p. 117; January, 2002, Thomas E. Luddy, review of *The Haitian Trilogy,* p. 105; July, 2002, Thomas E. Luddy, review of *Walker and the Ghost Dance,* p. 81.

Literary Review, spring, 1986.

London Magazine, December, 1973-January, 1974; February-March, 1977.

Los Angeles Times, November 12, 1986.

Los Angeles Times Book Review, April 4, 1982; May 21, 1985; April 6, 1986; October 26, 1986; September 6, 1987; January 20, 1991; October 20, 1996.

Nation, February 12, 1977; May 19, 1979; February 27, 1982.

National Review, November 3, 1970; June 20, 1986, James W. Tuttleton, review of *Collected Poems: 1948-1984,* p. 51.

New Criterion, March, 1998, Mark Steyn, review of *Capeman,* p. 38.

New Leader, March 11, 1991, Phoebde Pettingell, review of *Omeros,* p. 15; January 13, 1997, review of *Homage to Robert Frost;* September 8, 1997, review of *The Bounty.*

New Republic, November 20, 1976; March 17, 1982; January 23, 1984; March 24, 1986, J.D. McClatchy, review of *Collected Poems,* p. 36; October 29, 1990, Christopher Benfey, review of *Omeros,* p. 36; December 28, 1992; December 15, 1997, review of *The Bounty;* March 30, 1998, review of *Capeman.*

New Statesman, March 19, 1982; August 15, 1997, review of *The Bounty.*

New Statesman & Society, October, 16, 1992; July 21, 1995.

Newsweek, October 19, 1992.

New York, August 14, 1972; February 16, 1998.

New Yorker, March 27, 1971; June 26, 1971; December 12, 1992; February 9, 1998.

New York Review of Books, December 31, 1964; May 6, 1971; June 13, 1974; October 14, 1976; May 31, 1979; March 4, 1982; November 10, 1983; March 27, 1997.

New York Times, March 21, 1979; August 21, 1979; May 30, 1981; May 2, 1982; January 15, 1986; December 17, 1986; October 9, 1992; June 1, 1995; November 13, 1997.

New York Times Book Review, September 13, 1964; October 11, 1970; May 6, 1973; October 31, 1976; May 13, 1979; January 3, 1982; April 8, 1984; February 2, 1986; December 20, 1987; October 7, 1990; October 6, 1996; June 29, 1997.

New York Times Magazine, May 23, 1982; November 9, 1997.

Observer (London, England), October 11, 1992; February 14, 1999.

Paris Review, winter, 1986.

Poetry, February, 1972; December, 1973; July, 1977; December, 1984; June, 1986; August, 1998; August, 1999, review of *What the Twilight Says,* p. 286; April, 2001, Paul Breslin, review of *Tiepolo's Hound,* p. 38.

Progressive, June, 1998, review of *Capeman.*

Publishers Weekly, July 15, 1996, review of *Homage to Robert Frost;* May 26, 1997, review of *The Bounty;* August 31, 1998; February 7, 2000, review of *Tiepolo's Hound,* p. 69.

Research in African Literature, summer, 1994, Patrick Hogan, review of *Dream on Monkey Mountain,* p. 103; spring, 2003, Edward Baugh, "Derek Walcott and the Centering of the Caribbean Subject," p. 151.

Review, winter, 1974.

Sewanee Review, January, 1999, review of *What the Twilight Says,* p. R25.

South Carolina Review, fall, 1999, review of *Omeros,* p. 142.

Spectator (London, England), May 10, 1980.

Third World Quarterly, October, 1988.

Time, March 15, 1982; October 11, 1992; October 31, 1994, p. 78; July 14, 1997, Pico Iyer, review of *The Bounty,* p. 85; January 19, 1998; April 3, 2000, Paul Gray, "Islands in the Stream: Poet Derek Walcott Spins a Luminous Meditation on Visual Art," p. 81.

Times Literary Supplement, December 25, 1969; August 3, 1973; July 23, 1976; August 8, 1980; September 8, 1980; September 24, 1982; November 9, 1984; October 24, 1986; October 1, 1999, review of *What the Twilight Says,* p. 25.

Tribune Books (Chicago, IL), November 8, 1987.

TriQuarterly, winter, 1986.

Twentieth-Century Literature, summer, 2001, Charles W. Pollard, "Traveling with Joyce: Derek Walcott's Discrepant Cosmopolitan Modernism," p. 197; fall, 2001, Robert D. Hamner, review of *The Odyssey: A Stage Version,* p. 374.

Village Voice, April 11, 1974.
Virginia Quarterly Review, winter, 1974; summer, 1984; summer, 1999, review of *What the Twilight Says,* p. 84.
Vogue, January, 1998.
Wall Street Journal, October 9, 1992.
Washington Post Book World, February 21, 1982; April 13, 1986; November 11, 1990; April 26, 1995.
Western Humanities Review, spring, 1977.
World Literature Today, spring, 1977; summer, 1979; summer, 1981; winter, 1985; summer, 1986; winter, 1987; winter, 1989; winter, 1997; winter, 1998, review of *The Bounty,* p. 191; spring, 1999, review of *What the Twilight Says,* p. 339; autumn, 2000, Jim Hannan, review of *Tiepolo's Hound,* p. 797.
World Literature Written in English, April, 1973; April, 1977; November, 1977; spring, 1986; spring, 1987.
Yale Review, October, 1973.
Yomiuri Shimbun/Daily Yomiuri, August 22, 2000, "Walcott Turns an Artistic Eye to Colonialism in Epic Poem," p. YOSH12474972.

ONLINE

Academy of American Poets Web site, http://www.poets.org/ (June 3, 2003), author biography.
Boston University Web site, http://www.bu.edu/writing/faculty/ (June 3, 2003), Derek Walcott faculty profile.
Nobel e-Museum Web site, http://www.nobel.se/literature/laureates/ (June 3, 2003), author biographical material and interview.
Richmond Review Online, http://www.richmondreview.co.uk/ (June 3, 2003), Amanda Jeremin Harris, review of *Tiepolo's Hound.*

* * *

WALCOTT, Derek Alton
See WALCOTT, Derek

* * *

WALKER, Alice 1944-
(Alice Malsenior Walker)

PERSONAL: Born February 9, 1944, in Eatonton, GA; daughter of Willie Lee and Minnie Tallulah (Grant) Walker; married Melvyn Rosenman Leventhal (a civil rights lawyer), March 17, 1967 (divorced, 1976); children: Rebecca. *Ethnicity:* "Black." *Education:* Attended Spelman College, 1961-63; Sarah Lawrence College, B.A., 1965.

ADDRESSES: Home—Berkeley, CA. *Agent*—c/o Author Mail, Random House, 201 E. 50th St., New York, NY 10022.

CAREER: Writer. Wild Trees Press, Navarro, CA, cofounder and publisher, 1984-88. Has been a voter registration worker in Georgia, a worker in Head Start program in Mississippi, and on staff of New York City welfare department. Writer in residence and teacher of black studies at Jackson State College, 1968-69, and Tougaloo College, 1970-71; lecturer in literature, Wellesley College and University of Massachusetts—Boston, both 1972-73; distinguished writer in Afro-American studies department, University of California, Berkeley, spring, 1982; Fannie Hurst Professor of Literature, Brandeis University, Waltham, MA, fall, 1982. Lecturer and reader of own poetry at universities and conferences. Member of board of trustees of Sarah Lawrence College. Consultant on black history to Friends of the Children of Mississippi, 1967. Coproducer of film documentary *Warrior Marks,* directed by Pratibha Parmar, with script and narration by Walker, 1993.

AWARDS, HONORS: Bread Loaf Writer's Conference scholar, 1966; first prize, *American Scholar* essay contest, 1967; Merrill writing fellowship, 1967; MacDowell Colony fellowship, 1967, 1977-78; National Endowment for the Arts grant, 1969, 1977; Radcliffe Institute fellowship, 1971-73; Ph.D., Russell Sage College, 1972; National Book Award nomination and Lillian Smith Award from the Southern Regional Council, both 1973, both for *Revolutionary Petunias and Other Poems;* Richard and Hinda Rosenthal Foundation Award, American Academy and Institute of Arts and Letters, 1974, for *In Love and Trouble: Stories of Black Women;* Guggenheim fellowship, 1977-78; National Book Critics Circle Award nomination, 1982, and Pulitzer Prize and American Book Award, both 1983, all for *The Color Purple;* Best Books for Young Adults citation, American Library Association, 1984, for *In Search of Our Mother's Gardens: Womanist Prose;* D.H.L., University of Massachusetts, 1983; O. Henry Award, 1986, for "Kindred Spirits"; Langston Hughes Award, New York City College, 1989; Nora Astorga Leadership Award, 1989; Fred Cody Award for lifetime achievement, Bay Area Book Reviewers Association, 1990; Freedom to Write Award, PEN West, 1990; California Governor's Arts Award, 1994; Literary Ambassador Award, University of Oklahoma Center for Poets and Writers, 1998.

WRITINGS:

POETRY

Once: Poems (also see below), Harcourt (San Diego, CA), 1968.

Five Poems, Broadside Press (Highland Park, MI), 1972.

Revolutionary Petunias and Other Poems (also see below), Harcourt (San Diego, CA), 1973.

Goodnight, Willie Lee, I'll See You in the Morning (also see below), Dial (New York, NY), 1979.

Horses Make a Landscape Look More Beautiful, Harcourt (San Diego, CA), 1984.

Alice Walker Boxed Set—Poetry: Good Night, Willie Lee, I'll See You in the Morning; Revolutionary Petunias and Other Poems; Once, Poems, Harcourt (San Diego, CA), 1985.

Her Blue Body Everything We Know: Earthling Poems, 1965-1990 Complete, Harcourt (San Diego, CA), 1991.

A Poem Traveled down My Arm: Poem and Drawings, Random House (New York, NY), 2002.

Absolute Trust in the Goodness of the Earth: New Poems, Random House (New York, NY), 2003.

FICTION; NOVELS, EXCEPT AS NOTED

The Third Life of Grange Copeland, Harcourt (San Diego, CA), 1970.

In Love and Trouble: Stories of Black Women, Harcourt (San Diego, CA), 1973.

Meridian, Harcourt (San Diego, CA), 1976.

You Can't Keep a Good Woman Down (short stories), Harcourt (San Diego, CA), 1981.

The Color Purple, Harcourt (San Diego, CA), 1982.

Alice Walker Boxed Set—Fiction: The Third Life of Grange Copeland, You Can't Keep a Good Woman Down, and In Love and Trouble, Harcourt (San Diego, CA), 1985.

The Temple of My Familiar, Harcourt (San Diego, CA), 1989.

Possessing the Secret of Joy, Harcourt (San Diego, CA), 1992.

Everyday Use, edited by Barbara Christian, Rutgers University Press (New Brunswick, NJ), 1994.

By the Light of My Father's Smile, Random House (New York, NY), 1998.

The Way Forward Is with a Broken Heart, Random House (New York, NY), 2000.

Now Is the Time to Open Your Heart: A Novel, Random House (New York, NY), 2004.

FOR CHILDREN

Langston Hughes: American Poet (biography), Crowell (New York, NY), 1973, revised edition, illustrated by Catherine Deeter, HarperCollins (New York, NY), 2002.

To Hell with Dying, illustrations by Catherine Deeter, Harcourt (San Diego, CA), 1988.

Finding the Green Stone, Harcourt (San Diego, CA), 1991.

There Is a Flower at the Tip of My Nose Smelling Me, HarperCollins (New York, NY), 2006.

NONFICTION

In Search of Our Mothers' Gardens: Womanist Prose, Harcourt (San Diego, CA), 1983.

Living by the Word: Selected Writings, 1973-1987, Harcourt (San Diego, CA), 1988.

(With Pratibha Parmar) *Warrior Marks: Female Genital Mutilation and the Sexual Blinding of Women,* Harcourt (San Diego, CA), 1993.

Alice Walker Banned, with introduction by Patricia Holt, Aunt Lute Books (San Francisco, CA), 1996.

Anything We Love Can Be Saved: A Writer's Activism, Random House (New York, NY), 1997.

(With Francesco Mastalia and Alfonse Pagano) *Dreads: Sacred Rites of the Natural Hair Revolution,* Artisan (New York, NY), 1999.

(With others) *Letters of Love and Hope: The Story of the Cuban Five,* Consortium (New York, NY), 2005.

OTHER

(Editor) *I Love Myself when I'm Laughing . . . and Then Again when I Am Looking Mean and Impressive: A Zora Neale Hurston Reader,* introduction by Mary Helen Washington, Feminist Press (New York, NY), 1979.

The Same River Twice: Honoring the Difficult; A Meditation of Life, Spirit, Art, and the Making of the film "The Color Purple," Ten Years Later, Scribner (New York, NY), 1996.

Contributor to anthologies, including *Voices of the Revolution,* edited by Helen Haynes, E. & J. Kaplan (Philadelphia, PA), 1967; *The Best Short Stories by Negro Writers from 1899 to the Present: An Anthology,* edited by Langston Hughes, Little, Brown (Boston, MA), 1967; *Afro-American Literature: An Introduction,* Harcourt (San Diego, CA), 1971; *Tales and Stories for Black Folks,* compiled by Toni Cade Bambara, Zenith Books (New York, NY), 1971; *Black Short Story Anthology,* compiled by Woodie King, New American Library (New York, NY), 1972; *The Poetry of Black America: An Anthology of the Twentieth Century,* compiled by Arnold Adoff, Harper (New York, NY), 1973; *A Rock against the Wind: Black Love Poems,* edited by Lindsay Patterson, Dodd (New York, NY), 1973; *We Be Word Sorcerers: Twenty-five Stories by Black Americans,* edited by Sonia Sanchez, Bantam (New York, NY), 1973; *Images of Women in Literature,* compiled by Mary Anne Ferguson, Houghton Mifflin (Boston, MA), 1973; *Best American Short Stories: 1973,* edited by Margaret Foley, Hart-Davis, 1973; *Best American Short Stories, 1974,* edited by M. Foley, Houghton Mifflin (Boston, MA), 1974; *Chants of Saints: A Gathering of Afro-American Literature, Art and Scholarship,* edited by Michael S. Harper and Robert B. Stepto, University of Illinois Press (Chicago, IL), 1980; *Midnight Birds: Stories of Contemporary Black Women Authors,* edited by Mary Helen Washington, Anchor Press (New York, NY), 1980; and *Double Stitch: Black Women Write about Mothers and Daughters,* edited by Maya Angelou, HarperCollins (New York, NY), 1993.

Contributor to numerous periodicals, including *Negro Digest, Denver Quarterly, Harper's, Black World, Essence, Canadian Dimension,* and the *New York Times.* Contributing editor, *Southern Voices, Freedomways,* and *Ms.*

ADAPTATIONS: The Color Purple was made into a feature film directed by Steven Spielberg, Warner Bros., 1985.

SIDELIGHTS: Alice Walker "is one of the country's best-selling writers of literary fiction," according to Renee Tawa in the *Los Angeles Times.* "More than ten million copies of her books are in print." Walker has become a focal spokesperson and symbol for black feminism and has earned critical and popular acclaim as a major American novelist and intellectual. Her literary reputation was secured with her Pulitzer Prize-winning third novel, *The Color Purple,* which was transformed into a popular film by Steven Spielberg. Upon the release of the novel in 1982, critics sensed that Walker had created something special. " *The Color Purple* . . . could be the kind of popular and literary event that transforms an intense reputation into a national one," according to Gloria Steinem of *Ms.* Judging from the critical enthusiasm for *The Color Purple,* Steinem's words have proved prophetic. Walker "has succeeded," as Andrea Ford noted in the *Detroit Free Press,* "in creating a jewel of a novel." Peter S. Prescott presented a similar opinion in a *Newsweek* review. "I want to say," he commented, "that *The Color Purple* is an American novel of permanent importance, that rare sort of book which (in Norman Mailer's felicitous phrase) amounts to 'a diversion in the fields of dread.'"

Jeanne Fox-Alston and Mel Watkins both felt that the appeal of *The Color Purple* is that the novel, as a synthesis of characters and themes found in Walker's earlier works, brings together the best of the author's literary production in one volume. Fox-Alston, in Chicago's *Tribune Books,* remarked: "Celie, the main character in Walker's third . . . novel, *The Color Purple,* is an amalgam of all those women [characters in Walker's previous books]; she embodies both their desperation and, later, their faith." Watkins stated in the *New York Times Book Review:* "Her previous books . . . have elicited praise for Miss Walker as a lavishly gifted writer. *The Color Purple,* while easily satisfying that claim, brings into sharper focus many of the diverse themes that threaded their way through her past work."

Walker was born in Eatonton, Georgia, a southern town where most African Americans toiled at the difficult job of tenant farming. Her writing reflects these roots, where black vernacular was prominent and the stamp of slavery and oppression were still present. When she was eight, Walker was accidentally shot in the eye by a brother playing with his BB gun. Her parents, who were too poor to afford a car, could not take her to a doctor for several days. By that time, her wound was so bad that she had lost the use of her right eye. This handicap eventually aided her writer's voice, because she withdrew from others and became a meticulous observer of human relationships and interaction.

An excellent student, Walker was awarded a scholarship to Spelman College in 1961. The civil rights movement attracted her, and she became an activist. In 1963 she decided to continue her education at Sarah Lawrence College in New York, where she began to work seriously on writing poems, publishing several in a college journal. After graduation, she moved to Mississippi to teach and continue her social activism, and she met and married Melvyn Leventhal, a Jewish civil rights lawyer. The two became the only legally married interracial couple living in Jackson, Mississippi. After their divorce in 1976, Walker's literary output increased.

Walker coined the term "Womanist" to describe her philosophical stance on the issue of gender. As a Womanist, which is different from a feminist, she sees herself as someone who appreciates women's culture, emotions, and character. Her work often reflects this stance, and, paradoxically, the universality of human experience. Walker's central characters are almost always black women; Walker, according to Steinem, "comes at universality through the path of an American black woman's experience . . . . She speaks the female experience more powerfully for being able to pursue it across boundaries of race and class." This universality is also noted by Fox-Alston, who remarked that Walker has a "reputation as a provocative writer who writes about blacks in particular, but all humanity in general."

However, many critics recognize a particularly black and female focus in Walker's writings. For example, in her review of *The Color Purple,* Ford suggested that the novel transcends "culture and gender" lines but also refers to Walker's "unabashedly feminist viewpoint" and the novel's "black . . . texture." Walker does not deny this dual bias; the task of revealing the condition of the black woman is particularly important to her. Thadious M. Davis, in his *Dictionary of Literary Biography* essay, commented: "Walker writes best of the social and personal drama in the lives of familiar people who struggle for survival of self in hostile environments. She has expressed a special concern with exploring the oppressions, the insanities, the loyalties and the triumph of black women."

Walker's earlier books—novels, volumes of short stories, and poems—have not received the same degree of attention, but neither have they been ignored. Gloria Steinem pointed out that *Meridian,* Walker's second novel, "is often cited as the best novel of the civil rights movement, and is taught as part of some American history as well as literature courses." In *Everyday Use,* Barbara Christian found the title story— first published in Walker's collection *In Love and Trouble: Stories of Black Women*— to be "pivotal" to all of Walker's work in its evocation of black sisterhood and black women's heritage of quilting. William Peden, writing in *The American Short Story: Continuity and Change, 1940-1975,* called this same collection "a remarkable book." David Guy's commentary on *The Color Purple* in the *Washington Post Book World* included this evaluation: "Accepting themselves for what they are, the women [in the novel] are able to extricate themselves from oppression; they leave their men, find useful work to support themselves." Watkins further explained: "In *The Color Purple* the role of male domination in the frustration of black women's struggle for independence is clearly the focus."

Some reviewers criticize Walker's fiction for portraying an overly negative view of black men. Katha Pollitt, for example, in the *New York Times Book Review,* called the stories in *You Can't Keep a Good Woman Down* "too partisan." The critic added: "The black woman is always the most sympathetic character." Guy noted: "Some readers . . . will object to her overall perspective. Men in [*The Color Purple*] are generally pathetic, weak and stupid, when they are not heartlessly cruel, and the white race is universally bumbling and inept." Charles Larson, in his *Detroit News* review of *The Color Purple,* pointed out: "I wouldn't go as far as to say that all the male characters [in the novel] are villains, but the truth is fairly close to that." However, neither Guy nor Larson felt that this emphasis on women is a major fault in the novel. Guy, for example, while conceding that "white men . . . are invisible in Celie's world," observed: "This really is Celie's perspective, however—it is psychologically accurate to her—and Alice Walker might argue that it is only a neat inversion of the view that has prevailed in western culture for centuries." Larson also noted that by the end of the novel, "several of [Walker's] masculine characters have reformed."

This idea of reformation, this sense of hope even in despair, is at the core of Walker's vision. In spite of the brutal effects of sexism and racism suffered by the characters of her short stories and novels, critics note what Art Seidenbaum of the *Los Angeles Times* called Walker's sense of "affirmation . . . [that] overcomes her anger." This is particularly evident in *The Color Purple,* according to several reviewers. Ford, for example, asserted that the author's "polemics on . . . political and economic issues finally give way to what can only be described as a joyful celebration of human spirit—exulting, uplifting and eminently universal." Prescott discovered a similar progression in the novel. He wrote: "[Walker's] story begins at about the point that most Greek tragedies reserve for the climax, then . . . by immeasurable small steps . . . works its way toward acceptance, serenity and joy."

Davis referred to this idea as Walker's "vision of survival" and offered a summary of its significance in Walker's work. "At whatever cost, human beings have the capacity to live in spiritual health and beauty; they may be poor, black, and uneducated, but their inner selves can blossom." This vision, extended to all humanity, is evident in Walker's collection *Living by the Word: Selected Writings, 1973-1987.* Although "her original interests centered on black women, and especially on the ways they were abused or underrated," *New York Times Book Review* contributor Noel Perrin believed that "now those interests encompass all creation." Judith Paterson similarly observed in *Tribune Books* that in *Living by the Word,* "Walker casts her abiding obsession with the oneness of the universe in a question: Do creativity, love and spiritual wholeness still have a chance of winning the human heart amid political forces bent on destroying the universe with poisonous chemicals and nuclear weapons?" Walker explores this question through journal entries and essays that deal with Native Americans, racism in China, a lonely horse, smoking, and response to the criticism leveled against both the novel and the film version of *The Color Purple.* Many of these treatments are personal in approach, and Jill Nelson found many of them trivial. Writing in the *Washington Post Book World,* Nelson commented, "*Living by the Word* is fraught with . . . reaches for commonality, analogy and universality. Most of the time all Walker achieves is banality." But Derrick Bell differed, noting in his *Los Angeles Times Book Review* critique that Walker "uses carefully crafted images that provide a universality to unique events." The critic further asserted that *Living by the Word* "is not only vintage Alice Walker: passionate, political, personal, and poetic, it also provides a panoramic view of a fine human being saving her soul through good deeds and extraordinary writing."

Harsh criticisms of Walker's work crested with the 1989 publication of her fourth novel, *The Temple of My Familiar.* The novel, featuring several of the characters of *The Color Purple,* reflects concerns hinted at in that novel and confronted directly in *Living by the Word:* racism, a reverence for nature, a search for spiritual truths, and the universality referred to by reviewers Nelson and Bell. But according to David Gates in his *Newsweek* review, the novel "is fatally ambitious. It encompasses 500,000 years, rewrites Genesis and the Beatitudes and weighs in with mini-lectures on everything from Elvis (for) to nuclear waste (against)." David Nicholson, writing in the *Washington Post Book World,* felt that *The Temple of My Familiar* "is not a novel so much as it is an ill-fitting collection of speeches . . . a manifesto for the Fascism of the New Age . . . . There are no characters, only types representative of the world Walker lives in or wishes could be." In a similar vein, *Time* reviewer Paul Grey noted that "Walker's relentless adherence to her own sociopolitical agenda makes for frequently striking propaganda," but not for good fiction. Though generally disliked even by sympathetic critics, the novel has its defenders. Novelist J.M. Coetzee, writing in the *New York Times Book Review,* implored the reader to look upon the novel as a "fable of recovered origins, as an exploration of the inner lives of contemporary black Americans as these are penetrated by fabulous stories," and Bernard W. Bell, writing in the *Chicago Tribune,* felt that the novel is a "colorful quilt of many patches," and that its "stylized lovers, remembrances of things past, bold flights of fantasy and vision of a brave new world of cultural diversity and cosmic harmony challenge the reader's willingness to suspend disbelief."

A *Publishers Weekly* reviewer of Walker's 1991 children's story *Finding the Green Stone* said that "the tone is ethereal and removed . . . while the writing style, especially the dialogue, is stiff and didactic." But for Walker's collected poems, *Her Blue Body Everything We Know: Earthling Poems, 1965-1990 Complete,* a *Publishers Weekly* reviewer had high praise, characterizing Walker as "composed, wry, unshaken by adversity," and suggesting that her "strong, beautiful voice" beckons us "to heal ourselves and the planet."

Critics gave high praise to Walker's controversial fifth novel, *Possessing the Secret of Joy,* about the practice of female genital mutilation in certain African, Asian, and Middle Eastern cultures. Writing in the *Los Angeles Times Book Review,* Tina McElroy Ansa said that taking on such a taboo subject shows Walker's depth and range. The critic also felt that her portrait of the suffering of Tashi—a character from *The Color Purple*—is "stunning." "The description of the excision itself and its after effect is graphic enough to make one gag," but is the work of a thoughtful, impassioned artist, rather than a sensationalist, noted Charles R. Larson in the *Washington Post Book World.* And Donna Haisty Winchell wrote in her *Dictionary of Literary Biography* essay that *Possessing the Secret of Joy* is "much more concise, more controlled, and more successful as art" than *The Temple of My Familiar* and demonstrates an effective blend of "art and activism."

Walker's concerns about the international issue of female genital mutilation prompted her to further explore the issue, both on film and in the book *Warrior Marks: Female Genital Mutilation and the Sexual Blinding of Women,* written with documentary film director Pratibha Parmar. According to a *Publishers Weekly* contributor, *Warrior Marks* is a "forceful account" of how the two filmed a documentary on the ritual circumcision of African women.

In 1996 Walker produced *The Same River Twice: Honoring the Difficult; A Meditation of Life, Spirit, Art, and the Making of the film "The Color Purple," Ten Years Later.* The book focuses mainly on Walker's feelings about, and struggles with, the filming of *The Color Purple.* While having the book transformed into a film by Steven Spielberg was a high point in her life, it was also riddled with difficulties. First, Spielberg rejected Walker's screenplay of the book and implemented one with which Walker was not happy. In addition, the film itself was met with controversy and attacks on Walker's ideas—some people thought she had attacked the character of black people in general and black men specifically. Also at the time, Walker's mother was critically ill, while Walker herself was suffering from a debilitating illness that turned out to be Lyme disease. Included in the book are fan letters, reviews, and Walker's original version of the script. Francine Prose in Chicago's *Tribune Books* found fault with the book, feeling that Walker's protests about how things did not go her way ring of artistic posturing: "Walker seems to have so lost touch with the lives and sensibilities of ordinary humans that she apparently cannot hear how her complaints . . . might sound to the less fortunate, who have been less generously favored by greatness."

In 1998 Walker's sixth novel, *By the Light of My Father's Smile,* was published, a book again focusing on female sexuality. The main characters are the Robinsons, a husband-and-wife team of anthropologists, and the story is told in flashback. Unable to secure funding for research in Mexico in the 1950s, the husband poses as a minister to study the Mundo, a mixed black and Indian tribe. The couple brings along their young daughter to this new life in the Sierra Madre. Sexuality is at the heart of the story, though the father reacts violently upon discovering that his daughter has become involved with a Mundo boy. This reaction has repercussions throughout the novel. Again, Walker experiments with points of view, even recounting the action through the eyes of the recently deceased patriarch of the Robinson clan. According to Prose, reviewing the novel in the *New York Times Book Review,* this novel deals with the "damaging ways in which our puritanical culture suppresses women's sexuality." However, Prose felt that in focusing on polemics, Walker's book became "deeply mired in New Age hocus-pocus and goddess-religion baloney." Prose also complained of "passages of tortuously infelicitous prose." Similarly, Nedhera Landers, writing in the *Lambda Book Report,* was disappointed to find "almost every character to be a two-dimensional stereotype."

Regardless of such criticism, however, Walker's literary reputation is secure. She continues to write in a variety of genres, from fiction to nonfiction and poetry. In 1997's *Anything We Love Can Be Saved: A Writer's Activism,* she details her own political and social struggle, while in the critically acclaimed short-story collection *The Way Forward Is with a Broken Heart,* she employs fiction in a "quasi-autobiographical reflection" on her own past, including her marriage to a Jewish civil rights lawyer, the birth of her daughter, and the creative life she built after her divorce. For Jeff Guinn, writing for the *Knight Ridder/Tribune News Service,* the thirteen stories plus epilogue of this collection "beautifully leavened the universal regrets of middle age with dollops of uplifting philosophy." A contributor for *Publishers Weekly* described the collection as a reflection on the "nature of passion and friendship, pondering the emotional trajectories of lives and loves." This same reviewer found the collection, despite some "self indulgence," to be both "strong . . . [and] moving." Adele S. News-Horst, reviewing the book in *World Literature Today,* found that it is "peopled by characters who are refugees, refugees from the war over civil rights, from the 'criminal' Vietnam-American War, and from sexual oppression." News-Horst further commented that the "stories are neither forced nor unnatural, and there is a sense of truth in all of them." And Linda Barrett Osborne, writing in the *New York Times Book Review,* called *The Way Forward* a "touching and provocative collection."

The versatile Walker returned to poetry with her 2003 collection *Absolute Trust in the Goodness of the Earth,* her first verse collection in more than a decade. Walker had, she thought, given up writing, taking time off to study Tibetan Buddhism and explore the Amazon. Inspired by the terrorist attacks of September 11, 2001, however, she began writing poems. Though just a few poems in *Absolute Trust* deal with the attacks on New York and Washington, D.C., the tragedy let Walker know that she was not yet done with writing. Guinn described the verse in the new collection as "choppy, with sparse clumps of words presented in odd, brisk rhythms." Such devices resulted, Guinn thought, in occasional "sophisticated thought in simple, accessible form." Short lines in free verse are the skeletons of most of the poems in the collection, many of them dealing with "social and environmental justice, and America's blinding ethnocentrism," as Kelly Norman Ellis described them in *Black Issues Book Review.* Ellis further praised the poems in the collection as "psalms about the human capacity for great good and . . . for unimagined brutality." A contributor for *Publishers Weekly* also commended this work, concluding that "readers across the country who cherished Walker's earlier poems will find in this new work exactly what they've awaited."

Walker returns to the literary form for which she is best known with her seventh novel, *Now Is the Time to Open Your Heart,* the tale of a successful African American female novelist, Kate, and her search for new meaning as she approaches sixty. In a long-time relationship with the artist Yolo, Kate decides to voyage down the Colorado River and then down the Amazon, on trips of self-discovery. Yolo meanwhile goes on his own quest, to Hawaii, and to the woman he once loved. Both Kate and Yolo are changed by their experiences. Some reviewers found this novel full of trite philosophizing.

For example, Ellen Flexman, writing in *Library Journal,* while allowing that Walker "has some interesting insights on the power of stories and the nature of spirit," also felt that such revelations are "buried amid improbably situations and characters who have read too many bad books on spirituality." Flexman also noted that it "is difficult to take any of the characters seriously." Similarly, a contributor for *Publishers Weekly* called the novel an "inflated paean to the self," while a *Kirkus Reviews* critic complained of "the underlying smug preachiness, the unconvincing experiences, and the idiosyncratic thinking [that] make this more a self-indulgent fantasy than an intellectually provocative tale." Other reviewers were more sympathetic in their conclusions. Debby Waldman, writing in *People,* noted that the book might "strike some readers as New Age hooey," but that "Walker's evocative prose will please her fans." Likewise, Susan McHenry, writing in *Black Issues Book Review,* noted that she "started this novel skeptically, fearing a New Age ramble." However, McHenry found "reading this book a richly rewarding journey." And *Booklist* critic Vanessa Bush praised this "dreamlike novel [that] incorporates the political and spiritual consciousness and emotional style for which [Walker] is known and appreciated."

BIOGRAPHICAL AND CRITICAL SOURCES:

BOOKS

Allan, Tuzyline Jita, *Womanist and Feminist Aesthetics: A Comparative Review,* Ohio University Press (Athens, OH), 1995.

Bestsellers '89, Issue 4, Gale (Detroit, MI), 1989.

Black Literature Criticism, Volume 1, Gale (Detroit, MI), 1992.

Christian, Barbara, editor, *Everyday Use,* Rutgers University Press (New Brunswick, NJ), 1994.

Contemporary Literary Criticism, Gale (Detroit, MI), Volume 5, 1976, Volume 6, 1976, Volume 9, 1978, Volume 19, 1981, Volume 27, 1984, Volume 46, 1988, Volume 58, 1990, Volume 103, 1998.

Contemporary Novelists, 7th edition, St. James Press (Detroit, MI), 2001.

Dictionary of Literary Biography, Gale (Detroit, MI), Volume 6: *American Novelists since World War II, Second Series,* 1980, Volume 33: *Afro-American Fiction Writers after 1955,* 1984, Volume 143: *American Novelists since World War II, Third Series,* 1994.

Evans, Mari, editor, *Black Women Writers, 1950-1980: A Critical Evaluation,* Anchor (New York, NY), 1984.

Johnson, Yvonne, *The Voices of African American Women: The Use of Narrative and Authorial Voice in the Works of Harriet Jacobs, Zora Neale Hurston, and Alice Walker,* P. Lang (New York, NY), 1995.

Kaplan, Carla, *The Erotics of Talk: Women's Writing and Feminist Paradigms,* Oxford University Press (New York, NY), 1996.

Kramer, Barbara, *Alice Walker: Author of "The Color Purple,"* Enslow (Berkeley Heights, NJ), 1995.

O'Brien, John, *Interviews with Black Writers,* Liveright (New York, NY), 1973.

Peden, William, *The American Short Story: Continuity and Change, 1940-1975,* 2nd revised and enlarged edition, Houghton Mifflin (Boston, MA), 1975.

Prenshaw, Peggy W., editor, *Women Writers of the Contemporary South,* University Press of Mississippi (Jackson, MS), 1984.

St. James Guide to Young Adult Writers, 2nd edition, St. James Press (Detroit, MI), 1999.

Short Story Criticism, Volume 5, Gale (Detroit, MI), 1990.

Walker, Alice, *The Same River Twice: Honoring the Difficult; A Meditation of Life, Spirit, Art, and the Making of the film "The Color Purple," Ten Years Later,* Scribner (New York, NY), 1996.

PERIODICALS

Booklist, October 15, 2003, Vanessa Bush, review of *Now Is the Time to Open Your Heart,* p. 358.

Black Issues Book Review, March-April, 2003, Kelly Norman Ellis, review of *Absolute Trust in the Goodness of the Earth: New Poems,* p. 38; May-July, 2004, Susan McHenry, "The Gifts of the Grandmother Spirit," p. 44.

Bookseller, April 23, 2004, "Alice Walker," p. 29.

Chicago Tribune, April 23, 1989, Bernard W. Bell, review of *The Temple of My Familiar.*

Detroit Free Press, August 8, 1982, Andrea Ford, review of *The Color Purple*; July 10, 1988; January 4, 1989.

Detroit News, September 15, 1982, Charles Larson, review of *The Color Purple.*

Kirkus Reviews, December 15, 2003, review of *Now Is the Time to Open Your Heart,* p. 1422.

Knight Ridder/Tribune News Service, February 7, 2001, Ira Hadnot, review of *My Way Forward Is with a Broken Heart,* p. K1172; February 13, 2002, Sue Corbett, review of *Langston Hughes: American Poet,* p. K4900; March 12, 2003, Jeff Guinn, review of *Absolute Trust in the Goodness of the Earth,* p. K2933.

Lambda Book Report, December, 1998, Nedhera Landers, review of *By the Light of My Father's Smile,* p. 30.

Language Arts, November, 2002, Junko Yokota and Mingshui Cai, review of *Langston Hughes,* p. 152.

Library Journal, December, 1998, Nann Blaine Hilyard, review of *By the Light of My Father's Smile,* p. 172; November 15, 2003, Ellen Flexman, review of *Now Is the Time to Open Your Heart,* p. 100.

Los Angeles Times, April 29, 1981, article by Art Seidenbaum; April 18, 2003, Renee Tawa, "Alice Walker Ceased Writing, Then Started Anew. Don't Ask, Just Appreciate Wisdom Gained," p. E30.

Los Angeles Times Book Review, May 29, 1988, Derrick Bell, review of *Living by the Word: Selected Writings, 1973-1987*; July 5, 1992, Tina McElroy Ansa, review of *Possessing the Secret of Joy,* p. 4.

Ms., June, 1982, Gloria Steinem, "Do You Know This Woman? She Knows You," p. 35.

Newsweek, June 21, 1982, Peter S. Prescott, review of *The Color Purple,* p. 676; April 24, 1989, David Gates, review of *The Temple of My Familiar,* p. 74.

New York Times Book Review, May 24, 1981, Katha Pollitt, review of *You Can't Keep a Good Woman Down,* p. 9; July 25, 1982, Mel Watkins, review of *The Color Purple,* p. 7; June 5, 1988, Noel Perrin, review of *Living by the Word,* p. 42; April 30, 1989, J.M. Coetzee, review of *The Temple of My Familiar,* p. 7; October 4, 1998, Francine Prose, review of *By the Light of My Father's Smile,* p. 18; December 10, 2000, Linda Barrett Osborne, review of *The Way Forward Is with a Broken Heart,* p. 32.

People, May 3, 2004, Debby Waldman, review of *Now Is the Time to Open Your Heart,* p. 45.

Publishers Weekly, March 1, 1991, review of *Her Blue Body Everything We Know: Earthling Poems, 1965-1990 Complete,* p. 64; October 25, 1991, review of *Finding the Green Stone,* p. 66; October 25, 1993, review of *Warrior Marks: Female Genital Mutilation and the Sexual Blinding of Women,* p. 49; October 5, 1998, review of *By the Light of My Father's Smile,* p. 44; September 11, 2000, review of *The Way Forward Is with a Broken Heart,* p. 71; November 19, 2001, review of *Langston Hughes,* pp. 67-68; January 20, 2003, review of *Absolute Trust in the Goodness of the Earth,* p. 77; November 17, 2003, review of *Now Is the Time to Open Your Heart,* p. 38.

Time, May 1, 1989, Paul Grey, review of *The Temple of My Familiar,* p. 69.

Tribune Books (Chicago, IL), August 1, 1982, Jeanne Fox-Alston, review of *The Color Purple*; July 17, 1988, Judith Paterson, review of *Living by the Word*; January 21, 1996, Francine Prose, review of *The Same River Twice,* p. 5.

Washington Post Book World, July 25, 1982, David Guy, review of *The Color Purple*; May 29, 1988, Jill Nelson, review of *Living by the Word*; May 7, 1989, David Nicholson, review of *The Temple of My Familiar,* p. 3; July 5, 1992, Charles R. Larson, review of *Possessing the Secret of Joy,* p. 1.

World Literature Today, spring, 2001, Adele S. News-Horst, review of *The Way Forward Is with a Broken Heart,* pp. 335- 336.

* * *

WALKER, Alice Malsenior
See WALKER, Alice

* * *

WALKER, Margaret 1915-1998
(Margaret Abigail Walker)

PERSONAL: Born July 7, 1915, in Birmingham, AL; died November 30, 1998, in Chicago, IL; daughter of Sigismund C. (a Methodist minister) and Marion (a music teacher; maiden name, Dozier) Walker; married Firnist James Alexander, June 13, 1943 (deceased); children: Marion Elizabeth, Firnist James, Sigismund Walker, Margaret Elvira. *Education:* Northwestern University, B.A., 1935; University of Iowa, M.A., 1940, Ph.D., 1965. *Religion:* Methodist.

CAREER: Worked as a social worker, newspaper reporter, and magazine editor; Livingstone College, Salisbury, NC, member of faculty, 1941-42; West Virginia State College, Institute, WV, instructor in English, 1942-43; Livingstone College, professor of English, 1945-46; Jackson State College, Jackson, MS, professor beginning 1949, professor emeritus of English, director of Institute for the Study of the History, Life, and Culture of Black Peoples, 1968—. Lecturer, National Concert and Artists Corp. Lecture Bureau, 1943-48. Visiting professor in creative writing, Northwestern University, spring, 1969. Staff member, Cape Cod Writers Conference, Craigville, MA, 1967 and 1969. Participant, Library of Congress Conference on the Teaching of Creative Writing, 1973.

MEMBER: National Council of Teachers of English, Modern Language Association, Poetry Society of America, American Association of University Professors, National Education Association, Alpha Kappa Alpha.

AWARDS, HONORS: Yale Series of Younger Poets Award, 1942, for *For My People;* named to Honor Roll of Race Relations, the New York Public Library, 1942; Rosenthal fellowship, 1944; Ford fellowship for study at Yale University, 1954; Houghton Mifflin Literary fellowship, 1966; Fulbright fellowship, 1971; National Endowment for the Humanities, 1972; Doctor of Literature, Northwestern University, 1974; Doctor of Letters, Rust College, 1974; Doctor of Fine Arts, Dennison University, 1974; Doctor of Humane Letters, Morgan State University, 1976.

WRITINGS:

POETRY

For My People, Yale University Press (New Haven, CT), 1942.

Ballad of the Free, Broadside Press (Detroit, MI), 1966.

Prophets for a New Day, Broadside Press (Detroit, MI), 1970.

October Journey, Broadside Press (Detroit, MI), 1973.

This Is My Century, University of Georgia Press (Athens, GA), 1989.

PROSE

Jubilee (novel), Houghton Mifflin (Boston, MA), 1965.

How I Wrote "Jubilee," Third World Press (Chicago, IL), 1972.

(With Nikki Giovanni) *A Poetic Equation: Conversations between Nikki Giovanni and Margaret Walker,* Howard University Press (Washington, DC), 1974.

Richard Wright: Daemonic Genius, Dodd (New York, NY), 1987.

How I Wrote Jubilee and Other Essays on Life and Literature, edited by Maryemma Graham, Feminist Press at The City University of New York (New York, NY), 1990.

On Being Female, Black, and Free: Essays by Margaret Walker, 1932-1992, University of Tennessee Press (Knoxville, TN), 1997.

Conversations with Margaret Walker, edited by Maryemma Graham, University Press of Mississippi (Jackson, MI), 2002.

OTHER

Contributor to *Black Expression,* edited by Addison Gayle, Weybright & Tally (New York, NY), 1969; *Many Shades of Black,* edited by Stanton L. Wormley and Lewis H. Fenderson, Morrow (New York, NY), 1969; Stephen Henderson's *Understanding the New Black Poetry: Black Speech and Black Music as Poetic References,* Morrow (New York, NY), 1973, and *The Furious Flowering of African American Poetry,* edited by Joanne V. Gabbin, University Press of Virginia (Charlottesville, VA), 1999.

Also contributor to numerous anthologies, including Adoff's *Black Out Loud,* Weisman and Wright's *Black Poetry for All Americans,* and Williams' *Beyond the Angry Black.* Contributor of articles to periodicals including *Mississippi Folklore Register* and *Southern Quarterly.*

SIDELIGHTS: When *For My People* by Margaret Walker won the Yale Series of Younger Poets Award in 1942, "she became one of the youngest Black writers ever to have published a volume of poetry in this century," as well as "the first Black woman in American literary history to be so honored in a prestigious national competition," noted Richard K. Barksdale in *Black American Poets between Worlds, 1940-1960.* Walker's first novel, *Jubilee,* is notable for being "the first truly historical black American novel," reported *Washington Post* contributor Crispin Y. Campbell. It was also the first work by a black writer to speak out for the liberation of the black woman. The cornerstones of a literature that affirms the African folk roots of black American life, these two books have also been called visionary for looking toward a new cultural unity for black Americans that will be built on that foundation.

The title of Walker's first book, *For My People,* denotes the subject matter of "poems in which the body and spirit of a great group of people are revealed with vigor and undeviating integrity," wrote Louis Untermeyer in the *Yale Review.* Here, in long ballads, Walker draws sympathetic portraits of characters such as the New Orleans sorceress Molly Means; Kissie Lee, a tough young woman who dies "with her boots on switching blades"; and Poppa Chicken, an urban drug dealer and pimp. Other ballads give a new dignity to John Henry, killed by a ten-pound hammer, and Stagolee, who kills a white officer but eludes a lynch mob. In an essay for *Black Women Writers (1950-1980): A Critical Evaluation,* Eugenia Collier noted, "Using . . . the language of the grass-roots people, Walker spins yarns of folk heroes and heroines: those who, faced with the terrible obstacles which haunt Black people's very existence, not only survive but prevail—with style." Soon after it appeared, the book of ballads, sonnets, and free verse found a surprisingly large number of readers, requiring publishers to authorize three printings to satisfy popular demand.

"If the test of a great poem is the universality of statement, then 'For My People' is a great poem," remarked Barksdale. The critic explained in Donald B. Gibson's *Modern Black Poets: A Collection of Critical Essays* that the poem was written when "world-wide pain, sorrow, and affliction were tangibly evident, and few could isolate the Black man's dilemma from humanity's dilemma during the depression years or during the war years." Thus, the power of resilience presented in the poem is a hope Walker holds out not only to black people, but to all people, to "all the Adams and Eves." As she once remarked, "Writers should not write exclusively for black or white audiences, but most inclusively. After all, it is the business of all writers to write about the human condition, and all humanity must be involved in both the writing and in the reading."

Jubilee, a historical novel, is the second book on which Walker's literary reputation rests. It is the story of a slave family during and after the Civil War, and it took her thirty years to write. During these years, she married a disabled veteran, raised four children, taught full time at Jackson State College in Mississippi, and earned a Ph.D. from the University of Iowa. The lengthy gestation, she believes, partly accounts for the book's quality. As she told Claudia Tate in *Black Women Writers at Work,* "Living with the book over a long period of time was agonizing. Despite all of that, *Jubilee* is the product of a mature person," one whose own difficult pregnancies and economic struggles could lend authenticity to the lives of her characters. "There's a difference between writing about something and living through it," she said in the interview; "I did both."

The story of *Jubilee*'s main characters Vyry and Randall Ware was an important part of Walker's life even before she began to write it down. As she explains in *How I Wrote "Jubilee,"* she first heard about the "slavery time" in bedtime stories told by her maternal grandmother. When old enough to recognize the value of her family history, Walker took initiative, "prodding" her grandmother for more details, and promising to set down on paper the story that had taken shape in her mind. Later on, she completed extensive research on every aspect of the black experience touching the Civil War, from obscure birth records to information on the history of tin cans. "Most of my life I have been involved with writing this story about my great-grandmother, and even if *Jubilee* were never considered an artistic or commercial success I would still be happy just to have finished it," she claims.

Soon after *Jubilee* was published in 1966, Walker was given a fellowship award from Houghton Mifflin. Granting that the novel is "ambitious," *New York Times Book Review* contributor Wilma Dykeman deemed it "uneven." Arthur P. Davis, writing in *From the Dark Tower: Afro-American Writers, 1900-1960,* suggested that the author "has crowded too much into her novel." On the other hand, Abraham Chapman of the *Saturday Review* appreciated the author's "fidelity to fact and detail" as she "presents the little-known everyday life of the slaves," their music, and their folkways. In the *Christian Science Monitor,* Henrietta Buckmaster commented, "In Vyry, Miss Walker has found a remarkable woman who suffered one outrage after the other and yet emerged with a humility and a mortal fortitude that reflected a spiritual wholeness." Dykeman felt that, "In its best episodes, and in Vyry, 'Jubilee' chronicles the triumph of a free spirit over many kinds of bondages." Later critical studies of the book emphasize the importance of its themes and its position as the prototype for novels that present black history from a black perspective. Roger Whitlow claimed in *Black American Literature: A Critical History,* "It serves especially well as a response to white 'nostalgia' fiction about the antebellum and Reconstruction South."

Walker's next book to be highly acclaimed was *Prophets for a New Day,* a slim volume of poems. Unlike the poems in *For My People,* which, in a Marxist fashion, names religion an enemy of revolution, remarked Collier, *Prophets for a New Day* "reflects a profound religious faith. The heroes of the sixties are named for the prophets of the Bible: Martin Luther King is Amos, Medgar Evars is Micah, and so on. The people and events of the sixties are paralleled with Biblical characters and occurrences. . . . The religious references are important. Whether one espouses the Christianity in which they are couched is not the issue. For the fact is that Black people from ancient Africa to now have always been a spiritual people, believing in an existence beyond the flesh." One poem in *Prophets* that harks back to African spiritism is "Ballad of Hoppy Toad" with its hexes that turn a murderous conjurer into a toad. Though Collier felt that Walker's "vision of the African past is fairly dim and romantic," the critic went on to say that this poetry "emanates from a deeper area of the psyche, one which touches the mythic area of a collective being and reenacts the rituals which define a Black collective self." Perhaps more importantly, in all the poems, observed Collier, Walker depicts "a people striking back at oppression and emerging triumphant."

Much of Walker's responsiveness to the black experience, communicated through the realism of her work, can be attributed to her growing up in a southern home environment that emphasized the rich heritage of black culture. Walker was born on July 7, 1915, in Birmingham, Alabama, to the Reverend Sigismund C. Walker and Marion Dozier Walker. The family moved to New Orleans when Walker was a young child. A Methodist minister who had been born near Buff Bay, Jamaica, Walker's father was a scholar who bequeathed to his daughter his love of literature—the classics, the Bible, Benedict de Spinoza, Arthur Schopenhauer, the English classics, and poetry. Similarly, Walker's musician mother played ragtime and read poetry to her, choosing among such varied authors and works as Paul Laurence Dunbar, John Greenleaf Whittier's "Snowbound," the Bible, and Shakespeare. At age eleven Walker began reading the poetry of Langston Hughes and Countee Cullen. Elvira Ware Dozier, her maternal grandmother, who lived with her family, told Walker stories, including the story of her own mother, a former slave in Georgia. Before she finished college at Northwestern University in Evanston, Illinois, in the early 1930s, Walker had heard James Weldon Johnson read from *God's Trombones* (1927), listened to Marian Anderson and Roland Hayes sing in New Orleans, and, in 1932, heard Hughes read his poetry in a lecture recital at New Orleans University, where her parents then taught. She met Hughes in 1932, and he encouraged her to continue writing poetry. Her first poem was published in *Crisis* in 1934.

As a senior at Northwestern in 1934, Walker began a fruitful association with the Works Progress Administration (WPA). She lived on Chicago's North Side and worked as a volunteer on the WPA recreation project. The project directors assigned her to associate with so-called delinquent girls, mainly shoplifters and prostitutes, in order to determine if Walker's different background and training might have a positive influence on them. She became so fascinated by an Italian-black neighborhood that she eventually chose it as the setting and title for a novel that she began writing (but never published), *Goose Island.* On Friday, March 13, 1936, Walker received notice to report to the WPA Writer's Project in Chicago as a full-time employee. Classified as a junior writer—her salary was eighty-five dollars a month—her work assignment was the Illinois Guide Book. Other writers on the project were Nelson Algren, Jacob Scher, James Phelan, Sam Ross, Katherine Dunham, Willard Motley, Frank Yerby, Fenton Johnson, and Richard Wright. In 1937 the WPA office allowed her to come into the downtown quarters only twice weekly so that she might remain at home working on her novel.

Perhaps her most rewarding interaction with a writer at the project was Walker's friendship with Wright, a liaison that, while it lasted, proved practical and beneficial to both fledgling writers. Before she joined the project, Walker had met Wright in Chicago in February, 1936, when he had presided at the writer's section of the first National Negro Congress. Walker had attended solely to meet Hughes again, to show him the poetry she had written since their first meeting four years earlier. Hughes refused to take her only copy of the poems, but he introduced her to Wright and insisted that he include Walker if a writer's group organized. Wright then introduced her to Arna Bontemps and Sterling A. Brown, also writers with the WPA.

Although Wright left Chicago for New York at the end of May, neither his friendship with Walker nor their literary interdependence ended immediately. Walker provided him, in fact, with important help on *Native Son* (1940), mailing him—as he requested—newspaper clippings about Robert Nixon, a young black man accused of rape in Chicago, and assisting Wright in locating a vacant lot to use as the Dalton house address when Wright returned to Chicago briefly the next year. Furthermore, Walker was instrumental in acquiring for him a copy of the brief of Nixon's case from attorney Ulysses S. Keyes, the first black lawyer hired for the case. Together, Wright and Walker visited Cook County jail, where Nixon was incarcerated, and the library, where on her library card they checked out a book on Clarence Darrow and two books on the Loeb-Leopold case, from which, in part, Wright modeled Bigger's defense when he completed his novel in the spring of 1939.

Walker began teaching in the 1940s. She taught at North Carolina's Livingstone College in 1941 and West Virginia State College in 1942. In 1943 she married Firnist James Alexander. In that year, too, she began to read her poetry publicly when she was invited by Arthur P. Davis to read "For My People" at Richmond's Virginia Union University, where he was then teaching. After the birth of the first of her four children in 1944, Walker returned to teach at Livingstone for a year. She also resumed the research on her Civil War novel in the 1940s. She began with a trip to the Schomburg Center in 1942. In 1944 she received a Rosenwald fellowship to further her research. In 1948 Walker was unemployed, living in High Point, North Carolina, and working on the novel. By then she clearly envisioned the development of *Jubilee* as a folk novel and prepared an outline of incidents and chapter headings, the latter which were supplied by the stories of her grandmother. In 1949 Walker moved to Jackson, Mississippi, and began her long teaching career at Jackson State College (now Jackson State University).

The fictional history of Walker's great-grandmother, here called Vyry, *Jubilee* is divided into three sections:

the antebellum years in Georgia on John Dutton's plantation, the Civil War years, and the Reconstruction era. Against a panoramic view of history Walker focuses the plot specifically on Vyry's life as she grows from a little girl to adulthood. In the first section Vyry, the slave, matures, marries and separates from Randall Ware, attempts to escape from slavery with her two children, and is flogged. The second section emphasizes the destruction of war and the upheaval for slaveowner and slaves, while the last section focuses on Vyry as a displaced former slave, searching for a home.

Walker said her research was done "to undergird the oral tradition," and *Jubilee* is primarily known for its realistic depiction of the daily life and folklore of the black slave community. Although there are also quotes from Whittier and the English romantic poets, she emphasizes the importance of the folk structure of her novel by prefacing each of the fifty-eight chapters with proverbial folk sayings or lines excerpted from spirituals. The narrative is laced with verses of songs sung by Vyry, her guardian, or other slaves. A portion from a sermon is included. The rhymes of slave children are also a part of the narrative. A conjuring episode is told involving the overseer Grimes, suggesting how some folk beliefs were used for protection. Vyry provides a catalogue of herbs and discusses their medicinal and culinary purposes.

In response to Walker's Civil War story, Guy Davenport commented in *National Review* that "the novel from end to end is about a place and a people who never existed." For him Walker had merely recalled all the elements of the southern myth, writing a lot of "tushery that comes out of books, out of Yerby and Margaret Mitchell." He further found "something deeply ironic in a Negro's underwriting the made-up South of the romances, agreeing to every convention of the trade." More justly, Chapman in the *Saturday Review* found "a fidelity to fact and detail" in the depictions of slave life that was better than anything done before. Lester Davis, a contributor to *Freedomways,* decided that one could overlook the "sometimes trite and often stilted prose style" because the novel is "a good forthright treatment of a segment of American history about which there has been much hypocrisy and deliberate distortion." He found the "flavor of authenticity . . . convincing and refreshing."

Walker's *How I Wrote "Jubilee,"* a history of the novel's development from her grandmother's oral history, is an indirect response to those critics who compared *Jubilee* with books like Mitchell's *Gone with the Wind* (1936) and who accused Walker of sustaining the southern myth from the black perspective. She answers her detractors by citing the references and historical documents she perused over several years in order to gird her oral story with historical fact.

Walker's volume of poetry *Prophets for a New Day* was published in 1970. She called *Prophets for a New Day* her civil rights poems, and only two poems in the volume, "Elegy" and "Ballad of the Hoppy Toad," are not about the civil rights movement. Walker begins the volume with two poems in which the speakers are young children; one eight-year-old demonstrator eagerly waits to be arrested with her group in the fight for equality, and a second one is already jailed and wants no bail. Her point is that these young girls are just as much prophets for a new day as were Nat Turner, Gabriel Prosser, Denmark Vesey, Toussaint L'Ouverture, and John Brown. In "The Ballad of the Free" Walker establishes a biblical allusion and association as an integral part of the fight to end racism: "The serpent is loosed and the hour is come / The last shall be first and the first shall be none / The serpent is loosed and the hour is come."

The title poem, "Prophets for a New Day," and the seven poems that follow it invite obvious comparisons between the biblical prophets and the black leaders who denounced racial injustice and prophesied change during the civil rights struggle of the 1960s. For example, several prophets are linked to specific southern cities marked by racial turmoil: in "Jeremiah," the first poem of the series, Jeremiah "is now a man whose names is Benjamin / Brooding over a city called Atlanta / Preaching the doom of a curse upon the land." Among the poems, other prophets mentioned include "Isaiah," "Amos," and "Micah," a poem subtitled "To the memory of Medgar Evers of Mississippi."

In *For My People* Walker urged that activity replace complacency, but in *Prophets for a New Day* she applauds the new day of freedom for black people, focusing on the events, sites, and people of the struggle. Among the poems that recognize southern cities associated with racial turbulence are "Oxford Is a Legend," "Birmingham," "Jackson, Mississippi," and "Sit-Ins." Of these, the latter two, claim reviewers, are the most accomplished pieces. "Sit-Ins" is a recognition of "those first bright young to fling their . . . names across pages / Of new Southern history / With courage and faith, convictions, and intelligence."

BIOGRAPHICAL AND CRITICAL SOURCES:

BOOKS

African American Writers, Thomson Gale (Detroit, MI), 2nd edition, 2000, Volume 2, pp. 759-771.

Bankier, Joanna, and Dierdre Lashgari, editors, *Women Poets of the World,* Macmillan (New York, NY), 1983.

Baraka, Amiri, *The Black Nation,* Getting Together Publications, 1982.

Contemporary Literary Criticism, Thomson Gale (Detroit, MI), Volume 1, 1973; Volume 2, 1976.

Contemporary Southern Writers, St. James Press (Detroit, MI), 1999.

Davis, Arthur P., *From the Dark Tower: Afro-American Writers, 1900 to 1960,* Howard University Press (Washington, DC), 1974.

Emanuel, James A., and Theodore L. Gross, editors, *Dark Symphony: Negro Literature in America,* Free Press (New York, NY), 1968.

Evans, Mari, editor, *Black Women Writers (1950-1980): A Critical Evaluation,* Anchor/Doubleday (New York, NY), 1982.

Gayle, Addison, editor, *The Black Aesthetic,* Doubleday (New York, NY), 1971.

Gibson, Donald B., editor, *Modern Black Poets: A Collection of Critical Essays,* Prentice-Hall (Englewood Cliffs, NJ), 1983.

Henderson, Ashyia, editor, *Contemporary Black Biography,* Volume 29, Thomson Gale (Detroit, MI), 2001.

Jackson, Blyden, and Louis D. Rubin Jr., *Black Poetry in America: Two Essays in Historical Interpretation,* Louisiana State University Press (Baton Rouge, LA), 1974.

Jones, John Griffith, in *Mississippi Writers Talking,* Volume II, University of Mississippi Press (Jackson, MS), 1983.

Kent, George E., *Blackness and the Adventure of Western Culture,* Third World Press (Chicago, IL), 1972.

Lee, Don L., *Dynamite Voices I: Black Poets of the 1960s,* Broadside Press (Detroit, MI), 1971.

Miller, R. Baxter, editor, *Black American Poets between Worlds, 1940-1960,* University of Tennessee Press (Knoxville, TN), 1986.

Mitchell, Angelyn, editor, *Within the Circle: An Anthology of African American Literary Criticism from the Harlem Renaissance to the Present,* Duke University Press (Durham, NC), 1994.

Modern Black Writers, Thomson Gale (Detroit, MI), 2nd edition, 1999, pp. 758-762.

Pryse, Marjorie, and Hortense J. Spillers, editors, *Conjuring: Black Women, Fiction, and Literary Tradition,* Indiana University Press (Bloomington, IN), 1985.

Redmond, Eugene B., *Drumvoices: The Mission of Afro-American Poetry-A Critical Evaluation,* Doubleday (New York, NY), 1976.

Tate, Claudia, editor, *Black Women Writers at Work,* Continuum, 1983.

Walker, Margaret, *How I Wrote "Jubilee,"* Third World Press (Chicago, IL), 1972.

Whitlow, Roger, *Black American Literature: A Critical History,* Nelson Hall, 1973.

PERIODICALS

African American Review, summer, 1993, Jerry W. Ward Jr., "Black South Literature: Before Day Annotations (for Blyden Jackson)," p. 315.

Atlantic Monthly, December, 1942.

Black World, December, 1971; December, 1975.

Booklist, July, 1997, Alice Joyce, review of *On Being Female, Black, and Free: Essays by Margaret Walker, 1932-1992,* p. 1794; February 15, 1998, Brad Hooper, review of *Jubilee,* p. 979.

Book Week, October 2, 1966.

Callaloo, May, 1979.

Christian Science Monitor, November 14, 1942; September 29, 1966; June 19, 1974; January 22, 1990, Laurel Shaper, "One woman's world of words; 'Jubilee' author draws on her racial experience to craft works of concern and compassion".

CLA Journal, December, 1977.

Ebony, February, 1949.

Freedomways, summer, 1967.

Library Journal, November 1, 1989, Fred Muratori, review of *This Is My Century: New and Collected Poems,* p. 92; January 1990, Molly Brodsky, review of *Jubilee and Other Essays on Life and Literature,* p. 110; June 15, 1997, Ann Burns, review of *On Being Female, Black, and Free: Essays by Margaret Walker, 1932-1992,* p. 69.

Mississippi Quarterly, fall, 1988; fall, 1989.

National Review, October 4, 1966.

Negro Digest, February, 1967; January, 1968.

New Republic, November 23, 1942.

New York Times, November 4, 1942.

New York Times Book Review, August 2, 1942; September 25, 1966.

Publishers Weekly, April 15, 1944; March 24, 1945.

Saturday Review, September 24, 1966.

Times Literary Supplement, June 29, 1967.

Washington Post, February 9, 1983.

Yale Review, winter, 1943.

ONLINE

Internet Poetry Archive, http://www.ibiblio.org/ipa/walker/ (October 24, 2003).

Modern American Poetry, http://www.english.uiuc.edu/maps/ (October 27, 2003).

University of Mississippi, http://www.olemiss.edu/ (April 17, 2003), Jon Tucker, "Margaret Walker Alexander."

Voices from the Gaps, Women Writers of Color, http://voices.cla.umn.edu/ (December 9, 1999), Danye A. Pelichet, Shanese Baylor, and Kinitra D. Brooks, "Dr. Margaret Abigail Walker Alexander."

* * *

WALKER, Margaret Abigail
See WALKER, Margaret

* * *

WALLACE, David Foster 1962-

PERSONAL: Born February 21, 1962, in Ithaca, NY; son of James Donald (a teacher) and Sally (a teacher; maiden name, Foster) Wallace. *Education:* Amherst College, A.B. (summa cum laude), 1985; University of Arizona, M.F.A., 1987; graduate study at Harvard University. *Politics:* "Independent." *Hobbies and other interests:* Tennis.

ADDRESSES: Office—Department of English, Pomona College, 333 North College Way, Claremont, CA 91711. *Agent*—Frederick Hill Associates, 1842 Union St., San Francisco, CA 94123.

CAREER: Writer. Illinois State University, Bloomington-Normal, associate professor of English, 1993-2002; Pomona College, Claremont, CA, Roy Edward Disney Professor in Creative Writing, 2002—. Judge of 1997 O. Henry Awards, 1997.

AWARDS, HONORS: Whiting Writers' Award, Mrs. Giles Whiting Foundation, 1987; Yaddo residency fellowship, 1987, 1989; John Traine Humor Prize, *Paris Review,* 1988, for "Little Expressionless Animals;" National Endowment for the Arts fellowship, 1989; Illinois Arts Council Award for Nonfiction, 1989, for "Fictional Futures and the Conspicuously Young;" Quality Paperback Book Club's New Voices Award in Fiction, 1991, for *Girl with Curious Hair;* Pulitzer Prize nomination in nonfiction, 1991, for *Signifying Rappers;* National Magazine Award finalist, 1995, for "Ticket to the Fair," and 1997, for "David Lynch Keeps His Head;" Lannan Foundation Award for Literature, 1996, 2000; MacArthur Foundation fellowship, 1997-2002; named Outstanding University Researcher, Illinois State University, 1998, 1999.

WRITINGS:

The Broom of the System, Viking (New York, NY), 1987.

Girl with Curious Hair (short stories and novellas; includes "Little Expressionless Animals," "My Appearance," "Westward the Course of Empire Takes Its Way," "Lyndon," "John Billy," and "Everything Is Green"), Penguin (New York, NY), 1988.

(With Mark Costello) *Signifying Rappers: Rap and Race in the Urban Present* (nonfiction), Ecco Press (New York, NY), 1990.

Infinite Jest, Little, Brown (Boston, MA), 1996.

A Supposedly Fun Thing I'll Never Do Again: Essays and Arguments, Little, Brown (Boston, MA), 1997.

Brief Interviews with Hideous Men, Little, Brown (Boston, MA), 1999.

Up Simba! (e-book), i.Publish.com, 2000.

Everything and More: A Compact History of Infinity, Atlas Book (New York, NY), 2003.

Oblivion, Little, Brown (New York, NY), 2004.

Contributor of short fiction and nonfiction to numerous periodicals, including *Contemporary Fiction, Harper's,* and *New Yorker.* Short fiction included in anthologies, including *Best American Sportswriting 1997,* Houghton Mifflin, 1997. Contributing editor, *Harper's,* 1995.

SIDELIGHTS: Hailed as the "Generation-X"s answer to John Barth, John Irving, Thomas Pynchon, and Don Delillo, American writer David Foster Wallace is an author whose talent leaves critics groping for the proper artistic comparison. Filmmaker David Lynch, and even comic David Letterman have all been invoked as readers tackle the sardonic humor and complicated style that have led Wallace to be cited as the late twentieth-century's first avant-garde literary hero. Wallace, according to Frank Bruni in his *New York Times Magazine* profile, "is to literature what Robin Williams or perhaps Jim Carrey is to live comedy: a creator so maniacally energetic and amused with himself that he often follows his riffs out into the stratosphere, where he orbits all alone."

In his debut novel, *The Broom of the System,* Wallace uses a variety of writing techniques and points of view to create a bizarre, stylized world which, despite its strangeness, resonates with contemporary American images. Set in Cleveland on the edge of the state-constructed Great Ohio Desert—also known as G.O.D.—the novel follows Lenore Beadsman's search for her ninety-two-year-old great-grandmother, also named Lenore Beadsman, who has disappeared from her nursing home. In attempting to find her childhood mentor, the younger Lenore encounters a bewildering assemblage of characters with names such as Rick Vigorous, Biff Diggerence, Candy Mandible, and Sigurd Foamwhistle. It is significant that the elder Lenore was a student of language philosopher Ludwig Wittgenstein, since *The Broom of the System* has been viewed as an elaborate exploration of the relationship between language and reality. Wallace orchestrates Lenore's coming of age through the use of innovative plotting and language. The character's search for her great-grandmother then becomes the search for her own identity.

Critics have praised the skill and creativity evident in Wallace's experimental *bildungsroman.* Rudy Rucker, writing in *Washington Post Book World,* judged *The Broom of the System* to be a "wonderful book" and compared Wallace in particular to novelist Thomas Pynchon. Despite finding the novel to be "unwieldy" and "uneven" in parts, *New York Times* reviewer Michiko Kakutani commended Wallace's "rich reserves of ambition and imagination" and was impressed by his "wealth of talents." *New York Times Book Review* critic Caryn James liked the novel's "exuberance" and maintained that *The Broom of the System* "succeeds as a manic, human, flawed extravaganza."

In Wallace's second work, a collection of short stories titled *Girl with Curious Hair,* the author employs a mix of facts, fiction, and his own distinctive use of language to make observations about American culture. "Little Expressionless Animals," one of several stories that deals with American television, reveals a plan by the producers of the game show *Jeopardy!* to oust a long-time champion because of their sensitivity to her continuing lesbian love affair. The difference between appearance and reality is the subject of "My Appearance," the story of an actress's tranquilizer-induced nervous ramblings while she is waiting to do a guest appearance on the David Letterman show. In the title story, "Girl with Curious Hair," a young, Ivy League-trained corporate lawyer reveals the roots of his sadistic sexual impulses when he reflects on a Keith Jarrett concert he once attended with a group of violent punk rockers.

To reviewers, Wallace's imagination and energy are enticing. Wallace "proves himself a dynamic writer of extraordinary talent," asserted Jenifer Levin in *New York Times Book Review,* commenting that the writer "succeeds in restoring grandeur to modern fiction." Writing in Chicago's *Tribune Books,* Douglas Seibold commended Wallace's "irrepressible narrative energy and invention" claiming that, "as good a writer as he is now, he is getting better."

The buildup given to Wallace through his first books served as an appetizer to the hype that surrounded his 1996 novel, *Infinite Jest*—a work that, in the words of *Chicago Tribune* writer Bruce Allen, might well "confirm the hopes of those who called Wallace a genius and, to a lesser extent, the fears of those who think he's just an overeducated wiseacre with a lively prose style." The book is massive—over 1,000 pages—and the publicity upon its release was no less so. On the heels of wide-scale publicity, *Infinite Jest* became *de rigueur* as a book that literary fans bought and displayed, but would not—or could not—spend much time reading, according to reviewers. Some of the reason lies in the volume's heft and some in Wallace's dense prose style, peppered for the occasion with numerous pharmacological references that are partly responsible for the novel's 900 footnotes.

Infinite Jest is set in the not-too-distant future, in a date unspecified except as "the Year of the Depend Adult Undergarment," corporate sponsors having taken over the calendar. The United States is now part of the Organization of North American Nations—read ONAN—and has sold off New England to Canada to be used as a toxic waste dump. Legless Quebeçoise separatists have taken to terrorism in protest; what is more, President Limbaugh has just been assassinated. The book's title refers to a lethal movie—a film so entertaining that those who see it may be doomed to die of pleasure.

Into this fray steps the Incandenza brothers: tennis ace Hal, football punter Orin, and the less-gifted Mario. The boys have endured a tough childhood—their father "having committed suicide by hacking open a hole in a microwave door, sealing it around his head with duct tape and making like a bag of Orville Redenbacher," as *Nation* reviewer Rick Perlstein noted. The brother's adventures in this bizarre society fuel the novel's thick and overlapping storylines. Readers looking for a traditional linear ending, however, are in for a surprise: Those who manage to "stay with the novel until the pages thin will come to realize that Wallace has no intention of revealing whether *les Assassins des Fauteuils Rollents* succeed or fail in their quest," Perlstein continued. "Nor whether . . . Orin will master his awful desires . . . or whether Hal Incandenza will sacrifice himself to the Oedipal grail. Readers will turn the last page, in other words, without learning anything they need to know to secure narrative succor."

For the most part, critical reaction to *Infinite Jest* mixed admiration with consternation. "There is generous intelligence and authentic passion on every page, even the overwritten ones in which the author seems to have had a fit of graphomania," noted *Time*'s R.Z. Sheppard. Paul West, writing in *Washington Post Book World,* came prepared for Pynchon but came away with the opinion that "there is nothing epic or infinite about [the novel], although much that's repetitious or long." As West saw it, "the slow incessant advance of Wallace's prose is winningly physical, solid and even, more personable actually than the crowd of goons, ditzes, inverts, junkies, fatheads and doodlers he populates his novel with."

Indeed, noted Kakutani, "the whole novel often seems like an excuse for [Wallace] to simply show off his remarkable skills as a writer and empty the contents of his restless mind." Kakutani's *New York Times* review went on to laud "some frighteningly vivid accounts of what it feels like to be a drug addict, what it feels like to detox and what it feels like to suffer a panic attack." In the crowd of ideas and characters, the critic concluded, "Somewhere in the mess, . . . are the outlines of a splendid novel, but as it stands the book feels like one of those unfinished Michelangelo sculptures: you can see a godly creature trying to fight its way out, but it's stuck there, half excavated, unable to break completely free."

Kakutani had more encouraging words for Wallace's 1997 release, *A Supposedly Fun Thing I'll Never Do Again: Essays and Arguments.* This nonfiction collection "is animated by [the author's] wonderfully exuberant prose, a zingy, elastic gift for metaphor and imaginative sleight of hand, combined with a taste for amphetaminelike stream-of-consciousness riffs." *Supposedly Fun Thing* covers Wallace's observations on cultural themes, such as the influence television has on new fiction. It also contains recollections of the author's childhood in the Midwest, thoughts on tennis—Wallace was a highly ranked player in his youth—and even a tour of the Illinois State Fair. While finding some aspects of the collection flawed, Kakutani ultimately praised *A Supposedly Fun Thing I'll Never Do Again* as a work that "not only reconfirms Mr. Wallace's stature as one of his generation's pre-eminent talents, but it also attests to his virtuosity, an aptitude for the essay, profile and travelogue, equal to the gifts he has already begun to demonstrate in the realm of fiction."

Inspired by the author's interest in mathematic systems, Wallace's 2003 work, *Everything and More: A Compact History of Infinity,* focuses on nineteenth-century German mathematician Georg F.L.P. Cantor, a man who pioneered set theory in between stays at mental hospitals. Dubbing his work a "piece of pop technical writing," Wallace explores the theoretical history of the concept of infinity, from its roots in ancient paradoxes through its interpretation by scientists such as Galileo, as well as Plato and hosts of other philosophers, to today's theoretical mathematics. While *New Yorker* contributor Jim Holt noted that, with its author's limited mathematical understanding but contagious enthusiasm for his subject, *Everything and More* "is sometimes as dense as a math textbook, though rather more chaotic," is effective as a "purely literary experience." In *Library Journal,* Christopher Tinney praised the book as "classic DFW: engaging, self-conscious, playful, and often breathless," while John Green cited *Everything and More* as "a brilliant antidote both to boring math textbooks and to pop-culture math books that emphasize the discoverer over the discovery." Noting Wallace's characteristic "discursive style," a *Publishers Weekly* contributor praised the volume "as weird and wonderful as you'd expect," adding that, "had he not pursued a career in literary fiction, it's not difficult to imagine Wallace as a historian of science, producing quirky and challenging volumes . . . every few years." Praising *Everything and More* as "inspiring," Troy Patterson added in *Entertainment Weekly* that Wallace's "straightforward engagement with ultimate abstractions and unambiguous truths offers a heady pleasure distinct from that of fiction."

Wallace's first short-story collection in five years, *Oblivion,* "fashions complex tales rife with shrewd metaphysical inquiries, eviscerating social critiques, and twisted humor," according to Donna Seaman in *Booklist.* Charles Matthes for the *Knight Ridder/Tribune News Service* shared a similar sentiment, but also felt the stories were "soulless" and maintained that the "verbal tics and tricks soon grow tedious." However, Joel Stein from *Time* described the eight tales contained in the book as "breathtakingly smart."

BIOGRAPHICAL AND CRITICAL SOURCES:

BOOKS

Boswell, Marshall, *Understanding David Foster Wallace,* University of South Carolina Press (Columbia, SC), 2003.

Burn, Stephen, *David Foster Wallace's Infinite Jest: A Reader's Guide,* Continuum (New York, NY), 2003.

Contemporary Literary Criticism, Thomson Gale (Detroit, MI), Volume 50, 1988, Volume 114, 1999.

PERIODICALS

American Scholar, winter, 2004, Allen Paulos, review of *Everything and More: A Compact History of Infinity,* p. 147.

Asia Africa Intelligence Wire, June 27, 2004, Brad Quinn, review of *Oblivion.*

Booklist, October 15, 2003, John Green, review of *Everything and More: A Compact History of Infinity,* p. 366; May 15, 2004, Donna Seaman, review of *Oblivion,* p. 1600.

Boston Globe, October 26, 2003, Caleb Crain, interview with Wallace.

Chicago Tribune, March 24, 1996, Bruce Allen, review of *Infinite Jest.*

Comparative Literature Studies, summer, 2001, Timothy Jacobs, "American Touchstone," p. 215.

Critique, fall, 2001, p. 3.

Entertainment Weekly, October 10, 2003, Troy Patterson, review of *Everything and More,* p. 127; June 18, 2004, review of *Oblivion,* p. 89.

Kirkus Reviews, May 1, 2004, review of *Oblivion,* p. 422.

Knight Ridder/Tribune News Service, June 16, 2004, Charles Matthews, review of *Oblivion,* p. K3330.

Library Journal, November 1, 2003, Christopher Tinney, review of *Everything and More,* p. 120.

Los Angeles Times, February 11, 1996; March 18, 1996.

Los Angeles Times Book Review, February 1, 1987.

Nation, March 4, 1996, Rick Perlstein, review of *Infinite Jest.*

New Yorker, November 3, 2003, Jim Holt, review of *Everything and More,* p. 84.

New York Review of Books, February 10, 2000.

New York Times, December 27, 1986; February 13, 1996; February 4, 1997.

New York Times Book Review, March 1, 1987; November 5, 1989; March 3, 1996.

New York Times Magazine, March 24, 1996, Frank Bruni, "The Grunge American Novel," p. 38.

Publishers Weekly, October 13, 2003, review of *Everything and More,* p. 71.

Science News, December 6, 2003, review of *Everything and More,* p. 367.

Time, February 19, 1996; October 30, 2000, p. 94; June 7, 2004, Joel Stein, review of *Oblivion,* p. 123.

Tribune Books (Chicago, IL), January 21, 1990, Douglas Seibold, review of *Girl with Curious Hair.*

Washington Post Book World, January 11, 1987; August 6, 1989; March 24, 1996.

Wilson Quarterly, winter, 2004, Charles Seife, review of *Everything and More,* p. 124.

Wired, October, 2003, Bruce Schecter, review of *Everything and More,* p. 76.

ONLINE

David Foster Wallace Unoffical Web site, http://www.davidfosterwallace.com/ (November 19, 2003).

Salon.com, http://www.salon.com/ (April 24, 2004), interview with Wallace.

*   *   *

WALLEY, Byron
See CARD, Orson Scott

*   *   *

WARE, Chris 1967-

PERSONAL: Born December 28, 1967, in Omaha, NE; son of M.B. Haberman and Doris Ann Ware (a newspaper reporter); married, 1997; wife's name Marina. *Education:* Attended Skanregan School of Painting and Sculpture, 1989; University of Texas—Austin, B.F.A. (painting), 1990.

ADDRESSES: Home—Chicago, IL. *Agent*—c/o Fantagraphics Books, 7563 Lake City Way, Seattle, WA 98115.

CAREER: Author and illustrator of comic strips. *The Ragtime Ephemeralist,* publisher.

AWARDS, HONORS: Harvey Award for Best New Series and Special Award for Excellence in Presentation, 1995; Harvey Award for Best Letterer and Special Award for Excellence in Presentation, 1996; Harvey Awards for Best Colorist, Best Single Issue or Story, and Special Award for Excellence in Presentation, 1997; Harvey Award for Best Colorist and Special Award for Excellence in Presentation, and Ignatz Awards for Outstanding Series and Outstanding Comic, all 1998; Harvey Award for Excellence in Presentation,

1999, Harvey Awards for Best Letterer, Best Colorist, and Special Award for Excellence in Presentation, and Ignatz Awards for Outstanding Comic and Outstanding Story, all 2000; Harvey Award for Best Continuing or Limited Series, 2001, all for "Acme Novelty Library"; Harvey Award for Best Graphic Album of Previously Published Work and Special Award for Excellence in Presentation, and First Book Award, *Guardian,* all 2001, all for *Jimmy Corrigan: The Smartest Kid on Earth.*

WRITINGS:

Jimmy Corrigan: The Smartest Kid on Earth, Pantheon Books (New York, NY), 2000.

Jimmy Corrigan: The Smartest Kid on Earth: Souvenir Book of Views, Fantagraphics Books (Seattle, WA), 2000.

The Acme Novelty Datebook: Sketches and Diary Pages in Facsimile, 1986-1995, Drawn and Quarterly (Montreal, Ontario, Canada), 2003.

The Acme Novelty Library, Pantheon Books (New York, NY), 2005.

Contributor to *McSweeney's Quarterly Concern* Volume 13, McSweeney's (San Francisco, CA), 2005. Author of comic strips "I Guess," in *Raw,* Volume 2, number 3; "Quimby the Mouse"; "Big Tex"; "Rocket Sam"; "Jimmy Corrigan: The Smartest Kid on Earth"; "Blab!"; and "Rusty Brown." Editor and publisher of *The Ragtime Ephemeralist,* 1998—. Author of "Acme Novelty Library" comic book series, Fantagraphics, 1993—. Ware's work has appeared in the *New York Times* and *New City.*

SIDELIGHTS: Dubbed the Emily Dickinson of comics by one fan, cartoonist Chris Ware is the creative force behind several comic strips, including "Quimby the Mouse," "Big Tex," "Rocket Sam," and "Jimmy Corrigan: The Smartest Kid on Earth." While all of these have been collected and published in self-designed periodicals, the "Jimmy Corrigan" strips were also released as 2000's *Jimmy Corrigan: The Smartest Kid on Earth,* the first graphic novel ever to win a major British literary award when it received the London *Guardian*'s First Book Award. Ware's precisely detailed, warmly colored artwork has been compared to Islamic miniatures, Mayan glyphs, and Egyptian hieroglyphs. "The pictures are ideograms," Ware told Beth Nissen writing for *CNN.com,* "drawn words, if that makes any sense. The pictures tell the story—I'm a terrible writer." A meticulous draftsman, Ware has commented that creating just two pages of story takes about twenty hours to write and draw, another ten hours to ink, and then a further four to color. But these pages take only about twelve seconds to read.

Gary Groth, writing in *Comics Journal,* has divided Ware's work into three "untidy and overlapping" categories: "the doggedly visual gamesmanship, . . . ; the bigfoot humor, laced with irony, black humor and *pastiche* . . . ; the tragi-comic world of Jimmy Corrigan. It's the last that seems to me the most substantial and it's here that Ware's investigation into how formal visual properties impart meaning comes into play most successfully." Other critics have offered similar assessments. Jonathan Goldstein, for example, writing in the *New York Times,* called *Jimmy Corrigan* a "great work of art, deep and moving, pretty much unlike anything that's come before it." "Ware's book is arguably the greatest achievement of the form [of the graphic novel], ever," declared Dave Eggers in the *New York Times Book Review.* And *Time*'s Andrew Arnold called *Jimmy Corrigan* a "haunting and unshakable book [that] will change the way you look at your world."

"Drawing was the only way I had of distinguishing myself," Ware told Nissen, "of trying to impress people—impress people with my one pathetic ability. There's nothing less impressive than a scrawny kid with poofy hair, drawing superheroes." Ware was raised in Omaha, Nebraska, by his mother, a newspaper reporter, and his maternal grandparents, and did not know his father, who abandoned the family when Ware was a baby. His grandmother was an important person in Ware's life. "She and I spent whole days together every week, as I preferred being indoors to being out," Ware told Groth. "I liked going on errands with her, and drawing at the desk that she had set up in the basement of their house. She had it divided right down the middle so I would have half of it to work at and she had the other half." Ware's grandfather and mother were both journalists, and thus he was introduced to the world of printing at an early age. Comics were also an early passion for young Ware, who got his first taste for the medium through a stack of back copies kept in his grandmother's basement. For a few years, Ware took art lessons at the Joslyn Art Museum in Omaha, and he also learned rudimentary drawing techniques from watching a PBS television program. Soon he was trying to copy the pictures he admired in the comics. "I would just find panels I liked and try to figure out how they were making all those thick and thin lines," Ware recalled to Groth. "I'd try to do it with a pencil, because I had no idea they were using a brush or a pen."

Like many teenagers of his generation, Ware enjoyed popular music and television shows. He developed an interest in ragtime piano music, and he took up the piano, though he eventually decided against pursuing a career in music. When he moved from a private high school to a public one, he began to hang out with kids who were reading so-called "underground" comics. When a friend started drawing his own "alternative" comics for fun, Ware did the same. Largely, however, Ware "grew up bullied," as he told Nissen. "As a kid, I was, shall we say, not the favored one. Kids were threatening me all the time. I ate lunch by myself. I had some friends I talked to on the weekends—but they wouldn't talk to me at school. And I wasn't good at games—I was about as physical as an inert gas." Ware's nickname at the time was "Albino" because of his pasty complexion. Drawing became a refuge for him. "Ware came through it all," Nissen commented, "with an enduring empathy for the ridiculed, the awkward, the maladept."

While studying painting at the University of Texas—Austin, Ware drew comic strips for the student newspaper, the *Daily Texan.* A friend on the paper introduced Ware to older comic strips, and soon the fledgling cartoonist was immersing himself in the history of the medium. "Comics haven't really developed much since about 1920," Ware told Chip Kidd in an interview for *Print* magazine posted on the Random House Web site. "If one wants to tell stories that have the richness of life, their vocabulary is extremely limited. It's like trying to use limericks to make literature." Ware took note of the early masters, including Winsor McCay and his "Little Nemo," Frank King and the "Gasoline Alley" strips, George Herriman's "Krazy Kat," and, of course, "Superman." The omnivorous Ware also took inspiration from the mundane: the Sears catalogue, advertising from the first half of the twentieth century, and old newspaper comic strips. Each of these sources and traditions later came to play in Ware's own artwork. McCay had "Impeccable craftsmanship," Ware told Kidd, adding that the early twentieth-century cartoonist was "firmly rooted in the principles of realism and Renaissance perspective, invariably to stunning effect." From King he saw the power of a "real-time chronicle of American domesticity," and Herriman's "Krazy Kat" simply awed him. "A masterpiece. A world unto itself, eluding strict explanation." Such a world unto itself would present itself to Ware, as well.

In 1987, when he was a sophomore, Ware received a call from Art Spiegelman, publisher of the avant-garde comic book *RAW;* this call was a boost to Ware, as Spiegelman gave him four pages in the next issue of *RAW,* and then another assignment after that. One early strip in *RAW* became emblematic of the Ware style: "I Guess" draws on his childhood memories growing up with his journalist mom and his grandparents. In the story, the protagonist is a somewhat odd-looking superhero who had to deal with the slings and arrows of domestic life rather than super-villains. With his alternate takes on growing up in America, Ware was soon on his way to a certain degree of underground reknown.

As Neil Strauss noted in the *New York Times,* Ware "might never have hit his stride in illustrating but for an event that took place a couple of years later. He was working on what he describes as a pretentious, conceptual comic when his girlfriend dumped him." Depressed by the event, Ware trashed everything he was working on and started improvising with some stories he had in his sketchbooks. These "mostly wordless and action-free tales of a potato-shaped character" bear a "remarkable resemblance to Mr. Ware," Strauss commented. In these stories and sketches "one can see the beginnings of an immense vocabulary of loneliness, economical use of space, and dark humor," according to Strauss. The prototype of Jimmy Corrigan had come to be.

Alongside toying with this new character, Ware continued to improvise, playing with other artwork, experimenting with cartoons that are virtual flow charts, deeply intricate visual displays of plotting. Some of his comics "were crammed with as many as 300 panels on a single page," wrote Strauss, "an attempt . . . to create a comic that could be read like musical notes on a score." Other early cartoons from Ware include "Quimby the Mouse," "Big Tex," and "Rocket Sam."

In 1993, Ware moved from Austin to Chicago, and felt more isolated than ever. At this time he began to focus on the semi-autobiographical comic strip "Jimmy Corrigan: The Smartest Kid on Earth," which he published in a local alternative weekly, *New City.* Corrigan appears as the quintessential loser, although Ware told Groth, "It's not my goal to present a deliberately dark view of life." Instead, according to Ware, he is simply presenting life in a "realistic" manner, even if the result seems ironic or cruelly humorous. Ware, who thinks popular culture falsely misleads people into believing they should be happy all of the time, draws from events in his own life and the lives of others for material. Jimmy Corrigan, like his creator, grew up without a father. The story line follows Jimmy as he learns of the existence of this absent father, as he tries to become independent of his domineering mother, as he establishes a relationship with an African-American stepsister he never knew he had. One of the centerpieces of the strip is the story within a story of his grandfather, also named

Jimmy Corrigan, who himself was abandoned at the 1893 World's Columbian Exhibition in Chicago. Age thirty-six, Jimmy works long hours in a silent cubicle, calls his mother daily, and is terrified by women.

When Ware set out to draw his weekly comic strip, he did not plan the work in detail ahead of time. Instead he used a semi-improvisational method, explaining to Groth: "I'll have a vague idea and start working on the strip, and before I know it, by the time I'm to the bottom of the page, it's gone somewhere completely different from where I'd thought it might." As for technique, Ware has explored a number of different styles in his comics. "I could point to elements in my stuff that I've picked and chosen from hundreds of cartoonists," Ware told Groth. As an artist, he is constantly trying to push the boundaries of comic-strip language; through page layout, the rhythms of the panels, the framing of characters and their faces, and the amount and position of text, Ware tries to find new ways of visually communicating emotions and sensations not traditionally associated with this American art form.

The "Jimmy Corrigan" strip became so popular that Ware soon had two full pages every week, and he also launched the "Acme Novelty Library" to publish the collected volumes of this venture. Fantagraphics in Seattle, Washington, picked up on these, and published the first number in 1993. Over the course of the series, Ware developed stories within stories for his hapless hero. "The compact imagery, the compacted plot and subplots, make *Corrigan* more akin to a novel by [William] Faulkner or [Charles] Dickens than to 'The Adventures of Spiderman,'" wrote Nissen. Ware spent hours not only drawing each strip, but also researching. For the story of the grandfather abandoned in 1893, Ware researched art and architecture books of the period during a long convalescence after he broke both his legs in 1995. "I guess my graphic style draws from the past," Ware told Nissen. "Turn-of-the-[twentieth]-century—I prefer things from that era. The style then seemed to have more respect for the viewer. What was presented was something hand-made, something crafted with care and skill."

After seven years of weekly strips and more than a dozen volumes in the "Acme Novelty Library" series, Ware—who initially thought he might have enough material for a few months of the strip—published the entire collection as the graphic novel *Jimmy Corrigan: The Smartest Kid on Earth.* The book jacket itself attests to the care with which the project was mounted: it folds out to a poster-size diagram of the multiple story lines of Jimmy Corrigan, and is a piece of artwork in itself. With an initial printing of 25,000, the book went back for subsequent printings as word-of-mouth and rave reviews boosted sales.

A reviewer for *Publishers Weekly* called the book "graphically inventive" and "wonderfully realized." It is a graphic novel that "follows the sad fortunes of four generations of phlegmatic, defeated men while touching on themes of abandonment, social isolation, and despair within the sweeping depiction of Chicago's urban transformation over the course of a century," according to this same reviewer. It is hardly the usual comic book fare. Arnold, writing in *Time,* also applauded the depth in Ware's book, calling it a "graphic version of the anomie found in a Raymond Carver short story, with a social-historical sweep and unexpected, if fleeting, grace notes. And that may be this melancholy book's uplifting message: even in the most emotionally barren settings, there is still something not to deaden us but to make us stronger."

Other reviewers added to the praise. "Clearly," wrote Stephen Weiner in *Library Journal,* "Ware is one of today's premier cartoonists." *Booklist*'s Gordon Flagg noted Ware's antecedents in McCay and in turn-of-the-twentieth-century advertising images, and how the cartoonist transforms these into "something new, evocative, and affecting." Flagg further commented that Ware's "daunting skill transforms a simple tale into a pocket epic and makes Jimmy's melancholy story the stuff of cartoon tragedy." Laura J. Kloberg, writing in *National Forum,* concluded that Ware's "use of color, the rhythm of the panels, attention to details and details within details, and the repetition of themes—keep the reader interested in a story that on the surface is mundane. The many layers of history and images keep the mind engaged. It is ultimately a very complex tale, one that bears rereading. I loved the interconnectedness of it all." And Phil Daoust, reviewing the book in the *Guardian,* called *Jimmy Corrigan* "a rare and uplifting example of an artistic vision pushed to the limits."

The unpretentious, unaffected Ware is not only a maker of books, but also is a collector of ragtime ephemera, having played piano since he was a teenager. He publishes *The Ragtime Ephemeralist,* "a fascinating, dryly amusing periodical . . . devoted to ragtime," according to David Wondrich, writing in the *New York Times.* Ware told Wondrich that with his publication he "aims to provide a dense sense of the whole era, not simply a dissected examination of the music apart from it." In his periodical, he publishes newly rediscovered sheet music and articles on ragtime composers, both known and obscure. He also includes pictures of performers, minstrels, banjo players, and pianists from the time. "You cannot read *The Ephemeralist* without beginning to understand just how intimately ragtime is bound up with the perennial issue in American music, race," wrote Wondrich.

Ware has also continued his comic book odyssey in other avenues since putting the final "The End" to Corrigan's adventures. In 2001 he brought out the fifteenth number in his "Acme Novelty Library," titling it *The Big Book of Jokes,* and its publication ensured, according to Arnold, writing in *Time.com,* that Ware's reputation will "remain intact." Arnold described the issue as large enough to reach the "proportions of menus at Italian family-style restaurants," at ten inches wide and eighteen inches tall. Ware reprises some characters, such as Quimby the mouse, but also deals with new ones, such as Rusty Brown "a nasty collector of pop-cultural detritus," according to Arnold, who "lives in filth but owns the complete summer '87 Happy Meal toy series." Arnold concluded, "Those who have never picked up a copy of Chris Ware's 'Acme Novelty Library' owe it to themselves to do so. His dedication to the holistic experience of a single comic book issue has vastly increased the prestige of the medium."

Strauss, writing in the *New York Times,* noted that in the 1990s, "Thanks in part to Mr. Ware's 'Acme Novelty Library,' alternative comics have been slowly but steadily moving out of their underground niche" Yet despite all the critical fuss, fan response, and even interest from Hollywood, Ware has remained "profoundly unimpressed with himself," explained a contributor to the *Guardian.* "Beside the towering reputations of his comic-strip heroes—Art Spiegelman, Frank King, George Herriman—Ware says he feels 'like a real hayseed.'"

BIOGRAPHICAL AND CRITICAL SOURCES:

PERIODICALS

Book, January, 2001, James Sullivan, review of *Jimmy Corrigan: The Smartest Kid on Earth,* p. 66.

Booklist, February 15, 1998; November 15, 2000, Gordon Flagg, review of *Jimmy Corrigan,* p. 598.

Bookseller, December 7, 2001, review of *Jimmy Corrigan,* p. 7.

Chicago, February, 1998, pp. 68-72.

Comics Journal, December, 1997, Gary Groth, pp. 15-16, 119-171.

Creative Review, July, 2001, review of *Jimmy Corrigan,* p. 66.

Entertainment Weekly, February 23, 2001, p. 156.

Graphis, May-June, 2000, review of *Jimmy Corrigan,* p. 13.

Guardian (London, England), July 21, 2001, Phil Daoust, "Daddy, I Hardly Knew You"; December 7, 2001; "I Still Have Overwhelming Doubt about My Ability," pp. G4-G5.

Library Journal, November 15, 2000, Stephen Weiner, review of *Jimmy Corrigan,* p. 64; November 1, 2003, Steve Ratieri review of *Acme Novelty Date Book,* Volume 1: *1986-1995,* p. 62.

National Forum, summer, 2001, Laura J. Kloberg, review of *Jimmy Corrigan,* p. 44.

New York Times, January 21, 2001, David Wondrich, "Ragtime: No Longer a Novelty in Sepia," p. 2; April 4, 2001, Neil Strauss, "Graphic Tales Mine His Own Life and Heart," p. E1; February 8, 2002, Jonathan Goldstein, "Notes from Chicago."

New York Times Book Review, November 26, 2000, Dave Eggers, "After Wham! Pow! Shazam!," p. 7.

Print, July-August, 2002, Christopher Hawthorne, "Hard Ware," p. 24.

Publishers Weekly, September 4, 2000, review of *Jimmy Corrigan,* p. 87; July 19, 2004, review of *McSweeney's Quarterly Concern,* p. 146.

Time, September 11, 2000, Andrew Arnold, "Right Way, Corrigan," p. 116.

Wall Street Journal, October 20, 2000, Andrew Horton, "Beyond Archie and Spidey," p. W10.

ONLINE

CNN.com, http://europe.cnn.com/ (October 3, 2000), Beth Nissen, "A Not-so-Comic Comic Book."

Fantagraphics Books Web Site, http://www.fantagraphics.com/ (April 17, 2002), "Chris Ware."

Galerie Lambiek, http://www.lambiek.net/ (April 17, 2002).

Indy Online, http://www.indymagazine.com/ (April 17, 2002), Travis Fristoe and Chris Waldronn, interview with Ware.

Metroactive.com, http://www.metroactive.com/ (November 9-15, 2000), Richard von Busack, "One Hundred Years of Solitude."

Random House Web site, http://www.randomhouse.com/ (April 17, 2002), Chip Kidd, "Please Don't Hate Him" (originally printed in *Print* magazine).

This American Life Web site, http://www.thislife.org/ (April 17, 2002), "Chris Ware."

Time Online, http://www.time.com/ (November 27, 2001), Andrew Arnold, "The Depressing Joy of Chris Ware."

* * *

WARREN, Robert Penn 1905-1989

PERSONAL: Born April 24, 1905, in Guthrie, KY; died of cancer, September 15, 1989, in Stratton, VT; son of Robert Franklin (a businessman) and Anna Ruth (Penn) Warren; married Emma Brescia, September 12, 1930 (divorced, 1950); married Eleanor Clark (a writer), December 7, 1952; children: (second marriage) Rosanna Phelps, Gabriel Penn. *Education:* Vanderbilt University, B.A. (summa cum laude), 1925; University of California—Berkeley, M.A., 1927; Yale University, graduate study, 1927-28; Oxford University, B.Litt., 1930. *Politics:* Democrat.

CAREER: Poet, novelist, essayist, playwright, educator, literary critic, and editor. Southwestern Presbyterian University (now Southwestern at Memphis), Memphis, TN, assistant professor of English, 1930-31; Vanderbilt University, Nashville, TN, acting assistant professor, 1931-34; Louisiana State University, Baton Rouge, assistant professor, 1934-36, associate professor, 1936-42; University of Minnesota, Minneapolis, professor of English, 1942-50; Yale University, New Haven, CT, professor of playwrighting in School of Drama, 1950-56, professor of English, 1961-73, professor emeritus, 1973-89. Visiting lecturer, State University of Iowa, 1941; Jefferson Lecturer, National Endowment for the Humanities, 1974. Staff member of writers conferences, University of Colorado, 1936, 1937, and 1940, and Olivet College, 1940. Consultant in poetry, Library of Congress, 1944-45.

MEMBER: American Academy of Arts and Letters (member of board), Academy of American Poets (chancellor), American Academy of Arts and Sciences, American Philosophical Society, Modern Language Association (honorary fellow), Century Club (New York).

AWARDS, HONORS: Rhodes Scholar, Oxford University, 1928-30; Caroline Sinkler Prize, Poetry Society of South Carolina, 1936, 1937, and 1938; Levinson Prize, *Poetry* magazine, 1936; Houghton Mifflin literary fellowship, 1936; Guggenheim fellowship, 1939-40 and 1947-48; Shelley Memorial Prize, 1942, for *Eleven Poems on the Same Theme;* Pulitzer Prize for fiction, 1947, for *All the King's Men;* Southern Prize, 1947; Robert Meltzer Award, Screen Writers Guild, 1949; Union League Civic and Arts Foundation Prize, *Poetry* magazine, 1953; Sidney Hillman Award, 1957, Edna St. Vincent Millay Memorial Award, American Poetry Society, 1958, National Book Award, 1958, and Pulitzer Prize for poetry, 1958, all for *Promises: Poems, 1954-1956;* Irita Van Doren Award, *New York Herald Tribune,* 1965, for *Who Speaks for the Negro?;* Bollingen Prize in poetry, Yale University, 1967, for *Selected Poems: New and Old, 1923-1966;* National Endowment for the Arts grant, 1968. Van Wyck Brooks Award for poetry, National Medal for Literature, and Henry A. Bellaman Prize, all 1970, all for *Audubon: A Vision;* award for literature, University of Southern California, 1973; Golden Rose Trophy, New England Poetry Club, 1975; Emerson-Thoreau Medal, American Academy of Arts and Sciences, 1975; Copernicus Prize, American Academy of Poets, 1976; Wilma and Robert Messing Award, 1977; Pulitzer Prize for poetry, 1979, for *Now and Then: Poems, 1976-1978;* Harriet Monroe Award for poetry, 1979, for *Selected Poems: 1923-1975;* MacArthur Foundation fellowship, 1980; Commonwealth Award for Literature, 1980; Hubbell Memorial Award, Modern Language Association, 1980; Connecticut Arts Council award, 1980; Presidential Medal of Freedom, 1980; National Book Critics Circle Award nomination, 1980, and American Book Award nomination, 1981, both for *Being Here: Poetry, 1977-1980;* poetry prize nomination, *Los Angeles Times,* 1982, for *Rumor Verified: Poems, 1979-1980;* creative arts award, Brandeis University, 1984; named first Poet Laureate of the United States, 1986; National Medal of Arts, 1987. Honorary degrees from University of Louisville, 1949, Kenyon College, 1952, University of Kentucky, 1955, Colby College, 1956, Swarthmore College, 1958, Yale University, 1959, Bridgeport University, 1965, Fairfield University, 1969, Wesleyan University, 1970, Harvard University, 1973, Southwestern at Memphis, 1974, University of the South, 1974, University of New Haven, 1974, Johns Hopkins University, 1977, Monmouth College, 1979, New York University, 1983, Oxford University, 1983, and Arizona State University.

WRITINGS:

POETRY

Thirty-Six Poems, Alcestis Press, 1935.

Eleven Poems on the Same Theme, New Directions (New York, NY), 1942.

Selected Poems: 1923-1943, Harcourt (New York, NY), 1944.

Brother to Dragons: A Tale in Verse and Voices, Random House (New York, NY), 1953, revised edition published as *Brother to Dragons: A Tale in Verse and Voices—A New Version,* 1979.

Promises: Poems, 1954-1956, Random House (New York, NY), 1957.

You, Emperors and Others: Poems, 1957-1960, Random House (New York, NY), 1960.

Selected Poems: New and Old, 1923-1966, Random House (New York, NY), 1966.

Incarnations: Poems, 1966-1968, Random House (New York, NY), 1968.

Audubon: A Vision, Random House (New York, NY), 1969.

Or Else: Poems, 1968-1974, Random House (New York, NY), 1974.

Selected Poems, 1923-1975, Random House (New York, NY), 1976.

Now and Then: Poems, 1976-1978, Random House (New York, NY), 1978.

Being Here: Poetry, 1977-1980, Random House (New York, NY), 1980.

Rumor Verified: Poems, 1979-1980, Random House (New York, NY), 1981.

Chief Joseph of the Nez Perce, Random House (New York, NY), 1983.

New and Selected Poems, 1923-1985, Random House (New York, NY), 1985.

(Author of introduction and contributor with the Academy of American Poets) *Sixty Years of American Poetry: Celebrating the Anniversary of the Academy of American Poets,* preface by Richard Wilbur, wood engravings by Barry Moser, revised edition of *Fifty Years of American Poetry,* Harry N. Abrams (New York, NY), 1996.

The Collected Poems of Robert Penn Warren, edited by John Burt, Louisiana State University Press (Baton Rouge, LA), 1998.

Selected Poems of Robert Penn Warren, edited by John Burt, Louisiana State University Press (Baton Rouge, LA), 2001.

FICTION

Night Rider (novel), Houghton Mifflin (Boston, MA), 1939, reprinted, Vintage Books (New York, NY), 1979, abridged edition, edited and introduced by George Mayberry, New American Library (New York, NY), 1950.

At Heaven's Gate (novel), Harcourt (New York, NY), 1943, reprinted, New Directions (New York, NY), 1985, abridged edition, edited and introduced by George Mayberry, New American Library (New York, NY), 1949.

All the King's Men (also see below; novel), Harcourt (New York, NY), 1946, with a forword by Joseph Blotner, 1996, restored edition, edited by Noel Polk, 2001.

Blackberry Winter (novelette), Cummington Press, 1946.

The Circus in the Attic, and Other Stories (short stories), Harcourt (New York, NY), 1947, reprinted, 1968.

World Enough and Time (novel), Random House (New York, NY), 1950, reprinted, Vintage Books (New York, NY), 1979.

Band of Angels (novel), Random House (New York, NY), 1955, reprinted, Louisiana State University Press (Baton Rouge, LA), 1994.

The Cave (novel), Random House (New York, NY), 1959.

The Gods of Mount Olympus (adaptations of Greek myths for young readers), Random House (New York, NY), 1959.

Wilderness: A Tale of the Civil War (novel), Random House (New York, NY), 1961.

Flood: A Romance of Our Time (novel), Random House (New York, NY), 1964.

Meet Me in the Green Glen (novel), Random House (New York, NY), 1971.

A Place to Come To (novel), Random House (New York, NY), 1977.

NONFICTION

John Brown: The Making of a Martyr, Payson & Clarke, 1929, reprinted, Scholarly Press (New York, NY), 1970.

(With others) *I'll Take My Stand: The South and the Agrarian Tradition,* Harper (New York, NY), 1930.

(Author of critical essay) Samuel Taylor Coleridge, *The Rime of the Ancient Mariner,* illustrated by Alexander Calder, Reynal & Hitchcock, 1946, reprinted, Folcroft (Folcroft, PA), 1971.

Segregation: The Inner Conflict in the South, Random House (New York, NY), 1956, reprinted, University of Georgia Press (Athens, GA), 1994.

Remember the Alamo!, Random House (New York, NY), 1958.

Selected Essays, Random House (New York, NY), 1958.

How Texas Won Her Freedom: The Story of Sam Houston and the Battle of San Jacinto (booklet), San Jacinto Museum of History, 1959.

The Legacy of the Civil War: Meditations on the Centennial, Random House (New York, NY), 1961, reprinted, Harvard University Press (Cambridge, MA), 1983.

Who Speaks for the Negro?, Random House (New York, NY), 1965.

A Plea in Mitigation: Modern Poetry and the End of an Era (lecture), Wesleyan College (Middletown, CT), 1966.

Homage to Theodore Dreiser (criticism), Random House (New York, NY), 1971.

Democracy and Poetry, Harvard University Press (Cambridge, MA), 1975.

Jefferson Davis Gets His Citizenship Back (essay), University of Kentucky Press (Lexington, KY), 1980.

New and Selected Essays, Random House (New York, NY), 1989.

Selected Letters of Robert Penn Warren, Volume One: The Apprentice Years, 1924-1934. edited with an introduction by William Bedford Clark, Louisiana State University Press (Baton Rouge, LA), 2000.

WITH CLEANTH BROOKS

Selected Letters of Robert Penn Warren, Volume Two: The "Southern Review" Years, 1935-1942, compiled by William Bedford Clark, Louisiana State University Press (Baton Rouge, LA), 2001

(Editors, with John T. Purser) *An Approach to Literature,* Louisiana State University Press (Baton Rouge, LA), 1936, 5th edition, Prentice-Hall (Englewood Cliffs, NJ), 1975.

(Editors) *Understanding Poetry: An Anthology for College Students,* Holt (New York, NY), 1938, 4th edition, 1976.

(Editors) *Understanding Fiction,* Crofts (New York, NY), 1943, 2nd edition, Appleton-Century-Crofts (New York, NY), 1959, shortened version of 2nd edition published as *Scope of Fiction,* 1960, 3rd edition published under original title, Prentice-Hall (Englewood Cliffs, NJ), 1979.

Modern Rhetoric, Harcourt (New York, NY), 1949, published as *Fundamentals of Good Writing: A Handbook of Modern Rhetoric,* 1950, 2nd edition published under original title, 1958, 4th edition, 1979.

(Editors) *An Anthology of Stories from the Southern Review,* Louisiana State University Press (Baton Rouge, LA), 1953.

(And R.W.B. Lewis) *American Literature: The Makers and the Making* (criticism), two volumes, St. Martin's (New York, NY), 1974.

Cleanth Brooks and Robert Penn Warren: A Literary Correspondence, edited by James A. Grimshaw, Jr., University of Missouri Press (Columbia, MO), 1998.

EDITOR

A Southern Harvest: Short Stories by Southern Writers, Houghton (Boston, MA), 1937, reprinted, N.S. Berg, 1972.

(With Albert Erskine) *Short Story Masterpieces,* Dell (New York, NY), 1954, 2nd edition, 1958, reprinted, 1989.

(With Albert Erskine) *Six Centuries of Great Poetry,* Dell (New York, NY), 1955.

(With Albert Erskine) *A New Southern Harvest,* Bantam (New York, NY), 1957.

(With Allen Tate) Denis Devlin, *Selected Poems,* Holt (New York, NY), 1963.

Faulkner: A Collection of Critical Essays, Prentice-Hall (Englewood Cliffs, NJ), 1966.

Randall Jarrell, 1914-1965, Farrar, Straus (New York, NY), 1967.

John Greenleaf Whittier's Poetry: An Appraisal and a Selection, University of Minnesota Press (Minneapolis, MN), 1971.

Selected Poems of Herman Melville, Random House (New York, NY), 1971.

Katherine Anne Porter: A Collection of Critical Essays, Prentice-Hall (Englewood Cliffs, NJ), 1979.

The Essential Melville, Ecco Press (Hopewell, NJ), 1987.

(Author of introduction) *Sixty Years of American Poetry: Celebrating the Anniversary of the Academy of American Poets,* Harry N. Abrams (New York, NY), 1996.

PLAYS

Proud Flesh (in verse), produced in Minneapolis, MN, 1947, revised prose version produced in New York, NY, 1948.

(With Erwin Piscator) *Blut auf dem Mond: Ein Schauspiel in drei Akten* (adaptation of Warren's novel *All the King's Men;* produced in 1947; produced in Dallas, TX, as *Willie Stark: His Rise and Fall,* 1958; produced on Broadway, 1959), Lechte, 1956.

All the King's Men (adaptation of Warren's novel of same title; produced Off-Broadway at East 74th St. Theatre), Random House (New York, NY), 1960.

Ballad of a Sweet Dream of Peace: An Easter Charade (produced in New York City at Cathedral of St. John the Divine), music by Alexei Haieff, Pressworks, 1981.

(With others) *The Grotesque in Art and Literature: Theological Reflections,* edited by J.L. Adams and W. Yates, W.B. Eerdmans (Grand Rapids, MI), 1997.

OTHER

A Robert Penn Warren Reader, Random House (New York, NY), 1987.

Portrait of a Father, University Press of Kentucky (Lexington, KY), 1988.

Contributor to numerous publications, including *Virginia Quarterly Review, Southern Review, Mademoiselle, Sewanee Review, New Republic, Poetry, American Review, Harvard Advocate, Nation, American Scholar, New York Times Book Review, Holiday, Fugitive, Botteghe Oscure, Yale Review,* and *Saturday Review.* Cofounding editor, *Fugitive,* 1922-25; founder and editor, with Cleanth Brooks, *Southern Review,* 1935-42; advisory editor, *Kenyon Review,* 1938-61.

The complete papers of Robert Penn Warren are collected at Yale University's Beinecke Rare Book and Manuscript Library.

ADAPTATIONS: Two of Robert Penn Warren's novels have been made into films: *All the King's Men,* Columbia Pictures, 1949; and *Band of Angels,* Warner Brothers, 1956. *All the King's Men* also served as the basis for an opera by Carlisle Floyd, *Willie Stark,* broadcast on television, and was adapted as a play by Adrian Hall, *All the King's Men,* presented by Trinity Repertory Company, Providence, RI, April, 1987.

SIDELIGHTS: Described by *Newsweek* reviewer Annalyn Swan as "America's dean of letters and, in all but name, poet laureate," Robert Penn Warren was among the last surviving members of a major literary movement that emerged in the American South shortly after World War I. A distinguished poet, novelist, critic, and teacher, he won virtually every major award given to writers in the United States and was the only person to receive a Pulitzer Prize in both fiction (once) and poetry (twice). He also achieved a measure of commercial success that eludes many other serious artists. In short, as Hilton Kramer once observed in the *New York Times Book Review,* Warren "has enjoyed the best of both worlds. . . . Few other writers in our history have labored with such consistent distinction and such unflagging energy in so many separate branches of the literary profession. He is a man of letters on the old-fashioned, outsize scale, and everything he writes is stamped with the passion and the embattled intelligence of a man for whom the art of literature is inseparable from the most fundamental imperatives of life."

Literature did not always play a central role in Warren's life, however. As he once recalled in an interview with John Baker published in *Conversations with Writers:* "I didn't expect to become a writer. My ambition was to be a naval officer and I got an appointment to Annapolis. . . . Then I had an accident. I couldn't go—an accident to my eyes—and then I went to [Vanderbilt University] instead, and I started out in life there as a chemical engineer. That didn't last but three weeks or so, because I found the English courses so much more interesting. History courses were also interesting, but the chemistry was taught without imagination."

The freshman English teacher Warren found so fascinating was fellow Southerner John Crowe Ransom, "a real, live poet, in pants and vest, who had published a book and also fought in the war. . . . As a man, he made no effort to charm his students, but everything he said was interesting." Ransom, recognizing that Warren was no ordinary English student, encouraged the young man to enroll in one of his more advanced courses. He also invited Warren to join the "Fugitives," a group of Vanderbilt teachers and students as well as several local businessmen who had been meeting informally since around 1915 to discuss trends in American life and literature. By 1922, the year Warren joined, many of the Fugitives' discussions focused on poetry and critical theory, Warren's favorite subjects at the time. "In a very important way," Warren recalled, "that group was my education."

The Fugitives drifted apart in the mid-1920s, about the same time Warren graduated from Vanderbilt and headed west to continue his education at the University of California in Berkeley. After receiving his M.A. from there in 1927, Warren attended Yale University and then England's Oxford University where, as he described, he "stumbled on" writing fiction. Homesick and weary of devoting his days and nights to working on his dissertation, Warren, at the request of one of the editors of the literary annual *American Caravan,* agreed to compose a novelette based on the folk tales he had heard as a boy in Kentucky. As he later remarked to Baker, his contribution to the annual received "some pleasant notices in the press," and soon publishers were asking him to write novels.

Though Warren did indeed write several novels during the next decade—only one of which, *Night Rider,* was published—most of his time and effort was spent trying to earn a living. Returning to Tennessee in 1930 after completing his studies at Oxford, he briefly served on the faculty of Southwestern Presbyterian University (now Southwestern at Memphis) before obtaining a teaching position at Vanderbilt. From there Warren went to Louisiana State University in 1934, teaming up with friend and fellow faculty member Cleanth Brooks to write a series of immensely successful and influential textbooks, including *An Approach to Literature and Understanding Poetry.* Based on the authors' class notes and conversations, these books have been largely responsible for disseminating the theories of the New Criticism to several generations of college students and teachers. According to Helen McNeil in the *Times Literary Supplement,* Warren and Brooks helped to establish the New Criticism as "an orthodoxy so powerful that contemporary American fiction and poetry are most easily defined by their rebellion against it."

The New Criticism—a method of analyzing a work of art that focuses attention on the work's intrinsic value as an object in and of itself, more or less independent of outside influences (such as the circumstances of its composition, the reality it creates, the effect it has on readers, and the author's intention) grew out of discussions Warren had participated in first as a member of the Fugitives, then as an Agrarian. (The Agrarians were former Fugitives who banded together again in the late 1920s to extol the virtues of the rural South and to promote an agrarian as opposed to an industrial economy). Despite his close association with the Agrarians and his key role in publicizing their theories, Warren did not consider himself to be a professional critic. As he later explained to Baker: "I have only two roles, essentially: poetry and fiction—and only a certain kind of fiction. . . . A real critic, like Cleanth Brooks or I.A. Richards, has a system. . . . He's concerned with that, primarily. I'm not." Warren continued, "I'm interested in trying to understand this poem or that poem, but I'm not interested in trying to create a system. I'm interested in a different kind of understanding, you might say, a more limited kind of understanding. I'm interested in my enjoyment, put it that way, more than anything else. I've certainly written some criticism, but I usually take it from my class notes. I'm just not a professional critic. That business is just something that happens. . . . But writing fiction, poetry, that's serious—that's for keeps."

Poetry and fiction were thus Warren's main concerns throughout his long career, with poetry having edged out fiction as the author's preferred genre since the mid-1950s. He saw nothing unusual in the fact that he made notable contributions to both, remarking to Baker that "a poem for me and a novel are not so different. They start much the same way, on the same emotional journey, and can go either way. . . . At a certain level an idea takes hold. Now it doesn't necessarily come with a form; it comes as an idea or an impulse. . . . I've started many things in one form and shifted to another. . . . The interesting topics, the basic ideas in the poems and the basic ideas in the novels are the same."

For the most part, these "basic ideas" in Warren's poetry and fiction sprang from his Southern Agrarian heritage. Observed Marshall Walker in *London Magazine:* "Warren began as an enlightened conservative Southerner. Like his close associates, John Crowe Ransom, Donald Davidson, Allen Tate, Andrew Lytle, he was acutely aware of the gulf widening between an America that moved further into slavery to material progress and a minority of artists and intellectuals, self-appointed custodians of traditional values. . . . Agrarians, with Ransom in the lead, were determined to re-endow nature with an element of horror and inscrutability and to bring back a God who permitted evil as well as good—in short, to give God back his thunder."

Despite his reliance on history for material, Warren balked at being labeled an "historical novelist." "I just happened to encounter stories that had the right germ of an idea for a novel," he once stated in a *Saturday Review* article. "I should hope that the historical novel would be a way of saying something about the present." To this end, he often changes the actual historical focus of a story to concentrate on peripheral characters whose behavior reveals more about the ethical or dramatic issues *behind* the facts. Therefore, maintained Everett Wilkie and Josephine Helterman in the *Dictionary of Literary Biography,* Warren's "main obsession is knowledge," not history. Explained the critics: "His works reflect the many forms in which he himself . . . found knowledge. . . . [His] wisdom is the wisdom of interpretation; his main question, 'How is one to look at life?' From an elaboration of the complex forces which shape both our lives and our perceptions, he shows us history as a living force which can yet tell us something about ourselves."

For Warren, this process of self-discovery was painful, yet the opposite state—ignorance—was brutish. In his book *The Poetic Vision of Robert Penn Warren,* Victor Strandberg declared that the contemplation of this passage from innocence to maturity is "the crucial center" of Warren's career. With this theme in mind, wrote Strandberg, Warren typically divides his characters into two groups: "those who refuse passage into a polluted and compromised adult environment" and "those who accept passage into the world's stew." In all Warren's writing, the "most negative characters are those who reject the osmosis of being, while his spiritual guides are those who accept it," Strandberg observed.

The "action" in most of Warren's work consists primarily of an idealistic narrator's search for his or her identity in an atmosphere of confusion and/or corruption. This search eventually leads to recognition of the world's fallen state and, consequently, of the self's "innate depravity," to use Strandberg's phrase. In an attempt to overcome the sense of alienation caused by these "warring parts of the psyche," a typical Warren character undergoes a period of intense self-examination that ideally results in a near-religious experience of conversion, rebirth, and a mystical feeling of oneness with God. This in turn opens the door to further knowledge, not only about the self but about the world as well. Though the search for identity may not always end in success, noted Strandberg, "the craving to recreate that original felicity [that existed before the Fall] is one of mankind's deepest obsessions, in Warren's judgment."

Most observers have found Warren's language, style, and tone to be perfectly suited to his subject matter. His language, for example, is a lyrical mixture of earthiness and elegance, of the folk speech of Kentucky and Tennessee and what James Dickey referred to in the *Saturday Review* as a "rather quaintly old-fangled scholastic vocabulary." Richard Jackson offered a similar description in the *Michigan Quarterly Review:* "[Warren's] idiom . . . is at once conversational and lyric, contemporary and historic, profane and sacred. It is a language in which he can slip easily from necessary precept to casual observation, cosmic vision to particular sighting." According to *Sewanee Review* writer Calvin Bedient, Warren's poetry is written "in a genuinely expansive, passionate style. Look at its prose ease and rapidity oddly qualified by log-piling compounds, alliteration, successive stresses, and an occasional inversion something rough and serviceable as a horse-blanket yet fancy to—and you wonder how he ever came up with it. It is excitingly massive and moulded and full of momentum. Echoes of Yeats and Auden still persist, but it is wonderfully peculiar, homemade."

Charles H. Bohner was equally impressed by Warren's forceful and exuberant style. "There is about his art the prodigality of the writer who exercises his verbal gifts for the sheer magic of the effects he can produce," noted the critic in his book-length study of Warren. "[His] language is robust and rhetorical. He likes his adjectives and nouns to go in pairs, reinforcing one another, begetting rhythm and resonance. When a comparison catches his fancy, his first metaphor is likely to suggest another, and he piles image on image as he warms to his task. . . . About all of Warren's work there is a gusto and masculine force, a willingness to risk bathos and absurdity. . . . He has always seemed driven to explore the boundaries of his art, to push the possibilities of his form to its outer limits."

Though Warren drew extensively from his own past for the language, settings, and themes that appear in both his fiction and poetry, he approached all of this familiar material somewhat objectively and analytically, as if he were contemplating them from a distance, either far from home or, more frequently, much later in time. Warren's preoccupation with time and how the passage of years affects memory reveals itself in his extensive use of flashbacks to illustrate the often ironic nature of the relationship between the past and the present. Critics have also found the abundance of background detail in his work to be evidence of his near-obsession with time. According to James H. Justus in the *Sewanee Review,* for instance, one of the hallmarks of Warren's prose is his practice of including "periods of closely observed details strung out in an evocative rhetoric which invites nostalgia for a specific time and place or which invokes awe for a mythic history that seems to explain national and even human urges." And as Paul West asserted in his book *Robert Penn Warren:* "[No] writer has worked harder than Warren to substantiate narrative through close, doting observation of the physical, emotional world. He sees it, makes the page tremble with it. . . . His 'texture of relations'—to his past, to his work, to familiars and strangers—is something he fingers endlessly; and in the long run it is the feel, not the feel's meaning, that he communicates." Despite the fact that Warren is popularly known as the author of *All the King's Men,* a novel loosely based on the life of Louisianan politician Huey "Kingfish" Long, he thought of himself primarily as a poet. "I started as a poet and I will probably end as a poet," he once commented in the *Sewanee Review.* "If I had to choose between my novels and my *Selected Poems,* I would keep the *Selected Poems* as representing me more fully, my vision and my self."

After emerging from a ten-year-long period of "poet's block" in 1954, Warren devoted most of his creative energies to writing verse. Unlike his pre-1944 poetry, which sprang from either the contemplation of complex metaphysical concepts or the ballads and narratives native to his region, Warren's later poetry was inspired by a mood, a natural event, or a memory that often took shape as "a moralized anecdote," to use Warren's own words. It is a highly personal and often autobiographical, but by no means confessional, poetry. In fact, maintained Kramer, Warren's verse "is so unlike that of most other poets claiming our attention . . . that it requires a certain adjustment of the eye and the ear, and of that other faculty—call it the moral imagination—to which Mr. Warren's verse speaks with so much urgency and that of so many other poets nowadays does not. We are a long way, in this poetry, from the verse snapshot and the campy valentine—a long way, too, from the verse diaries, confessions and dirty laundry lists that have come to occupy such a large place in our poetic literature . . . [His] is a poetry haunted by the lusts and loves of the flesh, filled with dramatic incident, vivid landscapes and philosophical reflection—a poetry of passion recollected in the tragic mode. It teems with experience, and with the lessons and losses of experience."

The natural world plays a prominent role in Warren's poetry, providing him with much of his inspiration and imagery. But according to Wilkie in his *Dictionary of Literary Biography* essay, the poet's fascination with nature does not mean he believed man can turn to nature for answers to age-old questions about life and death. "Warren argues repeatedly that the natural world is not a sympathetic or reliable guide to interpreting human life and that man's affairs are a matter of indifference to the rest of creation," asserted the critic. "Only man's pride or ignorance allows him to impute to the natural world any concern with his comings and goings."

Though Warren did not deny that man is an integral part of nature, what he celebrated in his poetry was the trait that sets man apart from nature—namely, his ability (and desire) to seek knowledge in his quest "to make sense out of life." As a result, reported Peter Stitt in the *Southern Review,* "Warren's poems are a resounding testament to man, to nature, and to poetry itself. . . . Among contemporary poets, it has been Robert Penn Warren's task to discover how the void at man's heart may be filled. Though revolutionary for our age, Warren's answer places him at the heart of the great tradition in English and American poetry."

In a strictly artistic sense, too, Warren worked within this great tradition in English and American poetry. Explained Strandberg: "With respect to the ageless elements of poetic technique—command of metaphor, control of tone and diction, powers of organization, mastery of sound effects, and the like—each phase of Warren's career has evinced a 'morality of style' that is true to the classic standard." As Harold Bloom observed in the *New Leader:* Warren "ranks with . . . Frost, Stevens, Hart Crane, Williams, Pound, Eliot. . . . [He] is that rarest kind of major poet: he . . . never stopped developing from his origins up to his work-in-progress." Swan agreed, adding, "The progression is striking—from the impersonal tone, inspired by Eliot, of the early poems . . . to the more personal, more intense free-verse style that began with *Promises: Poems, 1954-1956* . . . to the majestic reverie of the late poems." Warren's later poetry is noted for its rambling conversational rhythm, due in part to what Edward L. Stewart referred to in the *Washington Post Book World* as its "wide range of conventional but loose-limbed, free but masterfully controlled verse patterns." Warren favored very long and very short lines, the use of which creates an irregular meter and sentences that seem to wind down the page, "run[ning] forward, as it were, into experience," as Bedient explained in *Parnassus.* The overall tone is one of reflection and meditation, though not in a passive sense, wrote Alan Williamson, another *Washington Post Book World* critic. "In the whiplash of [Warren's] long line, the most ordinary syntax becomes tense, muscular, searching," commented Williamson. "His ear is formidable, though given to strong effects rather than graceful ones." *Times Literary Supplement* writer Jay Parini also found that "power is the word that comes to mind" when reading Warren's work—power that is expressed in the "raw-boned, jagged quality" of his verse.

Not all reviewers have agreed that Warren's work deserves unqualified praise. The focus of most negative criticism is on the author's attitude toward his material; though Warren tackled unquestionably important themes, they believe his treatment of those themes bordered on the bombastic. As Leslie Fiedler explained in a volume of his collected essays, a Warren poem can be "bombastic in the technical sense of the word: [there is] a straining of language and tone toward a scream which can no longer be heard, the absolute cry of bafflement and pain. Such a tone becomes in Warren . . . ridiculous on occasion, ridiculous whenever we lapse from total conviction."

In his book *Contemporaries,* Alfred Kazin pointed out that "all [of Warren's] work seems to deal with the Fall of Man. And if in reading [him] I have come to be more wary of his handling of this theme, it is because of the nostalgia it conveys, the strident impatient language with which it is expressed, the abstract use to which it is put. . . . Warren tends to make rhetoric of his philosophy." Bedient expressed a similar thought in the *Sewanee Review,* commenting that Warren "seems bitten by the Enormity of it all. He *will* have mystery." As a result, concluded Bedient, his philosophical musings are "sometimes truly awkward and sometimes pseudo-profound."

A few reviewers attribute Warren's occasional awkwardness to the very quality that has made him such a noteworthy figure in American literature: his versatility. Eric Bentley, for one, speculated that Warren's dual role as both artist *and* critic hindered his ability to "submerge himself in the artist." Continued Bentley in a *Kenyon Review* article: "Trite as it is . . . to stigmatize an author as a dual personality, I cannot help pointing to a duality in Warren that may well constitute his major problem: it is his combination of critical and creative power. I am far from suggesting that the critical and the creative are of their nature antithetic and I am fully ready to grant that what makes Warren remarkable among American writers is his double endowment. The problem lies precisely in his being so two-sidedly gifted; he evidently finds it endlessly difficult to combine his two sorts of awareness."

Noting in the *Virginia Quarterly Review* that "Warren has dedicated his career to proving the indivisibility of the critical and the creative imaginations," David M. Wyatt went on to state: "Such a habit of mind stations Warren on the border between . . . the artist who works from experience and the critic who works toward meaning. . . . His works constantly talk about themselves. . . . His characters are placed out of themselves, the bemused or obsessive spectators of their own wayward acts. . . . [Warren] thus joins that central American tradition of speakers—Emerson, Thoreau, Henry Adams, Norman Mailer—who are not only the builders but the interpreters of their own designs."

Parnassus reviewer Rachel Hadas maintained that Warren's difficulties stem from "nothing as simple as a lack of talent." Explained Hadas: "Part of the problem seems to be an inordinate ambition for grandeur; part is what feels to me like haste. If Warren were in less of a hurry to chronicle each dawn dream, birdsong, and memory as it occurred, a process of distillation just might be allowed to take place. Mostly, though, it's a matter of the poet's judgment of his own work. . . . [Warren exhibits an] inability or unwillingness to recognize and settle for the nature of his particular genius. . . . [He], has an imagination of generous proportions. It embraces history, human drama, perhaps above all the beauty of the natural world; it is capable at times of both beauty of form *and* splendor of color. . . . But Warren cannot do everything well. He is *not* an original thinker or a visionary poet; in his handling of condensed lyric, as well as of abstraction, he can be embarrassingly inept." In effect, declared Bedient, also writing in *Parnassus,* "[Warren] has failed to be ruthless toward himself, and his weaknesses loom oppressively in the reflected brilliance of his accomplishments."

Many critics, of course, disagree with these evaluations of Warren's poetry. In another *Parnassus* article, for instance, Paul Mariani wrote: "I could quarrel with certain things in Warren I find alien to my own sense of poetics: a sometimes loose, rambling line, a nostalgia verging on obsession, a veering towards philosophical attitudinizing, the mask of the redneck that out-rednecks the redneck. But I would rather leave such critical caveats for others. There is enough [in his poetry] to praise, and I am thankful to have been given to drink, if not out of those too rare 'great depths,' then at least from a spring sufficiently deep, sufficiently clear." Monroe K. Spears reported in the *Sewanee Review* that Warren's failings "are hard for me to specify; I find his attitudes and themes—moral, psychological, and religious—so congenial that it is difficult for me to regard the poetry with proper detachment. Sometimes the themes are perhaps a little too explicit, not very fully dramatized; and there is a danger in the fact that they are basically few, though combined and varied in many ways." Nevertheless, continued Spears, "Warren's later poetry seems to me to embody most of the special virtues of 'open' poetry—accessibility, immediate emotional involvement, wide appeal—and to resist the temptations to formlessness and to moral exhibitionism, self-absorption, and sentimentality that are the chief liabilities of that school."

Even Bentley admitted that Warren, despite his faults, "is worth a dozen petty perfectionists." And as poet and critic James Dickey observed in his book *Babel to Byzantium:* "Opening a book of poems by Robert Penn Warren is like putting out the light of the sun, or like plunging into the labyrinth and feeling the thread break after the first corner is passed. One will never come out in the same Self as that in which one entered. When he is good, and often even when he is bad, you had as soon read Warren as live. He gives you the sense of poetry as a thing of final importance to life: as a way or *form* of life. . . . Warren's verse is so deeply and compellingly linked to man's ageless, age-old drive toward self-discovery, self-determination, that it makes all discussion of line endings, metrical variants, and the rest of poetry's paraphernalia appear hopelessly beside the point."

One point critics have agreed on, however, is the extraordinary nature of Warren's contribution to literature.

In his critical study of the author, Bohner declared that "no other American literary figure of the twentieth century has exhibited greater versatility than Robert Penn Warren. . . . While arguments about his preeminence in any one field would be ultimately inconclusive, his total accomplishment . . . surpasses that of any other living writer." Marshall Walker had similar words of praise for Warren in the *London Magazine,* calling him "America's most distinguished man of letters in the European sense of a writer involved with books and human kind and at ease in a variety of *genres.* . . . The range of his achievement testifies to the scope and commitment of Warren's human sympathies. Each intellectual act, whether formally poem, novel, or one of the interviews with black leaders in *Who Speaks for the Negro?* is of the nature of a poem, according to his own definition of the poem as 'a way of getting your reality shaped a little better'. . . . Underlying the energy, even the violence that is part of Warren's metaphor of the world as well as of the world itself, is a concern to visualize the meaning of common experience and, without artistic concessions, to make this meaning available in a body of work which, with astonishing success, unites metaphysical and social themes in a single vision."

Writing in the *Saturday Review,* Dickey suggested Warren's depth rather than his range should be celebrated. Warren is "direct, scathingly honest, and totally serious about what he feels," Dickey began. "He plunges as though compulsively into the largest of subjects: those that seem to cry out for capitalization and afflatus and, more often than not in the work of many poets, achieve only the former. . . . He is a poet of enormous courage, with a highly individual intelligence." But above all, concluded Dickey, Warren "looks, and refuses to look away. . . . [He] wounds deeply; he strikes in at blood-level and gut-level, with all the force and authority of time, darkness, and distance themselves, and of the Nothingness beyond nothingness, which may even be God."

BIOGRAPHICAL AND CRITICAL SOURCES:

BOOKS

Authors in the News, Volume 1, Thomson Gale (Detroit, MI) 1976.

Berger, Walter, *A Southern Renascence Man: Views of Robert Penn Warren,* Louisiana State University Press (Baton Rouge, LA), 1984.

Blotner, Joseph Leo, *Robert Penn Warren: A Biography,* Random House (New York, NY), 1997.

Bohner, Charles H., *Robert Penn Warren,* Twayne (Boston, MA), 1964.

Bradbury, John, *The Fugitives,* University of North Carolina Press (Chapel Hill, NC), 1958, pp. 172-255.

Brooks, Cleanth, *The Hidden God,* Yale University Press (New Haven, CT), 1963.

Burt, John, *Robert Penn Warren and American Idealism,* Yale University Press (New Haven, CT), 1988.

Casper, Leonard, *Robert Penn Warren: The Dark and Bloody Ground,* University of Washington Press (Seattle, WA), 1960.

Casper, Leonard, *The Blood-Marriage of Earth and Sky: Robert Penn Warren's Later Novels,* Louisiana State University Press (Baton Rouge, LA), 1997.

Clark, William Bedford, editor, *Critical Essays on Robert Penn Warren,*Twayne (Boston, MA), 1981.

Concise Dictionary of American Literary Biography: Broadening Views, 1968-88, Thomson Gale (Detroit, MI) 1989.

Contemporary Literary Criticism, Thomson Gale (Detroit, MI) Volume 1, 1973, Volume 4, 1975, Volume 6, 1976, Volume 8, 1978, Volume 10, 1979, Volume 13, 1980, Volume 18, 1981, Volume 39, 1986, Volume 53, 1989, Volume 59, 1990.

Conversations with Writers, Thomson Gale (Detroit, MI) 1977.

Corrigan, Lesa Carnes, *Poems of Pure Imagination: Robert Penn Warren and the Romantic Tradition,* Louisiana State University Press (Baton Rouge, LA), 1999.

Cowan, Louise, *The Fugitive Group,* Louisiana State University Press (Baton Rouge, LA), 1959.

Cowley, Malcolm, editor, *Writers at Work: The Paris Review Interviews,*Viking (New York, NY), 1959.

Cullick, Jonathan S., *Making History: The Biographical Narratives of Robert Penn Warren,* Louisiana State University Press (Baton Rouge, LA), 2000.

Dickey, James, *Babel to Byzantium,* Farrar, Straus (New York, NY), 1968.

Dictionary of Literary Biography, Thomson Gale (Detroit, MI) Volume 2: *American Novelists since World War II,* 1978, Volume 48: *American Poets, 1880-1945, Second Series,* 1986.

Dictionary of Literary Biography Yearbook, Thomson Gale (Detroit, MI), *1980,* 1981, *1989,* 1990.

Ferriss, Lucy, *Sleeping with the Boss: Female Subjectivity and Narrative Pattern in the Fiction of Robert Penn Warren,* Louisiana State University Press (Baton Rouge, LA), 1997.

Fiedler, Leslie, *The Collected Essays of Leslie Fiedler,* Volume 1, Stein & Day (New York, NY), 1971.

Gray, Richard, *The Literature of Memory: Modern Writers of the American South,* Johns Hopkins University Press (Baltimore, MD), 1977.

Gray, Richard, editor, *Robert Penn Warren: A Collection of Critical Essays,* Prentice-Hall (Englewood Cliffs, NJ), 1980.

Grimshaw, James A., Jr., *Robert Penn Warren: A Descriptive Bibliography 1922-1979,* University Press of Virginia (Charlottesville, VA), 1981.

Grimshaw, James A., Jr., editor, *Robert Penn Warren's Brother to Dragons: A Discussion,* Louisiana State University Press (Baton Rouge, LA), 1983.

Grimshaw, James A., Jr., *Time's Glory: Original Essays on Robert Penn Warren,* University of Central Arkansas Press, 1986.

Grimshaw, James A., Jr., *Understanding Robert Penn Warren,* University of South Carolina Press (Columbia, SC), 2001.

Justus, James H., *The Achievement of Robert Penn Warren,* Louisiana State University Press (Baton Rouge, LA), 1981.

Kazin, Alfred, *Contemporaries,* Atlantic-Little, Brown (Boston, MA), 1962.

Koppelman, Robert S., *Robert Penn Warren's Modernist Spirituality,* University of Missouri Press (Columbia, MO), 1995.

Litz, A. Walton, editor, *Modern American Fiction: Essays in Criticism,* Oxford University Press (New York, NY), 1963.

Longley, John L., Jr., editor, *Robert Penn Warren: A Collection of Critical Essays,* New York University Press (New York, NY), 1965.

Nakadate, Neil, editor, *Robert Penn Warren: Critical Perspectives,* University Press of Kentucky (Lexington, KY), 1981.

Newquist, Roy, editor, *Conversations,* Rand McNally (New York, NY), 1967.

Rubin, Louis D., Jr., *Writers of the Modern South: The Faraway Country,* University of Washington Press (Seattle, WA), 1963.

Short Story Criticism, Thomson Gale (Detroit, MI) Volume 4, 1990.

Snipes, Katherine, *Robert Penn Warren,* Ungar (New York, NY), 1983.

Strandberg, Victor H., *The Poetic Vision of Robert Penn Warren,* University Press of Kentucky (Lexington, KY), 1977.

Szczesiul, Anthony, *Racial Politics and Robert Penn Warren's Poetry,* University Press of Florida (Gainesville, FL), 2002.

Van O'Connor, William, editor, *Forms of Modern Fiction,* Indiana University Press (Bloomington, IN), 1959.

Watkins, Floyd C., and John T. Hiers, editors, *Robert Penn Warren Talking: Interviews 1950-1978,* Random House (New York, NY), 1980.

Watkins, Floyd C., *Then and Now: The Personal Past in the Poetry of Robert Penn Warren,* University Press of Kentucky (Lexington, KY), 1982.

West, Paul, *Robert Penn Warren,* University of Minnesota Press (Minneapolis, MN), 1964.

PERIODICALS

America, November 14, 1987, p. 359.

Chicago Tribune, September 10, 1978; April 7, 1985; June 1, 1987.

Chicago Tribune Book Review, October 14, 1979; September 7, 1980; February 28, 1982.

Christian Science Monitor, September 4, 1946.

Commonweal, October 4, 1946.

Detroit News, February 15, 1981.

Hudson Review, summer, 1977.

Kenyon Review, summer, 1948.

London Magazine, December, 1975-January, 1976.

Los Angeles Times, March 19, 1981.

Los Angeles Times Book Review, September 7, 1980; October 19, 1980; January 17, 1982; July 30, 1986.

Michigan Quarterly Review, fall, 1978.

Mississippi Quarterly, winter, 1958, pp. 19-28; winter, 1970-71, pp. 47-56; winter, 1971-72, pp. 19-30; spring, 2002, p. 231.

Nation, August 24, 1946.

New Leader, January 31, 1977.

New Republic, September 2, 1946.

Newsweek, August 25, 1980; March 10, 1986.

New Yorker, August 24, 1946; December 29, 1980.

New York Times, August 18, 1946; December 16, 1969; March 2, 1977; June 2, 1981; March 27, 1983; April 24, 1985; October 6, 1986.

New York Times Book Review, June 25, 1950; January 9, 1977; November 2, 1980; May 12, 1985.

Parnassus, fall-winter, 1975; summer, 1977; spring-summer, 1979.

People, March 17, 1986.

San Francisco Chronicle, August 18, 1946.

Saturday Review, June 24, 1950; August 20, 1955; August, 1980.

Saturday Review of Literature, August 17, 1946.

Sewanee Review, spring, 1970; spring, 1974; spring, 1975; summer, 1977; spring, 1979; summer, 1980.

Southern Literary Journal, spring, 2002, pp. 73, 153; fall, 2003, p. 90.

Southern Review, spring, 1976; winter, 1980, pp. 18-45; autumn, 2002, pp. 849, 913.

Studies in the Novel, 1970, pp. 325-354.

Style, summer, 2002.

Time, August 18, 1975.

Times Literary Supplement, November 28, 1980; January 29, 1982; February 17-23, 1989.
Virginia Quarterly Review, summer, 1977.
Washington Post, May 2, 1980; September 23, 1989.
Washington Post Book World, March 6, 1977; October 22, 1978; September 30, 1979; August 31, 1980; October 4, 1981; June 26, 1983; April 30, 1989.
Yale Review, autumn, 1946.

* * *

WARSHOFSKY, Isaac
See SINGER, Isaac Bashevis

* * *

WASSERSTEIN, Wendy 1950-2006

PERSONAL: Born October 18, 1950, in Brooklyn, NY; died of cancer, January 30, 2006, in New York, NY; daughter of Morris W. (a textile manufacturer) and Lola (a dancer; maiden name, Schleifer) Wasserstein; children: Lucy Jane. *Education:* Mount Holyoke College, B.A., 1971; City College of the City University of New York, M.A., 1973; Yale University, M.F.A., 1976.

CAREER: Dramatist, actress, and screenwriter. Teacher at Columbia University and New York University, New York, NY. Actress in plays, including *The Hotel Play,* 1981. Member of artistic board of Playwrights Horizons; board member of WNET (public television affiliate) and MacDowell Colony.

MEMBER: Dramatists Guild (member of steering committee and women's committee), British-American Arts Association (board member), Dramatists Guild for Young Playwrights.

AWARDS, HONORS: Joseph Jefferson Award, *Dramalogue* Award, and Inner Boston Critics Award, all for *Uncommon Women and Others;* grant for playwriting, Playwrights Commissioning Program of Phoenix Theater, c. 1970s; Hale Mathews Foundation Award; Guggenheim fellowship, 1983; grant for writing and for studying theater in England, British-American Arts Association; grant for playwriting, American Playwrights Project, 1988; Pulitzer Prize for drama, Antoinette Perry ("Tony") Award for best play, League of American Theatres and Producers, Drama Desk Award, Outer Critics Circle Award, Susan Smith Blackburn Prize, and award for best new play, New York Drama Critics' Circle, all 1989, all for *The Heidi Chronicles;* Outer Critics Circle Award and Tony Award nomination for best play, both 1993, both for *The Sisters Rosensweig.*

WRITINGS:

PLAYS

Any Woman Can't, produced off-Broadway, 1973.
Happy Birthday, Montpelier Pizz-zazz, produced in New Haven, CT, 1974.
(With Christopher Durang) *When Dinah Shore Ruled the Earth,* produced in New Haven, CT, 1975.
Uncommon Women and Others (also see below; produced as a one-act in New Haven, CT, 1975; revised and enlarged two-act version produced off-Broadway, 1977), Avon (New York, NY), 1978.
Isn't It Romantic (also see below; produced off-Broadway, 1981; revised version produced off-Broadway, 1983), Doubleday (New York, NY), 1984.
Tender Offer (one-act), produced off-off Broadway, 1983.
The Man in a Case (one-act; adapted from the short story by Anton Chekhov), written as part of *Orchards* (anthology of seven one-act plays adapted from short stories by Chekhov; produced off-Broadway, 1986), Knopf (New York, NY), 1986.
Miami (musical), produced off-Broadway, 1986.
The Heidi Chronicles (also see below; produced off-Broadway, 1988, produced on Broadway, 1989), Dramatists Play Service (New York, NY), 1990.
The Heidi Chronicles, and Other Plays (contains *Uncommon Women and Others, Isn't It Romantic,* and *The Heidi Chronicles*), Harcourt (San Diego, CA), 1990.
The Sisters Rosensweig (produced at Mitzi E. Newhouse Theater, Lincoln Center, October 22, 1992), Harcourt (New York, NY), 1993.
An American Daughter, Harcourt (New York, NY), 1997.
Psyche in Love (one-act), produced at the TriBeCa Theater Festival (New York, NY), 2004.
Third, produced at the Mitzi E. Newhouse Theater, Lincoln Center (New York, NY), 2005.

TELEVISION PLAYS

Uncommon Women and Others (adapted from Wasserstein's play), Public Broadcasting Service (PBS), 1978.
The Sorrows of Gin (adapted from the short story by John Cheever), PBS, 1979.

OTHER

Bachelor Girls (comic essays), Knopf (New York, NY), 1990.

Pamela's First Musical (children's picture book), illustrated by Andrew Jackness, Hyperion (New York, NY), 1996.

Shiksa Goddess; or, How I Spent My Forties: Essays, Knopf (New York, NY), 2001.

Old Money, Harcourt (New York, NY), 2002.

Also author of television plays *"Drive," She Said,* PBS, and of sketches for *Comedy Zone* (series), Columbia Broadcasting System, Inc. (CBS), 1984. Author of unproduced film scripts, including (with Christopher Durang) "House of Husbands," adapted from the short story "Husbands"; and a script adapted from the novel *The Object of My Affection* by Stephen McCauley. Contributor of articles to periodicals, including *Esquire, New York Times,* and *New York Woman.* Contributing editor, *New York Woman.*

SIDELIGHTS: "Serious issues and serious people can be quite funny," Wendy Wasserstein once stated in the *New York Times,* and the dramatist made her living expressing that philosophy. In her best-known plays—*Uncommon Women and Others, Isn't It Romantic,* and *The Heidi Chronicles*—Wasserstein spotlights college-educated women of the postwar baby boom who came of age in the late 1960s as feminism was redefining U.S. society. Such women, she suggests, have been torn between a newfound spirit of independence and the traditional values of marriage and motherhood they were taught as children. While portraying the struggles of her characters with deep sympathy, Wasserstein imbues her plays with a comic tone. "On some level, I'm terribly earnest," she told Sylvie Drake of the *Los Angeles Times.* "I almost have to look at problems with a sense of humor." Wasserstein has held the attention of theater critics since the late 1970s, when *Uncommon Women* opened to favorable reviews in New York City; a few years later, according to *New York Times* contributor Michiko Kakutani, she had "won recognition as one of this country's most talented young playwrights." In 1989 Wasserstein received the Pulitzer Prize in drama for *The Heidi Chronicles,* cementing her reputation as one of America's top playwrights.

Born into a New York City family in 1950, Wasserstein attended schools, such as New England's Mount Holyoke College, that were women-only and marked by social conservatism. She rebelled against these schools' traditions of propriety, preferring to cultivate a lively sense of humor. "I always thought in terms of getting by on being funny," she said in the *New York Times.* Wasserstein did graduate work at New York's City University, studying creative writing under playwright Israel Horovitz and novelist Joseph Heller before earning a master's degree in 1973. That year saw Wasserstein's first professional production: the play *Any Woman Can't,* a bitter farce about a woman's efforts to dance her way to success in a male-dominated environment. The show was presented by a small, experimental theater group, Playwrights Horizons, that would later prosper and play a major role in Wasserstein's career.

When Wasserstein graduated from City University, she was unsure of her future. The emergent women's movement brought the prospect of a career in law or business, but Wasserstein was not enthusiastic about these professions. She was drawn to a career as a playwright, a tenuous life made ever more so by the growing popularity of television and film. She applied to two prestigious graduate programs—Columbia Business School and Yale Drama School—was accepted by both, and opted for Yale. The leader of Yale's drama program was Robert Brustein, renowned in the U.S. theater community as an advocate of professional discipline and artistic creativity. Under his leadership, according to *Horizon*'s Steve Lawson, Yale became "the foremost theatrical training ground in the country." Brustein "felt that theater was as important as law or medicine," Wasserstein later told the *New York Times,* adding that such a guiding attitude "gave you high standards to maintain." Her classmates at Yale included Christopher Durang and Albert Innaurato, both of whom would become award-winning playwrights, and actress Meryl Streep.

Wasserstein's work at Yale evolved from broad mockery to more subtle portrayals of character. Of her student plays, two are forthright satires: *Happy Birthday, Montpelier Pizz-zazz* shows the social maneuvers at a college party, and *When Dinah Shore Ruled the Earth,* written with Durang, mocks a beauty pageant. But in *Uncommon Women and Others*—which Wasserstein began as her Yale master's thesis—the characters are more complex; and the humor, more low-keyed, is threaded through with tension.

Uncommon Women is about a fictional group of Mount Holyoke students who trade quips about men and sex while wondering about their own futures with a mixture of hope and apprehension. As the play makes clear, when feminism reached college campuses in the late

1960s it expanded women's horizons but filled them with uncertainty. The character Rita dominates the play as an outspoken aspiring novelist. As a student she tells her friends that "when we're thirty we're going to be pretty amazing," but she eventually hopes for a "Leonard Woolf" who will, like Virginia Woolf's husband, support her while she perfects her writing. Holly, dubbed "imaginative" and "witty" by the *Nation*'s Harold Clurman, makes a pathetic effort to find a husband on the eve of graduation by phoning a young doctor she once met. He has since married and has forgotten all about her. Surrounding the central characters, each of whom struggles to define herself, are other young women whose self-assurance seems vaguely unsettling by contrast. Leilah, self-contained and inscrutable, makes a cold peace with the world, deciding to become an anthropologist and marry a man from the Middle East. Susie is a booster for outmoded college traditions; Carter, a stereotypical genius who seems guaranteed of success. The play's opening and closing scenes show the central characters at a reunion luncheon a few years after college. Most seem confused and unfulfilled. Rita now asserts that by the age of forty-five they will all be "amazing." Chekhov, Wasserstein later revealed, inspired Rita's funny-sad refrain.

Uncommon Women was first presented at Yale in 1975 as a one-act play. Then Wasserstein rewrote the play in a two-act version and prepared it for the professional stage, receiving encouragement along the way from both Playwrights Horizons and the Eugene O'Neill Playwrights Conference. The finished work received widespread attention from reviewers when it premiered in 1977 under the auspices of Phoenix Theater, a troupe that spotlighted new American plays. While *Time* reviewer T.E. Kalem found Wasserstein's characters "stereotypical," Richard Eder in the *New York Times* wrote that "if the characters . . . represent familiar alternatives and contradictions, Miss Wasserstein has made each of them most real." *New Yorker* contributor Edith Oliver dubbed the work "a collage of small scenes" rather than a "play." Nonetheless, she found the result a "wonderful, original comedy" in which "every moment is theatrical," adding that "for all [the characters'] funny talk and behavior, they are sympathetically drawn." In conclusion, Oliver declared Wasserstein "an uncommon young woman if ever there was one." *Uncommon Women* soon reached national television as part of public television's *Theatre in America* series.

Wasserstein began her next major work, *Isn't It Romantic,* as she approached the age of thirty in the late 1970s. Observing that many women her own age were suddenly planning to marry, she pondered the reasons for such a choice, including the possibility that women might marry simply because it was expected of them. "Biological time bombs were going off all over Manhattan," she told the *Washington Post.* "It was like, it's not wild and passionate, but it's *time.*" *Isn't It Romantic,* observed *Nation* reviewer Elliott Sirkin, "has the kind of heroine the whole world thinks of as a New Yorker: Janie [Blumberg], a bright, plump, emotionally agitated young Jewish woman, who insults herself with sophisticated quips" while resisting the entreaties of an earnest but boring young doctor. Janie's mother, outgoing and energetic, urges her daughter to get married. In contrast to the Blumbergs are Janie's best friend, Harriet—an emotionally restrained Anglo-Saxon, more attractive and successful than Janie—and Harriet's mother, cooler and more successful yet. The play consists of many short scenes, abundant with comic one-liners, that explore how and why women choose a husband, a career, or a way of life. As the play ends, Janie, shocked to realize that Harriet is about to marry a man she does not love, pointedly refuses to move in with her own boyfriend.

When the original version of *Isn't It Romantic* premiered at the Phoenix Theater in 1981, a number of reviewers found that the play's episodic structure and Wasserstein's flair for jokes distracted from the issues that inspired the work. Wasserstein is "better at parts than at wholes, more gag-than goal-oriented," wrote *New York* 's John Simon. He suggested that the first draft was encumbered by "Yale Drama School or Christopher Durang humor, which consists of scrumptious, scattershot bitchiness that . . . refus[es] to solidify into shapeliness." However, Simon concluded, Wasserstein "has a lovely forte: the comic-wistful line. . . . This could be a vein of gold, and needs only proper engineering to be efficiently mined."

As Wasserstein established her theater career, she became clearly identified with Playwrights Horizons, which also attracted Durang, Innaurato, and several other well-educated writers of the same generation. Under the growing influence of Andre Bishop, who joined the organization as an administrator in 1975, Playwrights became "the most critically acclaimed off-off-Broadway group since Joseph Papp's Public Theater began in 1967," according to John Lombardi in the *New York Times.* What the dramatists at Playwrights Horizons "really have in common," Bishop explained to Lombardi, "is that they are all extremely literate and extremely intelligent, two qualities that don't necessarily go together." He continued: "They come at the world from a humorous angle that is rooted in an angry desire for truth." Bishop wanted the organization and its writers to have lasting professional ties, and it developed such a relationship with Wasserstein. After producing the revised version of *Isn't It Romantic,* Playwrights Horizons commissioned Wasserstein's next full-length work, *Miami,* a musical comedy about a teenage boy on vacation with his family in the late 1950s. The show received a limited run at the group's theater in early 1986. More successful was Wasserstein's subsequent full-length play, *The Heidi Chronicles,* which received its New York debut at Playwrights in late 1988.

The Heidi Chronicles was inspired by a single image in Wasserstein's mind: a woman speaking to an assembly of other women, confessing her growing sense of unhappiness. The speaker evolved into Dr. Heidi Holland, an art history professor who finds that her successful, independent life has left her alienated from men and women alike. Most of the play consists of flashbacks that capture Heidi's increasing disillusionment. Starting as a high-school student, she experiences, in turn, the student activism of the late 1960s, the feminist consciousness-raising of the early 1970s, and the tough-minded careerism of the 1980s. Friends disappoint her: a feminist activist becomes an entertainment promoter, valuing the women's audience for its market potential; a boyfriend becomes a manipulative and selfish magazine editor; a gay male friend tells her that in the 1980s, when gays are dying of AIDS, her unhappiness is a mere luxury. Heidi remains subdued until the play's climactic scene, when she addresses fellow alumnae from a private school for girls. "We're all concerned, intelligent, good women," she tells her old classmates, as quoted in the *New York Times.* "It's just that I feel stranded. And I thought the whole point was that we wouldn't feel stranded. I thought the point was we were all in this together." At the end of the play Heidi adopts a baby and poses happily with the child in front of an exhibition of works by Georgia O'Keeffe, an acclaimed woman artist.

Reviewers debated how well the play reflects the reality of Heidi's—and Wasserstein's—generation. In *Village Voice,* Alisa Solomon suggested that the playwright lacks sympathy with the aspirations of feminism. In *New York* John Simon felt the characters are oversimplified, averring that "Heidi's problem as stated—that she is too intellectual, witty, and successful for a mere hausfrau—just won't wash." Mimi Kramer, however, wrote in the *New Yorker* that "Wasserstein's portrait of womanhood always remains complex." Kramer found "generosity in the writing," contending that no character in the play "is made to seem ludicrous or dismissible." Praising Wasserstein's skill as a dramatist, the critic declared that the playwright "never states anything that can be inferred. . . . She condemns these young men and women simply by capturing them in all their charm and complexity, without rhetoric or exaggeration." *The Heidi Chronicles* became Wasserstein's first show to move to a Broadway theater; soon afterwards, the play brought its author the Pulitzer Prize.

In 1990 Wasserstein published *Bachelor Girls,* a collection of humorous essays that had been originally published in *New York Woman* magazine. *Booklist* reviewer Ilene Cooper compared Wasserstein to Fran Lebowitz, whose humor also turns on the trials of being a single Jewish woman in New York City. According to Cooper, the great difference is that Wasserstein's "wit is gently filtered rather than raw and rough." She noted, however, that "that doesn't mean she pulls her punches." *Time* contributor Margaret Carlson was less generous in her assessment of *Bachelor Girls,* stating that "the territory Wasserstein covers has been strip-mined by those who preceded her. . . . A piece about the split between women who shave their legs and those who don't would have to come up with some dazzling insights to merit another look." Carlson believed that Wasserstein's best work is most evident in the last piece in the book, a one-act play. A *Publishers Weekly* reviewer was also lukewarm, terming the collection only "semi-humorous," but a *Los Angeles Times Book Review* writer deemed it a "very funny blend of self-deprecation, pride and bemusement."

In her next play Wasserstein again entertains audiences with humor underlaid with seriousness. *The Sisters Rosensweig* "looks at the lives of women who are weighing priorities and deciding which doors to open and deciding which gently to close," reported Linda Simon in the *Atlanta Journal-Constitution.* The play is set in London, where fifty-four-year-old Sara is celebrating her birthday with her two younger sisters. Twice divorced and having long since abandoned any hope of real romance in life, she is surprised when love suddenly seems possible after all. "With her focus on the hidden yearnings and emotional resistance of the women, . . . [Wasserstein's] obvious debt is to Noel Coward," Simon noted, adding that *The Sisters Rosensweig* "is very much a drawing room comedy." Mel Gussow, in the *New York Times,* found echoes of Chekhov in Wasserstein's work: "Overlooking the play is the symbolic figure of Anton Chekhov, smiling. Although the characters do not directly parallel those in *The Three Sisters,* the comparison is intentional. . . . Wasserstein does not overstate the connection but uses it like background music while diverting her attention to other cultural matters."

In earlier plays, Wasserstein frequently presented remarkable women who, despite their gifts, feel their op-tions closing down with the passing of the years. In *The Sisters Rosensweig* the playwright presents images of strong, intelligent, middle-aged women whose lives are still full of possibilities. Several reviewers have characterized it as Wasserstein's most hopeful play. Discussing the process of aging with Claire Carter for *Parade,* Wasserstein noted that she found turning forty to be a liberating experience. "Before turning forty, I got very depressed," she mused. "I kept making lists of things I had to do before forty. I drove myself crazy. Then after I turned forty, I thought, 'I don't have to do these things.' I was much happier after that."

Wasserstein's much-anticipated play *An American Daughter* debuted in 1997. A satire on the manners and mores of "official" Washington, DC, it is peopled by a host of recognizable political animals, from a crusty southern senate baron to a closeted gay conservative. At the center of the storm of comings and goings is Dr. Lyssa Dent Hughes, an upright feminist physician nominated to become the next U.S. surgeon general. Confirmation problems ensue when it is revealed that Hughes forgot to show up for jury duty some years before. Many reviewers found the play muddled, the comedy weighed down by political pretension. "Wasserstein has little to say, and that little is false," wrote Stefan Kanfer in the *New Leader,* deriding *An American Daughter* for its shallow characters and "sitcom soul." The play's "brisk satire gives way to whiny venting and windy summations that have marred earlier Wasserstein plays," wrote the *Seattle Times*'s Misha Berson, who still found some of Wasserstein's political quipping trenchant and breezy.

In the 1990s Wasserstein took a major step by becoming a single parent, echoing the actions of the narrator of *The Heidi Chronicles.* An account of her daughter's birth is one of several autobiographical subjects broached in the 2001 essay collection *Shiksa Goddess; or, How I Spent My Forties.* Her relationship with her perfectionist mother, and her struggle to come to terms with her sister's death are also covered in these essays, which were deemed "highly readable" by Misha Berson in the *Seattle Times.* Despite the serious nature of some of the topics in the book, Wasserstein writes in a "breezy, splashy style," noted Penelope Mesic in *Book Magazine.* "Mildly funny, good-natured and ephemeral, these essays reveal that Wasserstein's overwhelming strength and weakness is the same: She is totally in touch with contemporary society." Wasserstein gently pokes fun at prominent gentiles who discover their Jewish roots in the title piece, claiming to have found some Episcopalians in her past and exploring her newfound culture. While such pieces were deemed "silly" by Jack Helbig in *Booklist,* the critic went on to note that Wasserstein's reflections on fertility, family ties, and death are "riveting and sometimes searing," and her observations on the state of writing and theater are "sharp and pungent." A *Publishers Weekly* writer also found the author's writing on childbirth and death to be imbued "with notable humor and heartbreaking poignancy."

While Wasserstein has proven her ability as an essayist and a screenwriter, she remains best known for her plays. A writer for *Contemporary Dramatists* summed up her strengths as "her ability to create characters who laugh at themselves while questioning others. She serves as a role model for women who wish to be successful in the New York theater venue. All of her plays are quirky and interesting and offer strong roles for women."

BIOGRAPHICAL AND CRITICAL SOURCES:

BOOKS

Contemporary Dramatists, St. James Press (Detroit, MI), 1999.

Contemporary Literary Criticism, Volume 32, Thomson Gale (Detroit, MI), 1985.

Dictionary of Literary Biography, Volume 228: *Twentieth-Century American Dramatists, Second Series,* Thomson Gale (Detroit, MI), 2000.

Feminist Writers, St. James Press (Detroit, MI), 1996.

Newsmakers 1991, Thomson Gale (Detroit, MI), 1991.

PERIODICALS

Advocate, May 27, 1997, James Oseland, review of *An American Daughter,* p. 90.

American Book Review, November-December, 1989, p. 4.

America's Intelligence Wire, May 5, 2003, Rick Weiss, "Wendy Wasserstein's Moldy Chronicles."

Architectural Digest, February, 1998, "Wendy Wasserstein: A Second Act for the Playwright's Central Park West Apartment," p. 30.

Atlantic Journal-Constitution, May 23, 1993, p. N10.

Back Stage, April 18, 1997, David Sheward, review of *An American Daughter,* p. 60; March 26, 1999, Roger Armbrust, "Wasserstein: Arts Not Elitist, but Democratic," p. 3; December 15, 2000, Julius Novick, review of *Old Money,* p. 48; February 16, 2001, Simi Horwitz, "Direct from Chekhov to Wasserstein," p. 19.

Back Stage West, September 10, 1998, Judy Richter, review of *An American Daughter,* p. 17; September 24, 1998, J. Brenna Guthrie, review of *The Sisters Rosensweig,* p. 13; October 8, 1998, Terri Roberts, review of *The Sisters Rosensweig,* p. 16.

Booklist, March 15, 1990, p. 1413; June 1, 1998, Jack Helbig, review of *An American Daughter,* p. 1709; May 1, 2001, Jack Helbig, review of *Shiksa Goddess,* p. 1647.

Book Magazine, May, 2001, Penelope Mesic, review of *Shiksa Goddess; or, How I Spent My Forties,* p. 73.

Boston Globe, February 1, 1990, p. 69; March 3, 1991, p. B1; March 8, 1991, p. 25; March 22, 1991, p. 78; April 1, 1993, p. 61; January 27, 1994, p. 45; October 9, 1994, section 13, p. 7.

Chicago, August, 1998, Penelope Mesic, review of *An American Daughter,* p. 27.

Chicago Tribune, October 12, 1985; November 10, 1985; April 24, 1990, section 5, p. 3; October 21, 1990, section 6, p. 1; March 15, 1992, section 13, p. 22; November 30, 1992, section 5, p. 1; October 9, 1994, section 13, p. 7.

Christian Science Monitor, April 30, 1986; April 30, 1991, p. 12; November 5, 1992, p. 13; November 15, 1994, p. 14.

Entertainment Weekly, June 20, 1997, Mark Harris, review of *An American Daughter,* p. 28; May 1, 1998, review of *The Object of My Affection,* p. 42.

Harper's Bazaar, April, 1994, p. 120.

Horizon, February, 1978.

Los Angeles Magazine, September, 1994, p. 140.

Los Angeles Times, January 31, 1984; October 28, 1984; October 30, 1984; December 17, 1988; October 15, 1990, p. F1; September 20, 1991, p. F20; July 31, 1994, section CAL, p. 45; December 29, 1994, p. F1.

Los Angeles Times Book Review, August 25, 1991, p. 10; May 30, 1993, p. 6.

Nation, December 17, 1977; February 18, 1984; May 1, 1989, pp. 605-606; October 16, 1995, p. 443.

New Leader, December 7, 1994, p. 22; April 7, 1997, Stefan Kanfer, review of *An American Daughter,* p. 22.

New Statesman, June 26, 1998, Gerald Kaufman, review of *The Object of My Affection,* p. 51.

Newsweek, March 20, 1989, pp. 76-77.

New York, June 29, 1981; January 2, 1989, pp. 48-49; March 27, 1989, pp. 66, 68; June 13, 1994, p. 72; November 7, 1994, p. 102; April 28, 1997, John Simon, review of *An American Daughter,* p. 105; December 18, 2000, John Simon, review of *Old Money,* p. 178.

New Yorker, April 14, 1997, Nancy Franklin, "The Time of Her Life," p. 62; December 5, 1977; June 22, 1981; June 13, 1983; December 26, 1983; December 26, 1988, pp. 81-82; November 14, 1994, p. 130; March 6, 1995, p. 132; December 25, 2000, John Lahr, review of *Old Money,* p. 166.

New York Post, November 22, 1977; December 16, 1983; April 23, 1986; December 12, 1988.

New York Times, November 22, 1977; May 24, 1978; June 23, 1978; December 27, 1978; June 8, 1979; February 15, 1981; May 24, 1981; June 15, 1981; June 28, 1981; July 17, 1983; December 16, 1983; January 1, 1984; January 3, 1984; February 26, 1984; June 13, 1984; January 3, 1986; March 28, 1986; April 23, 1986; January 11, 1987; August 30, 1987; January 24, 1988; June 8, 1988; December 11, 1988; December 12, 1988, p. C13; February 19, 1989; March 12, 1989; October 9, 1989, pp. C13, 16; January 24, 1991, p. C15; October 18, 1992, section 2, pp. 1, 24; October 23, 1992, p. C3; November 1, 1992, section 2, p. 5; December 6, 1992, section 9, p. 12; February 13, 1994, section 2, p. 5; May 23, 1994, p. C14; October 16, 1994, section 2, p. 5; October 27, 1994, p. C15; May 2, 1995, p. 37.

Parade, September 5, 1993, p. 24.

People, March 26, 1984.

Publishers Weekly, March 2, 1990, p. 68; April 23, 2001, review of *Shiksa Goddess,* p. 60.

Rolling Stone, April 30, 1998, Peter Travers, review of *The Object of My Affection,* p. 73.

Seattle Times, May 1, 1997; June 20, 2001, Misha Berson, "Wasserstein: Motherhood at Sixty Brings New Outlook."

Time, December 5, 1977; December 26, 1983; March 27, 1989, pp. 90-92; April 16, 1990, p. 83; April 20, 1998, Richard Schickel, review of *The Object of My Affection,* p. 81.

Variety, April 14, 1997, Greg Evans, review of *An American Daughter,* p. 100.

Village Voice, December 20, 1988.

Vogue, May, 1998, John Powers, review of *The Object of My Affection,* p. 154.

Wall Street Journal, December 16, 1988.

Washington Post, May 3, 1985; May 6, 1985; March 22, 1991, p. F3; November 12, 1991, p. D4; March 13, 1994, pp. G1, G6-G7.

Washington Times, May 10, 2003, Jayne M. Blanchard, review of *An American Daughter,* p. D3.

Wine Spectator, April 30, 1998, Mervyn Rothstein, interview with Wasserstein, p. 361.

* * *

WATKINS, Gloria Jean
See HOOKS, bell

WATSON, James D. 1928-
(James Dewey Watson)

PERSONAL: Born April 6, 1928, in Chicago, IL; son of James D. (a businessman) and Jean (Mitchell) Watson; married Elizabeth V. Lewis (an architectural historian), March 28, 1968; children: Rufus Robert, Duncan James. *Education:* University of Chicago, B.S., 1947; Indiana University, Ph.D., 1950. *Hobbies and other interests:* Tennis.

ADDRESSES: Home—Bungtown Rd., Cold Spring Harbor, NY 11724. *Office*—Cold Spring Harbor Laboratory, P.O. Box 100, Cold Spring Harbor, NY 11724. *E-mail*—pubaff@cshl.org.

CAREER: Research scientist and educator; co-discoverer, with Francis H.C. Crick and Maurice H.F. Wilkins, a double-helical structure of DNA. University of Copenhagen, Copenhagen, Denmark, Merck Fellow of National Research Council, 1950-51; Cambridge University, Cavendish Laboratory, Cambridge, England, research fellow, 1951-52, engaged in bio-chemical research with Crick, 1955-56; California Institute of Technology, Pasadena, senior research fellow in biology, 1953-55; Harvard University, Cambridge, MA, assistant professor, 1956-58, associate professor, 1958-61, professor of molecular biology, 1961-76; Cold Spring Harbor Laboratory, Cold Spring Harbor, NY, member of board of trustees, 1965—, director, 1968-94, president, 1994—. National Center for Human Genome Research, National Institutes of Science, director, 1989-92. DNA Sciences, member, board of directors, 2000—. Consultant, President Kennedy's scientific advisory committee.

MEMBER: American Academy of Arts and Sciences, National Academy of Sciences, Royal Danish Academy, American Society of Biological Chemists, American Association for Cancer Research, American Philosophical Society, Royal Society (London, England), Athenaeum Club (London), Piping Rock Club (New York), Academy of Sciences (Russia), Oxford University, National Academy of Sciences (Ukraine), University College Galway, Institute of Biology (London, England), Tata Institute of Fundamental Research (Bombay, India).

AWARDS, HONORS: (Corecipient, with Francis H.C. Crick) John Collins Warren Prize, Massachusetts General Hospital, 1959; Eli Lilly Award, 1960; (with Crick and Maurice H.F. Wilkins) Albert Lasker Award, American Public Health Association, 1960; (with Crick) Research Corporation Prize, 1962; (with Crick and Wilkins) Nobel Prize in medicine and physiology, 1962; honorary fellow, Clare College, Cambridge, 1967; John J. Carty Gold Medal, National Academy of Sciences, 1971; President Medal of Freedom, 1977; Guggenheim fellowship, 1983; Kaul Foundation Award for Excellence, 1992; Copley Medal of the Royal Society, 1993; Charles A. Dana Distinguished Achievement Award in Health, 1994; Lomonosov Medal, Russian Academy of Sciences, 1995; National Medal of Science awarded by President Clinton, 1997. D. Sc., University of Chicago, 1961, Indiana University, 1963, Long Island University, 1970, Adelphi University, 1972, Brandeis University, 1973, Albert Einstein College of Medicine, 1974, Hofstra University, 1976, Harvard University, 1978, Rockefeller Foundation, 1980, Clarkson College of Technology, 1981, State University of New York, 1983, Rutgers University, 1988, and Bard College, 1991; LL. D., University of Notre Dame, 1965; honorary M.D., Buenos Aires University, 1986.

WRITINGS:

The Molecular Biology of the Gene (textbook), W.A. Benjamin (New York, NY), 1965, 5th revised edition, Benjamin-Cummings (Menlo Park, CA), 2003.

The Double Helix: A Personal Account of the Discovery of the Structure of DNA, Atheneum (New York, NY), 1968, critical edition edited by Gunther S. Stent, Norton (New York, NY), 1980.

(Editor, with H.H. Hiatt and J.A. Winsten) *Origins of Human Cancer,* Cold Spring Harbor Laboratory Press (Plainview, NY), 1977.

(With John Tooze) *The DNA Story: A Documentary History of Gene Cloning,* W.H. Freeman (San Francisco, CA), 1981.

(With John Tooze and David T. Kurtz) *Recombinant DNA: A Short Course,* W.H. Freeman (San Francisco, CA), 1983, 2nd edition, 1992.

(Editor, with Kiyoshi Mizobuchi and Itaru Watanabe) *Nucleic Acid Research: Future Development,* Academic Press (New York, NY), 1983.

Recognition and Regulation in Cell-Mediated Immunity, edited by J. Marbrook, Dekker (New York, NY), 1985.

Landmarks of Twentieth-Century Genetics: A Series of Essays (bound with *Houses for Science: A Pictorial History of Cold Spring Harbor Laboratory,* by wife, Elizabeth L. Watson), Cold Spring Harbor Laboratory Press (Cold Spring Harbor, NY), 1991.

(Editor, with John Cairns and Stent) *Phage and the Origins of Molecular Biology,* Cold Spring Harbor Laboratory Press (Cold Spring Harbor, NY), 1992.

A Passion for DNA: Genes, Genomes, and Society, with an introduction, afterword, and annotations by Walter B. Gratzer, Cold Spring Harbor Laboratory Press (Cold Spring Harbor, NY), 2000, revised edition with three new essays by the author, 2001.

Genes, Girls, and Gamow: After the Double Helix (memoir), Oxford University Press (New York, NY), 2001.

(With Andrew Berry) *DNA: The Secret of Life,* Knopf (New York, NY), 2003.

Also author, with others, of *The Molecular Biology of the Cell,* 1983, 2nd edition, 1989. Author of forewords, *Arnold O. Beckman: 100 Years of Excellence* by Arnold Thackray, Chemical Heritage Foundation, 2000; and *The Road to Stockholm: Nobel Prizes, Science, and Scientists* by Istvan Hargittai, Oxford University Press, 2002. Also author of scientific papers and contributor to abstracts of professional meetings and symposia. Watson promoted the Genetic Information Nondiscrimination Act of 2003, in *Science,* October 31, 2003.

Some of Watson's work has been translated into German and Spanish.

ADAPTATIONS: An abridged version of *DNA: The Secret of Life* was recorded for Random House Audio, 2003.

WORK IN PROGRESS: Collaborated on a five-part series on DNA, "The Secret of Life," for broadcast on the Public Broadcasting Service (PBS).

SIDELIGHTS: By the age of twenty-five, James D. Watson had already earned both his Ph.D. and a place in the annals of science. At Cambridge University, he and his somewhat older British colleagues, physicist/biologist Francis H.C. Crick and biochemist Maurice H.F. Wilkins, devised the now-famous double-helical, or "spiral staircase," model of the molecular structure of DNA (deoxyribonucleic acid)—the substance that transmits genetic data from one generation to the next—and postulated its method of duplicating and conveying genetic information. For their groundbreaking work, which was first published by Watson and Crick in the British scientific journal *Nature* on May 30, 1953, and which has been called the most important biochemical breakthrough of the twentieth century, the three men shared the 1962 Nobel Prize in medicine and physiology.

In terms of competitive motivation, the discovery of the double-helical construction of DNA involved the research of scientists around the world, as Watson relates in *The Double Helix: A Personal Account of the Discovery of the Structure of DNA.* Watson chronicles the activities involved in the discovery, including such nonscientific elements as personality interaction, recreation, and ambition. In addition to describing the actual scientific work performed toward the discovery of DNA, Watson explores much of the "behind the scenes" events and occurrences that transpired during the discovery process, some of it unflattering to other scientists. Due to its personal content and subsequent negative reaction from many members of the scientific community, *The Double Helix* encountered difficulties in finding a publisher. When Harvard University Press was initially approached, Watson's colleagues Crick and Wilkins refused to sign a release for the book's publication. Crick even threatened litigation, and after numerous legal maneuverings and consultations with other professionals, Harvard president Nathan Pusey ordered the press to drop the book. Undaunted, Watson submitted his book to Atheneum, which published a small printing, as did *Atlantic Monthly.* The book eventually became a best-seller despite the controversy.

P.B. Medawar predicted in 1968 in the *New York Review of Books* that *The Double Helix* "will be an enormous success, and deserves to be so—a classic in the sense that it will go on being read. . . . Many of the things Watson says about the people in his story will offend them, but his own artless candor excuses him, for he betrays in himself faults graver than those he professes to discern in others." A reviewer for the *Times Literary Supplement* observed that the book "does indeed show us, if it really needs showing, that scientists are human; but it also shows us that James D. Watson is more human than most."

Robert K. Merton noted in the *New York Times Book Review* that the book "provides for the scientist and the general reader alike a fascinating case-history in the psychology and sociology of science as it describes the events that led up to one of the great biological discoveries of our time. I know of nothing quite like it in all the literature about scientists at work." *New York Times* critic Elliot Fremont-Smith thought *The Double Helix* "is a thrilling book from beginning to end—delightful, often funny, vividly observant, full of suspense and mounting tension, and so directly candid about the brilliant and abrasive personalities and institutions involved and the folkways, noble and eccentric, of scientists, that it has already stirred up a hornet's nest of controversy and miffed feelings." A *Times Literary Supplement* reviewer maintained that "the book is vividly written; it has flashes of wit and of insight; and it succeeds remarkably well in creating the suspense that a good detective story requires." *Nation* contributor J. Bronowski commented that *The Double Helix* contains "a quality of innocence and absurdity that children have when they tell a fairy story. The style is shy and sly, bumbling and irreverent, artless and good-humored and mischievous." Watson authored a second autobiography in 2001, *Genes, Girls, and Gamow: After the Double Helix,* which tells of his life, both personal and scientific, after the discovery of DNA.

The mid-1970s saw the emergence of early concerns about the safety and ethics of gene cloning, and Watson's position as a codiscoverer of DNA situated him as an expert in the possible ramifications of his research. He stated publicly that genetic engineering carried no risks, in the face of public fears that recombinant DNA experiments could accidentally produce some mutated, rogue organism, which might then be inadvertently released from a laboratory with potentially damaging results to humanity. Scientists placed a moratorium on biogenetic research, with eventual government safety regulations implemented. The persuasive arguments of scientists such as Watson combined with experiments in gene cloning research have resulted in the relaxation of federal guidelines and gradual acceptance of the safety of bioengineering. *The DNA Story: A Documentary History of Gene Cloning,* written by Watson and John Tooze, "is a collection of speeches, papers, letters and newspaper clippings about the genetic engineering debate and its various political and scientific manifestations," Lee Dembart reported in the *Los Angeles Times Book Review.* Dembart suggested that "if Watson and Tooze had presented private letters and other heretofore unknown material, their book would be more welcome." *Washington Post Book World* reviewer Rae Goodell noted, however, that "the very premise that recombinant DNA technology is safe, and that concerns have all but disappeared, is far from universally accepted among biologists, policy-makers, and observers. . . . Furthermore, Watson and Tooze largely ignore the broader, long-range ethical and political problems posed by DNA technology as it begins to have a major impact on the economy, agriculture, energy supplies and the treatment of human diseases and shortcomings."

The science surrounding genetics has continued to evolve and Watson has continued to be one of the most prominent people in the field, serving for a brief time as the director of the Human Genome Project of the National Institutes of Health and enjoying a long tenure as head of the Cold Spring Harbor Laboratory, which provides education in molecular biology. Genetic science has also been controversial, as witnessed by debates over genetic manipulation and cloning at the beginning of the twenty-first century.

Watson deals with controversies from the 1970s and succeeding decades, as well as scientific advances and his career experiences, in *A Passion for DNA: Genes, Genomes, and Society,* a collection of thirty years' worth of essays. Of the fears about recombinant DNA, he writes, "in retrospect, recombinant DNA may rank as the safest revolutionary technology ever developed," having failed to cause the disease or environmental damage predicted by its detractors. He also discusses newer fears, especially those that genetic manipulation could be employed to create a sort of master race or that testing for genetic predisposition for certain disorders could be used to invade people's privacy or discriminate against them. He issues a call "to keep government out of genetic decisions, and leave matters to the individuals involved," as Mark Ridley related in the *Times Literary Supplement,* but endorses a role for government in preventing forced genetic testing. Furthermore, Watson details his general beliefs about the politics of genetics. "He disagrees with right-wing religious critics, who dislike genetics for interfering with God's work and encouraging abortions," Ridley reported. "He also disagrees with the fork-tongued ideologues of the Left, who argue that genes are relatively unimportant in human affairs." As David W. Hodo remarked in the *Journal of the American Medical Association:* "Watson comes across as generally liberal but not left wing. . . . [His] historical writings on 'eugenic horrors,' not only in Nazi Germany but in this country, address the reality of science (or pseudoscience) run amok." James F. Crow, a contributor to the *Quarterly Review of Biology,* stated that "there is much good biology and history in this book," which is written "in Watson's frank, uninhibited style." Ridley found the essays "highly readable" and "non-technical in style"; he noted that "Watson knows how to tell a story." Hodo concluded: "*A Passion for DNA* is one of the finest books on science that I have ever read . . . a scientific primer, history lesson, review of microbiology, study of mentoring, and most fascinating memoir, absorbable in multiple brief essays, fulfilling Dr. Watson's desire to write like a novelist."

After fifty years, the discovery of DNA still fascinates, though its full significance might not yet be understood, suggests Watson in *DNA: The Secret of Life,* which he coauthored with Andrew Berry. The book begins with the race to discover DNA's structure, and following chapters recount the revolutionary changes in biology that ensued from the decoding of the genetic alphabet and grammar. The chapter "Out of Africa" outlines the impact of DNA analysis on what we know about human evolution and migrations, and "Genetic Fingerprinting" tells the story of how DNA analysis has entered the legal system. Though Watson believes genetic knowledge and gene manipulation have hazards, they are small ones, and hold the key to providing solutions to most social problems. To that end, he urges readers to shed their fear of genetic technology and submit their DNA samples to the government.

In his review of *DNA: The Secret of Life* in *American Scientist,* Jon Beckwith found that the work is "a rich source both for budding scientists and for the general public interested in science." *Washington Post Book World* contributor David Brown wrote that thanks to genetic research we've embarked on a steep road to self-discovery, and "for people who want to get the most out of the trip, Watson's book is a good place to start." University of Chicago professor of ecology Jerry Coyne remarked in the *New York Times* that in spite of his excessive DNA chauvinism, which would have us provide our DNA to public databanks, "we are lucky that a major architect of a revolution in biology should also be blessed with, or perhaps born with, the ability to bring that revolution to life in such an arresting way."

BIOGRAPHICAL AND CRITICAL SOURCES:

BOOKS

Bankston, John, *Francis Crick and James Watson: Pioneers in DNA Research* (juvenile biography), Mitchell Lane (Bear, DE), 2002.

Devine, Elizabeth, and others, editors, *Thinkers of the Twentieth Century: A Biographical, Bibliographical, and Critical Dictionary,* Thomson Gale (Detroit, MI), 1983.

McElheny, Victor, *Watson and DNA: Making a Scientific Revolution,* Perseus (Cambridge, MA), 2003.

PERIODICALS

American Scientist, July-August, 2003, review of *DNA: The Secret of Life,* and *Watson and DNA: Making a Scientific Revolution,* by Victor McElheny, p. 354; May-June, 2004, review of *Inspiring Science: Jim Watson and the Age of DNA,* edited by John R. Inglis, p. 286.

Book World, February 18, 1968.

Business Week, July 19, 2004, Catherine Arnst, "The Great Innovators," p. 20.

Chicago Tribune, January 24, 1981; January 30, 2004, William Mullen, "His Chicago DNA: Genetic Pioneer James Watson Recalls a South Side Education," p. 81.

Choice, October, 2003, review of *DNA: The Secret of Life,* p. 354.

Christian Century, August 21, 1968, p. 1065.

Hudson Review, summer, 1968, pp. 396-398.

Journal of the American Medical Association, January 17, 2001, David W. Hodo, review of *A Passion for DNA: Genes, Genomes, and Society,* p. 342.

Library Journal, March 1, 2004, review of *DNA: The Secret of Life,* p. 39.

Life, March 1, 1968, p. 8.

Los Angeles Times Book Review, February 7, 1982, p. 13.

Nation, March 18, 1968, pp. 381-382.

Nature, October 25, 2001, Horace Freeland Judson, review of *Girls, Genes, and Gamow: After the Double Helix,* p. 775.

New England Journal of Medicine, August 3, 2000, Donald A. Chambers, review of *A Passion for DNA,* p. 370.

New Yorker, April 13, 1968, pp. 172-182.

New York Review of Books, March 28, 1968, pp. 3-5.

New York Times, February 19, 1968; April 10, 1983.

New York Times Book Review, February 25, 1968, section 7, pp. 1, 41-42, 45; December 1, 1968; February 24, 2002, Barbara Ehrenreich, "Double Helix, Single Guy," p. 6; June 15, 2003, review of *DNA: The Secret of Life,* p. 7, 11.

New York Times Magazine, August 18, 1968, pp. 26-27, 29, 34, 41, 44; February 3, 2002, Amy Barrett, "Weird Science" (interview), p. 9.

Omni, May, 1984.

Quarterly Review of Biology, June, 2001, James F. Crow, review of *A Passion for DNA,* p. 232; March, 2004, Elof Axel Carlson, review of *DNA: The Secret of Life,* p. 51.

Saturday Review, March 16, 1968, pp. 36, 86.

Science, October 7, 1983; April 18, 2003, review of *DNA: The Secret of Life,* p. 432.

Technology and Culture, April, 2004, Neil M. Cowan, review of *Watson and DNA,* by Victor K. McElheny, p. 457.

Time, February 23, 1968, p. 98; October 3, 1983, p. 67.

Times Literary Supplement, May 23, 1968; August 3, 2001, Mark Ridley, "Gene Genie," p. 6; October 19, 2001, Sydney Brenner, review of *Girls, Genes, and Gamow,* p. 6.

Virginia Quarterly Review, spring, 2004, Edward J. Larson, "Wonderful Life," p. 72.

Washington Post Book World, January 24, 1982, pp. 1-2; May 18, 2003, David Brown, "Code Breakers," review of *DNA: The Secret of Life,* p. T10.

* * *

WATSON, James Dewey

See WATSON, James D.

WATSON, John H.
See FARMER, Philip José

* * *

WATSON, Larry 1947-

PERSONAL: Born 1947, in Rugby, ND; son of a sheriff; married; wife's name Susan; children: two daughters. *Education:* University of North Dakota, B.A., M.A.; University of Utah, Ph.D.

ADDRESSES: Office—c/o Author Mail, Pocket Books, Simon & Schuster, 1230 Avenue of the Americas, New York, NY 10020. *E-mail*—readermail@larry-watson.com.

CAREER: Fiction writer and poet. University of Wisconsin, Stevens Point, professor of English and creative writing, c. 1979-2003. Marquette University, Milwaukee, WI, visiting professor, 2003—.

AWARDS, HONORS: National Education Association creative writing fellowship, 1987; Milkweed National Fiction Prize, 1993, for *Montana 1948.*

WRITINGS:

In a Dark Time (novel), Scribner (New York, NY), 1980.
Montana 1948 (novel), Milkweed Editions (Minneapolis, MN), 1993.
Justice (novel), Milkweed Editions (Minneapolis, MN), 1995.
White Crosses (novel), Pocket Books (New York, NY), 1997.
Laura (novel), Pocket Books (New York, NY), 2000.
Orchard, Random House (New York, NY), 2003.

Also author of poetry collection *Leaving Dakota,* 1983.

ADAPTATIONS: Several of Watson's novels have been adapted as audiobooks.

SIDELIGHTS: The novels and poems of Larry Watson reflect his familiarity with the landscape and people of the western plains. Watson himself was born and raised in North Dakota and is the son and grandson of small-town sheriffs. Perhaps not surprisingly, his fiction is marked by "tight human ties, tough terrain, and pre-'60s ethos," as noted by Norman Oder in *Publishers Weekly.* The author himself admitted to *Publishers Weekly,* "I sometimes feel I'm working the dark side of Lake Wobegon." That may be the case, but Watson has emerged to become a mainstream writer who "captures smalltown life with searing acuity and vigorous heart," in the words of another *Publishers Weekly* reviewer.

Watson's 1993 novel, *Montana 1948,* is set in Bentrock, Montana, a fictional town only a dozen miles from both the Canadian and North Dakotan borders. This challenging countryside is the home of David Hayden, son of the local sheriff, who over the course of one summer observes conflict and violence within his community and his own family. *Nation* reviewer Chris Faatz applauded what he termed an "utterly mesmerizing story." Ellen Akin, writing for the *New York Times Book Review,* noted Watson's approach to his fiction: "A story, for this author, isn't necessarily what *happens;* it's that, of course, but also everything that came before and made what happens inevitable, or at least likely, as well as anything that might inform a reader about all the other stories this one touches." *Montana 1948* won the Milkweed National Fiction Prize and was one of Milkweed Edition's biggest-selling titles, going through more than six printings.

In 1995, Watson's *Justice* was published. This novel details the history of the Haydens and Bentrock leading to the events of *Montana 1948.* In the book, the Hayden sons, Frank and Wesley, take a disastrous camping trip that ultimately sets the stage for an exploration of the family history, dating from 1899. Kathleen Hughes of *Booklist* praised the novel as "an engrossing story of love, familial relationships, and secrets."

Watson's 1997 novel *White Crosses* concerns the efforts of Jack Nevelsen, sheriff of Bentrock, to prevent a scandal from erupting in the small town in the wake of two deaths. While Phil Hanrahan, in the Milwaukee *Journal Sentinel,* found the book's main character uninteresting, he noted, "still, there's a neat symmetry at the [novel's] end. . . . And the book's small-town tragic arc feels true and right."

Laura, published in 2000, presents a departure for Watson. Set initially in Vermont and later in Minnesota, the novel explores a man's thirty-year obsession with a self-destructive poet named Laura Coe Pettit. Paul Finley, the protagonist, first meets Laura when she accidentally blunders into his room while attempting to seduce his father. From that chance meeting at age eleven, Paul becomes fascinated with Laura, although he rarely sees her. Inevitably, this obsession takes a toll on Paul's relationships with other women in his life. A *Publishers Weekly* reviewer cited *Laura* for its "sharp dialogue and gorgeous, piquant language." Also praising the novel, *Washington Post Book World* contributor Howard Frank Mosher concluded: "Ultimately, the human heart has always been Larry Watson's principal territory. In its hard-won affirmation of the resilience of family love in the face of the darker forces of human nature, *Laura* is a beautifully realized work of fiction by a courageous and clear-eyed writer."

Praised by *Entertainment Weekly* reviewer Emily Mead as "technically flawless and quietly unnerving," *Orchard* draws readers back to 1950s Wisconsin, as Sonja House, a Norwegian-born housewife mourning the death of her young son secretly begins to pose for neighborhood painter Ned Weaver. Despite being married, the egotistical Weaver has gained a well-deserved reputation as a ladies' man, yet for Sonja his personable warmth fills a void left by her farmer husband's inability to relate to her grief. For Weaver's part, Sonja's aloofness is by turns challenging and fascinating, but the growing interrelationship between painter and subject ultimately has tragic consequences for all four adults involved. Watson's "sentences and chapters unfurl with a sense of inevitability," noted a *Publishers Weekly* contributor, adding that the novel's "narrative possesses an uncommon integrity." Praising *Orchard* as an "arresting" work that raises "telling questions about the value of permanence in art," Maureen Neville added in *Library Journal* that the author imbues his protagonists with "distinctive, almost archetypal traits." Praising Watson for his continuing shift to more contemporary settings, *Booklist* reviewer Bill Ott hailed *Orchard* as "another fine effort from a master of plainspoken prose."

BIOGRAPHICAL AND CRITICAL SOURCES:

PERIODICALS

Booklist, September 1, 1993, p. 38; January 15, 1994, p. 866; March 15, 1994, p. 1350; January 1, 1995, p. 801; January 1, 1996, p. 739; July, 2003, Bill Ott, review of *Orchard,* p. 1868.

Christian Science Monitor, December 3, 1993, p. 12.

Entertainment Weekly, August 15, 2003, Emily Mead, review of *Orchard,* p. 82.

Journal Sentinel (Milwaukee, WI), May 8, 1997.

Kirkus Reviews, November 15, 1994, p. 1494; May 15, 2003, review of *Orchard,* p. 713.

Kliatt, July, 1993, p. 816; May, 1995, p. 11; July, 1996, p. 24.

Library Journal, September 15, 1993, pp. 107-108; January, 1994, p. 61; June 15, 1994, p. 120; December, 1994, p. 135; March 1, 2003, Maureen Neville, review of *Orchard,* p. 121.

Los Angeles Times Book Review, October 10, 1993, p. 2; April 30, 1995, p. 13.

Nation, December 27, 1993, pp. 808-809.

New York Times Book Review, December 12, 1993, p. 22; January 29, 1995, pp. 14-15; August 17, 1997, Ruth Coughlin, review of *White Crosses,* p. 16; September 3, 2000, Bruce Allen, review of *Laura,* p. 14.

Publishers Weekly, July 12, 1993, pp. 69-70; November 28, 1994, pp. 42-43; January 23, 1995, Norman Oder, "Larry Watson: 'I'm Working the Dark Side of Lake Wobegone,'" pp. 48-49; March 13, 1995, p. 67; July 3, 1995, p. 22; March 18, 1996, p. 64; April 3, 2000, review of *Laura,* p. 59; May 5, 2003, review of *Orchard,* p. 193.

School Library Journal, September, 1995, p. 235; December, 1995, p. 25.

Times Literary Supplement, August 18, 1995, p. 20.

Washington Post Book World, November 7, 1993, p. 11; September 3, 2000, Howard Frank Mosher, "Poetic License," p. 6.

Western American Literature, winter, 1995, pp. 387.

Writer, July, 2004, Ronald Kovach, "Hearts in Conflict: Larry Watson Weaves Fine Novels from Emotional Tension" (interview), p. 20.

* * *

WATSON, Richard F.
See SILVERBERG, Robert

* * *

WAYS, C.R.
See BLOUNT, Roy, Jr.

* * *

WELDON, Fay 1931-

PERSONAL: Born September 22, 1931, in Alvechurch, Worcestershire, England; daughter of Frank Thornton (a physician) and Margaret (a writer; maiden name, Jepson) Birkinshaw; married briefly and divorced in her early twenties; married Ronald Weldon (an antique dealer), 1962 (divorced, 1994); married Nick Fox (a poet); children: (first marriage) Nicholas; (second marriage) Daniel, Thomas, Samuel. *Education:* University of St. Andrews, M.A., 1954.

ADDRESSES: Agent—c/o Casarotto Co., Ltd., National House, 62/66 Wardour St., London W1V 3HP, England.

CAREER: Novelist, playwright, television and radio scriptwriter. Worked as a propaganda writer for the British Foreign Office and as a market researcher for the *Daily Mirror,* London, England. Advertising copywriter for various firms in London; creator of the slogan "Go to work on an egg." Former member of the Art Council of Great Britain's literary panel and of the GLA's film and video panel; chair of the judges' panel for the Booker McConnell Prize, 1983.

AWARDS, HONORS: Society of Film and Television Arts award for best series, 1971, for "On Trial" episode of *Upstairs, Downstairs* television series; Writer's Guild award for best radio play, 1973, for *Spider;* Giles Cooper Award for best radio play, 1978, for *Polaris;* Booker McConnell Prize nomination, National Book League, 1979, for *Praxis;* Society of Authors' traveling scholarship, 1981; D.Litt., University of St. Andrew's, 1989.

WRITINGS:

NOVELS

The Fat Woman's Joke (also see below), MacGibbon & Kee (London, England), 1967, published as . . . *And the Wife Ran Away,* McKay (New York, NY), 1968.
Down among the Women, Heinemann (London, England), 1971, St. Martin's Press (New York, NY), 1972.
Female Friends, St. Martin's Press (New York, NY), 1974.
Remember Me, Random House (New York, NY), 1976.
Words of Advice, Random House (New York, NY), 1977, published as *Little Sisters,* Hodder & Stoughton (London, England), 1978.
Praxis, Summit Books (New York, NY), 1978.
Puffball, Hodder & Stoughton (London, England), 1979, Summit Books (New York, NY), 1980.
The President's Child, Hodder & Stoughton (London, England), 1982, Doubleday (New York, NY), 1983.
The Life and Loves of a She-Devil, Hodder & Stoughton (London, England), 1983, Pantheon (New York, NY), 1984.
The Shrapnel Academy, Viking (New York, NY), 1986.
The Hearts and Lives of Men, Viking (New York, NY), 1987.
The Rules of Life, HarperCollins (New York, NY), 1987.
Leader of the Band, Viking (New York, NY), 1988.
The Heart of the Country, Viking (New York, NY), 1988.
The Cloning of Joanna May, Viking (New York, NY), 1990.
Darcy's Utopia, Viking (New York, NY), 1991.
Life Force, Viking (New York, NY), 1992.
Trouble, Viking (New York, NY), published as *Affliction,* HarperCollins (London, England), 1993.
Splitting, Atlantic Monthly Press (New York, NY), 1995.
Worst Fears, Atlantic Monthly Press (New York, NY), 1996.
Big Girls Don't Cry, Atlantic Monthly Press (New York, NY), 1997.
Growing Rich, Penguin (New York, NY), 1998.
Rhode Island Blues, Atlantic Monthly Press (New York, NY), 2000.
The Bulgari Connection, Grove/Atlantic (New York, NY), 2001.
Mantrapped, Grove/Atlantic (New York, NY), 2005.

PLAYS

Permanence (produced in the West End at Comedy Theatre, 1969), published in *Mixed Blessings: An Entertainment on Marriage,* Methuen (New York, NY), 1970.
Time Hurries On, published in *Scene Scripts,* edited by Michael Marland, Longman (London, England), 1972.
Words of Advice (one-act; produced in Richmond, England, at Orange Tree Theatre, 1974), Samuel French (New York, NY), 1974.
Friends, produced in Richmond at Orange Tree Theatre, 1975.
Moving House, produced in Farnham, England, at Redgrave Theatre, 1976.
Mr. Director, produced at Orange Tree Theatre, 1978.
Action Replay (produced in Birmingham, England, at Birmingham Repertory Studio Theatre, 1979; produced as *Love among the Women* in Vancouver, British Columbia, at City Stage, 1982), Samuel French, 1980.

I Love My Love, produced in Exeter, England, at Northcott Theatre, 1981.
Woodworm, first produced as *After the Prize,* off-Broadway at Phoenix Theatre, 1981; produced in Melbourne, Australia, at Playbox Theatre, 1983.

Also author of *Watching Me, Watching You,* a stage adaptation of four of her short stories; *Jane Eyre,* a stage adaptation of the novel by Charlotte Brontë, 1986; and *The Hole in the Top of the World,* 1987.

TELEVISION PLAYS

The Fat Woman's Tale, Granada Television, 1966.
Wife in a Blond Wig, British Broadcasting Corp. (BBC-TV), 1966.
Office Party, Thames Television, 1970.
"On Trial" (episode in *Upstairs, Downstairs* series), London Weekend Television, 1971.
Hands, BBC-TV, 1972.
Poor Baby, ATV Network, 1975.
The Terrible Tale of Timothy Bagshott, BBC-TV, 1975.
Aunt Tatty (dramatization based on an Elizabeth Bowen short story), BBC-TV, 1975.
"Married Love" (part of Marie Stopes's *Six Women* series), BBC-TV, 1977.
Pride and Prejudice (five-part dramatization based on the novel by Jane Austen), BBC-TV, 1980.
"Watching Me, Watching You" (episode in *Leap in the Dark* series), BBC-TV, 1980.
Life for Christine, Granada Television, 1980.
Little Miss Perkins, London Weekend Television, 1982.
Loving Women, Granada Television, 1983.
The Wife's Revenge, BBC-TV, 1983.

Also author of *Big Women,* a four-part series, for Channel 4 television, and over twenty-five other teleplays for BBC-TV and independent television networks.

RADIO PLAYS

Housebreaker, BBC Radio 3, 1973.
Mr. Fox and Mr. First, BBC Radio 3, 1974.
The Doctor's Wife, BBC Radio 4, 1975.
"Weekend" (episode in *Just before Midnight* series), BBC Radio 4, 1979.
All the Bells of Paradise, BBC Radio 4, 1979.
Polaris, American Broadcasting Co. (ABC Radio), 1980, published in *Best Radio Plays of 1978: The Giles Cooper Award Winners,* Eyre Methuen, 1979.
The Hearts and Lives of Men, BBC Radio 4, 1996.

Also author of *Spider,* 1972, and *If Only I Could Find the Words,* BBC.

OTHER

(Editor, with Elaine Feinstein) *New Stories 4: An Arts Council Anthology,* Hutchinson, 1979.
Watching Me, Watching You (short stories; also includes the novel *The Fat Woman's Joke*), Summit Books (New York, NY), 1981.
Letters to Alice on First Reading Jane Austen (nonfiction), Michael Joseph, 1984, Carroll & Graf (New York, NY), 2000.
Polaris and Other Stories, Hodder & Stoughton (London, England), 1985.
Moon over Minneapolis; or, Why She Couldn't Stay (short stories), Viking (New York, NY), 1992.
So Very English, Serpent's Tail, 1992.
Wicked Women: A Collection of Short Stories, Flamingo (London, England), 1995, Atlantic Monthly Press (Boston, MA), 1997.
Godless in Eden: A Book of Essays, Flamingo, 1999.
Auto da Fay (memoir), Grove (New York, NY), 2003.
Mantrapped (nonfiction), Grove Press (New York, NY), 2005.

Also author of children's books, including *Wolf the Mechanical Dog,* 1988, *Party Puddle,* 1989, and *Nobody Likes Me,* 1997.

ADAPTATIONS: The Life and Loves of a She-Devil was adapted into the film *She-Devil* in 1989, written by Barry Strugatz and Mark R. Burns, directed by Susan Seidelman, starring Roseanne Barr and Meryl Streep.

SIDELIGHTS: After her parents divorced when she was only five, Fay Weldon grew up in New Zealand with her mother, sister, and grandmother. Returning to England to attend college, she studied psychology and economics at St. Andrews in Scotland. As a single mother in her twenties, Weldon supported herself and her son with a variety of odd jobs until she settled into a successful career as a copywriter. After marrying in the early sixties, Weldon had three more sons, underwent psychoanalysis as a result of depression, and subsequently abandoned her work in advertising for freelance creative writing. Her first novel, *The Fat Woman's Joke,* appeared in 1967 when she was thirty-six years old. Since that time she has published numerous novels, short stories, and plays for the theater, television, and radio. Throughout this work, Weldon's "major subject is the experience of women," wrote Agate Nesaule Krouse in *Critique.* "Sexual initiation, marriage, infidelity, divorce, contraception, abortion, motherhood, housework, and thwarted careers . . . all receive attention." Products of a keen mind concerned with women's issues, Weldon's novels have been labeled "feminist" by many reviewers. Yet, Weldon's views are her own and are not easily classified. In fact, feminists have at times taken exception to her portrayal of women, accusing the author of perpetuating traditional stereotypes.

Weldon's fiction fosters disparate interpretations because its author sees the complexity of the woman's experience. As Susan Hill noted in *Books and Bookmen,* Weldon has "the sharpest eyes for revealing details which, appearing like bubbles on the surface, are clues to the state of things lying far, far below." Weldon accepts feminist ideology as a liberating force, but she also understands its limitations. Thus, what emerges from Weldon's writing is more than an understanding of women's issues; she appreciates the plight of the individual woman. She told Sybil Steinberg in an interview in *Publishers Weekly,* "Women must ask themselves: What is it that will give me fulfillment? That's the serious question I'm attempting to answer."

Weldon's early novels, especially *Down among the Women, Female Friends,* and *Remember Me,* gained recognition both for their artistry and their social concerns. "Vivid imagery, a strong sense of time and place, memorable dialogue, complex events, and multiple characters that are neither confusing nor superficially observed," characterize these novels according to Krouse, making them "a rich rendering of life with brevity and wit." In her writing, John Braine added in *Books and Bookmen,* Fay Weldon "is never vague. . . . She understands what few novelists understand, that physical details are not embellishments on the story, but the bricks from which the story is made." And, like few other novelists, especially those that deal with women's issues, observed Braine, "she possesses that very rare quality, a sardonic, earthy, disenchanted, slightly bitter but never cruel sense of humour."

Although each of these books possesses elements typical of a Weldon novel, they focus on different aspects of the female experience and the forces that influence them. *Down among the Women* reflects how three generations of women, each the product of a different social climate, react to the same dilemma. Krouse found that in this book Weldon creates "a work whose very structure is feminist." She added in her *Critique* review, "The whole novel could profitably be analyzed as a definition of womanhood: passages describing how one has to live 'down among the women' contrast with anecdotes of male behavior." The image of womanhood offered here is not ideal, but as Krouse commented, Weldon's ability to blend "the terrible and the ridiculous is one of the major reasons why a novel filled with the pain endured by women . . . is neither painfully depressing nor cheerfully sentimental."

As its title suggests, *Female Friends* examines relationships among women, how the companionship of other women can be comforting to a woman wearied by the battle of the sexes. "The most radical feminist could not possibly equal the picture of injustice [Weldon] paints with wry, cool, concise words," wrote L.E. Sissman in the *New Yorker.* Sissman found that "the real triumph of *Female Friends* is the gritty replication of the gross texture of everyday life, placed in perspective and made universal; the perfectly recorded dialogue, precisely differentiated for each character; the shocking progression of events that, however rude, seem real." Weldon does not overlook the injustices committed by women in this day-to-day struggle, however. Ultimately, her characters suggest, women are responsible for their own lives. As Arthur Cooper concluded in *Newsweek,* Weldon "has penetrated the semidarkness of the semiliberated and shown that only truth and self-awareness can set them free."

Remember Me is the story of one man's impact on the lives of three women and how the resentment of one of those women becomes a disruptive force even after her death. This novel suggests that elements beyond the control of the individual often dictate her actions. "Scores of . . . coincidences . . . emphasize the theme that chance, misunderstanding, and necessarily limited knowledge play a significant part in human life," observed Krouse. Human frailties, Krouse added, body functions, pain, sickness "and death are recurrent images underscoring human mortality." Phyllis Birnbaum, writing in the *Saturday Review,* stated, "Precise satire, impassioned monologue, and a sense of limited human possibility make this novel a daring examination of twentieth-century discontent."

By the time she had written her sixth novel, *Praxis* (the fifth, *Words of Advice,* appeared in 1977), Weldon was considered, as Susan Hill put it, "an expert chronicler of the minutiae of women's lives, good at putting their case and pleading their cause." Kelley Cherry pointed out in the Chicago *Tribune Books* that *Praxis* is a novel about endurance. The central character, Praxis Duveen, must endure in a world filled with "just about every kind of manipulation and aggression that men use to get women where they want them," observed Katha Pollitt in the *New York Times Book Review,* "and just about every nuance of guilt and passivity that keeps women there." Struggling against most of the catastrophes that can befall a woman, Praxis does emerge, revealing according to Hill, that even though "Weldon's women are victims, they do have many compensatory qualities—toughness, resilience, flexibility, inventiveness, patience, nerve."

A novel in which so many misfortunes plague one character runs the risk of becoming unbelievable. Yet, Cherry wrote, "The writing throughout is brisk and ever so slightly off the wall—sufficiently askew to convey the oddness of events, sufficiently no-nonsense to make that oddness credible." And, concluded Pollitt, "As a narrative it is perhaps too ambitious, but as a collection of vignettes, polemics, epigrams, it is often dazzling, pointing up the mad underside of our sexual politics with a venomous accuracy for which wit is far too mild a word."

In her next novel, *Puffball,* "Weldon mixes gynecology and witchcraft to concoct an unusual brew," Joan Reardon noted in the *Los Angeles Times Book Review.* Here, more than before, Weldon confronts the woman's condition on a physical level, focusing on pregnancy. "Weldon has the audacity to include technical information on fertility, conception, and fetal development as an integral part of the story," commented Lorallee MacPike in *Best Sellers.* "She makes the physical process preceding and during pregnancy not only interesting but essential to the development of both story and character."

In the eyes of some reviewers such as Joan Reardon, however, the technical information weakens the novel. She wrote that in *Puffball,* "perspicacity has given way to whimsy and 'the pain in my soul, my heart, and my mind' has become a detailed analysis of the pituitary system." Moreover, some feminists faulted this book for its old-fashioned images of women; as Anita Brookner pointed out in the *Times Literary Supplement,* "superficially, it is a great leap backwards for the stereotype feminist. It argues in favour of the old myths of earth and motherhood and universal harmony: a fantasy for the tired businesswoman." Yet a reviewer for the *Atlantic* found that "the assertion of the primacy of physical destiny that lies at the center of *Puffball* gives the book a surprising seriousness and an impressive optimism."

In *The President's Child,* Weldon breaks new ground, exploring the impact of political intrigue on individual lives. Her next novel, however, is reminiscent of *Praxis.* Like Praxis, the protagonist of Weldon's ninth novel, *The Life and Loves of a She-Devil,* is buffeted by the injustice of her world. Yet, whereas Praxis endures, Ruth gets revenge. Losing her husband to a beautiful romance novelist, tall, unattractive Ruth turns against husband, novelist, and anyone else who gets in her way. Unleashing the vengeance of a she-devil, she ruins them all; the novelist dies and the husband becomes a broken man. In the end, having undergone extensive surgery to make her the very image of her former competitor, she begins a new life with her former husband. "What makes this a powerfully funny and oddly powerful book is the energy that vibrates off the pages," wrote Carol E. Rinzler in the *Washington Post Book World.* Weldon has created in *She-Devil,* Sybil Steinberg noted in *Publishers Weekly,* a "biting satire of the war between the sexes, indicting not only the male establishment's standards of beauty and feminine worthiness, but also women's own willingness . . . to subscribe to these standards."

Seeing Ruth's revenge as a positive response to the injustice of the male establishment, some reviewers were disappointed by her turnaround at the novel's end. As Michiko Kakutani pointed out in the *New York Times,* "Her final act—having extensive plastic surgery that makes her irresistible to men—actually seems like a capitulation to the male values she says she despises." Weldon is aware of the contradictions suggested by her story; she discussed this issue in her interview with Sybil Steinberg: "The first half of the book is an exercise in feminist thought. . . . It's the feminist manifesto really: a woman must be free, independent and rich. But I found myself asking, what then? . . . I think women are discovering that liberation isn't enough. The companionship of women is not enough. The other side of their nature is unfulfilled."

"Central to many of [Weldon's] plots is the rise of the Nietzschean superwoman," contended Daniel Harris in prefacing his review of the author's 1993 novel *Trouble* in the *Los Angeles Times Book Review.* Paralleling Weldon's own rise to literary acceptance from her former career as a lowly advertising copywriter, Harris characterized such women as emerging "out of the seething multitudes of hungry romantic careerists just waiting for their chance to advance up a hierarchical power structure that Weldon describes as the equivalent among women of a food chain." Annette Horrocks, the pregnant protagonist of *Trouble* is just such a woman, the second wife of a chauvinistic businessman who becomes threatened when his wife publishes a novel. In a twist, the husband runs, not into the arms of yet another manipulative woman, but into the clutches of a pair of pseudo-therapists, who convince him that Annette is his enemy. The novel was faulted by some for being uncharacteristic Weldon. "The characters are thin, the plot maniacally unreal, the dialogue brisk and bleak," noted *Observer* critic Nicci Gerrard, maintaining that *Trouble* contains too large a dose of its author's personal anger.

Weldon's twentieth novel, *Splitting,* finds the author returned to form, according to Bertha Harris in the *New York Times Book Review.* Seventeen-year-old former rock star Angelica White is determined to become the perfect female companion in order to endear herself to dissolute but wealthy Sir Edwin Rice and obtain a marriage commitment. She discards her image as the rock queen Kinky Virgin, doffs the nose rings and the spectacularly colored hair, and becomes overweight, drug-abusing Edwin's helpmate. "In effect, Angelica's troubles begin when she resolves that it's 'time to give up and grow up,'" according to Harris. Soon the typical flock of avaricious females descend on Angelica, breaking up her home and causing her to fracture into four separate personalities. Ultimately banished from the Rice estate, her money having long since been usurped by her husband, Angelica ultimately avenges herself through the savvy, recklessness, and sense of fun created by her multiple selves. "The splitting device works shamelessly well," explained Kate Kellaway in the *Observer.* "Weldon uses it as a way of exploring and rejoicing in the theatricality of women, their volatility, their love of disguise, of fancy dress, of playing different parts." As the author has one of Angelica's new selves say, "Women tend to be more than one person at the best of times. Men just get to be the one."

Weldon has since continued her pace, not only with novels such as 1996's *Worst Fears,* but also with a short story collection, appropriately titled *Wicked Women,* which she published in 1995. In *Worst Fears,* a widowed woman suddenly realizes that her life has not in fact been the rosy picture she imagined it. Snubbed by her friends, and lacking sympathy in favor of her husband's mistress, Alexandra soon finds that such deception by the living is nothing compared to the deceptions practiced on her by her now dead husband. Left with nothing, she plans her revenge in true Weldon fashion in a novel in which the author "has filed down a few sharp edges," according to *New York Times Book Review* critic Karen Karbo, ". . . and that makes it one of her best novels yet." Variations on this traditional Weldon theme are also played out in the sixteen short stories in *Wicked Women.* While noting that the collection is somewhat uneven in effectiveness, *Spectator* reviewer Susan Crosland hastened to add, "When the seesaw swings up, Fay Weldon is on form: sparkling, sharply observing, insights delivered with a light touch that puts us in a good mood, however dark the comedy. And one of the great things about short stories is that you can pick and chose."

Writing for the *Knight-Ridder/Tribune News Service,* Jean Blish Siers stated: "Perhaps the funniest of all Fay Weldon's very funny novels, *Big Girls Don't Cry* tackles the feminist movement head-on with the wry, ironic comedy for which Weldon is famous." This 1997 volume is also typical of Weldon's work in that its story is presented episodically, with short paragraphs and scenes often delivered in a temporally fragmented fashion. "It is a tapestry Weldon weaves," observed a critic for the online publication *The Complete Review,* "and the story does come together very well. Weldon's succinct style, with few wasted words, her dialogue brutally honest and straightforward, her explanations always cutting to the quick make for a powerful reading experience. Not everyone likes their fiction so direct, but we approve heartily and recommend the book highly." The plot of *Big Girl's Don't Cry* moves from the early seventies to the present and concerns five women who found a feminist publishing house called Medusa. As the novel opens we meet Zoë, a young mother in a loveless marriage, the beautiful Stephanie, the sexy Layla, the intellectual Alice, and Nancy, who has just broken off an unsatisfying engagement. While the publishing house thrives over the next three decades, the women's lives evolve dramatically. Husbands and friends change; children are abandoned; internecine conflicts sometimes plague the five while at other times they must rally in support of one another. "In the end," noted Siers, "the five—older but not much wiser—must face the consequences of decisions made a quarter-century earlier." A *Complete Review* critic commented: "The characters are all very human, and while they profess idealism Weldon ruthlessly shows how difficult it is to live up to it." Siers concluded: "Weldon never paints simple pictures of right and wrong. The men might be pigs, but they simply don't know any better. The women might mean well, but they blunder ahead with little thought of ramifications."

In 1999 Weldon's collection of essays *Godless in Eden* was published. Therein she covers a wide range of topics and examines a variety of controversial issues, including sex and society, the feminization of politics, the Royal Family, therapy, her own life and loves, and the changing roles of men and women in the contemporary world.

Weldon's understanding of the individual woman, living in a world somewhere between the nightmare of male chauvinism and the feminist ideal, has allowed her to achieve a balance in her writing. "She has succeeded in uniting the negative feminism, necessarily evident in novels portraying the problems of women, with a positive feminism, evident in the belief that change or equilibrium is possible," wrote Agate Nesaule Krouse. For this reason, "[Weldon] speaks for the female experience without becoming doctrinaire," noted *New York Times Book Review* contributor Mary Cantwell, "and without the dogged humorlessness that has characterized so much feminist writing." Having found an audience for her writing—insights into the condition of woman, shaped by her intelligence and humor—Fay Weldon has risen to prominence in literary circles. Writing in the *Times Literary Supplement,* Anita Brookner called Weldon "one of the most astute and distinctive women writing fiction today."

BIOGRAPHICAL AND CRITICAL SOURCES:

BOOKS

Barreca, Regina, *Fay Weldon's Wicked Fictions,* University Press of New England (Lebanon, NH), 1994.

Contemporary Literary Criticism, Volume 122, Thomson Gale (Detroit, MI), 2000.

Dictionary of Literary Biography, Volume 194: *British Novelists since 1960, Second Series,* Thomson Gale (Detroit, MI), 1998.

Dowling, Finuala, *Fay Weldon's Fiction,* Fairleigh Dickinson University Press (Madison, NJ), 1998.

Faulks, Lana, *Fay Weldon,* Twayne (Boston, MA), 1998.

PERIODICALS

Atlantic Monthly, August, 1980.

Best Sellers, October, 1980.

Booklist, May 1, 1995, p. 1554; June 1, 1995, p. 1804; May 1, 1996, p. 1470.

Books and Bookmen, January, 1977; March, 1979; May, 1979.

Critique, December, 1978.

Entertainment Weekly, June 16, 1995, p. 57.

Knight-Ridder/Tribune New Service, January 20, 1999, Jean Blish Siers, review of *Big Girls Don't Cry.*

Library Journal, February 15, 1995, p. 198; April 15, 1995, p. 117; March 15, 1996, p. 110; May 15, 1996, p. 85.

Los Angeles Times Book Review, September 7, 1980; April 19, 1987; April 10, 1988; December 18, 1988; June 4, 1989; June 25, 1995, pp. 3, 9.

New Statesman and Society, February 11, 1994, p. 40; January 5, 1996, p. 39.

Newsweek, November, 1974; December 4, 1978.

New Yorker, March 3, 1975; November, 1978.

New York Times, November 24, 1981; December 21, 1981; August 21, 1984; October 29, 1988; May 31, 1989; March 16, 1990.

New York Times Book Review, June 11, 1995, p. 48; June 9, 1996, p. 19.

Observer (London, England), February 13, 1994; May 7, 1995.

Publishers Weekly, January 13, 1984; August 24, 1984.

Saturday Review, December, 1976.

Spectator, March 1, 1980; July 1, 1981; October 2, 1982; February 12, 1994, pp. 29-30; May 13, 1995, pp. 39-40.

Times Literary Supplement, September 10, 1971; February 22, 1980; May 22, 1981; September 24, 1982; January 20, 1984; July 6, 1984; August 9, 1985; February 13, 1987; July 15, 1988; February 18, 1994.

Tribune Books, November 12, 1978; September 28, 1980; February 14, 1982; March 13, 1988; November 20, 1988; June 18, 1989; March 18, 1990.

Washington Post Book World, November 3, 1974; September 30, 1984; July 14, 1985; May 10, 1987; April 24, 1988; November 13, 1988; April 1, 1990.

ONLINE

Complete Review, http://www.complete-review.com/ (August 8, 2000), review of *Big Girls Don't Cry and Big Women.*

Fay Weldon, http://redmood.com/ (August 8, 2000).

HomeArts: Fay Weldon, http://homearts.com/ (August 8, 2000), "Fay Weldon."

* * *

WELLS, Rebecca

PERSONAL: Born in Rapides, LA; father a self-employed businessperson; married Tom Schworer (a photographer). *Education:* Louisiana State University, B.A.; attended Naropa Institute, Boulder, CO.

ADDRESSES: Agent—Jonathan Dolger Agency, 49 E. 96th St., No. 9B, New York, NY 10128.

CAREER: Playwright, actress, and writer.

MEMBER: Performing Artists for Nuclear Disarmament (Seattle, WA; chapter founder, 1982).

AWARDS, HONORS: Western States Book Award for fiction, 1992, for *Little Altars Everywhere;* Adult Trade ABBY Award, 1999, for *Divine Secrets of the Ya-Ya Sisterhood.*

WRITINGS:

PLAYS

Splittin' Hairs (one-woman show), first produced at Seattle Repertory Theater in Seattle, WA; later toured the United States, 1983–84.

Gloria Duplex, first produced at Empty Space Uncommon Theatre in Seattle, WA, 1986–87.

NOVELS

Little Altars Everywhere, Broken Moon Press (Seattle, WA), 1992.

Divine Secrets of the Ya- Ya Sisterhood, HarperCollins (New York, NY), 1996.

Ya-Yas in Bloom, HarperCollins (New York, NY), 2005.

Also author and performer of *Little Altars and Devine Secrets,* a performance piece based on the author's novels *Divine Secrets of the Ya-Ya Sisterhood* and *Little Altars Everywhere.*

ADAPTATIONS: Divine Secrets of the Ya-Ya Sisterhood, a film based on the book by the same name and the book *Little Altars Everywhere* and written and directed by Callie Khouri, was released by Warner Brothers, 2002; *Ya-Yas in Bloom* has been adapted as an audio book, Books on Tape, 2005.

SIDELIGHTS: Rebecca Wells is the author of the best-selling novels, *Little Altars Everywhere* and *Divine Secrets of the Ya-Ya Sisterhood,* both of which center on loyalty among women in the South. Born in the rural parish of Rapides, Louisiana, and raised on a plantation, Rebecca Wells worked briefly as a waitress at Yellowstone National Park, studied writing with the poet Allen Ginsberg, then began a career in off-Broadway theater in New York before writing her first book. *Little Altars Everywhere* is a 1992 novel set in a small Louisiana town in the early 1960s, and stars the Walkers, led by the flamboyant Vivi and her outdoorsy husband, Shep, and their children, Siddalee, Little Shep, Lulu, and Baylor. In the first part of the book, Siddalee narrates several chapters, telling engaging and interesting stories about her family, and later in the book, the other children have their say. Their stories hint at misconduct and drunkenness, abuse and hidden terrors, and even thirty years after the events took place, the family is still scarred. M.J. McAteer, in the *Washington Post Book World,* described the book as "a funny, eloquent and sad novel—her first—that easily leaps regional bounds." Mary B. Stuart, a reviewer for the *Curled Up with a Good Book* Web site, described *Little Altars Everywhere* as "a poignant, humorous, sad, heart-warming, heart-breaking novel that may very well, over time, be deemed an American classic, and a wonderful achievement by Rebecca Wells."

Divine Secrets of the Ya-Ya Sisterhood, published in 1996, tells the story of four aging Southern belles from Louisiana who have been friends ever since 1932, when they disrupted a Shirley Temple look-alike contest. The women made their first appearance in *Little Altars Everywhere,* and Vivi, the mother of the children in that book, is one of them. Her daughter Siddalee asks her mother about her friendships with the other women. Vivi gives her an old scrapbook about her friends, the "Ya-Yas," and the stories that unfold from this gift illuminate their past and their present relationship. *Booklist* contributor Donna Seaman called the book "a wonderfully irreverent look at life in small-town Louisiana from the thirties on up to the present through the eyes of the Ya-Yas, a gang of merry, smart, brave, poignant, and unforgettable goddesses." A *Publishers Weekly* contributor was distracted by the "superficial characterization and forced colloquialisms," but most other critics responded to Wells's characterization with enormous enthusiasm. According to Sarah Van Boven in *Newsweek,* women all over the country have formed over a dozen "Ya-Ya clubs" of their own. Van Boven quoted fans as saying: "It gives me comfort just to see it up there on the shelf," and "It's inspiring to see the Ya-Yas reveling in their nonfamilial bond."

When *Divine Secrets of the Ya-Ya Sisterhood* was first released, the publisher did not view it or attempt to market it as a best-seller, but it became one through word of mouth. When women started coming to Wells's book signings with stacks of copies for their mothers, sisters, and friends, she herself was surprised. "I didn't write the book because I had a group of friends like the Ya-Yas," she told Van Boven. "I think I wrote it because I wanted one." Readers identify deeply with the close-knit friends and the complicated mother-daughter relationship. At a reading, a fan once asked Wells if she was Sidda and her mother was Vivi. Before Wells could answer, another fan said, "No, I'm Sidda and my mother is Vivi." "The biggest blessing of the book has been meeting so many women who are loyal to each other," Wells told a writer for *People.* When asked how she feels about her characters inspiring women to "smoke, drink and never think," Wells replied, "Well, that's just one part of the book. I say, 'Go, girl.'"

Ya-Yas in Bloom is a follow up to *Divine Secrets of the Ya-Ya Sisterhood.* The former, like the latter, includes many stories from the women's pasts and tales of modern-day irreverence that the group so actively pursues. Among the stories recalled are the Walker family's trip to see the Beatles perform in 1965 and Vivi's confrontation with a nun who teaches her son first grade. Many of the stories also focus on the Ya-Yas' children. Although the stories are generally upbeat, the author takes a more serious tone with the tale about Myrtis's daughter—Myrtis's daughter kidnaps one of the Ya-Yas' grandchildren.

Critics greeted the follow-up novel with glowing reviews, and their comments highlighted the strengths that can be found in most of Wells's writings. A *Publishers Weekly* contributor commented that the author "still charms when she focuses on the redemptive power of family love and the special bond that comes from genuine, long-lived friendship." Writing on the *Bookreporter.com* Web site, Bronwyn Miller noted: "Through all their trials and tribulations . . . the Petit Ya-Yas, learn to face adversity with grit, determination and—most importantly—a sense of style." Miller next went on to conclude that reading the novel "feels like visiting with old friends."

BIOGRAPHICAL AND CRITICAL SOURCES:

PERIODICALS

Booklist, June 1, 1996, Donna Seaman, review of *Divine Secrets of the Ya-Ya Sisterhood,* p. 1674.

Books, summer, 1999, review of *Divine Secrets of the Ya-Ya Sisterhood,* p. 21; summer, 2001, review of *Little Altars Everywhere,* p. 21.

Christian Century, July 3, 2002, John Petrakis, movie review of *Divine Secrets of the Ya-Ya Sisterhood,* p. 43.

Daily Variety, May 10, 2002, Todd McCarthy, movie review of *Divine Secrets of the Ya-Ya Sisterhood,* p. 2.

Newsweek, July 6, 1998, Sarah Van Boven, review of *Divine Secrets of the Ya-Ya Sisterhood,* p. 71.

Observer (London, England), June 6, 1999, review of *Divine Secrets of the Ya-Ya Sisterhood,* p. 13.

People Weekly, October 5, 1998, "Divine Write," interview with author, p. 87.

Publishers Weekly, June 29, 1992, review of *Little Altars Everywhere,* p. 58; April 8, 1996, review of *Divine Secrets of the Ya-Ya Sisterhood,* p. 57; February 22, 1999, Daisy Maryles, "Ya-Ya begins Two, Too," p. 20; February 14, 2005, review of *Ya-Yas in Bloom,* p. 53; April 11, 2005, Daisy Maryles. "Yay-Yays for Ya-Yas," p. 20.

Romance Reader, February 4, 1999, review of *Divine Secrets of the Ya-Ya Sisterhood.*

Tribune Books (Chicago, IL), August 3, 1997, review of *Divine Secrets of the Ya-Ya Sisterhood,* p. 8.

Washington Post Book World, September 6, 1992, M.J. McAteer, review of *Little Alters Everywhere,* p. 9.

Women's Journal, July, 2001, review of *Little Altars Everywhere,* p. 16.

ONLINE

BookPage.com, http://www.bookpage.com/ (October 28, 2003), interview with Wells.

Bookreporter.com, http://www.bookreporter.com/ (March 9, 2006), Bronwyn Miller, review of *Ya-Yas in Bloom.*

Curled Up with a Good Book Web site, http://www.curledup.com/ (October 27, 2003), Mary B. Stuart, review of *Little Altars Everywhere;* Denise M. Clark, review of *Divine Secrets of the Ya-Ya Sisterhood.*

January Magazine Online, http://www.januarymagazine.com/ (October 27, 2003), Monica Stark, review of *Divine Secrets of the Ya-Ya Sisterhood.*

Rebecca Wells Home Page, http://www.ya-ya.com/ (March 9, 2006).

SouthCoast Today Online, http://www.southcoasttoday.com/ (March 9, 2006), Shana McNally, "You'd Know If You're 'Ya-Ya.'"

* * *

WELTY, Eudora 1909-2001
(Michael Ravenna, Eudora Alice Welty)

PERSONAL: Born April 13, 1909, in Jackson, MS; died of pneumonia, July 23, 2001, in Jackson, MS; daughter of Christian Webb (an insurance company president) and Chestina (Andrews) Welty. *Education:* Attended Mississippi State College for Women (now Mississippi University for Women), 1926-27; University of Wisconsin, B.A., 1929; attended Columbia University Graduate School of Business, 1930-31.

CAREER: Worked for newspapers and radio stations in Mississippi during early depression years, and as a publicity agent for the state office of the Works Progress Administration (WPA). Was briefly a member of the *New York Times Book Review* staff, in New York, NY. Honorary consultant in American letters, Library of Congress, beginning 1958.

MEMBER: American Academy and Institute of Arts and Letters.

AWARDS, HONORS: Guggenheim fellowship, 1942; O. Henry Award, 1942, 1943, 1968; National Institute of Arts and Letters, 1944, grant in literature, 1972, Gold Medal for fiction writing; William Dean Howells Medal from American Academy of Arts and Letters, 1955, for *The Ponder Heart;* Creative Arts Medal for fiction, Brandeis University, 1966; Edward MacDowell Medal, 1970; National Book Award nomination in fiction, 1971, for *Losing Battles*; Christopher Book Award, 1972, for *One Time, One Place: Mississippi in the Depression; A Snapshot;* National Institute of Arts and Letters Gold Medal, 1972; Pulitzer Prize in fiction, 1973, for *The Optimist's Daughter;* National Medal for Literature, 1980; *The Collected Stories of Eudora Welty* was named an American Library Association notable book for 1980; Presidential Medal of Freedom, 1980; American Book Award, 1981, for *The Collected Stories of Eudora Welty,* 1984, for *One Writer's Beginnings;* Common Wealth Award for Distinguished Service in Literature from Modern Language Association of America, 1984; National Book Critics Circle Award and *Los Angeles Times* Book Prize nominations, both 1984, for *One Writer's Beginnings;* Reader of the Year Award from Mystery Writers of America, 1985; National Medal of Arts, 1987; Chevalier de l'Ordre des Arts et des Lettres, 1987; National Book Foundation Medal, 1991; Helmerich Distinguished Author Award and Cleanth Brooks Letters (France), 1991; Frankel Prize, National Endowment for the Humanities, 1992; PEN/Malamud Award for excellence in the short story, 1993; inducted into National Women's Hall of Fame, 2000. D. Litt. from University of North Carolina, University of the South, Washington University, Smith College, University of Wisconsin, Western College for Women, Millsaps College, Yale University, Harvard University, and University of Dijon (France).

WRITINGS:

A Curtain of Green (short stories), with a preface by Katherine Anne Porter, Doubleday (Garden City, NY), 1941, published as *A Curtain of Green, and Other Stories,* Harcourt (New York, NY), 1964.

The Robber Bridegroom (novella), Doubleday (New York, NY), 1942.

The Wide Net, and Other Stories, Harcourt (New York, NY), 1943.

Delta Wedding (novel), Harcourt (New York, NY), 1946.

Music from Spain, Levee Press (Greenville, MS), 1948.

Short Stories (address delivered at University of Washington), Harcourt (New York, NY), 1949.

The Golden Apples (connected stories), Harcourt (New York, NY), 1949.

Selected Stories (contains all of the short stories in *A Curtain of Green,* and *The Wide Net, and Other Stories*), introduction by Katherine Anne Porter, Modern Library (New York, NY), 1953.

The Ponder Heart (novel), Harcourt (New York, NY), 1954.

The Bride of Innisfallen, and Other Stories, Harcourt (New York, NY), 1955.

Place in Fiction (lectures for Conference on American Studies in Cambridge, England), House of Books (New York, NY), 1957.

John Rood (catalog of sculpture exhibition), (New York, NY), 1958.

Three Papers on Fiction (addresses), Smith College (Northampton, MA), 1962.

The Shoe Bird (juvenile), Harcourt (New York, NY), 1964.

Thirteen Stories, edited and introduction by Ruth M. Vande Kieft, Harcourt (New York, NY), 1965.

A Sweet Devouring (nonfiction), Albondocani Press (New York, NY), 1969.

Losing Battles (novel), Random House (New York, NY), 1970.

A Flock of Guinea Hens Seen from a Car (poem), Albondocani Press (New York, NY), 1970.

One Time, One Place: Mississippi in the Depression; A Snapshot Album, illustrated with photographs by Welty, Random House (New York, NY), 1971, revised edition, University Press of Mississippi (Jackson, MS), 1996.

The Optimist's Daughter (novelette), Random House (New York, NY), 1972.

The Eye of the Story (selected essays and reviews), Random House (New York, NY), 1978.

Miracles of Perception, The Library (Charlottesville, VA), 1980.

The Collected Stories of Eudora Welty, Harcourt (New York, NY), 1980.

One Writer's Beginnings (lectures; includes *Beginnings*), Harvard University Press (Cambridge, MA), 1984.

Morgana: Two Stories from "The Golden Apples," University Press of Mississippi (Jackson, MS), 1988.

Photographs, University Press of Mississippi (Jackson, MS), 1989.

Eudora Welty's "The Hitch-hikers," edited by Larry Ketron, Dramatists Play Service (New York, NY), 1990.

(Editor, with Ronald A. Sharp) *The Norton Book of Friendship,* Norton (New York, NY), 1991.

A Worn Path, Creative Education (Mankato, MN), 1991.

(Author of text) *Beginnings: For Solo Voice and Piano or Chamber Orchestra* (score), music by Luigi Zaninelli, Shawnee Press (Delaware Gap, PA), 1992.

A Writer's Eye: Collected Book Reviews, edited by Pearl A. McHaney, University Press of Mississippi (Jackson, MS), 1994.

Stories, Essays, and Memoir, Library of America (New York, NY), 1998.

Complete Novels, Library of America (New York, NY), 1998.

The First Story, University Press of Mississippi (Jackson, MS), 1999.

(Contributor and photographer) *Country Churchyards,* University Press of Mississippi (Jackson, MS), 2000.

On Writing, Modern Library (New York, NY), 2002.

Contributor to *Southern Review, Atlantic, Harper's Bazaar, Manuscript, New Yorker,* and other periodicals. Also contributor of articles under pseudonym, Michael Ravenna, to *New York Times Book Review.* Author of introduction of *Novel-Writing in an Apocalyptic Time,* by Walker Percy, Faust, 1986; *The Democratic Forest,* by William Eggleston, Doubleday, 1989; and *The Capers Papers,* by Charlotte Capers, University Press of Mississippi, 1992.

ADAPTATIONS: The Ponder Heart was adapted for the stage and first produced on Broadway in 1956, and was adapted as an *opera bouffe* and produced in 1982; *The Robber Bridegroom* was adapted for the stage as a musical and first produced in 1978; "The Hitch-hikers" was adapted for the stage in 1986; "Lily Daw and the Three Ladies" was adapted for the stage.

SIDELIGHTS: With the publication of *The Eye of the Story* and *The Collected Stories,* Eudora Welty achieved the recognition she has long deserved as an important contemporary American fiction writer. Her position was confirmed in 1984 when her autobiographical *One Writer's Beginnings* made the best-seller lists with sales exceeding 100,000 copies. During the early decades of her career, she was respected by fellow writers but often dismissed by critics as a regionalist, a miniaturist, or an oversensitive "feminine" writer. The late 1970s and 1980s, however, saw a critical reevaluation of her work. Michael Kreyling affirmed in *Eudora Welty's Achievement of Order* that the value of her work is not that it is "primarily regional writing, or even excellent regional writing, but [that it conveys] the vision of a certain artist who must be considered with her peers—[Virginia] Woolf, [Elizabeth] Bowen, and [E. M.] Forster."

Marked by a subtle, lyrical narrative state, Welty's work typically explores the intricacies of the interior life and the small heroisms of ordinary people. In an article appearing in *Eudora Welty: Critical Essays,* Chester E. Eisinger described the writer's unique combination of realistic and modernist traditions: "Her work reflects the careful disorder of Chekhovian fiction and the accurate yet spontaneous rendering of detail that belonged to [Anton Chekhov's] slice of life technique. It reflects the modernism, . . . that characterized Woolf's fiction: The door she opened for Welty, she herself had passed through with [James] Joyce, [Franz] Kafka, [Marcel] Proust, [Robert] Musil, and the other twentieth-century makers of experimental, avant-garde fiction."

Raised in a close-knit bookish family, Welty and her two brothers had a happy childhood. Welty's education in the Jackson schools was followed by two years at Mississippi State College for Women between 1925 and 1927, and then by two more years at the University of Wisconsin and a B.A. in 1929. Her father, who believed that she could never earn a living by writing stories, encouraged her to study advertising at the Columbia University Graduate School of Business in New York during 1930-1931.

Welty returned to Jackson, Mississippi, in 1931 after her father's sudden death. To support herself, Welty first tried various small jobs with local newspapers and with radio station WJDX, which her father had started in the tower of his insurance building. Then, in 1933, she was offered a position as a publicity agent for the Works Progress Administration (WPA). "I did reporting, interviewing," she explained to Jean Todd Freeman in an interview collected in *Conversations with Eudora Welty.* "It took me all over Mississippi, which is the most important thing to me, because I'd never seen it. . . .

[The experience] was the real germ of my wanting to become a real writer, a true writer." It was at this time that Welty learned the art of seeing and capturing significant moments in the lives of ordinary people. She took hundreds of photographs of Mississippians of all social classes, capturing them at work and at leisure with their friends and families. In 1989, the majority of these photographs, along with an interview with the author and a foreword by Reynolds Price, were published as *Photographs.* Stuart Wright, writing in *Sewanee Review,* noted that Welty's photographs were indeed "the work of an amateur," but added that the photographs "have immense charm and naturalness attests to the honesty behind her motives and passion."

Welty's job gave her a first-hand look at the Depression-struck lives of rural and small-town people in a state that had always been the poorest in the nation. She captured their struggles and triumphs in stories, beginning with "Death of a Traveling Salesman," which was published in the literary magazine *Manuscript* in 1936. Other stories followed during the next five years, including some of her most famous—"Why I Live at the P.O.," "Powerhouse," "A Worn Path," "Petrified Man," "Lily Daw and the Three Ladies." Six stories were accepted by *Southern Review* between 1937 and 1939 and earned her the friendship and admiration of writers Albert Erskine, Robert Penn Warren, Katherine Anne Porter, and Ford Madox Ford. In a 1949 *Kenyon Review* essay Warren commented on the contrast between "the said, or violent, or warped" subjects of the stories and a tone that is "exhilarating, even gay, as though the author were innocently delighted . . . with the variety of things that stories could be and still be stories." In 1941 a collection of these stories was published as *A Curtain of Green* with a preface by Katherine Anne Porter. As Ruth Vande Kieft explained in *Eudora Welty,* the stories "are largely concerned with the mysteries of the inner life, the enigma of man's being—his relation to the universe; what is secret, concealed, inviolable in any human being, resulting in distance or separation between human beings; the puzzles and difficulties we have about our own feelings, our meaning, and our identity."

Welty's first sustained experiment with folk materials appeared in 1942 as *The Robber Bridegroom,* a bold fusing of Mississippi history, tall tale, and fairytales of mysterious seducers drawn from British and Germanic sources as well as from the Greek story of Cupid and Psyche. Here, as Carol Manning explained in *With Ears Opening Like Morning Glories: Eudora Welty and the Love of Storytelling,* the innocent tone of the narrative counteracts the dire stuff of robberies, murders, and the depredations of a cruel stepmother. To many early reviewers the result seemed pure magic. Alfred Kazin claimed in a review for the *New York Herald Tribune Books* that Welty had captured "the lost fabulous innocence of our departed frontier, the easy carelessness, the fond bragging and colossal buckskin strut." Although some commentators found it lacking in substance, Kreyling defended the book as a valuable addition to the pastoral tradition in American literature: "Welty seems to be saying that the dream of a pastoral paradise on Earth is always one step ahead of the dreamers; it is, sadly, only possible in a dream world removed from contact with human flesh and imperfections. But still worth dreaming."

Welty continued to experiment with such materials in her next collection, *The Wide Net, and Other Stories.* Here she explored the interrelationships of everyday Mississippi life with the timeless themes and patterns of myth, creating for her apparently ordinary characters a universality that links them with all times and cultures. In an essay appearing in *Eudora Welty: Critical Essays,* Garvin Davenport believed each story in the book presented "at least one character who confronts or encounters a situation which is in some way dark, mysterious or dreamlike. Each such encounter contributes to an awakening or renewal—sometimes only temporarily—of that character's potential for emotional enrichment and experiential meaning."

Welty's first novel, *Delta Wedding,* marks a significant change in her focus. Welty shifts from the dreamlike atmosphere of *The Wide Net* to the ordinary milieu of family life in the Mississippi Delta. Many of the circumstances of the Fairchild family in *Delta Wedding* recall those of the Ramsay family in Woolf's *To the Lighthouse.* The center of the Fairchild family is a mother of eight who continually ministers to her husband, her children, and a wider circle of relatives and friends. The novel is organized around domestic imagery of cooking and eating, wedding preparations, and diplomatic maneuvers to avert conflicts and soothe hurt feelings so that the wedding, on which the work centers, can occur.

The narrative technique in *Delta Wedding* is similar to Woolf's in its use of multiple perspectives. In Welty's case the observers are all female, from nine-year-old Laura McRaven, a visiting cousin, to the mother, Ellen Fairchild, and her many daughters. In an interview collected in *Conversations with Eudora Welty,* the writer told Jo Brans that the world of *Delta Wedding* is a matriarchy but that it is not at all hostile to men. Men, instead, are the objects of loving attention and perform the occasional acts of heroism that are necessary to protect the charmed and fertile pastoral world of the plantation. Chief among these men is Uncle George Fairchild, who reenacts in modern form the mythic rescue of a maiden from a dragon by St. George. In this case, the dragon is an approaching train, and George Fairchild's rush to pull his niece from the track symbolically expresses his function for the whole Fairchild family. Manning argued that with *Delta Wedding* "the Southern family and community replace the isolated individual and the abnormal one as Welty's favorite focus."

Delta Wedding was followed in 1949 by *The Golden Apples,* a closely related group of stories that functions almost as a novel. *The Golden Apples* depicts several families in the little town of Morgana, Mississippi, during the 1930s or early 1940s, focusing particularly on the defiant and talented Virgie Rainey, who rejects the conventional life of a Southern lady and creates an independent existence for herself while helping her widowed mother run her dairy farm. Fertility myths weave through these stories with particular attention given to the Pan-like figure of King Maclain, who wanders in and out of town seducing maidens like a mythical satyr and then disappearing in almost a twinkling of cloven hooves. But the main emphasis remains on the lives of the townspeople—the growing pains of children, the tragicomic disappointment of the fierce German music teacher Miss Eckhart, the near-drowning of an orphan girl at summer camp, and then the aging of the community and blighting of the lives of many characters who began as children full of possibility in the early stories. In a *PMLA* essay, Patricia Yeager emphasized Welty's subversive exploration to traditional gender distinctions in these stories, arguing that she deliberately transgresses masculine and feminine symbolic boundaries in order to call them into question. For Yeager, "the most interesting and persistent rhetorical strategy Welty employs is to continually shift the figure and ground of her story, allowing male discourse and female desire to contrast with, to comment on, and to influence each other as each becomes the ground on which the figure of the other begins to interact."

Welty's next book, *The Ponder Heart,* is a comic tour de force that concentrates many of her favorite themes in the dramatic events of an eccentric Southern gentleman's life. Set in the small town of Clay, Mississippi, *The Ponder Heart* is ostensibly an examination of the "heart" or character of Uncle Daniel Ponder, narrated by his spinster niece Edna Earle. Uncle Daniel is one of Welty's typical male heroes who unaccountably marries a selfish and brassy lower-class girl. In a tone combining sympathy and outrage, Edna Earle describes her uncle's wooing of seventeen-year-old Bonnie Dee Peacock in a dime store, their elopement, her desertion, return, death and burial, and Uncle Daniel's trial for murder. Playful use of cliche, giddy inversion of social conventions, and the juxtaposition of kindly motives and silly disasters prevent the story from ever moving outside the realm of farce. When Uncle Daniel literally tickles his wife to death in an attempt to distract her from her fear of a thunderstorm, readers can only laugh and recognize the ridiculous dimensions of the most painful human experiences.

In 1955, Welty published another collection of short stories, *The Bride of Innisfallen, and Other Stories,* experimenting with a more allusive style. Three of the stories—"Circe," "Going to Naples," and "The Bride of Innisfallen"—are set in Europe and lack the vivid sense of place that gives solidity to most of Welty's fiction. The other four stories operate in familiar Mississippi settings. With the exception of "The Burning," a cryptic account of the burning of a plantation by Yankee soldiers during the Civil War, most continue Welty's comedy of small-town manners: adulterous trysts are foiled by rain and curious children ("Ladies in Spring") or by heat and spiritual fatigue ("No Place for You, My Love"), and a visiting niece offers bemused observations on and childhood memories of her Mississippi relatives' social milieu ("Kin").

Welty received the Pulitzer Prize for her novel *The Optimist's Daughter.* The sparest of her novels, it recounts an adult daughter's return to Mississippi to be with her elderly father during an eye operation and then to preside over his funeral a few weeks later. As Laurel Hand confronts her memories of both parents, she comes to understand the pain of her mother's dying years and their effect on her father. Laurel is reconciled to her father's unwise second marriage to a ruthless young woman, and at the same time finally recognizes her own grief for the husband she has lost many years before. Welty's exploration of grief in *The Optimist's Daughter,* which was in part a working-out of her own losses during the 1960s, contains many autobiographical elements, particularly in the portrait of Laurel's mother. But the novel is also a close fictional examination of the interdependence of child and parents. In an interview collected in *Conversations with Eudora Welty,* Welty told Martha van Noppen that she "tried to give that feeling of support and dependence that just ran in an endless line among the three of them [mother, father, and daughter]." Finally, Laurel Hand works through her grief to achieve a calmer and more practical accommodation with the past.

On Writing was Welty's last publication before her death in 2001. The book contains seven essays written to help readers better understand literature. Writing for the *Knight Ridder/Tribune News Service,* Jay Goldin described some of the essays as "grand, sweeping," and "overarching." According to Goldin, Welty "examines literature with the same gimlet eye that, in creating her fictional world, she so often turned on life." Goldin noted that only a few of Welty's ideas in the book are original, but believed "that makes them no less valid."

Welty's fictional chronicle of Mississippi life adds a major comic vision to American literature, a vision that affirms the sustaining power of community and family life and at the same time explores the need for solitude. In his 1944 essay, Robert Penn Warren aptly identified these twin themes in Welty's work as love and separateness. While much of modern American fiction has emphasized alienation and the failure of love, Welty's stories show how tolerance and generosity allow people to adapt to each other's foibles and to painful change. Welty's fiction particularly celebrates the love of men and women, the fleeting joys of childhood, and the many dimensions and stages of women's lives. Welty spent her life in Jackson, Mississippi, in the house her family built when she was sixteen. "I am a writer who came of a sheltered life," Welty noted in her autobiography. "A sheltered life can be a daring life as well. For all serious daring starts from within."

BIOGRAPHICAL AND CRITICAL SOURCES:

BOOKS

Abadie, Ann J., and Louis D. Dollarhide, editors, *Eudora Welty: A Form of Thanks,* University Press of Mississippi (Jackson, MS), 1979.

Aevlin, Albert J., *Welty: A Life in Literature,* University Press of Mississippi (Jackson, MS), 1987.

Appel, Alfred, Jr., *A Season of Dreams: The Fiction of Eudora Welty,* Louisiana State University Press (Baton Rouge, LA), 1965.

Authors and Artists for Young Adults, Volume 48, Thomson Gale (Detroit, MI), 2003.

Balakian, Nona, and Charles Simmons, editors, *The Creative Present,* Doubleday (Garden City, NY), 1963.

Bloom, Harold, editor,*Eudora Welty,* Chelsea House (New York, NY), 1986.

Bryant, Joseph A., Jr., *Eudora Welty,* University of Minnesota Press (Minneapolis, MN), 1968.

Carson, Barbara Harrell, *Eudora Welty: Two Pictures at Once in Her Frame,* Whitston (Troy, NY), 1992.

Champion, Laurie, *The Critical Response to Eudora Welty's Fiction,* Greenwood Press (Westport, CT), 1994.

Concise Dictionary of American Literary Biography, Volume 5: *The New Consciousness, 1941-1968,* Thomson Gale (Detroit, MI), 1987.

Contemporary Literary Criticism, Thomson Gale (Detroit, MI), Volume 1, 1973, Volume 2, 1974, Volume 5, 1976, Volume 14, 1980, Volume 22, 1982, Volume 33, 1985.

Contemporary Novelists, St. James Press (Detroit, MI), 2001.

Contemporary Southern Writers, St. James Press (Detroit, MI), 1999.

Conversations with Writers II, Thomson Gale (Detroit, MI), 1978.

Cowie, Alexander, *American Writers Today,* Radiojaenst, 1956.

Desmond, John F., editor, *A Still Moment: Essays on the Art of Welty,* Scarecrow Press (New York, NY), 1978.

Devlin, Albert J., *Welty's Chronicle: A Story of Mississippi,* University Press of Mississippi (Jackson, MS), 1983.

Dictionary of Literary Biography, Thomson Gale (Detroit, MI), Volume 2: *American Novelists since World War II,* 1978, Volume 102: *American Short Story Writers, 1910-1945, Second Series,* 1991, Volume 143: *American Novelists since World War II, Third Series,* 1994.

Dictionary of Literary Biography Documentary Series, Volume 12, Thomson Gale (Detroit, MI), 1995.

Dictionary of Literary Biography Yearbook: 1987, Thomson Gale (Detroit, MI), 1988.

Encyclopedia of World Biography, Thomson Gale (Detroit, MI), 1998.

Encyclopedia of World Literature in the Twentieth Century, Ungar (New York, NY), 1981-1993.

Evans, Elizabeth, *Eudora Welty,* Ungar (New York, NY), 1981.

Gretlund, Jan Norby, *Eudora Welty's Aesthetics of Place,* Associated University Presses (Cranbury, NJ), 1994.

Gygax, Franziska, *Serious Daring from Within: Female Narrative Strategies in Eudora Welty's Novels,* Greenwood Press (Westport, CT), 1990.

Harrison, Suzan, *Eudora Welty and Virginia Woolf: Gender, Genre, and Influence,* Louisiana State University Press (Baton Rouge, LA), 1996.

Howard, Zelma Turner, *The Rhetoric of Welty's Short Stories,* University Press of Mississippi (Jackson, MS), 1973.

Jones, Anne Goodwyn, *Tomorrow Is Another Day: The Woman Writer in the South, 1859-1936,* Louisiana State University Press (Baton Rouge, LA), 1981.

Kreyling, Michael, *Eudora Welty's Achievement of Order,* Louisiana State University Press (Baton Rouge, LA), 1980.

Manning, Carol, *With Ears Opening Like Morning Glories: Eudora Welty and the Love of Storytelling,* Greenwood Press (Westport, CT), 1985.

Mark, Rebecca, *The Dragon's Blood: Feminist Intertextuality in Eudora Welty's "The Golden Apples,"* University Press of Mississippi (Jackson, MS), 1994.

Marrs, Suzanne, *Eudora Welty: A Biography,* Harcourt (New York, NY), 2005.

Mortimer, Gail L., *Daughter of the Swan: Love and Knowledge in Eudora Welty's Fiction,* University of Georgia Press (Athens, GA), 1994.

Newsmakers, Thomson Gale (Detroit, MI), 2002.

Pingatore, Diana R., *A Reader's Guide to the Short Stories of Eudora Welty,* Prentice-Hall (Englewood Cliffs, NJ), 1996.

Polk, Noel, *Eudora Welty: A Bibliography of Her Work,* University Press of Mississippi (Jackson, MS), 1994.

Prenshaw, Peggy Whitman, editor, *Eudora Welty: Critical Essays,* University Press of Mississippi (Jackson, MS), 1979.

Prenshaw, Peggy Whitman, editor, *Conversations with Eudora Welty,* University Press of Mississippi (Jackson, MS), 1984.

Prenshaw, Peggy Whitman, editor, *More Conversations with Eudora Welty,* University Press of Mississippi (Jackson, MS), 1996.

Randisi, Jennifer Lynn, *A Tissue of Lies: Eudora Welty and the Southern Romance,* University Press of America (Lanham, MD), 1982.

Ruas, Charles, *Conversations with American Writers,* Knopf (New York, NY), 1985.

St. James Guide to Horror, Ghost, and Gothic Writers, St. James Press (Detroit, MI), 1998.

Schmidt, Peter,*The Heart of the Story: Welty's Short Fiction,* University Press of Mississippi (Jackson, MS), 1991.

Short Story Criticism, Thomson Gale (Detroit, MI), Volume 1, 1988, Volume 27, 1998.

Trouard, Dawn, editor, *Eudora Welty: Eye of the Storyteller,* Kent State University Press (Kent, OH), 1990.

Turner, W. Craig, and Lee Emling Harding, editors, *Critical Essays on Eudora Welty,* G.K. Hall (Boston, MA), 1989.

Vande Kieft, Ruth, *Eudora Welty,* Twayne (New York, NY), 1962.

Westling, Louise, *Sacred Groves and Ravaged Gardens: The Fiction of Eudora Welty, Carson McCullers, and Flannery O'Connor,* University of Georgia Press (Athens, GA), 1985.

PERIODICALS

American Book Collector, January-February, 1981.

Booklist, June 1, 1994, p. 1775; November 1, 1994, p. 530; April 15, 1996, p. 1409; May 15, 2000, Brad Hooper, "Country Churchyards," 1727.

Bulletin of Bibliography, January, 1956; January, 1960; January, 1963; September, 1963.

Chicago Tribune, December 20, 1984.

Chicago Tribune Book World, April 1, 1982.

Christian Science Monitor, January 21, 1999, review of *Complete Novels,* and review of *Stories, Essays, and Memoir,* p. 16.

Critique, winter, 1964-65.

English Journal, January, 1990.

Globe and Mail (Toronto), March 24, 1984.

Harper's Magazine, February, 1990.

Kenyon Review, spring, 1944.

Kirkus Reviews, June 15, 1998, review of *Stories, Essays and Memoir,* p. 845.

Knight Ridder/Tribune News Service, September 4, 2002, Jay Goldin, review of *On Writing.*

Library Journal, March 1, 1994, p. 89; September 1, 1994, p. 230; April 1, 1995, p. 142; September 15, 1998, Michael Rogers, review of *Complete Novels,* p. 118; July, 2002, Michael Rogers, review of *On Writing,* p. 128.

Los Angeles Times, November 13, 1987.

Los Angeles Times Book Review, October 18, 1998, review of *Stories, Essays and Memoir,* p. 7.

Mississippi Quarterly, fall, 1973; fall, 1984.

New Republic, March 8, 1999, review of *Stories, Essays, and Memoir,* p. 40, review of *Complete Novels,* p. 40.

Newsweek, August 6, 2001, "Southern Lady, World-Class Storyteller," p. 60.

New Yorker, February 19, 1996, p. 36.

New York Herald Tribune Books, October 25, 1942.

New York Times, February 18, 1984; March 1, 1985; April 22, 1990.

New York Times Book Review, November 1, 1942; April 12, 1970; February 19, 1984; November 22, 1998, review of *Stories, Essays, and Memoir,* p. 18, review of *Complete Novels* p. 18.

Notes on Mississippi Writers, number 2, 1985.

Observer, July 26, 1998, review of *Collected Stories,* p. 14.

PMLA: Publications of the Modern Language Association of America, October, 1984.

Quill and Quire, May, 1999, review of *The Optimist's Daughter,* p. 35.

Sarasota Herald Tribune, Barbara Peters Smith, "A Death Like a Relative's Passing" p. A19.

Saturday Review, December, 1984.
Sewanee Review, July-September, 1952; summer, 1990.
Shenandoah, spring, 1969.
Southern Humanities Review, summer, 1980.
Southern Living, February, 1990; October, 1995, p. 104.
Southern Review, autumn, 1972.
Southwest Review, summer, 1981.
Times Literary Supplement, August 12, 1994, December 4, 1998, review of *Stories, Essays, and Memoir,* p. 4.
Twentieth Century Literature, winter, 1982.
U.S. News and World Report, August 18, 1986; February 15, 1993.
Washington Post Book World, October 25, 1998, review of *Stories, Essays, and Memoir,* p. 3, review of *Complete Novels,* p. 16; June 17, 2001, review of *One Writer's Biography,* p. 15.

ONLINE

Eudora Welty Newsletter, http://www.gsu.edu/~wwwewn/ (August 1, 2001).
Mississippi Writers Page, http://www.olemiss.edu/depts/english/ms-writers/ (June 3, 2003), "Eudora Welty."
Salon.com, http://www.salon.com/ (April 13, 1999), "Happy Birthday, Miss Welty."

* * *

WELTY, Eudora Alice
See WELTY, Eudora

* * *

WEST, Edwin
See WESTLAKE, Donald E.

* * *

WEST, Owen
See KOONTZ, Dean R.

* * *

WEST, Paul 1930-

PERSONAL: Born February 23, 1930, in Eckington, England; son of Alfred Massick and Mildred (Noden) West; came to United States, 1961; became citizen, 1971; married Diane Ackerman (a poet and naturalist); children: Amanda Klare. *Education:* University of Birmingham, B.A. (with first honors), 1950; Oxford University, graduate study, 1950-53; Columbia University, M.A., 1953. *Hobbies and other interests:* Music, swimming, travel, and astronomy.

ADDRESSES: *Agent*—Elaine Markson, 44 Greenwich Avenue, New York, NY 10011.

CAREER: Memorial University of Newfoundland, St. John's, Newfoundland, Canada, assistant professor, then associate professor of English, 1957-62; Pennsylvania State University, University Park, associate professor, 1963-69, professor of English and comparative literature, 1969-95, senior fellow of Institute for Arts and Humanistic Studies, 1969-95, professor emeritus, 1995—. Visiting professor, University of Wisconsin, 1956-66; Pratt Lecturer, Memorial University of Newfoundland, 1970; Crawshaw Professor of English, Colgate University, 1972; Virginia Woolf Lecturer, University of Tulsa, 1972; Melvin Hill Distinguished Visiting Professor of Humanities, Hobart and William Smith Colleges, 1974; distinguished writer-in-residence, Wichita State University, 1982; writer-in-residence, University of Arizona, 1984; visiting professor of English, Cornell University, 1987—; visiting professor and novelist-in-residence, Brown University, 1992. Judge, CAPS fiction panel, 1975. *Military service:* Royal Air Force, 1954-57; became flight lieutenant.

MEMBER: Authors League of America, Authors Guild.

AWARDS, HONORS: Canada Council senior fellowship, 1959; Guggenheim fellowship, 1962-63; listed in Books of the Year by *New York Times,* 1969, for *Words for a Deaf Daughter,* 1970, for *I'm Expecting to Live Quite Soon,* 1971, for *Caliban's Filibuster,* and 1986, for *Rat Man of Paris;* Best Books of the Year, *Time,* 1969, for *Words for a Deaf Daughter; Paris Review* Aga Khan Prize for fiction, 1974; National Endowment for the Humanities fellowship, 1975; National Endowment for the Arts fellowships, 1980, 1985; Heinz fiction prize, 1980 and 1986; Hazlitt Memorial Award for Excellence in Arts (Literature), 1981; Governor of Pennsylvania's award for excellence in the arts, 1981; American Academy and Institute of Arts and Letters award in literature, 1985, 1986; Pushcart Prize, 1987; named Literary Lion by New York Public Library, 1987; National Book Award, and Best American Essays award, 1990; nominated for Medicis, Femina, and Meilleur Livre prizes, and Grand Prix Halperine-Kaminsky (France), 1993; Lannan Prize for Fiction, 1993, for *Love's Mansion;* Distinguished Teaching

Award, Graduate Schools of the North-East, 1995; Chevalier de l'Ordre des Arts et des Lettres (France), 1996; National Book Critics Circle Award nomination for fiction, 1996, for *The Tent of Orange Mist;* Art-of-Fact Award, State University of New York, 2000.

WRITINGS:

The Fantasy Poets: Number Seven, Fantasy Press (Oxford, England), 1952.
The Growth of the Novel, Canadian Broadcasting Corporation (BBC) (Toronto, Ontario, Canada), 1959.
The Fossils of Piety: Literary Humanism in Decline, Vantage Press (New York, NY), 1959.
The Spellbound Horses (poems), Ryerson (Toronto, Ontario, Canada), 1960.
Byron and the Spoiler's Art, St. Martin's (New York, NY), 1960.
A Quality of Mercy (novel), Chatto & Windus (London, England), 1961.
I, Said the Sparrow (memoirs), Hutchinson (London, England), 1963.
(Editor) *Byron: A Collection of Critical Essays,* Prentice-Hall (Englewood Cliffs, NJ), 1963.
The Modern Novel, two volumes, Hillary (New York, NY), 1963, 2nd edition, 1965.
Robert Penn Warren, University of Minnesota Press (Minneapolis, MN), 1964.
The Snow Leopard (poems), Hutchinson (London, England), 1964, Harcourt (New York, NY), 1965.
Tenement of Clay (novel), Hutchinson (London, England), 1965, McPherson & Co. (Kingston, NY), 1993.
Alley Jaggers (first novel in trilogy), HarperCollins (New York, NY), 1966.
The Wine of Absurdity: Essays on Literature and Consolation, Pennsylvania State University Press (University Park, PA), 1966.
Words for a Deaf Daughter (biography), HarperCollins (New York, NY), 1969, expanded edition with new preface by West published as *Words for a Deaf Daughter* [and] *Gala* (novel; also see below), Dalkey Archive (Normal, IL), 1993.
I'm Expecting to Live Quite Soon (second novel in trilogy), HarperCollins (New York), 1970.
Caliban's Filibuster (novel), Doubleday (New York, NY), 1971.
Bela Lugosi's White Christmas (third novel in trilogy), HarperCollins (New York, NY), 1972.
Colonel Mint, Dutton (New York, NY), 1973.
Gala, HarperCollins (New York, NY), 1976.
The Very Rich Hours of Count von Stauffenberg (historical novel), HarperCollins (New York, NY), 1980.
Out of My Depths: A Swimmer in the Universe (nonfiction), Doubleday (New York, NY), 1983.
Rat Man of Paris (novel), Doubleday (New York, NY), 1986.
Sheer Fiction (essays), McPherson & Co. (Kingston, NY), 1987, Volume 2, 1991, Volume 3, 1994.
The Universe, and Other Fictions (short fiction), Overlook Press (Woodstock, NY), 1988.
The Place in Flowers Where Pollen Rests (novel), Doubleday (New York, NY), 1988.
Lord Byron's Doctor (biographical novel), Doubleday (New York, NY), 1989.
Portable People (character sketches), drawings by Joe Servello, British American Publishers (Latham, NY), 1990.
The Women of Whitechapel and Jack the Ripper (historical novel), Random House (New York, NY), 1991.
Love's Mansion (novel), Random House (New York, NY), 1992.
(Adaptor) *Duets: Photographs by James Kiernan,* Random House (New York, NY), 1994.
The Tent of Orange Mist (novel), Scribner (New York, NY), 1995.
A Stroke of Genius: Illness and Self-Discovery (autobiographical memoir), Viking (New York, NY), 1995.
My Mother's Music (memoir), Viking (New York, NY), 1996.
Sporting with Amaryllis (historical novel), Overlook (New York, NY), 1997.
Terrestrials: A Novel of Aviation, Scribner (New York, NY), 1997.
Life with Swan (novel), Scribner (New York, NY), 1999.
OK: The Corral, the Earps and Doc Holliday, Scribner (New York, NY), 2000.
The Secret Lives of Words, Harcourt (New York, NY), 2000.
The Dry Danube: A Hitler Forgery, New Directions (New York, NY), 2000.
Master Class: Scenes from a Fiction Workshop, Harcourt (New York, NY), 2001.
A Fifth of November, New Directions (New York, NY), 2001.
Oxford Days: An Inclination, British American Publishers (Latham, NY), 2002.
Cheops: A Cupboard for the Sun, New Directions (New York, NY), 2002.
The Immensity of Here and Now: A Novel of 911, Voyant (Ramsay, NJ), 2003.
My Father's War: A Memoir, McPherson & Co (Kingston, NY), 2005.

Regular contributor to *Washington Post Book World, Boston Phoenix,* and *New York Times Book Review.*

Also contributor of essays, poems, and reviews to periodicals, including *TriQuarterly, New Statesman, Iowa Review,Parnassus, Conjunctions, Quimera* (Barcelona, Spain), *Nation, Kenyon Review, Sinn und Form, Partisan Review, Washington Post, New York Times, Harper's, Gentlemen's Quarterly, Paris Review,New Directions Literary Anthology, Yale Review,* and *Chelsea.* Fiction critic, *New Statesman,* 1959-60.

SIDELIGHTS: Paul West's writings span the genres of poetry, essay, criticism, biography, and the novel. Although his work in each genre has received critical praise, West favors the novel form for expression and experimentation. As *Dictionary of Literary Biography* contributor Brian McLaughlin noted, "It is as a fiction writer that he seems most happy, for there he can demonstrate at one and the same time the strength of the critic and the grace of the poet." *Book World* contributor Diane Johnson likewise commented that one of the most positive aspects of West's work "is his faith in the novel as an art form, as a dignified production of the human mind, capable of rendering, in its infinite variety, social comment, philosophic statement, comedy, pain, all of which West can do—impressively." Within West's novels, the author takes the guise of a variety of characters, including Jack the Ripper, the Rat Man of Paris, and his deaf daughter. West even reflects upon his parents' courtship and love life before he was born.

In his historical novel *The Very Rich Hours of Count von Stauffenberg,* for example, West portrays von Stauffenberg, a key figure in the anti-Nazi movement who orchestrated an unsuccessful plot to bomb Adolph Hitler's office in 1944. Von Stauffenberg was executed, and many of his conspirators were tortured and killed. "On these bones," wrote Frederick Busch in the *New York Times Book Review,* "Mr. West lays a flesh of living words: Dead dreams—of self, love, nobility, military service—are the stuff of his narrative." Written as a fictional memoir, the novel reveals the various facets of von Stauffenberg's character and chronicles his transformation from a moderate supporter of Hitler to an activist against him. In a preface to the novel, West explains the genesis of *The Very Rich Hours of Count von Stauffenberg:* "I was devouring books about the bomb plot against Hitler, some grand, some shoddy, many of them giving details the others omitted, and almost all of them contradicting one another until I felt that some of what I was reading was fiction already and that a fictional attempt of my own—say an historical impersonation—might go."

The novel was indeed a critical success. As *Partisan Review* contributor Ronald Christ commented: "Having resisted the temptation to write an account, or indictment, Paul West has written instead a novel . . . that never forgets language and the sensibility it issues from as the real protagonist. The richness of West's prose is the real wealth here, and it is, like Stauffenberg's hours, loaded with all the treasures of a 'truant mind.'" *Washington Post Book World* reviewer Joe David Bellamy similarly observed that "There is little attention to conventional plotting and suspense, to the aspects that could have made the novel 'a thriller.' But a rich, textured style and metaphorical inventiveness are the dividends." In *Contemporary Novelists,* Elmer Borklund pronounced the book simply "West's finest novel."

West's novel *Rat Man of Paris,* like *The Very Rich Hours of Count von Stauffenberg,* is based on a historical figure. Inspired by stories of a man who haunted the boulevards of Paris at the end of World War II, flashing a rat at passersby, West began to "[fill] in the blanks" of Rat Man's life, as he explained to *Publishers Weekly* interviewer Amanda Smith. West's Rat Man is Etienne Poulsifer, and he carries a fox stole, not a rat. The stole is one of the few belongings Rat Man was able to take with him after his family and their entire village were burned alive by the Nazis. This event, reminiscent of the actual German extermination of the French village of Oradour, has shaped Rat Man's existence. Observed *New York Times Book Review* contributor Lore Segal: *Rat Man of Paris* "addresses the large question of our time: How does one live one's daily life in the span between past atrocity and atrocity to come? What happens to the wound that does not heal, that will not scar over?" Despite Rat Man's various eccentricities—he also bathes with his clothes on and hangs his soiled sheets out his window in the hope that the police will, according to *Los Angeles Times* critic Richard Eder, "arrest and launder them"—Rat Man attracts a lonely high school teacher, Sharli, who views him as "another of her pupils: bigger, heavier, and more of a liability, to be sure, yet a fount of promise so long as he is able to take his time." West described Rat Man in *Publishers Weekly* as "a parallel man, a man of distance who has a very uncertain relationship with civilization. He doesn't quite know what it is and where he belongs in it, and he's amazed that people think he *does* belong in it." When Rat Man discovers that a Nazi war criminal has been extradited to France, he wrongly assumes that the convict is responsible for murdering the villagers. As an attempt at vengeance, Rat Man outfits himself like a Nazi and walks the streets of Paris carrying a sign with the Nazi's picture on it and wheeling the "rat" about in a pram. Rat Man becomes, like his real-life counterpart, a local celebrity, but his renown ends when he is injured by a sniper's bullet. As Eder commented: "Up until the shooting, West's fable is compassionate and chilling. His Poulsifer, victim and avenger, has a questioning and original humanity. And then it all fogs over." Expressing a similar opinion, *Newsweek* reviewer Peter S. Prescott argued that "*Rat Man of Paris* achieves its quite dazzling effects early on and then settles down to work variations on them. The effect isn't one of motion or of answers obtained, but of a faint glow."

West's 1988 novel, *The Place in Flowers Where Pollen Rests,* is set in a Hopi settlement in northeastern Arizona, and is told in various narrative voices, including those of George, Oswald, their deceased relatives, and Sotuqnangu, a mythical Hopi spirit. George The Place In Flowers Where Pollen Rests is a doll carver; his nephew Oswald Beautiful Badger Going Over The Hill wants to be a Hollywood actor. When Oswald leaves the community, he ends up as a pornographic movie star, and enlists for a tour of duty in Vietnam. Oswald, as Thomas R. Edwards revealed in a *New York Times Book Review* article on *The Place in Flowers Where Pollen Rests,* "tries to live up to his name by deserting his birthplace" and his people in favor of the White occidental world. But for Oswald, the "Anglo world . . . both attracts and nauseates," and he returns to his Hopi people when "the horrors of White America come closer to destroying him."

Much critical attention focused on the textual complexity of *The Place in Flowers Where Pollen Rests.* For John Calvin Batchelor, writing in the *Washington Post Book World,* West is "a writer's writer who aggressively goes too far, thinks too much, turns too many metaphors and explores too much strangeness for the casual reader." Steven Moore likewise found the novel challenging, but commented that the textual intricacy conveys "not only the Hopi culture but its linguistic structure as well." In his critique of the novel for the *Review of Contemporary Fiction,* Moore argued that *The Place in Flowers Where Pollen Rests* requires careful, slow reading, in order that "the reader can better appreciate the detailed, visceral texture of the places West describes." *Los Angeles Times Book Review* commentator Hartman H. Lomawaima, though, quarreled with West's portrayal of Hopi life, deeming it superficial and inaccurate: "West's Hopis, in their shallowness, one-dimensionality, and simple-mindedness, owe nothing to Hopi culture. Perhaps this is inevitable, given West's incomplete knowledge of Hopi life. But this is scarcely to excuse him." The Hopis, Lomawaima noted, consider many activities of daily living within the realm of artistry, while West's protagonist, George, is "an artist in the narrower European sense," and the novel becomes "yet another stereotypical account of a provincial artist rebelling against his benighted home community" rather than something that truly reflects Hopi culture.

In the 1989 biographical novel *Lord Byron's Doctor,* West focuses on the small group of people who spent the summer of 1816 with the exiled George Gordon, Lord Byron, focusing specifically on John William Polidori. Polidori, the least famous member of the group which included Mary Wollstonecraft Godwin, Percy Bysshe Shelley, and Byron's mistress and Mary Godwin's stepsister, Claire Clairmont, was a "young physician traveling as the club-footed Byron's secretary and medical adviser. He also had a five-hundred-pound commission from a London publisher to report on the poet's adventures," noted R.Z. Sheppard in a *Time* review of the novel. *Lord Byron's Doctor* is West's version of the events written about in Polidori's diary, including the love/hate relationship between the doctor and Byron, the sexual exploits of Byron and Shelley, and Polidori's suicide. Pointing out that the author is a Byron scholar, Moore explained in the *Review of Contemporary Fiction* that West has fleshed out "Polidori's skeletal diary in a robust early-nineteenth-century style . . . [creating] a penetrating psychological portrait of Lord Byron's Doctor."

"Through Polidori, West compiles a lurid case history on the cruelty of genius," maintained Sheppard, who sees the author as "one of the most vigorous and inviting literary talents still punching away in semiobscurity." Moore concluded that *Lord Byron's Doctor* is a "stylistic tour de force of nineteenth-century eloquence, slang and technical jargon; and a wholly successful recreation of that crucial year in literary history when Romantic yearnings confronted the darker recesses of the unconscious, wreaking havoc in the personal lives of their creators, but also giving birth to poetry and monsters that haunt us still."

West chose another infamous historical figure for the focus of his 1991 novel. In *The Women of Whitechapel and Jack the Ripper,* he revisits the fall of 1888 to explain the murders of five London prostitutes. The story begins some years prior, when Queen Victoria's grandson, Prince Eddy, and the painter and Prince Eddy's chaperon, Walter Richard Sickert, are spending much of their time at London brothels. Sickert introduces Prince Eddy to the poor, young Annie Crook, the two fall in love, and soon after, Annie becomes pregnant. The pregnancy becomes the precipitating event to a savage conspiracy involving the royal family.

When the queen learns of the affair, she and the prime minister, Lord Salisbury, arrange to have Annie kidnapped and taken to the royal family's personal physician, Sir William Gull, who lobotomizes and permanently hospitalizes her. One of Annie's friends, Marie Kelly, and a few of her fellow prostitutes at Whitechapel, send a blackmail letter to the queen, demanding Annie's release and a sum of money to keep the matter quiet. The queen then sets Gull loose to hunt the prostitutes down and silence them, and Sickert is taken along to identify the women who signed the letter. Gull is eventually held in a private psychiatric hospital, and Sickert, who became increasingly entranced by the murders, takes into his own care Alice Margaret, the daughter of Prince Eddy and Annie.

The Women of Whitechapel is "superbly written and intricately choreographed, a work both sensational and serious," wrote Sven Birkerts in the *New Republic.* "But what finally remains vivid, long after the novel has shrunk down to its afterimage in the mind, is the feverish abandon of Gull and the descriptions of his myriad mutilations." "The passages are raw and uninhibited; they transmit perfectly Sickert's fascinated repulsion," Birkerts added. "The visual precision is a triumph of artistic detachment, even as it horrifies." West's "prose glistens with bright ideas and boldly inventive turns of phrase," commented Dan Cryer in *Newsday.* Josh Rubins, critiquing for the *New York Times Book Review,* had a similar view, finding that West's "specialty is filling in the missing details—psychological and otherwise—through verbally exquisite interior monologues or provocatively vivid evocations of unfamiliar milieus." Chicago *Tribune Books* commentator Vance Bourjaily called West "possibly our finest living stylist in English."

In the Lannan Prize-winning *Love's Mansion,* West's 1992 semi-autobiographical novel, the author explores the life of his own parents before his conception. Albert Mobilio argued in the *Voice Literary Supplement* that only an author like West, who "dotes on the minds of assassins, madmen, and murderers . . . might be . . . adequately girded to peer under the sheets on his parents' wedding night. In *Love's Mansion* . . . he does just that, pulling back the covers on both how he came to be, and how memory comes to life." *Love's Mansion* is the story of Clive Moxon, a novelist in his mid-fifties who asks his ninety-four-year-old mother, Hilly, about her relationship with his father. The novel recounts Clive's father Harry's adventure in World War I, from which he returns blind. Despite this handicap, upon his return, he and Hilly get married. Joseph Coates noted in Chicago *Tribune Books:* "Both of them know it's a misalliance, each having 'made a new demand on life' that excludes the other without having the resources to enforce it. Harry is an existentialist before his time, wanting nothing better than a life of continental vagrancy and sensuality; Hilly wanting a life in art." Over time, as Jonathan Yardley commented in the *Washington Post Book World,* their "marriage seems an enormous barrier to what used to be their affection." Yardley summarized: "Hilly, determined over Harry's objections to have a child, at last becomes pregnant with Clive and then with a daughter, Kotch. However improbable a family they may be, a family is what they are: a small mansion with four rooms, but a mansion all the same."

With *The Tent of Orange Mist,* noted a *Publishers Weekly* critic, West's "versatility and imagination are again evident." Scald Ibis, a sixteen year old, becomes the property of Colonel Hayashi as her home is turned into a brothel for Japanese soldiers during the assault and occupation of Nanking, China. West's story of severe and unspeakable violence becoming commonplace, which was nominated for the National Book Critics Circle fiction award, came highly recommended by Robert E. Brown, who, in *Library Journal* called the work "both moving and intriguing. . . . An affecting novel." Commenting that West explores and "illuminates the consciousness of each of his . . . characters—especially Scald Ibis' struggle to come to terms with her pillaged youth," *Booklist* reviewer Donna Seaman lauded West's "scorching insights into the consequences of evil." In the *New York Times Book Review,* however, John David Morley had a different take. Despite deeming *The Tent of Orange Mist* a "most arresting thesis" and West a "gifted writer," Morley faulted the novel on credibility: "that Scald Ibis should become reconciled to her fate with such savvy and bounce—is so far removed from experience that it is impossible to participate in the book's jollity. Victims of rape under the threat of imminent murder simply do not behave like this." Though allowing that West's narrative does wear "thin in spots," Seaman nonetheless concluded that West writes with "mind-stopping clarity and power." Richard Eder, writing in the *Los Angeles Times Book Review,* referred to the book as "a small masterpiece" and argued that "West has never written anything so risky and triumphant."

One of West's most widely read books—and considered by some to be one of his most eloquently written—is *Words for a Deaf Daughter,* a biography of his daughter, Mandy, born deaf and suffering from a brain dysfunction. Like the characters in some of West's novels, Mandy is an outsider. People turn away from her in the street because, according to West, "they don't like a universe that's absurd," related Claire Tomalin in the *New Statesman.* Mandy is destructive yet obsessed with order and symmetry. She will fly into a rage because of a missing button or crooked barrette, for example, yet she will happily paint her face green, chew cigarettes, and cut her hair at random. Her parents hope that Mandy will, with encouragement, develop fully, and the book is written in anticipation that she will one day be able to read about the early years of her life.

Borklund described *Words for a Deaf Daughter* as "the astonishing account of West's infinitely patient attempts to understand the world in which Mandy is enclosed but not, if he can help it, defeated." As Chaim Potok observed in the *New York Times Book Review:* "Trapped, by whatever it is that traps people, into a potential horror and hell, West converted the trap into a doorway to a world filled with the strange fruit of nonverbal communication and creative silence." *Time* critic R.Z. Sheppard commented that "West writes joyfully for a can-be Mandy, but obviously adores Mandy as is. . . . A lifelong slave of words and reasons, [West] envies the intensity with which Mandy perceives the world nonverbally through her four acute senses." *Commentary* contributor Johanna Kaplan, however, found West's optimistic, celebratory portrait of Mandy disturbing. She disputed West's description of Mandy's handicaps as a special gift. "For whom is it a gift?" the critic asked. "Not Mandy, clearly, for so cut off is she from the ordinary and essential means of human interchange that to try to understand the function of everyday objects, to give them some kind of place in what is for her an especially confusing world, she must 'smell at a pencil newly sharpened, inhaling from the beechwood its own sour-soot bouquet, or trace with addicted fingers the corrugations on the flat of a halved cabbage before eating it raw.'"

Words for a Deaf Daughter was reprinted in 1993 in a volume that also included a new introduction by West and a reprint of his 1976 novel *Gala.* As Borklund observed, "*Words for a Deaf Daughter* is 'fact'; *Gala* is 'fiction,' or, as West puts it, 'the scenario of a wish-fulfillment,' in which the adolescent Mandy comes to visit her father in America and finally speaks to him. The importance of this wish-fulfillment is central to West's fiction." West commented to Amanda Smith in *Publishers Weekly:* "*Words for a Deaf Daughter* was written a long time ago, and it's a sort of hard and fast and settled book. Maybe the sense of the outsider, the dispossessed prince or princess, the pariah, the person who is shunned or spurned for whatever unjust reason—maybe this is a gathering pattern in one's work over twenty years. I'm sure one could make a good case, but I don't think in those terms. If I did, I wouldn't be able to write."

West's autobiographical work *A Stroke of Genius: Illness and Self-Discovery* explores his experience with several diseases, including migraine headaches, heart disease, and diabetes, and his stroke, which forced him to accept a pacemaker implant to regulate his heartbeat. In the *Los Angeles Times Book Review,* D.T. Max remarked that West "must have been, without doubt, a nightmarish patient. As feckless as any autodidact, he reads and rereads the diagnostic manual with a fervor born of terror." Max praised *Stroke of Genius* despite finding that West buries disease itself under an "avalanche of prose." Still, in West's book, the reader is allowed closer to the trauma of disease than in other memoirs of a similar nature, "not because West is braver—he is a complete chicken—but because he is franker," Max concluded. Dwight Garner noted in a *Nation* review that West focuses on his "generation's ingrained existentialism," which argues against passivity and leads "happily" to "a simple dignity in being a 'critic, fighter, and perfectionist to the end.'" Alexander Theroux, in a Chicago *Tribune Books* critique of *Stroke of Genius,* quoted West's explanation for his preoccupation with his illness: "I ponder such matters in much the same spirit as I memorize the names of all the actors when a movie's final credits roll—not because I care who they are, but because I want to show myself I am still competent."

After *A Stroke of Genius,* West published another memoir, *My Mother's Music.* Set mainly during World War II, the book focuses on how West's mother, who gave piano lessons to help support the working-class family, inspired her son and encouraged his aspirations. West shows himself as an "awkward kid" who "finds in 'Mommy' a haven, a soul mate and (eventually) an exacting mentor, who plies him with good books and high standards and goads him toward scholarships and success," related David Sacks in the *New York Times Book Review.* In this exploration of his mother's awakening him to "the music in words," however, West's language is so dense that he fails to provide a "satisfying portrait" of either himself or his mother, in the opinion of a *Publishers Weekly* critic. Sacks had some reservations about the work as well, noting that the emphasis on West and his mother, at the expense of other family members or friends, "can become monotonous," and that West fails to explain how it felt to leave his mother when he emigrated from England to the United States. "Still, *My Mother's Music* stands as a bold, touching, entertaining work," Sacks concluded.

In *Sporting with Amaryllis,* West, as in many of his other novels, uses an historical character as his protagonist. In this case it is the great seventeenth-century English poet John Milton. West imagines Milton in his youth, suspended for a term from Cambridge

University—the suspension may have in fact occurred—and meeting a young woman he calls Amaryllis—named after a character in one of Virgil's works—who takes him on a wild sexual adventure and serves as his muse. The book's title is taken from Milton's poem "Lycidas," in which he ponders if it might not be better "to sport with Amaryllis in the shade" than to dedicate oneself to taxing work. West's language in this novel is earthy and explicit, regarding not only sex but other bodily processes, and sometimes "rises to rather uncomfortable levels," according to a *Publishers Weekly* reviewer, who nonetheless pronounced the book "a rich feast for lovers of ornate and stylish prose." To *New York Times Book Review* contributor Tony Tanner, though, *Sporting with Amaryllis* is "pretentious, distasteful and futile" and is "counterfactual—in spades." In *American Scholar,* however, Morris Freedman observed that the "shocking material so early in West's book can easily put one off, except that it serves to prepare the reader to see young Milton without the filter of a sterilizing idolatry." He allowed that some of Milton's admirers will not care for the portrait of their hero as a randy youth, "but one doesn't have to swallow a word of West's flamboyant writing to find it piquant."

Terrestrials: A Novel of Aviation takes West's readers through a far different story, one of American espionage agents who are actually space aliens who have come to believe they are human earthlings. They survive nightmarish ordeals following a plane crash in an African desert, only to be harassed by government investigators on their return. Along the way the agents, Booth and Clegg, reflect on World War II's Battle of Britain and the history of aviation in general. "West's theme is the unreality of the present—except insofar as you can contrive to live it as myth," remarked Lorna Sage in the *New York Times Book Review.* The book, she noted, is also a meditation on male bonding; Booth and Clegg are "basically interested only in each other and in the elusive essence of flight." In *Terrestrials'* universe, she noted, "a woman can play only a flaming goddess or a 'solace figment,' an accurate phrase for the role female characters are often assigned in fiction, with a lot less honesty." Sage concluded that *Terrestrials* "isn't [West's] best book—it gives off too acrid a scent of labor and loneliness for that—but it's a moving tribute to two-dimensional masculinity." The novel contains West's trademark dense prose, which may discourage some readers, remarked a *Publishers Weekly* critic, who added that "the persistent, however, will savor the way West, an accomplished stylist, explores the dilemma of Booth and Clegg: knowledgeable yet unknowing . . . puzzling out the mystery of their terrestrial lives."

The 1999 novel *Life with Swan* is closer to home for West, although space travel again figures in the plot. This novel is a portrait of a marriage, with the husband and wife based on West and his wife, poet and nature writer Diane Ackerman. The fictional wife's name, Ariada Mencken, is an anagram of Ackerman's; her nickname is Swan, and the book is narrated by her husband. Like their real-life models, Mencken and her husband are involved in academia and literature, and they are friends with a scientist, Raoul Bunsen—based on West and Ackerman's friend the late Carl Sagan. Bunsen arranges for them to attend the launches of various space missions, which they find fascinating and an inspiration for their writing. The book also provides a detailed look at other aspects of the couple's life and makes clear how much Swan's husband adores her. "Not the most engrossing of plots, perhaps, but *Life with Swan* is a book whose effect depends more on its atmosphere and language than its story," reflected Roger Kimball in the *New York Times Book Review.* "At bottom, it is an extended invitation to admire the narrator and his inamorata." A *Publishers Weekly* reviewer found the novel "rather touching, though a bit too pleased with itself." Kimball summed it up by saying, "People who like this sort of thing will find this the sort of thing they like. The rest of us, alas, are out of luck."

Throughout his career West has been fascinated with historical events and figures—Cheops, Hitler, Lord Byron, Jack the Ripper, Guy Fawkes—and has used them as a springboard for his fiction. His work *The Immensity of the Here and Now* examines the history surrounding the events of September 11, 2001. The drama of the World Trade Center bombings sets the stage for the story of two friends, both damaged physically and emotionally, and chronicles how the events of 9/11 affect them. In *Booklist* Seaman commented that "West, an intrepid and adroit prospector of the psyche, provides an atomizing rumination on the emotional shock waves of 9/11."

West clearly relishes words and "attests to his obsession in a piquantly entertaining celebration of the evolution of language," noted Seaman in *Booklist,* reviewing West's *The Secret Lives of Words.* In this volume the author describes the etymology of 400 common and obscure words, and says that words are living testimony to "human ingenuity and the bizarre twists we permit our minds to make." He shows his passion for words and their impact in *Master Class: Scenes from a Fiction Workshop,* in which he describes the interactions he had with his M.F.A. students. David Madden quoted West in the *Review of Contemporary Fiction,* as saying: "The idea is to make the arrangement of the prose unrecognizable . . . then restore each [word] to its proper place in the pattern." Madden wrote that *Master Class* "offers a unique glimpse into West's own aesthetic."

BIOGRAPHICAL AND CRITICAL SOURCES:

BOOKS

Contemporary Literary Criticism, Volume 96, Thomson Gale (Detroit, MI), 1997.

Contemporary Novelists, St. James Press (Detroit, MI), 1996.

Dictionary of Literary Biography, Volume 14: *British Novelists since 1960,* Thomson Gale (Detroit, MI), 1983.

Madden, David, *Understanding Paul West,* University of South Carolina Press (Columbia, SC), 1994.

PERIODICALS

American Scholar, winter, 1998, p. 176.

Booklist, August, 1994, p. 2017; August, 1995, p. 1929; November 1, 1996; January 1, 1999; May 1, 2000, Donna Seaman, review of *The Secret Lives of Words,* p. 1634; September 1, 2003, Donna Seaman, review of *The Immensity of the Here and Now: A Novel of 911,* p. 63.

Book World, May 28, 1972.

Commentary, January, 1971.

Commonweal, September 30, 1966; December 9, 1977.

Critique, fall, 1998, David Madden, "Indoctrination for Pariahdom: Liminality in the Fiction of Paul West," p. 49.

Harper's, October, 1970.

Kirkus Reviews, December 15, 1992, p. 1534; October 1, 1996.

Library Journal, September 15, 1988, p. 95; May 1, 1993, p. 119; August, 1995, p. 121; February 1, 1999; August, 2002, Henry Corrigan, review of *Oxford Days,* p. 96; October 15, 2003.

Los Angeles Times, March 21, 1983; February 12, 1986.

Los Angeles Times Book Review, October 9, 1988, pp. 2, 15; September 10, 1989, p. 3; September 6, 1992, review of *Love's Mansion,* p. 3; May 7, 1995, p. 1; September 10, 1995, p. 3.

Nation, January 8, 1977; March 20, 1995, pp. 391-394.

New Republic, August 19, 1972; May 6, 1991, p. 37.

Newsday, April 21, 1991.

New Statesman, August 29, 1969, review of *Words for a Deaf Daughter.*

Newsweek, August 31, 1970; March 10, 1986.

New Yorker, October 24, 1970; August 25, 1980.

New York Times Book Review, May 3, 1970; September 27, 1970; September 10, 1972; July 3, 1977; November 9, 1980; February 16, 1986; September 11, 1988, p. 7; May 12, 1991, p. 11; October 18, 1992, review of *Love's Mansion;* July 11, 1993, p. 20; September 20, 1993, p. 16; September 3, 1995, p. 17; May 12, 1996; April 6, 1997; October 19, 1997; March 14, 1999.

Partisan Review, summer, 1982.

Publishers Weekly, February 28, 1986; July 29, 1988, p. 219; July 21, 1989, p. 50; January 18, 1993, p. 464; July 11, 1994, p. 72; July 3, 1995, p. 48; April 1, 1996, p. 63; October 6, 1996, p. 59; August 11, 1997, p. 383; December 14, 1998, p. 56.

Review of Contemporary Fiction, fall, 1988, p. 156; fall, 1989, p. 215; spring, 1991 (special Paul West issue); fall, 2000, Irving Malin, review of *The Dry Danube,* p. 144; spring, 2002, David Madden, review of *Master Class,* p. 149; fall, 2003, David Madden, review of *Cheops,* p. 129.

Sewanee Review, spring, 1993, p. 300.

Southern Review, winter, 1979.

Time, September 7, 1970; September 11, 1989, p. 82.

Times Literary Supplement, January 21, 1965; October 16, 1969, review of *Words for a Deaf Daughter;* April 23, 1971; January 28, 1972; June 8, 1973; February 6, 1981; November 8, 1991, p. 31.

Tribune Books (Chicago, IL), April 14, 1991, p. 1; October 18, 1992, p. 5; February 19, 1995, p. 13.

Voice Literary Supplement, September, 1992, p. 15.

Washington Post Book World, April 26, 1970; August 23, 1970; January 2, 1977; August 3, 1980; February 2, 1986; September 18, 1988, p. 3; September 27, 1992, p. 3.

ONLINE

Center for Book Culture Web site, http://www.centerforbookculture.org/ (August 26, 2004), David Madden, interview with West.

* * *

WESTLAKE, Donald E. 1933-
(John B. Allan, Curt Clark, Tucker Coe, Timothy J. Culver, J. Morgan Cunningham, Allen Marshall, Richard Stark, Edwin West, Donald Edwin Westlake)

PERSONAL: Born July 12, 1933, in New York, NY; son of Albert Joseph (a salesman) and Lillian Marguerite (Bounda) Westlake; married Nedra Henderson, August 10, 1957 (divorced, 1966); married Sandra Foley, April 9, 1967 (divorced, 1975); married Abigail Adams, May 18, 1979; children: Sean Alan, Steven Albert, Tod,

Paul Edwin; stepchildren: Adrienne Adams, Patrick Adams, Katharine Adams. *Education:* Attended Champlain College and State University of New York at Binghamton.

ADDRESSES: Agent—c/o Author Mail, Mysterious Press, 1271 Avenue of the Americas, New York, NY 10020.

CAREER: Worked at odd jobs prior to 1958 ("the same list as every other writer, except that I was never a short-order cook"); associate editor at literary agency, 1958-59; writer, 1959—. *Military service:* U.S. Air Force, 1954-56 ("no awards, by mutual agreement").

AWARDS, HONORS: Edgar Allan Poe Award from Mystery Writers of America, 1967, for *God Save the Mark;* Academy Award nomination, 1990, for screenplay adaptation of *The Grifters,* based on Jim Thompson's novel; Edgar Allan Poe Grand Master Award from Mystery Writers of America, 1992.

WRITINGS:

The Mercenaries, Random House (New York, NY), 1960.

Killing Time, Random House (New York, NY), 1961.

361, Random House (New York, NY), 1962.

Killy, Random House (New York, NY), 1963.

Pity Him Afterwards, Random House (New York, NY), 1964.

The Fugitive Pigeon, Random House (New York, NY), 1965.

The Busy Body, Random House (New York, NY), 1966.

The Spy in the Ointment, Random House (New York, NY), 1966.

God Save the Mark, Random House (New York, NY), 1967, Forge (New York, NY), 2004.

Philip, Crowell (New York, NY), 1967.

(Compiler, with Philip Klass) *Once against the Law,* Macmillan (New York, NY), 1968.

The Curious Facts preceding My Execution, and Other Fictions, Random House (New York, NY), 1968.

Who Stole Sassi Manoon?, Random House (New York, NY), 1968.

Somebody Owes Me Money, Random House (New York, NY), 1969.

Up Your Banners, Macmillan (New York, NY), 1969.

Adios, Scheherezade, Simon & Schuster (New York, NY), 1970.

I Gave at the Office, Simon & Schuster (New York, NY), 1971.

Under an English Heaven, Simon & Schuster (New York, NY), 1971.

Cops and Robbers (also see below), M. Evans (New York, NY), 1972.

(With Brian Garfield) *Gangway,* M. Evans (New York, NY), 1972.

Help, I Am Being Held Prisoner, M. Evans (New York, NY), 1974.

Two Much, M. Evans (New York, NY), 1975.

A Travesty, M. Evans (New York, NY), 1975.

Brothers Keepers, M. Evans (New York, NY), 1975.

Dancing Aztecs, M. Evans (New York, NY), 1976, published as *A New York Dance,* Hodder & Stoughton (London, England), 1979.

Enough!, M. Evans (New York, NY), 1977.

Nobody's Perfect, M. Evans (New York, NY), 1977.

Castle in the Air, M. Evans (New York, NY), 1980.

Kahawa, Viking (New York, NY), 1982, reprinted, Mysterious Press (New York, NY), 1995.

Levine, Mysterious Press (New York, NY), 1984.

A Likely Story, Penzler Books (New York, NY), 1984.

High Adventure, Mysterious Press (New York, NY), 1985.

(With wife, Abby Westlake) *High Jinx,* Macmillan (New York, NY), 1987.

(With Abby Westlake) *Transylvania Station,* Macmillan (New York, NY), 1987.

Trust Me on This, Mysterious Press (New York, NY), 1988.

Tomorrow's Crimes (includes *Anarchaos,* a novel, and other stories published between 1961-84), Mysterious Press (New York, NY), 1989.

Sacred Monster, Mysterious Press (New York, NY), 1989.

Humans, Mysterious Press (New York, NY), 1992.

Baby, Would I Lie?: A Romance of the Ozarks, Mysterious Press (New York, NY), 1994.

Smoke, Mysterious Press (New York, NY), 1995.

What's the Worst That Could Happen?, Mysterious Press (New York, NY), 1996.

The Ax, Mysterious Press (New York, NY), 1998.

The Hook, Mysterious Press (New York, NY), 2000.

Money for Nothing, Mysterious Press (New York, NY), 2003.

The Road to Ruin, Mysterious Press (New York, NY), 2004.

Thieves' Dozen, Mysterious Press (New York, NY), 2004.

"JOHN A. DORTMUNDER" CRIME SERIES

The Hot Rock, Simon & Schuster (New York, NY), 1970.

Bank Shot, Simon & Schuster (New York, NY), 1972.
Jimmy the Kid, M. Evans (New York, NY), 1974.
Why Me? (also see below), Viking (New York, NY), 1983.
Good Behavior, Mysterious Press (New York, NY), 1986.
Drowned Hopes (also see below), Mysterious Press (New York, NY), 1990.
Don't Ask, Mysterious Press (New York, NY), 1993.
Watch Your Back!, Mysterious Press (New York, NY), 2005.

UNDER PSEUDONYM JOHN B. ALLAN

Elizabeth Taylor: A Fascinating Story of America's Most Talented Actress and the World's Most Beautiful Woman, Monarch, 1961.

UNDER PSEUDONYM TUCKER COE

Kinds of Love, Kinds of Death, Random House (New York, NY), 1966.
Murder among Children, Random House (New York, NY), 1968.
Wax Apple, Random House (New York, NY), 1970.
A Jade in Aries, Random House (New York, NY), 1971.
Don't Lie to Me, Random House (New York, NY), 1972.

UNDER PSEUDONYM RICHARD STARK

The Hunter (also see below), Pocket Books (New York, NY), 1963, published as *Point Blank,* Berkley (New York, NY), 1973, reprinted under original title with a new introduction by the author, Gregg Press, 1981.
The Man with the Getaway Face (also see below), Pocket Books (New York, NY), 1963, published as *The Steel Hit,* Coronet (London, England), 1971, Berkley (New York, NY), 1975.
The Outfit (also see below), Pocket Books (New York, NY), 1963.
The Mourner (also see below), Pocket Books (New York, NY), 1963.
The Score (also see below), Pocket Books (New York, NY), 1964.
The Jugger, Pocket Books (New York, NY), 1965.
The Seventh (also see below), Pocket Books (New York, NY), 1966, also published as *The Split,* Allison & Busby (London, England), 1984.
The Handle, Pocket Books (New York, NY), 1966, published as *Run Lethal,* Berkley (New York, NY), 1966.
The Damsel, Macmillan (New York, NY), 1967.
The Dame, Macmillan (New York, NY), 1967.
The Rare Coin Score, Fawcett (New York, NY), 1967.
The Green Eagle Score, Fawcett (New York, NY), 1967.
The Black Ice Score, Fawcett (New York, NY), 1968.
The Sour Lemon Score, Fawcett (New York, NY), 1969.
The Blackbird, Macmillan (New York, NY), 1969.
Deadly Edge, Random House (New York, NY), 1971.
Slayground, Random House (New York, NY), 1971.
Lemons Never Lie, World Publishing 1971.
Plunder Squad, Random House (New York, NY), 1972.
Butcher's Moon, Random House (New York, NY), 1974.
Stark Mysteries (contains *The Hunter, The Man with the Getaway Face, The Outfit, The Mourner, The Score,* and *The Seventh*), G.K. Hall, 1981.
Comeback, Mysterious Press (New York, NY), 1997.
Backflash, Mysterious Press (New York, NY), 1999.
Flashfire, Mysterious Press (New York, NY), 2000.
Firebreak, Mysterious Press (New York, NY), 2001.
Breakout, Mysterious Press (New York, NY), 2002.
Nobody Runs Forever, Mysterious Press (New York, NY), 2004.

SCREENPLAYS

(With Michael Kane) *Hot Stuff,* Columbia, 1979.
The Stepfather, New Century/Vista, 1986.
The Grifters, Miramax, 1990.

Also author of screenplays *Cops and Robbers,* upon which Westlake based the novel, and *Why Me?,* based on the novel.

OTHER

(Editor) *Murderous Schemes: An Anthology of Classic Detective Stories,* Oxford University Press (New York, NY), 1996.

Contributor to anthologies. Author of science fiction, sometimes under the pseudonym Curt Clark. Author of books under the pseudonyms Timothy Culver, J. Morgan Cunningham, Alan Marshall, and Edwin West.

ADAPTATIONS: Many novels by the author, either under the name Donald E. Westlake or pseudonym Richard Stark, have been made into films, including: *The Jugger,* adaptation produced in France as *Made in the USA,* 1966; *The Busy Body,* film produced by Paramount, 1967; *The Hunter,* adaptation produced as *Point Blank,* Metro-Goldwyn-Mayer, 1967; *The Score,* adaptation produced in France as *Mise en Sac,* 1967; *The Seventh,* adaptation produced as *The Split,* Metro-Goldwyn-Mayer, 1968; *The Hot Rock,* film released by Twentieth Century-Fox, 1972; *Bank Shot,* film produced by United Artists, 1974; *The Outfit,* film produced by Metro-Goldwyn-Mayer, 1974; *Jimmy the Kid,* film produced by New World, 1982; *Slayground,* film produced by Universal, 1984; *Two Much,* adaptation produced in France as *Le Jumeau;* and *What's the Worst That Could Happen?,* Metro-Goldwyn-Mayer, 2001. *Drowned Hopes* has been recorded on audio cassette and released by Dove Audio, 1992.

SIDELIGHTS: "The Neil Simon of the crime novel" is how Donald E. Westlake was described by *New York Times Book Review* critic Newgate Callendar. It is a title Westlake earned through such popular books as *The Hot Rock, Bank Shot,* and *Two Much,* all characteristic of the author's talent for combining laughs with thrills in his fiction. In a Westlake tale, criminals and law enforcement officers are equally incompetent, and daring felonies fall prey to bad timing, bad weather, and bad luck. The author's plots revolve around the offbeat: "Who else could write a book about a man who pretends to be twins in order to marry a pair of identical heiresses?" asked Sheldon Bart in another *New York Times Book Review* article.

Westlake's first published books were more conventional crime novels; funny cops-and-robbers stories were not considered marketable. He had been working on a running character named Parker, a thief who "handles frustration very badly—he gets annoyed and kills everybody," according to Westlake in Bart's article. The "Parker" books, written under Westlake's pseudonym Richard Stark, are no less than "the best caper novels ever written," in the opinion of *Austin Chronicle* writer Jesse Sublett. These tales crackle with "lean and mean prose and chapters that flash back and forward to drive a narrative that zips along at whiplash speed despite the infinite convolutions of the heists, take-downs, betrayals and general mayhem of the plot."

The character of Parker, furthermore—"cold as an iceberg, sure as lightning"—is one that stands out, in Sublett's view, thanks to a professional demeanor that does not bend to the chaos that inevitably surrounds him. Some of Parker's rules of the trade: "Never have sex when working on a caper. (Before and after is a different story.)" And, "During a takeover job, learn and use the first names of the people you're holding at gunpoint. It boosts their ego and makes them easier to deal with."

When the author realized the comic potential in a no-win criminal, Westlake created another character, John Dortmunder, and starred him in a gem-stealing caper, *The Hot Rock.* So successful was this character, who, noted *Newsweek* writer David Lehman, "makes burglar seem synonymous with bungler," that Westlake continued Dortmunder's adventures in several subsequent novels, including *Bank Shot* and *Jimmy the Kid.*

Critics and fans of Westlake's work are quick to point out that his comic novels are as intricately plotted as any serious thriller. In a *Los Angeles Times* review of *Why Me?,* a book in which Dortmunder is once again the hapless victim of his own crime, Carolyn See found that "the characterization . . . is flawless, if unregenerately silly. And the plot is absolutely masterful, so that a dozen pleasing little details making you smile, even giggle, as they first slide by, are discovered in Chapter 29 to have been part of an elaborate literary setup, making you laugh till the tears come."

To Jerome Charyn, writing in the *New York Times Book Review,* Westlake's novels "are quite different from the classical mystery and espionage novels of Graham Greene and John le Carré. . . . [The author] shoves cartoons at us, instead of characters we might love, fear or despise. There are no murderous boy gangsters [or] pathetic drunken spies. . . . But we do have energized masks that babble at us in all sorts of crazy tongues, come alive for a minute, then return to their normal frozen position. This allows Westlake to push his narrative along at a tremendous pace, and supply his masks with the marvelous illogic of a cartoon world."

Westlake departed from the crime novel format with his works *A Likely Story* and *Trust Me on This.* A farce about the world of publishing and one writer's attempt to market his Christmas book, *A Likely Story* almost did not get published. *Washington Post* critic Alan Ryan found no small irony in the fact that "all the big-time New York publishers turned this book down. Why? Because it wasn't a crime novel, because it was different from Westlake's previous books, and—one assumes—because they didn't think it was funny and/or didn't think it would sell." But even writing out of his usual genre, "Westlake knows what he's doing," continued Ryan. "[His] comic eye is hilariously perceptive and ruthlessly unsparing. The result is likely the funniest book of the year."

In *Trust Me on This,* aspiring journalist Sara Joslyn lands a job with *The Weekly Galaxy* tabloid and is soon immersed in the world of madcap reportage. The bulk of the book involves the *Galaxy* crew invading Martha's Vineyard to cover a movie star's wedding. William A. Henry III, writing in *Time,* stated: "Rather than mock the already preposterous, Westlake explores the mentality that capable, rational people would need in order to crank out such stuff." Henry described *Trust Me* as "perhaps the most beguiling beheading of journalists since Evelyn Waugh's *Scoop,*" and called the work "a frantic, inventive story with lots of good dialogue." In *Newsweek,* reviewer Peter S. Prescott proclaimed: "Donald E. Westlake writes a comic novel so well it's a wonder he bothers with crime at all."

Westlake returned to his "Dortmunder" series with the publication of *Good Behavior.* In this novel, the clever thief crash-lands in a Manhattan convent, the sanctuary of a sisterhood of nuns vowed to silence. They persuade Dortmunder to rescue Sister Mary Grace, a tycoon's daughter who has been spirited away by her father and held prisoner in a high-security skyscraper's penthouse. Dortmunder and crew attempt to save the girl, but in typical fashion, their plans go haywire when they confront mercenaries training for the overthrow of a South American dictatorship. Writing in the *Washington Post Book World,* Jean M. White emphasized: "In the midst of these antics, Westlake never allows his comedy to slide into silly farce or buffoonery," and Callendar remarked in the *New York Times Book Review:* "He has a wonderful feeling for the absurd, revels in farce and slapstick, [and] piles complication upon complication" on the hapless burglars.

Drowned Hopes, another Dortmunder caper, pits the ill-fated crook against ex-cellmate Tom Jimson, who plans to blow up a dam, endangering thousands of lives, to retrieve his hidden loot, now buried under fifty feet of water. In the Chicago *Tribune Books,* Kevin Moore observed that "Westlake, the Mel Brooks of mayhem, has great fun making it all much more complicated than that." About the "Dortmunder" novels, Katherine Dunn commented in the *New York Times Book Review,* "These are hard-nosed but never hard-boiled romps, with a hero you could trust to babysit but wouldn't ask to polish the silver." Dunn gave high marks to *Drowned Hopes,* claiming that "Westlake's lean prose and dead-pan delivery are engaging, as always. His psychology is sharp and his characters colorful."

A later work, *Sacred Monster,* unfolds as a lengthy interview with a drunken, drug-using Hollywood superstar. Charles Champlin, in the *Los Angeles Times Book Review,* deemed the book "a sparkling little set-piece," and commented that "Westlake's ingenuity in spinning out his tale and working his sleight-of-hand finale is an audacious treat." *Tomorrow's Crimes* gathers Westlake's previously unpublished 1967 novel, *Anarchaos,* and nine shorter science fiction-mystery stories. Gary Dretzka, in the Chicago *Tribune Books,* called the stories "fast, thought-provoking studies" of humankind in a universe disrupted by the inherited evils of corporate and individual greed and a deteriorating environment. Despite minor reservations, Randall Short, in the *New York Times Book Review,* determined that "devotees of either genre can look forward to a smooth, satisfying read."

In *Humans,* God orders the angel Ananayel to bring about the Apocalypse. Ananayel enlists five human agents to assist him, but the bringer of doom is drawn off course by a growing concern for humanity, as well as his battle with X, the force who wishes to perpetuate humanity's suffering for his own demonic pleasure. Garry Abrams, in the *Los Angeles Times Book Review,* suggested that "a major purpose of the book" may be "to satirize the cleverness and conventions of the typical thriller through the stereotypes of an earlier, more faithful era," but he pointed out: "In [its] final section, *Humans* becomes more and more like the standard thriller it parodies. . . . The climax also is something of a whimper, considering the buildup." The *New York Times Book Review's* Michael Upchurch felt that Westlake's "narrative building blocks include . . . a labyrinthine plot and an unnerving insight into the depths of human behavior. The writing isn't as crisp as it could be, however, and the author has a persistently hokey side to him that may seem simply sophomoric to some readers." Upchurch did note that the human agents, "with their sense of rage and helplessness . . . give *Humans* a compelling urgency that, in its best passages, outweighs its obvious gimmicks," and found that "in bringing his characters to the brink of oblivion, Donald Westlake zeroes in on what is most precious about life. The ride may be bumpy in terms of technique but the view is, in unexpected ways, divine." Howard Waldrop, writing in the *Washington Post Book World,* declared: "This is a book that in many ways hurts, when so many others don't work up emotions in the reader at all. It's about the way the world mangles (and always has) the good and bad indifferently." He concluded: "We get a few glimpses, true ones, of the Third World hells that have been created because no one gives a damn one way or the other. It does these things in a frightening, sometimes funny, and unpreachy way."

Westlake returns to the character of Sara Joslyn and the seamy world of tabloid journalism with his novel *Baby, Would I Lie?* Sara is now working for a weekly newsmagazine, *Trend: The Magazine for the Way We Live This Instant,* and is sent to Branson, Missouri, to cover the trial of Ray Hanson, a country-western star accused of murder. Ronald C. Miller, writing for *The Armchair Detective,* called *Baby, Would I Lie?* "a comedic cornucopia . . . [that] lampoons journalists, contemporary music, entrepreneurs, and the IRS, among others." Charles Champlin in the *Los Angeles Times Book Review* termed it "a deliciously nutty sequel" to *Trust Me on This,* and "the funniest mystery of the year." Michael Lewis, reviewer for the *New York Times Book Review* was less complimentary. Although praising "Mr. Westlake's usually fine work," he felt that the novel's "humor . . . seems more like an excuse for the absence of any real mystery and its mystery an apology for the fact that it isn't very funny." He concluded, "In the end, the book's real satire is of itself."

Smoke lampoons the tobacco industry and resurrects the concept of the Invisible Man, but as Don Sandstrom warned in *The Armchair Detective,* "Do not dismiss [Westlake's protagonist] Freddie Noon as another invisible man like H.G. Wells's Doctor Griffin, Thorne Smith's George Kirby, or . . . H.F. Saint's Nick Holloway. This is a Westlake production." Gary Dretzka, writing for Chicago's *Tribune Books,* called *Smoke* "the kind of novel mystery fans will pass along to the unconverted as an example of just how enjoyable genre writing can be." In the *Washington Post Book World,* Kathi Malo characterized it as "one of his best books in years." And Terry Teachout, writing for the *New York Times Book Review,* compared Westlake to P.G. Wodehouse and said of *Smoke,* "Squirrel it away for emergency use the next time you find yourself stuck in an airport lounge with a departure time of maybe. The bartender may resent the fact that you're too busy laughing to order another drink, but you'll definitely feel better in the morning."

Between 1998 and 2000, Westlake wielded *The Ax* and *The Hook,* two thrillers that take a decidedly grim view of the effects of modern society. In *The Ax,* described by D. Keith Mano in his *New York Times Book Review* article as "pretty much flawless," downsized executive Burke Devore decides—literally—to kill off the competition as he strives to reestablish himself in the paper business. While a *Kirkus Reviews* writer noted a lack of "any sense of cumulative horror or revulsion" in Devore's systematic assassinations, the review also acknowledged Westlake's expertise in the genre as he "rises effortlessly to the challenge of varying these executions [and] keeping up the tension."

With *The Hook,* Westlake again examines the lengths one will go to in order to strike it rich in a competitive society. This time, famous novelist Bryce Proctorr, facing a deadline and a severe case of writer's block, meets up with old friend Wayne Prentice, a struggling writer who happens to have a promising manuscript in his hands. The two strike a Faustian bargain—Prentice will let Proctorr submit the novel as his own, and the two will split the hefty book advance. But the deal is more complex: Wayne must also kill Bryce's wife, who would stand to devour Proctorr's profits in messy divorce proceedings. "Like *The Ax,*" remarked *Kirkus Reviews, The Hook* shows the often-genial Westlake "at his dourest." And while the novel's "opening conceits are clever," wrote *New York Times Book Review* contributor Valerie Sayers, the author "doesn't play it for the satire; [instead] he concentrates on building suspense with as many twists and bends as a plot can endure." Craig Shufelt, writing in *Library Journal,* also concluded that though *The Hook* "is not a comfortable read—there are no heroes to cheer for"—Westlake still earns plaudits for producing a book "this reader was unable [put] down."

To Sublett, "the bulk of Westlake's work [since the early 1970s] proved that he's just as good at being soft-boiled and biting and satirical as he is at being dark and suspenseful." In some of the author's most successful works, "he had already pushed the envelope just about as far as it could be pushed. Push it a little farther, the envelope turns inside out, and the payoff for a suspenseful setup isn't a sock in the jaw . . . but a tickled funny bone." In quoting the author, Sublett pointed out that "the line between noir suspense and dark comedy is a fine one. Or as Westlake says, 'It's the other side of the same street.'"

BIOGRAPHICAL AND CRITICAL SOURCES:

BOOKS

Contemporary Authors Autobiography Series, Volume 13, Thomson Gale (Detroit, MI), 1991.

Contemporary Literary Criticism, Thomson Gale (Detroit, MI), Volume 7, 1977, Volume 33, 1985.

PERIODICALS

Armchair Detective, spring, 1995, p. 206; winter, 1996, p. 106.
Austin Chronicle, December 29, 1997, "No Prozac for the Wicked."
Booklist, August, 1995, p. 1911; January 1, 2000, review of *The Hook.*
Connoisseur, December, 1989.
Entertainment Weekly, February 28, 1992; April 2, 1993; May 12, 1995, p. 59.
Film Quarterly, winter, 1987.
Harper's, September, 1988.
Kirkus Reviews, May 15, 1997, review of *The Ax;* January 15, 2000, review of *The Hook,* p. 88.
Library Journal, July, 1994, p. 130; November 1, 1994, p. 126; January, 1995, p. 158; February 1, 2000, review of *The Hook,* p. 120.
Los Angeles Times, February 28, 1983; August 7, 1985.
Los Angeles Times Book Review, April 25, 1981; July 13, 1986; May 8, 1988; June 4, 1989; April 15, 1990; March 1, 1992; September 11, 1994, p. 18.
Ms., June, 1986.
National Review, February 16, 1973.
New Republic, December 13, 1975.
New Statesman, January 10, 1986.
Newsweek, February 21, 1983; April 22, 1985; July 18, 1988; September 5, 1994.
New York, July 3 1989.
New Yorker, August 15, 1988.
New York Times, March 5, 1982; February 24, 2000, review of *The Hook,* p. B9.
New York Times Book Review, November 19, 1972; June 3, 1973; July 14, 1974; May 18, 1975; October 31, 1976; October 2, 1977; April 13, 1980; May 16, 1982; January 9, 1983; June 22, 1986; July 10, 1988; July 30, 1989; October 15, 1989; April 8, 1990; April 14, 1991; June 28, 1992; September 11, 1994, p. 20; October 8, 1995, p. 3; March 19, 2000, "Publish or Perish."
Observer (London, England), February 9, 1986.
People, November 6, 1989; October 24, 1994.
Publishers Weekly, January 17, 2000, review of *The Hook,* p. 43.
Saturday Review, May 29, 1971; September 25, 1971.
Spectator, January 29, 1977.
Time, July 22, 1974; August 8, 1988.
Times Literary Supplement, September 24, 1971; December 7, 1979.
Tribune Books (Chicago, IL), April 25, 1982; November 9, 1986; October 1, 1989; April 1, 1990; October 1, 1995, p. 4.
Wall Street Journal, September 30, 1994.
Washington Post, December 24, 1984; July 23, 1985.
Washington Post Book World, May 18, 1986; March 22, 1992; March 29, 1992; December 17, 1995, p. 11.
West Coast Review of Books, September 1986; Volume 13, number 6, 1988.

ONLINE

Donald Westlake Home Page, http://www.donaldwestlake.com/ (October 16, 2004).

* * *

WESTLAKE, Donald Edwin
See WESTLAKE, Donald E.

* * *

WHITE, Edmund 1940-
(Edmund Valentine White, III)

PERSONAL: Born January 13, 1940, in Cincinnati, OH; son of Edmund Valentine II (an engineer) and Delilah (a psychologist; maiden name, Teddlie) White. *Education:* University of Michigan, B.A., 1962.

ADDRESSES: Office—Princeton University, Department of Creative Writing, 185 Nassau St., Princeton, NJ 08544. *Agent*—Amanda Urban, ICM, 40 West 57th St., New York, NY 10019. *E-mail*—ewhite@mail.princeton.edu.

CAREER: Time, Inc., Book Division, New York, NY, staff writer, 1962-70; *Saturday Review,* New York, NY, senior editor, 1972-73; Johns Hopkins University, Baltimore, MD, assistant professor of writing seminars, 1977-79; Columbia University School of the Arts, New York, NY, adjunct professor of creative writing, 1981-83; New York Institute for the Humanities, executive director, 1982-83; Brown University, Providence, RI, professor of English, 1990-92; Princeton University, Princeton, NJ, professor in creative writing, 1998—. Instructor in creative writing at Yale University, New Haven, CT, New York University, New York, NY, and George Mason University, Fairfax, VA. Member of jury, Booker Prize, 1989.

MEMBER: American Academy of Arts and Letters (member of awards committee, 1999-2000), American Academy of Arts and Sciences.

AWARDS, HONORS: Hopwood Awards, University of Michigan, 1961 and 1962, for fiction and drama; Ingram Merrill grants, 1973 and 1978; Guggenheim fellow, 1983; American Academy and Institute of Arts and Letters award for fiction, 1983; citation for appeal and value to youth from Enoch Pratt Free Library's Young Adult Advisory Board, 1988, for *The Beautiful Room Is Empty;* chevalier, Ordre des Arts et Lettres (France), 1993; National Book Critics Circle award for biography, 1994, for *Genet: A Biography;* honorary doctorate, State University of New York at Oneonta, 2000, Deauville Festival prize (France), 2000; Ferro-Grumley Award, Publishing Triangle, 2003, for *The Married Man.*

WRITINGS:

NOVELS

Forgetting Elena, Random House (New York, NY), 1973.

Nocturnes for the King of Naples, St. Martin's Press (New York, NY), 1978.

A Boy's Own Story, Dutton (New York, NY), 1982, with new introduction by White, 1994.

Caracole, Dutton (New York, NY), 1985.

The Beautiful Room Is Empty, Knopf (New York, NY), 1988.

The Farewell Symphony, Knopf (New York, NY), 1997.

The Married Man, Knopf (New York, NY), 2000.

Fanny: A Fiction, Ecco/HarperCollins (New York, NY), 2003.

OTHER

Blue Boy in Black (play), produced Off-Broadway, 1963.

(With Peter Wood) *When Zeppelins Flew,* Time-Life (Alexandria, VA), 1969.

(With Dale Browne) *The First Men,* Time-Life (Alexandria, VA), 1973.

(With Charles Silverstein) *The Joy of Gay Sex: An Intimate Guide for Gay Men to the Pleasures of a Gay Lifestyle,* Crown (New York, NY), 1977.

States of Desire: Travels in Gay America, Dutton (New York, NY), 1980.

(With others) *Aphrodisiac* (short stories), Chatto & Windus (London, England), 1984.

(With Adam Mars-Jones) *The Darker Proof: Stories from a Crisis,* New American Library/Plume (New York, NY), 1988.

(Editor) *The Faber Book of Gay Short Fiction,* Faber & Faber (Winchester, MA), 1991.

(Compiler) *The Selected Writings of Jean Genet,* Ecco Press (New York, NY), 1993.

Genet: A Biography, Knopf (New York, NY), 1993.

The Burning Library: Essays, edited by David Bergman, Knopf (New York, NY), 1994.

Skinned Alive: Stories, Knopf (New York, NY), 1995.

Our Paris: Sketches from Memory, Knopf (New York, NY), 1995.

Marcel Proust ("Penguin Lives" series), Viking (New York, NY), 1999.

The Flaneur: A Stroll through the Paradoxes of Paris ("The Writer and the City" series), Bloomsbury (New York, NY), 2001.

(Editor) *Loss within Loss: Artists in the Age of AIDS,* University of Wisconsin Press (Madison, WI), 2001.

Arts and Letters, Cleis Press (San Francisco), 2004.

Also author of *Argument for Myth.* Contributor to anthologies, including *The Fabric of Memory: Ewa Kuryluk: Cloth Works, 1978-1987,* Northwestern University Press, 1987. Contributor of articles and reviews to *New York Times,* London *Observer, Los Angeles Times, Architectural Digest, Artforum International, Home and Garden, Mother Jones, New York Times Book Review, Savvy Woman, Southwest Review,* and other periodicals. Editor, *Saturday Review* and *Horizon;* contributing editor, *Vogue.*

SIDELIGHTS: American author Edmund White has produced highly acclaimed novels, insightful nonfiction on gay society, and semi-autobiographical novels that combine the best features of fiction and nonfiction. Known as a "gay writer," White also belongs among those writers whose literary reputations transcend simplistic labels. William Goldstein explained in *Publishers Weekly,* "To call Edmund White merely a gay writer is to oversimplify his work and his intentions. Although that two-word label . . . aptly sums up White's status, the first word no doubt helps obscure the fact that the second applies just as fittingly." White's studies of the gay lifestyle and changing attitudes about homosexuality in America, including the impact of AIDS on the gay community, are considered important contributions to late twentieth-century social history. Though male homosexuality is the subject of his nonfiction, White offers insights into human behavior in general, according to reviewers. *Nation* contributor Carter Wilson commented, "White is to be envied not only for his productivity . . . but because he is a gifted writer who has staked himself a distinguished claim in the rocky territory called desire."

Critics praised White's first novel, *Forgetting Elena,* for its satiric and insightful look at social interaction as well as for its elegant prose. A first-person narrative of an amnesia victim struggling to determine his identity and the identities of those around him, *Forgetting Elena* exposes the subtle entrapments of social hierarchy and etiquette. White told *Library Journal* that the novel's premise illustrates the "sinister" aspects of life in an artistically obsessed society. In such a culture, he explained, "Every word and gesture would . . . convey a symbolic meaning. Ordinary morality would be obscured or forgotten. People would seek the beautiful and not the good—and, perhaps, cut free from the ethics, the beautiful would turn out to be merely pretty." Setting the novel's action at a fictitious resort reminiscent of New York's Fire Island, White creates, in the words of *Nation* contributor Simon Karlinsky, "a semiology of snobbery, its complete sign system." Karlinsky stated that "what might at first seem to be merely a witty parody of a particular subculture's foibles and vagaries actually turns out to be something far more serious and profound. . . . He has produced a parable about the nature of social interaction that transcends any given period and applies to the human predicament at large."

Most critics consider *Forgetting Elena* a highly accomplished first novel. Karlinsky called the work "an astounding piece of writing—profound, totally convincing and memorable." Alan Friedman likewise praised the book in *New York Times Book Review,* though not without qualifications. Friedman wrote, "There is something so unfailingly petty about the narrator's apprehensions . . . and something so oppressive about his preoccupations . . . that it is often difficult to be receptive to the book's genuine wonders." Friedman nevertheless concluded that this "tale of a sleuth who strives to detect the mystery of the self" is "an astonishing first novel, obsessively fussy, yet uncannily beautiful."

Nocturnes for the King of Naples, White's second novel, won acclaim for its discerning treatment of human values and relationships. As John Yohalem explained in *New York Times Book Review, Nocturnes* "is a series of apostrophes to a nameless, evidently famous dead lover, a man who awakened the much younger, also nameless narrator . . . to the possibility of sexual friendship. It was an experience that the narrator feels he did not justly appreciate," Yohalem continued, "and that he has long and passionately—and fruitlessly—sought to replace on his own terms." David Shields wrote in *Chicago Tribune,* "Because of the speaker's final realization of the impossibility of ever finding a ground for satisfaction, a home, this book is more than a chronicle of sorrow and regret. It becomes, rather, a true elegy in which sorrow and self-knowledge combine and transform into a higher form of insight. This higher insight is the artistic intuition of the mortality of human things and ways."

While Doris Grumbach suggested in *Washington Post Book World* that White "will seem to the careful reader to be the poet of the burgeoning homosexual literature," she also noted, "The music of White's prose is seductive. It is of course possible that a tone-deaf, a melody-indifferent reader might turn his back on White's homoerotic narrative." However, she added, White's prose in *Nocturnes* promises satisfaction to "the lover of good fictional writing who is open to this most subtle exploration of the many ways of love, desertion, loss, and regret."

Caracole goes back to an earlier century and retrieves a more elaborate fictional form. Christopher Lehmann-Haupt observed in *New York Times* that White has "certainly conceived a nineteenth century plot steeped in the conventions of romanticism" when he writes of two country lovers forcibly separated who turn to sexual escapades in a large city. The resulting story is a "puzzling melange of comic opera and sleek sensuality," added the reviewer. *New York Times Book Review* contributor David R. Slavitt described *Caracole* as "a grand fantasy. . . . Shrewdness and self-awareness ooze from every intricate sentence, every linguistic arabesque and hothouse epigram." Slavitt concluded that *Caracole* "is, provokingly, a challenge to taste, which is likely to vary from one reader to another or even from moment to moment in the same reader."

White's novel *The Married Man,* called his "most readable novel" by David Bergman in *Review of Contemporary Fiction,* is about the relationship between Austin, an American writer living in Paris, and Julien, a younger married architect Austin meets in a gym and with whom he forges an alliance. The pair travel together and eventually return to Providence, Rhode Island where Austin is to teach a class. Austin is HIV positive, but healthy, and Julien promises to care for him until the end, but it is Julien who wastes away from AIDS, whereupon Austin discovers that Julien's life had been one of secrets and lies. "What is most interesting, however," wrote Alice Truax in *New York Times Book Review,* "is not the revelations themselves but how little the facts really matter: if Julien deceived Austin, Austin also collaborated in his deception. After all, it was that subtle blend of shared illusions and private realities that had nourished the marriage and made it possible—and White seems to be suggesting, perhaps the same can be said of most marriages." Like Julien in the book, White's own lover, Frenchman Hubert Sorin, died in Morocco of AIDS at age thirty-three. *The Married Man* is loosely based on White's years with Sorin.

In *Fanny: A Fiction* White presents what *People* reviewer Bella Stander dubbed a "witty and richly imagined" fictional biography of early nineteenth-century Scottish-born protofeminist Frances "Fanny" Wright. Purportedly authored by Frances "Fanny" Trollope—mother to more famous author Anthony Trollope—the novel is written in a style that mimics Trollope's perfunctory, sometimes harsh, and often unknowingly humorous prose. In the novel, Wright has founded Nashoba, a utopian colony of freed slaves located in Tennessee, and it is here she invites her struggling writer friend, in the hopes that the visit will provide literary inspiration for her *Domestic Manners of the Americans.* At the core of the book is middle-aged Fanny, whom Wright describes as "a funny little snaggle-toothed old woman with ratty hair," along with three of her six children and a French artist, joins Wright on the trip to America, a trip that sets the stage for the rest of the novel. As *New Statesman* contributor Carmen Callil described it, Wright "sails first class, while the Trollope family suffers amid the vomit and creaking of steerage. Nothing improves on arrival; Fanny Trollope's adventures lead her to be disappointed with—and even to hate—America, a place where men pass the day spitting at walls, where utopians and democrats pontificate about about God and indulge in an 'acrobatic Christianity,' which includes demonic treatment of their slaves." Although Callil noted that White's inclusion of a "plethora of historical detail" can sometimes be overwhelming, *Fanny* "captures with an amusing cattiness both Trollope's sharpness of tongue and Wright's self-delusion," noted Penelope Mesic in her *Book* review, while in *Publishers Weekly* a reviewer noted that "Trollope's struggle to maintain her own little bit of interior civilization is a joy to witness."

White's concern about AIDS has left its mark on his writing, particularly his short fiction, collected in *The Darker Proof* and *Skinned Alive: Stories.* Among the eight tales in the latter collection, several feature "gay love and loss in the shadow of AIDS" as a central motif, commented Maxine Chernoff in Chicago's *Tribune Books.* In "Running on Empty," a man returns to his hometown in Texas after traveling in Europe and confronts his worsening illness. "Palace Days" offers a love triangle in which one character is dying of AIDS while another, though healthy, is coping with the recent discovery that he is HIV-positive. And in "An Oracle," a man grieving for his dead lover falls in love with a young man while traveling in Greece.

"What Edmund White conjures here is a serious, sustained look at how AIDS measures and shapes the meaning of our existence," commented *Los Angeles Times Book Review* contributor Michael Bronski. While noting that the stories dealing with AIDS are "rarely somber," *New York Times Book Review* commentator Morris Dickstein wrote that "in the best stories . . . the author sometimes gives way to a sadness that reverberates more deeply than in anything else he has written." "White is never ponderous but vastly compassionate, and has the grace to be humorous in his compassion," remarked Alberto Manguel in the London *Observer.* James Woods, reviewing *Skinned Alive* for *London Review of Books,* commended "the scattered gorgeousness" in White's writing and concluded that the collection "shows us that for all his confusions, White has lost none of his artistry." As Chernoff observed, White's "subject is the human condition, no matter our sexual practices, and our final estrangement from each other, despite our efforts to hold on."

White's nonfiction on gay life in America is considered by many to be as compelling as his fiction. *The Joy of Gay Sex: An Intimate Guide for Gay Men to the Pleasures of a Gay Lifestyle,* published in the late 1970s, attempted to make the topic less mysterious for curious heterosexuals and to provide useful information for gay men. In 1980 White published *States of Desire: Travels in Gay America.* A documentary on segments of homosexual life in fifteen major American cities, *States of Desire* contains interviews, autobiographical reminiscences, and accounts of cultural and entertainment centers for gays. According to Ned Rorem in *Washington Post Book World, States of Desire* "poses as a documentary . . . on our national gay bourgeoisie. Actually it's an artist's selective vision . . . of human comportment which is and is not his own, mulled over, distilled, then spilled onto the page with a melancholy joy."

The Joy of Gay Sex and *States of Desire* qualified White as one of the first prominent spokespersons for gay men in America. He knew that publishing these works would engage him in politics to some extent. He explained in a *Paris Review* interview, "It was a political act for me to sign *The Joy of Gay Sex* at the time. The publisher could not have cared less, but for me it was a big act of coming out. Charles Silverstein, my co-author, and I were both aware that we would be addressing a lot of people and so in that sense we were spokesmen. We always pictured our ideal reader as someone who thought he was the only homosexual in the world. *States of Desire* was an attempt to see the varieties of gay experience and also to suggest the enormous range of gay life to straight and gay people—to show that gays aren't just hairdressers, they're also petroleum engineers and ranchers and short-order cooks."

Since the 1980s White has continued his role as a social historian on the homosexual experience in America. He writes with particular authority about the gay liberation movement because he has been an active participant in it since the Stonewall riot in New York City in 1969. Police had raided the discotheque and the gay men fought back in what is now seen as the official beginning of the campaign for homosexual rights. "The riot itself I considered a rather silly event at the time," he recalled in his *Paris Review* interview; "it seemed more Dada than Bastille, a kind of romp. But I participated in that and then was active from the very beginning in gay liberation. We had these gatherings which were patterned after women's and ultimately, I think, Maoist consciousness-raising sessions. Whether or not our sessions accomplished anything for society, they were certainly useful to all of us as a tool for changing ourselves." Before that time, he explained, gay men tended to think of themselves as primarily heterosexual except for certain sexual habits—"but we weren't homosexuals as people. Even the notion of a homosexual culture would have seemed comical or ridiculous to us, certainly horrifying."

White believes that gay writers should recognize the historical significance of the AIDS epidemic in the context of the larger culture in which they live. In *Rolling Stone* he noted: "No American phenomenon has been as compelling since the Vietnam War, which itself involved most of the same themes. Although obviously a greater tragedy, the war nevertheless took place on a different continent and invited a more familiar political analysis. We knew how to protest the war. In the rancorous debates over AIDS, all the issues are fuzzy and the moral imperatives all questions."

White maintains that while the tragedy of AIDS has caused the gay liberation movement some daunting setbacks, it has not been the only factor in the movement's mixed success. He explained in *Mother Jones:* "Gay liberation grew out of the progressive spirit of the 1960s—a strange and exhilarating blend of socialism, feminism and the human potential movement. Accordingly, what gay leaders in the late 1960s were anticipating was the emergence of the androgyne [a kind of person neither specifically masculine nor feminine], but what they got was the superbutch stud [a muscle-bound type whose homosexuality is a heightened form of masculine aggression]; what they expected was a communal hippie freedom from possessions, but what has developed is the acme of capitalist consumerism. Gays . . . consume expensive vacations, membership in gyms and discos, cars, elegant furnishings, clothes, haircuts, theater tickets and records. . . . Unfortunately, today this rampant and ubiquitous consumerism not only characterizes gay spending habits but also infects attitudes toward sexuality: gays rate each other quantitatively according to age, physical dimensions and income; and all too many gays consume and dispose of each other, as though the act of possession brought about instant obsolescence." White pointed out that finding a solution to this problem, as it is for the AIDS epidemic, is important not only for gays, but for all Americans.

Many of the essays in which White explores the intersection of homosexuality, culture, and AIDS are collected in *The Burning Library: Essays.* Consisting of forty pieces, many of them previously published, the collection chronicles White's literary and personal odyssey from the pre-Stonewall period to the sexually liberating 1970s and into the devastation wrought by AIDS in the 1980s and 1990s. Noting the "unparalleled stylistic elegance deployed" in these essays, *Observer* reviewer Jonathan Keates characterized White as being "armed with [a] . . . deep moral awareness and the . . . ability to charm the socks off the reader even while retailing unpalatable truths." Writing in *Los Angeles Times,* Chris Goodrich called *The Burning Library* "strikingly traditional, a writer's attempt to fathom his own identity and that of the subculture in which he works and lives."

Times Literary Supplement contributor Neil Powell claimed that the more personal essays in *The Burning Library* are stronger than those in which White discusses other writers and their works. Commented Powell, "White's admirable capacity for sympathetic understanding not only inhibits his critical judgment but actually weakens the case being argued." Goodrich, focusing on the more personal essays, noted that White's "reflections on AIDS are uncommonly thoughtful." Keates concurred, writing that White's "own HIV-positive status might have fueled him with accusatory hysteria and recrimination. Instead . . . he has challenged mortality with these noble fragments."

In addition to his social commentary, White has also made his mark as a biographer, and his interest and familiarity with French culture are evident in both *Genet:*

A Biography and *Marcel Proust.* White spent seven years researching and writing the biography of acclaimed writer Jean Genet, interviewing those who knew Genet and examining Genet's literary output. He chronicles the writer's early hardships—being abandoned by his parents and becoming a ward of the state—his adolescent initiation into stealing, which became a lifelong addiction, his first burst of literary creativity during the 1940s, which resulted in five novels and secured his fame, and his turbulent personal life, marked by his homosexuality and his apparent brutish ways towards friends and lovers alike. Noting Genet's legendary habit of falsifying the events of his life, *New York Review of Books* reviewer Tony Judt commended White for attempting "to unravel the threads that Genet so assiduously knotted and crossed in his various writings and interviews."

Critical reaction to *Genet* was mostly positive, with several reviewers calling the biography a definitive work. Writing in Chicago's *Tribune Books,* Thomas McGonigle said that "White has written a wonderfully readable account of a thoroughly repulsive individual," adding that the author "brings to bear on the life of Genet a grand literary sensibility." Similarly, *Los Angeles Times Book Review* contributor Daniel Harris called the work "an extraordinarily lucid biography" and noted, "White delights in ferreting out Genet's most compromising secrets." Some reviewers criticized White for focusing too heavily on Genet's homosexuality as a means of interpreting his life and literary output. Judt, for instance, stated that occasionally White falls "victim to his own anachronistic concern with sexual preference as a key to aesthetic appreciation." Writing in *New York Times Book Review,* Isabelle de Courtivron concurred, noting that "at times White comes perilously close to reducing his subject's complex works to an overinterpretation in light of" Genet's homosexuality. Nevertheless, added the critic, White's work "is so meticulously researched and detailed, his understanding and illumination of the works is so rich, that the book ultimately succeeds in resisting the nagging temptation of reductionism." *New York Times Book Review* contributor Margo Jefferson concluded by saying that White "presents the life meticulously, reads Genet's work intelligently and writes beautifully." Reflecting the positive critical opinion of the book, *Genet* was awarded the National Book Critics Circle award for biography in 1994.

White's biography of French writer Marcel Proust is one of the first in the "Penguin Lives" series that *New York Times Book Review* contributor Peter Ackroyd said "bear[s] testimony to the fact that biographical narratives can aspire to art rather than to history." Ackroyd described the volume as issuing "from imagination and intuition as much as from scholarship and research." Ackroyd continued, "White explores the pathology of a man who was passionate and yet oblique, rhetorical and secretive; sentimental and yet clearsighted, innocent and depraved—a great writer condemned as a flaneur and a gossip who wrote a masterpiece. It requires the skill and intuition of an imaginative artist to make these aspects cohere within a single and living portrait."

In addition to his accomplished fiction and nonfiction, White has produced several semi-autobiographical works that bring together the best features of both kinds of writing, beginning with *A Boy's Own Story,* a first-person narrative of a homosexual boy's adolescence during the 1950s. As a *Harper's* reviewer described it, *A Boy's Own Story* "is a poignant combination of the two genres . . . written with the flourish of a master stylist." The main conflict in this psychological novel is the narrator's battle against negative judgments from society and from within. Emotional turmoil related to homosexuality, though prominent in the novel, is only one difficulty among many related to coming of age, *Harper's* reviewer observed. *A Boy's Own Story* "is an endearing portrait of a child's longing to be charming, popular, powerful, and loved, and of his struggles with adults . . . told with . . . sensitivity and elegance."

More than one reviewer has called *A Boy's Own Story* a "classic" work. Comparing White to James Baldwin, Herman Wouk, and Mary McCarthy, Thomas M. Disch wrote in *Washington Post Book World* that the novel "represents the strongest bid to date by a gay writer to do for his minority experience what the writers above did for theirs—offer it as a representative, all-American instance." *New York Times Book Review* contributor Catharine R. Stimpson found the book "as artful as [White's] earlier novels but more explicit and grounded in detail, far less fanciful and elusive. . . . Balancing the banal and the savage, the funny and the lovely, he achieves a wonderfully poised fiction." *Voice Literary Supplement* columnist Eliot Fremont-Smith concluded, "*A Boy's Own Story* seems intended to be liberating, as well as touching and clever and smart. It is something else as well: unsettling to the willing heart. This makes it a problem, with no happy solution guaranteed, which defines what's wrong with the book. But also what's right, what intrigues." Lehmann-Haupt called the work "superior fiction," adding: "Somehow . . . White does succeed in almost simultaneously elevating and demeaning his self-history. And these extremes of epiphany and emptiness are what is most universal about this haunting Bildungsroman."

In *The Beautiful Room Is Empty,* the sequel to *A Boy's Own Story,* the narrator alternately revels in his homosexuality and rejects himself for it. Psychoanalysis and increasing surrender to sensual activity escalate the young man's battle for self-acceptance. Though his sexuality troubles him, the excitement and audacity of his experiences with gay men in public restrooms seems a needed respite from the blandness of his suburban life. While recreating these scenes, White evokes both humor and terror. The gay characters easily upstage the others in the book with their outspoken opinions, witty banter, and daring sexual exploits, while "White takes us through [the narrator's] unsentimental education like an indulgent pal, making graceful introductions, filling in with pungent details, saving his harshest judgments for himself," Vince Aletti wrote in *Voice Literary Supplement.* Sometimes the adolescent makes bold moves—as when he shouts "Gay is good!" in a Greenwich Village demonstration. At other times, he acts out his self-loathing, as when he seduces his music teacher and betrays him to the authorities. By depicting both kinds of behavior, the narrator helps White to evoke "the cautious emergence of a gay consciousness" taking place in the surrounding culture, Aletti said.

Some readers did not see how one could come away from *The Beautiful Room Is Empty* with a good feeling about homosexuality. In answer to these critics, White explained in a *Village Voice* interview that his role is not that of a propagandist, but that of a historian. He said, "I like to describe the way people actually are. Some rather young people don't see the historical point of *The Beautiful Room Is Empty.* . . . I was trying to point out that people were even more oppressed [in the 1960s] than they are today." Addressing the topic again in a *Publishers Weekly* interview, the author said, "I feel it wouldn't be true to the experience of the characters if I showed them gliding blissfully through, when it was obviously a painful thing coming out in a period before gay liberation." A *Time* reviewer concluded, "In the era of AIDS, White's novel is a fiercely remembered plea not to push gays back into the closet."

The title of White's *The Farewell Symphony,* is taken from a Haydn symphony that ends with the orchestra leaving the stage, until only the violin remains. Another autobiographical work, it follows his life from the 1970s to the 1990s, from New York to his expatriation, first in Rome, then in Paris. It also follows his success as a writer, and his friends, including those he has lost to AIDS. Kent D. Wolf wrote in *Review of Contemporary Fiction* of the first time period covered by the book, saying, "White's apparent nonstop sexfest . . . seems to defy logic; at one point the narrator does some math and figures he had over 3,000 partners between 1962 and 1982. . . . Putting all calculators . . . aside, amidst all this kissing is plenty of telling." The narrator writes of his growing success as a writer, of his father's death, and his sister's coming to terms with her lesbianism. A *Publishers Weekly* reviewer felt the book is best enjoyed "for its luminous snapshots of New York, Paris, and Rome, and of the vital parade of men—dowdy, forbiddingly gorgeous, sylph-like, ephebic, closeted, defiantly and militantly out that crowd its pages." *Booklist* contributor Whitney Scott called White "an older, maturer talent reflecting on the sweeping power of friendship, caring, and love in all its aspects."

Discussing the role of writer, White believes that originality is the creative writer's foremost concern. As he explained to interviewer Larry McCaffery in *Alive and Writing: Interviews:* "There are two ways of looking at literature. One is to feel that there is one great Platonic novel in the sky that we're all striving toward. I find that view to be very deadening, finally, and certainly it's a terrible view for a teacher or a critic to hold. The other view is that each person has a chance to write his or her own book in his or her own voice; maturing as an artist occurs when you find your own voice, when you write something that *only you* could have written. That's the view I have."

In a *Paris Review* interview White described the two impulses—toward fiction and nonfiction—between which he balances his writing, saying, "Writers can use literature as a mirror held up to the world, or they can use writing as a consolation for life (in the sense that literature is preferable to reality). I prefer the second approach, although clearly there has to be a blend of both. If the writing is pure fantasy it doesn't connect to any of our real feelings. But if it's grim realism, that doesn't seem like much of a gift. I think literature should be a gift to the reader, and that gift is in idealization. I don't mean it should be a whitewashing of problems, but something ideally energetic. Ordinary life is *blah,* whereas literature at its best is bristling with energy."

At a time when books by gay writers are not as widely read as he hopes they will be, White, who once had a novel rejected by twenty-two different publishers, admits to being thrilled by the recognition his writing has received. "I know I'll always be doing this," he told *Publishers Weekly,* "and I know that I'll never make a living from my writing; but that's fine. It's enough to be published. . . . I don't have very exalted notions of what a writer's life should be like." Concurrent with his career as an author, White has taught creative writing at several East Coast universities, including Johns Hopkins, Columbia, and Yale. His reviews and profiles appear frequently in *Vogue* and other magazines. He also writes travel articles, and, from his home in Paris, reports on contemporary trends in art and politics, and French social history.

BIOGRAPHICAL AND CRITICAL SOURCES:

BOOKS

Barber, Stephen, *Edmund White: The Burning World,* St. Martin's Press (New York, NY), 1999.

Contemporary Literary Criticism, Thomson Gale (Detroit, MI), Volume 27, 1984, Volume 110, 1999.

Dictionary of Literary Biography, Volume 227: *American Novelists Since World War II, Sixth Series,* Thomson Gale (Detroit, MI), 2000.

Gay and Lesbian Biography, St. James Press (Detroit, MI), 1997.

McCaffery, Larry, *Alive and Writing: Interviews,* University Press of Illinois (Champaign, IL), 1987.

PERIODICALS

Advocate, October 5, 1993; September 16, 1997, Sarah Schulman, "The White Party" (interview), p. 61; January 20, 1998, review of *The Farewell Symphony,* p. 102; March 2, 1999, Robert Plunket, review of *Marcel Proust,* p. 65; June 20, 2000, David Bahr, "French Lessons," p. 137, Robert Plunket, review of *The Married Man,* p. 138; April 10, 2001, David Bahr, review of *Loss within Loss: Artists in the Age of AIDS,* p. 66.

American Prospect, May 7, 2001, David L. Kirp, review of *Loss within Loss,* p. 51.

Artforum, January, 1987.

Bloomsbury Review, January, 1998, review of *The Farewell Symphony,* p. 20.

Book, November-December, 2003, Penelope Mesic, review of *Fanny: A Fiction,* p. 86.

Booklist, October 1, 1994; June 1, 1995, p. 732; November 1, 1995, p. 453; September 15, 1997, Whitney Scott, review of *The Farewell Symphony,* p. 211; December 1, 1998, Bryce Christensen, review of *Marcel Proust,* p. 646; May 1, 2000, Donna Seaman, review of *The Married Man,* p. 1654; February 15, 2001, Whitney Scott, review of *Loss within Loss,* p. 1105, Brad Hooper, review of *The Flaneur: A Stroll through the Paradoxes of Paris,* p. 1113; September 15, 2003, Michael Spinella, review of *Fanny,* p. 212.

Chicago Tribune, December 10, 1978; April 6, 1980; February 14, 1994; December 1, 1998, review of *Marcel Proust,* p. 646.

Entertainment Weekly, October 10, 2003, John Freeman, review of *Fanny,* p. 127.

Gay & Lesbian Review, fall, 2000, Christopher Hennessy, "'I See My Life as a Novel as I'm Leading It'" (interview), p. 26, Martha E. Stone, "Sketches from Memory," p. 53; winter, 2000, Nick Radel, "Travels of Young Edmund," p. 48; May, 2001, Karl Woelz, "Epitaph to a Genre," p. 43; September, 2001, p. 43; July-August, 2003, Chris Freeman, interview with White, p. 10.

Harper's, March, 1979; October, 1982; May, 1987.

Journal of European Studies, July, 2003, p. 161.

Kirkus Reviews, October 15, 1998, review of *Marcel Proust,* p. 1522; January 1, 2002, review of *The Flaneur,* p. 44.

Lambda Book Report, June, 2000, Robert Gluck, "The Whole Man in Love," p. 15; March, 2001, Jameson Currier, "The Price We Paid," p. 14.

Library Journal, February 15, 1973; October 1, 1994, p. 82; June 15, 1995, p. 95; November 15, 1995, p. 92; February 1, 1996, p. 75; September 15, 1997, Eric Bryant, review of *The Farewell Symphony,* p. 104; January, 1999, Diane G. Premo, review of *Marcel Proust,* p. 98; May 15, 2000, Brian Kenney, review of *The Married Man,* p. 127; February 15, 2001, Ravi Shenoy, review of *The Flaneur,* p. 190; March 15, 2001, Krista Ivy, review of *Loss within Loss,* p. 83.

Life, fall, 1989, Edmund White, "Residence on Earth: Living with AIDS in the '80s."

London Review of Books, April 17, 1986; March 3, 1988; June 10, 1993, p. 3; August 24, 1995, p. 12.

Los Angeles Times, January 12, 1994, p. C7; September 19, 1997, Charlotte Innes, "He's a Pillar to Some, a Source of Strife for Others" (interview), p. 1.

Los Angeles Times Book Review, May 4, 1980; April 3, 1982; November 21, 1993, p. 1; July 16, 1995, p. 4; December 14, 1997, Michael Frank, review of *The Farewell Symphony,* p. 5; January 22, 1999, Michael Frank, review of *Marcel Proust,* p. 6.

Mother Jones, June, 1983.

Nation, January 5, 1974; March 1, 1980; November 13, 1982; November 16, 1985; April 9, 1988; January 3, 1994; August 28, 1995, p. 214; October 20, 1997, Alfred Corn, review of *The Farewell Symphony,* p. 35.

New Republic, February 21, 1994; July 12, 1999, Andre Aciman, "Inversions," p. 35.

New Statesman, March 14, 1986; January 29, 1988; June 17, 1994, p. 38; February 26, 1999, Charlotte Raven, review of *Marcel Proust,* p. 53; September 1, 2003, Carmen Callil, review of *Fanny,* p. 37.

New Yorker, February 8, 1999, review of *Marcel Proust,* p. 80.

New York Review of Books, October 21, 1993, p. 15; March 18, 1999, Roger Shattuck, review of *Marcel Proust,* p. 10; August 10, 2000, John Banville, review of *The Married Man,* p. 42.

New York Times, January 21, 1980; December 17, 1982; September 8, 1985; March 17, 1988; December 8, 1993, p. C23.

New York Times Book Review, March 25, 1973; December 10, 1978; February 3, 1980; October 10, 1982; September 15, 1985; March 20, 1988; November 7, 1993; October 23, 1994, p. 18; July 23, 1995, p. 6; December 3, 1995, p. 50; September 14, 1997, Christopher Benfey, review of *The Farewell Symphony,* p. 11; November 1, 1998, review of *The Farewell Symphony,* p. 36; January 10, 1999, Peter Ackroyd, "Biography: The Short Form," p. 4; July 2, 2000, Alice Truax, "An Ideal Husband," p. 5; April 8, 2001, Angeline Goreau, "A Walker in the Cité," p. 7.

Observer (London, England), March 16, 1986; December 14, 1986; January 24, 1988; November 13, 1988; June 20, 1993; June 19, 1994; June 14, 1995; July 12, 1998, review of *The Farewell Symphony,* p. 18; February 28, 1999, Robert McCrum, "Books: Home to Proust," p. 11; August 8, 1999, Stephen Barber, "Arts: Edmund White Went to a Bath House for Sex, and Found a Whole New World—of Art, Love and Loss," p. 5; February 4, 2001, Peter Conrad, review of *The Flaneur,* p. 16.

Paris Review, fall, 1988 (interview).

People, November 3, 2003, Bella Stander, review of *Fanny,* p. 54.

Publishers Weekly, September 24, 1982 (interview); March 21, 1994, p. 8; April 17, 2000, review of *The Married Man,* p. 48; January 8, 2001, review of *The Flaneur,* p. 54; February 5, 2001, review of *Loss within Loss,* p. 82; August 11, 2003, review of *Fanny,* p. 37.

Review of Contemporary Fiction, fall, 1996, "Edmund White Speaks with Edmund White;" spring, 1998, Kent D. Wolf, review of *The Farewell Symphony,* p. 224; spring, 2001, David Bergman, review of *The Married Man,* p. 187; fall, 2003, David Bergman, review of *Fanny,* p. 127.

Rolling Stone, December 19, 1985.

Spectator, March 5, 1988; May 10, 1997, Alain de Botton, review of *The Farewell Symphony,* p. 35; March 20, 1999, Jonathan Keates, review of *Marcel Proust,* p. 69; February 24, 2001, Euan Cameron, review of *The Flaneur,* p. 36.

Time, April 11, 1988; July 30, 1990; December 27, 1993.

Times Literary Supplement, September 5, 1980; August 19, 1983; January 22, 1988; July 1, 1994, p. 13; March 17, 1995, p. 20; May 2, 1997, Nicholas Jenkins, review of *The Farewell Symphony,* p. 23; May 21, 1999, review of *Marcel Proust,* p. 8; March 17, 2000, Sylvia Brownrigg, review of *The Married Man,* p. 21; April 6, 2001, John Stokes, review of *The Flaneur,* p. 31.

Tribune Books (Chicago, IL), October 24, 1993, p. 3; August 13, 1995, p. 4.

Village Voice, January 28, 1980; June 28, 1988 (interview).

Vogue, February, 1984; November, 1984; May, 1985; January, 1986; July, 1986; July, 1987.

Voice Literary Supplement, December, 1982; April, 1988; June, 1988; March, 2001, Richard Klein, "Wander, Lust."

Washington Post Book World, November 12, 1978; December 10, 1978; January 27, 1980; October 17, 1982; October 6, 1985; April 3, 1988; February 28, 1999, Greg Varner, "Passionate Lives," p. 4; June 11, 2000, Michael Dirda, "In Health and in Sickness," p. 1.

ONLINE

Beatrice, http://www.beatrice.com/ (April 24, 2004), Ron Hogan, "Beatrice Interview: Edmund White."

Edmund White Home Page, http://www.edmundwhite.com/ (May 3, 2004).

Gay.com, http://www.gay.com/ (October 1, 2001), "Edmund White Discusses *The Married Man,* Life, and Love."

PlanetOut, http://www.planetout.com/ (October 1, 2001), Lawrence Chua, "Interview with Edmund White."

Thebestofmen.com, http://thebestofmen.com/ (October 21, 2001), "Fiction."

* * *

WHITE, Edmund Valentine, III
See WHITE, Edmund

* * *

WHITE, Phyllis Dorothy James
See JAMES, P.D.

WIDEMAN, John Edgar 1941-

PERSONAL: Born June 14, 1941, in Washington, DC; son of Edgar and Bette (French) Wideman; married Judith Ann Goldman, 1965; children: Daniel Jerome, Jacob Edgar, Jamila Ann. *Ethnicity:* Black. *Education:* University of Pennsylvania, B.A., 1963; New College, Oxford, England, B.Phil., 1966.

ADDRESSES: *Office*—Department of English, University of Massachusetts, Amherst Campus, Bartlett Hall, Amherst, MA 01003. *E-mail*—jwhoops@english.umass.edu.

CAREER: Howard University, Washington, DC, teacher of American literature, summer, 1965; University of Pennsylvania, Philadelphia, PA, 1966-74, began as instructor, professor of English, 1974, director of Afro-American studies program, 1971-73; University of Wyoming, Laramie, WY, professor of English, 1974-1986; University of Massachusetts—Amherst, Amherst, MA, professor of English, 1986—, named Distinguished Professor, 2001. Made U.S. Department of State lecture tour of Europe and the Near East, 1976; Phi Beta Kappa lecturer, 1976; visiting writer and lecturer at numerous colleges and universities; has also served as administrator/teacher in a curriculum planning, teacher-training institute sponsored by National Defense Education Act. Assistant basketball coach, University of Pennsylvania, 1968-72. National Humanities Faculty consultant in numerous states; consultant to secondary schools across the country, 1968—.

MEMBER: Association of American Rhodes Scholars (member of board of directors and of state and national selection committees), American Studies Association (council, 1980-81), Modern Language Association, American Academy of Arts and Sciences, Phi Beta Kappa.

AWARDS, HONORS: Kent fellow, and Writers' Workshop, University of Iowa, 1966; named member of Philadelphia Big Five Basketball Hall of Fame, 1974; Young Humanist fellow, 1975—; PEN/Faulkner Award for fiction, 1984, for *Sent for You Yesterday;* National Book Award nomination, 1984, for *Brothers and Keepers;* D. Litt., University of Pennsylvania, 1985; Du Sable Museum Prize for Non-fiction, 1985; John Dos Passos Prize for Literature, Longwood College, 1986; National Magazine Editors Prize for Short Fiction, 1987; Lannan Literary fellowship for fiction, 1991; PEN/Faulkner Award and American Book Award, Before Columbus Foundation, 1991, both for *Philadelphia Fire;* MacArthur fellow, MacArthur Foundation, 1993; James Fenimore Cooper Prize for historical fiction, 1996, for *The Cattle Killing;* Rea Prize for short fiction, Dungannon Foundation, 1998; *Readers' Digest*/Lila Wallace grant, 1999; O Henry Award for best short story of the year, 2000; New England Book Award for literary excellence, New England Booksellers Association, 2001, for *Hoop Roots: Basketball, Race, and Love;* Nonfiction Honor Book, Black Caucus Award, American Library Association, 2002, for *Hoop Roots: Basketball, Race, and Love;* grant, National Endowment Humanities; Chancellor's Medal, University of Massachusetts.

WRITINGS:

NOVELS

A Glance Away, Harcourt (New York, NY), 1967.
Hurry Home, Harcourt (New York, NY), 1970.
The Lynchers, Harcourt (New York, NY), 1973.
Hiding Place, Avon (New York, NY), 1981.
Sent for You Yesterday, Avon (New York, NY), 1983.
Reuben, Henry Holt (New York, NY), 1987.
Philadelphia Fire, Henry Holt (New York, NY), 1990.
A Glance Away, Hurry Home, and The Lynchers: Three Early Novels by John Edgar Wideman, Henry Holt (New York, NY), 1994.
The Cattle Killing, Houghton Mifflin (Boston, MA), 1996.
Two Cities, Houghton Mifflin (Boston, MA), 1998.

COLLECTIONS

Damballah (short stories), Avon (New York, NY), 1981.
The Homewood Trilogy (includes *Damballah, Hiding Place,* and *Sent for You Yesterday*), Avon (New York, NY), 1985.
Fever (short stories), Henry Holt (New York, NY), 1989.
The Stories of John Edgar Wideman, Pantheon Books (New York, NY), 1992, published as *All Stories Are True,* Vintage Books (New York, NY), 1993.
God's Gym (short stories), Houghton Mifflin, (Boston, MA), 2005.

OTHER

Brothers and Keepers (memoirs), Henry Holt (New York, NY), 1984.

Fatheralong: A Meditation on Fathers and Sons, Race and Society, Pantheon (New York, NY), 1994.

(With Mumia Abu-Jamal) *Live from Death Row,* Addison Wesley (New York, NY), 1995.

(With Bonnie Tusmith) *Conversations with John Edgar Wideman,* University Press Of Mississippi (Jackson, MS), 1998.

Hoop Roots: Basketball, Race, and Love (memoir), Houghton Mifflin (Boston, MA), 2001.

(Editor) *My Soul Has Grown Deep: Classics of Early African-American Literature,* Running Press (Philadelphia, PA), 2001.

(Editor) *20: The Best of the Drue Heinz Literature Prize,* University of Pittsburgh Press (Pittsburgh, PA), 2001.

Contributor of articles, short stories, book reviews, and poetry to periodicals, including *American Poetry Review, Negro Digest, Black American Literature Forum, Black World, American Scholar,Gentleman's Quarterly, New York Times Book Review, North American Review,* and *Washington Post Book World.* Also author of introduction, *Every Tongue Got to Confess: Negro Folktales from the Gulf States,* edited by Zora Neale Hurston and Carla Kaplan, HarperCollins, 2001.

SIDELIGHTS: John Edgar Wideman has been hailed by Don Strachen in the *Los Angeles Times Book Review* as "the black Faulkner, the softcover Shakespeare." Such praise is not uncommon for this author, whose novel *Sent for You Yesterday* was selected as the 1984 PEN/Faulkner Award winner over works by Bernard Malamud, Cynthia Ozick, and William Kennedy. Wideman attended Oxford University in 1963 on a Rhodes scholarship, earned a degree in eighteenth-century literature, and later accepted a fellowship at the prestigious University of Iowa Writers' Workshop. Yet this "artist with whom any reader who admires ambitious fiction must sooner or later reckon," as a *New York Times* contributor called him, began his college career not as a writer, but as a basketball star. "I always wanted to play pro basketball—ever since I saw a ball and learned you could make money at it," he told Curt Suplee in the *Washington Post.* Recruited by the University of Pennsylvania, Wideman first studied psychology, attracted by the "mystical insight" that he told Suplee he thought the subject would yield. When his subjects of study instead "turned out to be rats" and clinical experiments, Wideman changed his major to English, while continuing to be mainly concerned with basketball. He played well enough to earn a place in the Philadelphia Big Five Basketball Hall of Fame but, he told Suplee, as his time at the university drew to a close, "I knew I wasn't going to be able to get into the NBA (National Basketball Association). What was left?"

The Rhodes scholarship answered that question. Wideman began to concentrate on his writing rather than sports and did so with such success that his first novel, *A Glance Away,* was published just a year after he earned his degree from Oxford. The story of a day in the life of a drug addict, *A Glance Away* reflects the harsh realities that Wideman saw and experienced during his youth in Homewood, Pittsburgh's ghetto. And, though the author later resided in other locales, including Wyoming, his novels continued to describe black urban experiences. He explained to Suplee, "My particular imagination has always worked well in a kind of exile. It fits the insider-outside view I've always had. It helps to write away from the center of the action."

Wideman's highly literate style is in sharp contrast to his gritty subject matter, and while reviews of his books have been generally favorable, some critics initially expressed the opinion that such a formal style was not appropriate for his stories of street life. Anatole Broyard praised *The Lynchers* in his *New York Times* review, stating: "Though we have heard the themes and variations of violence before in black writing, *The Lynchers* touches us in a more personal way, for John Edgar Wideman has a weapon more powerful than any knife or gun. His weapon is art. Eloquence is his arsenal, his arms cache. His prose, at its best, is a black panther, coiled to spring." But Broyard went on to say that the book is not flawless: "Far from it. Mr. Wideman ripples too many muscles in his writing, often cannot seem to decide whether to show or snow us. . . . [He] is wordy, and *The Lynchers* is as shaky in its structure as some of the buildings his characters inhabit. But he can *write,* and you come away from his book with the feeling that he is, as they say, very close to getting it all together." In the *New York Times,* John Leonard commented on the extensive use of literary devices in *The Lynchers:* "Flashback, flashforward, first person, third person, journals, identity exchange, interior monologue, dreams (historical and personal), puns, epiphanies. At times the devices seem a thicket through which one must hack one's weary way toward meanings arbitrarily obscure, a vegetable indulgence. But John Edgar Wideman is up to much more than storytelling. . . . He is capable of moving from ghetto language to [Irish writer James] Joyce with a flip of the page."

Saturday Review critic David Littlejohn agreed that Wideman's novels are very complex, and in his review of *Hurry Home* he criticized those who would judge this author as a storyteller: "Reviewers . . . are probably more responsible than anyone else for the common delusion that a novel is somehow contained in its discernible, realistic plot. . . . *Hurry Home* is primarily an experience, not a plot: an experience of words, dense, private, exploratory, and non-progressive." Littlejohn described *Hurry Home* as a retelling of an American myth, that of "the lonely search through the Old World" for a sense of cultural heritage, which "has been the pattern of a hundred thousand young Americans' lives and novels." According to Littlejohn, Wideman's version is "spare and eccentric, highly stylized, circling, allusive, antichronological, far more consciously symbolic than most versions, than the usual self-indulgent and romantic works of this genre—and hence both more rewarding and more difficult of access." Reviewing the same book in the *New York Times Book Review,* Joseph Goodman stated: "Many of its pages are packed with psychological insight, and nearly all reveal Mr. Wideman's formidable command of the techniques of fiction. Moreover, the theme is a profound one—the quest for a substantive sense of self. . . . The prose, paratactic and rich with puns, flows as freely as thought itself, giving us . . . Joycean echoes. . . . It is a dazzling display. . . . We can have nothing but admiration for Mr. Wideman's talent."

Enthusiastic reviews such as these established Wideman's reputation as a major talent in the literary world. When his fourth and fifth books—*Damballah,* a collection of short stories, and *Hiding Place,* a novel—were issued originally as paperbacks, some critics, such as John Leonard and Mel Watkins, reacted with indignation. Leonard's *New York Times* review used extensive quotes from the books to demonstrate Wideman's virtuosity, and stated, "That [these] two new books will fall apart after a second reading is a scandal." Watkins's *New York Times Book Review* article on the two books, which were published simultaneously, had special praise for the short-story volume, and ended with a sentiment much like Leonard's on the books' binding. "In freeing his voice from the confines of the novel form," Watkins wrote, "[Wideman] has written what is possibly his most impressive work. . . . Each story moves far beyond the primary event on which it is focused. . . . Mr. Wideman has used a narrative laced with myth, superstition and dream sequences to create an elaborate poetic portrait of the lives of ordinary black people. . . . These books once again demonstrate that John Wideman is one of America's premier writers of fiction. That they were published originally in paperback perhaps suggests that he is also one of our most underrated writers." Actually, it was the author himself who had decided to bring the books out as original paperbacks. His reasons were philosophical and pragmatic. "I spend an enormous amount of time and energy writing and I want to write good books, but I also want people to read them," he explained to Edwin McDowell in the *New York Times.* Wideman's first three novels had been slow sellers "in spite of enormously positive reviews," he told Suplee, and it was his hope that the affordability of paperbacks would help give him a wider readership, particularly among "the people and the world I was writing about. A $15.95 novel had nothing to do with that world."

Damballah and *Hiding Place* were both set in Homewood, and in 1983 he published a third book with the same setting, titled *Sent for You Yesterday.* Critics were enthusiastic. "In this hypnotic and deeply lyrical novel, Mr. Wideman again returns to the ghetto where he was raised and transforms it into a magical location infused with poetry and pathos," wrote Alan Cheuse in the *New York Times Book Review.* "The narration here makes it clear that both as a molder of language and a builder of plots, Mr. Wideman has come into his full powers. He has the gift of making 'ordinary' folks memorable." Stated Garett Epps in the *Washington Post Book World,* "Wideman has a fluent command of the American language, written and spoken, and a fierce, loving vision of the people he writes about. Like the writing of William Faulkner, Wideman's prose fiction is vivid and demanding—shuttling unpredictably between places, narrators and times, dwelling for a paragraph on the surface of things, then sneaking a key event into a clause that springs on the reader like a booby trap. . . . *Sent for You Yesterday* is a book to be savored, read slowly again and again."

When he ventured into nonfiction for the first time with his book *Brothers and Keepers,* Wideman continued to draw inspiration from the same source, Homewood. In this book, Wideman comes to terms with his brother Robby, younger by ten years, whose life was influenced by the street, its drugs, and its crime. The author wrote, "Even as I manufactured fiction from the events of my brother's life, from the history of the family that had nurtured us both, I knew something of a different order remained to be extricated. The fiction writer was a man with a real brother behind real bars [serving a life sentence in a Pennsylvania penitentiary]." In his review in the *Washington Post Book World,* Jonathan Yardley called *Brothers and Keepers* "the elder Wideman's effort to understand what happened, to confess and examine his own sense of guilt about his brother's fate (and his own)." The result, according to the reviewer, is "a depiction of the inexorably widening chasm that divides middle-class black Americans from the black underclass." Wideman's personal experience, added Yardley, also reveals that for the black person, "moving out of the ghetto into the white world is a process that requires excruciating compromises, sacrifices and denials, that leaves the person who makes the journey truly at home in neither the world he has entered nor the world he has left."

Wideman has, however, made a home for himself in literary circles, and at the same time has learned much about the nature of success. When *Sent for You Yesterday* won the PEN/Faulkner Award—the only major literary award in the United States to be judged, administered, and largely funded by writers—Wideman told Suplee he felt "warmth. That's what I felt. Starting at the toes and filling up. A gradual recognition that it could be real." The author maintained that if such an honor "doesn't happen again for a long time—or never happens again—it really doesn't matter," because he "learned more and more that the process itself was important, learned to take my satisfaction from the writing" during the years of comparative obscurity. "I'm an old jock," he explained. "So I've kind of trained myself to be low-key. Sometimes the crowd screams, sometimes the crowd doesn't scream."

The narrator of Wideman's novel *Reuben* provides inexpensive legal aid to residents of Homewood. One of Reuben's clients is Kwansa, a young black prostitute whose husband, a recovering drug addict, kidnaps and seeks legal custody of their illegitimate child as revenge against her. Another customer is Wally, an assistant basketball coach at a local white university who seeks Reuben's counsel for two reasons, one being the killing of a white man in Chicago and the other being his fear that he will be blamed for the illegal recruiting practices of his department. Reviewing the book in *Washington Post Book World,* Noel Perrin characterized Wideman's novels as myths. "In the end," Perrin wrote, "one sees that all the shocks—the murders, the fantasies, burnings, strong words—all of them amount to a kind of metaphor for the psychic damage that human beings do to each other and that is no less hurtful than spread-eagled beating, just less visible to the outer eye."

In *Philadelphia Fire,* Wideman brings together two stories, combining fact in fiction. In the first, he describes the events in Philadelphia when the police, under the direction of black mayor Wilson Goode, bombed the headquarters of an organization known as Move, a group that had defied city eviction notices and was armed with weapons. The police bombing killed six adults and five children, destroyed fifty-three homes, and left 262 people homeless. Wideman's novel begins with a quote by William Penn, the founder of Pennsylvania, stating his dream that the town would "never be burnt, and always be wholesome." As Chicago *Tribune Books* reviewer Paul Skenazy pointed out, *Philadelphia Fire* tries to make sense of the changes that have occurred since Penn's statement, changes that include poverty and racism, changes that resulted in the burning of the Philadelphia neighborhood. The other story being told in the book is that of Wideman's relationship with a son who has received a life sentence for murder. "Few pages of prose," Skenazy said, "carry as much pain as do Wideman's thoughts on his son, his words to him in prison, his feelings of confusion as a father." Skenazy concluded that *Philadelphia Fire* is "about a person, and a nation, losing its grip, destroying the very differences and dissonance that provide spirit, beauty, life." Rosemary L. Bray in the *New York Times Book Review* concurred; "the author takes his readers on a tour of urban America perched on the precipice of hell," Bray wrote, "a tour in which even his own personal tragedy is part of the view."

The Stories of John Edgar Wideman combined several earlier story collections, including *Damballah, Fever,* and *All Stories Are True.* Michael Harris wrote in the *Los Angeles Times Book Review* that a comparison between Wideman and Faulkner makes sense, "because of the scope of Wideman's project, his ear for voices, . . . and the way he shows the present as perpetually haunted by the past." *New York Times Book Review* contributor Michael Gorra also believed the Faulkner comparison is apt. "It is appropriate," Gorra wrote, "because both are concerned with the life of a community over time. It is appropriate because they both have a feel for the anecdotal folklore through which a community defines itself, because they both often choose to present their characters in the act of telling stories, and because in drawing on oral tradition they both write as their characters speak, in a language whose pith and vigor has not yet been worn into cliche." It is Gorra's conclusion that "the more you read John Edgar Wideman, the more impressive he seems."

Fatheralong: A Meditation on Fathers and Sons, Race and Society, like *Philadelphia Fire* and the Homewood stories, juxtaposes Wideman's personal life with larger issues. Mel Watkins in the *New York Times Book Review* referred to it as a hybrid of memoir and "a meditation on fatherhood, race, metaphysics, time and the afterlife." Wideman explores his strained relationship with his father and his troubles with his own son, and then frames them in the context of all father-son relationships as well as America's racist legacy. A *Village Voice* critic found the sections on Wideman's son, Jacob, to be his "most artful work. The Jacob sections overshadow simply because they're so much better written, their subject more emotionally grasped than any other." Mitchell Duneier in the *Los Angeles Times Book Review* called *Fatheralong* "a masterpiece of sociological speculation, constructed with such an abundance of wisdom as to compensate for its lack of evidence regarding questions to which there are no easy answers." In the Chicago *Tribune Books,* Michael Boynton, calling the work "part memoir, part manifesto," concluded that "*Fatheralong* is an odd, sad book. Filled with flashes of insight told in Wideman's distinctive prose-poetry, it is at once personal and essentially opaque. . . . It leaves the reader wanting to know more, hoping that its author will one day find the key he has been looking for."

Wideman returned to fiction with his novel, *The Cattle Killing.* In it, he weaves together memories from his narrator's childhood in Philadelphia with the plight of blacks in the city in the late eighteenth century, and the story of the South African Xhosa tribe, pulling together threads of history, religion, and race to form his story. The complex story met with somewhat mixed reviews, with critics finding flaws in the novel's coherence but praising Wideman's imaginative storytelling powers.

Sven Birkerts of the *New York Times Book Review* offered the negative point of view, claiming that the author "ventured beyond his readers" with *The Cattle Killing,* adding, "Filaments of story, of precious sense, are woven like bits of rag into a rug of shimmering but also perplexing suggestiveness." A more positive assessment came from Joyce Carol Oates in the *New York Review of Books,* who described the book as "purposefully framed by contemporary American black voices." She added, "*The Cattle Killing* juxtaposes lyrical, parable-like tales with presumably authentic historical accounts. . . . Boldly, the author indicates little distinction between voices, times, or settings." While "the result is a novel frequently difficult to assess," Oates recommended that readers approach the book "as a kind of music, an obsessive beat in the author's head, a nightmare from which he yearns . . . to be awakened. It is a work of operatic polyphony that strains to break free of linguistic constraints into theatrical spectacle."

An improvisational tone characterized the style of *Two Cities.* In this novel—set in the Philadelphia and Pittsburgh of the title—the author tells the story of Kassima, who has had her share of hard luck with men. As the story opens, she is tentatively stepping back into a social life after the grief of losing two sons to gang-related crime and an imprisoned husband to AIDS. She may have found happiness after meeting Robert Jones, a middle-aged man whose own difficult past has given him a rare wisdom. But after Robert nearly loses his life in a close call with a gun-wielding young man, "Kassima is so terrorized by the prospect of another loss that she abandons her nascent attachment and returns to protective mourning," according to Richard Bernstein, writing in the *New York Times.* Kassima finds a kindred spirit in Mr. Mallory, an elderly World War II veteran who boards at her home. When he dies, she turns to Robert for emotional help.

"This is the essential story," said Bernstein, "but Mr. Wideman weaves a tapestry of American life tightly around it, telling stories reminiscent of the Homewood trilogy." In his review, Bernstein found *Two Cities* to be as "angry and intemperate" as it was infused with "stylistic virtuosity."

My Soul Has Grown Deep: Classics of Early African American Literature, edited by Wideman, is a collection of twelve writings by well-known and lesser known eighteenth-and nineteenth-century writers such as Phyllis Wheatley, Sojourner Truth, W.E.B. Dubois, and Booker T. Washington. *Library Journal* reviewer Karen S.E. Lempert praised Wideman for "providing a depth and breadth of content and editorial expertise rarely found" in this type of collection. Because of Wideman, wrote Donna Seamen in *Booklist,* "these eloquent and inspiring messages of hope will continue to be heard across the land and around the world."

Hoop Roots: Basketball, Race, and Love, said Wideman in an interview with Lisa Baker in the *African American Review,* is "really a study of race and culture—using sport as a way of getting people's attention." *Hoop Roots* follows Wideman's "lifelong love affair with basketball," commented David L. Ulin in the *Atlantic Monthly,* at times, "yielding to reflections on family, racial tension, memory, and the nebulous territory of storytelling itself." A *Publishers Weekly* called the book a "brilliant tribute to basketball, survival and families linked by blood, joy, and tragedy." This reviewer concluded that *Hoop Roots* "is as exhilarating as a few fast and furious hours on the court." Tracy Grant, a reviewer for *Black Issues Book Review,* found the book a challenge to read because of Wideman's "stream-of-consciousness writing style," but commented that "*Hoop Roots* demonstrates Wideman's unique voice and his true gift for capturing a slice of black life from the past."

"John Edgar Wideman is unafraid to experiment with many voices," declared Opal Palmer Adisa in *Reference Guide to American Literature.* "He has pushed his fiction to embrace both European and African American aesthetic traditions. Some aspect of his life is at the center of all of his works. He probes, relentless in his attempt to understand the social machine that seems so controlling and leaves so many people feeling powerless." As Adisa concluded, while the author's experimental techniques "might not always provide clarity, his works nonetheless cause one to look beyond the surface."

BIOGRAPHICAL AND CRITICAL SOURCES:

BOOKS

African American Almanac, 8th edition, Thomson Gale (Detroit, MI), 2000.

Black Literature Criticism, Thomson Gale (Detroit, MI), 1992.

Contemporary Black Biography, Volume 5, Thomson Gale (Detroit, MI), 1994.

Contemporary Literary Criticism, Thomson Gale (Detroit, MI), Volume 5, 1976, Volume 34, 1985, Volume 36, 1986, Volume 67, 1992, Volume 122, 2000.

Dictionary of Literary Biography, Thomson Gale (Detroit, MI), Volume 33: *Afro-American Fiction Writers after 1955,* 1984, Volume 143: *American Novelists since World War II,* 3rd series, 1994.

In Black and White: A Guide to Magazine Articles, Newspaper Articles, and Books concerning Black Individuals and Groups, 3rd edition, Thomson Gale (Detroit, MI), 1985.

Major Twentieth-Century Writers, 2nd edition, Thomson Gale (Detroit, MI), 1999.

Mbalia, Doreatha D., *John Edgar Wideman: Reclaiming the African Personality,* Associated University Presses (Cranbury, NJ), 1995.

Modern American Literature, Volume 3, 5th edition, St. James Press (Detroit, MI), 1999.

Modern Black Writers, St. James Press (Detroit, MI), 2000.

Notable Black American Men, Thomson Gale (Detroit, MI), 1999.

O'Brien, John, editor, *Interviews with Black Writers,* Liveright, 1973.

Reference Guide to American Literature, 4th edition, St. James Press (Detroit, MI), 2000.

Reference Guide to Short Fiction, 2nd edition, St. James Press (Detroit, MI), 1999.

Wideman, John Edgar, *Brothers and Keepers,* Henry Holt (New York, NY), 1984.

Wideman, John Edgar, *Philadelphia Fire,* Henry Holt (New York, NY), 1990.

PERIODICALS

African American Review, fall, 1992, Jessica Lustig, "Home: An Interview with John Edgar Wideman," pp. 453-457; summer, 1998, review of *The Cattle Killing,* p. 362; winter, 1998, Madhu Dubey, review of *Philadelphia Fire,* pp. 579-595; summer, 2000, Lisa Baker, "Storytelling and Democracy (in the Radical Sense): A Conversation with John Edgar Wideman," p. 263.

American Book Review, March-April, 1988, Harold Jaffe, "Rage," pp. 8-14; November, 1999, review of *Two Cities,* p. 4.

American Literature, March, 1999, "Conversation with John Edgar Wideman," p. 214.

American Scholar, autumn, 1967.

Atlantic Monthly, November, 2001, David L. Ulin, review of *Hoop Roots: Basketball, Race, and Love.*

Black American Literature Forum, spring/summer, 1986, John Bennion, "The Shape of Memory in John Edgar Wideman's *Sent for You Yesterday,*" pp. 143-150.

Black Scholar, spring, 1998, Mumia Abu-Jamal, review of *Brothers and Keepers,* pp. 75-79.

Black Issues Book Review, November-December 2001, Tracy Grant, review of *Hoop Roots,* p. 69.

Bloomsbury Review, January, 1999, review of *Two Cities,* p. 19.

Book, September, 2001, "John Edgar Wideman" (interview), p. 12.

Booklist, August, 1994, p. 1987; September 15, 1994, Joseph Keppler, review of *All Stories Are True,* p. 153; February 15, 1998, review of *The Cattle Killing,* p. 979; July, 1998, review of *Two Cities,* p. 1832; September 1, 2001, Wes Lukowsky, review of *Hoop Roots,* p. 38; September 15, 2001, Donna Seaman, review of *My Soul Has Grown Deep: Classics of Early African American Literature,* p. 180.

Callaloo, fall, 1985, Jacqueline Berben, "Beyond Discourse: The Unspoken versus Words in the Fiction of John Edgar Wideman," pp. 525-534; winter, 1990, author interview, pp. 47-61; summer, 1999, special issue devoted to Wideman, pp. 629-665.

Chicago Tribune Books, November 29, 1987, Gary Dretzka, "Haunting Novel of Rage and Love Packs a Punch," p. 6.

Christian Science Monitor, October 23, 1990, Shawn Smith, "Like Steam from a City Grate," p. 15; July 10, 1992.

CLA Journal, March, 1985, James Coleman, "Going Back Home: The Literary Development of John Edgar Wideman," pp. 326-343; March, 1990, Matthew Wilson, "The Circles of History in John Edgar Wideman's 'The Homewood Trilogy,'" pp. 239-259.

Contemporary Literature, fall, 1991, Ashraf H.A. Rushdy, "Fraternal Blues: John Edgar Wideman's *Homewood Trilogy,*" pp. 312-345.

Ebony, September, 2001, review of *Hoop Roots,* p. 22.

Esquire, September, 1998, review of *Two Cities,* p. 60.

Essence, October, 2001, Patrick Henry Bass, "Take Note," p. 70.

Hollins Critic, December, 1992, James Robert Saunders, "Exorcizing the Demons: John Edgar Wideman's Literary Response," pp. 1-10.

Interview, September, 2001, Patrick Giles, "Looking at Life from the Free Throw Line," p. 102.

Journal of Negro History, January, 1963.

Kenyon Review, spring, 1992, Jan Clausen, "Native Fathers," pp. 44-55.

Kirkus Reviews, August 1, 1996, p. 1092; July 15, 1998, review of *Two Cities,* p. 998.

Library Journal, March 1, 1994, Peter Joseph, review of *All Stories Are True,* p. 134; September 15, 1994, Michael A. Lutes, review of *Fatheralong: A Meditation on Fathers and Sons, Race and Society,* p. 85; July, 1996, Barbara Hoffert, review of *The Cattle Killing,* p. 164; November 1, 1998, review of *Two Cities,* p. 101; March 1, 1999, Michael Rogers, review of *Hiding Place* and *Damballah,* p. 116; October 15, 2001, Nathan Ward, review of *Hoop Roots,* p. 84; September 15, 2001, Karen E.S. Lempert, review of *My Soul Has Grown Deep,* p. 80; March 1, 2002, "ALA Awards at Midwinter," p. 18.

London Review of Books, November 27, 1997, Michael Wood, "Living in the Enemy's Dream," pp. 25-26.

Los Angeles Times, November 11, 1987.

Los Angeles Times Book Review, April 17, 1983; December 23, 1984, Ron Finney, "To Repair the Two Relations," p. 6; December 29, 1985; September 30, 1990; September 13, 1992; December 25, 1994, p. 2; September 27, 1998, review of *Two Cities,* p. 11.

Michigan Quarterly Review, winter, 1975.

Nation, January 1, 1990, Randall Kenan, review of *Fever,* pp. 25-27; October 28, 1996, Gene Seymour, "Dream Surgeon," pp. 58-60.

Negro Digest, May, 1963.

New Republic, July 13 and 20, 1992, Sven Birkerts, "The Art of Memory," pp. 42-44.

New Statesman, September 1, 1995, Ian Sansom, review of *Fatheralong,* p. 34.

Newsweek, May 7, 1970; October 1, 1990, Jack Kroll, review of *Philadelphia Fire,* p. 90.

New Yorker, October 1, 1998, review of *Two Cities,* p. 109.

New York Magazine, October 1, 1990, Rhoda Koenig, review of *Philadelphia Fire,* p. 66.

New York Review of Books, May 11, 1995, Darryl Pinckney, "Aristocrats," pp. 27-34; March 27, 1997, Joyce Carol Oates, "Troubles I've Seen," pp. 39-40.

New York Times, April 2, 1970; May 15, 1973; November 27, 1981; May 16, 1984; October 29, 1984; September 4, 1986; July 21, 1992; September 28, 1998, Richard Bernstein, "Finding Hope and Refuge on Bitter Urban Streets," p. E8.

New York Times Book Review, September 10, 1967; April 19, 1970; April 29, 1973; April 11, 1982, Mel Watkins, review of *Hiding Place,* pp. 6, 21; May 15, 1983, Alan Cheuse, review of *Sent for You Yesterday,* pp. 13, 41; November 4, 1984; January 13, 1985; December 15, 1985, C. Gerald Fraser, review of *A Glance Away,* p. 32; May 11, 1986, review of *Hurry Home,* p. 42; November 30, 1986, Patricia T. O'Conner, review of *The Lynchers,* p. 38; November 8, 1987, Walter Kendrick, review of *Reuben,* p. 3; October 16, 1988; December 10, 1989, Susan Fromberg Schaeffer, review of *Fever,* p. 1, and Rosemary L. Bray, "The Plague became the Fire," p. 30; September 30, 1990, Rosemary L. Bray, review of *Philadelphia Fire,* p. 7; October 14, 1990; November 17, 1991; June 14, 1992, Michael Gorra, "The Choral Voice of Homewood," p. 13; November 13, 1994, Mel Watkins, "A Son's Notes," p. 11; November 3, 1996, Sven Birkerts, "The Fever Days," p. 20; January 4, 1998, review of *The Cattle Killing,* p. 24; October 10, 1999, review of *Two Cities,* p. 36; December 5, 1999, review of *Two Cities,* p. 105; November 4, 2001, Will Blythe, "Benching Himself," p. 35; November 11, 2001, review of *Hoop Roots,* p. 30.

Progressive, July, 1999, Dean Bakopoulos, review of *Two Cities,* p. 44.

Publishers Weekly, August 12, 1996, p. 63; August 3, 1998, review of *Two Cities,* p. 72; June 8, 1998, "$30,000 Rea Prize to Wideman," p. 19; July 16, 2001, review of *Hoop Roots,* p. 167.

Revue française D'Etudes, April-June, 1991, Jacqueline Berben, "Promised Land and Wasteland in John Edgar Wideman's Recent Fiction," pp. 259-270.

Saturday Review, October 21, 1967; May 2, 1970.

Shenandoah, winter, 1974.

Sports Illustrated, November 19, 2001, Charles Hirshberg, "Books: A Basketball Tome That's Too Ambitious, Even for the Supposed Thinking Man," p. R3.

Tikkun, March-April, 1995, Mark Shechner, "Men Will Be Men," pp. 80-82.

Time, October 1, 1990; October 5, 1998, review of *Two Cities,* p. 88; November 19, 2001, "*Hoop Roots* by

John Edgar Wideman," p. 143; October 1, 1990, R.T. Sheppard, review of *Philadelphia Fire,* p. 90.
Times (London), December 6, 1984.
Times Literary Supplement, December 21, 1984; January 16, 1987; August 5, 1988; August 23, 1991, "Cos I'm a So-o-oul Man," pp. 19-20.
Tribune Books (Chicago), December 23, 1984; November 29, 1987; October 28, 1990; November 24, 1991; October 23, 1994, p. 8.
Village Voice, October 25, 1994.
Virginia Quarterly Review, spring, 1995, Sanford Pinsker, "The Moose on the Family Dinner Table," pp. 369-372.
Washington Post, May 10, 1984; May 12, 1984.
Washington Post Book World, July 3, 1983; September 29, 1996, Paul West, "Too Great a Sacrifice," p. 5; October 4, 1998, review of *Two Cities,* p. 5.
Whole Earth Review, summer, 1995, p. 78.
World Literature Today, winter, 1998, Jacqueline Brice-Finch, review of *The Cattle Killing,* p. 137.

* * *

WIESEL, Elie 1928-
(Eliezer Wiesel)

PERSONAL: Born September 30, 1928, in Sighet, Romania; immigrated to the United States, 1956, naturalized U.S. citizen, 1963; son of Shlomo (a grocer) and Sarah (Feig) Wiesel; married Marion Erster Rose, 1969; children: Shlomo Elisha. *Education:* Attended Sorbonne, University of Paris, 1948-51. *Religion:* Jewish.

ADDRESSES: *Office*—University Professors, Boston University, 745 Commonwealth Ave., Boston, MA 02215; and Elie Wiesel Foundation for Humanity, 529 Fifth Ave., Ste. 1802, New York, NY 10017. *Agent*—Georges Borchardt, 136 East 57th St., New York, NY 10022.

CAREER: Foreign correspondent at various times for *Yedioth Ahronoth,* Tel Aviv, Israel, *L'Arche,* Paris, France, and *Jewish Daily Forward,* New York, NY, 1949—; City College of the City University of New York, New York, NY, distinguished professor, 1972-76; Boston University, Boston, MA, Andrew Mellon professor in the humanities, 1976—, professor of philosophy, 1988—; cofounder with wife, Marion, of Elie Wiesel Foundation for Humanity, 1986—. Whitney Humanities Center, Yale University, New Haven, CT, Henry Luce visiting scholar in Humanities and Social Thought, 1982-83; Florida International University, Miami, distinguished visiting professor of literature and philosophy, 1982. Chair, United States President's Commission on the Holocaust, 1979-80, U.S. Holocaust Memorial Council, 1980-86. On advisory board of over seventy organizations.

MEMBER: Amnesty International, PEN, Writers Guild of America, Author's Guild, American Academy of Arts and Sciences (fellow), Jewish Academy of Arts and Sciences, European Academy of Arts and Sciences, Foreign Press Association (honorary lifetime member), Writers and Artists for Peace in the Middle East, Royal Norwegian Society of Sciences and Letters, Universal Academy of Cultures, Paris (founding president), Phi Beta Kappa.

AWARDS, HONORS: Prix Rivarol, 1963; Remembrance Award, 1965, for *The Town beyond the Wall* and all other writings; William and Janice Epstein Fiction Award, Jewish Book Council, 1965, for *The Town beyond the Wall;* Jewish Heritage Award, 1966, for excellence in literature; Prix Medicis, 1969, for *Le Mendiant de Jerusalem;* Prix Bordin, French Academy, 1972; Eleanor Roosevelt Memorial Award, 1972; American Liberties Medallion, American Jewish Committee, 1972; Frank and Ethel S. Cohen Award, Jewish Book Council, 1973, for *Souls on Fire;* Martin Luther King, Jr. Award, City College of the City University of New York, 1973; Faculty Distinguished Scholar Award, Hofstra University, 1973-74; Joseph Prize for Human Rights, Anti-Defamation League of B'nai B'rith, 1978; Zalman Shazar Award, State of Israel, 1979; Jabotinsky Medal, State of Israel, 1980; Prix Livre-International, 1980, and Prix des Bibliothecaires, 1981, both for *Le Testament d'un poete juif assassine;* Anatoly Scharansky Humanitarian Award, 1983; Congressional Gold Medal, 1985; humanitarian award, International League for Human Rights, 1985; Freedom Cup award, Women's League of Israel, 1986; Nobel Peace Prize, 1986; Medal of Libery Award, 1986; Special Christopher Book Award, 1987; achievement award, Artists and Writers for Peace in the Middle East, 1987; Profiles of Courage award, B'nai B'rith, 1987; Human Rights Law Award, International Human Rights Law Group, 1988; Presidential medal, Hofstra University, 1988; Human Rights Law award, International Human Rights Law Group, 1988; Bicentennial medal, Georgetown University, 1988; Janus Korczak Humanitarian award, NAHE, Kent State University, 1989; Count Sforza award in Philanthropy Interphil, 1989; Lily Edelman award for Excellence in Continuing Jewish Education, B'nai B'rith International, 1989; George Washington award, American Hungarian Foundation, 1989; Bicentennial medal, New York University, 1989; Humanitarian award Human Rights Campaign Fund, 1989; International Brotherhood award, C.O.R.E., 1990; Frank Weil award for distinguished contribution to the advancement of North American Jewish culture, Jewish Community Centers Association of North America, 1990; first Raoul Wallenberg medal, University of Michigan, 1990; Award of Highest Honor, Soka University, 1991; Facing History and Ourselves Humanity award, 1991; La Medaille de la Ville de Toulouse, 1991; Fifth Centennial Christopher Columbus medal, City of Genoa, 1992; first Primo Levi award, 1992; Ellis Island Medal of Honor, 1992; Presidential Medal of Freedom Literature Arts award, National Foundation for Jewish Culture, 1992; Ellis Island Medal of Honor, 1992; Guardian of the Children award, AKIM USA, 1992; Bishop Francis J. Mugavero award for religious and racial harmony, Queens College, 1994; Golden Slipper Humanitarian award, 1994; Interfaith Council on the Holocaust Humanitarian award, 1994; Crystal award, Davos World Economic Forum, 1995; first Niebuhr award, Elmhurst College, 1995; President's Award, Quinnipiac College, 1996; Golden Plate Award, American Academy of Achievement, 1996; Lotos Medal of Merit, Lotos Club, 1996; Guardian of Zion Award, Bar-Ilan University, 1997; Canterbury Medalist, Beckett Fund for Religious Liberty, 1998; American Bar Association Annual Award, 1998; Rabbi Marc H. Tannenbaum Award for the Advancement of Interreligious Understanding, 1998; Yitzhak Rabin Peacemaker Award, Merrimack College, 1998; Aesop Prize, Children's Folklore Section, American Folklore Society, for *King Solomon and His Magic Ring,* 1999; Raoul Wallenberg International Humanitarian Award, American Jewish Joint Distribution Committee, 1999; Mathilde Schechter Award, Women's League for Conservative Judaism, 2000; Manhattan Award, National Arts Club, 2000; Benediction Medal, Delbarton School, 2001; Humanitarian of the Year Award, New York Society of Association Executives, 2002; Dean's Medal, Walsh School of Foreign Service, Georgetown University, 2002; Emma Lazarus Statue of Liberty Award, American Jewish Historical Society, 2002; Lifetime Visionary Award, Israeli Film Festival, New York, 2002; named Humanitarian of the Century, Council of Jewish Organizations; recipient of over 100 honorary degrees; Oprah Book Club selection, for *Night;* honors established in his name: Elie Wiesel Award for Holocaust Research, University of Haifa; Elie Wiesel Chair in Holocaust Studies, Bar-Ilan University; Elie Wiesel Endowment Fund for Jewish Culture, University of Denver; Elie Wiesel Distinguished Service Award, University of Florida; Elie Wiesel Awards for Jewish Arts and Culture, B'nai B'rith Hillel Foundations; Elie Wiesel Chair in Judaic Studies, Connecticut College; Elie Wiesel Prize in Ethics, Elie Wiesel Foundation for Humanity.

WRITINGS:

Un Di Velt Hot Geshvign (title means "And the World Has Remained Silent"), [Buenos Aires], 1956, abridged French translation published as *La Nuit* (also see below), foreword by Francois Mauriac, Editions de Minuit (Paris, France), 1958, translation by Stella Rodway published as *Night* (also see below), Hill & Wang (New York, NY), 1960.

L'Aube (also see below), Editions du Seuil (Paris, France), 1961, translation by Frances Frenaye published as *Dawn* (also see below), Hill & Wang (New York, NY), 1961.

Le Jour (also see below), Editions du Seuil (Paris, France), 1961, translation by Anne Borchardt published as *The Accident* (also see below), Hill & Wang (New York, NY), 1962.

La Ville de la chance, Editions du Seuil (Paris, France), 1962, translation by Stephen Becker published as *The Town beyond the Wall,* Atheneum (New York, NY), 1964, new edition, Holt (New York, NY), 1967.

Les Portes de la foret, Editions du Seuil (Paris, France), 1964, translation by Frances Frenaye published as *The Gates of the Forest,* Holt (New York, NY), 1966.

Le Chant des morts, Editions du Seuil (Paris, France), 1966, translation published as *Legends of Our Time,* Holt (New York, NY), 1968.

The Jews of Silence: A Personal Report on Soviet Jewry (originally published in Hebrew as a series of articles for newspaper *Yedioth Ahronoth*), translation and afterword by Neal Kozodoy, Holt (New York, NY), 1966, 2nd edition, Vallentine, Mitchell, 1973.

Zalmen; ou, la Folie de Dieu (play), 1966, translation by Lily and Nathan Edelman published as *Zalmen; or, The Madness of God,* Holt (New York, NY), 1968.

Le Mendiant de Jerusalem, 1968, translation by the author and L. Edelman published as *A Beggar in Jerusalem,* Random House (New York, NY), 1970.

La Nuit, L'Aube, [and] *Le Jour,* Editions du Seuil (Paris, France), 1969, translation published as *Night, Dawn,* [and] *The Accident: Three Tales,* Hill & Wang (New York, NY), 1972, reprinted as *The Night Trilogy: Night, Dawn, The Accident,* Farrar, Straus (New York, NY), 1987, translation by Stella Rodway published as *Night, Dawn, Day,* Aronson (New York, NY), 1985.

Entre deux soleils, Editions du Seuil (Paris, France), 1970, translation by the author and L. Edelman published as *One Generation After,* Random House (New York, NY), 1970.

Celebration Hassidique: Portraits et legendes, Editions du Seuil (Paris, France), 1972, translation by wife, Marion Wiesel, published as *Souls on Fire: Portraits and Legends of Hasidic Masters,* Random House (New York, NY), 1972.

Le Serment de Kolvillag, Editions du Seuil (Paris, France), 1973, translation by Marion Wiesel published as *The Oath,* Random House (New York, NY), 1973.

Ani maamin: A Song Lost and Found Again (cantata), music composed by Darius Milhaud, Random House (New York, NY), 1974.

Celebration Biblique: Portraits et legendes, Editions du Seuil (Paris, France), 1975, translation by Marion Wiesel published as *Messengers of God: Biblical Portraits and Legends,* Random House (New York, NY), 1976.

Un Juif aujourd'hui: Recits, essais, dialogues, Editions du Seuil (Paris, France), 1977, translation by Marion Wiesel published as *A Jew Today,* Random House (New York, NY), 1978.

(With others) *Dimensions of the Holocaust,* Indiana University Press (Bloomington, IN), 1977.

Four Hasidic Masters and Their Struggle against Melancholy, University of Notre Dame Press (Notre Dame, IN), 1978.

Le Proces de Shamgorod tel qu'il se deroula le 25 fevrier 1649: Piece en trois actes, Editions du Seuil (Paris, France), 1979, translation by Marion Wiesel published as *The Trial of God (As It Was Held on February 25, 1649, in Shamgorod): A Play in Three Acts,* Random House (New York, NY), 1979, reprinted, Schocken Books (New York, NY), 1995.

Images from the Bible, illustrated with paintings by Shalom of Safed, Overlook Press (New York, NY), 1980.

Le Testament d'un poete Juif assassine, Editions du Seuil (Paris, France), 1980, translation by Marion Wiesel published as *The Testament,* Simon & Schuster (New York, NY), 1981.

Five Biblical Portraits, University of Notre Dame Press (Notre Dame, IN), 1981.

Somewhere a Master, Simon & Schuster (New York, NY), 1982, reprinted as *Somewhere a Master: Further Tales of the Hasidic Masters,* Summit Books (New York, NY), 1984.

Paroles d'etranger, Editions du Seuil (Paris, France), 1982.

The Golem: The Story of a Legend As Told by Elie Wiesel (fiction), illustrated by Mark Podwal, Summit Books (New York, NY), 1983.

Le Cinquieme Fils, Grasset (Paris, France), 1983, translation by M. Wiesel published as *The Fifth Son,* Summit Books (New York, NY), 1985.

Against Silence: The Voice and Vision of Elie Wiesel, three volumes, edited by Irving Abrahamson, Holocaust Library, 1985.

Signes d'exode, Grasset (Paris, France), 1985.

Job ou Dieu dans la tempete, Grasset (Paris, France), 1986.

Le Crepuscule au loin, Grasset (Paris, France), 1987, translation by Marion Wiesel published as *Twilight,* Summit Books (New York, NY), 1988, reprinted, Schocken Books (New York, NY), 1995.

(With Albert H. Friedlander) *The Six Days of Destruction,* Paulist Press (Mahwah, NJ), 1989.

L'Oublie: Roman, Editions du Seuil (Paris, France), 1989.

(With Philippe-Michael de Saint-Cheron) *Evil and Exile,* translated by Jon Rothschild, University of Notre Dame Press (Notre Dame, IN), 1990.

From the Kingdom of Memory: Reminiscences, Summit Books (New York, NY), 1990.

The Forgotten (novel), translated by Stephen Becker, Summit Books (New York, NY), 1992.

(With Salomon Malka) *Monsieur Chouchani: L'Enigme d'un maitre du XX siecle: Entretiens avec Elie Wiesel, suivis d'une enquete,* J.C. Lattes (Paris, France), 1994.

Tous les fleuves vont a la mer: Memoires, Editions du Seuil (Paris, France), 1994, published as *All Rivers Run to the Sea: Memoirs,* Knopf (New York, NY), 1995.

(With Francois Mitterrand) *Memoire a deux voix,* Jacob (Paris, France), 1995, published as *Memoir in Two Voices,* Arcade (New York, NY), 1996.

Das Gegenteil von Gleichgueltigkeit ist Erinnerung: Versuche zu Elie Wiesel, edited by Dagmar Mensink and Reinhold Boschki, Matthias-Gruenewald-Verlag (Mainz, Germany), 1995.

Jorge Semprun, *Semprun, Wiesel: Se taire est impossible,* Editions Mille et une nuits (Paris, France), 1995.

(Author of foreword) Robert Krell and Marc I. Sherman, editors, *Medical and Psychological Effects of Concentration Camps on Holocaust Survivors,* Transaction Publishers (New Brunswick, NJ), 1997.

Ethics and Memory, with a preface by Wolf Lepenies, W. de Gruyter (New York, NY), 1997.

Celebration prophetique: Portraits et legendes, Editions du Seuil (Paris, France), 1998.

Alan Rosen, editor, *Celebrating Elie Wiesel: Stories, Essays, Reflections,* University of Notre Dame Press (Notre Dame, IN), 1998.

King Solomon and His Magic Ring, paintings by Mark Podwal, Greenwillow Books (New York, NY), 1999.

Ekkehard Schuster and Reinhold Boschert-Kimmig, *Hope against Hope: Johann Baptist Metz and Elie*

Wiesel Speak Out on the Holocaust, translated by J. Matthew Ashley, Paulist Press (New York, NY), 1999.

And the Sea Is Never Full: Memoirs, 1969—, translated from the French by Marion Wiesel, Knopf (New York, NY), 1999.

(With Richard D. Heffner) *Conversations with Elie Wiesel,* edited by Thomas J. Vinciguerra, Schocken Books (New York, NY), 2001.

The Judges, Knopf (New York, NY), 2002.

After the Darkness, Schocken Books (New York, NY), 2002.

Elie Wiesel: Conversations, edited by Robert Franciosi, University of Mississippi Press (Jackson, MS), 2002.

Also author of *A Song for Hope,* 1987, and *The Nobel Speech,* 1987.

Contributor to numerous periodicals.

SIDELIGHTS: In the spring of 1944, the Nazis entered the Transylvanian village of Sighet, Romania, until then a relatively safe and peaceful enclave in the middle of a war-torn continent. Arriving with orders to exterminate an estimated 600,000 Jews in six weeks or less, Adolf Eichmann, chief of the Gestapo's Jewish section, began making arrangements for a mass deportation program. Among those forced to leave their homes was fifteen-year-old Elie Wiesel, the only son of a grocer and his wife. A serious and devoted student of the Talmud and the mystical teachings of Hasidism and the Cabala, the young man had always assumed he would spend his entire life in Sighet, quietly contemplating the religious texts and helping out in the family's store from time to time. Instead, along with his father, mother, and three sisters, Wiesel was herded onto a train bound for Birkenau, the reception center for the infamous death camp Auschwitz.

For reasons he still finds impossible to comprehend, Wiesel survived Birkenau and later Auschwitz and Buna and Buchenwald; his father, mother, and youngest sister did not (he did not learn until after the war that his older sisters also survived). With nothing and no one in Sighet for him to go back to, Wiesel boarded a train for Belgium with four hundred other orphans who, like him, had no reason or desire to return to their former homes. On orders of General Charles de Gaulle, head of the French provisional government after World War II, the train was diverted to France, where border officials asked the children to raise their hands if they wanted to become French citizens. As Wiesel (who at that time neither spoke nor understood French) recalled in the *Washington Post,* "A lot of them did. They thought they were going to get bread or something; they would reach out for anything. I didn't, so I remained stateless."

Wiesel chose to stay in France for a while, settling first in Normandy and later in Paris, doing whatever he could to earn a living: tutoring, directing a choir, translating. Eventually he began working as a reporter for various French and Jewish publications. But he could not quite bring himself to write about what he had seen and felt at Auschwitz and Buchenwald. Doubtful of his—or of anyone's—ability to convey the horrible truth without diminishing it, Wiesel vowed never to make the attempt.

The young journalist's self-imposed silence came to an end in the mid-1950s, however, after he met and interviewed the Nobel Prize-winning novelist Francois Mauriac. Deeply moved upon learning of Wiesel's tragic youth, Mauriac urged him to speak out and tell the world of his experiences, to "bear witness" for the millions of men, women, and children whom death, and not despair, had silenced. The result was *Night,* the story of a teen-age boy plagued with guilt for having survived the camps and devastated by the realization that the God he had once worshipped so devoutly allowed his people to be destroyed. For the most part autobiographical, it was, stated Richard M. Elman in the *New Republic,* "a document as well as a work of literature—journalism which emerged, coincidentally, as a work of art."

Described by the *Nation*'s Daniel Stern as "undoubtedly the single most powerful literary relic of the holocaust," *Night* is the first in a series of nonfiction books and autobiographical novels this "lyricist of lamentation" has written that deal, either directly or indirectly, with the Holocaust. "He sees the present always refracted through the prism of these earlier days," commented James Finn in the *New Republic.* The *New York Times*'s Thomas Lask agreed, stating: "For [more than] twenty-five years, Elie Wiesel has been in one form or another a witness to the range, bestiality, and completeness of the destruction of European Jewry by the Germans. . . . Auschwitz informs everything he writes—novels, legends, dialogues. He is not belligerent about it, only unyielding. Nothing he can say measures up to the enormity of what he saw, what others endured." Writing in *Nonfiction Classics for Students,* Kelly Winters explained that Wiesel tells his story in *Night* using simple, direct statements: "The story is told in an extremely understated, tight style. Wiesel does not tell the reader what to think; he simply presents events as plainly as possible and lets them speak for themselves. The events, such as the mass killing of babies who are thrown into a flaming furnace, or the hanging of children, are so horrifying that Wiesel does not need to belabor them or to express his own terror or anger directly; his taut style and emotional restraint make them even more believable and frightening."

Other novels by Wiesel about the Jewish experience during and after the Holocaust include *Dawn* and *The Accident,* which were later published together with *Night* in *The Night Trilogy: Night, Dawn, The Accident.* Like *Night,* the other two books in the trilogy have concentration camp survivors as their central characters. *Dawn* concerns the experiences of one survivor just after World War II who joins the Jewish underground efforts to form an independent Israeli state; and *The Accident* is about a man who discovers that his collision with an automobile was actually caused by his subconscious, guilt-ridden desire to commit suicide. "Wiesel's writings after *Night* have been attempts to reclaim faith in language, in humanity, in God, and in himself," explained Jane Elizabeth Dougherty in an essay for *Novels for Students.* "In *Night,* faith seems an incredible burden, a hindrance to survival, and yet it remains the only way in which the Jews can survive the horrors of the Holocaust. In the context of the concentration camp universe, Wiesel suggests that the only thing more dangerous than faith is disbelief."

In two of Wiesel's later novels, *The Testament* and *The Fifth Son,* the author also explores the effects of the Holocaust on the next generation of Jews. Some critics, such as *Globe and Mail* contributor Bronwyn Drainie, have questioned the validity of the author's belief that children of Holocaust survivors would be "as morally galvanized by the Nazi nightmare as the survivors themselves." But, asserted Richard F. Shepard in the *New York Times,* even if the feelings of these children cannot be generalized, "the author does make all of us 'children' of that generation, all of us who were not there, in the sense that he outlines for us the burdens of guilt, of revenge, of despair."

Indeed, the Holocaust and the Jewish religious and philosophical tradition involve experiences and beliefs shared by a great many people, including other writers. But as Kenneth Turan declared in the *Washington Post Book World,* Elie Wiesel has become "much more than just a writer. He is a symbol, a banner, and a beacon, perhaps *the* survivor of the Holocaust. . . . He seems to own the horror of the death camps, or, rather, the horror owns him." But it is a moral and spiritual, not a physical, horror that obsesses Wiesel and obliges him to compose what Dan Isaac of the *Nation* called "an angry message to God, filled with both insane rage and stoical acceptance; calculated to stir God's wrath, but careful not to trigger an apocalypse." Explained Isaac's *Nation* colleague Laurence Goldstein: "For Elie Wiesel memory is an instrument of revelation. Each word he uses to document the past transforms both the work and the memory into an act of faith. The writings of Elie Wiesel are a journey into the past blackened by the Nazi death camps where the charred souls of its victims possess the sum of guilt and endurance that mark the progress of man. It is a compulsive, fevered, single-minded search among the ashes for a spark that can be thrust before the silent eyes of God himself."

Unlike those who dwell primarily on the physical horror, then, Wiesel writes from the perspective of a passionately religious man whose faith has been profoundly shaken by what he has witnessed. As Goldstein remarked, "He must rediscover himself. . . . Although he has not lost God, he must create out of the pain and numbness a new experience that will keep his God from vanishing among the unforgettable faces of the thousands whose bodies he saw." According to Maurice Friedman of *Commonweal,* Wiesel is, in fact, "the most moving embodiment of the Modern Job": a man who questions—in books that "form one unified outcry, one sustained protest, one sobbing and singing prayer"—why the just must suffer while the wicked flourish. This debate with God is one of the central themes of what a *Newsweek* critic referred to as Wiesel's "God-tormented, God-intoxicated" fiction.

In addition to his intense preoccupation with ancient Jewish philosophy, mythology, and history, Wiesel displays a certain affinity with modern French existentialists, an affinity Josephine Knopp believed is a direct consequence of the Holocaust. Wrote Knopp in *Contemporary Literature:* "To the young Wiesel the notion of an 'absurd' universe would have been a completely alien one. . . . The traditional Jewish view holds that life's structure and meaning are fully explained and indeed derive from the divinely granted Torah. . . . Against this background the reality of Auschwitz confronts the Jew with a dilemma, an 'absurdity' which cannot be dismissed easily and which stubbornly refuses to dissipate of its own accord. . . . The only possible response that remains within the framework of Judaism is denunciation of God and a demand that He fulfill His contractual obligation [to protect those who worship Him]. This is the religious and moral context within which Wiesel attempts to apprehend and assimilate the events of the Holocaust. [He seeks] to reconcile Auschwitz with Judaism, to confront and perhaps wring meaning from the absurd." In a more recent novel, *Twilight,* Wiesel explores this absurdity—in this case, he goes so far as to call it madness—of the universe. Again, the protagonist is a Jew, who begins to wonder, as *New York Times* reviewer John Gross explained, whether "it is mad to go on believing in God. Or perhaps . . . it is God who is mad: who else but a mad God could have created such a world?"

The strong emphasis on Jewish tradition and Jewish suffering in Wiesel's works does not mean that he speaks only to and for Jews. In fact, maintained Robert McAfee Brown in *Christian Century,* "writing out of the particularity of his own Jewishness . . . is how [Wiesel] touches universal chords. He does not write about 'the human condition,' but about 'the Jewish condition.' Correction: in writing about the Jewish condition, he thereby writes about the human condition. For the human condition is not generalized existence; it is a huge, crazy-quilt sum of particularized existences all woven together."

To Stern, this time commenting in the *Washington Post Book World,* it seemed that "Wiesel has taken the Jew as his metaphor—and his reality—in order to unite a moral and aesthetic vision in terms of all men." Manes Sperber of the *New York Times Book Review* expressed a similar view, stating that "Wiesel is one of the few writers who, without any plaintiveness, has succeeded in revealing in the Jewish tragedy those features by which it has become again and again a paradigm of the human condition."

According to Michael J. Bandler in the *Christian Science Monitor,* Wiesel conveys his angry message to God "with a force and stylistic drive that leaves the reader stunned." Concise and uncluttered, yet infused with a highly emotional biblical mysticism, the author's prose "gleams again and again with the metaphor of the poet," wrote Clifford A. Ridley in the *National Observer.* Though it "never abandons its tender intimacy," reported Sperber, "[Wiesel's] voice comes from far away in space and time. It is the voice of the Talmudic teachers of Jerusalem and Babylon; of medieval mystics; of Rabbi Nachman of Bratzlav whose tales have inspired generations of Hasidim and so many writers." As Lask observed, "[Wiesel] has made the form of the telling his own. The surreal and the supernatural combine abrasively with the harsh fact; the parable, the rabbinic tale support and sometimes substitute for narrative. The written law and oral tradition support, explain and expand the twentieth-century event." Goldstein, noting the author's "remarkably compassionate tone," declared that "he writes with that possessive reverence for language that celebrates, as much as describes, experience. The written word becomes a powerful assertion, the triumph of life over death and indifference. . . . Words carved on gravestones, legend torn from the pit where millions of broken bodies lie. This is the inheritance which Elie Wiesel brings to us. His voice claims us with its urgency. His vision lights the mystery of human endurance."

Several critics, however, felt Wiesel's prose does not quite live up to the demands of his subject. Jeffrey Burke, for example, commenting in the *New York Times Book Review,* stated that the author occasionally "slips into triteness or purple prose or redundancy," and a reviewer for the *New Yorker* found that Wiesel becomes "nearly delirious" in his intensity. *Newsweek*'s Geoffrey Wolff believed that Wiesel's work at times "suffers from unnecessary confusions, linguistic cliches, dense and purple thickets, and false mystifications. Ideas tend to hobble about . . . on stilts. . . . The language, seeking to transport us to another world, collapses beneath the weight of its burden much too often." Burke concluded: "No one can or would deny the seriousness and necessity of Elie Wiesel's role as witness. . . . It is natural that such a mission would remain uppermost in the writer's mind, but that the requirements of art should proportionately diminish in significance is not an acceptable corollary. [Wiesel tends] to sacrifice the demands of craft to those of conscience."

In defense of Wiesel, Turan stated that "his is a deliberate, elegant style, consciously elevated and poetic, and if he occasionally tries to pack too much into a sentence, to jam it too full of significance and meaning, it is an error easy to forgive." Elman, this time writing in the *New York Times Book Review,* also found that "some of Wiesel's existentialist parables are deeply flawed by an opacity of language and construction, which may confirm that 'the event was so heavy with horror . . . that words could not really contain it.' But Wiesel's work is not diminished by his failure to make his shattering theme—God's betrayal of man—consistently explicit." Thus, according to Jonathan Brent in the *Chicago Tribune Book World,* Wiesel is "the type of writer distinguished by his subject rather than his handling of it. . . . Such writers must be read not for themselves but for the knowledge they transmit of events, personalities, and social conditions outside their fiction itself. They do not master their material esthetically, but remain faithful to it; and this constitutes the principal value of their work."

Few agree with these assessments of Wiesel's stylistic abilities, but many support Brent's conclusion that the author is almost compulsively faithful to his subject. As Lawrence L. Langer observed in the *Washington Post Book World:* "Although Elie Wiesel has announced many times in recent years that he is finished with the Holocaust as a subject for public discourse, it is clear . . . that the Holocaust has not yet finished with him. Almost from his first volume to his last, his writing has been an act of homage, a ritual of remembrance in response to a dreadful challenge 'to unite the language of man with the silence of the dead'. . . . If Elie Wiesel returns compulsively to the ruins of the Holocaust world, it is not because he has nothing new to say. . . . [It is simply that] the man he did not become besieges his imagination and compels him to confirm his appointments with the past that holds him prisoner."

Wiesel expresses what *Commonweal*'s Irving Halpern called "the anguish of a survivor who is unable to exorcise the past or to live with lucidity and grace in the present" in the book *Night,* his first attempt to bear witness for the dead. Wiesel wrote: "Never shall I forget that night, the first night in camp, which has turned my life into one long night, seven times cursed and seven times sealed. Never shall I forget that smoke. Never shall I forget the little faces of the children, whose bodies I saw turned into wreaths of smoke beneath a silent blue sky. Never shall I forget those flames which consumed my Faith forever. Never shall I forget that nocturnal silence which deprived me, for all eternity, of the desire to live. Never shall I forget those moments which murdered my God and my soul and turned my dreams to dust. Never shall I forget these things, even if I am condemned to live as long as God Himself. Never."

Concern that the truths of the Holocaust, and memories in general, might in time be forgotten has often fueled Wiesel's writing. In comparing his many works, Wiesel remarked to *Publishers Weekly* interviewer Elizabeth Devereaux, "What do they have in common? Their commitment to memory. What is the opposite of memory? Alzheimer's disease. I began to research this topic and I discovered that this is the worst disease, that every intellectual is afraid of this disease, not just because it is incurable, which is true of other diseases, too. But here the identity is being abolished." From this realization Wiesel created *The Forgotten,* a novel in which a Holocaust survivor fears he is losing his memories to an unnamed ailment. He beseeches his son to listen and remember as he recounts the events of his life. The dutiful son embarks for Romania to recover the details of his father's experience, including the death of his family at the hands of the Nazis and his role as an Eastern European partisan and freedom fighter for the establishment of Israel. Though Wiesel told Devereaux that this novel is "less autobiographical" than his others, *The Forgotten* contains recognizable allusions to his own life and work in references to the one-word titles of his first three novels and similarities between the father's childhood village and Wiesel's own. As Frederick Busch observed in the *New York Times Book Review,* Wiesel "intends to warn us that many of the survivors of the Holocaust are dying, that the cruel truth of the war against the Jews might one day be lost or clouded." Citing the author's "characteristic blend of petition, contemplative discourse, and devotion to Jewish tradition," Jonathan Dorfman wrote in a *Chicago Tribune* review, "*The Forgotten* is ample proof that . . . Wiesel remains a writer of significance and high merit."

The novel *The Judges* is a moral fable that deals with issues of justice and truth. An airplane is forced to land unexpectedly due to bad weather. Once on the ground, five of the passengers are taken captive by a strange figure who calls himself "the Judge." In a series of probing, intimate questions, the Judge forces the prisoners to face their own deepest selves, their beliefs and values. A *Publishers Weekly* critic explained that "each character, caught in the facts of his or her past and oriented toward future projects, must confront a present threat that crystallizes their existences." "Courageous and profoundly philosophical," Patrick Sullivan wrote in the *Library Journal,* "this novel skillfully explores moral questions that have never been more relevant."

Wiesel produced the first volume of his projected two-volume personal memoirs with *All Rivers Run to the Sea,* spanning the years from his childhood to the 1960s. He begins by recollecting the haunting premonition of a well-known rabbi which foretold the young Wiesel's future greatness, though it predicted that neither Wiesel nor his mother would live to know of his acclaim. In the reminiscence and anecdote that follows, Wiesel revisits his early village life, postwar orphanage and education in France, initiation as a professional journalist, and involvement in events surrounding the birth of Israel. As James E. Young noted in the *New Leader,* Wiesel devotes only twenty pages of the book to his concentration camp experiences. "Wiesel's memoir is not about what happened during those eleven months," Young wrote, "but about how they shaped his life afterward, how they have been remembered, how he has lived in their shadow." Despite Wiesel's confessed over-sensitivity to criticism and painful episodes of self-doubt, critics noted that his memoir reveals little about the author's personal life that is not evident in his previous works. Daphne Merkin wrote in the *New York Times Book Review,* "If the reader finishes this book with an impression that the public and private Elie Wiesel seem to dance around each other without ever really connecting, the author has foreseen this: 'Some see their work as a commentary on their life; for others it is the other way around. I count myself among the latter. Consider this account, then, as a kind of commentary.'" Wiesel concluded, as quoted by Vivian Gornick in the *Nation:* "The aim of the literature I call testimony is to disturb. I disturb the believer because I dare to put questions to God. I disturb the miscreant because I refuse to break with the religious and mystical universe that has shaped my own. Most of all, I disturb those who are comfortably settled within a system—be it political, psychological, or theological."

And the Sea Is Never Full continues Wiesel's life story since 1969. His activities as an activist promoting the memory of the Holocaust and of spreading the word about human rights violations in the Soviet Union are covered in great detail. As Pierre L. Horn noted in *World Literature Today,* "The emphasis is on Wiesel the public figure rather than the private man." Alvin H. Rosenfeld, writing in the *New Leader,* explained that "while this is a book of often vivid autobiographical reflection, it is also something more—an anguished probing of the links between memory and traumatic event, memory and justice, memory and the quest for a common morality." A critic for *Publishers Weekly* stated: "Wiesel's writing is as fluid and evocative as ever, and his storytelling skills turn the events of his own life into a powerful series of morality plays."

In 1996 *Memoir in Two Voices,* which Wiesel coauthored with his friend, former French president Francois Mitterrand, was published. The volume offers a glimpse into the life of the former leader, who served as France's president from 1981 to 1995; the topics covered are driven by Wiesel's questions, which are intended to elicit explanations from Mitterrand. The book was characterized by a *Publishers Weekly* reviewer as containing insights into Mitterrand's personal life that were "as fascinating for their revelations as they [were] for their silences," indicating that the book did not probe as deeply into the mind of the French leader as the critic would have liked. Bonnie Smothers, reviewing *Memoir in Two Voices* for *Booklist,* assessed the section of the book in which Wiesel questions Mitterrand about the leader's knowledge of the Nazis' treatment of Jews during World War II as providing "a very enlightening exchange" between the two authors, and called the volume as a whole "a very special book, powerful at times, always provoking the reader's inner thoughts."

Many years after *Night,* Wiesel is still torn between words and silence. "You must speak," he told a *People* interviewer, "but how can you, when the full story is beyond language?" Furthermore, he once remarked in the *Washington Post,* "there is the fear of not being believed, . . . the fear that the experience will be reduced, made into something acceptable, perhaps forgotten." But as he went on to explain in *People:* "We [survivors] believe that if we survived, we must do something with our lives. The first task is to tell the tale." In short, concluded Wiesel, "The only way to stop the next holocaust—the nuclear holocaust—is to remember the last one. If the Jews were singled out then, in the next one we are all victims." For his enduring efforts to keep the memory of the Holocaust alive so that such a tragedy would not repeat itself ever again, Wiesel was awarded the Nobel Peace Prize in 1986. In a *New York Times* article on the event, James M. Markham quoted Egil Aarvik, chair of the Norwegian Nobel Committee: "Wiesel is a messenger to mankind. . . . His message is one of peace, atonement and human dignity. His belief that the forces fighting evil in the world can be victorious is a hard-won belief . . . repeated and deepened through the works of a great author." Speaking of Wiesel's fiction, Albert H. Friedlander in *Contemporary World Writers* concluded: "Each new book by Wiesel is filled with the concern for humanity which earned him the Nobel Peace prize. Each book is a letter addressed both to humanity and God. When one understands this, one begins to understand Elie Wiesel and his message."

BIOGRAPHICAL AND CRITICAL SOURCES:

BOOKS

Authors and Artists for Young Adults, Volume 7, Thomson Gale (Detroit, MI), 1991.

Authors in the News, Volume 1, Thomson Gale (Detroit, MI), 1976.

Berenbaum, Michael, *Elie Wiesel: God, the Holocaust, and the Children of Israel,* Behrman House, 1994.

Cohen, Myriam B., *Elie Wiesel: Variations sur le Silence,* Rumeur des ages, 1988.

Contemporary Authors Autobiography Series, Volume 4, Thomson Gale (Detroit, MI), 1986.

Contemporary Issues Criticism, Volume 1, Thomson Gale (Detroit, MI), 1982.

Contemporary Literary Criticism, Thomson Gale (Detroit, MI), Volume 3, 1975, Volume 5, 1976, Volume 11, 1979, Volume 37, 1986.

Contemporary World Writers, 2nd edition, St. James Press (Detroit, MI), 1993.

Davis, Colin, *Elie Wiesel's Secretive Texts,* University Press of Florida Press (Gainesville, FL), 1994.

Dictionary of Literary Biography, Volume 83: *French Novelists since 1960,* Thomson Gale (Detroit, MI), 1989.

Dictionary of Literary Biography Yearbook: 1987, Thomson Gale (Detroit, MI), 1988.

Lazo, Caroline Evensen, *Elie Wiesel,* Macmillan (New York, NY), 1994.

Newsmakers 1998, Thomson Gale (Detroit, MI), 1998.

Nonfiction Classics for Students, Volume 4, Thomson Gale (Detroit, MI), 2002.

Novels for Students, Thomson Gale (Detroit, MI), 1998.

Pariser, Michael, *Elie Wiesel: Bearing Witness,* Millbrook Press, 1994.

Rosenfeld, Alvin, *Confronting the Holocaust,* Indiana University Press (Bloomington, IN), 1978.

Schuman, Michael, *Elie Wiesel: Voice from the Holocaust,* Enslow (Springfield, NJ), 1994.

Sibelman, Simon P., *Silence in the Novels of Elie Wiesel,* St. Martin's Press (New York, NY), 1995.

Stern, Ellen Norman, *Elie Wiesel: A Voice for Humanity,* Jewish Publication Society (Philadelphia, PA), 1996.

Wiesel, Elie, *Night,* translated by Stella Rodway, Hill & Wang (New York, NY), 1960.

PERIODICALS

America, November 19, 1988.

Atlantic, November, 1968.

Best Sellers, March 15, 1970; May, 1981.

Booklist, February 15, 1994, p. 1100; September 1, 1995, p. 96; July, 1996, Bonnie Smothers, review of *Memoir in Two Voices,* p. 1798.

Book Week, May 29, 1966.

Chicago Tribune Book World, October 29, 1978; March 29, 1981; May 3, 1992.

Christian Century, January 18, 1961; June 17, 1970; June 3, 1981.

Christian Science Monitor, November 21, 1968; February 19, 1970; November 22, 1978.

Commentary, June, 1996, p. 64.

Commonweal, December 9, 1960; January 6, 1961; March 13, 1964; October 14, 1966.

Contemporary Literature, spring, 1974.

Detroit Free Press, April 12, 1992.

Detroit News, April 4, 1992.

Globe and Mail (Toronto, Ontario, Canada), April 20, 1985; August 6, 1988.

Library Journal, February 15, 1994, p. 202; December, 1995, p. 120; June 1, 2002, Patrick Sullivan, review of *The Judges,* p. 198.

London Times, September 3, 1981.

Los Angeles Times Book Review, June 19, 1988.

Nation, October 17, 1966; February 24, 1969; March 16, 1970; January 5, 1974; December 25, 1995, p. 839.

National Observer, February 2, 1970.

National Review, June 12, 1981.

New Choices, December-January, 1993, p. 64.

New Leader, December 30, 1968; June 15, 1981; December 18, 1995, p. 17; December 13, 1999, Alvin H. Rosenfeld, review of *And the Sea Is Never Full,* p. 13.

New Republic, July 5, 1964; December 14, 1968.

Newsweek, May 25, 1964; February 9, 1970.

New York, December 11, 1995, p. 72.

New Yorker, March 18, 1961; January 9, 1965; August 20, 1966; July 6, 1970; July 12, 1976.

New York Herald Tribune Lively Arts, January 1, 1961; April 30, 1961.

New York Review of Books, July 28, 1966; January 2, 1969; May 7, 1970.

New York Times, December 15, 1970; March 10, 1972; April 3, 1981; April 16, 1984; March 21, 1985; October 15, 1986; June 10, 1988; December 5, 1995, p. B2.

New York Times Book Review, July 16, 1961; April 15, 1962; July 5, 1964; January 21, 1979; April 12, 1981; August 15, 1982; April 30, 1989; April 19, 1992, p. 8; December 17, 1995, p. 7.

People, October 22, 1979.

Publishers Weekly, April 6, 1992; October 16, 1995, p. 49; October 23, 1995, p. 33; January 15, 1996, p. 320; May 20, 1996, p. 245; November 8, 1999, review of *And the Sea Is Never Full,* p. 53; July 15, 2002, review of *The Judges,* p. 55.

Saturday Review, December 17, 1960; July 8, 1961; July 25, 1964; May 28, 1966; October 19, 1968; January 31, 1970; November 21, 1970.

Tikkun, July-August, 1999, "An Interview with Elie Wiesel," pp. 33-35.

Time, March 16, 1970; May 8, 1972; July 12, 1976; December 25, 1978; April 20, 1981.

Times Literary Supplement, August 19, 1960; November 20, 1981; June 6, 1986.

TV Guide, February 15, 1969.

Washington Post, October 26, 1968; February 6, 1970; November 15, 1986; November 4, 1989.

Washington Post Book World, October 20, 1968; January 18, 1970; August 8, 1976; October 29, 1978; April 12, 1981; May 29, 1988.

World Literature Today, summer, 2000, Pierre L. Horn, review of *And the Sea Is Never Full,* p. 630; summer-autumn, 2002, Pierre L. Horn, review of *Conversations with Elie Wiesel,* p. 101.

ONLINE

Elie Wiesel Foundation for Humanity Web site, http://www.eliewieselfoundation.org/ (June 25, 2003).

* * *

WIESEL, Eliezer
See WIESEL, Elie

* * *

WILBUR, Richard 1921-
(Richard Purdy Wilbur)

PERSONAL: Born March 1, 1921, in New York, NY; son of Lawrence Lazear (a portrait artist) and Helen Ruth (Purdy) Wilbur; married Mary Charlotte Hayes Ward, June 20, 1942; children: Ellen Dickinson, Christopher Hayes, Nathan Lord, Aaron Hammond. *Education:* Amherst College, A.B., 1942; Harvard University, A.M., 1947. *Politics:* Independent. *Religion:* Episcopal. *Hobbies and other interests:* Tennis, herb gardening, walking.

ADDRESSES: *Home*—87 Dodwells Rd., Cummington, MA 01026; 715R Windsor Ln., Key West, FL 33040. *Agent*—(Theatrical) Gilbert Parker, William Morris Agency, 1325 Avenue of the Americas, New York, NY 10019.

CAREER: Harvard University, Cambridge, MA, Society of Fellows, junior fellow, 1947-50, assistant professor of English, 1950-54; Wellesley College, Wellesley, MA, associate professor of English, 1955-57; Wesleyan University, Middletown, CT, professor of English, 1957-77; Smith College, Northampton, MA, writer-in-residence, 1977-86; Library of Congress, Washington, DC, Poet Laureate of the United States, 1987-88. Lecturer at colleges, universities, and Library of Congress. U.S. State Department cultural exchange representative to the USSR, 1961. *Military service:* U.S. Army, Infantry, 1943-45; became staff sergeant.

MEMBER: American Academy and Institute of Arts and Letters (president, 1974-76; chancellor, 1976-78), American Academy of Arts and Sciences, PEN, Academy of American Poets (chancellor emeritus), Dramatists' Guild, Modern Language Association (honorary fellow), American Society of Composers, Authors, and Publishers, Authors League of America, Century Club, Chi Psi.

AWARDS, HONORS: Harriet Monroe Memorial Prize, *Poetry* magazine, 1948, 1978; Oscar Blumenthal Prize, *Poetry* magazine, 1950; M.A., Amherst College, 1952; Guggenheim fellowships, 1952-53, 1963; Prix de Rome fellowship, American Academy of Arts and Letters, 1954; Edna St. Vincent Millay Memorial Award, 1957; Pulitzer Prize for poetry and National Book Award for poetry, both 1957, for *Things of This World;* Boston Festival Award, 1959; Ford Foundation fellowship for drama, 1960; Melville Cane Award, 1962; co-recipient, Bollingen Prize for translation, Yale University Library, 1963, for *Tartuffe,* and for poetry, 1971, for *Walking to Sleep;* Sarah Josepha Hale Award, 1968; Creative Arts Award, Brandeis University, 1971; Prix Henri Desfeuilles, 1971; Shelley Memorial Award, 1973; *Book World*'s Children's Spring Book Festival award, 1973, for *Opposites: Poems and Drawings;* PEN translation prize, 1983, for *Moliere: Four Comedies;* St. Botolph's Club Foundation Award, 1983; Drama Desk Award, 1983; Chevalier, Ordre des Palmes Academiques, 1983; named Poet Laureate of the United States, Library of Congress, 1987-88; Taylor Poetry Award, *Sewanee Review* and University of the South, 1988; Bunn Award, 1988; Washington College Literature Award, 1988; National Book Critics Circle Award nomination, 1988, *Los Angeles Times* Book Prize, 1988, and Pulitzer Prize for poetry, 1989, all for *New and Collected Poems;* St. Louis Literature Award, 1988; Gold Medal for Poetry, American Academy and Institute of Arts and Letters, 1991; Edward MacDowell medal, 1992; National Arts Club Medal of Honor for Literature, 1994; National Medal of the Arts, 1994; PEN/Manheim Medal for Translation, 1994; Milton Center prize, 1995; Academy American Achievement award, 1995; Robert Frost Medal, Poetry Society of America, 1996; T.S. Eliot Award, 1996; recipient of numerous honorary degrees, including L.H.D., Lawrence College (now Lawrence University of Wisconsin), 1960, Washington University, 1964, Williams College, 1975, University of Rochester, 1976, and Carnegie-Mellon University, 1980, State University of New York, Potsdam, 1986, Skidmore College, 1987, University of Lowell, 1990; Litt.D., Amherst College, 1967, Clark University, 1970, American International College, 1974, Marquette University, 1977, Wesleyan University, 1977, Lake Forest College, 1982, Smith College, 1996, and Sewanee University, 1996.

WRITINGS:

The Beautiful Changes and Other Poems, Reynal, 1947.

Ceremony and Other Poems, Harcourt (Boston), 1950.

Things of This World: Poems (also see below), Harcourt, 1956.

Poems, 1943-1956, Faber (London), 1957.

(With Robert Hillyer and Cleanth Brooks) *Anniversary Lectures,* U.S. Government Printing Office (Washington, DC), 1959.

(With Louise Bogan and Archibald MacLeish) *Emily Dickinson: Three Views* (criticism), Amherst College Press, 1960.

Advice to a Prophet, and Other Poems, Harcourt, 1961.

Loudmouse (juvenile), illustrated by Don Almquist, Collier (London), 1963, Harcourt (New York City), 1982.

The Poems of Richard Wilbur, Harcourt, 1963.

(Translator) Philippe de Thaun, *The Pelican from a Bestiary of 1120* (poem), privately printed, 1963.

Prince Souvanna Phouma: An Exchange between Richard Wilbur and William Jay Smith (poem), limited edition, Phoenix Book Shop, 1968.

Walking to Sleep: New Poems and Translations, Harcourt, 1969.

Digging to China: Poem (Child Study Association book list; first published in *Things of This World*), Doubleday (Garden City, NY), 1970.

(Self-illustrated) *Opposites: Poems and Drawings* (children's poems), Harcourt, 1973.

Seed Leaves: Homage to R. F. (poem), limited edition, David R. Godine, 1974.

Responses: Prose Pieces, 1953-1976, Harcourt, 1976, expanded edition published by Story Line Press (Ashland, OR), 2000.

The Mind-Reader: New Poems, Harcourt, 1976.

Seven Poems, Abbatoir Editions, 1981.

(Translator) *The Whale and Other Uncollected Translations,* BOA Editions, 1982.

New and Collected Poems, Harcourt, 1988.

Conversations with Richard Wilbur, edited by William Butts, University Press of Mississippi, 1990.

(Self-illustrated) *More Opposites* (children's poems), Harcourt, 1991.

A Game of Catch, illustrations by Barry Moser, Harcourt, 1994.

Runaway Opposites, selections illustrated by Henrik Drescher, Harcourt, 1995.

(Translator) Baudelaire, *L'invitation au voyage, or Invitation to the Voyage: A Poem from the Flowers of Evil, 1854,* Little, Brown (Boston), 1997.

The Catbird's Song: Prose Pieces, 1963-1995, Harcourt, 1997.

The Disappearing Alphabet (children's fiction), illustrated by David Diaz, Harcourt (San Diego), 1998.

Mayflies: New Poems and Translations, Harcourt (New York City), 2000.

Opposites, More Opposites, and a Few Differences (contains *Opposites* and *More Opposites*), edited by Diane D'Andrade, Harcourt, 2000.

The Pig in the Spigot (children's fiction), illustrated by J. Otto Seibold, Harcourt (San Diego), 2000.

Collected Poems: 1943-2004, Harcourt (San Diego, CA), 2005.

PLAYS

(Translator) Moliere, *The Misanthrope: Comedy in Five Acts, 1666* (also see below; produced in Cambridge, MA, by the Poet's Theatre, October 25, 1955; produced off-Broadway at Theatre East, November 12, 1956), Harcourt, 1955.

(Lyricist with John Latouche, Dorothy Parker, Lillian Hellman, and Leonard Bernstein) Voltaire, *Candide: A Comic Operetta Based on Voltaire's Satire* (musical; based on adaptation by Lillian Hellman; music by Leonard Bernstein; produced on Broadway at Martin Beck Theatre, December 1, 1956; produced on the West End at Saville Theatre, April 30, 1959), Random House, 1957.

(Translator) Moliere, *Tartuffe: Comedy in Five Acts, 1669* (also see below; produced in Milwaukee, WI, at Fred Miller Theatre, January, 1964; produced on Broadway at ANTA Theatre, January 14, 1965), Harcourt, 1963.

(Translator) Moliere, *The Misanthrope* [and] *Tartuffe,* Harcourt, 1965.

(Translator) Moliere, *The School for Wives: Comedy in Five Acts, 1662* (produced on Broadway at Lyceum Theatre, February 16, 1971), Harcourt, 1971.

(Translator) Moliere, *The Learned Ladies: Comedy in Five Acts, 1672* (produced in Williamstown, MA, at the Williamstown Festival Theatre, 1977), Harcourt, 1978.

(Translator) Jean Racine, *Andromache: Tragedy in Five Acts, 1667,* Harcourt, 1982.

(Translator) *Moliere: Four Comedies,* Harcourt, 1982.

(Translator) Racine, *Phaedra,* Harcourt, 1986.

(Translator) Moliere, *The School for Husbands* (also see below), Harcourt, 1992.

(Translator) *The Imaginary Cuckold* (also see below), Dramatists Play Service, 1993.

(Translator) Moliere, *The School for Husbands & Sganarelle, or The Imaginary Cuckold,* Harcourt, 1994.

(Translator) Moliere, *Amphitryon,* Dramatists Play Service (New York City), 1995.

(Translator) Moliere, *Don Juan,* Dramatists Play Service (New York City), 1998, published as *Don Juan: Comedy in Five Acts, 1665,* Harcourt, 2001.

EDITOR

(With Louis Untermeyer and Karl Shapiro) *Modern American and Modern British Poetry,* revised abridged edition, Harcourt, 1955.

A Bestiary (anthology), Pantheon, 1955.

(And author of introduction and notes) Edgar Allan Poe, *Complete Poems,* Dell, 1959.

(Editor, with others) *Major Writers of America,* Harcourt, 1962.

(With Alfred Harbage, and author of introduction) William Shakespeare, *Poems,* Penguin, 1966, revised edition published as *Shakespeare, the Narrative Poems and Poems of Doubtful Authenticity,* 1974.

(And author of introduction) Poe, *The Narrative of Arthur Gordon Pym,* David R. Godine, 1974.

(And author of introduction) Witter Bynner, *Selected Poems,*Farrar, Straus, 1978.

OTHER

(Contributor) Gygory Kepes, editor, *The New Landscape in Art and Science,* Paul Theobald, 1955.

Poems (recording), Spoken Arts, 1959.

(Contributor) Don C. Allen, editor, *The Moment of Poetry,* Johns Hopkins Press, 1962.

(Lyricist) *On Freedom's Ground* (cantata; music by William Schuman), produced in New York City at the Lincoln Center for the Statue of Liberty Centennial, October, 1986.

(Author of foreword) Rollie McKenna, *A Life in Photography,* efKnopf (New York City), 1991.

Also recorded *Richard Wilbur Reading His Own Poems,* for Caedmon, and additional readings for the Archive of Recorded Poetry and Literature, Library of Congress. Translator of *The Funeral of Bobo,* by Joseph Brodsky, for Ardis. Work represented in anthologies. Contributor of critical reviews to periodicals. General editor, "Laurel Poets" series, for Dell; former member of poetry board, Wesleyan University Press.

SIDELIGHTS: Richard Wilbur "is a poet for all of us, whose elegant words brim with wit and paradox," announced Librarian of Congress Daniel J. Boorstin when the poet succeeded Robert Penn Warren to become the second poet laureate of the United States. Elizabeth Kastor further quoted Boorstin in her *Washington Post* article: "He is also a poet's poet, at home in the long tradition of the traveled ways of the great poets of our language. . . . His poems are among the best our country has to offer." The second poet laureate has won the Pulitzer Prize and National Book Award for his collection *Things of This World: Poems* in 1957 and a second Pulitzer for *New and Collected Poems,* among other numerous awards for his poetry. His translations of French verse, especially Voltaire's *Candide* and the plays of Moliere and Jean Racine, are also highly regarded by critics; his translation of Moliere's *Tartuffe* won the 1971 Bollingen Prize.

The son of a commercial artist, Wilbur was interested in painting as a youth; but he eventually opted to pursue writing as his avocation, a decision he attributes to the influence of his mother's father and grandfather, both of whom were editors. As a student, Wilbur wrote stories, editorials, and poems for his college newspaper and magazine, but, as the poet commented in *Twentieth-Century Authors: A Biographical Dictionary of Modern Literature:* "It was not until World War II took me to Cassino, Anzio, and the Siegfried Line that I began to versify in earnest. One does not use poetry for its major purposes, as a means to organize oneself and the world, until one's world somehow gets out of hand." Witnessing war firsthand has had a major effect on Wilbur's poetry. "Many of his first poems had a common motive," wrote Richard L. Calhoun in the *Dictionary of Literary Biography,* "the desire to stress the importance of finding order in a world where war had served as a reminder of disorder and destruction."

Because of this motivation, Wilbur's first collection, *The Beautiful Changes and Other Poems,* contains "more poetic exercises on how to face the problems of disorder and destruction than laments over the losses occasioned by the war," noted Calhoun. The poems in this book, according to Donald L. Hill in his *Richard Wilbur,* also demonstrate "a pervasive good humor, a sweetness of spirit, unusual among the major poets of the century." This approach that Wilbur uses in his poetry has caused some critics of his early work to charge the poet with avoiding tragic themes by covering them with purely aesthetic verse. James Dickey, for example, wrote in his book, *Babel to Byzantium,* that one has "the feeling that the cleverness of phrase and the delicious aptness of Wilbur's poems sometimes mask an unwillingness or inability to think or feel deeply; that the poems tend to lapse toward highly sophisticated play." John Reibetanz speculated in *Modern Poetry Studies* that this is because "for Richard Wilbur, the sights offered by World War II contradict and threaten his most basic beliefs, as we can infer them from his writings: that love is more powerful than hatred; that nature is a source of values and of reassurance; and that there is a strong creative urge in both man and nature which constantly seeks and finds expression in images of graceful plenitude." "But in the 1940's," Reibetanz concluded, "the utter disparity between what he saw and what he wished to see made him run for cover."

The explanation for his choice of subjects and preference for a light-hearted tone in his poetry is, in Wilbur's view, not so much a matter of running from reality as it is a matter of affirming a philosophical conviction. "I feel that the universe is full of glorious energy," he explained in an interview with Peter Stitt in the *Paris Review,* "that the energy tends to take pattern and shape, and that the ultimate character of things is comely and good. I am perfectly aware that I say this in the teeth of all sorts of contrary evidence, and that I must be basing it partly on temperament and partly on faith, but that's my attitude." Robert B. Shaw commented in *Parnassus: Poetry in Review* that while "it is true that some of Wilbur's earlier poems veer with disconcerting abruptness from the naturalistic to the esthetic. . . . He has never, in fact, avoided negative subject matter as completely as some critics have charged." The critic later asserts that several poems in his third collection, *Things of This World,* deal directly with humane and political issues.

While Wilbur obdurately composed reflective, optimistic poetry, using traditional patterns of rhyme and meter, the changing poetic movements that flowed by him caused his image to change over the years. "His poetry was judged too impersonal for the early 1960s," noted Calhoun; "it was not politically involved enough during the literary protests against the war in Vietnam in the later 1960s, and, in the 1970s, not sufficiently postmodernist." Calhoun does note that Wilbur's poems of the 1960s show experimentation, "but in comparison with what other poets, Robert Lowell and John Berryman for example, were doing by 1961, the experimentation is comparatively minor." His skill at using rhyme and meter is acknowledged among critics like *London Magazine* reviewer Roy Fuller, who believed that "Wilbur is excellent at inventing stanza forms, and his stanzas rhyming in pairs are particularly effective.""His intricately patterned poems reflect the discovery of patterns of natural beauty," adds Shaw.

Wilbur's insistence on formalism, critics soon found, was naturally suited to his work in translating French poetry and plays. Speaking of his "tactful, metrical and speakable translation of verse drama,"*Hudson Review* critic Alan Shaw commented: "Wilbur's [translations] are almost the solitary example of this kind in English. And it is precisely, I think, because he has stood somewhat apart from the tradition on English-language poetry in this century . . . that he has been able to achieve this." He concluded that "Richard Wilbur's translations of classic French drama are among the undiscovered treasure of our recent literature." The expertise and importance of the poet's translations of plays by Moliere, Voltaire, and Racine has been little questioned by reviewers. "The rendition [of Moliere's *The Misanthrope*], delightful and literate, made Moliere accessible for the first time to a wide American audience and was the start of a lucrative sideline for the poet," wrote David H. Van Biema in *People.* Compared to other translators, *Saturday Review* contributor John Ciardi believed that "instead of cognate-snapping, as the academic dullards invariably do, [in his translation of *The Misanthrope*] Wilbur has found English equivalents for the turn and nuance of the French, and the fact that he has managed to do so in rhymed couplets that not only respect themselves as English poetry but allow the play to be staged . . . with great success is testament enough."

Analyzing the laureate's book *New and Collected Poems, Los Angeles Times Book Review* contributor Joshua Odell believed these newer poems "clearly show a continued evolution in style from an ornate elegance found particularly in Wilbur's first collection, *The Beautiful Changes,* toward a simple, direct and crisp verse." Still, poems like those in *The Mind Reader* manage "to stand up against every kind of poetic chic," according to Bruce Michelson in *Southern Review.* And as some critics have noted, the changes in Wilbur's poetry have not affected the basic philosophy his verses have always shown. "He seems to be seeking even firmer and more affirmative statements of the need for order and responsibility; and his tone in the later poems is more confident, more self-assured," asserted Calhoun. This is a need that Wilbur feels all poets should attempt to meet in their work. In his book, *Responses: Prose Pieces, 1953-1976,* the laureate declared: "Every poet is impelled to utter the whole of the world that is real to him, to respond to that world in some spirit, and to draw all its parts toward some *coherence.*"

In addition to his adult-oriented poetry, Wilbur has also published a number of works for children. These include a trio of word-play books devoted to synonyms and antonyms: 1973's *Opposites,* 1991's *More Opposites,* and 1995's *Runaway Opposites.*Self-illustrated, these books offer amusing poems devoted to words with opposite meanings. Another of Wilbur's works for children is *A Game of Catch,* first published in the *New Yorker* in 1953 and reprinted as a separate volume in 1994. The story revolves around three boys and a seemingly innocuous game of catch. When two of the boys refuse to let the third boy play, the outsider climbs a tree and turns the tables on his adversaries using mind games.

Released in 1997, *The Catbird's Song: Prose Pieces 1963-1995* contains a variety of essays by Wilbur that Barbara O'Hara for *Library Journal* described as "thoughtful, engaging, and persuasive." Mary Maxwell for *Boston Review* wrote that readers "may be surprised by melancholy undercurrents swelling below the book's expectedly sane and sunny acumen." While a *Publishers Weekly* reviewer commented that "[Wilbur] wrote unerring prose even when his muse is out of town." He wrote another children's title, *The Disappearing Alphabet,* in 1998, with illustrations by David Diaz. The book contains twenty-six poems, one for each letter, on what would happen if each one letter of the alphabet did not exist. A critic for *Kirkus Reviews* writes that the book is "an enchanting picture book. . . . a sly and beautiful upending of the world of letters." Jennifer M. Brabander of *Horn Book* noted that "Wilbur's poems are filled with small, satisfying surprises." The reviewer for *Publishers Weekly* called the work an "inventively witty book" with "plenty of brain-tickling words to grow on and a plethora of visual puns." David Sacks of the *New York Times* wrote of the book: "The overall result is charming."

Another volume of poetry and translations was released in 2000, titled *Mayflies: New Poems and Translations.* It was his first book of poetry since his 1989 title *New and Collected Poems* and it reinforced his standing as an exceptional poet. Not only does it contain Wilbur's original poetry, it also holds a few of his translations of poetry by such poets as Moliere and Dante. Ray Olson for *Booklist,* describing Wilbur as "a sublime formal poet," wrote that "this is the work of a master." Echoing that sentiment, a critic for *Publishers Weekly* related: "Wilbur remains America's reigning master of poems in traditional forms, creating flawless, balanced, charming, and even profound couplets, sonnets, sapphics, and intricately custom-made stanzas." Jill Pelaez Baumgaertner of *Christian Century* wrote that Wilbur "is arguably America's greatest living poet."

BIOGRAPHICAL AND CRITICAL SOURCES:

BOOKS

Bixler, Francis, *Richard Wilbur: A Reference Guide,* Macmillan, 1991.

Concise Dictionary of American Literary Biography, Supplement: Modern Writers, 1900-1998, Thomson Gale (Detroit), 1998.

Contemporary Literary Criticism, Thomson Gale, Volume 3, 1975, Volume 6, 1976, Volume 9, 1978, Volume 14, 1980, Volume 53, 1989.

Cummins, Paul F., *Richard Wilbur: A Critical Essay,* Eerdmans, 1971.

Dickey, James, *Babel to Byzantium,* Farrar, Straus, 1968.

Dictionary of Literary Biography, Volume 5: *American Poets since World War II,* Thomson Gale, 1980.

Edgecombe, Rodney Stenning, *A Reader's Guide to the Poetry of Richard Wilbur,* University of Alabama Press, 1995.

Hill, Donald L., *Richard Wilbur,* Twayne, 1967.

Hougen, John B., *Ecstasy within Discipline: The Poetry of Richard Wilbur,* Scholars Press, 1994.

Hungerford, Edward, editor, *Poets in Progress,* Northwestern University Press, 1962, new edition, 1967.

Jarrell, Randall, *Poetry and the Age,* Knopf, 1953.

Jarrell, Randall, *The Third Book of Criticism,* Farrar, Straus, 1969.

Kunitz, Stanley, and Vineta Colby, *Twentieth-Century Authors: A Biographical Dictionary of Modern Literature,* H.W. Wilson, 1955.

Michelson, Bruce, *Wilbur's Poetry: Music in a Scattering Time,* University of Massachusetts Press, 1991.

Nemerov, Howard, editor, *Poets on Poetry,* Basic Books, 1966.

Salinger, Wendy, editor, *Richard Wilbur's Creation,* University of Michigan Press (Ann Arbor), 1983.

Rosenthal, M. L., *The Modern Poets,* Oxford University Press, 1965.

PERIODICALS

America, October 15, 1994, p. 18.

Booklist, November 15, 1998, Michael Cart, review of *The Disappearing Alphabet,* p. 585; March 1, 2000, Ray Olson, review of *Mayflies,* p. 1190.

Boston Review, summer, 1998, review of *The Catbird's Song.*

Christian Century, May 24, 2000, Pelaez Jill Baumgaertner, review of *Mayflies,* p. 607.

Hollins Critic, April, 1977.

Horn Book, September-October, 1998, Jennifer M. Brabander, review of *The Disappearing Alphabet,* p. 618.

Hudson Review, summer, 1969; summer, 1987.

Kirkus Reviews, September 15, 1998, review of *The Disappearing Alphabet.*

Library Journal, April 15, 1997, Barbara O'Hara, review of *The Catbird's Song,* p. 83.
London Magazine, July, 1957.
Los Angeles Times, March 17, 1983; April 18, 1987; October 13, 1987.
Los Angeles Times Book Review, July 31, 1988; October 9, 1988.
Modern Poetry Studies, Volume 2, numbers 1 and 2, 1982.
Nation, November 3, 1956.
National Review, September 2, 1988.
New Republic, June 5, 1976; March 24, 1982, Brad Leithauser, "Reconsideration: Richard Wilbur—America's Master of Formal Verse," pp. 28-31.
New York, February 13, 1995, p. 102.
New Yorker, December 12, 1994, p. 122.
New York Times, January 28, 1983; April 18, 1987, Irvin Molotsky, "Richard Wilbur Is Named Nation's Poet Laureate," p. 26; March 14, 1999, David Sacks, review of *The Disappearing Alphabet,* p. 30; April 16, 2000, David Kirby, review of *Mayflies.*
New York Times Book Review, December 14, 1969; December 26, 1982; April 18, 1987; May 29, 1988; August 27, 1995, p. 27.
Paris Review, winter, 1977.
Parnassus: Poetry in Review, spring/summer, 1977.
People, October 5, 1987.
Publishers Weekly, August 2, 1991, p. 60; March 13, 1995, p. 68; February 10, 1997, review of *The Catbird's Song,* p. 72; August 17, 1998, review of *The Disappearing Alphabet,* p. 70; February 7, 2000, review of *Mayflies,* p. 69.
Saturday Review, August 18, 1956.
School Library Journal, September, 1992, p. 272; April, 1994, p. 132; May, 1995, p. 117.
Sewanee Review, spring, 1978.
Shenandoah, fall, 1965.
Southern Review, summer, 1973; April, 1975, Raymond Oliver, "Verse Translation and Richard Wilbur," pp. 318-330; July, 1979.
Southwest Review, summer, 1973.
Time, November 19, 1984.
Times (London), July 15, 1989.
Times Literary Supplement, May 20, 1977; September 15-21, 1989, p. 999.
Tribune Books (Chicago), July 24, 1988.
Twentieth Century Literature, winter, 1995, Philip White, "'Walking to Sleep' and Richard Wilbur's Quest for a Rational Imagination," pp. 249-265.
Variety, January 3, 1994, p. 58; May 30, 1994, p. 58; February 16, 1995, p. 82.
Virginia Quarterly Review, summer, 1990, Peter Harris, "Forty Years of Richard Wilbur: The Loving Work of an Equilibrist," pp. 412-425.
Wall Street Journal, April, 2000, p. W10.
Washington Post, July 25, 1976; October 6, 1987.

WILBUR, Richard Purdy
See WILBUR, Richard

* * *

WILLIAMS, Charles Kenneth
See WILLIAMS, C.K.

* * *

WILLIAMS, C.K. 1936-
(Charles Kenneth Williams)

PERSONAL: Born November 4, 1936, in Newark, NJ; son of Paul Bernard and Dossie (Kasdin) Williams; married Sarah Dean Jones, June, 1966 (divorced, 1975); married Catherine Mauger (an editor), April 13, 1975; children: (first marriage) Jessica Anne; (second marriage) Jed Mauger. *Education:* University of Pennsylvania, B.A., 1959. *Hobbies and other interests:* Piano, guitar, drawing.

ADDRESSES: Home—82, Rue d'Hauteville, 75010 Paris, France; 71 Leigh Ave., Princeton, NJ 08542. *E-mail*—ckwilliams@compuserve.com.

CAREER: Poet. Columbia University, New York, NY, professor of writing, 1981-85; George Mason University, Fairfax, VA, professor of literature, 1982-95. Visiting professor of literature, Beaver College, Jenkintown, PA, 1975, Drexel University, Philadelphia, PA, 1976, University of California at Irvine, 1978, Boston University, 1979-80, Brooklyn College, 1982-83; Franklin and Marshall College, Lancaster, PA, Mellon visiting professor of literature, 1977; Halloway lecturer at University California—Berkeley, 1986; lecturer at Princeton University, Princeton, NJ, 1996—.

MEMBER: PEN, Poetry Society of America.

AWARDS, HONORS: Guggenheim fellowship, 1974; Pushcart Press Prize, 1982, 1983, and 1987; National Endowment for Arts fellowships, 1985 and 1993; National Book Critics Circle Award, 1987, for *Flesh and Blood;* Morton Dauwen Zabel Prize, American Academy of Arts and Letters, 1989; Harriet Monroe Prize, 1993; Lila Wallace-*Reader's Digest* grantee, 1993; Pulitzer Prize for poetry, 2000, for *Repair*; National Book Award for poetry, 2003, for *The Singing*; Ruth Lilly Poetry Prize, *Poetry* magazine, 2005.

WRITINGS:

POEMS

A Day for Anne Frank, Falcon Press (Philadelphia, PA), 1968.

Lies, Houghton Mifflin (Boston, MA), 1969.

I Am the Bitter Name, Houghton Mifflin (Boston, MA), 1972.

With Ignorance, Houghton Mifflin (Boston, MA), 1977.

The Lark, the Thrush, the Starling, Burning Deck (Providence, RI), 1983.

Tar, Random House (New York, NY), 1983.

Flesh and Blood, Farrar, Straus (New York, NY), 1987.

Poems 1963- 1983, Farrar, Straus (New York, NY), 1988.

Helen, Orchises Press (Washington, DC), 1991.

A Dream of Mind, Farrar, Straus (New York, NY), 1992.

Selected Poems, Farrar, Straus (New York, NY), 1994.

New & Selected Poems, Bloodaxe, 1995.

The Vigil, Farrar, Straus (New York, NY), 1996.

Repair, Farrar, Straus (New York, NY), 1999.

Love about Love, Ausable Press (Keene, NY), 2001.

The Singing, Farrar, Straus (New York, NY), 2003.

Collected Poems, 1963-2006, Farrar, Straus (New York, NY), 2006.

TRANSLATOR

(With Gregory Dickerson) Sophocles, *Women of Trachis,* Oxford University Press (New York, NY), 1978.

Euripides, *Bacchae,* Farrar, Straus (New York, NY), 1990.

(With Renata Gorczynski and Benjamin Ivry) Adam Zagajewski, *Canvas,* Farrar, Straus (New York, NY), 1991.

(With John Montague and Margaret Grissom) *Selected Poems of Francis Ponge,* Wake Forest University Press (Winston-Salem, NC), 1994.

EDITOR

(And author of introduction) Paul Zweig, *Selected and Last Poems,* Wesleyan University Press (Middletown, CT), 1989.

(And author of introduction) Gerard Manly Hopkins, *The Essential Hopkins,* Ecco (Hopewell, NJ), 1993.

Also contributing editor of *American Poetry Review,* 1972—.

OTHER

Poetry and Consciousness (criticism), University of Michigan Press (Ann Arbor, MI), 1998.

Misgivings: My Mother, My Father, Myself (memoir), Farrar, Straus (New York, NY), 2000.

SIDELIGHTS: Hailed by poet Paul Muldoon in the *Times Literary Supplement* as "one of the most distinguished poets of his generation," C.K. Williams has created a highly respected body of work, including not only several collections of original poems but volumes of translations, editions of poem collections, a book of criticism, and a memoir. Readers and critics alike esteem him as an original stylist. His characteristic line is extraordinarily long, almost prose-like, and emphasizes characterization and dramatic development. His early work focused on overtly political issues, such as the Vietnam War and social injustice. Though often admired, this scathing material was sometimes considered "ruthless, even cruel," as reported in a retrospective sketch in the *New York Times* in 2000. In his more later work, Williams shifted from a documentary style toward a more introspective approach, writing descriptive poems that reveal the states of alienation, deception, and occasional enlightenment that exist between public and private lives in modern urban America.

Williams's early poetry was first promoted by other poets. His second book, *Lies,* was published upon the recommendation of confessional poet Anne Sexton who, according to Allan M. Jalon in the *Los Angeles Times,* called Williams "the Fellini of the written word," and the book received strong critical acclaim. M.L. Rosenthal, reviewing the book in *Poetry,* described it as a collection of poems that portrays "psychic paralysis despite the need to make contact with someone." Fred Moramarco in *Western Humanities Review* noted that the poems "sound the grim notes of [William Blake's] *Songs of Experience,*" where "paradox is a quality central to almost each poem in the volume." The final poem in the book, "A Day for Anne Frank," which had been published separately a year earlier, was praised by Alan Williamson in *Shenandoah* as "a surprisingly moving poem, one of the best in the book."

Williams's next three books all met with continued critical success. *I Am the Bitter Name,* the title of which, as Jascha Kessler pointed out in *Poetry,* "is meant . . .

to stand for Death," is largely a collection of protest poems about the fear and hatred nurtured by America's involvement in the Vietnam War, culminating in a long, final poem, "In the Heart of the Beast," about the shooting of students at Kent State University by the Ohio National Guard. In this poem, John Vernon stated in *Western Humanities Review,* "the language is like a whip that lashes out."

Williams's *With Ignorance,* however, shows the first development of the poet's trademark style, where, as James Atlas explained in *Nation,* "the lines are so long that the book had to be published in a wide-page format, like an art catalogue," giving the poetry "an eerie incantatory power." Indeed, these long lines, which have drawn comparisons to the work of Whitman and Ginsberg, have generated much critical comment throughout Williams's career.

Flesh and Blood exhibits a change in format, but not in subject matter. The book is a collection of eight-line poems, each poem of twenty or twenty-five syllables and printed two poems to a page, making them comparable, as Michael Hofmann suggested in the *Times Literary Supplement,* to "[Robert] Lowell's sonnets, or [John] Berryman's Dreamsongs." The poems' subjects, the critic pointed out, are "the by-now familiar gallery of hobos and winos, children and old people, lovers and invalids; the settings, typically, public places, on holidays, in parks, on pavements and metro-stations." Edward Hirsch, writing in the *New York Times Book Review,* commented that while these poems "lack the narrative scope and sheer relentless force of Mr. Williams's longer poems . . . together they have a strong cumulative energy and effectiveness." Hirsch described Williams's poetry as having a "notational, ethnographic quality" that presents "single extended moments intently observed." Even though these poems sometimes read "like miniature short stories, sudden fictions," Hirsch continued, they always present people in situations where they are "vulnerable, exposed, on the edge." The book won Williams the National Book Critics Circle Award in 1987.

Poems 1963-1983 collects selections from *Lies* and *I Am the Bitter Name,* and reproduces both *With Ignorance* and *Tar* in their entirety. Muldoon called it "the book of poems I most enjoyed this year," finding Williams to have "an enviable range of tone" and to be "by turns tender and troubling." Hofmann claimed that the book "has as much scope and truthfulness as any American poet since Lowell and Berryman."

A Dream of Mind received mixed reviews. William Logan criticized the book in the *New York Times Book Review* as one in which Williams's long- line style has "decayed" from his earlier works into "continual repetition, pointless variation and the automatic cloning of phrases," making the poems "little Xerox machines of technique" in which Williams is "most successful when purely voyeuristic, less when confessional, and least when meditative." Lawrence Norfolk, however, writing in the *Times Literary Supplement,* lauded Williams for his "stubbornness or refusal to turn away" from "uncomfortable or harrowing realities," such as those presented in "Helen," a husband's account of his wife's decline and death. Michael Dirda, writing in the *Washington Post Book World,* favorably judged Williams's "often plain language" that "keeps the reader fascinated as much by his storytelling power as by his telling phrases."

Selected Poems replaces the early poems with work from *Flesh and Blood* and *A Dream of Mind,* and contains thirteen new poems. Ashley Brown, in *World Literature Today,* suggested that "Williams has learned from [French novelist Marcel] Proust how to make the power of memory operate to maximum effect." Williams, in a *Los Angeles Times* interview with Jalon, stated that he believes "the drama of American poetry is based very much on experience. It's coming out of all the different cultures. We're an enormous nation and we have an enormous poetry." Stephen Dobyns, writing in *Washington Post Book World,* described a characteristic Williams poem as one in which there are "variations of meaning pushing toward the increasingly precise."

A *Publishers Weekly* contributor, in a review of *The Vigil,* observed that Williams's "stanzas extend to and from the book spine like knobby, elongated hands grabbing for God, for relief from pain and for love," while Ray Olson, writing in *Booklist,* found the poet's long line "an admirable instrument indeed . . . an Offenbach Baracole of a line." On the *Boston Review* Web site, Richard Howard related Williams's lines to color-field painting, pointing out that such a technique creates a "field" so wide that it cannot be taken in by the viewer/reader, but instead takes the viewer/reader in. Though Howard found that "The lines [in *The Vigil*] have to array some of the most garish and clunky language assayed in recent poetry" and employ a "clattering languor and . . . mock-Jamesian cadences," he appreciated their suitability for narration and description, if not for philosophical or intellectual matters. "So vivid are Williams's successes with immediacy of sensation and of narration, so overwhelming his virtuosity . . . in revving up his chosen, his imposed machine," Howard concluded, "that I am most of the time transfixed by his gift." However, Brian Phillips, reviewing

Williams's eighth collection, *Repair,* in *New Republic,* commented that "his long poetic line often dips its toe testingly into the waters of the prosaic," showing that line breaks work efficiently but "cannot be said to have much of a felt impact on the aesthetic experience of reading the poem."

The poet's later work, particularly in *Repair,* has developed an increasingly intimate tone. *Repair,* which won Williams the Pulitzer prize for poetry in 2000, is often personal and introspective, the poems consider such subjects as the birth of the poet's grandson, the death of a friend's child, love, or something as mundane as the flowered house dresses worn by his mother and the women of her generation. Yet Williams also included powerfully social material, such as the title poem, in which he points a righteous finger at a tyrant whose "henchmen had disposed of enemies . . . by hammering nails into their skulls/ . . . —how not to be annihilated by it?—the preliminary tap . . . /the way you do with your nail when you're fixing something, making something, shelves, a bed." *Boston Globe* critic Cathleen Calbert cited this poem as an example of "the Jewish sense of tikkun olam (to repair or make whole the world)," noting that "there is a deathly meaning to this kind of 'fixing something,' which Williams will not smooth over." Despite finding *Repair* an extremely bleak book, Calbert admired its "exact, bewildering, slant rendering of raw emotion and careful thought" and its unflinching honesty. Phillips, however, found the book often prosaic and almost didactic, suggesting that the poet's "inspections of motive and meaning seem more fit to offer moral instruction than to summon aesthetic intensity." Acknowledging Willliams's skills at observation and description, though, Phillips observed that "his work reflects the moral self-questioning of Herbert, the plain-spokenness and the yearning toward nature of Wordsworth, the foul rag-and-bone shop of the heart of the later Yeats." In addition to winning the Pulitzer, *Repair* was a finalist for the National Book Award.

Though his praise for *Repair* was qualified, Phillips expressed wholehearted admiration for Williams's prose memoir, *Misgivings: My Mother, My Father, Myself.* "In his memoir, Williams plumbs few deep truths," he observed, "but he emerges as one of the most authoritative psychologists (or pop-psychologists) in contemporary prose." The book presents mostly painful memories of Williams's authoritarian and emotionally cold father and his ineffective mother. In each chapter, the poet sketches a memory, then sharply questions his parents—both deceased—on their behavior. In the process, according to Phillips, Williams "creates an increasingly vivid portrait of both parents, who become fully realized and plausible human beings." A contributor to *Publishers Weekly,* however, faulted Williams for only "faint attempts to be sympathetic to his parents," and dismissed the memoir as a "tedious" list of grievances that "come off as both petty and inflated." David Kirby, writing in the *Library Journal,* praised the volume for its poetic nuance, complex understanding, and powerful emotional images.

In his volume of poems *The Singing,* which won the National Book Award in 2003, the author "continues in his new collection to give voice to fleeting moments of domestic rapture and despair that seem to always arrive wrapped in mortality," noted a *Publishers Weekly* contributor. Williams's long-lined poems appear in the collection often, although other poetic forms are also present. While the theme most often detected in the work addresses that of aging and death, the topic of love is also addressed. Reviews of the collection were positive; a *Booklist* contributor commended Williams's "bracing command of language." Averill Curdy, commenting on *The Singing* in a *Poetry* magazine round table discussion, noted that the author "is one of the poets of his generation who is still singing, who hasn't retreated into a pokey nostalgia or silence. His poems remain vital to me in their attempt to address the contemporary world, and I find the attempt itself moving."

BIOGRAPHICAL AND CRITICAL SOURCES:

BOOKS

Clark, LaVerne Harrell, editor, *Focus 101,* Heidelberg Graphics (Chico, CA), 1979.

Contemporary Literary Criticism, Gale (Detroit, MI), Volume 33, 1985, Volume 56, 1989.

Contemporary Poets, fifth edition, St. James Press (Detroit, MI), 1991.

Dictionary of Literary Biography, Volume 5: *American Poets since World War II,* Gale (Detroit, MI), 1980.

Hamilton, Ian, editor. *Oxford Companion to Twentieth-Century Poetry in English,* Oxford University Press (New York, NY), 1994.

Williams, C.K., *Misgivings: My Mother, My Father, Myself,* Farrar, Straus (New York, NY), 2000.

PERIODICALS

America, October 30, 1993, Andrew J. Krivak, "Dante's Inferno: Translations by Twenty Contemporary Poets," p. 17.

American Poetry Review, May-June, 1994, Alan Williamson, "Poems including Politics," p. 17.

Booklist, June 15, 1992, Frances Woods, review of *A Dream of Mind,* p. 1803; October 1, 1994, Elizabeth Gunderson, review of *Selected Poems,* p. 232; December 1, 1996, Ray Olson, review of *The Vigil,* p. 640; January 1, 2004, review of *The Singing,* p. 774.

Boston Globe, September 12, 1999, Cathleen Calbert, review of *Repair,* p. C1.

Critical Survey, May, 1997, Maurice Rutherford, review of *The Vigil,* p. 164.

Economist, September 6, 1997, review of *Vigil,* p. S19; March 18, 2000, "Whose Voice Is It Anyway?," p. 14.

Georgia Review, winter, 1983, p. 894; fall, 1993, Judith Kitchen, review of *A Dream of Mind,* p. 578.

Hudson Review, winter, 1988, Robert McDowell, review of *Flesh and Blood,* pp. 680-681; summer, 1995, Thomas M. Disch, review of *Selected Poems,* p. 339.

Library Journal, October 1, 1983, review of *Tar,* p. 1880; May 1, 1987, Thom Tammaro, review of *Flesh and Blood,* p. 72; June 1, 1990, p. 130; May 1, 1992, Louis McKee, review of *A Dream of Mind,* p. 86; June 1, 1999, Rochelle Ratner, review of *Repair,* p. 120; March 1, 2000, David Kirby, review of *Misgivings,* p. 92; January 1, 2001, Fred Muratori, review of *Love about Love,* p. 112.

Los Angeles Times, March 7, 1993, Allan M. Jalon, "The Poet as Witness," p. 30.

Los Angeles Times Book Review, January 22, 1984, Clayton Eshleman, review of *Tar,* p. 3.

Nation, June 18, 1977, James Atlas, review of *With Ignorance,* pp. 763-766; May 30, 1987, Dan Bogen, review of *Flesh and Blood,* pp. 734-736.

New Republic, August 17, 1992, Edward Hirsch, review of *A Dream of Mind,* p. 46; January 25, 1993, Robert Pinsky, review of *Canvas,* p. 43; September 18, 2000, Brian Phillips, review of *Repair* and *Misgivings,* p. 42.

New Statesman & Society, December 23, 1988, Robert Sheppard, review of *Flesh and Blood,* p. 36; December 4, 1992, David Herd, review of *A Dream of Mind,* p. 40.

New Yorker, January 11, 1993, review of *A Dream of Mind,* p. 111.

New York Times, October 4, 2000, Alan Riding, "An American Bard in Paris Stokes the Poetic Home Fires," p. E1.

New York Times Book Review, November 27, 1983, Louis Simpson, review of *Tar,* p. 13; August 23, 1987, Edward Hirsch, review of *Flesh and Blood,* p. 20; March 13, 1988, p. 34; November 15, 1992, William Logan, review of *A Dream of Mind,* p. 15; October 8, 2000, Laura Ciolkowski, review of *Misgivings,* p. 23.

Parnassus, August, 1990, Sherod Santos, reviews of *Poems: 1963-1983* and *Flesh and Blood,* p. 115; fall, 1993, Bill Marx, review of *Canvas,* p. 100.

Partisan Review, summer, 1991, Michael Collier, review of *Poems: 1963-1983,* p. 565.

Poetry, November, 1971, M.L. Rosenthal, review of *Lies,* pp. 99-104; February, 1973, Jascha Kessler, review of *I Am the Bitter Name,* pp. 292-303; September, 1984, Bruce Bawer, review of *Tar,* pp. 353-355; February, 1988, Linda Gregerson, review of *Flesh and Blood,* pp. 431-433; April, 1989, J.D. McClatchy, review of *Poems: 1963- 1983,* p. 29; December, 1993, Ben Howard, review of *A Dream of Mind,* p. 164; May, 1997, Bruce Murphy, review of *Selected Poems,* p. 95; August, 1999, Christian Whitman, review of *Poetry and Consciousness,* p. 286; August, 2001, Ian Tromp, reviews of *Poetry and Consciousness* and *Repair,* p. 288; October, 2004, Dan Chiasson and Averill Curdy, review of *The Singing Poems,* p. 53.

Publishers Weekly, July 22, 1983, review of *Tar,* p. 126; May 11, 1992, review of *A Dream of Mind,* p. 58; August 29, 1994, review of *Selected Poems,* p. 66; November 25, 1996, review of *The Vigil,* p. 71; March 13, 2000, review of *Misgivings,* p. 72; October 27, 2003, review of *The Singing,* p. 59.

Salmagundi, spring- summer, 1997, Frederick Pollack, review of *The Vigil,* p. 205.

Shenandoah, summer, 1970, Alan Williamson, review of *Lies,* pp. 89- 93.

Times Literary Supplement, December 2, 1988, Paul Muldoon, review of *Poems: 1963-1983,* p. 1342; January 20, 1989, Michael Hofmann, review of *Flesh and Blood,* p. 59; February 12, 1993, Lawrence Norfolk, review of *A Dream of Mind,* p. 11; October 8, 1993, Michael Parker, review of *Canvas;* October 3, 1997, Jamie McKendrick, review of *The Vigil,* p. 25; March 10, 2000, William Logan, review of *Repair,* p. 23.

TriQuarterly, winter, 1988, Reginald Gibbons, review of *Flesh and Blood,* pp. 224-225; spring-summer, 1991, Alan Shapiro, "In Praise of the Impure," p. 5.

Virginia Quarterly Review, winter, 1992, review of *A Dream of Mind,* p. 27; winter, 1993, review of *A Dream of Mind,* p. S27.

Washington Post, July 23, 2000, Debra Dickerson, "The Parent Trap," p. X06.

Washington Post Book World, January 3, 1993, Michael Dirda, review of *A Dream of Mind,* p. 10; July 30, 1995, Stephen Dobyns, review of *Selected Poems,* p. 8.

Western Humanities Review, spring, 1970, Fred Moramarco, review of *Lies,* pp. 201-207; winter, 1973, John Vernon, review of *I Am the Bitter Name,* pp. 101-10.

World Literature Today, autumn, 1989, Michael Leddy, review of *Poems: 1963-1983,* p. 685; winter, 1989, Ashley Brown, review of *Flesh and Blood,* p. 104; autumn, 1992, Joachim T. Baer, review of *Canvas,* p. 746; spring, 1993, Bernard F. Dick, review of *A Dream of Mind,* p. 387; autumn, 1997, Ashley Brown, review of *The Vigil,* p. 794.

Yale Review, October 1999, Carol Muske, review of *Repair,* p. 154.

ONLINE

Boston Review, http://bostonreview.net/ (February 1, 2001), Richard Howard, review of *The Vigil.*

Online News Hour, http://www.pbs.org/newshour/ (April 19, 2000), Jim Lehrer, interview with C.K. Williams.

Princeton University News, http://www.princeton.edu/ (February 1, 2001), author profile.

* * *

WILLIAMS, Juan 1954-

PERSONAL: Born April 10, 1954, in Colon, Panama; son of Rogelio L. (an accountant) and Alma Geraldine (a secretary; maiden name, Elias) Williams; married Susan Delise (a social worker), July 1, 1978; children: Antonio Mason, Regan Almina. *Education:* Haverford College, B.A., 1976.

ADDRESSES: Home—607 Whittier St. NW, Washington, DC 20012. *Office*—Washington Post, 1150 15th St. NW, Washington, DC 20071. *Agent*—Raphael Sagalyn, Inc., 7201 Wisconsin Ave., Ste. 675, Bethesda, MD 20814.

CAREER: Senior correspondent on *National Public Radio,* panelist on television program *Fox News Sunday,* and cohost of *America's Black Forum.* Contributor of commentaries to radio and television programs, including National Public Radio broadcasts, *NewsHour with Jim Lehrer,* and *Nightline. Washington Post,* Washington, DC, columnist and reporter. Onetime panelist on *Capital Gang Sunday* and former cohost of *Crossfire.*

AWARDS, HONORS: Front Page Award from Washington-Baltimore Newspaper Guild and award from Education Writers of America, both 1979, both for series on public schools in Washington, DC; named columnist of the year by *Washingtonian,* 1982; DuSable Museum Award, 1985, for political writing; Washington, DC, Emmy Award for documentary writing, 1989, for *From Riot to Recovery;* Bill Pryor Award for investigative reporting; Outstanding Book Award from Myers Center for the Study of Human Rights in the United States; Best National Book Award from *Time* magazine; American Association of University Women, award for political commentary; honorary doctorates from Haverford College and State University of New York.

WRITINGS:

Eyes on the Prize: America's Civil Rights Years, 1954-1965, Viking (New York, NY), 1987.

Thurgood Marshall: American Revolutionary, Times Books (New York, NY), 1998.

My Soul Looks Back in Wonder: Voices of the Civil Rights Experience, AARP/ Sterling (New York, NY), 2004.

I'll Find a Way or Make One: A Tribute to Historically Black Colleges, Amistad/ HarperCollins (New York, NY), 2004.

Also author of television documentaries, including *This Far by Faith: African-American Spiritual Journeys,* which he coauthored with Quinton Dixie; *Politics: The New Black Power, Marian Anderson, A. Philip Randolph: For Jobs and Freedom;* and *No One Dies Alone.* Contributor to newspapers, including *New York Times,* and periodicals, including *Atlantic, Ebony, Fortune,* and *New Republic.*

SIDELIGHTS: Each chapter of Juan Williams's book *Eyes on the Prize: America's Civil Rights Years, 1954-1965* deals with a specific event or series of events from the civil rights movement of the 1950s and 1960s. The book—produced in conjunction with a six-part public television series of the same title—provides a tribute to the thousands of ordinary people who participated in a movement that was physically strenuous, socially daring, and at times life-threatening. The author has concentrated on the memorable events, such as sit-ins, voting rights campaigns, and bus boycotts, but he does not neglect the lesser-known individuals who have faded from public memory. The book is dedicated to the men and women who lost their lives in the struggle. Roy Reed wrote in the *Washington Post Book World:* "The book is rich in detail on how the movement started, gained momentum and finally engulfed the political system and changed it." *Nation* contributor Fred

Powledge pronounced the book "not just a coffee-table adjunct to the TV series . . . [but] a worthy addition to the library of the concerned reader-viewer."

Williams once stated "I became interested in civil rights because of my work as a White House correspondent for the *Washington Post* during a period of strife between President Ronald Reagan's administration and civil rights groups. I gathered material for the book from extensive interviews, some taped and used in the public television series. Born in 1954, I was too young to participate in the civil rights movement but am inspired by it nonetheless. At the same time, I believe I'm sufficiently dispassionate about the events to see them as historically valuable evidence of democracy at work in modern America. That perspective makes me part of a new generation of black writers who feel less compelled to be advocates and, instead, simply recount the truth of the black American triumph."

In *Thurgood Marshall: American Revolutionary,* Williams chronicles the major role played in black American progress by Marshall, the prominent civil rights lawyer who in 1967 became the first black U.S. Supreme Court justice. As the lead attorney for the National Association for the Advancement of Colored People (NAACP) from 1938 to 1961, Marshall was involved in many court battles against racial discrimination. The most famous case was *Brown* v. *Board of Education,* which led to the Supreme Court's ruling in 1954 that racially segregated schools were inherently unequal, and it is the "literal and figurative center" of Williams's book, noted Gene Seymour in the *Nation.* Williams also recounts Marshall's work in many lesser-known civil rights cases and his term on the Supreme Court, where he served until 1991, and had a consistent record of favoring individual liberties. Williams deals with the less admirable aspects of Marshall's life and character as well: his decision to discuss alleged Communist activities in the civil rights movement with FBI director J. Edgar Hoover; his animosity toward many black leaders, including Martin Luther King Jr.; his increasing irascibility toward the end of his years on the court; and reports that he was a heavy drinker, an unfaithful husband, and a sexual harasser.

"Juan Williams's biography will provide grist to both celebrants and detractors" of Marshall, observed Randall Kennedy in the *New Republic.* Kennedy remarked that "For the most part, Williams strikes a praising tone," crediting Marshall with ending governmentally sanctioned segregation and putting him in the company of King and Malcolm X as one of the twentieth century's three most important African-American freedom fighters. However, the critic faulted Williams as too credulous regarding stories of Marshall's sexual misconduct: "All that exists, so far, are rumors. . . . A rumor marks the beginning of a biographer's work, not the end." Kennedy found Williams's detailing of Marshall's career as a lawyer "excellent," but deemed the account of his Supreme Court years wanting. "He and his law clerks produced scores of important opinions," Kennedy related. "Williams pays relatively little attention to that work. In a book that is about 400 pages long, only about seventy pages are devoted to Marshall's career as a Justice, and those pages are painfully thin."

Similarly, *National Review* commentator John O. McGinnis called the biography "at its weakest in its discussion of Marshall's years on the Court. Williams does not have a command of constitutional jurisprudence and frequently turns complex legal issues into political cartoons." Seymour asserted that "one needn't be a legal scholar to suspect that the book leaves plenty of room for deeper inquiry into Marshall's arguments, decisions and dissents." He also thought the report of Marshall's dealings with Hoover "disquieting" and longed for more information about what Marshall told Hoover and "who—or what—was hurt by his disclosures." But Ruth Conniff, writing in the *Progressive,* praised Williams as taking "a thoughtful, unflinching look at Marshall's 'intense, unpublicized dance'" with Hoover. She noted that Williams faced some difficulties in researching his book; for one thing, his public support for Clarence Thomas, the black conservative tapped to succeed Marshall on the Supreme Court, led the NAACP Legal Defense Fund to deny him use of the organization's records. "In spite of such obstacles," she contended, "he has written a terrifically engaging biography." David J. Garrow, reviewing for the *Washington Monthly,* wrote that the volume's "shortcomings detract surprisingly little from what overall is an excellent and important book." He further stated, "Williams's book leaves a definitive account of Marshall's Supreme Court service for some subsequent author, but his portrait of Marshall the man is rich and valuable, even if he fails to plumb fully some of the most fascinating complexities of Marshall's life."

In *This Far by Faith: Stories from the African American Religious Experience,* Williams, along with coauthor Quinton Dixie, provide narratives that testify to the significance of the religious movement in the African-American community, from slavery up to the civil rights movement, when "God's power to transform society [had] no greater example," the authors maintain unapologetically. According to a reviewer in the *Christian Science Monitor,* Williams and Dixie are "masters at placing black worship in the context of U.S. history" and "cover vast information without burying the reader in excessive detail." Vicki Hyman of the *News & Observer,* wrote that Williams told her some people were disappointed in the book because they hoped for less history and more inspirational stories. But, Hyman observes, "if the readers didn't glean an ounce of spiritual guidance from these tales, then they weren't paying attention."

In *My Soul Looks Back in Wonder: Voices of the Civil Rights Experience,* Williams looks back more than fifty years to the present day to tell the stories of men and women who were on the front lines of the civil rights movement. Carolyn McKinstry remembers witnessing the bombing of the 16th Street Baptist church by the Ku Klux Klan in 1963. Dr. Alvin Poussant, a professor of psychiatry at Harvard University, recalls the brutally suppressed march with Martin Luther King, Jr. in Canton, Mississippi, when Stokely Carmichael raised his fist and cried out, "Black Power! Black Power!" Feminist Diane Brownmiller discusses sit-in tactics she learned during Mississippi's Freedom Summer in 1964. In a review of the book for the *Washington Post,* Alicia Young stated that while few of the narrators have a sense of actually changing the world around them, "they force us to weigh whether outward indicators of success even matter, since they never really thought to live their lives in any other way." A reviewer for the *U.S. Newswire* said, "This book will radically transform the way you think about freedom and how it was won."

BIOGRAPHICAL AND CRITICAL SOURCES:

BOOKS

Williams, Juan, and Quinton Dixie, *This Far by Faith: Stories from the African-American Religious Experience,* Morrow (New York, NY), 2003.

PERIODICALS

America, April 10, 1999, p. 32.
Christian Science Monitor, November 25, 2003, review of *This Far by Faith.*
Economist, October 17, 1998.
Nation, January 31, 1987, p. 120; January 25, 1999, p. 36.
National Review, December 7, 1998, p. 62.
New Republic, April 5, 1999, p. 38.
News & Observer, April 19, 2004, review of *This Far by Faith,* p. C1.
New York Times Book Review, January 25, 1987, p. 20.
Progressive, December, 1998, p. 40.
Time, October 28, 1991, p. 30; October 5, 1998, p. 88.
U.S. Newswire, April 20, 2004, review of *My Soul Looks Back in Wonder: Voices of the Civil Rights Experience.*
Washington Monthly, November, 1998, p. 42.
Washington Post Book World, January 11, 1987; February 14, 1988; July 13, 2004, review of *My Soul Looks Back in Wonder.*

* * *

WILLIAMS, Tennessee 1911-1983 (Thomas Lanier Williams)

PERSONAL: Born Thomas Lanier Williams, March 26, 1911, in Columbus, MS; choked to death, February 24, 1983, in New York, NY; son of Cornelius Coffin (a traveling salesperson) and Edwina (Dakin) Williams. *Education:* Attended University of Missouri, 1931-33, and Washington University, St. Louis, MO, 1936-37; University of Iowa, A.B., 1938. *Religion:* Originally Episcopalian; converted to Roman Catholicism, 1969.

CAREER: Playwright, novelist, short story writer, and poet; full-time writer, 1944-83. International Shoe Co., St. Louis, MO, clerical worker and manual laborer, 1934-36; worked various jobs, including waiter and hotel elevator operator, New Orleans, LA, 1939; worked as teletype operator, Jacksonville, FL, 1940; worked various jobs, including waiter and theater usher, New York, NY, 1942; worked as screenwriter for Metro-Goldwyn-Mayer, 1943. Codirector of his play *Period of Adjustment,* 1959.

MEMBER: Dramatists Guild, National Institute of Arts and Letters, American Society of Composers, Authors, and Publishers (ASCAP), Alpha Tau Omega.

AWARDS, HONORS: Third prize, *Smart Set* magazine essay contest, 1927; Group Theatre Award, 1939, for *American Blues;* Rockefeller Foundation fellowship, 1940; grant, American Academy and National Institute of Arts and Letters, 1943; New York Drama Critics Circle Award, Donaldson Award, and Sidney Howard Memorial Award, all 1945, all for *The Glass Menagerie;* New York Drama Critics Circle Award, Pulitzer

Prize, and Donaldson Award, all 1948, all for *A Streetcar Named Desire;* Antoinette Perry ("Tony") Award, 1951, for *The Rose Tattoo;* elected to National Institute of Arts and Letters, 1952; New York Drama Critics Circle Award and Pulitzer Prize, both 1955, Tony Award nomination for best play, 1956, and London *Evening Standard* Award, 1958, all for *Cat on a Hot Tin Roof;* New York Drama Critics Circle Award and Tony Award nomination for best play, both 1962, and first place for best new foreign play, London Critics' Poll, 1964-65, all for *The Night of the Iguana;* creative arts medal, Brandeis University, 1964-65; National Institute of Arts and Letters Gold Medal, 1969; first centennial medal, Cathedral of St. John the Divine, 1973; elected to Theatre Hall of Fame, 1979; Kennedy Honors Award, 1979; Common Wealth Award for Distinguished Service in Dramatic Arts, 1981; Tony Award nomination for best play, 1999, for *Not about Nightingales.*

WRITINGS:

PLAYS

Cairo, Shanghai, Bombay! (comedy), produced in Memphis, TN, by Memphis Garden Players, 1935.

Headlines, produced in St. Louis, MO, at Wednesday Club Auditorium, 1936.

Candles to the Sun (produced in St. Louis, MO, at Wednesday Club Auditorium, 1936), published as *Candles to the Sun: A Play in Ten Scenes,* New Directions Publishing (New York, NY), 2004.

The Magic Tower, produced in St. Louis, MO, 1936.

The Fugitive Kind (also see below; produced in St. Louis, MO, at Wednesday Club Auditorium, 1937), edited and with an introduction by Allean Hale, New Directions Publishing (New York, NY), 2001.

Spring Song, produced in Iowa City, IA, at the University of Iowa, 1938.

The Long Goodbye (also see below), produced in New York, NY, at New School for Social Research, 1940.

Battle of Angels (also see below; produced in Boston, MA, at Wilbur Theatre, 1940), New Directions Publishing (New York, NY), 1945.

Stairs to the Roof, produced in Pasadena, CA, at Playbox, 1944.

The Glass Menagerie (also see below; first produced in Chicago, IL, at Civic Theatre, 1944; produced on Broadway, 1945; revived in New York, NY on March 22, 2005 at the Ethel Barrymore Theater), Random House (New York, NY, 1945, published as *The Glass Menagerie: Play in Two Acts,* Dramatists Play Service (New York, NY), 1948, edited, with an introduction by Allean Hale, New Directions Publishing (New York, NY), 2000.

(With Donald Windham) *You Touched Me!: A Romantic Comedy in Three Acts* (produced on Broadway, 1945), Samuel French (New York, NY), 1947.

Twenty-seven Wagons Full of Cotton (also see below; part of triple bill titled *All in One*; produced on Broadway, 1955), published in *The Best One-Act Plays of 1944,* New Directions Publishing (New York, NY), 1945.

This Property Is Condemned (also see below), produced Off-Broadway at Hudson Park Theatre, 1946.

Moony's Kids Don't Cry (also see below; produced in Los Angeles, CA, at Actor's Laboratory Theatre, 1946), published in *The Best One-Act Plays of 1940,* edited by Margaret Mayorga, Dodd (New York, NY), 1940.

Portrait of a Madonna (also see below), produced in Los Angeles, CA, 1946; produced in New York, NY as part of *Triple Play,* 1959.

The Last of My Solid Gold Watches (also see below), produced in Los Angeles, CA, at Actor's Laboratory Theatre, 1946.

Twenty-seven Wagons Full of Cotton, and Other One-Act Plays (includes *The Long Goodbye, This Property Is Condemned, Portrait of a Madonna, The Last of My Solid Gold Watches, Auto-da-Fe, The Lady of Larkspur Lotion, The Purification, Hello from Bertha, The Strangest Kind of Romance*, and *Lord Byron's Love Letter* [also see below]), New Directions Publishing (New York, NY), 1946, 3rd expanded edition with preface by Williams (contains two new plays, *Talk to Me Like the Rain and Let Me Listen* and *Something Unspoken;* also see below), 1953.

Lord Byron's Love Letter (also see below), produced in New York, NY, 1947; revised version produced in London, England, 1964.

Auto-da-Fe, produced in New York, NY, 1947.

The Lady of Larkspur Lotion, produced in New York, NY, 1947; produced in London, England, 1968.

Summer and Smoke (first produced in Dallas, TX, 1947; produced on Broadway, 1948; revised as *Eccentricities of a Nightingale*, produced in Washington, DC, 1966), New Directions Publishing (New York, NY), 1948, published as *Summer and Smoke: Play in Two Acts,* Dramatists Play Service (New York, NY), 1950, published as *The Eccentricities of a Nightingale, and Summer and Smoke: Two Plays,* New Directions Publishing, 1964.

A Streetcar Named Desire (also see below; first produced on Broadway, 1947), New Directions Publishing (New York, NY), 1947, with preface by Williams, 1951, revised edition published as *A Streetcar Named Desire: A Play in Three Acts,* Dramatists Play Service (New York, NY), 1953, with foreword by Jessica Tandy and introduction by Williams, Limited Editions Club, 1982, edition with introduction by Williams, New American Library (New York, NY), 1984.

American Blues: Five Short Plays (contains *Moony's Kids Don't Cry, The Dark Room, The Case of the Crushed Petunias, The Long Stay Cut Short; or, The Unsatisfactory Supper,* and *Ten Blocks on the Camino Real;* also see below), Dramatists Play Service (New York, NY), 1948, reprinted, 1976.

The Rose Tattoo (also see below; produced in New York, NY, 1951), with preface by Williams, New Directions Publishing (New York, NY), 1951.

Camino Real: A Play (also see below; expanded version of *Ten Blocks on the Camino Real;* produced in New York, NY, 1953), with foreword and afterword by Williams, New Directions Publishing (New York, NY), 1953.

Cat on a Hot Tin Roof (also see below; first produced on Broadway, 1955), with preface by Williams, New Directions Publishing (New York, NY), 1955, published as *Cat on a Hot Tin Roof: A Play in Three Acts,* Dramatists Play Service (New York, NY), 1958.

Three Players of a Summer Game (first produced in Westport, CT, 1955), Secker & Warburg (London, England), 1960.

(Librettist) Raffaello de Banfield, *Lord Byron's Love Letter: Opera in One Act,* Ricordi, 1955.

The Case of the Crushed Petunias, produced in Cleveland, OH, 1957; produced in New York, NY, 1958.

Orpheus Descending: A Play in Three Acts (also see below; revision of *Battle of Angels;* produced in New York, NY, 1957; produced Off-Broadway, 1959), New Directions Publishing (New York, NY), 1959.

Orpheus Descending, with Battle of Angels: Two Plays, preface by Williams, New Directions Publishing (New York, NY), 1958.

A Perfect Analysis Given by a Parrot: A Comedy in One Act (also see below), Dramatists Play Service (New York, NY), 1958.

The Rose Tattoo [and] *Camino Real,* introduced and edited by E. Martin Browne, Penguin (New York, NY), 1958.

Garden District: Two Plays; Something Unspoken, and Suddenly Last Summer (also see below; produced Off-Broadway at York Playhouse, 1958), Secker & Warburg (London, England), 1959.

Suddenly Last Summer, New Directions Publishing (New York, NY), 1958.

Talk to Me Like the Rain and Let Me Listen, first produced in Westport, CT, 1958; produced in New York, NY, 1967.

I Rise in Flame, Cried the Phoenix: A Play about D.H. Lawrence (first produced Off-Broadway, 1958), note by Frieda Lawrence, New Directions Publishing (New York, NY), 1951.

Sweet Bird of Youth (first produced in New York, NY, 1959), with foreword by Williams, New Directions Publishing (New York, NY), 1959, revised edition, Dramatists Play Service (New York, NY), 1962.

Period of Adjustment; High Point over a Cavern: A Serious Comedy (first produced in Miami, FL, 1959; produced on Broadway, 1960), first published in *Esquire,* New Directions Publishing (New York, NY), 1960, published as *Period of Adjustment; or, High Point Is Built on a Cavern: A Serious Comedy,* Dramatists Play Service (New York, NY), 1961.

The Purification, produced Off-Broadway at Theatre de Lys, 1959.

The Night of the Iguana (also see below; based on Williams's short story; short version first produced in Spoleto, Italy, 1960; expanded version produced on Broadway, 1961), New Directions Publishing (New York, NY), 1961.

Hello from Bertha, produced in Bromley, England, 1961.

To Heaven in a Golden Coach, produced in Bromley, England, 1961.

The Milk Train Doesn't Stop Here Anymore (also see below; one-act version produced in Spoleto, Italy, 1962; expanded version produced on Broadway, 1963; revision produced on Broadway at Brooks Atkinson Theatre, 1964), New Directions Publishing (New York, NY), 1964.

Slapstick Tragedy (contains *The Mutilated* and *The Gnaediges Fraulein;* also see below), first produced on Broadway, 1966.

The Dark Room, produced in London, England, 1966.

The Mutilated: A Play in One Act, Dramatists Play Service (New York, NY), 1967.

The Gnaediges Fraulein: A Play in One Act, Dramatists Play Service (New York, NY), 1967, revised as *The Latter Days of a Celebrated Soubrette,* produced in New York, NY, 1974.

Kingdom of Earth: The Seven Descents of Myrtle (first published in *Esquire* as one-act *Kingdom of Earth,* 1967, expanded as *The Seven Descents of Myrtle,* produced on Broadway at Ethel Barrymore Theatre, 1968, revised as *Kingdom of Earth,* produced in Princeton, NJ, 1975), New Directions Publishing (New York, NY), 1968, published as *The Kingdom of Earth (The Seven Descents of Myrtle): A Play in Seven Scenes,* Dramatists Play Service (New York, NY), 1969.

The Two-Character Play (first produced in London, England, 1967; revision produced as *Out Cry* in Chicago, IL, 1971; produced on Broadway, 1973), New Directions Publishing (New York, NY), 1969.

In the Bar of a Tokyo Hotel (first produced Off-Broadway, 1969), Dramatists Play Service (New York, NY), 1969.

The Strangest Kind of Romance, produced in London, England, 1969.

(With others) *Oh! Calcutta!,* produced Off-Broadway, 1969.

The Frosted Glass Coffin and *A Perfect Analysis Given by a Parrot,* produced in Key West, FL, 1970.

The Long Stay Cut Short; or, The Unsatisfactory Supper (also see below), produced in London, England, 1971.

I Can't Imagine Tomorrow [and] *Confessional,* produced in Bar Harbor, ME, 1971.

Small Craft Warnings (produced Off-Broadway, 1972), New Directions Publishing (New York, NY), 1972.

The Red Devil Battery Sign (produced in Boston, MA, 1975; revised version produced in Vienna, Austria, 1976), New Directions Publishing (New York, NY), 1988.

Demolition Downtown: Count Ten in Arabic, produced in London, England, 1976.

This Is (An Entertainment), produced in San Francisco, CA, 1976.

Vieux Carre (produced on Broadway, 1977), New Directions Publishing (New York, NY), 1979, with introduction by Robert Bray, 2000.

A Lovely Sunday for Creve Coeur (first produced under title *Creve Coeur* in Charleston, SC, 1978; produced Off-Broadway, 1979), New Directions Publishing (New York, NY), 1980.

Clothes for a Summer Hotel: A Ghost Play (produced on Broadway, 1980), Dramatists Play Service (New York, NY), 1981.

Steps Must Be Gentle: A Dramatic Reading for Two Performers, Targ Editions, 1980.

It Happened the Day the Sun Rose, Sylvester & Orphanos (New York, NY), 1981.

Something Cloudy, Something Clear (first produced Off-Off Broadway, 1981), introduction by Eve Adamson, New Directions Publishing (New York, NY), 1995.

The Remarkable Rooming-House of Mme. Le Monde, Albondocani Press, 1984.

Not about Nightingales (first produced in London, England, 1998), edited and with an introduction by Allean Hale, foreword by Vanessa Redgrave, New Directions Publishing (New York, NY), 1998.

Spring Storm, edited and with an introduction by Dan Isaacs, New Directions Publishing (New York, NY), 1999.

Also author of *Me, Vashya, Kirche, Kutchen und Kinder, Life Boat Drill, Will Mr. Merriwether Return from Memphis?, Of Masks Outrageous and Austere,* and *A House Not Meant to Stand.* Also author of television play *I Can't Imagine Tomorrow.* Contributor to anthologies and to periodicals, including *Esquire.*

Williams's plays appear in numerous foreign languages, and many continue to be staged in theaters worldwide.

COLLECTIONS

Four Plays (contains *The Glass Menagerie, A Streetcar Named Desire, Summer and Smoke*, and *Camino Real*), Secker & Warburg (London, England), 1956.

Five Plays (contains *Cat on a Hot Tin Roof, The Rose Tattoo, Something Unspoken, Suddenly Last Summer,* and *Orpheus Descending*), Secker & Warburg (London, England), 1962.

Three Plays: The Rose Tattoo, Camino Real, Sweet Bird of Youth, New Directions Publishing (New York, NY), 1964.

Baby Doll: The Script for the Film, Something Unspoken, and *Suddenly Last Summer,* Penguin (New York, NY), 1968.

The Night of the Iguana [and] *Orpheus Descending,* Penguin (New York, NY), 1968.

The Milk Train Doesn't Stop Here Anymore [and] *Cat on a Hot Tin Roof,* Penguin (New York, NY), 1969.

Dragon Country: A Book of Plays, New Directions Publishing (New York, NY), 1970.

Battle of Angels, The Glass Menagerie [and] *A Streetcar Named Desire,* New Directions Publishing (New York, NY), 1971.

Cat on a Hot Tin Roof, Orpheus Descending, [and] *Suddenly Last Summer,* New Directions Publishing (New York, NY), 1971.

The Eccentricities of a Nightingale, Summer and Smoke, The Rose Tattoo, [and] *Camino Real,* New Directions Publishing (New York, NY), 1971.

The Theatre of Tennessee Williams, New Directions Publishing (New York, NY), Volume 1, 1971, Volume 2, 1971, Volume 3, 1971, Volume 4, 1972, Volume 5, 1976, Volume 6, 1981, Volume 7, 1981.

Three by Tennessee Williams, New American Library (New York, NY), 1976.

Cat on a Hot Tin Roof, The Milk Train Doesn't Stop Here Anymore, [and] *The Night of the Iguana,* Penguin (New York, NY), 1976.

Selected Plays, illustrations by Jerry Pinkney, Franklin Library (Franklin Center, PA), 1977.

Tennessee Williams: Eight Plays, introduction by Harold Clurman, Doubleday (New York, NY), 1979.

Selected Plays, illustrations by Herbert Tauss, Franklin Library (Franklin Center, PA), 1980.

Ten by Tennessee (ten one-act plays), produced in New York, NY, at Lucille Lortel Theatre, May, 1986.

Plays (two volumes), Library of America (New York, NY), 2000

8 by Tenn (eight one-act plays), produced in Hartford, CT, 2003.

SCREENPLAYS

(With Gore Vidal) *Senso, Luchino Visconti,* c. 1949.

(With Oscar Saul) *The Glass Menagerie,* Warner Bros., 1950.

A Streetcar Named Desire, Twentieth Century-Fox, 1951.

(With Hal Kanter) *The Rose Tattoo,* Paramount, 1955.

Baby Doll (Warner Bros., 1956), published as *Baby Doll: The Script for the Film,* New American Library (New York, NY), 1956, published as *Baby Doll; The Script for the Film, incorporating the Two One-Act Plays Which Suggested It: Twenty-seven Wagons Full of Cotton and The Long Stay Cut Short; or, The Unsatisfactory Supper,* New Directions Publishing (New York, NY), 1956.

(With Gore Vidal) *Suddenly Last Summer,* Columbia, 1959.

(With Meade Roberts) *The Fugitive Kind* (based on *Orpheus Descending;* United Artists, 1959), Signet (New York, NY), 1960.

Boom (based on *The Milk Train Doesn't Stop Here Anymore*), Universal, 1968.

Stopped Rocking and Other Screenplays (contains *All Gaul Is Divided, The Loss of a Teardrop Diamond, One Arm,* and *Stopped Rocking*), introduction by Richard Gilman, New Directions Publishing (New York, NY), 1984.

A Streetcar Named Desire: A Screen Adaptation Directed by Elia Kazan, Irvington, 1989.

Baby Doll and Tiger Tail, New Directions Publishing (New York, NY), 1991.

Also author, with Paul Bowles, of *The Wanton Countess* (English-language version), filmed 1954.

SHORT STORIES

One Arm, and Other Stories (includes "The Night of the Iguana"), New Directions Publishing (New York, NY), 1948.

Hard Candy: A Book of Stories, New Directions Publishing (New York, NY), 1954.

Man Brings This up Road: A Short Story, Street & Smith (New York, NY), 1959.

Three Players of a Summer Game, and Other Stories, Secker & Warburg (London, England), 1960, reprinted, Dent (London, England), 1984.

Grand, House of Books (New York, NY), 1964.

The Knightly Quest: A Novella and Four Short Stories, New Directions Publishing (New York, NY), 1967.

Eight Mortal Ladies Possessed: A Book of Stories, New Directions Publishing (New York, NY), 1974.

Collected Stories, introduction by Gore Vidal, New Directions Publishing (New York, NY), 1985.

Contributor of short stories to *Esquire.*

OTHER

The Roman Spring of Mrs. Stone (novel), New Directions Publishing (New York, NY), 1950, reprinted, 1993.

In the Winter of Cities: Poems, New Directions Publishing (New York, NY), 1956.

(Author of introduction) Carson McCullers, *Reflections in a Golden Eye,* Bantam (New York, NY), 1961.

Glass Menagerie [and] *The Street Car Named Desire Notes,* Cliffs Notes, 1965.

Memoirs, Doubleday (New York, NY), 1975.

Moise and the World of Reason (novel), Simon & Schuster (New York, NY), 1975.

Tennessee Williams's Letters to Donald Windham, 1940-1965, edited with commentary by Windham, [Verona], 1976, Holt (New York, NY), 1977, reprinted, University of Georgia Press (Athens, GA), 1996.

Androgyne, Mon Amour: Poems, New Directions Publishing (New York, NY), 1977.

Where I Live: Selected Essays, edited by Christine R. Day and Bob Woods, introduction by Day, New Directions Publishing (New York, NY), 1978.

Conversations with Tennessee Williams, edited by Albert J. Devlin, University Press of Mississippi (Jackson, MS), 1986.

Five o'Clock Angel: Letters of Tennessee Williams to Maria St. Just, 1948-1982, Alfred A. Knopf (New York, NY), 1990.

The Notebook of Trigorin: A Free Adaptation of Anton Chekhov's "The Sea Gull," edited and with an introduction by Allean Hale, New Directions Publishing (New York, NY), 1997.

The Selected Letters of Tennessee Williams, edited by Albert J. Devlin and Nancy M. Tischler, New Directions Publishing (New York, NY), 2000.

The Collected Poems of Tennessee Williams, edited by David E. Roessel and Nicholas Rand Moschovakis, New Directions Publishing (New York, NY), 2002.

A collection of Williams's manuscripts and letters is located at the Humanities Research Center of the University of Texas at Austin. "Blue Song," a previously undiscovered 17-line poem written in Williams's exam book for his Greek final at Washington University in St. Louis, was discovered in 2005 by Washington University professor Henry Schvey in Williams's papers at the Faulkner House Books in New Orleans.

ADAPTATIONS: Cat on a Hot Tin Roof was filmed in 1958; *The Roman Spring of Mrs. Stone* was filmed by Warner Bros. in 1961; *Sweet Bird of Youth* was filmed in 1962; *Period of Adjustment* was filmed in 1962; *This Property Is Condemned* was filmed by Paramount in 1966; *I Can't Imagine Tomorrow* and *Talk to Me Like the Rain and Let Me Listen* were televised together under the title *Dragon Country,* by New York Television Theatre, 1970; an adaptation of *The Seven Descents of Myrtle* was filmed by Warner Bros. in 1970 under the title *The Last of the Mobile Hot-Shots; Summer and Smoke: Opera in Two Acts,* Belwin-Mills, 1972, was adapted from Williams's play, with music by Lee Hoiby and libretto by Lanford Wilson; *The Glass Menagerie* was filmed by Burt Harris for Cineplex Odeon in 1987; *A Streetcar Named Desire* was filmed for ABC-TV in 1984; *Cat on a Hot Tin Roof* was filmed for International TV Group in 1984; *Summer and Smoke* was filmed for NBC-TV in 1989. Several works by Williams have been adapted as sound recordings.

SIDELIGHTS: The production of his first two Broadway plays, *The Glass Menagerie* and *A Streetcar Named Desire*, secured Tennessee Williams's place, along with Eugene O'Neill and Arthur Miller, as one of America's major playwrights of the twentieth century. Critics, playgoers, and fellow dramatists recognized in Williams a poetic innovator who, refusing to be confined in what Stark Young in the *New Republic* called "the usual sterilities of our playwriting patterns," pushed drama into new fields, stretched the limits of the individual play and became one of the founders of the so-called "New Drama." Praising *The Glass Menagerie* "as a revelation of what superb theater could be," Brooks Atkinson in *Broadway* asserted that "Williams's remembrance of things past gave the theater distinction as a literary medium." Twenty years later, Joanne Stang wrote in the *New York Times* that "the American theater, indeed theater everywhere, has never been the same" since the premier of *The Glass Menagerie.* Four decades after that first play, C.W.E. Bigsby in *A Critical Introduction to Twentieth-Century American Drama* termed it "one of the best works to have come out of the American theater." *A Streetcar Named Desire* became only the second play in history to win both the Pulitzer Prize and the New York Drama Critics Circle Award. Eric Bentley, in *What Is Theatre?,* called it the "master-drama of the generation." "The inevitability of a great work of art," T.E. Kalem stated in Albert J. Devlin's *Conversations with Tennessee Williams,* "is that you cannot imagine the time when it didn't exist. You can't imagine a time when *Streetcar* didn't exist."

More clearly than with most authors, the facts of Williams's life reveal the origins of the material he crafted into his best works. The Mississippi in which Thomas Lanier Williams was born March 26, 1911, was in many ways a world that no longer exists, "a dark, wide, open world that you can breathe in," as Williams nostalgically described it in Harry Rasky's *Tennessee Williams: A Portrait in Laughter and Lamentation.* The predominantly rural state was dotted with towns such as Columbus, Canton, and Clarksdale, in which he spent his first seven years with his mother, his sister, Rose, and his maternal grandmother and grandfather, an Episcopal rector. A sickly child, Tom was pampered by doting elders. In 1918, his father, a traveling salesman who had often been absent—perhaps, like his stage counterpart in *The Glass Menagerie,* "in love with long distances"—moved the family to St. Louis. Something of the trauma they experienced is dramatized in the 1945 play. The contrast between leisurely small-town past and northern big-city present, between protective grandparents and the hard-drinking, gambling father with little patience for the sensitive son he saw as a "sissy," seriously affected both children. While Rose retreated into her own mind until finally beyond the reach even of her loving brother, Tom made use of that adversity. St. Louis remained for him "a city I loathe," but the South, despite his portrayal of its grotesque aspects, proved a rich source to which he returned literally and imaginatively for comfort and inspiration. That background, his homosexuality, and his relationships—painful and joyous—with members of his family, were the strongest personal factors shaping Williams's dramas.

During the St. Louis years, Williams found an imaginative release from unpleasant reality in writing essays, stories, poems, and plays. After attending the University of Missouri, Washington University—from which he earned a B.A. in 1938—and the University of Iowa, he returned to the South, specifically to New Orleans, one of two places where he was for the rest of his life to feel at home. Yet a recurrent motif in his plays involves flight and the fugitive, who, Lord Byron insists in *Camino Real: A Play,* must keep moving, and the flight from St. Louis initiated a nomadic life of brief stays in a variety of places. Williams fled not only uncongenial atmospheres but a turbulent family situation that had culminated in a decision for Rose to have a prefrontal lobotomy in an effort to alleviate her increasing psychological problems. (Williams's works often include absentee fathers, enduring—if aggravating—mothers, and dependent relatives; and the memory of Rose appears in some character, situation, symbol or motif in almost every work after 1938.) He fled as well some part of himself, for he had created a new persona—Tennessee Williams the playwright—who shared the same body as the proper young gentleman named Thomas with whom Tennessee would always be to some degree at odds.

In 1940, Williams's *Battle of Angels* was staged by the Theatre Guild in an ill-fated production marred as much by faulty smudge pots in the lynching scene as by Boston censorship. Despite the abrupt out-of-town closing of the play, Williams was now known and admired by powerful theater people. During the next two decades, his most productive period, one play succeeded another, each of them permanent entries in the history of modern theater: *The Glass Menagerie, A Streetcar Named Desire, Summer and Smoke, The Rose Tattoo, Camino Real, Cat on a Hot Tin Roof, Orpheus Descending, Suddenly Last Summer, Sweet Bird of Youth,* and *The Night of the Iguana.* Despite increasingly adverse criticism, Williams continued his work for the theater for two more decades, during which he wrote more than a dozen additional plays containing evidence of his virtues as a poetic realist. In the course of his long career he also produced three volumes of short stories, many of them as studies for subsequent dramas; two novels, two volumes of poetry; his memoirs; and essays on his life and craft. His dramas made that rare transition from legitimate stage to movies and television, from intellectual acceptance to popular acceptance. Before his death in 1983, he had become the best-known living dramatist; his plays had been translated and performed in many foreign countries, and his name and work had become known even to people who had never seen a production of any of his plays. The persona named Tennessee Williams had achieved the status of a myth.

Williams drew from the experiences of his persona. He saw himself as a shy, sensitive, gifted man trapped in a world where "mendacity" replaced communication, brute violence replaced love, and loneliness was, all too often, the standard human condition. These tensions "at the core of his creation" were identified by Harold Clurman in his introduction to *Tennessee Williams: Eight Plays* as a terror at what Williams saw in himself and in America, a terror that he must "exorcise" with "his poetic vision." In an interview collected in *Conversations with Tennessee Williams,* Williams identified his main theme as a defense of the Old South attitude—"elegance, a love of the beautiful, a romantic attitude toward life"—and "a violent protest against those things that defeat it." An idealist aware of what he called in a *Conversations* interview "the merciless harshness of America's success-oriented society," he was ironically, naturalistic as well, conscious of the inaccessibility of that for which he yearned. He early developed, according to John Gassner in *Theatre at the Crossroads: Plays and Playwrights of the Mid-Century American Stage,* "a precise naturalism" and continued to work toward a "fusion of naturalistic detail with symbolism and poetic sensibility rare in American playwriting." The result was a unique romanticism, as Kenneth Tynan observed in *Curtains,* "which is not pale or scented but earthy and robust, the product of a mind vitally infected with the rhythms of human speech."

Williams's characters endeavor to embrace the ideal, to advance and not "hold back with the brutes," a struggle no less valiant for being vain. In *A Streetcar Named Desire* Blanche's idealization of life at Belle Reve, the DuBois plantation, cannot protect her once, in the words of the brutish Stanley Kowalski, she has come "down off them columns" into the "broken world," the world of sexual desire. Since every human, as Val Xavier observes in *Orpheus Descending,* is sentenced "to solitary confinement inside our own lonely skins for as long as we live on earth," the only hope is to try to communicate, to love, and to live—even beyond despair, as *The Night of the Iguana* teaches. The attempt to communicate often takes the form of sex (and Williams has been accused of obsession with that aspect of human existence), but at other times it becomes a willingness to show compassion, as when in *The Night of the Iguana* Hannah Jelkes accepts the neuroses of her fellow creatures and when in *Cat on a Hot Tin Roof,* Big Daddy understands, as his son Brick cannot, the attachment between Brick and Skipper. In his preface to *Cat on a Hot Tin Roof* Williams might have been describing his characters' condition when he spoke of "the outcry of prisoner to prisoner from the cell in solitary where each is confined for the duration of his life." "The marvel is," as Tynan stated, that Williams's "abnormal" view of life, "heightened and spotlighted and slashed with bogey shadows," can be made to touch his audience's more normal views, thus achieving that "miracle of communication" Williams believed to be almost impossible.

Some of his contemporaries—Arthur Miller notably—responded to the modern condition with social protest, but Williams, after a few early attempts at that genre, chose another approach. Williams insisted in a *Conversations* interview that he wrote about the South not as a sociologist: "What I am writing about is human nature. . . . Human relations are terrifyingly ambiguous." Williams chose to present characters full of uncertainties, mysteries, and doubts. Yet Arthur Miller himself wrote in *The Theatre Essays of Tennessee Williams* that although Williams might not portray social reality, "the intensity with which he feels whatever he does feel is so deep, is so great" that his audiences glimpse another kind of reality, "the reality in the spirit." Clurman likewise argued that though Williams was no "propagandist," social commentary is "inherent in his portraiture." The inner torment and disintegration of a character like Blanche in *A Streetcar Named Desire* thus symbolize the lost South from which she comes and with which she is inseparably entwined. It was to that lost world and the unpleasant one which succeeded it that Williams turned for the majority of his settings and material.

Like that of most Southern writers, Williams's work exhibits an abiding concern with time and place and how they affect men and women. "The play is memory," Tom proclaims in *The Glass Menagerie;* and Williams's characters are haunted by a past that they have difficulty accepting or that they valiantly endeavor to transform into myth. Interested in yesterday or tomorrow rather than in today, painfully conscious of the physical and emotional scars the years inflict, they have a static, dreamlike quality, and the result, Tynan observed, is "the drama of mood." The Mississippi towns of his childhood continued to haunt Williams's imagination throughout his career, but New Orleans offered him, he told Robert Rice in the 1958 *New York Post* interviews, a new freedom: "The shock of it against the Puritanism of my nature has given me a subject, a theme, which I have never ceased exploiting." (That shabby but charming city became the setting for several stories and one-act plays, and *A Streetcar Named Desire* derives much of its distinction from French Quarter ambience and attitudes; as Stella informs Blanche, "New Orleans isn't like other cities," a view reinforced by Williams's 1977 portrait of the place in *Vieux Carre.*) Atkinson observed, "Only a writer who had survived in the lower depths of a sultry Southern city could know the characters as intimately as Williams did and be so thoroughly steeped in the aimless sprawl of the neighborhood life."

Williams's South provided not only settings but other characteristics of his work—romanticism; a myth of an Arcadian existence now disappeared; a distinctive way of looking at life, including both an inbred Calvinistic belief in the reality of evil eternally at war with good, and what Bentley called a "peculiar combination of the comic and the pathetic." The South also inspired Williams's fascination with violence, his drawing upon regional character types, and his skill in recording Southern language—eloquent, flowery, sometimes bombastic. Moreover, Southern history, particularly the lost cause of the U.S. Civil War and the devastating Reconstruction period, imprinted on Williams, as on such major Southern fiction writers as William Faulkner, Flannery O'Connor, and Walker Percy, a profound sense of separation and alienation. Williams, as Thomas E. Porter declared in *Myth and Modern American Drama,* explored "the mind of the Southerner caught between an idyllic past and an undesirable present," commemorating the death of a myth even as he continued to examine it. "His broken figures appeal," Bigsby asserted, "because they are victims of history—the lies of the old South no longer being able to sustain the individual in a world whose pragmatics have no place for the fragile spirit." In a *Conversations* interview the playwright commented that "the South once had a way of life that I am just old enough to remember—a culture that had grace, elegance. . . . I write out of regret for that."

Williams's plays are peopled with a large cast that J.L. Styan termed, in *Modern Drama in Theory and Practice,* "Garrulous Grotesques"; these figures include "untouchables whom he touches with frankness and mercy," according to Tynan. They bear the stamp of their place of origin and speak a "humorous, colorful, graphic" language, which Williams in a *Conversations* interview called the "mad music of my characters." "Have you ever known a Southerner who wasn't long-winded?" he asked; "I mean, a Southerner not afflicted with terminal asthma." Among that cast are the romantics who, however suspect their own virtues may be, act out of belief in and commitment to what Faulkner called the "old verities and truths of the heart." They include fallen aristocrats hounded, Gerald Weales observed in *American Drama since World War II,* "by poverty, by age, by frustration," or, as Bigsby called them in his 1985 study, "martyrs for a world which has already slipped away unmourned"; fading Southern belles such as Amanda Wingate and Blanche DuBois; slightly deranged women, such as Aunt Rose Comfort in an early one-act play and in the film "Baby Doll"; dictatorial patriarchs such as Big Daddy; and the outcasts (or "fugitive kind," the playwright's term later employed as the title of a 1960 motion picture). Many of these characters tend to recreate the scene in which they find themselves—Laura with her glass animals shutting out the alley where cats are brutalized, Blanche trying to subdue the ugliness of the Kowalski apartment with a paper lantern; in their dialogue they frequently poeticize and melodramatize their situations, thereby surrounding themselves with protective illusion, which in later plays becomes "mendacity." For also inhabiting that dramatic world are more powerful individuals, amoral representatives of the new Southern order, Jabe Torrance in *Battle of Angels,* Gooper and Mae in *Cat on a Hot Tin Roof,* Boss Finley in *Sweet Bird of Youth,* enemies of the romantic impulse and as destructive and virtueless as Faulkner's Snopes clan. Southern though all these characters are, they are not mere regional portraits, for through Williams's dramatization of them and their dilemmas and through the audience's empathy, the characters become everyman and everywoman.

Although traumatic experiences plagued his life, Williams was able to press "the nettle of neurosis" to his heart and produce art, as Gassner observed. Williams's family problems, his alienation from the social norm resulting from his homosexuality, his sense of being a romantic in an unromantic, postwar world, and his sensitive reaction when a production proved less than successful all contributed significantly to his work. Through the years he suffered from a variety of ailments, some serious, some surely imaginary, and at certain periods he overindulged in alcohol and prescription drugs. Despite these circumstances, he continued to write with a determination that verged at times almost on desperation, even as his new plays elicited progressively more hostile reviews from critics.

An outgrowth of this suffering is the character type "the fugitive kind," the wanderer who lives outside the pale of society, excluded by his sensitivity, artistic bent, or sexual proclivity from the world of "normal" human beings. Like Faulkner, Williams was troubled by the exclusivity of any society that shuts out certain segments because they are different. First manifested in Val of *Battle of Angels* (later rewritten as *Orpheus Descending*) and then in the character of Tom, the struggling poet of *The Glass Menagerie* and his shy, withdrawn sister, the fugitive kind appears in varying guises in subsequent plays, including Blanche DuBois, Alma Winemiller (*Summer and Smoke*), Kilroy (*Camino Real*), and Hannah and Shannon (*The Night of the Iguana*). Each is unique but they share common characteristics, which Weales summed up as physical or mental illness, a preoccupation with sex, and a "combination of sensitivity and imagination with corruption." Their abnormality suggests, the critic argued, that the dramatist views the norm of society as being faulty itself. Even characters within the "norm" (Stanley Kowalski, for example) are often identified with strong sexual drives. Like D.H. Lawrence, Williams indulged in a kind of phallic romanticism, attributing sexual potency to members of the unintelligent lower classes and sterility to aristocrats. Despite his romanticism, however, Williams's view of humanity was too realistic for him to accept such pat categories. "If you write a character that isn't ambiguous," Williams said in a *Conversations* interview, "you are writing a false character, not a true one." Though he shared Lawrence's view that one should not suppress sexual impulses, Williams recognized that such impulses are at odds with the romantic desire to transcend and that they often lead to suffering like that endured by Blanche DuBois. Those fugitive characters who are destroyed, Bigsby remarked, often perish "because they offer love in a world characterized by impotence and sterility." Thus phallic potency may represent a positive force in a character such as Val or a destructive force in one like Stanley Kowalski; but even in *A Streetcar Named Desire* Williams acknowledges that the life force, represented by Stella's baby, is positive. There are, as Weales pointed out, two divisions in the sexual activity Williams dramatizes: "desperation sex," in which characters such as Val and Blanche "make contact with another only tentatively, momentarily" in order to communicate; and the "consolation and comfort" sex that briefly fulfills Lady in *Orpheus Descending* and saves Serafina in *The Rose Tattoo.* There is, surely, a third kind, sex as a weapon, wielded by those like Stanley; this kind of sex is to be feared, for it is often associated with the violence prevalent in Williams's dramas.

Beginning with *Battle of Angels,* two opposing camps have existed among Williams's critics, and his detractors sometimes have objected most strenuously to the innovations his supporters deemed virtues. His strongest advocates among established drama critics, notably Stark Young, Brooks Atkinson, John Gassner, and Walter Kerr, praised him for realistic clarity; compassion and a strong moral sense; unforgettable characters, especially women, based on his keen perception of human nature; dialogue at once credible and poetic; and a pervasive sense of humor that distinguished him from O'Neill and Miller.

Not surprisingly, it was from the conservative establishment that most of the adverse criticism came. Obviously appalled by this "upstart crow," George Jean Nathan, dean of theater commentators when Williams made his revolutionary entrance onto the scene, sounded notes often to be repeated. In *The Theatre Book of the Year, 1947-1948,* he faulted Williams's early triumphs for "mistiness of ideology . . . questionable symbolism . . . debatable character drawing . . . adolescent point of view . . . theatrical fabrication," obsession with sex, fallen women, and "the deranged Dixie damsel." Nathan saw Williams as a melodramatist whose attempts at tragedy were as ludicrous as "a threnody on a zither." Subsequent detractors—notably Richard Gilman, Robert Brustein, Clive Barnes, and John Simon—taxed the playwright for theatricality, repetition, lack of judgment and control, excessive moralizing and philosophizing, and conformity to the demands of the ticket-buying public. His plays, they variously argued, lacked unity of effect, clarity of intention, social content, and variety; these critics saw the plays as burdened with excessive symbolism, violence, sexuality, and attention to the sordid, grotesque elements of life. Additionally, certain commentators charged that Elia Kazan, the director of the early masterpieces, virtually rewrote *A Streetcar Named Desire* and *Cat on a Hot Tin Roof.* A particular kind of negative criticism, often intensely emotional, seemed to dominate evaluations of the plays produced in the last twenty years of Williams's life.

Most critics, even his detractors, have praised the dramatist's skillful creation of dialogue. Bentley asserted that "no one in the English-speaking theater" created better dialogue, that Williams's plays were really "*written*—that is to say, set down in living language." Ruby Cohn stated in *Dialogue in American Drama* that Williams gave to American theater "a new vocabulary and rhythm," and Clurman concluded, "No one in the theater has written more melodiously. Without the least artificial flourish, his writing takes flight from the naturalistic to the poetic." Even Mary McCarthy, no ardent fan, stated in *Theatre Chronicles: 1937-1962* that Williams was the only American realist other than Paddy Chayevsky with an ear for dialogue, knew speech patterns, and really heard his characters. There were, of course, objections to Williams's lyrical dialogue, different as it is from the dialogue of O'Neill, Miller, or any other major American playwright. Bentley admitted to finding his "fake poeticizing" troublesome at times, while Bigsby insisted that Williams was at his best only when he restrained "over-poetic language" and symbolism with "an imagination which if melodramatic is also capable of fine control." However, those long poetic speeches or "arias" in plays of the first twenty-five years of his career became a hallmark of the dramatist's work.

Another major area of contention among commentators has been Williams's use of symbols, which he called in a *Conversations* interview "the natural language of drama." Laura's glass animals, the paper lantern and cathedral bells in *A Streetcar Named Desire,* the legless birds of *Orpheus Descending,* and the iguana in *The Night of the Iguana,* to name only a few, are integral to the plays in which they appear. Cohn commented on Williams's extensive use of animal images in *Cat on a Hot Tin Roof* to symbolize the fact that all the Pollitts, "grasping, screeching, devouring," are "greedily alive." In that play, Big Daddy's malignancy effectively represents the corruption in the family and in the larger society to which the characters belong. However, Weales objected that Williams, like *The Glass Menagerie* 's Tom, had "a poet's weakness for symbols," which can get out of hand; he argued that in *Suddenly Last Summer,* Violet Venable's garden does not grow out of the situation and enrich the play. Sometimes, Cohn observed, a certain weakness of symbolism "is built into the fabric of the drama."

Critics favorable to Williams have agreed that one of his virtues lay in his characterization. Those "superbly actable parts," Atkinson stated, derived from his ability to find "extraordinary spiritual significance in ordinary people." Cohn admired Williams's "Southern grotesques" and his knack for giving them "dignity," although some critics have been put off by the excessive number of such grotesques, which contributed, they argued, to a distorted view of reality. Commentators have generally concurred in their praise of Williams's talent in creating credible female roles. "No one in American drama has written more intuitively of women," Clurman asserted; Gassner spoke of Williams's "uncanny familiarity with the flutterings of the female heart." Kerr in *The Theatre in Spite of Itself* expressed wonder at such roles as that of Hannah in *The Night of the Iguana,* "a portrait which owes nothing to calipers, or to any kind of tooling; it is all surprise and presence, anticipated intimacy. It is found gold, not a borrowing against known reserves." Surveying the "steamy zoo" of Williams's characters with their violence, despair, and aberrations, Stang commended the author for the "poetry and compassion that comprise his great gift." *Compassion* is the key word in all tributes to Williams's characterization. It is an acknowledgment of the playwright's uncanny talent for making audiences and readers empathize with his people, however grotesque, bizarre, or even sordid they may seem on the surface.

Although they have granted him compassion, some of his detractors maintain that Williams does not exhibit a clear philosophy of life, and they have found unacceptable the ambiguity in judging human flaws and frailties that is one of his most distinctive qualities. For them, one difficulty stems from the playwright's recognition of and insistence on portraying the ambiguity of human activities and relationships. Moral, even puritanical, though he might be, Williams never seems ready to condemn any action other than "deliberate cruelty," and even that is sometimes portrayed as resulting from extenuating circumstances.

In terms of dramatic technique, those who acknowledge his genius disagree as to where it has been best expressed. For Jerold Phillips, writing in the *Dictionary of Literary Biography Documentary Series,* Williams's major contribution lay in turning from the Ibsenesque social problem plays to "Strindberg-like explorations of what goes on underneath the skin," thereby freeing American theater from "the hold of the so-called well-made play." For Allan Lewis in *American Plays and Playwrights of the Contemporary Theatre,* he was a "brilliant inventor of emotionally intense scenes" whose "greatest gift [lay] in suggesting ideas through emotional relations." His preeminence among dramatists in the United States, Jean Gould wrote in *Modern American Playwrights,* resulted from a combination of poetic sensitivity, theatricality, and "the dedication of the artist." If, from the beginning of his career, there were detractors who charged Williams with overuse of melodramatic, grotesque, and violent elements that produced a distorted view of reality, Kerr, in *The Theatre in Spite of Itself,* termed him "a man unafraid of melodrama, and a man who handles it with extraordinary candor and deftness."

Other commentators have been offended by what Bentley termed Williams's "exploitation of the obscene": his choice of characters—outcasts, alcoholics, the violent and deranged and sexually abnormal—and of subject matter—incest, castration, and cannibalism. Williams justified the "sordid" elements of his work in a *Conversations* interview when he asserted that "we must depict the awfulness of the world we live in, but we must do it with a kind of aesthetic" to avoid producing mere horror.

Another negative aspect of Williams's art, some critics argued, was his theatricality. Gassner asserted in *Directions in Modern Theatre and Drama* that Kazan, the director, avoided flashy stage effects called for in Williams's text of *The Glass Menagerie,* but that in some plays Kazan collaborated with the playwright to exaggerate these effects, especially in the expressionistic and allegorical drama *Camino Real.* In a *Conversations* interview, Williams addressed this charge, particularly as it involved Kazan, by asserting, "My cornpone melodrama is all my own. I want excitement in the theater. . . . I have a tendency toward romanticism and a taste for the theatrical."

Late in his career, Williams was increasingly subject to charges that he had outlived his talent. Beginning with *Period of Adjustment,* a comedy generally disliked by critics, there were years of rejection of play after play. By the late 1960s, even the longtime advocate Atkinson observed that in "a melancholy resolution of an illustrious career" the dramatist was producing plays "with a kind of desperation" in which he lost control of content and style. Lewis, accusing Williams of repeating motifs, themes, and characters in play after play, asserted that in failing "to expand and enrich" his theme, he had "dissipated a rare talent." Gilman, in a particularly vituperative review titled "Mr. Williams, He Dead," included in his *Common and Uncommon Masks: Writings on Theatre, 1961-1970,* charged that the "moralist," subtly present in earlier plays, was "increasingly on stage." Even if one granted a diminution of creative powers, however, the decline in Williams's popularity and position as major playwright in the 1960s and 1970s can be attributed in large part to a marked change in the theater itself. Audiences constantly demanded variety, and although the early creations of the playwright remained popular, theatergoers wanted something different, strange, exotic. One problem, Kerr pointed out, was that Williams was so good, people expected him to continue to get better; judging each play against those which had gone before denied a fair hearing to the new creations.

The playwright's accidental death came when his career, after almost two decades of bad reviews and of dismissals of his "dwindling talents," was at its lowest ebb since the abortive 1940 production of *Battle of Angels.* Following Williams's death, however, the inevitable reevaluation began. Bigsby, for example, found in a reanalysis of the late plays more than mere vestiges of the strengths of earlier years, especially in *Out Cry,* an experimental drama toward which Williams felt a particular affection. Some of those who had been during his last years his severest critics acknowledged the greatness of his achievement. Even Simon, who had dismissed play after play as valueless repetitions created by an author who had outlived his talent, acknowledged in *New York* that he had underestimated the playwright's genius and significance. Williams was, finally, viewed by formerly skeptical observers, as a rebel who broke with the rigid conventions of drama that had preceded him, explored new territory in his quest for a distinctive form and style, created characters as unforgettable as those of Charles Dickens, Nathaniel Hawthorne, or William Faulkner, and lifted the language of the modern stage to a poetic level unmatched in his time.

Posthumous publications of Williams's writings—correspondence and plays among them—show the many sides of this complex literary legend. *Five o'Clock Angel: Letters of Tennessee Williams to Maria St. Just,*

1948-1982 takes its title from the name the author gave to Russian-born actress and socialite Maria Britneva, later Maria St. Just, "the confidante Williams wrote to in the evening after his day's work—his 'Five o'Clock Angel,' as he called her in a typically genteel, poetic periphrasis," noted Edmund White in a piece for the *New York Times Book Review.* These letters, White added, allow readers "to see the source of everything in his work that was lyrical, innocent, loving, and filled with laughter." Among the other Williams works published posthumously is *Something Cloudy, Something Clear.* A play first produced in 1981 and published in 1995, *Something Cloudy, Something Clear* recounts the author's homosexual relationship with a doomed dancer in Provincetown. Homosexuality—this time in a violent context—also takes center stage in *Not about Nightingales,* a tale of terror in a men's prison. Actress Vanessa Redgrave reportedly played a key role in bringing this early play—written circa 1939—to the London stage in 1998.

Whatever the final judgment of literary historians on the works of Tennessee Williams, certain facts are clear. He was, without question, the most controversial American playwright, a situation unlikely to change as the debate over his significance and the relative merits of individual plays continues. Critics, scholars, and theatergoers do not remain neutral in regard to the man or his work. He is also the most quotable of American playwrights, and even those who disparage the highly poetic dialogue admit the uniqueness of the language he brought to modern theater. In addition, Williams has added to dramatic literature a cast of remarkable, memorable characters and has turned his attention and sympathy toward people and subjects that, before his time, had been considered beneath the concern of serious authors. With "distinctive dramatic feeling," Gassner said in *Theatre at the Crossroads,* Williams "made pulsating plays out of his visions of a world of terror, confusion, and perverse beauty." As a result, Gassner concluded, Williams "makes indifference to the theater virtually impossible."

BIOGRAPHICAL AND CRITICAL SOURCES:

BOOKS

Atkinson, Brooks, *Broadway,* revised edition, Macmillan (New York, NY), 1974.

Bentley, Eric, *What Is Theatre?,* Atheneum (New York, NY), 1968.

Bernstein, Samuel J., *The Strands Entwined: A New Direction in American Drama,* Northeastern University Press (Boston, MA), 1980.

Bigsby, C.W. E., *Confrontation and Commitment: A Study of Contemporary American Drama 1959-1966,* University of Missouri Press (Columbia, MO), 1968.

Bigsby, C.W. E., *A Critical Introduction to Twentieth-Century American Drama,* three volumes, Cambridge University Press (New York, NY), 1985.

Cohn, Ruby, *Dialogue in American Drama,* Indiana University Press (Bloomington, IN), 1971.

Crandell, George W., *Tennessee Williams: A Descriptive Bibliography,* University of Pittsburgh Press (Pittsburgh, PA), 1995.

Devlin, Albert J., editor, *Conversations with Tennessee Williams,* University Press of Mississippi (Jackson, MS), 1986.

Dictionary of Literary Biography, Volume 7: *Twentieth-Century American Dramatists,* Thomson Gale (Detroit, MI), 1981.

Dictionary of Literary Biography Documentary Series, Volume 4, Thomson Gale (Detroit, MI), 1984.

Fleche, Anne, *Mimetic Disillusion: Eugene O'Neill, Tennessee Williams, and U.S. Dramatic Realism,* University of Alabama Press (Tuscaloosa, AL), 1997.

Gassner, John, *Theatre at the Crossroads: Plays and Playwrights of the Mid-Century American Stage,* Henry Holt (New York, NY), 1960.

Gassner, John, *Directions in Modern Theatre and Drama,* Henry Holt (New York, NY), 1966.

Gilman, Richard, *Common and Uncommon Masks: Writings on Theatre, 1961-1970,* Random House (New York, NY), 1971.

Gould, Jean, *Modern American Playwrights,* Dodd (New York, NY), 1966.

Griffin, Alice, *Understanding Tennessee Williams,* University of South Carolina Press (Columbia, SC), 1995.

Kerr, Walter,*The Theatre in Spite of Itself,* Simon & Schuster (New York, NY), 1963.

Kerr, Walter, *Journey to the Center of Theatre,* Alfred A. Knopf (New York, NY), 1979.

Leverich, Lyle, *Tenn: The Timeless World of Tennessee Williams,* Crown Publishers (New York, NY), 1997.

Lewis, Allan, *American Plays and Playwrights of the Contemporary Theatre,* Crown Publishers (New York, NY), 1965.

Martin, Robert A., editor, *Critical Essays on Tennessee Williams,* Prentice Hall International (Tappan, NJ), 1997.

McCann, John S., *The Critical Reputation of Tennessee Williams: A Reference Guide,* G.K. Hall (Boston, MA), 1983.

McCarthy, Mary, *Theatre Chronicles: 1937-1962,* Farrar, Straus, & Giroux (New York, NY), 1963.

Miller, Arthur, *The Theatre Essays of Tennessee Williams,* edited by Robert A. Martin, Penguin (New York, NY), 1978.

Nathan, George Jean, *The Theatre Book of the Year, 1947-1948, 1948, 1948-1949,* Alfred A. Knopf (New York, NY), 1949.

O'Connor, Jacqueline, *Dramatizing Dementia: Madness in the Plays of Tennessee Williams,* Bowling Green State University Popular Press (Bowling Green, OH), 1997.

Porter, Thomas E., *Myth and Modern American Drama,* Wayne State University Press (Detroit, MI), 1969.

Rasky, Harry, *Tennessee Williams: A Portrait in Laughter and Lamentation,* Dodd (New York, NY), 1986.

Simon, John, *Acid Test,* Stein & Day (New York, NY), 1963.

Styan, J.L., *Modern Drama in Theory and Practice,* Volume 1, Cambridge University Press (New York, NY), 1981.

Tynan, Kenneth, *Curtains,* Atheneum (New York, NY), 1961.

Weales, Gerald, *American Drama since World War II,* Harcourt, Brace (New York, NY), 1962.

Williams, Edwina Dakin, as told to Lucy Freeman, *Remember Me to Tom,* Putnam (New York, NY), 1963.

Williams, Tennessee, *The Glass Menagerie,* Random House (New York, NY), 1945, published as *The Glass Menagerie: Play in Two Acts,* Dramatists Play Service (New York, NY), 1948.

Williams, Tennessee, *Camino Real: A Play,* foreword and afterword by Williams, New Directions Publishing (New York, NY), 1953.

Williams, Tennessee, *Cat on a Hot Tin Roof,* preface by Williams, New Directions Publishing (New York, NY), 1955, published as *Cat on a Hot Tin Roof: A Play in Three Acts,* Dramatists Play Service (New York, NY), 1958.

Williams, Tennessee, *Orpheus Descending: A Play in Three Acts,* New Directions Publishing (New York, NY), 1959.

Williams, Tennessee, *The Theatre of Tennessee Williams,* New Directions Publishing (New York, NY), Volume 1, 1971, Volume 2, 1971, Volume 3, 1971, Volume 4, 1972, Volume 5, 1976, Volume 6, 1981, Volume 7, 1981.

Williams, Tennessee, *Tennessee Williams: Eight Plays,* introduction by Harold Clurman, Doubleday (New York, NY), 1979.

PERIODICALS

Booklist, September 15, 1995, Jack Helbig, review of *Something Cloudy, Something Clear,* p. 131.

Library Journal, September 1, 1995, Ming-ming Shen Kuo, review of *Something Cloudy, Something Clear,* p. 178; October 15, 1995, Denise A. Garofalo, review of *The Migrants,* p. 100.

New Republic, Volume 112, 1945; June 17, 1996, Robert Brustein, review of *The Night of the Iguana,* p. 26.

New York, March 14, 1983, John Simon, "Poet of the Theater," p. 76; November 28, 1994, John Simon, review of *The Glass Menagerie,* p. 75; May 15, 1995, John Simon, review of *The Rose Tattoo,* p. 59; October 23, 1995, John Simon, review of *Garden District,* p. 60.

New Yorker, July 18, 1994, John Lahr, "Fugitive Mind," p. 68; November 21, 1994, John Lahr, review of *The Glass Menagerie,* p. 124; December 19, 1994. John Lahr, "The Lady and Tennessee," p. 76; May 15, 1995, Nancy Franklin, review of *The Rose Tattoo,* p. 100; April 8, 1996, Nancy Franklin, review of *Night of the Iguana,* p. 103.

New York Post, April 21-May 4, 1958, Robert Rice, interview with Williams.

New York Times Book Review, May 27, 1990, Edmund White, review of *Five o'Clock Angel: Letters of Tennessee Williams to Maria St. Just, 1948-1982,* p. 1.

Southern Living, March, 1996, Wanda Butler, "A Weekend Named Desire," p. 26.

Time, December 5, 1994, William Tynan, review of *The Glass Menagerie,* p. 94.

World Literature Today, winter, 1992, Phillip C. Kolin, "Tennessee Williams: Fugitive Kind," p. 133.

ONLINE

Mississippi Writers Page, http://www.olemiss.edu/mwp/ (April 26, 2004), "Tennessee Williams."

* * *

WILLIAMS, Thomas Lanier
See WILLIAMS, Tennessee

* * *

WILLIS, Charles G.
See CLARKE, Arthur C.

WILSON, August 1945-2005 (Frederick August Kittel)

PERSONAL: Born Frederick August Kittel, April 27, 1945, in Pittsburgh, PA; died October 2, 2005, in Seattle, WA, of liver cancer; son of Frederick August (a baker) and Daisy (a cleaning woman; maiden name, Wilson) Kittel; stepfather, David Bedford; married Brenda Burton (divorced), 1969; married Judy Oliver (a social worker; divorced), 1981; married Constanza Romero (a costume designer), 1994; children: (first marriage) Sakina Ansari; (third marriage) Azula Carmen. *Ethnicity:* Black.

CAREER: Writer. Black Horizons on the Hill (theater company) Pittsburgh, PA, cofounder (with Rob Penny), scriptwriter, and director, 1968-78; Science Museum of Minnesota, St. Paul, MN, scriptwriter, 1979.

AWARDS, HONORS: Award for best play, New York Drama Critics Circle, and Tony Award nomination, League of New York Theatres and Producers, both 1985, and Whiting Writers' Award from the Whiting Foundation, 1986, all for *Ma Rainey's Black Bottom;* Outstanding Play Award, American Theatre Critics, Drama Desk Outstanding New Play Award, and New York Drama Critics Circle Best Play Award, all 1986, all for *Fences;* Pulitzer Prize for drama, Tony Award for best play, and award for best Broadway play, Outer Critics Circle, all 1987, all for *Fences;* John Gassner Award for best American playwright from Outer Critics Circle, 1987; named Artist of the Year by *Chicago Tribune,* 1987; Literary Lion Award, New York Public Library, 1988; New York Drama Critics Circle Best Play award, and Tony Award nomination for best play, both 1988, both for *Joe Turner's Come and Gone*; Drama Desk Outstanding New Play Award, New York Drama Critics Circle Best Play Award, Tony Award nomination for Best Play, American Theatre Critics Outstanding Play Award, and Pulitzer Prize for drama, all 1990, all for *The Piano Lesson;* Black Filmmakers Hall of Fame Award, 1991; Tony Award nomination for best play, and American Theatre Critics' Association Award, both 1992, both for *Two Trains Running;* Clarence Muse Award, 1992; New York Drama Critics Circle Award and Tony Award nomination for best play, 1996, both for *Seven Guitars;* recipient of Bush and Guggenheim Foundation fellowships; Tony Award nomination, 2001, for *King Hedley II;* Tony Award nomination, 2005, for *Gem of the Ocean.*

WRITINGS:

PLAYS

Recycle, produced in Pittsburgh, PA, 1973.

The Homecoming, produced 1989.

The Coldest Day of the Year, produced 1989.

Jitney! (two-act play; produced in Pittsburgh, PA, by Black Horizons Theatre Company, 1978; revised version produced in Atlanta, GA, at the Alliance Theatre Company, 1999; in Los Angeles, CA, at Mark Taper Forum, 2000; in New York, NY, at Second Stage, 2000), Overlook Press (Woodstock, NY), 2001.

Fullerton Street, produced 1980.

Black Bart and the Sacred Hills, produced in St. Paul, MN, at Penumbra Theatre, 1981.

The Mill Hand's Lunch Bucket, produced in New York, NY, 1983.

Ma Rainey's Black Bottom (produced in New Haven, CT, at the Yale Repertory Theatre, 1984; on Broadway at the Cort Theatre, October, 1984), in *Three Plays,* University of Pittsburgh Press (Pittsburgh, PA), 1991, by New American Library (New York, NY), 1985.

Fences (produced in New Haven, CT, at Yale Repertory Theatre, 1985; on Broadway at 46th Street Theatre, March, 1987), in *Three Plays,* University of Pittsburgh Press (Pittsburgh, PA), 1991, by New American Library (New York, NY), 1988.

Joe Turner's Come and Gone (produced in New Haven, CT, at Yale Repertory Theatre, 1986; on Broadway at Barrymore Theatre, March, 1988; revival production in New York, NY, at Royale Theater, 2003), in *Three Plays* University of Pittsburgh Press (Pittsburgh, PA), 1991, by New American Library (New York, NY), 1988.

(And author of teleplay) *The Piano Lesson* produced in New Haven, CT, at Yale Repertory Theatre, 1987; produced on Broadway at Walter Kerr Theatre, 1990; teleplay produced by Hallmark Hall of Fame, CBS television special, 1995), New American Library (New York, NY), 1990.

Two Trains Running (produced in New Haven, CT, at Yale Repertory Theatre, 1990; in Washington, DC, at John F. Kennedy Center for the Performing Arts, 1991; at Walter Kerr Theatre, 1992), New American Library/Dutton (New York, NY), 1993.

Seven Guitars (produced in Chicago, IL, at Goodman Theatre, 1995; at Walter Kerr Theatre, 1996), Dutton (New York, NY), 1996.

King Hedley II, produced in Pittsburgh, PA, at Pittsburgh Public Theatre, 2000; produced on Broadway at Virginia Theatre, 2001.

Gem of the Ocean, produced in Chicago, IL, at Goodman Theatre, 2003; produced on Broadway at Walter Kerr Theatre, 2004.

Radio Golf, produced in New Haven, CT, at Yale Repertory Theatre, 2005.

BOOKS

(Author of preface) *August Wilson: Three Plays* (contains *Ma Rainey's Black Bottom, Fences,* and *Joe Turner's Come and Gone*), afterword by Paul C. Harrison, University of Pittsburgh Press (Pittsburgh, PA), 1991.

The Ground on Which I Stand, Theatre Communications Group (New York, NY), 2000.

Contributor to play *Urban Blight.* Author of the book for a stage musical about jazz musician Jelly Roll Morton. Work represented in *A Game of Passion: The NFL Literary Companion,* Turner, 1994; *Selected from Contemporary American Plays,* 1990; and *The Poetry of Black America.* Contributor to periodicals, including *American Theatre, Black Lines* and *Connection.*

SIDELIGHTS: August Wilson, who was born Frederick August Kittel, has been hailed since the mid-1980s as an important talent in the American theater. He spent his childhood in poverty in Pittsburgh, Pennsylvania, where he lived with his parents and five siblings. Though he grew up in a poor family, Wilson felt that his parents withheld knowledge of even greater hardships they had endured. "My generation of blacks knew very little about the past of our parents," he told the *New York Times* in 1984. "They shielded us from the indignities they suffered." Wilson's goal is to illuminate that shadowy past with plays that focus on black issues. *Ma Rainey's Black Bottom, Fences, Joe Turner's Come and Gone, The Piano Lesson, Two Trains Running,* and *Seven Guitars* are part of this ambitious project.

Wilson has noted that his real education began when he was sixteen years old. Disgusted by the racist treatment he endured in the various schools he had attended until that time, he dropped out and began educating himself in the local library. Working at menial jobs, he also pursued a literary career and successfully submitted poems to black publications at the University of Pittsburgh. In 1968 he became active in the theater by founding—despite lacking prior experience—Black Horizons on the Hill, a theater company in Pittsburgh. Recalling his early theater involvement, Wilson described himself to the *New York Times* as "a cultural nationalist . . . trying to raise consciousness through theater."

According to several observers, however, Wilson found his artistic voice—and began to appreciate the black voices of Pittsburgh—after he moved to St. Paul, Minnesota, in 1978. In St. Paul Wilson wrote his first play, *Jitney!,* a realistic drama set in a Pittsburgh taxi station. *Jitney!,* noted for the fidelity with which it portrayed black urban speech and life, had a successful engagement at a small theater in Pittsburgh. Wilson followed *Jitney!* with another play, *Fullerton Street,* but this work failed to strengthen his reputation.

Wilson then resumed work on an earlier unfinished project, *Ma Rainey's Black Bottom,* a play about a black blues singer's exploitation of her fellow musicians. This work, whose title role is named after an actual blues singer from the 1920s, is set in a recording studio in 1927. In the studio, temperamental Ma Rainey verbally abuses the other musicians and presents herself—without justification—as an important musical figure. But much of the play is also set in a rehearsal room, where Ma Rainey's musicians discuss their abusive employer and the hardships of life in racist America.

Ma Rainey's Black Bottom earned Wilson a trip to the O'Neill Theatre Center's National Playwrights Conference. There Wilson's play impressed director Lloyd Richards from the Yale Repertory Theatre. Richards worked with Wilson to refine the play, and when it was presented at Yale in 1984 it was hailed as the work of an important new playwright. Frank Rich, who reviewed the Yale production in the *New York Times,* acclaimed Wilson as "a major find for the American theater" and cited Wilson's ability to write "with compassion, raucous humor and penetrating wisdom."

Wilson enjoyed further success with *Ma Rainey's Black Bottom* after the play came to Broadway later in 1984. *Chicago Tribune* contributor Richard Christiansen reviewed the Broadway production as "a work of intermittent but immense power" and commended the "striking beauty" of the play's "literary and theatrical poetry." Christiansen added that "Wilson's power of language is sensational" and that *Ma Rainey's Black Bottom* was "the work of an impressive writer." The London *Times*'s Holly Hill agreed, calling Wilson "a promising new playwright" and hailing his work as "a remarkable first play."

Wilson's subsequent plays include the Pulitzer Prize-winning *Fences,* which is about a former athlete who forbids his son to accept an athletic scholarship, and *Joe Turner's Come and Gone,* which concerns an ex-convict's efforts to find his wife. Like *Ma Rainey's Black Bottom,* these plays underwent extensive rewriting. Guiding Wilson in this process was Lloyd Richards, dean of Yale's drama school and director of the school's productions of Wilson's plays. "August is a wonderful poet," Richards told the *New York Times* in 1986. "A wonderful poet turning into a playwright." Richards added that his work with Wilson involved "clarifying" each work's main theme and "arranging the material in a dynamic way."

Both *Fences* and *Joe Turner's Come and Gone* were praised when they played on American stages. The *New York Times*'s Frank Rich, in his review of *Fences,* wrote that the play "leaves no doubt that Mr. Wilson is a major writer, combining a poet's ear for vernacular with a robust sense of humor (political and sexual), a sure instinct for cracking dramatic incident and passionate commitment to a great subject." And in his critique of *Joe Turner's Come and Gone,* Rich speculated that the play "will give a lasting voice to a generation of uprooted black Americans." Rich contended that the work was "potentially its author's finest achievement yet" and described it as "a teeming canvas of black America . . . and a spiritual allegory."

Wilson is intensely passionate about portraying the truth of the black experience, about being the voice of the ghetto. While he did not set out to create his plays in a series, it became clear to him that his plays in combination were creating a twentieth-century history of the black experience in America. "I'm taking each decade," Wilson said, "and looking at one of the most important questions that blacks confronted in that decade and writing a play about it. Put them all together, and you have a history."

In 1990 Wilson claimed his second Pulitzer Prize, this time for *The Piano Lesson.* Set during the Great Depression of the 1930s, this drama pits brother against sister in a contest to decide the future of a treasured heirloom—a piano, carved with African-style portraits by their grandfather, an enslaved plantation carpenter. The brother wants to sell it to buy land, while the sister adamantly insists that the instrument carries too much family history to part with. Acclaim for the play was widespread, although some commentators were put off by the supernatural elements that came to play in the climax of this otherwise realistic piece. "When ghosts begin resolving realistic plays, you can be sure the playwright has failed to master his material," wrote Robert Brustein in the *New Republic.* Brustein also found the play overlong and repetitious, and asserted that Wilson's focus on the effects of racism was limiting him artistically. Others praised the work unreservedly, however, including Clive Barnes of the *New York Post.* He declared, "This is a play in which to lose yourself—to give yourself up . . . to August Wilson's thoughts, humors and thrills, all caught in a microcosm largely remote for many of us from our own little worlds, yet always talking the same language of humanity." Frank Rich of the *New York Times* wrote that Wilson has given "miraculous voice" to the black experience, and William A. Henry III of *Time* dubbed the play's piano "the most potent symbol in American drama since Laura Wingfield's glass menagerie" in the Tennessee Williams classic. Barnes concluded, "This is a wonderful play that lights up man. See it, wonder at it, and recognize it." Wilson later adapted *The Piano Lesson* for a *Hallmark Hall of Fame* television production. It was judged a success by John J. O'Connor, who wrote in the *New York Times:* "If anything, *The Piano Lesson* is even more effective in this shortened version."

Two Trains Running continued Wilson's projected ten-play cycle about black American history. The play, which came to Broadway in 1992, is set in a run-down diner on the verge of being sold. Reactions by the diner's regular patrons to the pending sale make up the body of the drama. Some critics, such as the *New Yorker*'s Mimi Kramer, found the play less subtle and dramatic than its predecessors, but *Newsweek*'s David Ansen praised the "musical eloquence" of Wilson's language, which he felt enhanced a "thematically rich" work. And Henry wrote in *Time* that *Two Trains Running* is a "delicate and mature" play that shows Wilson "at his lyrical best."

Two Trains Running was followed by *Seven Guitars.* Set in the 1940s, it recounts the tragic story of blues guitarist Floyd Barton, whose funeral opens the play. Action then flashes back to recreate the events of Floyd's last week of life. *Seven Guitars* was the first major production of a Wilson play without the direction of Richards, who was forced to abandon the project due to illness. The task of directing fell to Walter Dallas, whose staging at the Goodman Theatre in Chicago William Tynan characterized as "skillful" in a *Time* review. Yet the critic's overall assessment was mixed. "Part bawdy comedy, part dark elegy, part mystery," he wrote, "August Wilson's rich new play, *Seven Guitars,* nicely eludes categorization. . . . But though full and strong in its buildup, the play loses its potency as it reaches its climax. . . . Though Floyd is as charming and sympathetic a protagonist as we could want, the surprising truth is that his death has little effect on us. We leave the theater entertained and admiring but not truly moved." Vincent Canby differed markedly in his judgment, writing in the *New York Times,* "Though the frame of *Seven Guitars* is limited and employs only seven characters, Mr. Wilson writes so vividly that the play seems to have the narrative scope and depth of a novel. When the curtain comes down, it's difficult to remember which characters you've actually seen and which you have come to know only through stories recollected on stage. . . . *Seven Guitars* plays with such speed that you begin the journey one minute, and the next thing you know, you're leaving the theater on a high."

Further praise came from *Newsweek* reviewer Jack Kroll, who called *Seven Guitars* "a kind of jazz cantata for actors," with "a gritty, lyrical polyphony of voices that evokes the character and destiny of these men and women who can't help singing the blues even when they're just talking." The play, he continued, "bristles with symbolism" and with "anguished eloquence." Kroll found the protagonist's death "shocking, unexpected, yet inevitable" and the characters overall "not victims, wallowing in voluptuous resentment," but "tragic figures, bursting with the balked music of life."

Not long after *Seven Guitars* opened, Wilson gave a keynote address to the Theatre Communications Group National Conference. The address, titled "The Ground on Which I Stand," was first published in *American Theatre* in 1996. Wilson's remarks created critical controversy and feud. According to Jonathan Little, writing for the *Dictionary of Literary Biography,* this address "can be read as the culminating manifesto of his personal politics, his aesthetics, and his vision for the future." A series of responses and counterattacks appeared in print both from Wilson and from critic Robert Brustein, leading to the culmination of a debate on January 27, 1997, at the New York City Town Hall. Little reported that critical reaction to the debate was mixed with both plaudits and criticisms given to the arguments made by both men.

In 2001, Wilson's ninth play in his cyclic history opened on Broadway for a surprisingly brief twelve-week run. *King Hedley II* is a dark retrospective,drawing upon the life of title character King Hedley, an ex-convict attempting to rebuild his life in 1990s Pittsburgh. Hedley, who first appeared as "a cracked old man who sees ghosts" in *Seven Guitars* (a technique the playwright uses often, according to Ashyia Henderson in *Contemporary Black Biography*), deals with his past while figuring out how to go "legit" in the midst of the brutality of a black ghetto. The play depicts the decline of the black family and the prevalence of violence and guns in contemporary inner-city neighborhoods.

Discussing Wilson's body of work, Lawrence Bommer stated in the *Chicago Tribune,* "August Wilson has created the most complete cultural chronicle since Balzac wrote his vast 'Human Comedy,' an artistic whole that has grown even greater than its prize-winning parts." As for the playwright, he has repeatedly stressed that his first objective is simply getting his work produced. "All I want is for the most people to get to see this play," he told the *New York Times* while discussing *Joe Turner's Come and Gone.* Wilson added, however, that he was not opposed to having his works performed on Broadway. He told the *New York Times* that Broadway "still has the connotation of Mecca" and asked, "Who doesn't want to go to Mecca?"

In September of 2005, Wilson announced that he had been diagnosed with liver cancer. He died shortly after he made his illness known to the public.

BIOGRAPHICAL AND CRITICAL SOURCES:

BOOKS

Bogumil, Mary L. *Understanding August Wilson,* University of South Carolina Press (Columbia, SC), 1998.

Contemporary Dramatists, St. James Press (Detroit, MI), 1999.

Contemporary Literary Criticism, Thomson Gale (Detroit, MI), Volume 39, 1996, Volume 50, 1988, Volume 63, 1991.

Contemporary Theatre, Film, and Television, Volume 40, Thomson Gale (Detroit, MI), 2002.

Dictionary of Literary Biography, Volume 228: *Twentieth-Century American Dramatists, Second Series,* Thomson Gale (Detroit, MI), 2000.

Elkins, Marilyn, editor, *August Wilson: A Casebook,* Garland (New York, NY), 1994.

Encyclopedia of World Biography, 2nd edition, Thomson Gale (Detroit, MI), 1998.

Flowers, Betty Sue, *A World of Ideas: Conversations with Thoughtful Men and Women about American Life Today and the Ideas Shaping Our Future,* Doubleday (New York, NY), 1989.

Hartigan, Karelisa V., editor, *Within the Dramatic Spectrum,* University Press of America (Lanham, MD), 1986.

Herrington, Joan, *I Ain't Sorry for Nothin' I Done: August Wilson's Process of Playwrighting,* Limelight Editions (New York, NY), 1998.

International Dictionary of Theatre, Volume 2: *Playwrights,* St. James Press (Chicago, IL), 1993.

King, Bruce, editor, *Contemporary American Theatre,* St. Martin's Press (New York, NY), 1991.

Nadel, Alan, editor, *May All Your Fences Have Gates: Essays on the Drama of August Wilson,* University of Iowa Press (Iowa City, IA), 1994.

Notable Black Men, Thomson Gale (Detroit, MI), 1998.

Pereira, Kim, *August Wilson and the African-American Odyssey,* University of Illinois Press (Urbana, IL), 1995.

Shannon, Sandra Garrett, *The Dramatic Vision of August Wilson,* Howard University Press (Washington, DC), 1995.

Wolfe, Peter, *August Wilson,* Twayne (New York, NY), 1999.

PERIODICALS

African American Review, winter, 1993, Jay Plumb, "Blues History and the Dramaturgy of August Wilson," pp. 561-567; winter, 1995, Qun Wang, "Blues, History, and the Dramaturgy of August Wilson," pp. 605-613; spring, 1996, p. 99; fall, 2001, review of *Joe Turner's Come and Gone,* p. 471.

American Theatre, October, 1996, Robert Brustein, "Subsidized Separatism," pp. 100-101; March 1997, Stephen Nunns, "Wilson, Brustein, and the Press," pp. 17-19.

Black American Literature Forum, spring, 1991, Sandra G. Shannon, review of *Ma Rainey's Black Bottom,* pp. 135-136, 143-145.

Black Scholar, spring, 1995, Alice Mills, "The Walking Blues: An Anthropological Approach to the Theater of August Wilson," pp. 30-35.

Chicago Tribune, October 15, 1984; June 8, 1987; December 17, 1987; December 27, 1987, pp. 4-5; January 20, 1993, p. 20; January 24, 1993, section 13, pp. 8-9; January 26, 1993, section 1, p. 16; January 15, 1995, section 13, pp. 16-17, 21.

Christian Science Monitor, October 16, 1984, Hilary Davies, "August Wilson—A New Voice for Black American Theater," pp. 29-30; March 27, 1987, Hillary DeVries, "A Street-Corner Scribe of Life in Black America" (interview), p. 1, 8; March 30, 1988, p. 21.

Ebony, January, 1985; November, 1987, Alex Poinsett, "August Wilson: Hottest New Playwright," pp. 68, 70, 72, 74; September, 2001, Charles Whitaker, "Is August Wilson America's Greatest Playwright?" (interview), p. 80.

Esquire, April, 1989, Chip Brown, "The Light in August," pp. 116, 118, 120, 122-127.

Essence, August, 1987, Brent Staples, "August Wilson," pp. 51, 111, 113.

Los Angeles Times, November 24, 1984; November 7, 1986; April 17, 1987; June 7, 1987; June 8, 1987; June 9, 1987; February 6, 1988.

Maclean's, May 28, 1990, p. 62; May 18, 1992, pp. 56-57.

Massachusetts Review, spring, 1988, pp. 87-97.

MELUS, fall, 1989, Sandra G. Shannon, "The Good Christian's Come and Gone: The Shifting Role of Christianity in August Wilson Plays," pp. 127, 141-142.

Nation, April 18, 1987, p. 518; June 1, 1990, pp. 832-833; June 8, 1992, pp. 799-800; December 8, 1984, Paul Berman, review of *Ma Rainey's Black Bottom,* p. 626-628.

New Republic, May 21, 1990, Robert Brustein, "The Lesson of *The Piano Lesson,*" pp. 28-30.

Newsmakers, Issue 2, Thomson Gale (Detroit, MI), 2002.

Newsweek, April 6, 1987; April 11, 1988, p. 82; April 27, 1992, p. 70; February 6, 1995, p. 60.

New York, April 6, 1987, pp. 92-94; May 7, 1990, pp. 82-83.

New Yorker, April 6, 1987, p. 81; April 11, 1988, p. 107; April 30, 1990, p. 85; April 27, 1992, p. 85; February 3, 1997, Henry Louis Gates, Jr., "The Chitlin Circuit," pp. 44-55.

New York Post, March 28, 1988; April 17, 1990.

New York Times, April 11, 1984; April 13, 1984; October 12, 1984; October 22, 1984, p. C15; May 5, 1985, p. 80; May 6, 1986; May 14, 1986; May 19, 1986, p. C11; June 20, 1986; March 27, 1987, p. C3; April 5, 1987, pp. 1, 39; April 9, 1987; April 17, 1987; May 7, 1987; December 10, 1987; December 11, 1987; March 27, 1988, pp. 1, 34; March 28, 1988, p. C15; January 30, 1989, p. 69; April 17, 1990, p. C13; March 10, 1991, section 2, pp. 5, 17; January 25, 1995, pp. C13-C14; February 3, 1995, p. D26; February 5, 1995, section 2, pp. 1, 5; February 7, 2003.

New York Times Book Review, March 3, 1996, p. 22.

New York Times Magazine, March 15, 1987, Samuel Freedman, "A Voice from the Streets," pp. 36-50; June 10, 1987, pp. 36, 40, 49, 70.

People, May 13, 1996, p. 63.

Theater, fall-winter, 1984, pp. 50-55; summer-fall, 1986, pp. 64; summer-fall, 1988, Mei-Ling Ching, review of *Joe Turner's Come and Gone, Fences,* and *The Piano Lesson,* pp. 69-71; fall, 1991, Lisa Wilde, review of *Two Trains Running,* pp. 73-74.

Theatre Journal, December, 1994, pp. 468-476.

Time, April 6, 1987, p. 81; April 27, 1987; April 11, 1988, pp. 77-78; January 30, 1989, p. 69; April 27, 1992, pp. 65-66; February 6, 1995, p. 71.

Times (London, England), November 6, 1984; April 18, 1987; April 24, 1987.

Tribune Books (Chicago, IL), February 9, 1986, pp. 12-13.
Variety, February 26, 1996, p. 175.
Vogue, August, 1988, pp. 200, 204.
Washington Post, May 20, 1986; April 15, 1987; June 9, 1987; October 4, 1987; October 9, 1987.

ONLINE

A & E Biography Web site, http://www.biography.com/ (November 18, 2003), "August Wilson."
Black Collegian Online, http:/ www.black-collegian.com/ (November 18, 2003), "August Wilson."
CNN.com, http://www.cnn.com/ (November 18, 2003) James Earl Jones, "Playwright: August Wilson. His Poetic Plays about African-American Life Offer Plainspoken Truths That Transcend Race."
PostGazette, http://www.post-gazette.com/ (November 18, 2003), Chris Rawson, "August Wilson: A Timeline."
Syracuse University Web site, http://provost.syr.edu/lectures/ (November 18, 2003), "August Wilson."

* * *

WILSON, Dirk
See POHL, Frederik

* * *

WILSON, Edward O. 1929-
(Edward Osborne Wilson, Jr.)

PERSONAL: Born June 10, 1929, in Birmingham, AL; son of Edward O., Sr. (an accountant) and Inez (Freeman) Wilson; married Irene Kelley, October 30, 1955; children: Catherine Irene. *Education:* University of Alabama, B.S., 1949, M.S., 1950; Harvard University, Ph. D., 1955.

ADDRESSES: Office—Museum of Comparative Zoology, Harvard University, Cambridge, MA 02138.

CAREER: Harvard University, Cambridge, MA, assistant professor of biology, 1956-58, associate professor of zoology, 1958-64, professor of zoology, 1964-76, Frank B. Baird Jr. Professor of Science, 1976-94, Pellegrino Professor, 1994-97, then Pellegrino University Professor Emeritus and research professor, beginning 1997, curator in entomology at Museum of Comparative Zoology, 1972-97, then honorary curator, 1997—; writer. Member of selection committee, J.S. Guggenheim Foundation, 1982-89. Trustee of Marine Biological Laboratory, Woods Hole, MA, 1976-80. Member of board of directors, World Wildlife Fund, 1983-94, Organization for Tropical Studies, 1984—, New York Botanical Gardens, 1991—, American Museum of Natural History, 1992—, American Academy of Liberal Education, 1993—, and Conservation International, 1997—.

MEMBER: World Wildlife Fund (member of advisory council, 1977—), Deutsche Akademie Naturforsch (fellow), Society for the Study of Evolution, British Ecological Society (honorary life member), Royal Society (London, England), Finnish Academy of Science and Letters, Russian Academy of Natural Science, Royal Society of Science (Uppsala), American Philosophical Society (fellow), American Genetics Association (honorary life member), National Academy of Sciences, American Academy of Arts and Sciences (fellow), Entomological Society of America (honorary life member), Zoological Society of London (honorary life member), Netherlands Society of Entomology (honorary life member), Academy of Humanism (honorary life member).

AWARDS, HONORS: Cleveland Award, American Association for the Advancement of Science, 1969; Mercer Award, Ecological Society of America, 1971; Founders Memorial Award, Entomological Society of America, 1972; Distinguished Service Award, American Institute of Biological Sciences, 1976; National Medal of Science, 1977; Leidy Medal, Academy of Natural Sciences, 1979; Pulitzer Prize in general nonfiction, 1979, for *On Human Nature,* and 1991 for *Ants;* Sesquicentennial Medal, University of Alabama, 1981; Distinguished Humanist Award, American Humanist Association, 1982; Tyler Ecology Prize, 1984; Richard M. Weaver Award for Scholarly Letters, Ingersoll Foundation, 1989; Crafoord Prize, Royal Swedish Academy, 1990; Prix d'Institute de la Vie (Paris), 1990; Revelle Medal, 1990; Gold Medal, Worldwide Fund for Nature, 1990; National Wildlife Association Award and Sir Peter Kent Conservation Prize, both 1991, both for *The Diversity of Life;* Hawkins Award, Outstanding Professional or Reference Work, American Publishers Association, 1991, for *The Ants;* National Wildlife Federation Achievement Award, 1992; Wildlife Society Book Award, 1993, for *The Diversity of Life;* Shaw Medal, Missouri Botanical Garden, 1993; International Prize in Biology, Japanese government, 1993; Eminent Ecologist Award, Ecological Society of America, 1994; Distinguished Achievement Award, Educational Press Association of America, 1994; 1994 Award for Increasing the Public Understanding of Science, Council of Scientific Society Presidents, 1994; AAAS Award for Public Understanding of Science and Technology, American Association for the Advancement of Science, 1994; David Ingalls Award for Excellence, Cleveland Museum of Natural History, 1995; Audubon Medal, Audubon Society, 1995; John Hay Award, Orion Society, 1995; *Los Angeles Times* Book Prize for science and technology, and Benjamin Franklin Award, Publishers Marketing Association, both 1995, both for *Naturalist;* Phi Beta Kappa Prize, and Science, and Science Book of the Year (Germany), both 1995, both for *Journey to the Ants;* Certificate of Distinction, Council of the XX International Congress of Entomology, 1996; first recipient, Edward Osborne Wilson Naturalist Award, American Society of Naturalists, 1997; William Procter Prize for Scientific Achievement, Sigma Xi, 1997; Benjamin Franklin Medal, American Philosophical Society, 1998; Deutsche Umweltstiftung prize, 1998, for *The Diversity of Life;* Clarence Cason Award, University of Alabama, 1999; Humanist of the Year citation, American Humanist Association, 1999; King Faisal International Prize for Science, 2000; Kistler Prize, Foundation for the Future, 2000; J.C. Phillips Memorial Medal, World Conservation Union, 2000; recipient of numerous other awards and honorary degrees.

WRITINGS:

(With R.H. MacArthur) *The Theory of Island Biogeography,* Princeton University Press (Princeton, NJ), 1967, with a new preface by the author, 2001.

(With Robert W. Taylor) *The Ants of Polynesia,* Hawaii Museum Department of Entomology (Honolulu, HI), 1967.

The Insect Societies, Belknap Press (Cambridge, MA), 1971.

(With W.H. Bossert) *A Primer of Population Biology,* Sinauer Associates (Sunderland, MA), 1971.

(Coauthor) *Life on Earth,* Sinauer Associates (Sunderland, MA), 1973, 2nd edition 1978.

(Author of introduction) *Ecology, Evolution and Population Biology: Readings from Scientific American,* Freeman (London, England), 1974.

Sociobiology: The New Synthesis, Belknap Press (Cambridge, MA), 1975, 25th anniversary edition, 2000.

(Author of introduction, with Thomas Eisner) *Animal Behavior: Readings from Scientific American,* Freeman (London, England), 1975.

(Author of introduction, with Thomas Eisner) *The Insects: Readings from Scientific American,* Freeman (London, England), 1977.

(Coauthor) *Life: Cells, Organisms, Populations,* Sinauer Associates (Sunderland, MA), 1977.

(With George F. Oster) *Caste and Ecology in Social Insects,* Princeton University Press (Princeton, NJ), 1978.

On Human Nature, Harvard University Press (Cambridge, MA), 1978, with new preface, 2004.

(With Charles J. Lumsden) *Genes, Mind, and Culture: The Coevolutionary Process,* Harvard University Press (Cambridge, MA), 1981.

(With Charles J. Lumsden) *Promethean Fire: Reflections on the Origin of the Mind,* Harvard University Press (Cambridge, MA), 1983.

Biophilia: The Human Bond to Other Species, Harvard University Press (Cambridge, MA), 1984.

(Editor) *Biodiversity,* National Academy Press (Washington, DC), 1988.

(With Bert Holldobler) *The Ants,* (Cambridge, MA Press), 1990.

Success and Dominance in Ecosystems: The Case of the Social Insects, Ecology Institute (Luhe, Germany), 1990.

The Diversity of Life, Belknap Press (Cambridge, MA), 1992, new edition, W.W. Norton (New York), 1999.

(Editor, with Stephen R. Kellert) *The Biophilia Hypothesis,* Island Press (Washington, DC), 1993.

(With Bert Holldobler) *Journey to the Ants: A Story of Scientific Exploration,* (Cambridge, MA), 1994.

Naturalist (autobiography), Island Press (Washington, DC), 1994, illustrated by Laura Simonds Southworth, Warner Books (New York, NY), 1995.

In Search of Nature, Island Press (Washington, DC), 1996.

(Editor, with others) *Biodiversity II: Understanding and Protecting Our Biological Resources,* Joseph Henry (Washington, DC), 1997.

Consilience: The Unity of Knowledge, Knopf (New York, NY), 1998.

Biological Diversity: The Oldest Human Heritage, New York State Museum (Albany, NY), 1999.

(With Dan L. Perlman) *Conserving Earth's Biodiversity with E.O. Wilson* (CD-ROM), Island Press (Washington, DC), 2000.

Pheidole in the New World: A Dominant, Hyperdiverse Ant Genus, Harvard University Press (Cambridge, MA), 2001.

The Future of Life, Knopf (New York, NY), 2002.

Contributor of over 350 articles to scientific and popular journals. Coeditor, *Theoretical Population Biology,* 1971-74, *Behavioral Ecology and Sociobiology,* 1975-98, and *Psyche,* 1958—.

ADAPTATIONS: The Ants was adapted as the model for *SimAnt,* a computer game created by Maxis Company, 1991.

SIDELIGHTS: Prior to 1975, Edward O. Wilson was primarily known as one of America's foremost experts on the insect world, his specialty being the study of ants and their social behavior. As a noted professor of entomology at Harvard University, Wilson produced several books on insect culture and physiology before becoming, as Peter Gwynne described him in *Newsweek,* "one of the most visible and articulate spokesmen for sociobiology, the controversial scientific discipline whose purpose is to examine the biological bases of behavior." The author of two Pulitzer Prize-winning works of nonfiction and the recipient of the National Medal of Science, Wilson has become, in the words of *Los Angeles Times Book Review* critic Jonathan Weiner, "one of the preeminent evolutionary biologists of our time." In 1996 *Time* magazine named him one of the twenty-five most influential contemporary Americans, and John Simmons, in *The Scientific 100,* ranked him among the one hundred most influential scientists of all time.

Sociobiology: The New Synthesis, which Wilson published in 1975, is considered a groundbreaking book. The first detailed study of the emerging science of sociobiology, it catapulted its author to both fame and controversy. The most debated tenet of sociobiology is that all human behavior is genetically based, or, as Wilson once put it, that "genes hold culture on a leash." This position aroused heated debate in both the scientific and cultural communities. Some of its critics, questioning Wilson's methodology, dismissed his work as "so-so biology," while others have gone so far as to label sociobiology "dangerously racist," according to *Time,* because "the new science would give comfort to the supporters of psychologist Arthur Jensen, a leading proponent of another controversial theory: that racial differences in IQs have a genetic basis." Many critics questioned Wilson's biological explanation of such social behaviors as altruism and religious activity, and accused him and other sociobiologists of advocating the idea of eugenics, the so-called "purifying" of races by genetic control of breeding.

Despite such controversy, many scholars perceived *Sociobiology* to be a work of exceptional relevance and importance. While the *Humanist* published an article by Nathaniel S. Lehrman decrying sociobiology as "Wilson's Fallacy," the magazine went on to name Wilson its 1982 Distinguished Humanist and, in 1999, Humanist of the Year. "Many challenges have been made to Wilson's sociobiology, particularly as it applies to humans," explained Frederick Edwords on the *American Humanist Web site,* "but it seems that many of the challenges are railings at some of Wilson's *conclusions*—not his evidence or reasons. Wilson has linked humans and human behavior more closely to the genes than many people feel comfortable with. He has compared human social structure to animal societies. He has found selfish roots in altruistic behavior." Edwords went on to say that "because many of Wilson's carefully arrived at conclusions have seemed to burst a few bubbles, or have seemed to threaten a few ideals, Wilson has been persecuted to some extent. But he has stood by his ideas, stood firm on his facts."

In a *New York Review of Books* review of *Sociobiology,* C.H. Waddington cited Wilson's "extraordinarily ambitious aim" in outlining the synthesis, and added that the biologist "has been astoundingly successful in achieving [that aim]. This book will undoubtedly be for many years to come a major source of information about all aspects of our knowledge of social behavior in animals. . . . It has also some of the clearest discussions yet written about the recent advances in general population biology and demography." *New York Times Book Review* critic John Pfeiffer noted that Wilson "falters somewhat in presenting the human story" of sociobiology in his book, and that the author "can also be faulted for his vision of the future." But Pfeiffer concluded that *Sociobiology* "may be regarded as an evolutionary event in itself, announcing for all who can hear that we are on the verge of breakthroughs in the effort to understand our place in the scheme of things."

Decades after the initial publication of *Sociobiology* controversy continued to rage. Some scientists criticized the book as reductionist; others denounced it on political grounds. At a meeting of the American Association for the Advancement of Science in 1978, a woman doused Wilson with a pitcher of cold water as protestors shouted "Wilson, you're all wet!" Others picketed Wilson's lectures, urged their peers to disrupt his classes, and published lengthy denunciations of what they perceived to be his racist, sexist, and classist views. Yet, as Michael Ruse put it in *Reason* in 1999, "A work that offended so many had to be saying something right." By the time *Sociobiology* was reissued in its twenty-fifth-anniversary edition, its thesis had become the foundation for much new behavioral research and new discoveries, especially in DNA research, had lent credence to Wilson's argument. As Ken Ringle noted in the *Washington Post* in 1998, "Today sociobiology is not only an accepted branch of science but one of its driving forces. The Animal Behavior Association in the 1980s voted Wilson's once-controversial work the most important such book ever."

Wilson continued to explore the synthesis of ideas in his 1978 book, *On Human Nature,* which he describes as "not a work *of* science," but rather "a work *about* science, and about how far the natural sciences can penetrate into human behavior before they will be transformed into something new." *On Human Nature* "takes up in a philosophical way where *Sociobiology* left off," observed William McPherson in a *Washington Post Book World* review. "It is a vastly ambitious attempt to bring the 'two cultures' of science and the humanities together." As with the earlier book, some of Wilson's hypotheses in *On Human Nature* met with skepticism from the scientific community. Colin Beer, writing in the *New York Times Book Review,* pointed to a passage from the work which reveals Wilson's prediction that a "durable foundation for peace" might be found by creating "a confusion of cross-finding loyalties to prevent the formation of the kinds of group loyalties that give rise to aggressive behavior." Beer responded that "it is doubtful whether this solution, in itself, would be sufficient to make human aggression, in all its forms, a thing of the past. But the argument that [the author] uses here is typical of his tactics throughout most of the book: it is quietly persuasive rather than belligerently coercive, and it appeals to plausible possibility rather than logical necessity. At least to readers of good will, most of the conclusions will seem reasonable interpretations of the evidence—so much so that many may be left wondering what all the fuss has been about."

Wilson's "most grandiose and least appealing scheme is to replace conventional religion with a mythology based on scientific materialism and incorporating a more objectively chosen value system," noted Nicholas Wade in *New Republic.* "Gee-whiz wonders from the scientific textbooks—evolution, the Big Bang and so forth—would replace religious awe and the sense of the sacred. This false touch makes the reader wonder if Wilson here hasn't slipped too far afield." However, Wade concluded that *On Human Nature* "is a splendid departure from the dead-hand canons of the scientific 'literature.' Clarity, precision and boldness distinguish Wilson's attempt to complete the Darwinian revolution. He is dealing with matters that lie mostly beyond the reach of present scientific methods, and perhaps for that reason has chosen to present his ideas in a way that makes them accessible to the public at large as well as to his scientific peers." And despite the controversy surrounding its subject matter, *On Human Nature* was awarded the 1979 Pulitzer Prize in general nonfiction. Wilson told the *Washington Post*'s Megan Rosenfeld that the honor is "an affirmation that this is an important new area of thought. It's not necessarily a certification that I'm right, but an affirmation that this is an important thing we should be talking about."

In 1981 Wilson and theoretical physicist Charles J. Lumsden collaborated on *Genes, Mind, and Culture: The Coevolutionary Process.* Extending the theory of sociobiology, the two scientists described what they labeled the "gene-culture coevolution," a process by which human genetic makeup "helps guide and create culture, while culture in turn operates directly on the genes," according to *Harper's* reviewers James L. Gould and Carol Grant Gould. Two years later Wilson and Lumsden produced *Promethean Fire: Reflections on the Origin of the Mind,* a layperson's book on the subject.

One example of the authors' gene-culture theory can be seen in their detailed study of the incest taboo, included in *Promethean Fire.* According to Wilson and Lumsden, the incest taboo, historically considered a cultural phenomenon, has actually been genetically programmed into humans as a reaction against the mentally and physically deformed offspring that incestuous unions can produce. Thus, the cultural taboo against familial sexual relations is an outgrowth of the genetic rule. "The authors also point out how easily (and in some cases even spontaneously) certain deep, long-lasting phobias appear [to such ancient terrors as snakes, spiders, and thunderstorms, for instance], while determined attempts on the part of parents to instill fear of the real threats of modern-day life (electrical outlets, knives, and busy streets) rarely succeed, at least at the phobia level," noted the *Harper's* critics. "Surely this argues for a type of genetic programming that could have a role in culture."

Sociologist Howard Kaye, reviewing *Promethean Fire* for *Commentary,* found fault with the authors' conclusions: "Although Lumsden and Wilson view their theory as orthodox science, certain questionable assumptions about mind and culture and an extreme reductionism mar their thought and inflate their claims. . . . Observers of men in society have always known that no human culture, not even our own, is a supermarket of discrete and competing cultural products—row upon row of hymns, gods, cuisines, clothing styles, styles of life—to which each individual is uniformly exposed, and from which he selects according to genetically prescribed preferences and abhorrences," Kaye contended. "Rather, each culture has done the shopping for us, circumscribing the chaos of possibility and ordering our choices to make our lives possible and meaningful. . . . Only an a-priori reductionism could lead one to conclude that *all* human choices and tendencies [are] governed by epigenetic rules." However, James and Carol Gould maintained that "Sociobiology is rapidly unraveling many of the mysteries of animal societies. In doing so, it will give us invaluable insights into why we humans organize ourselves as we do, act as we do, perhaps even think as we do. To the extent that this sort of armchair speculation, bolstered by anthropological anecdote and mathematical calculation of probabilities, can encourage new ways of looking at our own evolution and the genetic constraints on our behavior, Lumsden and Wilson have done a service in making their theories accessible to the thinking public in *Promethean Fire*."

In 1992's *The Diversity of Life,* Wilson explores the meaning of an offshoot of ecology known as *biodiversity*—the underlying relationships existing between all life forms that result in the creation and perpetuation of healthy virgin ecosystems. Praising Wilson for his "elegant and ingratiating literary style," *Washington Post Book World* critic T.H. Watkins hailed *The Diversity of Life* as "a book that will enlighten the uninformed, correct the misinformed and serve as a beacon of lucidity in the wilderness." Beginning with the discussion of what he terms the "fundamental unit" species—or, in reference to its unique DNA code, a "living genetic library"—Wilson goes on to discuss the elaborate system of checks and balances that functions within the processes of evolution, adaptation, colonization, reproduction, migration, and transmogrification. Cautioning readers about the devastating ecological consequences of humankind's continued destruction of such sensitive ecosystems, Wilson devotes the second section of his book to conservation: humans' moral dilemma as it relates to the stewardship of life on earth. "If there is danger in the human trajectory," he warns, "it is not so much in the survival of our own species as in the fulfillment of the ultimate irony of organic evolution: that in the instant of achieving self-understanding through the mind of man, life has doomed its most beautiful creations. And thus humanity closes its door on its past."

Wilson considers *The Ants,* his second Pulitzer prize winner, to be his "magnum opus," not only because the book itself weighed seven and a half pounds, but because it brings together for the first time all the knowledge and widely scattered information now known about ants. Working with fellow myrmecologist and Harvard faculty member Bert Holldobler, Wilson organizes a monumental amount of information about everything from ant evolution and history to ant communication and social structures. *Journey to the Ants: A Story of Scientific Exploration,* published four years later, once again united Wilson and Holldobler. A layperson's introduction to the amazing variation existing within the ant kingdom, *Journey* also provides a revealing look at the motivations of those who have devoted their lives to the study of these surprisingly social creatures.

Wilson's attraction to biology, evolution, and ecology grew from his fascination, as a young boy, with the natural wonders surrounding the many places were he and his family lived, from the rural Alabama countryside to Washington, DC, where Wilson discovered the treasures contained in both the National Zoo and the Smithsonian Institution. The scientist's *biophilia*—what he describes as "the innate tendency to focus on life and lifelike processes"—is the subject of several books, including *Biophilia: The Human Bond to Other Species,* and *Naturalist.*

"No one can doubt [that Wilson] is powerfully drawn to other creatures, but he wants to make some larger points: human attraction to other living things is innate, and this natural affinity should serve as the philosophical basis for a new conservation ethic," assessed *New York Times Book Review* critic Sarah Boxer, in her review of *Biophilia.* While Wilson's "attempt to promote conservation is noble and appealing," Boxer contended that he "loses the thread of his main argument" when he "flits from a reverie about time scales to a reminiscence about his work in biogeography."

Psychology Today writer Wray Herbert cited a specific example of Wilson's biophilic notions. Pointing to "an appreciation of the 'savanna gestalt,'" Herbert explained that "early humans evolved on the African savannas, presumably because tree-studded open land overlooking water offered the optimal environment for survival; this predisposition became ingrained, Wilson argues [in *Biophilia*], and today is reflected in our esthetics [in designs like] malls, gardens and cemeteries." "It's hard not to like this little book. . . . and it's hard not to like Wilson after having read it," concluded Herbert, adding that *Biophilia* "is a very personal statement. Mixing bits of autobiography with meditations on nature, he has put together a poetic rather than a scientific argument; he offers biophilia as an article of faith, making only a half-hearted effort to prove it for what he calls his 'determined critics.'"

"What happened, what we *think* happened in distant memory, is built around a small collection of dominating images," Wilson wrote in *Naturalist,* a personal memoir of his own evolution from young boy to biologist. The only child of an alcoholic father, the biologist eventually attended military school, channeling his developing intellect, self-discipline, reverence for single-mindedness of purpose, and interest in nature into a passion for the study of insects. "Wilson emerges not only as a gifted scientist, but also as a likable, passionate, eloquent person," noted Jared Diamond, reviewing *Naturalist* in the *New York Review of Books.* William Howarth had equal praise for the work in the *Washing-*

ton Post Book World: "What distinguishes Wilson's story is its handsome prose, honed by years of practice into a concise and sly discourse. Among literary scientists, no one since Rachel Carson has more effectively joined humble detail to a grand vision of life processes and structures." Unlike Wilson's previous works, *Naturalist* is illuminating on a personal as well as an instructional level. "It is still possible to realize the romantic ideal of exploration that many of us harbor in childhood, and then abandon as impractical," Diamond added. "By explaining how Wilson realized that ideal, his book helps us to understand one of the brighter trajectories in twentieth-century intellectual life."

"Wilson's critics want certain things—like beauty and morality—kept mysterious," wrote Herbert, of the negative response to some of Wilson's more controversial theories; "they are angered by what they perceive as a reductionist view of human culture. And like Darwin, Wilson has tendered an idea that is shocking in its simplicity, which if correct will demand a basic revision of what it is to be human." Wilson's fascination with synthesis—a unifying relationship among seemingly disparate things—found what many critics considered its most ambitious articulation in *Consilience: The Unity of Knowledge.* As its subtitle indicates, the 1998 book argues for the necessity of seeing all knowledge, from all disciplines, as part of one coherent scientific system. And as with *Sociobiology,* the book stimulated much controversy.

Tzvetan Todorov, in the *New Republic,* attacked the book on several levels. He found its argument lacking in unity, its philosophical understanding incorrect, and its central argument wrong. Todorov objected to the idea of any unifying system, stating that "Surely [any attempt to remedy overspecialization in the sciences] does not mean that all boundaries must be erased. Surely the nature of knowledge differs with the object of knowledge." Finding fault with almost every major point in *Consilience* and making a direct allusion to Adolph Hitler's use of Social Darwinism in Nazi Germany, Todorov emphasized that "it is even less desirable to seek to unite knowledge and action," and added that "what is original in Wilson's book is indefensible, and what is true in it is banal."

Other criticism of the book, however, was less hostile. Among the most common of the complaints against *Consilience* was that the book oversimplifies complex matters. Physicist Jeremy Bernstein, writing in *Commentary,* noted that the reductionist laws of hard sciences doubtless made it "irresistible to apply the lessons thereby learned to, essentially, everything . . . [Wilson] genuinely feels that once we know enough about physics, chemistry, and biology, there will be nothing on earth we cannot explain." John Dupre, in *Science,* wrote that "the central thesis of the book is vague, the arguments presented generally difficult to discern, and many of the opinions expressed are quite eccentric." Daniel J. Kevles, in the *New York Times Book Review,* suggested that much of Wilson's argument is "overstated," but concluded that *Consilience* "is an evangelic book, an arresting exposition of Wilson's religion of science and a kind of sermon—forceful in delivery if shaky in substance—intended to assist in the reform of the world."

Despite such criticisms, however, *Consilience* received much extravagant praise. Psychologist Steven Pinker lauded it, in a *Slate* review, as an "excellent" work that "provides superb overviews of Western intellectual history and of the current state of understanding in many academic disciplines." Freeman Dyson, writing in the *New England Journal of Medicine,* hailed the work as "a major contribution to philosophy" and the articulation of a "great and noble vision, portrayed with eloquence and passion." "The questions that the book raises are important," Dyson noted, "whether Wilson's answers turn out to be right or not." Though *Humanist* reviewer Michael Werner admitted that *Consilience* "reaches too far at times," he deemed it "audacious, prophetic, and bound to become a recurrent touchstone to test intellectual progress in the twenty-first century." Werner concluded that, though imperfect, *Consilience* is a book "of wide scholarship, wisdom, and hope, whose overreaching is easily overlooked as a courageous testament of one who tests how close to the sun he can fly."

Wilson looks to the health of the planet in *The Future of Life,* and posits that conservation of all resources is the only way to avoid apocalyptic extinction. Humankind has been selfish in its appropriation of more than its share of natural resources, and has thus disturbed the ecological balance. The biologist maintains that environmental destruction is a consequence of mankind's greed, and Kevin Shapiro, in his review of *The Future of Life,* noted that "Recorded history has been an unmitigated disaster for the biosphere, and it will continue to be . . . so long as our quest for material comfort and security takes precedence over our sense of kinship with the natural world." In a review of the book, a *Science News* contributor wrote that "Wilson makes an impassioned and compelling plea for saving species while giving a balanced account of the current state of affairs. . . . He focuses on solutions that can provide economic prosperity for all people, especially those that have to rely on our most fragile ecosystems in order to sustain themselves."

BIOGRAPHICAL AND CRITICAL SOURCES:

BOOKS

Barlow, Connie, editor, *From Gaia to Selfish Genes: Selected Writings in the Life Sciences,* MIT (Cambridge, MA), 1991.

Contemporary Authors Autobiography Series, Volume 16, Thomson Gale (Detroit, MI), 1985.

Segerstrale, Ullica, *Defenders of the Truth: The Battle for Science in the Sociobiology Debate and Beyond,* Oxford University Press (New York, NY), 2000.

Simmons, John, *The Scientific 100: A Ranking of the Most Influential Scientists, Past and Present,* Kensington Publishing Corporation, Citadel Press (New York, NY), 1996.

Wright, Robert, *Three Scientists and Their Gods: Looking for Meaning in an Age of Information,* Times Books (New York, NY), 1988.

PERIODICALS

American Scholar, summer, 1998, p. 143.

Atlantic, March, 1998.

Audubon, January-February, 1996, p. 92; November-December, 1998, p. 90; November, 1999, p. 64.

Bioscience, June, 1999, p. 487; October, 2000, Brian Shmaefsky review of *Conserving Earth's Biodiversity,* p. 920; November, 2003, Fred Powledge, "Island Biogeography Lasting Impact," p. 1032.

Boston Globe, April 11, 1991, p. 29; September 15, 1992, p. 1; October 9, 1994; November 6, 1994, p. B20.

Business Week, April 20, 1998, p. 15.

Christian Century, November 4, 1998, p. 1027.

Christian Science Monitor, May 29, 1990, p. 13; October 22, 1992, p. 11; December 5, 1994, p. 13.

Commentary, October, 1983; June, 1998, p. 62; April, 2002, review of *The Future of Life,* p. 65.

Commonweal, July 17, 1998, p. 23.

Discover, March 1996, p. 66.

Economist, July 11, 1998, p. S15.

Forbes, September 21, 1998, p. 110.

Harper's, June, 1983.

Humanist, July-August, 1981; September-October, 1982; March, 1999, p. 44.

Insight on the News, June 8, 1998, p. 42.

Journal of the American Medical Association, October 28, 1998, p. 1455.

London Review of Books, April 22, 1993, p. 20; July 20, 1995, pp. 26-27; October 29, 1998.

Los Angeles Times, August 12, 1988, p. V4; October 16, 1994, p. E2.

Los Angeles Times Book Review, December 17, 1984; September 5, 1993, p. 7; October 23, 1994, p. 4; December 10, 1995.

National Review, May 4, 1998, p. 49; June 19, 2000.

New England Journal of Medicine, July 16, 1998.

New Republic, November 11, 1983; April 27, 1998, p. 29.

New Scientist, August 22, 1998.

Newsweek, October 16, 1978; June 22, 1998, p. 59, p. 61.

New York Review of Books, August 7, 1975; October 12, 1978; November 5, 1992, pp. 3-6; January 12, 1995, pp. 16-19; April 23, 1998, pp. 14-17.

New York Times, December 18, 1978; September 21, 1989; August 20, 1991, p. C1; September 22, 1992, p. C4; October 1, 1992, p. C17.

New York Times Book Review, July 27, 1975; October 18, 1981; November 26, 1981; April 24, 1983; October 7, 1984; July 29, 1990, p. 6; October 4, 1992, p. 1; October 16, 1994, pp. 15-17; April 26, 1998.

New York Times Magazine, May 30, 1993, p. 24.

Omni, February, 1979.

OnEarth, fall, 2002, Philip Connors review of *The Future of Life,* p. 39.

Psychology Today, November, 1984; September-October, 1998, p. 50.

Quarterly Review of Biology, June, 2003, Michael Simon review of *The Future of Life,* p. 208.

Reason, August-September 1998, p. 79; December 1999, p. 20.

Saturday Night, September, 1983.

Science, January 10, 1997, p. 175; May 29, 1998, p. 1395; October, 2000, Brian Shmaefsky review of *Conserving Earth's Biodiversity,* p. 920; April 4, 2003, T.R. Schultz review of *Pheidole in the New World,* p. 57.

Science News, April 27, 2003, review of *The Future of Life,* p. 271.

Scientific American, June, 1998, p. 97.

Skeptical Inquirer, July-August, 1998, p. 47.

Time, June 17, 1996, p. 72; August 1, 1977; June 17, 1996; April 20, 1998, p. 15; April 26, 2000, p. 54.

Times Literary Supplement, August 13, 1993, pp. 5-6.

Tribune Books (Chicago, IL), November 5, 1978; March 16, 1990; November 25, 1992, p. 3; December 18, 1994, p. 6.

Utne Reader, July-August, 1998, p. 95.

Washington Post, May 4, 1979; April 10, 1991, p. B1; June 11, 1998.
Washington Post Book World, October 8, 1978; October 15, 1978; March 25, 1990, p. 4; September 27, 1992, pp. 1, 13; December 12, 1993, p. 8; October 16, 1994, p. 4.

ONLINE

Actionbioscience.org, http://www.actionbioscience.org/ (August 8, 2004), "Speciation and Biodiversity: A Interview with Edward O. Wilson."
American Humanist Web site, http://www.american humanist.org/ (August 8, 2004).
Slate, http://www.slate.com/ (March 31, 1998).

* * *

WILSON, Edward Osborne, Jr.
See WILSON, Edward O.

* * *

WINTERSON, Jeanette 1959-

PERSONAL: Born August 27, 1959, in Manchester, England; daughter of a factory worker and Constance (Brownrigg) Winterson. *Education:* St. Catherine's College, Oxford, M.A., 1981.

ADDRESSES: *Home*—Gloucestershire, England; and London, England. *Agent*—International Creative Management, 40 West 57th St., New York, NY 10019. *E-mail*—c/o Hschroder@icmtalent.com.

CAREER: Writer.

AWARDS, HONORS: Whitbread Award for best first novel, Booksellers Association of Great Britain and Ireland, and Publishing for People Award, both 1985, both for *Oranges Are Not the Only Fruit;* John Llewellyn Rhys Memorial Prize, British Book Trust, 1987, for *The Passion;* E.M. Forster Award, American Academy of Arts and Letters, 1989, for *Sexing the Cherry;* Golden Gate Award, San Francisco International Film Festival, 1990, and FIPA d'Argent Award, Cannes Film Festival, 1991, both for *Oranges Are Not the Only Fruit* (screenplay); Lambda Literary Award for Lesbian Fiction, 1994, for *Written on the Body;* International Fiction Award, Festival Letteratura Mantova, 1998.

WRITINGS:

NOVELS

Oranges Are Not the Only Fruit (also see below), Pandora Press (London, England), 1985, Atlantic Monthly Press (New York, NY), 1987.
Boating for Beginners, illustrations by Paula Youens, Methuen (London, England), 1985.
The Passion, Bloomsbury (London, England), 1987, Atlantic Monthly Press (New York, NY), 1988.
Sexing the Cherry, Bloomsbury (London, England), 1989, Atlantic Monthly Press (New York, NY), 1990.
Written on the Body, J. Cape (London, England), 1992, Knopf (New York, NY), 1993.
Art and Lies: A Piece for Three Voices and a Bawd, Knopf (New York, NY), 1995.
Gut Symmetries, Knopf (New York, NY), 1997.
The.PowerBook, J. Cape (London, England), 2000.

OTHER

(Editor) *Passionfruit* (stories), Pandora Press (London, England), 1986.
Fit for the Future: The Guide for Women Who Want to Live Well, Pandora Press (London, England), produced 1986.
Oranges Are Not the Only Fruit (television screenplay; adapted from Winterson's novel; produced 1991), published in *Great Moments in Aviation; and Oranges Are Not the Only Fruit: Two Filmscripts,* Vintage (London, England), 1994.
Great Moments in Aviation (screenplay; produced 1993), published in *Great Moments in Aviation; and Oranges Are Not the Only Fruit: Two Filmscripts,* Vintage (London, England), 1994.
Art Objects: Essays on Ecstasy and Effrontery, Knopf (New York, NY), 1995.
The World and Other Places, Knopf (New York, NY), 1998.
(Author of introduction) Jonathan Swift, *Gulliver's Travels,* Oxford University Press (New York, NY), 1999.
The King of Capri (for children), illustrations by Jane Ray, Bloomsbury Children's Books (New York, NY), 2003.

WORK IN PROGRESS: An Internet project for the BBC.

SIDELIGHTS: Jeanette Winterson is an English writer who has drawn attention due to the radical nature of both her literary works and her sexuality. A *Contemporary Novelists* contributor noted that Winterson "is often described as one of the most controversial yet innovative fiction writers in contemporary English literature," while Laura Miller commented in *Salon.com* that Winterson "has a reputation as a holy terror, a lesbian desperado and a literary genius." A *Gay and Lesbian Biography* writer affirmed that Winterson "has challenged the conventions of the novel form," and Ann Hancock observed in *Dictionary of Literary Biography* that the outspoken author is "the most visible lesbian writer in mainstream British culture." Kelleher Jewett, meanwhile, acknowledged Winterson in a *Nation* review, as "one of England's hottest . . . writers and London's most celebrated literary lesbian."

Winterson began her literary career in 1985 with *Oranges Are Not the Only Fruit,* a novel about an adopted daughter's ties to her mother, a religious fanatic. The heroine, Jeanette, is raised to perceive sin as ever present, and she blindly adheres to her mother's plans for her to become a missionary. A social outsider, Jeanette serves her mother's organization, Society for the Lost, and regularly participates in church functions and activities, including prayer meetings and the dispensation of materials at street corners. But she also falls in love with another church member, Melanie, with whom she enjoys sexual relations. After discovering the affair, Jeanette's mother openly humiliates the lovers at a church service. Jeanette ultimately enters into another lesbian love affair, then comes to realize that she must make some important decisions about her life.

Oranges Are Not the Only Fruit, which won England's Whitbread Prize for best first novel in 1985, earned Winterson substantial acclaim as a novelist. Joseph Olshan, in his review for Chicago's *Tribune Books,* hailed the author's literary debut as a "daring, unconventionally comic novel" and he deemed it "penetrating." Another reviewer, John Clute, wrote in *New Statesman* of Winterson's "brisk, glittering, vengeful accuracy . . . for detail and character and the taut strength of her handling of material." Equally impressed, Sarah Gold commented in *Washington Post* that *Oranges Are Not the Only Fruit* is "a strikingly quirky, delicate and intricate work," and Roz Kaveney praised it in *Times Literary Supplement* as an "excellent" novel. In *Contemporary Popular Writers* the novelist received recognition for her handling of the heroine's lesbianism. "Though some critics have chided Winterson for not exploring the issue of lesbian identity," wrote the book's essayist, "the fact that Jeanette's lesbianism is simply one fact of her life and not the central issue in [the novel] . . . is one of its most positive attributes."

Winterson followed *Oranges Are Not the Only Fruit* with *Boating for Beginners,* a novel—as David Lodge noted in *New York Review of Books*—that "transfers the story of Noah to our own commercialized and media-ridden times." Lodge described the novel as "an extremely funny travesty" and added that "the comedy is often blasphemous, [but] it is based on affection for as well as familiarity with the Bible."

In 1987 Winterson received the John Llewellyn Rhys Memorial Prize for *The Passion,* an historical novel wherein a cook from Napoleon Bonaparte's army befriends a woman whose husband sold her to a cruel soldier after discovering her affair with another woman. The cook and the woman eventually undertake a treacherous trek across the wintery Russian landscape in an effort to reach Venice, where the heroine hopes to regain her sense of self. *Chicago Tribune* reviewer Alan Cheuse found *The Passion* a compelling, powerful work. "If you require strong medicine for your heart before bedtime," Cheuse advised, "take this novel in a few large doses." David Lodge, meanwhile, declared in *New York Review of Books* that the novel "represents a remarkable advance in boldness and invention" when contrasted with Winterson's earlier works.

Sexing the Cherry is a fantastical historical work about a young man's magical adventures in seventeenth-century England. Found floating down the Thames River as a newborn, the hero—Jordan—is raised by Dog-Woman, a foul-smelling, pock-marked giantess. Jordan eventually leaves his squalid home, which is inhabited by more than two dozen dogs, and sets sail with a botanist determined to bring rare plants back to England. The hero's travels take him to magical realms, including a land of flying princesses. He falls in love with the youngest of these females and expends considerable energy, and imagination, in attempting to meet her. Dog-Woman, meanwhile, affords a second narration, fighting in military conflicts and opposing religious injustices. Her path eventually crosses with that of the wandering Jordan, and the novel culminates in some surprising and timely revelations.

Sexing the Cherry won praise as a provocative, entertaining, and occasionally experimental novel. *Los Angeles Times* reviewer Richard Eder contrasted the novel with James Joyce's *Finnegan's Wake,* and *New York*

Times critic Michiko Kakutani deemed it "wonderfully inventive." Kakutani added that Winterson "possesses the ability to combine the biting satire of [Jonathan] Swift with the ethereal magic of [Gabriel] García Márquez, the ability to reinvent old myths even as she creates new ones of her own." Another critic, Nancy Wigston, likened *Sexing the Cherry* to works of Swift and Italian novelist Italo Calvino, and she claimed, in her Toronto *Globe and Mail* appraisal, that the book "shows an astonishing imagination at work." Wigston contended that "Winterson combines the outlook of a philosopher with the energy of a catapult," and further declared that *Sexing the Cherry* "sparkles with youthful virtuosity." Michael Gorra, meanwhile, wrote in *New York Times Book Review* that *Sexing the Cherry* "fuses history, fairy tale and metafiction into a fruit that's rather crisp, not terribly sweet, but of a memorably startling flavor."

In Winterson's *Written on the Body,* an unnamed narrator recalls a love affair with a married woman, Louise. The novel focuses on the nature of physical passion and the meaning of desire, and it includes both straightforward narrative and prose poems in which the narrator honors Louise. In addition, as Terry L. Allison related in *Gay and Lesbian Literature,* in her fiction Winterson "removes some of the familiarity of gendered and sexed roles in lovemaking." Andree Pages, writing in *American Book Review,* criticized the novel as "overly dramatic and unconvincing at times" and commented that "the plot is often unnecessarily baroque." Despite these criticisms, Pages called Winterson "an amazing writer" and noted that in *Written on the Body* she "achieves a real depth of feeling, a savoring of sex and the body and life itself." Aurelie Jane Sheehan, meanwhile, found the novel "funny and sexy." Asserting that the narrator is a woman, Sheehan added, in her *Review of Contemporary Fiction* appraisal, that *Written on the Body* "is a joy even in its most serious moments."

The novel *Art and Lies: A Piece for Three Voices and a Bawd* offers three loosely connected plot lines centering around characters named Handel, Sappho, and Picasso, all of whom assume multiple identities. Ann Hancock, writing in *Dictionary of Literary Biography,* described the novel as "a complete departure from realism." Julie Burchill proved less diplomatic, contending in *Spectator,* "This is *not* beautiful writing, despite its frantic claims to the title." She added that *Art and Lies* constitutes "a garish, artificial, bejewelled mechanical nightingale of a prose style." Mary Scott expressed similar disapproval, claiming in *New Statesman and Society* that "the one voice in which all the narrators eventually speak becomes dominant" and adding that "it isn't very pleasant and it swiftly destroys the book's power." *Times Literary Supplement* contributor Lorna Sage accorded the novel a more positive assessment, characterizing it as "safely good." Sage also noted: "Winterson writes beautifully about the value of *lightness,* about the thrills you can engineer for yourself if you stop trying to represent the world."

In 1997 Winterson published her seventh novel, *Gut Symmetries,* which relates the sometimes grim, sometimes fantastical aspects of a love triangle in which a husband and wife conduct separate affairs with a young woman. Ann Hancock, in an essay for *Dictionary of Literary Biography,* expressed reservations about the novel's "incorporation of contemporary scientific theory," but nonetheless conceded that "Winterson's talent for evoking the physicality of passionate feeling is impressive" and added that "the lyricism of Winterson's descriptive writing can be masterful." Similarly, Christopher Paddock wrote in *Review of Contemporary Fiction,* "*Gut Symmetries* proves its author's dynamic sense of language." Paddock acknowledged the novel as "a solid addition to an already stellar body of work." Less favorably inclined, Rhonda Johnson concluded in *Entertainment Weekly* that *Gut Symmetries* degenerates into "self-conscious posturing," while a *Publishers Weekly* reviewer contended that it "drifts too far from the loamy shores of the heart and gut."

Winterson takes further experimentation in *The.PowerBook,* her novel about an e-mail writer who creates online identities for customers who thereupon find themselves, as a *Boston Herald* reviewer wrote, undergoing experiences that leave them "profoundly changed." Kate Kellaway, writing in the London *Observer,* remarked that the novel "looks like an Apple Mac manual," and she added that "sometimes [it] reads like a DIY bible." At her Internet home page, Winterson noted the experimental nature of *The.PowerBook:* "The shape of the book, its structure, its language, is a different way of working." Elaine Showalter cautioned in *Guardian,* however, that "*The.PowerBook* is not a playful postmodern experiment" but a novel that "uses the metaphor of email to discuss sexual freedom and power." Reviewer E. Jane Dickson described *The.PowerBook* in the London *Independent* as "a heaving, millennial effort of a novel," while David Galef concluded in *New York Times Book Review* that Winterson "should stop e-mailing and get back to work."

In addition to writing novels, Winterson has completed several screenplays, a children's book, a book on women's health issues, and the collection *Art Objects: Es-*

says on Ecstasy and Effrontery. While a *Kirkus Reviews* contributor dubbed *Art Objects* "self-important," Michael Dirda averred in *Washington Post Book World* that the work shows its author's characteristic—and welcome—tendency to provoke, adding: "Anyone who values literature will want to keep these essays around, to argue with, marvel at, find consolation in."

BIOGRAPHICAL AND CRITICAL SOURCES:

BOOKS

Allen, Carolyn, *Following Djuna: Women Lovers and the Erotics of Loss,* Indiana University Press (Bloomington, IN), 1996.

Contemporary Novelists, 7th edition, St. James Press (Detroit, MI), 2001.

Contemporary Popular Writers, St. James Press (Detroit, MI), 1997.

Dictionary of Literary Biography, Volume 207: *British Novelists since 1960, Third Series,* Thomson Gale (Detroit, MI), 1999, pp. 301-308.

Gay and Lesbian Biography, St. James Press (Detroit, MI), 1997.

Gay and Lesbian Literature, St. James Press (Detroit, MI), 1994, pp. 422-424.

PERIODICALS

American Book Review, March, 1995, Andree Pages, review of *Written on the Body,* p. 19.

Boston Herald, November 10, 2000, review of *The. PowerBook,* p. 50.

Chicago Tribune, July 5, 1988, Alan Cheuse, review of *The Passion.*

Entertainment Weekly, May 9, 1997, Rhonda Johnson, review of *Gut Symmetries,* p. 77.

Globe and Mail (Toronto, Ontario, Canada), March 31, 1990, Nancy Wigston, review of *Sexing the Cherry.*

Guardian (Manchester, England), August 27, 2000, Kate Kellaway, "She's Got the Power"; September 2, 2000, Elaine Showalter, "Eternal Triangles."

Independent (London, England), September 2, 2000, E. Jane Dickson, "Dot.com Dominatrix."

Kirkus Reviews, December 15, 1995, review of *Art Objects: Essays on Ecstasy and Effrontery,* p. 1761.

Library Journal, December, 2001, Nancy Pearl and Catherine Ritchie, "Out of the Closet: Gay Literature," p. 212.

Los Angeles Times, May 3, 1990, Richard Eder, review of *Sexing the Cherry.*

Magazine of Fantasy and Science Fiction, April, 1995, p. 34.

Nation, February 12, 1996, Kelleher Jewett, review of *Art Objects,* p. 30.

New Statesman, April 12, 1985, John Clute, review of *Oranges Are Not the Only Fruit,* p. 25; July 1, 1994, Mary Scott, review of *Art and Lies,* p. 38.

New York Review of Books, September 29, 1988, David Lodge, review of *The Passion,* pp. 25-26.

New York Times, April 27, 1990.

New York Times Book Review, November 8, 1987, p. 26; April 29, 1990, Michael Gorra, review of *Sexing the Cherry,* p. 24; February 14, 1993, p. 10; March 26, 1995, p. 14; February 25, 1996, p. 20; November 19, 2000, David Galef, review of *The. PowerBook.*

Observer (London, England), August 27, 2000, Kate Kellaway, "She's Got the Power."

Publishers Weekly, March 17, 1997, review of *Gut Symmetries,* p. 76.

Review of Contemporary Fiction, fall, 1993, Aurelie Jane Sheehan, review of *Written on the Body,* p. 208; fall, 1997, review of *Gut Symmetries,* p. 225.

Spectator, June 25, 1994, Julie Burchill, review of *Art and Lies: A Piece for Three Voices and a Bawd,* p. 26.

Times Literary Supplement, March 22, 1985, p. 326; November 1, 1985, p. 1228; June 17, 1994, p. 22.

Tribune Books (Chicago, IL), November 8, 1987, Joseph Olshan, review of *Oranges Are Not the Only Fruit.*

Washington Post, October 1, 1987, Sarah Gold, review of *Oranges Are Not the Only Fruit.*

Washington Post Book World, May 13, 1990, p. 9; March 24, 1996, Michael Dirda, review of *Art Objects,* p. 3.

ONLINE

Jeanette Winterson Home Page, http://www.jeanettewinterson.com/ (April 25, 2004).

Salon.com, http://www.salon.com/ (April, 1997), Laura Miller, "Rogue Element."

* * *

WOLF, Naomi 1962-

PERSONAL: Born November 12, 1962, in San Francisco,CA; daughter of Leonard (an English professor) and Deborah (a psychotherapist) Wolf; married David Shipley (a magazine editor), 1993; children: one daughter. *Education:* Yale University, B.A.,1984; attended New College, Oxford, 1984-87. *Religion:* Jewish. *Hobbies and other interests:* Rollerblading.

ADDRESSES: Agent—John Brockman, John Brockman Associates Inc., 5 E. 59th St., New York, NY 10022.

AWARDS, HONORS: Academy of American Poets prize, twice.

WRITINGS:

The Beauty Myth: How Images of Beauty Are Used against Women, Chatto & Windus (London, England) 1990, William Morrow (New York, NY), 1991.

Fire with Fire: The New Female Power and How It Will Change the Twenty-first Century, Random House (New York, NY), 1993.

Promiscuities: The Secret Struggle for Womanhood, Random House (New York, NY), 1997.

Misconceptions: Truth, Lies, and the Unexpected on the Journey to Motherhood, Doubleday (New York, NY), 2001.

The Treehouse: Eccentric Wisdom from My Father on How to Live, Love, and See, Simon and Schuster (New York, NY), 2005.

Contributor to numerous periodicals and newspapers, including *George, New Republic, Ms., Glamour, New York Times,* and *Wall Street Journal.*

SIDELIGHTS: Naomi Wolf is the author of the groundbreaking 1991 book *The Beauty Myth: How Images of Beauty Are Used against Women* and three other bestsellers, all of which deal with the role of women in western society. During the 1990s, the literary success of this poet-turned-author enabled her to emerge as a media celebrity and one of America's most influential, high-profile, and controversial feminists. Wolf, who also frequently lectures on college campuses, served for a time as a political consultant to 2000 Democratic presidential candidate Al Gore, and sometimes appears on television talk shows, has set an ambitious task for herself: to make feminism relevant to a new generation of young women. In attempting to do so, she has argued that women must reshape society by asserting themselves and making effective use of their political and economic power.

Scott Shuger, reviewing Wolf's 1997 book *Promiscuities: The Secret Struggle for Womanhood* for the journal *Washington Monthly,*described the author as a "third wave" feminist. As Shuger explained, the first wave of modern feminists, represented by women such as Betty Friedan, Germaine Greer, and Gloria Steinem, raised awareness of the problems and inequalities that women face in the world. The second wave, which included such militants as Andrea Dworkin and Susan Brownmiller, viewed men as the enemy. In Shuger's opinion, Wolf is representative of an influential segment of the third wave of feminism. "[Her] basic approach has always been more on the order of 'women can fashion solutions, and can ally with me to do so,'" he wrote. Other observers have been less accepting. For example, outspoken feminist literary critic Camille Paglia has attacked Wolf, sarcastically referring to the author as "Little Miss *Pravda*"—an allusion that equates her to the Moscow newspaper that once was the propaganda "voice" of the old Soviet Union's despotic government.

Wolf was the younger of two children born to Leonard Wolf, an English professor at San Francisco State University, and Deborah Wolf, a psychoanalyst. Leonard Wolf was of Eastern European and Orthodox Jewish background, and Wolf recalls in her 1997 book *Promiscuities* that her parents made her and her older brother Aaron attend synagogue and Hebrew school. Leonard and Deborah Wolf, whose approach to life was liberal and permissive, encouraged their children to experience the world around them. The Wolf family lived in the famous Haight-Ashbury neighborhood, one of the birthplaces of the free-love, "flower power" counterculture that came to symbolize the 1960s. This had a profound impact on young Naomi Wolf; as she recalled in *Promiscuities,* "the city made us feel that we were not alive if we were not being sexual."

Wolf lost her virginity at age fifteen while high on LSD and for a time in her early teens became obsessed with her body image in a negative way. She was in junior high when she developed anorexia, dropping more than twenty pounds and suffering serious health problems as a result. "Adolescent starvation was for me a prolonged reluctance to be born into woman if that meant assuming a station of beauty," Wolf wrote in her 1990 book *The Beauty Myth.*

Despite these problems, Wolf was a straight-A student. She did well in high school and then earned a bachelor of arts degree in English literature from Yale University in 1984. After winning a Rhodes scholarship, she spent three years (1984-87) studying in England at Oxford University. During this period, Wolf wrote poetry for the *Voice Literary Supplement, Verse,* and other small literary journals in England and the United States.

The author recalled in a 1991 interview with a reporter for *Publishers Weekly* that she also used her time at New College, Oxford, to work on a doctoral thesis about how male and female writers in the nineteenth and twentieth centuries "used beauty differently—male writers often used beauty not to illuminate, but to silence women characters." Doing so gave Wolf new insights into the systemic discrimination that she and other women faced in the male-dominated world of academia. Then, one day she overheard someone comment that she had won her Rhodes scholarship because of her looks. "I had an image of the documents I had presented to the committee—my essay, a book of poems I had written, letters of recommendation—and the whole of it being swept away by that one sentence," Wolf told a *Time* magazine interviewer in 1991.

In the end, Wolf never finished her Oxford degree. However, as Lynn Darling noted in an article in *Harper's Bazaar,* Wolf did become a writer "who can hold her own in any angels-on-the-head-of-a-pin academic debate." She twice won prizes from the American Academy of Poets, and she turned her thesis into a book manuscript that was sold to publishers in both England and the United States.

Wolf's first book, *The Beauty Myth: How Images of Beauty Are Used against Women,* caused a sensation when it was published in London in the fall of 1990 and in New York the following spring. *The Beauty Myth* was widely reviewed. It also generated a flurry of media interest and sparked spirited debates on college campuses both in England and across North America. Wolf's views have always been as topical as they are controversial. She noted in a 1991 interview with *Publishers Weekly* that although *The Beauty Myth* was widely reviewed in England, "the reaction [to it]was emotional—very few people actually grappled with the thesis."

Some of the critics who did deal with the substance of Wolf's argument noted that her thesis echoes a Marxist notion: that western industrial society, which Karl Marx maintained is inherently exploitive, requires an underpaid working class in order to thrive and prosper. In modern times, Wolf theorizes, our male-dominated society has shunted women into a "pink-collar ghetto" of low-paying, service sector jobs. The author maintains that women have not only gone along with this exploitation, they have furthered it by subscribing to "the beauty myth."

Wolf argues that women in Western society labor under an unrealistic ideal of body image and beauty, one that dictates that women must be slim, physically attractive, and subservient to men. She explores the negative effects of social pressures on women to be "beautiful," examining such topics as anorexia, cosmetic surgery, makeup, and impractical clothing. Seventy-five percent of all plastic-surgery patients are female, she points out, while more than fifty billion dollars are spent each year on cosmetics, dieting products, and exercise.

According to Wolf, appearance—or, more precisely, the unlikely standard by which female appearance is judged in western society—has, in effect, become a repressive force by which feminism itself is significantly thwarted. "I contend that this obsession with beauty in the Western world . . . is, in fact, the last way men can defend themselves against women claiming power,"she explained in a 1991 interview with a reporter from *People* magazine. Wolf regards "economic necessity" as a principal reason that such an impractical ideal—or, indeed, any ideal at all—is imposed. "Over and over in the course of women's history, the female ideals that form just happen to be ones that serve what the economy needs at the moment," she told *People.* "There's no male conspiracy. There's doesn't need to be."

Wolf argues that both sexes are diminished by these unreasonable expectations, for men as well as women are obliged to conform to an extraordinary and unrealistic standard of beauty. She terms the seemingly increased reinforcement of this standard an "epidemic." *The Beauty Myth* was Wolf's effort to raise reader awareness and effect positive social change. "What I've tried to do," she explained in the *Publishers Weekly* interview, "is make an argument so powerful that by the end the reader either has to find a situation we take for granted intolerable and take steps to change it—or kill the messenger."

In the three years that Wolf spent researching *The Beauty Myth* she gathered statistical background information and studied the works of such feminist writers as Germaine Greer, Ann Hollander, and Betty Friedan. Ironically, as *Time* magazine reported at the time, "Pioneer feminist Betty Friedan dismisse[d] the book as an 'obsolete rehash' and criticize[d] Wolf for dwelling on superficialities rather than coming to grips with the modern-day political challenges that confront females."

Other critics argued that the basic premise of Wolf's book is flawed because it emphasizes "the beauty myth" as the cause of women's problems. For instance, writing in the *New York Review of Books,* Diane Johnson commented that Wolf "ultimately attributes all social evils . . . to the frenzied thrashings of threatened manhood, and here it is possible that she has not cast her net wide enough." Meanwhile, *National Review* writer Mary G. Gotschall faulted *The Beauty Myth* for its pessimistic tone, but also praised Wolf for her "excellent writing and wonderful breadth of scholarship." Gotschall hailed *The Beauty Myth* as "a provocative new feminist tract which should take its place alongside such polemics as Betty Friedan's *The Feminine Mystique."* Margo Jefferson wrote in the *New York Times Book Review* that Wolf's book "shows us yet again how much we need new ways of seeing."

In addition to generating enormous media interest, *The Beauty Myth* won a mass readership and made best-seller lists in England, Canada, and the United States. The *New York Times* named it one of the seventy most influential books of the twentieth century. Wolf told *People* magazine that she received many letters from teenagers and young women who told her that her book was "the most true thing about their generation they've read." The author also alluded to the controversy *The Beauty Myth*generated when she noted in her *People* interview: "I'm trying to seize this culture by its collar and say 'Stop! Look what you're doing!' To the extent that people get angry, I know I've done a good job."

Wolf's second book, *Fire with Fire: The New Female Power and How it Will Change the Twenty-First Century,* was every bit as provocative as *The Beauty Myth.* "In part, it was a critique of second-wave feminism, accusing it of becoming too rigid in its views and calling on feminists to broaden their self definition," Judith Harlan wrote in *American Women Writers: A Critical Reference Guide.* "Wolf presented the idea of 'power feminism,' arguing that the time had come for women to embrace their political power . . . . She urged women, too, to eschew 'victim feminism' and to acknowledge, celebrate, and build their own power in business and in all of life's realms." Reviewer Karen Lehrman commented in the *New Republic,* "[Wolf's] central point is that the women's movement should now be seen as a big tent open to all kinds of women, that individual feminists should feel free to exercise their own 'line-item veto.' At the same time, however, she maintains that women must seize 'power' with a 'concerted, unified effort.'"

Like *The Beauty Myth, Fire with Fire* touched a nerve with reviewers. Many judged the book from an ideological perspective; others attacked Wolf herself for everything from her personal appearance to her relatively privileged background and her political views. Writing in *Christian Century,* reviewer Helen M. Sterk commented, "With the publication of *Fire with Fire,* Wolf takes her place among a new crop of antifeminist-feminists such as Kate Roiphe and Camille Paglia."-*Commonweal* reviewer Clare Collins wrote, "In the end, Wolf's philosophy comes down to this: For women to enjoy true equality they must usurp the economic stranglehold of men. Certainly this is true, at least in one sense. However, I can't but think that the very audience who needs this message the most, the poor and disenfranchised, is least likely to benefit from Wolf's brand of feminism with a smiling but still elitist face."

Some reviewers and media pundits also seized upon Wolf's use of the term "victim feminism" and then chided her for having used it. However, the author explained to *Publishers Weekly* that in doing so she had meant to "acknowledge that women are victimized." Instead, anti- feminists have seized upon her words and used them in ways that Wolf had not foreseen. "The term has come to mean the equivalent of whining and has been used against established feminists ever since," noted Judith Harlan. Reviewing *Fire with Fire* for *Nieman Reports,* Jack Kammer stated, "[Wolf] displays courage and candor in expressing sentiments she surely knew would bring stinging reproach from her feminist allies." He added, "perhaps the most admirable part of *Fire with Fire* is its analysis of 'victim feminism.' . . . [the author's] antidote for this 'hierarchy of miserable saintliness' is 'power feminism'—robust, creative, and fun. Such freshness raises the anticipation that Wolf might provide a breakthrough in feminist thought. But that hope is dashed by her stale analysis of male power in government and media."

Wolf's third book, *Promiscuities: The Secret Struggle for Womanhood,* also dealt with issues relating to women and power, "this time focusing on the sexuality and coming-of-age stories of young women,"as Judith Harlan observed. "Wolf shares reminiscences of her own and those of old friends about their sexuality during the confusing teen years, and attempts to generalize from them." *Entertainment Weekly* reviewer Vanessa Friedman described *Promiscuities* as "a touchy-feely analysis of women's sexual coming of age." The reviewer continued, "The central premise . . . is that girls become women through their sexual experiences and that society has not grappled with that transition in any meaningful way."

As was the case with Wolf's earlier books, *Promiscuities* became an immediate best seller, although once again the reviews were mixed. On the one hand, critics such as Laura Shapiro of *Newsweek* hailed the work as "Wolf's most successful . . . more original than *The Beauty Myth* and more genuinely reflective than her political analysis in *Fire with Fire*. . . . what she proves here, for the first time, is that she's a writer." Reviewer Anne Gottleib of the *Nation* praised Wolf's abilities as "a good storyteller, with an imaginative empathy and an eye for the sensuous, emotionally telling detail." Gottleib concluded that although "Wolf ultimately overreaches," she "is definitely onto something. Female sexuality and who controls it, is central to the problem of women's power, both subjective and social." On the other hand, *New York Times* reviewer Michiko Kakutani allowed that while there are "some interesting topics in this book," Wolf is "a frustratingly inept messenger: a sloppy thinker and incompetent writer." Writing in the British publication *New Statesman,* Eve Pollard commented, "By pinpointing the time when girls 'become women' as the moment they lose their virginity, [Wolf] enters an unreal world. That may have been how it was in Haight-Ashbury, but she doesn't pause to consider that this transition could well be different and somewhat earlier for a girl who lives in poverty, squalor, or hunger—or suffers inadequate or absentee parenting."

The subject matter of Wolf's fourth book, published in 2001, was another exploration of the themes and events of her own life. She had married David Shipley, executive editor of the *New Republic,* in 1993, and *Misconceptions: Truth, Lies, and the Unexpected on the Journey to Motherhood* is Wolf's first-person account and exploration of motherhood and the birth of her daughter. Reviewer Rebecca Abrams of *New Statesman* described the book as "mummy lit," typical of "an amassing body of fiction and nonfiction" that deals with motherhood. "Taken individually, these books vary greatly in style, approach, and quality; taken together, they represent something substantial and unignorable."

A *Publishers Weekly* reviewer wrote that Wolf "attempts to employ her fiercely confident and uncompromising, rip-the-lid-off style to tell the painful truth of motherhood in contemporary America." *New York Times* reviewer Claire Dederer wrote, "Wolf's goal is not to write a small, personal book. It is, as with her previous writing, to link her experience to larger cultural and social forces. Her books can be boiled down to a simple calculus of woman acted upon by society." Dederer concluded, "In the context of memoir, Wolf's personal writing no longer seems self-indulgent. It seems vital, and in a sense radical, in the tradition of 1970s feminists who sought to speak to every aspect of women's lives. In fact, her autobiographical testimony has a stringently moral quality, an intelligence not found in her social critique." Reviewer Bonnie Schiedel of *Chatelaine* magazine had a similar assessment. "*Misconceptions* is eye-opening, irritating, and tender, but it will make you see motherhood in a new light," she wrote.

As has been the case with all of Wolf's books, many reviews were colored by the politics of the debate over feminism and reproductive rights. However, with publication of *Misconceptions* there came something of a shift in Wolf's public image; suddenly, liberal critics, who had usually been supportive of her ideas, began to join the attacks on her. "Certainly the most offensive and dangerous part of the book is Wolf's decision to cave in completely on reproductive rights," Susan Douglas and Meredith Michaels stated in an article in the *Nation.*

If Wolf has been bothered by any of the criticisms that have been thrown her way, she has not let it show. In fact, the evidence is that Wolf relishes the intellectual challenge of defending herself and her writings. In a question-and-answer session that appeared in the British newspaper the *Guardian,* one reader asked Wolf how she copes with "the constant derision of your ideas." Her response was succinct: "To me, it is much more important to do what we all can to work for social justice than it is to get sidetracked by ridicule, which is the anti-feminists' oldest and most boring weapon." In an interview with a reporter from *Newsweek,* Wolf touched on the same theme when she explained, "Women are the majority now, but we're not going to get power by being nice girls."

Yet Wolf's next book, *The Treehouse: Eccentric Wisdom from My Father on How to Live, Love, and See,* is unconcerned with power or politics. A marked departure from her previous work, the book is a noncontroversial exploration of her father's wisdom as it pertains to fostering creativity. *Library Journal* reviewer Kathryn R. Bartelt called the book "lyrical, insightful, and poignant."

BIOGRAPHICAL AND CRITICAL SOURCES:

BOOKS

American Women Writers: A Critical Reference Guide, Volume 4, 2nd edition, St. James Press (Detroit, MI), 2000.

Feminist Writers, St. James Press (Detroit, MI), 1996.

Newsmakers Gale (Detroit, MI), 1994.

Wolf, Naomi, *Promiscuities: The Secret Struggle for Womanhood,*Random House (New York, NY), 1997.

PERIODICALS

Book, November- December, 2001, Stephanie Foote, review of *Misconceptions: Truth, Lies, and the Unexpected on the Journey to Motherhood,* p. 66.

Booklist, May 1, 1997, Sonna Seaman, review of *Promiscuities: The Secret Struggle for Womanhood,* p. 1459-60; September 1, 2001, Mary Frances Wilkens, review of *Misconceptions,* p. 29; March 1, 2005, Mary Frances Wilkens, review of *The Treehouse: Eccentric Wisdom from My Father on How to Live, Love, and See,* p. 1101.

Chatelaine, November, 2001, Bonnie Schiedel, "Three Books People Are Talking About," p. 26.

Choice, May 1994, C. Adamsky, review of *Fire with Fire: The New Female Power and How it Will Change the Twenty-First Century,* p. 1511.

Christian Century, July 13, 1994, Helen Sterk, review of *Fire with Fire,* pp. 694-695.

Christian Science Monitor, September 27, 2001, Marilyn Gardner, "The Baby Myth: Naomi Wolf Critiques a Culture Determined to Make Pregnancy Difficult," p. 19.

Commonweal, February 25, 1994, Clare Collins, review of *Fire with Fire,* pp. 22-23.

Entertainment Weekly, July 20, 1997, Vanessa V. Friedman, review of *Promiscuities,* pp. 65-66.

Guardian, September 11, 2001, "Naomi Wolf Answers Your Questions."

Harper's Bazaar, November, 1993, article by Lynn Darling; May, 1997, Cynthia Kling, "Remembrance of Past Sex," pp. 114-115.

Human Life Review, summer, 1996, "A Conversation with Naomi Wolf," pp. 65- 86.

Library Journal, March 1, 1994, Miriam Kahn, review of audio version of *Fire with Fire,* p. 138; June 15, 1997, Rose M. Cichy, review of *Promiscuities,* p. 88; September 1, 2001, Barbara M. Bibel, review of *Misconceptions,* p. 218; April 1, 2005, Kathryn R. Bartelt, review of *The Treehouse,* p. 95.

Nation, January 31, 1994, Kio Stark, review of *Fire with Fire,* pp. 137- 141; June 9, 1997, Annie Gottleib, review of *Promiscuities,* pp. 25-27; November 26, 2001, Susan J. Douglas and Meredith Michaels, "The Belly Politics," p. 26.

National Review, July 8, 1991, pp. 42-44; October 23, 1995, J. O'Sullivan, "Regrets Only," p. 6; June 2, 1997, Ellen Wilson Fielding, review of *Promiscuities,* pp. 54-56.

New Republic, March 14, 1994, Karen Lehrman, review of *Fire with Fire,* pp. 40-45; October 16, 1995, Naomi Wolf, "Our Bodies, our Souls: Rethinking Pro-Choice Rhetoric," p. 26.

New Statesman, May 9, 1997, Eve Pollard, review of *Promiscuities,* p. 45; September 17, 2001, Rebecca Abrams, "More Mummy Lit," p. 55.

Newsweek, November 15, 1993; June 16, 1997, Laura Shapiro, review of *Promiscuities,* p. 55.

New York Review of Books, January 16, 1992, p. 13.

New York Times, June 10, 1997, Michiko Kakutani, review of *Promiscuities,* p. C13.

New York Times Book Review, May 19, 1991, p. 11; June 8, 1997, Courtney Weaver, review of *Promiscuities;* October 7, 2001, Claire Dederer, review of *Misconceptions,* p. 30.

Nieman Reports, spring, 1994, Jack Kammer, review of *Fire with Fire,* pp. 107-108.

off our backs, May, 1994, Ann Menasche, review of *Fire With Fire,* p. 9; December 1994, Karla Mantilla, *Fire With Fire,* pp. 1-5.

People, June 24, 1991, pp. 117-21.

Publishers Weekly, February 15, 1991, Maria Simon, "Cry Wolf: Morrow Explores the Burdens of Beauty," p. 64; March 1, 1991, p. 68; May 5, 1997, review of *Promiscuities,* p. 186; June 30, 1997, W. Smith, "Naomi Wolf: Confessions of a Feminist," pp. 56-57; August 20, 2001, review of *Misconceptions,* p. 73; February 28, 2005, review of *The Treehouse,* p. 48.

Time, March 4, 1991, Emily Mitchell, "The Bad Side of Looking Good," p. 68.

Times (London, England), June 30, 1997, Ginia Bellafante, review of *Promiscuities,* p. 71; September 10, 2001, Erica Wagner, "Welcome to Motherhood, Parents," p. S8.

US Weekly, September 17, 2001, Janet Steen, review of *Misconceptions,* p. 90.

Wall Street Journal, June 6, 1997, Elizabeth Powers, review of *Promiscuities,* p. 17.

Washington Monthly, June, 1997, Scott Shuger, review of *Promiscuities,* pp. 49-51.

Washington Post, November 5, 1999, Ann Gerhart, "Who's Afraid of Naomi Wolf? The List Is Growing since the Promiscuities Author Turned Gore Advisor," p. C01.

Women's Review of Books, February 1994, Lesley Hazelton, review of *Fire with Fire,* pp. 1-3; July 1997, Julie Phillips, review of *Promiscuities,* pp. 34-35.

ONLINE

Salon.com, http://www.salon.com/ (November 1, 1999), Jake Tapper, "I Am Woman, Hear Me Gore."

WOLFE, Gene 1931-
(Gene Rodman Wolfe)

PERSONAL: Born May 7, 1931, in Brooklyn, NY; son of Roy Emerson (in sales) and Mary Olivia (Ayers) Wolfe; married Rosemary Frances Dietsch, November 3, 1956; children: Roy II, Madeleine, Therese, Matthew. *Education:* Attended Texas A&M University, 1949-52; University of Houston, B.S.M.E., 1956. *Religion:* Roman Catholic.

ADDRESSES: Home—P.O. Box 69, Barrington, IL 60011. *Agent*—Virginia Kidd, Box 278, Milford, PA 18337.

CAREER: Project engineer with Procter & Gamble, 1956-72; *Plant Engineering Magazine,* Barrington, IL, senior editor, 1972-84; writer. *Military service:* U.S. Army, 1952-54; received Combat Infantry badge.

MEMBER: Science Fiction Writers of America.

AWARDS, HONORS: Nebula Award, Science Fiction Writers of America (SFWA), 1973, for novella *The Death of Doctor Island*; Chicago Foundation for Literature Award, 1977, for *Peace;* Rhysling Award, 1978, for poem "The Computer Iterates the Greater Trumps"; Nebula Award nomination, SFWA, 1979, for novella *Seven American Nights;* Illinois Arts Council award, 1981, for short story "In Looking-Glass Castle"; World Fantasy Award, 1981, for *The Shadow of the Torturer,* 1996, for life achievement; Nebula Award, SFWA, and *Locus* Award, both 1982, both for *The Claw of the Conciliator;* British Science Fiction Award, 1982; British Fantasy Award, 1983; *Locus* Award, 1983, for *The Sword of the Lictor;* John W. Campbell Memorial Award, Science Fiction Research Association, 1984, for *The Citadel of the Autarch;* World Fantasy Award, 1989, for collection *Storeys from the Old Hotel*; Nebula Award nomination, SFWA, 1993, for *Nightside the Long Sun;* Nebula Award nomination, SFWA, 2005, for *The Knight;* Mythopoeic Fantasy Award nomination, Mythopoeic Society, 2005, for *The Knight* and *The Wizard.*

WRITINGS:

SCIENCE FICTION/FANTASY

Operation ARES, Berkley Publishing (New York, NY), 1970.

The Fifth Head of Cerberus (three novellas), Scribner (New York, NY), 1972, reprinted, Orb, 1994.

(With Ursula K. LeGuin and James Tiptree, Jr.) *The New Atlantis, and Other Novellas of Science Fiction,* edited by Robert Silverberg, Hawthorn (New York City), 1975.

The Devil in a Forest (juvenile), Follett, 1976, reprinted, Orb, 1996.

The Island of Doctor Death and Other Stories and Other Stories, Pocket Books (New York, NY), 1980, reprinted, Orb, 1997.

The Shadow of the Torturer (first book in "The Book of the New Sun" tetralogy), Simon & Schuster (New York, NY), 1980.

Gene Wolfe's Book of Days (short stories), Doubleday (New York, NY), 1981.

The Claw of the Conciliator (second book in "The Book of the New Sun" tetralogy), Simon & Schuster, 1981.

The Sword of the Lictor (third book in "The Book of the New Sun" tetralogy), Simon & Schuster, 1982.

The Citadel of the Autarch (fourth book in "The Book of the New Sun" tetralogy), Simon & Schuster, 1983.

The Wolfe Archipelago (short stories), Ziesing Bros. (Willimantic, CT), 1983.

Plan(e)t Engineering, New England Science Fiction Association, 1984.

Free Live Free, Ziesing Bros., 1984, new edition, Tor Books (New York, NY), 1985.

Soldier of the Mist, Tor Books, 1986.

The Urth of the New Sun (sequel to "The Book of the New Sun" tetralogy), Tor Books, 1987.

There Are Doors, Tor Books, 1988.

Storeys from the Old Hotel (short stories), Kerosina, 1988, reprinted, Orb, 1995.

Endangered Species (short stories), Tor Books, 1989.

Seven American Nights (bound with *Sailing to Byzantium,* by Silverberg), Tor Books, 1989.

Soldier of Arete (sequel to *Soldier of the Mist*), St. Martin's (New York, NY), 1989.

Pandora by Holly Hollander, Tor Books, 1990.

Castleview, Tor Books, 1991.

Castle of Days, Tor Books, 1992, reprinted, Orb, 1995.

Nightside the Long Sun, Tor Books, 1993.

Lake of the Long Sun, Tor Books, 1993, reprinted, Doherty, 1994.

Sword and Citadel, Orb, 1994.

Calde of the Long Sun, Tor Books, 1994.

Shadow & Claw (contains *The Shadow of the Torturer,* and *The Claw of the Conciliator*), Orb, 1994.

Exodus from the Long Sun, Tor Books, 1995.

In Green's Jungles, Tor, 2000.

Strange Travelers, Tor, 2000.

Return to the Whorl, Tor (New York, NY), 2001.
Innocents Aboard: New Fantasy Stories, Tor (New York, NY), 2004.
The Knight, Tor (New York, NY), 2004.
The Wizard, Tor (New York, NY), 2004.
Starwater Strains, Tor (New York, NY), 2005.

OTHER

Peace (novel), Harper (New York, NY), 1975, reprinted Tor, 1995.
The Castle of the Otter (essays), Ziesing Bros., 1982.
Bibliomen, Cheap Street (New Castle, VA), 1984.
Empires of Foliage and Flower, Cheap Street, 1987.
For Rosemary (poetry), Kerosina, 1988.

Contributor of stories to anthologies, including awards anthologies *Best SF: 70,* 1970, *Nebula Award Stories 9, The Best SF of the Year #3,* and *Best SF: 73,* all 1974. Also contributor of short stories to *Omni, New Yorker, Isaac Asimov's Science Fiction Magazine,* and other publications.

SIDELIGHTS: "With the publication of his tetralogy *The Book of the New Sun,* Gene Wolfe has entered the ranks of the major contemporary writers of science fiction," Pamela Sargent asserted in *Twentieth-Century Science Fiction Writers.* The series is set on Earth and takes place far in the future in a society reminiscent of medieval Europe in its social structure where long-forgotten technologies appear magical. When Severian, an apprentice torturer, is exiled from his guild for aiding the suicide of a prisoner he loves, a journey of discovery is inaugurated that culminates in Severian's elevation to Autarch, ruler of Urth. "The far-future world of Urth through which Wolfe's characters move is a world of beauty and horror, one in which humanity's great accomplishments are not only past, but also nearly forgotten, and in which the lack of resources makes the knowledge that remains nearly useless," noted Sargent. Severian, however, possesses perfect recall, making his retrospective narration fecund with detail and meaning. As Thomas D. Clareson commented in his *Dictionary of Literary Biography* essay, Severian's account is "a rich tapestry rivaling any imaginary world portrayed in contemporary science fiction"; he called the series of books "one of the high accomplishments of modern science fiction."

Critics have particularly admired the realism with which Wolfe presents his imaginary society. *London Tribune* contributor Martin Hillman, for example, declared that "in the evocation of the world, and the unsettling technologies, creatures, and behavioural rules within it," Wolfe's tetralogy "is streets ahead of most tales featuring sword-bearing heroes." "Wolfe is not only deft at creating a whole and strange new world," Tom Hutchinson of the London *Times* claimed, "he also, disturbingly, makes us understand a different way of thinking." This vivid depiction of a remote civilization, however, has not prevented the author from creating a comprehensive portrayal of Severian's character. "Although Wolfe has created an epic stage and although he permits his protagonist to travel extensively through the world," Clareson commented in *Extrapolation,* "the emphasis is never upon external action for the sake of action; rather, the four novels become increasingly a study of Severian's reactions and musings. The result," the critic concluded, "is that Gene Wolfe has created one of the richest and most complex characterizations in the field of fantasy and science fiction." Peter Nicholls agreed, stating in a *Washington Post Book World* article that Severian "is perhaps the most extraordinary hero in the history of the heroic epic, and none of his confrontations are without surprises."

While *The Book of the New Sun* series has been celebrated for the vividness of its descriptions, reviewers also commend Wolfe's intricate imagery. "In fact, there are two 'Books of the New Sun,'" Nicholls argued. "Out in the open is the wonderfully vivid and inventive story of a brave and lonely hero; below is the sea of allusion and juxtaposition . . . [and] a pungent debate on ontology, eschatology and the metaphysics of time." Contributing to the series' profundity, C.N. Manlove suggested in *Kansas Quarterly,* is Wolfe's literary skill: "The author creates his images with such apparent effortlessness that they seem to have been come upon, to have been always there, rather than to have been invented. Every stage of Severian's journey is accompanied by a startling new image or landscape." "With great urgency, layer after layer," John Clute similarly maintained in the *Washington Post Book World,* Wolfe "has created a world radiant with meaning, a novel that makes sense in the end only if it is read as an attempt to represent the Word of God."

It is this layering of image and meaning that has led critics such as Algis Budrys to praise the overall literary quality of Wolfe's series: "As a piece of literature, the work is simply overwhelming," Budrys related in the *Magazine of Fantasy and Science Fiction.* "Severian is a character realized in a depth and to a breadth we have never seen in SF before," the critic explained, adding that "as craftsmanship and as literature, what were talking about are attributes that are world-class as *prose,* not 'just' as SF." As Thomas M. Disch noted in the *Washington Post Book World:* "Gene Wolfe has managed to do what no science fantasy author has done heretofore—he's produced a work of art that can satisfy adult appetites and in which even the most fantastical elements register as poetry rather than as penny-whistle whimsy. Furthermore, he's done this without in any way sacrificing the showmanship and splashy colors that auger a popular success." "In a triumph of imagination, [Wolfe] creates a truly alien social order that the reader comes to experience from within," concluded *New York Times Book Review* critic Gerald Jonas. "The result does not make for easy reading. But once into it, there is no stopping—and you will not quickly forget Severian or his world." Although the author leaves room for future volumes, a *Booklist* reviewer proposed that "it is not necessary that we see any more for this series to loom as a major landmark of contemporary American literature. . . . Wolfe has wrought a genuine marvel here."

While *The Urth of the New Sun* continues Severian's story, it is "neither afterthought nor reprise," *Times Literary Supplement* reviewer Colin Greenland remarked. Nevertheless, Roz Kaveney wrote in the *Washington Post Book World,* "this volume makes of the whole work a palimpsest, in which moments from an underlay of earlier versions of reality crop up suddenly, producing seeming inconsistencies. . . . *The Urth of the New Sun* makes of the whole sequence a more perfect work by showing us [these] inconsistencies before ironing them out." The novel traces the journey of Severian, now Autarch, as he travels to a high galactic court to petition for the "new sun" that will renew Urth. While the concept of one person representing his race to a higher authority is a common science fiction convention, a *Washington Post Book World* critic noted that "as usual, Wolfe takes this old chestnut and makes it into something very rich and very strange."

Kaveney likewise claimed that "Gene Wolfe's career has thus far been dedicated to making us see in a new light some of what we had thought of as the stock habits of science fiction and fantasy." In *Free Live Free,* for example, "Wolfe extends his freedom in another direction, embracing for his own purposes that problematic mix of nonscientific lore and dreams of power known as the occult," commented Jonas. The result, says the critic, is a series of "character studies," something "rare in science fiction." *Soldier of the Mist* is also innovative in its account of Latro, a soldier of ancient Greece whose memory is wiped clean every time he sleeps—payment for having seen the gods; Latro's condition necessitates the keeping of a journal in which he records each day's events—with each new day he must read the journal and relearn his life. Guided by his text and various gods, Latro journeys to regain his memory. Wolfe continues Latro's story in *Soldier of Arete,* in which Latro becomes embroiled in the political and military rivalry between Greece and Sparta. John Calvin Batchelor observed in the *Washington Post Book World* that *Soldier of the Mist,* while difficult reading, is "a work of consequence." The author "is a master of science fiction," Batchelor concludes, "and for the best of all reasons, vaulting ambition."

Some of Wolfe's novels are set in contemporary American society and present the intrusion of fantastic elements into mundane reality. A subtle example of this is *Pandora by Holly Hollander,* a murder mystery narrated by a teenage girl named Pandora. The investigation focuses on the contents of a mysterious box, and, as Faren Miller observed in *Locus,* while everything in the novel "has an explanation in human fear, curiosity, passion, or greed. . . , the little things, the offbeat details, manage to give a sparkle of fairytale to the book." In contrast, *Castleview* is an out-and-out fantasy in which the longtime residents of Castleview, Illinois, have all seen visions of a medieval castle floating in air. In the course of the novel, in which the reader follows the arrival to town of Will E. Shields, new owner of the local auto dealership, figures from Arthurian legend appear along with the fictional feline Puss-in-Boots and increasing numbers of dead bodies from bizarre accidents.

Although Wolfe became famous for his novels, the "Urth" series in particular, his literary reputation is also bolstered by his short fiction, notably the collections *Storeys from the Old Hotel*—a highly accessible gathering of imaginative fiction—and *Endangered Species*—a somewhat more challenging volume of philosophically inclined tales. As Clareson asserted in an *Extrapolation* review of *Gene Wolfe's Book of Days,* the collection "is another cornerstone in emphasizing how important a writer Gene Wolfe has been throughout his surprising brief career. His stature becomes apparent by reading a number of his works. Only in that way does one realize the skill and subtlety with which he brings a fresh perspective to established themes and situations." *Gene Wolfe's Book of Days* was recently republished in a volume entitled *Castle of Days* that also includes the essay collection *The Castle of the Otter* as well as previously unpublished fiction and nonfiction. Clareson contended in his *Dictionary of Literary Biography* essay that Wolfe is "a major figure whose stories and novels must be considered among the most important science fiction published in the 1970s. He will undoubtedly become increasingly significant in the 1980s because he skillfully uses the materials of science fiction and fantasy to explore the themes which dominate contemporary fiction." "Gene Wolfe is a writer for the thinking reader," Sargent similarly stated; "he will reward anyone searching for intelligence, crafted prose, involving stories, and atmospheric detail. He is the heir of many literary traditions—pulp stories, fantasy, adventure stories of all kinds, and serious literature—and he makes use of all of them," she continued. "His work can be read with pleasure many times; new discoveries are made with each reading, and the stories linger in one's mind."

In the early 1990s, Wolfe started a new multivolume series to rival "The Book of the New Sun." Occasionally referred to as the "Starcrosser's Planetfall" series, the series includes the novels *Nightside the Long Sun, Lake of the Long Sun, Calde of the Long Sun,* and *Exodus from the Long Sun.* The main character of the series is a cleric named Patera Silk whose universe comprises the vast interior of the cylindrical starship Whorl, an environment lighted by a "long sun" that runs the length of the cylinder. The society inside the Whorl is roughly medieval, but there are numerous elements of high—albeit decaying—technology. Silk's adventure begins when he prophesies the existence of a god, the Outsider, who is not one of the nine who rule the Whorl.

Tom Easton, reviewing *Nightside the Long Sun* in *Analog Science Fiction and Fact,* commented that "Wolfe is a master of style and texture." Similarly, Gerald Jonas of the *New York Times Book Review* noted, "Sentence by sentence, Mr. Wolfe writes as well as anyone in science fiction today." "His writing is stamped by extraordinary grace," added Easton in a review of the series' second volume, *Lake of the Long Sun.* "It flows so smoothly and clearly and evocatively that one is hardly aware that one is reading and not living."

Wolfe commented: "The books and stories I write are what are usually called escapist, in the pejorative sense. They do not teach the reader how to build a barbecue, or get a better job, or even how to murder his mother and escape detection. I have never understood what was wrong with escape. If I were in prison, or aboard a sinking vessel, I would escape if I could. I would try to escape from East Germany or the U.S.S.R., if I were unfortunate enough to find myself in one of those places. My work is intended to make life—however briefly—more tolerable for my readers, and to give them the feeling that change is possible, that the world need not always be as it is now, that their circumstances may be radically changed at any time, by their own act or God's."

BIOGRAPHICAL AND CRITICAL SOURCES:

BOOKS

Andre-Driussi, Michael, *Lexicon Urthus: A Dictionary for the Urth Cycle,* Sirius Fiction (San Francisco), 1994.

Contemporary Authors Autobiography Series, Volume 9, Thomson Gale (Detroit), 1989.

Contemporary Literary Criticism, Volume 25, Thomson Gale, 1983.

Dictionary of Literary Biography, Volume 8: *Twentieth Century American Science Fiction Writers,* Thomson Gale, 1981.

Gordon, Joan, *Gene Wolfe,* Borgo (San Bernardino, CA), 1986.

Lane, Daryl, William Vernon, and David Carson, editors, *The Sound of Wonder: Interviews from "The Science Fiction Radio Show,"* Volume 2, Oryx (Phoenix, AZ), 1985.

Twentieth-Century Science Fiction Writers, St. James Press (Detroit), 1986.

PERIODICALS

Analog Science Fiction & Fact, August, 1990, p. 143; June, 1991, p. 178; April, 1993, p. 160; June, 1994, p. 161; February, 1995, p. 159.

Booklist, July 1, 1975; November 1, 1982; August, 1989; November 15, 1992; September 15, 1994, p. 118.

Chicago Tribune Book World, June 8, 1980; June 14, 1981.

Extrapolation, summer, 1981; fall, 1982.

Kansas Quarterly, summer, 1984.

Library Journal, November 15, 1990, p. 95; December, 1992, p. 191; August, 1994, p. 139; September 15, 1994, p. 94.

Locus, March, 1989; February, 1990; November, 1990; January, 1993; December, 1993; August, 1994.

London Tribune, April 24, 1981.

Los Angeles Times Book Review, April 3, 1983; July 29, 1990.

Magazine of Fantasy and Science Fiction, April, 1971; May, 1978; June, 1981; September, 1994, p. 16.

New York Times Book Review, July 13, 1975; September 12, 1976; May 22, 1983; November 24, 1985; July 2, 1989; May 13, 1990; May 9, 1993, p. 20; January 2, 1994, p. 22; September 11, 1994, p. 46.

Publishers Weekly, September 8, 1989; November 9, 1992.

Science Fiction Review, summer, 1981.

Times (London), April 2, 1981.
Times Literary Supplement, May 18, 1973; January 15, 1988.
Washington Post Book World, May 25, 1980; March 22, 1981; July 26, 1981; January 24, 1982; January 30, 1983; November 24, 1985; October 26, 1986; October 27, 1987; August 28, 1988; April 30, 1989; January 31, 1993; December 26, 1993; October 23, 1994.

* * *

WOLFE, Gene Rodman
See WOLFE, Gene

* * *

WOLFE, Thomas Kennerly Jr.
See WOLFE, Tom

* * *

WOLFE, Tom 1931-
(Thomas Kennerly Jr. Wolfe)

PERSONAL: Born March 2, 1931, in Richmond, VA; son of Thomas Kennerly (a scientist and business executive) and Helen (Hughes) Wolfe; married Sheila Berger (art director of *Harper's* magazine), 1978; children: Alexandra, Thomas. *Education:* Washington and Lee University, B.A. (cum laude), 1951; Yale University, Ph.D., 1957. *Hobbies and other interests:* Window shopping.

ADDRESSES: *Home*—New York, NY. *Agent*—International Creative Management, 40 West 57th St., New York, NY 10019.

CAREER: Writer, journalist, social commentator, and artist. *Springfield Union,* Springfield, MA, reporter, 1956-59; *Washington Post,* Washington, DC, reporter and Latin American correspondent, 1959-62; *New York Herald Tribune,* New York, NY, reporter and writer for *New York* Sunday magazine (now *New York* magazine), 1962-66, contributing editor, 1968-76; *New York World Journal Tribune,* New York, NY, writer, 1966-67; *Esquire* magazine, New York, NY, contributing editor, 1977—; *Harper's* magazine, New York, NY, contributing artist, 1978-81. *Exhibitions:* Has exhibited drawings in one-man shows at Maynard Walker Gallery, 1965, and Tunnel Gallery, 1974.

AWARDS, HONORS: Washington Newspaper Guild awards for foreign news reporting and for humor, both 1961; Society of Magazine Writers award for excellence, 1970; D.F.A., Minneapolis College of Art, 1971; Frank Luther Mott research award, 1973; D.Litt., Washington and Lee University, 1974; named Virginia Laureate for literature, 1977; American Book Award and National Book Award, both 1980, for *The Right Stuff;* Harold D. Vursell Memorial Award for excellence in literature, American Institute of Arts and Letters, 1980; Columbia Journalism Award, 1980; citation for art history from National Sculpture Society, 1980; L.H.D., Virginia Commonwealth University, 1983, and Southampton College, 1984; John Dos Passos Award, 1984; Gari Melchers Medal, 1986; Benjamin Pierce Cheney Medal from Eastern Washington University, 1986; Washington Irving Medal for literary excellence from Nicholas Society, 1986; D.F.A., School of Visual Arts, 1987; L.H.D., Randolph-Macon College, Manhattanville College, 1988, and Longwood College, 1989; D.Litt., St. Andrews Presbyterian College, and John Hopkins University, 1990, University of Richmond, 1993; Quinnipiac College, St. Louis Literary award, 1990, presidential award, 1993; D.H.L., Duke University, 2002; *Chicago Tribune* literary prize, 2003.

WRITINGS:

(Self-illustrated) *The Kandy-Kolored Tangerine-Flake Streamline Baby* (essays), Farrar, Straus & Giroux (New York, NY), 1965.
The Electric Kool-Aid Acid Test, Farrar, Straus & Giroux (New York, NY), 1968.
The Pump House Gang (essays), Farrar, Straus & Giroux (New York, NY), 1968, published as *The Mid-Atlantic Man and Other New Breeds in England and America,* Weidenfeld & Nicolson (London, England), 1969.
Radical Chic and Mau Mauing the Flak Catchers (essays), Farrar, Straus & Giroux (New York, NY), 1970.
(Editor, with E.W. Johnson, and contributor) *The New Journalism* (anthology), Harper & Row (New York, NY), 1973.
(Self-illustrated) *The Painted Word,* Farrar, Straus & Giroux (New York, NY), 1975.
(Self-illustrated) *Mauve Gloves & Madmen, Clutter & Vine, and Other Short Stories* (essays), Farrar, Straus & Giroux (New York, NY), 1976.
The Right Stuff (also see below), Farrar, Straus & Giroux (New York, NY), 1979.
(Self-illustrated) *In Our Time* (essays), Farrar, Straus & Giroux (New York, NY), 1980.

From Bauhaus to Our House, Farrar, Straus & Giroux (New York, NY), 1981.

(Self-illustrated) *The Purple Decades: A Reader* (collection), Farrar, Straus & Giroux (New York, NY), 1982.

The Bonfire of the Vanities (novel; also see below), Farrar, Straus & Giroux (New York, NY), 1987.

Two Complete Books (contains *The Right Stuff* and *The Bonfire of the Vanities*), Wings (Belfast, ME), 1994.

A Man in Full (novel), Farrar, Straus & Giroux (New York, NY), 1998.

Hooking Up (essays), Farrar, Straus & Giroux (New York, NY), 2000.

I Am Charlotte Simmons (novel), Farrar, Straus & Giroux (New York, NY), 2004.

Contributor to *The New York Spy,* edited by Alan Rinzler, David White, 1967; and to *Marie Cosindas, Color Photographs,* edited by Susan Feldman, New York Graphic Society (New York, NY), 1978. Contributor of numerous articles to periodicals, including *Esquire, Harper's,* and *Rolling Stone.* Cofounder of literary quarterly *Shenandoah.*

ADAPTATIONS: The Right Stuff was adapted for a film of the same title, Warner Bros., 1983; *Bonfire of the Vanities,* directed by Brian DePalma and starring Tom Hanks, Melanie Griffith, and Bruce Willis, was filmed and released in 1990.

SIDELIGHTS: "Those of you who are not aware of Tom Wolfe should—really—do your best to acquaint yourselves with him," wrote William F. Buckley in the *National Review.* "He is probably the most skillful writer in America. I mean by that he can do more things with words than anyone else." Satirist, caricaturist, social critic, coiner of phrases ("Radical Chic," "good ol' boy," "The Me Decade"), Wolfe has become known as a leading chronicler of American trends. His painstaking research and detailed accounts have made him a widely respected reporter; at the same time, his unorthodox style and frequently unpopular opinions have resulted in a great deal of controversy. Leslie Bennetts in the *Philadelphia Bulletin* has called him "a professional rogue," who has "needled and knifed at the mighty of every description, exposing in print the follies and foibles of superstars from Leonard Bernstein to the Hell's Angels. Gleefully ripping off every shred of disguise from anyone's pretensions, Wolfe has performed his dissections in *New York* Magazine, *Esquire,* and *Rolling Stone,* not to mention his earlier years on the *New York Herald Tribune* and the *Washington Post.*"

Considering Wolfe's body of work, Richard A. Kallan declared in *Dictionary of Literary Biography:* "Wolfe's writings have produced penetrating social and cultural insights, raised intriguing journalistic questions, and suggested the vast potential of nonfictional writing when exercised by a stylistically inventive, perceptive author committed to investigative reporting. For these accomplishments, Tom Wolfe ranks as one of the premier literary journalists in America."

Wolfe is generally recognized as one of the leaders in the branch of writing known as "New Journalism." Bennetts explained that while Wolfe did not invent the movement, "he at least became its stentorian spokesman and most flamboyant practitioner." *Fort Lauderdale Sun-Sentinel* writer Margo Harakas believed that there are "only a handful of standouts among [New Journalists]—Jimmy Breslin, Gay Talese, Hunter Thompson, and of course, Wolfe, with his explosive punctuation, name brand detailing, and kaleidoscopic descriptions." In a *Writer's Digest* article, Wolfe defines New Journalism as "the use by people writing nonfiction of techniques which heretofore had been thought of as confined to the novel or to the short story, to create in one form both the kind of objective reality of journalism and the subjective reality that people have always gone to the novel for." The techniques employed in New Journalism, then, include a number of devices borrowed from traditional fiction writing: extensive dialogue; shifting points of view; scene-by-scene construction; detailed descriptions of setting, clothes, and other physical features; complex character development; and, depending on the reporter and the subject, varying degrees of innovation in the use of language and punctuation.

Wolfe's association with New Journalism began in 1963, when he wrote his first magazine article, a piece on custom automobiles. He had become intrigued with the strange subculture of West Coast car customizers and was beginning to see these individuals as folk artists worthy of serious study. He convinced *Esquire* magazine to send him to California, where he researched the story, interviewed a number of subjects and, observed Harakas, "racked up a $750 tab at the Beverly Wilshire Hotel (picked up by *Esquire,* of course)." Then, having returned to New York to write the article, he found that standard journalistic techniques, those he had employed so successfully during his years of newspaper work for the *Washington Post* and the *New York Herald Tribune,* among others, could not adequately describe the bizarre people and machines he had encountered in California.

Stymied, he put off writing the story until finally he called Byron Dobell, his editor at *Esquire,* and admitted that he was unable to finish the project. Dobell told him to type up his notes so that the magazine could get another writer to do the job. In the introduction to *The Kandy-Kolored Tangerine-Flake Streamline Baby,* Wolfe writes: "About 8 o'clock that night I started typing the notes out in the form of a memorandum that began, 'Dear Byron.' I started typing away, starting right with the first time I saw any custom cars in California." In an attempt to provide every possible detail for the writer who was to finish the piece, Wolfe wrote in a stream-of-consciousness style, including even some of his most garbled notes and random thoughts. "I wrapped up the memorandum about 6:15 A.M., and by this time it was forty-nine pages long. I took it over to *Esquire* as soon as they opened up, about 9:30 A.M. About 4 P.M. I got a call from Byron Dobell. He told me they were striking out the 'Dear Byron' at the top of the memorandum and running the rest of it in the magazine."

It is the style developed during the writing of the custom car article—his unique blend of "pop" language and creative punctuation—that for many years remained Wolfe's trademark. He was a pioneer in the use of what several reviewers refer to as an "aural" style of writing, a technique intended to make the reader come as close as possible to experiencing an event first-hand. Wilfrid Sheed, in the *New York Times Book Review,* suggested that Wolfe tries to find "a language proper to each subject, a special sound to convey its uniqueness"; and *Newsweek* Jack Kroll felt that Wolfe is "a genuine poet" among journalists, who is able "to get under the skin of a phenomenon and transmit its metabolic rhythm . . . . He creates the most vivid, most pertinent possible dimension of his subject." F.N. Jones, in a *Library Journal* article, described Wolfe's prose as "free-flowing colorful Joycean, quote-slang, repetitive, cult or class jargon with literary and other reverberations."

Wolfe's style, combined with solid reporting and a highly critical eye, quickly gained a large audience for his magazine pieces. When his first book, *The Kandy-Kolored Tangerine-Flake Streamline Baby,* a collection of twenty-two of his best essays, was published in 1965, William James Smith wrote in *Commonweal:* "Two years ago [Tom Wolfe] was unknown and today those who are not mocking him are doing their level best to emulate him. Magazine editors are currently flooded with Zonk articles written, putatively, in the manner of Wolfe and, by common account, uniformly impossible . . . . None of his parodists—and even fewer of his emulators—has successfully captured much of the flavor of Wolfe . . . . They miss the spark of personality that is more arresting than the funny punctuation. Wolfe has it, that magical quality that marks prose as distinctively one's own."

In *The Kandy-Kolored Tangerine-Flake Streamline Baby,* Wolfe analyzes, caricatures, and satirizes a number of early-1960s American trends and pop culture heroes. His essays zero in on the city of Las Vegas, the Peppermint Lounge, demolition derbies, fashion, art galleries, doormen, nannies, and such personalities as Murray the K, Phil Spector, Baby Jane Holzer, and Muhammed Ali (then Cassius Clay). "He knows everything," wrote Kurt Vonnegut in the *New York Times Book Review.* "I do not mean he *thinks* he knows everything. He is loaded with facile junk, as all personal journalists have to be—otherwise, how can they write so amusingly and fast? . . . Verdict: Excellent book by a genius who will do anything to get attention."

What Wolfe has done, according to *Commonweal* contributor Smith, "is simply to describe the brave new world of the 'unconscious avant-garde' who are shaping our future, but he has described this world with a vividness and accuracy that makes it something more than real." In a *New Republic* article, Joseph Epstein expressed the opinion that Wolfe "is perhaps most fatiguing when writing about the lower classes. Here he becomes Dr. Wolfe, Department of American Studies, and what he finds attractive about the lower orders, as has many an intellectual slummer before him, is their vitality. At bottom, what is involved here is worship of the Noble Savage . . . . Wolfe is much better when he writes about New York City. Here he drops his studied spontaneity, eases up on the rococo, slips his doctorate, and takes on the tone of the reasonably feeling New Yorker who has not yet been knocked insensate by the clatter of that city." A *Newsweek* writer concluded that "partly, Wolfe belongs to the old noble breed of poet-journalists, like Ben Hecht, and partly he belongs to a new breed of supereducated hip sensibilities like Jonathan Miller and Terry Southern, who see the complete human comedy in everything from a hair-do to a holocaust."

In *The Electric Kool-Aid Acid Test,* Wolfe applies his distinctive brand of journalism to novelist Ken Kesey and his "Merry Pranksters," a West Coast group dedicated to LSD and the pursuit of the psychedelic experience. Joel Lieber said in *Nation* that in this book, Wolfe "has come as close as seems possible, with words, at re-creating the entire mental atmosphere of a scene in which one's understanding is based on feeling rather than verbalization . . . [The book] is nonfiction told as experimental fiction; it is a genuine feat and a landmark in reporting style." Lawrence Dietz, in a *National Review* article, called *The Electric Kool-Aid Acid Test* "the best work Wolfe has done, and certainly the most profound and insightful book that has been written about the psychedelic life . . . . [He] has elicited a history of the spread of LSD from 1960 (when Kesey and others got their first jolts in lab experiments) to 1967, when practically any kid with five dollars could buy some kind of trip or other." Dietz observed that Wolfe displays "a willingness to let accuracy take the place of the hysterical imprecations that have passed for reportage in most magazine articles and books" on this subject.

Kallan noted that *The Electric Kool-Aid Acid Test* demonstrates "a frequent characteristic of Wolfe's style," namely, "a repetition of a single metaphor to synthesize his thesis." Kallen added that Wolfe "notes Kesey's battle cry, 'You're either on the bus or off the bus.'" As Kallen explained, the bus symbolizes "the entire trip, the quest for personal growth and self-discovery. To say one is either on the bus or off the bus is to say he is either committed to the search for identity or he is not."

Radical Chic and Mau Mauing the Flak Catchers was made up of two lengthy essays. The first, "Radical Chic," elicited by far the most critical commentary. It deals with a fund-raising party given by Leonard Bernstein in his Park Avenue apartment in 1970, to raise money for the Black Panthers. Wolfe was at the party, and he became aware of the incongruity of the scene, distinguished, according to Melvin Maddocks in the *Christian Science Monitor,* by "white liberals nibbling caviar while signing checks for the revolution with their free hand." Thomas R. Edwards wrote in the *New York Times Book Review:* "For Wolfe, the scene in the Bernsteins' living room demonstrates his pet sociological thesis, here called *nostalgie de la boue,* the aristocrat's hankering for a proletarian primitivism. He shows us cultivated parvenu Jews, torn between cherished new 'right wing' lifestyles and the 'left wing' politics of their own oppressive history, ludicrously confused about how to take the black revolution."

A *Times Literary Supplement* reviewer commented that Wolfe "both defends and exonerates the Bernsteins, that is—their motives were sound, liberal, serious, responsible—while cocking an almighty snook at 'the essential double-track mentality of Radical Chic—*nostalgie de la boue* and high protocol' that can entertain Afro hair-styles with Roquefort cheese savouries in a Park Avenue duplex . . . . Such is this dazzling piece of trapeze work by the most practised social stuntman of them all."

Many reviewers were critical of *Radical Chic and Mau Mauing the Flak Catchers.* As William F. Buckley explained in the *National Review,* Wolfe "has written a very, very controversial book, for which he has been publicly excommunicated from the company of the orthodox by the bishops who preside over the *New York Review of Books.*" Edwards felt that Wolfe "humiliates and degrades everyone concerned, his pre-potent but child-like and shiftless blacks no less than his gutless, time-serving, sexually-fearful white bureaucrats." Timothy Foote noted in a *Time* article: "When a *Time* reporter recently asked a minister of the Panther Party's shadow government about the truthfulness of Wolfe's *Radical Chic* account, the reply was ominous: 'You mean that dirty, blatant, lying, racist dog who wrote that fascist disgusting thing in *New York* magazine?'" Yet despite objections to the book, Foote insisted, the fact remains that it "is generally so accurate that even some of the irate guests at the Bernsteins' later wondered how Wolfe—who in fact used shorthand—managed to smuggle a tape recorder onto the premises."

Christopher Lehmann-Haupt, writing in the *New York Times,* noted that "Radical Chic" first appeared as a magazine article, wrote: "When the news got out that it would be published as a book eventually, one began to prepare a mental review of it. One had certain questions—the usual Tom Wolfe questions: Where exactly was Wolfe located when all those things occurred? Just how did he learn Leonard Bernstein's innermost fantasies? At exactly what points did Wolfe's imagination impinge on his inferences, and his inferences on his facts?" The book, Lehmann-Haupt concluded, "represents Wolfe at his best, worst, and most. It has his uncanny eye for life-styles; his obsessive lists of brand names and artifacts; his wicked, frequently cruel, cartoon of people's physical traits; his perfect mimicry of speech patterns. Once again, Wolfe proves himself the complete chameleon, capable of turning any color. He understands the human animal like no sociologist around."

The Painted Word is another of Wolfe's more controversial works. T. O'Hara, in a *Best Sellers* review, introduced the book's thesis: "About 10,000 people constitute the present art world. Artists, doing what they must to survive, obey orders and follow the gospel as written by the monarchs." Among these monarchs, in Wolfe's opinion, are three influential and well-respected art critics: Clement Greenberg, Harold Rosenberg, and Leo Steinberg (the "kings of cultureburg," according to Wolfe). In a *Time* article, Robert Hughes suggested that "the New York art world, especially in its present decay, is the easiest target a pop sociologist could ask for. Most of it is a wallow of egotism, social climbing and power brokerage, and the only thing that makes it tolerable is the occasional reward of experiencing a good work of art in all its richness, complexity and difficulty." Hughes continued: "Take the art from the art world, as Wolfe does, and the matrix becomes fit for caricature. Since Wolfe is unable to show any intelligent response to painting, caricature is what we get . . . . Wolfe seems to know virtually nothing about the history of art, American or European."

New York Times art critic John Russell, writing in the *New York Times Book Review,* stated: "If someone who is tone-deaf goes to Carnegie Hall every night of the year, he is, of course, entitled to his opinion of what he has listened to, just as a eunuch is entitled to his opinion of sex. But in the one case, as in the other, we on our side are entitled to discount what they say. Given the range, the variety and the degree of accomplishment represented by the names on Mr. Wolfe's list [including artists such as Pollock, de Kooning, Warhol, Newman, Rauschenberg, and Stella], we are entitled to think that if he got no visual reward from any of them . . . the fault may not lie with the art."

As Ruth Berenson of the *National Review* pointed out, however, response to the book is generally dependent on the extent to which an individual is involved in the world of modern art. She maintained that *The Painted Word* "will delight those who have long harbored dark suspicions that modern art beginning with Picasso is a put-on, a gigantic hoax perpetrated on a gullible public by a mysterious cabal of artists, critics, dealers, and collectors aided and abetted by *Time* and *Newsweek.* Those who take modern art somewhat more seriously will be disappointed."

In *From Bauhaus to Our House,* Wolfe does to modern architecture what he did to modern art in *The Painted Word,* and the response was similar: Readers close to the subject tended to resent the intrusion by an "outsider," while those further from the subject often enjoyed the author's perspective. *New York Times* architecture critic Paul Goldberger, in a *New York Times Book Review* article, wrote: "Mr. Wolfe wants to argue that ideology has gotten in the way of common sense . . . . We are told how the International Style became a 'compound'—a select, private, cult-like group of ideologues . . . . whose great mission, as Mr. Wolfe sees it, was to foist modern design upon an unwilling world . . . . The problem, I think . . . is that Tom Wolfe has no eye. He has a wonderful ear, and he listens hard and long, but he does not seem to see . . . . He does precisely what he warns us against; he has listened to the words, not looked at the architecture."

In a *Washington Post Book World* review, *Post* architecture critic Benjamin Forgey said that *Bauhaus* "is a case of crying Wolfe for one more time. *Bauhaus* is distinguished by the same total loathing of modern culture that motivated *The Painted Word.* . . . Wolfe's explanation is that modernism has been a conspiracy. In place of the New York critics who foisted abstract art upon us, we have the European giants of architecture . . . . and their abject American followers." Forgey felt that "there is some truth in this, but it makes for a thin book and a narrow, limited history of architecture in the twentieth century."

New York Times literary critic Lehmann-Haupt made the point that even many architects have been unhappy with the structures created by proponents of the Bauhaus school. Thus, according to Lehmann-Haupt, "Wolfe has not really come up with anything very startling when he laments the irony that four-fifths of the way into the American Century . . . what we still see inflicted upon us [are] the anti-bourgeois, socialist, proworker ideas that arose from 'the smoking rubble of Europe after the Great War.' But the explication of this notion is done with such verve and hilarity by Mr. Wolfe that its substance almost doesn't seem to matter." John Brooks, in a review for Chicago's *Tribune Books,* called the book "a readable polemic on how in our architecture over the past few decades things have gone very much as they have in the other visual arts—a triumph of conformity over true innovation . . . *From Bauhaus to Our House* is lucidly and for the most part gracefully written."

In 1979 Wolfe published the book that many critics consider his finest piece of extended journalism: *The Right Stuff,* a 1980 National Book award-winning study of the early years of the U.S. space program. At one point in the book Wolfe attempts to define the "ineffable quality" from which the title is taken: "It obviously involved bravery. But it was not bravery in the simple sense of being willing to risk your life . . . . any fool could do that . . . . No, the idea . . . seemed to be that a man should have the ability to go up in a hurtling piece of machinery and put his hide on the line and then have the moxie, the reflexes, the experience, the coolness, to pull it back in the last yawning moment—and then to go up again *the next day,* and the next day, and every next day."

The main characters in the book are, of course, the first U.S. astronaut team: Scott Carpenter, Gordon Cooper, John Glenn, Gus Grissom, Wally Schirra, Alan Shepard, and Deke Slayton. Wolfe assiduously chronicles their early careers as test pilots, their private lives, their selection for the astronaut program and their subsequent medical processing and training. But, as *Commonweal* correspondent Thomas Powers pointed out, *The Right Stuff* "is not a history; it is far too thin in dates, facts and source citations to serve any such pulse. It is a work of literature which must stand or fall as a coherent text, and its subject is not the Mercury program itself but the impulse behind it, the unreflecting competitiveness which drove the original astronauts to the quite extraordinary lengths Wolfe describes so vividly." That the author goes beyond mere reportage of historical fact was confirmed by Mort Sheinman in a *Chicago Tribune* article: "*The Right Stuff* is a dazzling piece of work, something that reveals much about the nature of bravery and celebrity and—yes—patriotism."

Time writer R.Z. Sheppard said that the book "is crammed with inside poop and racy incident that nineteen years ago was ignored by what [Wolfe] terms the 'proper Victorian gents' of the press. The fast cars, booze, astro groupies, the envies and injuries of the military caste system were not part of what Americans would have considered the right stuff. Wolfe lays it all out in brilliantly stated Op Lit scenes." Christopher Lehmann-Haupt wrote in the *New York Times* wrote, "What fun it is to watch Mr. Wolfe put the antiseptic space program into the traces of his inimitable verbal cadenzas."

Former test pilot and astronaut Michael Collins (a member of the *Gemini 10* flight and command module pilot on the Apollo 11 moon flight) wrote in a *Washington Post Book World* review: "I lived at Edwards [Air Force Base, site of the Air Force Flight Test Center] for four years, and, improbable as some of Tom's tales seem, I know he's telling it like it was. He is the first gifted writer to explore the relationship between test pilots and astronauts—the obvious similarities and the subtle differences."

In a review of *The Right Stuff* for the *Lone Star Book Review,* Martha Heimberg noted that for the most part, "Wolfe's reporting, while being marvelously entertaining writing, has also represented a telling and trustworthy point of view. His is one of those finely critical intelligences that can detect the slightest pretention or falsification in an official posture or social pose. And, when he does, he goes after the hypocrisy—whether large or small, left or right—with all the zeal of the dedicated reformer." Like Collins, Heimberg felt that *The Right Stuff* "represents a departure for the satirist whose observant eye and caustic pen have impaled on the page a wide range of American social phenomena." She concluded that "the book represents a tremendous accomplishment and a new direction for a writer who figures among the top stylists of his generation."

By the mid-1980s Wolfe had a new ambition for his writing. As he told the *New York Times:* "I was curious, having spouted off so much about fiction and nonfiction, and having said that the novelists weren't doing a good job, to see what would happen if I tried it. Also, I guess I subconsciously had the suspicion that maybe, what if all this to-do I've made about nonfiction is because I really, secretly think I can't do a novel. So I said, well, I've got to prove this to myself." The result was *The Bonfire of the Vanities,* a novel about New York City in the 1980s.

The Bonfire of the Vanities ignited a veritable firestorm of critical commentary. Some hailed the novel as a stellar example of what fiction about late-twentieth-century America should be; others derided it as exaggerated, stereotyped, and even mean-spirited. Much of the negative analysis centered on the novel's depiction of race relations, stemming from the implication of a smug Wall Streeter named Sherman McCoy in the hit-and-run traffic death of a young black man. But race is only one of the novel's huge themes; it also takes on, in the words of *Boston Globe* reviewer Mark Feeney, "money . . . politics, the courts, Wall Street, the press: New York at its grandest and most wretched." Many critics felt that Wolfe's treatment of African Americans in the book is insensitive at best. As Feeney observed, "they comprise either a great silent majority . . . or, worst of all, self-aggrandizing hustlers" whose inner lives Wolfe never begins to reveal. "Cheap accusations of racism are almost as contemptible as racism itself," Feeney concluded, adding that "a novel as good as *The Bonfire of the Vanities*—as vivid, as acute, as deeply intelligent—should not have its rancid streak, however narrow, pass unnoticed." Wolfe, however, defended his take on race. "There's been the occasional murmur that there's something wrong with my depiction of these various ethnic and racial elements, these hostilities," he admitted in an interview with Gail Caldwell in the *Boston Globe.*"To which I say, anyone who doesn't think this is exactly the way it is, you go out and take a look, and come back with your notes and tell me what you saw. And I think you'll come back with the same picture I did."

Washington Post Book World reviewer Jonathan Yardley was among those who found Wolfe's picture in *The Bonfire of the Vanities* to be stunningly accurate. He called the book "a superb human comedy and the first novel ever to get contemporary New York, in all its arrogance and shame and heterogeneity and insularity, exactly right." This opinion stood the test of time; in a later *Washington Post Book World* piece on Wolfe's second novel, Yardley declared *Bonfire* to be "the benchmark American novel of the 1980s, a book that added phrases to the language . . . and significantly altered the way Americans, or at least those who read books and take them seriously, see themselves and their country. It was a book the popularity and influence of which are beyond measure."

After *The Bonfire of the Vanities* became a major best-seller, Wolfe issued what he called a "literary manifesto" in *Harper's* magazine, prompting expected controversy from the literary establishment. He urged fellow novelists to abandon the esoteric literary experiments that have characterized fiction for much of the twentieth century and use realism to chronicle the bizarre and astounding world around them. "At this weak, pale, tabescent moment in the history of American literature," he wrote, "we need a battalion, a brigade, of Zolas to head out into this wild, bizarre, unpredictable, hog-stomping baroque country of ours and reclaim its literary property."

Wolfe attempted such a task in his sprawling second novel, *A Man in Full.* It presents the same vast canvas as *Bonfire* and confronts the same themes—greed, power, race, class—this time against the backdrop of 1990s Atlanta, where, as *Los Angeles Times* critic Richard Eder observed, "boom is shadowed by bust and the party-givers rub shoulders with the party-poopers: in this case a bank collection team that coldly asset-strips a real estate tycoon with debts of more than half a billion dollars." The novel's plot centers on Charlie Croker, the man to which the title refers—an uncouth ex-college-football star who has made a fortune in shady real estate deals and has elbowed his way into the upper echelons of Atlanta society. Now, however, Charlie is in deep trouble: he's late in paying back the millions he borrowed to finance even grander ambitions. As Charlie scrambles to save face and fortune, a vast array of secondary characters are drawn into the mix, including high-ranking members of "White Establishment" Atlanta: Roger White II, a member of the black elite disparagingly known as "Roger Too White" behind his back; Fareek "the Cannon" Fanon, a star athlete at Georgia Tech who grew up in one of Atlanta's toughest neighborhoods and is handling his success with obnoxious arrogance; Conrad Hensley, an unskilled worker laid off from Croker's wholesale food business; and mild-mannered Raymond Peepgass, an ambitious underling at the bank that is threatening to destroy Croker. Eder enjoyed Wolfe's "comically squalid and megalomaniacal characters, drawn with an acutely detailed realism that blurs into hyper reality," and pointed out that the author "works into a coolly penetrating understanding of the life of some of America's underclasses and the way in which even hope is stacked against them." Yet even so, in Eder's view, Wolfe's sympathy "fights a losing battle with his irony." Accusing Wolfe of heartlessness an d some "incoherence of intent and tone," Eder concluded that his huge novel is too cold and unwieldy to succeed as satire. John Leonard, in the *Nation,* chastised Wolfe as "a right-wing Andy Warhol" whose satire of gay issues in the novel reveals even more nastiness than in *The Bonfire of the Vanities.*

Others, however, felt that the flaws in *A Man in Full* are relatively insignificant compared to its strengths. "The novel contains passages as powerful and as beautiful as anything written not merely by contemporary American novelists but by any American novelist," declared Michael Lewis in the *New York Times Book Review.* Yardley hailed the novel as "an expansive, energetic, ambitious, bumptious book, flawed in much the same way its predecessor was, but big in the same way, too." The novel's triumph, according to *New Criterion* writer James Bowman, is its ability to "put the circus of business and civic life in late twentieth-century America into a moral context which does not sound foreign or artificial in spite of its provenance in ancient Rome." And Matthew Cooper in *Washington Monthly* observed that "this is an extraordinary novel: for its comedy, for its scope, for the way it evokes the Clinton '90s, a time and place of prosperity but relative unease. *Bonfire of the Vanities* was a warmup act. *A Man in Full* represents Wolfe at his best."

Wolfe returned to the essay form in *Hooking Up,* a collection of miscellaneous pieces on topics from neuroscientific breakthroughs to the contemporary art scene, and including a response to the criticism of *A Man in Full.* A *Publishers Weekly* reviewer deemed the book "arch, vengeful and incisive as ever," while *South Florida Sun-Sentinel* critic Chauncey Mabe commented that it shows Wolfe "at his best and at his worst, often in the same piece." To quote Malcolm Jones in *Newsweek,* "Wolfe may have made millions off his fiction, but at heart he is and always will be a reporter. 'Hooking Up' provides a great introduction to Wolfe the nonfiction stylist."

Although there can be no question that Wolfe has achieved a reputation as a superb stylist and skillful reporter, no discussion of Wolfe would be complete without some mention of his famous wardrobe. *Philadelphia Bulletin* writer Leslie Bennetts tells of an encounter with the author when he lectured at Villanova University: "The legendary sartorial splendors were there, of course: the gorgeous three-piece creamy white suit he has been renowned for . . . not to mention the navy suede shoes, dark as midnight, or the jaunty matching suede hat, or the sweeping midnight cashmere coat of the exact same hue, or the crisp matching tie on which perched a golden half-moon pin to complement the glittering gold watch chain that swung gracefully from the milky vest." Wolfe told Bennetts that he began wearing the white suits in 1962: "That was when I had a white suit made, started wearing it in January, and found it annoyed people tremendously. Even slight departures in dress at that time really spun people out. So I liked it. It's kind of a harmless form of aggression, I guess." But Wolfe's mode of dress has also been an important part of his journalism, serving as a device to distance him from his subject. He told Susan Forrest of the *Fort Lauderdale News:* "A writer can find out more if he doesn't pretend to be hip . . . . If people see you are an outsider, they will come up and tell you things. If you're trying to be hip, you can't ask a lot of naive questions." This technique has been effective for Wolfe in interviewing stock car racers, Hell's Angels, and—particularly—astronauts. He feels that at least part of the success of *The Right Stuff* was due to the fact that he did not try to get too close to that inner circle. Wolfe told Janet Maslin in the *New York Times Book Review:* "I looked like Ruggles of Red Gap to them, I'm sure . . . . But I've long since given up on the idea of going into a situation trying to act like part of it."

A writer for *Time* called Wolfe's form of dress "a splendiferous advertisement for his individuality. The game requires a lot of reverse spin and body English but it boils down to antichic chic. Exclaims Wolfe proudly: 'I own no summer house, no car, I wear tank tops when I swim, long white pants when I play tennis, and I'm probably the last man in America to still do the Royal Canadian Air Force exercises.'"

Wolfe's next novel, *I Am Charlotte Simmons,* takes on the American university. Much like his previous works, however, the book focuses on the status-based interplay of its characters. The title character is an Appalachian honor student who earns a scholarship to the exclusive (yet fictional) Dupont University. Her religious country upbringing has left Charlotte ill-prepared for Wolfe's version of the college experience. The three men she dates at Dupont are male archetypes, the jock, the frat-guy, and the intellectual. The plot thus revolves around Charlotte's relationships with these men, the men's relationship to one another, and the conflict between the characters' baser desires and supposedly higher minds.

Many critics felt that the book was not as successful as Wolfe's other efforts. Wolfe is renowned for his aural writing, yet critics lamented the curse-laden dialogue and felt the country patois of Charlotte and her family was overwrought. Sam Leith, writing in *Spectator* noted that this resulted in "patronising descriptions of Charlotte's hick family." Critics also felt the characters were too stereotypical, and that Charlotte was not a fully realized character. According to *Village Voice* critic Joy Press, Wolfe "defines" his protagonist "more by which guys are in love with her than by anything that springs out of her mouth."

Nevertheless, one of the most intriguing aspects of the book is the juxtaposition of the university as a place of ideas that is simultaneously a place of debauchery. Stereotypical or not, "each of the characters discovers that, for better or worse, ideas really do move the world," noted Sam Schulman in *Commentary.* While Wolfe may be known for a journalistic style that illuminates American subcultures, Schulman noted that the author departs from this tradition. He stated, "Wolfe's earlier novels were about human passions and frailties, illuminated against a sharply observed social background. *I Am Charlotte Simmons,* is different. It is a novel of ideas, a philosophical novel."

"Whatever his future literary offerings, Wolfe thus far has delivered a bursting portfolio of provocative observations and thoughts," mused Kallan. "When students of American culture look back on the last third of the twentieth century, Wolfe may well be the person toward whom they turn. More than any other fiction or nonfiction writer, he has recorded in detail the popular mentality of the period. For this reason his essays seem certain to be restudied. Already, signs of reevaluation and discussion of his work are evident: once criticism focused on Wolfe's writing style and his school of journalism, but now it looks more to the meaning and implications of his message." In *Commentary,* Midge Decter commended Wolfe for his "enormous intelligence and cultivation," adding that, over the course of the author's career "it all began to come together: the fearless inquiring mind, the wicked eye, and the cooling—though never to be really cooled —prose." The critic concluded that, especially as a novelist, Wolfe has "finally broken through from a very high order of shrewdness to a deep and truly affecting intelligence."

BIOGRAPHICAL AND CRITICAL SOURCES:

BOOKS

Authors in the News, Volume 2, Gale (Detroit, MI), 1976.

Bellamy, Joe David, editor, *The New Fiction: Interviews with Innovative American Writers,* University of Illinois Press (Champaign, IL), 1974.

Bestsellers 89, Issue 1, Gale (Detroit, MI), 1989.

Contemporary Literary Criticism, Gale (Detroit, MI), Volume 1, 1973, Volume 2, 1974, Volume 9, 1978, Volume 15, 1980, Volume 35, 1985, Volume 51, 1989.

Dennis, Everette E., *The Magic Writing Machine: Student Probes of the New Journalism,* School of Journalism, University of Oregon (Eugene, OR), 1971.

Dictionary of Literary Biography, Gale (Detroit, MI), Volume 152: *American Novelists since World War II, Fourth Series,* 1995, pp. 299-307, Volume 185: *American Literary Journalists, 1945-1995, First Series,* 1997, pp. 334-342.

Fact and Fiction: The New Journalism and the Nonfiction Novel, University of North Carolina Press (Chapel Hill, NC), 1977.

Hellmann, John, *Fables of Fact: The New Journalism as New Fiction,* University of Illinois Press (Urbana, IL), 1981.

McKeen, William, *Tom Wolfe,* Prentice Hall (Englewood Cliffs, NJ), 1995.

Scura, Dorothy, editor, *Conversations with Tom Wolfe,* University Press of Mississippi (Jackson, MS), 1990.

Wolfe, Tom, *The Kandy-Kolored Tangerine-Flake Streamline Baby* (essays), self illustrated, Farrar, Straus & Giroux (New York, NY), 1965.

Wolfe, Tom, *A Man in Full,* Farrar, Straus & Giroux (New York, NY), 1998.

PERIODICALS

America, February 5, 1977; April 2, 1988; January 30, 1999, Ronald Wendling, review of *A Man in Full,* p. 29.

American Journalism Review, October, 1994, pp. 40-46.

American Journal of Sociology, November, 1983, pp. 739-741.

American Libraries, July-August, 1990, p. 644.

American Spectator, January, 1999, John O. O'Sullivan, review of *A Man in Full,* p. 64.

Atlantic, October, 1979; December, 1987.

Best Sellers, August, 1975.

Booklist, October 1, 2000, Brad Hooper, review of *Hooking Up,* p. 291.

Books and Art, September 28, 1979.

Books in Canada, April, 1988.

Boston Globe, October 18, 1987, Mark Feeney, review of *The Bonfire of the Vanities,* p. A11; November 13, 1987, Gail Caldwell, "Vanities, the Novel, & Wolfe: The Social Chronicler Turns His Hand to Fiction," p. 51.

Business Week, November 23, 1987.

Chicago Tribune, September 9, 1979; September 15, 1979; January 16, 1983; November 4, 1987.

Christian Science Monitor, November 17, 1970; November 3, 1987.

Chronicle of Higher Education, November 13, 2004, Elaine Showalter, review of *I Am Charlotte Simmons,* p. B14.

Columbia Journalism Review, winter, 1966, pp. 29-34; July-August, 1972, pp. 45-47.

Commentary, March, 1971; May, 1977; February, 1980; February, 1988; February 1999, Christopher Caldwell, review of *A Man in Full,* p. 61; January, 2001, Midge Decter, review of *Hooking Up,* p. 62; January, 2005, Sam Schulman review of *I Am Charlotte Simmons,* p. 67.

Commonweal, September 17, 1965; December 20, 1968; March 3, 1978; October 12, 1979; February 26, 1988; May 7, 1999, Rand Richards Cooper, "Tom Wolfe, Material Boy," p. 11.

Communication Monographs, number 46, 1979, pp. 52-62.

Critical Studies in Mass Communication, March, 1984, pp. 51-65.

Detroit News, October 14, 1979; November 9, 1980.

Economist, December 22, 1990, p. 120.

Encounter, September, 1977.

Entertainment Weekly, November 1, 1999, Jeff Gordinier, "The 100 Greatest Entertainers," p. 93; November 10, 2000, Benjamin Svetkey, review of *Hooking Up,* p. 78.

Esquire, September, 2000, Sven Birkerts, "Tom Wolfe. (What?) Tom Wolfe. (Can't Hear You.) Tom Wolfe!!!!," p. 118.

Fort Lauderdale Sentinel, April 22, 1975.

Globe and Mail (Toronto), December 5, 1987.

Guardian Weekly, February 21, 1988.

Harper's, February, 1971; November, 1989; January, 1990.

Journal of American Culture, summer, 1990, pp. 39-50; fall, 1991.

Journal of Popular Culture, summer, 1974, pp. 71-79; summer, 1975; fall, 1984, pp. 111-115.

Library Journal, August, 1968; February 15, 1995, p. 199; February 1, 1999, Barbara Valle, review of *A Man in Full,* p. 137; November 15, 2000, Nathan Ward, review of *Hooking Up,* p. 70.

Listener, February 11, 1988.

London Review of Books, February 18, 1988.

Lone Star Book Review, November, 1979.

Los Angeles Times, October 19, 1979; November 22, 1987; October 12, 1989.

Los Angeles Times Book Review, November 2, 1980; October 25, 1981; October 17, 1982; January 23, 1983; October 25, 1987; November 8, 1998, Richard Eder, review of *A Man in Full,* p. 2.

Nation, March 5, 1977; November 3, 1977; January 28, 1991, p. 100; January 11, 1999, John Leonard, review of *A Man in Full,* p. 32.

National Review, August 27, 1968; January 26, 1971; August 1, 1975; February 19, 1977; December 18, 1987; November 23, 1998, Richard Lowry, review of *A Man in Full,* p. 50.

New Criterion, January, 1999, James Bowman, review of *A Man in Full,* p. 67.

New Leader, January 31, 1977.

New Republic, July 14, 1965; December 19, 1970; November 23, 1987.

New Statesman, February 12, 1988.

New Statesman & Society, November 20, 1998, William Geordiades, review of *A Man in Full,* p. 49.

Newsweek, June 28, 1965; August 26, 1968; June 9, 1975; September 17, 1979; October 26, 1987; December 28, 1998, Malcolm Jones and Ray Sawhill, review of *A Man in Full,* p. 82; March 15, 1999, "Crying Wolfe," p. 8; November 13, 2000, Malcolm Jones, "Ace Reporter," p. 84.

New York, September 21, 1981; March 21, 1988; January 7, 1991, p. 64.

New Yorker, February 1, 1988; January 25, 1999, Rebecca Mead, review of *A Man in Full,* p. 26.

New York Review of Books, August 26, 1965, pp. 3-5; February 3, 1966, pp. 18-24; December 17, 1970; June 26, 1975; January 20, 1977; October 28, 1979; November 4, 1982; February 4, 1988; February 8, 2001, Benjamin DeMott, review of *Hooking Up,* p. 22.

New York Times, November 25, 1970; May 27, 1975; November 26, 1976; September 14, 1979; October 9, 1981; December 20, 1981; October 13, 1987; October 22, 1987; November 21, 1987; December 31, 1987; January 3, 1988; March 11, 1988; October 28, 1998, Michiko Kakutani, review of *A Man in Full.*

New York Times Book Review, June 27, 1965, pp. 4, 38; August 18, 1968; November 29, 1970; December 3, 1972; June 15, 1975; December 26, 1976; October 28, 1979; October 11, 1981; October 10, 1982; November 1, 1987; November 8, 1998, Michael Lewis, review of *A Man in Full;* November 5, 2000, Maureen Down, review of *Hooking Up,* p. 45; November 28, 2004, Jacob Weisberg, review of *I Am Charlotte Simmons,* p. 13.

Observer (London, England), February 7, 1988.

Partisan Review, number 3, 1969, pp. 535-544; number 2, 1974.

People, December 24, 1979; November 23, 1987; November 20, 2000, review of *Hooking Up.*

Philadelphia Bulletin, February 10, 1975.

Publishers Weekly, August 6, 1999, "Keeping the Wolfe at the Door," p. 315; October 2, 2000, review of *Hooking Up,* p. 69; November 13, 2000, "Look, Ma, No Title," p. 22.

Punch, February 12, 1988.

Rolling Stone, August 21, 1980; November 5-December 10, 1987.

Saturday Review, September 15, 1979; April, 1981.

Southern Cultures, summer, 1999, John Shelton Reed, review of *A Man in Full,* p. 92.

South Florida Sun-Sentinel, November 15, 2000, Chauncey Mabe, review of *Hooking Up.*

Spectator, February 13, 1988; November 13, 2004, Sam Leith, review of *I Am Charlotte Simmons,* p. 42.

Time, September 6, 1968; December 21, 1970; June 23, 1975; December 27, 1976; September 29, 1979; November 9, 1987; February 13, 1989; November 27, 1989.

Times (London, England), February 11, 1988; February 13, 1989; April 22, 1989.

Times Literary Supplement, October 1, 1971; November 30, 1979; November 26, 1980; March 18, 1988.

Tribune Books (Chicago, IL), December 7, 1980; October 25, 1981; January 16, 1983; August 2, 1987; October 18, 1987.

U.S. News and World Report, November 23, 1987; December 25, 1989, p. 117.

Village Voice, September 10, 1979; November 17, 2004, Joy Press, review of *I Am Charlotte Simmons,* p. C79.

Wall Street Journal, October 29, 1987.

Washington Monthly, March, 1988; December, 1998, Matthew Cooper, review of *A Man in Full,* p. 36.

Washington Post, September 4, 1979; October 23, 1980; March 27, 1988; October 17, 1989.

Washington Post Book World, September 9, 1979; November 23, 1980; November 15, 1981; November 7, 1982; October 25, 1987; November 1, 1998, Jonathan Yardley, review of *A Man in Full,* p. 3.

Writer's Digest, January, 1970.

ONLINE

Tom Wolfe Home Page, http://www.tomwolfe.com/ (January 30, 2001).

* * *

WOLFF, Tobias 1945-
(Tobias Jonathan Ansell Wolff)

PERSONAL: Born June 19, 1945, in Birmingham, AL; son of Arthur Saunders (an aeronautical engineer) and Rosemary (Loftus) Wolff; married Catherine Dolores

Spohn (a clinical social worker), 1975; children: Michael, Patrick, Mary Elizabeth. *Education:* Oxford University, B.A. (with first-class honors), 1972, M.A., 1975; Stanford University, M.A., 1978.

ADDRESSES: Office—Department of English, Stanford University, Stanford, CA 94305-2087. *Agent*—Amanda Urban, International Creative Management, 40 West 57th St., New York, NY 10019.

CAREER: Stanford University, Stanford, CA, Jones Lecturer in Creative Writing, 1975-78; Syracuse University, Syracuse, NY, Peck Professor of English, 1980-97; Stanford University, Stanford, CA, Ward W. and Priscilla B. Woods Professor of English, 1997—. Member of faculty at Goddard College, Plainfield, VT, and Arizona State University, Tempe. Former reporter for *Washington Post. Military service:* U.S. Army, 1964-68 (Special Forces, 1965-67); served in Vietnam; became first lieutenant.

MEMBER: PEN, Associated Writing Programs.

AWARDS, HONORS: Wallace Stegner fellowship in creative writing, 1975-76; National Endowment for the Arts fellowship in creative writing, 1978 and 1985; Mary Roberts Rinehart grant, 1979; Arizona Council on the Arts and Humanities fellowship in creative writing, 1980; Guggenheim fellowship, 1982; St. Lawrence Award for Fiction, 1982, for *In the Garden of the North American Martyrs;* PEN/Faulkner Award for Fiction, 1985, for *The Barracks Thief;* Rea Award for short story, 1989; *Los Angeles Times* Book Prize for biography, and National Book Critics Circle Award finalist, both 1989, and Ambassador Book Award of the English-speaking Union, all for *This Boy's Life: A Memoir;* Whiting Foundation Award, 1990; Lila Wallace-*Reader's Digest* Award, 1993; Lyndhurst Foundation Award, 1994; National Book Award finalist, and Esquire-Volvo-Waterstone's Prize for Nonfiction (England), both 1994, and *Los Angeles Times* Book Award for biography finalist, 1995, all for *In Pharaoh's Army: Memories of the Lost War;* National Book Critics Circle Award nomination in fiction category, and *Los Angeles Times* Book Award nomination, both 2003, and PEN/Faulkner Award nomination in fiction category, John Gardner Memorial Book Award, and Northern California Book Award, all 2004, all for *Old School.*

WRITINGS:

Ugly Rumours, Allen & Unwin (London, England), 1975.

In the Garden of the North American Martyrs (short stories), Ecco Press (New York, NY), 1981, published as *Hunters in the Snow* (also see below), J. Cape (London, England), 1982.

(Editor) *Matters of Life and Death: New American Stories,* Wampeter (Green Harbor, ME), 1982.

The Barracks Thief (novella; also see below), Ecco Press (New York, NY), 1984, published as *The Barracks Thief and Other Stories,* Bantam (New York, NY), 1984.

Back in the World (short stories; also see below), Houghton Mifflin (Boston, MA), 1985.

(Editor) *A Doctor's Visit: The Short Stories of Anton Chekhov,* Bantam (New York, NY), 1987.

The Stories of Tobias Wolff (contains *Hunters in the Snow, Back in the World,* and *The Barracks Thief*), Picador (London, England), 1988.

This Boy's Life: A Memoir, Atlantic Monthly Press (New York, NY), 1989.

(Editor) *The Picador Book of Contemporary American Stories,* Picador (London, England), 1993.

(Editor and author of introduction) *The Vintage Book of Contemporary American Short Stories,* Random House (New York, NY), 1994.

In Pharaoh's Army: Memories of the Lost War (memoir), Knopf (New York, NY), 1994.

(Editor) *Best American Short Stories,* Houghton Mifflin (Boston, MA), 1994.

The Night in Question: Stories, Knopf (New York, NY), 1996.

(Editor and author of introduction) *Writers Harvest 3,* Dell (New York, NY), 2000.

Old School (novel), Knopf (New York, NY), 2003.

Contributor to periodicals, including *Atlantic, New Yorker, Granta, Story, Esquire,* and *Antaeus.*

ADAPTATIONS: This Boy's Life: A Memoir was made into the movie *This Boy's Life,* 1993, produced by Art Linson, directed by Michael Caton-Jones, starring Robert De Niro as Wolff's stepfather, Ellen Barkin as Wolff's mother, and Leonardo DiCaprio playing Wolff as a teenager.

SIDELIGHTS: Tobias Wolff, a short story writer, novelist, memoirist, editor, and journalist, has received critical acclaim since the publication of his first collection of short stories in 1981. Both *Los Angeles Times* book reviewer James Kaufman and *New Statesman* contributor Bill Greenwell labeled the stories collected in *In the Garden of the North American Martyrs* "impressive," and Chicago's *Tribune Books* writer Bruce Allen deemed Wolff's work "one of the most acclaimed short-story collections within memory." In the twelve tales that comprise *In the Garden of the North American Martyrs,* according to *Nation* reviewer Brina Caplan, Wolff "scrutinizes the disorders of daily living to find significant order; in the best of [these] stories . . . he informs us not only of what happened but of why it had to happen as it did. . . . Distant in age, class and geography, [his characters] have in common lives crowded with the results of previous choices." *Best Sellers* reviewer James C. Dolan advised readers to "relax and enter into the sometimes comic, always compassionate world of ordinary people who suffer twentieth-century martyrdoms of growing up, growing old, loving and lacking love, living with parents and lovers and wives and their own weaknesses."

Among the characters of *In the Garden of the North American Martyrs*—all of whom, claimed Alane Rollings in Chicago's *Tribune Books,* readers can "care for"—are a teenage boy who tells morbid lies about his home life, a timid professor who, in the first genuine outburst of her life, pours out her opinions in spite of a protesting audience, a prudish loner who gives an obnoxious hitchhiker a ride, and an elderly couple on a golden anniversary cruise who endure the offensive conviviality of the ship's social director. Rollings concluded that Wolff's "ironic dialog, misfit heroes, and haphazard events play beautifully off the undercurrent drift of the searching inner mood which wins over in the end." *New York Times Book Review* critic Le Ann Schreiber admired Wolff's avoidance of "the emotional and stylistic monotone that constricts so many collections of contemporary short stories," pointing out that "his range, sometimes within the same story, extends from fastidious realism to the grotesque and the lyrical. . . . He allows [his] characters scenes of flamboyant madness as well as quiet desperation, moments of slap-happiness as well as muted contentment." In addition, observing that the time covered by the collection's stories varies from a few hours to two decades, Schreiber declared Wolff's vision "so acute" and his talent "so refined" that "none of them seems sketchy" and that, in fact, they evoke our "amazed appreciation."

Wolff's novella *The Barracks Thief* won the prestigious PEN/Faulkner Award as the best work of fiction of 1984. Linda Taylor maintained in her review of the work for the *Times Literary Supplement* that *The Barracks Thief* "is a book to be taken in all at once: the ingenuousness of the narration and the vulnerability of the characters are disarmingly seductive." Narrated retrospectively by one of three paratroopers stationed at Fort Bragg, North Carolina, during the Vietnam years, the story focuses on an event that leaves a lasting impression on the trio. Assigned to guard a nearby ammunition dump on a steamy Fourth of July evening in 1967, they face the threat of an approaching forest fire. The temptation to allow the dump to ignite and explode proves exhilarating and unites them in a bond of friendship. "The world of *The Barracks Thief* contains no answers," observed *New York Times* reviewer Walter Kendricks. "We are left to make up our own minds whether it is better to die spectacularly or to dribble on for decades in safe conventionality." Kendricks also hailed Wolff's "boundless tolerance for the stupid sorrow of ordinary human entanglements" and his "command of eloquent detail." *America* critic Andre Dubus concluded, "If words on paper could make sounds, you would hear me shouting now, urging you to read this book."

Wolff's 1985 short-story collection, *Back in the World,* derives its title from the expression used by servicemen during the Vietnam War to refer to post-war life at home in the United States. The experience of returning home, however, proves more disillusioning than hopeful to the veterans in Wolff's stories. Feeling alienated from society and powerless to change their circumstances, his characters capitulate to whatever life deals them, only briefly—if at all—challenging fate. They seek relief from their cheerless, detached existence in drugs, casual sex, and, as *Tribune Books* contributor Allen saw it, "contriving falsely romantic or interesting versions of themselves and their experiences." *New York Times* reviewer Michiko Kakutani noted that Wolff suggests for these people "the power of some kind of redemption in their fumbling efforts to connect with one another, and even in their sad attempts to shore up their dignity with their pipe dreams and clumsy fictions." This "power of . . . redemption," according to Kakutani, "enables these characters to go on, and it is also what invests these stories with the burnished glow of compassion."

This Boy's Life: A Memoir "is about growing up, as inevitably any such memoir must be," commented Jonathan Yardley in the *Washington Post Book World.* The autobiographical work addresses Wolff's teenage years, when he and his mother moved from Florida to Utah to Washington State to escape her abusive boyfriend. Wolff had lost contact with his father and brother—fellow writer Geoffrey Wolff, author of *The Duke of Deception: Memories of My Father,* an autobiography about his youth spent with their father—following his parents' divorce. In Washington his mother remarried, and Wolff experienced difficulties with his new stepfather. Yardley remarked that, in part, *This Boy's Life* "is the story of what happens to a child when the peculiarities of a mother's romance place him at the mercy of a man who is neither his father nor his protector, but it is not a self-pitying lament and it is not really a tale of abuse and neglect."

New York Times Book Review critic Joel Conarroe praised the literary quality of the book, noting that *This Boy's Life* "reads very much like a collection of short stories, each with its own beginning, middle and end. Lifted from their context, the individual chapters would be at home in the fiction pages of any good magazine." Francine Prose made a similar observation in the *New York Times Magazine:* "Its strategy is novelistic," she noted of the book; "details have been altered, events ordered and edited, to give Wolff's memoir the shape of fiction." Prose added that Wolff "admits to having omitted things from *This Boy's Life*—real events he chose to leave out lest the true account of his life seem too markedly patterned and shaped. 'It would have seemed too contrived,' he says. 'Too much like a novel.'"

Some critics viewed Wolff's acclaimed memoir *In Pharaoh's Army: Memories of the Lost War* as a logical continuation of *This Boy's Life.* However, the author told Nicholas A. Basbanes in a *Publishers Weekly* interview that the book is not a sequel. "I'm a really different person in the new book," Wolff said. "I see it as a story about a young man going off to war, and the kind of moral transformations that take place." The book, which was nominated for the National Book Award in 1994 and received England's Esquire-Volvo-Waterstone's Prize for Nonfiction, recounts Wolff's one-year Vietnam tour of duty in thirteen chapters, or "episodes." Paul Gray commented in *Time* that each of the thirteen chapters "reads like a rigorously boiled-down short story, but the effects never seem artificial or contrived." Gray called the book a "terse, mesmerizing memoir."

While *In Pharaoh's Army* focuses on events that took place during the Vietnam War, as Basbanes noted in *Publishers Weekly,* readers who are "in search of riveting battle scenes will have to look elsewhere; of far greater moment is the maturation of Tobias Wolff. The immature lieutenant who arrives in the war zone returns home as a man ready to spend four years at Oxford University . . . and to begin his life as a writer." Judith Coburn observed in the *Washington Post Book World* that throughout the work Wolff "tells stories, awful, hilarious stories, often at his own expense, of what it was like day-to-day, trying to get by." Although Wolff does not write specifically of atrocity and carnage, critics infer abominations from the very simplicity of his stories. Richard Eder suggested in the *Los Angeles Times Book Review* that "because there was no actual horror, we see more clearly what underlay the horror." While Bawer, in the *New York Times Book Review,* questioned the "limitations" of Wolff's literary style applied to the horrors and intensity of war, he nonetheless stated: "There is a great deal of precise, evocative writing here." Gray commented in *Time* that the war taught Wolff "how to portray life as both desperately serious and perfectly absurd."

The Night in Question collects fourteen short stories in which Wolff's characters search for the essence of life that lies hidden beneath quotidian surfaces. To quote Jay Parini in the *New York Times Book Review,* these protagonists search for "something authentic, something they can unmistakably call their own." Moral judgment is sometimes compromised in these tales, as in "The Chain," where an attack by a vicious dog precipitates an act of revenge that backfires. "Storytellers appear everywhere in the collection," wrote Christopher Lehmann-Haupt in the *New York Times.* "Often they are troublemakers, the enemies of the prevailing moral order. . . . One might even say that the most significant conflict in these stories is that between the moralists and the ironists." A *Kirkus Reviews* contributor noted that "Understatement, irony, and surprising juxtapositions are the key ingredients of these generally accomplished and resonant fictions—the best of which are certainly among the most accomplished being written in our time." Parini concluded that readers of *The Night in Question* "will be stirred by Mr. Wolff's marvelous stories, by their pure unexpectedness and—perhaps most of all—by their music."

Wolff moved to longer fiction in 2003 with his award-winning novel *Old School.* In this book—written, memoir-fashion, in the first person—he deals with growing up and dishonesty, themes that have also resonated throughout his stories as well as his several memoirs. The unnamed protagonist of the novel is an aspiring writer attending a prestigious East Coast boarding school that solicits well-known writers to visit. The year is 1960, when certain literary celebrities held an almost godlike mystique, and none was perhaps more godlike than Ernest Hemingway. It is also an era when the narrator's hidden truth—that he is Jewish—would put him at a disadvantage if it were known, and developing his writing has become a way for him, as Wolff writes, "to escape the problems of blood and class"; writers are beyond politics. His desperation to meet Papa Hemingway in a private conference—a privilege competed for via an essay contest—is thus great, and as he fears exposing his inferior self through his essay he resorts to plagiarism and is ultimately expelled.

Wolff's "hero is cast out of paradise" at the close of *Old School,* wrote *America* contributor John B. Breslin, adding that, "Like the prodigal, he will make his return, in time, as a successful and legitimate writer." Praising the novel as an effective *bildungsroman,* Breslin also commented on the sociological underpinnings of Wolff's novel, particularly the depiction of the mid-twentieth-century prep-school world. While the narrator's teachers and administrators challenge him to excel in the closed world of literature, where words become currency, his insecurities and fear of exposure also illustrate "the unspoken prejudices and self-satisfaction" of this cloistered environment. In another sense, *Old School* "is a nuanced portrayal of a young man falling—and staying—in love with words," as Amy Weldon maintained in her review for the *Carolina Quarterly,* echoing the opinion of Francine Prose who found the novel to be primarily a story of a developing intellect. "Not a word is wasted in this spare, brilliant novel about the way that reading changes and forms our lives," Prose wrote of *Old School* in *People,* "and about how one learns to become a writer—and a conscious human being."

In addition to his writing, Wolff serves as a professor of English and creative writing at Stanford University. In an interview posted on the *Stanford University Web site,* he commented upon the role teaching plays in his working life. "The greater world doesn't really much care whether you write or not," he said. "It doesn't care about the things that I care most about, and here I am surrounded by people who love writing, who devote their lives to literature and teaching literature and to seeing it as a way of understanding the world and understanding oneself that no other thing can quite afford. That's a very privileged position to be in. Teaching allowed me the time to do my own writing in a way that nothing I'd ever done before had. At a certain point I probably could have lived on my writing and stopped teaching. But I think my life would feel a little empty without it because of the intellectual heat I experience with brilliant young writers and the unexpectedness of what goes on in workshops." "I've learned at least as much from my students as they've learned from me," he concluded. "I know that's a cliché, but it happens in my case to be absolutely true."

BIOGRAPHICAL AND CRITICAL SOURCES:

BOOKS

Hannah, James, *Tobias Wolff: A Study of the Short Fiction,* Twayne (Boston, MA), 1996.

PERIODICALS

America, September 8, 1984, Andre Dubus, review of *The Barracks Thief;* March 22, 2004, John B. Breslin, review of *Old School,* p. 24.

American Heritage, November, 1994, review of *In Pharaoh's Army,* p. 120.

Atlantic, December, 2003, pp. 128-129.

Best Sellers, November, 1981, James C. Dolan, review of *In the Garden of North American Martyrs.*

Bloomsbury Review, March-April, 1995, p. 13.

Booklist, September 1, 1994, p. 2; January 1, 2004, p. 778.

Boston Review, December, 1985.

Carolina Quarterly, winter, 2004, Amy Weldon, review of *Old School,* p. 60.

Entertainment Weekly, November 7, 2003, p. 38; November 21, 2003, p. 90.

Esquire, October, 1994, p. 133.

Globe and Mail (Toronto, Ontario, Canada), February 8, 1986.

Hudson Review, summer, 1982; autumn, 1986.

Kirkus Reviews, August 16, 1996, review of *The Night in Question;* September 1, 2003, p. 1100.

Kliatt, May, 2004, Janet Julian, review of *Old School,* p. 54.

Library Journal, November 1, 2003, pp. 126-127.

Life, September, 1990, p. 95.

Los Angeles Times Book Review, January 3, 1982; November 17, 1985; January 8, 1989, p. 3; November 5, 1989, p. 12; June 6, 1993, p. 15; October 16, 1994, pp. 3, 10.

Mosaic, March, 1999, p. 149.

Nation, February 6, 1982, Brina Caplan, review of *In the Garden of North American Martyrs,* p. 152.

New Leader, November-December, 2003, pp. 37-39.

New Statesman, July 23, 1982, p. 22; August 12, 1983, p. 27; February 9, 2004, Helen Brown, review of *Old School,* p. 52.

Newsweek, January 23, 1989, p. 64; October 24, 1994, p. 78.

New York, April 12, 1993, p. 58.

New York Times, November 25, 1981; October 2, 1985, p. 27; October 28, 1985; October 30, 1985; January 12, 1989; October 3, 1996, Christopher Lehmann-Haupt, "Seizing the Imagination with Moral Questions."

Papers on Language and Literature, spring, 2003, p. 144.

New York Times Book Review, November 15, 1981, p. 11; June 2, 1982; October 17, 1982, p. 45; October 20, 1985, p. 9; October 5, 1986, p. 58; January 15, 1989, p. 1; November 27, 1994, p. 10; November 3, 1996, Jay Parini, "Interior Archeology."

New York Times Magazine, February 5, 1989, Francine Prose, review of *This Boy's Life,* p. 22.

People, October 7, 1985; Janurary 12, 2004, Francine Prose, review of *Old School,* p. 47.

Publishers Weekly, August 29, 1994, p. 55; October 24, 1994, pp. 45-46; August 5, 1996; October 13, 2003, p. 57.
School Library Journal, April, 2004, p. 182.
Seattle Times, December 3, 2003, Michael Upchurch, review of *Old School.*
Time, December 2, 1985, p. 99; February 6, 1989, p. 70; October 31, 1994, p. 81; December 1, 2003, p. 98.
Times (London, England), May 4, 1989; May 11, 1989.
Times Literary Supplement, March 14, 1975, p. 269; July 30, 1982, p. 815; January 24, 1986; November 6, 1987, p. 1227; May 13, 1988, p. 532; May 12, 1989.
Tribune Books (Chicago, IL), October 18, 1981; December 8, 1985; January 22, 1989.
Village Voice, January 31, 1989.
Virginia Quarterly Review, spring, 1982.
Wall Street Journal, January 3, 1989.
Washington Post Book World, December 26, 1982, p. 12; November 3, 1985, p. 5; January 22, 1989, p. 3; November 6, 1994, pp. 3, 12.
Writer's Digest, August, 1989, p. 52.

ONLINE

Continuum Online, http://www.alumni.utah.edu/continuum/ (summer, 1998), Anne Palmer Peterson, "Talking with Tobias Wolff."
New York State Writers Institute Web site, http://www.albany.edu/ (August 16, 2004), "Tobias Wolff."
Salon.com, http://www.salon.com/ (December, 1996), Joan Smith interview with Wolff.
Stanford University Web site, http://www.stanford.edu/ (October 16, 1998), "A Conversation with Tobias Wolff."

* * *

WOLFF, Tobias Jonathan Ansell
See WOLFF, Tobias

* * *

WOODIWISS, Kathleen E. 1939-
(Kathleen Erin Woodiwiss)

PERSONAL: Born June 3, 1939, in Alexandria, LA; daughter of Charles Wingrove, Sr., and Gladys (Coker) Hogg; married Ross Eugene Woodiwiss (a U.S. Air Force major), July 20, 1956 (divorced); children: Sean Alan, Dorren James, Heath Alexander. *Education:* Attended schools in Alexandria, LA. *Politics:* Republican.

ADDRESSES: Home—Princeton, MN. *Office*—c/o Avon Books, 1350 Avenue of the Americas, New York, NY 10019.

CAREER: Writer. Worked as a model in fashion shows in Tokyo, Japan.

WRITINGS:

The Flame and the Flower, Avon (New York, NY), 1972.
The Wolf and the Dove, Avon (New York, NY), 1974.
Shanna, Avon (New York, NY), 1977.
Ashes in the Wind, Avon (New York, NY), 1979.
A Rose in Winter, Avon (New York, NY), 1982.
Come Love a Stranger, Avon (New York, NY), 1984.
So Worthy My Love, Avon (New York, NY), 1989.
Forever in Your Embrace, Avon (New York, NY), 1992, author's preferred edition, 1999.
(With others) *Three Weddings and a Kiss* (anthology), Avon (New York, NY), 1995.
(Editor and contributor) *Married at Midnight,* Avon (New York, NY), 1996.
Petals on the River, Avon (New York, NY), 1997.
A Season beyond a Kiss, Avon (New York, NY), 2000.
The Reluctant Suitor, Morrow (New York, NY), 2003.

ADAPTATIONS: The Flame and the Flower, So Worthy My Love, Petals on the River, and *A Season beyond a Kiss* have been recorded on audio cassette.

WORK IN PROGRESS: A medieval romance set in England and Scotland.

SIDELIGHTS: A pioneering writer of romance fiction, Kathleen E. Woodiwiss's first novel is generally credited with creating the subgenre known as "erotic historical" romance. When *The Flame and the Flower* was published in 1972, the field of romance writing was dominated by "contemporary gothics" produced by writers such as Mary Stewart, Victoria Holt, and Phyllis Whitney. *The Flame and the Flower* differed from its predecessors in that it was substantially longer, but also because it contained lengthy, often detailed passages describing the sexual encounters of the hero and heroine. The immediate success of *The Flame and the Flower* cleared the way for writers like Rosemary Rogers and Laura McBain, authors who, along with Woodiwiss, have helped to make the historical romance an enormously popular form. *The Flame and the Flower* has gone through eighty printings and has sold over four million copies.

The novels following *The Flame and the Flower* continued to be ground-breakers and assured Woodiwiss a large and loyal readership. *Shanna,* Woodiwiss's third book, made publishing history by becoming the first historical romance released in a trade paperback edition, and it went on to sell over three million copies and spend a full year on the *New York Times* bestseller list. In 1979 Avon published *Ashes in the Wind* with a first printing of one-and-a-half million copies; the publisher backed the book with a huge promotional campaign, including full-page advertisements in national women's magazines and commercials on network television. The publicity paid off almost immediately as *Ashes in the Wind* sold over two million copies and went into a third printing within a month of its release. The 2000 release *A Season beyond a Kiss* was launched with a first printing of seven hundred thousand copies and was the first romance novel to top the *Publishers Weekly* paperback bestseller list. In total, over thirty-six million copies of Woodiwiss's books have been sold worldwide.

Historical romances vary in some respects but share fundamental similarities. Settings are typically exotic and frequently change from continent to continent. Heroes are characteristically handsome and commanding, while heroines are beautiful and sensitive. Often innocent, the heroine is usually introduced to the hero with whom she falls in love. *The Flame and the Flower* clearly embodies the traditions of its genre. The heroine, Heather, is a teenager throughout the narrative, which begins in England around 1800 and eventually moves to the American Carolinas. A beautiful and decorous girl who becomes the ward of a cruel aunt, Heather is mistaken for a harlot by an attractive Yankee who, in turn, is forced to marry her. After many adventures, the pair work out their initial hatred for each other and fall in love. *The Flame and the Flower* also maintains the traditional structural relationship of males as dominant over and protective of females.

Where *The Flame and the Flower* and other Woodiwiss novels break with tradition is in their frank depiction of the sexual relationship between the hero and the heroine. While her books contain occasional sexual passages, Woodiwiss says that she is "insulted when my books are called erotic," as she maintained in a *Cosmopolitan* interview. "I don't think people who say that have read my books. I believe I write love stories. With a little spice. Some of the other current romances are a bit savage, though. They make sex dirty. It's embarrassing to read them. But women are looking for the love story. I get a lot of fan mail, and they tell me that." Janice Radway, writing in *Twentieth-Century Romance and Historical Writers,* saw the erotic passages in Woodiwiss's novels as being integral parts of "complex plots which all focus on the *gradual* development of love between the two principal characters. Unlike many writers of this subgenre who keep the heroine and the hero apart until the final pages of the novel, Woodiwiss brings them into contact early in the tale. Having established their initial attraction for each other, she then shows how love develops between two extraordinary individuals, emphasizes that the relationship must be cultivated carefully, and demonstrates that compromise, tenderness, and generosity are necessary to maintain it."

Just such a relationship is presented in Woodiwiss's 1979 novel, *Ashes in the Wind.* This tale features the heroine Alaina MacGaren, a seventeen-year-old orphan who must leave her home in central Louisiana for New Orleans when a rumor is started that she is a traitor. In order to keep her identity a secret, Alaina assumes a number of disguises, including that of a street urchin, a penniless widow, and a hospital volunteer. In the midst of these many identities, the life of surgeon Captain Cole Lattimer becomes entangled with Alaina's, and the two overcome adversity to find a deep and lasting love. Although *Washington Post Book World* contributor Maude McDaniel found *Ashes in the Wind* to be filled with silly characters, a formulaic plot, and awful writing, she went on to conclude, "Actually, I rather enjoyed" the novel. And a *Publishers Weekly* contributor maintained that Woodiwiss "has fashioned her heroine in a picaresque tradition. Readers will find Alaina's spunky ingenuity refreshing."

In Woodiwiss's 1989 romance, *So Worthy My Love,* Maxim Seymour, another alleged traitor, this time to Queen Elizabeth, is thought to be dead. The young man, hated by the noble Radborne family, is actually hiding in Germany, desperately wanting his beloved, Arabella Radborne, to be with him. Sending his men to kidnap her, Maxim is surprised when they bring back Arabella's beautiful cousin Elise by mistake. Unable to let Elise go, the two battle each other defiantly until they realize that they are actually in love. Woodiwiss "provides ripe descriptions" in *So Worthy My Love,* stated a *Publishers Weekly* contributor, adding, "This long romance by a veteran of the genre delivers well-paced, well-structured diversion."

In 1998 Woodiwiss wrote a long-awaited sequel to her first novel, *The Flame and the Flower,* titled *The Elu-*

sive Flame. Woodiwiss picks up the story with Heather and Brandon Birmingham's son, Beauregard, who is a sea captain. The novel tells of Beau's romance with the orphan Cerynise, their tempestuous relationship, their troubles with London scoundrels who have stolen Cerynise's rightful inheritance, and their eventual triumph over all ordeals during a "melodramatic climax in a storm-buffeted house," as a *Publishers Weekly* critic put it. Melanie Duncan, writing in *Booklist,* stated, "Woodiwiss set the standard for excellence in romance novels with *The Flame and the Flower* . . . a standard that current authors still try to meet, and fans have waited 25 years for this wonderful sequel." *The Elusive Flame* enjoyed a first printing of 800,000 copies.

A Season beyond a Kiss, published in 2000, brought back the Birmingham family for the third time. Brandon's younger brother, Jeffrey, has just wed beautiful Raelynn Barrett. Their marriage hits upon rocky times almost immediately when Jeff is accused of getting a young girl pregnant. Despite Jeff's claims of innocence, Raelynn, who wants to believe him, is not sure if he can be trusted. When the young girl in question is murdered, Jeff is found in possession of the murder weapon. He must now try to prove his innocence while going up against a mysterious conspiracy and a vicious murderer.

Woodiwiss published her first hardcover novel, *The Reluctant Suitor,* in 2003. Sixteen years ago, James Colton Wyndham's parents betrothed him to an unattractive young woman, Adriana Elynn Sutton, without either his or Adriana's consent. James ran away, but finally, sixteen years later, he returns. Adriana is still unmarried, and James is thus bound by the terms of the betrothal to court Adriana for three months; at that point, he will be allowed to break the agreement. Adriana has grown to be beautiful, but, fearful of another rejection, she still wants nothing to do with James. Like Woodiwiss's other books, John Charles noted in *Booklist, The Reluctant Suitor* contains "an arrogantly handsome hero, a beautiful naive heroine, [and] a nicely developed cast of scheming secondary characters." *Library Journal* reviewer Kristin Ramsdell also commented on Woodiwiss's "intriguing" supporting cast, "including an especially despicable villain."

Although Woodiwiss's novels are enormously successful with the public, they are generally ignored by "serious" reviewers. This situation does not seem to bother Woodiwiss, however, nor does it make her wish to change her approach to writing. "I never started out to win any prizes for my writing," she related in her interview with Judy Klemesrud in the *New York Times Book Review.* "I wanted to appease a hunger for romantic novels, and that is what I shall continue to do." Woodiwiss similarly pointed out that her books are only an attempt to give readers "enjoyment. Escape. I would like to be able to give the reader a time period of relaxation and pleasure, a time of being able to put the worries and everything aside and just enjoy and relax." She told Giovanna Breu in *People* that her books "are fairy tales. They are an escape for the reader, like an Errol Flynn movie."

For an interview with Woodiwiss, See *Contemporary Authors New Revisions,* Volume 23.

BIOGRAPHICAL AND CRITICAL SOURCES:

BOOKS

Falk, Kathryn, *Love's Leading Ladies,* Pinnacle (New York, NY), 1982.

Twentieth-Century Romance and Historical Writers, 2nd edition, St. James (Detroit, MI), 1990.

PERIODICALS

Booklist, September 15, 1998, Melanie Duncan, review of *The Elusive Flame,* p. 214; July, 2000, Mary McCay, review of *A Season beyond a Kiss* (audiobook), p. 2054; February 15, 2003, John Charles, review of *The Reluctant Suitor,* p. 1058.

Cosmopolitan, February, 1978, interview with Kathleen E. Woodiwiss.

Kirkus Reviews, February 1, 2003, review of *The Reluctant Suitor,* p. 180.

Library Journal, May 15, 1974, p. 1410; February 15, 1995, Jodi L. Israel, review of *Petals on the River,* p. 198; July, 2001, Jodi L. Israel, review of *A Season Beyond a Kiss* (audiobook), p. 149; February 15, 2003, Kristin Ramsdell, review of *The Reluctant Suitor,* p. 124.

New York Times Book Review, November 4, 1979, Judy Klemesrud, interview with Kathleen E. Woodiwiss.

People, February 7, 1983, Giovanna Breu, "Romance Writer Kathleen Woodiwiss Is Passionate about Horses—and Happy Endings," pp. 75-76.

Publishers Weekly, January 21, 1974, p. 88; January 31, 1977; May 30, 1977; September 3, 1979, review of *Ashes in the Wind,* p. 94; October 22, 1982, review of *A Rose in Winter,* p. 51; August 25, 1989, review of *So Worthy My Love,* p. 57; August 24, 1998, Daisy Maryles, "Fanning the Flames," p. 19; August 31, 1998, review of *The Elusive Flame,* p. 50; March 20, 2000, Daisy Maryles and Dick Donahue, "The Flame 28 Years Later," p. 21; February 17, 2003, review of *The Reluctant Suitor,* p. 56.

Romance Reader, August 28, 1998, review of *The Elusive Flame.*

Village Voice, May 9, 1977.

Washington Post Book World, April 9, 1972, p. 9; October 7, 1979, Maude McDaniel, review of *Ashes in the Wind,* pp. 9, 14.

West Coast Review of Books, January, 1983, p. 42.

ONLINE

Kathleen E. Woodiwiss Home Page, http://www.kathleenewoodwiss.com/ (August 14, 2004).

* * *

WOODIWISS, Kathleen Erin
See WOODIWISS, Kathleen E.

* * *

WOODSON, Jacqueline 1964-

PERSONAL: Born February 12, 1964, in Columbus, OH; daughter of Jack and Mary Ann Woodson; children: Toshi. *Education:* Adelphi University, B.A., 1985; also attended New School for Social Research.

ADDRESSES: *Home*—Brooklyn, NY. *Agent*—c/o Charlotte Sheedy Literary Agency, 65 Bleecker St., 12th Fl., New York, NY 10012. *E-mail*—letters@jacquelinewoodson.com.

CAREER: Freelance writer, 1997—. Goddard College, Plainfield, VT, M.F.A. Writing Program, associate faculty member, 1993-95; New School University, Eugene Lang College, New York, NY, associate faculty member, 1994; Vermont College, Montpelier, VT, M.F.A. program, associate faculty member, 1996. Writer in residence, National Book Foundation, 1995, 1996. Has also worked as an editorial assistant, and as a drama therapist for runaway children in East Harlem, New York, NY.

MEMBER: Alpha Kappa Alpha.

AWARDS, HONORS: MacDowell Colony fellowship, 1990 and 1994; Fine Arts Work Center, Provincetown, MA, fellow, 1991-92; *Kenyon Review* Award for literary excellence in fiction, 1992 and 1995; Best Books for Young Adults citation, American Library Association (ALA), 1993, for *Maizon at Blue Hill; Publishers Weekly* Best Book citation, 1994; Jane Addams Children's Book Award, 1995 and 1996; Coretta Scott King Honor Book, ALA, 1995, for *I Hadn't Meant to Tell You This,* and 1996, for *From the Notebooks of Melanin Sun; Granta* Fifty Best American Authors under 40 Award, 1996; Lambda Literary Award for best fiction and best children's fiction, 1996; Lambda Literary Award, children/young adult, 1998, for *The House You Pass on the Way; Booklist* Editor's Choice citation; American Library Association Best Books citation; American Film Institute award; Best Books for Young Readers citation, ALA, 2000, and Bulletin Blue Ribbon Book citation, both for *If You Come Softly; Los Angeles Times* Book Award for young adult fiction, Coretta Scott King Book Award, 2001, Best Book for Young Adults, ALA, for *Miracle's Boys;* Time of Wonder Award, 2001, International Reading Association (IRA) Teacher's Choice citation, 2002, Best Book citation, *School library Journal, Booklist* Editor's Choice selection, ALA Notable Book, Riverbank Review Book of Distinction citation, and Texas Blue Bonnet List citation, all for *The Other Side;* nominee for National Book Award in young people's literature category, 2002, *Booklist* Editor's Choice selection, 2002, Best Book for Young Adults, ALA, 2003, Best Book citation, *School library Journal,* and Bank Street Best Children's Books of the Year, all for *Hush; Boston Globe-Horn Book* Award nominee in fiction and poetry category, 2003, IRA-CBC Children's Choice selection, 2004, National Book Award finalist, Coretta Scott King Honor, Best Book citation, *School library Journal,* all for *Locomotion*; named *Child* magazine Best of 2004, Caldecott Medal nominee, 2005, Charlotte Zolotow Award Honor Book, 2005, ALA Notable Book, and *Booklist* Editor's Choice selection, all for *Coming on Home Soon;* Top Ten Best Books for Young Adults selection, Young Adult Library Services Association, 2005, for *Behind You; Booklist* Editor's Choice selection, and Best Children's Books citation, *Kirkus Reviews,* both 2005, both for *Show Way.*

WRITINGS:

FOR CHILDREN

Martin Luther King, Jr. and His Birthday (nonfiction), illustrated by Floyd Cooper, Silver Burdett (Parsippany, NJ), 1990.

We Had a Picnic This Sunday Past, illustrated by Diane Greenseid, Hyperion (New York, NY), 1997.

The Other Side, illustrated by Earl B. Lewis, Putnam (New York, NY), 2001.

Our Gracie Aunt, illustrated by Jon J. Muth, Hyperion (New York, NY), 2002.

Coming on Home Soon, illustrated by E.B. Lewis, Putnam (New York, NY), 2004.

Show Way, illustrated by Hudson Talbott, Putnam (New York, NY), 2005.

FICTION; FOR YOUNG ADULTS

Last Summer with Maizon (first book in trilogy), Delacorte (New York, NY), 1990.

The Dear One, Delacorte (New York, NY), 1991, Putnam (New York, NY), 2004.

Maizon at Blue Hill (second book in trilogy), Delacorte (New York, NY), 1992.

Between Madison and Palmetto (third book in trilogy), Delacorte (New York, NY), 1993.

Book Chase ("Ghostwriter" series), illustrated by Steve Cieslawski, Bantam (New York, NY), 1994.

I Hadn't Meant to Tell You This, Delacorte (New York, NY), 1994.

From the Notebooks of Melanin Sun, Scholastic, Inc. (New York, NY), 1995.

The House You Pass on the Way, Delacorte (New York, NY), 1997.

If You Come Softly, Putnam (New York, NY), 1998.

Lena, Delacorte (New York, NY), 1998.

Miracle's Boys, edited by Nancy Paulsen, Putnam (New York, NY), 2000.

Sweet, Sweet Memory, illustrated by Floyd Cooper, Hyperion (New York, NY), 2000.

Visiting Day, illustrated by James Ransome, Scholastic (New York, NY), 2002.

Hush, Putnam (New York, NY), 2002.

Locomotion, Putnam (New York, NY), 2003.

Behind You, Putnam (New York, NY), 2004.

OTHER

(With Catherine Saalfield) *Among Good Christian Peoples* (video), A Cold Hard Dis', 1991.

Autobiography of a Family Photo (novel), New American Library/Dutton (New York, NY), 1994.

(Editor) *A Way out of No Way: Writing about Growing Up Black in America* (short stories), Holt (New York, NY), 1996.

(Editor, with Norma Fox Mazer) *Just a Writer's Thing: A Collection of Prose and Poetry from the National Book Foundation's 1995 Summer Writing Camp,* National Book Foundation (New York, NY), 1996.

Contributor to short-story collection *Am I Blue?,* edited by Marion Dane Bauer, HarperTrophy, 1994; contributor to *Just a Writer's Thing: A Collection of Prose & Poetry from the National Book Foundation's 1995 Summer Writing Camp,* edited by Norma F. Mazer, National Book Foundation, 1996. Also contributor to periodicals, including *American Voice, American Identities: Contemporary Multi-Cultural Voices, Common Lives Quarterly, Conditions, Essence, Horn Book, Kenyon Review* and *Out/Look.* Member of editorial board, Portable Lower East Side/*Queer City.*

SIDELIGHTS: Award-winning author Jacqueline Woodson is equally proficient in the novel format, verse, and picture books. She writes about "invisible" people: young girls, minorities, homosexuals, the poor, all the individuals who are ignored or forgotten in mainstream America. They are the people, as the author wrote in a *Horn Book* article, "who exist on the margins." An African American and lesbian herself, Woodson knows first-hand what it is like to be labeled, classified, stereotyped, and pushed aside. Nevertheless, her stories are not intended to champion the rights of minorities and the oppressed. Rather, they celebrate people's differences. Her characters are not so much striving to have their rights acknowledged as they are struggling to find their own individuality, their own value as people. "I feel compelled to write against stereotypes," Woodson further remarked, "hoping people will see that some issues know no color, class, sexuality. No—I don't feel as though I have a commitment to one community—I don't want to be shackled this way. I write from the very depths of who I am, and in this place there are all of my identities."

Woodson's sense of not really belonging to one community might be grounded in her childhood. During her adolescent years, she moved back and forth between South Carolina and New York City, and "never quite felt a part of either place," according to a *Ms.* article by Diane R. Paylor. But Woodson began to feel "outside of the world," as she explained in *Horn Book,* even before her teen years. The turning point for her came when Richard Nixon resigned the presidency in 1974 and Gerald Ford took his place instead of George McGovern. "McGovern was my first 'American Dream.' Everyone in my neighborhood had been pulling for him." When Ford stepped into the Oval Office, Woodson felt that she and all of black America had been abandoned. "The word *democracy* no longer existed for me. I began to challenge teachers, and when they couldn't give me the answers I wanted, I became sullen, a loner. I would spend hours sitting underneath the porch, writing poetry and anti-American songs."

Writing soon became Woodson's passion. In the fifth grade, she was the literary editor of her school's magazine. "I used to write on everything," she commented for a Bantam Doubleday Dell Web site. "It was the thing I liked to do the most. I never thought I could have a career as a writer—I always thought it was something I would have to do on the side." Her seventh-grade English teacher encouraged Woodson to write and convinced her that she should pursue whatever career she felt would make her happiest. Deciding that writing was, indeed, what she wanted to do, Woodson endeavored "to write about communities that were familiar to me and people that were familiar to me. I wanted to write about communities of color. I wanted to write about girls. I wanted to write about friendship and all of these things that I felt like were missing in a lot of the books that I read as a child."

Woodson has always had a deep empathy for young girls, who often suffer from low self-esteem in their preteen and adolescent years. "I write about black girls because this world would like to keep us invisible," she wrote in *Horn Book.* "I write about *all* girls because I know what happens to self-esteem when we turn twelve, and I hope to show readers the number of ways in which we are strong." Woodson's first published book, *Last Summer with Maizon,* begins a trilogy about friends Margaret and Maizon. Set in the author's hometown of Brooklyn, the story tells of two eleven-year-olds who are the closest of friends. Their friendship is strained, however, when Margaret's father dies of a heart attack and Maizon goes to boarding school on a scholarship. While her friend is away, Margaret, who is the quieter of the two, discovers that she has a talent for writing. She also finds comfort in her family, who support her in her attempt to deal with her father's death. Maizon, meanwhile, finds that she does not like the almost all-white Connecticut boarding school and returns home after only three months. Glad to be with her loved ones again, Maizon, along with Margaret, goes to a gifted school in her own neighborhood.

Critics praised *Last Summer with Maizon* for its touching portrayal of two close friends and for its convincing sense of place. Julie Blaisdale, writing in *School Librarian,* also lauded the work for its "positive female characters . . . who provide the enduring sense of place and spiritual belonging" in the tale. Roger Sutton of the *Bulletin of the Center for Children's Books,* while generally commending the book, found fault with the way Margaret eases her sadness by writing poetry. "Although underdeveloped," Sutton concluded, "this story will appeal to readers who want a 'book about friends.'" Similarly, *Horn Book* writer Rudine Sims Bishop commented on the story's "blurred focus," but asserted that "the novel is appealing in its vivid portrayal of the characters and the small community they create."

Woodson continues Margaret and Maizon's stories with *Maizon at Blue Hill* and *Between Madison and Palmetto.* The former is not really a sequel but, rather, an "equal" to the first book in the trilogy. *Maizon at Blue Hill* focuses on what happens to Maizon while she is at the Connecticut boarding school. Maizon, who is a very bright girl, likes the academic side of Blue Hill, but she is worried about fitting in socially. Most of the other girls are white and are either snobbish or, at least, not eager to be her friend. Although she is welcomed by a small clique of other black students, Maizon sees this group as rather elitist, too. She decides to return to Brooklyn, where she can comfortably just be herself. An American Library Association Best Book for young adults, *Maizon at Blue Hill* has been acclaimed for its strong and appealing characters. "More sharply written than its predecessor, this novel contains some acute characterization," remarked Roger Sutton in the *Bulletin of the Center for Children's Books.* Noting that the issues about self-esteem and identity that are addressed in the story spring appropriately from the characters rather than vice versa, *Voice of Youth Advocates* contributor Alice F. Stern asserted: "We are in the hands of a skilled writer here . . . . Woodson is a real find."

The last book in the trilogy, *Between Madison and Palmetto,* picks up where the first book left off, with Maizon and Margaret entering eighth grade at the academy. Again, Woodson covers a lot of ground in just over one hundred pages, including Margaret's bout with bulimia, issues of integration as the two girls' neighborhood begins to change and white families move in, and the testing of Margaret and Maizon's friendship as Maizon spends more time with another girl, named Carolyn. A *Publishers Weekly* reviewer applauded Woodson's gift with characterization, but noted that the effect is "somewhat diluted by the movie-of-the-week problems." In another *Voice of Youth Advocates* review, Alice F. Stern acknowledged that Woodson has "a lot of ground to cover," but noted that "she manages admirably." A *Kirkus Reviews* critic described *Between Madison and Palmetto* as a fine portrayal of a "close- knit community . . . [that] comes nicely to life."

In her *Horn Book* article, Woodson grouped her books into two categories: her "good" books, which deal with relationships between family members and friends, and her more controversial books, which address issues of alcoholism, teenage pregnancy, homosexuality, and other issues that skirt the delicate problem of what is "appropriate" for children to read. She reflected on how, after writing her second book, *The Dear One,* the speaking invitations she had formerly received suddenly stopped coming. "Even after *Maizon at Blue Hill,* another relatively 'nice book,' school visits were few and far between. Yet I often wonder, If every book had been like *Last Summer with Maizon,* and I was a young woman with a wedding band on my hand, would I get to visit schools more often?"

The central character of *The Dear One* is twelve-year-old Feni, a name meaning "The Dear One" in Swahili. Feni lives in an upper-class African-American home and basks in her family's attention. This all changes, however, when fifteen-year-old Rebecca is invited by Feni's mother to stay with them. Rebecca, the daughter of an old college friend, is a troubled, pregnant teenager from Harlem. Feni becomes jealous because she is no longer the center of attention. "But gradually and believably, with the patient support of Feni's mother and a lesbian couple who are longstanding family friends, the two girls begin to develop mutual trust and, finally, a redemptive friendship," related *Twentieth-Century Children's Writers* contributor Michael Cart.

The Dear One is a unique book in that it deals with tensions not between blacks and whites but between poor and wealthy blacks. Woodson gives a sympathetic portrayal of Rebecca, who is uncomfortable living in what she considers to be a mansion, and who is also reluctant to change her lifestyle. She misses her boyfriend and her family back in Harlem; she envies Feni and resents the privileges Feni has been given. The novel also offers a fresh perspective on adult relationships. As Hazel S. Moore noted in *Voice of Youth Advocates,* "The lesbian couple seems to be intact, while the straight couples have divorced and suffered." Marion and Bernadette, the lesbian couple, provide Feni with wise advice to add to the support she receives from her mother.

Taking things a step further than *The Dear One, I Hadn't Meant to Tell You This* explores a relationship that spans both race and class when Marie, a girl from a well-to-do black family, befriends Lena, whom Marie's father considers to be "white trash." Both girls have problems: Marie's mother has abandoned her family, and Lena is the victim of her father's sexual molestations. Told from Marie's point of view, the book details the twelve-year-old's internal conflicts as she tries to think of how she can help Lena. In the end, Lena, who has been able to find no other viable solutions to her problem, runs away from home, and Marie must accept the fact that there is nothing she can do about her friend's tragedy. Woodson has been praised by critics for not resolving her story with a pat conclusion. Cart commented: "Woodson's refusal to impose a facile resolution on this heartbreaking dilemma is one of her singular strengths as a writer." "Woodson's novel is wrenchingly honest and, despite its sad themes, full of hope and inspiration," concluded a *Publishers Weekly* reviewer.

In *Lena,* Woodson picks up Lena's own story after she leaves Marie. Lena plans to hitchhike with her little sister Dion to Pine Mountain, Kentucky—their mother's birthplace—in an effort to escape their father's abuse. "In the first novel, the girls' friendship sustained them across racial barriers in a desolate world," declared Hazel Rochman in *Booklist,* "but here everything has a glowingly happy ending." "The great appeal here," the reviewer concluded, "is the survival story. After cold and danger, we feel the elemental luxury of shelter: warmth, cleanliness, breakfast, privacy." "Writing in Lena's voice, striking for its balance of tough-mindedness and tenderness," stated a critic in *Publishers Weekly,* "Woodson conveys the love that the protective heroine feels for her sister as well as the compassion of strangers."

Another Woodson novel, *If You Come Softly,* also explores the issue of race. The book tells of the budding relationship between two fifteen-year-olds: a black boy named Jeremiah, and Ellie, a Jewish girl. "The intensity of their emotions will make hearts flutter, then ache," stated a *Publishers Weekly* reviewer, "as evidence mounts that Ellie's and Jeremiah's 'perfect' love exists in a deeply flawed society." "This, like every story I've written, from *Last Summer with Maizon* to *I Hadn't Meant to Tell You This* to *From the Notebooks of Melanin Sun,* is my story," Woodson wrote in a *Horn Book* essay on writing outside one's own cultural group. "While I have never been Jewish, I have always been a girl. While I have never lived on the Upper West Side, I have lived for a long time in New York. While I have never been a black male, I've always been black. But most of all, like the characters in my story, I have felt a sense of powerlessness in my lifetime. And this is the room into which I can walk and join them."

The issue of homosexuality, which had been peripheral in Woodson's earlier books, comes to the forefront in *From the Notebooks of Melanin Sun* and *The House*

You Pass on the Way. Thirteen-year-old Melanin Sun, the central character in the former novel, has a close relationship with his mother, whom he admires as a single working mother who is also putting herself through law school. Their bond is strained, however, when Melanin's mother tells him that she is a lesbian and that she is in love with a white woman. This development makes Melanin question his relationship with his mother, as well as making him wonder about his own sexuality. Torn between his emotional need for his mother and his fear about what her lesbianism implies, Melanin goes through a tough time as his friends also begin to abandon him. Gossip in the neighborhood that Melanin's mother is "unfit" also spreads, making matters even worse. Again, Woodson offers no clear-cut resolution to the story, but by the novel's end Melanin has begun to grow and understand his mother. Critics praised Woodson's portrayal of Melanin's inner conflicts as being right on the money. As Lois Metzger wrote in the *New York Times Book Review,* "Ms. Woodson, in this moving, lovely book, shows you Melanin's strength and the sun shining through." "Woodson has addressed with care and skill the sensitive issue of homosexuality within the family . . . [without] becoming an advocate of any particular attitude," asserted *Voice of Youth Advocates* critic Hazel S. Moore. In *The House You Pass on the Way,* fourteen-year-old Evangeline, the middle child in a mixed-race family, struggles with feelings of guilt and dismay over her awakening sexual orientation. "A provocative topic," noted a *Kirkus Reviews* critic, "treated with wisdom and sensitivity, with a strong secondary thread exploring some of the inner and outer effects of biracialism."

The plight of three orphaned brothers in New York is presented in Woodson's Coretta Scott King Award-winning novel, *Miracle's Boys.* Lafayette, the youngest of the three, tells the story in a "voice that's funny, smart, and troubled," according to *Booklist* critic Rochman. Ty'ree, the oldest brother, has given up his educational possibilities to raise his younger brothers, but faces conflict at every turn from the middle brother, Charlie, who has just returned from a correctional institution for robbing a candy story and now is in gang trouble once again. The boys also carry the sad memory of their dead mother, Milagro; Charlie blames Lafayette, or Laff as he is called, for her death. But through it all the brothers try to stay together, healing their grief as best as they can. A contributor for *Horn Book* praised Lafayette's narrative voice, noting that it "maintains a tone of sweet melancholy that is likely to hold the attention of thoughtful young teens." Likewise, a reviewer for *Publishers Weekly* called the novel an "intelligently wrought, thought-provoking story," and Edward Sullivan, writing in *School Library Journal,* found this "story of tough, self- sufficient young men to be powerful and engaging."

In her 2002 novel *Hush,* Woodson explores the loss of a child's identity when a young girl and her family are forced into the witness protection program. Toswiah Green's father is a black policeman in Denver. Her life is perfect: a wonderful home, caring parents, and cool friends. But when her father chooses to testify against fellow policemen—white—whom he witnessed shooting and killing an unarmed black teen, the lives of the entire family are turned upside down. The white community and his fellow cops turn against Green, and the family must enter the witness protection program, move to another state, and assume new identities. "Woodson's taut, somber novel examines complex themes," wrote Lynda Jones in *Black Issues Book Review.* Such themes as racism, self-identity, the class system, and ethical imperatives are dealt with in the journal that Toswiah—who takes the assumed name of Evie Thomas—keeps. "Woodson shows that while Evie's situation is extreme, everyone has to leave home and come to terms with many shifting identities," commented Rochman in a *Booklist* review. Jennifer M. Brabander, reviewing *Hush* in *Horn Book,* also lauded the story, concluding that Woodson's "poetic, low-key, yet vivid writing style perfectly conveys the story's atmosphere of quiet intensity." Reviewing the same novel in *School Library Journal,* Sharon Grover called it a "complex coming-of-age story," and Claire Rosser, writing in *Kliatt,* declared Woodson to be "one of the best novelists we have in the Y[oung] A[dult] field." Rosser further asserted that Woodson "brings poetry to her prose and always a deep understanding of emotional upheaval."

Woodson brings much the same sensibility to her picture books for younger readers, presenting subjects not usually examined in books for children. These include titles such as *The Other Side,* a "story of friendship across race," according to *Booklist* critic Rochman; *Sweet, Sweet Memory* is the tale of a little girl whose grandmother has died, and one that "will resonate with those who have lost someone dear," as Ilene Cooper observed in *Booklist; Our Gracie Aunt* is the story of two children whose mother is in the hospital and who must go into foster care; and *Visiting Day* is a "poignant picture book," according to a *Publishers Weekly* reviewer, that tells an intergenerational tale about a young girl and her grandmother who go to visit the father in jail. As Rochman noted in *Booklist,* "Woodson brings children close to those whose stories are seldom told." Woodson turns to poetry for her "sad but hopeful" story *Locomotion,* as a critic for *Publishers Weekly* called the book. Young Lonnie tells his story of loss and redemption in sixty poems in various styles from sonnet to haiku. *Horn Book*'s Brabander concluded that "Woodson's finely crafted story of heartbreak and hope won't let [readers] go."

Woodson's picture book *Show Way* is perhaps her most autobiographical work yet; it is a fictionalized tale of Woodson's family history that ends with a picture of Woodson's daughter, Toshi. *Show Way* begins in pre-Civil War America when a young girl is sold away from her parents to a new plantation. The girl learns to sew "Show Way" quilts that tell stories and also contain secret symbols that show the way to freedom in the North. The narrative then follows the girl's female descendents for several generations, culminating with the author and her daughter. The images in the book predominantly mirror the Show Way quilts; each picture tells part of the family's story. Critics praised to book's format as an effective approach to the topic and *School Library Journal* critic Mary N. Oluonye called the story's combined elements "perfectly executed." In addition, *Booklist* contributor Hazel Rochman noted that *Show Way* "will move many readers to explore their own family roots."

Although most of her works, like *Show Way,* have been aimed at preteen and teenage audiences, Woodson has also written a novel for adults, *Autobiography of a Family Photo,* which addresses issues of sexuality and sexual behavior for a more mature audience. However, its short length and central coming-of-age theme put *Autobiography of a Family Photo* within the reach of young adult audiences. Told in a series of vignettes spanning the 1960s and 1970s, the novel is a reminiscence related by an unnamed narrator. Her family has many problems, including her parents' troubled marriage, her brother Carlos's inclination to be sexually abusive, her brother Troy's struggles with homosexuality that compel him to go to Vietnam, and other difficulties. Despite all of this, the narrator survives adolescence, undergoing a "compelling transformation," according to Margot Mifflin in an *Entertainment Weekly* review. However, some critics have contended that the vignettes fail to form a unified whole. A *Kirkus Reviews* contributor, for example, commented: "Chapters build on each other, but the information provided is too scanty to really create any depth." Catherine Bush, writing in the *New York Times Book Review,* complained that the novel focuses too much on the narrator's growing sexual awareness. "I found myself wishing that the narrator's self-awareness and longing could be defined less exclusively in sexual terms," Bush remarked. Bush concluded, however, that "even in these restrictive terms, the novel is the best kind of survival guide: clear-eyed, gut true."

Woodson has never backed away from portraying truths about life in modern American society. She has written her "good" books about friendship and family that deal with safe, acceptable topics, but she clearly does not shy away from controversial subjects like homosexuality and sexual abuse. Woodson has asserted that she is not trying to force any kind of ideology on her readers, but rather is interested in all kinds of people, especially the socially rejected. "One of the most important ideas I want to get across to my readers," Woodson emphasizes, "is the idea of feeling like you're okay with who you are." "Death happens," Woodson told Samiya A. Bashir in *Black Issues Book Review.* "Sexual abuse happens. Parents leave. These things happen every day and people think that if they don't talk about it, then it will just go away. But that's what makes it spread like the plague it is. People say that they're censoring in the guise of protecting children, but if they'd open their eyes they'd see that kids are exposed to this stuff every day, and we need a venue by which to talk to them about it and start a dialogue. My writing comes from this place, of wanting to change the world. I feel like young people are the most open."

BIOGRAPHICAL AND CRITICAL SOURCES:

BOOKS

Children's Literature Review, Volume 49, Gale (Detroit, MI), 1998.

Gay and Lesbian Literature, Volume 2, St. James Press (Detroit, MI), 1998.

St. James Guide to Young Adult Writers, 2nd edition, St. James Press (Detroit, MI), 1999.

Twentieth-Century Children's Writers, 4th edition, St. James Press (Detroit, MI), 1995.

Writers for Young Adults, Scribner (New York, NY), 2000.

PERIODICALS

Black Issues Book Review, May, 2001, Samiya A. Bashir, "Tough Issues, Tender Minds," p. 78; March-April, 2002, Lynda Jones, review of *Hush,* p. 67; July-August, 2002, Lynda Jones, review of *Our Gracie Aunt,* p. 75.

Book, March-April, 2003, Kathleen Odean, review of *Hush,* p. 37.

Booklist, February 1, 1999, Hazel Rochman, review of *Lena,* p. 970; February 15, 2000, Hazel Rochman, review of *Miracle's Boys,* p. 1102; February 15,

2001, Hazel Rochman, review of *Miracle's Boys,* p. 1149; February 15, 2001, Hazel Rochman, review of *The Other Side,* p. 1154; February 15, 2001, Ilene Cooper, review of *Sweet, Sweet Memory,* p. 1158; January 1, 2002, Hazel Rochman, review of *Hush,* p. 851; January 1, 2002, review of *The Other Side,* p. 769; February 15, 2002, Stephanie Zvirin, reviews of *Hush* and *The Other Side,* p 1034; September 1, 2002, Hazel Rochman, review of *Our Gracie Aunt,* p. 137; January 1, 2003, review of *Hush,* p. 798; September 15, 2005, Hazel Rochman, review of *Show Way,* p. 63.

Bulletin of the Center for Children's Books, October, 1990, Roger Sutton, review of *Last Summer with Maizon,* pp. 49-50; December, 1992, Roger Sutton, review of *Maizon at Blue Hill,* p. 128; September, 1998, Janice M. DelNegro, review of *We Had a Picnic This Sunday Past,* p. 40; April, 1999, Deborah Stevenson, review of *Lena,* p. 298; February, 2001, Janice M. DelNegro, review of *The Other Side,* p. 211; May, 2001, Janice M. DelNegro, review of *Sweet, Sweet Memory,* p. 357; Deborah Stevenson, review of *Coming on Home Soon,* p. 272.

Childhood Education, summer, 2003, Sharon White-Williams, review of *Visiting Day,* p. 247.

Entertainment Weekly, April 21, 1995, Margot Mifflin, review of *Autobiography of a Family Photo,* pp. 50-51.

Horn Book, September, 1992, Rudine Sims Bishop, "Books from Parallel Cultures: New African-American Voices," pp. 616-620; November-December, 1995, Jacqueline Woodson, "A Sign of Having Been Here," pp. 711-715; May-June, 1999, Kristi Beavin, review of *I Hadn't Meant to Tell You This* (audio version), p. 358; March-April, 2000, review of *Miracle's Boys,* p. 203; January-February, 2002, Jennifer M. Brabander, review of *Hush,* p. 87; November-December, 2002, Roger Sutton, review of *Visiting Day,* p. 743; March-April, 2003, Jennifer M. Brabander, review of *Locomotion,* pp. 219-220.

Kirkus Reviews, December 1, 1993, review of *Between Madison and Palmetto,* p. 1532; October 1, 1994, review of *Autobiography of a Family Photo,* pp. 1307-1308; July 1, 1997, review of *The House You Pass on the Way,* p. 1038; September 15, 2002, review of *Visiting Day,* p. 1403; November 15, 2002, review of *Locomotion,* p. 1704.

Kliatt, January, 1999, Paula Rohrlick, review of *Lena,* pp. 10-11; January, 2002, Claire Rosser, review of *Hush,* p. 8; March, 2002, Claire Rosser, review of *Miracle's Boys,* p. 20.

Ms., November- December, 1994, Diane R. Paylor, "Bold Type: Jacqueline Woodson's 'Girl Stories,'" p. 77; July, 1995, p. 75.

New York Times Book Review, February 26, 1995, Catherine Bush, "A World without Childhood," p. 14; July 16, 1995, Lois Metzger, review of *From the Notebooks of Melanin Sun,* p. 27.

Publishers Weekly, November 8, 1993, review of *Between Madison and Palmetto,* p. 78; April 18, 1994, review of *I Hadn't Mean to Tell You This,* p. 64; June 22, 1998, review of *If You Come Softly,* p. 92; December 14, 1998, review of *Lena,* p. 77; April 17, 2000, review of *Miracle's Boys,* p. 81; December 4, 2000, review of *The Other Side,* p. 73; March 4, 2002, review of *Our Gracie Aunt,* p. 79; September 16, 2002, review of *Visiting Day,* p. 68; November 25, 2002, review of *Locomotion,* pp. 68-69.

Reading Teacher, November, 2002, review of *The Other Side,* pp. 257- 258.

School Librarian, November, 1991, Julie Blaisdale, review of *Last Summer with Maizon,* p. 154.

School Library Journal, May, 2000, Edward Sullivan, review of *Miracle's Boys,* p. 178; January, 2001, Catherine T. Quattlebaum, review of *The Other Side,* p. 112; April, 2001, Marianne Saccardi, review of *Sweet, Sweet Memory,* p. 126; August, 2001, Jacqueline Woodson, "Miracles," p. 57; August, 2001, Julie Cummins, "Offstage or Upstaged?," p. 9; February, 2002, Sharon Grover, review of *Hush,* p. 138; September, 2002, Susan Pine, review of *Visiting Day,* pp. 208-209; December, 2002, Anna DeWind, review of *Our Gracie Aunt,* p. 114; September, 2003, Grace Oliff, review of *Visiting Day,* p. 86; August, 2005, Blair Christolon, review of *Coming on Home Soon,* p. 50; November, 2005, Mary N. Oluonye, review of *Show Way,* p. 111.

Voice of Youth Advocates, October, 1991, Hazel S. Moore, review of *The Dear One,* p. 236; October, 1992, Alice F. Stern, review of *Maizon at Blue Hill,* p. 235; June, 1994, Alice F. Stern, review of *Between Madison and Palmetto,* p. 95; October, 1995, Hazel S. Moore, review of *From the Notebooks of Melanin Sun,* p. 227; February, 2001, review of *Miracle's Boys,* p. 400.

ONLINE

Bantam Doubleday Dell, http://www.bdd.com/ (April 8, 1997), "Jacqueline Woodson."

BookPage.com, http://www.bookpage.com/ (February, 2003), Heidi Henneman, "Poetry in Motion."

Jacqueline Woodson Home Page, http://www.jacquelinewoodson.com/ (February 16, 2006).

WOUK, Herman 1915-

PERSONAL: Surname is pronounced "woke"; born May 27, 1915, in New York, NY; son of Abraham Isaac (an industrialist in the power laundry field who started as an immigrant laundry laborer at $3 a week) and Esther (Levine) Wouk; married Betty Sarah Brown, December 9, 1945; children: Abraham Isaac (deceased), Nathaniel, Joseph. *Education:* Columbia University, B.A. (with honors), 1934. *Religion:* Jewish. *Hobbies and other interests:* Judaic scholarship, Zionist studies, travel (especially in Israel).

ADDRESSES: Agent—c/o Author Mail, Little, Brown & Co., 3 Center Plaza, Ste. 100, Boston, MA 02108.

CAREER: Gag writer for radio comedians, New York City, 1934-35; scriptwriter for Fred Allen, 1936-41; U.S. Treasury Department, "dollar-a-year-man," writing and producing radio plays to promote war bond sales, 1941; self-employed writer, 1946—. Visiting professor, Yeshiva University, 1953-57; scholar in residence, Aspen Institute of Humanistic Studies, 1973-74; lectured in China, 1982. Trustee, College of the Virgin Islands, 1962-69; member of board of directors, Washington National Symphony, 1969-71, and Kennedy Center Productions, 1974-75; member of advisory council, Center for U.S.-China Arts Exchange, 1981-87. *Military service:* U.S. Navy, 1942-46; served on Pacific Ocean aboard two destroyer-minesweepers, U.S.S. Zane and U.S.S. Southard; became lieutenant; received four campaign stars and Presidential Unit Citation.

MEMBER: International Platform Association (Ralph Waldo Emerson award, 1981), Authors Guild, PEN, Dramatists Guild, Reserve Officers Association of the United States, Writers Guild of America East, Century Club (New York City), Bohemian Club (San Francisco); Cosmos Club, Metropolitan Club (both Washington, DC).

AWARDS, HONORS: Richard H. Fox Prize, 1934; Pulitzer Prize in fiction, 1952, for *The Caine Mutiny: A Novel of World War II;* Columbia University Medal of Excellence, 1952; L.H.D., Yeshiva University, 1955; LL.D., Clark University, 1960; Litt.D., American International University, 1979, Ph.D., Bar-Ilan University, 1990; Alexander Hamilton Medal, Columbia College Alumni Association, 1980; American Book Award nomination, 1981, for *War and Remembrance;* Ralph Waldo Emerson Award, International Platform Association, 1981; University of California—Berkeley Medal, 1984; Golden Plate Award, American Academy of Achievement, 1986; *Washingtonian* Book Award, 1986, for *Inside, Outside,* Yad Vashem KaZetnik award, 1990.

WRITINGS:

Aurora Dawn; or, The True History of Andrew Reale, Containing a Faithful Account of the Great Riot, Together With the Complete Texts of Michael Wilde's Oration and Father Stanfield's Sermon (novel; Book-of-the-Month Club selection), Simon & Schuster (New York, NY), 1947, reprinted, Pocket Books (New York, NY), 1983.

The City Boy: The Adventures of Herbie Bookbinder and His Cousin, Cliff (novel; Reader's Digest Condensed Book Club selection; Family Book Club selection; Book-of-the-Month Club alternate selection), Simon & Schuster (New York, NY), 1948, published as *The City Boy,* Doubleday (New York, NY), 1952, published as *City Boy: The Adventures of Herbie Bookbinder,* Doubleday (New York, NY), 1969.

The Caine Mutiny: A Novel of World War II (Reader's Digest Condensed Book Club selection; Literary Guild alternate selection), Doubleday (New York, NY), 1951, reprinted, Franklin Library (Franklin Center, PA), 1977, published as *The Caine Mutiny,* Dell (New York, NY), 1966.

Marjorie Morningstar (novel; Reader's Digest Condensed Book Club selection; Book-of-the-Month Club selection), Doubleday (New York, NY), 1955, reprinted, Pocket Books (New York, NY), 1977.

This Is My God (nonfiction; Reader's Digest Condensed Book Club selection; Book-of-the-Month Club alternate selection), Doubleday (New York, NY), 1959, published as *This Is My God: The Jewish Way of Life,* 1970, revised edition, Collins (London, England), 1973.

Youngblood Hawke (novel; Reader's Digest Condensed Book Club selection; Book-of-the-Month Club selection), Doubleday (New York, NY), 1962.

Don't Stop the Carnival (novel; Book-of-the-Month Club selection), Doubleday (New York, NY), 1965.

The "Lomokome" Papers, Pocket Books (New York, NY), 1968.

The Winds of War (novel; Literary Guild selection; Reader's Digest Condensed Book Club selection), Little, Brown (Boston, MA), 1971.

War and Remembrance (novel; sequel to *The Winds of War;* Literary Guild selection; Reader's Digest Condensed Book Club selection), Little, Brown (Boston, MA), 1978.

Inside, Outside (novel; Book-of-the-Month Club selection), Little, Brown (Boston, MA), 1985.
The Hope, Little, Brown (Boston, MA), 1994.
The Glory, Little, Brown (Boston, MA), 1994.
The Will to Live on: This Is Our Heritage, Cliff Street Books (New York, NY), 2000.
A Hole in Texas, Little, Brown (Boston, MA), 2004.

PLAYS

The Traitor (two-act; first produced on Broadway at Forty-Eighth Street Theater, April 4, 1949), Samuel French (New York, NY), 1949.
Slattery's Hurricane (screenplay; produced by Twentieth Century-Fox, 1949), Permabooks, 1956.
The Caine Mutiny Court-Martial (two-act; based on his novel *The Caine Mutiny;* first produced in Santa Barbara, CA, 1953; produced on Broadway at Plymouth Theater, January 20, 1954), Doubleday (New York, NY), 1954, reprinted, Pocket Books (New York, NY), 1974.
Nature's Way (two-act comedy; first produced on Broadway at Coronet Theater, October 15, 1957), Doubleday (New York, NY), 1958, reprinted, Samuel French (New York, NY), 1977.

Also author of screenplay "The Winds of War," ABC-TV, 1983, and co-author of screenplay "War and Remembrance," ABC-TV, 1988.

ADAPTATIONS: The Caine Mutiny was filmed by Columbia in 1954, starring Humphrey Bogart as Captain Queeg; *The City Boy* was made into a motion picture by Columbia in 1950; Warner Bros. filmed *Marjorie Morningstar* and *Youngblood Hawke* in 1958 and 1964, respectively. A television adaptation of *The Caine Mutiny Court Martial,* with Barry Sullivan, Lloyd Nolan, and Frank Lovejoy, aired on "Ford Star Jubilee" in 1955; *The Winds of War* and *War and Remembrance* were adapted as television miniseries airing on ABC-TV in 1983 and 1988, respectively.

SIDELIGHTS: An American novelist and playwright of Russian-Jewish heritage, Herman Wouk received the 1952 Pulitzer Prize in fiction for *The Caine Mutiny: A Novel of World War II* and has since published several other bestsellers, including *The Winds of War* and *War and Remembrance.* The *Atlantic*'s Edward Weeks called him a compelling narrator "who uses large canvases and who, without much fuss for style or symbolism, drives his story ahead with an infectious belief in the people he is writing about." According to a reviewer for *Time,* Wouk's chief significance is that "he spearheads a mutiny against the literary stereotypes of rebellion—against three decades of U.S. fiction dominated by skeptical criticism, sexual emancipation, social protest, and psychoanalytic sermonizing." He remains, wrote Pearl K. Bell in *Commentary,* "an unembarrassed believer in such 'discredited' forms of commitment as valor, gallantry, leadership, patriotism." Because of the reaffirmation of traditional values in his works, Wouk has enjoyed wide readership but has also been accused by some critics of pandering to popular prejudice.

Wouk began writing fiction in 1943 while on sea duty on the Pacific Ocean, and he later used his Navy experience aboard the U.S.S. *Zane* and U.S.S. *Southard* as background for his third novel, *The Caine Mutiny* (which is not autobiographical). The book is not concerned with battles at sea but with adherence to appointive authority. The conflict centers around Lieutenant Commander Philip Francis Queeg, who, according to W.J. Stuckey in *The Pulitzer Prize Novels,* "manifests a professional incompetence that will probably remain unparalleled in or out of fiction." When it appears that Queeg is too terrified to issue the necessary orders to save the ship during a typhoon, Lieutenant Maryk, the ship's executive officer, is persuaded by Lieutenant Keefer and his followers to seize control. Maryk is subsequently tried for making a mutiny but is acquitted through the efforts of Lieutenant Barney Greenwald, an adept trial lawyer. Ironically, at a party celebrating Maryk's acquittal, Greenwald tells Maryk that it is he, Maryk, (and not Queeg) who is morally guilty, for he deserted a military system that had, despite its flaws, protected America from foreign fascists.

Several critics considered Wouk's treatment of the military affair insightful and carefully constructed. Harry Gilroy, for example, wrote in the *New York Times* that Wouk "has a profound understanding of what Navy men should be, and against some who fell short of the mark he has fired a deadly broadside." Edmund Fuller pointed out in his *Man in Modern Fiction* that the book's ability "to view the problem within the inescapable military premise without oversimplifying it" distinguishes *The Caine Mutiny* from other World War II novels. Discussing the justification of the mutiny in his *In My Opinion,* Orville Prescott commented that it is "the crux of [the novel, and] Mr. Wouk develops it extremely well, with racy wit and genial humor, with lively pace and much ingenuity of incident and with unexpected subtlety." Similarly, a reviewer for the *Times Literary Supplement* concluded: "So convincingly has Mr. Wouk created his officers, so subtly has he contrived the series of incidents that culminate in the final drama, that, given both the characters and the situations, the climax is perfectly acceptable."

Stuckey, however, saw the climax as "the unwarranted whitewash" of Queeg: "Throughout three-fourths of the novel, Captain Queeg is a thoroughly incompetent and badly frightened man. However, toward the close of the book Wouk springs a wholly unprepared-for surprise: Queeg, he tells us, is not really the incompetent everyone thinks him; he is the victim of ambitious and cowardly subordinates. . . . While it is easy to understand the reason for Lieutenant Greenwald's emotional defense of the United States Navy, it is difficult to see why he—an intelligent trial lawyer, we are told—defends an incompetent American ship's captain who had not served in the Atlantic and who, if he had encountered Nazi warships, would have fled in terror. Greenwald's only defense of Queeg is that he was a member of the regular navy. It would make as much sense to defend a doctor guilty of malpractice on the grounds that he engaged in a humane calling. . . . The war in Europe and Hitler's treatment of the Jews had nothing to do with Queeg's or Maryk's innocence or guilt."

Eric Bentley found the same weakness in "The Caine Mutiny Court Martial," Wouk's play based on the court martial sequence of the novel. Discussing the theme that the important thing is not to save a particular ship but to preserve the authority of commanders, Bentley wrote in the *New Republic:* "There is a good point here, and there must surely be a good play in it—a play that would show up the sentimentality of our prejudice against commanders and in favor of mutineers. If, however, Mr. Wouk wanted to write such a play, he chose the wrong story and told it in the wrong way, for we spend three quarters of the evening hoping that Queeg—the commander—will be found insane and the mutineers vindicated. When, in the very last scene, Mr. Wouk explains that this is not the right way to take the story, it is too late. We don't believe him. At best we say that he is preaching at us a notion that ought to have been dramatized. And no amount of shock technique—not even the reiterated image of Jews melted down for soap—can conceal the flaw."

Marjorie Morningstar, Wouk's fourth novel, also focuses on rebellion, but in a civilian context. The book traces the life of a beautiful, intelligent girl who renounces the values and authority of her hard-working Jewish parents only to end up, years later, affirming them as a suburban matron and community servant. E.W. Foell noted in the *Christian Science Monitor* that Wouk "has not flinched at what he sees in his characters' thoughts, [but] many of his readers are likely to." A *Time* critic wrote that, indeed, "Wouk [sets] teeth on edge by advocating chastity before marriage, suggesting that real happiness for a woman is found in a home and children, cheering loud and long for the American middle class and blasting Bohemia and Bohemians. Wouk is a Sinclair Lewis in reverse." Reviewing the book in the *New York Times,* Maxwell Geismar believed that "here as in *The Caine Mutiny* [the conflict] is settled by a final bow to the red-tape of a bureaucracy or to the properties of a social class, under the impression that these are among the eternal verities. *Marjorie Morningstar* is very good reading indeed. But to this reviewer at least the values of true culture are as remote from its polished orbit as are, at base, the impulses of real life."

Leslie A. Fiedler, however, sees the most popular novel of 1955 as untraditional in one regard. In *Love and Death in the American Novel,* Fiedler called *Marjorie Morningstar* "the first fictional celebration of the mid-twentieth-century detente between the Jews and middle-class America." He explained: "In the high literature of Europe and, more slowly, in that of the United States, gentile and Jew have joined forces to portray the Jewish character as a figure representing man's fate in . . . an age of rootlessness, alienation, and terror, in which the exiled condition so long thought peculiar to the Jew comes to seem the common human lot. . . . Wouk [suggests] . . . that the Jew was never . . . the rootless dissenter, . . . but rather the very paragon of the happy citizen at home . . . in short, Marjorie Morningstar."

After *Marjorie Morningstar,* Wouk interrupted his career as a novelist to write a short, clear account of the Jewish faith from a personal viewpoint—something he had been thinking of doing for years. Dedicated to the memory of his grandfather, Mendel Leib Levine, a rabbi from Minsk, *This Is My God* was published in 1959 and became a best-seller. Then, with *Youngblood Hawke* and *Don't Stop the Carnival,* Wouk returned to writing fiction, but he also began work on a second ambition: a panoramic novel of World War II.

Wouk first considered doing a global war novel in 1944, according to *Time*'s Timothy Foote. Later, *The Caine Mutiny* "threatened to sprawl in that direction," noted Foote, "with more home-front material and a subplot in Europe. Wisely, Wouk cut it back and waited." Having begun reading standard histories in 1962, Wouk moved to Washington two years later to utilize the National Archives and Library of Congress, as well as to interview surviving military leaders. His quest for information also led him to England, France, Italy, Germany, Poland, Czechoslovakia, Israel, Iran, and the Soviet Union. Due to the scope of his task, Wouk ended up writing not one but two novels: *The Winds of War* and a sequel, *War and Remembrance.* "Since both have been best sellers, it is likely that more Americans have learned about, or remembered, the war through Wouk's account than from any other single source in the last decade," claimed Michael Mandelbaum in the *Political Science Quarterly.*

Generally praised by critics for their depth and accuracy of detail, the two books may be described as the history of the Second World War seen through the eyes of an American family and their immediate friends and contacts. *The Winds of War* takes Commander Victor "Pug" Henry and his family from the invasion of Poland to the attack on Pearl Harbor, Hawaii, and *War and Remembrance* details their experiences from Pearl Harbor to the dropping of the atomic bomb on Hiroshima, Japan. Over the course of the war, Henry serves as a special presidential envoy; meets Hitler, Stalin, Churchill, and Mussolini; is in Hawaii the day after the attack on Pearl Harbor; is present at the summit meetings off Nova Scotia in 1940 and in Tehran in 1943; is in London during the Battle of Britain; accompanies the Harriman-Beaverbrook mission to Moscow in 1941; participates in the battles of Midway, Guadalcanal, and Leyte Gulf; tours the Russian front in 1944; and even comes in contact with people working on the Manhattan Project. What he fails to witness, members of his family see: the invasion of Poland, the war in North Africa, the fall of Singapore, and the horrors of Auschwitz.

In reviewing the two books, critics often point out that this technique of depicting the effects of war on ordinary people (some of whom rub shoulders with the high and mighty) is a familiar one. Timothy Foote, among others, suggested that Wouk's opus is reminiscent of *War and Peace*—though not of the same quality—and that Wouk's aim is "nothing less than to do for the middle-class American vision of World War II pretty much what [Leo] Tolstoy did for the Battle of Borodino." More often, however, reviewers like Granville Hicks of the *New York Times Book Review* cited the resemblance between "Pug" Henry and Upton Sinclair's Lanny Budd: "Like Lanny, Pug becomes a kind of secret Presidential agent. In this role, he turns up at most of the places where history is being made."

Several critics charged that the technique results in characterization that is purely functional. Though Hicks admited that Wouk has "the gift of compelling narrative," he felt that the characters in *The Winds of War,* "even Pug Henry, are never living human beings. Although [Wouk] tries to give these men and women some semblance of reality by involving them in more or less complicated love affairs, they remain essentially observers and reporters." Similarly, Pearl K. Bell, reviewing *War and Remembrance* in *Commentary,* described the characters as "not merely trivial but offensively so. Time and again, Wouk the student of history writes a brilliantly evocative account of battle—he has mastered every maneuver, knows exactly how submarines, aircraft carriers, battleships, destroyers, dive bombers work, how the vast machinery of war was deployed during a particular operation—only to return with a dismaying thump to his super-Lanny Budd hero, Captain (eventually Admiral) Victor (Pug) Henry." Foote is willing "to forgive Henry, and the author, the narrative necessities that shoot [Henry] hither and yon and miraculously equip him with the Russian and German necessary to do his work for Wouk, F.D.R., and the reader. [But] not so the other Henrys. The wife who would worry about getting her hair done on the day of Armageddon, a wayward daughter caught up in the sleazy radio industry in New York, two naval-officer sons, all are conventional appurtenances, without the emotional or dynastic depth to support a drama on the scale of World War II."

Nevertheless, Michael Mandelbaum asserted that Wouk's aim was to create something not purely fictional and that his "hybrid literary genre" of historical romance "turns out to be singularly appropriate." Reviewing *The Winds of War* in the *Midwest Quarterly,* Richard R. Bolton wrote: "Critics who have castigated the book for failing in various ways as a *novel* have seemingly overlooked the author's description of it as a romance. That form is older, and adheres to rather different standards, than the novel. Much criticism directed at the book's emphasis of incident and plot over deep character development, or its unfashionably detailed descriptions of people's appearances, becomes immaterial if one accepts Wouk's idea of what *The Winds of War* is—a historical romance, with a didactic purpose. That purpose is to dramatize the author's ideas about his themes—how the 'curse' emerged, how we might constructively understand it, and how 'men of good will' have been involved with it."

A major theme of the two books, according to Mandelbaum, "centers on the German question. Why did the Germans do it? Why did they cause so much trouble? Why, especially, did they behave in such brutal, aggressive fashion? These questions arise again and again, and Wouk has different characters give different answers—[geopolitical, political, cultural, historical]. Together they make for a symposium on the central puzzle of the twentieth century." Mandelbaum suggested that at the heart of the German question is the fate of the Jews under the Third Reich, the description of which "gives the two books their enduring message, a message that neither plain fiction nor standard history could convey as forcefully. It is not, [however,] the only, nor perhaps the primary, message that the author intends."

Wouk widens the scope of the story by presenting a German perspective on the war through excerpts of General Armin von Roon's *World Empire Lost,* an imaginary treatise based on actual writings of German generals. Bolton claimed that von Roon's views, "and (in places) Henry's 'later' comments on them, jolt the reader out of enough preconceptions to make him more receptive to Wouk's own explanations of why things turned out as they did, or (more important) *how* they might have been made to turn out better." Bolton surmised that, according to Wouk, World War II was a "natural" disaster in that it arose from fallible human nature: "Human cruelty, of which war is the most massive and spectacular manifestation, occurs not because most people are cruel, but because most people are weak or lazy, or too wishful to perceive in time what truly cruel people like the Nazis are about. . . . Given that fallibility, World War II, and possibly other wars since, probably could not have been avoided." But, he continued, "given also the availability of enough men with the training and virtues of Victor Henry—the truly 'best' in Wouk's view, those who do not lack conviction—that war, and possibly others since, could have been ameliorated, at least. It was not ameliorated, because democratic societies, notably ours, have little stomach for the unpleasant facts that are a military professional's daily fare."

Thus, Bolton discerns a thematic relation to *The Caine Mutiny:* "Captain Henry can be seen as the fulfillment and justification of Lt. Barney Greenwald's unexpected and much discussed encomium to Regular Navy officers in the post-trial scene of *The Caine Mutiny.* Greenwald pays his tributes not so much to the *Caine*'s fallen captain as to what-Queeg-could-have-been . . . —the selfless and dedicated guardian of a reckless and unappreciative nation's safety. In Henry, Wouk presents a man who really *is* what Queeg could only try, pretend, or fail to be, the 'compleat' and admirable United States Navy officer." Pearl K. Bell believed that Wouk's traditionalist support of the military career man will strike many "as at best naive, at worst absurdly out of touch with the Catch-22 lunacy of all war, including the war against Hitler. [However,] it is precisely to confute such facile and ahistorical cynicism that Wouk devotes so large and sober a part of his novel to the Final Solution and the ideological poison that overwhelmed the German people during Hitler's twelve years of power."

In Wouk's eyes, men like Victor Henry, wrote Bolton, have instincts and habits that "predispose them to be builders and preservers. . . . 'Constructive' rather than creative, they build things that are not particularly original, but are for Wouk the cement of civilization—families, homes, churches, firms, and especially, professional reputations. What repels Capt. Henry first about Nazi racism is that it destroys these things, and judges men on factors other than their accomplishments. Only after learning of the *Einsatzgruppen*'s atrocities does he react to Nazi racism with more visceral rage." Referring to the one-word Hebrew epigraph of *The Winds of War,* "Remember!," Bolton concluded: "Part of remembering, in Wouk's sense, would be to emulate Victor Henry and to listen, early and attentively, to those men who live in his tradition. If we do not, the author suggests, . . . it becomes too easy to look away, to make excuses while the massacres begin, while terrorism becomes pardonable."

Wouk's 1985 novel, *Inside, Outside,* "comes as close to being an outright autobiography as he is likely to write," declared John Eisenhower in the *Chicago Tribune Book World.* It tells of a Jewish man who, like Wouk, was born in New York City in 1915, the son of immigrant parents who established a commercial laundry business. Like Wouk, protagonist Israel David Goodkind—"Yisroelke" to his friends and family on the "inside"—worked as a gag writer, although Goodkind becomes a lawyer rather than a novelist. Goodkind is, however, writing his memoirs, which transforms Wouk's novel into "a paean to the American Jewish experience," according to *Diversion* contributor Sybil S. Steinberg. Unifying the novel, which deals by turns with Goodkind's present reality as a speech writer for U.S. President Richard Nixon and with Goodkind's childhood and relatives, is the tension between the "inside" (which includes Jewish religious life, values, and heritage as well as the search for identity for Jew or gentile) and the "outside" (secular American life).

The novel—Wouk's first in seven years—received mixed reviews. Critics such as Steinberg praised the "breezy, humorous style" in which it is written and cited its compassion and wisdom. Eisenhower wrote, it is "an easy-to-read, informative tale that . . . provides an enlightening perspective on Jewish attitudes." He singled out one scene in which "Jews of varying persuasions . . . exchange views and insults" and concluded that "that scene alone, which illuminates so much of the current Jewish dilemma, gives this novel the right to be regarded as Wouk's most significant work since 'The Caine Mutiny.'" In contrast, Christopher Lehmann-Haupt of the *New York Times* found the novel "remarkably predictable" and, "worst of all, . . . smug." Others criticized the book for superficiality and expressed reservations about what Bill Wine in the *Philadelphia Inquirer* deemed "the failure of Wouk's storytelling proclivities to break out. The narrative, though carefully wrought, somehow registers as out of kilter, as if the seemingly appropriate admixture of memories, insights, observations and descriptions were really a convenience embraced by a writer unable to find a handle on his material." Nonetheless, Wine approvingly concluded that, "on the whole, *Inside, Outside* is an entertaining X-ray of being Jewish in America." Novelist James Michener, reviewing the book in the *New York Times Book Review,* judged it "ambitious," lauding its segments as "compact, beautifully focused and often hilarious." Among the critics who acknowledged faults, several, like Steinberg, still maintained that "the universality of [the] theme . . . lifts this novel above the level of inbred American Jewish experience. For *Inside, Outside* is about anyone who must reconcile private and public commitments. It is about living a good life on many levels, and while it makes no pretension of being profound, it is funny, wise, and kind."

Nearly a decade later Wouk produced two expansive historical novels on the founding of the modern state of Israel. *The Hope* picks up at the end of the Second World War and recounts the creation and early development of Israel through the lives of several military men and their families. The central character is Zev Barak, an Israeli officer who participates in the 1948 War of Independence, the 1956 Suez Campaign, and the Six Day War of 1967, and who is privy to political and diplomatic intrigue involving David Ben-Gurion, Yitzhak Rabin, and Menachem Begin. In *The Glory,* the sequel, Wouk continues his story of Israel's struggle for nationhood through the experiences of the Barak family, covering the period from 1967 to the early 1980s.

Though finding weakness in Wouk's characterizations and obtuse rendering of military action in *The Hope, People* reviewer Sara Nelson noted that "Wouk has invented plenty of behind-the-scenes machinations that make for frequent page turning—as well as educational reading." *Washington Post Book World* contributor Webster Schott similarly found the narrative of *The Hope* compelling despite "literary lapses." According to Schott, "burning Jewish pride or chauvinism . . . animates Wouk's novel. It is not an emotion likely to lead to epiphany in fiction but it makes for heroic storytelling, especially when all the wars are for survival and all the military odds are unfavorable." Irving Abrahamson wrote of *The Hope* in the Chicago *Tribune Books,* "Though Wouk serves up a full cast of characters and keeps the pot constantly boiling with their largely unfulfilled love affairs, his primary aim is to describe the heroic aspects of Israel's rebirth and to trace Israel's part in the game of power politics played out by Britain, France, Russia and America in the Middle East."

Despite noting melodramatic elements in both novels, *Booklist* reviewer Gilbert Taylor praised *The Glory* for Wouk's ability to "humanize these intense events" while incorporating major historical figures. Relying on authentic sources for his material, Wouk provides several pages of historical notes in *The Hope* and claims to have quoted Arab leaders directly from historical records and contemporary journalism. "Though underappreciated by literary types," wrote Arnold Beichman in the *National Review,* "Herman Wouk is one of our outstanding historical novelists."

BIOGRAPHICAL AND CRITICAL SOURCES:

BOOKS

Beichman, Arnold C., *Herman Wouk: The Novelist as Social Historian,* Transaction Books (Somerset, NJ), 1984.

Bentley, Eric, *The Dramatic Event: An American Chronicle,* Horizon Press (New York, NY), 1954.

Contemporary Literary Criticism, Thomson Gale (Detroit, MI), Volume 1, 1973, Volume 9, 1978, Volume 38, 1986.

Dictionary of Literary Biography Yearbook: 1982, Thomson Gale (Detroit, MI), 1983.

Fiedler, Leslie A., *Love and Death in the American Novel,* Stein & Day (New York, NY), 1966.

Fuller, Edmund, *Man in Modern Fiction: Some Minority Opinions on Contemporary American Writing,* Random House (New York, NY), 1958.

Geismar, Maxwell, *American Moderns from Rebellion to Conformity,* Hill & Wang (New York, NY), 1958.

Hyman, Stanley Edgar, *Standards: A Chronicle of Books for Our Time,* Horizon Press (New York, NY), 1966.

Mazzeno, Laurence W., *Herman Wouk,* Macmillan (London, England), 1994.

Prescott, Orville, *In My Opinion,* Bobbs-Merrill (Indianapolis, IN), 1952.

Sarner, Harvey, *A Checklist of the Works of Herman Work,* Brunswick Press (Fredericton, New Brunswick), 1995.

Stuckey, W.J., *The Pulitzer Prize Novels,* University of Oklahoma Press (Norman, OK), 1966.

PERIODICALS

Antioch Review, Volume 16, 1956.

Atlantic, August, 1951; October, 1955; December, 1971.

Booklist, December 15, 1994, p. 715.

Book Week, March 7, 1965.

Boston Sunday Globe, March 24, 1985.

Chicago Sunday Tribune, March 18, 1951.

Chicago Tribune, February 6, 1983; September 12, 1988.

Chicago Tribune Book World, November 14, 1971; March 24, 1985.

Christian Science Monitor, September 1, 1955; September 24, 1959; May 24, 1962; October 23, 1978.

College English, Volume 17, 1956.

Commentary, December, 1978.

Critic, August, 1965.

Detroit Free Press, February 6, 1983; April 7, 1985.

Detroit News, January 24, 1985.

Diversion, May, 1985.

Economist, November 20, 1971.

Entertainment Weekly, January 14, 1994, p. 49.

Globe and Mail (Toronto, Ontario, Canada), June 15, 1985.

Library Journal, February 15, 1994, p. 204; June 15, 1995, p. 110.

Life, June, 1962; November 19, 1971.

Los Angeles Times Book Review, March 3, 1985; May 8, 1986; December 12, 1993, p. 3.

Midwest Quarterly, July, 1975.

National Review, January 23, 1995, p. 72.

New Republic, February 15, 1954; September 3, 1955; June 11, 1962; October 14, 1978.

Newsweek, March 9, 1965; November 29, 1971; October 9, 1978; February 7, 1983.

New York, August 30, 1971.

New York Herald Tribune Book Review, March 18, 1951; September 4, 1955; May 20, 1962.

New York Herald Tribune Weekly Book Review, April 20, 1947; August 29, 1948.

New York Times, April 20, 1947; August 29, 1948; March 18, 1951; September 4, 1955; September 27, 1959; January 2, 1983; January 21, 1983; January 30, 1983; February 5, 1983; February 6, 1983; March 7, 1985.

New York Times Book Review, September 16, 1951; May 20, 1962; November 14, 1971; November 12, 1978; March 10, 1985; January 9, 1994, p. 10.

Parade, February 6, 1983.

Partisan Review, Volume 20, 1953.

People, January 24, 1994, p. 27.

Philadelphia Inquirer, April 14, 1985.

Publishers Weekly, February 7, 1972; June 10, 1996, p. 47.

San Francisco Chronicle, March 24, 1985.

Saturday Review, February 6, 1954; September 3, 1955; September 26, 1959; May 19, 1962; November 27, 1971.

Saturday Review of Literature, April 19, 1947; August 21, 1948; March 31, 1951.

Time, April 9, 1951; September 5, 1955; May 18, 1962; March 5, 1965; November 22, 1971; October 16, 1978; February 7, 1983; February 28, 1983; April 1, 1985.

Times Literary Supplement, November 9, 1951.

Times (London, England), March 2, 1985.

Tribune Books (Chicago, IL), December 26, 1993, p. 5.

USA Today, March 22, 1985.

Vogue, February 15, 1952.

Washingtonian, March, 1986.

Washington Post, April 29, 1985; May 31, 1986.

Washington Post Book World, October 8, 1978; March 10, 1985; December 12, 1993, p. 3.

* * *

WRIGHT, Charles 1935-
(Charles Penzel Wright, Jr.)

PERSONAL: Born August 25, 1935, in Pickwick Dam, TN; son of Charles Penzel and Mary Castleman (Winter) Wright; married Holly McIntire, April 6, 1969; children: Luke Savin Herrick. *Education:* Davidson College, B.A., 1957; University of Iowa, M.F.A., 1963; graduate study, University of Rome, 1963-64. *Politics:* Democrat. *Religion:* Episcopalian.

ADDRESSES: Home—940 Locust Ave., Charlottesville, VA 22901-4030. *Office*—Department of English, Bryan Hall, University of Virginia, Charlottesville, VA 22903.

CAREER: University of California, Irvine, 1966-83, began as assistant professor, became professor of English; University of Virginia, Charlottesville, Souder Family Professor of English, 1983—. Fulbright lecturer in Venice, Italy, 1968-69, distinguished visiting professor, Universita Degli Studi, Florence, Italy, 1992. *Military service:* U.S. Army, Intelligence Corps, 1957-61.

MEMBER: PEN American Center, Fellowship of Southern Writers, Academy of American Poets (chancellor), American Academy and Institute of Arts and Letters, American Academy of Arts and Sciences.

AWARDS, HONORS: Fulbright scholar at University of Rome, 1963-65; Eunice Tietjens Award, *Poetry* magazine, 1969; Guggenheim fellow, 1975; Melville Cane Award, Poetry Society of America, and Edgar Allan Poe Award, Academy of American Poets, both 1976, both for *Bloodlines;* Academy-Institute Award, American Academy and Institute of the Arts, 1977; PEN translation award, 1979; Ingram Merrill fellow, 1980 and 1993; National Book Award in poetry (cowinner), 1983, for *Country Music: Selected Early Poems;* National Book Critics Circle Award nomination in poetry, 1984, for *The Other Side of the River;* Brandeis Creative Arts Citation for poetry, 1987; Merit Medal, American Academy and Institute Arts and Letters, 1992; Ruth Lilly Poetry Prize, 1993; fellow, American Academy of Arts and Letters, 1995; Lenore Marshall Poetry Prize, Academy of American Poets, 1996; Wood Prize, *Poetry* magazine, 1996; Book Prize, *Los Angeles Times,* and National Book Critics Circle Award for poetry, both 1997, and Pulitzer Prize for Poetry, Ambassador Book Award, and Premio di Poesia, Antico Fattore, all 1998, all for *Black Zodiac;* fellow, American Academy of Arts and Sciences, 2002.

WRITINGS:

POETRY

Six Poems, David Freed, 1965.

The Dream Animal (chapbook), House of Anansi (Toronto, Ontario, Canada), 1968.

Private Madrigals, limited edition, Abraxas Press (Madison, WI), 1969.

The Grave of the Right Hand, Wesleyan University Press (Middletown, CT), 1970.

The Venice Notebook, Barn Dream Press (Boston, MA), 1971.

Hard Freight (also see below), Wesleyan University Press (Middletown, CT), 1973.

Bloodlines (also see below), Wesleyan University Press (Middletown, CT), 1975.

China Trace (also see below), Wesleyan University Press (Middletown, CT), 1977.

Colophons, limited edition, Windhover (New York, NY), 1977.

Wright: A Profile, with interview and critical essay by David St. John, Grilled Flowers Press (Iowa City, IA), 1979.

Dead Color, limited edition, Meadow Press, 1980.

The Southern Cross (also see below), Random House (New York, NY), 1981.

Country Music: Selected Early Poems (includes *Hard Freight, Bloodlines,* and *China Trace*), Wesleyan University Press (Middletown, CT), 1982.

Four Poems of Departure, limited edition, Trace Editions (Portland, OR), 1983.

The Other Side of the River (also see below), Random House (New York, NY), 1984.

Five Journals (also see below), limited edition, Red Ozier Press (New York, NY), 1986.

Zone Journals (includes *Five Journals*; also see below), Farrar, Straus (New York, NY), 1988.

The World of the Ten Thousand Things: Poems, 1980-1990 (includes *The Southern Cross, The Other Side of the River,* and *Zone Journals*), Farrar, Straus (New York, NY), 1990.

Xionia, Windhoven Press (Iowa City, IA), 1990.

Chickamauga (also see below), Farrar, Straus (New York, NY), 1995.

Black Zodiac (also see below), Farrar, Straus (New York, NY), 1997.

Appalachia (also see below), Farrar, Straus (New York, NY), 1998.

Negative Blue: Selected Later Poems (includes *Chickamaunga, Black Zodiac,* and *Appalachia*), Farrar, Straus (New York, NY), 2000.

A Short History of the Shadow, Farrar, Straus (New York, NY), 2002.

Buffalo Yoga, Farrar, Straus (New York, NY), 2004.

OTHER

The Voyage, Patrician Press, 1963.

Backwater, Golem Press (Boulder, CO), 1973.

(Translator) Eugenio Montale, *The Storm,* Field Editions, 1978.

(Translator) Eugenio Montale, *Motets,* Windhover (New York, NY), 1981.

(Translator) Dino Campana, *Orphic Songs,* Field Editions, 1984.

Halflife: Improvisations and Interviews, 1977-1987, University of Michigan Press (Ann Arbor, MI), 1988.

Quarter Notes: Improvisations and Interviews, University of Michigan Press, 1995 (Ann Arbor, MI).

Selected writings have been recorded by the Library of Congress Archive of Recorded Poetry and Literature and the Modern Poetry Association.

SIDELIGHTS: Pulitzer Prize-winning poet Charles Wright creates verse that is a "strange alchemy, a fusion of the direct, understated lyrics of ancient Chinese poets like Tu Fu and Wang Wei, the lush language of nineteenth-century Jesuit Gerard Manley Hopkins, and the allusive, rhetorical movement—the 'gists and piths'—of Ezra Pound's Cantos," according to Ted Genoways in the *Southern Review.* Wright is a notable American poet whose reputation has increased steadily with each poetry collection he has published. From his early collection *The Grave of the Right Hand* to lauded works such as *The Other Side of the River, Zone Journals, Chickamauga, Black Zodiac, Appalachia, Negative Blue: Selected Later Poems,* and *A Short History of the Shadow,* Wright has worked in a style that creates a feeling of immediacy and concreteness by emphasizing objects and personal perspective. Wright's literary perseverance has resulted in what David Young described in *Contemporary Poets* as "one of the truly distinctive bodies of poetry created in the second half of the twentieth century." Many critics believe that Wright's childhood in rural Tennessee remains a vital force in his writing, for he shows a typically southern concern for the past and its power. Young, for example, wrote in his *Contemporary Poets* piece that Wright's "Southern heritage makes him both a powerful storyteller and a writer unafraid of ornate, carnivalesque language." Yet Wright reaches beyond his southern roots, creating images of landscapes from Italy to Virginia in what Genoways typified as a "search for transcendence in the landscape of the everyday." According to Genoways, "Wright's poems yearn for the ideal, but are tempered by a suspicion of futility."

Wright began writing poetry while serving in Italy with the U.S. Army. While there, as Wright recalled in George F. Butterick's essay in the *Dictionary of Literary Biography Yearbook: 1982,* he "began using Ezra Pound's Italian Cantos first as a guide book to out-of-the-way places, then as a reference book and finally as a 'copy' book." Writing in *Contemporary Poets,* Young noted Pound's influence on Wright. "It might be said," Young speculated, "that Wright is reconstituting Pound's failed program along new and successful lines: more centered, less bookish, more ready to mend what is broken and relinquish authority in areas where it will not hold firm." But Young concluded that Wright's "post-modern temper is more that of a listener and observer: attentive, modest, but firmly committed to a music that realizes poetry's highest aims, the aims of Dante."

Ezra Pound's influence is readily evident in *The Grave of the Right Hand,* Wright's first major collection. These poems "have the polished clarity one would expect from a master of the plain style," *Georgia Review* contributor Peter Stitt observed. "They are obviously meant to speak to the reader, to communicate something he can share." At the same time, *The Grave of the Right Hand* is the most symbolic of all Wright's works, with images of gloves, shoes, hands, and hats recurring throughout. Through these images, the poet introduces what will become his recurring themes, which Butterick summarized as "mortality, the uses of memory, the irrepressible past, states of being, personal salvation, the correspondence between nature and the spiritual work, and, most broadly, the human condition."

Wright is credited with finding his own voice in *Hard Freight,* which Peter Meinke called in a *New Republic* review "less Poundian, less hard-edged, than his first book, *The Grave of the Right Hand.*" *Poetry* reviewer John L. Carpenter likewise applauded Wright for reaching for his own style in *Hard Freight:* "It is less incisive and less deliberate than the first book, but it is more experimental, less ironclad and defensive." It is in this volume that the poet first exhibits his technique of creating poetry by compiling catalogs of fragmented images. It is a device which requires "that the reader assist in the creative activity," found *Washington Post Book World* contributor Edward Kessler. "[Wright's]; almost spastic writing can at times be enlivening and fascinating, like watching the changing fragments of a kaleidoscope."

But this technique is not appreciated by all critics, some of whom find it excessive. As Sally M. Gall declared in *Shenandoah:* "[Wright]; frantically piles up details, images, similes, and metaphors as if sheer quantity can replace quality of perception. His catalogues can be perniciously boring rather than enlightening." Kessler, however, disagreed with this assessment, stating that Wright's "senses are awake, and even when he cannot quite bring his *things* of the world into a satisfying shape, his fragments are rife with suggestions. This man is feeling his way toward a personal definition."

Bloodlines bears similarities to *Hard Freight,* but many reviewers felt that Wright's voice is even stronger in this later volume. *Yale Review* contributor J.D. McClatchy, for instance, observed, "Charles Wright has come completely home in *Bloodlines,* a book that confirms and emphasizes his reputation." Carol Muske also noted the power of this collection in *Parnassus: Poetry in Review:* "[Wright] is on the move. His poems fairly explode from the page in hurly-burly refrain, elliptical syntax, and giddy shifts that recall Hopkins." McClatchy added that Wright "recreates not aspects but images of his past experiences—prayer meetings, sexual encounters, dreams—mingling memory and fantasy. The poems are suffused with remembered light."

Hard Freight, Bloodlines, and *China Trace* comprise what Wright considers to be a poetic trilogy. Explained Kathleen Agena in *Partisan Review,* "Like Wallace Stevens, Wright has conceived of his work as a whole. Individual poems are arresting but none of them quite has its meaning alone. The poems elucidate and comment on each other, extending and developing certain key metaphors and images." In *China Trace,* Wright again considers universal connections to the past. According to Butterick, the poet describes this collection as "a book of Chinese poems that don't sound like Chinese poems and aren't Chinese poems but are *like* Chinese poems in the sense that they give you an idea of one man's relationship to the endlessness, the ongoingness, the everlastingness of what's around him, and his relationship to it as he stands in the natural world."

Works such as *Zone Journals* and the collection *The World of the Ten Thousand Things* reflect Wright's "departure from his earlier crystalline short lyrics that aimed for inevitability of effect," Helen Vendler observed in the *New Republic.* These journal poems "weave diverse thematic threads into a single autobiographical fabric" which can be read as a single work, Richard Tillinghast wrote in the *New York Times Book Review.* "Freed from the stringencies of unity and closure demanded by the sort of poem most readers are used to, Mr. Wright is at liberty to spin out extended meditations that pick up, work with, lay aside and return again to landscapes, historical events and ideas." With his "subtle cadences" and "famously 'good ear,'" the critic added, Wright "continues to reveal himself as a poet of great purity and originality."

Writing in *Poetry* about *Chickamauga,* David Baker observed that Wright uses abstractions to sustain the oblique. Of Wright's style, he commented, "Almost nothing ever happens in a Charles Wright poem. This is his central act of restraint, a spiritualist's abstinence, where meditation is not absence but an alternative to action and to linear, dramatic finality." David Mason admitted in the *Hudson Review,* however, that Wright's poetry disappointed him. Mason found that Wright's "ideas are uninteresting, his poems undramatic; his language is only intermittently charged or lyrical." He further remarked, "There is plenty of meditative near-spirituality in *Chickamauga,* but it's all air and light, history without the details." According to James Longenbach in the *Yale Review,* Wright's career seems to change with *Chickamauga,* as he tries to constrain his writing. "Wright seems to feel that all he can do is spin new variations on a limited number of subjects and scenes [in *Chickamauga,*]," wrote the critic, although the work is "a beautiful book, bearably human yet in touch with the sublime."

Agena contended that Wright's power comes from his faith in "the mad sense of language" and his willingness to abandon himself to it. She summarized: "When Charles Wright's poems work, which is most of the time, the poetic energies seem to break the membrane of syntax, exploding the surface, reverberating in multiple directions simultaneously. . . . It seems to happen by accident, as if Wright simply sets the words in motion and they, playing a game according to their own rules, write the poem."

But Wright's greatest accomplishment, according to Butterick, "is the imagistic narrative." Butterick added, "How he activates and propels the line of images . . . is his special genius, his ability to drive spirit into the matter of words." William Logan, meanwhile, wrote in the *New York Times Book Review,* "[Wright's]; best work has always been founded in the hard-edged fact, not the gauze of metaphysics," and he praised Wright's "individuality and seriousness, his gorgeous images and taste for experiment." As a result, the critic concluded, "for twenty years, [Wright]; has written to a consistently high and exacting standard."

Wright continued to impress readers and reviewers with *Black Zodiac,* which secured a host of awards, including the Pulitzer Prize for poetry and the National Book Critics Circle Award, following its appearance in 1997. Donna Seaman wrote in *Booklist* that Wright is "wholly in his element in these gleaming pages," while Robert Ellis Hosmer, Jr. hailed the volume in an *America* review as "an intriguing, occasionally very difficult but immensely rewarding collection." Lee Oser, meanwhile, reported in *World Literature Today* that Wright "writes very well" and acknowledged that he "clears some serious ground." Barbara Hoffert, in her *Library Journal* review, heartily endorsed *Black Zodiac,* declaring that its "luscious jumble of language simply must be experienced firsthand," and James Longenbach, in a *Nation* appraisal, described the collection as "haunted, elegiac" and deemed it Wright's "most richly satisfying single book."

Wright's following collection, *Appalachia,* inspired further praise and appreciation. *Library Journal* reviewer

Hoffert reported that in this volume Wright mines his themes in "new and exciting ways," while *Booklist* critic Seaman called Wright "a philosopher-poet with a gift for whimsical imagery." Fred Muratori, another *Library Journal* reviewer, affirmed that *Appalachia* constitutes an "animated collection," while a *Kirkus Reviews* critic deemed the volume "characteristic" of Wright's poetic pursuits.

If *China Trace* completed the first of Wright's trilogies, *Appalachia* completed the third such trilogy sequence, along with *Chickamauga* and *Black Zodiac,* as Wright revealed to Genoways. The middle sequence consists of *The Southern Cross, The Other Side of the River,* and *Zone Journals.* "It's an odd sequence," the poet commented. "All three trilogies do the same thing, and they have essentially the same structure. Past, present, future: yesterday, today, tomorrow." And just as the earlier trilogies were ultimately gathered into larger volumes—the first sequence in *Country Music* and the second in *The World of Ten Thousand Things*—so too was the third sequence collected in the year 2000 volume *Negative Blue: Selected Later Poems.* Writing in *World Literature Today,* Ashley Brown called this final installment "one of the most ambitious poems of our time," while a contributor for *Publishers Weekly* noted that Wright gathers a "decade's worth of striking descriptions and laid-back meditation" in the collection, which concludes with seven new poems. For this reviewer, Wright's own career makes a unified poem, a "continual, often compelling exploration of seeing, thinking and the dialectic between them." Taken together, Wright's three trilogies have been referred to as "The Appalachian Book of the Dead."

Wright followed up *Negative Blue* with *A Short History of the Shadow,* a "moody, winning collection," according to a *Publishers Weekly* reviewer. Here Wright serves up a sampling of many of his traditional themes: evocations of Blue Ridge landscapes, tips of the hat to his favorite poets, as well as a genial recognition of the "fleetingness of all things," as the same contributor mentioned. Muratori, writing in *Library Journal,* pointed out Wright's "signature style: slow pace and passive imagery," both at work in these "gravely wistful" poems. Oser, writing in *World Literature Today,* noted that Wright and his peers are "the last generation that did not have its brains softened by television." Oser went on to note that in *A Short History of the Shadow,* Wright "sounds an extended note of suffering, loitering among landscapes that show a spiritual kinship to Hardy's, though the major influence remains, as ever, Pound." For William Logan, writing in the *New Criterion,* however, the poems of *A Short History of the Shadow,* compared to those of his three trilogies that took a quarter-century to finish, "are written in the sketchy, hither-thither manner, like the musings of a man waking from anaesthesia, into which Wright's hard early style has gradually softened." Logan further noted that Wright's "specialty is romantic vision," and that he "finds the sublime in the unlikeliest of places." Yet in the end, Logan felt that despite the fact that Wright is "one of our most talented poets, . . . too many of these poems skim the surface of the poet's impressions the way a cook skims fat." Jay Parini, reviewing the collection in the *Nation,* was more positive in his evaluation. Parini felt the poems in *A Short History of the Shadow* harkened back to Wright's "middle period," beginning with *The Other Side of the River.* Parini went on to note that Wright "fetches the reader's attention with compelling aphorisms, with phrases arranged to crate a subtle, alluring music." Wright is, Parini further suggested, "all ears, all eyes, sifting the world that falls before him with astonishing freshness, thinking shallowly so he can see and hear profoundly."

Through his numerous collection of poetry and particularly his "Appalachian Book of the Dead" sequence, Wright has consistently proved that he is, as Parini and other critics maintain, "among the best poets" of his generation. Yet Wright remains stoic about such achievements: it is not the poet, but the poems, as he concluded to Genoways. "One wants one's work to be paid attention to, but I hate personal attention. I just want everyone to read the poems. I want my poetry to get all the attention in the world, but I want to be the anonymous author."

BIOGRAPHICAL AND CRITICAL SOURCES:

BOOKS

Andrews, Tom, *The Point Where All Things Meet: Essays on Charles Wright,* Oberlin College Press (Oberlin, OH), 1995.

Contemporary Literary Criticism, Thomson Gale (Detroit, MI), Volume 6, 1976, Volume 13, 1980, Volume 28, 1984.

Contemporary Poets, 5th edition, St. James Press (Chicago, IL), 1991.

Dictionary of Literary Biography, Volume 165: *American Poets since World War II, Fourth Series,* Thomson Gale (Detroit, MI), 1996.

Dictionary of Literary Biography Yearbook: 1982, Thomson Gale (Detroit, MI), 1983.

Friebert, Stuart, and David Young, editors, *A Field Guide to Contemporary Poetry and Poetics,* Longman (New York, NY), 1980.

Ingersoll, Earl W., and others, editors, *Post-Confessionals: Conversations with American Poets of the Eighties,* Fairleigh Dickinson University Press (Madison, NJ), 1989.

Perkins, David, *A History of Modern Poetry,* Harvard University Press (Cambridge, MA), 1987.

Vendler, Helen, *The Music of What Happens,* Harvard University Press (Cambridge, MA), 1988.

PERIODICALS

America, December 20, 1997, Robert Ellis Hosmer, Jr., review of *Black Zodiac,* pp. 24-26.

Booklist, April 15, 1997, Donna Seaman, review of *Black Zodiac,* p. 1337; November 1, 1998, Donna Seaman, review of *Appalachia,* p. 466.

Hudson Review, spring, 1996, David Mason, review of *Chickamauga,* p. 166.

Kirkus Reviews, October 1, 1998, review of *Appalachia,* p. 94.

Library Journal, April 15, 1997, Barbara Hoffert, review of *Black Zodiac;* October 1, 1998, Fred Muratori, review of *Appalachia,* p. 94; April 1, 1999, Barbara Hoffert, review of *Appalachia,* p. 9; April, 2003, Fred Muratori, review of *A Short History of the Shadow,* pp. 112-113.

Nation, April 14, 1997, James Longenbach, review of *Black Zodiac;* May 20, 2002, Jay Parini, review of *A Short History of the Shadow,* p. 30.

New Criterion, June, 2002, William Logan, review of *A Short History of the Shadow,* pp. 75-82.

New Republic, November 24, 1973, Peter Meinke, review of *Hard Freight.*

Parnassus: Poetry in Review, spring-summer, 1976, Carol Muske, review of *Bloodlines.*

Poetry, April, 1996, David Baker, review of *Chickamauga,* p. 33.

Publishers Weekly, April 24, 2000, review of *Negative Blue: Selected Later Poems,* p. 81; February 25, 2003, review of *A Short History of the Shadow,* p. 56.

Shenandoah, fall, 1974, Sally M. Gall, review of *Hard Freight.*

Southern Review, spring, 2000, Ted Genoways, "An Interview with Charles Wright," pp. 442-452.

Washington Post Book World, May 5, 1974, Edward Kessler, review of *Hard Freight.*

World Literature Today, autumn, 1997, Lee Oser, review of *Black Zodiac;* autumn, 2000, Ashley Brown, review of *Negative Blue: Selected Later Poems,* p. 821; spring, 2003, Lee Oser, review of *A Short History of the Shadow,* pp. 105-106.

Yale Review, autumn, 1975, J.D. McClatchy, review of *Bloodlines;* October, 1995, James Longenbach, review of *Chickamauga,* p. 144.

ONLINE

Poets.org, http://www.poets.org/ (November 11, 2003), "Charles Wright: The Academy of American Poets."

University of Virginia News Online, http://www.virginia.edu/ (May 9, 2002), "Poet Charles Wright Is Named to American Academy of Arts."

* * *

WRIGHT, Charles Penzel, Jr.
See WRIGHT, Charles

* * *

WRIGHT, Judith 1915-2000 (Judith Arundell Wright)

PERSONAL: Born May 31, 1915, in Armidale, New South Wales, Australia; died of a heart attack, June 25, 2000, in Canberra, Australia; daughter of Phillip Arundell (a farmer and university administrator) and Ethel Mabel (Bigg) Wright; married Jack Philip McKinney (a philosophical writer), 1962 (died, 1966); children: Meredith Anne. *Education:* Attended New South Wales Correspondence School, New England Girls' School, and University of Sydney. *Politics:* "Swing voter." *Hobbies and other interests:* Gardening.

CAREER: Poet, writer, and activist. J. Walter Thompson (advertising agency), Sydney, Australia, secretary, 1938-39; University of Sydney, Sydney, secretary, 1940-42; Australian Universities Commission, Brisbane, Australia, clerk, 1943-46; University of Queensland, Brisbane, statistician, 1946-49. Part-time lecturer in Australian literature at various Australian universities. President, Wildlife Preservation Society of Queensland, 1962-74; member, Committee of Inquiry into the National Estate, Australia, 1973-74; secretary, Aboriginal Treaty Committee, 1978-83.

MEMBER: Society of Authors (Australia; council member), Australian Academy of the Humanities (fellow).

AWARDS, HONORS: Grace Leven Prize, 1953; D.Litt., University of New England, Armidale, Australia, 1963, Monash University, 1977, University of Sydney, 1977,

Australian National University, 1980, University of New South Wales, 1985, Griffith University, 1988, and University of Melbourne, 1988; *Encyclopedia Britannica* Award, 1964; Robert Frost Medallion, Fellowship of Australian Writers, 1975; Asan World Prize, Asan Memorial Association, 1984; New South Wales Premier's Special Prize for Poetry, 1991; Queen's Gold Medal for Poetry, 1992; Human Rights Poetry Award, 1994; establishment of The Judith Wright Centre of Contemporary Arts (Brisbane, Queensland, Australia), 2001.

WRITINGS:

Kings of the Dingoes (juvenile), illustrated by Barbara Albiston, Oxford University Press (Melbourne, Australia), 1958.

The Generations of Men, illustrated by Alison Forbes, Oxford University Press (Melbourne, Australia), 1959, revised edition, Harper (New York, NY), 1995.

The Day the Mountains Played (juvenile), Jacaranda, 1960, Boolarong, 1988.

Range the Mountains High (juvenile), Lansdowne Press, 1962, 3rd edition, 1971.

Charles Harpur (biography and criticism), Lansdowne Press, 1963.

Country Towns (juvenile), Oxford University Press (Melbourne, Australia), 1963.

Preoccupations in Australian Poetry (history and criticism), Oxford University Press (Melbourne, Australia), 1965, new edition, 1966.

The Nature of Love (short stories), Sun Books (Melbourne, Australia), 1966.

The River and the Road (juvenile), Lansdowne Press, 1966, revised edition, 1971.

Henry Lawson, Oxford University Press (Melbourne, Australia), 1967.

Because I Was Invited, Oxford University Press (Melbourne, Australia), 1975.

The Coral Battleground (documentary), Thomas Nelson (Australia), 1977.

The Cry for the Dead, Oxford University Press (Melbourne, Australia), 1981.

We Call for a Treaty, William Collins/John M. Fontana (London, England), 1985.

Born of the Conquerors: Selected Essays, Aboriginal Studies Press, 1991.

Going on Talking, Butterfly Books, 1992.

Tales of a Great Aunt: A Memoir, Ett Imprint (Bondi Junction, New South Wales), 1998.

Half a Lifetime (autobiography), edited by Patricia Clarke, Text Publishing (Melbourne, Australia), 1999.

Also contributor to periodicals, including *Honi Soit,Bulletin's Red Page,* and *Meanjin.*

POETRY

The Moving Image, Meanjin, 1946, revised edition, 1953.

Woman to Man, Angus & Robertson (Sydney, Australia) 1949, 2nd edition, 1955.

The Gateway, Angus & Robertson (Sydney, Australia) 1953.

The Two Fires, Angus & Robertson (Sydney, Australia) 1955.

Birds, Angus & Robertson (Sydney, Australia) 1962, 3rd edition, 1978.

Five Senses: Selected Poems, Angus & Robertson (Sydney, Australia) 1963, revised edition, 1972.

City Sunrise, limited edition, Shapcott Press, 1964.

The Other Half, Angus & Robertson (Sydney, Australia) 1966.

Collected Poems, Angus & Robertson (Sydney, Australia) 1971, 2nd edition, 1975.

Alive: Poems 1971-1972, Angus & Robertson (Sydney, Australia) 1973.

Fourth Quarter, and Other Poems, Angus & Robertson (Sydney, Australia) 1976.

The Double Tree: Selected Poems, Houghton Mifflin (Boston, MA), 1978.

Phantom Dwelling, Angus & Robertson (Sydney, Australia) 1985.

A Human Pattern: Selected Poems, Angus & Robertson (Sydney, Australia) 1990.

Collected Poems, 1942-1985, Angus & Robertson (Sydney, Australia) 1994.

EDITOR

Australian Poetry, Angus & Robertson (Sydney, Australia) 1948.

(And author of introduction) *A Book of Australian Verse,* Oxford University Press (Melbourne, Australia), 1956, 2nd revised edition, 1968.

(And author of introduction) *New Land, New Language: An Anthology of Australian Verse,* Oxford University Press (Melbourne, Australia), 1957.

Judith Wright (selected poetry), Angus & Robertson (Sydney, Australia) 1963.

Shaw Neilson (biography and selected poetry), Angus & Robertson (Sydney, Australia) 1963.

(With Andrew Thomson) *The Poet's Pen,* Jacaranda, 1965.

John Shaw Neilson, *Witnesses of Spring: Unpublished Poems of Shaw Neilson,* Angus & Robertson (Sydney, Australia) 1970.

SIDELIGHTS: A well-known author and poet in Australia, Judith Wright was "outrageously neglected" outside of her native land, according to *London Magazine* critic D.M. Thomas. After years of publishing her verse in Australian periodicals, as well as in books in her homeland and abroad, Wright accumulated much critical attention in Australia for her distinctly endemic poetry. One Australian reviewer, *Meanjin* contributor Elizabeth Vassilieff, considered Wright to be "the most interesting of Australian poets, with no exceptions." "Her poetry has the touch and feel of [Australia]," noted another *Meanjin* reviewer, S. Musgrove, "for she knows that man . . . must not lose that immediate contact" with the land. But although her poetry gained her the most attention, Ken Goodwin wrote in his *A History of Australian Literature* that Wright, "in both poetry and prose, presents a wide panorama of the interests of the socially conscious present-day Australian."

Wright's prose writing included children's stories, which she originally composed for her daughter, as well as criticism, the biographical novel *The Generations of Men,* and an historical work, *The Cry for the Dead.* The latst two books concern the author's own ancestors; Wright's grandfather, Albert Wright, figures prominently in both books, and the author borrowed much of her material for these books from her grandfather's diary. Next to other comparable novels, critics viewed these retrospects on life in nineteenth-century Australia favorably. One "never has the feeling . . . that he is watching an artificial period-piece or costume melodrama," remarked *Meanjin* contributor Russel Ward. *New Statesman* critic V.S. Pritchett observed, too, that in *The Generations of Men* Wright "is also free of that family complacency which affects so many writers when they are describing their pioneer forebears." In another review of this book, Leonie Kramer wrote in *Southerly:* "Wright has shown herself to be a biographer of rare sensitivity." Kramer concluded that the author's "prose transmits particularly well the atmosphere of the times, and the arid beauty of the country."

Both books not only tell the story of the author's family, but also that of the land itself. Albert Wright's diary became a helpful source in this regard, for, as Goodwin described, "his book tells less of the official story than of the disastrous neglect of proper land-management procedures and the story of the brutal extermination of Aborigines." The tragic waste which these practices have brought to Australia is a concern in much of Wright's poetry as well. As a result, several of the author's poems are meditations "on the problem of how to give meaning to, or discover meaning in, this 'flowing and furious world,'" stated *Australian Quarterly* critic R.F. Brissenden, quoting a poem from Wright's *Five Senses: Selected Poems.*

Maintaining a respect for the timelessness of the land throughout her work, Wright expressed in such poetry collections as *Alive: Poems 1971-1972* and *Fourth Quarter, and Other Poems* a horror "at the efficiency with which her fellow countrymen are raping their country," wrote Peter Porter in the London *Observer.* Having been raised on a "station," or ranch, as a child, and being active as an adult in the conservation movement in Australia, Wright maintained a strong bond with her surroundings, which is evident in her poetry. She had, asserted Arthur Murphy in *Southerly,* an ability "to merge herself with all natural forces, delving deep into the almost inexpressible in verse of highly wrought formation and full content." But although several critics, such as one *Times Literary Supplement* reviewer, felt that her poems "about people, landscapes, and animals are good when she describes her subjects directly," Val Vallis remarked in the *Times Literary Supplement* that "the most commonly heard objection to her poetry as it progressed was that its author had gone too philosophical." *Carleton Miscellany* critic Keith Harrison, however, noted that even though one might see some "occasional vagueness" in Wright's sometimes metaphysical poems, "the strengths of her work far outweigh the faults."

Some of these strengths, declared Elyne Mitchell in *Southerly,* include "vivid imagery, lovely songs of creation and of a creator, poems of philosophic journey, of the integration of dark and light, [and] of rebirth." Wright was a poet, who, as S.E. Lee characterized her in *Southerly,* was "a rare combination of metaphysical thinker . . . and down-to-earth realist." Her "best poems then," concluded Lee, "integrate the intellect, passion, imagination and common sense of the thinker-mystic-poet-country wife." What is evident in both Wright's prose and poetry is "her bond to her native land and its once pastoral wilderness," asserted Margaret Gibson in the *Library Journal.*

Wright died of a heart attack in Canberra on June 25, 2000. Since 1976 she had been living in the nearby town of Braidwood and had maintained a peaceful existence where she focused on Aboriginal and environmental causes and her writing. A writer for the *Times* of London described her as representing "a generation and a section of Australian society which deplored the ravages of a materialistic culture on that vast and beautiful yet ecologically vulnerable land. . . . Wright became perhaps the best-known poet in Australia." In the *Age,* an editorial writer expressed that "Wright was not only a remarkable poet, she was a fine human being." Goodwin summarized the author's career this way: "Her lifelong quest [was] to define Australia as a land, a nation and a metaphysical entity, in language that [shows] awareness of contemporary overseas writing in English but also [recognizes] the unique environment and society of Australia." Veronica Brady, a biographer of Wright, stated to the *Canberra Times* upon Wright's death: "'It's very sad but in a sense, with somebody like Judith Wright, the spirit doesn't die.'"

BIOGRAPHICAL AND CRITICAL SOURCES:

BOOKS

Brady, Veronica, *South of My Days: A Biography of Judith Wright,* Angus & Robertson (Sydney, Australia), 1998.

Contemporary Literary Criticism, Thomson Gale (Detroit, MI), Volume 11, 1979, Volume 53, 1989.

Contemporary Poets, 6th edition, St. James Press (Detroit, MI), 1996.

Goodwin, Ken, *A History of Australian Literature,* St. Martin's Press (New York, NY), 1986.

Hope, A. D., *Judith Wright,* Oxford University Press (Melbourne, Australia), 1975.

Kramer, L., editor, *The Oxford History of Australian Literature,* Oxford University Press (Melbourne, Australia), 1982.

Poetry Criticism, Volume 14, Thomson Gale (Detroit, MI), 1996.

Strauss, Jennifer, *Judith Wright,* Oxford University Press (Melbourne, Australia), 1995.

Walker, Shirley, *Flame and Shadow: A Study of Judith Wright's Poetry,* University of Queensland Press, 1991.

Walker, Shirley, *The Poetry of Judith Wright,* Edward Arnold, 1980.

Walker, Shirley, *Judith Wright,* Oxford University Press (Melbourne, Australia), 1981.

Walker, Shirley, *Vanishing Edens: Responses to Australia in the Works of Mary Gilmore, Judith Wright, and Dorothy Hewett,* Foundation for Australian Literary Studies, 1992.

PERIODICALS

American Poetry Review, September-October, 1980.

Australian Literary Studies, October, 2003, p. 178.

Australian Quarterly, March, 1964.

Carleton Miscellany, summer, 1980.

Library Journal, June 15, 1978.

London Magazine, May, 1967.

Meanjin, September, 1946; March, 1950; June, 1960; December, 1962.

New Statesman, September 5, 1959.

Observer (London, England), May 7, 1978.

Quadrant, October, 1999, Clement Semmler, review of *Half a Lifetime,* p. 82; May 2001, p. 9.

Southerly, Volume 11, number 3, 1950; Volume 16, number 1, 1955; Volume 17, number 2, 1956; Volume 20, number 9, 1959; Volume 23, number 2, 1963; Volume 27, number 1, 1967; Volume 61, number 1, spring 2001, pp. 78, 82, 160.

Times Literary Supplement, September 10, 1964; April 9, 1976; October 15, 1982; November 27, 1987.

ONLINE

Judith Wright Centre, http://www.judithwrightcentre.com/ (October 26, 2003).

* * *

WRIGHT, Judith Arundell
See WRIGHT, Judith

X-Y

XINGJIAN, Gao 1940-
(Gao Xingjian)

PERSONAL: Born January 4, 1940, in Ganzhou, Jiangxi Province, China; immigrated to France, 1987; naturalized French citizen; son of a bank official and an actress. *Education:* Attended Beijing Foreign Languages Institute, 1957-62.

ADDRESSES: Home—Paris, France. *Agent*—c/o Author Mail, Éditions de l'Aube, 13 pl Andre Masson, 84240 La Tour-d'Aigues, France.

CAREER: Writer. Beijing People's Art Theatre, resident playwright, 1981-87; China Reconstructs and Chinese Writers Association, translator; worked as a farm laborer and teacher.

AWARDS, HONORS: Chevalier de l'Ordre des Arts et des Letters, Government of France, 1992; Nobel Prize for literature, Swedish Academy, 2000; honorary literary doctorate from Chinese University in Hong Kong, 2001.

WRITINGS:

IN ENGLISH TRANSLATION

Ink Paintings, Taipei Fine Arts Museum, 1995.

The Other Shore: Plays by Gao Xingjian (includes *The Other Shore, Between Life and Death, Dialogue and Rebuttal, Nocturnal Wanderer,* and *Weekend Quartet;* also see below), translated by Gilbert C.F. Fong, Chinese University Press (Hong Kong, China), 1999.

Soul Mountain (novel), translated by Mabel Lee, HarperCollins (Australia), 1999, HarperCollins (New York, NY), 2000.

One Man's Bible (novel), translated by Mabel Lee, published in Taiwan, 1999, published as *Le Livre d'un homme seul,* Éditions de l'Aube (La Tour d'Aigues, France), 2000, published by HarperCollins (New York, NY), 2002.

Return to Painting, translated by Nadia Benabid, Perennial (New York, NY), 2002.

Buying a Fishing Rod for My Grandfather (stories), translated by Mabel Lee, HarperCollins (New York, NY), 2004.

OTHER

Juedui zinghao (play; title means "The Alarm Signal"), 1982.

Chezhan (play; title means "Bus Stop"), 1983.

Ye ren (play; title means "Wild Man"), 1985.

Dialoguer-interloquer (two-act play; title means "Dialogue and Rebuttal"), M.E.E.T. (Saint-Nazaire, France), 1992.

Le Somnambule (title means "The Sleepwalker"), Editions Lansman (Carnières-Morlanwelz, France), 1994.

La Montagne de l'âme, Éditions de l'Aube (La Tour d'Aigues, France), 1995.

Au plus près du reel: Dialogues sur l'écriture (1994-1997), Éditions de l'Aube (La Tour d'Aigues, France), 1997.

Une canne à pèche pour mon grand-père, Éditions de l'Aube (La Tour d'Aigues, France), 1997.

Also author of *You zhi ge zi jiao hong chun er, Xian dai xiao shuo ji qiao chu tan* and *You zhi ge zi jiao hong chun er,* all c. 2003.

SIDELIGHTS: Gao Xingjian is a Chinese writer who received the Nobel Prize for literature in 2000. Olivier Burckhardt, writing in *Quadrant,* affirmed that Gao "has been described as the leading dramatist of avant-garde Chinese theatre; an author who has forged new paths in Chinese prose writing; and a painter of international repute." Phillip Adams acknowledged Gao, in *Late Night Live,* as "one of China's best known dissidents" and a figure who is "regarded as being at the fore of avant garde Chinese/French literature." Sarah Lyall, meanwhile, wrote in the *New York Times* that Gao "is best known for daring plays that combine a modernist sensibility with traditional elements from Chinese drama."

Gao was born in 1940, a time of turbulence in China, and spent his childhood evading the Japanese forces that had invaded his homeland. During this period, as Bruno Roubicek related in *Asian Theatre Journal,* Gao "came into intimate contact with the cultures and performing arts of remote regions of China." Following the withdrawal of Japanese troops, Gao entered a Chinese university and began studying the works of European playwrights such as Bertolt Brecht. He then found work as a translator with both *China Reconstructs,* a journal, and the Chinese Writers Association.

During this period Gao began producing a sizeable body of literary work, but fear of government authorities compelled him to destroy these writings. In the repressive Cultural Revolution that ensued, Gao worked on farms and served as a teacher in some of China's less developed regions. While laboring in these rural areas he persevered as a writer, but was forced to destroy these writings as well. Marilyn August, in the *Bergen Record,* disclosed that Gao "burned his early writings to save himself from communist zealots."

In 1981 Gao obtained an appointment to the Beijing People's Art Theatre; and, during the next few years, he proved an accomplished, if controversial, playwright. Among his works from this period are *Juedui zinghao,* which Roubicek described in *Asian Theatre Journal* as a play about "the psychology of a youth who turns to crime," and *Chezhan,* in which citizens consider their plight as they await a bus. Among the characters in *Chezhan* is Glasses, described by Kevin Hodgson, writing in *Road to East Asia,* as "a short-sighted pseudo-intellectual who recognizes his plight but has no vision and consequently no incentive to emancipate himself from oppression." Another critic, Jessica Martin, wrote in the same journal that "Glasses presents himself as an intellectual with a vast expanse of knowledge at his disposal," but added that "it is questionable whether or not he knows what he is talking about." William Tay, writing in *Worlds Apart: Recent Chinese Writing and Its Audiences,* acknowledged *Chezhan* for its "aspects of inarticulation, incomprehensibility, and non sequitur" and added that such elements render the characters "comical."

Chezhan drew recognition as a pioneering work in Chinese theatre, but it also proved troubling to authorities. Gao continued to divide audiences with *Ye ren,* in which an ecologist attempts to promote forest conservation to peasants. As with Chezhan, the use of both European avant-garde techniques and traditional Chinese elements in *Ye ren* impressed some theatergoers, while its thematic obscurity and lack of closure outraged others. Xiaomei Chen noted in a *Comparative Literary Studies* essay that Gao considered *Ye ren* "an attempt to realize his ideal of establishing a 'modern theater' by drawing on traditional Chinese operas."

Gao left China in 1987. The next year, as Chinese troops crushed a student rebellion at Tiananmen Square, Gao dropped his membership in the Communist party and established residency in Paris, where he began writing in French. He also began publishing various works in English translation. These English-language volumes include *The Other Shore,* which contains such works as *The Other Shore, Between Life and Death, Dialogue and Rebuttal, Nocturnal Wanderer,* and *Weekend Quartet.*

Gao also published *Soul Mountain,* which Lyall described in the *New York Times* as "a long, impressionistic work that arose from a . . . walking tour Gao took along the Yangtze River." Lyall added that the novel constitutes "a hodgepodge of literary styles and techniques, with a variety of narrators and interwoven tales of people Gao met on his journey." Writing in the same publication, Richard Eder found *Soul Mountain* "often bewildering and considerably uneven," but he conceded that it provides "a fascinating account of [China]." Eder called Gao "a gifted, angry writer." After receiving the Nobel Prize for literature, Gao conceded that he would probably not return to his homeland. "I don't consider myself to have cut myself off from my roots," he told Paisley Rekdal in a *New York Times Magazine* interview. "But China remains an authoritarian state, and I don't plan on returning while I'm alive."

Gao's novel *One Man's Bible,* first published in Taiwan in 1999 and translated into English in 2003, combines a fictionalized description of Gao's life under the Chinese Communist regime with reflections on writing, living in exile, and political oppression and how the human spirit can ultimately triumph. Written in his typical stream-of-consciousnesses style, the story jumps back and forth in time as a writer living in Taiwan recalls his life under China's oppressive Cultural Revolution under Chairman Mao. Shirley N. Quan, writing in *Library Journal,* noted that that "Gao's liberal shifting from second to third person, mixed with a sprinkling of dialog throughout, add to the novel's complexity and make it a difficult work." *Review of Contemporary Fiction* contributor Jason Picone felt that Gao's lack of providing an historical context for the story could leave some readers confused, especially concerning the violence and betrayals that occur in the novel. Pointing out that much of the story is told between the lovemaking sessions between the narrator and his lover, Piccone also noted, "Even though Gao's intense eroticism makes a strange bedfellow for the revelations concerning China's bitter past, this unique pairing gives the book a tenderness and desperation it might otherwise lack."

In 2004 a collection of Gao's past short stories, primarily published in Chinese between 1983 and 1991, was translated into English and published as *Buying a Fishing Rod for My Grandfather.* The collection contains six short stories that Janet St. John, writing in *Booklist,* called "richly diverse." One of the favorite stories among book reviewers was the story titled "The Accident," about a father on a bicycle and his young son in an attached baby buggy who are hit by a bus with tragic consequences. Noting that the collection offers readers "a sample of Nobel-winner Gao's sharp, poetic early work," a *Publishers Weekly* contributor wrote of "The Accident" that it "explores the simultaneous enormity and anonymity of death." In the title story, the narrator recalls the destruction of his grandfather's village and the lake where they used to fish together, using both his memory and his daydreams to reveal the tale. In a review in *Library Journal,* Shirley N. Quan commented, "As a whole, the collection is a fast read, but the literary nature of Gao's writing makes it a challenge." St. John noted, "For variety of content, stylistic experimentation, graceful language, and poignant insight, Xingjian is a writer who does it all beautifully."

"One of the qualities that place Gao Xingjian squarely in the ranks of the most respected Nobel laureates is the universal appeal of his works, which are distinctively Chinese and yet transcend national boundaries," noted Sylvia Li-Chun Lin in *World Literature Today.* "Unlike so many modern and contemporary Chinese writers, who seem 'obsessed with China,' Gao, though drawing his inspiration from Chinese culture, nevertheless ponders more fundamental issues of human existence."

BIOGRAPHICAL AND CRITICAL SOURCES:

BOOKS

Goldblatt, Howard, editor, *Worlds Apart: Recent Chinese Writing and Its Audience,* M.E. Sharpe (Armonk, NY), 1990.

PERIODICALS

Asian Theatre Journal, fall, 1990, Gao Xingjian, "Wild Man," pp. 184-239.

Bergen Record, October 13, 2000, Marilyn August, "Chinese Exile Gao Xingjian Wins Nobel Prize for Literature."

Booklist, December 15, 2000, Donna Seaman, review of *Soul Mountain,* p. 762; February 1, 2004, Janet St. John, review of *Buying a Fishing Rod for My Grandfather,* p. 949.

Comparative Literature Studies, fall, 1992, Xiaomei Chen, "A Wildman Between Two Cultures," pp. 397-417.

Library Journal, August, 2002, Shirley N. Quan, review of *One Man's Bible,* p. 142; February 1, 2004, Shirley N. Quan, review of *Buying a Fishing Rod for My Grandfather,* p. 126.

Newsweek International, February 12, 2001, Mahlon Meyer, "Too Eager to Toe the Line?," p. 77.

New York Times, October 13, 2000, Sarah Lyall, "Exiled Chinese Writer Wins Nobel Prize in Literature"; December 18, 2000, Richard Eder, "A Dreamlike Chinese Journey Haunted by Past and Present."

Publishers Weekly, December 11, 2000, review of *Soul Mountain,* p. 65; January 12, 2004, review of *Buying a Fishing Rod for My Grandfather,* p. 36.

Quadrant, April, 2000, Olivier Burckhardt, "The Voice of One in the Wilderness."

New York Times Magazine, December 10, 2000, "Questions for Gao Xingjian," p. 51.

Review of Contemporary Fiction, spring, 2003, Jason Picone, review of *One Man's Bible,* p. 152.

World Literature Today, Winter, 2001, Sylvia Li-Chun Lin, "Between the Individual & the Collective," p. 12.

ONLINE

Age, http://www.theage.com/ (August 8, 2001).

Late Night Live, http://www.abc.net/ (August 8, 2001).

Road to East Asia, http://www.yorku.ca/ (August 8, 2001).

* * *

YOLEN, Jane 1939-
(Jane Hyatt Yolen)

PERSONAL: Born February 11, 1939, in New York, NY; daughter of Will Hyatt (an author and publicist) and Isabelle (a social worker, puzzle-maker, and homemaker; maiden name, Berlin) Yolen; married David W. Stemple (a retired professor of computer science and ornithologist), September 2, 1962; children: Heidi Elisabet, Adam Douglas, Jason Frederic. *Education:* Smith College, B.A., 1960; University of Massachusetts, M.Ed., 1976; also completed course work for doctorate in children's literature at the University of Massachusetts. *Politics:* Liberal Democrat. *Religion:* Jewish/Quaker. *Hobbies and other interests:* "Folk music and dancing, reading, camping, politics, all things Scottish."

ADDRESSES: Home—Phoenix Farm, 31 School St., Box 27, Hatfield, MA 01038, and Wayside, 96 Hepburn Gardens, St. Andrews, Fife, Scotland KY16 9LN. *Agent*—Elizabeth Harding, Curtis Brown, Ltd., 10 Astor Place, New York, NY 10003. *E-mail*—JaneYolen@aol.com.

CAREER: Saturday Review, New York, NY, production assistant, 1960-61; Gold Medal Books (publishers), New York, NY, assistant editor, 1961-62; Rutledge Books (publishers), New York, NY, associate editor, 1962-63; Alfred A. Knopf, Inc. (publishers), New York, NY, assistant juvenile editor, 1963-65; full-time professional writer, 1965—. Editor of imprint, Jane Yolen Books, for Harcourt Brace Jovanovich, 1988-98. Teacher of writing and lecturer, 1966—; has taught children's literature at Smith College. Chairman of board of library trustees, Hatfield, MA, 1976-83; member of Arts Council, Hatfield.

MEMBER: Society of Children's Book Writers (member of board of directors, 1974—), Science Fiction Writers of America (president, 1986-88), Children's Literature Association (member of board of directors, 1977-79), Science Fiction Poetry Association, National Association for the Preservation and Perpetuation of Storytelling, Western New England Storyteller's Guild (founder), Bay State Writers Guild, Western Massachusetts Illustrators Guild (founder), International Kitefliers Association, Smith College Alumnae Association.

AWARDS, HONORS: Boys' Club of America Junior Book Award, 1968, for *The Minstrel and the Mountain;* Lewis Carroll Shelf Award, 1968, for *The Emperor and the Kite,* and 1973, for *The Girl Who Loved the Wind;* Best Books of the Year selection, *New York Times,* 1968, for *The Emperor Flies a Kite; World on a String: The Story of Kites* was named an American Library Association (ALA) Notable Book, 1968; Chandler Book Talk Reward of Merit, 1970; Children's Book Showcase of the Children's Book Council citations, 1973, for *The Girl Who Loved the Wind,* and 1976, for *The Little Spotted Fish;* Golden Kite Award, Society of Children's Book Writers, 1974, ALA Notable Book, 1975, and National Book Award nomination, 1975, all for *The Girl Who Cried Flowers and Other Tales;* Golden Kite Honor Book, 1975, for *The Transfigured Hart,* and 1976, for *The Moon Ribbon and Other Tales;* Christopher Medal, 1978, for *The Seeing Stick,* and 2000, for *How Do Dinosaurs Say Goodnight?*; Children's Choice from the International Reading Association and the Children's Book Council, 1980, for *Mice on Ice,* and 1983, for *Dragon's Blood;* LL.D., College of Our Lady of the Elms, 1981; Parents' Choice Awards, Parents' Choice Foundation, 1982, for *Dragon's Blood,* 1984, for *The Stone Silenus,* and 1989, for *Piggins* and *The Three Bears Rhyme Book; School Library Journal* Best Books for Young Adults citations, 1982, for *The Gift of Sarah Barker,* and 1985, for *Heart's Blood;* Garden State Children's Book Award, New Jersey Library Association, 1983, for *Commander Toad in Space;* CRABbery Award from Acton Public Library (MD), 1983, for *Dragon's Blood; Heart's Blood* was selected one of ALA's Best Books for Young Adults, 1984; Mythopoeic Society's Fantasy Award, Adult Novel, 1985, for *Cards of Grief,* 1993 for *Briar Rose,* and 1998 for children's novels *The Young Merlin Trilogy: Passager, Hobby, Merlin;* Daedelus Award, 1986, for fantasy and short fiction; *The Lullaby Songbook* and *The Sleeping Beauty* were each selected one of Child Study Association of America's Children's Books of the Year, 1987; World Fantasy Award, 1988, for *Favorite Folktales from around the World;* Kerlan Award for "singular achievements in the creation of children's literature," 1988; Parents' Choice Silver Seal Award, Jewish Book Council Award, and Sydney Taylor Award, all 1988, Golden Sower Award from the Nebraska Library Association, 1989, and Charlotte Award from New York State Reading Association, all for *Piggins;* Smith College Medal, 1990; Skylark Award, New England Science Fiction Association, 1990; Regina Medal for body of writing in children's literature, 1992; Mythopoetic Fantasy Award, Adult, 1993, for *Briar Rose;* Keene State College Children's Literature Festival Award, 1995 and Children's Book Award, 1998; Maud Hart Lovelace Award, 1996, for *The Devil's Arithmetic;* Nebula Award, Best Short Story, 1997, for *Sister Emily's Lightship,* and 1998, for *Lost Girls;* Literary Lights for Children Award, Boston Library, 1998; H.D.L., Keene State College, 1998; Anna V. Zarrow Award, 1999; Remarkable Women Award, 1999; California Young Reader Medal, young adult category, 2001, for *Armageddon Summer;* National Outdoor Book Awards, children's category, 2002, for *Wild Wings;* Network 2003 ORACLE Award for outstanding contributions to the literary body of storytelling, 2003; honorary doctorate, Smith College, 2003; Parents' Choice Gold Medal for *Sword of the Rightful King,* 2004; honorary doctorate, Bay Path College, 2004. Fifteen of Yolen's books have been selected by the Junior Literary Guild. In addition, *The Emperor and the Kite* was named a Caldecott Medal Honor Book, 1968, for its illustrations by Ed Young, and *Owl Moon* received the Caldecott Medal, 1988, for its illustrations by John Schoenherr.

WRITINGS:

FOR CHILDREN; PICTURE BOOKS AND FICTION

The Witch Who Wasn't, illustrated by Arnold Roth, Macmillan (New York, NY), 1964.

Gwinellen, the Princess Who Could Not Sleep, illustrated by Ed Renfro, Macmillan (New York, NY), 1965.

The Emperor and the Kite, illustrated by Ed Young, World Publishing (Cleveland, OH), 1967, Philomel Books (New York, NY), 1988.

The Minstrel and the Mountain: A Tale of Peace, illustrated by Anne Rockwell, World Publishing (Cleveland, OH), 1967.

Isabel's Noel, illustrated by Arnold Roth, Funk & Wagnalls (New York, NY), 1967.

Greyling: A Picture Story from the Islands of Shetland, illustrated by William Stobbs, World Publishing (Cleveland, OH), 1968, new edition, illustrated by David Ray; Philomel Books (New York, NY), 1991.

The Longest Name on the Block, illustrated by Peter Madden, Funk & Wagnalls (New York, NY), 1968.

The Wizard of Washington Square, illustrated by Ray Cruz, World Publishing (Cleveland, OH), 1969.

The Inway Investigators; or, The Mystery at McCracken's Place, illustrated by Allan Eitzen, Seabury (New York, NY), 1969.

Hobo Toad and the Motorcycle Gang, illustrated by Emily McCully, World Publishing (Cleveland, OH), 1970.

The Seventh Mandarin, illustrated by Ed Young, Seabury (New York, NY), 1970.

The Bird of Time, illustrated by Mercer Mayer, Crowell (New York, NY), 1971.

The Girl Who Loved the Wind, illustrated by Ed Young, Crowell (New York, NY), 1972.

The Girl Who Cried Flowers and Other Tales, illustrated by David Palladini, Crowell (New York, NY), 1974.

The Boy Who Had Wings, illustrated by Helga Aichinger, Crowell (New York, NY), 1974.

The Adventures of Eeka Mouse, illustrated by Myra McKee, Xerox Education Publications (Middletown, CT), 1974.

The Rainbow Rider, illustrated by Michael Foreman, Crowell (New York, NY), 1974.

The Little Spotted Fish, illustrated by Friso Henstra, Seabury (New York, NY), 1975.

The Transfigured Hart, illustrated by Donna Diamond, Crowell (New York, NY), 1975, Magic Carpet Books/Harcourt Brace (San Diego, CA), 1997.

Milkweed Days, photographs by Gabriel Amadeus Cooney, Crowell (New York, NY), 1976.

The Moon Ribbon and Other Tales, illustrated by David Palladini, Crowell (New York, NY), 1976.

The Seeing Stick, illustrated by Remy Charlip and Demetra Maraslis, Crowell (New York, NY), 1977.

The Sultan's Perfect Tree, illustrated by Barbara Garrison, Parents' Magazine Press (New York, NY), 1977.

The Hundredth Dove and Other Tales, illustrated by David Palladini, Crowell (New York, NY), 1977.

Hannah Dreaming, photographs by Alan R. Epstein, Museum of Fine Art (Springfield, MA), 1977.

The Lady and the Merman, illustrated by Barry Moser, Pennyroyal, 1977.

Spider Jane, illustrated by Stefan Bernath, Coward (New York, NY), 1978.

The Simple Prince, illustrated by Jack Kent, Parents' Magazine Press (New York, NY), 1978.

No Bath Tonight, illustrated by Nancy Winslow Parker, Crowell (New York, NY), 1978.

The Mermaid's Three Wisdoms, illustrated by Laura Rader, Collins (New York, NY), 1978.

Dream Weaver and Other Tales, illustrated by Michael Hague, Collins (New York, NY), 1979, reissued as *Dream Weaver,* 1989.

Spider Jane on the Move, illustrated by Stefan Bernath, Coward (New York, NY), 1980.

Mice on Ice, illustrated by Lawrence DiFiori, Dutton's Children's Books (New York, NY), 1980.

Shirlick Holmes and the Case of the Wandering Wardrobe, illustrated by Anthony Rao, Coward (New York, NY), 1981.

The Acorn Quest, illustrated by Susanna Natti, Harper (New York, NY), 1981.

Brothers of the Wind, illustrated by Barbara Berger, Philomel Books (New York, NY), 1981.

Sleeping Ugly, illustrated by Diane Stanley, Coward (New York, NY), 1981.

The Boy Who Spoke Chimp, illustrated by David Wiesner, Knopf (New York, NY), 1981.

Uncle Lemon's Spring, illustrated by Glen Rounds, Dutton's Children's Books (New York, NY), 1981.

(Reteller) *The Sleeping Beauty,* illustrated by Ruth Sanderson, Knopf (New York, NY), 1986.

Owl Moon, illustrated by John Schoenherr, Philomel Books (New York, NY), 1987.

Dove Isabeau, illustrated by Dennis Nolan, Harcourt Brace (San Diego, CA), 1989.

Baby Bear's Bedtime Book, illustrated by Jane Dyer, Harcourt Brace (San Diego, CA), 1990.

Sky Dogs, illustrated by Barry Moser, Harcourt Brace (San Diego, CA), 1990.

(Reteller) *Tam Lin: An Old Ballad,* illustrated by Charles Mikolaycak, Harcourt Brace (San Diego, CA), 1990.

Elfabet: An ABC of Elves, illustrated by Lauren Mills, Little, Brown (Boston, MA), 1990.

Letting Swift River Go, illustrated by Barbara Cooney, Little, Brown (Boston, MA), 1990.

The Dragon's Boy, Harper (New York, NY), 1990.

Wizard's Hall, Harcourt Brace (San Diego, CA), 1991.

Hark! A Christmas Sampler, illustrated by Tomie dePaola, music by Adam Stemple, Putnam (New York, NY), 1991.

(Reteller) *Wings,* Harcourt Brace (San Diego, CA), 1991.

All Those Secrets of the World (autobiographical fiction), illustrated by Leslie Baker, Little, Brown (Boston, MA), 1991.

Encounter, illustrated by David Shannon, Harcourt Brace (San Diego, CA), 1992.

Eeny, Meeny, Miney Mole, illustrated by Kathryn Brown, published by Harcourt Brace (San Diego, CA), 1992.

Mouse's Birthday, illustrated by Bruce Degen, Putnam (New York, NY), 1993.

Hands, illustrated by Chi Chung, Sundance Publishing (White Plains, NY), 1993, also published as *Hands: Big Book,* 1993.

Beneath the Ghost Moon, illustrated by Laurel Molk, Little, Brown (Boston, MA), 1994.

Honkers, illustrated by Leslie Baker, Little, Brown (Boston, MA), 1993.

Travelers Rose, Putnam (New York, NY), 1993.

Grandad Bill's Song, illustrated by Melissa Bay Mathis, Philomel Books (New York, NY), 1994.

And Twelve Chinese Acrobats (autobiographical fiction), illustrated by Jean Gralley, Philomel Books (New York, NY), 1994.

Good Griselle, illustrated by David Christiana, Harcourt Brace (San Diego, CA), 1994.

The Girl in the Golden Bower, illustrated by Jane Dyer, Little, Brown (Boston, MA), 1994.

Old Dame Counterpane, illustrated by Ruth Tietjen Councell, Putnam (New York, NY), 1994.

(Reteller) *Little Mouse and Elephant: A Tale from Turkey,* illustrated by John Segal, Simon & Schuster (New York, NY), 1994.

(Reteller) *The Musicians of Bremen: A Tale from Germany,* illustrated by John Segal, Simon & Schuster (New York, NY), 1994.

The Ballad of the Pirate Queen, illustrated by David Shannon, Harcourt Brace (San Diego, CA), 1995.

Before the Storm, illustrated by Georgia Pugh, Boyds Mills Press (Honesdale, PA), 1995.

(Reteller) *A Sip of Aesop,* illustrated by Karen Barbour, Blue Sky Press (New York, NY), 1995.

Merlin and the Dragons, illustrated by Ming Li, Dutton's Children's Books (New York, NY), 1995.

The Wild Hunt, illustrated by Francisco Mora, Harcourt Brace (San Diego, CA), 1995.

(With daughter, Heidi Elisabet Yolen Stemple) *Meet the Monsters,* illustrated by Patricia Ludlow, Walker (New York, NY), 1996.

Nocturne, illustrated by Anne Hunter, Harcourt Brace (San Diego, CA), 1997.

Child of Faerie, Child of Earth, illustrated by Jane Dyer, Little, Brown (Boston, MA), 1997.

Miz Berlin Walks, illustrated by Floyd Cooper, Philomel Books (New York, NY), 1997.

(Reteller) *Once upon a Bedtime Story: Classic Tales,* illustrated by Ruth Tietjen Councell, 1997.

The Sea Man, illustrated by Christopher Denise, Putnam (New York, NY), 1997.

Twelve Impossible Things before Breakfast (short stories), Harcourt Brace (San Diego, CA), 1997.

House, House, illustrated with photographs by the Howes Brothers and Jason Stemple, Marshall Cavendish (New York, NY), 1998.

King Long Shanks, illustrated by Victoria Chess, Harcourt Brace (San Diego, CA), 1998.

(Reteller) *Pegasus, the Flying Horse,* illustrated by Ming Li, Dutton's Children's Books (New York, NY), 1998.

The Book of Fairy Holidays, illustrated by David Christiana, Blue Sky Press (New York, NY), 1998.

Raising Yoder's Barn, illustrated by Bernie Fuchs, Little, Brown (Boston, MA), 1998.

(Reteller) *Prince of Egypt,* Dutton's Children's Books (New York, NY), 1998.

(Compiler with Linda Mannheim) *The Liars' Book,* illustrated by Kevin Hawkes, Blue Sky Press, 1998.

(With Heidi E.Y. Stemple) *Mary Celeste: An Unsolved Mystery from History,* illustrated by Roger Roth, Simon & Schuster (New York, NY), 1999.

Moonball, illustrated by Greg Couch, Simon & Schuster (New York, NY), 1999.

How Do Dinosaurs Say Goodnight?, illustrated by Mark Teague, Blue Sky Press (New York, NY), 2000.

Off We Go!, illustrated by Laurel Molk, Little, Brown (Boston, MA), 2000.

Harvest Home, illustrated by Greg Shed, Harcourt Brace (San Diego, CA), 2000.

Where Have the Unicorns Gone?, illustrated by Ruth Sanderson, Simon & Schuser (New York, NY), 2000.

Welcome to the River of Grass, illustrated by Laura Regan, Putnam (New York, NY), 2000.

The Hurrying Child, illustrated by Stephen T. Johnson, Silver Whistle Books (San Diego, CA), 2001.

Firebird, illustrated by Vladimir Vagin, HarperCollins (New York, NY), 2002.

The Sea King, illustrated by Stefan Czernecki, Crocodile Books (Brooklyn, NY), 2003.

My Brothers' Flying Machine: Wilbur, Orville, and Me, paintings by Jim Burke, Little, Brown (New York, NY), 2003.

How Do Dinosaurs Get Well Soon?, illustrated by Mark Teague, Blue Sky Press (New York, Ny), 2003.

Hoptoad, illustrated by Karen Lee Schmidt, Silver Whistle Books, (San Diego, CA), 2003.

The Flying Witch, illustrated by Vladimir Vagin, HarperCollins (New York, NY), 2003.

Meow: Cat Stories from around the World, illustrated by Hala Wittwer, HarperCollins (New York, NY), 2004.

How Do Dinosaurs Count to Ten?, illustrated by Mark Teague, Blue Sky Press (New York, NY), 2004.

"GIANTS" SERIES; ILLUSTRATED BY TOMIE DEPAOLA

The Giants' Farm, Seabury (New York, NY), 1977.

The Giants Go Camping, Seabury (New York, NY), 1979.

"COMMANDER TOAD" SERIES; ILLUSTRATED BY BRUCE DEGEN

Commander Toad in Space, Coward (New York, NY), 1980.

Commander Toad and the Planet of the Grapes, Coward (New York, NY), 1982.

Commander Toad and the Big Black Hole, Coward (New York, NY), 1983.

Commander Toad and the Dis-Asteroid, Coward (New York, NY), 1985.

Commander Toad and the Intergalactic Spy, Coward (New York, NY), 1986.

Commander Toad and the Space Pirates, Putnam (New York, NY), 1987.

Commander Toad and the Voyage Home, Putnam (New York, NY), 1998.

"ROBOT AND REBECCA" SERIES

The Robot and Rebecca: The Mystery of the Code-Carrying Kids, illustrated by Jurg Obrist, Knopf (New York, NY), 1980, student book club edition illustrated by Catherine Deeter, Random House (New York, NY), 1980.

The Robot and Rebecca and the Missing Owser, illustrated by Lady McCrady, Knopf (New York, NY), 1981.

"PIGGINS" SERIES; ILLUSTRATED BY JANE DYER

Piggins, Harcourt Brace (San Diego, CA), 1987.

Picnic with Piggins, Harcourt Brace (San Diego, CA), 1988.

Piggins and the Royal Wedding, Harcourt Brace (San Diego, CA), 1988.

"YOUNG MERLIN" TRILOGY

Passager, Harcourt Brace (San Diego, CA), 1996.

Hobby, Harcourt Brace (San Diego, CA), 1996.

Merlin, Harcourt Brace (San Diego, CA), 1997.

"TARTAN MAGIC" SERIES

The Wizard's Map, Harcourt Brace (San Diego, CA), 1998.

The Pictish Child, Harcourt Brace (San Diego, CA), 1999.

The Bagpiper's Ghost, Harcourt Brace (San Diego, CA), 2002.

FOR CHILDREN; NONFICTION

Pirates in Petticoats, illustrated by Leonard Vosburgh, McKay (New York, NY), 1963.

World on a String: The Story of Kites, World Publishing (Cleveland, OH), 1968.

Friend: The Story of George Fox and the Quakers, Seabury (New York, NY), 1972.

(Editor, with Barbara Green) *The Fireside Song Book of Birds and Beasts,* illustrated by Peter Parnall, Simon & Schuster (New York, NY), 1972.

The Wizard Islands, illustrated by Robert Quackenbush, Crowell (New York, NY), 1973.

Ring Out! A Book of Bells, illustrated by Richard Cuffari, Seabury (New York, NY), 1974.

Simple Gifts: The Story of the Shakers, illustrated by Betty Fraser, Viking (New York, NY), 1976.

(Compiler) *Rounds about Rounds,* music by Barbara Green, illustrated by Gail Gibbons, Watts (New York, NY), 1977.

The Lap-Time Song and Play Book, musical arrangements by son Adam Stemple, illustrated by Margot Tomes, Harcourt Brace (San Diego, CA), 1989.

A Letter from Phoenix Farm (autobiography), illustrated with photographs by son Jason Stemple, Richard C. Owen (Katonah, NY), 1992.

Jane Yolen's Songs of Summer, musical arrangements by Adam Stemple, illustrated by Cyd Moore, Boyds Mills Press (Honesdale, PA), 1993.

Welcome to the Green House, illustrated by Laura Regan, Putnam (New York, NY), 1993.

Jane Yolen's Old MacDonald Songbook, illustrated by Rosekrans Hoffman, Boyds Mills Press (Honesdale, PA), 1994.

Sing Noel, musical arrangements by Adam Stemple, illustrated by Nancy Carpenter, Boyds Mills Press (Honesdale, PA), 1996.

Milk and Honey: A Year of Jewish Holidays, illustrated by Louise August, musical arrangements by Adam Stemple, Putnam (New York, NY), 1996.

Welcome to the Sea of Sand, illustrated by Laura Regan, Putnam (New York, NY), 1996.

Welcome to the Ice House, illustrated by Laura Regan, Putnam (New York, NY), 1998.

Tea with an Old Dragon: A Story of Sophia Smith, Founder of Smith College, illustrated by Monica Vachula, Boyds Mills Press (Honesdale, PA), 1998.

(With Heidi E.Y. Stemple) *The Wolf Girls: An Unsolved Mystery from History,* illustrated by Roger Roth, Simon & Schuster (New York, NY), 2000.

(With Heidi E.Y. Stemple) *Roanoke: The Lost Colony: An Unsolved Mystery from History,* illustrated by Roger Roth, Simon & Schuster (New York, NY), 2003.

The Perfect Wizard: Hans Christian Andersen, illustrated by Denis Nolan, Dutton's Children's Books (New York, NY), 2004.

FOR CHILDREN; POETRY

See This Little Line?, illustrated by Kathleen Elgin, McKay (New York, NY), 1963.

It All Depends, illustrated by Don Bolognese, Funk & Wagnalls (New York, NY), 1970.

An Invitation to the Butterfly Ball: A Counting Rhyme, illustrated by Jane Breskin Zalben, Parents' Magazine Press (New York, NY), 1976, Caroline House (Honesdale, PA), 1991.

All in the Woodland Early: An ABC Book, illustrated by Jane Breskin Zalben, Collins, 1979, Caroline House (Honesdale, PA), 1991.

How Beastly! A Menagerie of Nonsense Poems, illustrated by James Marshall, Philomel Books (New York, NY), 1980.

Dragon Night and Other Lullabies, illustrated by Demi, Methuen (New York, NY), 1980.

(Editor) *The Lullaby Songbook,* musical arrangements by Adam Stemple, illustrated by Charles Mikolaycak, Harcourt Brace (San Diego, CA), 1986.

Ring of Earth: A Child's Book of Seasons, illustrated by John Wallner, Harcourt Brace (San Diego, CA), 1986.

The Three Bears Rhyme Book, illustrated by Jane Dyer, Harcourt Brace (San Diego, CA), 1987.

Best Witches: Poems for Halloween, illustrated by Elise Primavera, Putnam (New York, NY), 1989.

Bird Watch, illustrated by Ted Lewin, Philomel Books (New York, NY), 1990.

Dinosaur Dances, illustrated by Bruce Degen, Putnam (New York, NY), 1990.

(Compiler) *Street Rhymes around the World,* illustrated by seventeen artists, Wordsong (Honesdale, PA), 1992.

Jane Yolen's Mother Goose Songbook, musical arrangements by Jason Stemple, illustrated by Rosekrans Hoffman, Boyds Mill Press, 1992.

(Compiler) *Weather Report,* illustrated by Annie Gusman, Boyds Mills Press (Honesdale, PA), 1993.

Mouse's Birthday, illustrated by Bruce Degen, Putnam (New York, NY), 1993.

Raining Cats and Dogs, illustrated by Janet Street, Harcourt Brace (San Diego, CA), 1993.

What Rhymes with Moon?, illustrated by Ruth Tietjen Councell, Philomel Books (New York, NY), 1993.

(Compiler and contributor) *Alphabestiary: Animal Poems from A to Z,* illustrated by Allan Eitzen, Boyds Mills Press (Honesdale, PA), 1994.

Sacred Places, illustrated by David Shannon, Harcourt Brace (San Diego, CA), 1994.

Animal Fare: Zoological Nonsense Poems, illustrated by Janet Street, Harcourt Brace (San Diego, CA), 1994.

The Three Bears Holiday Rhyme Book, illustrated by Jane Dyer, Harcourt Brace (San Diego, CA), 1995.

Water Music: Poems for Children, illustrated with photographs by Jason Stemple, Boyds Mills Press (Honesdale, PA), 1995.

(Compiler) *Mother Earth, Father Sky: Poems of Our Planet,* illustrated by Jennifer Hewitson, Boyds Mills Press (Honesdale, PA), 1996.

O Jerusalem, illustrated by John Thompson, Scholastic Books (New York, NY), 1996.

Sea Watch: A Book of Poetry, illustrated by Ted Lewin, Putnam (New York, NY), 1996.

(Compiler and contributor) *Sky Scrape/City Scape: Poems of City Life,* illustrated by Ken Condon, Boyds Mills Press (Honesdale, PA), 1996.

(Compiler) *Once upon Ice and Other Frozen Poems,* illustrated with photographs by Jason Stemple, Boyds Mills Press (Honesdale, PA), 1997.

Snow, Snow: Winter Poems for Children, illustrated with photographs by Jason Stemple, Wordsong (Honesdale, PA), 1998.

The Originals: Animals That Time Forgot, illustrated by Ted Lewin, Philomel Books (New York, NY), 1998.

Color Me a Rhyme: Nature Poems for Young People, photographs by Jason Stemple, Wordsong/Boyds Mills Press (Honesdale, PA), 2000.

(With Heidi E.Y. Stemple) *Dear Mother, Dear Daughter: Poems for Young People,* illustrated by Gil Ashby, Wordsong/Boyds Mills Press (Honesdale, PA), 2001.

Wild Wings: Poems for Young People, photographs by Jason Stemple, Wordsong/Boyds Mills Press (Honesdale, PA), 2002.

Horizons: Poems As Far As the Eye Can See, photographs by Jason Stemple, Wordsong/Boyds Mills Press (Honesdale, PA), 2002.

Least Things: Poems about Small Natures, photographs by Jason Stemple, Wordsong/Boyds Mills Press (Honesdale, PA), 2003.

FOR YOUNG ADULTS; FICTION

(With Anne Huston) *Trust a City Kid,* illustrated by J.C. Kocsis, Lothrop, 1966.

(Editor) *Zoo 2000: Twelve Stories of Science Fiction and Fantasy Beasts,* Seabury (New York, NY), 1973.

The Magic Three of Solatia, illustrated by Julia Noonan, Crowell (New York, NY), 1974.

(Editor and contributor) *Shape Shifters: Fantasy and Science Fiction Tales about Humans Who Can Change Their Shape,* Seabury (New York, NY), 1978.

The Gift of Sarah Barker, Viking (New York, NY), 1981.

Neptune Rising: Songs and Tales of the Undersea Folk (story collection), illustrated by David Wiesner, Philomel Books (New York, NY), 1982.

The Stone Silenus, Philomel Books (New York, NY), 1984.

Children of the Wolf, Viking (New York, NY), 1984.

(Editor and contributor, with Martin H. Greenberg and Charles G. Waugh) *Dragons and Dreams,* Harper (New York, NY), 1986.

(Editor and contributor, with Martin H. Greenberg and Charles G. Waugh) *Spaceships and Spells,* Harper (New York, NY), 1987.

The Devil's Arithmetic, Viking (New York, NY), 1988.

(Editor and contributor, with Martin H. Greenberg) *Werewolves: A Collection of Original Stories,* Harper (New York, NY), 1988.

The Faery Flag: Stories and Poems of Fantasy and the Supernatural, Orchard Books (New York, NY), 1989.

(Editor and contributor, with Martin H. Greenberg) *Things That Go Bump in the Night,* Harper (New York, NY), 1989.

(Editor and contributor) *2041 AD: Twelve Stories about the Future by Top Science Fiction Writers* (anthology), Delacorte Press (New York, NY), 1990, reprinted as *2041,* Delacorte Press (New York, NY), 1991.

(Editor and contributor, with Martin H. Greenberg) *Vampires,* HarperCollins (New York, NY), 1991.

Here There Be Dragons (original stories and poetry), illustrated by David Wilgus, Harcourt Brace (San Diego, CA), 1993.

Here There Be Unicorns (stories and poetry), illustrated by David Wilgus, Harcourt Brace (San Diego, CA), 1994.

Here There Be Witches (stories and poetry), illustrated by David Wilgus, Harcourt Brace (San Diego, CA), 1995.

(Editor and contributor) *Camelot: A Collection of Original Arthurian Tales,* illustrated by Winslow Pels, Putnam (New York, NY), 1995.

(Editor, with Martin H. Greenberg, and contributor) *The Haunted House: A Collection of Original Stories,* illustrated by Doron Ben-Ami, HarperCollins (New York, NY), 1995.

Here There Be Angels (stories and poetry), illustrated by David Wilgus, Harcourt Brace (San Diego, CA), 1996.

Here There Be Ghosts (stories and poetry), illustrated by David Wilgus, Harcourt Brace (San Diego, CA), 1998.

(With Bruce Coville) *Armageddon Summer,* Harcourt Brace (San Diego, CA), 1998.

Not One Damsel in Distress: World Folktales for Strong Girls, Silver Whistle Books (San Diego, CA), 2000.

Boots and the Seven Leaguers: A Rock-and-Troll Novel, Harcourt Brace (San Diego, CA), 2000.

(Editor and contributor) *Sherwood: A Collection of Original Robin Hood Stories,* illustrated by Dennis Nolan, Philomel Books (New York, NY), 2000.

Sword of the Rightful King: A Novel of King Arthur, Harcourt Brace (San Diego, CA), 2003.

Mightier Than the Sword: World Folktales for Strong Boys, illustrated by Paul Colón, Harcourt Brace (San Diego, CA), 2003.

"YOUNG HEROES" SERIES; FICTION

(With Robert J. Harris) *Odysseus in the Serpent Maze,* HarperCollins (New York, NY), 2001.

(With Robert J. Harris) *Hippolyta and the Curse of the Amazons,* HarperCollins (New York, NY), 2002.

(With Robert J. Harris) *Atalanta and the Arcadian Beast,* HarperCollins (New York, NY), 2003.

(With Robert J. Harris) *Jason and the Gorgon's Blood,* HarperCollins (New York, NY), 2004.

"STUART" QUARTET; FICTION

Queen's Own Fool, Philomel Books (New York, NY), 2001.

(With Robert J. Harris) *Girl in a Cage,* Philomel Books (New York, NY), 2002.

Prince across the Water, Philomel Books (New York, NY), 2004.

"PIT DRAGON" SERIES; FICTION

Dragon's Blood: A Fantasy, Delacorte Press (New York, NY), 1982, Harcourt Brace (Orlando, FL), 2004.

Heart's Blood, Delacorte Press (New York, NY), 1984, Harcourt Brace (Orlando, FL), 2004.

A Sending of Dragons, illustrated by Tom McKeveny, Delacorte Press (New York, NY), 1987, Harcourt Brace (Orlando, FL) 2004.

FOR ADULTS; FICTION

Cards of Grief (science fiction), Ace Books (New York, NY), 1984.

Sword and the Stone, Pulphouse (Eugene, OR), 1991.

Briar Rose, Tor Books (New York, NY), 1992.

The Books of Great Alta (includes *Sister Light, Sister Dark, White Jenna,* and *The One Armed Queen*) Tor (New York, NY), 1997.

COLLECTIONS

Merlin's Booke (short stories), illustrated by Thomas Canty, Ace Books (New York, NY), 1982.

Tales of Wonder (short stories), Schocken (New York, NY), 1983.

Dragonfield and Other Stories (story collection), Ace Books (New York, NY), 1985.

Storyteller, New England Science Fiction Association Press (Cambridge, MA), boxed edition illustrated by Merle Insinga, 1992

(With Nancy Willard) *Among Angels* (poetry), illustrated by S. Saelig Gallagher, Harcourt Brace (San Diego, CA), 1995.

Sister Emily's Lightship and Other Stories, (science fiction), Tor Books (New York, NY), 2000.

The Radiation Sonnets (poetry collection) Algonquin Books (Chapel Hill, NC), 2003.

ANTHOLOGIES

(Editor) *Favorite Folktales from around the World,* Pantheon Books (New York, NY), 1986.

(Editor and contributor, with Martin H. Greenberg) *Xanadu,* Tor Books (New York, NY), 1993.

(Editor and contributor, with Martin H. Greenberg) *Xanadu Two,* Tor Books (New York, NY), 1994.

(Editor and contributor, with Martin H. Greenberg) *Xanadu Three,* Tor Books (New York, NY), 1995.

(Editor) *Gray Heroes: Elder Tales from around the World,* Penguin Books (New York, NY), 1998.

(With Heidi E.Y. Stemple) *Mirror, Mirror,* Viking (New York, NY), 2000.

(With Shulamith Oppenheim) *The Fish Prince and Other Stories: Mermen Folk Tales,* illustrated by Paul Hoffman, Interlink Books (New York, NY), 2001.

NOVELTY

Time for Naps, illustrated by Hiroe Nakata, Little Simon (New York, NY), 2002.

Animal Train, illustrated by Hiroe Nakata, Little Simon (New York, NY), 2002.

Bedtime for Bunny: A Book to Touch and Feel, illustrated by Norton Parker, Little Simon (New York, NY), 2002.

"WHITE JENNA" SERIES; FICTION

Sister Light, Sister Dark, Tor Books (New York, NY), 1988.

White Jenna, Tor Books (New York, NY), 1989.

The One-armed Queen, with music by son Adam Stemple, Tor Books (New York, NY), 1998.

FOR ADULTS; NONFICTION

Writing Books for Children, The Writer (Boston, MA), 1973, revised edition, 1983.

Touch Magic: Fantasy, Faerie and Folklore in the Literature of Childhood, Philomel Books (New York, NY), 1981, revised edition, August House, 2000.

Guide to Writing for Children, The Writer (Boston, MA), 1989.

Take Joy: A Book for Writers, Kalmbach Trade Press (Waukesha, WI), 2003.

Also author of the play *Robin Hood,* a musical with music by Barbara Greene first produced in Boston, MA, 1967, and of the chapbook *The Whitethorn Wood.* Ghostwriter of a number of books for Rutledge Press that were distributed by other publishing houses, including *One, Two, Buckle My Shoe,* a counting rhyme book published by Doubleday, and a series of activity books. Editor of books, including *A Plague of Sorcerers* by Mary Frances Zambreno, *Appleblossom* by Shulamith L. Oppenheim, *Jeremy Thatcher, Dragon Hatcher* by Bruce Coville, *The Jewel of Life* by Anna Kirwan-Vogel, *The Patchwork Lady* by Mary K. Whittington, and *The Red Ball* by Joanna Yardley, all Harcourt Brace, 1991. Contributor to many books, including *Dragons of Light,* edited by Orson Scott Card, Ace Books, 1981; *Elsewhere,* edited by Terri Windling and Mark Alan Arnold, Ace Books, Volume 1, 1981, Volume 2, 1982; *Hecate's Cauldron,* edited by Susan Schwartz, DAW Books, 1982; *Heroic Visions,* edited by Jessica Amanda Salmonson, Ace Books, 1983; *Faery!,* edited by Windling, Ace Books, 1985; *Liavek,* edited by Will Shetterly and Emma Bull, Ace Books, 1985; *Moonsinger's Friends,* edited by Susan Schwartz, Bluejay, 1985; *Imaginary Lands,* edited by Robin McKinley, Greenwillow, 1985; *Don't Bet on the Prince: Contemporary Feminist Fairy Tales in North America and England,* by Jack Zipes, Methuen, 1986; *Liavek: Players of Luck,* edited by Will Shetterly and Emma Bull, Ace Books, 1986; *Liavek: Wizard's Row,* edited by Will Shetterly and Emma Bull, Ace Books, 1987; *Visions,* by Donald R. Gallo, Delacorte, 1987; *Liavek: Spells of Binding,* edited by Will Shetterly and Emma Bull, Ace Books, 1988; *Invitation to Camelot,* by Parke Godwin, Ace Books, 1988; and *The Unicorn Treasury,* by Bruce Coville, Doubleday, 1988, and dozens more. Author of introduction for *Cut from the Same Cloth: American Women of Myth, Legend, and Tall Tale,* collected and told by Robert D. San Souci, Philomel Books, 1993; *Best-Loved Stories Told at the National Storytelling Festival,* National Storytelling Association, 1996; and *Fearless Girls, Wise Women, and Beloved Sisters: Heroines in Folktales from around the World* by Kathleen Ragan, Norton, 1998. Yolen has also written songs and lyrics for folksingers, some of which have been recorded. Her papers are housed at the Kerlan Collection, University of Minnesota.

Author of column "Children's Bookfare" for *Daily Hampshire Gazette* during the 1970s. Contributor of articles, reviews, poems, and short stories to periodicals, including *Chicago Jewish Forum, Horn Book, Isaac Asimov's Science Fiction Magazine, Language Arts, Los Angeles Times, Magazine of Fantasy and Science Fiction, New Advocate, New York Times, Parabola, Parents' Choice, Washington Post Book World, Wilson Library Bulletin,* and *Writer.* Member of editorial board, *Advocate* (now *New Advocate*) and *National Storytelling Journal,* until 1989. Some of Yolen's books have been translated into twenty-one languages, including Afrikaans and Xhosa, and have been published in many countries, including Australia, Austria, Brazil, Denmark, England, France, Germany, Japan, South Africa, Spain, and Sweden. She also writes as Jane H. Yolen.

ADAPTATIONS: The Seventh Mandarin was produced as a motion picture by Xerox Films, 1973; *The Emperor and the Kite* was produced as a filmstrip with cassette by Listening Library, 1976; *The Bird of Time* was adapted as a play and first produced in Northampton, MA, 1982; *The Girl Who Cried Flowers and Other Tales* was released on audio cassette by Weston Woods, 1983; *Dragon's Blood* was produced as an animated television movie by Columbia Broadcasting System (CBS), 1985, and shown on *CBS Storybreak; Commander Toad in Space* was released on audio cassette by Listening Library, 1986; *Touch Magic . . . Pass It On,* a selection of Yolen's short stories, was released on audio cassette by Weston Woods, 1987; *Owl Moon* was produced as a filmstrip with cassette by Weston Woods, 1988, and as both a read-along cassette, 1990, and a video; *Owl Moon* was also adapted as part of the video

Owl Moon and Other Stories produced by Children's Circle; *Piggins and Picnic with Piggins* was released on audio cassette by Caedmon, 1988; *Best of Science Fiction and Fantasy* was released on audio cassette by NewStar Media, 1991; *Merlin and the Dragons* was released on audio cassette by Lightyear Entertainment, 1991, was produced as a video by Coronet, 1991, and was released as *What's a Good Story? Merlin and the Dragon* with commentary by Yolen; *Greyling* was released on audio cassette by Spoken Arts, 1993; *Hands* was released on audio cassette by Sundance Publishing, 1993; *Beneath the Ghost Moon* was produced as a video by Spoken Arts, 1996; *Wizard's Hall* was released on audio cassette by "Words Take Wines," narrated by Yolen, 1997. Recorded Books has also issued audio cassettes of three of Yolen's books: *Briar Rose,The Devil's Arithmetic,* and *Good Griselle.* Yolen is the subject of the audio cassette *The Children's Writer at Work—Jane Yolen,* produced by Real Life Productions; in addition, she is the subject of the videos *Good Conversation: A Talk with Jane Yolen,* produced by Weston Woods, and *The Children's Writer at Work,* produced by Reel Life, 1997. *The Devil's Arithmetic* was the inspiration for a TV movie broadcast on Showtime, which won two Emmys.

SIDELIGHTS: Dubbed "the American Hans Christian Andersen" by editor/publisher Ann K. Beneduce and "a modern equivalent of Aesop" by Noel Perrin in the *New York Times Book Review,* Jane Yolen is considered a gifted, versatile author who has developed a stellar reputation as a fantasist while contributing successfully to many other genres. An exceptionally prolific writer, she is the creator of approximately three hundred books for children and young adults and approximately twenty-five for adults. Yolen has written fiction for young adults and adults as well as poetry, criticism, and books on the art of writing and the genre of fantasy for an adult audience. She has also edited and compiled a number of works for both younger and older readers and has also contributed to several collections and anthologies. As a writer of juvenile literature, Yolen addresses her books to an audience ranging from preschool through high school and has written works ranging from picture books and easy readers to young adult novels. She is the creator of realistic fiction, mysteries, verse, animal tales, concept books, historical fiction, humorous stories, and lyrical prose poems, as well as informational books on such subjects as kites, bells, the Shakers, the Quakers, and the environment. Several of Yolen's books have been published in series, and she is particularly well known for the "Pit Dragon" series of young adult fantasy novels in which she created a mythological world based around cockfighting dragons on an arid planet. A folksinger and storyteller, Yolen has created several works that reflect her love of music and oral folklore, including compilations of international songs, rhymes, and stories. Several of the author's books are autobiographical or incorporate elements from her life or the lives of her family, and her three children all contribute to her works—daughter Heidi Elisabet as a writer and sons Adam and Jason as a musical arranger and photographer, respectively.

Yolen is perhaps best known as a writer of original folk and fairy tales and fables with a strong moral core. She has received special recognition for her literary fairy tales, works in the tradition of Oscar Wilde and Laurence Housman that combine familiar fantasy motifs with contemporary elements and philosophical themes. As a fantasist, Yolen is noted for creating elegant, eloquent tales with deep psychological insights that evoke a timeless sense of wonder while having relevance to contemporary life. She includes figures such as dragons, unicorns, witches, and mermaids as characters, and her stories often revolve around shape-shifters, animals who have the ability to transform into humans or humans into animals. As a writer, Yolen invests her works with images, symbols, and allusions as well as with wordplay—especially puns—and metaphors. She is considered an exceptional prose stylist whose fluid, musical writing is both polished and easy to read aloud.

As a writer of nonfiction, the author is credited for capturing the spirit of her subjects as well as for the enthusiasm with which she invests her books. Although her fiction is occasionally criticized for unlikely plots and sketchy characterizations and her fairy tales are sometimes considered too mannered, Yolen is generally praised as a writer of consistent quality whose books are evocative, moving, and enjoyable. Peter D. Sieruta of *Children's Books and Their Creators* stated: "With a confident writing style and inexhaustible imagination, Jane Yolen has proven herself one of the most prolific and diverse creators in the field of children's literature." In Yolen's entry in *Twentieth-Century Children's Writers,* Marcia G. Fuchs commented: "Faerie, fiction, fact, or horrible fantasy, Yolen's lyrical and magical tales are indeed tales to read and to listen to, to share, to remember, and to pass on." Jane Langton, herself a noted writer of fantasy, stated in the *New York Times Book Review* that Yolen's fables "are told with sober strength and native wit. They are simple and perfect, without a word too much." Writing in *Teaching and Learning Literature,* Lee Bennett Hopkins toasted the author: "May the pen of Yolen never run dry. The world of children's literature has been, and will continue to be, richer for her vast talents."

Writing in the *Fourth Book of Junior Authors and Illustrators (FBJAI),* Yolen said, "I come from a long line of storytellers. My great-grandfather was the Reb, the storyteller in a small village in Finno-Russia, my father an author, my mother a mostly unpublished writer." Yolen once remarked CA: "My father's family were merchants and storytellers (some called them well-off liars!). My mother's family were intellectuals. I seem to have gotten a bit of both, though not enough of either." Yolen's father publicized the sport of kite flying so successfully that, according to his daughter in he "forced a renaissance in kiting that is still going on"; in 1968 Yolen published *World on a String: The Story of Kites,* a well-received informational book about the subject. The author's mother quit her job as a social worker in order to raise Jane and her younger brother, Steven; in her free time, Isabelle Yolen wrote short stories and created crossword puzzles and double acrostics. Jane spent most of her childhood in New York City. She also spent summers in Virginia, the birthplace of her mother, and lived for a year and a half in California, where her father did publicity for Warner Brothers.

Yolen commented: "I was a writer from the time I learned to write." An early reader as well as a tomboy, Yolen played games in Central Park while being encouraged in her reading and writing by her teachers. "I was," she recalled "the gold star star. And I was also pretty impossibly full of myself. In first or second grade, I wrote the school musical, lyrics and music, in which everyone was some kind of vegetable. I played the lead carrot. Our finale was a salad. Another gold star." Yolen wrote in *FBJAI,* "If I had to point to my primary source of inspiration, it would be to the folk culture. My earliest readings were the folk tales and fairy stories I took home from the library by the dozens. Even when I was old enough to make the trip across Central Park by myself, I was still not too old for those folk fantasies." Yolen once reflected that she read "all the Andrew Lang fairy books as a child and any kind of fairy stories I could get my hands on. I vividly remember *Treasure Island* and the Louisa May Alcott books. All of the Alcott books, *Jo's Boys,* and even the Alcott books that nobody else had heard of, became part of my adolescent reading. I read *The Wind in the Willows* and the Mowgli stories. We didn't have 'young adult' fiction, so I skipped right into adult books which tended to be very morose Russian novels—my Dostoevsky phase—then I got hooked on Joseph Conrad. Adventure novels or lugubrious emotional books are what I preferred. Then I went back into my fairy tale and fantasy stage. Tolkien and C.S. Lewis, metaphysical and folkloric fantasy." In a transcript of a speech in *Judaica Librarianship,* Yolen commented that she was raised "on tales of King Arthur and Robin Hood. I was a fanatical reader of fantasy and magic, history and adventure." She also began to develop her musical abilities, singing with a friend and earning enough money by passing the hat to buy sodas and ice cream. In sixth grade, Yolen was accepted by Hunter, a girls' school for what were called "intelligently gifted" students. The author said: "With my gold stars and my writing ability, I expected to be a superior gift to Hunter. To my surprise—and horror—I was barely in the middle of my class and managed to stay there by studying extremely hard."

While at Hunter, Yolen commented: "Music became a mainstay in my life." Her father, who sang and played the guitar, introduced Yolen to folk songs. She wrote in *FBJAI,* "I went him some better in learning every old English, Scottish, Irish, and Appalachian love song and ballad I ever heard." Yolen starred as Hansel in the school production of Engelbert Humperdinck's opera *Hansel and Gretel,* played the piano, and wrote songs; in addition, she studied at Balanchine's American School of Ballet. She also developed her interest in writing. In eighth grade, Yolen wrote her first two books, a nonfiction book on pirates, and a novel about a trip across the West by covered wagon. She described this work, which is seventeen pages long and includes a plague of locusts, death by snake bite, and the birth of a baby on the trail, as "a masterpiece of economy." Her experience writing the novel helped Yolen to develop an appreciation for the short form. She acknowledged that short stories and poetry "have remained my first loves." During her twelfth and thirteenth summers, Yolen attended Indianbrook (now Farm and Wilderness), a Quaker camp in Vermont. Here, she said, "I learned about pacifism, swimming, storytelling, mucking out horse stalls, planting a garden, and kissing, not necessarily in that order."

After returning from her second summer at Indianbrook, Yolen moved with her family to Westport, Connecticut. As a student at Staples High School, she became captain of the girls' basketball team; news editor of the school paper; head of the Jewish Youth Group; vice president of the Spanish, Latin, and jazz clubs; a member of the school's top singing group; and a contributor to the school literary magazine. She also won a Scholastic Writing Award for one of her poems, a contest called "I Speak for Democracy," and her school's English prize. Before graduation, her class named Yolen "Best Voice for The Perfect Senior." A high school friend, Stella Colandrea, introduced Yolen to the Catholic Mass. "It was because of Stella's influence that I became enamored of different religions. My own Judaism and camp-discovered Quakerism were the most morally appealing, but the panoply of Catholic rites seem to have taken hold of my imagination and wind in and out of many of the elaborate religious rituals I write about in my fantasy tales. And, since I am an Arthurian buff and a lover of things medieval, knowing a bit about the church helps," Yolen stated. However, Yolen's greatest influence in high school was her cousin-in-law Honey Knopp, a pacifist and peace activist who held hootenannies at her home and gave Yolen a copy of *Journal* by George Fox, the founder of the Quaker faith. Fox later became the subject of Yolen's biography *Friend: The Story of George Fox and the Quakers.* The home that Honey Knopp shared with her husband, Burt, according to Yolen, "became my haven. Oh, I still went to basketball games and dances and parties, wisecracking with my friends and being outrageous. But Honey called out another side of me." Honey's influence is present in many of Yolen's most well-known books, such as *The Gift of Sarah Barker* and *The Transfigured Hart.*

After graduating from high school, Yolen attended Smith College, a prestigious institution for women in western Massachusetts. Going to Smith, Yolen "was a choice that would, all unknowingly, change my life. It made me aware of friendships possible—and impossible—with women. It created in me a longing for a particular countryside, that of New England. It charged me with a sense of leftsidedness, of an alien or changeling awareness. And it taught me, really, about poetry and literature and the written word." At Smith, Yolen majored in English and Russian literature and minored in religion. She ran several campus organizations, authored and performed in the class musicals, and wrote her final exam in American intellectual history in verse, receiving an A+ as her grade. She also wrote poetry: between her junior and senior year, one of Yolen's poems was published in *Poetry Digest,* and her verse was also published in other small literary magazines.

Although poetry was in her soul, Yolen decided to become a journalist. During the summer between her freshman and sophomore years, Yolen worked as a cub reporter for the *Bridgeport Sunday Herald.* "It was there," Yolen recalled, "I wrote my first signed pieces for a newspaper. My very first byline read 'by Joan Yolen.' I did not take it as a sign." Other vacations were spent as a junior counselor in New Jersey and working for *Newsweek* magazine as an intern; she also contributed to the *New Haven Register* and published an article on kites in *Popular Mechanics.* Yolen dismissed the idea of being a journalist when she found herself making up facts and writing stories off the top of her head; she also found that she was emotional when it came to interviewing the poor. "It became clear," she said, "that I was a fiction writer." However, Yolen did continue her musical pursuits, writing in *FB-JAI* that she "made an unhappy college career bearable by singing with a guitar-playing boyfriend at fraternity parties and mixers. We made a little money, a lot of friends, and imprinted hundreds of folk tunes on our hungry minds." After graduating from Smith, Yolen moved to New York City and worked briefly for *This Week* magazine and *Saturday Review* before launching her career as a freelance writer. She helped her father write his book *The Young Sportsman's Guide to Kite Flying* and did a number of small freelance jobs. Yolen took an apartment in Greenwich Village with two roommates. At a wild party there in the summer of 1960, she met her future husband, David Stemple, who was a friend of one of her roommates; the couple were married in 1962. Yolen has noted that one of her most popular books, *The Girl Who Loved the Wind,* is about her meeting with David, a computer expert and photographer who is Yolen's chief advisor on her books. "In it," she stated "a Persian girl is kept in a walled-in palace by an overprotective father until the day the wind leaps over the garden wall and sweeps her away into the wide, everchanging world."

Approached by an editor from the publisher Alfred A. Knopf, Yolen fibbed and said that she had a book-length manuscript ready for review. She recalled: "Caught in the web of this deceit, I, who always prided myself on my honesty, realized there was nothing to do but sit down at my typewriter and get something done quickly. Children's books! I thought. They'd be quickest and easiest." Yolen soon learned that writing books for children was not as quick and easy as she first thought. She collaborated with a high school friend, illustrator Susan Purdy, on several manuscripts, none of which were accepted by the editor at Knopf. Then, Yolen and Purdy sent their manuscripts to other publishers, but with no success. In 1961, Yolen became an assistant editor at Gold Medal Books, a paperback house known for its western novels and spy thrillers. She once commented: "I was famous for about a moment in publishing as the one who coined 'she was all things to two men' for some Gothic novel." Her father introduced Yolen to Eleanor Rawson, the vice president of David McKay Publishing Company. In turn, Rawson introduced the fledgling author to Rose Dobbs, the editor in charge of children's books. Yolen's first book, the nonfiction title *Pirates in Petticoats,* was followed by *See This Little Line?,* a picture book in rhyme that was published the same year.

After leaving Gold Medal Books, where she got to know such authors as Kurt Vonnegut and Harlan Ellison, Yolen became an associate editor at Rutledge Press, a small packaging house that created books and then sold them to larger publishing companies for distribution. Yolen became a ghostwriter for Rutledge, authoring several books—often concept and activity books—that were published under different names. While at Rutledge, Yolen met Frances Keene, an editor who became head of the children's book department at Macmillan. Yolen called Keene, who was to publish five of her books, "a great teacher as well as a fine editor. She taught me to trust my storytelling ability and to work against being too quick. . . . She also pushed me into delving deeply into folklore while at the same time recognizing my comedic talents." Yolen described her association with Keene as the "beginning of an editorial relationship that I *really* count as the start of my writing career." In 1963 Yolen became an assistant editor in the children's department at Knopf, where she met authors and illustrators such as Roald Dahl and Roger Duvoisin and learned about children's literature. She formed a writers' group with such aspiring authors and editors as Jean van Leeuwen, Alice Bach, and James Cross Giblin; one of the members of the group, Anne Huston, collaborated with Yolen on the realistic young adult novel *Trust a City Kid.*

In 1965 the Stemples decided to spend a year traveling. For nine months, they trekked across Europe and then sailed for Israel and Greece. Yolen recalled that bits and pieces "of our wanderings have already found their way into my stories." She added that "places and people we met were stored away in my memory, and months, even years, later were transformed into the magical landscape of my tales." While they were traveling, Yolen discovered that she was pregnant; Heidi Stemple arrived in 1966, shortly after her parents returned to America. David Stemple took a job at the University of Massachusetts Computer Center in Amherst, so he and Jane relocated to western Massachusetts. Adam Stemple was born in 1968 and Jason Stemple in 1970. During the late 1960s, Yolen met editor Ann K. Beneduce, whom the author described as "another seminal influence in my writing life." Yolen and Beneduce, who, according to the author, "produced book after book in the handsomest way possible," worked on approximately thirty books together.

The Emperor and the Kite, a picture book that was among the first of Yolen's works to be edited by Beneduce, is the first of the author's titles to receive major awards. The story outlines how Djeow Seow, the youngest and smallest daughter of an ancient Chinese emperor, saves her father after he is kidnapped by sending him a kite to which is attached a rope made of grass, vines, and strands of her hair. Writing in the *Dictionary of Literary Biography (DLB),* William E. Krueger noted that the story "is simply told in the folk tradition, with traditional motifs which provide an aura both of antiquity and of familiarity to the tale." The critic also observed the theme—"that those whom society considers deficient are capable and perhaps more proficient than others—recurs in subsequent tales." A critic in *Publishers Weekly* said that *The Emperor and the Kite* "is easily one of the most distinguished [books with Oriental backgrounds]—and distinguished proof that extravagance, intelligence, premeditated extravagance, always justifies itself." A reviewer in *Children's Book News* commented: "Here is a writer who delights in words and can use them in a controlled way to beautiful effect." In *The Girl Who Loved the Wind,* a picture book, again illustrated by Ed Young, a widowed merchant tries to protect his beautiful daughter from unhappiness but ends up making her a virtual prisoner. The wind visits her and sings to her about life, how it is always full of change and challenges. Finally, the merchant's daughter escapes with the wind into the world. Writing in *School Library Journal,* Marilyn R. Singer stated that Yolen "produced a treasure. The story has the grace and wisdom of a folk tale, the polish that usually comes from centuries of telling." Eleanor Von Schweinitz of *Children's Book Review* added that the author "has an especial gift for the invention of traditional-type tales and this is complemented by her rare ability to use language creatively. Here she has used the simple rhythms of the storyteller to conjure up the distinctive flavour of an Eastern tale." Yolen said that she wrote *The Girl Who Loved the Wind* "for myself, out of my own history. But recently I received a letter from a nurse who told me that she had read the story to a dying child, and the story had eased the little girl through her final pain. The story did that—not me. But if I can continue to write with as much honesty and love as I can muster, I will truly have touched magic—and passed it on."

When Yolen was sixteen, her aunt's sister by marriage, Honey Knopp, gave her a copy of the journal of George Fox, the founder of the Quakers. "Since then," Yolen commented "I've been interested in the Quakers." Yolen became a member of the Religious Society of Friends (Quakers) in 1971. The next year, she published another of her most well-received titles, *Friend: The Story of George Fox and the Quakers.* A biography of the seventeenth-century Englishman who founded the movement that came to be known as Quakerism as part of his own quest for religious freedom, the book is noted for portraying Fox—with his long hair and pronouncements in favor of women's rights and against war and slavery—as a kindred spirit to the young radicals of today. William E. Krueger of *DLB* called *Friend* "a quite readable biography, interesting and, in places, quite touching, without fictionalization." Writing in *Library Journal,* Janet G. Polacheck noted: "Even where the subject is not in great demand, this beautifully written, valuable biography is an essential purchase."

The Girl Who Cried Flowers and Other Tales, is a collection of five stories that, according to a reviewer in *Publishers Weekly,* "could be called modern folk-or fairy tales, since they boast all the usual ingredients—supernatural beings, inexplicable happenings, the struggle between good and evil forces." The critic concluded that Yolen's "artistry with words . . . makes a striking book." A critic in *Kirkus Reviews* called *The Girl Who Cried Flowers* a "showpiece, for those who can forego the tough wisdom of traditional fairy tales for a masterful imitation of the manner." Reflective of a clear moral tone, *The Girl Who Cried Flowers* is also considered notable for suggesting the close relationship of humanity and nature. William E. Krueger of *DLB* called the book "haunting in its mythic implications" and stated that "the tone and poetic elements are Yolen's unique contributions."

All in the Woodland Early is a concept book that teaches the alphabet through the author's verses and musical score. The book outlines a little boy's hunting expedition in the woods; each letter represents the animal, bird, or insect—both familiar and unfamiliar—for which he is searching. At the end of the last verse, readers discover that the boy is gathering the animals to play with him and a little girl. Yolen also provides music to go with her words. Writing in the *Washington Post Book World,* Jerome Beatty, Jr. said: "Count on versatile Jane Yolen to invent something special and intriguing." He summed up his review by saying: "So clever! It adds another dimension to a lesson in the ABCs, does it not?" A reviewer in *Publishers Weekly* called *All in the Woodland Early* "an outstanding alphabet book," while William E. Krueger of *DLB* called it a "beautifully composed book, reminiscent of cumulative nursery rhymes. . . . This work exhibits Yolen's delightful handling of image, verse, and music."

Commander Toad in Space is the first of her popular "Commander Toad" series for beginning readers that pokes fun at the popular "Star Wars" films—for example, Commander Toad's ship is called the *Star Warts*—and the "Star Trek" television series. Yolen's series is usually considered a humorous and entertaining way of introducing children to literature. In *Commander Toad in Space,* the brave captain and his frog crew discover a watery planet and an evil monster, Deep Wader, who is defeated by being engaged in a sing-along. Judith Goldberger of *Booklist* stated: "Any beginning-to-read book with brave space explorers, a ship named the *Star Warts,* and a monster who calls himself Deep Wader would be popular almost by definition. The bonus here is that the adventure of Commander Toad and his colleagues is a clever spoof and really funny reading." A reviewer in *School Library Journal* called the book a "hoppy combination of good story and clever media exploitation" before concluding: "This one holds water."

Simple Gifts: The Story of the Shakers is an informational book about the history of Shakerism, a millennium religion that grew out of Quakerism but has different beliefs. *The Gift of Sarah Barker* is a historical novel for young adults that is set in a Shaker community. The story features two teenagers, Abel and Sarah, who have grown up in the Society of Believers, a celibate religious community, and now find that they are sexually attracted to each other. As the young people struggle with their feelings, Yolen depicts the contradiction between the religious ecstasy of the Shakers—whose dances and celebrations gave the group their nickname—and the repressive quality of their lifestyle. Sarah and Abel decide to leave the community, but not before Sister Agatha, Sarah's abusive mother, commits suicide. Writing in *Children's Book Review Service,* Barbara Baker called *The Gift of Sarah Barker* "an absorbing tale" and a "jewel of a historical novel," while Stephanie Zvirin of *Booklist* stated: "Into the fabric of a teenage romance [Yolen] weaves complicated and disturbing—at times violent—undercurrents that add a dimension both powerful and provocative." Before writing *Sarah Barker,* Yolen interviewed some of the few remaining Shakers for background information. She also used her daughter, Heidi, who was becoming interested in boys, as the prototype for Sarah. Yolen "I kept wondering how, in a Shaker community, you could keep the boys away from a girl like Heidi or keep Heidi away from the boys. I imagined a Romeo and Juliet story within the Shaker setting."

Dragon's Blood: A Fantasy, is the first volume in her "Pit Dragon" series. High fantasy for young adults that incorporates elements of science fiction and is often compared favorably to the "Pern" books by Anne McCaffrey, the "Pit Dragon" series is acknowledged for Yolen's imaginative creation of a completely realized world. *Dragon's Blood* features Jakkin, a fifteen-year-old slave boy whose master is the best dragon breeder on the planet Austar IV, a former penal colony where inhabitants train and fight dragons domesticated by the early colonists. Jakkin steals a female dragon hatchling to train in secret for the gaming pits, a cockfighting ritual that contributes largely to the planet's economy. Hoping to win his freedom by raising a superior fighting dragon, Jakkin establishes an amazing mental link with his "snatchling," which he names Heart's Blood. The story ends with the dragon's first win; Jakkin—now free—learns that his master knew about his theft and that Akki, a bond girl training in medicine whom Jakkin loves, is his master's illegitimate daughter. Writing in *Horn Book,* Ann A. Flowers called *Dragon's Blood* an "original and engrossing fantasy," while Patricia Manning of *School Library Journal* said that the novel provides a "fascinating glimpse of a brand new world." Pauline Thomas of the *School Librarian* called the book "splendid entertainment," adding, "the author explains little, letting the reader work out the details of geography, natural history, social structure, and sexual mores. The result is remarkably convincing. Austar IV is a world as real as [Ursula K. Le Guin's] Earthsea."

In the second volume of the series, *Heart's Blood,* Jakkin is the new Dragon Master and Heart's Blood has given birth to five hatchlings. Jakkin becomes involved in Austar politics when he is asked to infiltrate rebel forces and rescue Akki. Becoming the pawns in a deadly game, Jakkin and Akki flee with Heart's Blood into the freezing cold of night, called Dark After. Cornered by the authorities after inadvertently blowing up a major arena, the trio fight for their lives. In the battle, Heart's Blood is killed. In order to survive the freezing temperatures, Jakkin and Akki enter her carcass; when they emerge, they have been given the gift of dragon's sight—telepathy—and the ability to withstand the cold. Charlotte W. Draper of *Horn Book* stated: "Rich in symbolism, eloquent in the evocation of a culture which carries within it the seeds of its own destruction, the book stretches the reader's conception of human capability." In *A Sending of Dragons,* the third volume in the series, Jakkin and Akki avoid capture by running into the wilderness with Heart's Blood's five babies. When they enter a hidden tunnel, the group encounter an underground tribe of primitives who have discovered the way to extract metals on Austar IV. Jakkin and Akki also learn that these people, who, like them, are bonded to dragons, have developed a bloody, terrifying ritual of dragon sacrifice. At the end of the novel, Akki, Jakkin, and Heart's Blood's fledglings escape with two of the primitive community's dragons. Confronted by their pursuers from above ground, they decide to return to the city and use their new knowledge to bring about an end to the feudalism and enslavement on Austar IV. A reviewer in *Publishers Weekly* stated: "Yolen's tightly plotted, adventurous trilogy constitutes superb storytelling. She incorporates elements of freedom and rebellion, power and control, love and friendship in a masterfully crafted context of a society sick with perversion." Writing in *School Library Journal,* Michael Cart said that, like the two volumes preceding it, the particular strengths of *A Sending of Dragons* are in "the almost encyclopedic detail which Yolen has lavished upon her fully realized alternative world of Austar IV, in her sympathetic portrayal of the dragons as both victims and telepathic partners, and in the symbolic subtext which enriches her narrative and reinforces her universal theme of the inter-dependency and unique value of all life forms."

One of Yolen's most highly acclaimed books is *The Devil's Arithmetic,* a young adult time-travel fantasy that is rooted in one of the darkest episodes of history. The novel features Hannah Stern, a twelve-year-old Jewish girl who is transported from contemporary New York to rural Poland in 1942 when she opens the door for Elijah during her family's Seder celebration. Captured by the Nazis, Hannah—now called Chaya—is taken to a death camp, where she meets Rivka, a spirited young girl who teaches her to fight against the dehumanization of the camp and tells her that some must live to bear witness. When Rivka is chosen to be taken to the gas chamber, Chaya, in an act of self-sacrifice, goes in her place; as the doors of the gas chamber close, Chaya—now Hannah again—is returned to the door of her grandparents' apartment, waiting for Elijah. Hannah realizes that her Aunt Eva is her friend Rivka and that she also knew her grandfather in the camp. A critic in *Kirkus Reviews* wrote of *The Devil's Arithmetic:* "Yolen is the author of a hundred books, many of which have been praised for their originality, humor, or poetic vision, but this thoughtful, compelling novel is unique among them." Writing in *Bulletin of the Center for Children's Books,* Roger Sutton noted that Yolen's depiction of the horrors in the camp "is more graphic than any we've seen in holocaust fiction for children before." Confirming that Yolen has brought the "time travel convention to a new and ambitious level," Cynthia Samuels of the *New York Times Book Review* concluded that "sooner or later, all our children must know what happened in the days of the Holocaust. *The Devil's Arithmetic* offers an affecting way to begin." Yolen, who has said that she wrote *The Devil's Arithmetic* for her own children, stated in her acceptance speech for the Sydney Taylor Book Award: "There are books one writes because they are a delight. There are books one writes because one is asked to. There are books one writes because . . . they are there. And there are books one writes simply because the book has to be written. *The Devil's Arithmetic* is this last kind of book. I did not just write it. The book itself was a mitzvah."

With *Encounter,* a picture book published to coincide with the five-hundredth anniversary of the discovery of America, Yolen created what is perhaps her most controversial work. Written as the remembrance of an elderly Taino Indian man, the story, which describes the first encounter of Native Americans with Columbus, depicts the man's experience as a small boy. The narrator awakens from a terrifying dream about three predatory birds riding the waves to see three anchored ships. Frightened yet fascinated by the strangers who come ashore, the boy tells his chief not to welcome the men, but he is ignored. The boy and several other Indians are taken aboard the ships as slaves. After he escapes by jumping overboard, the boy tries to warn other tribes, but to no avail; the Taino are wiped out. Calling *Encounter* an "unusual picture book," Carolyn Phelan of *Booklist* noted that "while the portrayal of Columbus as evil may strike traditionalists as heresy, he did hunger for gold, abduct native people, and ultimately (though unintentionally), destroy the Taino. This book effectively presents their point of view." Writing in the *New Advocate,* James C. Junhke called *Encounter* "among the most powerful and disturbing publications of the Columbus Quincentennial." Noting the "pioneering brilliance" of the book, the critic called Yolen's greatest achievement "the reversal of perspective. This book forces us to confront what a disaster it was for the Taino people to be discovered and destroyed by Europeans. Readers young and old will fervently wish never to be encountered by such 'strangers from the sky.'" Writing in response to Junhke's review in the same publication, Yolen said, "If my book becomes a first step towards the exploration of the meeting between Columbus and the indigenous peoples—and its tragic aftermath—then it has done its work, whatever its flaws, perceived or real." The author concluded, "We cannot change history. But we—and most especially our children—can learn from it so that the next encounters, be they at home, abroad, or in space, may be gentler and mutually respectful. It is a large hope but it is, perhaps, all that we have."

Yolen has a penchant for viewing popular versions of stories from a new perspective. Of *Sword of the Rightful King,* Kelly Milner Halls wrote in the *Denver Post:* "Master storyteller Jane Yolen deftly turns the popular myth upside down in this vibrant new look at Arthur's dubious destiny and the cast of characters who helped deliver it." In the book, Yolen ponders such questions as what if pulling the sword from the stone did not entitle the young Arthur to become king? Maybe the fable was created after the boy was crowned king as a public relations effort to gain the people's devotion? Maybe Merlin (Merlinnus, in the book) was simply manipulating Arthur for his own political gain? What if the brave knights of the round table were easily deceived? "The theme of power and belief becoming reality, while not new, is used to good effect here to properly explore the Authurian myths in a new light," commented Mike Jones in *SF.*

Companion book to *Not One Damsel in Distress: World Folktales for Strong Girls, Mightier Than the Sword* begins with a letter from Yolen to the "boys" in her life—her sons and grandsons. She writes, "being a hero [is] more than whomping and stomping the bad guy" and comments on the truth "that brains trump brawn almost every time; that being smart makes the battle shorter, the kingdom nearer, the victory brighter, and the triumph greater." The book consists of fourteen folktales in which, according to Susan Dove Lempke in *Horn Book* magazine, "boys solve their seemingly impossible problems not with force but with wit, trust, kindness and other virtues." Writing in the *Bulletin of the Center for Children's Books,* Janice M. Del Negro said that even so, there is still plenty of action in the tales, and the similarity many of them bear to already classic fables—such as "The Bremen Town Musicians" and "Puss in Boots"—"make this title valuable for comparative folktale curricula and collections."

Throughout her career, Yolen has woven bits and pieces of her personal history—and that of her family and friends—into her works. She was quoted in *DLB* as saying that she uses "these scraps the way a bird makes a nest and a mouse makes a house—snippet by snippet, leaf and bough and cotton batting and all." Several of the author's books are directly autobiographical. For example, *All Those Secrets of the World* is set during the two years that her father was away at war. Yolen recalls how, as a four-year-old, she watched her father depart by ship. The next day, Janie and her five-year-old cousin Michael see some tiny specks on the horizon while they are playing on the beach; the specks are ships. Michael teaches Janie a secret of the world, that as he moves farther away, he gets smaller. Two years later, when her father returns, Janie whispers Michael's secret after he tells her that she seems bigger: that when he was so far away, everything seemed smaller, but now that he is here, she is big. A reviewer in *Publishers Weekly* wrote: "Yolen here relates a bittersweet memory from an important period in her childhood. . . . This timely nostalgic story is told with simple grace, and Janie's thoughts and experiences are believably childlike." Phyllis G. Sidorsky of *School Library Journal* called *All Those Secrets of the World* an "affecting piece without an extraneous word and one that is particularly timely today."

And Twelve Chinese Acrobat is based on family stories about her father's older brother. Set in a Russian village in 1910, the book features Lou the Rascal, a charming troublemaker who keeps getting into scrapes. When Lou is sent to a military school in Kiev, the family—especially narrator Wolf, Lou's youngest brother (and Yolen's father)—is sad. Lou is expelled from military school. Months later, he surprises everyone by bringing home a troupe of twelve Chinese acrobats he met while working in a Moscow circus. The acrobats fascinate the locals with their descriptions of an exotic world far removed from the little village. When the acrobats leave the *shtel* in the spring, Lou's father, recognizing his son's managerial ability, sends him to America to find a place for the family. Writing in the *Bulletin of the Center for Children's Books,* Betsy Hearne said: "The relationship between the two brothers, Lou and Wolf, lends an immediate dynamic to the historical setting." The critic concluded that the compressed narrative, brief chapters, spacious format, large print, and "vivaciously detailed pen-and-ink illustrations dancing across almost every page [by Jean Gralley] make this a prime choice for young readers venturing into historical fiction for the first time, or, for that matter, considering a probe into their own family stories." A critic in *Kirkus Reviews* called *And Twelve Chinese Acrobats* a book "radiating family warmth, in words, art, and remembrance."

Yolen again drew on personal experience when her husband was diagnosed with an inoperable brain tumor in 2003. Suddenly finding her life spinning out of control, she attempted to combat the helpless sensation by each night retiring to her attic office to compose a sonnet. "It is such a rigid form that it imposes structure; it empowered me because then I had control," she told Eric Goldscheider of the *Boston Globe.* The result: forty-three sonnets written over the course of her husband's forty-three-day radiation regimen and released as *The Radiation Sonnets.* "Some of the poems are funny and some of the poems are just a cry for help," she told Goldscheider.

In an article for *Horn Book,* Yolen stated: "As a writer I am the empress of thieves, taking characters like gargoyles off Parisian churches, the *ki-lin* (or unicorn) from China, swords in stones from the Celts, landscapes from the Taino people. I have pulled threads from magic tapestries to weave my own new cloth." The author concluded, "Children's literature is about growth. Just as we do not put heavy weights on our children's heads to stunt their growth, we should not put weights on our writers' heads. To do so is to stunt story forever. Stories go beyond race, beyond religion—even when they are about race and religion. The book speaks to individuals in an individual voice. But then it is taken into the reader's life and recreated, re-invigorated, re-visioned. That is what literature is about."

Yolen mused that her life, "like anyone else's is a patchwork of past and present. . . . I can also see a pattern that might tell me my future—as long as I remain consistent. I consider myself a poet and a storyteller. Being 'America's Hans Christian Andersen' means trying to walk in much-too-large seven-league boots. I just want to go on writing and discovering my stories for the rest of my life because I know that in my tales I make public what is private, transforming my own joy and sadness into tales for the people. The folk."

During an interview for *Bookbird* with Eva-Maria Metcalf, Yolen discussed the relevance of folklore in her work. She commented: "Only in America do we seem to want to throw away the past and constantly rebuild afresh. We seem to think that there is no need to stand on the shoulders of giants. That we ARE the giants. Give me a moment of metaphor here. In Scotland, where I live half the year, the old stones from houses and churches, and cathedrals, become incorporated into new buildings. Harled over and whitewashed, they are still a reminder of how close to their own ghosts the Scots dwell. I believe that is a better way."

BIOGRAPHICAL AND CRITICAL SOURCES:

BOOKS

Authors and Artists for Young Adults, Volume 4, Thomson Gale (Detroit, MI), 1990, pp. 229-241.

Children's Literature Review, Volume 4, Thomson Gale (Detroit, MI), 1982, pp. 255-269; Volume 44, 1997, pp. 167-211.

de Montreville, Doris, and Elizabeth D. Crawford, editors, *Dictionary of Literary Biography,* Volume 52: *American Writers for Children since 1960: Fiction,* Thomson Gale (Detroit, MI), 1986, pp. 398-405.

Drew, Bernard A., *The One Hundred Most Popular Young Adult Authors,* Libraries Unlimited (Englewood, CO), 1996.

Roginski, Jim, *Behind the Covers: Interviews with Authors and Illustrators of Books for Children and Young Adults,* Libraries Unlimited (Englewood, CO), 1985.

St. James Guide to Fantasy Writers, St. James Press (Detroit, MI), 1996.

St. James Guide to Young Adult Writers, St. James Press (Detroit, MI), 1999.

Silvey, Anita, editor, *Children's Books and Their Creators,* Houghton Mifflin (Boston, MA), 1995, pp. 700-701.

Twentieth-Century Children's Writers, St. James Press (Detroit, MI), 1989, pp. 1075-1078.

Yolen, Jane, *Guide to Writing for Children,* The Writer (Boston, MA), 1989.

Yolen, Jane, *Touch Magic: Fantasy, Faerie, and Folktale in the Literature of Childhood,* Philomel Books (New York, NY), 1981.

Yolen, Jane, *Writing Books for Children,* The Writer (Boston, MA), 1973, revised edition, 1983.

PERIODICALS

Bookbird, May, 2003, Eva-Maria Metcalf, interview with Jane Yolen, pp. 52-55.

Booklist, November 15, 1980, Judith Goldberger, review of *Commander Toad in Space,* p. 464; May 15, 1981, Stephanie Zvirin, review of *The Gift of Sarah Barker,* p. 1250; March 1, 1992, Carolyn Phelan, review of *Encounter,* p. 1281.

Boston Globe, May 22, 2003, Eric Goldscheider, interview, "At Home with Jane Yolen," p. H2; June 8, 2003, Liz Rosenberg, "High-Flying Youths and Brave Patriots," review of *My Brothers' Flying Machine: Wilbur, Orville, and Me,* p. H.9.

Bulletin of the Center for Children's Books, October, 1988, Roger Sutton, review of *The Devil's Arithmetic,* pp. 23-24; June, 1995, Betsy Hearne, review of *And Twelve Chinese Acrobats,* p. 365; May 2003, Elizabeth Bush, review of *My Brothers' Flying Machine,* p. 379-380; July-August 2003, Janice M. Del Negro, review of *Mightier Than the Sword: World Folktales for Strong Boys,* p. 466; September 2003, Janice M. Del Negro, review of *Sword of the Rightful King: A Novel of King Arthur,* p. 41; September 2003, Elizabeth Bush, review of *Roanoke: The Lost Colony: An Unsolved Mystery from History,* p. 40-41.

Childhood Education, summer, 2003, Heather J.B. Arbuckle, review of *Wild Wings: Poems for Young People,* pp. 244-245.

Children's Book News, January-February, 1970, review of *The Emperor and the Kite,* pp. 23-24.

Children's Book Review, December, 1973, Eleanor Von Schweinitz, review of *The Girl Who Loved the Wind,* pp. 172-173.

Children's Book Review Service, June, 1981, Barbara Baker, review of *The Gift of Sarah Barker,* p. 100.

Denver Post, August 3, 2003, Kelly Milner Halls, review of *Sword of the Rightful King,* p. H2.

Horn Book, August, 1982, Ann A. Flowers, review of *Dragon's Blood,* pp. 418-419; April, 1984, Charlotte W. Draper, review of *Heart's Blood,* p. 206; November-December, 1994, Jane Yolen, "An Empress of Thieves," pp. 702-705; May-June 2003, Susan Dove Lempke, review of *Mightier than the Sword,* p. 362-363.

Judaica Librarianship, spring, 1989-winter, 1990, transcript of Yolen's acceptance speech for the Sydney Taylor Book Award, pp. 52-53.

Kirkus Reviews, July 15, 1974, review of *The Girl Who Cried Flowers and Other Tales,* p. 741; August 15, 1988, review of *The Devil's Arithmetic,* p. 1248; April 15, 1995, review of *And Twelve Chinese Acrobats,* p. 564.

Library Journal, June 15, 1972, Janet G. Polacheck, review of *Friend: The Story of George Fox and the Quakers,* p. 2245.

New Advocate, spring, 1993, James C. Juhnke and Jane Yolen, "An Exchange on *Encounter,*" pp. 94-96.

New York Times Book Review, November 20, 1977, Jane Langton, review of *The Hundredth Dove and Other Tales,* p. 30; November 13, 1988, Cynthia Samuels, "Hannah Learns to Remember," p. 62; November 8, 1992, Noel Perrin, "Bulldozer Blues," p. 54; August 10, 2003, Eric Nagourney, review of *How Do Dinosaurs Get Well Soon?,* p. 19.

Publishers Weekly, August 14, 1967, review of *The Emperor and the Kite,* p. 50; July 22, 1974, review of *The Girl Who Cried Flowers and Other Tales,* p. 70; January 11, 1980, review of *All in the Woodland Early,* p. 88; October 9, 1987, review of *A Sending of Dragons,* p. 90; March 22, 1991, review of *All Those Secrets of the World,* p. 80; April 14, 2003, Diane Robak, review of *Sword of the Rightful King;* August 4, 2003, review of *The Flying Witch,* p. 78.

School Librarian, December, 1983, Pauline Thomas, review of *Dragon's Blood,* p. 384.

School Library Journal, March, 1973, Marilyn R. Singer, review of *The Girl Who Loved the Wind,* p. 102; December, 1980, review of *Commander Toad in Space,* p. 66; September, 1982, Patricia Manning, review of *Dragon's Blood,* p. 146; January, 1988, Michael Cart, review of *A Sending of Dragons,* pp. 87-88; July, 1991, Phyllis G. Sidorsky, review of *All Those Secrets of the World,* p. 66.

SF, August, 2003, Mike Jones, review of *Sword of the Rightful King,* pp. 66-68.

Teaching and Learning Literature (TALL), November-December, 1996, Lee Bennett Hopkins, "O Yolen: A Look at the Poetry of Jane Yolen," pp. 66-68.

USA Today, April 24, 2003, Ayesha Court, review of *Mightier Than the Sword,* p. D.06.

Washington Post Book World, April 13, 1980, Jerome Beatty, Jr., "Herds of Hungry Hogs Hurrying Home," p. 10; July 13, 2003, review of *Sword of the Rightful King.*

ONLINE

Jane Yolen Home Page, http://www.janeyolen.com/ (August 21, 2004).

OTHER

The Children's Writer: Jane Yolen (video), ReelLife Productions, produced 1996.

Good Conversations: A Talk with Jane Yolen (video), Tom Podell Productions, produced 1998.

* * *

YOLEN, Jane Hyatt
See YOLEN, Jane

* * *

YORK, Simon
See HEINLEIN, Robert A.